Probability and Probability Distributions

PROBABILITY

Bayes's theorem

$$P(B_i|A) = \frac{P(B_i) \cdot P(A|B_i)}{P(B_1) \cdot P(A|B_1) + P(B_2) \cdot P(A|B_2) + \cdots + P(B_k) \cdot P(A|B_k)}$$

Conditional probability

$$P(A|B) = \frac{P(A \cap B)}{P(B)}$$

General addition rule

$$P(A \cup B) = P(A) + P(B) - P(A \cap B)$$

General multiplication rule

$$P(A \cap B) = P(B) \cdot P(A|B) \quad \text{or} \quad P(A \cap B) = P(A) \cdot P(B|A)$$

Mathematical expectation

$$E = a_1 p_1 + a_2 p_2 + \cdots + a_k p_k$$

PROBABILITY DISTRIBUTIONS

Binomial distribution

$$f(x) = \binom{n}{x} p^x (1 - p)^{n-x}$$

Mean of probability distribution

$$\mu = \sum x \cdot f(x)$$

Standard deviation of probability distribution

$$\sigma = \sqrt{\sum (x - \mu)^2 \cdot f(x)}$$

Continued inside back cover

Elementary Business Statistics

SIXTH EDITION

Elementary Business Statistics

The Modern Approach

John E. Freund
Arizona State University

Frank J. Williams
San Francisco State University

Benjamin M. Perles
Suffolk University

Prentice-Hall
Englewood Cliffs, New Jersey 07632

Library of Congress Cataloging-in-Publication Data

Freund, John E.
    Elementary business statistics: the modern approach/John E.
Freund, Frank J. Williams, Benjamin M. Perles.—6th ed.
        p. cm.
    Includes bibliographical references and index.
    ISBN 0-13-252958-0
        1. Commercial statistics.   I. Williams, Frank Jefferson.
II. Perles, Benjamin M.   III. Title.
HF1017.F73 1993
519.5′024658—dc20

Acquisitions Editor: Valerie Ashton

Production Editor: Eleanor Perz

Copy Editor: Sally Ann Bailey

Interior and Cover Designer: Nancy Field

Prepress Buyer: Trudy Pisciotti

Manufacturing Buyer: Patrice Fraccio

Supplements Editor: Lisamarie Brassini

Editorial Assistant: AnnMarie Dunn

 © 1993, 1988, 1982, 1977, 1972, 1964 by Prentice-Hall, Inc.
A Simon & Schuster Company
Englewood Cliffs, New Jersey 07632

Printed in the United States of America

10 9 8 7 6 5 4 3 2 1

ISBN 0-13-252958-0

Prentice-Hall International (UK) Limited, *London*
Prentice-Hall of Australia Pty. Limited, *Sydney*
Prentice-Hall Canada Inc., *Toronto*
Prentice-Hall Hispanoamericana, S.A., *Mexico*
Prentice-Hall of India Private Limited, *New Delhi*
Prentice-Hall of Japan, Inc., *Tokyo*
Simon & Schuster Asia Pte. Ltd., *Singapore*
Editora Prentice-Hall do Brasil, Ltda., *Rio de Janeiro*

Contents

CHAPTER 3

Summarizing Data: Statistical Descriptions **44**

CHAPTER 4

Possibilities, Probabilities, and Expectations **113**

CHAPTER 5

Some Rules of Probability **150**

CHAPTER 6

Decision Analysis* **200**

CHAPTER 7

Probability Distributions **253**

*This chapter is optional and can be omitted without loss of continuity.

*This chapter is optional and can be omitted without loss of continuity.

CHAPTER 12

Decision Making: Inferences About Standard Deviations   **453**

CHAPTER 13

Decision Making: Inferences About Proportions   **471**

CHAPTER 17

Decision Making: Correlation   **652**

CHAPTER 18

Quality Control   **686**

CHAPTER 19

Index Numbers   **723**

Contents   xi

CHAPTER 20

Time-Series Analysis   **759**

CHAPTER 21

Planning Business Research   **820**

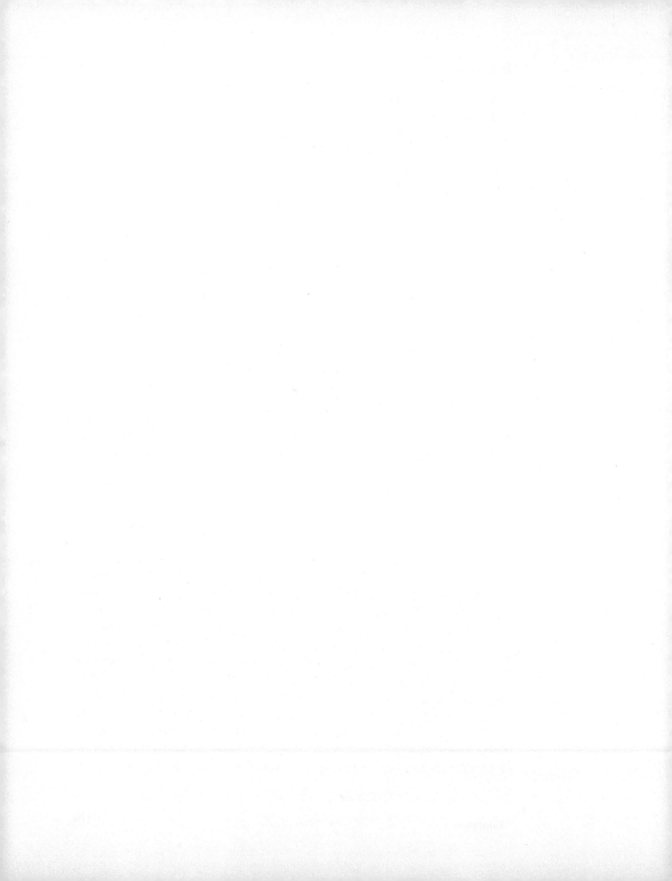

Preface

In the Preface to the first edition of this book (1964) it was noted that, in the past few decades, the development and application of new mathematical, statistical, and computer techniques had brought about radical changes in virtually all areas of business. The Preface noted that statistics itself had clearly shifted from a backward-looking discipline, concerned with describing the past in numerical terms, to a forward- and outward-looking action-oriented discipline. It was also stated that emphasis is now placed on decisions that must be made and their consequences for both current and future operations. Today, nearly 30 years after the first edition was published, it is apparent that this attitude toward statistics, called "the modern approach," has become the accepted way of life in the practice and teaching of business and economic statistics.

The aim in writing the first five editions of this book was to describe, as effectively as possible, the modern approach to decision making in the face of uncertainty. This objective also applies to the sixth edition, and is based upon additional years of valuable classroom experience. Over the years the authors have discussed both formally and informally, with hundreds of teaching faculty and thousands of students, the earlier ideas on how evolving modern business statistics could best be organized and presented at an elementary level of mathematical difficulty. The book has become widely used as a first course in statistics at both the undergraduate and graduate levels by students of business administration, public administration, and economics. Students and faculty around the world have taken time to share their experiences and thoughts about the book with the authors. The great extent to which the authors have relied upon this network of friends may not be evident to every reader, but their counsel and advice are reflected in almost every aspect of this sixth edition.

An English language soft-cover International Edition is available outside North America from Prentice-Hall International, Inc., and a Spanish language edition entitled Quinta Edicion, *Estadistica Para Administracion, Con Enfoque Moderno,* is available from Prentice-Hall Hispanoamericana. The contents of both of these editions are identical with those of the hardcover editions.

As in all prior revisions, the sixth edition introduces substantial changes in content, organization, language, notation, and format. The book contains well over 1,100 exercises, the majority of which have been changed. In many cases the change consists simply of merely substituting current data for older data, although the statistical concepts and level of difficulty remain unchanged. Over 280 Practice Exercises (a new concept in this edition) are printed in color throughout the textbook, and detailed solutions are found at the end of each chapter. As in prior editions, the answers to odd-numbered exercises are provided at the end of the book, but these are not detailed worked-out solutions. The book also contains nearly 240 worked-out examples, which are numbered sequentially in each chapter to provide easy reference for users. A set of review exercises is also provided at the end of each chapter.

Chapter 11, *Decision Making: Inferences About Means,* has been greatly revised, especially in the area of P-values (also known as p-values or prob values). P-values have been used increasingly in recent years and are often provided gratuitously in computer software solutions of certain statistical problems. We show that in testing hypotheses, the dual approach of basing decisions on test statistics, and also of basing decisions on P-values, can be used effectively. Exercises and examples in Chapter 11 and the following chapters are now solved by a five-step procedure (a new concept in this edition). This procedure organizes and systematizes the solution of these problems and is a useful aid to learning. The chapter has been augmented further by a new section on differences between means of paired data.

Much new information is also provided in Chapter 15, *Decision Making: Nonparametric Tests,* which adds the sign test (large samples); rank sums: the signed-rank test; rank sums: the U test for large samples and the inclusion of the one-sided alternative; tests of randomness: runs (large samples); and P-values for nonparametric tests.

Chapter 18, *Quality Control,* has been expanded to include W. Edwards Deming's 14 Points for Management. Also added is a new section concerning median and range control charts. Median charts avoid giving false out-of-control signals based upon occasional very large or very small values. Since the median chart is simple to calculate and use, it is especially valuable where quality control data are collected by mathematically unskilled workers on the shop floor.

As in previous editions of this book, many of the exercises and examples are drawn from real business and economic data that have been modified and scaled down to simplify the computational burden. As before, sections are numbered, formulas are boxed with descriptions in the margins, some of the more important formulas are listed on the end papers, and each chapter has a list of key terms.

The book contains enough material for a full year's work (six semester hours or nine quarter hours), and it permits a good deal of latitude in the selection of topics for shorter courses. The material on decision analysis is taken up as early as possible (in Chapters 6 and 8, immediately following the chapters on probability and probability distributions). However, Chapters 6 and 8 are optional and can be dropped out of the course without lack of continuity. Also, the special topics of index numbers, quality control, and time series are grouped together near the end of the book. These chapters can be taken up earlier, especially if offered in a one-semester course. Time-series analysis, however, is essentially a problem of curve fitting and can conveniently be studied following chapters on regression and correlation. Finally, probability is introduced informally in Chapter 4, and formally in Chapter 5, thus making it possible to omit the formal treatment and continue into decision analysis and inference without going into the more rigorous study of probability.

The authors are greatly indebted and express special thanks to Nancy Croll, director of the Computer Center, Suffolk University, who provided the computer printouts, to Barbara R. Perles who provided technical assistance, to Rita Ewer who helped with the proofreading, to Valerie Ashton, the executive editor, and to Eleanor Perz who was in charge of production.

The authors gratefully acknowledge the advice received from Lorna M. Daniells, Business Bibliographer Retired, Baker Library, Harvard Business School, and Marie Moisden, Department Head, Government Documents, Broward County Main Library, Florida, who contributed greatly to the revised Bibliography of the sixth edition.

In addition, the authors thank Professors Sue Simmons, the Citadel; Joan Whalen-Ayyappan, DeVry Institute of Technology; Ted H. Szatrowski, Rutgers University; Donald R. Barr, Naval Postgraduate School, Monterey, Calif.; Marcel Fulog, Kean College; Fike Zahroon, Moorhead State University; Rosa Oppenheim, Rutgers University; William J. Adams, Pace University; Gaston A. Mendoza, Fairleigh Dickenson University; Daniel D. Gordon, Salem State College; Constance H. McLaren, Indiana State University; Fred Tyler, Fordham University; John O. Stock, Lawrence Institute of Technology; Herbert Eskot, Northeastern University; and William Soule,

University of Maine, who reviewed the manuscript and offered many valuable suggestions. This revision of *Elementary Business Statistics: The Modern Approach* is entirely the work of Benjamin M. Perles.

The authors are also indebted to Professor E. S. Pearson and the *Biometrika* trustees for permission to reproduce parts of their *Biometrika Tables for Statisticians* used in our Tables III and IV; to the Addison-Wesley Publishing Co. to base Table VII on Table 11.4 of D. B. Owen's *Handbook of Statistical Tables;* to the editor of the *Annals of Mathematical Statistics* to reproduce the material in Table VIII; to the American Society for Testing Materials for permission to reproduce part of Table B2 of Supplement B to the ASTM *Manual on Quality Control of Materials;* to Prentice-Hall, Inc., for permission to base Table II on page 582 of Richard A. Johnson and D. W. Wichern, *Applied Multivariate Statistical Analysis;* to the American Cyanamid Company for permission to reproduce the table, Critical Values of *T,* from F. Wilcoxon and R. A. Wilcox, *Some Rapid Approximate Statistical Procedures,* Pearl River, New York, 1964; to G. P. Putnam's Sons, publishers, for permission to quote the 14 Points from Mary Walton, *Deming Management at Work,* New York, 1990; to the Massachusetts Institute of Technology, Center for Advanced Engineering Study, for permission to quote the 14 Points for Management from *Out of the Crisis,* Cambridge, 1982; and to Lotus Development Corporation and Minitab, Inc., for permission to use their software in preparing computer printouts. Some of the material concerning fractiles and exploratory data analysis and some of the formulas in the chapters on regression and correlation are adapted from John E. Freund's *Modern Elementary Statistics,* 8th edition, Prentice-Hall, Inc.

B.M.P.

Elementary Business Statistics

1

Introduction

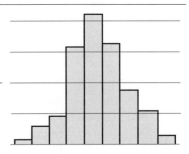

Everything dealing even remotely with the collection, processing, analysis, and interpretation of numerical data belongs to the domain of statistics. This includes, for example, calculating the average profit growth of a major chemical company over the past 10 years; collecting and presenting annually, for all companies listed on the New York Stock Exchange, their short-term debt as a percentage of their long-term debt; evaluating the effectiveness of two different safety programs aimed at reducing the number of lost-time injury accidents on a hazardous job; and analyzing the variations which occur from time to time in series of economic data (retail sales, consumer and wholesale prices, money supply, common stock prices, farm labor productivity, and so on).

The word "statistics" itself is used in several ways. In one connection it means a collection of data such as may be found in the financial pages of newspapers, or in the *Statistical Abstract of the United States.* And in another connection it means the totality of the methods employed in the collection, processing, analysis, and interpretation of any kind of data. In this latter sense, statistics is a branch of applied mathematics, and it is this field of mathematics which is the subject matter of this book.

In Section 1.1 we discuss the recent growth of statistics and the distinction between **descriptive statistics** and **statistical inference**. Section 1.2 contains a brief introduction to the role of statistics in business management.

1.1

Modern Statistics

One of the most remarkable phenomena of the past few decades has been the growth of statistical methods and statistical ideas. For many years, statistics was concerned mostly with the collection of data and their presentation in tables and charts; today, it has evolved to the extent that its impact is felt in almost every area of human endeavor. This is because modern statistics is directly concerned with the problem of decision making under uncertainty. Needless to say, there are elements of uncertainty in nearly everything we do.

The most important feature of the recent growth of statistics has been the shift in emphasis from methods which merely describe to methods which serve to make generalizations, or in other words, a shift in emphasis from **descriptive statistics** to **statistical inference**. By descriptive statistics we mean any treatment of data which is designed to summarize or describe some of their important features without attempting to infer anything that goes beyond the data. For instance, if the government of the United States reports on the basis of the decennial census counts that the population of the United States was 179,323,175 in 1960, 203,302,031 in 1970, 226,542,203 in 1980, and 248,709,783 in 1990, this belongs to the field of descriptive statistics. This would also be the case if we calculated the corresponding percentage growth from one decade to the next. It would *not* have been the case, however, if we used these data to predict the population of the United States in the year 2010 or the percentage growth from 1990 to the year 2010.

Descriptive statistics is an important branch of statistics, and it continues to be widely used in business and other areas of activity. In most cases, however, statistical information arises from samples (from observations made only on some of a large set of items), or from observations made on past happenings. Time, cost, or the impossibility of doing otherwise usually requires such a procedure, even though our real interest lies in the whole large set of items from which the sample came, and in future happenings, not in the past. Since generalizations of any kind lie outside the scope of descriptive statistics, we are led to the use of statistical inference in solving many problems of day-to-day operations and in making both short- and long-range plans. For instance, the methods of statistical inference are required to decide whether a large lot of 9-volt transistor batteries meets its manufacturer's guaranteed average useful life, to decide upon the minimum effective and maximum safe dose of a new anti-inflammatory agent in the treatment of painful local inflammations, to estimate the demand for new snow tires during the next snow season, or to predict the year 2005 demand for wood fibers for all uses in the United States.

At the very beginning of our study of statistics, however, we hasten to add that whenever we make a statistical inference—a generalization that goes beyond the limits of our observations—we must proceed with great caution. In fact, we must consider carefully whether it is possible to make any valid generalizations at all, and if it is, just how far we can go in generalizing. And yet, no matter how carefully we proceed, we may be entirely wrong in the generalizations and find ourselves in trouble. Indeed, one of the most basic problems of statistical inference is that of appraising the risks of making wrong generalizations, and perhaps doing the wrong thing on the basis of sample data. Calling attention here to statistical errors may seem like a negative way to begin our study, but in a very real way, the constant awareness of the possibility of erroneous conclusions and actions, and the desire to control them, direct the course of statistical investigations.

Reality is harsh and unyielding, and must be dealt with on its own terms. We live in a world filled with uncertainties and there is no way to eliminate completely the risks of wrong decisions. This being the case, our real problem is not how to eliminate them, but how to live with them intelligently. The sooner we realize this, the better off we are, and the better we can understand why statistics is a discipline worth studying. One of the main reasons for studying statistics is that it addresses itself directly to this universal problem of how to make intelligent decisions in the face of uncertainty, or more briefly, to the problem of decision making under uncertainty.

1.2

Statistics in Business Management

Modern statistics is highly refined and it is now making a great contribution to the solution of many problems of decision making in the face of uncertainty. Moreover, continuing substantial progress is being made in developing new methods to meet urgent practical needs in many different areas of activity. For example, in the fields of medicine and public health, the recently developed and rapidly growing science of biostatistics is applying powerful mathematical and statistical methods to the study of such fundamental problems connected with the growth, development, illnesses, and deaths of human populations as the harmful effects of air pollution, the relationship between diet and heart disease, and the relationship between smoking and lung cancer. In these areas, as in many others, statistical methods provide a framework for looking at problems in a systematic and logical way. As a matter of fact, these modern methods are in many cases absolutely essential to orderly and continued progress toward important goals.

There is hardly any area in which the impact of statistics has been felt more strongly than in business, where, as a daily way of life, decisions which affect profitability and continuity must be made at all levels of all kinds of businesses. Indeed, it would be hard to overestimate the contributions that statistical methods have made to the effective planning, operations, and control of business activities of all sorts. In the past 35 to 40 years the application of statistical methods has brought about drastic changes in all the major areas of business management: general management, research and development, finance, production, sales, advertising, and the rest. Of course, not all problems in these areas are of a statistical nature, but the list of those which can be treated either partly or entirely by statistical methods is very long. To illustrate, let us mention a few which might face a large multinational manufacturer.

In the general management area where long-range planning is of great concern, population trends in various countries must be forecast and their effects on consumer markets must be analyzed. In research and engineering, costs must be estimated for various projects, and manpower, skill, equipment, and time requirements must be anticipated. In the area of finance, the profit potentials of alternative capital investments must be determined, overall financial requirements must be projected, and capital markets must be studied so that sound long-range financing and investment plans can be developed.

In production, problems of a statistical nature arise in connection with such matters as plant layout and structure, plant size and location, inventory, production scheduling and control, maintenance, traffic and materials handling, and quality assurance. Enormous strides have been made in recent years in the application of statistics to the last area, that is, to sampling inspection and quality control. In the area of sales, many problems arise which require statistical solutions. For instance, sales must be forecast for both present and new products and for existing as well as new markets, channels of distribution must be determined, and requirements for sales forces must be estimated. In advertising, building successful campaigns can be a troublesome task. Budgets must be determined, allocations must be made to various media, and the effectiveness of the campaign must be measured (or predicted) by means of survey samples of public response and other statistical techniques.

So far we have been speaking of problems of a statistical nature which might typically be encountered by a large manufacturer. However, similar problems are faced, say, by a large railroad trying to make the best use of its thousands of freight cars; by a large rancher trying to decide how to feed his cattle so that their nutritional needs will be met at the lowest possible cost; by an open-end investment company trying to decide how much of its total assets should be kept in working cash balances and how much should be invested in common stocks and short-term notes; and by a large integrated gas company (which produces, processes, and transports natural gas, crude oil, and petroleum products) in planning its future conservation practices, transportation system, and energy sources development.

It is not at all necessary to refer to large organizations to find business applications of statistics. For small businesses, problems usually differ more in degree than in kind from those of their large competitors. Neither the largest supermarket nor the smallest neighborhood grocery store, for example, has unlimited capital or shelf space, and neither can afford to tie up these two assets in the wrong goods. The problem of utilizing capital and shelf space most effectively is as critical for the small store as it is for the large, and it is extremely shortsighted to think that modern management tools (including modern statistical techniques) are of value only to big business. In fact, they could hardly be needed more anywhere else than in small business, where each year thousands of operating units fail and many of the thousands of new units entering the field are destined to fail because of inadequate capital, overextended credit, overloading with the wrong stock, and, generally speaking, no knowledge of the market or the competition.

Although in this text our attention will be directed largely toward business statistics and our specific goal is to introduce the basic concepts and methods of statistics to the beginning student, the formal notions of statistics as a way of making rational decisions should really be part of any thoughtful person's equipment. After all, the employees and managers of business are not the only persons who must make decisions involving uncertainties and risks. Everyone must make decisions of this sort professionally or simply as part of everyday life. It is true that some of the choices we must make entail only matters of personal preference, say, whether to watch television or read a book. But, in many instances, there is the possibility of being wrong in the sense that there is an actual loss or penalty—possibly only a minor annoyance, but possibly something as serious as the loss of one's fortune, even one's life, or something between these extremes. The methods of modern statistics deal with decision problems involving risks not only in business and industry, and in everyday life, but also in such fields as medicine, physics, chemistry, agriculture, foods and nutrition, economics, psychology, education, politics, government, and ecology.

1.3

Use of Computers in Business Statistics

Computers have enabled modern business, government, and other organizations to store and process massive quantities of data. For example, the Internal Revenue Service uses computers to compile data relative to millions of tax returns; lawyers use the computer to search among the records of thousands of legal cases which may offer precedents useful in cases they are currently preparing; researchers use the computer to retrieve information from hundreds of data bases which yield current and historical statistics concerning business, economics, and government; and statisticians benefit from the capability of the computer to perform millions of calculations with speed and accuracy, often summarizing the solutions in interesting, colorful charts and tables.

Students who have studied computer languages can write their own programs to solve many of the exercises in this book, or they may prefer to use one or more of the available software packages which provide ready-made programs. In either case the student benefits from an interesting and useful experience.

It may be noted, however, that the use of the computer is not essential to the reader. Almost all of the exercises in this book can be solved with pencil and paper, but the use of an inexpensive hand-held calculator will reduce the amount of labor involved in many calculations. Some exercises are provided in which the use of a computer is recommended, and these are clearly marked.

1.4

A Word of Caution

The amount of statistical information that is disseminated to the public for one reason or another is almost beyond comprehension, and what part of it is "good" statistics and what part is "bad" statistics is anybody's guess. Certainly, all of it cannot be accepted uncritically. Sometimes entirely erroneous conclusions are based on sound data. For instance, a certain city once claimed to be the "nation's healthiest city," since its death rate was the lowest in the country. Even if we go along with their definition that healthy means "not dead," there is another factor that was not taken into account: since the city had no hospital, its citizens had to be hospitalized elsewhere, and their deaths were recorded in the cities in which death actually occurred. The following are some other non sequiturs based on otherwise sound statistical data: "Statistics show that there were fewer airplane accidents in 1920 than in 1992; hence, flying was safer in 1920 than in 1992." "Since there are more automobile accidents in the daytime than there are at night, it is safer to drive at night." "Recent statistics show that the average income per person in the United States is $16,444; thus, the average income for a family of five is $82,220."

Sometimes, identical data are made the basis for directly opposite conclusions, as in collective-bargaining disputes when the same data are used by one side to show that employees are getting rich and by the other side to show that they are on the verge of starvation. In view of examples such as these, it is understandable that some persons are inclined to feel that figures can be made to show pretty much what one wants them to show. Sadly, as we have just demonstrated, this may be uncomfortably close to the truth. We need to develop the ability to distinguish between "good" statistics and "bad" statistics, between statistical methods properly applied and statistical methods shamefully misapplied, and between statistical information correctly analyzed and interpreted and statistical information either intentionally or unintentionally perverted. We shall repeatedly remind the reader of this problem in special sections titled "A Word of Caution," which are given at the ends of many chapters.

To make one final point before beginning the formal study of statistics, let us make it clear that the sound statistical treatment of a problem consists of a good deal more than making a few observations, performing some calculations, and drawing some sort of conclusion. Questions as to how the data are collected and how the whole experiment or survey is planned are of basic importance. As elsewhere, we get "nothing for nothing" in statistics and unless proper care is taken in all phases of an investigation—from the conception and statement of the problem (sometimes, the hardest job of all) to the planning and design, through the stages of data collection, analysis, and interpretation—no useful or valid conclusion whatever may be reached. Generally speaking, no amount of fancy mathematical or statistical manipulation of data on the most expensive computer hardware in the world can salvage poorly designed surveys or experiments. Indeed, professional statisticians insist that even the simplest of sampling studies be rigidly conducted according to well-defined rules. There is no more justification for calling a study which does not conform to these rules "statistical" than there is for calling a barnacle a ship.

Summarizing Data:
Frequency Distributions

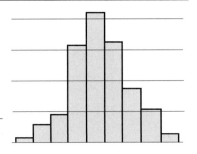

In recent years, business decisions have come to depend more and more on the analysis of very large sets of data. Small-business owners need information about the income patterns and population characteristics in the areas they serve; market research analysts must deal with the views expressed by thousands of shoppers; government statisticians must handle, analyze, and interpret voluminous data collected in censuses of various kinds; and the heads of large corporations must consider information relevant to many problems which would simply overwhelm them if it were not presented in a compact and usable form. This trend in the use of mass data is due partly to the increasing availability of high-speed computers (many current applications of statistical methods would have been practically impossible before the advent of modern data processing techniques) and partly to an increasing awareness of the need for scientific methods in business management. Of course, we do not always deal with very large sets of data; in many cases, they are prohibitively costly and hard to collect, but the problem of putting mass data into a usable form is so important that it requires special attention.

The most common method of summarizing mass data is to present them in condensed form in tables or charts, and the study of statistical presentation once took up most of the time in elementary statistics courses. Nowadays, the scope of statistics has grown to such an extent that much less time is devoted to this kind of work—in fact, we shall discuss it here only in this brief chapter.

Nevertheless, there has been a resurgence in the use of tables and charts, partly because of their ease of preparation on computers. Until recently, computer graphics were expensive luxuries, produced by highly trained experts on very costly equipment. But the introduction of easily operated devices, accompanied by a great drop in their price, has rapidly increased the popularity of computer graphics. The sheer availability of such low-cost graphics has greatly changed their level of utilization and presages greater use in the immediate future. Computer graphics can now be economically prepared by nonexperts, on mainframe and small computers, in a variety of formats, in black and white and in color.

2.1

Frequency Distributions

We can often gain much valuable information about a large set of data and get a good overall picture of it by grouping the data into a number of classes. For instance, the distribution of the population of the United States by age, as reported in the U.S. Department of Commerce, *Selected Population and Housing Characteristics for the United States, 1990,* may be summarized as follows:

Age (years)	Population (millions)
Under 5	18.4
5–17	45.2
18–24	26.7
25–44	80.8
45–64	46.4
65 and older	31.2
Total	248.7

Also, 2,439 complaints about comfort-related characteristics of an airline's planes may be presented as follows:

Nature of complaint	Number of complaints
Inadequate leg room	719
Uncomfortable seats	914
Narrow aisles	146
Insufficient carry-on facilities	218
Insufficient rest rooms	58
Miscellaneous other complaints	384
Total	2,439

Tables such as these are called **frequency distributions** (or simply **distributions**). The first one shows how the population is distributed among the chosen classes, and the second one shows how the complaints are distributed among the different categories. If, as in the first table, data are grouped according to numerical size, the resulting table is called a **numerical** or **quantitative distribution**. In contrast, if data are grouped into categories which differ in kind rather than in degree, as in the second table, the resulting table is called a **categorical** or **qualitative distribution**.

Frequency distributions present data in a relatively compact form, give a good overall picture, and contain information that is adequate for many purposes, but some things which can be determined from the original data cannot be determined from a distribution. For instance, from the first distribution we cannot find the exact value of the number of 4-year-old or 40-year-old persons in the population, or the exact average age of the entire population of 248.7 million persons. Similarly, from the second distribution we cannot tell how many of the complaints about uncomfortable seats were over the width of the seats, how many of the complaints about insufficient carry-on facilities were over particular size luggage, and so forth. Nevertheless, frequency distributions present **raw** (unprocessed) **data** in a more readily usable form, and the price we pay for this—the loss of certain information—is usually a fair exchange.

The construction of a numerical distribution consists essentially of three steps: (1) choosing the classes, (2) sorting (or tallying) the data into these classes, and (3) counting the number of items in each class. The last two of these steps are purely mechanical, so we shall discuss here only the first, the problem of choosing a suitable classification.

The two things that we must consider in choosing a classification scheme are the number of classes we should use to accommodate the data, and the range of values each class should cover, that is, from where to where each class should go. Both choices are essentially arbitrary, but the following rules are usually observed:

> **We seldom use fewer than 6 or more than 15 classes; the exact number we use in a given situation will depend on the nature, magnitude, and range of the data.**

Clearly, we would lose more than we gain if we group 5 observations into 12 classes with most of them empty, and we would lose a great deal of information if we group 10,000 measurements into 3 classes.

> **We always make sure that each item (measurement or observation) goes into one and only one class.**

To this end we must make sure that the smallest and largest values fall within the classification, that none of the values can fall into gaps between successive classes, and that successive classes do not overlap and contain some values in common.

> **Whenever possible, we make the classes the same length; that is, we make them cover equal ranges of values.**

If we can, we also make these ranges multiples of easy to work with numbers, such as 5, 10, or 100, for this facilitates constructing, reading, and using the distribution.

Since the ages in the population distribution of this section were all rounded to the nearest year, only the last of these rules was violated in constructing the frequency distribution. (Had the ages been given to the nearest month, however, a person who was 17 years 9 months old would have fallen between the second class and the third class, and we would have also violated the second rule.) Actually, the last rule was violated in several ways: The intervals from 5 to 17, 18 to 24, and 25 to 44 cover unequal ranges of values, and the first class has no specific lower limit and the last class has no specific upper limit.

In general, we refer to any class of the "less than," "or less," "more than," or "or more" type as an **open class**. If a set of data contains a few values which are much greater than or much smaller than the rest, open classes are quite useful in reducing the number of classes required to accommodate the data. However, we try to avoid them because they make it hard, if not impossible, to calculate values of concern, such as an average or a total.

As we have suggested, the appropriateness of a classification may depend on whether the data are rounded to the nearest dollar or to the nearest cent. It may also depend on whether the data are given to the nearest inch or to the nearest hundredth of an inch, to the nearest second or to the nearest millisecond, or whether they are rounded to the nearest percent or to the nearest tenth of a percent, and so on.

For instance, if we want to group the sizes of all sales, in dollars and cents, made by an office supply store on one day, we might use the classification

Size of sale (dollars)
0.00– 4.99
5.00– 9.99
10.00–14.99
15.00–19.99
20.00–24.99
etc.

Also, for the price-earnings ratios of common stocks given to the nearest tenth, we might use the classification

Price-earnings ratio
4.0– 5.9
6.0– 7.9
8.0– 9.9
10.0–11.9
12.0–13.9
etc.

Chapter 2   Summarizing Data: Frequency Distributions

and for the number of calls received per hour at a department store's switch-board, we might use the classification

Number of calls
0– 24
25– 49
50– 74
75– 99
100–124
etc.

To illustrate the construction of a frequency distribution, let us go through the actual steps of grouping a set of data.

EXAMPLE 2.1   Construct a distribution of the following scores which 150 applicants for secretarial positions in a large company made on a clerical aptitude test:

27	79	69	40	51	88	55	48	36	61
53	44	94	51	65	42	58	55	69	63
70	48	61	55	60	25	47	78	61	54
57	76	73	62	36	67	40	51	59	68
27	46	62	43	54	83	59	13	72	57
82	45	54	52	71	53	82	69	60	35
41	65	62	75	60	42	55	34	49	45
49	64	40	61	73	44	59	46	71	86
43	69	54	31	56	51	75	44	66	53
80	71	53	56	91	60	41	29	56	57
35	54	43	39	56	27	62	44	85	61
59	89	60	51	71	53	58	26	77	68
62	57	48	69	76	52	49	45	54	41
33	61	80	57	42	45	59	44	68	73
55	70	39	58	69	51	85	46	55	67

SOLUTION   Since the smallest of the scores is 13 and the largest is 94, it seems reasonable to choose the nine classes 10–19, 20–29, . . . , and 90–99, which satisfy the three rules for choosing a suitable classification. Performing the actual tally and counting the number of items in each class, we get the following frequency distribution:

Score	Tally	Frequency
10–19	/	1
20–29	/N/ /	6
30–39	/N/ ////	9
40–49	/N/ /N/ /N/ /N/ /N/ /N/ /	31
50–59	/N/ /N/ /N/ /N/ /N/ /N/ /N/ /N/ //	42
60–69	/N/ /N/ /N/ /N/ /N/ /N/ //	32
70–79	/N/ /N/ /N/ //	17
80–89	/N/ /N/	10
90–99	//	2
	Total	150

The numbers given in the right-hand column of this table, which show how many items fall into each class, are called the **class frequencies**. The smallest and largest values that can go into any given class are called its **class limits**, and for this distribution they are 10 and 19, 20 and 29, 30 and 39, . . . , and 90 and 99. More specifically, 10, 20, 30, . . . , and 90 are called the **lower class limits**, and 19, 29, 39, . . . , and 99 are called the **upper class limits**. ■

Using this terminology, we can now say that the choice of the class limits depends on the extent to which the numbers we want to group are rounded. If our data are prices rounded to the nearest dollar, the class $5–9 actually contains all prices between $4.50 and $9.50; and if our data are lengths rounded to the nearest tenth of an inch, the class 1.5–1.9 actually contains all lengths between 1.45 and 1.95 inches. These pairs of values are usually called **class boundaries** or **real class limits**.

For the distribution of clerical aptitude scores, the class boundaries are 9.5 and 19.5, 19.5 and 29.5, 29.5 and 39.5, . . . , and 89.5 and 99.5, namely, the midpoints between the respective class limits. Of course, these values must be, by their nature, "impossible" values which cannot occur among the data being grouped. To make sure of this, we have only to observe the extent to which the data are rounded; for instance, for the size-of-sales classification on page 12 the class boundaries are the impossible values −0.005, 4.995, 9.995, 14.995, and so on.

Numerical distributions also have what are called **class marks** and **class intervals**. Class marks are just the midpoints of the classes, and they are found by adding the lower and upper limits of a class (or its upper and lower boundaries) and dividing by 2. A class interval is simply the length of a class, or the range of values it can contain, and it is given by the difference between its class boundaries. If the classes of a distribution are all equal in length, their common class interval, which we call the **class interval of the distribution**, is also given by the difference between any two successive class marks.

EXAMPLE 2.2 Find the class marks and the class interval of the distribution of aptitude scores.

SOLUTION The class marks are $\frac{10 + 19}{2} = 14.5$, $\frac{20 + 29}{2} = 24.5$, . . . , and $\frac{90 + 99}{2} = 94.5$, and the class interval of the distribution is $24.5 - 14.5 = 10$. Note that the class interval is not given by the difference between the upper and lower limits of a class, which here is 9, not 10. ■

Sometimes it is preferable to present data in what is called a **cumulative frequency distribution**, or simply a **cumulative distribution**, which shows directly how many of the items are less than, or greater than, various values.

EXAMPLE 2.3 Convert the distribution of aptitude scores into a cumulative "or less" distribution.

SOLUTION Since none of the values is 9 or less, one of the values is 19 or less, $1 + 6 = 7$ of the values are 29 or less, $1 + 6 + 9 = 16$ of the values are 39 or less, . . . , the "or less" distribution is

Score	Cumulative frequency
9 or less	0
19 or less	1
29 or less	7
39 or less	16
49 or less	47
59 or less	89
69 or less	121
79 or less	138
89 or less	148
99 or less	150

Had we written "less than 10" instead of "9 or less," "less than 20" instead of "19 or less," "less than 30" instead of "29 or less," ..., and "less than 100" instead of "99 or less," we would have a cumulative "less than" distribution. If we cumulate the frequencies, beginning with the largest class, we get an "or more" distributuion if we designate the classes "10 or more," "20 or more," "30 or more," ..., and "100 or more"; or a "more than" distribution if we designate the classes "more than 9," "more than 19," "more than 29," ..., and "more than 99." ∎

Often, it is better to show what percentage of the items falls into each class of a distribution instead of showing the actual class frequencies. To convert a frequency distributiuon into a corresponding **percentage distribution**, we divide each class frequency by the total number of items grouped and multiply the quotient by 100.

EXAMPLE 2.4 Convert the distribution of the aptitude scores into a percentage distribution.

SOLUTION The first class contains $\frac{1}{150} \cdot 100 = 0.7$ percent of the data, the second class contains $\frac{6}{150} \cdot 100 = 4.0$ percent of the data, ..., and the ninth class contains $\frac{2}{150} \cdot 100 = 1.3$ percent of the data. Hence, the percentage distribution is

Score	Percentage
10–19	0.7
20–29	4.0
30–39	6.0
40–49	20.7
50–59	28.0
60–69	21.3
70–79	11.3
80–89	6.7
90–99	1.3

∎

So far we have discussed only the construction of numerical distributions, but the general problem of constructing categorical (or qualitative) distributions is somewhat the same. Here again we must decide how many categories (classes) to use and what kind of items each category is to contain, making sure that all the items are accommodated and that there are no ambiguities. Since the categories must often be chosen before any data are actually collected, it is prudent to include a category labled "others" or "miscellaneous."

For categorical distributions, we do not have to worry about such mathematical details as class limits, class boundaries, and class marks. On the other hand, there is often a serious problem with ambiguities and we must be very careful and explicit in defining what each category is to contain. For this reason, it is advisable, where possible, to use standard categories developed by the Bureau of the Census and other government agencies.

EXERCISES

(Exercises 2.1, 2.2, 2.3, and 2.4 are practice exercises. Their complete solutions are given on page 39.)

2.1   The daily number of tolls paid by vehicles on a certain toll road varied from 1,380 to 9,990. Indicate the limits of nine classes into which these tolls paid might be grouped.

2.2   The campus bookstore groups the value of its sales to students into a frequency distribution with the classes $0.00–9.99, $10.00–19.99, $20.00–29.99, $30.00–39.99, $40.00–49.99, $50.00–59.99, and $60.00 and over. Is it possible to determine from this distribution the number of sales in the amount of

(a) less than $40.00   (b) $40.00 or less

(c) more than $30.00   (d) $30.00 or more

2.3   The weights, in troy ounces, of 300 purchases of gold by a precious metals buyer have the classes 0.00–19.99, 20.00–39.99, 40.00–59.99, and 60.00–79.99. Find

(a) the class boundaries

(b) the class marks

(c) the class intervals

2.4   The class marks of a distribution of the daily number of emergency flights made by an air ambulance service company are 10.5, 18.5, 26.5, 34.5, and 42.5. Find

(a) the class boundaries

(b) the class limits

2.5 A set of measurements of the number of gallons of diesel fuel (given to the nearest tenth of a gallon) used by vehicles in a fleet of trucks is grouped into a table with the class boundaries of 9.95, 14.95, 19.95, 24.95, 29.95, 34.95, and 39.95. What are the lower and upper limits of the six classes, and what are their class marks?

2.6 To group the amounts of time it takes a typist to prepare a short, standardized collection letter, the following classifications were used: 1.0–1.9 minutes, 2.0–2.9 minutes, 2.9–3.9 minutes, and 3.9–5.9 minutes. Explain where difficulties might arise.

2.7 The following are the numbers of credit reports prepared by a credit reporting agency on 110 business days:

62	60	43	64	58	52	52	67	59	60	51
62	56	63	61	68	57	51	59	47	42	64
43	67	52	58	47	59	64	58	52	63	48
65	60	61	59	63	56	62	56	62	57	59
62	56	63	55	73	60	69	53	66	54	52
54	61	55	65	55	61	59	74	62	49	63
63	53	71	59	46	64	41	60	51	55	64
46	64	56	59	49	64	60	57	58	66	53
65	62	58	65	61	50	55	57	61	45	55
60	66	63	58	78	65	61	57	67	54	53

(a) Group these figures into a table having the classes 40–44, 45–49, 50–54, 55–59, 60–64, 65–69, 70–74, and 75–79.

(b) Convert the distribution of part (a) into a cumulative "less than" distribution.

2.8 A household appliance service and repair company received the following numbers of orders for service and repair daily during eight weeks of six working days each.

19	27	24	18	26	24	21	18
30	32	16	28	25	18	22	22
25	31	22	28	26	25	20	29
22	34	22	28	25	25	19	24
30	23	27	15	25	24	28	21
29	23	22	26	31	24	25	26

(a) Group these figures into a table having the classes 15–17, 18–20, 21–23, . . . , and 33–35.

(b) Convert the distribution of part (a) into a corresponding percentage distribution and also a cumulative "or more" percentage distribution.

2.9 A retail athletic shoe store sold the following numbers of pairs of athletic shoes daily during seven weeks of six working days each.

35	45	63	60	76	75	69
49	60	55	75	85	65	67
38	65	71	93	43	51	59
61	78	65	89	70	73	55
64	58	75	32	75	40	72
87	83	75	85	65	97	89

(a) Group these daily sales figures into a distribution having the classes 30–39, 40–49, 50–59, . . . , and 90–99.

(b) Convert the distribution of part (a) into a percentage distribution.

2.10 Convert the percentage distribution of part (b) of the preceding exercise into a cumulative "less than" percentage distribution.

2.11 An analysis of the 40 grades on a college transcript, where the possible grades were A, B, C, D, and F, revealed that the student had attained the following:

B	F	A	C	D	B	C	C	C	B
B	C	B	A	C	D	C	B	D	B
C	B	A	D	C	B	C	C	B	C
C	C	B	C	C	A	C	B	C	B

Construct a table showing the frequencies corresponding to the grades achieved by the student.

2.2

Stem-and-Leaf Plots[1]

In the preceding sections we directed our attention to the grouping of mass data, with the objective of putting such data into a manageable form. As we saw, this entailed some loss of information. In recent years, similar techniques have been proposed for the preliminary exploration of relatively small sets of data which yield a good overall picture of the data without any loss of information.

To illustrate, consider the number of collection letters mailed by a collection agency on 30 consecutive business days:

64	62	57	54	47	67	58	51	72	45
51	83	51	74	59	53	78	45	69	64
58	54	42	62	51	45	69	51	78	67

[1]Adapted from J. E. Freund and G. A. Simon, *Modern Elementary Statistics*, 8th ed. (Englewood Cliffs, N.J.: Prentice-Hall, Inc., 1992).

Proceeding as in Section 2.1, we can group these data into the following distribution:

Number of letters	Tally	Frequency
40–49	ⅣⅤ	5
50–59	ⅣⅤ ⅣⅤ Ⅱ	12
60–69	ⅣⅤ Ⅲ	8
70–79	ⅣⅣ	4
80–89	Ⅰ	1

where the tally shows the overall pattern of the data.

If we wanted to avoid the loss of information inherent in the foregoing table, we could replace the tally marks with the last digits of the corresponding scores, getting

```
40–49 | 7  5  5  2  5
50–59 | 7  4  8  1  1  1  9  3  8  4  1  1
60–69 | 4  2  7  9  4  2  9  7
70–79 | 2  4  8  8
80–89 | 3
```

This can also be written as

```
4* | 7  5  5  2  5
5* | 7  4  8  1  1  1  9  3  8  4  1  1
6* | 4  2  7  9  4  2  9  7
7* | 2  4  8  8
8* | 3
```

where * is a placeholder for 0, 1, 2, 3, 4, 5, 6, 7, 8, or 9 or simply as

```
4 | 7  5  5  2  5
5 | 7  4  8  1  1  1  9  3  8  4  1  1
6 | 4  2  7  9  4  2  9  7
7 | 2  4  8  8
8 | 3
```

In either of these final forms, the table is referred to as a **stem-and-leaf plot**—each line is a **stem** and each digit on a stem to the right of the vertical line is a **leaf**. To the left of the vertical line are the **stem labels**, which, in our example, are 4*, 5*, 6*, 7*, and 8* or 4, 5, 6, 7, and 8.

Essentially, a stem-and-leaf plot presents the same picture as the corresponding tally, yet it retains all the original information. For instance, if a stem-and-leaf plot has the stem

$$32* \mid 8 \quad 0 \quad 4 \quad 7 \quad 6$$

the corresponding data are 328, 320, 324, 327, and 326, and if a stem-and-leaf plot has the stem

$$8** \mid 12 \quad 92 \quad 00 \quad 29$$

with two-digit leaves, the corresponding data are 812, 892, 800, and 829.

In a **double-stem plot** the stem labels are subdivided as shown in the computer printout of Figure 2.1, which uses the collection letter data. In this printout the center column contains the stem labels 4, 4, 5, 5, 6, 6, 7, 7, and 8. The first of the 4's, 5's, 6's, 7's, and the 8 are stem labels for the leaves whose values are 0, 1, 2, 3, and 4, and the repeated stem labels are followed by leaves whose values are 5, 6, 7, 8, and 9. The left-hand column accumulates the count of the number of leaves from the top and from the bottom of the plot. The third row, for example, is preceded by 13, the accumulated number of leaves in the first three rows, and the sixth row is preceded by 9, the accumulated number of leaves shown in the last four rows. The paren-

```
MTB > SET C1
DATA> 64 62 57 54 47 67 58 51 72 45
DATA> 51 83 51 74 59 53 78 45 69 64
DATA> 58 54 42 62 51 45 69 51 78 67
DATA> END
MTB > STEM C1

Stem-and-leaf of C1          N  = 30
Leaf Unit = 1.0

      1        4 2
      5        4 5557
     13        5 11111344
     (4)       5 7889
     13        6 2244
      9        6 7799
      5        7 24
      3        7 88
      1        8 3
```

FIGURE 2.1
Computer printout for double-stem plot of the number of collection letters mailed

theses in the column denote the stem value to which the middle leaf (arranged in order of size) is attached, and the 4 within the parentheses denotes the number of leaves attached to this stem label. This arrangement highlights the partial ordering of data in stem-and-leaf plots—the data are ordered with respect to stem labels—and as we shall see in Chapter 3, this simplifies the determination of further descriptions.

The computer printout of Figure 2.1 designates that the software used in the computer to produce this double-stem plot is Minitab. This is one of several excellent computer packages which we can use for this purpose. Although the data are shown on the printout in several rows, the user can view these numbers as a lengthy list in one column, which has been labeled C1. The printout also provides the item, $N = 30$, which tells us the number of items which have been listed.

There are various ways in which stem-and-leaf plots can be modified to meet particular needs, but we shall not go into this in any detail, as it has been our objective only to present one of the relatively new techniques which come under the general heading of **exploratory data analysis**.

EXERCISES

(Exercises 2.12 and 2.16 are practice exercises. Their complete solutions are given on page 39.)

2.12 The distances in feet from home plate to the right-field walls in the 14 American League playing fields are 309, 302, 333, 341, 320, 325, 330, 315, 327, 310, 330, 316, 330, and 330. Construct a stem-and-leaf plot with the stem labels 30, 31, 32, 33, and 34.

2.13 The total number of overtime hours worked for each of 30 consecutive weeks by data processing personnel in an office was 252, 240, 244, 249, 224, 235, 235, 269, 216, 228, 230, 215, 236, 229, 221, 237, 253, 233, 228, 256, 210, 223, 222, 240, 231, 230, 244, 245, 255, and 230. Construct a stem-and-leaf plot with one-digit leaves.

2.14 The yields (in percent) of the 30 Dow Jones Industrial Average stocks provided in a recent issue of *The Wall Street Journal* were Alcoa, 4.09; Allied-Signal, 5.05; American Express, 2.90; AT&T, 2.83; Bethlehem Steel, 2.30; Boeing, 2.00; Chevron, 4.24; Coca-Cola, 1.88; Du Pont, 3.92; Exxon, 5.00; General Electric, 2.95; General Motors, 7.12; Goodyear, 4.48; IBM, 4.86; International Paper, 3.24; Kodak, 4.92; McDonald's, 0.96; Merck, 2.46; Minnesota Mining, 3.21; Navistar, 0.00; Philip Morris, 3.49; Primerica, 1.11; Procter & Gamble, 2.59; Sears, Roebuck, 5.39; Texaco, 5.38; Union Carbide, 4.44; United Technology, 3.10; USX Corp., 4.01; Westinghouse, 3.33; and Woolworth, 3.08. Construct a stem-and-leaf plot with the stem labels 0., 1., 2., 3., 4., 5., 6., and 7. (and, hence, with two-digit leaves).

2.15 List the data that correspond to the following items of stem-and-leaf plots:

(a) 9* $\vert$0 9 5 3 4

(b) 27 $\vert$8 4 7 5 1

(c) 6** $\vert$15 45 30 95 00

(d) 2.1 $\vert$4 8 7 7 5

2.16 A double-stem plot similar to that shown, and using the same data as that of the computer printout of Figure 2.1, can be prepared manually as shown here. We might use * as a placeholder for 0, 1, 2, 3, and 4, and • as a placeholder for 5, 6, 7, 8, and 9. We get

```
4*  | 2
4•  | 7  5  5  5
5*  | 4  1  1  1  3  4  1  1
5•  | 7  8  9  8
6*  | 4  2  4  2
6•  | 7  9  9  7
7*  | 2  4
7•  | 8  8
8*  | 3
```

where we doubled the number of stems by cutting the interval covered by each stem in half.

(a) Construct a double-stem plot with one-digit leaves for the data of Exercise 2.13.

(b) The numbers of automobile mufflers installed each day in 35 consecutive days by an automobile muffler shop are 41, 37, 52, 41, 46, 50, 47, 36, 44, 51, 37, 38, 44, 56, 30, 34, 28, 40, 39, 41, 40, 38, 36, 49, 43, 46, 31, 31, 43, 29, 31, 33, 46, 37, and 35. Construct a double-stem plot with one-digit leaves.

2.3

Graphical Presentations

When frequency distributions are constructed primarily to condense large sets of data and display them in an "easy to digest" form, it is usually advisable to present them graphically. The most common form of graphical presentation of statistical data is the **histogram**, an example of which is shown in Figure 2.2. The example portrays the clerical aptitude scores shown on page 13. A histogram is constructed by representing the measurements or observations which are grouped (the clerical aptitude scores) on the horizontal scale and indicating the class frequencies on the vertical scale.

Rectangles are constructed whose bases equal the class interval and whose heights are determined by the corresponding class frequencies. The markings on the horizontal scale can be the class limits, as in Figure 2.2, the class boundaries, or arbitrary key values. For easy readability, it is usually better to indicate the class limits, although the rectangles actually go from one class boundary to the next. Histograms cannot be used in connection with frequency distributions having open classes, and they must be used with extreme care if the class intervals are not all equal (see the discussion on page 32).

Histograms can be constructed directly from raw data using a computer package designed for data analysis. The computer printout of the data in Figure 2.2 shows a histogram of the distribution of clerical aptitude scores with the class marks 14.5, 24.5, 34.5, ..., and 94.5. In Figure 2.3, the word "MINITAB" and its abbreviation "MTB" designate that the computer software used here is Minitab. "SET IN C1" instructs the computer to accept the $N = 150$ items of data, treating them as though they were listed in one column. For convenience, the computer divided the "column" which shows all of the clerical aptitude scores of page 13. "HISTOGRAM OF C1, FIRST MIDPOINT AT 14.5, WIDTH OF 10," instructs the computer to print a histogram with 14.5 as its first class mark and with 10 as the class interval. Note that the frequency scale is horizontal so that the histogram is, so to speak, on its side. As we have defined the term, the result shown in Figure 2.3 is not a histogram. However, combining some of the features of Figures 2.7 and 2.10, it conveys the same idea.

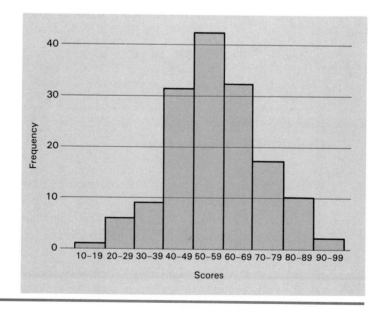

FIGURE 2.2
Histogram of the distribution of clerical aptitude scores

Chapter 2 Summarizing Data: Frequency Distributions

FIGURE 2.3
Computer printout
for histogram of the
distribution of
clerical aptitude
scores

```
OK, MINITAB
MTB > SET IN C1
DATA> 27 79 69 40 51 88 55 48 36 61
DATA> 53 44 94 51 65 42 58 55 69 63
DATA> 70 48 61 55 60 25 47 78 61 54
DATA> 57 76 73 62 36 67 40 51 59 68
DATA> 27 46 62 43 54 83 59 13 72 57
DATA> 82 45 54 52 71 53 82 69 60 35
DATA> 41 65 62 75 60 42 55 34 49 45
DATA> 49 64 40 61 73 44 59 46 71 86
DATA> 43 69 54 31 56 51 75 44 66 53
DATA> 80 71 53 56 91 60 41 29 56 57
DATA> 35 54 43 39 56 27 62 44 85 61
DATA> 59 89 60 51 71 53 58 26 77 68
DATA> 62 57 48 69 76 52 49 45 54 41
DATA> 33 61 80 57 42 45 59 44 68 73
DATA> 55 70 39 58 69 51 85 46 55 67
DATA> END
MTB > HISTOGRAM OF C1, FIRST MIDPOINT AT 14.5, WIDTH OF 10

Histogram of C1    N = 150

Midpoint    Count
   14.5        1   *
   24.5        6   ******
   34.5        9   *********
   44.5       31   *******************************
   54.5       42   ******************************************
   64.5       32   ********************************
   74.5       17   *****************
   84.5       10   **********
   94.5        2   **
```

An alternative, although less widely used form of graphical presentation, is the **frequency polygon**, shown in Figure 2.4. Here the class frequencies are plotted at the class marks and the successive points are connected by straight lines. Note that we added frequencies at both ends of the distribution in order to "tie down" the graph to the horizontal scale.

The computer printout of Figure 2.5 again shows a frequency polygon of the distribution of clerical aptitude scores. The 150 items of raw data were typed into the computer, which arranged the data into classes as instructed, plotted the points (outlined by small squares), and connected them with straight lines. In this example the data were not printed, the instructions to

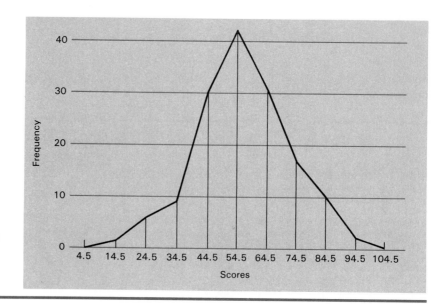

FIGURE 2.4
Frequency polygon
of the distribution
of the aptitude
scores

the computer not shown, and the end points not "tied down" to the base line.

If we apply the same technique to a cumulative distribution, we obtain what is called an **ogive**. However, the cumulative frequencies are not plotted

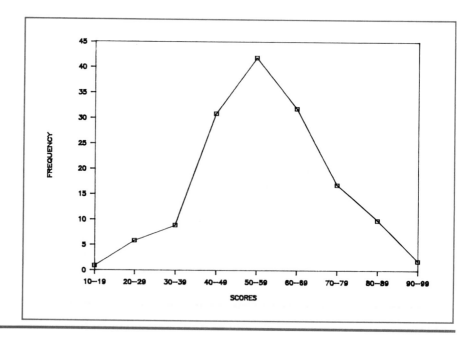

FIGURE 2.5
Computer printout
of frequency
polygon of the
distribution of
aptitude scores

Chapter 2   Summarizing Data: Frequency Distributions

at the class marks—it stands to reason that the frequency corresponding, say, to "29 or less" should be plotted at 29.5, the class boundary, since "29 or less" actually includes everything up to 29.5. Figure 2.6 shows an ogive corresponding to the "or less" distribution of the aptitude scores.

Although the visual appeal of histograms, frequency polygons, and ogives exceeds that of frequency tables, there are ways in which distributions can be presented even more dramatically and often more effectively. Two kinds of such pictorial presentations (often seen in newspapers, magazines, and reports of various kinds) are illustrated by the **pictograms** of Figures 2.7 and 2.8.

Categorical (or qualitative) distributions are often presented graphically as **pie charts** such as the one shown in Figure 2.9, where a circle is divided into sectors (pie-shaped pieces) which are proportional in size to the corresponding frequencies or percentages. To construct a pie chart, we first convert the distribution into a percentage distribution. Then, since a complete circle corresponds to 360° (degrees), we get the central angles of the various sectors by multiplying the percentages by 3.6.

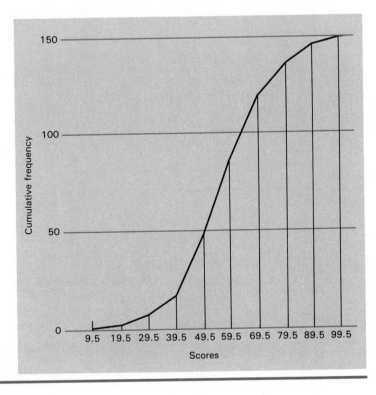

FIGURE 2.6
Ogive of the "or less" distribution of the aptitude scores

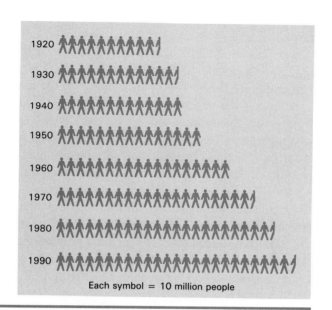

FIGURE 2.7
Pictogram of the population of the United States

Each symbol = 10 million people

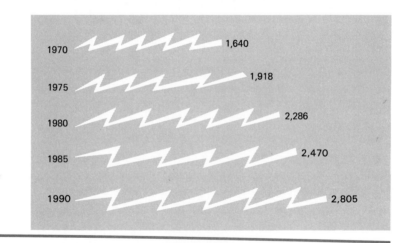

FIGURE 2.8
Electric energy production in the United States (billions of kilowatt-hours)

1970   1,640
1975   1,918
1980   2,286
1985   2,470
1990   2,805

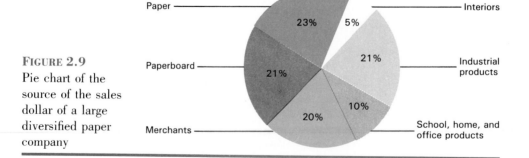

FIGURE 2.9
Pie chart of the source of the sales dollar of a large diversified paper company

Paper — 23%
Interiors — 5%
Industrial products — 21%
School, home, and office products — 10%
Merchants — 20%
Paperboard — 21%

(Exercises 2.17, 2.18, 2.19, 2.20, and 2.22 are practice exercises. Their complete solutions are given on page 39.)

2.17 When a machine in a factory is inoperative because of breakdowns or other difficulties during working hours, the condition is called "downtime." An efficiency expert measures durations of downtimes in minutes. Following is the frequency distribution of 200 downtimes which occurred in a factory during a week.

Time (minutes)	Number of downtimes
10–19	15
20–29	62
30–39	67
40–49	42
50–59	10
60–69	4
Total	200

Draw a histogram of this distribution.

2.18 Convert the distribution of the preceding exercise into a cumulative "less than" distribution and draw its ogive.

2.19 The following are daily numbers of automobiles rented by an automobile rental company in 90 business days.

Automobile rentals	Number of days
20–24	3
25–29	10
30–34	21
35–39	28
40–44	14
45–49	9
50–54	5
Total	90

(a) Draw a histogram of this distribution.

(b) Draw a frequency polygon of this distribution.

2.20 Convert the distribution of the preceding exercise into an "or more" distribution and draw its ogive.

2.21 A **bar chart** is a form of graphical presentation which is very similar to a histogram. In this kind of chart (see Figures 2.10 and 2.11) the heights of the bars are proportional to the class frequencies, but there is no pretense of having a continuous horizontal scale. Draw a bar chart of the distribution of

(a) Exercise 2.17

(b) Exercise 2.19

2.22 Draw a pie chart to display the information that in a recent year the retail shopping center sales in the six New England states were (in billions of dollars) Massachusetts, 13.5; Rhode Island, 2.3; Connecticut, 10.4; Maine, 2.3; New Hampshire, 2.2; and Vermont, 0.9. Total sales for all these states were $31.6 billion.

2.23 Of the $207 million total raised in a major university's fund drive, $117 million came from individuals and bequests, $24 million from industry and business, and $66 million from foundations and associations. Present this information in a pie chart.

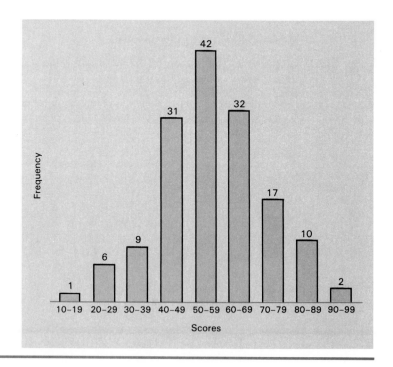

FIGURE 2.10
Bar chart of the distribution of clerical aptitude scores

Chapter 2   Summarizing Data: Frequency Distributions

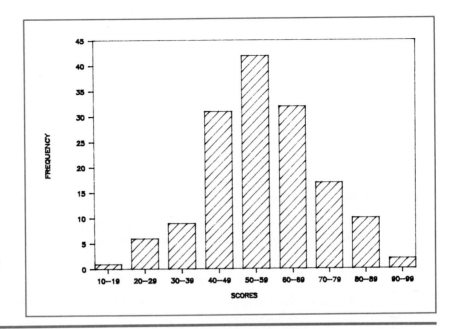

FIGURE 2.11
Computer printout of the bar chart of the distribution of clerical aptitude scores

2.24   With reference to Exercise 2.11 on page 19, present the distribution obtained in that exercise in the form of

(a) a bar chart (see Exercise 2.21)

(b) a pie chart

2.25   Graphs which are used in business reports, scientific reports, or similar presentations often include information such as a title, headnotes, footnotes, and source.

    The title is generally located above the graph and provides answers to three questions: what, where, and when. An example of a complete title is, ''Gold Production in the United States, 1986–1995.'' Another complete title is, ''Canadian Exports, 1993.''

    Headnotes are placed above the graph but below the title, and footnotes are placed below the graph. Headnotes and footnotes provide information which would otherwise not be apparent to the reader. Notes typically contain such comments as ''Not including Alaska and Hawaii''; ''Revised in 1992''; ''Persons of Hispanic origin may be of any race''; or ''Figures may not add due to rounding.'' Headnotes and footnotes may be referenced by numerals such as 1, 2, 3, ...; letters such as a, b, c, ...; or symbols such as * (asterisk or star), † (dagger), or ‡ (double dagger).

    The statement of source is important since the reader may want to identify the person or organization which collected the data. The source is usually found as the last line of material surrounding the graph, although sometimes the source is located directly under the title. Some typical source statements might be "Source: *The Wall Street Journal*, January 16, 1993" or "Source: *Monthly Labor Review*, November 1992, page 17."

    (a) Prepare a complete title for a graph of automobile production during the period 1990 through 1993. The graph is based upon data provided about the U.S. economy by the Federal Reserve Board.

    (b) Provide a hypothetical illustration of a headnote or footnote which might accompany the graph of part (a).

    (c) Why might a reader be interested in knowing the source of the automobile data?

2.26 Use a computer package and the tally of collection letters on page 20 to construct a stem-and-leaf plot with the stem labels 4, 5, 6, 7, and 8.

2.27 Use a computer package and the data of Exercise 2.16(b) to construct a double-stem plot with one-digit leaves.

2.28 Use a computer package to construct a bar chart with the classes 10–19, 20–29, ... , 60–69 from the data of Exercise 2.17.

2.29 Use a computer package and the data of Exercise 2.19 to construct a bar chart of this distribution.

2.4

A Word of Caution

    Intentionally or unintentionally, frequency tables, histograms, and other pictorial presentations are sometimes very misleading. Suppose, for instance, that when we grouped the clerical aptitude scores, we combined the two classes 60–69 and 70–79 into one class, the class 60–79. This new class has a frequency of 49, but in Figure 2.12 where we still use the heights of the rectangles to represent the class frequencies, we get the erroneous impression that this class contains about one-half of the scores (instead of one-third). This is due to the fact that when we compare the sizes of rectangles, triangles, and other plane figures, we instinctively compare their areas and not their sides. This does not matter when the class intervals are equal, but in Figure 2.12 the class 60–79 is twice as wide as the others, and we should compensate for this by dividing the height of the rectangle by 2. Figure 2.13 (where the vertical scale, which has lost its significance, has been omitted) shows the result of this adjustment. Now we get the correct impression that the class 60–79 contains nearly as many items as the two classes 50–59 and

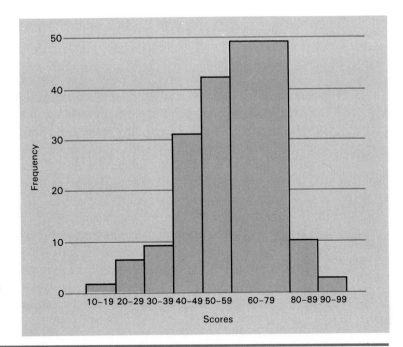

FIGURE 2.12
Incorrectly modified histogram of the distribution of the aptitude scores

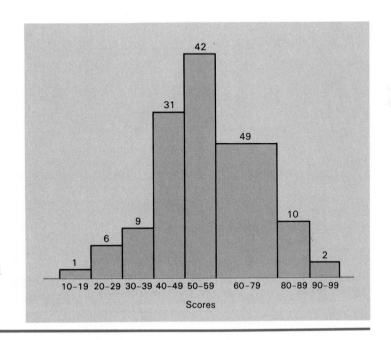

FIGURE 2.13
Correctly modified histogram of the distribution of the aptitude scores

80–89 combined. This is as it should be, since the frequency of the class 60–79 is 49 and the sum of the frequencies of the two classes 50–59 and 80–89 is 42 + 10 = 52.

This same difficulty arises in the construction of pictograms of the sort where the sizes of various objects are intended to illustrate and emphasize differences among the data. Suppose, for instance, we want to dramatize the fact that in a recent month, according to the U.S. Bureau of Labor Statistics, *Employment and Earnings Monthly,* the average hourly wage paid to construction workers was $13.01, while that paid to retail trade workers was $6.31. Since the amount paid to construction workers was about twice that paid to retail trade workers, we might be tempted to draw a picture such as the one in Figure 2.14, where the height and width of the wage dollar paid to construction workers are both twice the height and width of the wage dollar paid to retail trade workers. However, this gives the false impression that hourly wages paid to construction workers were four times as large (instead of two) as those paid to retail trade workers, and objectivity requires that we make the sides of the wage dollar paid to construction workers about $\sqrt{2} =$ 1.4 times or, more precisely, $\sqrt{\dfrac{13.01}{6.31}} = 1.4$ times the corresponding side of the wage dollar paid to retail trade workers, as in Figure 2.15.

Hourly wage dollars paid to retail workers

FIGURE 2.14 Misleading pictogram of average hourly wages paid to retail trade and construction workers

Hourly wage dollars paid to construction workers

Hourly wage dollars paid to retail workers

FIGURE 2.15
Corrected
pictogram of
average hourly
wages paid to retail
trade and
construction
workers

Hourly wage dollars paid to construction workers

2.5

Checklist of Key Terms

2.6

Review Exercises

2.30 The class marks for the ages of sales clerks employed in a department store are 19.5, 29.5, 39.5, 49.5, 59.5, and 69.5. What are the class limits of this distribution?

2.31 The daily numbers of airline tickets sold by a travel agent are grouped into a table with the classes 0–24, 25–49, 50–74, 75–99, and 100 or more. Is it possible to determine from this table the number of days on which there were

(a) at least 25 tickets sold

(b) more than 25 tickets sold

(c) at least 74 tickets sold

(d) at least 75 tickets sold

2.32 The offering prices of 50 yachts offered for sale by a yacht broker vary from $65,900 to $200,000. Write the class limits and also the class boundaries of a distribution with eight equal classes into which these prices might be grouped.

2.33 *Lot-for-lot ordering* is the simplest deterministic inventory ordering model. In this model items are purchased from a supplier (say, a wholesaler) in the exact amounts required for each time period. It is well suited for inventory items of high value or with a discontinuous demand. One hundred consecutive weekly purchases of diamond rings are made by a retail jeweler from a wholesaler to replenish the inventory sold to customers during the preceding week. The number of rings are

44	35	34	25	41	66	50	38	45	41
40	43	49	31	44	52	55	45	51	63
33	68	27	30	58	62	45	52	12	72
49	38	66	64	60	41	30	65	46	35
70	54	43	64	24	25	52	42	53	22
23	35	51	43	11	58	75	50	67	51
32	57	24	43	35	37	42	58	42	59
25	37	40	28	60	31	64	72	48	16
26	57	33	18	46	69	74	39	26	55
78	40	50	46	47	36	29	47	63	55

(a) Group these figures into a distribution having the classes 10–19, 20–29, 30–39, 40–49, 50–59, 60–69, and 70–79 rings.

(b) Draw a histogram of the distribution of part (a).

2.34 Convert the distribution of part (a) of the preceding exercise into a cumulative "less than" distribution and draw its ogive.

2.35 The daily number of photocopies made in an office are grouped into a table having the classes 0–49, 50–99, 100–149, and 150–199. Find

(a) the class boundaries

(b) the class marks

(c) the class interval

2.36 A newspaper company has grouped its daily number of classified advertisements printed into a table having the class boundaries 499.5–999.5, 999.5–1,499.5, 1,499.5–1,999.5, and 1,999.5–2,499.5. Find

(a) the corresponding class limits

(b) the class marks

(c) the class interval

2.37 The following are the shipping weights, in pounds, of 60 supposedly identical office desks.

Shipping weight	Number of desks
98– 98.9	8
99– 99.9	23
100–100.9	14
101–101.9	13
102–102.9	2

Draw a histogram of this distribution.

2.38 Convert the distribution of the preceding exercise into a cumulative "or more" distribution and draw its ogive.

2.39 To group data on the number of ships departing from a certain port for the month of July during the last 50 years, a harbor master uses the classes 0–5, 6–10, 12–17, 18–23, and 23–30. Explain where difficulties might arise.

2.40 The deadweight tonnage of the nonmilitary oceangoing merchant ships of the world is 602 million (deadweight tonnage is the carrying capacity of a ship in long tons of 2,240 pounds) and consists of the following types of ships: freighters, 118 million; bulk carriers, 228 million; and tankers, 256 million deadweight tons. Present this information in a pie chart.

2.41 A videotape rental company classifies its movies as comedy, special interest, drama, science fiction, horror, and action/adventure. A list of 50 movies rented to customers on a certain day shows that these movies are in the following categories: drama, drama, special interest, drama, drama, horror, comedy, comedy, special interest, action/adventure, action/adventure, drama, drama, horror, drama, horror, drama, drama, comedy, comedy, comedy, comedy, drama, horror, horror, comedy, action/adventure, drama, drama, action/adventure, science fiction, special interest, drama, action/adventure, drama, comedy, science fiction, science fiction, science fiction, comedy, action/adventure, horror, science fiction, comedy, drama, special interest, action/adventure, action/adventure, drama, and horror. Construct a categorical distribution showing the frequencies corresponding to the various movies which were rented, and present it pictorially in the form of a pie chart.

2.42 The pictogram of Figure 2.16 is intended to illustrate the fact that assets of mutual funds in the United States nearly tripled (actually increased 2.9 times) from 1984, when they were in the amount of $371 billion, to 1990, when they were in the amount of $1,069 billion.

(a) How should the pictogram be modified to convey a fair impression of the actual change?

(b) Suppose the assets of mutual funds had quadrupled during this period. How should the pictogram be modified to convey a fair impression of this change?

2.43 Following is a distribution of the number of hours billed during a week to 100 clients of an office cleaning service company.

Hours worked	Number of clients
0– 9	6
10–19	7
20–29	12
30–39	14
40–49	22
50–59	15
60–69	9
70–79	6
80–89	5
90–99	4

(a) Draw a histogram of this distribution.

(b) Draw a histogram of the modified distribution obtained by combining the classes 30–39, 40–49, 50–59 into one class.

2.44 The time required to complete a speed skating race is given to the nearest hundredth of a second, and the completion times of the contestants are grouped into a table whose classes have the boundaries 2:53.995, 2:54.995, 2:55.995, 2:56.995, 2:57.995, 2:58.995, 2:59.995, and 3:00.995 (where 2:53.995 is 2 minutes and 53.995 seconds). What are the lower and upper limits of each class?

 2.45 Use a computer package and the data of Exercise 2.23 to construct a pie chart of the distribution.

FIGURE 2.16
Value of assets held by U.S. mutual funds, 1984 and 1990

$370.7 billion
(1984)

$1,069.1 billion
(1990)

 2.46 Use a computer package and the data of Exercise 2.22 to construct a pie chart of retail shopping center sales in six New England states (in billions of dollars).

2.7

Solutions of Practice Exercises

2.1 The number of tolls paid varies from 1,380 to 9,990, and the difference between them is $9,990 - 1,380 = 8,610$. Each of the nine classes must, therefore, include $\frac{8,610}{9} = 956.7$ or more tolls. This suggests that we round up to 1,000. This is a multiple with which it is convenient to work. One possible set of class limits is therefore 1,000–1,999, 2,000–2,999, 3,000–3,999, 4,000–4,999, 5,000–5,999, 6,000–6,999, 7,000–7,999, 8,000–8,999, and 9,000–9,999.

2.2 (a) yes, (b) no, (c) no, (d) yes

2.3 (a) Deduct 0.005 from the lower limit of each class and add 0.005 to the upper limit of each class. The class boundaries are -0.005, 19.995, 39.995, 59.995, and 79.995. The upper boundary of each lower class is the same value as the lower boundary of the next higher class.

(b) Using class boundaries for calculations, the class marks are
$$\frac{-0.005 + 19.995}{2} = 9.995, \quad \frac{19.995 + 39.995}{2} = 29.995,$$

$$\frac{39.995 + 59.995}{2} = 49.995, \text{ and } \frac{59.995 + 79.995}{2} = 69.995. \text{ The same}$$

answers can be obtained using class limits for calculations and are
$$\frac{0.00 + 19.99}{2} = 9.995, \quad \frac{20.00 + 39.99}{2} = 29.995, \quad \frac{40.00 + 59.99}{2}$$

$$= 49.995, \text{ and } \frac{60.00 + 79.99}{2} = 69.995.$$

(c) Subtract the lower boundary of each class from the upper boundary of the class to obtain the class interval. In the largest class, for example, $79.995 - 59.995 = 20.000$. Performing the same calculation for each class, we find that all of the class intervals equal 20.000.

2.4 (a) The boundary between the first two classes is $\dfrac{10.5 + 18.5}{2} = 14.5$, be-

tween the second and third class is $\dfrac{18.5 + 26.5}{2} = 22.5$, between the

third and fourth class is $\dfrac{26.5 + 34.5}{2} = 30.5$, and between the fourth

and fifth class is $\dfrac{34.5 + 42.5}{2} = 38.5$. Since the difference between

successive boundaries is, say, $22.5 - 14.5 = 8.0$, the lower boundary of the first class is $14.5 - 8 = 6.5$ and the upper boundary of the fifth class is $38.5 + 8.0 = 46.5$

(b) Add 0.5 to the lower boundary and subtract 0.5 from the upper boundary to obtain the class limits for each class. The class limits are 7–14, 15–22, 23–30, 31–38, and 39–46.

2.12

30	9 2
31	5 0 6
32	0 5 7
33	3 0 0 0 0
34	1

2.16 (a)

21*	0
21•	6 5
22*	4 1 3 2
22•	8 9 8
23*	0 3 1 0 0

(b)

2•	8 9
3*	0 4 1 1 1 3
3•	7 6 7 8 9 8 6 7 5
4*	1 1 4 4 0 1 0 3 3
4•	6 7 9 6 6

```
23•   5 5 6 7              5*   2 0 1
24*   0 4 0 4             5•   6
24•   9 5
25*   2 3
25•   6 5
26*
26•   9
```

2.17 Histogram of 200 downtimes.

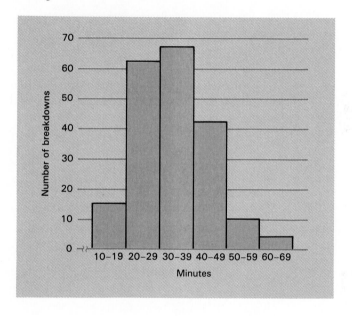

2.18

Time (minutes)	Number of breakdowns
Less than 10	0
Less than 20	15
Less than 30	77
Less than 40	144
Less than 50	186
Less than 60	196
Less than 70	200

Ogive of the cumulative "less than" distribution of 200 breakdowns.

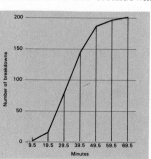

Section 2.7 Solutions of Practice Exercises   **41**

2.19 (a) Histogram of the distribution of the daily number of automobiles rented by an automobile company in 90 business days.

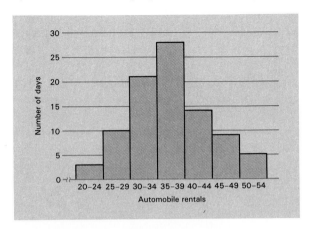

(b) Frequency polygon of the distribution of the daily number of automobiles rented by an automobile company in 90 business days.

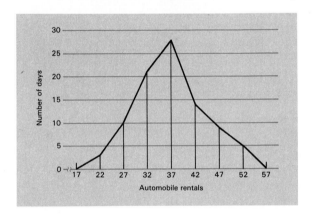

2.20

Automobile rentals	Number of days
20 or more	90
25 or more	87
30 or more	77
35 or more	56
40 or more	28
45 or more	14
50 or more	5
55 or more	0

Chapter 2   Summarizing Data: Frequency Distributions

Ogive of the cumulative distribution of the number of days and the corresponding volume of automobile rentals.

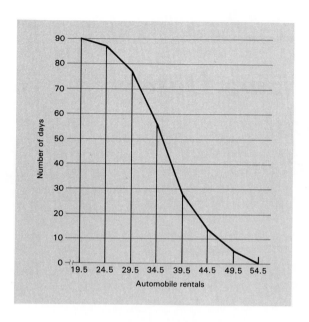

2.22 The central angles are 153.8°, 26.2°, 118.5°, 26.2°, 25.1°, and 10.2°.

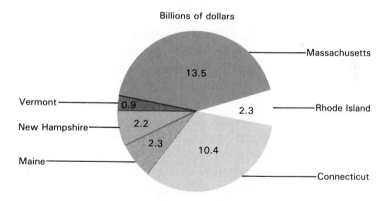

Summarizing Data: Statistical Descriptions

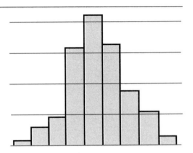

Descriptions of statistical data can be quite brief or quite elaborate, depending on what we intend to do with them. In any event, when we describe collections of data we try to say neither too little nor too much. On some occasions it may be satisfactory to present data just as they are, in raw form, and let them speak for themselves; on others, it may be necessary only to group a set of data and present its distribution in tabular or graphical form. Usually, though, data have to be summarized further by means of appropriate statistical descriptions, and in this chapter we shall concentrate on two special kinds of descriptive measures, called **measures of location** and **measures of variation**. The former are discussed in Sections 3.2 and 3.3, and the latter in Sections 3.5 and 3.6. The description of **grouped data** is treated in Section 3.8 and some further kinds of descriptions are presented in Section 3.9.

3.1

Populations and Samples

Before we study specific statistical descriptions, let us define the terms "population" and "sample." If a set of data consists of all conceivably possible (or hypothetically possible) observations of a certain phenomenon, we call it a **population**; if a set of data contains only a part of these observations, we call it a **sample**. We added the qualification "hypothetically possible" in the first definition to take care of such clearly hypothetical situations as where we look at the outcomes (heads or tails) of 10 tosses of a coin as a sample from the population which consists of all possible tosses of the coin, or where we look at five measurements of the length of a steel shaft as a sample from the population of all possible measurements of its length. In fact, we often look at the results of an experiment as a sample of what we would see if the experiment were repeated over and over again.

Although we are free to call any group of items a population, what we do in practice depends on the context in which the items are to be viewed. Suppose, for instance, that we are offered a lot of 500 ceramic tiles, which we may or may not buy depending on their strength. If we measure the breaking strength of 10 of these tiles in order to estimate the average breaking strength of all the tiles, these 10 measurements constitute a sample from the population which consists of the breaking strengths of all the tiles. Denoting the number of items in a finite population, the **population size**, by the letter N, and the number of items in a sample, the **sample size**, by the letter n, we could thus say that we have a sample of size $n = 10$ drawn from a population of $N = 500$. In another context, however, if we were considering entering into a long-term contract calling for the delivery of tens of thousands of such tiles, we would look upon the breaking strengths of the original 500 tiles only as a sample. Similarly, the complete set of figures for a recent year, giving the elapsed time between the application and the issuance of residential building permits in Atlanta, can be looked on as either a population or a sample. If we were interested only in the city of Atlanta and that particular year, we would consider these data to constitute a population; on the other hand, if we wanted to generalize about the time required for the issuance of residential building permits in the entire United States, in some other large cities, or in some other years, these data would constitute only a sample.

As we have used it here, the word "sample" has very much the same meaning as it has in everyday language. A newspaper considers the attitudes of 100 readers toward a proposed city-county sports complex to be a sample of the attitudes of all its readers toward the complex; and a homemaker considers a trial-size box of a new heavy-duty laundry detergent a sample of all the boxes of this detergent. Later, we shall use the word "sample" to refer only to sets of data which can reasonably serve as the basis for valid generalizations about the populations from which they came, and in this more technical sense many sets of data which are popularly called samples are not samples at all.

In this chapter we shall describe things statistically, but not make any generalizations. For future reference, though, it is important even here to distinguish between populations and samples. Thus, we shall use different symbols depending on whether we are describing populations or samples, and sometimes even different formulas.

3.2

Measures of Location: The Mean, the Median, and the Mode

It is often necessary to represent a set of data in terms of a single number which, in its way, is descriptive of the entire set. Exactly what sort of number we choose depends on the particular characteristic we want to describe. In one study, for example, we might be interested in the extreme (smallest and largest) values among the data; in another, in the value which is exceeded by only 10 percent of the values; and in still another, in the total of all the values. In this section, we shall consider those measures which somehow describe the center or middle of a set of data—the **measures of central location**.

Of the different measures of central location, by far the best known and the most widely used is the **arithmetic mean**, or simply the **mean**, which we define as follows:

The mean of n values is the sum of the values divided by n.

In everyday speech this value is often called the "average," and on occasion we shall call it that ourselves. But, as we shall see, there are other "averages" in statistics, and we cannot afford to speak loosely when there is any danger of ambiguity.

EXAMPLE 3.1 Given that during the 12 months of 1991 a state auditor charged 5, 2, 1, 3, 3, 8, 6, 7, 4, 1, 2, and 6 calls to her telephone credit card, find the mean, that is, the average number of charges per month.

SOLUTION The total for the 12 months is $5 + 2 + 1 + 3 + 3 + 8 + 6 + 7 + 4 + 1 + 2 + 6 = 48$, and therefore,

$$\text{mean} = \frac{48}{12} = 4 \qquad \blacksquare$$

Since we shall have occasion to calculate the means of many different sets of sample data, it will be convenient to have a simple formula that is always applicable. This requires that we represent the figures to be averaged by some general symbol such as x, y, or z. Choosing the letter x, we can refer to the n values in a sample as x_1 ("x sub one"), x_2, x_3, . . . , and x_n and write

$$\text{sample mean} = \frac{x_1 + x_2 + x_3 + \cdots + x_n}{n}$$

This formula is perfectly general, and it will take care of any set of sample data, but it can be made more compact by assigning the sample mean the special symbol $\bar{x}$ ("x bar") and using the Σ (Greek capital sigma) notation. In this notation we let Σx stand for "the sum of the x's," that is, for $x_1 + x_2 + x_3 + \ldots + x_n$. Thus, the mean, $\bar{x}$, of a set of sample values x_1, x_2, x_3, . . . , and x_n is given by the formula

Sample mean

$$\bar{x} = \frac{\Sigma x}{n}$$

If we refer to the measurements as y's or z's, we write their mean as $\bar{y}$ or $\bar{z}$. In the preceding formula, the term Σx does not state explicitly which values of x are to be added; let it be understood, however, that Σx always refers to the sum of all the x's under consideration. In the technical note of Section 3.10, the **sigma notation** is discussed in more detail.

The mean of population of N items is defined in the same way. It is the sum of the N items, $x_1 + x_2 + x_3 + \cdots + x_N$, or Σx, divided by N. Giving the population mean the special symbol μ where μ, or mu, is the Greek letter for lowercase "m", we write

Population mean

$$\mu = \frac{\sum x}{N}$$

with the reminder that in this formula $\sum x$ is now the sum of all N values of x which constitute the population. Also, to distinguish between descriptions of populations and descriptions of samples, statisticians not only use different symbols such as μ and $\bar{x}$, but they refer to descriptions of populations as **parameters** and descriptions of samples as **statistics**. Parameters are usually denoted by Greek letters.

The terminology and notation introduced here is illustrated by the following example:

EXAMPLE 3.2   A sample of $n = 5$ high-precision spring-driven motors is taken from a production lot of $N = 100,000$ such motors. The motors are wound and started, and their running times clocked at 3.50, 3.65, 3.55, 3.58, and 3.52 minutes. Find their mean running time.

SOLUTION   Substituting into the formula for $\bar{x}$, we have

$$\bar{x} = \frac{\sum x}{n} = \frac{3.50 + 3.65 + 3.55 + 3.58 + 3.52}{5} = 3.56 \text{ minutes}$$

and if these times constitute a sample in the technical sense (that is, a set of data from which valid generalizations can be made), we can estimate the mean running time μ of all the 100,000 motors as 3.56 minutes. Moreover, if the sample is a particular kind of sample called a "random sample," we can apply techniques we shall study later and say that we are reasonably sure that this estimate is in error by at most 0.073 minute (or about 4.4 seconds).   ■

The widespread use of the mean to describe the "middle" of a set of data is not accidental. Aside from the fact that it is a simple, familiar measure, the mean has the following desirable properties:

1. It can be calculated for any set of numerical data, so it always exists.

2. A set of numerical data has one and only one mean, so it is always unique.

3. It lends itself to further statistical treatment (for instance, the means of several sets of data can be combined into the overall mean of all the data).

4. It is relatively reliable in the sense that the means of many samples drawn from the same population usually do not fluctuate, or vary, as widely as other statistics used to estimate the population mean μ.

The fourth property is of fundamental importance in statistical inference.

There is another characteristic of the mean which, on the surface, seems desirable but may not be so:

5. It takes into account every item of the data.

However, samples sometimes contain very small or very large values which are so far removed from the main body of the data that the appropriateness of including them in the samples is questionable. When such values, called **outliers**, are averaged in with the other values, they can affect the mean to such an extent that its worth as a reasonable description of the "middle" of the data becomes debatable.

EXAMPLE 3.3   Five light bulbs burned out after lasting for 867, 849, 840, 852, and 822 hours of continuous use. Find the mean and also determine what the mean would be if the second value is recorded incorrectly as 489 instead of 849.

SOLUTION   For the original data we get

$$\bar{x} = \frac{867 + 849 + 840 + 852 + 822}{5} = \frac{4,230}{5} = 846$$

and with 489 instead of 849 we get

$$\bar{x} = \frac{867 + 489 + 840 + 852 + 822}{5} = \frac{3,870}{5} = 774$$

This illustrates how a careless error in recording a set of data can have a pronounced effect on the mean.   ■

Outliers resulting from such things as gross errors in recording data, gross errors in calculations, malfunctioning of equipment, or contamination can sometimes be identified as to their source and simply eliminated from the data before they are averaged. However, instead of omitting outliers and calculating a sort of **modified mean** in an attempt to avoid this difficulty, we can use another measure of location, called the **median**, to describe the "middle" of the data. Unlike the mean, the median is not easily affected by extreme values. By definition,

The median of a set of data is the value of the middle item (or the mean of the values of the two middle items) when the data are arrayed or ordered, that is, arranged in an increasing or decreasing order of magnitude.

Like the mean of a sample of n values of x, the **sample median**, which we denote $\tilde{x}$, can be used to estimate the population mean; in fact, this accounts for our main interest in this statistical measure.

If there is an odd number of items in a set of data, there is always a middle item whose value is the median.

EXAMPLE 3.4   Eleven large corporations reported that in 1992 they made cash donations to 9, 16, 11, 19, 11, 10, 13, 12, 6, 9, and 12 colleges. Find the median number of donations.

SOLUTION   Arranging these figures according to size, we get

$$6 \quad 9 \quad 9 \quad 10 \quad 11 \quad 11 \quad 12 \quad 12 \quad 13 \quad 16 \quad 19$$

and it can be seen that the median is 11.   ■

Generally speaking, the median of a set of n items, where n is odd, is the value of $\frac{n+1}{2}$th largest item. For instance, the median of 35 numbers is the value of the $\frac{35+1}{2} = 18$th largest item, and the median of 199 numbers is the value of the $\frac{199+1}{2} = 100$th largest item.

For a set of data containing an even number of items, there is no single middle item, and the median is defined as the mean of the values of the two middle items, but the formula $\frac{n+1}{2}$ still serves to locate the position of the median. For instance, for $n = 12$ we get $\frac{12+1}{2} = 6.5$, and the median is the mean of the values of the 6th and 7th largest items; also, for $n = 50$ we get $\frac{50+1}{2} = 25.5$, and the median is the mean of the values of the 25th and 26th largest items.

EXAMPLE 3.5   On 10 days, a bank had 18, 13, 15, 12, 8, 3, 7, 14, 16, and 3 foreign currency transactions. Find the median.

SOLUTION   Arranging these figures according to size, we get

3   3   7   8   12   13   14   15   16   18

and it can be seen that the median is 12.5, the mean of 12 and 13.   ∎

The mean of the numbers in this example is 10.9, and it should not come as a surprise that it differs from the median, which is 12.5. Each of these averages describes the middle of the data in its own way. The median is typical (central or average) in the sense that it splits the data into two parts so that the values of half the items are less than or equal to the median, and the values of the other half are greater than or equal to the median. The mean, on the other hand, is typical in the sense that if all the values were the same size (but their total is the same), they would all be equal to the mean. (Since $\bar{x} = \frac{\Sigma x}{n}$, it follows that $n \cdot \bar{x} = \Sigma x$ and, hence, that n values, each of size $\bar{x}$, have the same total as the actual n values of x.)

Like the mean, the median always exists and is unique for any set of data. It can also be used to define the middle of a number of objects, properties, or qualities which are not really quantitative in nature. For instance, we can rank a number of tasks according to their difficulty and then describe the middle (or median) one as being of "typical" difficulty. On the less desirable side, ordering large sets of data manually can be a very tedious job, and what is more serious from the standpoint of statistical inference, a sample median is usually not so reliable an estimate of the population mean as the (arithmetic) mean of the same data. The medians of many samples drawn from the same population usually vary more widely than the corresponding sample means.

The median may also be obtained from a **stem-and-leaf plot**.

EXAMPLE 3.6   Following are the numbers of packages mailed by a small mail-order company on 25 consecutive business days: 79, 39, 48, 85, 50, 56, 43, 31, 65, 61, 93, 68, 40, 48, 72, 25, 52, 54, 67, 55, 51, 47, 30, 74, and 42. Construct a stem-and-leaf plot with one-digit leaves and use it to find the median. Each line of the display is a **stem** and each piece of information on it is a **leaf**. In this case the tens digits are the **starting parts** of the lines and the units digits are the leaves.

SOLUTION   First constructing the stem-and-leaf plot, we get

```
2 | 5
3 | 9  1  0
4 | 8  3  0  8  7  2
5 | 0  6  2  4  5  1
6 | 5  1  8  7
7 | 9  2  4
8 | 5
9 | 3
```

Since the position of the median is $\dfrac{25 + 1}{2} = 13$ and 10 of the values fall on the first three stems, we must find the third smallest value on the fourth stem. As can be seen by inspection, it is 52. ∎

Another measure which is sometimes used to describe the center of a set of data is the **mode**, which is defined simply as the value that occurs with the highest frequency greater than 1. Its two main advantages are that it requires no calculations, only counting, and that it can be determined for qualitative as well as quantitative data.

EXAMPLE 3.7   The 12 sessions of a seminar in personal financial planning were attended by 22, 16, 20, 20, 15, 16, 12, 14, 16, 14, 11, and 16 persons. Find the mode.

SOLUTION   Among these numbers 22, 15, 12, and 11 occur once, 20 and 14 occur twice, and 16 occurs four times. Thus, 16 is the modal attendance, or the mode. ∎

Aside from the fact that the mode is an extremely poor measure of location in statistical inference, it also has the disadvantage that for some sets of data it may not exist and for others it may not be unique. For instance, there is no mode of the ages 19, 23, 29, 31, 25, and 22 (which are all different), and there are two modes, 9 and 14, of the dress sizes 7, 10, 14, 9, 9, 14, 9, 18, 16, 12, 11, 14, 14, 14, 9, 20, 9, and 11. The fact that a set of data has more than one mode (or is **bimodal**) is sometimes indicative of a lack of homogeneity in the data. For instance, the two modes of the dress sizes are accounted for by the fact that they are the sizes worn by nine mothers and their teenaged daughters.

Besides the mean, the median, and the mode, there are various other measures which describe in some way the middle or the center of a set of data. In addition to the **weighted mean** discussed in Section 3.3, there are the **geometric** and **harmonic means** given in Exercises 3.23 and 3.24 on page 63 and the **midrange**, which is mentioned on page 97.

The median is but one of many **fractiles** which divide data into two or more parts, as nearly equal as they can be made. Among them we also find **quartiles**, **deciles**, and **percentiles**, which are intended to divide data into four, ten, and a hundred parts. Until recently, fractiles were determined mainly for distributions of large sets of data, and in this connection we shall study them in Section 3.8.

We shall concern ourselves here mainly with a problem which has arisen in **exploratory data analysis**[1]—in the preliminary analysis of relatively small sets of data. It is the problem of dividing such data into four nearly equal parts, where we say "nearly equal" because there is no way in which we can divide a set of data into four equal parts for, say, $n = 27$ or $n = 33$. Statistical measures designed for this purpose have traditionally been referred to as the three **quartiles**, Q_1, Q_2, Q_3, and there is no argument about Q_2, which is simply the median. On the other hand, there is ample room for arbitrariness in the definition of Q_1 and Q_3.[2]

The following are some of the desirable properties we would like the quartiles Q_1 and Q_3 to have:

1. Q_1 is exceeded by three times as many values as it exceeds, and it is the other way around for Q_3.

2. There are as many values less than Q_1 as there are between Q_1 and Q_2, between Q_2 and Q_3, and greater than Q_3.

3. Half the data fall between Q_1 and Q_3.

It is assumed here that no two values are alike; otherwise, the wording would have to be changed as indicated on page 57.

To illustrate, consider the number of runs scored by the twelve baseball teams of the National League during the year 1990:

---

[1]Adapted from J. E. Freund and G. A. Simon, *Modern Elementary Statistics*, 8th ed. (Englewood Cliffs, N.J.: Prentice-Hall, Inc., 1992).

[2]A more complete discussion with several methods for calculation of fractiles may be found in J. E. Freund and B. M. Perles, "A New Look at Quartiles of Ungrouped Data," *The American Statistician*, Vol. 41, No. 3 (August 1987).

Team	Number of runs
Atlanta	682
Chicago	690
Cincinnati	693
Houston	573
Los Angeles	728
Montreal	662
New York	775
Philadelphia	646
Pittsburgh	733
San Diego	673
San Francisco	719
St. Louis	599

Arranging these figures according to size we get 573, 599, 646, 662, 673, 682, 690, 693, 719, 728, 733, and 775, and it can be seen that the dashed lines in the upper part of Figure 3.1 divide the data into four equal parts. If we let the midpoints between 646 and 662, 682 and 690, and 719 and 728 be the quartiles, we get $Q_1 = \dfrac{646 + 662}{2} = 654.0$, $Q_2 = \dfrac{682 + 690}{2} = 686.0$, and $Q_3 = \dfrac{719 + 728}{2} = 723.5$. Of course, Q_2 is also the median, and

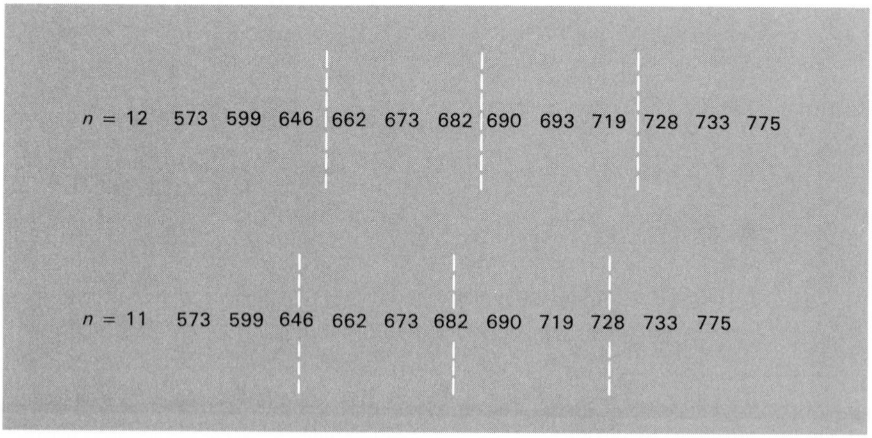

FIGURE 3.1 Quartiles for number of runs scored by baseball teams of National League, with and without pennant-winning team

Chapter 3   Summarizing Data: Statistical Descriptions

it can easily be verified that all three of the desirable properties listed for the quartiles are satisfied.

Everything worked nicely in this example because 12, the sample size, happened to be a multiple of 4. What can we do, though, when this is not the case? Suppose, for instance, that we did not want to include the pennant-winning Cincinnati baseball team, so that we were left with the following 11 numbers arranged according to size:

573   599   646   662   673   682   690   719   728   733   775

The median, or Q_2, is now 682, but what can we do about the other two dividing lines? If it is felt that the second of the three properties listed on page 53 is most relevant, the dividing lines can be drawn as in the lower part of Figure 3.1, so that $Q_1 = 646$, $Q_2 = 682$, and $Q_3 = 728$.

There are 2 values less than Q_1, two values between Q_1 and Q_2, two values between Q_2 and Q_3, and two values greater than Q_3; but Q_1 is exceeded by four times as many values as it exceeds and only 5 of the 11 values fall between Q_1 and Q_3.

In exploratory data analysis we look at the process of finding values which divide a set of data into four parts in a different way—as a process of folding. With reference to the first of our two examples, where the sample size was 12, suppose that in the upper part of Figure 3.1, or that of Figure 3.2, we fold the page along the dashed line on the left, along the dashed line on the right, and then along the dashed line in the middle. If we do this, the four parts into which we have divided the data will overlap. If we do this for our second example, where the sample size was 11, the four parts will not overlap if we fold the page along the dashed lines in the lower part of Figure 3.1.

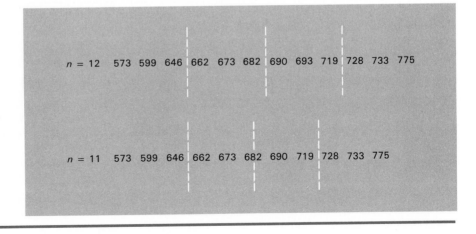

$n = 12$ 573   599   646   662   673   682   690   693   719   728   733   775

$n = 11$ 573   599   646   662   673   682   690   719   728   733   775

FIGURE 3.2
Hinges for number of runs scored by baseball teams of National League, with and without pennant-winning team

However, they will overlap if we move the dashed lines as in the lower part of Figure 3.2. The new dividing lines on the left and on the right are at the midpoints between 646 and 662, and 719 and 728, and we could write $Q_1 = \dfrac{646 + 662}{2} = 654.0$ and $Q_3 = \dfrac{719 + 728}{2} = 723.5$. Actually in exploratory data analysis these two values are referred to as **hinges**—the **lower hinge** is 654.0 and the **upper hinge** is 723.5. This terminology reflects the process of folding, which is used to divide the data into four parts.

Having introduced the concept of a hinge by means of an example, let us now give a formal definition. Assuming that no two values are alike (but see page 57), we write

> **The lower hinge is the median of all the values less than or equal to the median of the whole set of data; the upper hinge is the median of all the values greater than or equal to the median of the whole set of data.**

In practice we first find the position of one hinge, and then count as many places from the other end to find the position of the other hinge.

EXAMPLE 3.8   Nine furniture companies are listed among the *Fortune* 500 in 1991. This is a list of the 500 largest industrial corporations in the United States from *Fortune*, April 22, 1991. The following are the sales (in millions of dollars) of these nine companies for the year 1990.

Furniture company	Sales (millions of dollars)
HON Industries	668
INTERCO	2,224
Johnson Controls	4,515
Kimball International	620
La-Z-Boy Chair	595
Lear Seating	1,068
Leggett & Platt	1,089
Miller (Herman)	869
Sealy Holdings	642

Find the median and the two hinges.

SOLUTION   For $n = 9$ the median position is $\dfrac{9 + 1}{2} = 5$. Thus, the position of the lower hinge is $\dfrac{5 + 1}{2} = 3$, and the upper hinge is the third value from the other end. Arranging data according to size, we get (in millions)

595,   620,   642,   668,   869,   1,068,   1,089   2,224   4,515

and it can be seen that the lower hinge is 642, the median is 869, and the upper hinge is 1,089. Also, if we imagine dashed lines drawn through these values as in figure 3.2, we find that the four parts will, indeed, overlap.   ∎

If some of the values are alike, we may have to modify the definition of the hinges by replacing "less than or equal to the median" by "to the left of or at the median position" and "greater than or equal to the median" by "to the right of or at the median position." Otherwise, the procedure is exactly the same. For instance, in a certain restaurant the waiting time of patrons at nine tables before a waiter or waitress took their orders was 3, 3, 3, 3, 4, 4, 4, 4, and 5 minutes. Since the sample size is the same as in the preceding example, we find that the lower hinge, the third value, is 3; the median, the fifth value is 4; and the upper hinge, the third value from the right is 4.

Quartiles and hinges are not intended to be descriptive of the "middle" or "center" of a set of data, and we have given them here mainly because, like the median, they are fractiles and they are determined in more or less the same way. The midquartile, $\dfrac{Q_1 + Q_3}{2}$, has been used on occasion as a measure of central location, and presumably the mean of the two hinges could be used in the same way.

3.3

Measures of Location: The Weighted Mean

In averaging quantities it is often necessary to account for the fact that not all of them are equally important in the phenomenon being described. For instance, if a person makes three investments which return 7, 8, and 9 percent, the average return is $\dfrac{7 + 8 + 9}{3} = 8$ percent only if the person puts the same amount in each of the investments. In order to give quantities being averaged their proper degree of importance, it is necessary to assign them (relative importance) **weights**, and then calculate a **weighted mean**. In general, the weighted mean $\bar{x}_w$ of a set of numbers $x_1, x_2, x_3, \ldots$, and x_n, whose relative importance is expressed numerically by a corresponding set of numbers $w_1, w_2, w_3, \ldots$, and w_n, is given by

Weighted mean

$$\bar{x}_w = \frac{w_1 x_1 + w_2 x_2 + \cdots + w_n x_n}{w_1 + w_2 + \cdots + w_n} = \frac{\Sigma w \cdot x}{\Sigma w}$$

If all the weights are equal, this formula reduces to that of the ordinary (arithmetic) mean.

EXAMPLE 3.9   In the year 1989, corn, wheat, oats, barley, and soybeans brought average prices of 2.33, 3.72, 1.49, 2.42, and 5.60 dollars per bushel. Production of these crops in the United States was 7.53, 2.04, 0.37, 0.40, and 1.93 billions of bushels, respectively. What is the average price per bushel of these crops?

SOLUTION   Substituting $x_1 = 2.33$, $x_2 = 3.72$, $x_3 = 1.49$, $x_4 = 2.42$, and $x_5 = 5.60$, $w_1 = 7.53$, $w_2 = 2.04$, $w_3 = 0.37$, $w_4 = 0.40$, and $w_5 = 1.93$ into the formula for $\bar{x}_w$, we get

$$\bar{x}_w = \frac{7.53(2.33) + 2.04(3.72) + 0.37(1.49) + 0.40(2.42) + 1.93(5.60)}{7.53 + 2.04 + 0.37 + 0.40 + 1.93}$$

$$= \frac{37.461}{12.27} = \$3.05 \text{ per bushel}$$

The figure in the denominator, 12.27, is the total crop for the year 1989 in billions of bushels, and the figure in the numerator, 37.461, is the total value of the 1989 crop in billions of dollars. Also, if we average 2.33, 3.72, 1.49, 2.42, and 5.60 without using weights, we get

$$\bar{x} = \frac{2.33 + 3.72 + 1.49 + 2.42 + 5.60}{5} = \$3.11 \text{ per bushel}$$

In this example the difference between the weighted mean of $3.05 and the unweighted mean of $3.11 is relatively small. In many problems, however, the difference between the weighted and unweighted means can be very large, for reasons which should be apparent. ■

A special application of the formula for the weighted mean arises when we must find the overall mean, or **grand mean**, of k sets of data having the means $\bar{x}_1, \bar{x}_2, \bar{x}_3, \ldots$, and $\bar{x}_k$ and consisting of $n_1, n_2, n_3, \ldots$, and n_k measurements or observations. The result is given by

Grand mean of combined data

$$\bar{\bar{x}} = \frac{n_1\bar{x}_1 + n_2\bar{x}_2 + \cdots + n_k\bar{x}_k}{n_1 + n_2 + \cdots + n_k} = \frac{\Sigma n \cdot \bar{x}}{\Sigma n}$$

where the weights are the sizes of the samples, the numerator is the total of all the measurements or observations, and the denominator is the number of items in the combined samples.

EXAMPLE 3.10   In three separate weeks a discount store chain sold 475, 310, and 420 microwave ovens at average prices of \$490, \$520, and \$495. What is the average price of the ovens sold?

SOLUTION   Substituting $n_1 = 475$, $n_2 = 310$, $n_3 = 420$, $\bar{x}_1 = 490$, $\bar{x}_2 = 520$, and $\bar{x}_3 = 495$ into the formula for the grand mean of the combined data, we get

$$\bar{\bar{x}} = \frac{475(490) + 310(520) + 420(495)}{475 + 310 + 420}$$

$$= \frac{601,850}{1,205}$$

$$= \$499.46$$

or \$499 rounded to the nearest dollar. ■

EXERCISES

(Exercises 3.2, 3.3, 3.5, 3.7, 3.9, 3.10, 3.14, 3.15, 3.18, 3.22, 3.23, and 3.24 are practice exercises. Their complete solutions are given on page 106.)

3.1   Suppose that we are given complete information about the number of fires fought by a fire department in a certain month. These include 352 Class A fires (which involve combustible materials such as wood, paper, or coal), 38 class B fires (which involve flammable liquids such as gasoline, grease, or wax), and 21 Class C fires (which involve electrical fires as in electrical motors or wiring). Give an example of a problem in which we might consider these data to constitute

(a) a population

(b) a sample

3.2 Suppose we have the shoe sizes of all soldiers in an infantry company of the U.S. Army. Give an example of a situation in which the data might be looked upon as

(a) a population

(b) a sample

3.3 Following are the daily numbers of bunches of cut flowers sold by a florist during a 10-day period: 120, 122, 130, 138, 125, 160, 161, 101, 98, and 172. Find the mean of the daily numbers of bunches of cut flowers sold during the 10-day period.

3.4 During a five-year period the Front Street Mutual Fund paid the following dividends to a stockholder who had made an initial investment of $1 million: $89,782, $130,486, $95,413, $115,449, and $98,440. During the same period the Back Street Mutual Fund paid the following dividends to a stockholder who had also made an initial investment of $1 million: $125,486, $101,674, $89,814, $122,776, and $101,194. Which of the two mutual funds paid higher mean dividends?

3.5 A van is designed to carry loads of 2,000 pounds or less. Is the van overloaded if, at one time, it carries

(a) 11 football players who have an average weight of 210 pounds

(b) 5 football players who have an average weight of 210 pounds and 8 cheerleaders who have an average weight of 115 pounds

(c) 4 football players who have an average weight of 210 pounds, 4 cheerleaders who have an average weight of 115 pounds, and 4 members of the coaching staff who have an average weight of 175 pounds

3.6 Five equal-sized shipments of 4-inch-wide boards from a certain supplier yielded the following mean width of boards (measurements of lumber are made before seasoning and planing, so finished boards are narrower than the stated width): 3.32, 3.65, 3.58, 3.41, and 3.39 inches. Five similar shipments from another supplier yielded mean widths of 3.28, 3.64, 3.62, 3.40, and 3.71 inches. Find the mean width of the shipments of 4-inch boards from each of the two suppliers.

3.7 Wool fibers may be classified as combing, French combing, and clothing, according to fiber lengths (with commonly accepted lengths of over 2 inches, $1\frac{1}{4}$ to 2 inches, and less than $1\frac{1}{4}$ inches, respectively). A sample of eight specimens taken from a large shipment of the three grades of wool yields the following lengths measured to the nearest tenth of an inch.

Grade of wool	Length of fiber (inches)							
Combing	3.3	3.5	3.2	3.2	3.5	3.0	3.3	3.4
French combing	1.4	1.7	1.5	2.0	2.0	1.8	1.8	2.0
Clothing	1.1	1.2	0.9	1.0	0.9	1.2	1.0	1.2

Calculate the mean, the median, and the mode of each of the three samples.

3.8 An electric meter reader took a sample of six electric meter readings in an apartment building which has a large number of electric meters. The readings, in hundreds of kilowatt-hours, are 7.7, 8.0, 7.8, 8.3, 8.3, and 8.1. Find the mean, median, and mode of these data.

3.9 The value of sales in the 11 stores of a shopping mall, during a typical week, are $200,000, $150,000, $100,000, $90,000, $85,000, $84,000, $83,000, $81,000, $80,000, $78,000, and $78,000.

(a) Find the mean, median, and mode of these sales and comment on the suitability of each as a way of expressing store sales during a typical week.

(b) Find the hinges of the store sales.

3.10 A customs inspector examined the luggage of 20 persons who were entering the United States, and the time required for the inspections was 3.0, 2.0, 3.1, 2.0, 0.5, 5.0, 2.0, 1.1, 2.0, 1.9, 2.9, 1.8, 2.8, 2.8, 3.2, 2.7, 1.6, 1.6, 2.4, and 4.9 minutes. Find

(a) the mean

(b) the median

(c) the two hinges

(d) the mode of the time required for the inspections

3.11 The heights of 25 young blue spruce trees which are to be transplanted by a tree nursery are 13, 26, 42, 38, 35, 37, 42, 30, 59, 23, 57, 40, 46, 42, 18, 40, 21, 57, 28, 58, 42, 64, 55, 43, and 29 inches. Determine

(a) the median

(b) the two hinges

(c) the mode of the heights of these young nursery trees

3.12 A customer can make purchases from a specialty shop using a store charge account, bank credit card, cash, or check. A random sample of sales slips showed that customers used the following methods of purchase: charge account, charge account, cash, credit card, check, credit card, check, credit card, charge account, credit card, credit card, charge account, credit card, check, credit card, check, credit card, cash, charge account, charge account, credit card, charge account, charge account, credit card, charge account, cash, cash, charge account, credit card, check, credit card, credit card, charge account, cash, check, check, credit card, charge account, check, and cash. What is the modal choice of customers for making purchases?

3.13 The published profile of the freshman class at an eastern university provides the information that its typical freshman is 18 years of age, unmarried, comes from an upper-middle-income family, has never held full-time employment, and has a cumulative SAT score of 1,176 points. Comment on the statistical aspects of this statement.

3.14 The average amount of chemical pollution per acre of soil in the United States is well below the safety standards established by the Environmental Protection Agency, even in cities with major chemical factories. Comment on the statement that "there is therefore no danger to anyone from chemical pollution of the soil."

3.15 A bank has $1,500,000 of 30-year fixed mortgages outstanding at a mean interest rate of 10.2 percent; $1,000,000 of 15-year fixed mortgages outstanding at a mean interest rate of 9.9 percent; $750,000 of automobile loans outstanding at a mean interest rate of 12.0 percent; $250,000 of unsecured personal loans outstanding at a mean interest rate of 16.4 percent; and $500,000 of credit card debt at a mean interest rate of 17.8 percent. What is the overall mean interest rate received by the bank?

3.16 In a marketing experiment a supermarket chain of three stores sold lettuce, on a certain day, at a different price in each of its stores. One store sold 75 heads of lettuce at 98 cents; the second store sold 125 heads at 88 cents; and the third store, which had an advertised special, sold 300 heads at 69 cents. How much was the average price per head of lettuce sold by the supermarket chain?

3.17 With reference to the preceding exercise, how many additional heads of lettuce must be sold at 98 cents a head to raise the mean price of lettuce sold that day by the supermarket chain to 80 cents per head?

3.18 A portfolio of three public utility stocks was purchased at the following prices: 4,000 shares at $38\frac{1}{8}$; 10,000 shares at $28\frac{1}{4}$; and 6,000 shares at $42\frac{1}{2}$. Following an increase in value, these stocks now have a market price of $41\frac{3}{8}$, $29\frac{7}{8}$, and $46\frac{3}{4}$ per share, respectively. (Note: Stock prices are expressed in whole numbers which are dollars, and in eighths of a dollar, which are worth $12\frac{1}{2}$ cents each. Possible fractions are $\frac{1}{8}$, $\frac{1}{4}$, $\frac{3}{8}$, $\frac{1}{2}$, $\frac{5}{8}$, $\frac{3}{4}$, and $\frac{7}{8}$.)

(a) What was the average purchase price per share, rounded to the nearest eighth?

(b) How much is the average market value per share after the increase in price, rounded to the nearest eighth?

(c) How large is the average increase in value per share rounded to the nearest eighth?

3.19 During a month the 12 agents of the Star Real Estate Co. sold an average of $6\frac{1}{2}$ single-family homes, the 6 agents of the Sun Realty Corp. sold an average of 4 single-family homes, and the 2 agents of Moon Homes, Inc., sold an average of 5 single-family homes. What was the overall average of single family homes sold by these agents during the month?

3.20 A classroom section of 32 students of statistics received grades averaging 78 points on a standardized test, and another section of 48 students of statistics received grades averaging 84 points on the same test. What is the overall average of these grades rounded to the nearest point?

3.21 An analysis of response times of an emergency ambulance service to emergency calls disclosed that for 21 emergency calls where an ambulance arrived in 5 minutes or less, the arrival times averaged 3.6 minutes; for 37 emergency calls where an ambulance arrived in over 5 but not more than 10 minutes, the arrival time averaged 5.8 minutes; and 2 arrival times of over 10 minutes averaged 10.9 minutes. What is the average arrival time of an ambulance dispatched by this service?

3.22 A carload of stone taken from a quarry by the plug-and-feather method (where stone is split into definite shapes using wedges and other tools) contains pieces of stone which have a mean weight of 1,500 pounds and a total weight of 36,000 pounds. Another carload of stone produced by the explosive method (where stone is blasted into random shapes by explosives) contains pieces of stone which have a mean weight of 600 pounds and a total weight of 30,000 pounds. What is the mean weight of all the pieces of stone combined?

3.23 The **geometric mean** of a set of n positive numbers is the nth root of their product. If the numbers are all the same, the geometric mean equals the arithmetic mean, but otherwise the geometric mean is always less than the arithmetic mean. For example, the geometric mean of the numbers 1, 1, 2, and 8 is $\sqrt[4]{1 \cdot 1 \cdot 2 \cdot 8} = 2$, but their (arithmetic) mean is 3. The geometric mean is used mainly to average ratios, rates of change, and index numbers (see Chapter 19), and in practice it is usually calculated by making use of the fact that the logarithm of the geometric mean of a set of numbers equals the arithmetic mean of their logarithms.

(a) Find the geometric mean of 8 and 18.

(b) Find the geometric mean of 9, 8, and 24.

(c) If a quart of milk, a pound of butter, a dozen eggs, and a loaf of bread cost 12, 3, 4, and 9 percent more than they cost a year earlier, find the geometric mean of these percentages.

3.24 The **harmonic mean** of n numbers $x_1, x_2, x_3, \ldots$, and x_n is defined as n divided by the sum of the reciprocals of the n numbers, or $\dfrac{n}{\sum 1/x}$. The harmonic mean has limited usefulness, but it is appropriate in some special situations. For instance, if an aircraft flies 100 miles at 300 miles per hour and the next 100 miles at 600 miles per hour, it will not have averaged

$\dfrac{300\,+\,600}{2} = 450$ miles per hour. It will have flown a total of 200 miles in 30 minutes, so its average speed is 400 miles per hour.

(a) Verify that the harmonic mean of 300 and 600 is 400 so that it gives the appropriate "average" in this case.

(b) If an office manager spends $30.00 on pencils which cost $10 per gross (144 items per gross) and another $30.00 on pencils which cost $15.00 per gross, what is her average cost per gross?

(c) A dealer invests $5,000 in a certain stock at a price of $10.00 per share, $5,000 at $12.50 per share, and $5,000 at $8.00 per share. Use the harmonic mean to determine the average price per share of stock.

3.4

The Concept of Variability

One of the most important characteristics of a set of data is that the values are usually not all alike; indeed, the precise extent to which they are not alike, or vary among themselves, is of basic importance in statistics. Measures of central location describe one important aspect of a set of data— their middle or their "average"—but they tell us nothing about this other basic characteristic. Hence, we require ways of measuring the extent to which data are dispersed, or spread out, and the statistical measures which provide this information are called **measures of variation**. In the paragraphs that follow, we give three examples which we hope will illustrate the importance of these measures.

Suppose that we are considering buying some common stock in one of two food service companies in a large metropolitan area. Among other things, we are interested in their operating results, as measured by the net profit of each $1 sale during the past six years, and we find that both firms averaged a net profit of 4.8 cents on each $1 sale. From this it might appear that the operating results of the two firms are equally good and that a choice between them must depend on other investment considerations. However, these averages have obscured an interesting and important fact. Over the six-year period the net profits of one firm were

$$5.2, \quad 4.5, \quad 3.9, \quad 4.8, \quad 5.0, \quad \text{and} \quad 5.4 \text{ cents}$$

varying from 3.9 to 5.4, while the net profits of the other were

$$7.9, \quad 7.0, \quad -5.3, \quad 14.2, \quad -11.0, \quad \text{and} \quad 16.9 \text{ cents}$$

varying from -11.0 to 16.0. These figures show clearly that the first firm has turned in a very consistent operating performance, but that the other is a highly inconsistent, erratic sort of "feast or famine" performer. This wide variability in the second firm's operating results introduces an element of risk into its investment potential which cannot be observed from a comparison of the mean profit figures alone.

The concept of variability or dispersion is of fundamental importance in statistical inference (estimation, tests of hypotheses, forecasting, and so on). Suppose that we have a somewhat bent and worn coin and we wonder whether it is still balanced or "fair" and will, in the long run, fall heads about 50 percent of the times it is tossed. What can we say if we actually toss the coin 100 times and get 29 heads and 71 tails? Is there anything unusual or out of the ordinary about this result? Specifically, does the shortage of heads—only 29 where we might have expected 50—suggest that, in fact, the coin is not fair?

To answer these questions, we must have some idea of how a fair coin behaves when it is tossed, that is, some idea about the magnitude of the fluctuations, or variations, produced by the action of chance in the number of times, in 100 tosses, that a fair coin falls heads. Suppose that, to get this information, we take a brand new coin in mint condition—presumably a balanced coin—and toss it 100 times, then again 100 times, and repeat this procedure until we have 10 sets of 100 tosses each. Suppose, furthermore, that in these 10 sets we get 51, 54, 58, 56, 41, 49, 58, 53, 47, and 56 heads. The number of heads varies from 41 to 58, so we might conclude from these results that a discrepancy of about 10 heads from the expected 50 heads is not unusual but that a discrepancy of 21 heads is so large that we would hesitate to attribute it to chance. On the basis of this small experiment, it seems more reasonable to conclude that the original coin is not balanced and is behaving accordingly than that it is balanced and behaving in an unusual way.

For our third example, suppose that we want to estimate the true mean (net) weight of all cans of beef hash in a very large production lot put out by a food processor. To do this we take a random sample of three cans from the lot and find that their weights are 15.0, 14.8, and 15.2 ounces. The mean of this sample is $\bar{x} = 15.0$ ounces, and in the absence of any further information we may use this figure to estimate the actual mean weight of all the cans. But, obviously, the "goodness" of this estimate depends in a very real way on the population variability, that is, on the variability of the weights of all the cans in the entire lot. To illustrate this, let us consider the following two possibilities:

Case 1: The true mean weight is 15.1 ounces, the filling process is very consistent, and all the cans in the lot weigh somewhere between 14.8 and 15.4 ounces.

Case 2: The true mean weight is 15.1 ounces, but the filling process is very inconsistent, and the weights of the cans in the lot vary widely from 13.0 to 17.2 ounces.

If the population of weights whose mean we are estimating is the relatively homogeneous one described in case 1, we can be sure that the sample mean will not differ from the true mean by much, regardlesss of the size of the sample. In fact, a sample mean cannot possibly be off by more than 0.3 ounce, and off by that much only if the sample values are all 14.8 or all 15.4 ounces. The population described in case 2, however, is a much less homogeneous collection of weights, even though its mean is the same as that in case 1. If, by chance, the three sample weights chosen from the second population were all 13.0 or all 17.2 ounces, the sample mean would differ from the population mean (which we are estimating) by 2.1 ounces. Clearly, in order to judge the closeness of an estimate or the "goodness" of a generalization based on a sample, we must know something about the variability in the population from which the sample came.

The preceding three examples are intended to suggest how the concept of variability plays an important part in practically all aspects of statistics; specifically, we hope they illustrate the need for understanding and measuring chance variation. In later chapters we shall treat such problems more rigorously and in much more detail.

3.5

Measures of Variation: The Range

In the first of the examples given, we actually introduced one way of measuring variability when we gave the two extreme values of each set of data. More or less the same thing is accomplished by taking the difference between the two extremes; this statistical measure is called the **range**.

EXAMPLE 3.11   Four batteries have lifetimes of 6.2, 6.8, 6.0, and 6.4 hours. Find the range of these values.

SOLUTION   Since the largest value is 6.8 and the smallest value is 6.0, the range is $6.8 - 6.0 = 0.8$ hour.   ■

The range is easy to calculate and easy to understand, but despite these advantages it is not a very useful measure of variation. Its main shortcoming is that it tells us nothing about the dispersion of the data which fall between the two extremes. For instance, each of the following sets of data

Set 1:	5	17	17	17	17	17	17	17	17	17
Set 2:	5	5	5	5	5	17	17	17	17	17
Set 3:	5	6	8	10	11	14	14	15	16	17

has a range of $17 - 5 = 12$, but the dispersion is quite different in each case.

In some cases, where the sample size is quite small, the range can be an adequate measure of variation. For instance, it is used widely in industrial quality control, where it is necessary to keep a close check on the quality of raw materials and semifinished and finished products on the basis of many small samples taken at more or less regular intervals of time.

3.6

Measures of Variation: The Variance and the Standard Deviation

To define the **standard deviation**, by far the most useful measure of variation, let us observe that the dispersion of a set of data is small if the numbers are closely bunched about their mean and that it is large if the numbers are scattered widely about their mean. Hence, it would seem reasonable to measure the variation of a set of data in terms of the amounts by which the various numbers deviate from their mean. If a set of numbers x_1, $x_2, x_3, \ldots$, and x_N, constituting a population, has the mean μ, the differences $x_1 - \mu, x_2 - \mu, x_3 - \mu, \ldots$, and $x_N - \mu$ are called the **deviations from the mean**, and it seems that we might use their arithmetic mean as a measure of the variation in the population. Unfortunately, this will not do. Unless the x's are all equal, some of the deviations will be positive, some will be negative, and it can be shown that their sum. $\sum (x - \mu)$, and consequently also their mean, is always zero.

Since we are really interested in the magnitude of the deviations, and not in their direction, we might simply ignore their signs and define a measure of variation in terms of the absolute values of the deviations from the mean. Indeed, adding the values of the deviations from the mean as if they were all positive and dividing by their number gives an intuitively appealing measure of variation called the **mean deviation**. However, using precisely the same deviations from the mean there is another way to proceed which does not require absolute values and, hence, is preferable on theoretical grounds. The squares of the deviations from the mean cannot be negative; in fact, they are all positive unless x happens to coincide with the mean, in which case both $x - \mu$ and $(x - \mu)^2$ are equal to zero. Therefore, it seems reasonable to measure the variability of a set of data in terms of the squared deviations from the mean, and this leads us to define the **population variance** in the following way:

Population variance

$$\sigma^2 = \frac{\Sigma\,(x - \mu)^2}{N}$$

This measure of variation, denoted by σ^2 (where σ, or sigma, is the Greek letter for lowercase ''s''), is simply the mean of the squared deviations from the population mean μ, and it is sometimes called the **mean-square deviation**.

The variance of a set of data is an extremely important measure of variation, and it is used extensively in statistical work. By reason of squaring the deviations, however, the variance is not in the same unit of measurement as the data themselves and their mean—if the data are in inches, the variance is in inches squared; if the data are in pounds, the variance is in pounds squared; and so on. However, if we take the square root of the population variance, we get another measure of variability called the **population standard deviation**, or sometimes the **root-mean-square deviation**.

Population standard deviation

$$\sigma = \sqrt{\frac{\Sigma\,(x - \mu)^2}{N}}$$

The term ''root-mean-square deviation'' describes it precisely—it is the square root of the mean of the squared deviations from the population mean μ. Also, it is in the same unit of measurement as the original data.

It may seem logical to use the same formulas for a sample, with n and $\bar{x}$ substituted for N and μ, but this is not quite what we do. Instead of dividing the sum of the squared deviations from the sample mean $\bar{x}$ by n, we divide it by $n - 1$ and define the **sample standard deviation**, denoted by s, as

Sample standard deviation	$$s = \sqrt{\frac{\sum (x - \bar{x})^2}{n - 1}}$$

and its square, the **sample variance**, as

Sample variance	$$s^2 = \frac{\sum (x - \bar{x})^2}{n - 1}$$

In using $n - 1$ instead of n in the denominator of these two formulas, we are not just being arbitrary. There is a good reason for it, and it is explained in the technical note of section 3.11.

To calculate the sample standard deviation by the definition formula, we must (1) find $\bar{x}$, (2) determine the n deviations from the mean $x - \bar{x}$, (3) square these deviations, (4) add the squared deviations, (5) divide by $n - 1$, and (6) take the square root of the quantity arrived at in step 5. Square roots can be calculated by arithmetic or obtained by using most calculators.

EXAMPLE 3.12   The response times in a sample of six switches designed to activate an alarm system upon receiving a certain stimulus are 9, 8, 5, 11, 7, and 5 milliseconds. Calculate the standard deviation.

SOLUTION   We first calculate the mean

$$\bar{x} = \frac{9 + 8 + 5 + 11 + 7 + 5}{6} = 7.5$$

Then we set up the work required to find $\sum (x - \bar{x})^2$ in the following table:

x	$x - \bar{x}$	$(x - \bar{x})^2$
9	1.5	2.25
8	0.5	0.25
5	-2.5	6.25
11	3.5	12.25
7	-0.5	0.25
5	-2.5	6.25
45	0.0	27.50

Finally, we divide $\sum (x - \bar{x})^2$ by $6 - 1 = 5$ and take the square root of this quotient. We get

$$s = \sqrt{\frac{27.50}{5}} = \sqrt{5.5} = 2.3.$$ ∎

It was easy to calculate s in this example because the response times were whole numbers and their mean was exact to one decimal. Often, though, the calculations required by the formulas defining s and s^2 are quite cumbersome, and it may be better to use the following computing formula, which can be derived by applying the rules of summations given in the technical note of Section 3.10:

*Computing
formula for the
sample standard
deviation*

$$s = \sqrt{\frac{n(\sum x^2) - (\sum x)^2}{n(n - 1)}}$$

This formula gives the exact value of s, not an approximation, and its advantage is that we do not actually have to find all the deviations from the mean. Instead we calculate $\sum x$, the sum of the x's, $\sum x^2$, the sum of their squares, and substitute into the formula. Aside from its advantage in manual calculations, this formula for s (or a slight modification of it) is the one usually preprogrammed into electronic statistical calculators, and it is the one most easily programmed for solution on a digital computer.[3]

EXAMPLE 3.13   Use the computing formula for s to rework the preceding example.

SOLUTION   First, we calculate the two sums

$$\sum x = 9 + 8 + 5 + 11 + 7 + 5 = 45$$

and

$$\sum x^2 = 81 + 64 + 25 + 121 + 49 + 25 = 365$$

Then, substituting these sums and $n = 6$ into the formula, we find that

[3]The computing formula for s can also be used to find σ, provided that we substitute n for the factor $n - 1$ in the denominator before we replace s and n with σ and N, obtaining

$$\sigma = \sqrt{\frac{N(\sum x^2) - (\sum x)^2}{N^2}}$$

Chapter 3   Summarizing Data: Statistical Descriptions

$$s = \sqrt{\frac{6(365) - (45)^2}{6 \cdot 5}} = \sqrt{\frac{165}{30}} = \sqrt{5.5} = 2.3$$

and this agrees with the results we obtained before. ■

In Section 3.4 we showed that there are many ways in which knowledge of the variability of a set of data can be of importance. Another application arises in the comparison of numbers belonging to different sets of data. To illustrate, suppose that a large securities firm administers a battery of tests to all job applicants, and a particular applicant, A, scores 135 on the General Information (GI) test and 265 points on the Accounting and Finance (AF) test. At first glance it may seem that A did much better (nearly twice as well) in accounting and finance than in general information. However, if the mean score which thousands of applicants made on the GI test was 100 points with a standard deviation of 15 points, and the mean score which all these applicants made on the AF test was 250 points with a standard deviation of 30 points, we can argue that A's score on the GI test is

$$\frac{135 - 100}{15} = 2\frac{1}{3} \text{ standard deviations}$$

above the mean of the distribution of all the scores on this test, while her score on the AF test was only

$$\frac{265 - 250}{30} = \frac{1}{2} \text{ standard deviation}$$

above the mean of the distribution of all the scores on this test. Whereas the original scores cannot be meaningfully compared, these new scores, expressed in terms of standard deviations, can. Clearly, A rates much higher on her command of general information than she does on her knowledge of accounting and finance.

What we did in the example is convert raw scores into **standard units**, or **z-scores**. If x is a measurement belonging to a set of data having the mean $\bar{x}$ (or μ) and the standard deviation s (or σ), then its value in standard units, denoted by the letter z, is given by

Formula for converting to standard units

$$z = \frac{x - \bar{x}}{s} \quad or \quad z = \frac{x - \mu}{\sigma}$$

depending on whether the data constitute a sample or a population. In these units, z tells us how many standard deviations a value lies above or below the mean of the set of data to which it belongs. Standard units will be used frequently in later chapters.

3.7

Chebyshev's Theorem

In the argument that led to the definition of the standard deviation, we observed that the dispersion of a set of data is small if the values are bunched closely about their mean and that it is large if the values are scattered widely about their mean. Correspondingly, we can now say that if the standard deviation of a set of data is small, the values are concentrated near the mean, and if the standard deviation is large, the values are scattered widely about the mean. To present this argument on a less intuitive basis (after all, what is small and what is large?), let us refer to an important theorem called **Chebyshev's theorem**. This theorem states that

Chebyshev's
theorem

> *For any set of data (population or sample) and any constant k greater than 1, at least $1 - 1/k^2$ of the data must lie within k standard deviations on either side of the mean.*

Accordingly, we can be sure that at least $\frac{3}{4}$, or 75 percent, of the values in any set of data must lie between the mean minus 2 standard deviations and the mean plus 2 standard deviations; at least $\frac{8}{9}$, or about 88.9 percent, of the values in any set of data must lie between the mean minus 3 standard deviations and the mean plus 3 standard deviations and at least $\frac{24}{25}$, or 96 percent, of the values in any set of data must lie between the mean minus 5 standard deviations and the mean plus 5 standard deviations. Here we arbitrarily let $k = 2$, 3, and 5.

EXAMPLE 3.14   If all the 1-pound cans of coffee filled by a food processor have a mean weight of 16.00 ounces with a standard deviation of 0.02 ounce, at least what percentage of the cans must contain between 15.95 and 16.05 ounces of coffee?

SOLUTION Since k standard deviations, or $k(0.02)$, equals $16.05 - 16.00 = 16.00 - 15.95 = 0.05$, we find that $k = \dfrac{0.05}{0.02} = 2.5$. Thus, at least $1 - \dfrac{1}{(2.5)^2} = 1 - \dfrac{1}{6.25} = 0.84$, or 84 percent, of the cans must contain between 15.95 and 16.05 ounces of coffee. ∎

EXERCISES

(Exercises 3.25, 3.28, 3.34, 3.36, and 3.37 are practice exercises. Their complete solutions are given on page 106.)

3.25 The numbers of workers supervised by each of eight forepersons are 12, 15, 16, 12, 15, 17, 11, and 14. Calculate the standard deviation of this population of workers.

3.26 Following are the gains and losses (in thousands of dollars) of two commodities speculators for 10 business days.

Speculator 1:	6	4	2	−3	4	0	−2	5	4	5
Speculator 2:	3	2	0	−1	−4	3	5	6	5	5

(a) Calculate the standard deviation of each of these samples.

(b) Which speculator shows the more consistent performance?

3.27 A sample of seven taxicabs from a large fleet of taxicabs used the following amounts of gasoline in one day: 10.9, 19.3, 14.7, 13.8, 15.3, 11.4, and 12.6 gallons.

(a) Use the definition formula $s = \sqrt{\dfrac{\sum (x - \bar{x})^2}{n - 1}}$ to calculate the standard deviation of the number of gallons of gasoline used.

(b) Use the computing formula $s = \sqrt{\dfrac{n(\sum x^2) - (\sum x)^2}{n(n-1)}}$ to calculate the standard deviation of the number of gallons of gasoline used. The answer should be exactly the same as that obtained in part (a).

(c) An alternative formula is based on a notation which we shall find convenient to use in the study of linear regression. It is

$$s = \sqrt{\dfrac{S_{xx}}{n - 1}}$$

where $S_{xx} = \sum x^2 - \dfrac{1}{n} (\sum x)^2$. Use this formula to recalculate s for the gasoline consumption data. The answer should be exactly the same as those obtained in parts (a) and (b). It may be noted that the alternative computing formula shown here is obtained by simple algebraic manipulation of the computing formula used in part (b).

Section 3.7   Chebyshev's Theorem   73

3.28 In a recent year the birth rates (births per 1,000 of population) for the New England, Middle Atlantic, East North Central, West North Central, South Atlantic, East South Central, West South Central, Mountain, and Pacific regions of the United States were 15.0, 14.8, 15.1, 15.0, 15.4, 15.1, 17.2, 17.7, and 17.5, respectively. At the same time the death rates (deaths per 1,000 of population) were 9.4, 9.9, 8.9, 9.5, 9.2, 9.7, 8.1, 7.3, and 7.4, respectively.

(a) Find the ranges and standard deviations of the birth rates and death rates if we view these data as samples.

(b) Find the ranges and standard deviations of the birth rates and death rates if we view these data as populations.

3.29 The 12 tallest buildings in Montreal, Quebec, are 47, 43, 42, 40, 38, 36, 33, 32, 32, 32, 27, and 26 stories.

(a) Calculate the range and standard deviation for this sample of buildings.

(b) Recalculate the range and standard deviation after deleting the heights of the four tallest buildings.

3.30 No two manufactured products, although they may appear identical, are exactly alike because production processes contain many sources of product variation. Suppose that an automobile manufacturer carefully measures the distances between the centers of two mounting holes drilled in each of a sample of 10 automobile engine blocks, where the desired distances between centers is 2.50 centimeters. The measured distances are 2.52, 2.52, 2.51, 2.49, 2.50, 2.45, 2.53, 2.52, 2.48, and 2.48 centimeters. Calculate

(a) the mean

(b) the range

(c) the standard deviation

3.31 A sample of five cans of a brand of mixed nuts contained, by weight, the following percentages of various nuts.

	Can 1	Can 2	Can 3	Can 4	Can 5
Almonds	14.6	12.1	13.8	15.0	11.3
Brazil nuts	10.2	9.4	11.0	11.1	11.8
Cashews	30.7	31.4	34.0	31.6	29.1
Peanuts	24.3	26.1	23.3	22.5	27.1
Walnuts	20.2	21.0	17.9	19.8	20.7

Calculate the mean, range, and the standard deviation for each of the five types of nuts.

3.32 With reference to Exercise 3.3 on page 60, find the range and standard deviation of the sample of daily numbers of bunches of cut flowers sold by the florist.

3.33 With reference to Exercise 3.11 on page 61, find the range and standard deviation of this sample of 25 young blue spruce trees which are to be transplanted by a tree nursery.

3.34 If each item in a set of data has the same constant a added to it, the mean of this new set equals the mean of the original set plus the constant a, but the range and the standard deviation remain unchanged.

(a) Verify that for a sample consisting of the values $-3, 1, 0, 2, -2, 1$, and -6 the mean is -1, the range is 8, and the standard deviation is $\sqrt{8}$, and that after adding 6 to each value the mean becomes $-1 + 6 = 5$, but the range is still 8 and the standard deviation is still $\sqrt{8}$.

(b) Tests of the operating life for a sample of four incandescent electric light bulbs showed that they burned out at 980, 1,031, 968, and 1,053 hours of operation. The arithmetic mean of the sample is 1,008 and the standard deviation is 40.6. Show that if we subtract 100 hours from each item in the sample, the arithmetic mean of the sample is also reduced by 100, but the standard deviation is unchanged.

(c) Verify that the standard deviation which was calculated in Exercise 3.30(c) remains unchanged if we deduct 2.50 centimeters from each of the sample measurements of the distances between centers and recalculate as before.

3.35 If each item in a set of data is multiplied by the same positive constant b, the mean, range, and standard deviation of this new set equal the mean, range, and standard deviation of the original set multiplied by b.

(a) With reference to the seven sample values of part (a) of the preceding exercise, show that if each value is multiplied by 2, the mean becomes -2, the range becomes 16, and the standard deviation becomes $2\sqrt{8}$.

(b) A word processor with a *daisy wheel* prints characters one at a time like a typewriter. Tests of a sample of four such word processors show that their speeds are 46.1, 54.2, 51.0, and 52.7 characters per second, and that the standard deviation is 3.5 characters per second. Recalculate the standard deviation after multiplying each figure by 10 and then subtracting 510. Divide your answer by 10 and compare it with the standard deviation of the original data.

3.36 A movie theater whose average monthly attendance was 12,000 persons, with standard deviation of 2,000, increased its attendance in a certain month to 14,000 persons. An art museum whose average monthly attendance was 6,000 persons, with standard deviation of 500, increased its attendance during the same month to 7,000 persons. Can we conclude from the data that the increased attendance results for the movie theater were twice as good as those for the art museum?

3.37 A shipping company ships an average of 10,000 metric tons (1 MT = about 1.1 tons, or 2,000 pounds, or 1,000,000 grams) of freight monthly with a standard deviation of 800 metric tons. According to Chebyshev's theorem, in at least what percentage of the months will the company ship between 8,000 and 12,000 metric tons of freight?

3.38 The mean amount of time for chemical workers to vacate a chemical factory during a fire drill is 7 minutes with a standard deviation of 0.5 minutes. Use Chebyshev's theorem to determine at least what percentage of the time the chemical factory can be vacated during a fire drill

(a) between 6 and 8 minutes

(b) between 5 and 9 minutes

3.39 Suppose that the mean amount of time required by a technician to repair a videocassette recorder (VCR) is 30 minutes, with variance of 9 minutes^2.

(a) At least what fraction of the VCRs can the technician repair between 24 and 36 minutes?

(b) Between what two times, in minutes, can the technician repair at least $\dfrac{24}{25}$ of the VCRs?

3.40 For a certain library, the mean daily number of books which are returned overdue is 45 and the standard deviation is 6 books. Use Chebyshev's theorem to determine between what two numbers must lie

(a) at least $\dfrac{3}{4}$ of the daily number of books which are returned overdue

(b) at least $\dfrac{15}{16}$ of the daily number of books which are returned overdue

3.41 One characteristic of the standard deviation as a measure of variation is that it depends on the units of measurement. If, for instance, a set of measurements of the weights of containers of bleach have a standard deviation of 0.24 ounce, we would look at this variability in one light if the containers are "80-pound" containers, and in quite another light if they are "8-ounce" containers. What we need in a situation like this is a **measure of relative variation**, such as the **coefficient of variation**

$$V = \frac{s}{\bar{x}} \cdot 100 \qquad or \qquad V = \frac{\sigma}{\mu} \cdot 100$$

which expresses the standard deviation as a percentage of the mean.

(a) A sample of the mileages driven in a month (in thousands of miles) by four traveling salespersons shows mileages of 2.5, 3.4, 2.1, and 2.0. Find the coefficient of variation.

(b) A sample of the sales (in thousands of dollars) produced by the four traveling salespersons of part (a) shows 37.8, 63.6, 33.0, and 30.0. Find the coefficient of variation.

(c) By comparing the coefficients of variation (which are percentages) we can compare the dispersions of two or more sets of data pertaining to different kinds of measurements (say, height, weight, speed, age, and dollars). Compare the coefficients of variation obtained in parts (a) and (b) to judge which set of measurements is relatively more variable.

(d) A sample of the ages of five women members of an aerobics class showed the following ages in years to the nearest birthday: 22, 18, 26, 20, and 24. Their weights were 115, 159, 141, 137, and 130 pounds. Which of the two sets of data is relatively more variable?

3.8

The Description of Grouped Data

Published data are often available only in the form of a frequency distribution. For this reason, we shall discuss briefly the calculation of statistical descriptions from grouped data.

As we have already seen, the grouping of data entails some loss of information. Each item loses its identity, so to speak; we only know how many items there are in each class, so we must be satisfied with approximations. In the case of the mean and the standard deviation, we can usually get good approximations by assigning to each item falling into a class the value of the class mark. For instance, to calculate the mean or the standard deviation of the distribution of the aptitude scores on page 14, we treat the six values falling into the class 20–29 as if they were all 24.5, the nine values falling into the class 30–39 as if they were all 34.5, . . . , and the two values falling into the class 90–99 as if they were both 94.5. This procedure is usually quite satisfactory, since the errors which it introduces into the calculations will more or less "average out."

To write formulas for the mean and the standard deviation of a distribution with k classes, let us designate the successive class marks $x_1, x_2, x_3,$ . . . , x_k, and the corresponding class frequencies $f_1, f_2, f_3,$ . . . , and f_k. The total that goes into the numerator of the formula for the mean is the sum obtained by adding x_1 times f_1, x_2 times f_2, x_3 times f_3, . . . , and x_k times f_k, or $x_1f_1 + x_2f_2 + x_3f_3 + \cdots + x_kf_k$. Using again the $\sum$ notation, we write the formula for the mean of grouped sample data as

Mean of grouped data	$$\bar{x} = \frac{\sum x \cdot f}{n}$$

where $\sum x \cdot f$ represents, in words, the sum of the products obtained by multiplying each class mark by the corresponding class frequency. (If the data constitute a population instead of a sample, we substitute μ for $\bar{x}$ and N for n in this formula.)

Similarly, the total that goes into the numerator of the formulas defining the sample variance and the sample standard deviation is the sum obtained by adding $(x_1 - \bar{x})^2$ times f_1, $(x_2 - \bar{x})^2$ times f_2, $(x_3 - \bar{x})^2$ times f_3, . . . , and $(x_k - \bar{x})^2$ times f_k. Thus, for the sample standard deviation we write

Standard deviation of grouped data	$$s = \sqrt{\frac{\sum (x - \bar{x})^2 \cdot f}{n - 1}}$$

In the computing formulas for s and s^2 we replace $\sum x$ by $\sum x \cdot f$ and $\sum x^2$ by $\sum x^2 \cdot f$, so that the formula for s becomes

Computing formula for the standard deviation of grouped data	$$s = \sqrt{\frac{n(\sum x^2 \cdot f) - (\sum x \cdot f)^2}{n(n - 1)}}$$

EXAMPLE 3.15 Calculate the mean and the standard deviation of the distribution of aptitude scores on page 14.

SOLUTION To get $\sum x \cdot f$ and $\sum x^2 \cdot f$, we perform the calculations shown in the following table, where the first and third columns are copied from the original distribution, the second column contains the class marks, and the fourth and fifth columns contain the products $x \cdot f$ and $x^2 \cdot f$:

Chapter 3 Summarizing Data: Statistical Descriptions

Score	Class mark x	Frequency f	$x \cdot f$	$x^2 \cdot f$
10–19	14.5	1	14.5	210.25
20–29	24.5	6	147.0	3,601.50
30–39	34.5	9	310.5	10,712.25
40–49	44.5	31	1,379.5	61,387.75
50–59	54.5	42	2,289.0	124,750.50
60–69	64.5	32	2,064.0	133,128.00
70–79	74.5	17	1,266.5	94,354.25
80–89	84.5	10	845.0	71,402.50
90–99	94.5	2	189.0	17,860.50
		150	8,505.0	517,407.50

Then, substitution into the formulas yields

$$\bar{x} = \frac{8,505.0}{150} = 56.7$$

and

$$s = \sqrt{\frac{150(517,407.5) - (8,505.0)^2}{150 \cdot 149}} = 15.4 \qquad \blacksquare$$

It is apparent from this example that some heavy arithmetic may be required to find the mean or the standard deviation of a distribution. However, we can simplify this work by **coding** the class marks so that we have smaller numbers to work with. Provided the class intervals are all equal, this coding consists of assigning the value 0 to one of the class marks (in manual calculations, preferably at or near the center of the distribution), and representing all the class marks by means of successive integers. For instance, if a distribution has seven classes and the class mark of the middle class is assigned the value 0, the successive class marks of the distribution are assigned the values -3, -2, -1, 0, 1, 2, and 3.

Of course, when we code the class marks like this, we must account for it in the formulas for the mean and the standard deviation. Referring to the new (coded) class marks as u's, the formula for the mean of a distribution of sample data becomes

Mean of grouped data (with coding)

$$\bar{x} = x_0 + \frac{\sum u \cdot f}{n} \cdot c$$

where x_0 is the class mark in the original scale to which we assign 0 in the new scale, c is the class interval, n is the number of items grouped, and $\sum u \cdot f$ is the sum of the products obtained by multiplying each of the new class marks by the corresponding class frequency. Similarly, the formula for the standard deviation of a distribution of sample data becomes

Standard deviation of grouped data (with coding)

$$s = c \sqrt{\frac{n(\sum u^2 \cdot f) - (\sum u \cdot f)^2}{n(n-1)}}$$

where $\sum u^2 \cdot f$ is the sum of the products obtained by multiplying the squares of the new class marks by the corresponding class frequencies.

EXAMPLE 3.16   To demonstrate the simplification brought about by coding, recalculate the mean and the standard deviation of the distribution of the clerical aptitude scores.

SOLUTION   Arranging the work, as before, in a table, we get

Class mark x	u	f	$u \cdot f$	$u^2 \cdot f$
14.5	-4	1	-4	16
24.5	-3	6	-18	54
34.5	-2	9	-18	36
44.5	-1	31	-31	31
54.5	0	42	0	0
64.5	1	32	32	32
74.5	2	17	34	68
84.5	3	10	30	90
94.5	4	2	8	32
Totals		150	33	359

where the class mark 54.5 is taken to be 0 in the u scale (shown in the second column of the table). Of course, we could have used any class mark, for instance, 24.5, as the zero of the u scale, but the objective is to make the arithmetic as simple as possible.

Substituting $c = 10$, $x_0 = 54.5$, $n = 150$, $\sum u \cdot f = 33$, and $\sum u^2 \cdot f = 359$ into the preceding formulas for $\bar{x}$ and s, we get

$$\bar{x} = 54.5 + \frac{33}{150} \cdot 10 = 56.7$$

and

$$s = 10 \sqrt{\frac{150(359) - (33)^2}{150 \cdot 149}} = 15.4$$

These results are, as they should be, identical with the ones obtained earlier without coding. ∎

A disadvantage of grouping data, as we have repeatedly stated, is that this entails some loss of information. In the past this advantage was generally offset by the advantage of grouping data to reduce the amount of manual labor in performing calculations. The use of the computer, and of some calculators, eliminates the need for grouping for this purpose, even for large sets of data. In the computer printout of Figure 3.3, the mean and standard deviation of the distribution of the aptitude scores are calculated without

FIGURE 3.3
Computer printout
for mean and
standard deviation
of clerical aptitude
test scores

```
MTB > SET C1
DATA> 27 79 69 40 51 88 55 48 36 61
DATA> 53 44 94 51 65 42 58 55 69 63
DATA> 70 48 61 55 60 25 47 78 61 54
DATA> 57 76 73 62 36 67 40 51 59 68
DATA> 27 46 62 43 54 83 59 13 72 57
DATA> 82 45 54 52 71 53 82 69 60 35
DATA> 41 65 62 75 60 42 55 34 49 45
DATA> 49 64 40 61 73 44 59 46 71 86
DATA> 43 69 54 31 56 51 75 44 66 53
DATA> 80 71 53 56 91 60 41 29 56 57
DATA> 35 54 43 39 56 27 62 44 85 61
DATA> 59 89 60 51 71 53 58 26 77 68
DATA> 62 57 48 69 76 52 49 45 54 41
DATA> 33 61 80 57 42 45 59 44 68 73
DATA> 55 70 39 58 69 51 85 46 55 67
DATA> END
MTB > MEAN C1
   MEAN     =        56.667
MTB > STDEV C1
    ST.DEV. =        15.114
```

grouping, obtaining a mean and standard deviation which are very close to the answers of 56.7 and 15.4 obtained from the grouped data of the preceding example.

Computer printout of Figure 3.3 shown here is nearly identical to the computer printout of Figure 2.3 shown on page 25. The data are printed in the form "Set C1," previously explained on page 24. But in Figure 3.3 the instructions to the computer are MTB > MEAN C1 and MTB > STDEV C1. These instruct the Minitab software to calculate both the mean and the standard deviation at the same time. These are printed as 56.667 and 15.114, respectively.

As for the median of a set of grouped data, we cannot calculate the precise value of this measure because of the loss of identity which results from the act of grouping. To approximate it, we shall not assign the value of the class mark to each item falling within any given class; instead, we shall assume that the items lying within each class are spread evenly throughout the class. With this assumption, if the class containing the actual median had, say, 60 values and the median was the 59th largest, the median would be located very close to the upper class boundary instead of at the middle of the class. This entirely reasonable result leads us to define the median of a numerical distribution as the number which is such that half the total area of the rectangles of the histogram of the distribution lies to its left and the other half lies to its right (see Figure 3.4).

To find the dividing line between the two halves of a histogram (each of which represents $n/2$ of the items grouped), we must count $n/2$ of the items starting at one end of the distribution. How this is done is illustrated in the following example:

EXAMPLE 3.17   Find the median of the distribution of the clerical aptitude scores.

SOLUTION   Since $\dfrac{n}{2} = \dfrac{150}{2} = 75$, we must count 75 items starting at one end.

Counting from the smallest values (that is, beginning with the frequencies of the smallest class, 10–19), we find that $1 + 6 + 9 + 31 = 47$ of the values are less than 50, and $1 + 6 + 9 + 31 + 42 = 89$ are less than 60. Therefore, we must count $75 - 47 = 28$ more items beyond the 47 which are less than 50, and on the assumption that the 42 values of the 50–59 class are spread evenly throughout the class, we can do this by adding $\dfrac{28}{42}$ of the class interval, which is ten, to 49.5, the lower boundary of the class

Score	Frequency	Items included
10–19	1	0– 1
20–29	6	2– 7
30–39	9	8– 16
40–49	31	17– 47
50–59	42	48– 89
60–69	32	90–121
70–79	17	122–138
80–89	10	139–148
90–99	2	149–150
Total	150	

This gives us

$$\tilde{x} = 49.5 + \frac{28}{42} \cdot 10 = 56.2$$

for the median of this distribution. ∎

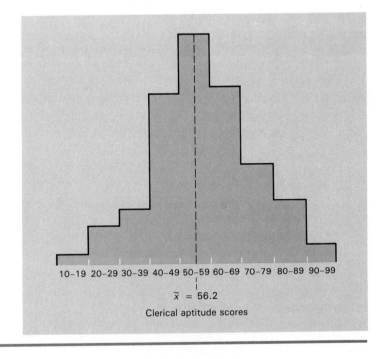

FIGURE 3.4
Median of a
distribution

10–19 20–29 30–39 40–49 50–59 60–69 70–79 80–89 90–99

$\tilde{x} = 56.2$

Clerical aptitude scores

In general, if L is the lower boundary of the class into which the median must fall, f its frequency, c is the class interval, and j is the number of items we still lack when we reach L, then the median of the distribution is given by the formula

Median of grouped data

$$\tilde{x} = L + \frac{j}{f} \cdot c$$

If we prefer, we can find the median of a distribution by starting to count at the other end and subtracting an appropriate fraction of the class interval from the upper boundary U of the median class. A general formula for the case where we start counting from the largest values, (that is, beginning with the frequencies of the largest class, 90–99) is given by

Alternate formula for the median of grouped data

$$\tilde{x} = U - \frac{j'}{f} \cdot c$$

where j' is the number of items we still lack when we reach U.

EXAMPLE 3.18   Use the alternate formula to find the median of the distribution of aptitude scores.

SOLUTION   Since $2 + 10 + 17 + 32 = 61$ of the values fall above 59.5, we need $75 - 61 = 14$ of the 42 values which fall into the next class to reach the median, and we write

$$\tilde{x} = 59.5 - \frac{14}{42} \cdot 10 = 56.2$$

The result is the same, of course.   ∎

The procedure we have just described for finding the median of a distribution can also be used to determine more general "positional measures" called **fractiles** or **quantiles**. By definition, a fractile, or quantile, is a value at or below which a given fraction of the data must lie. There are, for instance, the three **quartiles** Q_1, Q_2, and Q_3, which are such that 25 percent of the data is less than or equal to Q_1, 50 percent is less than or equal to Q_2, and 75 percent is less than or equal to Q_3. Also, there are the nine **deciles**,

Chapter 3   Summarizing Data: Statistical Descriptions

$D_1, D_2, \ldots$, and D_9, which are such that 10 percent of the data is less than or equal to D_1, 20 percent is less than or equal to D_2, and so on; and there are the 99 **percentiles**, $P_1, P_2, \ldots$, and P_{99}, which are such that 1 percent of the data is less than or equal to P_1, 2 percent is less than or equal to P_2, and so on. It should be clear from this that Q_2, D_5, and P_{50} are all equal to the median and that P_{25} equals Q_1 and P_{75} equals Q_3.

EXAMPLE 3.19   Referring again to the distribution of aptitude scores, find Q_1, D_9, and P_{15}.

SOLUTION   Using the formulas for the median and counting in each case the appropriate fraction of the number of items grouped in the distribution, we find that

$$Q_1 = 39.5 + \frac{21.5}{31} \cdot 10 = 46.4$$

$$D_9 = 79.5 - \frac{3}{17} \cdot 10 = 77.7$$

and

$$P_{15} = 39.5 + \frac{6.5}{31} \cdot 10 = 41.6 \qquad \blacksquare$$

To conclude this discussion of statistical descriptions of grouped data, let us point out that there exist fairly elaborate ways of defining the mode of a distribution. In most cases, however, all we need is the **modal class**, the class with the highest frequency; if a single number is preferred, we can define the mode of a distribution as the midpoint of the modal class.

3.9

Some Further Descriptions

Measures of location and measures of variation are fundamentally important statistical descriptions, but there are many other ways to describe statistical data. In this section we shall consider briefly the problem of describing the overall shape of a distribution.

Distributions of actual data can assume almost any shape or form, but most of those which arise in practice can be described fairly well by one or another of a few standard types. A very important one is the symmetrical

bell-shaped distribution shown in Figure 3.5. Indeed, there are theoretical reasons why, in many cases, distributions of actual data can be expected to follow this form very closely. The other two distributions of Figure 3.5 can still, by a stretch of the imagination, be called bell shaped, but they certainly cannot be called symmetrical. Distributions of this sort, having a pronounced "tail" on one side or the other, are said to be **skewed**; those with a tail on the left are **negatively skewed** and those with a tail on the right are **positively skewed**.

Distributions of incomes are often positively skewed because of the presence of some relatively high incomes that are not offset by correspondingly low ones. Since these values tend to affect the mean more than the median, the median is widely used to average incomes. For instance, the Bureau of the Census uses the median to measure household incomes (an important indicator of the nation's standard of living).

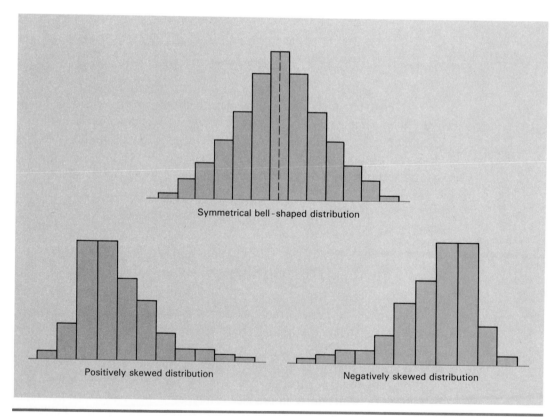

FIGURE 3.5 Bell-shaped distributions

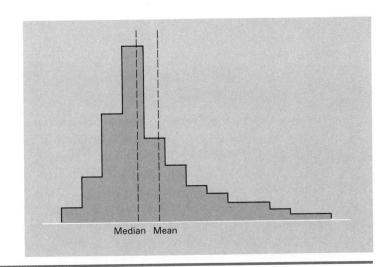

FIGURE 3.6
The median and the mean of a positively skewed distribution

Median Mean

For a perfectly symmetrical bell-shaped distribution such as the one in Figure 3.5, the values of the mean, median, and mode coincide, and they all lie on the axis of symmetry (the dashed vertical line which divides the histogram of the distribution into equal halves). But, as we have already observed, in a positively skewed distribution the median will generally be exceeded by the mean (see also Figure 3.6), and by the same token in a negatively skewed distribution the median will generally exceed the mean. A simple measure of the extent to which a distribution is skewed is based on this relationship between the median and the mean. Called the **Pearsonian coefficient of skewness**, its formula is

Pearsonian coefficient of skewness

$$SK = \frac{3\,(mean - median)}{standard\ deviation}$$

For a perfectly symmetrical distribution the value of *SK* is 0, and in general its value must fall between -3 and 3.

EXAMPLE 3.20 Find the Pearsonian coefficient of skewness for the distribution of the clerical aptitude scores.

SOLUTION Substituting into the formula the values of the mean, $\bar{x} = 56.7$, the median, $\tilde{x} = 56.2$, and the standard deviation, $s = 15.4$, we find that

$$SK = \frac{3(56.7 - 56.2)}{15.4} = 0.097$$

On the basis of this result we can say that the distribution is nearly symmetrical. ∎

Two other kinds of distributions which sometimes arise in practice are the **reverse J-shaped** and **U-shaped distributions**; as can be seen from the histograms of Figure 3.7, the names of these distributions quite literally describe their shape. Examples of such distributions may be found in Exercises 3.54 and 3.55.

A **box-and-whisker plot** or **boxplot** is another means of determining the shape of a distribution. It is especially useful where the sample size is small, and a histogram fails to reveal its shape. The box is a rectangular figure whose ends represent the lower hinge and upper hinge of the distribution. A line representing the median is drawn parallel to the hinges, dividing the box into two parts.

A line, or **whisker**, is drawn from the lowest value of the distribution to the lower hinge, and another whisker is drawn from the highest value of the distribution to the upper hinge. **Outliers** are values which are so far removed from the main body of data that they may well be due to extraneous causes such as errors of measurement or recording. Such outliers are usually omitted prior to drawing the whiskers. Caution should be exercised in the removal of outliers since they may well contain important data. Their removal is, nevertheless, justified where the purpose of the boxplot is to provide us with a better understanding of the shape of the data.

In judging the symmetry or skewness of a set of data we use the following criteria. If the line at the median is at or near the center of the box, this is an indication of symmetry of the data. If the line at the median is considerably closer to the lower hinge, this is an indication that the data are positively skewed, and if appreciably closer to the upper hinge, this is an indication that the data are negatively skewed. Similarly, the relative length

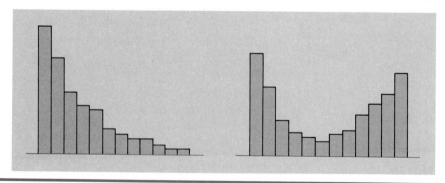

FIGURE 3.7
Histograms of reverse J-shaped and U-shaped distributions

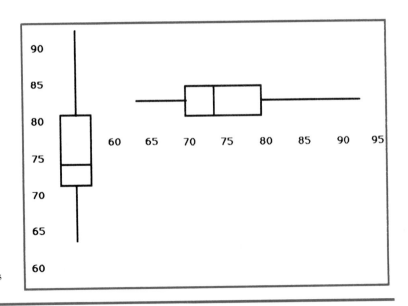

FIGURE 3.8
Boxplot for the
number of landings
of private aircraft

of the whiskers may be used as an indication of skewness. If the whisker extending from the upper hinge to the highest data point is appreciably longer than the whisker extending from the lower hinge to the lowest data point, this suggests that the data are positively skewed. On the other hand, if the whisker extending from the lower hinge is appreciably longer than the whisker extending from the upper hinge, this suggests the data are negatively skewed.

EXAMPLE 3.21 The following are the numbers of private aircraft which landed at an airport on 15 consecutive days: 85, 74, 67, 77, 71, 79, 82, 93, 73, 64, 77, 72, 70, 90, and 69. Draw a boxplot of these data.

SOLUTION Arranging the data according to size, we get

64   67   69   70   71   72   73   74   77   77   79   82   85   90   93

The smallest value in this array is 64 and the largest is 93. The median is the $\frac{n+1}{2} = \frac{15+1}{2} = 8$th item from either end of the array, which is 74. The lower hinge is the mean of the fourth and fifth smallest values, which is $\frac{70+71}{2} = 70.5$, and the upper hinge is the mean of the fourth and fifth largest values, which is $\frac{82+79}{2} = 80.5$. All of this information is summarized by the boxplots of Figure 3.8, which shows a boxplot in a vertical position

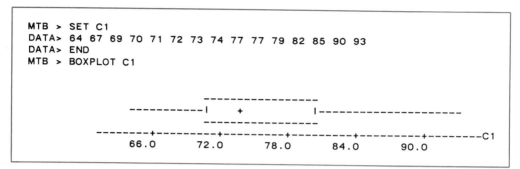

```
MTB > SET C1
DATA> 64 67 69 70 71 72 73 74 77 77 79 82 85 90 93
DATA> END
MTB > BOXPLOT C1


                                   ------------------
                        -----------I      +        I---------------------
                                   ------------------
            --------+---------+---------+---------+---------+--------C1
                  66.0      72.0      78.0      84.0      90.0
```

FIGURE 3.9 Computer printout of boxplot for the number of landings of private aircraft

and which also shows the same boxplot in a horizontal position. There is a strong indication that the data are positively skewed since the median is much closer to the lower hinge than it is to the upper hinge, and the whisker extending from the upper hinge is appreciably longer than the whisker extending from the lower hinge. A computer printout of the horizontal boxplot is shown in Figure 3.9. ■

EXERCISES

(Exercises 3.42, 3.43, 3.44, 3.46 and 3.53 are practice exercises. Their complete solutions are given on page 106.)

3.42 *The Wall Street Journal* Stock Market Data Bank reports the numbers of shares traded on the New York Stock Exchange in half-hourly intervals. Following are the combined numbers of shares traded (in millions of shares) at half-hourly intervals for three recent days.

Shares traded (in millions)	Numbers of half-hourly periods
5– 9	8
10–14	17
15–19	8
20–24	3
25–29	2
30–34	1

Find the mean and standard deviation of this distribution

(a) without coding

(b) with coding

3.43 With reference to the distribution of the preceding exercise, find

(a) the median

(b) the mode

3.44 Use the results of the two preceding exercises to calculate the Pearsonian coefficient of skewness for the distribution of shares traded on the New York Stock Exchange at half-hourly intervals.

3.45 Find the mean and standard deviation of a sample of ages of restaurant workers who are insured under a group health insurance policy.

Ages	Frequency
15–24	22
25–34	27
35–44	41
45–54	35
55–64	28
65–74	14
75–84	3

3.46 With reference to the distribution of the preceding exercise, find

(a) the median

(b) the quartiles Q_1 and Q_3

(c) the percentiles P_{90} and P_{95}

3.47 Use the results of the two preceding exercises to calculate the Pearsonian coefficient of skewness for the distribution of the ages of restaurant workers.

3.48 The marketing department of a household detergent manufacturing company summarized the sales results for a new detergent product following a major advertising campaign.

Cases sold (thousands)	Number of cities
Less than 5	12
5– 9	21
10–29	58
30–49	28
50–59	14
60–69	7
70 or more	10

(a) Find the median.

(b) Find the quartiles, Q_1 and Q_3.

(c) Can we calculate P_{95} for this distribution? Why or why not?

3.49 With reference to the distribution of automobile rentals in Exercise 2.19 on page 29, find

(a) the mean

(b) the median

(c) the sample standard deviation

(d) the Pearsonian coefficient of skewness

3.50 With reference to the distribution of downtimes in Exercise 2.17 on page 28, find

(a) the quartile Q_3

(b) the deciles D_2 and D_8

(c) the percentiles P_5 and P_{95}

3.51 Following is the distribution of a sample of the number of patient contacts made by volunteers who help patients in a hospital.

Patient contacts	Hospital volunteers
5– 9	8
10–14	11
15–19	19
20–24	25
25–29	18
30–34	14
35–39	10

Calculate

(a) the mean and the median

(b) the standard deviation

(c) the quartiles Q_1 and Q_3

(d) the deciles D_2 and D_8

(e) the percentiles P_{15} and P_{85}

3.52 Use the results of parts (a) and (b) of the preceding exercise to calculate the Pearsonian coefficient of skewness for the distribution of patient contacts by volunteers.

3.53 Sometimes we use the **midquartile** $\frac{1}{2}(Q_1 + Q_3)$ as a measure of central location instead of the median or the mean, the **semi-interquartile range** $\frac{1}{2}(Q_3 - Q_1)$ as a measure of variation instead of the standard deviation or

Chapter 3 Summarizing Data: Statistical Descriptions

the range, and the **coefficient** of **quartile variation** $\dfrac{Q_3 - Q_1}{Q_1 + Q_3} \cdot 100$ as a measure of relative variation instead of the coefficient of variation.

(a) Use the results of part (b) of Exercise 3.46 to calculate all these statistical measures for the distribution of ages of restaurant workers.

(b) Use the results of part (c) of Exercise 3.51 to calculate all these statistical measures for the distribution of patient contacts by hospital volunteers.

(c) Use the results of part (a) of Exercise 3.50 and the value of $Q_1 = 25.1$ to calculate all these statistical measures for the distribution of down-times.

3.54 Roll a pair of dice 120 times and construct a distribution showing how many times there were 0 sixes, how many times there was 1 six, and how many times there were 2 sixes. Draw a histogram of this distribution and describe its shape.

3.55 If a coin is flipped 5 times, the result may be represented by means of a sequence of H's and T's (for example, HHTTH), where H stands for *heads* and T for *tails*. Having obtained such a sequence of H's and T's, we can then check after each successive flip whether the number of heads exceeds the number of tails. For example, for the sequence HHTTH, heads is ahead after the first flip, after the second flip, after the third flip, not after the fourth flip, but again after the fifth flip; altogether, it is ahead 4 times. Repeat this experiment 50 times, and construct a histogram showing in how many cases heads was ahead altogether 0 times, 1 time, 2 times, . . . , and 5 times. Explain why the resulting distribution should be U shaped.

3.56 In a recent year, Bureau of Labor Statistics data disclosed that workers in all of the states and the District of Columbia had average pay increases of the following percentages (there were no decreases): 3.7, 0.1, 3.9, 3.0, 4.4, 3.1, 7.9, 5.8, 6.2, 4.5, 4.3, 7.1, 3.4, 6.1, 3.8, 3.7, 3.3, 3.0, 3.3, 5.2, 5.5, 7.4, 4.8, 5.0, 3.7, 3.5, 3.2, 4.0, 5.3, 6.9, 8.0, 2.8, 7.0, 4.3, 2.2, 4.5, 2.6, 4.0, 5.3, 7.1, 4.2, 3.1, 3.8, 3.3, 3.3, 5.3, 5.5, 3.5, 2.8, 7.4, and 1.5.

(a) Find the mean.

(b) Find the standard deviation of this population of pay increases.

(c) If the data are arranged in a frequency distribution with the classes 0.0–1.4, 1.5–2.9, 3.0–4.4, 4.5–5.9, 6.0–7.4, and 7.5–8.9, and the mean and standard deviation are recalculated, the answers are 4.46 percent and 1.60 percent, respectively. These are slightly different from the answers obtained in parts (a) and (b). Why are the answers not identical?

3.10

Technical Note (Summations)

In summation notation, $\sum x$ does not make it clear which, or how many, values of x are to be added. This is taken care of by the more explicit notation

$$\sum_{i=1}^{n} x_i = x_1 + x_2 + \cdots + x_n$$

where it is made clear that we are adding the x's whose subscripts i are 1, 2, . . . , n. We did not use this notation in the text, in order to simplify the overall appearance of the various formulas, assuming that it is clear in each case what x's we are referring to and how many there are.

Using the $\sum$ notation, we shall also have occasion to write such expressions as $\sum x^2$, $\sum xy$, $\sum x^2 f$, . . . , which, respectively, represent the sums

$$\sum_{i=1}^{n} x_i^2 = x_1^2 + x_2^2 + x_3^2 + \cdots + x_n^2$$

$$\sum_{j=1}^{m} x_j y_j = x_1 y_1 + x_2 y_2 + \cdots + x_m y_m$$

$$\sum_{i=1}^{n} x_i^2 f_i = x_1^2 f_1 + x_2^2 f_2 + \cdots + x_n^2 f_n$$

Working with two subscripts, we shall also have the occasion to evaluate **double summations** such as

$$\sum_{j=1}^{3} \sum_{i=1}^{4} x_{ij} = \sum_{j=1}^{3} (x_{1j} + x_{2j} + x_{3j} + x_{4j})$$
$$= x_{11} + x_{21} + x_{31} + x_{41} + x_{12} + x_{22} + x_{32} + x_{42}$$
$$+ x_{13} + x_{23} + x_{33} + x_{43}$$

To verify some of the formulas involving summations that are stated but not proved in the text, it will be convenient to use the following rules:

$$\text{Rule A:} \quad \sum_{i=1}^{n} (x_i \pm y_i) = \sum_{i=1}^{n} x_i \pm \sum_{i=1}^{n} y_i$$

$$\text{Rule B:} \quad \sum_{i=1}^{n} k \cdot x_i = k \cdot \sum_{i=1}^{n} x_i$$

$$\text{Rule C:} \quad \sum_{i=1}^{n} k = n \cdot k$$

The first of these rules states that the summation of the sum (or difference) of two terms equals the sum (or difference) of the individual summations, and it can be extended to the sum or difference of more than two terms. The second rule states that we can, so to speak, factor a constant out of a summation, and the third rule states that the summation of a constant is simply n times that constant. All these rules can be proved by actually writing out in full what each of the summations represents.

EXERCISES

(Exercises 3.57 and 3.58 are practice exercises. Their complete solutions are given on page 106.)

3.57 Write each of the following as summations:

(a) $x_1^2 + x_2^2 + \cdots + x_{10}^2$

(b) $y_1 + y_2 + \cdots + y_{12}$

(c) $y_5 z_5 + y_6 z_6 + \cdots y_n z_n$

(d) $2a_1 + 2a_2 + \cdots + 2a_n$

(e) $(a_1 - b_1) + (a_2 - b_2) + \cdots + (a_n - b_n)$

(f) $(a_3)^2 b_3 + (a_4)^2 b_4 + \cdots + (a_8)^2 b_8$

3.58 Write each of the following expressions without summation signs:

(a) $\sum_{i=1}^{3} x_i y_i$

(b) $\sum_{i=1}^{4} (a_i - b)$

(c) $\sum_{i=3}^{5} k a_i$

(d) $\sum_{i=3}^{6} y_i^2$

(e) $\sum_{j=2}^{7} (z_j - c)$

(f) $\sum_{j=4}^{8} (z_j - a_j)$

3.59 Given $a_1 = 3$, $a_2 = 5$, $a_3 = 8$, and $a_4 = 2$, evaluate

(a) $\sum a$

(b) $\sum a^2$

(c) $\sum (6 - a)$

(d) $\sum (a - 2)$

(e) $\sum (4a - 2)$

(f) $\sum 2(a - 3)$

3.60 Given

$$
\begin{array}{lllll}
a_1 = -2 & a_2 = 4 & a_3 = -1 & a_4 = 5 & a_5 = 1 \\
b_1 = -3 & b_2 = 3 & b_3 = 1 & b_4 = -2 & b_5 = 3 \\
c_1 = -4 & c_2 = 3 & c_3 = 1 & c_4 = -3 & c_5 = 2
\end{array}
$$

evaluate each of the following:

(a) $\displaystyle\sum_{i=1}^{4} c_i$ (c) $\displaystyle\sum_{i=1}^{3} c_i b_i$ (e) $\displaystyle\sum_{i=3}^{5} (a_i + c_i)$

(b) $\displaystyle\sum_{i=2}^{5} a_i$ (d) $\displaystyle\sum_{i=2}^{4} (c_i)^2$ (f) $\displaystyle\sum_{i=1}^{5} (c_i b_i)$

3.61 Given that $\displaystyle\sum_{i=1}^{6} x_i = 14$ and $\displaystyle\sum_{i=1}^{6} x_i^2 = 44$, find

(a) $\displaystyle\sum_{i=1}^{6} (x_i - 1)$ (b) $\displaystyle\sum_{i=1}^{6} (3x_i + 2)$ (c) $\displaystyle\sum_{i=1}^{6} (x_i + 4)^2$

3.62 Prove that

(a) $\displaystyle\sum_{i=1}^{n} (x_i - k) = \sum_{i=1}^{n} x_i - nk$

(b) $\displaystyle\sum_{i=1}^{n} (x_i - \bar{x}) = 0$, where $\bar{x}$ is the mean of the x_i

(c) $\displaystyle\sum_{i=1}^{n} (x_i - k)^2 = \sum_{i=1}^{n} x_i^2 - 2k \cdot \sum_{i=1}^{n} x_i + nk^2$

3.63 (a) Is it true in general that $\left(\displaystyle\sum_{i=1}^{n} x_i\right)^2 = \sum_{i=1}^{n} x_i^2$? (Hint: Determine whether the equation holds for $n = 2$.)

(b) Use the sigma notation with subscripts and limits of summation to write the formula for the sample mean, the weighted mean, and the grand mean of combined data.

3.11

Technical Note (Unbiased Estimators)

Ordinarily, the purpose of calculating a sample statistic (such as the mean, the standard deviation, or the variance) is to estimate the corresponding population parameter. If we actually took many samples from a population which has the mean μ, calculated the sample means $\bar{x}$, and then averaged all these estimates of μ, we should find that their average is very close to μ. However, if we calculated the variance of each sample by means of the formula $\sum (x - \bar{x})^2/n$, and then averaged all these estimates of σ^2, we would probably find that their average is less (perhaps substantially so) than σ^2. Theoretically, it can be shown that we can compensate for this by dividing by $n - 1$ instead of n in the formula s^2. Estimators which have the desirable property that their values will on the average equal the quantity they are supposed to estimate are said to be **unbiased**; otherwise, they are said to be **biased**. So, we say that $\bar{x}$ is an unbiased estimator of the population mean μ, and that s^2 is an unbiased estimator of the population variance σ^2. It does not follow from this, however, that s is also an unbiased estimator of σ; but when n is large the bias is small, so we can use s as an estimate of σ.

3.12

A Word of Caution

The fact that there is a certain amount of arbitrariness in the selection of statistical descriptions has led some persons to believe that they can take a set of data, commit some statistics, and prove almost anything they want. To put it more bluntly, a nineteenth-century British statesman once said that there are three kinds of lies: lies, damned lies, and statistics.

To show where such a criticism might be justified, suppose that a paint manufacturer asks his research department to ''prove'' that on the average a gallon of his paint covers more square feet than those of his two principal competitors. Suppose, furthermore, that the research department tests five cans of each brand, getting the following results (in square feet per gallon can):

$$\begin{array}{llllll}\text{Brand } A: & 505 & 516 & 478 & 513 & 503 \\ \text{Brand } B: & 512 & 486 & 511 & 486 & 510 \\ \text{Brand } C: & 496 & 485 & 490 & 520 & 484 \end{array}$$

If the manufacturer's own brand is brand A, the data analyst finds to his delight that the means of the three samples are 503, 501, and 495. He can, thus, claim that in actual tests a can of his employer's product covered on the average more square feet than those of his competitors.

If, however, the manufacturer's own brand is brand B, the analyst can no longer base the comparison on the sample means. The sample medians, though, are 505, 510, and 490, and this gives him the results he wants. The median is a perfectly respectable measure of the ''average'' or ''center'' of a set of data, and using the medians he can claim that his employer's product came out best in the test.

Finally, suppose that the manufacturer's own brand is brand C. After going down the list of various measures of central location, the analyst comes upon one he wants. The **sample midrange** is defined as the mean of the smallest and largest values in a sample, and the midranges of the three samples of this example are 497, 499, and 502. So, he can claim that brand *C*, his employer's product, scored on the average highest in the test.

The moral of this example is that if data are to be compared and special pleading or indoctrination is not to be indulged in, the method of comparison should be decided upon beforehand, or at least without actually looking at the data. All this is aside from the fact that comparisons based on samples are often far from conclusive. It is quite possible that whatever differences there may be among the three means (or three other descriptions) can be attributed entirely to chance.

Another point which must be remembered is that a statistical measure always describes a particular characteristic of a set of data and that it describes this characteristic in a special way. Whether this "special way" is appropriate for a given situation is something which will have to be examined individually in each case. Suppose, for instance, that we want to buy a house and that we are shown one in a neighborhood where, according to the broker, average family income is in excess of $60,000. This gives the impression of a relatively prosperous neighborhood, but it could well be a neighborhood where most families have incomes of less than $20,000 while one very wealthy family has an income of several hundred thousand dollars a year. In this kind of situation the mean is greatly affected by the one extreme value, and it would be much more informative to say here that the median family income is less than $20,000, mentioning, perhaps, the special situation created by the one wealthy family. Further examples of this kind may be found in *How to Lie with Statistics,* the book by D. Huff referred to in the bibliography at the end of this book.

3.13

Checklist of Key Terms

Arithmetic mean, 46
Bell-shaped distribution, 86
Biased estimator, 97
Bimodal, 52
Box-and-whisker plot, 88
Boxplot, 88
Chebyshev's theorem, 72
Coding, 79
Coefficient of quartile
   variation, 92

Coefficient of variation, 76
Decile, 84
Deviation from mean, 67
Fractile, 84
Geometric mean, 53, 63
Grand mean of combined data, 59
Grouped data, 44
Harmonic mean, 53, 63
Hinges, 56
Leaf, 51

3.14

Review Exercises

3.64 An environmental group collected the following amounts of newspaper for recycling (data in truckloads): 38, 26, 51, 42, 38, and 45. Calculate the mean, median, range, and variance of the number of truckloads of newspaper collected by this group.

3.65 Sand varies greatly in composition and size with grains larger than $\frac{1}{400}$ of an inch but less than $\frac{1}{12}$ of an inch. An abrasive company receives a shipment of sand whose grains have a mean diameter of 0.0500 inch and a variance of 0.0001 inch^2. At least what percent of the grains of sand must have sizes between

(a) 0.03 and 0.07 inch

(b) 0.025 and 0.075 inch

(c) 0.020 and 0.080 inch

3.66 The owner of an illuminated sign, with a large population of light bulbs, decides to replace all the bulbs after the sign has been illuminated for 1,000 hours. The standard unit corresponding to 1,000 burning hours for these bulbs is -3, and the population coefficient of variation is 2.5 percent. What is the population mean and standard deviation of these bulbs?

3.67 Railroad freight trains have an average of 70 cars (not including the locomotive and caboose), and the trains carry an average of 1,400 tons of freight per train. If the average train receives routine maintenance every 10,000 miles at a cost of $7,000,

(a) What is the average maintenance cost per car mile traveled?

(b) What is the average maintenance cost per ton mile (a ton mile is 1 ton of freight transported 1 mile)?

3.68   The numbers of sales prospects called and the percentages of sales made by five industrial equipment salespersons are

Salespersons	Sales prospects	Percentage of sales
A	50	18
B	36	25
C	70	20
D	40	30
E	75	24

What is the overall percentage of sales made by these salespersons?

3.69   The three following distributions show the sales of the 50 largest corporations in the United States for a recent year.

Distribution A		Distribution B		Distribution C	
Sales (billions)	Number of companies	Sales (billions)	Number of companies	Sales (billions)	Number of companies
$ 0– 9	18	$ 0– 9	18	$29 or less	43
10– 19	19	10–19	19	30–39	2
20– 29	6	20–29	6	40–49	1
30– 39	2	30–39	2	More than 49	4
40– 49	1	More than 39	5		
50– 59	1				
60– 69	2				
70– 79	0				
80– 89	0				
90– 99	0				
100–109	1				

Decide for each distribution whether it is possible to find the mean and the median.

3.70　The total annual payroll for four machine shops in a certain community is $1,448,000. The first machine shop has 10 employees at an annual average wage of $26,000, the second has 14 employees with an annual average wage of $32,000, the third has 11 employees with an annual average wage of $25,000, and the fourth has an unknown number of workers with an annual average wage of $31,000.

(a) How many workers are employed in the fourth machine shop?

(b) What is the overall annual average wage of the workers in the four machine shops?

3.71　The mileages read from the odometers of a sample of automobiles which were lubricated at an automobile service station are

Thousands of miles	Frequency
0– 9	20
10–19	28
20–29	36
30–39	49
40–49	58
50–59	42
60–69	30
70–79	20
80–89	12
90–99	5

Find the mean and standard deviation of this distribution.

3.72　With reference to the preceding exercise, find
(a) the median
(b) the quartiles Q_1 and Q_3

3.73　Use the results of Exercises 3.71 and 3.72 to find the Pearsonian coefficient of skewness for the distribution of the mileages of a sample of automobiles which were lubricated.

3.74　Determine the standard deviation of corporate earnings if a sample showed a mean corporate earnings rate of 14 percent and coefficient of variation of 10 percent.

3.75   The registrar of a college has calculated the grade point averages of its students for a certain year. Give one example each of a problem where the data might be looked on as

(a) a population

(b) a sample

3.76   After a few days of on-the-job experience, the output of three recently employed production workers increased by 4, 6, and 9 percent. Calculate the geometric mean of these production increases.

3.77   A comparison shopping service found that identical television sets were for sale in store 1, store 2, store 3, store 4, and store 5 at prices of $500, $549, $475, $425, and $450, respectively.

(a) Calculate the mean of these prices.

(b) What would be the average price per set if 3 were sold by store 1, 6 by store 2, 4 by store 3, none by store 4, and 1 by store 5?

(c) Use the harmonic mean to determine the average price of a television set if store 1 sold $9,000 of its sets and store 5 also sold $9,000 of its sets. Assume none was sold by stores 2, 3, and 4.

3.78   If $\sum\limits_{i=1}^{6} x_i = 24$ and $\sum\limits_{i=1}^{6} x_i^2 = 100$ for a sample of size $n = 6$, find

(a) the mean

(b) the standard deviation

3.79   The numbers of fluorescent light bulbs which were replaced by the maintenance department of a factory on 30 consecutive working days were 7, 8, 9, 7, 8, 7, 7, 7, 6, 8, 9, 9, 6, 7, 7, 8, 7, 8, 9, 9, 7, 8, 6, 7, 7, 8, 9, 8, 6, and 7. What is the modal number of fluorescent light bulbs which were replaced?

3.80   A random sample of the yields of essential oils from 10 one-ton lots of flower petals (by enfleurage and extraction, an old process used in perfume manufacturing) showed yields of 14.84, 12.02, 13.29, 12.95, 13.02, 11.91, 12.64, 13.25, 12.77, and 12.01 ounces of essential oils. Find the mean and median number of ounces of essential oils per ton of flower petals.

3.81   A wholesale greenhouse sells flats of 12 marigold plants for $1.25, flats of 12 petunia plants for $1.50, and flats of 12 pansy plants for $2.00. If a gardener spends $30.00 for marigolds, $30.00 for petunias, and $30.00 for pansies, use the harmonic mean to determine the average cost per dozen plants.

3.82   If the mean time it takes a production worker to assemble a metal cabinet is 5 minutes and the standard deviation is 20 seconds, what fraction of the worker's assembly times lies between 4 and 6 minutes?

3.83   Following is the distribution of the number of prescriptions filled daily by a pharmacy during 100 business days.

Prescriptions filled	Frequency
0– 4	3
5– 9	17
10–14	24
15–19	31
20–24	19
25–29	6

Find the mean, median, mode, and standard deviation of this distribution.

3.84 With reference to the distribution of the preceding exercise, find

(a) Q_1 and Q_3

(b) D_1 and D_9

(c) P_5 and P_{95}

3.85 A manufacturer of lacquer finishes estimates that it takes $\frac{1}{2}$ pint (16 ounces per pint) of lacquer to apply a finish to a certain size chest. To test this claim, the manufacturer of the chests applied 25 pints of lacquer to a production lot of 50 chests, but finished only 40 before the lacquer was exhausted.

(a) How much lacquer is required to apply a finish to a production lot of 50 chests?

(b) How much lacquer is required to apply a finish to each chest?

3.86 During a recent 12-month period, the inflation rates (consumer prices, year-to-year change) of the United States, Japan, West Germany, France, and Great Britain were 4.7 percent, 2.6 percent, 2.4 percent, 3.0 percent, and 9.8 percent, respectively. Calculate the mean, median, range, and standard deviation of this sample of inflation rates.

3.87 A study comparing actual delivery dates with scheduled delivery dates of raw materials revealed the following days early ($-$) and days late ($+$) information for a sample of seven deliveries: -4, -11, 0, $+1$, 0, -5, and -2.

(a) Find the mean, median, and range of the days early/days late information.

(b) Early deliveries of raw materials inventory may overcrowd limited storage space, while late deliveries can stop or delay production. The mean of the foregoing data is 3.3 days if $(+, -)$ signs are omitted. Explain how this is different from the mean calculated in part (a).

3.88 Comment on the statement that while 12 students seeking employment wrote to an average of 8 employers, 7 of them wrote to 15 or more employers.

3.89 Given a sample for which $\sum_{i=1}^{5} x_i = 4.1$ and $\sum_{i=1}^{5} x_i^2 = 3.39$ find

(a) $\sum_{i=1}^{5} (x_i + 4)$ (b) $\sum_{i=1}^{5} (3x_i - 1)$ (c) $\sum_{i=1}^{5} (x_i - 2)^2$

3.90 A sample of five experienced income tax preparers completed a federal income tax test problem in 25, 15, 22, 18, and 20 minutes. Also, a sample of eight trainees for income tax preparation completed the same federal income tax test problem in 55, 60, 53, 58, 54, 51, 63 and 62 minutes.

(a) Calculate the means, medians, and standard deviations of the two samples.

(b) Find the coefficients of variation for the two samples and determine which sample has the greater variation.

3.91 Shares of stock of a business machine corporation are purchased at a mean price of $100 per share, and shares of stock of a railroad corporation are purchased at a mean price of $25 per share. The mean price of all shares purchased is $50 per share.

(a) What fraction of the total number of shares of stock is railroad stock?

(b) If $15,000 is the total purchase price of the stock, how much is invested in railroad stock?

3.92 In Exercise 3.9 on page 61, the weekly sales of the 11 stores in a shopping mall are $200,000, $150,000, $100,000, $90,000, $85,000, $84,000, $83,000, $81,000, $80,000, $78,000, and $78,000, and the hinges of this series are $95,000 and $80,500. Show that these hinges, together with the median, which is $84,000, *do not satisfy even one* of the desirable properties for quartiles which we gave on page 53.

3.93 Which of the three properties of quartiles on page 53 are satisfied by the hinges and the median when

(a) $n = 13$

(b) $n = 14$

3.94 If we delete the words "or equal to" in the definition of hinges, it can be shown that we obtain statistical measures which, together with the median, will always satisfy the second of the three properties of quartiles which we gave on page 53. Verify that this is, indeed, the case for

(a) $n = 17$

(b) $n = 22$

3.95 Some statisticians and some computer packages use interpolation to determine the position of quartiles and other fractiles. If we refer to the statistical measures which divide a set of data into k parts as k-tiles, one formula which is sometimes used for the position of the ith k-tile is

$$i \cdot \frac{n+1}{k}$$

For instance, for the position of the first quartile of 30 values we substitute $i = 1$, $k = 4$, and $n = 30$, and get $1 \cdot \frac{30+1}{4} = 7\frac{3}{4}$. This means that we must go three-fourths of the way between the 7th and 8th values, and if these values happen to be 34 and 36, the $Q_1 = 34 + \frac{3}{4} (36 - 34) = 35.5$. The advantage of this approach is that it can be used to determine all kinds of fractiles, say, the percentiles which divide a set of data into a hundred parts.

(a) A college had 8, 3, 20, 5, 2, 8, 14, 2, 6, 10, 7, and 15 applicants for 12 different teaching positions. Use the method of interpolation just given to find Q_1 and Q_3.

(b) Use the method of interpolation just given to find Q_1 and Q_3 for the array, in inches, of the heights of 25 young blue spruce trees of Exercise 3.11 on page 61.

3.96   Use a computer package and the data of Exercise 3.10 to determine the mean, median, quartile 1, and quartile 3 of the times, in minutes, required for the inspections.

3.97   Use a computer package and the data of Exercise 3.12 to obtain the modal choice of customers method of payment when making purchases. Hint: Code the data using, for example, 1 to replace store charge account; 2 to replace bank credit card; 3 to replace cash; and 4 to replace check.

3.98   Use a computer package and the data of Exercise 3.10 to calculate the standard deviation of this population of people entering the United States.

3.99   Use a computer package and the data of Exercise 3.27 to calculate the standard deviation of the number of gallons of gasoline used by this sample of seven taxicabs.

3.100   Use a computer package and the data of Exercise 3.28 to
(a) find the range and standard deviations of the birth rates and death rates if we view these data as samples
(b) find the range and standard deviations of the birth rates and death rates if we view these data as populations

3.101   Use a computer package and the sample data for the 10 engine blocks of Exercise 3.30 to calculate
(a) the mean
(b) the range
(c) the standard deviation

3.102 Use the computer printout of Figure 3.9 and the data of Example 3.21 to verify the boxplot for the number of private aircraft that landed at an airport on 15 consecutive days.

3.15

Solutions of Practice Exercises

3.2 (a) If we are interested in the shoe sizes of all the soldiers in this infantry company of the U.S. Army at the time of measurement, this is a population.

(b) The measurements would be a sample if we wanted to generalize from them to shoe sizes of the soldiers at different times or to all the infantry companies in the U.S. Army.

3.3 Since $120 + 122 + 130 + 138 + 125 + 160 + 161 + 101 + 98 + 172 = 1,327$, the mean daily numbers of bunches of cut flowers is $\frac{1,327}{10} = 132.7$.

3.5 (a) Yes, since $11 \cdot 210 = 2,310$ pounds is greater than 2,000 pounds.

(b) No, since $(5 \cdot 210) + (8 \cdot 115) = 1,970$ pounds is less than 2,000 pounds.

(c) No, since $(4 \cdot 210) + (4 \cdot 115) + (4 \cdot 175) = 2,000$ pounds.

3.7

	Mean (inches)	Median (inches)	Mode (inches)
Combing	3.3	3.3	3.2, 3.3, 3.5
French combing	1.8	1.8	2.0
Clothing	1.1	1.0	1.2

Note that the calculation of the mean for French combing is $\frac{1.4 + 1.7 + 1.5 + 2.0 + 2.0 + 1.8 + 1.8 + 2.0}{8} = 1.775$, which is rounded to 1.8, and the median for clothing is 0.9, 0.9, 1.0, $\boxed{1.0, 1.1,}$ 1.2, 1.2, 1.2, which is $\frac{1.0 + 1.1}{2} = 1.05$, which is rounded to 1.0.

3.9 (a) Mean: Since $200,000 + 150,000 + 100,000 + 90,000 + 85,000 + 84,000 + 83,000 + 81,000 + 80,000 + 78,000 + 78,000 = 1,109,000$, the mean is $\frac{1,109,000}{11} = 100,818$ dollars, rounded to the nearest dollar.

Median: $\dfrac{n+1}{2} = \dfrac{11+1}{2} =$ 6th largest value, namely, \$84,000.

Mode: \$78,000, the value which occurs with the highest frequency (two times). The mean is unduly affected by the two largest values. The mode is unrepresentative and reflects only that two stores happen to have the same value of sales. The median, which is the center of the data, is most typical. The median is also fairly close to the value of the mean when the two largest values are excluded and the mean is recalculated.

(b) One hinge is the $\dfrac{6+1}{2} = 3.5$th item, and its value is $\dfrac{100,000 + 90,000}{2} = 95,000$. The other hinge is the 3.5th item from the other side, and its value is $\dfrac{80,000 + 81,000}{2} = \$80,500$.

3.10 (a) Since $3.0 + 2.0 + 3.1 + 2.0 + 0.5 + 5.0 + 2.0 + 1.1 + 2.0 + 1.9 + 2.9 + 1.8 + 2.8 + 2.8 + 3.2 + 2.7 + 1.6 + 1.6 + 2.4 + 4.9 = 49.3$, the mean is $\dfrac{49.3}{20} = 2.5$ minutes.

(b) Arranged according to size the values are 0.5, 1.1, 1.6, 1.6, 1.8, 1.9, 2.0, 2.0, 2.0, 2.0, 2.4, 2.7, 2.8, 2.8, 2.9, 3.0, 3.1, 3.2, 4.9, and 5.0, so that the median is the $\dfrac{20+1}{2} = 10.5$th value, namely, $\dfrac{2.0 + 2.4}{2} = 2.2$ minutes.

(c) The lower hinge is the $\dfrac{10+1}{2} = 5.5$th item, namely, $\dfrac{1.8 + 1.9}{2} = 1.85$. The upper hinge is the 5.5th item from the other side, and its value is $\dfrac{2.9 + 3.0}{2} = 2.95$ minutes.

(d) The mode is 2.0, the value which occurs with the highest frequency (four times).

3.14 Although the average amount of pollution may be trivial, dangerously high concentrations exist in specific areas. Some of these polluted areas exist in heavily populated areas.

3.15 $\dfrac{(10.2 \cdot 1.50) + (9.9 \cdot 1.00) + (12.0 \cdot 0.75) + (16.4 \cdot 0.25) + (17.8 \cdot 0.50)}{1.50 + 1.00 + 0.75 + 0.25 + 0.50}$

$= \dfrac{47.2}{4.00} = 11.8$ percent (denominators are in millions of dollars.)

3.18 (a) $\dfrac{(4,000 \cdot 38\frac{1}{8}) + (10,000 \cdot 28\frac{1}{4}) + (6,000 \cdot 42\frac{1}{2})}{4,000 + 10,000 + 6,000} = \dfrac{690,000}{20,000} = \$34\frac{1}{2}$ per share.

(b) $\dfrac{(4,000 \cdot 41\frac{3}{8}) + (10,000 \cdot 29\frac{7}{8}) + (6,000 \cdot 46\frac{3}{4})}{4,000 + 10,000 + 6,000} = \dfrac{744,750}{20,000} = \$37.2375$ or rounded to $\$37\frac{1}{4}$ per share.

Section 3.15   Solutions of Practice Exercises

(c) $37\frac{1}{4} - 34\frac{1}{2} = \$2\frac{3}{4}$.

3.22 $\dfrac{36,000}{1,500} = 24$ pieces of stone by plug and feather method, $\dfrac{30,000}{600} = 50$

pieces of stone by explosive method, so that the mean combined weight is
$\dfrac{36,000 + 30,000}{24 + 50} = 891.9$ pounds.

3.23 (a) $\sqrt{8 \cdot 18} = 12$

(b) $\sqrt[3]{9 \cdot 8 \cdot 24} = 12$

(c) $\sqrt[4]{12 \cdot 3 \cdot 4 \cdot 9} = 6$

3.24 (a) $\dfrac{2}{\dfrac{1}{300} + \dfrac{1}{600}} = 400$ miles per hour.

(b) $\dfrac{2}{\dfrac{1}{10} + \dfrac{1}{15}} = \$12$ per gross.

(c) $\dfrac{3}{\dfrac{1}{10} + \dfrac{1}{12.5} + \dfrac{1}{8}} = \$9.84$ per share.

3.25

x	$x - \mu$	$(x - \mu)^2$
12	-2	4
15	1	1
16	2	4
12	-2	4
15	1	1
17	3	9
11	-3	9
14	0	0
112		32

$\mu = \dfrac{112}{8} = 14$

$\sigma = \sqrt{\dfrac{\sum (x - \mu)^2}{N}}$

$= \sqrt{\dfrac{32}{8}} = 2$ workers

Alternatively, $\sum x = 12 + 15 + 16 + 12 + 15 + 17 + 11 + 14 = 112$ and
$\sum x^2 = 144 + 225 + 256 + 144 + 225 + 289 + 121 + 196 = 1,600$, so
that

$$\sigma = \sqrt{\dfrac{N(\sum x^2) - (\sum x)^2}{N^2}} = \sqrt{\dfrac{8(1,600) - (112)^2}{64}} = 2 \text{ workers}$$

3.28 (a) The ranges are $17.7 - 14.8 = 2.9$ births per 1,000 and $9.9 - 7.3 = 2.6$
deaths per 1,000. These answers apply whether the data are samples or
populations.

For the sample of birth rates, $\sum x = 15.0 + 14.8 + 15.1 + 15.0 + 15.4 + 15.1 + 17.2 + 17.7 + 17.5 = 142.8$ and $\sum x^2 = 225.00 + 219.04 + 228.01 + 225.00 + 237.16 + 228.01 + 295.84 + 312.29 + 306.25 = 2{,}276.60$, so that

$$s = \sqrt{\frac{9(2{,}277.60) - (142.8)^2}{9 \cdot 8}} = \sqrt{\frac{106.56}{72}} = 1.22 \text{ births per } 1{,}000$$

For the sample of deaths, $\sum x = 9.4 + 9.9 + 8.9 + 9.5 + 9.2 + 9.7 + 8.1 + 7.3 + 7.4 = 79.4$ and $\sum x^2 = 88.36 + 98.01 + 79.21 + 90.25 + 84.64 + 94.09 + 65.61 + 53.29 + 54.76 = 708.22$, so that

$$s = \sqrt{\frac{9(708.22) - (79.4)^2}{9 \cdot 8}} = \sqrt{\frac{69.62}{72}} = 0.98 \text{ deaths per } 1{,}000$$

(b) The ranges of the births and deaths are the same as those of the samples calculated in (a). For the population of births, $\sigma = \sqrt{\dfrac{106.56}{9 \cdot 9}} = 1.09$

births per 1,000. For the population of deaths, $\sigma = \sqrt{\dfrac{69.62}{9 \cdot 9}} = 0.93$

deaths per 1,000.

3.34 (a) Since $\sum x = -3 + 1 + 0 + 2 + (-2) + 1 + (-6) = -7$ and $\sum x^2 = 9 + 1 + 0 + 4 + 4 + 1 + 36 = 55$, we find that for the original data the

mean is $\dfrac{-7}{7} = -1$, the range is $2 - (-6) = 8$, and

$$s = \sqrt{\frac{7(55) - (-7)^2}{7 \cdot 6}} = \sqrt{8}$$

Since $\sum (x + 6) = 3 + 7 + 6 + 8 + 4 + 7 + 0 = 35$ and $\sum (x + 6)^2 = 9 + 49 + 36 + 64 + 16 + 49 + 0 = 223$, we find that after adding 6 to

each value the mean is $\dfrac{35}{7} = 5$, the range is $8 - 0 = 8$, and

$$s = \sqrt{\frac{7(223) - (35)^2}{7 \cdot 6}} = \sqrt{8}$$

(b) Since $\sum x = 980 + 1{,}031 + 968 + 1{,}053 = 4{,}032$ and $\sum x^2 = 960{,}400 + 1{,}062{,}961 + 937{,}024 + 1{,}108{,}809 = 4{,}069{,}194$, we find

that for the original data the mean is $\dfrac{4{,}032}{4} = 1{,}008$ operating hours and

$$s = \sqrt{\frac{4(4{,}069{,}194) - (4{,}032)^2}{4 \cdot 3}} = 40.6 \text{ operating hours}$$

Since $\sum (x - 100) = 880 + 931 + 868 + 953 = 3{,}632$ and $\sum (x - 100)^2 = 774{,}400 + 866{,}761 + 753{,}424 + 908{,}209 = 3{,}302{,}794$,

we find that after subtracting 100 from each value the mean is $\dfrac{3{,}632}{4} = 908$ operating hours and

$$s = \sqrt{\frac{4(3,302,794) - (3,632)^2}{4 \cdot 3}} = 40.6 \text{ operating hours}$$

(c) After we subtract 2.50 from each measurement, $\sum x = 0.02 + 0.02 + 0.01 + (-0.01) + 0.00 + (-0.05) + 0.03 + 0.02 + (-0.02) + (-0.02) = 0.00$ and $\sum x^2 = 0.0004 + 0.0004 + 0.0001 + 0.0001 + 0.0000 + 0.0025 + 0.0009 + 0.0004 + 0.0004 + 0.0004 = 0.0056$, we get

$$s = \sqrt{\frac{10(0.0056) - (0.0)^2}{10 \cdot 9}} = 0.025 \text{ centimeters}$$

3.36 No. The movie's attendance increased by $\dfrac{14,000 - 12,000}{2,000} = 1$ standard deviation, and the museum's attendance increased by $\dfrac{7,000 - 6,000}{500} = 2$ standard deviations.

3.37 $k \cdot 800 = 2,000$, so $k = 2.5$, and $1 - \dfrac{1}{k^2} = 1 - \dfrac{1}{2.5^2} = 0.84$ or 84 percent.

3.42 (a)

Shares traded (in millions)	Class mark	f	xf	x^2f
5– 9	7	8	56	392
10–14	12	17	204	2,448
15–19	17	8	136	2,312
20–24	22	3	66	1,452
25–29	27	2	54	1,458
30–34	32	1	32	1,024
		39	548	9,086

Since $\sum xf = 548$ and $\sum x^2f = 9,086$, we get $\bar{x} = \dfrac{548}{39} = 14.05$, which may be rounded to 14.0, and $s = \sqrt{\dfrac{39(9,086) - (548)^2}{39 \cdot 38}} = 6.04$, which may be rounded to 6.0.

(b)

Class mark	μ	f	μf	$\mu^2 f$
7	-2	8	-16	32
12	-1	17	-17	17
17	0	8	0	0
22	1	3	3	3
27	2	2	4	8
32	3	1	3	9
		39	-23	69

Since $\sum \mu f = -23$ and $\sum \mu^2 f = 69$, we get $\bar{x} = 17 + \dfrac{-23}{39} \cdot 5 = 14.0$, and

$$s = 5\sqrt{\dfrac{39(69) - (-23)^2}{39 \cdot 38}} = 6.0.$$

3.43 (a) Since $\dfrac{n}{2} = \dfrac{39}{2} = 19.5$, $L = 9.5$, $j = 19.5 - 8 = 11.5$, $f = 17$, and $c = 5$,

we get $\tilde{x} = 9.5 + \dfrac{11.5}{17} \cdot 5 = 12.9.$

(b) The midpoint of the modal class is $\dfrac{9.5 + 14.5}{2} = 12.$

3.44 $SK = \dfrac{3(14.0 - 12.9)}{6.0} = 0.55$

3.46 (a)

Ages	Frequency	Cumulative frequency in each class
15–24	22	0– 22
25–34	27	23– 49
35–44	41	50– 90
45–54	35	91–125
55–64	28	126–153
65–74	14	154–167
75–84	3	168–170
	170	

The median for this set of grouped data is the *value* of the $\dfrac{170}{2} = 85$th item.

We know that the 85th item lies between (is in the class) the ages 35–44 years because its cumulative frequencies (50–90) contain the 85th item. L, the lower boundary of the class, is 34.5; j, the number of items we lack when we reach L, is $85 - 49 = 36$; f is 41; and $c = 44.5 - 34.5 = 10$. So the value of the 85th item is

$$\tilde{x} = L + \dfrac{j}{f} \cdot c = 34.5 + \dfrac{85 - 49}{41} \cdot 10 = 43.3 \text{ years}$$

(b) Q_1 is the value of the $\dfrac{170}{4} = 42.5$ item.

The value of $Q_1 = 24.5 + \dfrac{42.5 - 22}{27} \cdot 10 = 32.1$ years.

Q_3 is the value of the $\dfrac{3}{4} \cdot 170 = 127.5$ item.

The value of $Q_3 = 54.5 + \dfrac{127.5 - 125}{28} \cdot 10 = 55.4$ years.

(c) P_{90} is the $\dfrac{90}{100} \cdot 170 = 153$ item.

The value of $P_{90} = 54.5 + \dfrac{153 - 125}{28} \cdot 10 = 64.5$ years.

P_{95} is the value of the $\dfrac{95}{100} \cdot 170 = 161.5$ item.

The value of $P_{95} = 64.5 + \dfrac{161.5 - 153}{14} \cdot 10 = 70.6$ years.

3.53 (a) $\dfrac{Q_1 + Q_3}{2} = \dfrac{32.1 + 55.4}{2} = 43.8$ years

$\dfrac{Q_3 - Q_1}{2} = \dfrac{55.4 - 32.1}{2} = 11.6$ years

$\dfrac{Q_3 - Q_1}{Q_1 + Q_3} \cdot 100 = \dfrac{55.4 - 32.1}{32.1 + 55.4} \cdot 100 = 26.6$ percent

(b) $\dfrac{Q_1 + Q_3}{2} = \dfrac{16.4 + 28.9}{2} = 22.6$ patient contacts

$\dfrac{Q_3 - Q_1}{2} = \dfrac{28.9 - 16.4}{2} = 6.25$ patient contacts

$\dfrac{Q_3 - Q_1}{Q_1 + Q_3} \cdot 100 = \dfrac{28.9 - 16.4}{16.4 + 28.9} \cdot 100 = 27.6$ percent

(c) $\dfrac{Q_1 + Q_3}{2} = \dfrac{25.1 + 40.9}{2} = 33.0$ minutes

$\dfrac{Q_3 - Q_1}{2} = \dfrac{40.9 - 25.1}{2} = 7.8$ minutes

$\dfrac{Q_3 - Q_1}{Q_1 + Q_3} \cdot 100 = \dfrac{40.9 - 25.1}{25.1 + 40.9} \cdot 100 = 23.9$ percent

3.57 (a) $\sum\limits_{i=1}^{10} x_i^2$ (b) $\sum\limits_{i=1}^{12} y_i$ (c) $\sum\limits_{i=5}^{n} y_i z_i$ (d) $2 \cdot \sum\limits_{i=1}^{n} a_i$

(e) $\sum\limits_{i=1}^{n} a_i - \sum\limits_{i=1}^{n} b_i$ (f) $\sum\limits_{i=3}^{8} a_i^2 b_i$

3.58 (a) $x_1 y_1 + x_2 y_2 + x_3 y_3$

(b) $a_1 + a_2 + a_3 + a_4 - 4b$

(c) $k(a_3 + a_4 + a_5)$

(d) $y_3^2 + y_4^2 + y_5^2 + y_6^2$

(e) $z_2 + z_3 + z_4 + z_5 + z_6 + z_7 - 6c$

(f) $z_4 + z_5 + z_6 + z_7 + z_8 - (a_4 + a_5 + a_6 + a_7 + a_8)$

4

Possibilities, Probabilities, and Expectations

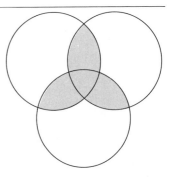

W̲e can hardly predict the outcome of a presidential election unless we know what candidates are running for office, and we cannot very well predict what recordings will be among the "top 10" unless we know at least which ones are on the market. More generally, we cannot make intelligent predictions or decisions unless we know at least what is possible, or to put it differently, we must know what is possible before we can judge what is probable. Thus, Sections 4.1 and 4.2 will be devoted to the problem of determining what is possible in given situations. Then, in Section 4.3 we shall learn how to judge also what is probable, and in Section 4.4 we shall introduce the related concept of a mathematical expectation.

4.1

Counting

The simple process of counting still plays an important role in business and economics. One still has to count 1, 2, 3, 4, . . . , for example, when taking inventory, when determining the number of damaged cases in a shipment of wines from France, or when preparing a report showing how many times certain stock market indexes went up during a given month. Sometimes, the process of counting can be simplified by using mechanical devices (for instance, when counting spectators passing through turnstiles) or by performing counts indirectly (for instance, by subtracting the serial numbers of invoices to determine the total number of sales). At other times, the process of counting can be simplified greatly by means of special mathematical techniques, such as the ones given in this chapter.

In the study of "what is possible," there are essentially two kinds of problems. First there is the problem of listing everything that can happen in a given situation, and then there is the problem of determining how many different things can happen (without actually constructing a complete list). The second kind of problem is especially important, because in many cases we really do not need a complete list, and hence, can save ourselves a great deal of work. Although the first kind of problem may seem straightforward and easy, this is not always the case.

EXAMPLE 4.1   Three applicants for real estate licenses in the state of Arizona are planning to take the required examination in October, and repeat it, if necessary, in November and December. If we are interested only in how many of the applicants pass the examination in each of the three months, how many different possibilities are there?

SOLUTION   Clearly, there are many. For instance, all three applicants might pass the examination in October; one might pass in October, another in December, and the third fail all three times; one might pass in November and the other two in December; and all three of the applicants might fail each month. Continuing this way carefully, we may determine that there are altogether 20 possibilities.   ■

To handle problems like Example 4.1 systematically, it helps to construct a **tree diagram** such as that of Figure 4.1. This diagram shows that for

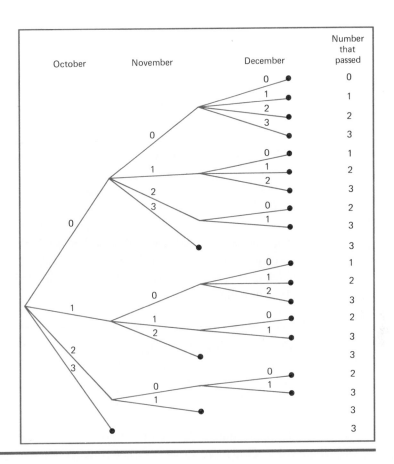

FIGURE 4.1
Tree diagram for
real estate license,
Example 4.1

October there are four possibilities (four branches), corresponding to 0, 1, 2, or 3 of the applicants passing the examination; for November there are four branches emanating from the top branch, three from the second branch, two from the third branch, and none from the bottom branch. Evidently, there are still four possibilities (0, 1, 2, or 3) when no one passes in October, but only three possibilities (0, 1, or 2) when one passes in October, two possibilities (0 or 1) when two pass in October, and there is no need to go on when all three of the applicants pass in October. The same sort of reasoning applies also to December, and (going from left to right) we find that there are altogether 20 different paths along the "branches" of the tree. In other words, there are 20 distinct possibilities in this situation. It can also be seen from this diagram that in 10 of the cases all three of the applicants pass the examination (sooner or later) during the three months, in 6 of the cases two of them pass, in 3 cases only one of them passes, and in 1 case none of the applicants passes.

EXAMPLE 4.2   A helicopter service connecting two airports has four pilots and three helicopters. In how many different ways can one pilot and one helicopter be assigned to a job?

SOLUTION   If we label the four pilots, *A, B, C,* and *D,* the three helicopters I, II, and III, and draw the tree diagram of Figure 4.2, we find that there are 12 different ways in all. The first path along the branches of the tree corresponds to the choice of pilot *A* and helicopter I, the second path corresponds to the choice of pilot *A* and helicopter II, . . . , and the 12th path corresponds to the choice of pilot *D* and helicopter III.   ■

The answer we got in Example 4.2 is $4 \cdot 3 = 12$, the product of the number of ways in which one pilot can be selected and the number of ways in which one helicopter can be selected. Generalizing from this example, let us state the following rule:

Multiplication of choices

> *If a choice consists of two steps, the first of which can be made in m ways and for each of these the second can be made in n ways, then the whole choice can be made in m · n ways.*

To prove this, we have only to draw a tree diagram similar to that of Figure 4.2. First there are *m* branches corresponding to the possibilities in the first step, and then there are *n* branches emanating from each of these branches to represent the possibilities in the second step. This leads to $m \cdot n$ paths along the branches of the tree diagram and, hence, $m \cdot n$ possibilities.

EXAMPLE 4.3   If a firm has 4 warehouses and 12 retail outlets, in how many different ways can it ship an item from one of the warehouses to one of the stores?

SOLUTION   Since m = 4 and $n = 12$, there are $4 \cdot 12 = 48$ ways.   ■

EXAMPLE 4.4   If a travel agency offers trips to 15 different cities, either by air, rail, or bus, in how many different ways can such a trip be arranged?

SOLUTION   Since $m = 15$ and $n = 3$, there are $15 \cdot 3 = 45$ ways.   ■

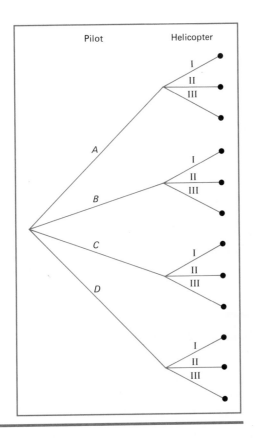

FIGURE 4.2
Tree diagram for
helicopter service
example

By use of appropriate tree diagrams, it is easy to generalize the fore-going rule so that it will apply to choices involving more than two steps. For k steps, where k is a positive integer, we arrive at the following rule:

Multiplication of
choices
(generalized)

> *If a choice consists of k steps, the first of which can be made in n_1,*
> *ways, for each of these the second can be made in n_2 ways, . . . , and*
> *for each of these the kth can be made in n_k ways, then the whole choice*
> *can be made in $n_1 \cdot n_2 \cdot \cdots \cdot n_k$ ways.*

EXAMPLE 4.5 If a new car buyer is faced with a choice of 5 body styles, 3 engines, and 10 colors, in how many different ways can he choose a body style, an engine, and a color for his car? Also, if the buyer can choose a car with or without automatic transmission, with or without air conditioning, and with or without bucket seats, how many different choices does the buyer have?

SOLUTION   For the first question, $n_1 = 5$, $n_2 = 3$, and $n_3 = 10$, so the buyer can choose his car in $5 \cdot 3 \cdot 10 = 150$ different ways. For the second question, $n_1 = 5$, $n_2 = 3$, $n_3 = 10$, $n_4 = 2$, $n_5 = 2$, and $n_6 = 2$, so there are altogether $5 \cdot 3 \cdot 10 \cdot 2 \cdot 2 \cdot 2 = 1{,}200$ different choices open to the buyer. ■

EXAMPLE 4.6   If a test consists of 10 multiple-choice questions, each providing three possible answers, in how many different ways can a student mark one answer to each question?

SOLUTION   Since $n_1 = 3$, $n_2 = 3$, ..., and $n_{10} = 3$, there are $3 \cdot 3 \cdot 3 \cdot 3 \cdot 3 \cdot 3 \cdot 3 \cdot 3 \cdot 3 \cdot 3 = 59{,}049$ ways. In one of the 59, 049 cases the answers will all be correct, and in $2 \cdot 2 \cdot 2 \cdot 2 \cdot 2 \cdot 2 \cdot 2 \cdot 2 \cdot 2 \cdot 2 = 1{,}024$ of them they will all be wrong. ■

4.2

Permutations and Combinations

The rule for the multiplication of choices and its generalization are often applied when several choices are made from one set and we are concerned with the order in which they are made.

EXAMPLE 4.7   In how many different ways can the judges choose the winner and the first runner-up from among the 10 finalists in a student essay contest?

SOLUTION   Since the winner can be chosen in $m = 10$ ways and the first runner-up must be one of the other $n = 9$ finalists, there are $10 \cdot 9 = 90$ ways. ■

EXAMPLE 4.8   In how many different ways can the 48 members of a college fraternity choose a president, a vice president, a secretary, and a treasurer?

SOLUTION   Since $n_1 = 48$, $n_2 = 47$, $n_3 = 46$, and $n_4 = 45$ (regardless of which officer is elected first, second, third, and fourth), there are $48 \cdot 47 \cdot 46 \cdot 45 = 4{,}669{,}920$ ways. ■

In general, if r objects are selected from a set of n objects, any particular arrangement (order) of these objects is called a **permutation**. For instance, 3 2 1 4 is a permutation of the first four positive integers; Vermont, Massachusetts, Connecticut is a permutation (a particular ordered arrangement) of three of the six New England states, and

Yankees, Orioles, Brewers, Red Sox, and
Tigers, Indians, Yankees, Brewers

are two different permutations (ordered arrangements) of four of the six baseball teams in the Eastern Division of the American League.

EXAMPLE 4.9 Determine the number of possible permutations of two of the five vowels, a, e, i, o, and u, and list them all.

SOLUTION Since $m = 5$ and $n = 4$, there are $5 \cdot 4 = 20$ permutations; they are

ae	ai	ao	au	ei	eo	eu	io	iu	ou
ea	ia	oa	ua	ie	oe	ue	oi	ui	uo	■

To find a formula for the total number of permutations of r objects selected from n distinct objects, such as the six baseball teams or the five vowels, we observe that the first selection is made from the whole set of n objects, the second selection is made from the $n - 1$ objects which remain after the first selection has been made, the third selection is made from the $n - 2$ objects which remain after the first two selections have been made, . . . , and the rth and final selection is made from the $n - (r - 1) = n - r + 1$ objects which remain after the first $r - 1$ selections have been made. Now, direct application of the generalized rule for the multiplication of choices shows that the total number of permutations of r objects selected from n distinct objects, which we shall denote $_nP_r$, is $n(n - 1)(n - 2) \cdot \cdots \cdot (n - r + 1)$.

Since products of consecutive integers occur in many problems relating to permutations and other kinds of special arrangements or selections, it is convenient to introduce here the **factorial notation**. In this notation, the product of all positive integers less than or equal to the positive integer n is called "n factorial" and is denoted by $n!$. Thus,

$$1! = 1$$
$$2! = 2 \cdot 1 = 2$$
$$3! = 3 \cdot 2 \cdot 1 = 6$$
$$4! = 4 \cdot 3 \cdot 2 \cdot 1 = 24$$
$$5! = 5 \cdot 4 \cdot 3 \cdot 2 \cdot 1 = 120$$
$$6! = 6 \cdot 5 \cdot 4 \cdot 3 \cdot 2 \cdot 1 = 720$$

and in general $n! = n(n-1)(n-2) \cdot \cdots \cdot 3 \cdot 2 \cdot 1$. Also, to make various formulas more generally applicable, we let $0! = 1$ by definition.

To express the formula for $_nP_r$ in terms of factorials, we note, for instance, that $15 \cdot 14 \cdot 13! = 15!$, $8 \cdot 7 \cdot 6 \cdot 5! = 8!$, $36 \cdot 35 \cdot 34 \cdot 33 \cdot 32 \cdot 31! = 36!$, and similarly,

$$_nP_r \cdot (n-r)! = n(n-1)(n-2) \cdot \cdots \cdot (n-r+1)(n-r)!$$
$$= n!$$

so that $_nP_r = \dfrac{n!}{(n-r)!}$. To summarize,

Number of permutations of n objects taken r at a time

> *The number of permutations of r objects selected from a set of n distinct objects is*
>
> $$_nP_r = n(n-1)(n-2) \cdot \cdots \cdot (n-r+1)$$
>
> *or, in factorial notation,*
>
> $$_nP_r = \frac{n!}{(n-r)!}$$

and we now have two expressions of the formula for $_nP_r$. Note that the first expression applies for $r = 1, 2, \ldots, n$, and the second for $r = 0, 1, 2, \ldots, n$.

EXAMPLE 4.10 Find the number of ways in which 3 of 10 real estate salespersons can be ranked first, second, and third according to market knowledgeability.

SOLUTION For $n = 10$ and $r = 3$ the first expression yields

$$_{10}P_3 = 10 \cdot 9 \cdot 8 = 720$$

and the second expression yields

$$_{10}P_3 = \frac{10!}{7!} = \frac{10 \cdot 9 \cdot 8 \cdot 7!}{7!} = 720 \qquad \blacksquare$$

EXAMPLE 4.11 Find the number of permutations of zero objects selected from a set of 25 distinct objects.

Chapter 4 Possibilities, Probabilities, and Expectations

SOLUTION   We cannot use the first expression here, but substituting $n = 25$ and $r = 0$ into the second expression, we get

$$_{25}P_0 = \frac{25!}{25!} = 1$$

This result may be trivial, but it shows that the factorial notation makes the formula for the number of permutations more generally applicable. ∎

To find the formula for the number of permutations of n distinct objects taken all together, we substitute $n = r$ into the second expression for $_nP_r$, getting $\dfrac{n!}{(n-n)!} = \dfrac{n!}{0!} = n!$ (since $0! = 1$ by definition). Hence,

Number of permutations of n objects taken all together

$$_nP_n = n!$$

EXAMPLE 4.12   Find the number of ways in which 9 teaching assistants can be assigned to 9 sections of a course and the number of ways in which 12 different package designs for a new product can be ranked in order of preference.

SOLUTION   For the 9 teaching assistants we get $9! = 362{,}880$, and for the 12 package designs we get $12! = 479{,}001{,}600$. ∎

There are many problems in which we want to know the number of ways in which r objects can be selected from a set of n objects, but we do not want to include in our count all the different orders in which the selection can be made. For instance, three persons, P, Q, and R, can be assigned to a three-person committee in $3! = 6$ different orders *(PQR, PRQ, QPR, QRP, RPQ, and RQP)*, but there is only one committee, not six.

To obtain a formula which applies to problems like this, let us consider the following 24 permutations of three of the first four letters of the alphabet:

abc	acb	bac	bca	cab	cba
abd	adb	bad	bda	dab	dba
acd	adc	cad	cda	dac	dca
bcd	bdc	cbd	cdb	dbc	dcb

Inspection of this table shows that if we do not count the different orders in which three letters are chosen from the four letters, a, b, c, and d, there are only four ways in which the selection can be made. These are shown in the first column—abc, abd, acd, and bcd. Each row of the table merely contains the 3! = 6 different permutations of the letters shown in the first column.

In general, there are $r!$ permutations of any r objects selected from a set of n distinct objects, so that the $_nP_r$ permutations of r objects selected from a set of n distinct objects contain each set of r objects $r!$ times. Therefore, to find the number of ways in which r objects can be selected from a set of n distinct objects, also called the number of **combinations** of n objects taken r at a time and denoted by $\binom{n}{r}$, we divide $_nP_r$ by $r!$, and we get

Number of combinations of n objects taken r at a time

> *The number of ways in which r objects can be selected from a set of n distinct objects is*
>
> $$\binom{n}{r} = \frac{n(n-1)(n-2) \cdot \cdots \cdot (n-r+1)}{r!}$$
>
> *or, in factorial notation,*
>
> $$\binom{n}{r} = \frac{n!}{r!(n-r)!}$$

For $n = 0$ to $n = 20$, the values of $\binom{n}{r}$ may be read from Table IX at the end of the book, where these quantities are called **binomial coefficients** (see Exercise 4.30 on page 128). Again, the first expression applies for $r = 1, 2, \ldots, n$ and the second for $r = 0, 1, 2, \ldots, n$.

EXAMPLE 4.13 Find the number of ways in which a person can select four stocks from a list of eight stocks (the number of combinations of eight things taken four at a time).

SOLUTION For $n = 8$ and $r = 4$, the first expression yields

$$\binom{8}{4} = \frac{8 \cdot 7 \cdot 6 \cdot 5}{4!} = 70$$

and the second expression yields

$$\binom{8}{4} = \frac{8!}{4!4!} = \frac{8 \cdot 7 \cdot 6 \cdot 5}{4 \cdot 3 \cdot 2 \cdot 1} = 70$$

∎

EXAMPLE 4.14 In how many ways can a dean choose 2 of 50 faculty members to review a student grade appeal?

SOLUTION For $n = 50$ and $r = 2$, the first expression yields

$$\binom{50}{2} = \frac{50 \cdot 49}{2!} = 1,225 \qquad \blacksquare$$

The result of Example 4.13, but not that of Example 4.14 can be read from Table IX, Binomial Coefficients.

EXAMPLE 4.15 In how many ways can 4 good switches and 2 defective switches be chosen from a lot containing 20 good and 5 defective switches?

SOLUTION The 4 good switches can be selected in $\binom{20}{4}$ ways, the 2 defective switches in $\binom{5}{2}$ ways, and by the multiplication of choices we have

$$\binom{20}{4} \cdot \binom{5}{2} = 4,845 \cdot 10 = 48,450$$

In this case we looked up the binomial coefficients in Table IX. $\blacksquare$

When r objects are selected from a set of n distinct objects, $n - r$ of the objects are left, and consequently there are as many ways of leaving (or selecting) $n - r$ objects from a set of n distinct objects as there are ways of selecting or leaving r objects. Symbolically, we write

Rule for binomial coefficients

$$\binom{n}{r} = \binom{n}{n - r} \qquad for\ r = 0, 1, 2, \ldots, n$$

Sometimes this rule serves to simplify details and sometimes it is needed in connection with the use of Table IX.

EXAMPLE 4.16 Determine the value of $\binom{85}{82}$.

SOLUTION To avoid having to write down the product $85 \cdot 84 \cdot 83 \cdot \cdots \cdot 4$ and cancel $82 \cdot 81 \cdot \cdots \cdot 4$, we can write directly (since binomial coefficients are symmetrical)

$$\binom{85}{82} = \binom{85}{3} = \frac{85 \cdot 84 \cdot 83}{3!} = 98,770 \qquad \blacksquare$$

EXAMPLE 4.17   Find the value of $\binom{17}{13}$.

SOLUTION $\binom{17}{13}$ cannot be looked up directly in Table IX, but $\binom{17}{17-13} = \binom{17}{4} = 2,380$ can.   ■

EXERCISES

(Exercises 4.1, 4.6, 4.7, 4.13, 4.15, 4.19, 4.23, 4.24, 4.26, and 4.27 are practice exercises. Their complete solutions are given on page 146.)

4.1   Equal numbers of motor vehicles turn north and turn south from the entrance ramps of a major highway. Draw a tree diagram which shows, for the next three motor vehicles approaching the highway, how many could turn north, and how many could turn south. In how many cases could there be

(a) exactly two vehicles that turn north

(b) exactly one vehicle that turns north

(c) exactly three vehicles that turn south

(d) exactly three vehicles that turn north

4.2   Suppose that a baseball player has been offered a $5,000 bonus if he hits at least one home run in each of four games of a six-game series. Four games have been played, and he has hit home runs in three games and failed to hit a home run in one game. Construct a tree diagram to show the number of ways in which he can earn the $5,000 bonus during the remaining games of the series.

4.3   (a) A caterer can serve zero, one, or two dinners in an evening. Construct a tree diagram which shows that there are six ways in which the caterer can serve exactly two dinners in three evenings.

(b) Using the tree diagram of part (a), count the number of ways the caterer can serve exactly five dinners in three evenings.

(c) Using the tree diagram of part (a), count the number of ways the caterer can serve exactly four dinners in three evenings.

4.4   There are four elevators in a 15-floor office building in which street level is the first floor. Elevator A stops at all floors on the way up and down. Elevator B stops at street level and all even-numbered floors on the way up, and at all floors on the way down. Elevator C stops at street level and all odd-numbered floors on the way up, and at all floors on the way down. Elevator D goes nonstop to the top floor on the way up and stops at all even-numbered floors and the street level on the way down.

(a) Draw a tree diagram showing the various ways a person can use one elevator to go from the street level to the 11th floor and use that same or a different elevator to return to the street level.

(b) Draw a tree diagram showing the various ways a person can use one elevator to go from the street level to the 11th floor and use a different elevator to return to the street level.

4.5 After preliminary orientation and training, junior executives of a certain national corporation are relocated to New York, Chicago, or Los Angeles to obtain practical experience. If assigned to New York, these junior executives can be placed in the offices of the Finance Department, Marketing Department, or Production Department. If assigned to Chicago, they can be placed in the offices of the Marketing Department or of the Production Department. If assigned to Los Angeles, they will be placed in the offices of the Marketing Department. Draw a tree diagram to show the six ways in which a junior executive can be relocated to obtain practical experience.

4.6 In a market study, heads of households are classified into six categories according to income, into five categories according to the extent of their education, and into four categories according to their place of residence. In how many different ways can the head of a household be classified?

4.7 An international investor wants to purchase one investment from among common stocks, preferred stocks, and bonds of six industries located in several countries. The investor can use a full-service broker or a discount broker and can buy with cash or on margin (margin purchases are partially financed by borrowing). If there are 288 choices to be made, how many countries is the investor considering?

4.8 If a national professional association is considering six hotels as possible sites for their national meeting next year, and also for the year thereafter, in how many ways can they select the hotels

(a) if the two consecutive national meetings are not to be held in the same hotel

(b) if the two consecutive national meetings may be held in the same hotel

4.9 A manager can evaluate a subordinate as outstanding, excellent, average, below average, or poor.

(a) In how many ways can a manager evaluate four subordinates as either excellent or outstanding (not using any other evaluation categories)?

(b) In how many ways can the manager evaluate four subordinates, using all five evaluation categories?

4.10 A customer can order a tailored shirt with choice of 12 materials, 10 shirt styles, 6 monogram styles, or no monogram. How many ways can a customer order a shirt?

4.11 In a research study of women who buy mutual fund shares, women interviewed were classified into seven categories of income, four categories of investment objectives, five categories of place of residence, and two categories of occupational status. In how many ways can a woman mutual fund buyer be classified?

4.12 A school of management has four finalists for a faculty position in the Accounting Department, three finalists for a position in the Finance Department, and two finalists for a position in the Marketing Department. In how many ways can the three positions be staffed from among the nine finalists?

4.13 An examination consists of 10 multiple-choice questions, each with 4 choices (1 of which is correct and 3 incorrect).
    (a) In how many ways can a student mark the answers to these questions if 1 choice is made for each of the 10 questions?
    (b) How many ways can the student get a perfect score (all correct) on this examination?
    (c) How many ways can the student mark the answers to these questions, marking all 10 questions incorrectly?

4.14 Mary's bicycle lock has a three-dial combination, with each dial having all whole numbers from 0 to 9. When each of the three dials displays the correct number, the lock opens. Mary has forgotten the number for the first dial. She remembers that the number for the second dial is between 0 and 5, inclusive and that the number for the third dial is between 6 and 9, inclusive. If Mary is correct, how many different combinations are possible, only one of which will open the lock?

4.15 The *Institutional Investor* ranks the top 10 institutions according to assets under management—the institution's own as well as those of their clients. In order of size these are Prudential Insurance Co., American Express Co., Metropolitan Life, Bankers Trust Co., Equitable Investment Corp., J. P. Morgan & Co., Citicorp, Wells Fargo & Co., Aetna Life Insurance Co., and Mellon Bank Corp.
    (a) How many permutations are there of 3 of these 10 institutions?
    (b) How many permutations are there of 2 of the 3 largest institutions?
    (c) List all the permutations of part (b).

4.16 Determine whether each of the following is true or false:
    (a) $9! = 9 \cdot 8 \cdot 7 \cdot 6!$
    (b) $5! \cdot 4! = 20!$
    (c) $5! + 5! = 10!$
    (d) $8! = \dfrac{9!}{9}$

4.17 The police have captured three suspected shoplifters and plan to interrogate all of them.

   (a) If the order of interrogations matters, in how many ways can the police question the suspected shoplifters?

   (b) If the order of interrogations does not matter, in how many ways can the police question the suspected shoplifters?

4.18 If 10 banks in a community offer differing interest rates on their certificates of deposit, in how many ways could the banks pay the highest, second highest, and third highest interest rates?

4.19 In how many ways can four potted plants be aligned on a windowsill?

4.20 In how many ways can a chief executive officer meet individually with five department heads at five different times?

4.21 The number of ways in which n distinct objects can be arranged in a circle is $(n-1)!$.

   (a) Present an argument to justify this formula.

   (b) In how many ways can 11 football players stand in a circular huddle (if it matters only who stands on whose left and right)?

   (c) In how many ways can five turquoises be set around a silver bracelet?

4.22 If among n objects r are alike and the others are all distinct, the number of permutations of these n objects taken altogether is $\dfrac{n!}{r!}$.

   (a) How many permutations are there of the letters in the word ''boss'' and how many in the word ''poolroom''?

   (b) How many permutations are there of the cans of soft drinks in a six-pack if there are three cans of cola, and one can each of ginger ale, root beer, and lemon-lime.

   (c) Justify the formula given in this exercise.

4.23 If among n objects r_1 are identical, another r_2 are identical, and the rest are all distinct, the number of permutations of these n objects taken all together is $\dfrac{n!}{(r_1! \cdot r_2!)}$.

   (a) How many permutations are there of the letters in the word ''seethes''?

   (b) In how many ways can the chief executive officer of Exercise 4.20 schedule six meetings if there are only two department heads, each of whom he will meet three times?

   (c) Generalize the formula so that it applies if among n objects r_1 are identical, another r_2 are identical, another r_3 are identical, and the rest are all distinct. In how many ways can the chief executive officer of part (b) schedule the six meetings if there are three department heads, each of whom he will meet two times?

(d) A retail clothing salesperson sold one jacket, two pairs of jeans, three sweaters, and four pairs of stockings. If these sales were made one at a time, in how many different sequences can these articles of clothing be sold?

4.24 Calculate the number of ways in which a shipper can choose 3 of 12 interstate trucking companies.

4.25 Calculate the number of ways that 4 soldiers in a group of 30 soldiers can volunteer for a hazardous assignment.

4.26 Among six men and four women accountants employed by an accounting firm, two will be offered promotions to positions as partners. In how many ways can the partnerships be offered to
(a) any two of the accountants
(b) two of the male accountants
(c) one male accountant and one female accountant
(d) zero male accountants

4.27 A manager must reduce the size of a work force by dismissing 3 typists and 2 data processors. In how many ways can this be done if among the 20 persons presently employed, 12 are typists, and the rest are data processors.

4.28 A shipment of 15 calves includes 1 that is diseased. In how many ways can a veterinarian choose 3 of the calves for examination so that
(a) the diseased calf is not included
(b) the diseased calf is included

4.29 Suppose that among the 15 calves of the preceding exercise, 2 are diseased. In how many ways can a veterinarian choose 3 of the calves for examination so that
(a) neither of the diseased calves is included
(b) one of the diseased calves is included
(c) both of the diseased calves are included

4.30 The quantity $\binom{n}{r}$ is called a binomial coefficient because it is, in fact, the coefficient of $a^{n-r}b^{r}$ in the binomial expansion of $(a + b)^{n}$. Verify that this is true for $n = 2, 3$, and 4, by expanding $(a + b)^{2}$, $(a + b)^{3}$, and $(a + b)^{4}$ and comparing the coefficients with the corresponding values of $\binom{n}{r}$ given in Table IX.

4.31 A table of binomial coefficients is easy to construct by following the pattern shown here, which is called Pascal's triangle.

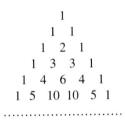

$$1$$
$$1 \quad 1$$
$$1 \quad 2 \quad 1$$
$$1 \quad 3 \quad 3 \quad 1$$
$$1 \quad 4 \quad 6 \quad 4 \quad 1$$
$$1 \quad 5 \quad 10 \quad 10 \quad 5 \quad 1$$

....

In this arrangement, each row begins with a 1, ends with a 1, and each other entry is given by the sum of the nearest two entries in the row immediately above.

(a) Use Table IX to verify that the third row of the triangle contains the values of $\binom{2}{r}$ for $r = 0$, 1, and 2, the fourth row contains the values of $\binom{3}{r}$ for $r = 0$, 1, 2, and 3, and the fifth row contains the values of $\binom{4}{r}$ for $r = 0$, 1, 2, 3, and 4.

(b) Construct the next two rows of the triangle and use Table IX to verify the results.

4.32 Verify the identity $\binom{n+1}{r} = \binom{n}{r} + \binom{n}{r-1}$ by expressing each of the binomial coefficients in terms of factorials. Explain why this identity justifies the method used in the construction of Pascal's triangle in the preceding exercise.

4.3

Probability

So far we have studied only what is possible in a given situation. In some instances we listed all possibilities, and in others we merely determined how many different possibilities there are. Now we shall go one step further and judge also what is probable and what is improbable.

The most common way of measuring the uncertainties connected with events (say, the success of a new product, the effectiveness of an advertising campaign, or the return of an investment) is to assign them **probabilities**; alternatively, we may specify the **odds** at which it would be fair to bet that the events will occur. In this section we shall see how probabilities are interpreted and their numerical values are determined; then in Section 4.4

and in Chapter 5 we shall see how they can be used to make choices, among different courses of action, which promise to be the most profitable, or otherwise most desirable. "Odds," will be defined later, in Section 5.3, where we shall also study the relationship between probabilities and odds.

Historically, the oldest way of measuring uncertainties is the **classical probability concept**. It was developed originally in connection with games of chance, and it lends itself most readily to bridging the gap between possibilities and probabilities. This concept applies only when all possible outcomes are equally likely, in which case we can say that

The classical probability concept

> *If there are n equally likely possibilities, one of which must occur and s are regarded as favorable, or as a "success," then the probability of a "success" is given by the ratio $\frac{s}{n}$.*

In the application of this rule, the terms "favorable" and "success" are used rather loosely—what is favorable to one player is unfavorable to his opponent, and what is a success from one point of view is a failure from another. Thus, the terms "favorable" and "success" can be applied to any particular kind of outcome, even if "favorable" means that a television set does not work, or a "success" means that someone caught the flu. This usage dates back to the days when probabilities were studied only in connection with games of chance.

EXAMPLE 4.18   What is the probability of drawing an ace at random from a well-shuffled deck of 52 playing cards?

SOLUTION   There are $s = 4$ aces among the $n = 52$ cards, so we get

$$\frac{s}{n} = \frac{4}{52} = \frac{1}{13}$$

    ■

EXAMPLE 4.19   What is the probability of rolling a 5 or a 6 with a balanced die?

SOLUTION   Since $s = 2$ and $n = 6$, we get

$$\frac{s}{n} = \frac{2}{6} = \frac{1}{3}$$

    ■

Although equally likely possibilities are found mostly in games of chance, this probability concept applies also in a great variety of situations where gambling devices are used to make **random selections**, say, when offices are assigned to sales agents by lot, when machine parts are chosen for inspection so that each part produced has the same chance of being selected, or when each family in a certain market area has the same chance of being included in a sample survey.

EXAMPLE 4.20 If 2 of 20 tires are defective and 4 of the 20 are randomly chosen for inspection, what is the probability that none of the defective tires will be chosen?

SOLUTION There are $\binom{20}{4} = 4{,}845$ equally likely ways of choosing 4 of the 20 tires by reason of the random selection. The number of favorable outcomes is the number of ways in which none of the defective tires and 4 of the nondefective tires can be selected, or $\binom{2}{0}\binom{18}{4} = 1 \cdot 3{,}060 = 3{,}060$, and it follows that the probability is

$$\frac{s}{n} = \frac{3{,}060}{4{,}845} = \frac{12}{19}$$ ∎

The values of the binomial coefficients $\binom{20}{4}$, $\binom{2}{0}$, and $\binom{18}{4}$ were read directly from Table IX.

The major shortcoming of the classical probability concept (where the possibilities must all be equally likely) is that there are many situations in which the possibilities that arise cannot be regarded as equally likely. This might be the case, for example, if we are concerned with the question whether there will be rain, sunshine, snow, or hail; when we wonder whether or not a person will receive a promotion; or when we want to predict the success of a new business or the behavior of the stock market.

Among the various other probability concepts, most widely held is the **frequency interpretation**, according to which

The frequency interpretation of probability

> *The probability of an event (happening or outcome) is the proportion of the time that events of the same kind will occur in the long run.*

If we say that the probability is 0.78 that a jet from San Francisco to Phoenix will arrive on time, we mean that such flights arrive on time 78 percent of the time. Also, if the Weather Service predicts that there is a 40 percent chance of rain (that the probability is 0.40 that it will rain), it means that under the same weather conditions it will rain 40 percent of the time. More generally, we say that an event has a probability of, say, 0.90, in the same sense in which we might say that our car will start in cold weather 90 percent of the time. We cannot guarantee what will happen on any particular occasion— the car may start and then it may not—but if we kept records over a long period of time, we should find that the proportion of "successes" is very close to 0.90.

In accordance with the frequency concept of probability, we estimate the probability of an event by observing what fraction of the time similar events have occurred in the past.

EXAMPLE 4.21   If records show that (over a period of time) 516 of 600 jets from Denver to Chicago arrived on time, what is the probability that any 1 jet from Denver to Chicago will arrive on time?

SOLUTION   Since in the past $\dfrac{516}{600} = 0.86$ of the flights arrived on time, we use this fraction as an estimate of the probability.   ■

EXAMPLE 4.22   If 687 of 1,854 freshmen who entered a men's college (over a number of years) dropped out before the end of their freshman year, what is the probability that a freshman entering this college will drop out before the end of his freshman year?

SOLUTION   Since in the past $\dfrac{687}{1,854} = 0.37$ of the freshmen dropped out before the end of their freshman year, we use this figure as an estimate of the probability.   ■

When probabilities are estimated in this way, it is only reasonable to ask just how good the estimates are. Later we shall answer this question in some detail, but for now let us refer to an important theorem called the **Law of Large Numbers**. Informally, this theorem may be stated as follows:

The Law of Large Numbers

If a situation, trial, or experiment is repeated again and again, the proportion of successes will tend to approach the probability that any one outcome will be a success.

To illustrate this law we might have flipped a balanced coin, say, 80 times and recorded the accumulated proportion of heads after every fifth flip. In fact, however, we ran a computer simulation of 80 flips of a coin as shown in Figure 4.3.

Letting the zeros represent heads and reading across the rows of the computer printout, we calculate the accumulated proportion of heads as $\frac{4}{5} = 0.80$, $\frac{8}{10} = 0.80$, $\frac{11}{15} = 0.73$, . . . , and $\frac{37}{80} = 0.46$. These results are shown in the graph of Figure 4.4 where the proportion of heads can be seen to fluctuate but comes close to $\frac{1}{2}$, the probability of heads for each flip of the coin.

In the frequency interpretation, the probability of an event is defined in terms of what happens to similar events in the long run, so let us consider briefly whether it is at all meaningful to talk about the probability of an event which can occur only once. For instance, can we assign a probability to the event that Ms. Barbara Smith's broken arm, broken for the first time, will heal within a month? If we put ourselves in the position of Ms. Smith's doctor, we could check medical records, discover that such fractures have healed within one month in, say, 39 percent of the thousands of reported cases, and apply this figure to Ms. Smith's arm. This may not be of much comfort to Ms. Smith, but it does provide a meaning for a probability statement concerning her arm: the probability that it will heal within a month is 0.39.

This illustrates that when we make a probability statement about a specific (nonrepeatable) event, the frequency concept of probability leaves us no choice but to refer to a set of similar events. As can well be imagined, however, this can easily lead to complications, since the choice of "similar"

```
MTB  >  BRANDOM 80 N=1 P=.5 C1
     80  BINOMIAL EXPERIMENTS WITH N =    1 AND P = 0.5000
        1       0     0     0      0     0     0     0      0     1
        0       0     1     1      0     0     0     1      0     0
        1       0     1     1      0     0     0     1      1     1
        1       1     1     1      0     0     1     0      0     0
        1       0     0     1      0     1     1     0      1     1
        1       0     0     0      1     1     0     1      1     0
        0       1     1     1      1     1     1     0      1     1
        1       1     1     1      1     0     1     0      1     1

     SUMMARY

     VALUE          FREQUENCY
       0               37
       1               43
```

FIGURE 4.3   Computer simulation of 80 flips of a balanced coin

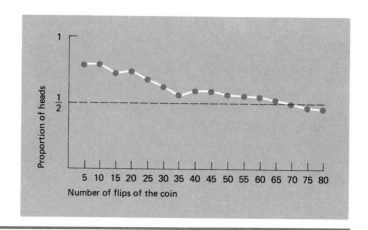

FIGURE 4.4
Graph illustrating
the Law of Large
Numbers

events is often neither obvious nor straightforward. For instance, with reference to Ms. Smith's arm, we might consider as ''similar'' only those cases where the fracture was in the same arm, or only those in which the patients were the same age as Ms. Smith, or only those in which the patients were also the same height and weight as Ms. Smith.

This shows that the choice of ''similar'' events is ultimately a matter of personal judgment, and it is by no means contradictory that we can arrive at different probabilities concerning the same event. It should be observed, however, that the more we narrow things down, the less information we have to estimate probabilities.

An alternative point of view, which is currently gaining in favor, is to interpret probabilities as **personal** or **subjective** evaluations. Such probabilities express the strength of one's belief with regard to the uncertainties that are involved, and they apply especially when there is little or no direct evidence, so that there really is no choice but to consider collateral (indirect) information, ''educated guesses,'' and perhaps intuition and other subjective factors. Subjective probabilities are sometimes determined by putting the issues in question on a ''put up or shut up'' basis, as will be explained in Sections 4.4 and 5.3.

EXERCISES

(Exercises 4.33, 4.36, and 4.38 are practice exercises. Their complete solutions are given on page 146.)

4.33   When a card is picked from a well-shuffled deck of 52 playing cards, what are the probabilities that it will be

(a) a black ace

(b) a club

(c) a 10 of any suit

4.34 If two babies are born at a hospital and B stands for boy, and G for girl, the four possibilities in the sequence of these two births are BB, GB, BG, GG. If it can be assumed that these possibilities are equally likely, what are the probabilities that zero, one, or two boys are born?

4.35 If H stands for heads and T for tails, the eight possible outcomes in three successive flips of a coin are HHH, HHT, HTH, THH, HTT, THT, TTH, and TTT. Assuming that these eight possibilities are equally likely, what are the probabilities of getting zero, one, two, or three heads?

4.36 If a window display of live kittens at a pet shop contains 8 Domestic Short-hair, 11 Siamese, 4 Persian, and 7 Angora kittens, what are the probabilities that 1 kitten selected at random will be

(a) Persian

(b) Domestic Shorthair or Angora

(c) Siamese

(d) neither Persian nor Siamese

4.37 If we roll a balanced die, what are the probabilities of getting

(a) a 3 or a 5

(b) an even number

4.38 If three cards are chosen from a well-shuffled deck of 52 playing cards, what are the probabilities of selecting

(a) 3 hearts

(b) no hearts

(c) 3 red cards

(d) no red cards

4.39 If 4 factories in a group of 24 factories in a certain community are violating environmental regulations and 6 are randomly selected for inspection, what is the probability that

(a) none of the violators will be selected for inspection

(b) all of the violators will be selected for inspection

4.40 Ten identical personal computers are in the inventory of a dealer, and one has a hidden defect. If 3 are to be shipped, and the computers are selected in such a way that each has the same probability of being shipped, find

(a) the total number of ways in which 3 of the 10 computers can be selected for shipment

(b) the number of ways in which 3 of 10 computers can be selected so that the one with the hidden defect will be included for shipment

(c) the probability that the computer with the hidden defect will be shipped

4.41 Alberta, British Columbia, and Quebec are 3 of 10 provinces of Canada. Assuming that the selection is random (that each set of 3 provinces has the same chance of being selected), what are the probabilities that a marketing campaign for a new product conducted in 3 of the 10 provinces of Canada will include

(a) Quebec

(b) British Columbia and Alberta

4.42 Among 296 registered guests of a hotel in a certain state, 114 guests were from out of state. Estimate the probability that a registered guest of this hotel is from out of state.

4.43 If a survey reveals that 1,487 of 1,994 visitors to a theme park are under 30 years of age, estimate the probability that a randomly selected visitor to this theme park is under 30 years of age.

4.44 If 340 of 395 executives in a firm have a college education, what is the probability that a randomly selected executive from this group does not have a college education?

4.45 Use a computer to simulate 80 flips of a balanced coin as in Figure 4.3 on page 133. Since the computer is in random mode, you should expect your numbers to be different from those of Figure 4.3. Plot the accumulated proportion of heads after each tenth flip as shown in Figure 4.4.

(a) Your plotted line, which shows the accumulated proportion of heads, should be expected to approach $\frac{1}{2}$ as the number of flips of the coin increases. Why?

(b) Use the figures of your computer simulation to calculate the proportion of tails after each fifth flip and plot, as before, on the graph of part (a). The resulting line will be the mirror image of the accumulated proportion of heads prepared for part (a). Verify that both plotted lines approach $\frac{1}{2}$ as the number of flips of the coin increases.

4.46 When we flip two coins at a time (we flipped one at a time in Figure 4.3) the theoretical probabilities of obtaining two heads, one head, and one tail, and two tails are 0.25, 0.50, and 0.25. Use the data of Figure 4.3 to simulate flips of two coins at a time by grouping the 80 coin flips by pairs, obtaining a sample of 40 pairs. Reading across the rows of the computer printout we obtain the pairs $10, 00, 00, \ldots, 10, 10, 11$. We thus have 10 pairs of heads, 17 pairs of one head and one tail, and 13 pairs of tails, yielding the probabilities $\frac{10}{40} = 0.25$, $\frac{17}{40} = 0.425$, and $\frac{13}{40} = 0.325$. Except for the pairs of heads (where $0.25 = 0.25$), the simulated proportions therefore differ noticeably from the theoretical probabilities.

(a) Have we disproved the Law of Large Numbers, given the noted differences between the simulated and theoretical probabilities?

(b) Repeat the experiment with a computer using a larger number of, say, 320 flips of a coin. Are the resulting proportions closer to the theoretical probabilities of 0.25, 0.50, and 0.25?

4.4

Mathematical Expectation

If an insurance agent tells us that a 45-year-old woman can expect to live 33 more years, this does not mean that anyone really expects a 45-year-old woman to live until her 78th birthday and then die the next day. Similarly, if we read that a person living in the United States can expect to eat 21.7 pounds of cheese and 233.1 eggs a year, it must be obvious that the word ''expect'' is not being used in its colloquial sense. Most persons do not eat 0.1 egg, and it would be surprising, indeed, if we found somebody who has actually eaten 21.7 pounds of cheese in a given year. So far as the first statement is concerned, some 45-year-old women will live another 12 years, some will live another 25 years, some will live another 50 years, . . . , and the life expectancy of ''33 more years'' must be interpreted as a particular kind of average called an **expected value**, or a **mathematical expectation**.

Originally, the concept of a mathematical expectation arose in connection with games of chance, and in its simplest form it is given by the product of the amount a player stands to win and the probability that he or she will win this amount.

EXAMPLE 4.23 What is our mathematical expectation if we stand to win $5 if and only if a balanced coin falls heads?

SOLUTION The coin is balanced, so the probability of heads is $\frac{1}{2}$ and our mathematical expectation is $5 \cdot \frac{1}{2} = \$2.50$. ∎

EXAMPLE 4.24 What is our mathematical expectation if we buy one of 1,000 raffle tickets issued for a prize, a color television set, worth $480?

SOLUTION   Since the probability that we will win is $\frac{1}{1,000}$, our mathematical expectation is $480 \cdot \frac{1}{1,000} = \$0.48$ or 48 cents. Thus, in a strictly monetary sense, it would be foolish to pay more than 48 cents for the ticket.   ■

In Examples 4.23 and 4.24 there was a single prize, but in each case there were two possible payoffs—$5 or $0 in the first example and $480 or $0 in the other. Indeed, in the second example we can argue that 999 of the tickets will not pay anything at all, 1 ticket will pay $480 (or the equivalent in merchandise), so that altogether the 1,000 tickets pay $480, or on the average 48 cents per ticket, which is the mathematical expectation.

To generalize the concept of a mathematical expectation, let us consider the following modification of the raffle of Example 4.24.

EXAMPLE 4.25   What is our mathematical expectation if we buy one of 1,000 raffle tickets for a first prize of a color television set worth $480, a second prize of a record player worth $120, and a third prize of a radio worth $40?

SOLUTION   Now we can argue that 997 of the tickets will not pay anything at all, one ticket will pay the equivalent of $480, another will pay the equivalent of $120, while a third will pay the equivalent of $40; altogether, the 1,000 raffle tickets will pay $480 + $120 + $40 = $640, or on the average 64 cents per ticket—this is the mathematical expectation of each ticket. Looking at the problem in a different way, we could argue that if the raffle were repeated many times, we would win nothing $\frac{997}{1,000} \cdot 100 = 99.7$ percent of the time and win each of the three prizes $\frac{1}{1,000} \cdot 100 = 0.1$ percent of the time. On the average, we would win

$$0(0.997) + 480(0.001) + 120(0.001) + 40(0.001) = \$0.64$$

or 64 cents, which is the sum of the products obtained by multiplying each amount by the corresponding proportion or probability.   ■

Generalizing from Example 4.25, let us now give the following definition:

> If the probabilities of obtaining the amounts a_1, a_2, . . . , or a_k are p_1, p_2, . . . , and p_k, then the mathematical expection is
>
> $$E = a_1 p_1 + a_2 p_2 + \cdots + a_k p_k$$

Each amount is multiplied by the corresponding probability, and the mathematical expectation, E, is given by the sum of all these products. It is important to keep in mind that the a's are positive when they represent profits, winnings, or gains (amounts which we receive) and that they are negative when they represent losses, penalties, or deficits (amounts which we must pay).

EXAMPLE 4.26   What is our mathematical expectation if we win \$5 if a balanced coin falls heads and lose \$5 if it falls tails?

SOLUTION   The amounts are $a_1 = 5$ and $a_2 = -5$, the probabilities are $p_1 = \frac{1}{2}$ and $p_2 = \frac{1}{2}$, and the mathematical expectation is

$$E = 5 \cdot \frac{1}{2} + (-5) \cdot \frac{1}{2} = 0 \qquad \blacksquare$$

Games, like this one, in which the mathematical expectation is zero and neither player is favored, are said to be **fair**, or **equitable**.

EXAMPLE 4.27   The probabilities are 0.24, 0.35, 0.29, and 0.12 that a speculator will be able to sell a subdivision lot within a year at a profit of \$12,500, at a profit of \$8,000, at a profit of \$1,000, or at a loss of \$2,500, respectively. What is his expected profit?

SOLUTION   Substituting $a_1 = 12{,}500$, $a_2 = 8{,}000$, $a_3 = 1{,}000$, $a_4 = -2{,}500$, $p_1 = 0.24$, $p_2 = 0.35$, $p_3 = 0.29$, and $p_4 = 0.12$ into the formula for E, we get

$$\begin{aligned} E &= 12{,}500(0.24) + 8{,}000(0.35) + 1{,}000(0.29) - 2{,}500(0.12) \\ &= \$5{,}790 \qquad \blacksquare \end{aligned}$$

In Examples 4.26 and 4.27, the a's were the dollar amounts or the cash equivalent of merchandise, and it is customary in that case to refer to the mathematical expectation as the **expected monetary value**, or EMV. However, the a's need not be monetary values at all. For instance, if we say that a child in the age group from 6 to 16 can expect to go to the dentist 1.9 times a year, we are actually referring to the result obtained by multiplying 0, 1, 2, 3, 4, . . . , by the probabilities that a child in this age group will visit a dentist that many times a year, and then adding all these products.

EXAMPLE 4.28 If the probabilities are 0.05, 0.17, 0.24, 0.19, 0.18, 0.09, 0.05, 0.02, and 0.01 that an airline office at a certain airport will receive 0, 1, 2, 3, 4, 5, 6, 7, or 8 complaints about its luggage handling on any one day, how many such complaints can be expected per day?

SOLUTION   The expected number is

$$E = 0(0.05) + 1(0.17) + 2(0.24) + 3(0.19) + 4(0.18)$$
$$+ 5(0.09) + 6(0.05) + 7(0.02) + 8(0.01)$$
$$= 2.91$$ ∎

It has been suggested that a person's behavior is rational if, when choosing between alternatives in situations involving uncertainties and risks, the person chooses the alternative having the highest mathematical expectation. This may seem to be a reasonable criterion for rational behavior and in many cases it is, but there are exceptions and they involve a number of difficulties which we shall discuss in Chapter 6 (see also Exercise 4.61 on page 142). For the moment, let us merely show how this decision-making criterion can be used to determine subjective probabilities.

EXAMPLE 4.29   Defending a liability suit against a client, a lawyer must decide whether to charge a straight fee of $1,500 or a contingent fee of $4,500, which she will get only if her client wins the case. How does she feel about her client's chances if she prefers the straight $1,500 fee?

SOLUTION   If she feels that the probability is p that her client will win and she accepts the contingent fee, her mathematical expectation is $4,500p + 0(1 - p) = 4,500p$. Since she feels that the certainty of getting $1,500 is preferable to a mathematical expectation of $4,500p$, we write

$$1,500 > 4,500p$$

which yields $p < \dfrac{1,500}{4,500}$ and, hence $p < \dfrac{1}{3}$. To narrow things down further, we might ask the lawyer if she would still prefer the straight $1,500 fee if the contingent fee were, say, $6,000 (see Exercise 4.58 on page 142). ∎

EXERCISES

(Exercises 4.47, 4.48, 4.50, 4.51, 4.53, and 4.59 are practice exercises. Their complete solutions are given on page 146.)

4.47 A supermarket offers its customers a free ticket in a drawing for a Thanksgiving turkey. If 200 tickets are entered in the drawing and the turkey is worth $25.00, what is the mathematical expectation of a customer who receives a free ticket?

4.48 An organization raises funds by selling 1,000 raffle tickets for a $200 first prize, $100 second prize, and five consolation prizes of $10 each. What is the mathematical expectation of a person who buys one of the tickets?

4.49 A gambler offers a player the following game with a well-shuffled deck of 52 ordinary playing cards.

    (a) A player bets $100 and randomly draws one card from the deck. If the card is a jack, queen, king, or ace the player wins $225, but if any other card is drawn, the player loses the game. Is this a fair game?

    (b) What is the mathematical expectation for this game if the gambler cheats and surreptitiously removes a winning card (a jack, queen, king, or ace) before the player draws a card?

4.50 (a) The five door prizes at a college sorority dance are a stuffed animal worth $20, a chit for a dinner worth $10, and three college pennants worth $5 each. If students presented 100 free tickets from which the winning ticket stubs are to be randomly drawn, what is the mathematical expectation for each ticket?

    (b) Is it worthwhile, in the monetary sense, to spend 50 cents for bus fare to get a free ticket for the drawing?

4.51 The two finalists in a golf tournament play 18 holes, with the winner getting $20,000 and the runner-up getting $12,000. What are the two players mathematical expectations if

    (a) they are evenly matched

    (b) their probabilities of winning are $\frac{3}{4}$ and $\frac{1}{4}$

4.52 If the two league champions are evenly matched, the probabilities that a "best of seven" basketball playoff will take 4, 5, 6, or 7 games are $\frac{1}{8}$, $\frac{1}{4}$, $\frac{5}{16}$, and $\frac{5}{16}$. Under these conditions, how many games can we expect such a playoff to last?

4.53 In evaluating the profitability of a business for the coming year, an investor feels that the probabilities are 0.05, 0.20, 0.30, and 0.45 that the business will earn profits of $1,000,000, $900,000, $800,000, and $700,000, respectively. According to the investor, what is the expected profit of the business?

4.54 A dealer purchased the entire contents of a bankrupt shoe store for $100,000. The probabilities that he will be able to sell the contents of the shoe store for $125,000, $110,000, $100,000, and $90,000 are 0.34, 0.26, 0.22, and 0.18. What is the dealer's expected gross profit?

4.55 The manager of an office knows that the probabilities of 0, 1, 2, 3, or 4 absentees on a given day are 0.21, 0.36, 0.25, 0.13, and 0.05. How many absentees can the manager expect on a given day?

4.56 A police chief uses the following table to summarize the probabilities of 0, 1, 2, 3, 4, 5, and 6 or more car thefts a day.

Car thefts reported	0	1	2	3	4	5	6 or more
Probability	0.23	0.34	0.26	0.12	0.04	0.01	negligible

How many car thefts can the police chief expect per day?

4.57 A grab bag contains 5 packages worth $1 apiece, 5 packages worth $3 apiece, and 10 packages worth $5 apiece. Is it rational to pay $4 for the privilege of selecting one of these packages at random?

4.58 A lawyer must decide whether to charge a straight fee of $1,500 or a contingent fee of $6,000, which she will get only if her client wins the case. How does the lawyer feel about the probability that her client will win if she prefers a contingent fee of $6,000 to the straight fee of $1,500?

4.59 A person must choose between a straight salary of $25,600 as a junior executive in the main office or a salary of $21,800 plus bonus of $7,600 if employed by the sales department and sales exceed her quota. Her objective is to maximize her income. How does she assess the probability of exceeding her sales quota if she accepts the sales position?

4.60 The owner of a one-hour dry cleaning service must decide whether to charge $6.00 to clean a suit of clothes or $7.50 with a "double your money back if not ready in one hour" guarantee. How does the owner feel about the chances that a person will actually ask for double his money back if
(a) he decides to charge $6.00 to clean a suit of clothes
(b) he decides to charge $7.50 with the guarantee
(c) he cannot make up his mind

4.61 A real estate speculator must choose between two investments, one of which is an investment in an apartment building and the other an investment in an office building. The apartment building promises a profit of $200,000 with a probability of 0.80, or a loss of $25,000 (from a high vacancy rate and declining rental income) with a probability of 0.20. The office building promises a profit of $300,000 with a probability of 0.50, or a loss of $50,000 with a probability of 0.50.

(a) Which investment should the speculator make if she wants to maximize her expected profit?

(b) Which investment should the speculator make if she is in financial difficulty and will go bankrupt unless she can make a profit of at least $250,000 on her next investment?

4.5

A Word of Caution

Many fallacies involving probabilities are due to inappropriate assumptions concerning the equal likelihood of events. Consider, for example, the following situation:

Among three identical file trays one contains two current records, one contains one current and one dead record, and the other contains two dead records. After taking one of these trays at random, a clerk randomly takes one record from it. If this record is a current one, what is the probability that the other record on this tray is also a current one?

Without giving the matter too much thought, it may seem reasonable to say that this probability is $\frac{1}{2}$. After all, the current record must have come from the first or second tray. For the first tray the other record is a current one, for the second tray the other record is a dead one, and it would seem reasonable to say that these two possibilities are equally likely. Actually, this is not the case. The correct value of the probability is $\frac{2}{3}$, and the reader can verify this by drawing an appropriate tree diagram. (When drawing such a tree diagram showing the six possible outcomes corresponding to which of the six records is actually chosen, it will be convenient to label the two current records on the first tray C_1 and C_2 and the two dead records on the third tray D_1 and D_2.)

4.6

Checklist of Key Terms

4.7

Review Exercises

4.62   If an accountant classifies the accounts receivable of a firm into four categories by size, three categories by age, and two categories by type of customer (governmental and commercial), in how many ways can these accounts receivable be classified?

4.63   If a collection agency plans to call 3 of 10 delinquent accounts on the telephone, in how many ways can the collection associate make these three calls?

4.64   The probabilities that a worker will leave his workstation 0, 1, 2, 3, or 4 times during a day are 0.25, 0.48, 0.20, 0.04, and 0.02. How many times can a worker be expected to leave his workstation during a day?

4.65   In how many ways can 6 wristwatches be arranged in a line inside a display case?

4.66   In how many ways can 4 videocassette movies be selected from a shelf on which there are 10 videocassette movies?

4.67   In a gubernatorial election Mr. Adams (R), Ms. Baker (D), and Mr. Cabot (R) are running for governor, and Ms. Davis (D), Mr. Evans (R), and Ms. Flynn (D) are running for lieutenant governor. (R) is an abbreviation for Republican party and (D) is an abbreviation for Democratic party.

    (a) Construct a tree diagram showing the nine possible outcomes.

    (b) According to the diagram of part (a), in how many ways can the governor and lieutenant governor be elected so that they will not be of the same political party?

4.68   In how many ways can nine audits be assigned to three accountants so that the first is responsible for four audits, the second is responsible for three audits, and the third is responsible for two?

4.69   An insurance company agrees to pay the promoter of an outdoor concert $100,000 if the concert is rained out. If the insurance company's actuary feels that $18,000 is a fair net premium for the risk, what does this tell us about the actuary's assessment of the probability that the concert will be rained out?

4.70   If 566 out of 923 voters in a certain community are in favor of issuing a school
       bond, estimate the probability that a randomly selected voter is opposed to the
       school bond issue.

4.71   In how many ways can the five finalists in a beauty contest, where the win-
       ners are determined by a panel of judges, win first, second, and third
       prize?

4.72   The employee benefits counselor of a firm offers a new employee a choice of
       six health insurance policies, three retirement annuity policies, and two life
       insurance policies. In how many different ways can the employee choose a
       health policy, a retirement annuity policy, and a life insurance policy?

4.73   If a real estate agent feels that the probabilities are $0.25, 0.45, 0.20, 0.08$, and
       0.02 that a house can be sold for $\$100,000, \$105,000, \$110,000, \$115,000$,
       or $\$120,000$, what is the real estate agent's mathematical expectation?

4.74   Determine whether each of the following is true or false:

       (a) $5! = \dfrac{10!}{2!}$

       (b) $\dfrac{3}{4!} + \dfrac{1}{4!} = 1$

       (c) $3! \times 2! = 6!$

       (d) $8! = 6! \times 56$

4.75   What is the probability of rolling a seven with a pair of balanced dice?

4.76   The decision to purchase land as a location for a new shopping mall has been
       narrowed down to five sites, A, B, C, D, and E. Draw a tree diagram which
       shows the number of different ways a decision can be made for a first choice
       and for an alternate choice.

4.77   (a) In how many ways can a customer purchase one or more of the following
            pieces of gold jewelry: a necklace, a bracelet, a ring, and a brooch?

       (b) In how many ways can a customer purchase zero or more of the pieces of
            gold jewelry listed in part (a)?

4.78   If we receive 90 cents each time we draw any ace, king, queen, or jack from a
       well-shuffled deck of 52 ordinary playing cards, how much should we pay
       back when we draw any other card so as to make the game fair?

4.79   In how many ways can a parking attendant park seven cars in a row?

4.80   A multiple-choice quiz contains five questions, each with four different
       answers.

       (a) How many ways can a student answer all the questions?

       (b) How many ways can the student get all the answers correct?

4.81   In how many ways can a student select 3 of 8 required courses and 2 of 10
       elective courses?

Section 4.7   Review Exercises   145

4.82 In a recent year 262 Democrats were elected to serve as members of Congress in the 435-member House of Representatives. Estimate the probability that a randomly selected congressional representative is a member of the Democratic party.

4.8

Solutions of Practice Exercises

4.1

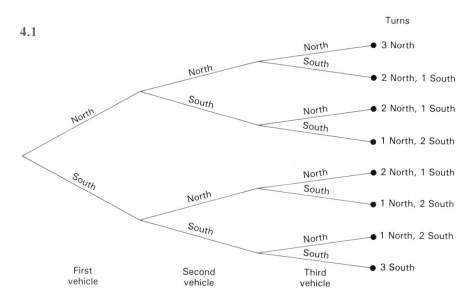

(a) 3   (b) 3   (c) 1   (d) 1

4.6 $6 \cdot 5 \cdot 4 = 120$ choices

4.7 $\dfrac{288}{3 \cdot 6 \cdot 2 \cdot 2} = 4$ countries

4.13 (a) $4^{10} = 1,048,576$ ways   (b) $1^{10} = 1$ way   (c) $3^{10} = 59,049$ ways

4.15 (a) $_{10}P_3 = \dfrac{10!}{(10 - 3)!} = \dfrac{10!}{7!} = 10 \cdot 9 \cdot 8 = 720$ permutations

(b) $_3P_2 = \dfrac{3!}{(3 - 2)!} = \dfrac{3!}{1} = 6$

(c) 1. Prudential Insurance Co., American Express Co., Metropolitan Life

2. Prudential Insurance Co., Metropolitan Life, American Express Co.
3. American Express Co., Prudential Insurance Co., Metropolitan Life
4. American Express Co., Metropolitan Life, Prudential Insurance Co.
5. Metropolitan Life, Prudential Insurance Co., American Express Co.
6. Metropolitan Life, American Express Co., Prudential Insurance Co.

4.19 $4 \cdot 3 \cdot 2 \cdot 1 = 24$

4.23 (a) $\dfrac{n!}{r_1! \cdot r_2!} = \dfrac{7!}{2! \cdot 3!} = \dfrac{5{,}040}{12} = 420$ permutations.

(b) $\dfrac{6!}{3!3!} = 20$ ways to schedule the 6 meetings.

(c) As in part (c) of Exercise 4.22 on page 127, if x is the number of permutations of n objects taken all together, of which r_1 are alike and the others distinct, we write $x \cdot r_1! = n!$. Now, if there is another set of r_2 objects that are alike, we have $x \cdot r_1! r_2! = n!$, and if there is a third set of r_3 objects that are alike we have $x \cdot r_1! r_2! r_3! = n!$. Continuing this argument, we can state in general that $x \cdot r_1! r_2! r_3! \cdot \ldots \cdot r_k! = n!$ when among n objects r_1 are alike, r_2 are alike, r_3 are alike, ... , and r_k are alike, and we get

$$x = \dfrac{n!}{r_1! r_2! \cdot \cdots \cdot r_k!}$$

for the number of permutations of n objects taken all together, of which r_1 are alike, r_2 are alike, ... , r_k are alike, and the others are all distinct.

The number of ways the chief executive officer can schedule the 3 department heads, each of whom he will meet twice, is $\dfrac{6!}{2!2!2!} = 90$.

(d) $\dfrac{10!}{2!3!4!} = \dfrac{3{,}628{,}800}{288} = 12{,}600$ sequences.

4.24 $\dfrac{12!}{3!(12 - 3)!} = \dfrac{12 \cdot 11 \cdot 10 \cdot 9!}{3 \cdot 2 \cdot 1 \cdot 9!} = 220$ ways.

4.26 (a) $\dbinom{10}{2} = \dfrac{10!}{2!(10 - 2)!} = 45$ ways.

(b) $\dbinom{6}{2} = \dfrac{6!}{2!(6 - 2)!} = \dfrac{6 \cdot 5 \cdot 4!}{2 \cdot 1 \cdot 4} = 15$ ways.

(c) $\dbinom{6}{1}\dbinom{4}{1} = \dfrac{6!}{1!(6-1)!} \cdot \dfrac{4!}{1!(4-1)!} = 6 \cdot 4 = 24$ ways.

(d) $\dbinom{6}{0}\dbinom{4}{2} = \dfrac{6!}{0!(6-0)!} \cdot \dfrac{4!}{2!(4-2)!} = 1 \cdot 6 = 6$ ways.

4.27 $\dbinom{12}{3}\dbinom{8}{2} = \dfrac{12!}{3!9!} \cdot \dfrac{8!}{2!6!} = 220 \cdot 28 = 6{,}160$ ways.

4.33 (a) $\dfrac{2}{52}$ (b) $\dfrac{13}{52}$ (c) $\dfrac{4}{52}$

4.36 (a) $\dfrac{4}{8+11+4+7} = \dfrac{4}{30} = 0.13$ (b) $\dfrac{8+7}{30} = \dfrac{15}{30} = 0.50$

     (c) $\dfrac{11}{30} = 0.37$ (d) $1 - \dfrac{11+4}{30} = 0.50$

4.38 (a) $\dfrac{\dbinom{13}{3}}{\dbinom{52}{3}} = \dfrac{286}{22{,}100} = 0.0129 \ \left(\text{or } \dfrac{13}{52} \cdot \dfrac{12}{51} \cdot \dfrac{11}{50} = 0.0129\right)$

     (b) $\dfrac{\dbinom{13}{0}\dbinom{39}{3}}{\dbinom{52}{3}} = \dfrac{9{,}139}{22{,}100} = 0.4135 \ \left(\text{or } \dfrac{39}{52} \cdot \dfrac{38}{51} \cdot \dfrac{37}{50} = 0.4135\right)$

     (c) $\dfrac{\dbinom{26}{3}}{\dbinom{52}{3}} = \dfrac{2{,}600}{22{,}100} = 0.1176 \ \left(\text{or } \dfrac{26}{52} \cdot \dfrac{25}{51} \cdot \dfrac{24}{50} = 0.1176\right)$

     (d) $\dfrac{\dbinom{26}{0}\dbinom{26}{3}}{\dbinom{52}{3}} = \dfrac{1(2{,}600)}{22{,}100} = 0.1176 \ \left(\text{or } \dfrac{26}{52} \cdot \dfrac{25}{51} \cdot \dfrac{24}{50} = 0.1176\right)$

4.47 $0 \cdot \dfrac{199}{200} + 25 \cdot \dfrac{1}{200} = \$0.125$

4.48 $0 \cdot \dfrac{993}{1{,}000} + 200 \cdot \dfrac{1}{1{,}000} + 100 \cdot \dfrac{1}{1{,}000} + 10 \cdot \dfrac{5}{1{,}000} = \$0.35$

4.50 (a) $-0 \cdot \dfrac{95}{100} + 20 \cdot \dfrac{1}{100} + 10 \cdot \dfrac{1}{100} + 5 \cdot \dfrac{3}{100} = \$0.45.$

     (b) No. The bus fare (50 cents) exceeds the expected value of the door prize (45 cents).

4.51 (a) $20{,}000 \cdot \tfrac{1}{2} + 12{,}000 \cdot \tfrac{1}{2} = \$16{,}000$ for both players.

(b) $20{,}000 \cdot \frac{3}{4} + 12{,}000 \cdot \frac{1}{4} = \$18{,}000$ for the better player and

$20{,}000 \cdot \frac{1}{4} + 12{,}000 \cdot \frac{3}{4} = \$14{,}000$ for the poorer player.

4.53 $0.05(1{,}000{,}000) + 0.20(900{,}000) + 0.30(800{,}000) + 0.45(700{,}000) = \$785{,}000$

4.59 $(21{,}800 + 7{,}600)p + 21{,}800(1 - p) > 25{,}600$, so that $p > \dfrac{3{,}800}{7{,}600} = 0.5$.

Some Rules of Probability

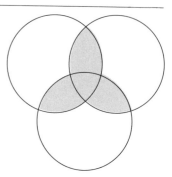

In the study of probability there are basically three kinds of questions: (1) What do we mean when we say, for example, that the probability of rain tomorrow is 0.80, that the probability that a new video rental shop will succeed is 0.35, or that the probability a candidate will be elected mayor is 0.60? (2) How are the numbers we call probabilities determined, or measured in actual practice? (3) What are the mathematical rules which probabilities must obey?

We have already studied the first two of these questions in Chapter 4. In the classical probability concept we are concerned with equally likely possibilities and count "favorable" outcomes; in the frequency interpretation we are concerned with proportions of "successes" in the long run and base our estimates on what happened in the past; and in the subjective probability concept we are concerned with a measure of a person's belief and we observe how the person will react in risk-taking situations.

In this chapter, after some preliminaries in Section 5.1 we shall study the question of what basic rules probabilities must obey, or how they must "behave." As we shall see in Section 5.2 there are essentially three of these rules, called the **postulates of probability**, and they must be obeyed regardless of whether we interpret probabilities in terms of equally likely possibilities, as proportions in the long run, or as subjective evaluations.

Then, in Section 5.3 we shall see how probabilities are related to **odds**, and in Section 5.4 we shall study the important concepts of **conditional probability** and **independence**.

5.1

Sample Spaces and Events

In statistics, a set of all possible outcomes of an experiment is called a **sample space** and it is usually denoted by the letter S. For instance, if a broker must choose 3 of 24 stocks to suggest to a client, the sample space consists of the $\binom{24}{3} = 2{,}024$ ways in which this choice can be made; if the dean of a college must assign 2 of 84 faculty members as advisors to a journalism club, the sample space consists of the $\binom{84}{2} = 3{,}486$ ways in which this can be done. Also, if we are concerned with the number of days it rains in Pittsburgh during the month of March, the sample space is the set

$$S = \{0,\ 1,\ 2,\ 3,\ 4,\ \ldots,\ 30,\ 31\}$$

To avoid misunderstandings about the terms "outcome" and "experiment," let us make it clear that they are used here in a very wide sense. For lack of a better term, "experiment" refers to any process of observation or measurement. Thus, an **experiment** may consist of determining the number of injury accidents in a large motor freight terminal in one year, it may consist of the simple process of noting whether a light is on or off, or it may consist of the complicated process of obtaining and evaluating data to predict Gross Domestic Product. The results one obtains from an experiment, whether they are instrument readings, counts, "yes" or "no" answers, or values obtained through extensive calculations, are called the **outcomes** of the experiment.

When we study the outcomes of an experiment, we usually identify the various possibilities with numbers, points, or other kinds of symbols, so that we can treat all questions concerning the outcomes mathematically, without having to go through long verbal descriptions of what has taken place, is taking place, or will take place. For instance, if there are eight applicants for a job and we let a, b, c, d, e, f, g, and h denote the events that it is offered to Arnold, Betty, Clark, and so on, then the sample space for this experiment is the set

$$S = \{a, b, c, d, e, f, g, h\}$$

The use of points rather than letters or numbers has the added advantage that it is easier to visualize the various possibilities, and perhaps discover some special features which several of the outcomes may have in common. For instance, if two contractors, among others, bid on two construction jobs and we are interested in how many jobs each of the two will get, we could write the six possible outcomes as (0, 0), (1, 0), (0, 1), (2, 0), (1, 1), and (0, 2). Here, (0, 1) represents the outcome that the first contractor gets neither job and the second gets one, and (1, 1) represents the outcome that each contractor gets one job. Geometrically, this situation may be pictured as in Figure 5.1, from which it is apparent, for instance, that they get the same number of jobs in two of the six possibilities and that, between them, they get both jobs in three of the six possibilities.

Usually, we classify sample spaces according to the number of elements, or points, which they contain. The ones we have studied so far in this section contained 2,024, 3,486, 32, 8, and 6 elements, and we call them all **finite**, since the number of possibilities is in each case finite, or fixed. In this chapter we shall consider only finite sample spaces, but in later chapters we shall consider also **infinite sample spaces**.

In statistics, any subset of a sample space is called an **event**, and usually is designated by a capital letter. By subset we mean any part of a set, including the set as a whole, and trivially, a set called the **empty set** and denoted by $\emptyset$, which has no elements at all. For instance, for the sample space of the number of days that it rains in Pittsburgh during the month of March,

$$A = \{15, 16, 17, 18, 19, 20\}$$

is the event that there will be from 15 to 20 rainy days, and

$$B = \{18, 19, 20, \ldots, 30, 31\}$$

is the event that there will be at least 18 rainy days. Also, with reference to Figure 5.1,

$$C = \{(1, 0), (0, 1)\}$$

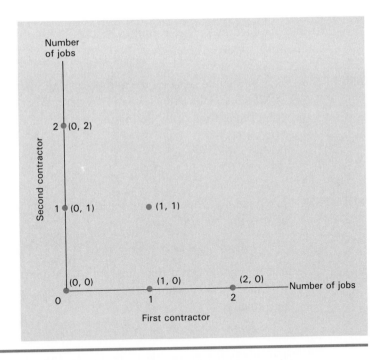

FIGURE 5.1
Outcomes of the two-contractor example

is the event that, between them, the two contractors get only one job,

$$D = \{(0, 0), (1, 0), (0, 1), (1, 1)\}$$

is the event that neither contractor gets both jobs, and

$$E = \{(1, 1)\}$$

is the event that each contractor gets one job.

Also, in the two-contractor example events C and E have no elements in common. Such events are called **mutually exclusive**, which means that they cannot both occur at the same time. Evidently, if, between them, the two contractors get only one job, each one cannot get one job. On the other hand, events D and E are not mutually exclusive since they both contain the outcome $(1, 1)$, where each contractor gets one job.

In many probability problems we are interested in events that can be expressed in terms of two or more events by forming **unions**, **intersections**, and **complements**. In general, the union of two events, X and Y, denoted by $X \cup Y$, is the event which consists of all the elements (outcomes) either in event X or in event Y, or in both; the intersection of two events X and Y, denoted by $X \cap Y$, is the event which consists of all the elements (outcomes) contained in both X and Y; and the complement of X, denoted by X', is the event which consists of all the elements (outcomes) of the sample space that are not contained in X. We usually read $\cup$ as "or," $\cap$ as "and," and X' as "not X."

EXAMPLE 5.1   For the sample space of the number of days that it rains in Pittsburgh in March and the events A and B as defined earlier, list the outcomes comprising each of the following events and also express the events in words:
(a) $A \cup B$ (c) B'
(b) $A \cap B$ (d) $A' \cap B'$

SOLUTION   (a) Since $A \cup B$ contains all the elements that are either in A or in B, or in both, we find that

$$A \cup B = \{15, 16, 17, \ldots, 30, 31\}$$

and this is the event that there will be at least 15 rainy days.
(b) Since $A \cap B$ contains all the elements that are in both A and B, we find that

$$A \cap B = \{18, 19, 20\}$$

and this is the event that there will be from 18 to 20 rainy days.
(c) Since B' contains all the elements of the sample space that are not in B, we find that

$$B' = \{0, 1, 2, \ldots, 16, 17\}$$

and this is the event that there will be fewer than 18 rainy days. (d) Since $A' \cap B'$ contains all the elements of the sample space that are neither in A nor in B, we find that

$$A' \cap B' = \{0, 1, 2, \ldots, 13, 14\}$$

and this is the event that there will be fewer than 15 rainy days.   ∎

Sample spaces and events, particularly relationships among events, are often pictured by means of **Venn diagrams** such as those of Figures 5.2 and 5.3. In each case, the sample space is represented by a rectangle, and events by circles or parts of circles within the rectangle. The tinted regions of the four Venn diagrams of Figure 5.2 represent the event X, the complement of event X, the union of events X and Y, and the intersection of events X and Y.

EXAMPLE 5.2   If X is the event that stock prices will go up and Y is the event that interest rates will go up, what events are represented by the tinted regions of the four Venn diagrams of Figure 5.2?

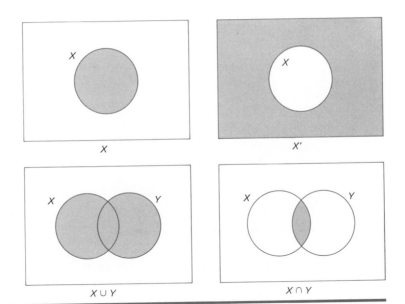

FIGURE 5.2
Venn diagrams

SOLUTION   The tinted region of the first diagram represents the event that stock prices will go up; the tinted region of the second diagram represents the event that stock prices will not go up; the tinted region of the third diagram represents the event that either stock prices or interest rates, or both, will go up; and the tinted region of the fourth diagram represents the event that stock prices and interest rates will both go up. ∎

When we deal with three events, we draw the circles as in Figure 5.3. In this diagram, the circles divide the sample space into eight regions, numbered 1 through 8, and it is easy to determine whether the corresponding events are in X or in X', in Y or in Y', and in Z or in Z'.

EXAMPLE 5.3   With reference to a newly designed engine, X represents the event that its gasoline consumption will be low, Y represents the event that its maintenance cost will be low, and Z represents the event that it can be sold at a profit. Express in words what events are represented by the following regions of the Venn diagram of Figure 5.3:
(a) region 4
(b) regions 1 and 3 together
(c) regions 3, 5, 6, and 8 together

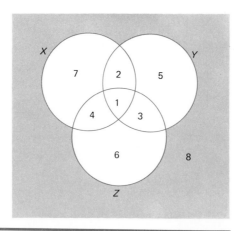

FIGURE 5.3
Venn diagram

SOLUTION (a) Since this region is contained in X and in Z but not in Y, it represents the event that the engine's gasoline consumption will be low, that it can be sold at a profit, but that its maintenance cost will not be low.

(b) Since this is the region common to Y and Z, it represents the event that the engine's maintenance cost will be low and that it can be sold at a profit.

(c) Since this is the entire region outside X, it represents the event that the engine's gasoline consumption will not be low. ■

EXERCISES

(Exercises 5.1, 5.2, 5.3, 5.4, 5.5, 5.6, 5.13, and 5.14 are practice exercises. Their complete solutions are given on page 195.)

5.1 The seven departments in a department store are assigned numbers 1 through 7 so that the sample space is the set $S = \{1, 2, 3, 4, 5, 6, 7\}$. If $X = \{1, 2, 3, 4\}$, $Y = \{3, 4, 5, 6, 7\}$, and $Z = \{5, 6, 7\}$, list the elements of the sample space comprising each of the following events and also express the events in words.

(a) $X \cup Z$

(b) $Y \cap Z$

(c) Z'

5.2 With reference to the illustration on page 152, suppose that there are eight applicants for a job and we let $a, b, c, d, e, f, g,$ and $h,$ denote the events that Arnold, Betty, Clark, David, Eric, Francis, George, or Hilda will be offered the job. If $A = \{b, d, f, h\}$, $B = \{c, g, h\}$, and $C = \{a, b, d\}$, list the elements of the sample space comprising each of the following events and also express the events in words.

(a) C'

(b) $B \cup C$

(c) $C \cap A$

(d) $B' \cap C$

5.3   To construct sample spaces for experiments in which we deal with categorical data, we often code the various alternatives by assigning them numbers. For instance, an accountant might code the entries relating to current assets of a firm as 1, 2, 3, 4, or 5 depending on whether the entry should be posted to cash, marketable securities, accounts receivable, inventory, or prepaid expenses. Express each of the following events in words:

(a) $K = \{1, 5\}$

(b) $L = \{3, 5\}$

(c) $M = \{1, 2, 3\}$

5.4   With reference to the preceding exercise, list the elements in the sample space comprising each of the following events and also express the events in words.

(a) K'

(b) $K \cup L$

(c) $K \cap L$

(d) $K \cap M$

5.5   With reference to the two-contractor illustration on page 152 and Figure 5.1 describe each of the following events in words:

(a) $F = \{(0, 0), (1, 1)\}$

(b) $G = \{(2, 0), (1, 1), (0, 2)\}$

(c) $H = \{(0, 0), (0, 1), (0, 2)\}$

5.6   With reference to the two-contractor illustration on page 152 and Figure 5.1 list the points of the sample space which comprise the following events:

(a) One of the contractors gets both jobs.

(b) The second contractor gets one job.

(c) The second contractor does not get either job.

5.7   An office hires up to four secretaries and three bookkeepers by the day from a temporary help contractor.

(a) Use two coordinates so that (1, 3), for example, represents the fact that on a certain day the office hires one secretary and three bookkeepers and (2, 0) represents the event that the office hires two secretaries and no bookkeepers. Draw a diagram similar to that of Figure 5.1 on page 153 showing the 20 points of the corresponding sample space.

(b) Describe in words the event which is represented by each of the following sets of points of the sample space: the event D, which consists of the points (2, 3), (3, 2), (3, 3), (4, 1), (4, 2), and (4, 3); the event E, which consists of the points (0, 0), (1, 1), (2, 2), and (3, 3); the event F, which consists of the points (0, 1), (0, 2), (0, 3), (1, 2), (1, 3), and (2, 3); and the event G, which consists of the points (0, 3), (1, 2), (2, 1), and (3, 0).

5.8   With reference to the preceding exercise, which of the following are mutually exclusive events:

(a) E and F

(b) E and G'

(c) D and F

(d) D and G

5.9   A boat rental firm has three boats for rent and has fishing guides available for hire.

(a) Using two coordinates so that (3, 0), for example, represents the event that three boats are rented and zero guides are hired and (2, 1) represents the event that two boats are rented and one guide is hired, draw a diagram similar to that of Figure 5.1 on page 153 showing the 10 points of the corresponding sample space.

(b) List the points which comprise the event H, that at least two of the rented boats have hired guides; the event I, that only one boat is rented; and the event J, that any boats that are rented have hired guides.

(c) With reference to part (b), list the points of the sample space which represent J' and $J \cap I$, and describe in words the corresponding events.

(d) With reference to part (b), which of the pairs of events, H and I, H and J, and I and J are mutually exclusive?

5.10   A fire insurance claims adjuster wants to inspect the fire-damaged sites of four policyholders. He may or may not be able to inspect all of them during the remaining two days of the week and will not inspect any one of these sites more than once.

(a) Using two coordinates so that (3, 1), for example, represents the event that he will inspect three sites on the first day and one on the second day, and (0, 4) represents the event that he will not visit any of these sites on the first day and will visit four sites on the second day, draw a diagram similar to that of Figure 5.1 on page 153, which shows the 15 possibilities.

(b) List the points of the sample space of part (a) which constitute the following events: event K that he will inspect all four of the sites during his visit, event L that he will inspect more of them on the first day than on the second day, event M that he will inspect at least three of the sites on the second day, and event Q that he will inspect only one of the sites during the two days.

(c) With reference to part (b), list the points of the sample space which comprise the events K', $K \cup M$, $K \cap L$, and $K' \cap M$.

5.11 With reference to the preceding exercise, which of the following are mutually exclusive events:

(a) K and M

(b) L and M

(c) Q and L

(d) Q and M

5.12 Which of the following pairs of events are mutually exclusive? Explain your answers.

(a) Weighing 95 pounds and being a heavyweight boxer

(b) Being in the police force and wearing civilian clothing

(c) Being 16 years old and voting in a national political election

(d) Walking and chewing gum at the same time

(e) Getting a speeding ticket while parked in a parking lot

(f) Drawing an ace of spades and a red card on a single draw from an ordinary deck of 52 playing cards

(g) A golfer getting a hole in one in two strokes

(h) Wearing athletic shoes and being an athlete

5.13 In Figure 5.4, U is the event that the unemployment rate will go down and I is the event that the inflation rate will go up. Explain in words what events are represented by regions 1, 2, 3, and 4.

5.14 With reference to the preceding exercise, what events are represented by

(a) regions 3 and 4 together

(b) regions 2 and 3 together

(c) regions 1, 2, and 3 together

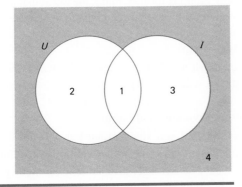

FIGURE 5.4
Venn diagram for
Exercise 5.13

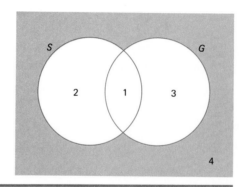

FIGURE 5.5
Venn diagram for
Exercise 5.15

5.15   In Figure 5.5, *S* is the event that an investor in the stock market hired an investment counselor, and *G* is the event that the investor made capital gains on her investments. Explain in words what events are represented by regions 1, 2, 3, and 4.

5.16   With reference to the preceding exercise, what events are represented by
       (a) regions 1 and 2 together
       (b) regions 1 and 3 together

5.17   With reference to the illustration on page 156 dealing with the newly designed engine and Figure 5.3, express in words what events are represented by the following regions of the Venn diagram:
       (a) region 2
       (b) regions 1 and 4 together
       (c) regions 2 and 5 together
       (d) regions 4, 6, and 7 together
       (e) regions 2, 5, 7, and 8 together

5.18   A conservation group is meeting to consider the possibility of establishing three study groups to examine the balance of nature between soil, water, and wildlife. Let *S* be the event that a soil study group is formed, *W* the event that a water study group is formed, and *L* the event that a wildlife study group is formed. With reference to the Venn diagram of Figure 5.6, list (by number) the region or combination of regions which represent the events that the conservation group
       (a) will establish a soil study group and a water study group, but will not establish a wildlife study group
       (b) will not establish a soil study group or water study group, but will establish a wildlife study group
       (c) will establish a soil study group but will not establish a water study group and will not establish a wildlife study group
       (d) will establish a soil study group or a water study group (or both) but not establish a wildlife study group

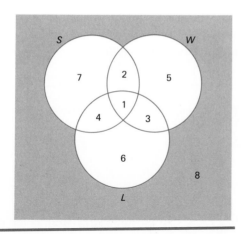

FIGURE 5.6
Venn diagram for
Exercise 5.18

5.19 With reference to the preceding exercise and the Venn diagram of Figure 5.6, express in words what events are represented by the following regions:

(a) region 1   (b) region 5

(c) region 8   (d) regions 3 and 5 together

(e) regions 1 and 4 together   (f) regions 3, 5, 6, and 8 together

5.20 Venn diagrams are often used to verify relationships among sets, subsets, or events, without requiring rigorous proofs based on a formal algebra of sets. We simply show that the expressions which are supposed to be equal are represented by the same region of a Venn diagram. Use Venn diagrams to show that

(a) $A \cup (A \cap B) = A$

(b) $(A \cap B) \cup (A \cap B') = A$

(c) $(A \cap B)' = A' \cup B'$ and $(A \cup B)' = A' \cap B'$

(d) $(A \cup B) = (A \cap B) \cup (A \cap B') \cup (A' \cap B)$

(e) $A \cap (B \cup C) = (A \cap B) \cup (A \cap C)$

5.2

Some Basic Rules

We turn now to the question of how probabilities must "behave," and we begin by stating the three basic postulates. To formulate these postulates and some of their immediate consequences, we shall continue the practice of denoting events by capital letters, and we shall write the probability of event

A as $P(A)$, the probability of event *B* as $P(B)$, and so forth. As before, we shall denote the set of all possible outcomes, the sample space, by the letter *S*. As we shall formulate them here, the three postulates of probability apply only when the sample space *S* is finite.

<table>
<tr><td>

First two postulates of probability

</td><td>

1 *The probability of any event is a positive real number or zero; symbolically, $P(A) \geq 0$ for any event A.*

2 *The probability of any sample space is equal to 1; symbolically, $P(S) = 1$ for any sample space S.*

</td></tr>
</table>

Let us justify these two postulates, as well as the one which follows, with reference to the classical probability concept and the frequency interpretation; in Section 5.3 we shall see to what extent the postulates are compatible also with subjective probabilities.

So far as the first postulate is concerned, the fraction s/n is always positive or zero, and so are percentages or proportions. The second postulate states indirectly that certainty is identified with a probability of 1; after all, one of the possibilities included in *S* must occur, and it is to this certain event that we assign a probability of 1. For equally likely outcomes, $s = n$ for the whole sample space and $s/n = n/n = 1$, and in the frequency interpretation, a probability of 1 implies that the event will occur 100 percent of the time, or in other words, that it is certain to occur.

In actual practice, we also assign a probability of 1 to events which are "practically certain" to occur. For instance, we would assign a probability of 1 to the event that at least one person will vote in the next presidential election and that among all new cars sold during any one model year at least one will be involved in an accident before it has been driven 12,000 miles.

The third postulate of probability is especially important, but it is not quite so obvious as the other two.

<table>
<tr><td>

Third postulate of probability

</td><td>

3 *If two events are mutually exclusive, the probability that one or the other will occur equals the sum of their probabilities. Symbolically,*

$$P(A \cup B) = P(A) + P(B)$$

for any two mutually exclusive events A and B.

</td></tr>
</table>

Chapter 5   Some Rules of Probability

For instance, if the probability that a manufacturer's raw material price index will go up during a certain month is 0.82 and the probability that it will remain unchanged is 0.13, then the probability that it will either go up or remain unchanged is $0.82 + 0.13 = 0.95$. Similarly, if the probability that a student will get an A in a course is 0.17 and the probability that she will get a B is 0.35 then the probability that she will get either an A or a B is $0.17 + 0.35 = 0.52$.

This postulate is also compatible with the classical probability concept and the frequency interpretation. In the classical concept, if s_1 of n equally likely possibilities constitute event A and s_2 others constitute event B, then these $s_1 + s_2$ equally likely possibilities constitute event $A \cup B$, and we have

$$P(A) = \frac{s_1}{n}, \quad P(B) = \frac{s_2}{n}, \quad P(A \cup B) = \frac{s_1 + s_2}{n},$$

and

$$P(A) + P(B) = P(A \cup B)$$

In accordance with the frequency interpretation, if one event occurs, say, 36 percent of the time, another event occurs 41 percent of the time, and they cannot both occur at the same time (they are mutually exclusive), then one or the other will occur $36 + 41 = 77$ percent of the time; this satisfies the third postulate.

By using the three postulates of probability, we can derive many further rules according to which probabilities must "behave"—some of them are easy to prove and some are not, but they all have important applications. Among the immediate consequences of the three postulates, we find that probabilities can never be greater than 1, that an event which cannot occur has the probability 0, and that the probabilities that an event will occur and that it will not occur always add up to 1. Symbolically,

Further rules of probability

$$
\begin{array}{ll}
P(A) \leq 1 & \textit{for any event } A \\
P(\varnothing) = 0 & \\
P(A) + P(A') = 1 \quad \textit{or} & P(A') = 1 - P(A)
\end{array}
$$

The first of these results simply expresses the fact that there cannot be more favorable outcomes than there are outcomes and that an event cannot occur more than 100 percent of the time. The second result expresses the fact that when an event cannot occur there are $s = 0$ favorable outcomes, and that such an event occurs 0 percent of the time. In actual practice, we also assign 0 probabilities to events which are so unlikely that we are "practically certain" they will not occur. For instance, we would assign a probability of 0 to the event that a monkey set loose on a typewriter will by chance type Plato's *Republic* word for word without a single mistake.

The third result can also be derived from the postulates of probability, but it can easily be seen that it is compatible with the classical probability concept and the frequency interpretation. In the classical concept, if there are s "successes" there are $n - s$ "failures," the corresponding probabilities are $\frac{s}{n}$ and $\frac{n-s}{n}$, and their sum is $\frac{s}{n} + \frac{n-s}{n} = 1$. In accordance with the frequency interpretation, if shipments arrive late 16 percent of the time, then they do not arrive late 84 percent of the time, the corresponding probabilities are 0.16 and 0.84, and their sum is 1.

The examples which follow illustrate how the postulates and the further rules are put to use in actual practice.

EXAMPLE 5.4 If A is the event that the price of a certain stock will remain unchanged on a given trading day and B is the event that its price will go up, $P(A) = 0.64$ and $P(B) = 0.21$, find

(a) $P(A')$

(b) $P(A \cup B)$

(c) $P(A \cap B)$

SOLUTION (a) From the third of the further rules, we find that $P(A') = 1 - P(A) = 1 - 0.64 = 0.36$; (b) since A and B are mutually exclusive, it follows from the third postulate that $P(A \cup B) = P(A) + P(B) = 0.64 + 0.21 = 0.85$; (c) since A and B are mutually exclusive, $A \cap B = \varnothing$ and it follows that $P(A \cap B) = 0$ in accordance with the second of the further rules. ∎

In problems like this, it often helps to draw a Venn diagram, fill in the probabilities associated with the various regions, and then read the answers directly off the diagram.

EXAMPLE 5.5 If C is the event that a certain lawyer will be in her office on a given afternoon and D is the event that she will be in court, $P(C) = 0.48$ and $P(D) = 0.27$, find the value of $P(C' \cap D')$, the probability that she will be neither in her office nor in court.

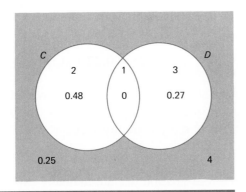

FIGURE 5.7
Venn diagram

SOLUTION   Drawing the Venn diagram as in Figure 5.7, we first put a 0 into region 1 because C and D are mutually exclusive events. It follows that the 0.48 probability of event C must go into region 2, the 0.27 probability of event D must go into region 3, and since the probability of the entire sample space must equal 1, we put $1 - (0.48 + 0.27) = 0.25$ into region 4. Since the event $C' \cap D'$ is represented by region 4, the region outside both circles, we find that $P(C' \cap D') = 0.25$. ∎

The third postulate applies only to two mutually exclusive events, but it can easily be generalized; repeatedly using this postulate, it can be shown that

Generalization of Postulate 3

If k events are mutually exclusive, the probability that one of them will occur equals the sum of their individual probabilities; symbolically

$$P(A_1 \cup A_2 \cup \cdots \cup A_k) = P(A_1) + P(A_2) + \cdots + P(A_k)$$

for any mutually exclusive events $A_1, A_2, \ldots,$ and A_k.

---

where, again, $\cup$ is usually read "or."

EXAMPLE 5.6   The probabilities that a woman will buy a new party dress at Macy's, Neiman-Marcus, or Lord & Taylor are $0.35, 0.22,$ and 0.18. What is the probability that she will buy the dress at one of these stores?

SOLUTION Since the three possibilities are mutually exclusive, direct substitution into the formula yields

$$0.35 + 0.22 + 0.18 = 0.75$$ ∎

EXAMPLE 5.7 If the probabilities that the Standard & Poor's Corporation will rate a company's stock A+, A, A−, or B+ are 0.10, 0.16, 0.31, and 0.36, what is the probability that the stock will get one of these ratings?

SOLUTION Since the four possibilities are mutually exclusive, direct substitution into the formula yields

$$0.10 + 0.16 + 0.31 + 0.36 = 0.93$$ ∎

The job of assigning probabilities to all possible events connected with a given situation can be very tedious, to say the least. If there are only five outcomes (or points) in a sample space S, there is $\binom{5}{0} = 1$ subset (the empty set) which contains no outcomes at all, there are $\binom{5}{1} = 5$ subsets which contain one outcome, $\binom{5}{2} = 10$ subsets which contain two outcomes, $\binom{5}{3} = 10$ subsets which contain three outcomes, $\binom{5}{4} = 5$ subsets which contain four outcomes, and there is $\binom{5}{5} = 1$ subset (the sample space itself) which contains all five outcomes. Thus, there are $1 + 5 + 10 + 10 + 5 + 1 = 32$ different subsets of a sample space with five outcomes, and as the number of outcomes increases slowly the number of subsets increases rapidly.

In general, if we let $a = 1$ and $b = 1$ in the binomial expansion of $(a + b)^n$, it follows directly that a sample space with n outcomes has 2^n different subsets, namely, that

$$\binom{n}{0} + \binom{n}{1} + \binom{n}{2} + \cdots + \binom{n}{n-1} + \binom{n}{n} = 2^n$$

where $\binom{n}{0}$, $\binom{n}{1}$, $\binom{n}{2}$, . . . , $\binom{n}{n-1}$, and $\binom{n}{n}$ are the numbers of subsets containing $0, 1, 2, \ldots, n - 1$, and n outcomes. As we saw in the preceding

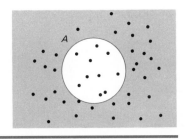

FIGURE 5.8
Sample space

paragraph, a sample space with $n = 5$ outcomes has $2^5 = 32$ different subsets; also, a sample space with $n = 20$ outcomes has $2^{20} = 1,048,576$ different subsets.

Fortunately, it is seldom necessary to assign probabilities to all possible events, and the following rule (which is a direct application of the foregoing generalization of the third postulate) makes it relatively easy to determine the probability of any event on the basis of the probabilities assigned to the individual outcomes (points) of the corresponding sample space.

Rule for calculating the probability of an event

> *The probability of any event A is given by the sum of the probabilities of the individual outcomes comprising A.*

This rule is illustrated in Figure 5.8, where the dots represent the individual (mutually exclusive) outcomes.

EXAMPLE 5.8   If the probabilities are 0.05, 0.14, 0.17, 0.33, 0.20, and 0.11 that a consumer testing service will rate a new lawn mower very poor, poor, fair, good, very good, or excellent, what are the possibilities that it will rate the lawn mower

(a) very poor or poor

(b) good, very good, or excellent

(c) poor, fair, good, or very good

SOLUTION   Adding the probabilities of the respective outcomes, we get (a) $0.05 + 0.14 = 0.19$, (b) $0.33 + 0.20 + 0.11 = 0.64$, and (c) $0.14 + 0.17 + 0.33 + 0.20 = 0.84$. ∎

EXAMPLE 5.9   Referring again to the two-contractor illustration of Figure 5.1 on page 153, suppose that the six points of the sample space have the probabilities shown in Figure 5.9. find the probabilities that

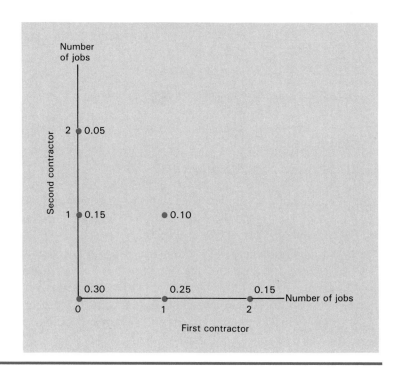

FIGURE 5.9
Sample space with probabilities

(a) the first contractor will not get either job

(b) between them, the two contractors will get both jobs

(c) the second contractor will get at most one job

SOLUTION (a) Adding the probabilities associated with the points $(0, 0)$, $(0, 1)$, and $(0, 2)$, we get $0.30 + 0.15 + 0.05 = 0.50$; (b) adding the probabilities associated with the points $(2, 0)$, $(1, 1)$, and $(0, 2)$, we get $0.15 + 0.10 + 0.05 = 0.30$; (c) adding the probabilities associated with the points $(0, 0)$, $(1, 0)$, $(2, 0)$, $(0, 1)$, and $(1, 1)$, we get $0.30 + 0.25 + 0.15 + 0.15 + 0.10 = 0.95$. ∎

If the individual outcomes are all equiprobable, the calculations are even simpler, for the rule immediately preceding leads to the formula $\dfrac{s}{n}$, which we introduced in Chapter 4 in connection with the classical probability concept.

Since the third postulate applies only to mutually exclusive events, it cannot be used, for example, to find the probability that at least one of two roommates will pass a final exam in economics, the probability that a person will break an arm or a rib in an automobile accident, or the probability that a customer will buy a shirt or a tie while shopping at Macy's. Both roommates can pass the exam, a person can break an arm and a rib, and a customer can buy both a shirt and a tie.

To find a formula for $P(A \cup B)$ which holds whether the events A and B are mutually exclusive or not, let us consider the Venn diagram of Figure 5.10, which concerns the appointment of a college president. The letter G stands for the event that the appointee will be a graduate of the given college, and the letter W stands for the event that the appointee will be a woman. It follows from the figures in the Venn diagram that

$$P(G) = 0.59 + 0.08 = 0.67$$
$$P(W) = 0.08 + 0.04 = 0.12$$

and

$$P(G \cup W) = 0.59 + 0.08 + 0.04 = 0.71$$

Here we added the probabilities because they represent mutually exclusive events (nonoverlapping regions of the Venn diagram).

Erroneously using the third postulate of probability to calculate $P(G \cup W)$, we get $P(G) + P(W) = 0.67 + 0.12 = 0.79$, which exceeds the correct value by 0.08. The error here results from adding $P(G \cap W)$ in twice, once in $P(G) = 0.67$ and once in $P(W) = 0.12$. However, we can correct for this by subtracting $P(G \cap W) = 0.08$ from $P(G) + P(W) = 0.79$, writing

$$P(G \cup W) = P(G) + P(W) - P(G \cap W)$$
$$= 0.67 + 0.12 - 0.08$$
$$= 0.71$$

This agrees, as it should, with the result which we obtained before.

Since the argument we used in this example holds for any two events A

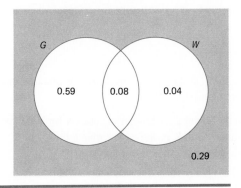

FIGURE 5.10
Venn diagram

and *B,* we can now state the following **general addition rule**, which applies whether *A* and *B* are mutually exclusive or not:

General addition rule

$$P(A \cup B) = P(A) + P(B) - P(A \cap B)$$

When *A* and *B* are mutually exclusive $P(A \cap B) = 0$ (since by definition the two events cannot both occur at the same time), and this formula reduces to that of the third postualte of probability. In this connection, the third postulate is also called the **special addition rule**.

EXAMPLE 5.10   If the probabilities are 0.20, 0.15, and 0.03 that a student will get a failing grade either in accounting or marketing, or in both, what is the probability that he will fail at least one of these subjects?

SOLUTION   Direct substitution into the foregoing formula yields

$$0.20 + 0.15 - 0.03 = 0.32 \qquad \blacksquare$$

EXAMPLE 5.11   If the probabilities are 0.87, 0.36, and 0.29 that a family randomly chosen as part of a sample survey in a large metropolitan area, owns a color television set, or a videocassette recorder, or both, what is the probability that a family in this area will own one, or the other, or both kinds of sets?

SOLUTION   Substituting these values into the formula for the general addition rule, we get

$$0.87 + 0.36 - 0.29 = 0.94 \qquad \blacksquare$$

The general addition rule can be generalized further so that it applies to more than two events (see, for example, Exercise 5.37 on page 174).

EXERCISES

(Exercises 5.21, 5.23, 5.24, 5.26, and 5.37 are practice exercises. Their complete solutions are given on page 195.)

5.21   In a plan to balance its budget, *C* stands for the event that the city will cut expenditures, and *R* is the event that the city will raise revenues. State in words what probabilities are expressed by
(a) $P(C')$ (b) $P(R')$
(c) $P(C \cup R)$ (d) $P(C \cap R)$
(e) $P(C' \cup R)$ (f) $P(C' \cap R)$

5.22 A business consultant is analyzing a troubled firm to determine the source of its failings. If F is the event that the firm has financial difficulties, M is the event that the firm has marketing problems, and A is the event that the firm uses questionable administrative practices, write in symbolic form the probabilities that the troubled firm

(a) has marketing problems and uses questionable administrative practices

(b) does not have financial difficulties but has marketing problems

(c) uses questionable administrative practices or has marketing problems

(d) does not have financial difficulties and does not have marketing problems

5.23 Explain why there must be a mistake in each of the following statements.

(a) The probability that a salesperson will make a sale is 0.78, and the probability that the salesperson will not is 0.32.

(b) The probability that a patient will have adequate hospitalization insurance is 0.41, and the probability that a patient will have no hospital insurance or inadequate coverage is 0.28.

(c) The probability that a trainee will answer all the true-false questions correctly on a training program quiz is 0.60, and the probability that the trainee will make no more than one mistake is 0.20.

(d) The probability that a corporate executive is very pleased with being transferred to a better assignment in a different city is 0.74, and the probability that the executive and his or her spouse are both very pleased with the transfer is 0.83.

(e) The probability that a speculative real estate transaction will earn a profit is better than even. The probability that it will incur a loss is 0.45, and the probability that it will break even is 0.10.

5.24 The probability that the president of a corporation will interview at most 6 candidates when selecting a new treasurer, or interview from 7 to 10 candidates for the position, are 0.65 and 0.20. Find the probabilities that the president will interview

(a) at least 7 candidates

(b) at most 10 candidates

(c) more than 10 candidates

5.25 If F and S are the events that a magazine publisher will launch a new fashion magazine or a new sports magazine, and $P(F) = 0.35$ and $P(S) = 0.25$, find the probability that the publisher

(a) will not launch the fashion magazine

(b) will launch the fashion magazine or the sports magazine

(c) will launch neither the fashion magazine nor the sports magazine

5.26 Given the mutually exclusive events A and B for which $P(A) = 0.37$ and $P(B) = 0.41$, find

(a) $P(A')$

(b) $P(B')$

(c) $P(A \cap B)$

(d) $P(A \cup B)$

(e) $P(A' \cup B')$

(f) $P(A' \cap B')$

5.27 The probabilities that members of a company pension plan are production personnel, office personnel, and first-line supervisory personnel are 0.57, 0.11, and 0.05. What is the probability that a member of the company pension plan is in one or the other of these three classifications?

5.28 The probabilities that a student will get an A, B, or a C in a management course are 0.06, 0.22, and 0.44.

(a) What is the probability that a student will get a grade of C or higher than a C?

(b) What is the probability that a student will get a grade which is lower than a C?

(c) What is the probability that a student will get a grade of C or lower than a C?

5.29 With reference to Figure 5.9 on page 168, find the probabilities that

(a) the first contractor will get only one job

(b) between them, the two contractors will get only one job

(c) neither contractor will get both jobs

5.30 The probabilities that an engineer will evaluate a new method of chemical waste disposal as poor, fair, adequate, very good, or excellent are 0.22, 0.21, 0.33, 0.19, and 0.05. Find the probabilities that the engineer will evaluate the new method of chemical waste disposal as

(a) fair or adequate

(b) at least fair

(c) at best fair

(d) neither poor nor excellent

5.31 The probabilities that 0, 1, 2, 3, 4, or at least 5 applicants for a carpenter's job will apply in response to a help wanted advertisement are 0.080, 0.090, 0.135, 0.165, 0.170, and 0.360. What are the probabilities that

(a) at most 3 persons will apply

(b) at least 2 persons will apply

(c) from 2 to 4 persons will apply

5.32 Given 2 events R and T for which $P(R) = 0.46$ and $P(T) = 0.32$ and $P(R \cap T) = 0.19$ (Figure 5.11), find

(a) $P(R')$

(b) $P(T')$

(c) $P(R \cup T)$

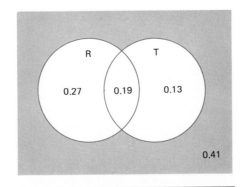

FIGURE 5.11
Venn diagram for
Exercise 5.32

(d) $P(R' \cap T)$

(e) $P(R' \cup T)$

(f) $P(R \cap T')$

5.33   The probabilities that a certain person will not complete a U.S. Individual Income Tax Return, or fail to mail it to the Internal Revenue Service on time, or both are $0.20, 0.15$, and 0.05. What is the probability that this person will fail to complete the income tax return or fail to mail it to the Internal Revenue Service on time?

5.34   The probability that a woman trying on a dress will ask to have it altered is 0.65, the probability that she will ask to have it delivered to her home is 0.32, and the probability that she will ask to have both done is 0.21. What is the probability that a woman shopping in this store will ask

(a) either to have the dress altered or to have it delivered to her home

(b) neither to have it altered nor to have it delivered to her home

5.35   Two magazine salespersons have daily sales quotas. The probability that the experienced salesperson will fail to achieve her daily sales quota is 0.10, the probability that the inexperienced salesperson will fail to achieve her daily

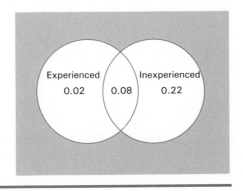

FIGURE 5.12
Venn diagram for
Exercise 5.35

quota is 0.30, and the probability that both will fail to achieve their sales quotas on a given day is 0.08 (Figure 5.12). What is the probability that

(a) either or both will fail to achieve their sales quotas on a given day

(b) only one salesperson fails to achieve her sales quota on a given day

5.36 A group of financiers is attempting to acquire control over an airline and over a steel manufacturer. They feel that the probabilities are 0.27, 0.18, and 0.14 that they will win control over the airline, the steel manufacturer, or both. What are the probabilities that they will win control over

(a) either the airline or the steel manufacturer

(b) neither the airline nor the steel manufacturer

(c) over the airline but not over the steel manufacturer

5.37 It can be shown that for any three events, A, B, and C, the probability that at least one of them will occur is given by $P(A \cup B \cup C) = P(A) + P(B) + P(C) - P(A \cap B) - P(A \cap C) - P(B \cap C) + P(A \cap B \cap C)$. Use this formula in the following problems:

(a) The probabilities that a person visiting a certain dentist will have his teeth cleaned; a cavity filled; a tooth extracted; his teeth cleaned and a cavity filled; his teeth cleaned and a tooth extracted; a cavity filled and a tooth extracted; or his teeth cleaned, a cavity filled, and a tooth extracted, are 0.47, 0.29, 0.22, 0.08, 0.06, 0.07, and 0.03. What is the probability that a person visiting this dentist will have at least one of these three things done?

(b) Suppose that if a person visits Disneyland, the probabilities that he will go on the Jungle Cruise; the Monorail; the Matterhorn ride; the Jungle Cruise and the Monorail; the Jungle Cruise and the Matterhorn ride; the Monorail and the Matterhorn ride; or the Jungle Cruise, the Monorail, and the Matterhorn ride, are 0.74, 0.70, 0.62, 0.52, 0.46, 0.44, and 0.34. What is the probability that a person visiting Disneyland will go on at least one of these three rides?

5.38 The following is a proof of the fact that $P(A) \leq 1$ for any event A: By definition A and A' represent mutually exclusive events and $A \cup A' = S$ (since A and A' together comprise all the points of the sample space S). So, we can write $P(A \cup A') = P(S)$, and it follows that

$$P(A) + P(A') = P(S) \qquad \text{step 1}$$
$$P(A) + P(A') = 1 \qquad \text{step 2}$$
$$P(A) = 1 - P(A') \qquad \text{step 3}$$
$$P(A) \leq 1 \qquad \text{step 4}$$

State which of the three postulates of probability justify the first, second, and fourth steps of this proof; the third step is simple arithmetic. Note also that in step 2 we actually proved that $P(A') = 1 - P(A)$.

5.3

Probabilities and Odds

If an event is twice as likely to occur as not to occur, we say that the **odds** are 2 to 1 that it will occur; if an event is three times as likely to occur as not to occur, we say that the odds are 3 to 1; if an event is 10 times as likely to occur as not to occur, we say that the odds are 10 to 1; and so forth. In general, the odds that an event will occur are given by the ratio of the probability that it will occur to the probability that it will not occur. Symbolically,

Formula relating odds to probabilities

> If the probability of an event is p, the odds for its occurrence are a to b, where a and b are positive values such that
>
> $$\frac{a}{b} = \frac{p}{1 - p}$$

It is customary to express odds as a ratio of two positive integers having no common factor, and if an event is more likely not to occur as to occur, to give the odds that it will not occur rather than the odds that it will occur.

EXAMPLE 5.12   What are the odds for the occurence of an event if its probability is

(a) $\frac{5}{9}$

(b) 0.85

(c) 0.20

SOLUTION   (a) By definition, the odds are $\frac{5}{9}$ to $1 - \frac{5}{9} = \frac{4}{9}$, or 5 to 4; (b) by definition, the odds are 0.85 to $1 - 0.85 = 0.15$, 85 to 15, or 17 to 3; (c) by definition, the odds are 0.20 to $1 - 0.20 = 0.80$, 20 to 80, or 1 to 4, but we say instead that the odds against the occurrence of the events are 4 to 1. ∎

In gambling, the word "odds" is also used to denote the ratio of the wager of one party to that of another. For instance, if a gambler says that he will give 3 to 1 odds on the occurrence of an event, he means that he is willing to bet $3 against $1 (or perhaps $30 against $10 or $1,200 against $400) that the event will occur. If such **betting odds** equal the odds that the event will occur, we say that the betting odds are **fair**.

EXAMPLE 5.13 Records show that $\frac{1}{12}$ of the trucks weighed at a certain checkpoint in Nevada are overloaded. If someone offers to bet $40 against $4 that the next truck weighed at this checkpoint is not overloaded, are these odds fair?

SOLUTION Since the probability is $1 - \frac{1}{12} = \frac{11}{12}$ that the truck is not overloaded, the odds are 11 to 1, and the bet would be fair if the person offered to bet $44 against $4 that the next truck weighed at the checkpoint is not overloaded. Thus, the original bet of $40 against $4 favors the person offering the bet; it is not fair. ■

The preceding discussion provides the groundwork for a way of measuring subjective probabilities. If a businessman feels that the odds on the success of a new clothing store are 3 to 2, this means that he is willing to bet (or considers it fair to bet), say, $300 against $200 that the new store will be a success. In this way, he is expressing his belief regarding the uncertainties connected with the success of the store. To convert the odds into a probability we solve the equation $\frac{a}{b} = \frac{p}{1-p}$ for p, and get the following result:

Formula relating probabilities to odds

> If the odds are a to b that an event will occur, the probability of its occurrence is
>
> $$p = \frac{a}{a+b}$$

EXAMPLE 5.14 Convert the businessman's 3-to-2 odds on the success of the new clothing store into a probability.

SOLUTION Substituting $a = 3$ and $b = 2$ into the formula for p, we get

$$p = \frac{3}{3+2} = \frac{3}{5}$$ ■

EXAMPLE 5.15 If an applicant for a managerial position feels that the odds are 7 to 4 that she will get the job, what probability does she assign to her getting the job?

SOLUTION   Substituting $a = 7$ and $b = 4$ into the formula for p, we get

$$p = \frac{7}{7 + 4} = \frac{7}{11}$$ ∎

Let us now see whether subjective probabilities, determined in this way, "behave" in accordance with the postulates of probability. Since a and b are positive quantities, $\frac{a}{a + b}$ cannot be negative, and this satisfies the first postulate. In connection with the second postulate, we note that the surer we are that an event will occur, the "better" odds we should be willing to give, say, 100 to 1, 1,000 to 1, or even 1,000,000 to 1. The corresponding probabilities are $\frac{100}{100 + 1} = 0.99$, $\frac{1,000}{1,000 + 1} = 0.999$, and $\frac{1,000,000}{1,000,000 + 1}$ $= 0.999999$, and it can be seen that the surer we are that an event will occur, the closer its probability will be to 1.

The third postulate of probability—$P(A \cup B) = P(A) + P(B)$ for any two mutually exclusive events A and B—does not necessarily apply to subjective probabilities, but proponents of the subjectivist point of view impose it as a **consistency criterion**. In other words, if a person's subjective probabilities "behave" in accordance with the third postulate, he is said to be **consistent**; otherwise, he is said to be **inconsistent** and his probability judgments cannot be taken seriously.

EXAMPLE 5.16   If an economist feels that the odds are 2 to 1 that the price of beef will go up during the next month, 1 to 5 that it will remain unchanged, and 8 to 3 that it will go up or remain unchanged, are the corresponding probabilities consistent?

SOLUTION   The probabilities that the price of beef will go up during the next month, that it will remain unchanged, and that it will go up or remain unchanged are $\frac{2}{2 + 1} = \frac{2}{3}$, $\frac{1}{1 + 5} = \frac{1}{6}$, and $\frac{8}{8 + 3} = \frac{8}{11}$. Since $\frac{2}{3}$ $+ \frac{1}{6} = \frac{5}{6} \neq \frac{8}{11}$, the probabilities are not consistent.   ∎

EXERCISES

(Exercises 5.39, 5.42, 5.43, 5.48, and 5.50 are practice exercises. Their complete solutions are given on page 195.)

Section 5.3   Probabilities and Odds   **177**

5.39 Convert each of the following probabilities to odds.

    (a) The probability that the last digit of a telephone number is 5, 6, 7, 8, 9, or 0 is $\frac{6}{10}$.

    (b) The probability of getting two heads in four flips of a balanced coin is $\frac{6}{16}$.

    (c) The probability of randomly selecting the letters alpha, delta, lambda, rho, tau, phi, psi, or omega from the 24 letters of the Greek alphabet is $\frac{8}{24}$.

    (d) The probability of drawing a spade from a well-shuffled deck of 52 ordinary playing cards is $\frac{13}{52}$.

5.40 If the probability is 0.75 that an applicant for a driver's license will pass the driving test, what are the odds that a randomly selected applicant will pass the driver's test?

5.41 If the probability is $\frac{1}{10}$ that a new art museum can pay its expenses from ticket sales revenues, what are the odds that the museum will be unable to pay its expenses from ticket sales revenues?

5.42 Convert each of the following odds to probabilities.

    (a) The odds are 5 to 3 that a supplier will deliver an order of automobile parts by the promised delivery date.

    (b) The odds against getting zero heads in eight flips of a balanced coin are 15 to 1.

5.43 The marketing manager feels that the odds are 5 to 1 against men using a certain hair spray which is presently being marketed to women. What subjective probability expresses his feelings about the hair spray being used by men?

5.44 The manager of a department store feels that the odds are 5 to 3 that the store will sell 100 ladies' coats during a sale, 7 to 2 against selling 120 coats during the sale, and 9 to 1 against selling 150 coats during the sale.

    (a) Find the corresponding probabilities that the department store will sell 100, 120, or 150 coats.

    (b) What is the expected number of coats the department store will sell?

5.45 A real estate broker is unwilling to bet $100 against $300 that he will sell a certain house within a week. What is his subjective probability that he can sell the house within a week? (Hint: The answer should read ''less than . . .''.)

5.46 Suppose that a passenger on an airplane is willing to bet a traveling companion $5 against $1, but not $8 against $1, that their plane will land at its destination on time. What personal probability does the passenger assign to the plane's landing at its destination on time? (Hint: The answer should read ''at least . . . but less than . . .''.)

5.47 A store detective is willing to bet $50 against $450, but not $60 against $440, that a newly installed security system will be successful in cutting shoplifting losses. What is the store detective's subjective probability that the newly installed security system will not be successful in cutting shoplifting losses? (Hint: The answer should read "greater than . . . but at most . . .".)

5.48 An auctioneer feels that the odds are 7 to 5 against selling a fine painting at auction for $1 million and 11 to 1 against selling the painting at auction for $2 million. Furthermore, the auctioneer feels that the odds are even (1 to 1) that the painting will be sold for $1 million or $2 million. Discuss the consistency of these subjective probabilities.

5.49 Two road building contractors are competing for the award of a contract to build a county road, and one of the contractors feels that the odds against their being awarded the contract are, respectively, 3 to 1 and 4 to 1. To be consistent, what odds should the contractor assign to the event that neither contractor will obtain the award?

5.50 A decathlon is a grueling contest of 10 events to determine the best track and field athlete. If an athlete feels that the odds are 2 to 1 that he can complete the decathlon, and 3 to 1 that he cannot complete this contest, can these odds be right? Explain.

5.4

Conditional Probabilities

It is often meaningless (or at least very confusing) to speak of the probability of an event without specifying the sample space on which the event is defined. For instance, if we ask for the probability that a lawyer makes more than $60,000 per year, we may well get many different answers, and they can all be correct. One of these might apply to all lawyers in the United States, another to lawyers handling only divorce cases, a third to corporation lawyers, another to lawyers handling only tax cases, and so on. Since the choice of the sample space (that is, the set of all possibilities under consideration) is by no means always self-evident, it is helpful to use the symbol $P(A|S)$ to denote the **conditional probability** of event A relative to the sample space S, or as we often call it "the probability of A given S." The symbol $P(A|S)$ makes it explicit that we are referring to a particular sample space S, and it is generally preferable to the abbreviated notation $P(A)$ unless the tacit choice of S is clearly understood.

To elaborate on the idea of a conditional probability, suppose that a consumer research organization has studied the service under warranty provided by the 200 tire dealers in a large city and that its findings are summarized in the following table:

	Good service under warranty	Poor service under warranty
Name-brand tire dealers	84	36
Off-brand tire dealers	38	42

Suppose, too, that a person randomly selects the name of one of these tire dealers. Since each of the dealers has the same chance, a probability of $\frac{1}{200}$, of being selected, the probability of choosing a name-brand dealer who provides good service under warranty is $\frac{84}{200} = 0.42$, and if we let N denote the selection of a name-brand tire dealer and G the selection of a tire dealer who provides good service under warranty, this probability can be written as

$$P(N \cap G) = 0.42$$

Also, it can be seen that the probability of choosing a name-brand tire dealer is

$$P(N) = \frac{84 + 36}{200} = 0.60$$

and that the probability of choosing a tire dealer who provides good service under warranty is

$$P(G) = \frac{84 + 38}{200} = 0.61$$

where all these probabilities were calculated by means of the formula $\frac{s}{n}$ for equally likely possibilities.

Suppose now that the person wants to limit the selection to name-brand dealers. This reduces the number of equally likely choices to $84 + 36 = 120$. Hence, the probability of choosing a dealer who provides good service under warranty given that he is a name-brand dealer is

$$P(G|N) = \frac{84}{120} = 0.70$$

Note that this conditional probability, 0.70, can also be written as

$$P(G|N) = \frac{\dfrac{84}{200}}{\dfrac{120}{200}} = \frac{P(N \cap G)}{P(N)}$$

which is the ratio of the probability of choosing a name-brand dealer who provides good service under warranty to the probability of choosing a name-brand dealer.

Generalizing from this example, let us now make the following definition of **conditional probability**, which applies to any two events A and B belonging to a given sample space S:

Definition of conditional probability

> *If $P(B)$ is not equal to zero, then the conditional probability of A relative to B, namely, the probability of A given B, is*
> $$P(A|B) = \frac{P(A \cap B)}{P(B)}$$

EXAMPLE 5.17 With reference to the tire dealers of the above illustration, what is the probability that an off-brand tire dealer will give good service under warranty?

SOLUTION As can be seen from the table, $P(G \cap N') = \dfrac{38}{200}$ and $P(N') = \dfrac{38 + 42}{200}$, so that substitution into the formula yields

$$P(G|N') = \frac{\dfrac{38}{200}}{\dfrac{38 + 42}{200}} = \frac{38}{38 + 42} = 0.475$$

Of course, the fraction $\dfrac{38}{38 + 42}$ could have been obtained directly from the second row of the table. ∎

Although we introduced the formula $P(A|B)$ by means of an example in which the possibilities were all equally likely, this is not a requirement for its use. The only restriction is that $P(B)$ must not equal zero.

Section 5.4 Conditional Probabilities   **181**

EXAMPLE 5.18   A paint manufacturer feels that the probability is 0.72 that the raw materials needed to fill an order will arrive on time, and the probability is 0.54 that the raw materials will arrive on time and the order will be filled on time. What is the probability that the order will be filled on time given that the raw materials arrive on time?

SOLUTION   If R and F denote the events that the raw materials will arrive on time and that the order will be filled on time, then $P(R) = 0.72$ and $P(F \cap R) = 0.54$. Substituting into the formula for conditional probabilities, we get

$$P(F|R) = \frac{P(F \cap R)}{P(R)} = \frac{0.54}{0.72} = 0.75 \qquad \blacksquare$$

To introduce another concept which is important in the study of probability, let us consider the following problem:

EXAMPLE 5.19   The probabilities that a student will fail accounting, art history, or both are $P(A) = 0.20$, $P(H) = 0.15$, and $P(A \cap H) = 0.03$. What is the probability that he will fail accounting given that he will fail art history?

SOLUTION   Substituting into the formula for conditional probabilities, we get

$$P(A|H) = \frac{P(A \cap H)}{P(H)} = \frac{0.03}{0.15} = 0.20 \qquad \blacksquare$$

What is special, and interesting, about this result is that $P(A|H) = P(A) = 0.20$; that is, the probability of event A is the same regardless of whether event H has occurred (occurs, or will occur).

In general, if $P(A|B) = P(A)$, we say that event A is **independent** of event B and since it can be shown that event B is independent of event A whenever event A is independent of event B, we say simply that A and B are independent whenever one is independent of the other. Intuitively, we might say that two events are independent if the probability of the occurrence of either is in no way affected by the occurrence or nonoccurrence of the other (see also Exercise 5.55 on page 186). If two events A and B are not independent, we say that they are **dependent**.

So far we have used the formula $P(A|B) = \dfrac{P(A \cap B)}{P(B)}$ only to calculate conditional probabilities, but if we multiply both sides of the equation by $P(B)$, we get the following formula, called the **general multiplication rule**, which enables us to calculate the probability that two events will both occur:

General multiplication rule

$$P(A \cap B) = P(B) \cdot P(A|B)$$

In words, this formula states that the probability that two events will both occur is the product of the probability that one of the events will occur and the conditional probability that the other event will occur given the first event has occurred (occurs, or will occur). It does not matter which event is referred to as *A* and which is referred to as *B,* so the preceding formula can also be written as

General multiplication rule

$$P(A \cap B) = P(A) \cdot P(B|A)$$

EXAMPLE 5.20   If we randomly select 2 hair dryers, 1 after the other, from a carton containing 12 hair dryers, 3 of which are defective, what is the probability that both of them will be defective?

SOLUTION   Since the selections are random, the probability that the first one we pick will be defective is $\frac{3}{12}$, and the probability that the second one we pick will be defective given that the first one was defective is $\frac{2}{11}$. Clearly, there are only 2 defective dryers among the 11 which remain after 1 defective dryer has been picked. Hence, the probability of getting 2 defective dryers is

$$\frac{3}{12} \cdot \frac{2}{11} = \frac{1}{22}$$

Using the same kind of argument we find that the probability of getting 2 good dryers is

$$\frac{9}{12} \cdot \frac{8}{11} = \frac{12}{22}$$

and it follows, by subtraction, that the probability of getting one good dryer and one defective dryer is $1 - \frac{1}{22} - \frac{12}{22} = \frac{9}{22}$.   ■

Section 5.4   Conditional Probabilities   **183**

When A and B are independent events, we can substitute $P(A)$ for $P(A|B)$ in the first of the two formulas for $P(A \cap B)$, or $P(B)$ for $P(B|A)$ in the second, and we obtain

Special multiplication rule

$$P(A \cap B) = P(A) \cdot P(B)$$

In words, the probability that two independent events will both occur is simply the product of their probabilities. This rule is sometimes used as the definition of independence; in any case, it may be used to determine whether two given events are independent.

EXAMPLE 5.21   What is the probability of getting two heads in two flips of a balanced coin?

SOLUTION   Since the probability of heads is $\frac{1}{2}$ for each flip and the two flips are independent, the probability is $\frac{1}{2} \cdot \frac{1}{2} = \frac{1}{4}$.   ■

EXAMPLE 5.22   If $P(C) = 0.65$, $P(D) = 0.40$, and $P(C \cap D) = 0.24$, are the events C and D independent?

SOLUTION   Since $P(C) \cdot P(D) = (0.65)(0.40) = 0.26 \neq 0.24$, the two events are not independent.   ■

EXAMPLE 5.23   What is the probability of getting two consecutive aces in two cards drawn at random from an ordinary deck of 52 playing cards if
(a) the first card is replaced before the second card is drawn
(b) the first card is not replaced before the second card is drawn

SOLUTION   (a) Since there are four aces among the 52 cards, we get

$$\frac{4}{52} \cdot \frac{4}{52} = \frac{1}{169}$$

(b) Since there are only three aces among the 51 cards which remain after one ace has been removed from the deck, we get

$$\frac{4}{52} \cdot \frac{3}{51} = \frac{1}{221}$$ ■

The distinction between the two parts of the preceding example is important in statistics, where we sometimes **sample with replacement** and sometimes **sample without replacement**.

The special multiplication rule can easily be generalized so that it applies to the occurrence of three or more independent events—again, we simply multiply all the individual probabilities together.

EXAMPLE 5.24   What is the probability of getting three heads in three flips of a balanced coin?

SOLUTION   The flips of the coin are independent and we get

$$\frac{1}{2} \cdot \frac{1}{2} \cdot \frac{1}{2} = \frac{1}{8}$$ ∎

EXAMPLE 5.25   What is the probability of first rolling four 3's and then another number in five rolls of a balanced die?

SOLUTION   Multiplying the five probabilities, we get

$$\frac{1}{6} \cdot \frac{1}{6} \cdot \frac{1}{6} \cdot \frac{1}{6} \cdot \frac{5}{6} = \frac{5}{7,776}$$ ∎

For three or more dependent events the multiplication rule becomes somewhat more complicated, as is illustrated in Exercise 5.69 on page 188.

Another important rule relating to conditional probability will be given in Section 8.1.

EXERCISES

(Exercises 5.51, 5.52, 5.56, 5.57, and 5.69(a) and (b) are practice exercises. Their complete solutions are given on page 195.)

5.51   If T is the event that an applicant for a secretarial position can type, H is the event that the applicant can take shorthand, and J is the event that the applicant gets the job, state in words what probabilities are expressed by

(a) $P(J|T)$
(b) $P(H|J)$
(c) $P(J|H')$
(d) $P(J'|T')$
(e) $P(J|T \cap H)$
(f) $P(J \cap T|H')$

5.52   If F is the event that a fast-food restaurant is franchised and G is the event that it has good profit prospects, express in symbolic form the probabilities that

(a) a franchised fast-food restaurant will also have good profit prospects

(b) a fast-food restaurant with good profit prospects will also be franchised

(c) a fast-food restaurant which is not franchised will have good profit prospects

(d) a fast-food restaurant which does not have good profit prospects will not be franchised either

5.53 If A and B are independent events and $P(A) = 0.30$ and $P(B) = 0.60$, find

(a) $P(A|B)$

(b) $P(A \cap B)$

(c) $P(A \cup B)$

(d) $P(A' \cap B')$

5.54 Given $P(A) = 0.4$, $P(B|A) = 0.3$, and $P(B'|A') = 0.2$, find

(a) $P(A')$

(b) $P(B|A')$

(c) $P(B)$

(d) $P(A \cap B)$

(e) $P(A|B)$

5.55 Given $P(A) = 0.30$, $P(B) = 0.50$, and $P(A \cap B) = 0.15$, verify that

(a) $P(A|B) = P(A)$

(b) $P(A|B') = P(A)$

(c) $P(B|A) = P(B)$

(d) $P(B|A') = P(B)$

5.56 The following table summarizes National Fire Protection Association data for a given year concerning the numbers of deaths and injuries caused by residential and nonresidential fires.

| | *(in thousands)* | |
	Deaths	*Injuries*
Residential	4.7	20.4
Nonresidential	1.2	7.8

If the name of a victim is chosen randomly, R represents the event that the person was involved in a residential fire, and D represents the event that the person died from the fire, find each of the following probabilities:

(a) $P(D')$ (b) $P(R)$

(c) $P(R \cap D')$ (d) $P(R \cup D)$

(e) $P(R' \cap D')$ (f) $P(R|D)$

(g) $P(D'|R)$ (h) $P(D|R')$

(i) $P(R'|D')$

5.57 With reference to the preceding exercise, suppose that the number of deaths had been doubled for both residential and nonresidential fires. Recalculate the probabilities (a) through (i) of that exercise with the number of deaths doubled.

5.58 A shoe manufacturer places an order for the leather required to produce a specified number of pairs of shoes for a fixed shipment date. The probability that the leather will be received promptly is 0.75. The probability that the leather will be received promptly and that the shoes will be manufactured by the fixed shipment date is 0.60. What is the probability that the shipment date will be met on time given that the leather is received on time?

5.59 The probability that a burglar alarm system will be installed in a warehouse is 0.90, and the probability that the burglar alarm will be installed and will decrease the number of burglaries is 0.60. What is the probability that if the burglar alarm is installed the number of burglaries will decrease?

5.60 If the probabilities are 0.45, 0.25, and 0.10 that an employee of a certain firm is a woman, a member of the credit union, or both, find the probabilities that

(a) an employee who is a woman will also be a member of the credit union

(b) an employee who is a member of the credit union will also be a woman

5.61 With reference to Example 5.19 on page 182 show that event H is also independent of event A, namely, that $P(H|A) = P(H) = 0.15$.

5.62 If $P(A) = 0.75$, $P(B) = 0.50$, and $P(A \cap B) = 0.25$, are events A and B independent?

5.63 If the probability that a firm's checking account can be balanced by its president is $\frac{1}{2}$ and that the checking account can be balanced by the firm's treasurer independently of the president is $\frac{2}{3}$, what is the probability that the checking account will be balanced if these two officers of the firm do, in fact, work on it independently?

5.64 Among 50 registration forms for students at a university, 30 were for students who were registered in the college of liberal arts, and 20 for students who were registered in the college of business administration. If two of the forms were lost by the registrar and their "selection" was random, what are the probabilities that

(a) both forms were for students registered in the college of liberal arts

(b) both forms were for students registered in the college of business administration

(c) one form was for a student registered in the college of liberal arts and the other form was for a student registered in the college of business administration

5.65 What is the probability of getting two 6's in two rolls of a balanced die?

5.66 What is the probability of getting six heads in six tosses of a balanced coin?

5.67 What is the probability of getting 4 spades in four random draws from an ordinary deck of 52 playing cards, if each card is replaced before the next card is drawn?

5.68 A seamstress frequently threads a needle (passes a thread through the eye of a needle) by making repeated attempts to thread the needle until she is successful. If the constant probability that she can thread the needle on each attempt is $\frac{2}{3}$, and it is assumed that each attempt is an independent event, what is the probability that

(a) she will not thread the needle on two attempts but will thread the needle on her third attempt.

(b) she will thread the needle within three attempts?

(In this example the set of all possible outcomes is not finite, and when this is the case we must modify the third postulate of probability so that it applies to the union of any number of mutually exclusive events; nevertheless, it is possible to solve this problem with the methods discussed in this chapter.)

5.69 The problem of determining the probability that any number of events will occur becomes more complicated when the events are not independent. For three events, A, B, and C, for example, the probability that they will all occur is obtained by multiplying the probability of A by the probability of A given B, and then multiplying the result by the probability of C given $A \cap B$. For instance, the probability of drawing (without replacement) three aces in a row from an ordinary deck of 52 playing cards is

$$\frac{4}{52} \cdot \frac{3}{51} \cdot \frac{2}{50} = \frac{1}{5,525}$$

Clearly, there are only 3 aces among the 51 cards which remain after the first ace has been drawn, and only 2 aces among the 50 cards which remain after the first 2 aces have been drawn.

(a) An Internal Revenue Service auditor has 10 income tax returns, 2 of which contain mistakes in arithmetic. If 2 of the 10 income tax returns are randomly selected for verification, what is the probability that both will be the returns which contain the mistakes in arithmetic?

(b) If a fire department inspector randomly tests 3 battery-operated smoke alarms in an apartment building which has 20 such smoke alarms, 8 of which have dead batteries, what is the probability that all of the smoke alarms tested will have dead batteries?

(c) If three of nine coal mines do not meet federal standards for employee safety and two are randomly selected for inspection, what is the probability that both will fail to meet the safety standards?

(d) If three flight attendants who will staff a flight are randomly selected from a group of three male and four female flight attendants, what is the probability that all of those selected will be of the same sex?

(e) The only supermarket in a small town offers two brands of frozen orange juice, brand A and brand B. Among its customers who buy brand A one week, 80 percent will buy brand A and 20 percent will buy brand B the next week, and among its customers who buy brand B one week, 40 percent will buy brand B and 60 percent will buy brand A the next week. To simplify matters, it will be assumed that each customer buys frozen orange juice once a week.

(1) What is the probability that a customer who buys brand A one week will buy brand B the next week, brand B the week after that, and brand A the week after that?

(2) What is the probability that a customer who buys brand B one week will buy brand B the next two weeks, and brand A the week after that?

(3) What is the probability that a customer who buys brand A in the first week of a month will also buy brand A in the third week of that month? (Hint: Add the probabilities associated with the two mutually exclusive possibilities corresponding to his buying brand A or brand B in the second week.)

(f) A department store which bills its charge account customers once a month has found that if a customer pays promptly one month, the probability is 0.90 that he will also pay promptly the next month; however, if a customer does not pay promptly one month, the probability that he will pay promptly the next month is only 0.50.

(1) What is the probability that a customer who pays promptly one month will also pay promptly the next three months?

(2) What is the probability that a customer who does not pay promptly one month will also not pay promptly the next three months and then make a prompt payment the month after that?

(3) What is the probability that a customer who pays promptly one month will also pay promptly the third month after that?

Parts (e) and (f) of this exercise deal with sequences of experiments, called

Markov chains, in which the outcome of each experiment depends only on what happened in the preceding experiment.

5.70 Ten blue automobiles and 8 gray automobiles are available for rental by an automobile rental company. If the company rents 2 of these cars and if these are independent events, what are the probabilities that

(a) both will be gray

(b) both will be blue

(c) one will be gray and one will be blue

(Hint: There are four possibilities. These are blue-blue, gray-gray, blue-gray, gray-blue.)

5.5

Checklist of Key Terms

5.6

Review Exercises

5.71 Convert each of the following probabilities to odds.

(a) The library of a medical supply company subscribes to four journals in medicine, one journal in chemistry, and one in biology. If the librarian randomly permits two subscriptions to expire, the probability that both will not be in medicine is $\frac{3}{5}$.

(b) If the office manager randomly selects four out of five clerical personnel to work overtime, the probability that any one person will be selected is $\frac{4}{5}$.

5.72 Computer experts are asked whether they prefer a certain model of an IBM computer to a competitive model of an Apple computer, whether they prefer the Apple computer to the IBM computer, or whether they have no preference, and these three alternatives are assigned the codes 1, 2, and 3.

    (a) Use two coordinates to represent, in order, the responses of two computer experts, and draw a diagram (similar to that of Figure 5.1) which shows the nine points of the sample space.

    (b) Describe in words the event which is represented by each of the following sets of points of the sample space of part (a): the event A, which consists of the points (1, 1), (1, 2), and (1, 3); the event B, which consists of the points (1, 2), (2, 2), and (3, 2); the event C, which consists of the points (1, 1), (1, 2), (2, 1), and (2, 2); and the event D, which consists of the points (1, 3), and (3, 1).

    (c) With reference to part (b), describe in words the events which are denoted by C', $A \cup B$, and $C \cap B$. Also list the points which comprise each of these three events.

5.73 With reference to part (b) of the preceding exercise, determine whether events A and C are mutually exclusive and also whether events B and D are mutually exclusive.

5.74 Seventy percent of the executive personnel of a computer software company have only one college degree and the remainder have two or more college degrees. Sixty percent of these executives are under 50 years of age, and the rest are 50 years of age or older. Of the executives who are under 50 years of age, $\frac{4}{5}$ have only one college degree and the rest have two or more degrees. If one executive is selected at random from all the executives of the company, what are the probabilities that this executive.

    (a) is under 50 years of age and has only one college degree

    (b) neither has two or more degrees nor is under 50 years of age

    (c) either has two or more college degrees or is under 50 years of age

    (d) has two or more degrees given that the executive is not under 50 years of age

5.75 If the probability is 0.25 that a guest at a hotel will use a charge card to pay the hotel bill, what is the probability that three guests, selected at random, will use charge cards to pay their bills.

5.76 If J is the event that a person will buy a ski jacket and S is the event a person is a skier, state in words what probabilities are expressed by

    (a) $P(J|S)$

    (b) $P(S'|J)$

    (c) $P(S|J')$

    (d) $P(J'|S)$

Section 5.6 Review Exercises

191

5.77 If $P(B) = 0.42$. $P(C) = 0.27$, and $P(B \cap C) = 0.1134$, are events B and C independent or dependent?

5.78 If 3 customers are randomly chosen from a group of 10 customers, 2 of whom have poor credit ratings

    (a) verify that the probability of choosing at least one customer who was a poor credit rating is $\frac{8}{15}$. (Hint: Use Table IX, Binomial Coefficients.)

    (b) Convert the probability of part (a) to odds.

5.79 Suppose that the numbers 1, 2, 3, 4, 5, 6, are used to code that a buyer thinks the wool fibers in a bolt of fabric are (1) sheep/lamb, (2) angora/cashmere, (3) camel, (4) alpaca, (5) llama, (6) vicuna. If $A = \{1, 2, 3, 4\}$ and $B = \{2, 3, 4, 5\}$, list the elements of the sample space comprising each of the following events, and also express the events in words.

    (a) A'

    (b) $A \cup B$

    (c) $A \cap B$

    (d) $A \cap B'$

5.80 If a military commander feels that 5 to 2 are fair odds that he can capture a hill, what subjective probability does he assign to this event?

5.81 If the probability that a family will purchase a condominium apartment, buy stock in a cooperative apartment building, or rent an apartment is $0.20, 0.10$, or 0.40, respectively, what is the probability that the family will consummate one of these transactions?

5.82 The probabilities that the maintenance department of a residential property management company will receive 0, 1, 2, 3, . . . , 7 or at least 8 requests for service each day are 0.02, 0.03, 0.05, 0.09, 0.17, 0.22, 0.20, 0.16, and 0.08. What are the probabilities that on a certain day the maintenance department will receive

    (a) at most 5 requests

    (b) at least 5 requests

    (c) from 5 to 7 requests

5.83 The probability that an accountant's report will be approved by the department head is 0.75, and the probability that the accountant's report will be approved by the treasurer as well as the department head is 0.50. What is the probability that the accountant's report will be approved by the treasurer given that it will be approved by the department head?

5.84 If the dots of Figure 5.8 on page 167 all represent equally likely outcomes, what is the probability of event A?

5.85 A sample of 360 executives was interviewed in a *Wall Street Journal* Gallup survey to determine whether there were differences in the ages of 207 senior executives of the *Fortune* 500 (largest 500 U.S. corporations listed in *Fortune* magazine) and 153 entrepreneurs (chief executives of 500 fastest-growing small companies in the United States listed in *Inc.* magazine). The dividing line used was 45 years of age for all executives.

	Fortune 500 senior executives	*Inc. chief executives*
Under 45 years of age	19	96
45 years of age or older	188	57

If the order in which the respondents were interviewed is random, F is the event that the first executive interviewed is a *Fortune* 500 senior executive, and A is the event that the first executive interviewed is under 45 years of age, determine each of the following probabilities directly from the entries and the row and column totals of the table.

(a) $P(F)$

(b) $P(A')$

(c) $P(F \cap A)$

(d) $P(F' \cap A')$

(e) $P(A|F)$

(f) $P(F'|A')$

5.86 With reference to the preceding exercise, verify that

(a) $P(A|F) = \dfrac{P(F \cap A)}{P(F)}$

(b) $P(F'|A') = \dfrac{P(F' \cap A')}{P(A')}$

5.87 Given $P(X) = 0.33$, and $P(Y) = 0.59$, and $P(X \cap Y) = 0$, find

(a) $P(X')$

(b) $P(Y')$

kc) $P(X \cup Y)$

(d) $P(X' \cap Y')$

5.88 A game of chance is played as follows. The player shuffles the 13 cards constituting the set of all the hearts in an ordinary deck of cards and then draws a card at random. If the card drawn is a 2, 3, . . . , 10, the game ends right there. However, if the card drawn is a jack, queen, king, or ace, the

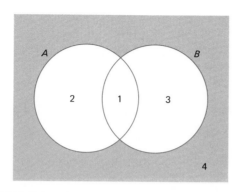

FIGURE 5.13
Venn diagram for
Exercise 5.89

player draws one more card without replacing the first card, after which the game concludes. If the player wins $2.00 for each jack, queen, king, or ace that she draws, and loses $1.00 for each 2, 3, . . . , 10 she draws, what is her expectation?

5.89 If A is the event that a bank is ranked among the largest 20 in the United States and B is the event that it is ranked among the largest 20 in the world, what events are represented by the four areas of the Venn diagram in Figure 5.13?

5.90 An antiquarian feels that the odds are 8 to 1 that a plainly built old chair with bun-shaped feet is not English Puritan. 5 to 1 that it is not Early American which is similarly designed, and 13 to 5 that it is neither English Puritan nor Early American. Are the corresponding probabilities consistent?

5.91 The probability that a suit will be sold during a sale is 0.60, and the probability that the suit will be returned or exchanged after it is sold is 0.10. What is the probability that the suit will be sold during the sale and then returned or exchanged?

5.92 Explain why there must be a mistake in each of the following statements:
   (a) The probability that a custom-tailored suit will require a second fitting is 0.85, and the probability that it will not is 0.10.
   (b) The probability that a depositor will lose his $1,000 savings account in an insolvent federally insured savings bank is -0.001.
   (c) The probability that a customer in an automobile showroom will buy a sedan is 0.60, but the customer is twice as likely to buy a sports car.

5.93 If a student answers the three questions on a true-false quiz by flipping a balanced coin, what is the probability that the student will answer all three questions correctly?

5.94 The probabilities are 0.25 that an indolent student will be late to class, 0.20 that the student will not understand the lecture, and 0.15 that the student will

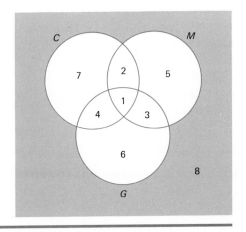

FIGURE 5.14
Venn diagram for
Exercise 5.95

come to class late and not understand the lecture. What is the probability that the student will be late to class or will not understand the lecture?

5.95 In Figure 5.14, C is the event that a mutual fund will invest in corporate bonds, M is the event a mutual fund will invest in municipal bonds, and G is the event that a mutual fund will invest in U.S. government bonds. Explain in words what events are represented by the following regions or combinations of regions:

(a) region 7
(b) regions 1 and 2 together
(c) regions 2 and 7 together
(d) regions 4, 6, and 7 together
(e) regions 7 and 8 together

5.96 A gambler invents a simple game where the dealer shuffles a short deck consisting of seven red cards and three black cards. A player is to draw two cards at random without replacement and wins $3 for each red card drawn. Show formally that the player should lose $7 for each black card drawn to make the game fair.

5.7

Solutions of Practice Exercises

5.1 (a) $X \cup Z = \{1, 2, 3, 4, 5, 6, 7\}$ represents all of the departments in the store.

(b) $Y \cap Z = \{5, 6, 7\}$ represents the departments of Z, all of which are included in Y, but are not included in X.

(c) $Z' = \{1, 2, 3, 4\}$ represents all of the departments in X, two of which are also included in Y.

5.2 (a) $\{c, e, f, g, h\}$ is the event that Clark, Eric, Francis, George, or Hilda is offered the job.

(b) $\{a, b, c, d, g, h\}$ is the event that Arnold, Betty, Clark, David, George, or Hilda is offered the job.

(c) $\{b, d\}$ is the event that Betty or David is offered the job.

(d) $\{a, b, d\}$ is the event that Arnold, Betty, or David is offered the job.

5.3 (a) The entry should be posted to cash or prepaid expenses.

(b) The entry should be posted to accounts receivable or prepaid expenses.

(c) The entry should be posted to cash, marketable securities, or accounts receivable.

5.4 (a) $K' = \{2, 3, 4\}$ is the event that the entry is posted to marketable securities, accounts receivable, or inventory.

(b) $K \cup L = \{1, 3, 5\}$ is the event that the entry is posted to cash, accounts receivable, or prepaid expenses.

(c) $K \cap L = \{5\}$ is the event that the entry is posted to prepaid expenses.

(d) $K \cap M = \{1\}$ is the event that the entry is posted to cash.

5.5 (a) The two contractors get equally many jobs.

(b) Between them, the two contractors get both jobs.

(c) The first contractor does not get either job.

5.6 (a) $\{(0, 2), (2, 0)\}$; (b) $\{(0, 1), (1, 1)\}$

(c) $\{(0, 0), (1, 0), (2, 0)\}$

5.13 Region 1 is the event that the unemployment rate will go down and the inflation rate will go up, region 2 is the event that the unemployment rate will go down and the inflation rate will not go up, region 3 is the event that the unemployment rate will not go down and the inflation rate will go up, and region 4 is the event that the unemployment rate will not go down and the inflation rate will not go up.

5.14 (a) The unemployment rate will not go down.

(b) The unemployment rate will go down or the inflation rate wil go up, but not both.

(c) The unemployment rate will go down, the inflation rate will go up, or both.

5.21 (a) $P(C')$ is the probability the city will not cut expenditures.

(b) $P(R')$ is the probability the city will not raise revenues.

(c) $P(C \cup R)$ is the probability the city will cut expenditures, or raise revenues, or both.

(d) $P(C \cap R)$ is the probability the city will cut expenditures and raise revenues.

(e) $P(C' \cup R)$ is the probability the city will not cut expenditures, or will raise revenues, or both.

(f) $P(C' \cap R)$ is the probability the city will not cut expenditures and will raise revenues.

5.23 (a) The sum of the probabilities exceeds 1; (b) the sum of the probabilities is less than 1; (c) the second probability cannot be less than the first; (d) the second probability cannot be greater than the first; (e) $0.50 + 0.45 + 0.10$ exceeds 1.

5.24 (a) $1 - 0.65 = 0.35$ (b) $0.65 + 0.20 = 0.85$ (c) $1 - (0.65 + 0.20) = 0.15$

5.26 (a) $1.00 - 0.37 = 0.63$ (b) $1.00 - 0.41 = 0.59$ (c) 0

      (d) $0.37 + 0.41 = 0.78$ (e) $1.00 - 0.78 = 0.22$ (f) 1

5.37 (a) $0.47 + 0.29 + 0.22 - 0.08 - 0.06 - 0.07 + 0.03 = 0.80$

      (b) $0.74 + 0.70 + 0.62 - 0.52 - 0.46 - 0.44 + 0.34 = 0.98$

5.39 (a) Odds are $\dfrac{6}{10}$ to $(1 - \dfrac{6}{10}) = 6$ to 4 or 3 to 2.

      (b) Odds are $\dfrac{6}{16}$ to $(1 - \dfrac{6}{16}) = 6$ to 10 or 3 to 5, which is 5 to 3 against the occurrence.

      (c) Odds are $\dfrac{8}{24}$ to $(1 - \dfrac{8}{24}) = 8$ to 16 or 1 to 2, which is 2 to 1 against the occurrence.

      (d) Odds are $\dfrac{13}{52}$ to $(1 - \dfrac{13}{52})$ or 13 to 39 or 1 to 3, which is 3 to 1 against the occurrence.

5.42 (a) The probability is $\dfrac{5}{5 + 3} = \dfrac{5}{8}$ or 0.625.

      (b) The probability is $\dfrac{15}{15 + 1} = \dfrac{15}{16}$ or 0.9375.

5.43 The probability that men will use the hair spray is $\dfrac{1}{1 + 5} = \dfrac{1}{6}$.

5.48 The probabilities are $\dfrac{5}{5 + 7} = \dfrac{5}{12}$, $\dfrac{1}{1 + 11} = \dfrac{1}{12}$, and $\dfrac{1}{1 + 1} = \dfrac{1}{2}$, and since

$\dfrac{5}{12} + \dfrac{1}{12} = \dfrac{1}{2}$, the probabilities are consistent.

5.50 The corresponding probabilities are $\dfrac{2}{2+1} = \dfrac{2}{3}$ and $\dfrac{3}{3+1} = \dfrac{3}{4}$, and since $\dfrac{2}{3}$

$+ \dfrac{3}{4} > 1$, the odds cannot be right.

5.51 (a) The probability that an applicant who can type will get the job
(b) The probability that an applicant who gets the job can take shorthand
(c) The probability that an applicant who cannot take shorthand will get the job
(d) The probability that an applicant who cannot type will not get the job
(e) The probability that an applicant who can type and take shorthand will get the job
(f) The probability that an applicant who cannot take shorthand can type and will get the job

5.52 (a) $P(G|F)$ (b) $P(F|G)$ (c) $P(G|F')$ and (d) $P(F'|G')$

5.56 (a) $P(D') = \dfrac{28.2}{34.1} = 0.83$ (f) $P(R|D) = \dfrac{4.7}{5.9} = 0.80$

(b) $P(R) = \dfrac{4.7 + 20.4}{34.1} = 0.74$ (g) $(P(D'|R) = \dfrac{20 \cdot 4}{4.7 + 20.4} = 0.81$

(c) $P(R \cap D') = \dfrac{20.4}{34.1} = 0.60$ (h) $P(D|R') = \dfrac{1.2}{1.2 + 7.8} = 0.13$

(d) $P(R \cup D) = \dfrac{4.7 + 20.4 + 1.2}{34.1} = 0.77$ (i) $P(R'|D') = \dfrac{7.8}{20.4 + 7.8} = 0.28$

(e) $P(R' \cap D') = \dfrac{7.8}{34.1} = 0.23$

(In thousands)

	D	D'	
R	4.7	20.4	25.1
R'	1.2	7.8	9.0
	5.9	28.2	

5.57 (a) $P(D') = \dfrac{28.2}{40} = 0.70$ (d) $P(R \cup D) = \dfrac{20.4 + 9.4 + 2.4}{40} = 0.80$

(b) $P(R) = \dfrac{29.8}{40} = 0.74$ (e) $P(R' \cap D') = \dfrac{7.8}{40} = 0.20$

(c) $P(R \cap D') = \dfrac{20.4}{40} = 0.51$ (f) $P(R|D) = \dfrac{9.4}{11.8} = 0.80$

(g) $P(D'|R) = \dfrac{20.4}{9.4 + 20.4} = 0.68$ (i) $P(R'|D') = \dfrac{7.8}{20.4 + 7.8} = 0.28$

(h) $P(D|R') = \dfrac{2.4}{2.4 + 7.8} = 0.24$

	Doubled D	D'	
R	9.4	20.4	29.8
R'	2.4	7.8	10.2
	11.8	28.2	

5.69 (a) $\dfrac{2}{10} \cdot \dfrac{1}{9} = \dfrac{1}{45} = 0.02$ (b) $\dfrac{8}{20} \cdot \dfrac{7}{19} \cdot \dfrac{6}{18} = \dfrac{21}{425} = 0.05$

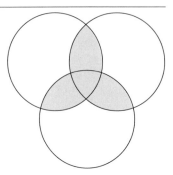

CHAPTER 6

*Decision Analysis**

T he approach to statistics as the art, or science, of decision making in the face of uncertainty is called **decision theory**. The initial impact of this very general approach to statistics, which dates back to the middle of this century, was largely on the theoretical level, but in the last few years it has become increasingly important in practical situations, especially in business applications.

Since the study of statistical decision theory is quite complicated mathematically, we shall introduce here only some of the most basic ideas. However, even these are extremely important, because the decision-theory approach has the positive advantage of forcing one to formulate problems clearly, to anticipate the various consequences of one's actions, to retain the relevant and eliminate the irrelevant, to place cash values on the consequences of one's actions, and so on. No matter how little or how far it is pursued, a systematic approach like this is bound to help.

After a brief introduction to basic concepts in Sections 6.1 and 6.2, Sections 6.3 through 6.5 are devoted to problems where the decision maker has **no information about relevant events over which he or she has no control**. In Sections 6.6 and 6.7 we learn what a decision maker might do when such events are controlled by a **competitor**, and in Sections 6.8 through 6.10

*This chapter is optional and can be omitted without loss of continuity.

200

we assume the decision maker has **some knowledge about the probabilities** that these events will occur. Finally, in Section 6.11 we introduce the concept of **utility**, which often plays an important role in decision making.

We have introduced this subject material early in the textbook since it follows the course sequence of large numbers of instructors. Some instructors prefer to include this material with the sequence of decision-making chapters which begins with Chapter 11.

6.1

Payoff Tables and Decision Trees

The first step in the mathematical analysis of any problem is to translate the problem into the language of mathematics, that is, express the given information in terms of equations, tables, graphs, charts, or other kinds of mathematical objects. In the analysis of decision problems, the first step usually consists of summarizing the given information in the form of a **payoff** table or in the form of a **decision tree**. To illustrate the former, suppose that a manufacturer of office equipment must decide whether to expand his plant capacity now or wait another year. His advisors tell him that if he expands now and economic conditions remain good, there will be a profit of $369,000; if he expands now and there is a recession, there will be a loss (negative profit) of $90,000; if he waits another year to expand and economic conditions remain good, there will be a profit of $180,000; and if he waits another year and there is a recession, there will be a small profit of $18,000. Schematically, this information can be presented in the following table:

	Expand now	Delay expansion
Economic conditions remain good	$369,000	$180,000
There is a recession	−$90,000	$18,000

The columns "Expand now" and "Delay expansion" represent the two actions the manufacturer can take, the two rows represent the economic conditions over which he has no control, and for each combination of actions and economic conditions the table shows the corresponding profit.

Borrowing from the language of **game theory**, we refer to the entries in the table, the various profits, as the **payoffs**, and to the table itself as a **payoff table**, or a **payoff matrix**. The advantage of the table should be obvious—it gives a much easier-to-grasp picture of the whole situation than the original lengthy verbal formulation. As in many other problems of decision making, the payoffs in our example are based on accounting data, but there are also situations where they follow directly from the formulation of the problem (see, for example, Exercise 6.3 on page 204).

In general, if a decision maker has the choice of k actions, $A_1, A_2, \ldots,$ and A_k, and their consequences depend on r events (possibilities, alternatives, or conditions), $E_1, E_2, \ldots,$ and E_r, over which he has no direct control, the corresponding payoffs are denoted $p_{11}, p_{12}, \ldots,$ and p_{rk}, with the first subscript being like that of event E and the second like that of action A. Thus, for $r = 3$ and $k = 4$ the payoff table would be

	A_1	A_2	A_3	A_4
E_1	p_{11}	p_{12}	p_{13}	p_{14}
E_2	p_{21}	p_{22}	p_{23}	p_{24}
E_3	p_{31}	p_{32}	p_{33}	p_{34}

The events E, over which the decision maker has no direct control, may reflect facts unavailable at the time the decision must be made; they may reflect the decision maker's ignorance; they may reflect unknown decisions made by a competitor; or they may reflect situations brought about by fate or chance. Because of the latter, the E's are often called **states of nature**.

To simplify our example, we based the payoffs on the opinions of advisors; in actual practice, if the values of the payoffs are not given, they must be determined from pertinent information (see, for example, Exercises 6.3, 6.4, and 6.6 on pages 204 and 205). Also, the payoffs are dollar profits in our example, but this need not be the case. They may also be losses, production costs, sales revenues, quantities produced or consumed, the IQs of job applicants, mileages, and so forth.

In the beginning of this section we said that decision trees, as well as payoff tables, are widely used in the analysis of decision problems. A decision tree is simply a tree diagram whose branches represent the A's (actions)

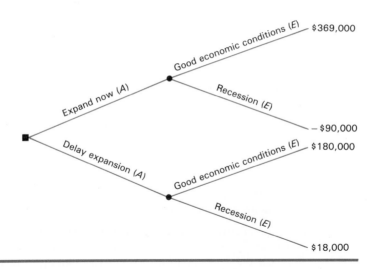

FIGURE 6.1
Decision tree

and the E's (events). Furthermore, to make it clear whether a branch represents an A or an E, branches representing A's emanate from small squares and branches representing E's emanate from small circles (see Figure 6.1). Also, the payoff associated with a given path along the branches of a decision tree is usually shown on the right, at the end of the path.

For the problem in which the manufacturer must decide whether to expand his plant capacity now or later, we drew the decision tree in Figure 6.1. However, there is really no advantage to constructing a decision tree in a simple problem like this: The payoff table is more compact and gives an easier-to-grasp picture of the whole situation. On the other hand, decision trees can be of great help in more complicated kinds of decision problems, for instance, in problems where it is hard even to enumerate all the decision maker's courses of action.

EXERCISES

(Exercises 6.1 and 6.4 are practice exercises. Their complete solutions are given on page 248.)

6.1 A private investigator is offered a straight fee of $1,000 to search for a missing person or a reward of $5,000 which she will get only if she locates the missing person.

(a) Construct a payoff table in which the payoffs are the amounts the private investigator receives.

(b) Draw a decision tree.

6.2 A frozen food manufacturer must decide whether to continue a marketing campaign for frozen soup. If the manufacturer continues the marketing campaign and frozen soup sales are high, this will be worth $50 million to the company; if the manufacturer continues the marketing campaign and frozen soup sales are low, this will entail a loss of $30 million; if the manufacturer does not continue the marketing campaign and frozen soup sales are high (but are lost to competing frozen food manufacturers), this will entail a loss of $20 million; and if the manufacturer does not continue the marketing campaign and frozen soup sales are low, this will be worth $5 million to the company (because funds allocated to the marketing campaign will not be spent).

(a) Construct a payoff table.

(b) Draw a decision tree.

6.3 A parcel delivery service wants to make an emergency delivery to an engineer who may be at any one of three construction sites which are located 5, 9, and 12 miles away from the delivery service terminal. The distance between the first two sites is 3 miles, that between the first and the third is 8 miles, and that between the second and the third is 6 miles. If the delivery service driver goes to the wrong site, she can find out where the engineer is located by asking the foreman at the job.

(a) Construct a payoff table showing the total mileage which must be driven, depending on where the driver goes first and where the delivery should be made.

(b) Draw a decision tree.

6.4 A street vendor can stock up to four pennants which are specially imprinted for sale at a major league baseball World Series. Any unsold pennants become worthless after the World Series games have been played and are discarded by the vendor. The unit cost of the pennants is $4, the selling price is $10, so the profit is $6 for each pennant sold. The vendor must decide whether to stock 1, 2, 3, or 4 pennants, and there may be a demand for 0, 1, 2, 3, 4, or 5 or more of them.

(a) Construct a payoff table in which the payoffs are the vendor's profits.

(b) Draw a decision tree.

6.5 A professional organization has decided to hold its annual meeting during the month of January and is deciding among the cities of Boston, New York, or Philadelphia as the site. Since the organization is interested in the temperatures of the three cities, it has obtained National Weather Service data for January which show that Boston has a mean low temperature of 23°F, a normal temperature of 30°F, and a mean high temperature of 36°F; New York has a mean low of 26°F, a normal of 32°F, and a mean high of 37°F; and Philadelphia has a mean low of 24°F, a normal of 31°F, and a mean high of 39°F.

(a) Using these degrees Fahrenheit as payoffs, construct a payoff table for this decision problem.

(b) Draw a decision tree.

6.6 A manufacturer produces an item consisting of two components, which must both work if the item is to function properly. The cost to the manufacturer of having one of the items returned for repairs is $12, the cost of inspecting one of the components is $10, and the cost of repairing a faulty component is $25. He can ship each item without inspection with the guarantee that each component will be put in perfect working condition at his factory in case it does not work; he can inspect both components and repair them if necessary; or he can randomly select one of the two components for inspection, repair it if necessary, and ship the item with the same guarantee as in the first case. Using the manufacturer's expected cost of inspecting, returning, and repairing an item as the payoffs, construct a payoff table for his choice among the inspection procedures.

6.2

Decision Making Under Certainty and Uncertainty

Although we shall be concerned here only with decision making under uncertainty, there also exist problems of **decision making under certainty**. Suppose, for instance, that a student wants to sell her car and she has two offers. The first offer consists of a payment of $3,550 now, and the second consists of three payments, $1,200 now, $1,200 six months from now, and $1,200 one year from now, and we assume that money earns interest at 10 percent. Even though the three payments total $3,600, their present value is only $3,433.77, which is less than $3,550. So, it would be to the student's advantage to accept the first offer, and that is all there is to this problem of decision making under certainty. All the pertinent facts are known in a problem like this, and a decision is reached after appropriate calculations.

In all the decision problems we shall study in this chapter, both the actions, the A's, open to the decision maker and the events, the E's, which are beyond the decision maker's control will be known and stated, and the payoffs, the p's, will either be given or can be calculated (as in the exercises preceding this section). So far as our work here is concerned, the uncertainties which the decision maker faces arise in connection with the E's; that is, we shall study problems in which we do not know how, by whom, under what circumstances, or with what probabilities the occurrences of the E's are controlled.

To cover these various possibilities, we shall divide our study of decision making into the following three parts:

1. We shall study problems in which the decision maker has no knowledge whatever about the E's, other than what they are.

2. We shall study problems in which the decision maker knows that the choice of the *E*'s is controlled by a competitor whose interests are diametrically opposed to those of the decision maker.

3. We shall study problems in which the decision maker has some idea about the probabilities of the occurrences of the different *E*'s.

The next three sections will be devoted to the first kind of problem; the other two kinds will be discussed after that.

6.3

Dominance and Admissibility

When a decision maker has no information about the *E*'s except that he knows what they are, it may be possible, nevertheless, to make a choice among the *A*'s, or at least eliminate some of the possibilities. Suppose, for instance, that we want to invest in one of four mutual funds, basing our choice on the ratings (from A high to F low) given to the performance of these funds in up markets and in down markets by *Forbes* magazine. The ratings shown in the following table are taken from a recent issue of that magazine:

	Fund I	Fund II	Fund III	Fund IV
Performance in up markets	A	B	C	D
Performance in down markets	F	F	B	C

Comparing the ratings of fund IV with those of the other three, we find that compared to funds I and II, fund IV is rated lower for up markets and higher for down markets (D is lower than A or B and C is higher than F), but compared to fund III, fund IV is rated lower for both markets (D is lower than C and C is lower than B). Thus, we say that the ratings of fund III

dominate those of fund IV, and that the selection of fund IV is **not admissible**; that is, fund IV should not be selected so long as fund III is available for investment. Similarly, comparing the ratings of fund II with those of funds I and III, we find that compared to fund III, fund II is rated higher for up markets and lower for down markets (B is higher than C and F is lower than B), but compared to fund I, fund II is never rated higher but it is rated lower for up markets (B is lower than A and one F is as low as the other). Thus, the ratings of fund I dominate those of fund II, and the selection of fund II is not admissible. As a result of this analysis, the decision problem has been simplified quite a bit—we have eliminated two funds from consideration and, instead of having to choose one of four mutual funds, we now have to choose only one of two, fund I or fund III. Evidently, this is as far as we can go in this way, since fund I is rated higher for up markets and fund III is rated higher for down markets (A is higher than C and B is higher than F).

In general, **one action of a decision maker is said to dominate a second action, and the second is said to be nonadmissible, if none of the payoffs of the second action is preferable to the corresponding payoff of the first, and at least one payoff of the first action is preferable to the corresponding payoff of the second.** If the columns representing the payoffs of two different actions are identical, there is no way to make a logical choice between the two actions and they may, in fact, be regarded as one so far as the decision analysis is concerned.

For instance, if after eliminating the nonadmissible funds II and IV in the preceding example we consider another fund, fund V rated C for up markets and B for down markets like fund III, we group funds III and V together as one action and arrive at the following payoff table:

	Fund I	Fund III or Fund V
Performance in up markets	A	C
Performance in down markets	F	B

The process of eliminating nonadmissible actions or discovering actions that are equivalent can be of great help, and it is usually the first step in the analysis of a decision-making problem.

6.4

The Maximin and Maximax Criteria

The basic problem of decision making is to find decision-making procedures, or **decision rules**, which meet certain criteria of desirability. If we knew or could calculate the mathematical expectations associated with the various actions open to us, it would seem reasonable to follow the rule of choosing whichever action is best for us, but for the time being we are assuming that we have no knowledge of the probabilities of the E's (the "states of nature" over which the decision maker has no control), and, hence, cannot calculate expectations of any kind. However, there are criteria which apply even in such cases, but they are based on the decision maker's *attitudes* rather than on straight economic considerations.

To illustrate one of these, let us return to the plant expansion example, where the payoff table is

	Expand now	Delay expansion
Economic conditions remain good	$369,000	$180,000
There is a recession	−$90,000	$18,000

Suppose now that the office equipment manufacturer is a confirmed pessimist, who always expects the worst to happen. Looking at the situation through dark-colored glasses, he finds that if he expands his plant capacity now, the worst that can happen is a loss of $90,000, and if he decides to delay the expansion, the worst that can happen is a profit of $18,000. A profit of $18,000 is definitely preferable to a loss of $90,000, so the pessimistic manufacturer would decide to delay expanding his plant capacity.

The criterion we have introduced in this example is called the **maximin criterion**, since it suggests that one maximize the minimum payoffs corresponding to the various actions. To apply this criterion, we look for the worst that can happen, namely, the smallest value of each column of the payoff table. Then we choose the column (action) which maximizes this minimum payoff.

EXAMPLE 6.1   Referring to the table on page 206 showing the four mutual funds, which one will we choose if we base our choice on the maximin criterion?

SOLUTION   The payoff table with the nonadmissible choices deleted is

	Fund I	Fund III
Performance in up markets	A	C
Performance in down markets	F	B

and we find that the lowest ratings are F for fund I and C for fund III. Since C exceeds F, it follows that the maximin criterion leads to the choice of fund III. By making this choice, the pessimistic decision maker protects himself against a fund rated lower than C in either an up or down market.   ∎

The maximin criterion applies only when the payoffs are quantities such as profits or benefits, which we want to make large. If the payoffs are quantities such as losses or costs, which we want to make small, we use the **minimax criterion** instead. To apply this criterion, we again look for the worst than can happen, in this case the largest value of each column of the payoff table. Then we choose the column (action) which minimizes this maximum payoff. For all practical purposes, though, the maximin and minimax criteria are equivalent, since minimizing maximum losses is the same as maximizing minimum profits.

Besides the maximin and minimax criteria, there are several other criteria which are based on the attitudes of the decision maker. Referring again to the office equipment manufacturer, let us suppose, for instance, that he is a confirmed optimist, who always expects the best to happen. Looking at his payoff table through rose-colored glasses, he finds that if he expands his plant capacity now, he might make a profit of $369,000, but if he decides to delay the expansion, the profit cannot be more than $180,000. A profit of $369,000 is preferable to a profit of $180,000, so the optimistic manufacturer would decide to expand his plant capacity right away.

The criterion illustrated in the preceding example is called the **maximax criterion**, since it requires that one maximize the maximum payoffs corresponding to the different actions. To apply this criterion, we look for the best that can happen, namely, the largest value of each column of the payoff table. Then we choose the column (action) which maximizes this maximum payoff.

EXAMPLE 6.2 Referring to the payoff table of Example 6.1, which mutual fund will we choose if we base our decision on the maximax criterion?

SOLUTION The payoff table with the nonadmissible choices deleted is

	Fund I	Fund III
Performance in up markets	A	C
Performance in down markets	F	B

and we find the highest ratings are A for fund I and B for fund III. Since A exceeds B, it follows that the maximax criterion leads to the choice of fund I. ■

Finally, there is also the **minimin criterion**, which an optimistic decision maker would use instead of the maximax criterion when the payoffs are losses, costs, or other quantities which he wants to make small.

6.5

Opportunity Losses

Decisions can also be based on a person's fear of not taking the best possible action open to him and missing, or losing, a good opportunity. For instance, if the office equipment manufacturer we have been discussing is this kind of person, he might argue that if he decided to expand his plant capacity now and there is a recession, he would have been better off by $18,000 - (-\$90,000) = \$108,000$ (the $18,000 profit he could have made plus the $90,000 he lost) if he had decided to delay. On the other hand, if he decided to delay the expansion of his plant capacity and economic conditions remain good, he would have been better off by $369,000 - \$180,000 =$

$189,000 (the $369,000 profit he could have made minus the $180,000 profit he made) if he had decided to expand right away. These quantities, usually called **opportunity losses** or **regrets** are shown in the following **opportunity-loss table**:

	Expand now	*Delay expansion*
Economic conditions remain good	$369,000 − $369,000 **0** No opportunity-loss	$369,000 − $180,000 **$189,000** loss
There is a recession	$18,000 − (−$90,000) **$108,000** loss	$18,000 − $18,000 **0** No opportunity-loss

To explain the two zeros, note that when the manufacturer decides to expand his plant capacity right away and economic conditions remain good, he has made the best possible decision and there is no loss of opportunity. This is also true if he decides to delay expanding his plant capacity and there is a recession.

In general, opportunity losses are calculated for each row of an opportunity-loss table as follows. If the payoffs are profits or other quantities which we want to make large, we subtract each value in a row from the largest value in the row; if the payoffs are losses or other quantities which we want to make small, we subtract the smallest value in a row from each value in the row.

EXAMPLE 6.3 An office manager is giving his assistant the choice of one of two brands of personal computers. Three computer dealers stock these computers. The office manager is preparing to take his assistant to one of these dealers and purchase the computer right there, on the spot. Since the assistant has not made up his mind which brand of computer he wants, the office manager does not know which dealer they should patronize. Construct the opportunity-loss table which corresponds to the following pay-off table, where the payoffs are the prices of the two computers at the three dealerships, A_1, A_2, and A_3 represent the office manager's decision to go to the first, second, or third dealer; and the E's represent the assistant's ultimate choice of the first or second brand of personal computer.

Payoff Table

	A_1 Dealer 1	A_2 Dealer 2	A_3 Dealer 3
E_1 Computer 1	$2,850	$2,530	$2,500
E_2 Computer 2	$3,450	$3,520	$3,600

SOLUTION   Since the first brand of computer is cheapest at the third dealer, the opportunity losses in the first row are $2,850 − $2,500 = $350, $2,530 − $2,500 = $30, and $2,500 − $2,500 = 0, and since the second brand of personal computer is cheapest at the first dealer, the opportunity losses in the second row are $3,450 − $3,450 = 0, $3,520 − $3,450 = $70, and $3,600 − $3,450 = $150. All this is summarized in the following opportunity-loss table:

Opportunity-Loss Table

	A_1 Dealer 1	A_2 Dealer 2	A_3 Dealer 3
E_1 Computer 1	$350	$30	$0
E_2 Computer 2	$0	$70	$150

■

Having learned how opportunity losses are calculated, let us now see how they may be used in making decisions. Since opportunity losses are quantities we want to make small, it seems that we could select either the minimax or minimin criterion and apply it to opportunity-loss tables. However, since opportunity losses are never negative and there is a zero in each row, the minimin criterion will generally not lead to a unique course of action. This leaves the minimax criterion for making decisions based on opportunity-loss tables, and according to this criterion we choose whichever action minimizes the maximum opportunity loss.

EXAMPLE 6.4   Continuing the preceding example, determine where the office manager should go so as to minimize his maximum loss of opportunity.

SOLUTION   We see from the opportunity-loss table that the maximum opportunity loss is $350 for A_1, $70 for A_2, and $150 for A_3. Since $70 is the smallest of the three, the minimax criterion leads the office manager to go to the second dealer. ∎

EXAMPLE 6.5   Use the opportunity-loss table on page 211 to determine what the office equipment manufacturer should do so as to minimize the maximum loss of opportunity.

SOLUTION   From the opportunity-loss table we see that the maximum opportunity loss is $108,000 if he expands his plant capacity now and $189,000 if he delays the expansion. Since the first of these figures is smaller than the second, the minimax criterion leads the manufacturer to expand his plant capacity now. ∎

EXERCISES

(Exercises 6.7, 6.9, 6.10, and 6.11 are practice exercises. Their complete solutions are given on page 248.)

6.7   The following payoff table shows the information obtained by two surveys of incomes of families residing within a 2-mile radius of three different locations being considered as a site for a new supermarket.

	Location 1	Location 2	Location 3
Survey 1	$33,500	$34,000	$32,400
Survey 2	$30,300	$35,100	$33,500

(a) If a supermarket chain is interested in acquiring one of these sites, and it prefers one in an area of high family income, which choice or choices are not admissible?

(b) With no information about the credibility of these surveys, is it possible to make a first choice and a second choice?

6.8   With reference to Exercise 6.5 on page 204, which choice of cities is inadmissible if the intent of the decision makers is to select the warmest city?

6.9   The values in the following table are the unit prices of a certain brand of flexible disks at three different computer supply stores in the city.

	Store A	Store B	Store C
$3\frac{1}{2}$-inch micro disks	$1.49	$1.25	$1.19
$5\frac{1}{4}$-inch flexible disks	$1.99	$2.25	$2.05
8-inch flexible disks	$2.75	$2.99	$2.49

An office boy has to go to one of these computer supply stores to buy a disk for his boss, but he cannot remember whether he is supposed to buy the $3\frac{1}{2}$-inch, $5\frac{1}{4}$-inch, or 8-inch disk. Hoping that he will recognize the correct disk when he sees it, but wanting to be economical with his boss's money, find

(a) which of the computer supply stores is inadmissible

(b) the computer supply store where he would go (after excluding the inadmissible store) if he applied the minimax criterion to the amount of money he would have to pay

6.10 With reference to the preceding exercise, construct an opportunity-loss table and find the computer supply store where the office boy should go so as to minimize his maximum loss of opportunity.

6.11 With reference to Exercise 6.1 on page 203, what should the private investigator do if she wants to

(a) maximize her minimum fee

(b) maximize her maximum fee

6.12 With reference to Exercise 6.3 on page 204, where should the parcel delivery service driver go if she wants to

(a) minimize the maximum distance she will have to drive

(b) minimize the minimum distance she will have to drive

(c) minimize her maximum loss of opportunity

6.13 With reference to Exercise 6.4 on page 204, how many of the pennants should the street vendor stock if he wants to

(a) maximize his minimum profit

(b) maximize his maximum profit

(c) minimize his maximum loss of opportunity

6.14 The proprietor of a health club that serves the needs of swimmers and non-swimmers wants to promote new memberships and is considering offering nonmembers a free trial day on the exercise machines, a free trial day in the swimming pool, or a free trial swimming lesson in the pool. He feels that the reactions of prospective members to these offers are shown in the following table, where the payoffs are in units of prospective member satisfaction. The proprietor must decide which one of the free trials to offer.

	Free trials		
	Exercise machines	Swimming pool	Swimming lesson
Swimmers	4	5	3
Nonswimmers	4	−3	−1

What action should be taken if the proprietor wants to

(a) maximize the minimum satisfaction of prospective members with the trial offers

(b) maximize the maximum satisfaction of prospective members with the trial offers

(c) minimize the health club's maximum loss of opportunity to provide satisfaction to prospective members with the trial offers

6.15 With reference to Exercise 6.6 on page 205, what inspection procedure should the manufacturer choose if he wants to

(a) minimize the maximum expected cost

(b) minimize the maximum expected loss of opportunity

6.16 Because of various difficulties, the supplier of glue used in the manufacture of a laminated fiberboard product can guarantee the manufacturer only that he will deliver on schedule the required quantity of either glue Q or glue R (but not some of both). Because of time requirements, however, the manufacturer must set up his production process prior to knowledge of which glue will be available with no later change possible if he is to meet contractual obligations. Both glues can be used with any one of six production methods open to the company, but for technical reasons the profit per piece differs substantially from one method to another for the same glue. The estimated unit profits (in cents) for methods 1 through 6 using glue Q are, respectively, 108, 158, 147, 172, 137, and 156, while the corresponding figures for glue R are 267, 128, 187, 207, 247, and 214.

(a) Construct a payoff table and eliminate the nonadmissible production methods.

(b) Which production method should the manufacturer use if he wants to maximize his minimum unit profit?

(c) Which production method should the manufacturer use if he wants to minimize his maximum loss of opportunity?

6.6

Decision Making Under Competition[1]

Let us now consider the case where the choice among the E's (the events over which the decision maker has no control) is made by a competitor. It is customary in this kind of problem to let the payoffs be the decision maker's losses, so that his gains will be represented by negative numbers. Furthermore, it will be assumed that whatever the decision maker gains, his competitor loses, and vice versa. In mathematics, this is called a **zero-sum two-person game**, where "game" is just a word meaning "competitive situation," the two persons are the decision maker and his competitor, and the "zero-sum" means that whatever one person loses the other person gains. In other words, in a zero-sum game there is no "cut for the house" as in professional gambling, and no capital is created or destroyed during the course of play.

To illustrate these ideas, suppose that a small town has two service stations which share the town's market for gasoline. The owner of station I is debating whether or not to give away table glasses to his customers as part of a promotional scheme, and the owner of station II is debating whether or not to give away kitchen knives. Their decisions will be based on the information (from similar situations elsewhere) that if station I gives away glasses and station II does not give away knives, station I's share of the market will increase by 12 percent; if station II gives away knives and station I does not give away glasses, station II's share of the market will increase by 16 percent; and if both stations give away the respective items, station II's share of the market will increase by 5 percent. Schematically, this information may be represented in the following payoff table.

		Station I, decision maker	
		A_1 no glasses	A_2 glasses
	E_1 no knives	0	-12
Station II, competitor	E_2 knives	16	5

[1]This section and Section 6.7 may be omitted without loss of continuity.

The zero represents the case where both owners decide not to give away these items, so that there is no change in their shares of the market. Also, station I's gain of 12 percent is denoted -12, for as we said, the payoffs are the decision maker's losses, and a loss of -12 percent is the same as a gain of 12 percent. In the foregoing scheme, we let the owner of station I play the role of the decision maker and the owner of station II the role of the competitor, but this is an arbitrary choice; their roles may be reversed and the signs of all the numbers changed accordingly.

The following tables restate the distribution of gains and losses from the view of the decision maker, and from the view of the competitor. The sums of the corresponding cells in the two tables (say, a gain of 12 percent plus a loss of 12 percent) must equal zero.

	Decision maker A_1	A_2
E_1	No change	Gain of 12 percent
E_2	Loss of 16 percent	Loss of 5 percent

	Competitor A_1	A_2
E_1	No change	Loss of 12 percent
E_2	Gain of 16 percent	Gain of 5 percent

In practice, of course, the second and third tables are not shown; only the first is used.

In decision making under competition, as in the cases which we studied earlier, the basic problem is to determine **optimum choices**, that is, choices which are in some respect the most desirable. This applies not only to the decision maker who must choose one of the A's, but also to the competitor who must choose one of the E's. Clearly, the decision maker must judge what the competitor might consider most profitable, and then account for this in making his decision. Also, it will be assumed that the decision maker as well as the competitor must make his choice without knowledge of what the other one has done or is planning to do, and once he has made his choice, it cannot be changed.

Having begun the analysis of a decision-making problem under competition by constructing a payoff table, we continue by looking for dominances and nonadmissible choices. We do this for the A's as well as the E's, for surely no thinking person would want to make a choice which is worse than another regardless of what the other person decides to do.

EXAMPLE 6.6   With reference to the preceding illustration, find the best choices for the two station owners.

SOLUTION   We see from the payoff table (with perceptions of the competitor) that it would be foolish of the owner of station II to choose E_1, regardless of the choice made by the owner of station I. Clearly, a 16 percent gain in the market share is preferable to no change, and a 5 percent gain is better than a 12 percent loss. Thus, E_1 is not admissible and we eliminate it from the payoff tables. Then we see from the payoff table (with perceptions of the decision maker) that it would be foolish of the owner of station I to choose A_1 since a 12 percent gain is better than no change, and a 5 percent loss is better than a 16 percent loss and, hence, A_2 dominates A_1. This leaves A_2 and E_2 as the optimum choices for the two owners.

We can, of course, arrive at the same conclusion by first viewing the table from the decision maker's perspective and determine that A_2 dominates A_1, and delete A_1, which is inadmissible. We can then view the table from the competitor's perspective, determining that E_2 dominates E_1, and eliminate E_1, which is inadmissible. As before, we are left with A_2 and E_2 as the optimum choices for the two owners.

Additionally, in the preceding scheme, we let the owner of station I play the role of the decision maker and the owner of station II the role of the competitor, but this is an arbitrary choice. Their roles may be reversed and the signs of all the numbers changed accordingly. In any event, the outcome of the problem favors the owner of station II, and this suggests that the owner of station 1 might well consider some other promotional scheme, but this is not part of the problem as formulated here.   ■

The process of discarding dominated alternatives can be of great help in solving problems of decision making under competition (that is, in finding optimum choices for the decision maker and his competitor), but what do we do when no dominances exist?

To illustrate this situation, let us consider a problem of decision making under competition which has the following payoff table:

		Decision maker		
		A_1	A_2	A_3
	E_1	-2	5	-3
Competitor	E_2	1	3	5
	E_3	-3	-7	11

The payoffs are the decision maker's losses, say, in dollars, which he wants to make small. Inspection shows that there are no dominances among the A's or the E's, but if we look at the problem from the decision maker's point of view, we might argue as follows. If he chooses A_1, the worst that can happen is that he loses \$1; if he chooses A_2, the worst that can happen is that he loses \$5, and if he chooses A_3, the worst that can happen is that he loses \$11. Looking at the problem from this rather pessimistic point of view, it would seem advantageous for the decision maker to minimize his maximum loss by choosing A_1; that is, it would be advantageous for him to apply the minimax criterion to the loss he might incur.

If we apply the same kind of argument to the competitor's choice, we find that if he chooses E_1, the most he can lose is \$3; if he chooses E_2, the worst that can happen is that he wins \$1; and if he chooses E_3, the most he can lose is \$7. Thus, the competitor would minimize his maximum losses (or maximize his minimum gain, which is the same thing) by choosing E_2.

The use of the minimax criterion in decision making under competition is really quite reasonable. By choosing A_1 in our example, the decision maker is assured that his competitor can win at most \$1, and by choosing E_2, the competitor makes sure that he actually does win this amount. A very important aspect of the results obtained in our example is that the choices are completely "spyproof" in the sense that neither the decision maker nor the competitor can profit from knowledge of the other's choice. Even if the decision maker announces publicly that he will choose A_1, it is still best for the competitor to choose E_2, and if the competitor announces publicly that he will choose E_2, it is still best for the decision maker to choose A_1.

The method we used here works nicely in our example—the minimax choices are spyproof—but this will not always be the case. Consider the following example.

EXAMPLE 6.7 Show that if the payoff corresponding to A_1 and E_1 is 3 instead of -2 in the preceding example, the minimax choices are not spyproof.

SOLUTION With this modification, the payoff table becomes

	Decision maker		
	A_1	A_2	A_3
E_1	3	5	-3
Competitor E_2	1	3	5
E_3	-3	-7	11

and it can be seen that the minimax criterion leads to the same choices as before, A_1 and E_2. However, they are no longer spyproof; if the competitor knows that the decision maker will use minimax criterion and choose A_1, he can switch to E_1 and thus assure himself a gain of \$3 instead of a gain of \$1. ■

Fortunately, there is a fairly easy way of deciding for any given problem whether minimax choices are spyproof. What we do is look for pairs of choices, called **saddle points**, for which the payoff entry is the smallest value in its row and also the largest value in its column. We cannot prove it here, but it can be shown that the choices which correspond to a saddle point are optimum choices, and if there is more than one saddle point in a given problem (see Exercise 6.19 on page 224), the corresponding payoffs will be the same and it does not matter which saddle point is used for making optimum choices among the A's and E's. When there is a saddle point, we say that the decision problem is **strictly determined**.

EXAMPLE 6.8   With reference to the payoff table on page 218, verify that the optimum choices constitute a saddle point.

SOLUTION   Since the entry corresponding to A_1 and E_2 is the smallest value in its row (1 is less than 3 or 5) and also the largest value in its column (1 is greater than -2 or -3), it follows from the definition that A_1 and E_2 constitute a saddle point. Note, however, that on the modified payoff table in the preceding example, the entry which corresponds to A_1 and E_2 is no longer the largest value in its column (1 is greater than -3 but less than 3), and A_1 and E_2 do not constitute a saddle point. ■

6.7

Randomized Decisions[2]

If there are no saddle points in a zero-sum two-person game, game theory has some other ideas on how the decision maker and the competitor should proceed in determining their optimum choices. To illustrate, let us consider the following problem of decision making under competition. A country has two missile bases, one with installations worth \$20 million and

[2]This section, based on the material in Section 6.6, may be omitted without loss of continuity.

the other with installations worth $100 million. It can defend only one of these bases against an attack by its enemy. The enemy, on the other hand, can attack only one of the bases, and can capture it only if the base is left undefended. In trying to decide which base to defend in the face of the uncertainty as to which base the enemy might attack, the defender considers its payoff in this (deadly) game to be the dollar worth of an installation lost to the enemy. If A_1 represents the decision to defend the smaller base and A_2 the decision to defend the larger base, and E_1 represents the decision to attack the smaller base and E_2 the decision to attack the larger base, the payoff table is

		Defending country	
		A_1	A_2
Attacking country	E_1	0	20
	E_2	100	0

where the units are in millions of dollars. Since the smallest value in each row is 0 and neither 0 is the largest value in its column, there is no saddle point. One might argue, though, that to the defending country a maximum loss of $20 million is preferable to a maximum loss of $100 million and, hence, that A_2 is preferable to A_1. However, if the attacking country knows that the defending country always uses minimax decision procedures, in this case A_2, it can take advantage of this by choosing E_1 and capturing the smaller base. This sounds fine, unless the defending country reasons that this is precisely what the attacking country intends to do and switches to A_1 and prepares to defend the smaller base. This argument can be continued ad infinitum. If the attacking country thinks that the defending country will try to outwit it by choosing A_1, it can, in turn, try to outwit the defending country by choosing E_2; if the defending country thinks that this is precisely what the attacking country will do, it can switch to A_2 and prepare to defend the larger base; and so on, and so on.

To avoid the possibility of being outguessed or outsmarted, it seems reasonable for each decision maker to mix up his decision deliberately in some way or other, and the best way to do this is to introduce an element of chance into the final choice.

To illustrate how this can be done, suppose that the defending country in the preceding example uses some kind of gambling device which leads it to choose A_1 with probability p, and to choose A_2 with probability $1 - p$. The

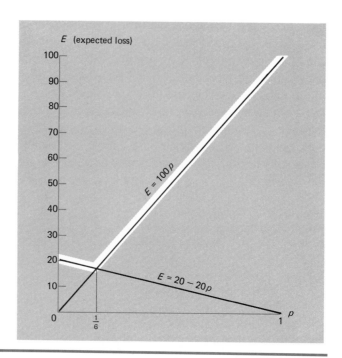

FIGURE 6.2
Expected loss of
decision maker

defenders can then argue as follows: If the enemy chooses E_1, the expected loss will be

$$E = 0 \cdot p + 20(1 - p) = 20 - 20p$$

and if the enemy chooses E_2, the expected loss will be

$$E = 100 \cdot p + 0(1 - p) = 100p$$

This situation is described graphically in Figure 6.2, where we have plotted the two lines whose equations are $E = 20 - 20p$ and $E = 100p$ for values of p from 0 to 1. (Actually, we drew the lines by connecting in both cases the two values of E which correspond to $p = 0$ and $p = 1$.)

To apply the minimax criterion to the expected loss of the defending country, observe from Figure 6.2 that the most the defenders can expect to lose (the larger of the two values of E for any given value of p, as indicated by the shading) is least where the two lines intersect, and to find the value of p which leads to this minimax expected loss, we must set $20 - 20p$ equal to $100p$, and solve for p. We have

Chapter 6   Decision Analysis

$$20 - 20p = 100p$$
$$20 = 120p$$

and, finally,

$$p = \frac{20}{120} = \frac{1}{6}$$

Therefore, in order to minimize the maximum expected loss, the defenders could do the following. Label one tag A_1 and five tags A_2, put the tags in an urn, and draw one of them from the urn at random; then if the tag drawn is A_1, take action A_1 (defend the smaller base); otherwise, take action A_2 (defend the larger base). This minimax criterion assures the defending country of holding its maximum expected loss to

$$E = 100 \cdot \frac{1}{6} = 16\frac{2}{3} \text{ million dollars}$$

and there is nothing the enemy can do about it. Observe that this expected loss is less than the possible loss of \$100 million the defenders are exposed to by the direct (nonchance) choice of A_1 and the possible loss of \$20 million they are exposed to by the direct choice of A_2.

If a decision maker's ultimate choice is left to chance, his overall decision procedure is referred to as **randomized** or **mixed**. If a decision maker chooses directly an action open to him without introducing an element of chance, his decision procedure is said to be **pure**. Of course, it may be hard to convince anyone that it makes any sense at all, much less is "best," to gamble with one's country's security, but if one really wants a decision procedure, or **strategy**, that is absolutely spyproof, there is no alternative. Although game theory has been used in analyzing complicated military problems and in playing war games on computers, it should be observed that the illustration we gave here pictures an "ivory tower" kind of situation. In warfare there seems always to be some intelligence and counterintelligence, no matter how little or how poor it is, and it is usually possible to change one's decision (adjust one's strategy) after it becomes known what one's opponent is doing or intends to do. This is certainly not the case, however, in all competitive business situations.

EXERCISES

(Exercises 6.17, 6.18, 6.20, 6.22, and 6.23 are practice exercises. Their complete solutions are given on page 248.)

6.17 Each of the following is a payoff for a problem of decision making under competition, with the payoffs being the losses of the decision maker, who has to choose among the columns. Eliminate all dominated choices and thus determine the best choice of each "player."

(a)

	A_1	A_2
E_1	5	7
E_2	3	-2

(c)

	A_1	A_2	A_3
E_1	2	-1	2
E_2	5	0	8
E_3	4	-7	6

(b)

	A_1	A_2
E_1	6	-4
E_2	4	1

(d)

	A_1	A_2	A_3
E_1	4	2	1
E_2	2	5	2
E_3	-1	3	1

6.18 Find the saddle point for each part of the preceding exercise.

6.19 Each of the following is the payoff table for a problem of decision making under competition, with the payoffs being the losses of the decision maker who has to choose among the columns. Find the saddle point or saddle points, and show that if there is more than one, it does not matter which one is selected.

(a)

	A_1	A_2	A_3
E_1	2	1	3
E_2	0	-2	-1
E_3	1	-1	-5

(b)

	A_1	A_2	A_3	A_4
E_1	-1	0	-2	5
E_2	0	0	0	-1
E_3	1	1	2	2
E_4	1	1	3	5

6.20 A certain type of computer is made by only two companies that share the market for the machine equally. Both would prefer not to introduce a new model at this time, but both suspect that the other is readying a new model and that if it is introduced some sales will be lost to the competitor. If neither brings out a new model or if both bring out new models, the status quo will be maintained and both will continue to get their same relative share of the market. If, however, one brings out a new model and the other does not, there will be a change of 10 percent in share of the market gained by the competitor with the new machine. What is the best strategy for the two companies to use with respect to the introduction of a new model?

6.21 Show that in the problem of decision making under competition given by the following payoff table, the maximin criterion leads the competitor to choose the second alternative:

Decision Maker

−2	200	200	200	200
0	0	0	0	0

Competitor

It has been suggested that in a situation like this, it would be wholly irrational for the competitor to choose the second alternative. Give examples where

(a) this suggestion would be reasonable

(b) this suggestion would not be reasonable

6.22 Two applicants are competing for a single job as sales associate in a retailing firm. Each can provide the firm with a transcript of grades, a resume of experience, or both, and the corresponding decreases in applicant A's probability of getting the job are shown in the following payoff table.

		Applicant A		
		Transcript	*Resume*	*Both*
	Transcript	−0.02	0.08	0.06
Applicant B	*Resume*	0.00	0.04	0.20
	Both	−1.10	−0.16	0.00

If they base their decisions on the minimax and maximin criteria, what should the two applicants do?

6.23 The following is the payoff table for a zero-sum two-person game, with the payoffs being the amounts player A loses to player B:

Player A

Player B	6	−5
	−4	4

(a) What randomized decision procedure should player A use so as to minimize his maximum expected loss?

(b) What randomized decision procedure should player B use so as to maximize his minimum expected gain?

6.24 Two persons agree to play the following game: The first writes either 1 or 4 on a slip of paper and at the same time the second writes either 0 or 3 on another slip of paper. If the sum of the two numbers is odd, the first wins this amount in dollars; otherwise, the second wins $2.

(a) Construct a payoff table in which the payoffs are the first person's losses.

(b) What randomized decision procedure should the first person use so as to minimize his maximum expected loss?

(c) What randomized decision procedure should the second person use so as to maximize his minimum expected gain?

6.25 Suppose that the manufacturer of Exercise 6.16 on page 215 has the choice of only three production methods for which the unit profits (in cents) using glue Q are, respectively, 120, 90, and 200. If the corresponding figures for glue R are 240, 175, and 180, what randomized decision procedure should the manufacturer use so as to maximize his minimum expected unit profit?

6.26 With reference to Exercise 6.2 on page 204, what randomized procedure should the frozen food manufacturer use if it wants to minimize the maximum expected loss? Explain under what conditions this procedure might be regarded as rational.

6.27 There are two gas stations in a certain block, and the owner of the first station knows that if neither station lowers its prices, he can expect a net profit of $100 on any given day. If he lowers his prices while the other station does not, he can expect a new profit of $140; if he does not lower his prices but the other station does, he can expect a net profit of $70; and if both stations participate in this "price war" he can expect a net profit of $80. The owners of the two stations decide independently what prices to charge on any given day, and it is assumed that they cannot change their prices after they discover those charged by the other.

(a) Should the owner of the first station charge his regular prices or should he lower them, if he wants to maximize his minimum net profit?

(b) Assuming that the foregoing profit figures apply also to the second station, how might the two owners collude so that each could expect a net profit of $105? (Note that this "game" is not zero sum, so that the prospect of collusion opens entirely new possibilities.)

The Bayes Decision Rule

Until now we have considered only problems in which the decision maker has no information about the probabilities of the events E over which he has no control. In practical business applications, however, decisions are ordinarily made by knowledgeable persons whose expertise enables them to assign valid (not to say correct) probabilities to the occurrences of the different events. These probability estimates are often based on subjective evaluations, collateral information, intuition, and other factors, which are all acquired prior to the time that the decision-making situation arises. We therefore refer to such probabilities as **prior probabilities**, and to decision analysis based on such probabilities as **prior analysis**, or as **decision making under risk**.

After assigning probabilities to the E's, we calculate mathematical expectations and base decisions on whichever action promises the maximum expected profit, the minimum expected cost, the maximum expected sales, the minimum expected spoilage, and so on. When we do this we are using the **Bayes decision rule**, named after the Reverend Thomas Bayes (1702–1761), and what we are doing is called **Bayesian decision making**. It is called this because in most real applications we base our decisions on prior information as well as direct sample evidence collected specially to aid in making the decisions, and combining these two kinds of evidence requires the use of Bayes formula, which we shall present in Chapter 8.

The following is an example of Bayesian decision making based on the values of the payoffs and prior probabilities of the events E over which the decision maker has no control.

EXAMPLE 6.9   Referring again to the example on page 201 where the payoff table was

	Expand now	Delay expansion
Economic conditions remain good	$369,000	$180,000
There is a recession	−$90,000	$18,000

find the decision which will maximize the manufacturer's expected profit if he feels (on the basis of relevant information available to him) that the odds on a recession are

(a) 2 to 1

(b) 3 to 2

SOLUTION (a) If the odds on a recession are 2 to 1, the probability of a recession is $\dfrac{2}{2+1} = \dfrac{2}{3}$ and the probability that economic conditions will remain good is $\dfrac{1}{1+2} = \dfrac{1}{3}$. Thus, if he expands his plant capacity right away, the expected profit is

$$369,000 \cdot \frac{1}{3} + (-90,000) \cdot \frac{2}{3} = \$63,000$$

and if the expansion is delayed, the expected profit is

$$180,000 \cdot \frac{1}{3} + 18,000 \cdot \frac{2}{3} = \$72,000$$

Since an expected profit of \$72,000 is obviously preferable to an expected profit of \$63,000, the Bayes decision rule leads the manufacturer to delay expanding his plant capacity.

(b) If the odds on a recession are 3 to 2, the probability of a recession is $\dfrac{3}{3+2} = \dfrac{3}{5}$ and the probability that economic conditions will remain good is $\dfrac{2}{2+3} = \dfrac{2}{5}$. Thus, if he expands his plant capacity right away, the expected profit is

$$369,000 \cdot \frac{2}{5} + (-90,000) \cdot \frac{3}{5} = \$93,600$$

and if the expansion is delayed, the expected profit is

$$180,000 \cdot \frac{2}{5} + 18,000 \cdot \frac{3}{5} = \$82,800$$

Here the Bayes decision rule leads the manufacturer to expand his plant capacity right away, which is the reverse of the decision arrived at in part (a). ∎

Example 6.9 illustrates that in Bayesian decision making we must be fairly sure that the prior probabilities are "correct" (or at least reasonably close). Just how sensitive our decisions are to changes (errors?) in the prior probabilities is a matter of **sensitivity analysis**, which we shall illustrate here by finding the "changeover point," namely, the value of the prior probability (of economic conditions remaining good) at which the manufacturer's choice of action would change from one to the other.

If we let p denote the probability that economic conditions will remain good, so that the probability is $1 - p$ that there will be a recession, the manufacturer's expected profit is

$$369,000p + (-90,000)(1 - p) = 459,000p - 90,000$$

if he expands his plant capacity right away, and it is

$$180,000p + (18,000)(1 - p) = 162,000p + 18,000$$

if the expansion is delayed. These two expected profits are represented by the two lines of Figure 6.3, and it can be seen that the second alternative is preferable (has the higher expected profit) up to the value of p where the two lines intersect, and that the first alternative is preferable for values of p

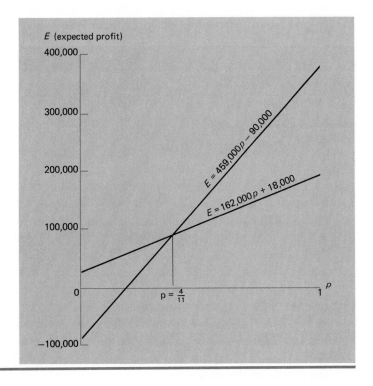

FIGURE 6.3
Diagram for
sensitivity analysis

greater than that. To find the value of p where the lines intersect, we equate the two expected profits, getting

$$459{,}000p - 90{,}000 = 162{,}000p + 18{,}000$$

and, hence, $297{,}000p = 108{,}000$ and $p = \dfrac{108{,}000}{297{,}000} = \dfrac{4}{11}$, or approximately 0.364. So, for $p = \dfrac{4}{11}$ the expected profit is the same regardless of whether or not the manufacturer decides to expand his plant capacity right away.

As the problem was originally formulated in part (a) of Example 6.9 on page 227, the manufacturer felt that the odds on a recession were 2 to 1 and, hence, assigned the probability $p = \dfrac{1}{3}$ to economic conditions remaining good. However, if this probability had been slightly higher (higher by more than $\dfrac{4}{11} - \dfrac{1}{3} = \dfrac{1}{33}$ or approximately 0.03), the manufacturer's decision would have gone the other way. Surely, this is not much of a margin for error.

Another question that comes to one's mind in Bayesian decision making is how sensitive it may be to changes in the payoffs. Indeed, this is a crucial factor in any kind of decision analysis (see, for example, Exercise 6.37 on page 236).

6.9

Expected Opportunity Losses

Earlier in this chapter, we suggested that decisions could be based on opportunity losses instead of the payoffs themselves and, in the absence of any prior information, used the minimax criterion to choose a course of action. Once again, opportunity losses are calculated for each row of an opportunity-loss table as follows: If the payoffs are profits or other quantities which we want to make large, we subtract each value in a row from the largest value in the row; if the payoffs are losses or other quantities which we want to make small, we subtract the smallest value in a row from each value in the row. Now, if we can assign prior probabilities to the "states of nature," we can proceed as in the preceding section and apply the Bayesian decision rule; that is, we can minimize the **expected opportunity loss**, also referred to as the **EOL**.

EXAMPLE 6.10 In Example 6.3 on page 211, the opportunity losses which the office manager faced in deciding where to buy the computer for his assistant are shown in the following table.

	Dealer 1 A_1	Dealer 2 A_2	Dealer 3 A_3
E_1	$350	$30	$0
E_2	$0	$70	$150

Which dealer should he go to to minimize the EOL if he feels that the odds are 4 to 1 that his assistant will decide on the brand 1 computer?

SOLUTION If he chooses the first dealer, the expected opportunity loss is

$$350(0.80) + 0(0.20) = \$280$$

if he chooses the second dealer, the EOL is

$$30(0.80) + 70(0.20) = \$38$$

and if he chooses the third dealer, the EOL is

$$0(0.80) + 150(0.20) = \$30$$

Thus, the EOL is least if he decides to go to the third dealer, and this should not come as a surprise—the prior probabilities strongly favor E_1, and for E_1 and A_3 (the third store) the opportunity loss is zero. ■

EXAMPLE 6.11 For the office equipment manufacturer problem on page 211, the opportunity-loss table is summarized as follows.

	A_1	A_2
E_1	0	$189,000
E_2	$108,000	0

Which decision will minimize the EOL if the prior probabilities of E_1 and E_2 are

(a) $\frac{1}{3}$ and $\frac{2}{3}$ (b) $\frac{2}{5}$ and $\frac{3}{5}$

SOLUTION (a) If the manufacturer decides to expand his plant capacity right away, the EOL is

$$0 \cdot \frac{1}{3} + 108{,}000 \cdot \frac{2}{3} = \$72{,}000$$

and if he delays, the EOL is

$$189{,}000 \cdot \frac{1}{3} + 0 \cdot \frac{2}{3} = \$63{,}000$$

and he will minimize his expected opportunity loss by deciding to delay.

(b) If he decides to expand his plant capacity right away, the EOL is

$$0 \cdot \frac{2}{5} + 108{,}000 \cdot \frac{3}{5} = \$64{,}800$$

and if he delays, the EOL is

$$189{,}000 \cdot \frac{2}{5} + 0 \cdot \frac{3}{5} = \$75{,}600$$

and he will minimize his expected opportunity loss by deciding to expand right away. ∎

In all these examples the decisions are identical with those arrived at earlier by applying the Bayes decision rule directly to the expected profits. This is by no means a coincidence, as it can be shown mathematically that minimizing the expected loss of opportunity will always lead to the same decision as maximizing the expected profit or minimizing the expected loss, as the case may be (see Exercise 6.38 on page 237). Therefore, the method of this section does not really present anything new, and we have given it here mainly because it is essential to understanding another important concept in decision analysis, which we shall introduce in the next section.

6.10

Expected Value of Perfect Information

In the two preceding sections we studied problems in which decisions were based on prior information, without considering the possibility of acquiring further information before making a decision. We shall see later how decisions may be based on prior information as well as direct sample evidence, but for the moment let us merely consider whether it is really worthwhile to delay a decision until we collect further information; more specifically, how much should we be willing to pay for such information?

Let us introduce first the concept of an **expected payoff with perfect information**, that is, the payoff we could expect, with reference to a given set of prior probabilities, if we were called upon to make such a decision an indefinitely large number of times and we always made the best possible decision.

EXAMPLE 6.12   In the office equipment manufacturer problem on page 201 the payoffs are

	Expand now	Delay expansion
Economic conditions remain good	$369,000	$180,000
There is a recession	−$90,000	$18,000

Find the expected payoff with perfect information when the prior probabilities of economic conditions remaining good and of there being a recession are $\frac{1}{3}$ and $\frac{2}{3}$.

SOLUTION   If economic conditions remain good, the optimum choice would be to expand the plant capacity right away, and if there is a recession, the optimum choice would be to delay the expansion. The corresponding payoffs are $369,000 and $18,000, so that for prior probabilities of $\frac{1}{3}$ and $\frac{2}{3}$ the expected payoff with perfect information is

$$369,000 \cdot \frac{1}{3} + 18,000 \cdot \frac{2}{3} = \$135,000 \qquad \blacksquare$$

The importance of knowing an expected payoff with perfect information is that it enables us to determine how much of an improvement perfect information is over merely knowing the prior probabilities of the E's. For instance, in the office equipment manufacturer Example 6.9, on page 227, based only on the prior probabilities $\frac{1}{3}$ and $\frac{2}{3}$, the maximum expected profit is $72,000. Since this is $135,000 − $72,000 = $63,000 less than the expected payoff with perfect information calculated earlier, it follows that the manufacturer should be willing to spend not more than $63,000 for additional information and spend that much only for perfect information.

As suggested by this discussion, we are really interested mostly in the difference between the expected payoff with perfect information and the optimum expected payoff based only on the prior probabilities. We call this difference the **expected value of perfect information**, or simply the **EVPI**. In practice, the EVPI can be determined without first calculating the expected payoff with perfect information. As the reader will be asked to demonstrate in Exercise 6.39 on page 237 (for the special case where there are only two choices A_1 and A_2 and two events E_1 and E_2), **the expected value of perfect information is always equal to the minimum expected opportunity loss**; that is, the EVPI is always equal to the smallest of the EOL's.

EXAMPLE 6.13 In the office equipment manufacturer problem on page 201, verify that the EVPI equals the smallest of the EOL's.

SOLUTION In the preceding discussion we showed that the EVPI = $63,000 and on page 000 we showed that for the same prior probabilities, $\frac{1}{3}$ and $\frac{2}{3}$, the two EOL's are $72,000 and $63,000. Thus, the EVPI is, indeed, equal to the smallest of the EOL's. ∎

The expected value of perfect information is an important concept in decision analysis, and it is sometimes referred to as the **cost of uncertainty**. It must be understood, though, that it depends on the choice of the prior probabilities, where even a small inaccuracy or misjudgment can have a pronounced effect (see Exercise 6.35 on page 236).

EXERCISES

(Exercises 6.28, 6.29, 6.35, and 6.38 are practice exercises. Their complete solutions are given on page 248.)

6.28 The manager of a store in a chain of department stores wants to set up a display of sterling silver flatware. If the silverware will not be advertised in the newspapers this week, it must be displayed in the wall showcase, but if advertised, it must be placed prominently on a counter in the front of the department. The costs incurred in preparing the silver for the wall showcase or counter display are $25 and $20, respectively. An additional $8 charge will result if the silverware must be moved from the wall showcase to the counter or vice versa.

(a) Construct a payoff table for this decision problem.

(b) If the manager feels that the odds are 3 to 1 that the silverware will not be advertised this week and he wants to minimize his expected cost, where should he display the silverware?

(c) If the manager is figuring his costs very closely, would it be worth $1.00 to telephone the advertising manager at corporate headquarters to find out whether the silverware will be advertised this week?

6.29 With reference to part (b) of the preceding exercise, how far off could the prior probabilities be without affecting the store manager's decision?

6.30 With reference to Exercise 6.2 on page 204,

(a) Find what decision would maximize the frozen food manufacturer's expected gain (or minimize its expected loss) if it is felt the probability of high sales is 0.25.

(b) At most, how much should the manufacturer be willing to spend to find out for certain whether the sales will be high or low?

6.31 With reference to the preceding exercise, how far off could the 0.25 probability be without affecting the decision?

6.32 With reference to Exercise 6.3 on page 204, which site should the parcel delivery driver go to first if she wants to minimize the expected mileage and feels that the prior probabilities for sites 1, 2, and 3 are 0.15, 0.55, and 0.30?

6.33 With reference to Exercise 6.4 on page 204, how many of the pennants should the vendor stock so as to maximize the expected profit if it is felt the prior probabilities of a demand for 0, 1, 2, 3, 4, or 5 or more pennants are 0.10, 0.15, 0.20, 0.25, 0.20, and 0.10?

6.34 A driver for a bus company which provides service to ski resorts in the mountains must decide whether to put tire chains on the bus. If it snows and he does not put the tire chains on, he will be displeased since the bus will skid without them; and if it does not snow, he will be displeased if he puts on the tire chains because of the wasted work involved in mounting them. On the other hand, the bus driver will be pleased if he puts on the tire chains and it snows, since the bus will operate more safely, and the bus driver will be neither pleased nor displeased if he does not put on the tire chains and it does not snow. To express all of this numerically, suppose that the payoffs in the following table are in units of displeasure, so that the negative value reflects pleasure.

	Puts chains on	Does not put chains on
Snows	−35	95
Does not snow	65	0

(a) What should the bus driver do to minimize his expected displeasure if he feels the probabilities of snow and no snow are 0.45 and 0.55, respectively?

(b) If the cash equivalent of a unit of displeasure is 20 cents, at most how much should he be willing to spend to find out whether or not it is going to snow?

(c) How much could the prior probabilities be off without affecting his decision?

6.35 With reference to Example 6.3 on page 211 concerning two brands of personal computers and the three dealers, find the EVPI when the prior probabilities are 0.80 and 0.20 by

(a) subtracting the expected payoffs with perfect information from the smallest of the expected prices for the three stores

(b) determining the smallest of the EOL's

Also, repeat part (b) when the prior probabilities are 0.70 and 0.30, and discuss the effect of this change in the prior probabilities.

6.36 A women's fashion store can buy 1,000 or 2,000 high-fashion bathing suits of a new style at a price of $20 each. If the store buys 1,000 bathing suits, it expects to sell all of them at $50 each even if this new style does not become very popular. If the store buys 2,000 bathing suits and the new style does not become very popular, it nevertheless expects to sell 1,000 bathing suits at $50 each and be forced to sell the remainder at a postseason sale price of $10 each. If the style becomes very popular, the store expects to sell 2,000 bathing suits at $50 each, but if it buys only 1,000 it will have to rebuy and pay $35 each for the additional bathing suits needed.

(a) If there is a 50-50 chance that the bathing suit style will not become very popular, how large should the initial order be to maximize the expected profit?

(b) Show that if we use the same probability as in part (a), minimizing the expected opportunity loss would lead to the same decision as maximizing the expected profit.

(c) Calculate first the expected profit with perfect information and then the expected value of perfect information, and verify that EVPI equals the expected opportunity loss corresponding to the optimum choice.

6.37 With reference to Example 6.9 on page 227, would the Bayes decision rule lead to different decisions if

(a) the $369,000 profit is replaced by a $450,000 profit and the prior probabilities of economic conditions remaining good or there being a recession are $\frac{1}{3}$ and $\frac{2}{3}$

(b) the $90,000 loss is replaced by a $135,000 loss and the prior probabilities of economic conditions remaining good or there being a recession are $\frac{2}{5}$ and $\frac{3}{5}$

6.38 The following is the payoff table of a decision problem in which the payoffs are profits, $b > a$, $c > d$, and the prior probabilities of E_1 and E_2 are p and $1 - p$:

	A_1	A_2
E_1	a	b
E_2	c	d

(a) Find an expression for the difference between the expected profits corresponding to A_1 and A_2.

(b) Construct an opportunity-loss table and find an expression for the difference between the expected opportunity losses corresponding to A_1 and A_2.

(c) Combining the results of parts (a) and (b), explain why maximizing the expected profit leads to the same decision as minimizing the expected opportunity loss.

6.39 To show that the expected value of perfect information equals the minimum expected loss of opportunity, refer to the decision problem of the preceding exercise.

(a) Find an expression for the expected profit with perfect information.

(b) Subtract the expected profits corresponding to A_1 and A_2 from the expression obtained in part (a) to show that the expected value of perfect information is either $(b - a)p$ or $(c - d)(1 - p)$, depending on whether A_1 or A_2 is the optimum selection.

(c) Based on the opportunity-loss table of part (b) of the preceding exercise, find expressions for the expected opportunity losses corresponding to A_1 and A_2.

(d) Use the results of part (b) and (c) to verify that the EVPI equals the minimum EOL.

6.11

Further Considerations: Utility

In all the problems in which we applied the Bayes decision rule, we assumed that it is rational to take whichever action maximizes expected profit, minimizes expected cost, minimizes expected opportunity loss, and so on. Of course, there are many situations where this kind of decision making is justified, but there are exceptions. Suppose, for example, that the office equipment manufacturer (see page 201) is in bad financial condition and feels that, unless he makes a profit in the next year, he will be forced to file for bankruptcy. This would make the $90,000 loss in the payoff table very heavy, and he might well decide to delay expanding his plant capacity in spite of the prior probabilities of $\frac{2}{5}$ and $\frac{3}{5}$ and expectations which tell him to do otherwise.

This illustrates the fact that the value, usefulness, or **utility** of a payoff may be greater or less than its cash equivalent, and it raises the question of how such intangibles might actually be measured. Of course, we could always ask a person directly how much something is worth to him, but "talk is cheap" and unless there is something at stake, it is hard to get meaningful answers.

To illustrate another way of measuring utilities, suppose that a football fan tells us that he would "give his right arm" for a ticket to a football game that has been sold out for weeks. Naturally, this is only a figure of speech, but it is meant to imply that the value which he attaches to a game ticket is very high. If we asked him to be more specific, he might say that he would be willing to pay $50 or perhaps even $100, but unless we can put this on a "put up or shut up" basis, it really does not have much significance. So, suppose that we make him the following proposition. If he will pay us $5.00, we will let him draw at random one of 10 sealed envelopes, nine of which contain a dollar bill and the tenth a ticket to the game. If he accepts this deal and we let U denote the value, or utility, which he assigns to the ticket, we can argue that his expected utility, $\frac{1}{10} \cdot U + \frac{9}{10} \cdot 1$, must be worth at least $5.00 to him. Symbolically,

$$\frac{1}{10} \cdot U + \frac{9}{10} \cdot 1 \geq 5$$

and this leads to $U + 9 \geq 50$ and, hence, to $U \geq 41$. We have arrived here at the result that the fan feels that the ticket to the game is worth at least $41 to him, and if we varied the odds, the contents of the envelopes, or the amount he is asked to pay, we could be more precise about it than that. For instance, if he is willing to pay $6 but not $7.50 in this situation, this would lead to $51 \leq U < $66 (see Exercise 6.40 on page 241).

In this example we assumed that $5 is worth five times as much as $1 and $50 is worth ten times as much as $5. Assumptions like this are often reasonable when we are dealing with fairly small amounts. It is a well-known fact, however, that the utility which a person assigns to a sum of money does not always equal its monetary value. Very often, the reason for this is that "the second $100 gain is worth less than the first," "the second $1,000 gain is worth less that the first," . . . , or that "the second $1,000 loss hurts more than the first." Of course, $100 is $100 and $1,000 is $1,000, but the value a person attaches to a sum of money will depend on how much a person already has or owes; in technical language, this is a matter of **marginal utility**.

To give an example, suppose that we offer someone the choice between an outright gift of $120 or a gamble on the flip of a fair coin which pays him $250 if it falls heads and nothing if it falls tails. Even though the mathematical expectation of the gamble is $250 \cdot \frac{1}{2} + 0 \cdot \frac{1}{2} = \$125$, which exceeds the dollar value of the outright gift, it would be surprising if a person actually chose the gamble. In some cases this reluctance to gamble may be based on moral or religious grounds, or on a person's general dislike of taking chances, but in others it simply reflects the fact that the first $120 is worth more to a person than the next $130.

To continue this argument, suppose that the gamble is modified so that the person wins the $250 if he draws at random a white bead from an urn containing 100 beads, some black and some white. If he feels that the value of the gamble equals the value of the outright gift of $120 when there are 60 white beads and 40 black beads in the urn, we can write

$$\frac{60}{60 + 40} \cdot U = 120$$

where U is the value, or utility, which the person attaches to $250. This leads to $U = \frac{5}{3} \cdot \$120$, and it tells us that the utility which the person assigns to $250 is only five-thirds the utility he assigns to $120. It would be misleading, though, to multiply out $\frac{5}{3} \cdot \$120$ and get $200, since the utility which a person attaches to $200 may not be five-thirds the utility he assigns to $120.

To avoid this difficulty, we introduce an artificial unit of utility and call it a **utile**. For instance, in our last example we could let $0 be 0 utiles and $120 be 1 utile, and we could then say that the person assigns $250 a utility of $\frac{5}{3} \cdot 1 = 1\frac{2}{3}$ utiles.

Proceeding with the example, suppose that we make the same person another offer; he will toss a fair coin and if it falls heads he wins and we will pay him $120, otherwise he loses and he will pay us $120. This is certainly a fair offer in a monetary sense, but suppose the person declines it because, to him, the possibility of losing $120 outweighs the possibility of winning $120. Instead, he makes us this counteroffer: he will match with us but if he loses he will pay us only $100, not $120. We would not accept this offer, but it does tell us something about the utility U which the person attaches to a loss of $100. Since he considers a bet of $100 against $120 fair and since his probabilities of winning and losing are both $\frac{1}{2}$, we can assign his winning $120 a utility of 1 utile, as before, and write

$$\frac{1}{2} \cdot U + \frac{1}{2} \cdot 1 = 0$$

Solving this equation for U, we get $U = -1$.

Continuing in this way, we could find the utilities, the numbers of utiles, which the person attaches to various other amounts, and thus arrive at a **utility curve** like the one shown in Figure 6.4.

When utilities are measured in this way, the concept of utility is closely interwoven with a person's eagerness or reluctance to take chances. For instance, if we are willing to bet $120 against someone's $100 on the flip of a balanced coin, we are the kind of person who is eager to bet even when the odds are against him (a compulsive gambler, perhaps), and our utility curve is like the one pictured in Figure 6.5. If we are willing to bet only when the

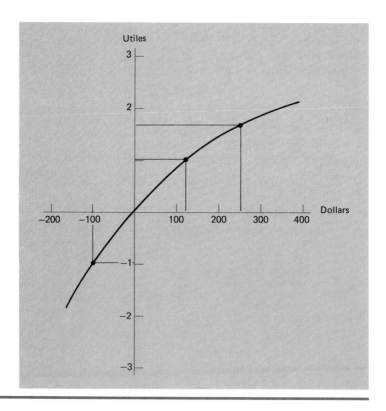

FIGURE 6.4
Utility curve for illustration

Chapter 6   Decision Analysis

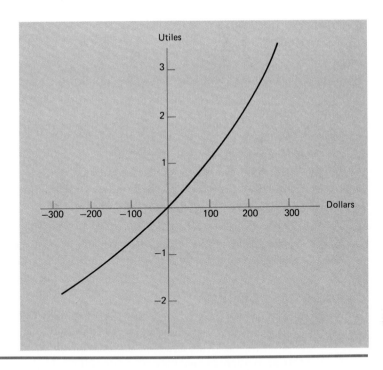

FIGURE 6.5
Utility curve for
person eager to
take chances

situation is fair to both parties in the monetary sense, we are said to be
neutral to risk, and our utility curve is a straight line.

We have introduced the concept of utility here mainly to make Bayesian decision making more generally applicable. Let us add, though, that the
construction of meaningful utility curves is usually a formidable task. A
Bayesian decision analysis based on maximizing one's expected utility is
illustrated in Exercise 6.49 on page 242.

EXERCISES

(Exercises 6.40, 6.41, and 6.49 are practice exercises. Their complete solutions are
given on page 248.)

6.40 With reference to the illustration on page 238, verify that if the fan is willing
to pay $6.00 but not $7.50 to play the game, the value he assigns to the ticket
is greater than or equal to $51 but less than $66.

6.41 Tom feels that it is a toss-up whether to accept a $15 cash gift or to cast a
single die and receive $6 if the outcome is a 1 or a 6 and a transistor radio if
the outcome is a 2, 3, 4, or 5. What value or utility does he assign to the
transistor radio?

6.42 A student would like to pass a course in accounting, but chances are practically hopeless unless she hires a private tutor. According to knowledgeable friends, tutoring will cost her $300 and will give her a 50-50 chance of receiving a passing grade. If the student assigns the utility U to passing the course and the utility $-\frac{1}{5}U$ to failing the course, find U if the student decides that it is just about worthwhile to spend the $300 on private tutoring.

6.43 Suppose that the person referred to on page 239 who attaches a utility of 1 utile to $120 is a used computer dealer who is willing to bid $120, but not more than $120, at an auction sale for a used computer which he can resell for $600 if he can find the right customer, but which is worthless if he cannot. If he believes that the probability he can resell the computer to the right customer is $\frac{1}{4}$, what utility does he assign to $600?

6.44 Suppose that the person referred to on page 240, who attaches a utility of -1 utile to a loss of $100, actually owes a business associate $100. To settle the debt he proposes a wager, which he considers fair, on the outcome of a game of golf which they will play. If he wins the game, the debt is canceled, but if he loses, he will pay the associate $300. Given the odds that he will win the game are 4 to 1, what utility does he assign to this $300 loss?

6.45 The person whose utility curve is given in Figure 6.4 takes a job which promises to pay her a fee of $100, $200, $300, or $400 with probabilities of $0.24, 0.32, 0.28$, and 0.16. Read the utilities corresponding to these amounts off the graph of Figure 6.4 and calculate the expected utility which the person assigns to this job.

6.46 Discuss under what conditions it would be wise for a person to have

(a) complete health insurance

(b) only major medical insurance with a $500 deductible

(c) no health insurance at all

6.47 Suppose that the utility which Ms. Brown assigns to the amount A (in dollars) is given by

$$U = A - 0.001A^2$$

for $-\$200 \leq A \leq \$200$. Calculate U for $A = -\$200, -\$100, -\$50, \$0, \$50, \$100$, and $\$200$, and sketch the graph of this utility curve.

6.48 Would Ms. Brown of the preceding exercise prefer to pay $100 outright for an oil painting or match the artist "double or nothing" for the painting using a balanced coin?

6.49 With reference to the office equipment manufacturer on page 201, suppose that he will be forced into bankruptcy if he cannot show a positive profit during the next year, and that he translates the payoffs into the utiles shown in the following table:

	Expand now	Delay expansion
Economic conditions remain good	30	20
There is a recession	−485	5

Which decision will maximize the manufacturer's expected utility, if he feels that the prior probabilities for economic conditions remaining good and there being a recession are $\frac{1}{3}$ and $\frac{2}{3}$?

6.50 With reference to the preceding exercise, show that expanding his plant capacity right away will maximize the manufacturer's expected utility so long as the prior probability of a recession is less than or equal to 0.02. Does it matter what he does when this prior probability is 0.02?

6.12

A Word of Caution

One of the greatest difficulties in applying the methods of this chapter (and more general methods) to realistically complex problems in statistics, business management, and economics is that we seldom know the exact values of all the risks that are involved. That is, we seldom know the exact values of the payoffs corresponding to the various eventualities, and we seldom have sufficient information about the values of all relevant probabilities. For instance, if a manufacturer must decide whether to market a new drug right away, how can he put a cash value on the damage that might be caused by not waiting for a more thorough evaluation of the side effects of the drug or on the lives that might be lost by not marketing the drug? Similarly, if a management consultant must decide whether to recommend that a new detergent be marketed or not marketed, how can he possibly take into account all the effects which his advice (good or bad) might have on himself, on the prospective marketer, and ultimately on the consumer of the product?

So far as the prior probabilities of the events over which the decision maker has no control are concerned, small changes (perhaps errors of judgment or differences of opinion) can lead to different decisions. Indeed, the problem of ''policing'' subjective probabilities—of deciding which ones are to be trusted and which ones are not and which ones are to be used and which ones are not—can pose serious difficulties in practical applications.

Nevertheless, there is much good to be said for decision theory and we repeat here what we said in the introduction to this chapter: ''The decision-theory approach has the positive advantage of forcing one to formulate problems clearly, to anticipate the various consequences of one's actions, to retain the relevant and eliminate the irrelevant, to place cash values on the consequences of one's actions, and so on. No matter how little or how far it is pursued, such a systematic approach is bound to help.''

6.13

Checklist of Key Terms

6.14

Review Exercises

6.51 A woman wants a set of buttons sewn on a jacket but is uncertain whether she wants gold or silver buttons. A tailor will sell and sew on a set of silver buttons for $9.00, and a gold set for $11.00. He has offered to exchange and replace whichever set is selected for an additional charge of $4.00 if the woman should change her mind. Construct a payoff table which shows the price the woman will pay for the buttons depending on whether she orders and keeps the gold set, the silver set, or changes her mind and replaces the set she has ordered with the other.

6.52 With reference to the preceding exercise, which set of buttons should the woman order if she wants to
   (a) minimize the maximum cost of the set of buttons
   (b) minimize the minimum cost of the set of buttons

6.53 With reference to Exercise 6.51, which set of buttons should the woman first order the tailor to sew on her jacket if she wants to minimize the cost and feels that
   (a) the odds are 5 to 1 that she will finally order the tailor to sew on the gold buttons
   (b) the odds are 2 to 1 that she will finally order the tailor to sew on the gold buttons
   (c) the odds are 3 to 1 that she will finally order the tailor to sew on the gold buttons

6.54 With reference to Exercise 6.51, what is the EVPI when the odds are 5 to 1 that she will finally order the tailor to sew on the gold buttons?

6.55 The investors in a new theater production must decide whether to provide additional funds for rewriting the script of the play. They know that if the script is rewritten and a well-known leading actress is hired, there will be a profit of $480,000; if the script is rewritten and they do not hire the leading actress, there will be a loss of $80,000; if the script is not rewritten and a leading actress is hired, there will be a profit of $220,000; and if the script is not rewritten and the leading actress is not hired, there will be a profit of $40,000 because of the money and time saved in not rewriting the script.
   (a) Construct a payoff table.
   (b) Construct a decision tree.

6.56 With reference to the preceding exercise, construct an opportunity-loss table and determine which decision of the investors will
   (a) minimize the maximum loss of opportunity
   (b) minimize the minimum loss of opportunity

6.57 Based on the opportunity-loss table of Exercise 6.56, what should the investors do if they feel that the prior probabilities of hiring a well-known leading actress are 0.30 and 0.70 and they want to minimize the EOL?

6.58 With reference to the preceding exercise, how much could the 0.30 prior probability be increased without changing the investors' decision?

6.59 Mr. Green has the choice of staying home and reading a good book or going to a party. If he goes to the party he might have a terrible time (to which he assigns a utility of 0), or he might have a wonderful time (to which he assigns a utility of 30 units). If he feels that the odds against his having a good time are 4 to 1 and he decides not to go, what can we say about the utility which he assigns to staying home and reading a good book?

6.60 Following are the ratings of selected 35mm single-lens-reflex cameras provided in a recent issue of *Consumer Reports*. Ratings are 1, 2, 3, 4, and 5, where 1 is the highest rating and 5 is the lowest.

	Pentax Super Program	Nikon FA	Canon AE-1 Program	Minolta X-570	Fujika AX-5	Yashika FX-D
Overall lens quality	1	1	2	3	3	3
Exposure consistency	2	2	1	2	4	2
Convenience	1	2	2	1	2	1

Based on these considerations only (that is, prices vary greatly), which choices of cameras are not admissible?

6.61 A traveler is considering the purchase of a reduced-fare airline ticket which costs $400 and must be purchased at least one month prior to the flight. The ticket is nonrefundable and if not used, the traveler loses $400. The price of a full-fare ticket is $500 which is fully refundable to the traveler, without penalty, if he does not take the flight.

(a) Construct a payoff table for this decision problem which shows the gains and losses incurred in buying a reduced-fare ticket as compared to a full-fare ticket.

(b) If the traveler feels that the probabilities are 0.90 and 0.10 that he will take the flight or not take the flight, what shold he do to maximize his expected gain?

(c) Construct an opportunity-loss table and use the probabilities of part (b) to determine at most how much the traveler should be willing to spend to find out for certain whether or not he will take the flight.

(d) Rework part (b) of this exercise with the probabilities 0.10 that the traveler will take the flight and 0.90 that he will not. What should the traveler do to maximize his expected gain?

6.62 In an unfriendly takeover attempt of a corporation the *acquiring corporation* wants to acquire another corporation and must decide whether to do so by direct negotiation (negotiations between the managements and boards of directors of the two corporations) or by a tender offer (an offer made directly to the shareholders, often through financial newspapers). The *defending corporation* must decide whether to expect the acquiring corporation will negotiate or make a tender offer and set up its defenses accordingly. Depending on these choices, the probabilities that the acquiring corporation will be successful in its takeover attempt in this specific situation are shown in the following table.

		Acquiring Corporation	
		Negotiate	Tender offer
Defending corporation	Negotiate	0.70	0.30
	Tender offer	0.40	0.50

(a) What randomized decision procedure will maximize the acquiring corporation's minimum expected probability of successfully acquiring the defending corporation?

(b) If the acquiring corporation uses the procedure of part (a) what is the probability that it will acquire the defending corporation?

6.63 The following is the payoff table for a zero-sum two-person game, with the payoffs being the amounts player A loses to player B:

	Player A	
Player B	3	-1
	-2	5

(a) What randomized decision procedure should player A use so as to minimize the maximum expected loss?

(b) What randomized decision procedure should player B use so as to maximize the minimum expected gain?

6.64 The following is the payoff table for a problem of decision making under competition, with the payoffs being the losses (in thousands of dollars) of the decision maker who must choose a column.

Decision maker

		A_1	A_2	A_3
	E_1	−2	−1	3
Competitor E_2		1	4	2
	E_3	0	5	−3

(a) Find the saddle point.

(b) Determine the column the decision maker should choose.

6.65 A television game show host offers a contestant a cash prize of $1,000 or a gamble on drawing a card from an ordinary deck of playing cards where she is to receive $200 if she draws a spade, a club, or a heart or a genuine diamond ring if she draws a diamond. If the contestant feels that it is a toss-up whether to accept the cash prize of $1,000 or to draw a card, what utility does she attach to the diamond ring?

6.15

Solutions of Practice Exercises

6.1 (a)

	Straight fee	Reward
Locates	$1,000	$5,000
Does not locate	$1,000	0

(b)

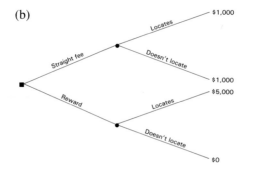

248

6.4 (a)

	Stock			
	1	*2*	*3*	*4*
0	−4	−8	−12	−16
1	6	2	−2	−6
Demand *2*	6	12	8	4
3	6	12	18	14
4	6	12	18	24
5 or more	6	12	18	24

(b)

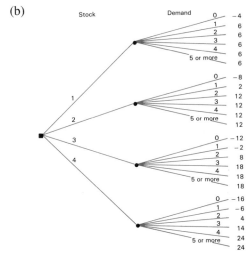

6.7 (a) Locations 1 and 3 are not admissible.

(b) Since locations 1 and 3 are not admissible, location 2 is first choice. It is not possible to make a second (or third) choice.

6.9 (a) Store B is inadmissible.

(b) Store C, where the minimax value is $2.49.

6.10

	Store A	Store C
$3\frac{1}{2}$-inch micro disks	0.30	0.00
$5\frac{1}{4}$-inch flexible disks	0.00	0.06
8-inch flexible disks	0.26	0.00

Store C since the minimax value is $0.06.

Section 6.15 Solutions of Practice Exercises

6.11 (a) Work on a straight fee (maximin is $1,000).

(b) Work on possibility of reward (maximax is $5,000).

6.17 (a) Eliminate E_2, then eliminate A_2 since a loss of 5 is preferable to a loss of 7. The best choices are A_1 and E_1.

(b) Eliminate A_1, then eliminate E_1 since a gain of 1 is preferable to a loss of 4. The best choices are A_2 and E_2.

(c) Eliminate A_1 and A_3, then eliminate E_1 and E_3 since 0 is preferable to a loss of 1 and a loss of 7. The best choices are A_2 and E_2.

(d) Eliminate A_2, then eliminate E_3, then eliminate A_1, then eliminate E_1 since a profit of 2 is preferable to a profit of 1. The best choices are A_3 and E_2.

6.18 (a) A_1 and E_1 (5 is the maximum of its column and the minimum of its row.

(b) A_2 and E_2 (1 is the maximum of its column and the minimum of its row)

(c) A_2 and E_2 (0 is the maximum of its column and the minimum of its row)

(d) A_3 and E_2 (the 2 in the third column is the maximum of its column and the minimum of its row)

6.20

One company

		No new model	New model
Other company	No new model	0	−10
	New model	10	0

There is a saddle point (optimum strategy) corresponding to both companies introducing the new model (the 0 in the second row is the maximum value of its column and the minimum value of its row).

6.22 The maximum values of the columns are 0.00, 0.08, and 0.20, and the minimum values of the rows are −0.02, 0.00, and −1.10; since there is a saddle point corresponding to the first column and the second row (0.00 is the maximum value of its column and the minimum value of its row), candidate A should send a transcript and candidate B should send a resume.

6.23 (a) $6p - 5(1 - p) = -4p + 4(1 - p)$, so that $10p = 9(1 - p) = 9 - 9p$, $19p = 9$, and $p = \dfrac{9}{19}$; A should choose his first strategy with probability $\dfrac{9}{19}$ and his second strategy with probability $\dfrac{10}{19}$.

(b) $6q - 4(1 - q) = -5q + 4(1 - q)$ so that $11q = 8(1 - q) = 8 - 8q$,

$19q = 8$, and $q = \dfrac{8}{19}$; B should choose his first strategy with probability $\dfrac{8}{19}$ and his second strategy with probability of $\dfrac{11}{19}$.

6.28 (a)

First display in

	Showcase	*Counter*
Showcase	25	28
Counter	33	20

Then in (to the left of the rows: Showcase / Counter)

(b) $25 \cdot \dfrac{3}{4} + 33 \cdot \dfrac{1}{4} = \$27$ for showcase, and $28 \cdot \dfrac{3}{4} + 20 \cdot \dfrac{1}{4} = \$26$ for the counter. He will minimize his expected cost by first placing the silverware on the counter.

(c) $25 \cdot \dfrac{3}{4} + 20 \cdot \dfrac{1}{4} = \$23.75$. Since $\$26.00 - \$23.75 = \$2.25$ exceeds $\$1.00$, it would be worthwhile to make the call.

6.29 $25p + 33(1 - p) = 28p + 20(1 - p)$, so that $p = \dfrac{13}{16} = 0.81$. Since the odds of part (a) were 3 to 1, which is a probability of $\dfrac{3}{3 + 1} = 0.75$, the manager could be off by at most $0.81 - 0.75 = 0.06$.

6.35 (a) The expectations are $2{,}850(0.8) + 3{,}450(0.2) = \$2{,}970$ if he goes to the first store, $2{,}530(0.8) + 3{,}520(0.2) = \$2{,}728$ if he goes to the second store and $2{,}500(0.8) + 3{,}600(0.2) = \$2{,}720$ if he goes to the third store. The expected payoff with perfect information is $2{,}500(0.8) + 3{,}450(0.2) = \$2{,}690$, and the expected value of perfect information is $2{,}720 - 2{,}690 = \$30$.

(b) Since the expected opportunity losses are $350(0.8) + 0(0.2) = \$280$, $30(0.8) + 70(0.2) = 38$, and $0(0.8) + 150(0.2) = \$30$, the smallest of these values, the EVPI, is $\$30$. When the prior probabilities are 0.7 and 0.3, the expected opportunity losses are $350(0.7) + 0(0.3) = \$245$, $30(0.7) + 70(0.3) = \$42$, and $0(0.7) + 150(0.3) = \$45$, and the smallest one corresponds to the second store instead of the third.

6.38 (a) The expected profits corresponding to A_1 and A_2 are $ap + c(1 - p)$ and $bp + d(1 - p)$, and their difference is $[ap + c(1 - p)] - [bp + d(1 - p)] = (a - b)p + (c - d)(1 - p)$.

(b)

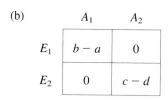

The expected opportunity losses corresponding to A_1 and A_2 are $(b - a)p + 0(1 - p) = (b - a)p$ and $0 \cdot p + (c - d)(1 - p) = (c - d)(1 - p)$, and their difference is $(b - a)p - (c - d)(1 - p) = -[(a - b)p + (c - d)(1 - p)]$.

(c) The difference between the expected opportunity losses is the negative of the difference between the expected profits, so, if we minimize the opportunity losses, we maximize the expected profits.

6.40 $0.1 \cdot U + 0.9 \cdot 1 \geq 6.00$, so that $U \geq \$51$; $0.1 \cdot U + 0.9 \cdot 1 < 7.50$, so that $U < \$66$.

6.41 $6\left(\dfrac{1}{3}\right) + U\left(\dfrac{2}{3}\right) = 15$ so that $U\left(\dfrac{2}{3}\right) = 13$ and $U = 19\dfrac{1}{2}$.

6.49 Since the expected utilities are $30 \cdot \dfrac{1}{3} - 485 \cdot \dfrac{2}{3} = -313.3$ and $20 \cdot \dfrac{1}{3} + 5 \cdot \dfrac{2}{3} = 10$, the decision would be to delay the expansion.

7

Probability Distributions

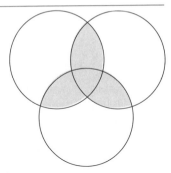

I n most statistical problems we are interested in only one aspect, or at most in a few aspects, of the outcomes of experiments. For example, a student who takes a true-false test may be interested only in how many questions he misses, since his grade depends on just this. A depositor in a federally insured savings bank may be interested only in the rate of interest currently paid by the bank and care nothing about the bank's earnings from loans, or the bank's earnings from investments in securities. Also, a grape hybridizer may be interested not only in the yield per acre of a new grape variety but also in the total acidity and the sugar content of the grapes. And an automotive engineer may be interested in both the durability and brightness of the headlights proposed for a new-model car.

In these cases the student, the depositor, the hybridizer, and the engineer are all interested in numbers that are associated with the outcomes of situations involving an element of chance, or more specifically, in the values taken on by **random variables**.

In the study of random variables, we are usually interested in the probabilities with which they take on the various values within their range, namely, in their **probability distributions**. The study of random variables and probability distributions in Sections 7.1 and 7.2 will be followed by the discussion of various special probability distributions in Sections 7.3 through 7.6, and the description of their most important features in Sections 7.7 through 7.9.

7.1

Random Variables

To be more explicit about the concept of a random variable, let us consider Figure 7.1, which, like Figure 5.9 on page 168 pictures the sample space for the example dealing with the two contractors who have bid on two jobs. Here, however, we have added another number to each point—the number 0 to the point (0, 0); the number 1 to the points (1, 0) and (0, 1); and the number 2 to the points (2, 0), (1, 1), and (0, 2). In this way, we have associated with each point of the sample space the total number of jobs which, between them, the two contractors will get.

Since associating numbers with the points of a sample space is just a way of defining a function over the points of the sample space, random variables are, strictly speaking, functions. Conceptually, though, most beginners find it easier to think of random variables simply as quantities

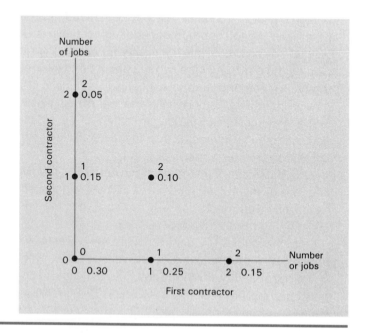

FIGURE 7.1

Sample space with values of random variable

Chapter 7   Probability Distributions

which can take on different values depending on chance. For instance, the number of speeding tickets issued each day on the freeway from Phoenix to Tucson is a random variable, and so are the annual production of soybeans in the United States, the number of persons visiting Disneyland each week, the number of defectives produced each day by a machine, and the number of classified ads in the Sunday edition of a metropolitan newspaper.

Random variables are usually classified according to the number of values which they can assume. In this chapter we shall limit our discussion to random variables called **discrete random variables** which can take on only a finite number of values, or a countable infinity of values (as many as there are whole numbers). Random variables will be taken up again in Chapter 9.

7.2

Probability Distributions

The tables in the illustrations which follow serve to show what we mean by a probability distribution. With reference to Figure 7.1, if we add the probabilities associated with the different points, we find that the random variable "the number of jobs which, between them, the two contractors will get" takes on the value 0 with probability 0.30, the value 1 with probability 0.25 + 0.15 = 0.40, and the value 2 with probability 0.15 + 0.10 + 0.05 = 0.30. All this is summarized in the following table:

Number of jobs	Probability
0	0.30
1	0.40
2	0.30

As this table shows, a probability distribution is a correspondence which assigns probabilities to the values of a random variable.

Another illustration is the probability distribution of the number of points which show in one roll of a fair die, for which we have the correspondence shown in the following table:

Number of points rolled with a die	Probability
1	$\frac{1}{6}$
2	$\frac{1}{6}$
3	$\frac{1}{6}$
4	$\frac{1}{6}$
5	$\frac{1}{6}$
6	$\frac{1}{6}$

Also, for four flips of a balanced coin there are the 16 equally likely possibilities, HHHH, HHHT, HHTH, HTHH, THHH, HHTT, HTHT, HTTH, THHT, THTH, TTHH, HTTT, THTT, TTHT, TTTH, and TTTT, and, counting the number of heads in each case and using the formula $\frac{s}{n}$ for equally likely possibilities, we get

Number of heads	Probability
0	$\frac{1}{16}$
1	$\frac{4}{16}$
2	$\frac{6}{16}$
3	$\frac{4}{16}$
4	$\frac{1}{16}$

Whenever possible, we try to write probability distributions in the form of mathematical formulas which enable us to calculate the probabilities associated with the various values of a random variable. For instance, for the previous illustration, the number of points which we roll with a fair die, where the probability is $\frac{1}{6}$ for each value of x, we can write

$$f(x) = \frac{1}{6} \qquad \text{for } x = 1, 2, 3, 4, 5, \text{ and } 6$$

Chapter 7   Probability Distributions

where $f(1)$ represents the probability of rolling a 1, $f(2)$ represents the probability of rolling a 2, and so on. We shall write the probability that a random variable takes on the value x as $f(x)$.

In the sections that follow, we shall see how other probability distributions can be expressed mathematically as formulas.

To conclude this introduction to probability distributions, let us state the following two general rules which the values of all probability distributions must obey:

> **Since the values of a probability distribution are probabilities, they must be numbers on the interval from 0 to 1.**

> **Since a random variable has to take on one of its values, the sum of all the values of a probability distribution must be equal to 1.**

7.3

The Binomial Distribution

There are many applied problems in which we are interested in the probability that an event will occur "x times in n trials." For instance, we may be interested in the probability of getting 34 responses to 300 mail questionnaires, the probability that 8 of 24 newly franchised travel agencies will go bankrupt within two years, or the probability that 132 of 400 television viewers (interviewed by a rating service) will recall what products were advertised on a given program. To borrow again from the language of games of chance, we say that in each of these examples we are interested in the probability of getting x **successes** and $n - x$ **failures** in n **trials**.

In the problems which we shall study in this section, it will always be assumed that the number of trials is fixed, that the probability of a success is the same for each trial, and that the trials are all independent. This means that the theory we shall develop will not apply, for example, if we are interested in the number of pairs of shoes a woman will try on before she finally buys a pair (where the number of trials is not fixed), if we check hourly whether traffic is congested at an important intersection (where the probability of congestion is not the same for each trial), or if we are interested in a student's passing in order French I, French II, French III, and French IV (where the trials are not indepedent).

To solve problems which do meet the conditions listed in the preceding paragraph, we use a formula obtained in the following way. If p and $1 - p$ are the probabilities of a success and a failure on any given trial, then the probability of getting x successes and $n - x$ failures in some specific order is $p^x(1 - p)^{n-x}$. In this product of p's and $(1 - p)$'s there is one factor p for each success, one factor $1 - p$ for each failure, and the x factors p and $n - x$ factors $1 - p$ are all multiplied together by virtue of the generalized multi-plication rule for more than two independent events. Since this probability applies to all points of the sample space which represent x successes and $n - x$ failures (in any specific order), we have only to count how many points of this kind there are, and then multiply $p^x(1 - p)^{n-x}$ by this number. Now, the number of ways in which we can select the x trials on which there is to be a success is $\binom{n}{x}$, the number of combinations of x objects selected from a set of n objects, and we have arrived at the following result:

Binomial distribution

The probability of getting x successes in n independent trials is

$$f(x) = \binom{n}{x}p^x(1 - p)^{n-x} \quad for \ x = 0,1,2,\dots, or \ n$$

where p is the constant probability of a success for each trial.

It is customary to say here that the number of successes in n trials is a random variable having the **binomial probability distribution** or simply the **binomial distribution**. The binomial distribution is called by this name because for $x = 0, 1, 2,\dots,$ and n, the values of the probabilities are the successive terms of the binomial expansion of $[(1 - p) + p]^n$.

EXAMPLE 7.1 Write the formula for the binomial distribution of the number of heads obtained in four flips of a balanced coin.

SOLUTION Substituting $n = 4$ and $p = \dfrac{1}{2}$ into the formula, we get

$$f(x) = \binom{4}{x}\left(\frac{1}{2}\right)^x\left(1 - \frac{1}{2}\right)^{4-x} = \binom{4}{x}\left(\frac{1}{2}\right)^4 = \frac{\binom{4}{x}}{16}$$

Chapter 7 Probability Distributions

for $x = 0, 1, 2, 3$, and 4. For instance, for $x = 2$ we get $f(2) =$ $\dfrac{\binom{4}{2}}{16} = \dfrac{6}{16}$, and for $x = 4$ we get $\dfrac{\binom{4}{4}}{16} = \dfrac{1}{16}$. ∎

EXAMPLE 7.2 If the probability is 0.20 that any one shoplifter will get caught, what is the probability that in a random sample of eight shoplifters three will get caught?

SOLUTION Substituting $x = 3$, $n = 8$, $p = 0.20$, and $\binom{8}{3} = 56$ into the formula, we get

$$f(3) = \binom{8}{3}(0.20)^3(1 - 0.20)^{8-3}$$
$$= 56(0.20)^3(0.80)^5$$
$$= 0.147$$ ∎

The following is an example in which we calculate all the probabilities of a binomial distribution.

EXAMPLE 7.3 A supermarket uses several cash registers to check out the orders of its customers but has assigned one cash register to an express lane which serves customers who have purchased only a small number of articles. The probability that a customer in this store will use the express lane is 0.20. Find the probability that among five randomly selected customers there are zero, one, two, three, four, or five who will use the express lane.

SOLUTION Substituting $n = 5$, $p = 0.20$, and $x = 0, 1, 2, 3, 4$, and 5 into the formula for the binomial distribution, we get

$$f(0) = \binom{5}{0}(0.20)^0(0.80)^5 = 0.328$$

$$f(1) = \binom{5}{1}(0.20)^1(0.80)^4 = 0.410$$

$$f(2) = \binom{5}{2}(0.20)^2(0.80)^3 = 0.205$$

$$f(3) = \binom{5}{3}(0.20)^3(0.80)^2 = 0.051$$

$$f(4) = \binom{5}{4}(0.20)^4(0.80)^1 = 0.006$$

$$f(5) = \binom{5}{5}(0.20)^5(0.80)^0 = 0.000$$

A histogram of this binomial distribution is shown in Figure 7.2. ■

In actual practice, binomial probabilities are seldom calculated by direct substitution into the formula. Sometimes we use approximations such as those discussed later, but more often we refer to special tables such as Table V at the end of the book or the more detailed tables listed in the bibliography. Table V is limited to the binomial probabilities for $n = 2$ to $n = 15$, and $p = 0.05, 0.1, 0.2, 0.3, 0.4, 0.5, 0.6, 0.7, 0.8, 0.9,$ and 0.95. Where values are omitted in the table, they are 0.0005 or less. The computer printout of Figure 7.3 shows binomial probabilities for a value not published in Table V. The letter N in the printout corresponds to n in Table V, P corresponds to p and K corresponds to x. The column headed P(X = K) in the printout corresponds to the column under the numerical probability of p in Table V; and the column headed P(X LESS OR = K) in the printout provides cumulative totals of the preceding P(X = K) column. The numbers

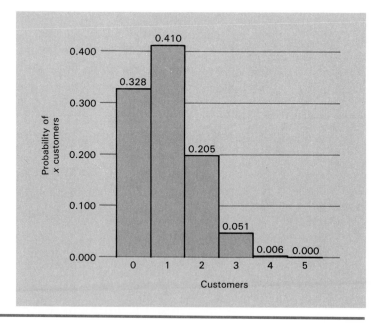

FIGURE 7.2
Histogram of binomial distribution with $n = 5$ and $p = 0.20$

```
MTB > BINOMIAL N=10 P=0.45

      BINOMIAL PROBABILITIES FOR N =   10   AND P = 0.450000

           K              P( X = K )              P(X LESS OR = K)
           0                0.0025                  0.0025
           1                0.0207                  0.0233
           2                0.0763                  0.0996
           3                0.1665                  0.2660
           4                0.2384                  0.5044
           5                0.2340                  0.7384
           6                0.1596                  0.8980
           7                0.0746                  0.9726
           8                0.0229                  0.9955
           9                0.0042                  0.9997
          10                0.0003                  1.0000
```

FIGURE 7.3
Computer printout
of the binominal
distribution with
$n = 10$ and
$p = 0.45$

in column 3 of the printout may not agree with the cumulative totals of the numbers in column 2 because of rounding.

EXAMPLE 7.4 Suppose that 30 percent of the shipments made by a United States pharmaceutical manufacturer go to Latin American countries. Use Table V to find the probabilities that

(a) at most 3 of 10 randomly selected shipments are destined for Latin America

(b) at least 7 of 10 randomly selected shipments are destined for Latin America

SOLUTION (a) For $n = 10$ and $p = 0.30$, the entries in Table V corresponding to $x = 0, 1, 2$, and 3 are $0.028, 0.121, 0.233$, and 0.267, and the probability that, at most, 3 of 10 shipments are destined for Latin America is

$$0.028 + 0.121 + 0.233 + 0.267 = 0.649$$

(b) For $n = 10$ and $p = 0.30$, the entries in Table V corresponding to $x = 7$ and 8 are $0.009 + 0.001$; the probability that $x = 9$ or $x = 10$ is, at most, 0.0005 for each (all values omitted in Table V are 0.0005 or less), so the probability that at least 7 of 10 shipments are destined for Latin America is $0.009 + 0.001 = 0.010$ (or as much as an additional thousandth). ■

EXAMPLE 7.5 If the probability is 0.05 that any one person will dislike the taste of a new mouthwash, what is the probability that at least 2 of 15 randomly selected persons will dislike it?

Section 7.3 The Binomial Distribution   261

SOLUTION Adding the tabled probabilities for $n = 15$, $p = 0.05$, and $x = 2, 3,$ 4, and 5, we get

$$0.135 + 0.031 + 0.005 + 0.001 = 0.172$$

The probabilities which have not been added here, those for $x = 6$, 7, 8,..., and 15, are all no greater than 0.0005 and they are not shown in Table V.

The same answer can be obtained even more readily by subtracting the probabilities for $x = 0$, and $x = 1$, from one, obtaining

$$1 - (0.463 + 0.366) = 0.171$$

The small difference between 0.171 and 0.172 is due to rounding in the table. ∎

EXAMPLE 7.6 Suppose that 45 percent of a large number of parcels shipped by a mailing service company were erroneously mailed with incorrect postage. Use the computer printout of Figure 7.3 to find the probability that in a randomly selected sample of 10 parcels

(a) none were mailed with incorrect postage

(b) all were mailed with incorrect postage

(c) exactly 5 were mailed with incorrect postage

(d) 5 or fewer were mailed with incorrect postage

(e) more than 5 were mailed with incorrect postage

(f) 5 or more were mailed with incorrect postage

SOLUTION (a) Locating the number $K = 0$ in the first column of the printout (Figure 7.3) and reading across the row, we find the answer 0.0025 in the second column.

(b) Locating the number $K = 10$ in the first column and reading across the row, we find the answer 0.0003 in the second column.

(c) Locating the number $K = 5$ in the first column and reading across the row, we find the answer 0.2340 in the second column.

(d) Locating the number $K = 5$ in the first column and reading across the row, we find the answer 0.7384 in the third column. Alternatively we can locate $K = 0, 1, 2, 3, 4$, and 5 in the first column and then add the corresponding probabilities in the second column, and we get $0.0025 + 0.0207 + 0.0763 + 0.1665 + 0.2384 + 0.2340 = 0.7384$.

(e) Subtracting 0.7384 obtained in part (d) from 1 we get $1 - 0.7384 = 0.2616$. Alternatively we can locate $K = 6, 7, 8, 9,$ and 10 in the first column and then add the corresponding probabilities in the second column, and we get $0.1596 + 0.0746 + 0.0229 + 0.0042 + 0.0003 = 0.2616$.

(f) Locating the number $K = 4$ in the first column and reading across the row, we find the probability 0.5044 in the third column, and subtracting this value from 1, we get $1 - 0.5044 = 0.4956$. Alternatively we can locate $K = 5, 6, 7, 8, 9,$ and 10 in the first column and then add the corresponding probabilities in the second column, and we get $0.2340 + 0.1596 + 0.0746 + 0.0229 + 0.0042 + 0.0003 = 0.4956$. ∎

EXERCISES

(Exercises 7.1, 7.3, 7.7, 7.8, 7.9, 7.10, and 7.15 are practice exercises. Their complete solutions are given on page 291.)

7.1   In each case, use the two general rules on page 257 to determine whether the given values can be looked upon as the values of a probability distribution of a random variable which can take on only the values 1, 2, 3, and 4 and explain your answers:

(a) $f(1) = 0.15, f(2) = 0.20, f(3) = 0.25, f(4) = 0.30$

(b) $f(1) = \dfrac{0}{11}, f(2) = \dfrac{2}{11}, f(3) = \dfrac{4}{11}, f(4)\ \dfrac{6}{11}$

(c) $f(1) = 0.21, f(2) = 0.26, f(3) = 0.36, f(4) = 0.17$

(d) $f(1) = 0.39, f(2) = 0.43, f(3) = 0.24, f(4) = -0.06$

(e) $f(1) = \dfrac{1}{3}, f(2) = \dfrac{1}{6}, f(3) = \dfrac{2}{9}, f(4) = \dfrac{5}{12}$

7.2   Use the two general rules on page 257 to determine whether the following can be probability distributions, defined in each case for the given values of x, and explain your answers:

(a) $f(x) = \dfrac{1}{5}$ for $x = 0, 1, 2, 3, 4, 5$

(b) $f(x) = \dfrac{x}{10}$ for $x = 0, 1, 2, 3, 4$

(c) $f(x) = \dfrac{x - 2}{5}$ for $x = 0, 1, 2, 3, 4, 5$

(d) $f(x) = \dfrac{x^2}{14}$ for $x = 0, 1, 2, 3$

Section 7.3   The Binomial Distribution   263

7.3 In a large shipment of tomatoes, 90 percent are green and therefore not ready for sale to retail customers. Find the probability that three of four tomatoes randomly selected from the shipment are green and not ready for sale to retail customers, by using

(a) the formula for the binomial distribution

(b) Table V

Use a computer printout of the binomial distribution with $n = 4$ and $p = 0.90$ to verify parts (a) and (b) of this exercise.

7.4 A multiple-choice test consists of five questions and four answers to each question (only one answer is correct). A student answers each question by picking a card from a deck of 52 playing cards and checking the first answer if he draws a spade, the second answer if he draws a club, the third answer if he draws a heart, and the fourth answer if he draws a diamond. The drawn card is replaced in the deck after each trial. Find the probability of getting

(a) exactly three correct answers

(b) no correct answers

(c) at least three correct answers

Use a computer printout of the binomial distribution with $n = 5$ and $p = 0.25$ to verify parts (a), (b), and (c) of this exercise.

7.5 If 4 in 5 customers at a certain shopping mall arrive by automobile, find the probability that 10 of 12 randomly selected customers will arrive by automobile using

(a) the formula for the binomial distribution

(b) Table V

Use a computer printout of the binomial distribution with $n = 12$ and $p = 0.8$ to verify parts (a) and (b) of this exercise.

7.6 A medical doctor knows from experience that 10 percent of her patients are late for their appointments. Find the probability that two of five randomly selected patients are late for their appointments by using

(a) the formula for the binomial distribution

(b) Table V

Use a computer printout of the binomial distribution with $n = 5$ and $p = 0.10$ to verify parts (a) and (b) of this exercise.

7.7 In the game of "chuck-a-luck" three dice are thrown and a player bets on the occurrence of a number which he can choose. He wins $1 if his number appears on only one die, $2 if his number appears on two dice, $3 if his number appears on all three dice, and he loses $1 if his number appears on none of the dice.

(a) Find the probabilities of his winning $1, $2, and $3, and the probability of his losing $1.

(b) Determine the player's mathematical expectation.

7.8 Sixty percent of the suits sold at a men's clothing store require alterations by the store's tailor. Find the probability that, at most, three of seven randomly selected suits sold will require alterations.

7.9 Find the constant probability that a salesperson will find any one buyer present in his office if the probability that all four of the buyers he plans to visit on a day are out of their offices equals $\frac{16}{81}$.

7.10 An airline claims that 95 percent of its flights arrive on time. Use Table V to find the probabilities that among 10 randomly selected flights

(a) at least 8 are on time

(b) from 7 to 9 are on time

(c) at most 9 are on time

7.11 A study has shown that 40 percent of all families in a large neighborhood have one or more videocassette recorders. Find the probabilities that among 15 families randomly selected in the area

(a) 10 have 1 or more VCRs

(b) more than 12 have VCRs

(c) at most 5 own VCRs

(d) from 6 to 9 own VCRs

7.12 In a survey of the workers of a large corporation, 30 percent of all employees said that they were dissatisfied with their working conditions. Find the probabilities that among 12 randomly selected employees who were surveyed

(a) none were dissatisfied with working conditions

(b) all were dissatisfied with working conditions

(c) 10 to 12 were dissatisfied with working conditions

(d) 6 or fewer were dissatisfied with working conditions

7.13 After examination of a large shipment of glassware which was badly packed for shipment, a claims adjuster states that 50 percent of the glassware is undamaged. Find the probablities that among 10 randomly selected glassware articles 0, 1, 2, ..., 9, or 10 will be undamaged, and draw a histogram of this distribution.

7.14 A fast-food restaurant owner wants to promote sales by offering a free contest ticket to each customer. She wants 80 percent of the tickets to be printed as ''prize winners'' and plans to award numerous small prizes such as a soft drink, an order of fries, or a hamburger to the winners. To test whether 80 percent of the tickets are prize winners, a market research organization decides to take 10 tickets at random from a large batch of tickets, reject the claim if fewer than 7 tickets are prize winners, and otherwise accept it. What are the probabilities that the market research organization will

(a) reject the claim even though it is true

(b) accept the claim when in reality only 50 percent of the contest tickets are printed as winners

Section 7.3   The Binomial Distribution   **265**

(c) accept the claim when in reality only 30 percent of the contest tickets were printed as winners

7.15 In some situations where the binomial distribution applies, we are interested in the probabilities that the first success will occur on any given trial. For this to happen on the xth trial, it must be preceded by $x - 1$ failures for which the probability is $(1 - p)^{x-1}$, and it follows that the probability that the first success will occur on the xth trial is

Geometric distribution

$$f(x) = p(1 - p)^{x-1} \qquad for\ x = 1, 2, 3, 4, \dots$$

This distribution is called the **geometric distribution** (because its successive values constitute a geometric progression) and it should be observed that there is a countable infinity of possibilities.[1] Using the formula for the geometric distribution, we find, for example, that in repeated rolls of a balanced die, the probability that the first 6 will occur on the fifth roll is

$$\frac{1}{6}\left(\frac{5}{6}\right)^{5-1} = \frac{625}{7,776}$$

(a) When playing a football game, the probability that a certain player will complete a pass is 0.60. What is the probability that this player will complete a pass for the first time on the third attempt?

(b) Suppose the probability is 0.30 that any given student in a large class can provide the answer to an assigned problem. What is the probability that the fourth student randomly selected by the instructor will be the first one who can provide the answer to the problem?

7.4

The Hypergeometric Distribution

In Chapter 5 we spoke of sampling "with replacement" to illustrate the multiplication rule for independent events, and of sampling "without replacement" to illustrate the rule for dependent events. Now, to introduce a

---

[1] As formulated in Chapter 5, the postulates of probability apply only when the sample space is finite. When the sample space is **countably infinite** (that is, when there are as many outcomes as there are whole numbers), as is the case here, the third postulate has to be modified so that for any sequence of mutually exclusive events $A_1, A_2, A_3, \dots$,

$$P(A_1 \cup A_2 \cup A_3 \cup \dots) = P(A_1) + P(A_2) + P(A_3) + \dots$$

probability distribution which applies when we sample without replacement, let us consider the following problem. A company ships automatic dishwashers in lots of 24. Before they are shipped, though, an inspector randomly selects 4 dishwashers from each lot, and the lot passes this inspection only if all 4 are in perfect condition; otherwise, each dishwasher is checked out individually and repaired, if necessary, at a considerable cost. Clearly, this kind of sampling inspection involves certain risks—it is possible for a lot to pass this inspection even though 12, or even 20, of the 24 dishwashers have serious defects, and it is possible for a lot to fail this inspection even though only one of the dishwashers has a slight defect. This raises many questions. For instance, it may be of special interest to know the probability that a lot will pass the inspection when, say, 4 of the dishwashers are not in perfect condition. This means that we shall have to find the probability of 4 successes (perfect dishwashers) in 4 trials, and we might be tempted to argue that since 20 of the dishwashers are in perfect condition, the probability of getting such a dishwasher is $\frac{20}{24} = \frac{5}{6}$, and hence the probability of "4 successes in 4 trials" is

$$f(4) = \binom{4}{4}\left(\frac{5}{6}\right)^4\left(1 - \frac{5}{6}\right)^{4-4} = 1\left(\frac{5}{6}\right)^4 = \frac{625}{1,296} = 0.482$$

This use of the binomial distribution is correct if sampling is with replacement and each dishwasher is replaced before the next one is selected; otherwise, the assumption of independence is violated. Clearly, if a dishwasher is randomly selected and not replaced, the probability that a second randomly selected dishwasher will be in perfect condition depends on whether or not the first one was in perfect condition.

However, in sampling inspection we seldom, if ever, sample with replacement. To get the correct answer for our problem when sampling is without replacement, we can argue as follows: There are altogether $\binom{24}{4}$ = 10,626 ways of selecting four of the 24 dishwashers, and they are all equiprobable since the selection is random. Among these, there are $\binom{20}{4}$ = 4,845 ways of selecting four of the 20 dishwashers in perfect condition, and it follows by the rule for equiprobable outcomes that the desired probability is $\frac{4,845}{10,626} = 0.456$.

To generalize the method used in the preceding example, suppose that n objects are to be chosen from a set of a objects of one kind (successes) and *b* objects of another kind (failures) and that we are interested in the probability of getting "*x* successes and *n* − *x* failures." Arguing as before, we can say that the *x* successes can be chosen in $\binom{a}{x}$ ways, the *n* − *x* failures can be chosen in $\binom{b}{n-x}$ ways, and, hence *x* successes and *n* − *x* failures can be chosen in $\binom{a}{x} \cdot \binom{b}{n-x}$ ways. Also, *n* objects can be chosen from the whole set of *a* + *b* objects in $\binom{a+b}{n}$ ways, and if we regard all these possibilities as equally likely, it follows that the probability of getting "*x* successes and *n* − *x* failures" is

Hypergeometric distribution

$$f(x) = \frac{\binom{a}{x} \cdot \binom{b}{n-x}}{\binom{a+b}{n}} \qquad \text{for } x = 0, 1, 2, \ldots, \text{ or } n$$

This is the formula for the **hypergeometric distribution**, and it applies only when *x* does not exceed *a* and *n* − *x* does not exceed *b*, since we cannot very well get more successes (or failures) than there are in the whole set.

EXAMPLE 7.7 Among a department store's 16 delivery trucks, 5 have worn brakes. If 8 trucks are randomly picked for inspection, what is the probability that this sample will include at least three trucks with worn brakes?

SOLUTION The probability we want to find is $f(3) + f(4) + f(5)$, where each term in this sum is to be calculated by means of the formula for the hypergeometric distribution with *a* = 5, *b* = 11, and *n* = 8. Substituting these values together with *x* = 3, then *x* = 4, and *x* = 5, we get

$$f(3) = \frac{\binom{5}{3} \cdot \binom{11}{5}}{\binom{16}{8}} = \frac{10 \cdot 462}{12{,}870} = 0.359$$

$$f(4) = \frac{\binom{5}{4} \cdot \binom{11}{4}}{\binom{16}{8}} = \frac{5 \cdot 330}{12,870} = 0.128$$

$$f(5) = \frac{\binom{5}{5} \cdot \binom{11}{3}}{\binom{16}{8}} = \frac{1 \cdot 165}{12,870} = 0.013$$

and the probability that the sample will include at least three trucks with worn brakes is

$$0.359 + 0.128 + 0.013 = 0.500 \qquad \blacksquare$$

In the beginning of this section we introduced the hypergeometric distribution with an example in which we first erroneously used the binomial distribution. The error was not large though—we got 0.482 instead of 0.456—and in actual practice the binomial distribution is often used to approximate the hypergeometric distribution. It is generally agreed that this approximation is satisfactory if n constitutes less than 5 percent of $a + b$. The main advantages of the approximation are that the binomial distribution has been tabulated much more extensively than the hypergeometric distribution and that it is generally easier to use.

7.5

The Poisson Distribution

If n is large and p is small, binomial probabilities are often approximated by means of the formula

Poisson distribution

$$f(x) = \frac{(np)^x \cdot e^{-np}}{x!} \qquad \text{for } x = 0, 1, 2, 3, \ldots$$

which is that for the **Poisson distribution**. Here the irrational number $e = 2.71828 \ldots$ is the base of the system of natural logarithms, and the values of e^{-np} may be read from Table X at the end of the book. For the Poisson distribution, the random variable x can take on the infinite set of values $x = 0, 1, 2, 3, \ldots$; practically speaking, though, this poses no problems, since the probabilities become negligible (very close to zero) after the first few values of x.

EXAMPLE 7.8 Records show that the probability is 0.00005 that a car will have a flat tire while driving through a certain tunnel. Use the Poisson approximation to the binomial distribution to find the probability that among 10,000 cars passing through this tunnel at least two will have a flat tire.

SOLUTION Subtract from 1 the probabilities that 0 or 1 of the cars will have a flat tire. Since $np = 10,000(0.00005) = 0.5$ and $e^{-0.5} = 0.607$ (see Table X), we find that

$$f(0) = \frac{(0.5)^0(0.607)}{0!} = 0.607$$

$$f(1) = \frac{(0.5)^1(0.607)}{1!} = 0.304$$

and the probability that at least two cars will have a flat tire is $1 - (0.607 + 0.304) = 0.089$. ∎

Poisson probabilities such as those obtained in the foregoing example can also be solved by reference to tables of Poisson probabilities, which may be found in handbooks of statistical tables or through the use of a computer. The printout of Figure 7.4 shows "POISSON PROBABILITIES FOR MEAN = 0.500," which is the same as our $np = 0.5$. Using this printout to solve Example 7.8, we find that the answer is $1 - 0.9098 = 0.0902$, where 0.9098 is the value in the right-hand column corresponding to $K = 1$. An

```
MTB > POISSON MU=.5


POISSON PROBABILITIES FOR MEAN = 0.500

         K        P(X = K)        P(X LESS OR = K)
         0         0.6065            0.6065
         1         0.3033            0.9098
         2         0.0758            0.9856
         3         0.0126            0.9982
         4         0.0016            0.9998
         5         0.0002            1.0000
```

FIGURE 7.4
Computer printout of the Poisson distribution with $np = 0.5$

alternative way of obtaining the answer is to locate $K = 2, 3, 4,$ and 5 in the first column of the printout and, reading across the rows to column 2, obtain the corresponding probabilities 0.0758, 0.0126, 0.0016, and 0.0002. The sum of these probabilities also equals 0.0902. The difference between the result using the printout and the result obtained in Example 7.8 is due to rounding.

The Poisson distribution has many important applications which have no direct connection with the binomial distribution. In these cases np is replaced by the parameter λ (Greek lowercase lambda) and we calculate the probability of getting x "successes" by means of the formula

Poisson distribution (with parameter λ)

$$f(x) = \frac{\lambda^x \cdot e^{-\lambda}}{x!} \qquad for\ x = 0, 1, 2, 3, \ldots$$

where the parameter λ is interpreted as the expected, or average, number of successes.

The formula applies in many situations where we can expect a fixed number of "successes" per unit time (or for some other kind of unit), say, when a bank can expect to receive 6 bad checks per day, when 1.6 accidents can be expected per day at a busy intersection, when 12 small pieces of meat can be expected in a frozen meat pie, when 5.2 imperfections can be expected per roll of cloth, when 0.3 complaint per visitor can be expected by the manager of a resort, and so on.

EXAMPLE 7.9 If a bank receives on the average $\lambda = 6$ bad checks per day, what is the probability that it will receive four bad checks on a given day?

SOLUTION Substituting $\lambda = 6$ and $x = 4$ into the formula, we get

$$f(4) = \frac{6^4 \cdot e^{-6}}{4!} = \frac{(1,296)(0.0025)}{24} = 0.135 \qquad \blacksquare$$

EXAMPLE 7.10 If $\lambda = 1.6$ accidents can be expected at a certain intersection per day, what is the probability that there will be three accidents at the intersection on a given day?

SOLUTION Substituting $\lambda = 1.6$ and $x = 3$ into the formula, we get

$$f(3) = \frac{1.6^3 \cdot e^{-1.6}}{3!} = \frac{(4.096)(0.202)}{6} = 0.138 \qquad \blacksquare$$

```
MTB > POISSON MU=1.6


POISSON PROBABILITIES FOR MEAN =   1.600
     K            P(X = K)          P(X LESS OR = K)
     0             0.2019             0.2019
     1             0.3230             0.5249
     2             0.2584             0.7834
     3             0.1378             0.9212
     4             0.0551             0.9763
     5             0.0176             0.9940
     6             0.0047             0.9987
     7             0.0011             0.9997
     8             0.0002             1.0000
     9             0.0000             1.0000
```

FIGURE 7.5
Computer printout
of the Poisson
distribution with
$np = 1.6$

The computer printout of Figure 7.5 is very much the same as that of Figure 7.4 except that we now use a mean of 1.6, corresponding to $\lambda = 1.6$ accidents expected at a certain intersection per day. Using the printout to solve this problem, we find that the answer is 0.1378, where 0.1378 is the value in the second column corresponding to $K = 3$, which refers to the probability that there will be 3 accidents at the intersection on a given day.

7.6

The Multinomial Distribution

An important generalization of the binomial distribution arises when there are more than two possible outcomes for each trial, the probabilities of the various outcomes remain the same for each trial, and the trials are independent. This is the case, for example, in repeated rolls of a die where each trial has six possible outcomes, when students are asked whether they like a certain recording, dislike it, or are indifferent toward it, or when a USDA inspector grades beef as prime, choice, good, commercial, or utility.

If there are k possible outcomes for each trial and their probabilities are $p_1, p_2, \ldots,$ and p_k, it can be shown that the probability of x_1 outcomes of the first kind, x_2 outcomes of the second kind, $\ldots,$ and x_k outcomes of the kth kind in n trials is given by

$$\frac{n!}{x_1!x_2!\cdot\ \cdots\ \cdot x_k!}\, p_1^{x_1} \cdot p_2^{x_2} \cdot\ \cdots\ \cdot p_k^{x_k}$$

This distribution is called the **multinomial distribution**.

EXAMPLE 7.11   If four clerks prepare all the billings in a company office and it has been determined that 40 percent of all erroneous billings are prepared by clerk A, 20 percent by clerk B, 10 percent by clerk C, and the rest by clerk D, what is the probability that among seven randomly selected erroneous billings two were prepared by A, one by B, one by C, and three by D?

SOLUTION   Substituting $n = 7$, $x_1 = 2$, $x_2 = 1$, $x_3 = 1$, $x_4 = 3$, $p_1 = 0.4$, $p_2 = 0.2$, $p_3 = 0.1$, and $p_4 = 0.3$ into the formula, we get

$$\frac{7!}{2! \cdot 1! \cdot 1! \cdot 3!}\,(0.4)^2(0.2)^1(0.1)^1(0.3)^3 = 0.036 \qquad \blacksquare$$

EXERCISES

(Exercises 7.16, 7.22, 7.25, 7.28, 7.31, and 7.32 are practice exercises. Their complete solutions are given on page 291.)

7.16   Among 14 new electric razors which are packaged for shipment, there are 6 in which the operating instructions brochure is not included. If 2 of these packaged razors are randomly selected for inspection, what are the probabilities that

(a) neither packaged razor contains the operating instructions brochure

(b) 1 packaged razor contains the operating instructions brochure

(c) both packaged razors contain the operating instructions brochure

7.17   Find the probability that an Internal Revenue Service auditor will get 3 tax returns with unallowable deductions if she randomly selects 5 returns from among 15 returns, 7 of which contain unallowable deductions.

7.18   A supplier has 20 female and 10 male mice, and 5 are randomly selected for sale to a laboratory. Find the probability distribution of the number of female mice selected and draw a histogram of this distribution.

7.19   Of 19 management trainees in a corporation, 11 are graduates of a college of business administration. If 6 are chosen for practical training in the production department, what is the probability that at least 4 of them are graduates of a college of business administration?

7.20   Among 14 women department store sales associates, 5 have one or more preschool children. If 2 of these employees are randomly selected, find the probabilities that

(a) neither has a preschool child

(b) 1 has at least one preschool child

(c) both have at least one preschool child

7.21   Among the repair jobs to 16 automobiles for ignition problems, 4 repairs were unsatisfactory, and the automobiles were returned to the service shop for completion of the job. Find the probability distribution of the number of unsatisfactory repairs in a random sample of 3 repair jobs taken without replacement from the 16 automobiles.

7.22   To pass a quality control inspection 2 microwave ovens are chosen from each lot of 10 microwave ovens, and the lot is passed only if neither microwave oven has any defects; otherwise each of the microwave ovens in the lot is checked. If the selection of microwave ovens is random, find the probabilities that a lot will

(a) pass inspection when 1 of the 10 microwave ovens is defective

(b) fail the inspection when 3 of the 10 microwave ovens are defective

(c) fail the inspection when 6 of the 10 microwave ovens are defective

7.23   A wholesaler has an inventory of 100 individually boxed portable radios which he believes to be black but 5 of which are white. If 3 of these radios are randomly selected and shipped to a customer, find the probability that the customer will receive exactly 1 white radio using

(a) the formula for the hypergeometric distribution

(b) the binomial distribution as an approximation

What is the error of the approximation of part (b)?

7.24   The portfolio of a global mutual fund includes 30 common stock positions in U.S. corporations and 50 stock positions of corporations outside the United States. If the stocks of 4 corporations are randomly selected for study, find the probability that 2 of them will be stocks of U.S. corporations and the other 2 will be stocks of corporations outside the United States, using

(a) the formula for the hypergeometric distribution

(b) the binomial distribution as an approximation

What is the error of the approximation of part (b)?

 7.25   One and one-half percent of the letters mailed from the mailroom of a company do not have the correct postage. Use the Poisson approximation to the binomial distribution to determine the probability that in a random sample of 200 letters, 2 do not have the correct postage. The values of e^{-x} are found in Table X. Verify your answer using a computer printout of the Poisson distribution with $np = 3.0$.

7.26 A mail-order firm knows from experience that 2.8 percent of its sales are exchanged by customers because they ordered the wrong size or color, changed their minds, and so forth. Use Table X and the Poisson approximation to the binomial distribution to determine the probability that among 225 orders, 6 will be exchanged. Verify your answer by using a computer printout of the Poisson distribution with $np = 6.3$.

7.27 The personnel department of a large company knows that the turnover rate (voluntary quits and terminations) of production workers is 1.7 percent per month. Use Table X to determine the approximate probablity that in a random sample of 300 workers, 8 will quit or be terminated during a month. Verify your answer by using a computer printout of the Poisson distribution with $np = 5.1$

7.28 The number of textbooks turned in each day to the lost and found department of a university is a random variable with $\lambda = 4.5$. Use Table X and the Poisson approximation to the binominal distribution to find the probabilities that on any given day the lost and found department will receive

(a) no books

(b) at least one book

(c) two books

(d) four books

Verify your answers by using a computer printout of the Poisson distribution with $\lambda = 4.5$.

7.29 The number of patients who are received per hour in the emergency room of a hospital is a random variable having the Poisson distribution with $\lambda = 3.5$. Use Table X and the Poisson approximation to the binomial distribution to find the probabilities that in any given hour the emergency room will receive

(a) no patients

(b) at least one patient

(c) two patients

(d) four patients

Verify your answers by using a computer printout of the Poisson distribution with $\lambda = 3.5$.

7.30 Suppose the number of telephone calls answered per minute by a telephone answering service is a random variable having the Poisson distribution with $\lambda = 1.7$. Use Table X and the Poisson approximation to the binomial distribution to find the probabilities that during a minute the answering service will answer

(a) no telephone calls

(b) one telephone call

Section 7.6   The Multinomial Distribution   **275**

(c) two telephone calls

(d) at least three telephone calls

Verify your answer by using a computer printout of the Poisson distribution with $\lambda = 1.7$.

7.31   Al, a salesperson for a tire company, claims he makes 50 percent of the tire sales for the company and that the other two salespersons, Bess and Chuck, make 30 percent and 20 percent. If Al is correct, what is the probability that among eight randomly selected sales slips four will credit Al with the sales, two will credit Bess with the sales, and two will credit Chuck with the sales?

7.32   In an effort to computerize its delivery schedule, a retail fuel oil company has developed a mathematical model to describe the oil delivery needs of its customers. Ideally for the customer and the company, deliveries should be made when the customer's tank is one-fourth full. Because of the assumptions made in the model, the company found that only 50 percent of the deliveries made were to tanks that were one-fourth full, 30 percent were made to tanks that were more than one-fourth full and less than one-half full, and 10 percent were made to tanks less than one-fourth full. What is the probability that among 10 randomly chosen deliveries five tanks will be one-fourth full, three will be more than one-fourth full but less than one-half full, one will be at least one-half full, and one will be less than one-fourth full?

7.7

The Mean of a Probability Distribution

When we say that an airline office at an airport can expect 2.91 complaints per day about its luggage handling, we are referring to the sum of the products obtained by multiplying 0, 1, 2, 3, 4, . . . , by the probabilities that it will receive 0, 1, 2, 3, 4, . . . , complaints on any one day. If we apply the same argument to the illustrations of Section 7.2, we find that, between them, the two contractors can expect to get

$$0(0.30) + 1(0.40) + 2(0.30) = 1$$

of the two jobs, the number of points we can expect in the roll of a die is

$$1 \cdot \frac{1}{6} + 2 \cdot \frac{1}{6} + 3 \cdot \frac{1}{6} + 4 \cdot \frac{1}{6} + 5 \cdot \frac{1}{6} + 6 \cdot \frac{1}{6} = 3\frac{1}{2}$$

and the number of heads we can expect in four flips of a balanced coin is

$$0 \cdot \frac{1}{16} + 1 \cdot \frac{4}{16} + 2 \cdot \frac{6}{16} + 3 \cdot \frac{4}{16} + 4 \cdot \frac{1}{16} = 2$$

Of course, we cannot actually roll a $3\frac{1}{2}$ with a die; as with all mathematical expectations, this figure must be looked upon as an average.

In general, if a random variable takes on the values $x_1, x_2, x_3, \ldots,$ and x_k, with the probabilities $f(x_1), f(x_2), f(x_3), \ldots,$ and $f(x_k)$, its expected value (or its mathematical expectation) is given by the quantity.

$$x_1 \cdot f(x_1) + x_2 \cdot f(x_2) + x_3 \cdot f(x_3) + \cdots + x_k \cdot f(x_k)$$

called the **mean of the random variable** or the **mean of its probability distribution**. The mean of a random variable is usually denoted by the Greek letter μ (lowercase mu), and using the Σ notation, we can write

*Mean of
probability
distribution*

$$\mu = \Sigma \, x \cdot f(x)$$

EXAMPLE 7.12   With reference to Example 7.3 on page 259, how many of five randomly selected supermarket customers can be expected to use the express lane to check out their order?

SOLUTION   Substituting $x = 0, 1, 2, 3, 4,$ and 5 and the probabilities in Example 7.3 into the formula $\mu = \Sigma \, x \cdot f(x)$, we get

$$\mu = 0(0.328) + 1(0.410) + 2(0.205) + 3(0.051) + 4(0.006)$$
$$+ 5(0.000)$$
$$= 0.997 \qquad \blacksquare$$

When a random variable can take on many different values, the calculation of μ usually becomes quite laborious. For instance, if we want to know how many among 800 customers entering a store can be expected to make a purchase, and the probability that any one of them will make a purchase is 0.40, we would first have to calculate the 801 probabilities corresponding to 0, 1, 2, . . . , and 800 of them making a purchase. However, if we think for a moment, we might argue that in the long run 40 percent of the customers make a purchase, 40 percent of 800 is 320, and, hence, we can expect 320 of the 800 customers to make a purchase. Similarly, if a balanced coin is flipped 1,000 times, we can argue that in the long run heads will come up 50 percent of the time and, hence, that we can expect $(1,000)(0.50) = 500$ heads. These two values are, indeed, correct, and it can be shown that, in general, there exists the special formula

Mean of binomial distribution

$$\mu = n \cdot p$$

for the mean of a binomial distribution. In words, the mean of a binomial distribution is simply the product of the number of trials and the probability of success on an individual trial.

EXAMPLE 7.13 With reference to Example 7.3, the manager of the supermarket wants to know the mean of the probability distribution of the number of customers among five randomly selected customers who use the express lane to check out their order.

SOLUTION Since we are dealing with a binomial distribution with $n = 5$ and $p = 0.20$, we have $\mu = n \cdot p = 5(0.20) = 1.00$. The small difference of 0.003 between this exact value and the value obtained in Example 7.12 is due to rounding the probabilities to three decimals in the earlier calculations. ■

EXAMPLE 7.14 Find the mean of the probability distribution of the number of heads obtained in four flips of a balanced coin.

SOLUTION For a binomial distribution with $n = 4$ and $p = \frac{1}{2}$, we get $\mu = 4 \cdot \frac{1}{2} = 2$, and this agrees with the result obtained in the beginning of this section. ■

It is important to remember, of course, that the formula $\mu = n \cdot p$ applies only to binomial distributions. Fortunately, there are other formulas for other distributions; for the hypergeometric distribution, for example, the formula for the mean is

Mean of hypergeometric distribution

$$\mu = \frac{n \cdot a}{a + b}$$

EXAMPLE 7.15   Among 16 delivery trucks, 5 have worn brakes. If 8 trucks are ran-
                domly picked for inspection, how many of them can be expected to
                have worn brakes?

SOLUTION   We have here a hypergeometric distribution with $a = 5, b = 11$, and
            $n = 8$, and substitution into the formula yields

$$\mu = \frac{8 \cdot 5}{5 + 11} = 2.5$$

This should not come as a surprise; half the trucks are selected and
half the ones with worn brakes are expected to be included in the
sample.   ■

Also, the mean of the Poisson distribution is simply $\mu = \lambda$. Formal
proofs of all these special formulas may be found in any textbook on mathematical statistics.

7.8

The Standard Deviation of a Probability Distribution

We saw in Chapter 3 that there are many cases in which we must
describe, in addition to the mean or some other measure of location, the
variability (spread, or dispersion) of a set of data. The most widely used
statistical measures of variation are the variance and its square root, the
standard deviation, which both measure variability by averaging the squared
deviations from the mean. For probability distributions, we measure variability in almost the same way, but instead of averaging the squared deviations from the mean, we calculate their expected value. If x is a value of
some random variable whose probability distribution has the mean μ, the
deviation from the mean is $x - \mu$, and we define the **variance of the probability distribution** as the expected value of the squared deviation from the
mean, that is, as

Variance of probability distribution

$$\sigma^2 = \sum (x - \mu)^2 \cdot f(x)$$

where the summation extends over all values assumed by the random variable. The square root of the variance defines the **standard deviation, σ, of a probability distribution**, and we write

Standard deviation of probability distribution

$$\sigma = \sqrt{\sum (x - \mu)^2 \cdot f(x)}$$

EXAMPLE 7.16   Use the probabilities obtained in Example 7.3 to determine the standard deviation of the probability distribution of the numbers of customers who will use the express lane to check out their orders at the supermarket.

SOLUTION   Here $\mu = 5(0.20) = 1.00$ customer, and using the formula $\sigma = \sqrt{\sum (x - \mu)^2 \cdot f(x)}$, we arrange the calculations as follows.

Number of customers	Probability	Deviation from mean	Squared deviation from mean	
x	$f(x)$	$(x - \mu)$	$(x - \mu)^2$	$(x - \mu)^2 f(x)$
0	0.328	-1	1	0.328
1	0.410	0	0	0
2	0.205	1	1	0.205
3	0.051	2	4	0.204
4	0.006	3	9	0.054
5	0.000	4	16	0

$$\sigma^2 = 0.791$$

The values in the column on the right were obtained by multiplying each squared deviation from the mean by its probability, and their sum is the variance of the distribution. Also $\sigma = \sqrt{0.791} = 0.89$. ■

The calculations in Example 7.16 were quite easy since the deviations from the mean were small whole numbers. If the deviations from the mean are large numbers, or if they are given to several decimals, it is usually worthwhile to simplify the calculations by using the computing formula for σ^2 given in Exercise 7.35 on page 284.

As in the case of the mean, the calculation of the variance or the standard deviation of a probability distribution can often be simplified when dealing with special kinds of probability distributions. For instance, for the binomial distribution we have the formula

Standard deviation of binomial distribution

$$\sigma = \sqrt{np(1 - p)}$$

EXAMPLE 7.17   Use this formula to verify the result obtained in Example 7.16.

SOLUTION   For a binomial distribution with $n = 5$ and $p = 0.20$, the formula $\sigma = \sqrt{np(1 - p)}$ yields

$$\sigma^2 = 5(0.20)(0.80) = 0.800$$

and this exact value differs from the result obtained in Example 7.16 by the rounding error of $0.800 - 0.791 = 0.009$.   ■

EXAMPLE 7.18   Find the variance of the probability distribution of the number of heads obtained in four flips of a balanced coin.

SOLUTION   The variance of the binomial distribution with $n = 4$ and $p = \dfrac{1}{2}$ is

$$\sigma^2 = 4 \cdot \frac{1}{2} \cdot \frac{1}{2} = 1$$ ■

There also exist special formulas for the standard deviation of other special distributions, and they may be found in more advanced texts.

7.9

Chebyshev's Theorem

Intuitively speaking, the variance and the standard deviation of a probability distribution measure its spread or its dispersion: When σ is small, the probability is high that we will get a value close to the mean, and when σ is large, we are more likely to get a value far away from the mean. This important idea is expressed rigorously in a theorem called **Chebyshev's theorem**, which we introduced in Chapter 3. For probability distributions, this theorem can be stated as follows:

> The probability that a random variable will take on a value within k standard deviations of the mean is at least
>
> $$1 - \frac{1}{k^2}$$

For instance, the probability of getting a value within two standard deviations of the mean (a value between $\mu - 2\sigma$ and $\mu + 2\sigma$) is at least $1 - \frac{1}{2^2} = \frac{3}{4}$, the probability of getting a value within five standard deviations of the mean (a value between $\mu - 5\sigma$ and $\mu + 5\sigma$) is at least $1 - \frac{1}{5^2} = \frac{24}{25}$, and so forth. When Chebyshev's theorem is used to illustrate the relationship between the standard deviation of a probability distribution and its spread or dispersion, k is often chosen more or less arbitrarily; k can be any positive number, although the theorem becomes trivial when k is 1 or less.

EXAMPLE 7.19 The number of telephone calls which an answering service receives between 10 A.M. and 11 A.M. is a random variable whose distribution has the mean $\mu = 26$ and the standard deviation $\sigma = 3\frac{1}{3}$. What does Chebyshev's theorem with $k = 3$, for instance, tell us about the number of telephone calls which the answering service may receive between 10 A.M. and 11 A.M.?

SOLUTION Since $\mu - 3\sigma = 26 - 3\left(3\frac{1}{3}\right) = 16$ and $\mu + 3\sigma = 26 + 3\left(\frac{1}{3}\right) = 36$,

we can assert with a probability of at least $1 - \frac{1}{3^2} = \frac{8}{9}$, or approximately 0.89, that the answering service will receive between 16 and 36 calls. ∎

EXAMPLE 7.20 What does Chebyshev's theorem with $k = 6$, for instance, tell us about the number of heads we may get in 400 flips of a balanced coin?

SOLUTION   For the binomial distribution with $n = 400$ and $p = \dfrac{1}{2}$, the mean

and the standard deviation are $\mu = n \cdot p = 400 \cdot \dfrac{1}{2} = 200$ and

$\sigma = \sqrt{np(1-p)} = \sqrt{400 \cdot \dfrac{1}{2} \cdot \dfrac{1}{2}} = 10$, so that $\mu - 6\sigma = 200 -$

$6 \cdot 10 = 140$ and $\mu + 6\sigma = 200 + 6 \cdot 10 = 260$. Thus, we can

assert with a probability of at least $1 - \dfrac{1}{6^2} = \dfrac{35}{36}$, or approximately

0.97, that we will get between 140 and 260 heads.   ∎

If we convert the numbers of heads into proportions, we can assert with
a probability of at least $\dfrac{35}{36}$ that the proportion of heads we get in 400 flips of
a balanced coin will lie between $\dfrac{140}{400} = 0.35$ and $\dfrac{260}{400} = 0.65$. To continue
this argument, the reader will be asked to show in Exercise 7.51 on page 286
that the probability is at least $\dfrac{35}{36}$ that for 10,000 flips of a balanced coin the
proportion of heads will lie between 0.47 and 0.53, and that for 1,000,000
flips of a balanced coin it will lie between 0.497 and 0.503. This provides
support for the **Law of Large Numbers**, which we mentioned in Section 4.3
in connection with the frequency interpretation of probability.

The probability statement which Chebyshev's theorem enables us to
make, though mathematically correct, is often unnecessarily weak—that is,
the probability is often unnecessarily small. For instance, in the preceding
example we showed that the probability of getting a value within six standard
deviations of the mean is at least 0.97, whereas the actual probability that
this will happen for a random variable having the binomial distribution with
$n = 400$ and $p = \dfrac{1}{2}$ is about 0.999999998.

EXERCISES

(Exercises 7.33, 7.34, 7.35, 7.38, 7.42, 7.43, 7.45, 7.48, and 7.49 are practice
exercises. Their complete solutions are given on page 291.)

7.33   The probabilities that zero, one, two, or three workers will be injured in a
factory during a month are 0.50, 0.30, 0.15, and 0.05. Find the mean and
variance of this probability distribution.

7.34 The following table gives the probabilities that zero, one, two, three, four, five, or six oceangoing oil tankers will be unloaded in a port per day.

Number of oil tankers	0	1	2	3	4	5	6
Probability	0.10	0.27	0.36	0.13	0.07	0.06	0.01

Calculate the mean and standard deviation of this distribution.

7.35 Using the rules for summations given in Section 3.10, we can derive the following shortcut formula for the variance of a probability distribution:

$$\sigma^2 = \sum x^2 \cdot f(x) - \mu^2$$

The advantage of this formula is that we do not have to work with the deviations from the mean. Instead, we subtract μ^2 from the sum of the products obtained by multiplying the square of each value of the random variable by the corresponding probability. Use this formula to find

(a) the variance of the probability distribution of Exercise 7.33

(b) the standard deviation of the probability distribution of Exercise 7.34

7.36 Use the formula of the preceding exercise to recalculate σ^2 and σ for the probability distribution of customers who use the express lane at the supermarket which is shown in Example 7.16 on page 280.

7.37 Find σ^2 for the distribution of the number of times a fair coin falls heads in four flips, using the probabilities on page 256 and

(a) the definition formula on page 280

(b) the shortcut formula of Exercise 7.35

Also compare the results with that obtained on page 281 with the special formula $\sigma^2 = np(1 - p)$.

7.38 Find the mean and the standard deviation of the number of points rolled with a balanced die.

7.39 Find the mean and standard deviation of the binomial distribution with $n = 7$ and $p = 0.20$ using

(a) the definition formulas for the mean and standard deviation of a probability distribution

(b) the special formulas for the mean and the standard deviation of a binomial distribution

7.40 A recent study done by the Center for Social Organization of Schools at Johns Hopkins University discloses that 60 percent of middle grades schools have 15 or more computers used by students or teachers. Find the mean and vari-

Chapter 7 Probability Distributions

ance of the distribution of the number of randomly selected middle grades schools (among eight middle grades schools that a computer salesperson plans to visit) using

(a) the definition formulas for the mean of a probability distribution and the shortcut formula for the variance given in Exercise 7.35

(b) the special formulas for the mean and the variance of a binomial distribution

7.41 Find the mean and the standard deviation of the distribution of each of the following random variables having binomial distributions:

(a) the number of tails obtained in 576 flips of a balanced coin

(b) the number of 3's obtained in 636 rolls of a balanced die

(c) the number of guests attending an awards banquet, among 750 invited, when the probability is 0.65 that any one of them will attend

(d) the number of customers who buy from a catalog, among 125 who requested the catalog, when the probability is 0.15 that any one of them will buy from the catalog

(e) the number of households, among 2,500 randomly selected households, who care for their own cars when (according to the Newspaper Advertising Bureau Inc.) the probability is 0.17 that a household will care for its own car, and 0.83 that it will be cared for by, say, a service station

7.42 If 5 of 18 boats in a marina cannot pass a Coast Guard safety inspection and 8 boats are randomly selected for inspection, the probabilities are $0.029, 0.196$, and 0.392 that 0, 1, or 2 of the 8 selected boats cannot pass inspection.

(a) Show that the probabilities are $0.294, 0.082$, and 0.006 that 3, 4, or 5 boats of the 8 cannot pass inspection.

(b) Using all these probabilities, calculate the mean of the distribution of the number of boats which cannot pass inspection that will be included among the 8.

(c) Compare the value obtained for μ in part (b) with the value of the mean, $\mu = 2.222$, obtained by the formula for the mean of a hypergeometric distribution.

7.43 With reference to the preceding exercise, find the variance of the distribution of the number of boats which cannot pass inspection and are among the 8 randomly selected boats.

7.44 Two of 15 paychecks prepared by the payroll department are calculated inaccurately and the rest are calculated accurately. If an auditor draws a random sample of 2 paychecks without replacement

(a) Find the probability distribution of the number of paychecks in the sample with inaccurate calculations.

(b) Use the probabilities obtained in part (a) to calculate the mean of this distribution and compare it with the value yielded by the special formula for the mean of a hypergeometric distribution.

7.45 The probabilities that the security police in an office building will respond to zero, one, two, three, four, or five emergencies in a day are 0.449, 0.360, 0.144, 0.038, 0.008, and 0.001. Calculate the mean of this Poisson distribution with $\lambda = 0.8$ and use the result to confirm (subject to an error due to rounding) the special formula $\mu = \lambda$ for the mean of a Poisson distribution.

7.46 Use the probabilities of the preceding exercise and the shortcut formula of Exercise 7.35 to calculate the variance of the given distribution, and use the result to confirm (subject to an error due to rounding) the special formula $\sigma^2 = \lambda$ for the variance of a Poisson distribution.

7.47 If the weekly number of residential sales made by a real estate brokerage office is a random variable having the Poisson distribution with $\lambda = 4$, the probabilities of 0, 1, 2, 3, . . . , or 12 residential sales are 0.018, 0.073, 0.147, 0.195, 0.195, 0.156, 0.104, 0.060, 0.030, 0.013, 0.005, 0.002, and 0.001.

   (a) Calculate the mean of this distribution and use the result to verify (subject to an error due to rounding) the special formula $\mu = \lambda$ for the mean of a Poisson distribution.

   (b) Calculate the standard deviation of this distribution, and use the result to verify (subject to an error due to rounding) the special formula $\sigma = \sqrt{\lambda}$ for the standard deviation of a Poisson distribution.

7.48 A traffic signal alternates regularly between red and green at 1-minute time intervals. When the signal is red, an approaching vehicle must stop, and when the signal is green, an approaching vehicle may go. If a certain vehicle reaches the signal at 36 randomly selected times, what does Chebyshev's theorem with $k = 3$ tell us about the number of times this vehicle must stop?

7.49 The daily number of flights of private aircraft departing from an airport per business day is a random variable with $\mu = 130$ and $\sigma = 10$. According to Chebyshev's theorem, with what probability can we assert that between 80 and 180 aircraft will depart from the airport on any given business day?

7.50 The monthly number of orders for wedding invitations processed by a printing company is a random variable with $\mu = 75$ and $\sigma = 4$.

   (a) What does Chebyshev's theorem with $k = 6$ tell us about the number of orders for wedding invitations processed in any given month?

   (b) According to Chebyshev's theorem, with what probability can we assert that the printer will process between 61 and 89 orders for wedding invitations per month?

7.51 Use Chebyshev's theorem to show that the probability is at least $\frac{35}{36}$ that

   (a) in 10,000 flips of a balanced coin there will be between 4,700 and 5,300 heads, and hence the proportion of heads will be between 0.47 and 0.53

(b) in 1,000,000 flips of a balanced coin there will be between 497,000 and 503,000 heads, and hence the proportion of heads will be between 0.497 and 0.503

7.10

A Word of Caution

When we use a specific probability distribution to describe a given situation, we must be sure that we are using the right model. For instance, we must make sure that we do not use the binomial distribution when we should be using the hypergeometric distribution, or that we do not use the Poisson distribution when we should be using some other distribution, unless, of course, we are intentionally making approximations. Specifically, we must always make sure that the assumptions underlying the distribution which we choose are actually met. Thus, it would be a mistake to use the binomial distribution to determine, say, the probability that there will be five rainy days at a given resort during the first two weeks in August, or the probability that 8 of 100 persons (whose ages range from 18 to 79) will be hospitalized at least once during the coming year. In the first case the successive trials are clearly not independent, and in the second case the probability of being hospitalized is not the same for each trial (person).

7.11

Checklist for Key Terms

7.12

Review Exercises

7.52 The manager of an apartment building complex knows that 12 percent of the tenants are late in making their monthly rental payments. Find the probability that in a random sample of eight tenants

(a) one tenant is late in paying his rent this month

(b) at least one tenant is late in paying his rent this month

7.53 If a florist has 10 geraniums on display, 7 in green flowerpots and the rest in white flowerpots, and a customer buys 6 of these potted plants, selecting them at random, what are the probabilities that she selects

(a) 4 geraniums in green flowerpots

(b) at least 4 geraniums in green flowerpots

7.54 In each case determine whether the given values can be looked upon as the values of a probability distribution of a random variable which can take on the values 1, 2, and 3, and explain your answers.

(a) $f(1) = \frac{1}{10}, f(2) = \frac{1}{5}, f(3) = \frac{7}{10}$

(b) $f(1) = 0.46, f(2) = 0.23, f(3) = 0.35$

(c) $f(1) = 0.63 + f(2) = -0.10 + f(3) = 0.47$

7.55 The probabilities that a real estate broker will sell zero, one, two, or three houses in a month are 0.43, 0.27, 0.23, and 0.07. Find the mean of this probability distribution.

7.56 Find the variance of the probability distribution of the preceding exercise.

7.57 If the probability is 90 percent that taxpayers subjected to a field audit by the Internal Revenue Service will have an upward adjustment of taxes (as reported by *The Wall Street Journal*), what is the probability that an IRS revenue agent will

(a) first conduct an audit of a taxpayer without making an upward adjustment, and then audit a second taxpayer who will receive an upward adjustment of taxes

(b) conduct two consecutive audits of taxpayers without upward adjustment, and then audit a third taxpayer who will receive an upward adjustment of taxes

(c) conduct three consecutive audits of taxpayers without upward adjustment, and then audit a fourth taxpayer who will receive an upward adjustment of taxes

7.58 A cage in a pet store contains 6 male and 14 female parakeets. If a sales associate randomly selects 2 birds from this cage, what is the probability that both are of the same sex?

7.59 Among 18 persons at an employee meeting of a firm, 6 are from the sales department. If 4 of the 18 are selected at random for a committee, find

(a) the probabilities that zero, one, two, three, or four are from the sales department

(b) the mean of this probability distribution

Verify the results of part (b) by using the special formula for the mean of such a distribution.

7.60 The owner of a greeting card shop knows from experience that the probabilities are 0.50, 0.30, and 0.20 that a shopper in her store will purchase no greeting cards, one greeting card, or two or more greeting cards. What is the probability that among eight shoppers in the store four will purchase no greeting cards, three will purchase one, and one will purchase two or more?

7.61 Find the mean and the variance of the binomial distribution with $n = 4$ and $p = 0.30$ using

(a) the formulas for the mean and the variance of a probability distribution

(b) the special formulas for the mean and the variance of a binomial distribution

7.62 The daily number of residential fires in a certain town has a Poisson distribution with $\lambda = 2.5$. Find the probability that on one randomly selected day there are at least two residential fires.

7.63 A student marks the 49 questions on a weekly true-false test by flipping a balanced coin and marking the question true for tails and false for heads.

(a) What does Chebyshev's theorem with $k = 3$ indicate about the number of correct answers he will obtain?

(b) What does Chebyshev's theorem say about the probability that between 10.5 and 38.5 answers will be correct?

7.64 Suppose that of all the franchise operations of a large fast-food franchisor, 60 percent are profitable. What is the probability that 6 of 10 randomly chosen franchise operations of this kind are profitable?

7.65 Ninety percent of all sales personnel in a national sales organization meet their sales quotas. What are the probabilities that in a random sample of 12 salespersons

(a) at most 9 salespersons meet their quotas

(b) from 8 to 10 salespersons meet their quotas

(c) at least 10 salespersons meet their quotas

7.66 Delivery records show that 2 percent of the chairs shipped by a factory to its dealers arrive in damaged condition. Use the formula for the Poisson approximation to the binomial distribution to determine the probability that among 90 chairs shipped to a dealer, 2 will arrive in damaged condition.

7.67 Suppose that a shopping center has determined that half of its customers reside within a 4-mile radius of its location. If 100 randomly selected customers are interviewed, with what probability can we state (according to Chebyshev's theorem) that between 40 and 60 of the customers will reside within a 4-mile radius?

7.68 Determine whether the following can be probability distributions (defined in each case only for the given values of x) and explain your answers:

(a) $f(x) = \dfrac{x + 1}{14}$ for $x = 1, 2, 3, 4$

(b) $f(x) = \dfrac{\binom{2}{x}}{4}$ for $x = 0, 1, 2$

(c) $f(x) = \dfrac{x^2 + 1}{18}$ for $x = 1, 2, 3$

7.69 If 5 of 20 mechanical toys in a carton are defective, find the probabilities that among 6 toys randomly selected from the carton

(a) 3 will be defective

(b) none will be defective

(c) 5 will be defective

(d) at least 1 will be defective

7.70 The owner of a used record store offers to sell an album that cost him $3 to a buyer for two bills chosen at random from the buyer's wallet, which contains one $5 bill and five $1 bills. Show that the odds are 2 to 1 that the owner will lose money on the sale but that, despite this, the owner expects to make 0.33\frac{1}{3}$. How can we explain this seeming contradiction?

7.71 A cash register contains 10 $20 bills, 3 of which are counterfeit.

(a) If the cashier randomly selects 3 $20 bills from this cash register, what is the probability that 0, 1, 2, or 3 are counterfeit?

(b) Using the answers calculated in part (a), how many counterfeits can the cashier expect to get when he takes 3 of the bills from the cash register?

(c) What are the odds against the cashier's getting zero counterfeits when he randomly selects 3 $20 bills from the cash register?

7.72 With reference to Exercise 7.3 on page 264, suppose that 85 percent of the tomatoes are green.

(a) Use a computer printout of the binomial distribution with $n = 4$ and $p = 0.85$ to verify that 0.368 is the probability that 3 of 4 tomatoes are green and not ready for sale to retail customers.

(b) Use the formula for the binomial distribution to verify the answer to part (a).

7.73 With reference to Exercise 7.11 on page 265, change the percentage of all families from 40 to 45. Use a computer printout of the binomial distribution with $n = 15$ and $p = 0.45$ to solve parts (a), (b), (c), and (d) of this exercise.

7.74 With reference to Exercise 7.12 on page 265, change the percentage of all employees from 30 percent to 33 percent. Use a computer printout of the binomial distribution with $n = 12$ and $p = 0.33$ to solve parts (a), (b), (c), and (d) of this exercise.

7.75 With reference to Exercise 7.13 on page 265, change the percentage of undamaged glassware from 50 to 58 to find the probabilities that $0, 1, 2, \ldots, 9$ or 10 randomly selected glassware articles are undamaged.

7.13

Solutions of Practice Exercises

7.1 (a) No; the sum of the probabilities is less than 1.

(b) No; the sum of the probabilities is greater than 1.

(c) Yes; the sum $= 1$, and none is negative.

(d) No; $f(4)$ is negative.

(e) No; the sum of the probabilities is greater than 1.

7.3 (a) $\binom{4}{3}(0.9)^3(0.1)^1 = 0.2916$ (b) 0.292

In left margin of Table V, find $n = 4$, $x = 3$ and go across line to answer under $p = 0.9$.

From computer solution

```
MTB > PDF;
SUBC> BINOMIAL N=4 P=.9.

    BINOMIAL WITH N =    4  P = 0.900000
        K            P( X = K)
        0              0.0001
        1              0.0036
        2              0.0486
        3              0.2916
        4              0.6561
MTB > STOP
```

(c) Probability of 3 tomatoes is read directly and is 0.2916.

7.7 The probability that a player's number occurs x times is $f(x) = \binom{3}{x}\left(\frac{1}{6}\right)^x\left(\frac{5}{6}\right)^{3-x}$ for $x = 0, 1, 2,$ or 3. Thus, the probability of his winning

$1 is $f(1) = \binom{3}{1}\left(\frac{1}{6}\right)\left(\frac{5}{6}\right)^2 = \dfrac{75}{216}$, the probability of his winning \$2 is $f(2)$

$= \binom{3}{2}\left(\frac{1}{6}\right)^2\left(\frac{5}{6}\right) = \dfrac{15}{216}$, the probability of his winning \$3 is $f(3) =$

$\binom{3}{3}\left(\frac{1}{6}\right)^3\left(\frac{5}{6}\right)^0 = \dfrac{1}{216}$, the probability of his losing \$1 is $f(0) =$

$\binom{3}{0}\left(\frac{1}{6}\right)^0\left(\frac{5}{6}\right)^3 = \dfrac{125}{216}$. Hence, the player's mathematical expectation is

$$1 \cdot \frac{75}{216} + 2 \cdot \frac{15}{216} + 3 \cdot \frac{1}{216} - 1 \cdot \frac{125}{216} = -\frac{17}{216} = -7.9 \text{ cents.}$$

7.8 From Table V, $0.002 + 0.017 + 0.077 + 0.194 = 0.290$. Alternatively, through the use of the formula for the binomial distribution

$$\binom{7}{0}(0.60)^0(0.40)^7 + \binom{7}{1}(0.60)^1(0.40)^6 + \binom{7}{2}(0.60)^2(0.40)^5 +$$

$$\binom{7}{3}(0.60)^3(0.40)^4 = 0.0016 + 0.0172 + 0.0774 + 0.1935 = 0.2897$$

7.9 $f(0) = \binom{4}{0}p^0(1-p)^4 = \dfrac{16}{81}$, so that $(1-p)^4 = \dfrac{16}{81}$, $1 - p = \dfrac{2}{3}$, and $p = \dfrac{1}{3}$.

7.10 Using Table V with $n = 10$ and $p = 0.95$
(a) $0.075 + 0.315 + 0.599 = 0.989$
(b) $0.010 + 0.075 + 0.315 = 0.400$
(c) $1.000 - 0.599 = 0.401$, or $0.001 + 0.010 + 0.075 + 0.315 = 0.401$

```
MTB > PDF;
SUBC> BINOMICAL N=10 P=.95.
   BINOMICAL WITH    N = 10   P = 0.950000
          K                  P( X = K)
          4                    0.0000
          5                    0.0001
          6                    0.0010
          7                    0.0105
          8                    0.0746
          9                    0.3151
         10                    0.5987
MTB > STOP
```

7.15 (a) $f(3) = 0.60(0.40)^{3-1} = 0.096$ (b) $f(4) = 0.30(0.70)^{4-1} = 0.103$

7.16 (a) $\dfrac{\binom{6}{0}\binom{8}{2}}{\binom{14}{2}} = \dfrac{1 \cdot 28}{91} = 0.308$ (b) $\dfrac{\binom{6}{1}\binom{8}{1}}{\binom{14}{2}} = \dfrac{6 \cdot 8}{91} = 0.527$

(c) $\dfrac{\binom{6}{2}\binom{8}{0}}{\binom{14}{2}} = \dfrac{15 \cdot 1}{91} = 0.165$

7.22 (a) $f(0) = \dfrac{\binom{1}{0}\binom{9}{2}}{\binom{10}{2}} = \dfrac{1 \cdot 36}{45} = 0.800$

(b) $f(1) + f(2) = \dfrac{\binom{3}{1}\binom{7}{1} + \binom{3}{2}\binom{7}{0}}{\binom{10}{2}} = \dfrac{3 \cdot 7 + 3 \cdot 1}{45} = 0.533$

Alternatively,

$$1 - \dfrac{\binom{3}{0}\binom{7}{2}}{\binom{10}{2}} = 1 - \dfrac{1 \cdot 21}{45} = 0.533$$

(c) $f(0) = \dfrac{\binom{6}{0}\binom{4}{2}}{\binom{10}{2}} = \dfrac{1 \cdot 6}{45} = 0.133$ and $1 - 0.133 = 0.867$

Alternatively,

$$f(1) + f(2) = \dfrac{\binom{6}{1}\binom{4}{1} + \binom{6}{2}\binom{4}{0}}{\binom{10}{2}} = \dfrac{6 \cdot 4 + 15 \cdot 1}{45} = 0.867$$

7.25 After solving for np, we then substitute $np = 3$ and $x = 2$ into the Poisson distribution formula found on page 269. The value of e^{-np} is read from Table X where the number corresponding to $np = 3$ is 0.050. Thus we get

$np = 200(0.015) = 3;\ f(2) = \dfrac{3^2 \cdot e^{-3}}{2!} = \dfrac{9(0.050)}{2} = 0.225.$

```
MTB > PDF;
SUBC> POISSON MU=3.0.

     POISSON WITH MEAN =    3.000
        K              P( X = K)
        0               0.0498
        1               0.1494
        2               0.2240
        3               0.2240
        4               0.1680
        5               0.1008
        6               0.0504
        7               0.0216
        8               0.0081
        9               0.0027
       10               0.0008
       11               0.0002
       12               0.0001
       13               0.0000
MTB > STOP
```

$f(2)$ is read directly and is 0.2240.

7.28 (a) $f(0) = \dfrac{4.5^0 \cdot e^{-4.5}}{0!} = \dfrac{1(0.011)}{1} = 0.011$ (b) $1 - 0.011 = 0.989$

(c) $f(2) = \dfrac{4.5^2 \cdot e^{-4.5}}{2!} = \dfrac{20.25(0.011)}{2} = 0.111$

(d) $f(4) = \dfrac{4.5^4 \cdot e^{-4.5}}{4!} = \dfrac{410.1(0.011)}{24} = 0.188$

From computer solution

```
MTB > PDF;
SUBC> POISSON MU=4.5.

     POISSON WITH MEAN =    4.500
        K              P( X = K)
        0               0.0111
        1               0.0500
        2               0.1125
        3               0.1687
        4               0.1898
        5               0.1708
        6               0.1281
        7               0.0824
        8               0.0463
        9               0.0232
       10               0.0104
       11               0.0043
       12               0.0016
       13               0.0006
       14               0.0002
       15               0.0001
       16               0.0000
MTB > STOP
```

(a) $f(0)$ is read directly and is 0.111.

(b) At least one book is $1 - f(0) = 1 - 0.0111 = 0.9889$.

(c) $f(2)$ is read directly and is 0.1125.

(d) $f(4)$ is read directly and is 0.1898.

7.31 Using the formula for the multinomial distribution on page 273 with $n = 8$, $x_1 = 4$, $x_2 = 2$, and $x_3 = 2$, we get

$$\frac{8!}{4!2!2!}(0.5)^4(0.3)^2(0.2)^2 = 0.094$$

7.32 $\dfrac{10!}{5!3!1!1!}(0.5)^5(0.3)^3(0.1)^1(0.1)^1 = 5,040(0.03125)(0.027)(0.01) = 0.042$

7.33 $\mu = 0(0.50) + 1(0.30) + 2(0.15) + 3(0.05) = 0.75$ injuries.
$\sigma^2 = (0 - 0.75)^2 (0.50) + (1 - 0.75)^2 (0.30) + (2 - 0.75)^2 (0.15) +$
$(3 - 0.75)^2(0.05) = 0.28125 + 0.01875 + 0.234375 + 0.253125 = 0.79$
injuries.

7.34 $\mu = 0(0.10) + 1(0.27) + 2(0.36) + 3(0.13) + 4(0.07) + 5(0.06) + 6(0.01)$
$= 0 + 0.27 + 0.72 + 0.39 + 0.28 + 0.30 + 0.06 = 2.02$ tankers.
$\sigma^2 = (0 - 2.02)^2(0.10) + (1 - 2.02)^2(0.27) + (2 - 2.02)^2(0.36) +$
$(3 - 2.02)^2(0.13) + (4 - 2.02)^2(0.07) + (5 - 2.02)^2(0.06) + (6 -$
$2.02)^2(0.01) = 0.408040 + 0.280908 + 0.000144 + 0.124852 + 0.274428$
$+ 0.532824 + 0.158404 = 1.7796$ and $\sigma = \sqrt{1.7796} = 1.33$ tankers.

7.35 (a) $\mu = 0.75$ injuries from Exercise 7.33, $\sum x^2 f(x) = 0^2(0.50) + 1^2(0.30) +$
$2^2(0.15) + 3^2(0.05) = 0.00 + 0.30 + 0.60 + 0.45 = 1.35$, and $\sigma^2 =$
$1.35 - (0.75)^2 = 0.79$ injuries.

(b) $\mu = 2.02$ tankers from Exercise 7.34, $\sum x^2 fx = 0^2(0.10) + 1^2(0.27) +$
$2^2(0.36) + 3^2(0.13) + 4^2(0.07) + 5^2(0.06) + 6^2(0.01) = 0.00 + 0.27$
$+ 1.44 + 1.17 + 1.12 + 1.5 + 0.36 = 5.86$, so that $\sigma = 5.86 - (2.02)^2$
$= 1.7796$ and $\sigma = \sqrt{1.7796} = 1.33$ tankers.

7.38 $\mu = 1 \cdot \dfrac{1}{6} + 2 \cdot \dfrac{1}{6} + 3 \cdot \dfrac{1}{6} + 4 \cdot \dfrac{1}{6} + 5 \cdot \dfrac{1}{6} + 6 \cdot \dfrac{1}{6} = 3.5$, and

$\sum x^2 f(x) = 1^2 \cdot \dfrac{1}{6} + 2^2 \cdot \dfrac{1}{6} + 3^2 \cdot \dfrac{1}{6} + 4^2 \cdot \dfrac{1}{6} + 5^2 \cdot \dfrac{1}{6} + 6^2 + \dfrac{1}{6} = \dfrac{91}{6}$,

so that $\sigma^2 = \dfrac{91}{6} - 3. 5^2 = \dfrac{35}{12}$ and $\sigma = \sqrt{\dfrac{35}{12}} = 1.71$.

7.42 (a) $f(3) = \dfrac{\binom{5}{3}\binom{13}{5}}{\binom{18}{8}} = 0.294;\ f(4) = \dfrac{\binom{5}{4}\binom{13}{4}}{\binom{18}{8}} = 0.082;\ f(5) = \dfrac{\binom{5}{5}\binom{13}{3}}{\binom{18}{8}}$

$= 0.006$

(b) $0(0.029) + 1(0.196) + 2(0.392) + 3(0.294) + 4(0.082) + 5(0.006) =$
2.220

(c) $\mu = \dfrac{n \cdot a}{a + b} = \dfrac{8 \cdot 5}{5 + 13} = 2.22$

7.43 $\sum x^2 f(x) = 0^2(0.029) + 1^2(0.196) + 2^2(0.392) + 3^2(0.294) +$
$4^2(0.082) + 5^2(0.006) = 5.872$, and using $\mu = 2.22$ from the preceding exercise, we get $\sigma^2 = 5.872 - (2.22)^2 = 0.944$ boats (squared).

7.45 $\mu = 0(0.449) + 1(0.360) + 2(0.144) + 3(0.038) + 4(0.008) + 5(0.001) =$
0.799, which is very close to $\lambda = 0.8$.

7.48 $\mu = 36(0.5) = 18$ and $\sigma = \sqrt{36(0.5)(0.5)} = 3$. The probability is at least $1 - \dfrac{1}{3^2} = \dfrac{8}{9} = 0.89$ that the vehicle will stop between $18 - 3 \cdot 3 = 9$ and $18 + 3 \cdot 3 = 27$ times.

7.49 $k = \dfrac{130 - 80}{10} = \dfrac{180 - 130}{10} = 5$; the probability is at least $1 - \dfrac{1}{k^2} = 1 - \dfrac{1}{25} = \dfrac{24}{25} = 0.96$.

8

Bayes's Theorem and the Revision of Probabilities*

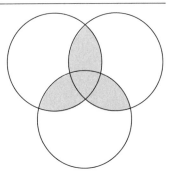

Although the symbols *P(A|B)* and *P(B|A)* may look alike, conceptually there is a great difference between the probabilities which they represent. For instance, if *A* is the event that Christmas retail sales are high in a given metropolitan area in a given year and *B* is the event that the weather is good, then *P(A|B)* is the probability that retail sales are high given that the weather is good, but *P(B|A)* is the probability that the weather is good given that sales are high. Also, if *A* is the event that a man committed a certain crime of embezzlement and *B* is the event that he is convicted of the crime, then *P(A|B)* is the probability that the man actually committed the crime given that he is convicted of it, but *P(B|A)* is the probability that he is convicted of the crime given that he committed it.

There are many problems in statistics which involve such pairs of conditional probabilities, and in Section 8.1 we shall introduce a very important formula, that of **Bayes's theorem**, which enables us to express the mathematical relationship between probabilities of the form *P(A|B)* and *P(B|A)*. Then, in Sections 8.2 and 8.3 we shall see how Bayes's theorem may be applied in statistical inference and decision making.

*This chapter is optional and can be omitted without loss of continuity.

8.1

Bayes's Theorem

In order to find a formula which expresses $P(B|A)$ in terms of $P(A|B)$ for any two events A and B, let us equate the two expressions for $P(A \cap B)$ on page 183. We have

$$P(A) \cdot P(B|A) = P(B) \cdot P(A|B)$$

and, hence,

$$P(B|A) = \frac{P(B) \cdot P(A|B)}{P(A)}$$

after dividing the expressions on both sides of the equation by $P(A)$.

EXAMPLE 8.1   The loan officer of a bank knows that 5 percent of all loan applicants are bad risks, 92 percent of all loan applicants who are bad risks are also rated bad risks by a credit advisory service, and 2 percent of all loan applicants who are not bad risks are rated bad risks by the service. What is the probability that a loan applicant who is rated a bad risk by the service is actually a bad risk?

SOLUTION   Let A denote the event that the service rates a loan applicant a bad risk, B the event that a loan applicant is in fact a bad risk, and B' the event that the loan applicant is not a bad risk. We can translate the given percentages into probabilities and write $P(B) = 0.05$, $P(A|B) = 0.92$, and $P(A|B') = 0.02$.

Before we can calculate $P(B|A)$ by means of the formula given, we will first have to determine $P(A)$, and to this end let us look at the tree diagram of Figure 8.1. Here A is reached either along the branch which passes through B or along the branch which passes through B' so the probabilities of reaching A are $(0.05)(0.92) = 0.046$ and $(1 - 0.05)(0.02) = 0.019$. Since the possibilities represented by the two branches are mutually exclusive, we get $P(A) = 0.046 + 0.019 = 0.065$, and substitution into the formula for $P(B|A)$ yields

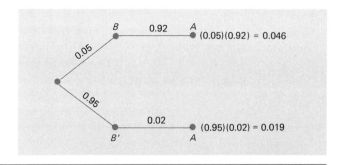

FIGURE 8.1
Tree diagram for
calculating $P(A)$ in
Example 8.1

$$P(B|A) = \frac{P(B) \cdot P(A|B)}{P(A)} = \frac{(0.05)(0.92)}{0.065} = 0.71$$

This is the probability that a loan applicant, rated a bad risk by the service, actually is a bad risk. ∎

With reference to the tree diagram of Figure 8.1 we can say that $P(B|A)$ is the probability that event A is reached via the upper branch of the tree, and its value is given by the ratio of the probability associated with that branch to the sum of the probabilities associated with both branches of the tree. This argument can be generalized to the case where there are more than two branches leading to an event A. With reference to Figure 8.2 we can say that $P(B_i|A)$ is the probability that event A is reached via the ith branch of the tree (for $i = 1, 2, \ldots,$ or k), and it can be shown that the value of this probability is given by the ratio of the probability associated with the ith branch to the sum of the probabilities associated with all the branches leading to A. Symbolically, this result, called **Bayes's theorem**, is given by

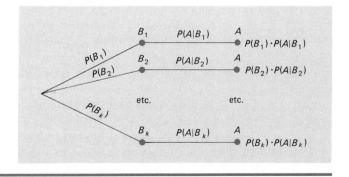

FIGURE 8.2
Tree diagram for
Bayes's theorem

Bayes's theorem

> If B_1, B_2, . . . , and B_k are mutually exclusive events one of which must occur, then
> $$P(B_i|A) = \frac{P(B_i) \cdot P(A|B_i)}{P(B_1) \cdot P(A|B_1) + P(B_2) \cdot P(A|B_2) + \ldots + P(B_k) \cdot P(A|B_k)}$$
> for $i = 1, 2, \ldots, $ or k.

The expression in the denominator here actually equals $P(A)$. $P(B_1) \cdot P(A|B_1)$ is the probability of reaching A via the first branch, $P(B_2) \cdot P(A|B_2)$ is the probability of reaching A via the second branch, . . . , $P(Bk) \cdot P(A|B_k)$ is the probability of reaching A via the kth branch, and the sum of all these probabilities equals $P(A)$. This rule, or procedure, for calculating $P(A)$ is often called the **rule of elimination** or the **rule of total probability**.

EXAMPLE 8.2 A management consultant is asked for her opinion as to why an executive's dissatisfied secretary quit her job. Unable to get any direct information about the secretary, she takes the following data from a large-scale corporate morale and motivation study: Among all dissatisfied secretaries, 20 percent are dissatisfied mainly because they dislike their work, 50 percent because they feel they are underpaid, and 30 percent because they dislike their boss. Furthermore, the corresponding probabilities that they will quit are 0.60, 0.40, and 0.90. Based on these figures, what are the probabilities that the secretary quit because of the work, because of the pay, or because of the boss?

SOLUTION Picturing this situation in Figure 8.3, we find that the probabilities associated with the three branches of the tree are $(0.20)(0.60) = 0.12$, $(0.50)(0.40) = 0.20$, and $(0.30)(0.90) = 0.27$, and that their sum is 0.59. Consequently, the probabilities that a dissatisfied secretary has quit because of the work, the pay, or the boss, are $\frac{0.12}{0.59} = 0.20$, $\frac{0.20}{0.59} = 0.34$, and $\frac{0.27}{0.59} = 0.46$. It follows that the secretary is most likely to have quit because of dislike for the boss.

To solve this problem by means of Bayes's formula, without reference to a tree diagram, we let A denote the event that a dissatisfied secretary quits, and B_1, B_2, and B_3 denote the events that she is dissatisfied with the work, the pay, or the boss. We can thus write $P(B_1) = 0.20$, $P(B_2) = 0.50$, $P(B_3) = 0.30$, $P(A|B_1) = 0.60$, $P(A|B_2) = 0.40$, and $P(A|B_3) = 0.90$, and the formula yields

Chapter 8   Bayes's Theorem and the Revision of Probabilities

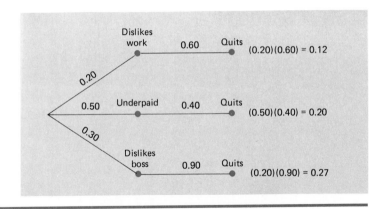

FIGURE 8.3
Tree diagram for
Example 8.2

$$P(B_1|A) = \frac{(0.20)(0.60)}{(0.20)(0.60) + (0.50)(0.40) + (0.30)(0.90)} = \frac{0.12}{0.59}$$

$$= 0.20$$

The other two probabilities, $P(B_2|A) = 0.34$ and $P(B_3|A) = 0.46$, are obtained in the same way. ∎

As the two examples of this section show, Bayes's formula is a relatively simple mathematical formula. The conditional probabilities calculated by means of the formula are sometimes called "probabilities of causes." In the preceding example we calculated the probabilities that the secretary was "caused" to quit because of dislike of the work, the pay, or the boss.

EXERCISES

(Exercises 8.1, 8.4, 8.6, 8.7, and 8.9 are practice exercises. Their complete solutions are given on page 318.)

8.1 A careful analysis of the causes for absences in a certain factory shows that the probability that an employee will be absent because of substance abuse is 0.03; the probability that the factory manager correctly attributes the absence to substance abuse is 0.80, and the probability that the factory manager incorrectly attributes an absence to substance abuse is 0.05. What is the probability that an absence attributed to substance abuse by the factory manager is actually due to substance abuse?

8.2 Use the information on the tree diagram of Figure 8.4 to determine the values of
(a) $P(B|A)$
(b) $P(B|A')$

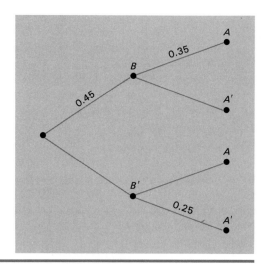

FIGURE 8.4
Tree diagram for
Exercise 8.2

8.3   At a certain computer sales company it is known, from past experience, that the probability is 0.76 that a new sales associate who has attended the company's sales training program will meet his or her sales quota. The corresponding probability is 0.25 for a new sales associate who has not attended the sales training program. If 80 percent of all new sales associates attend the training program, what is the probability that a new sales associate will meet his or her sales quota?

8.4   Two executives of a company are being considered for the position of chief executive officer. If Mr. Action is nominated by one director, the probability that he will be elected by the board of directors is $\frac{4}{5}$, provided that Ms. Bright is not nominated by another director. The probability that Ms. Bright will be nominated is $\frac{1}{4}$ and the probability that Mr. Action will be elected if Ms. Bright is nominated is $\frac{3}{4}$.

(a) What is the probability that Mr. Action will be elected?

(b) If Mr. Action is elected, what is the probability that Ms. Bright was not nominated?

8.5   A guest at a picnic randomly selects two cans of soda pop from a six-pack of brand X, which contains four cans of cola and two cans of ginger ale, or from a six-pack of brand Y, which contains two cans of cola and four cans of ginger ale. But the guest is three times as likely to select brand Y than brand X.

(a) What is the probability that both cans selected by the guest are ginger ale?

(b) If both cans selected by the guest are ginger ale, what is the probability that they are selected from brand Y?

(c) If the guest selects at least one can of cola, what is the probability that the soda pop is taken from brand X?

8.6 In the bookkeeping department of a firm, Anne, Betty, and Carl prepare 0.55, 0.30, and 0.15 of the statements, respectively, which are mailed to customers following final verification. If 0.6 percent of the statements prepared by Anne, 0.4 percent of the statements prepared by Betty, and 1.0 percent of the statements prepared by Carl are inaccurate, what are the probabilities that an inaccurate statement, detected at final verification, was prepared by

(a) Anne

(b) Betty

(c) Carl

8.7 A self-employed mason knows from experience that 45 percent of his contracts for brickwork are for common (American) bond, 35 percent for English bond, and 20 percent for Flemish bond. Bonding provides various patterns which arrange the bricks to lap over each other in order to stagger the vertical joints. Also, 60 percent of the mason's contracts for common bond are for residential construction, 35 percent of the contracts for English bond are for residential construction, and 40 percent of the contracts for Flemish bond are for residential construction. If the mason signs a contract to provide brickwork for a residence, what are the odds that the job is not for common bond?

8.8 Four employees of a wholesale toy company (James, Karen, Lillian, and Michael) make forecasts of sales for each of hundreds of different toys. These four employees make substantial errors in forecasting sales of the toys 4 times in 100, 6 times in 100, 12 times in 100, and 18 times in 100, respectively, and they make 25, 45, 20, and 10 percent, respectively, of all the company's sales forecasts for toys. If a substantial error is made in the sales forecast for a particular toy, what are the probabilities that the error was made by James, Karen, Lillian, or Michael?

8.9 [From I. Miller and J. E. Freund, *Probability and Statistics for Engineers*, 3rd ed. (Englewood Cliffs, N.J.: Prentice-Hall, Inc., 1985).] An explosion in a Liquefied Natural Gas storage tank in the process of being repaired could have occurred as the result of static electricity, malfunctioning electrical equipment, an open flame in contact with the liner, or purposeful action (industrial sabotage). Interviews with engineers who were analyzing the risks involved led to estimates that such an explosion would occur with probability 0.25 as a result of static electricity, 0.20 as a result of malfunctioning electrical equipment, 0.40 as a result of an open flame, and 0.75 as a result of purposeful action. These interviews also yielded subjective estimates of the probabilities of the four causes of 0.30, 0.40, 0.15, and 0.15, respectively. Based on all this information, what is the most likely cause of the explosion?

Prior Probabilities and Posterior Probabilities

There are many situations in which we assign probabilities to events on the basis of whatever information or feelings we have about their likelihoods at the time. Later, however, we may get additional information which forces us to revise our earlier appraisals. Sometimes we learn or observe something which causes us to assign even higher probabilities to events we already considered very likely to happen; at other times we find that we must assign a probability of zero to an event which, at one time, we had felt was reasonably sure to happen. The mechanics of making logical revisions of earlier probability assignments is the subject matter of this section.

Suppose, for instance, that Adam and Brown are planning to form a corporation to build and operate a number of automatic car washes and that Adam feels that there is a 50-50 chance that any new unit will show a profit for the first year, but Brown feels that the odds on this are 2 to 1. Suppose, furthermore, that we may want to invest some money in this corporation and, hence, we would like to know who is right. If a business consultant feels that in view of Adam's experience he is three times as likely to be right as Brown, the consultant is, in fact, assigning the event B_1 that Adam is right the probability $P(B_1) = \dfrac{3}{4}$ and the event B_2 that Brown is right the probability $P(B_2) = \dfrac{1}{4}$. Since the entire operation is still in the planning stage, we have no direct information about the performance of the units, and we refer to $P(B_1) = \dfrac{3}{4}$ and $P(B_2) = \dfrac{1}{4}$ as the **prior probabilities** of events B_1 and B_2.

Now suppose that the corporation opens six new units and five of them show a profit for the first year and the sixth shows a loss. How does that affect our feelings about B_1 (that Adam is right) and B_2 (that Brown is right)? If we let A denote the event that five of the six new units show a first-year profit, the answer to this question is given by the probabilities $P(B_1|A)$ and $P(B_2|A)$. For two mutually exclusive events, one of which must occur, Bayes's formula becomes

$$P(B_1|A) = \frac{P(B_1) \cdot P(A|B_1)}{P(B_1) \cdot P(A|B_1) + P(B_2) \cdot P(A|B_2)}$$

and

$$P(B_2|A) = \frac{P(B_2) \cdot P(A|B_2)}{P(B_1) \cdot P(A|B_1) + P(B_2) \cdot P(A|B_2)}$$

In order to find these we must first calculate the binomial probabilities $P(A|B_1)$ and $P(A|B_2)$, and then substitute the results together with the prior probabilities $P(B_1)$ and $P(B_2)$ into Bayes's formula. To find $P(A|B_1)$ we substitute $x = 5$, $n = 6$, and $p = \frac{1}{2}$ (corresponding to the 50-50 chance of first-year profit suggested by Adam) into the formula for the binomial distribution, and we get

$$P(A|B_1) = \binom{6}{5}\left(\frac{1}{2}\right)^5\left(1 - \frac{1}{2}\right)^{6-5} = \frac{3}{32}$$

Similarly, to find $P(A|B_2)$ we substitute $x = 5$, $n = 6$, $p = \frac{2}{3}$ (corresponding to the 2 to 1 odds on a first-year profit) into the formula for the binomial distribution, and we get

$$P(A|B_2) = \binom{6}{5}\left(\frac{2}{3}\right)^5\left(1 - \frac{2}{3}\right)^{6-5} = \frac{64}{243}$$

Finally, substituting $P(B_1) = \frac{3}{4}$, $P(B_2) = \frac{1}{4}$, $P(A|B_1) = \frac{3}{32}$, and $P(A|B_2) = \frac{64}{243}$ into Bayes's formula, we find that

$$P(B_1|A) = \frac{\dfrac{3}{4} \cdot \dfrac{3}{32}}{\dfrac{3}{4} \cdot \dfrac{3}{32} + \dfrac{1}{4} \cdot \dfrac{64}{243}} = \frac{2{,}187}{4{,}235} = 0.52$$

It follows that $P(B_2|A) = 1 - 0.52 = 0.48$.

The probabilities $P(B_1|A)$ and $P(B_2|A)$ are called the **posterior probabilities** of events B_1 and B_2, and it is important to note how we have combined the direct evidence (five of the six new car washes showed a first-year profit) with the original subjective evaluation of the consultant.

Note also how the weight of the direct evidence has given increased merit to Brown's claim. Whereas his claim was originally assigned a probability of $\frac{1}{4}$, is now assigned a probability of 0.48, or almost $\frac{1}{2}$.

EXAMPLE 8.3 Three engineers agree that the number of times a newly designed desktop computer will malfunction in a week of normal use is a random variable having a Poisson distribution, but they disagree on the expected (or mean) number of such malfunctions per week. The first engineer's calculations lead him to assert that the expected value is $\lambda = 1.4$, the second says it is $\lambda = 2.0$, and the third says it is $\lambda = 3.1$. These are the expected values for Exercise 8.16 on page 313. If the three engineers are highly competent men whose judgments, in our considered opinion, are equally valid, and if in an experiment the computer actually malfunctions four times during one week of normal use, what posterior probabilities should we assign to the values of λ suggested by the three engineers?

SOLUTION If B_1 is the event that the first engineer is right, B_2 the event that the second engineer is right, and B_3 the event that the third engineer is right, the prior probabilities of these events are $P(B_1) = P(B_2) = P(B_3) = \frac{1}{3}$, since we feel that these judgments are equally valid. The lambda, λ, of the Poisson distribution formula is the expected number of occurrences of a random event, while the actual observed number of occurrences of the random event is x. Then if A is the event that the computer malfunctions four times in a week of normal use, substitution of $x = 4$ and the three suggested values of λ into the formula for the Poisson distribution, $f(x) = \dfrac{\lambda^x \cdot e^{-\lambda}}{x!}$, yields

$$P(A|B_1) = \frac{(1.4)^4 \cdot e^{-1.4}}{4!} = 0.040$$

$$P(A|B_2) = \frac{(2.0)^4 \cdot e^{-2.0}}{4!} = 0.090$$

and

$$P(A|B_3) = \frac{(3.1)^4 \cdot e^{-3.1}}{4!} = 0.173$$

Substituting now in Bayes's formula, we find that for the first engineer the posterior probability is

$$P(B_1|A) = \frac{\frac{1}{3}(0.040)}{\frac{1}{3}(0.040) + \frac{1}{3}(0.090) + \frac{1}{3}(0.173)} = 0.13$$

Replacing the numerator by the second term in the denominator, we get $P(B_2|A) = 0.30$; then replacing it by the third term, we get $P(B_3|A) = 0.57$.

The effect of the additional information gained in the experiment is to increase the weight assigned originally to the third engineer's claim and to decrease the weights assigned to the claims of the others. This should not really come as a surprise. After the computer was observed to malfuntion four times in one week, it seems entirely reasonable to give more weight to the claim of the engineer whose expectation was closest. ∎

In the first example of this section we assumed that either Adam or Brown was right, and in the second example we assumed that one or another of the three engineers was right; no other possibilities were even considered to exist. This may not seem reasonable. Why, for instance, couldn't the probability of a first-year profit for one of the new car washes be $\frac{4}{5}$ instead of either $\frac{1}{2}$ or $\frac{2}{3}$? And why couldn't the computer malfunction on the average 3.5 times a week instead of 1.4, 2.0, or 3.1 times? The answer is that assumptions of this sort are necessary in order to make the kind of analysis we have described. Of course, we used only two alternatives in the first example and three in the second to simplify the calculations; in actual practice, we may use 10 alternatives, 25 alternatives, or even more as the need may be.

8.3

Posterior Analysis

In Chapter 6 we introduced the Bayes decision rule, and we used it to maximize expected profits, minimize expected costs, or minimize expected opportunity losses, using only prior probabilities in each case. Now, if we combine prior information with direct sample evidence as in the preceding section, we can use the posterior probabilities instead of the prior probabilities, and we refer to this as **posterior analysis**.

Let us consider a very large company which routinely pays thousands of invoices submitted by its suppliers. They are collected in batches of 1,000 before payment is made, and since the company often receives erroneous invoices (the prices, the quantities, and the extensions have all been known to be in error on occasion), it must decide whether or not to have each invoice in a batch checked (or verified). Clearly, the proportion of erroneous invoices will vary from batch to batch, and for the sake of simplicity let us assume that for any given batch it can take on only the values $p = 0.001, p = 0.010$, or $p = 0.020$. Also, the company's statistical studies show that on the average an erroneous invoice overcharges the company by $5, and it is known that it costs $45 to eliminate all errors from a batch of 1,000 invoices by means of a computer.

All this information is summarized in the following payoff table, where the entries in the second column show that it costs the company $45 to check and eliminate all errors from a batch of 1,000 invoices regardless of how many of them are in error. The entries in the first column are the expected costs (overcharges) which result from not checking a batch before payment is made. If $p = 0.001$, the expected number of erroneous invoices per batch is $(1,000)(0.001) = 1$, and hence, the expected cost (overcharge) is $1 \cdot 5 = \$5$. Similarly, for $p = 0.010$ the expected number of erroneous invoices per batch is $(1,000)(0.010) = 10$, and for $p = 0.020$ it is $(1,000)(0.020) = 20$, so the corresponding expected costs are $10 \cdot 5 = \$50$ and $20 \cdot 5 = \$100$.

| | | Cost or expected cost per batch | |
		Without checking	With checking
	0.001	$5	$45
Proportion of invoices containing errors	0.010	$50	$45
	0.020	$100	$45

In this problem, as in some of those in Chapter 6, there are certain advantages to working with opportunity losses instead of payoffs; for one thing, the minimum expected opportunity loss, the minimum EOL, equals the expected value of perfect information, the EVPI, which we also call the cost of uncertainty. To convert the payoff table into an opportunity-loss

Chapter 8 Bayes's Theorem and the Revision of Probabilities

table, we subtract from both entries in each row the smaller of the two, and we get

		Opportunity losses	
		Without checking	*With checking*
	0.001	0	$40
Proportion of invoices containing errors	0.010	$5	0
	0.020	$55	0

Now, if the value of p were known for each batch before it is decided whether or not it should be checked, there is no real problem and the right decision is obvious. When $p = 0.001$ the company should pay the invoices without having the batch checked, and when $p = 0.010$ or $p = 0.020$, the company should have each invoice checked before payment is made. In either case this minimizes the expected cost or the expected loss of opportunity.

In practice, of course, the value of p is not known in advance. This is precisely why there is a problem, and this is where the importance of probability in decision making becomes evident. If someone felt "pretty sure" that $p = 0.001$ for a given batch (that is, if he assigned $p = 0.001$ a very high subjective probability for this batch), he would not have the batch checked; conversely, if someone felt "pretty sure" that $p = 0.020$ for a given batch, he would have it checked. Since different "feelings" about a correct value of p can affect the decision on whether or not to have a batch checked, let us look more closely into the problem of assigning probabilities to the different values which p can take on.

One way to handle this problem is to assign objective, rather than subjective, prior probabilities—if they can be found—to the various events (in our example, the three possible values of p). Suppose that the company maintains a set of records extending back over a long period of time, and suppose that we find from these records that in 70 percent of all the many batches checked p was 0.001, in 20 percent of them p was 0.010, and in the remaining 10 percent p was 0.020. If we use 0.70, 0.20, and 0.10 as the prior probabilities of the three values of p, we find that the expected opportunity loss associated with the decision not to check the batch is

$$\$0(0.70) + \$5(0.20) + \$55(0.10) = \$6.50$$

and the expected opportunity loss associated with the decision to check the batch is

$$\$40(0.70) + \$0(0.20) + \$0(0.10) = \$28.00$$

Thus, the expected opportunity loss is minimized by deciding not to check the batch, and the expected value of perfect information is $6.50. This figure is the maximum amount the company should be willing to spend in collecting more information before making the final decision as to whether or not to have the entire batch checked.

If no further information having a bearing on this problem can be obtained, this procedure would seem to provide a reasonable solution. However, it may be observed that the weights assigned to the possible values of p (the prior probabilities, that is) are based on historical data which tell us what happened in the past but tell us nothing directly about the particular batch which is of concern. What we would like to do, if possible, is take a sample of the 1,000 invoices contained in the batch, observe the number of erroneous invoices, and revise the prior probabilities in the light of this direct evidence. So let us suppose that 25 invoices are randomly selected (at negligible cost) from the batch in question, and that only one of them contains an error. If we let A denote the event of getting one erroneous invoice in the sample of 25 invoices, B_1 denote the event that the actual proportion of erroneous invoices in the lot is 0.001, and B_2 and B_3 denote the events that the proportions are 0.010 and 0.020, we first want to determine the probabilities $P(A|B_1)$, $P(A|B_2)$, and $P(A|B_3)$, and then use Bayes's formula to find the posterior probabilities $P(B_1|A)$, $P(B_2|A)$, and $P(B_3|A)$. The sampling here is without replacement, as is usually the case, so the exact values of the first three probabilities are given by the formula for the hypergeometric distribution. However, since the sample of 25 invoices constitutes only a small portion of the entire batch, we can use the binomial distribution to approximate these probabilities, and we get

$$P(A|B_1) = \binom{25}{1}(0.001)^1(0.999)^{24} = 0.0244$$

$$P(A|B_2) = \binom{25}{1}(0.010)^1(0.990)^{24} = 0.1965$$

$$P(A|B_3) = \binom{25}{1}(0.020)^1(0.980)^{24} = 0.3080$$

Combining these probabilities with the prior probabilities $P(B_1) = 0.70$, $P(B_2) = 0.20$, and $P(B_3) = 0.10$, and substituting into Bayes's formula, we get

$$P(B_1|A) = \frac{(0.70)(0.0244)}{(0.70)(0.0244) + (0.20)(0.1965) + (0.10)(0.3080)}$$

$$= \frac{0.01708}{0.08718} = 0.196$$

$$P(B_2|A) = \frac{(0.20)(0.1965)}{0.08718} = 0.451$$

and

$$P(B_3|A) = \frac{(0.10)(0.3080)}{0.08718} = 0.353$$

Finally, using these posterior probabilities with the opportunity-loss table, we find that the expected opportunity loss associated with the decision not to check the batch is

$$\$0(0.196) + \$5(0.451) + \$55(0.353) = \$21.67$$

and the expected opportunity loss associated with the decision to check the batch is

$$\$40(0.196) + \$0(0.451) + \$0(0.353) = \$7.84$$

Thus, the posterior analysis shows that the expected opportunity loss is minimized by deciding to check the entire batch, and that the expected value of perfect information is $7.84.

It may seem surprising that the expected value of perfect information has increased from $6.50 without the sample data to $7.84 with the added information. This is due to the fact that the sample evidence does not support the prior considerations, where most of the weight (a probability of 0.70) was given to $p = 0.001$. The proportion of erroneous invoices in the sample was $\frac{1}{25} = 0.04$, which exceeds even $p = 0.020$, and the posterior analysis has, in fact, reversed the decision we arrived at by means of the prior analysis. If there had been no erroneous invoices among the 25 in the sample, this would have offered support for the prior considerations, the decision would not have been reversed, and the expected value of perfect information would have been reduced to $4.55 (see Exercise 8.15).

(Exercises 8.10, 8.11, 8.14, 8.17, 8.18, and 8.19 are practice exercises. Their complete solutions are given on page 318.)

8.10 In planning the inventory requirements for a new sporting goods store, the first partner claims that only one out of five tennis rackets sold will be of the high-priced deluxe model, while the second partner claims that it would be correct to, say, two out of five. In the past the two partners have been about equally reliable, so that in the absence of direct information we would assign their judgments equal weight. What posterior probabilities would we assign if it were found that among the first 10 customers who purchased a tennis racket, 3 purchased the deluxe model?

8.11 In a marketing study for a new ethnic food product, three consultants disagree about the percentage of consumers who will find the taste of the product too spicy. The first consultant claims that 30 percent of adult consumers will find the product too spicy, the second claims that 20 percent of adult consumers will find the product too spicy, and the third consultant claims that only 10 percent of adult consumers will find the product too spicy.

(a) If the president of the food product manufacturing company feels that the first consultant is 6 times as reliable as the third consultant and that the second consultant is 3 times as reliable as the third consultant, what prior probabilities should the president assign to their claims?

(b) If an actual taste test is performed and 2 of 10 adult consumers find that the taste of the product is too spicy, what posterior probabilities should the president apply to the claims of the consultants? [Hint: Use Table V, letting $n = 10$ and $x = 2$, with probabilities 0.3, 0.2 and 0.1 to find $P(A|B_1)$, $P(A|B_2)$, and $P(A|B_3)$, respectively.]

8.12 Discussing the sale of a grand piano, one dealer expresses the feeling that a newspaper advertisement should produce seven serious inquiries about the piano, a second dealer feels that it should produce three serious inquiries, and a third dealer feels that it should produce five.

(a) If in the past the second dealer has been twice as reliable as the first, and the first has been three times as reliable as the third, what prior probabilities should we assign to their claims?

(b) How would these probabilities be affected if the advertisement actually produced two inquiries and it can be assumed that the number of inquiries is a random variable having the Poisson distribution with $\lambda = 7$, $\lambda = 3$, or $\lambda = 5$ according to the three claims?

8.13 A used furniture dealer expects to receive a shipment of four wooden chairs, and, on the basis of past experience with similar shipments, she feels that the probabilities that zero, one, two, three, or four of them will require repairs are 0.35, 0.20, 0.10, 0.10, and 0.25. If the dealer obtains a randomly selected chair from this lot, and it turns out that the chair requires repairs, what posterior probabilities should she assign to the possibilities that zero, one, two, three, or all four of the chairs will require repairs?

8.14 The manager of an athletic shoe store knows, from experience, that the probabilities that a pair of a certain brand of sneakers will have zero, one, or two blemished sneakers are, respectively, 0.90, 0.08, 0.02. If he randomly selects a pair of these sneakers from his shelves and then randomly selects one of the two sneakers and finds that it is blemished, what is the probability that the other sneaker is blemished?

8.15 If there had been no errors in any of the 25 invoices in the illustration on page 310, the binomial probabilities $P(A|B_1)$, $P(A|B_2)$, and $P(A|B_3)$ would have been 0.975, 0.778, and 0.604, with A denoting the event of getting zero erroneous invoices.

(a) Calculate the corresponding posterior probabilities.

(b) Use the posterior probabilities obtained in part (a) and the opportunity-loss table on page 309 to determine the expected opportunity losses and verify that the Bayes decision rule leads to the decision not to check the entire batch of invoices.

(c) Verify that the expected value of perfect information is reduced to $4.55.

8.16 With reference to Example 8.3 on page 306, suppose that someone wants to buy one of the desktop computers, but only if the expected number of break-downs is less than 2.5 per week. Would he buy the computer if he based his decision on

(a) a prior analysis using the prior probabilities given on page 306

(b) a posterior analysis using the posterior probabilities given on page 306

8.17 A woman bidding at an auction must decide whether to bid $50 for a sealed carton containing five crystal goblets. The goblets are worth $20 each to the bidder if they are perfect, but are worthless if they are cracked, chipped, or broken. Based on prior experience and observation the bidder assigns prior probabilities of 0.1, 0.2, 0.3, 0.2, 0.1, and 0.1 to the events that zero, one, two, three, four, or five goblets are cracked, chipped, or broken.

(a) Although examination of the goblets is impossible, should the bidder offer $50 for the carton of goblets if she wants to minimize her expected loss of opportunity?

(b) If the auctioneer randomly selects a goblet for inspection by the bidder, who finds that it is perfect, should the bidder offer $50 for the carton of goblets if she wants to minimize her expected loss of opportunity?

(c) How did the inspection of the goblet by the bidder in part (b) affect the cost of uncertainty?

8.18 With reference to the preceding exercise, suppose the woman at the auction found it necessary to increase her bid to $60 or to drop out of the competition for the crystal goblets, while everything else remains unchanged.

(a) If it is not possible for the woman to inspect the goblets, should she bid $60 for them if she wants to minimize her expected loss of opportunity?

(b) If the auctioneer randomly selects two goblets for inspection by the woman who observes that both of them are cracked and therefore worthless, should she bid $60 for the goblets if she wants to minimize her loss of opportunity?

(c) How did the inspection of part (b) affect the cost of uncertainty?

8.19 A bookstore near a college campus expects a shipment of a certain mathematics textbook to arrive in time for the beginning of the school year. If the books arrive on time, the bookstore can sell them for a profit of $1,800. But if the books arrive late (after the beginning of the school year), the bookstore will lose $600. The proprietor of the bookstore knows from experience that the odds are 4 to 1 against a shipment of books arriving late.

(a) If another book dealer offers the proprietor of the bookstore a $1,000 profit for this shipment of mathematics books (regardless of whether the shipment arrives on time), what should the proprietor do to minimize the EOL?

(b) The bookstore proprietor knows from experience that half the shipments of mathematics books that are not late arrive before mid-August. If the shipment of mathematics books has not arrived before mid-August and the offer of part (a) is repeated, what should the bookstore proprietor do to minimize the EOL?

8.20 A manufacturing firm has produced 500 electrical switches which are component parts of electrical coffee pots the firm manufactures. The firm assigns probabilities of 0.55, 0.35, and 0.10 to the events that the proportion of defective switches in the lot is $p = 0.01, 0.09$, or 0.10. The switches can be installed in the coffee pots directly, without inspection, but each defective switch costs $2.50 to replace with a good one upon final inspection of the pots. Alternatively, the switches can be inspected before they are installed in the plots at a cost of $0.0475 per switch, and all the defective switches found can be discarded and replaced with good ones. The inspected lots used in the manufacture of coffee pots are presumed to be 99 percent free of defective switches.

(a) In the absence of additional information, what should the company do to minimize its EOL?

(b) Suppose that the manufacturer makes a preliminary inspection of the switches prior to making a decision. Specifically, suppose that the manufacturer inspects at a negligible cost a sample of 25 switches and finds one defective switch in the sample. Should the company put the lot directly into production or have the entire lot inspected so as to minimize its EOL? (Use the Poisson approximation to the probabilities of finding one defective in the sample of 25 switches.)

(c) How did the information supplied by the sample affect the EVPI?

8.4

Check List of Key Terms

Bayes's theorem, 297, 299	Prior probabilities, 304
Posterior analysis, 307	Rule of elimination, 300
Posterior probabilities, 305	Rule of total probability, 300

8.5

Review Exercises

8.21 The records of a credit manager for a furniture store show that of all the credit applications rejected by the store, 75 percent are from the east side of town and the rest are from the west side. The records also show that 6 percent of the applications received from the east side of town are rejected and 10 percent of the applications received from the west side of town are rejected. If it is known that a credit application was rejected, what is the probability that the application was received from

(a) the west side of town

(b) the east side of town

8.22 A canning company wants to build a cannery in a truck farming area. Experience in other locations suggests that if only 5 percent of the farmers in the area contract to sell their produce to the cannery, then it will lose $300,000 per year; if 10 percent of the farmers contract to sell to the cannery, it will make a profit of $500,000 per year; and if 30 percent of the farmers in the area contract to sell to the cannery, it will make a profit of $1,300,000 per year. Also, the buyer for the canning company feels that the probabilities are 0.50, 0.40, and 0.10 that 5, 10, or 30 percent of the farmers in the area will contract to sell their produce to the company.

(a) In view of these data, should the canning company build the cannery if it wants to minimize its expected loss of opportunity?

(b) Suppose that, in a random sample of 10 farmers in the area, not one farmer says that he or she will contract to sell the farm's produce to the cannery. Find the posterior probabilities associated with the three percentages.

(c) Using also the sample information, should the canning company build the cannery if it wants to minimize its expected loss of opportunity?

(d) How did the information of part (b) affect the cost of uncertainty?

8.23 A blanket manufacturing company produces identical blankets in its three mills, 25 percent from Mill No. 1, 35 percent from Mill No. 2, and the remainder from Mill No. 3. Four percent of the blankets from Mill No. 1, 6 percent from Mill No. 2, and 8 percent from Mill No. 3 are slightly imperfect and are labeled "Seconds." If a blanket labeled "Second" is selected by a customer, what is the probability that it was produced by Mill No. 3?

8.24 In planning for anticipated employee turnover in a large office, the office manager of the company claims that 3 out of 5 newly hired personnel will stay with the office for more than one year, while the personnel manager of the company claims that it would be correct to say 7 out of 10. In the past, the two managers have been about equally reliable in their predictions, so that in the absence of direct information, we would assign their judgments equal weight. What posterior probabilities would we assign to their claims if we found that 9 out of 10 newly hired office personnel stayed with the office for more than one year?

8.25 On page 201 we gave an illustration where a manufacturer of office equipment must decide whether to expand his plant capacity now or wait at least another year, and where the payoff's corresponding to the events "economic conditions remain good" and "there is a recession" are as shown in the following table:

	Expand now	Delay expansion
Economic conditions remain good	$369,000	$180,000
There is a recession	−$90,000	$18,000

Also, in Example 6.11 on page 231 we showed that if he feels that the odds on a recession are 2 to 1, he will minimize the EOL if he delays expanding the capacity of his plant. Now suppose that the manufacturer consults an expert who, in the past, has made correct predictions 80 percent of the time when economic conditions remained good, but only 50 percent of the time when there were recessions.

(a) If the expert tells him that economic conditions will remain good, how will this affect the probabilities which the manufacturer assigns to the two events?

(b) Based on the probabilities of part (a), what should the manufacturer do so as to minimize the expected loss of opportunity?

8.26   At a firing range where an experimental guided missile is being tested for accuracy, 12 percent of all the missiles are inaccurate. When tested, 95 percent of all the inaccurate missiles will fail the test, but 4 percent of the missiles which are not inaccurate will also fail. What is the probability that an experimental guided missile which fails the test is actually inaccurate?

8.27   A store manager feels that 60 percent of the customers of her store are college students, while the merchandise buyer for the store feels that only 40 percent of the customers are college students. If, originally, we assign these assessments equal weight, how would this assignment be affected if a random sample shows that 7 of 12 customers are college students?

8.28   A shoplifter arrested by a security guard has stolen a randomly selected ring from one of the three trays in a display case. The first tray contains 30 genuine diamond rings and 10 inexpensive synthetic diamond rings, the second tray contains 20 genuine and 20 inexpensive synthetic diamond rings, and the third tray contains 10 genuine and 30 inexpensive synthetic diamond rings. The genuine and synthetic rings are indistinguishable from one another except upon close inspection by experts. Because of their locations in the display case the security guards believe that the shoplifter is twice as likely to have stolen the ring from the first tray as from the second tray and twice as likely to have stolen the ring from the second tray as from the third tray. If the ring is synthetic, the shoplifter will be charged with petty larcency, and if the ring is genuine, the shoplifter will be charged with grand larceny, a much more serious crime.

(a) What is the probability that the shoplifter will be charged with petty larceny?

(b) If the ring which has been stolen has a synthetic diamond, what is the probability that it comes from the first tray?

8.29   The prior probabilities are 0.60, 0.30, and 0.10 that 0, 1, or 2 cookies in a box of 10 cookies are broken. If 2 of the cookies in the box are randomly selected and it is found that neither is broken, how will this affect the probabilities that 0, 1, or 2 of the cookies in the box are broken?

8.30   The safety inspector for an insurance company feels that the probability is 0.70 that any one of several factories in a certain city will meet the insurance company's safety requirements. The head of the city's development commission feels that this probability is 0.90, and a labor relations expert feels that it is 0.60.

(a) If the mayor of the city feels that in this matter the safety inspector for the insurance company is six times as reliable as the labor relations expert, while the head of the city's development commission is three times as reliable as the labor relations expert, what prior probabilities would he apply to the three claims?

(b) If five of the factories are inspected and only two meet the insurance company's safety requirements, how does this affect the probabilities obtained in part (a)?

8.31   A coin dealer offers to sell us a lot of 20 foreign silver coins, which we know contains either 10 percent, 20 percent, or 30 percent counterfeit coins. From past experience we consider the first of these three possibilities to be three times as likely as the second and the second to be three times as likely as the third. The coins are priced to us at $20 each, and we can resell all good coins for $25 each and all counterfeits (as curios) for $2 each.

(a) If no inspection is possible, what should we do in order to minimize our expected opportunity loss? Buy the lot? Not buy the lot? What is the expected value of perfect information?

(b) Suppose that the dealer makes us the following offer: Before deciding whether or not to buy the lot, we can inspect three of the coins drawn at random from the lot. The cost of this inspection is $5, which the dealer will return to us if we buy the lot but keep if we do not buy the lot. If we accept the dealer's offer and find two counterfeits among the three coins inspected, what should we do in order to minimize our expected opportunity loss? Buy the lot? Not buy the lot?

8.6

Solutions of Practice Exercises

8.1   If A is the event that an absence is attributed by the factory manager to substance abuse and B is the event that the absence is due to substance abuse, we are given $P(B) = 0.03$, $P(A|B) = 0.80$, and $P(A|B') = 0.05$, so probability of $B' = 0.97$ and

$$P(B|A) = \frac{(0.03)(0.80)}{(0.03)(0.80) + (0.97)(0.05)} = \frac{0.024}{0.024 + 0.0485} = 0.331$$

8.4   If A is the event that Mr. Action is elected and B is the event that Ms. Bright is nominated, we are given $P(A|B') = \frac{4}{5}$, $P(B) = \frac{1}{4}$, and $P(A|B) = \frac{3}{4}$.

(a) $P(A) = P(B) \cdot P(A|B) + P(B') \cdot P(A|B') = \dfrac{1}{4} \cdot \dfrac{3}{4} + \left(1 - \dfrac{1}{4}\right)\left(\dfrac{4}{5}\right) = \dfrac{63}{80}$

(b) $P(B'|A) = \dfrac{P(B') \cdot P(A|B')}{P(A)} = \dfrac{\dfrac{3}{4} \cdot \dfrac{4}{5}}{\dfrac{63}{80}} = \dfrac{16}{21}$

8.6 Letting A correspond to Anne, B to Betty, and C to Carl, the data may be summarized in a diagram.

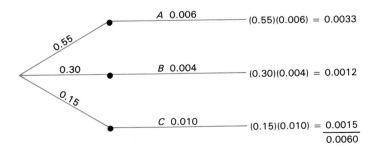

As can be seen from the diagram,

(a) $\dfrac{0.0033}{0.0060} = 0.55$ prepared by Anne

(b) $\dfrac{0.0012}{0.0060} = 0.20$ prepared by Betty

(c) $\dfrac{0.0015}{0.0060} = 0.25$ prepared by Carl

8.7 If B_1 is the event that the contract is for common bond, B_2 is the event that the contract is for English bond, B_3 is the event that the contract is for Flemish bond, and A is the event that a contract is for residential construction, we are given $P(B_1) = 0.45$, $P(B_2) = 0.36$, $P(B_3) = 0.20$, $P(A|B_1) = 0.60$, $P(A|B_2) = 0.35$, and $P(A|B_3) = 0.40$, and we get

$$P(B_1|A) = \dfrac{(0.45)(0.60)}{(0.45)(0.60) + (0.35)(0.35) + (0.20)(0.40)} = \dfrac{0.27}{0.4725} = \dfrac{4}{7}$$

Also, the probability that the contract is not for common bond is $1 - \dfrac{4}{7} = \dfrac{3}{7}$, and the odds are $\dfrac{3}{7}$ to $\dfrac{4}{7}$, or 3 to 4, that the contract is not for common bond.

8.9 If B_1, B_2, B_3, and B_4 are the events that an explosion in an LNG storage tank occurs as a result of static electricity, malfunctioning electrical equipment, an open flame, or purposeful action, and A is the event that there is an explosion in such a tank, then

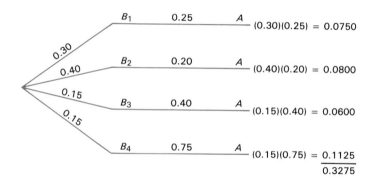

B_1 0.25 A $(0.30)(0.25) = 0.0750$

B_2 0.20 A $(0.40)(0.20) = 0.0800$

B_3 0.40 A $(0.15)(0.40) = 0.0600$

B_4 0.75 A $(0.15)(0.75) = 0.1125$

0.3275

and the probabilities of the four alternatives are $\dfrac{0.0750}{0.3275} = 0.229$, $\dfrac{0.0800}{0.3275} =$ 0.244, $\dfrac{0.0600}{0.3275} = 0.183$, and $\dfrac{0.1125}{0.3275} = 0.344$. Purposeful action is the most likely cause.

8.10   If B_1 is the event that the first partner is right and $p = 0.20$, B_2 is the event that the second partner is right and $p = 0.40$, and A is the event that 3 out of 10 rackets sold were deluxe models, we are given $P(B_1) = P(B_2) = \frac{1}{2}$, and we find from Table V that $P(A|B_1) = 0.201$ and $P(A|B_2) = 0.215$. Therefore,

$$P(B_1|A) = \frac{\frac{1}{2}(0.201)}{\frac{1}{2}(0.201) + \frac{1}{2}(0.215)} = 0.48 \qquad \text{and} \qquad P(B_2|A) = 1 - 0.48 = 0.52$$

8.11   (a) If B_1, B_2, and B_3 are the events that consultant 1, consultant 2, and consultant 3 are right, $P(B_1) = 6 \cdot P(B_3)$ and $P(B_2) = 3 \cdot P(B_3)$, so that $6 \cdot P(B_3) + 3 \cdot P(B_3) + P(B_3) = 1$ and $P(B_3) = 0.10$.   Therefore, $P(B_1) = 6(0.10) = 0.60$, $P(B_2) = 3(0.10) = 0.30$, and $P(B_3) = 0.10$.

(b) If A is the event that 2 of 10 adult consumers find the taste too spicy, we find from Table V that $P(A|B_1) = 0.233$, $P(A|B_2) = 0.302$, and $P(A|B_3) = 0.194$, so that

$$P(B_1|A) = \frac{(0.60)(0.233)}{(0.60)(0.233) + (0.30)(0.302) + (0.10)(0.194)} = \frac{0.1398}{0.2498} = 0.560$$

$$P(B_2|A) = \frac{(0.30)(0.302)}{0.2498} = 0.363$$

$$P(B_3|A) = \frac{(0.10)(0.194)}{0.2498} = 0.078$$

8.14   If B_1, B_2, and B_3 are the events that zero, one, or two of the sneakers are blemished, and A is the event that the chosen sneaker is blemished, then $P(B_1) = 0.90$, $P(B_2) = 0.08$, $P(B_3) = 0.02$, $P(A|B_1) = 0$, $P(A|B_2) = \frac{1}{2}$, and $P(A|B_3) = 1$, and substitution into Bayes's formula yields

$$P(B_3|A) = \frac{(0.02)(1)}{(0.90)(0) + (0.08)(0.5) + (0.02)(1)} = \frac{0.02}{0.06} = 0.33$$

8.17 (a) Opportunity losses are calculated in the following table for, say, the event that the carton contains two defective goblets, as $3 \cdot 20 - 50 = \$10$ if she does not bid and as 0 if she bids.

		Bid $50	Don't bid
	0	0	50
	1	0	30
Number of	2	0	10
defective			
goblets	3	10	0
	4	30	0
	5	50	0

Thus, the expected opportunity losses are $10(0.20) + 30(0.10) + 50(0.10) = \$10$ if she bids and $50(0.1) + 30(0.2) + 10(0.3) = \$14$ if she does not bid for the goblets, and she should decide to bid.

(b) If B_1, B_2, B_3, B_4, B_5, and B_6 are the events that zero, one, two, three, four, or five of the goblets are cracked, chipped, or broken, and A is the event that the goblet inspected is perfect, then $P(B_1) = 0.1$, $P(B_2) = 0.2$, $P(B_3) = 0.3$, $P(B_4) = 0.2$, $P(B_5) = 0.1$, $P(B_6) = 0.1$, $P(A|B_1) = 1.0$, $P(A|B_2) = 0.8$, $P(A|B_3) = 0.6$, $P(A|B_4) = 0.4$, $P(A|B_5) = 0.2$, and $P(A|B_6) = 0$, and substitution into Bayes's formula yields

$$P(B_1|A) = \frac{(0.1)(1.0)}{(0.1)(1.0) + (0.2)(0.8) + (0.3)(0.6) + \cdots + (0.1)(0.0)}$$

$$= \frac{0.1}{0.54} = 0.185$$

$$P(B_2|A) = \frac{(0.2)(0.8)}{0.54} = 0.296$$

$$P(B_3|A) = \frac{(0.3)(0.6)}{0.54} = 0.333$$

$$P(B_4|A) = \frac{(0.2)(0.4)}{0.54} = 0.148$$

$$P(B_5|A) = \frac{(0.1)(0.2)}{0.54} = 0.037$$

$$P(B_6|A) = \frac{(0.1)(0.0)}{0.54} = 0.00$$

The expected opportunity losses are $10(0.148) + 30(0.037) + 50(0.0) = 2.59$ if she bids and $50(0.185) + 30(0.296) + 10(0.333) = 21.46$ if she does not bid, and she should bid for the goblets.

(c) It is reduced by $10 - 2.59 = \$7.41$.

8.18 (a) The opportunity losses are

		Bid $60	Don't bid
	0	0	40
	1	0	20
Number of	2	0	0
defective			
goblets	3	20	0
	4	40	0
	5	60	0

and the expected opportunity losses are $20(0.2) + 40(0.1) + 60(0.1) = 14$ if she bids and acquires the goblets and $40(0.1) + 20(0.2) = 8$ if she does not bid for the goblets. Therefore, she should not bid.

(b) If C is the event that both goblets are cracked, then $P(C|B_1) = 0$, $P(C|B_2) = 0$, $P(C|B_3) = \dfrac{2}{5} \cdot \dfrac{1}{4} = 0.1$, $P(C|B_4) = \dfrac{3}{5} \cdot \dfrac{2}{4} = 0.3$, $P(C|B_5) = \dfrac{4}{5} \cdot \dfrac{3}{4} = 0.6$, and $P(C|B_6) = \dfrac{5}{5} \cdot \dfrac{4}{4} = 1$, and substitution into Bayes's formula yields

$$P(B_1|C) = \frac{(0.1)0}{(0.1)0 + (0.2)0 + (0.3)(0.1) + (0.2)(0.3) + \cdots + (0.1)1}$$

$$= \frac{0}{0.25} = 0$$

$$P(B_2|C) = \frac{(0.2)0}{0.25} = 0$$

$$P(B_3|C) = \frac{(0.3)(0.1)}{0.25} = 0.12$$

$$P(B_4|C) = \frac{(0.2)(0.3)}{0.25} = 0.24$$

$$P(B_5|C) = \frac{(0.1)(0.6)}{0.25} = 0.24,$$

$$P(B_6|C) = \frac{(0.1)1}{0.25} = 0.40$$

The expected opportunity losses are $20(0.24) + 40(0.24) + 60(0.40) = 38.4$ if she bids for the goblets and $40(0.0) + 20(0.0) = 0$ if she does not bid. Therefore, she should not bid.

(c) It is reduced by $\$8.00 - \$0.00 = \$8.00$.

8.19 (a) The opportunity losses are

	Accepts offer	Rejects offer
Arrives on time	800	0
Arrives late	0	1,600

and the expected opportunity losses are $800(0.8) + 0(0.2) = \$640$ if the proprietor accepts the offer and $0(0.8) + 1,600(0.2) = \$320$ if the proprietor rejects it. The proprietor should reject the offer since $320 is less than $640.

(b) If B_1 is the event that the shipment of books arrives on time, B_2 is the event that the shipment arrives late, and A is the event that the shipment has not arrived by mid-August, then $P(B_1) = 0.8$, $P(B_2) = 0.2$, $P(A|B_1) = 0.5$, and $P(A|B_2) = 1$, and substitution into Bayes's formula yields

$$P(B_1|A) = \frac{(0.8)(0.5)}{(0.8)(0.5) + (0.2)(1)} = \frac{0.4}{0.6} = \frac{2}{3} \quad \text{and} \quad P(B_2|A) = 1 - \frac{2}{3} = \frac{1}{3}$$

The expected opportunity losses are $800 \cdot \frac{2}{3} + 0 \cdot \frac{1}{3} = 533.33$ if the proprietor accepts the offer and $0 \cdot \frac{2}{3} + 1,600 \cdot \frac{1}{3} = 533.33$ if the proprietor rejects it. Since the outcomes are exactly equal, it makes no difference financially whether the proprietor accepts or rejects the offer.

CHAPTER **9**

The Normal Distribution

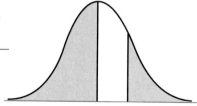

Continuous sample spaces arise whenever we deal with quantities that are measured on a continuous scale—for instance, when we measure the speed of a car, the net weight of a package of frozen food, the purity of a product, or the amount of tar in a cigarette. In cases like these there exist continuums of possibilities, and in practice what we are really interested in are probabilities associated with intervals or regions, not individual numbers or points, of a sample space. For instance, we might want to know the probability that at a given time a car is moving between 60 and 65 miles per hour (not at exactly 62.8 miles per hour), or that a package of frozen food weighs more than 7.95 ounces (not exactly 8.006 ounces).

In this chapter we shall learn how to determine, and work with, probabilities relating to continuous sample spaces and continuous random variables. The concept of a **continuous distribution** will be introduced in Section 9.1, followed by that of a **normal distribution** in Section 9.2. Various applications of the normal distribution will be discussed in Sections 9.3 and 9.4.

9.1

Continuous Distributions

In histograms, the frequencies, percentages, or proportions associated with the various classes are given by the heights of the rectangles or by their areas if the class intervals are all equal; this is true also for histograms showing the probabilities associated with the values of discrete random variables. In the continuous case, we also represent probabilities by means of areas, as is illustrated in Figure 9.1, but instead of areas of rectangles, we use areas under continuous curves. The first diagram of Figure 9.1 represents the probability distribution of a random variable which takes on only the values 0, 1, 2, . . . , 9, and 10, and the probability that it will take on the value 3, for example, is given by the area of the white region. The second diagram refers to a continuous random variable which can take on any value on the interval from 0 to 10, and the probability that it will take on a value on the interval from 2.5 to 3.5 is given by the area of the white region under the curve. Similarly, the area of the dark region under the curve gives the probability that it will take on a value greater than 8.

Continuous curves such as the one shown in the right-hand diagram of Figure 9.1 are the graphs of functions called **probability densities**, or informally, **continuous distributions**. A probability density is characterized by the following:

> The area under the curve between any two values *a* and *b* (see Figure 9.2) gives the probability that a random variable having the continuous distribution will take on a value on the interval from *a* to *b*.

It follows from this that the total area under the curve (representing the certainty that a random variable must take on one of its values) is always equal to 1.

For instance, if we approximate a family income distribution with a smooth curve as in Figure 9.3, we can determine what proportion of the incomes falls into any given interval (or the probability that the income of a family, chosen at random, will fall into the interval) by looking at the corresponding area under the curve. By comparing the area of the white region of Figure 9.3 with the total area under the curve (representing 100 percent),

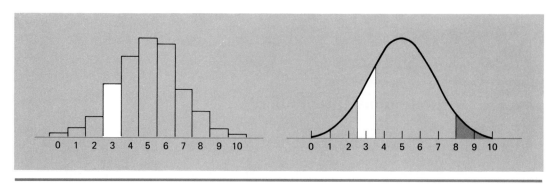

FIGURE 9.1   Histogram of probability distribution and graph of continuous distribution

we can judge by eye that roughly 10 to 12 percent of the families have incomes of $30,000 or more. Similarly, it can be seen that about 40 to 45 percent of the families have incomes of $15,000 or less.

Statistical descriptions of continuous distributions are as important as descriptions of probability distributions or distributions of observed data, but most of them including the mean and the standard deviation, cannot be defined without the use of calculus. Nevertheless, we can always picture a continuous distribution as being approximated by a histogram of a probability distribution whose mean and standard deviation can be calculated (see Figure 9.4). Then, if we choose histograms with narrower and narrower classes, the means and the standard deviations of the corresponding probability distributions will approach the mean and the standard deviation of the continuous distribution. Actually, the mean and the standard deviation of a continuous distribution measure the same properties as the mean and the standard deviation of a probability distribution—the expected value of a

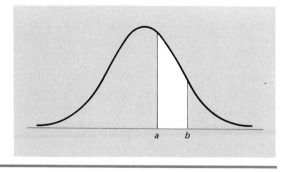

FIGURE 9.2
Continuous
distribution

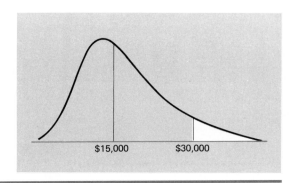

FIGURE 9.3
Curve approximating family income distribution

$15,000 $30,000

random variable having the given distribution, and the expected value of the squared deviation from the mean. More intuitively, the mean μ of a continuous distribution is a measure of its "center" or "middle," and the standard deviation σ of a continuous distribution is a measure of its dispersion or spread.

9.2

The Normal Distribution

Among the many continuous distributions used in statistics, the **normal distribution** is by far the most important. Its study dates back to eighteenth-century investigations into the nature of experimental errors. It was observed that discrepancies between repeated measurements of the same physical

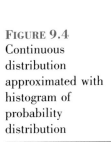

FIGURE 9.4
Continuous distribution approximated with histogram of probability distribution

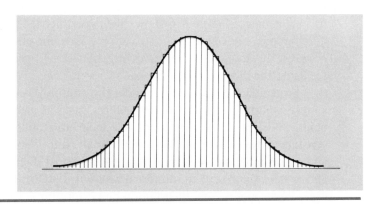

FIGURE 9.5
Normal distribution

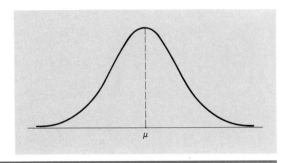

quantity displayed a surprising degree of regularity; their patterns (distribution), it was found, could be closely approximated by a certain kind of continuous distribution curve, referred to as the **"normal curve of errors"** and attributed to the laws of chance.

The graph of a normal distribution is a bell-shaped curve that extends indefinitely in both directions. Although this may not be apparent from a small drawing such as Figure 9.5, the curve comes closer and closer to the horizontal axis without ever reaching it, no matter how far we go from the mean in either direction. Fortunately, it is seldom necessary to extend the tails of a normal distribution very far because the area under that part of the curve lying more than four or five standard deviations away from the mean is for most practical purposes negligible.

An important feature of a normal distribution is that its mathematical equation is such that we can determine the area under the curve between any two points on the horizontal scale if we know its mean and its standard deviation; in other words, there is one and only one normal distribution with a given mean μ and a given standard deviation σ.

Since the equation of the normal distribution depends on μ and σ, we get different curves and, hence, different areas for different values of μ and σ. For instance, Figure 9.6 shows the superimposed graphs of two normal distributions, one having $\mu = 10$ and $\sigma = 5$ and the other having $\mu = 20$ and $\sigma = 10$. The area under the curve, say, between 12 and 15, is obviously not the same for the two distributions.

In practice, we find areas under the graph of a normal distribution, or simply a normal curve, in special tables, such as Table I at the end of the book. As it is physically impossible, and also unnecessary, to construct separate tables of normal-curve areas for all conceivable pairs of values of μ and σ, we tabulate these areas only for a normal distribution having $\mu = 0$ and $\sigma = 1$, the so-called **standard normal distribution**. Then, we obtain areas under any normal distribution by performing a simple change of scale

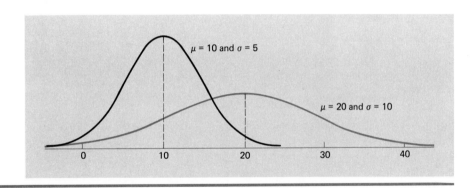

FIGURE 9.6
Two normal
distributions

(see Figure 9.7), in which we convert the units of measurement in the original, or *x*-scale, into **standard units**, **standard scores**, or **z-scores**, by means of the formula

Standard units

$$z = \frac{x - \mu}{\sigma}$$

In this new scale, the *z*-scale, *z* simply tells us how many standard deviations the corresponding *x*-value lies above or below the mean of its distribution.

The entries in Table I are the areas under the standard normal curve between the mean $z = 0$ and $z = 0.00, 0.01, 0.02, \ldots, 3.08$, and 3.09, and also $z = 4.00$, $z = 5.00$, and $z = 6.00$. In other words, the entries in Table I

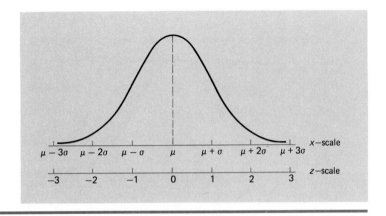

FIGURE 9.7
Change of scale

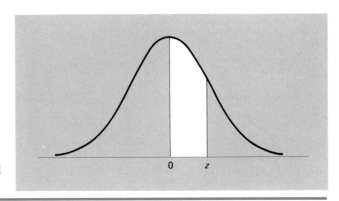

FIGURE 9.8
Tabulated areas
under the graph of
the standard normal
distribution

are areas under the standard normal distribution like the white area in Figure 9.8. Table I has no entries corresponding to negative values of z, for these are not needed by virtue of the symmetry of any normal curve about its mean.

EXAMPLE 9.1   Find the area under the standard normal curve between $z = -1.20$ and $z = 0$.

SOLUTION   As can be seen from Figure 9.9, the area under the curve between $z = -1.20$ and $z = 0$ equals the area under the curve between $z = 0$ and $z = 1.20$. So, we look up the entry for $z = 1.20$ and get 0.3849. ■

Questions concerning areas under normal distributions arise in various ways, and the ability to find any desired area quickly can be a big help. Although the table gives only areas between the mean $z = 0$ and selected

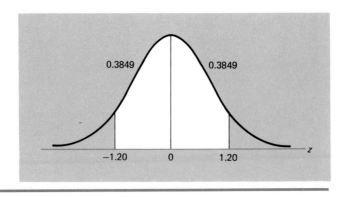

FIGURE 9.9
Area under normal
curve

Chapter 9   The Normal Distribution

positive values of z, we often have to find areas to the left or to the right of given positive or negative values of z, or areas between two given values of z. This is easy, provided we remember exactly what areas are represented by the entries in Table I, and also that the standard normal distribution is symmetrical about $z = 0$, so that the area to the left of $z = 0$ and the area to the right of $z = 0$ are both equal to 0.5000.

EXAMPLE 9.2   If a random variable has the standard normal distribution, what are the probabilities that it will take on a value
     (a) less than 1.64
     (b) greater than -0.47
     (c) greater than 0.76
     (d) less than -1.35
     (e) between 0.95 and 1.36
     (f) between -0.45 and 0.65

SOLUTION   For each part see Figure 9.10. (a) The probability that the random variable will take on a value less than 1.64 (the area to the left of $z = 1.64$) is 0.5000 plus the entry in Table I corresponding to $z = 1.64$, or $0.5000 + 0.4495 = 0.9495$; (b) the probability that it will take on a value greater than -0.47 (the area to the right of $z = -0.47$) is 0.5000 plus the entry in Table I corresponding to $z = 0.47$, or $0.5000 + 0.1808 = 0.6808$; (c) the probability that it will take on a value greater than 0.76 is 0.5000 minus the entry in Table I corresponding to $z = 0.76$, or $0.5000 - 0.2764 = 0.2236$; (d) the probability that it will take on a value less than -1.35 is 0.5000 minus the entry in Table I corresponding to $z = 1.35$, or $0.5000 - 0.4115 = 0.0885$; (e) the probability that it will take on a value between 0.95 and 1.36 is the difference between the entries in Table I corresponding to $z = 1.36$ and $z = 0.95$, or $0.4131 - 0.3289 = 0.0842$; (f) the probability that it will take on a value between -0.45 and 0.65 is the sum of the entries in Table I corresponding to $z = 0.45$ and $z = 0.65$, or $0.1736 + 0.2422 = 0.4158$.   ■

EXAMPLE 9.3   For the two normal curves of Figure 9.6, find the area under the curve between 12 and 15 for the distribution with
     (a) $\mu = 10$ and $\sigma = 5$
     (b) $\mu = 20$ and $\sigma = 10$

SOLUTION   (a) The values of z corresponding to $x = 12$ and $x = 15$ are

$$z = \frac{12 - 10}{5} = 0.40 \quad \text{and} \quad z = \frac{15 - 10}{5} = 1.00$$

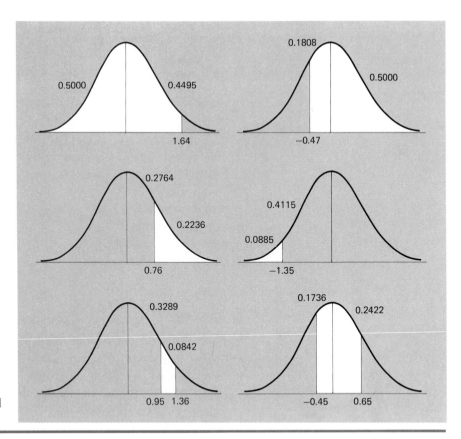

FIGURE 9.10
Areas under normal distributions

the corresponding entries in Table I are 0.1554 and 0.3413, and the area under the curve between 12 and 15 (the area of the white region of the upper diagram of Figure 9.11) is $0.3413 - 0.1554 = 0.1859$;

(b) The values of z corresponding to $x = 12$ and $x = 15$ are

$$z = \frac{12 - 20}{10} = -0.80 \qquad \text{and} \qquad z = \frac{15 - 20}{10} = -0.50$$

the corresponding entries in Table I are 0.2881 and 0.1915, and the area under the curve between 12 and 15 (the area of the white region of the lower diagram of Figure 9.11) is $0.2881 - 0.1915 = 0.0966$. ■

There are also problems in which we are given areas under normal curves and asked to find the corresponding values of z. The results of the example that follows will be used extensively in subsequent chapters.

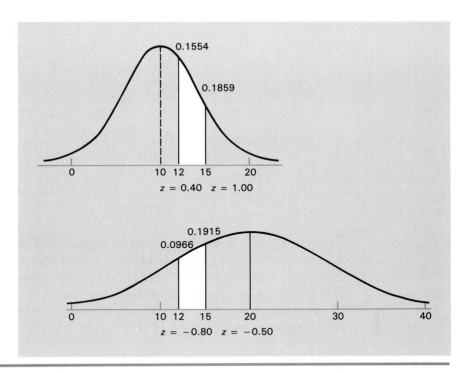

FIGURE 9.11
Areas under normal
distributions

EXAMPLE 9.4 If z_α denotes the value of z for which the area under the standard normal curve to its right is equal to α (Greek lowercase alpha), find

(a) $z_{0.01}$

(b) $z_{0.05}$

SOLUTION (a) It can be seen from Figure 9.12 that $z_{0.01}$ corresponds to an entry of $0.5000 - 0.0100 = 0.4900$ in Table I; since the nearest entry is 0.4901 corresponding to $z = 2.33$, we have $z_{0.01} = 2.33$; (b) also from Figure 9.12, $z_{0.05}$ corresponds to an entry of $0.5000 - 0.0500 = 0.4500$ in Table I; since the two nearest entries are 0.4495 and 0.4505 corresponding to $z = 1.64$ and $z = 1.65$, we have $z_{0.05} = 1.645$. ∎

Table I also enables us to show that for reasonably symmetrical bell-shaped distributions, about 68 percent of the values fall within one standard deviation of the mean, about 95 percent fall within two standard deviations of the mean, and over 99 percent fall within three standard deviations of the mean. These figures are for normal distributions, and in parts (a), (b), and (c) of Exercise 9.6 on page 335 the reader will be asked to show that 0.6826 of

FIGURE 9.12
Diagram for
determination of z_α

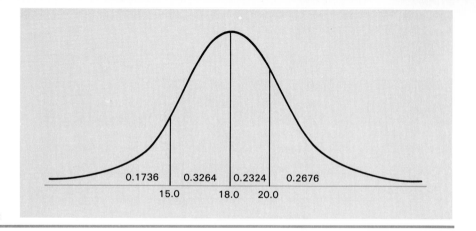

the area under the standard normal distribution falls between $z = -1$ and $z = 1$, that 0.9544 of the area falls between $z = -2$ and $z = 2$, and that 0.9974 of the area falls between $z = -3$ and $z = 3$. The results of parts (d) and (e) of Exercise 9.6 also show that, although the "tails" extend indefinitely in both directions, the area under a standard normal curve beyond $z = 4$ or $z = 5$ is negligible.

EXERCISES

(Exercises 9.1, 9.2, 9.5, 9.7, 9.8, 9.10, and 9.11 are practice exercises. Their complete solutions are given on page 350.)

9.1 Suppose that a continuous random variable takes on values on the interval from 3 to 9 and that the graph of its distribution is a horizontal line (Figure 9.13). Such a distribution is called a **uniform density**.

(a) What is the probability represented by the shaded region of Figure 9.13?

(b) What is the probability that the random variable will take on a value less than 7?

(c) Is the probability in part (b) the same as the probability that the random variable will take on a value less than or equal to 7?

(d) What is the probability that the random variable will take on a value between 3.6 and 7.8?

9.2 Find the area under the standard normal curve which lies

(a) between $z = 0$ and $z = 0.89$

(b) between $z = -1.82$ and $z = 0$

(c) to the right of $z = 0.45$

(d) to the right of $z = 3.09$

(e) to the left of $z = -1.13$

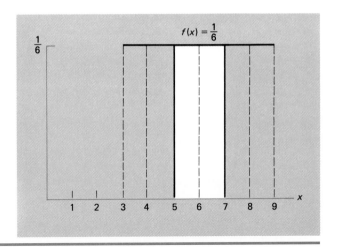

FIGURE 9.13
Uniform density

9.3   Find the area under the standard normal curve which lies
(a) between $z = -0.63$ and $z = 0.63$
(b) between $z = -0.84$ and $z = 1.23$
(c) between $z = 0.26$ and $z = 0.97$
(d) between $z = -0.42$ and $z = -1.00$

9.4   Find the area under the standard normal curve which lies
(a) between $z = -0.86$ and $z = 0.86$
(b) to the right of $z = -2.00$
(c) to the left of $z = -2.00$
(d) between $z = 1.41$ and $z = 1.45$
(e) to the right of $z = 0.22$
(f) between $z = -2.34$ and $z = -0.39$

9.5   Find z if the normal curve area
(a) between 0 and z is 0.4854
(b) to the left of z is 0.9962
(c) to the right of z is 0.7642
(d) to the right of z is 0.2514
(e) to the left of z is 0.0885

9.6   Find the normal-curve area between $-z$ and z if
(a) $z = 1.00$
(b) $z = 2.00$
(c) $z = 3.00$
(d) $z = 4.00$
(e) $z = 5.00$

Section 9.2   The Normal Distribution

9.7 Verify that

(a) $z_{0.005} = 2.575$

(b) $z_{0.025} = 1.96$

9.8 A random variable has a normal distribution with the mean $\mu = 50$ and the standard deviation $\sigma = 5.2$. What are the probabilities that the random variable will take on a value

(a) less than 55.2

(b) greater than 60.3

(c) between 52 and 57.2

(d) between 40 and 65

9.9 A normal distribution has the mean $\mu = 200$. If 70 percent of the area under the curve lies to the left of 220, find

(a) the area to the left of 200

(b) the area to the right of 220

(c) the area between 200 and 220

(d) the standard deviation

(e) the area between 200 and 225

(f) the area to the right of 225

9.10 A random variable has a normal distribution with the standard deviation $\sigma = 9.0$. If the probability that the random variable will take on a value less than 84.0 is 0.8413, what is the probability that it will take on a value greater than 80.0?

9.11 Another continuous distribution, called the **exponential distribution**, has many important applications. If a random variable has an exponential distribution with mean μ, the probability that it will take on a value between 0 and any given positive value x is $1 - e^{-x/\mu}$ (see Figure 9.14). Here e is the constant which appears also in the formula for the Poisson distribution, and values of $e^{-x/\mu}$ can be obtained directly from Table X.

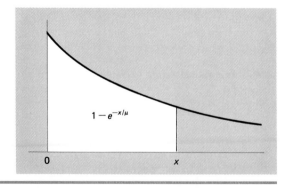

FIGURE 9.14
Exponential distribution

Chapter 9 The Normal Distribution

(a) Find the probabilities that a random variable having an exponential distribution with $\mu = 10$ will take on a value between 0 and 4, a value greater than 6, and a value between 8 and 12.

(b) The lifetime of a certain kind of battery is a random variable which has an exponential distribution with a mean of $\mu = 200$ hours. What is the probability that such a battery will last at most 100 hours? Between 400 and 600 hours?

(c) In a certain brokerage house, the time a customer has to wait for confirmation of a transaction has an exponential distribution with $\mu = 30$ minutes. What is the probability that a customer will have to wait between 12 and 36 minutes for such a confirmation?

9.3

Applications of the Normal Distribution

Let us now consider some applied problems in which we shall assume that the distributions of the data, or the distributions of the random variables under consideration, can be approximated closely with normal curves.

EXAMPLE 9.5   The lengths of the sardines received by a certain cannery have a mean of 4.62 inches and a standard deviation of 0.23 inch.

(a) What percentage of all these sardines is longer than 5.00 inches?

(b) What percentage of the sardines is between 4.35 and 4.85 inches long?

SOLUTION   (a) The answer to this question is given by the area of the white region of Figure 9.15, that is, the area to the right of 5.00 inches, and

$$z = \frac{5.00 - 4.62}{0.23} = 1.65$$

Since the entry in Table I corresponding to $z = 1.65$ is 0.4505, we find that $0.5000 - 0.4505 = 0.0495$, so 4.95 percent of the sardines is longer than 5.00 inches.

(b) The answer is given by the area of the white region of Figure 9.16, the area under the curve between

$$z = \frac{4.35 - 4.62}{0.23} = -1.17 \quad \text{and} \quad z = \frac{4.85 - 4.62}{0.23} = 1.00$$

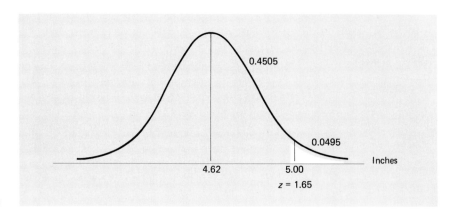

FIGURE 9.15
Normal distribution

The corresponding entries in Table I are 0.3790 for $z = 1.17$ and 0.3413 for $z = 1.00$, and $0.3790 + 0.3413 = 0.7203$. Hence, a little more than 72 percent of the sardines are between 4.35 and 4.85 inches long. ∎

EXAMPLE 9.6   The actual amount of instant coffee which a filling machine puts into "6-ounce" cans varies from can to can, and it may be looked upon as a random variable having a normal distribution with a standard deviation of 0.04 ounce. If only 2 percent of the cans are to contain less than 6 ounces of coffee, what must the mean fill of these cans be?

SOLUTION   We are given $\sigma = 0.04$, $x = 6.00$, and a normal curve area (that of the white region of Figure 9.17), and we are asked to find μ. Since

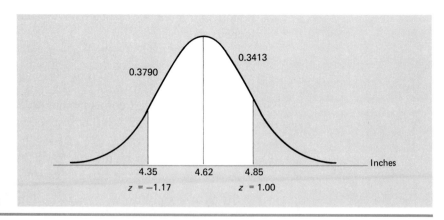

FIGURE 9.16
Normal distribution

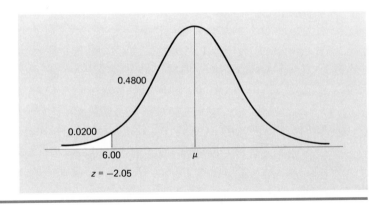

FIGURE 9.17
Normal distribution

the value of z for which the entry in Table I comes closest to $0.5000 - 0.0200 = 0.4800$ is 2.05, we have

$$-2.05 = \frac{6.00 - \mu}{0.04}$$

and, solving for μ, we get

$$6.00 - \mu = (-2.05)(0.04) = -0.082$$

and then

$$\mu = 6.00 + 0.082 = 6.08 \text{ ounces} \qquad \blacksquare$$

Although, strictly speaking, the normal distribution applies to continuous random variables, it is often used to approximate distributions of **discrete** random variables, which can take on only a finite number of values or as many values as there are positive integers. This yields quite satisfactory results in many situations, provided that we make the **continuity correction** illustrated in the following example.

EXAMPLE 9.7   A baker knows that the daily demand for whole pecan pies is a random variable with a distribution which can be approximated closely by a normal distribution with the mean $\mu = 43.3$ and the standard deviation $\sigma = 4.6$. What is the probability that the demand for these pies will exceed 50 on any given day?

SOLUTION   The answer is given by the area of the white region of Figure 9.18; the area to the right of 50.5, not 50. The reason for this is that the number of pies the baker sells is a whole number. Hence, if we want to approximate this demand distribution with a normal curve, we

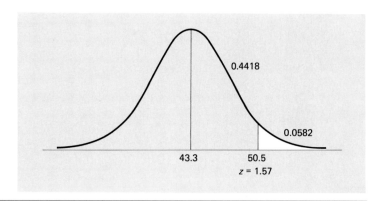

FIGURE 9.18
Normal distribution

must "spread" the values of this discrete random variable over a continous scale, and we do this by representing each whole number k by the interval from $k - \frac{1}{2}$ to $k + \frac{1}{2}$. For instance, 20 is represented by the interval from 19.5 to 20.5, 25 is represented by the interval from 24.5 to 25.5, 50 is represented by the interval from 49.5 to 50.5, and the probability of a demand greater than 50 is given by the area under the curve to the right of 50.5. Accordingly, we get

$$z = \frac{50.5 - 43.3}{4.6} = 1.57$$

and it follows from Table I that the area of the white region of Figure 9.18—the probability of a demand for more than 50 pecan pies—is $0.5000 - 0.4418 = 0.0582$. ∎

9.4

The Normal Approximation to the Binomial Distribution

The normal distribution is sometimes introduced as a continous distribution which provides a very close approximation to the binomial distribution when n, the number of trials, is very large and p, the probability of a success on an individual trial, is close to 0.50. Figure 9.19 shows the histograms of binomial distributions having $p = 0.50$ and $n = 2, 5, 10,$ and 25, and it can be seen that with increasing n these distributions approach the symmetrical bell-shaped pattern of the normal distribution. In fact, a normal

Chapter 9   The Normal Distribution

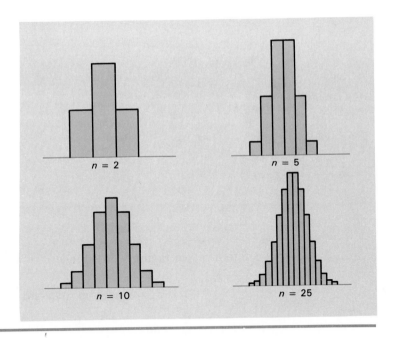

FIGURE 9.19
Binomial
distributions with
$p = 0.50$

curve with the mean $\mu = np$ and the standard deviation $\sigma = \sqrt{np(1-p)}$ can often be used to approximate a binomial distribution even when n is fairly small and p differs from 0.50 but is not too close to either 0 or 1. A good rule of thumb is to use this approximation only when np and $n(1-p)$ are both greater than 5.

The following examples illustrate the normal approximation to the binomial distribution.

EXAMPLE 9.8   Find the exact probability of getting 4 heads in 12 flips of a balanced coin and also the normal approximation to this binomial probability.

SOLUTION   To find the exact value, we substitute $n = 12$, $x = 4$, and $p = \frac{1}{2}$ into the binomial formula, getting

$$f(4) = \binom{12}{4}\left(\frac{1}{2}\right)^4\left(1 - \frac{1}{2}\right)^{12-4} = 495 \cdot \left(\frac{1}{2}\right)^{12}$$
$$= \frac{495}{4,096}$$
$$= 0.1208$$

To find the normal-curve approximation to this probability, we use the continuity correction and represent 4 heads by the interval

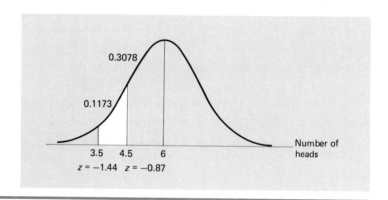

FIGURE 9.20

Normal-curve
approximation to
binomial
distribution

from 3.5 to 4.5 (see Figure 9.20). Since $\mu = 12 \cdot \dfrac{1}{2} = 6$ and $\sigma = \sqrt{12 \cdot \dfrac{1}{2} \cdot \dfrac{1}{2}} = 1.732$, we have in standard units $z = \dfrac{3.5 - 6}{1.732} = -1.44$ for $x = 3.5$ and $z = \dfrac{4.5 - 6}{1.732} = -0.87$ for $x = 4.5$ The corresponding entries in Table I are 0.4251 and 0.3078, and the approximate probability is $0.4251 - 0.3078 = 0.1173$, only 0.0035 smaller than the exact probability. ∎

The normal-curve approximation to the binomial distribution is particularly useful in problems where we would otherwise have to use the formula for the binomial distribution repeatedly to obtain the values of many different terms.

EXAMPLE 9.9 What is the probability of getting at least 12 replies to questionnaires mailed to 100 persons, when the probability is 0.18 that any one of them will reply?

SOLUTION If we tried to solve this problem by using the formula for the binomial distribution, we would have to find the sum of the probabilities corresponding to 12, 13, 14, . . . , and 100 replies or subtract from 1 the sum of the probabilities of 0, 1, 2, . . . , and 11 replies. This would obviously involve a tremendous amount of work, but using the normal-curve approximation, we need only find the white area of Figure 9.21, the area to the right of 11.5. We are again using the continuity correction according to which 12 is represented by the interval from 11.5 to 12.5, 13 is represented by the interval 12.5 to 13.5, and so on.

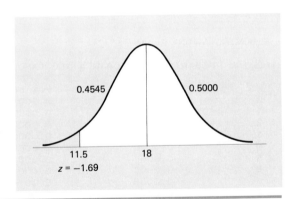

FIGURE 9.21
Normal-curve
approximation to
binomial
distribution

Since $\mu = 100(0.18) = 18$ and $\sigma = \sqrt{100(0.18)(0.82)} = 3.84$, we find that in standard units $x = 11.5$ becomes

$$z = \frac{11.5 - 18}{3.84} = -1.69$$

and that the probability is $0.4545 + 0.5000 = 0.9545$. This means that among many mailings of 100 questionnaires we can expect to get at least 12 replies about 95 percent of the time, provided the probability that any one person will reply is 0.18. The actual value of the probability, to four decimal places, is 0.9605, so the error of the approximation is only 0.0060. ∎

To verify the error of the approximation made in this example, let us refer to the computer printout of Figure 9.22, which shows the actual binomial probabilities for $n = 100$ and $p = 0.18$ as well as the cumulative "or less" probabilities. Since "at least 12 replies" is 1 minus the probability of 11 or less, we find that the desired probability is $1 - 0.0395 = 0.9605$, where 0.0395 is the value in the right-hand column of the printout corresponding to $K = 11$. Thus, the error of the normal approximation, as before, is only $0.9605 - 0.9545 = 0.0060$.

EXERCISES

(Exercises 9.12, 9.15, 9.16, 9.17, 9.20, 9.21, and 9.26 are practice exercises. Their complete solutions are given on page 350.)

9.12 A bank manager has determined from experience that the time required for a security guard to make his rounds in a bank building is a random variable having an approximately normal distribution with $\mu = 18.0$ minutes and $\sigma =$

FIGURE 9.22
Computer printout
of the binomial
distribution with
$n = 100$ and
$p = 0.18$

```
MTB > BINOMIAL N=100 P=.18

     BINOMIAL PROBABILITIES FOR N = 100   AND P = 0.180000

        K              P( X = K )            P(X LESS OR = K)
        0               0.0000                 0.0000
        1               0.0000                 0.0000
        2               0.0000                 0.0000
        3               0.0000                 0.0000
        4               0.0000                 0.0000
        5               0.0001                 0.0001
        6               0.0003                 0.0004
        7               0.0009                 0.0014
        8               0.0024                 0.0038
        9               0.0054                 0.0092
       10               0.0108                 0.0200
       11               0.0194                 0.0395
       12               0.0316                 0.0711
       13               0.0470                 0.1181
       14               0.0641                 0.1823
       15               0.0807                 0.2630
       16               0.0941                 0.3571
       17               0.1021                 0.4592
       18               0.1033                 0.5626
       19               0.0979                 0.6605
       20               0.0870                 0.7475
       21               0.0728                 0.8203
       22               0.0574                 0.8777
       23               0.0427                 0.9204
       24               0.0301                 0.9504
       25               0.0201                 0.9705
       26               0.0127                 0.9832
       27               0.0076                 0.9909
       28               0.0044                 0.9952
       29               0.0024                 0.9976
       30               0.0012                 0.9989
       31               0.0006                 0.9995
       32               0.0003                 0.9998
       33               0.0001                 0.9999
```

3.2 minutes. What are the probabilities that a security guard will complete his rounds of the bank building in

(a) less than 15 minutes

(b) 15 to 20 minutes

(c) more than 20 minutes

9.13   The trees in a forest have a mean height of 39.5 feet with a standard deviation of 2.2 feet. Assuming that the distribution of these trees has roughly the shape of a normal distribution, find

(a) what percentage of the trees are less than 38 feet tall

(b) what percentage are at least 40 feet tall

(c) what percentage of the trees are between 38 and 40 feet tall

(d) the height below which are the shortest 30 percent of the trees

(e) the height above which are the tallest 30 percent of the trees

9.14   The time required by a mechanic in a bicycle shop to assemble a certain type of bicycle may be looked upon as a random variable with a mean distribution of 20.5 minutes and a standard deviation of 2.3 minutes. Find the probabilities that the time required to assemble a bicycle is

(a) at least 20 minutes

(b) at most 19.0 minutes

(c) between 20.0 and 21.0 minutes

(d) between 18.0 and 20 minutes

9.15   A crossword puzzle enthusiast has exactly 30 minutes to complete a puzzle each day during her morning commute on the train. She knows from experience that the puzzle published in newspaper A takes an average of 25.2 minutes to complete with a standard deviation of 3.9 minutes. The puzzle published in newspaper B also takes an average of 25.2 minutes to complete, but it has a standard deviation of 1.9 minutes. What is the probability that she will complete the puzzle if she buys

(a) newspaper A

(b) newspaper B

9.16   With reference to the filling machine of Example 9.6 on page 338, show that if the variability of the machine is reduced so that $\sigma = 0.025$ ounce, this will lower the required average amount of coffee per can to $\mu = 6.05$ ounces, yet keep about 98 percent of the weights above 6 ounces.

9.17   The owner of an automobile towing service company knows that the number of towing service calls the company makes each day is a random variable having approximately a normal distribution with the mean 36.2 and the standard deviation 5.1. What are the probabilities that in any given day the company will make

(a) exactly 30 towing service calls

(b) at most 30 towing service calls

9.18   The daily number of lost books returned to the lost and found department of a college is a random variable having approximately a normal distribution with the mean $\mu = 11.3$ and the standard deviation $\sigma = 2.6$. During how many days of a 192 day academic year can the lost-and-found department expect to get between 6 and 12 returned lost books?

9.19   A department store salesclerk knows that the number of sales she will make on a business day is a random variable having approximately a normal distribution with $\mu = 24.9$ and $\sigma = 4.1$. Find the probabilities that during a business day the salesclerk will make

(a) more than 25 sales

(b) fewer than 20 sales

9.20 Use the normal-curve approximation to find the probability of getting 7 heads in 14 flips of a balanced coin, and compare the result with the value given in Table V.

9.21 If 15 percent of the mortgage loan applications received by a savings and loan association are refused, what is the probability that among 160 loan applications at least 30 will be refused?

9.22 What is the probability that fewer than 25 walkers out of 500 walkers will fail to finish a walkathon for a charitable event, if the probability is 0.06 that any one walker will not finish?

9.23 A television station claims that its late evening news program regularly has 35 percent of the total viewing audience. If this claim is correct, what is the probability that among 500 late evening viewers, more than 200 will be watching the station's news program?

9.24 A videocassette recorder manufacturer knows that, on the average, 4 percent of the VCRs made by the firm will require repairs before their warranties expire. What is the probability that among 1,000 VCRs shipped by the manufacturer, at least 30 will require repairs before their warranties expire?

9.25 To avoid accusations of sexism in a college class equally populated by male and female students, the professor flips a balanced coin to decide whether to call upon a male or female student to answer a question directed to the class. If the professor does this 75 times during the semester what is the probability that a male student will be called upon
(a) more than 44 times
(b) fewer than 31 times

9.26 To illustrate the Law of Large Numbers which we mentioned in connection with the frequency interpretation of probability and also on page 283, find the probabilities that the proportion of heads will be anywhere from 0.49 to 0.51 when a balanced coin is flipped
(a) 100 times
(b) 10,000 times

9.5

A Word of Caution

Although the normal distribution is the only continuous distribution which we have discussed in any detail in this chapter, we hope that this will not give the erroneous impression that the normal distribution is the only continuous distribution that matters in the study of statistics. The exponential distribution is an important one, too, and in later chapters we shall meet several other continuous distributions, among them the *t* **distribution** the **chi-square distribution**, and the *F* **distribution**, which play important roles in problems of statistical inference.

It is true that the normal distribution plays a fundamental role in many statistical problems, but it is also true that its indiscriminate use can lead to very misleading results. There are various ways in which we can decide whether or not a distribution of observed data fits the overall pattern of a normal curve; one of these will be described in Chapter 13, Exercise 13.57.

9.6

Checklist of Key Terms

Continuity correction,   339
Continuous distribution,   325
Discrete random variables,   339
Exponential distribution,   336
Normal approximation to binomial
   distribution,   340
Normal curve of errors,   328

Normal distribution,   327
Probability density,   325
Standard normal distribution,   328
Standard scores,   329
Standard units,   329
Uniform density,   334

9.7

Review Exercises

9.27 The weights of a large shipment of bronze castings are random variables which have a normal distribution with $\mu = 50.25$ pounds and $\sigma = 0.63$ pounds. What is the probability that a casting selected from this shipment will weigh

(a) less than 49.00 pounds

(b) more than 50.50 pounds

(c) between 50.00 and 51.00 pounds

9.28 Use the normal-curve approximation to find the probability of getting 10 heads in 12 flips of a balanced coin and compare the results with the value given in Table V.

9.29 Find the area under the standard normal curve which lies
  (a) between $z = 0$ and $z = 0.83$
  (b) to the left of $z = 1.48$
  (c) to the right of $z = -2.1$
  (d) to the right of $z = 2.1$
  (e) to the left of $z = -1.00$

9.30 A random variable has a normal distribution with the mean $\mu = 102.9$ and the standard deviation $\sigma = 4.7$. What are the probabilities that this random variable will take on a value
  (a) less than 110.1
  (b) greater than 95.6
  (c) between 104.5 and 105.0
  (d) between 98.7 and 105.0

9.31 Find the values of
  (a) $z_{0.02}$
  (b) $z_{0.10}$

9.32 If 75 percent of the applicants for a job in a manufacturing company can pass a manual dexterity test, what is the probability that among 150 applicants at least 100 will pass the test?

9.33 Suppose that a continuous random variable takes on values on the interval from 0 to 4 and that the graph of its distribution, called a **triangular density**, is given by the line of Figure 9.23. Find the probabilities that the random variable will take on a value
  (a) less than 1
  (b) greater than 2
  (c) between 1.5 and 2.5

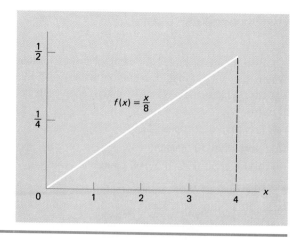

FIGURE 9.23
Triangular density

Chapter 9   The Normal Distribution

9.34 The head of the personnel department of a company knows from experience that the number of production workers who are absent because of illness each day is a random variable with the mean $\mu = 41.3$ and the standard deviation $\sigma = 4.9$. Assuming that the number of absences for illness has roughly the shape of a normal distribution, find the probabilities that there will be in one day

(a) more than 50 absences

(b) at least 50 absences

(c) between 40 and 50 absences, not inclusive

9.35 A random variable has a normal distribution with the standard deviation $\sigma = 3.75$. If the probability is 0.9961 that the random variable will take on a value less than 145.6, what is the probability that it will take on a value between 125.8 and 129.0?

9.36 If 40 percent of the orders shipped by a restaurant supply company are shipped C.O.D. (cash on delivery), what is the probability that among 90 orders shipped, more than 40 are C.O.D.?

9.37 Find the area under the standard normal curve which lies

(a) between $z = 0$ and $z = -1.95$

(b) between $z = -0.75$ and $z = 0.75$

(c) between $z = 0.50$ and $z = 0.75$

(d) between $z = -2.2$ and $z = 0.5$

(e) between $z = -2.2$ and $z = -0.5$

9.38 Under an incentive plan, workers are paid at a set rate per unit for all units produced per day up to a certain quota, after which a bonus rate is paid. If the number of units produced is a random variable having approximately a normal distribution with the mean $\mu = 80$ units and the standard deviation $\sigma = 5$ units, find the probability that the number of units produced by a worker during a day will

(a) equal or exceed the quota of 83 units per day

(b) be 90 or more units per day

(c) be from 83 to 90 units inclusive

9.39 Find z if the normal-curve area

(a) between 0 and z is 0.3944

(b) to the right of z is 0.2709

(c) to the right of z is 0.9793

(d) between $-z$ and z is 0.9876

9.40 The average time required for a boat to sail to destination A is 65 minutes with a standard deviation of 8 minutes, and the average time required to sail to destination B is 85 minutes with a standard deviation of 9 minutes. Assuming normal distributions, what proportion of the time will the trip to destination A take longer than the average time to sail to destination B; and what proportion of the time will the trip to destination *B* take less time than the average time to destination *A*?

 9.41 Repeated experiments of a seed company show that the probability a certain type of flower seed will not germinate (begin to grow) when planted is 0.18. If a package of 100 seeds is planted, determine the probability that

(a) exactly 12 seeds will not germinate

(b) at least 12 seeds will not germinate

(c) fewer than 12 seeds will not germinate

(d) 12 or fewer seeds will not germinate

Use the computer printout of Figure 9.22 on page 344 to solve this exercise.

9.8

Solutions of Practice Exercises

9.1   (a) There are six rectangles of equal area under the horizontal line, two of the rectangles lie between $x = 5$ and $x = 7$; $\frac{2}{6} = \frac{1}{3}$ or 0.33.

(b) Four rectangles lie between $x = 3$ and $x = 7$; $\frac{4}{6} = \frac{2}{3} = 0.67$.

(c) It does not matter whether $x = 7$ is included.

(d) $(7.8 - 3.6)\frac{1}{6} = \frac{4.2}{6} = 0.70$.

9.2   (a) 0.3133   (b) 0.4656   (c) $0.5000 - 0.1736 = 0.3264$
(d) $0.5000 - 0.4990 = 0.0010$ (e) $0.5000 - 0.3708 = 0.1292$

9.5   (a) 2.18   (b) 2.67   (c) -0.72 (d) 0.67   (e) -1.35

9.7   (a) $0.5000 - 0.005 = 0.4950$. The two nearest entries in Table I are 0.4949 and 0.4951 corresponding to $z = 2.57$ and $z = 2.58$; thus, by interpolation, $z_{0.005} = 2.575$.

(b) The entry in Table I, $0.5000 - 0.0250 = 0.4750$, corresponds to 1.96; thus, $z_{0.025} = 1.96$.

9.8   (a) Since $z = \dfrac{55.2 - 50}{5.2} = 1$, the probability is $0.3413 + 0.5000 = 0.8413$.

(b) Since $z = \dfrac{60.3 - 50}{5.2} = 1.98$, the probability is 0.4761. The probability that the random variable will take on a value greater than 60.3 is $0.5000 - 0.4761 = 0.0239$.

(c) Since $z = \dfrac{52 - 50}{5.2} = 0.38$ and $z = \dfrac{57.2 - 50}{5.2} = 1.38$, the corresponding entries in Table I are 0.1480 and 0.4162 and the probability is $0.4162 - 0.1480 = 0.2682$.

(d) Since $z = \dfrac{40 - 50}{5.2} = -1.92$ and $z = \dfrac{65 - 50}{5.2} = \dfrac{15}{5.2} = 2.88$, the probability is $0.4726 + 0.4980 = 0.9706$.

9.10 Since the entry corresponding to $0.8413 - 0.5000 = 0.3413$ is $z = 1.00$, $1.00 = \dfrac{84 - \mu}{9}$ and $\mu = 84 - 9(1.00) = 75$; also $z = \dfrac{80 - 75}{9} = 0.56$ and the corresponding area $= 0.2123$. The probability is $0.5000 - 0.2123 = 0.2877$.

9.11 (a) $1 - e^{-4/10} = 1 - e^{-0.4} = 1 - 0.670 = 0.330$, $1 - (1 - e^{-6/10}) = e^{-0.6} = 0.549$, and $(1 - e^{-12/10}) - (1 - e^{-8/10}) = e^{-0.8} - e^{-1.2} = 0.449 - 0.301 = 0.148$.

(b) $1 - e^{-100/200} = 1 - e^{-0.5} = 1 - 0.607 = 0.393$, and $(1 - e^{-600/200}) - (1 - e^{-400/200}) = e^{-2.0} - e^{-3.0} = 0.135 - 0.050 = 0.085$.

(c) $(1 - e^{-36/30}) - (1 - e^{-12/30}) = e^{-0.4} - e^{-1.2} = 0.670 - 0.301 = 0.369$.

9.12 (a) $z = \dfrac{15.0 - 18.0}{3.2} = -0.94$, and the probability is $0.5000 - 0.3264 = 0.1736$.

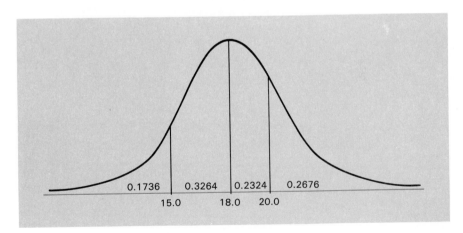

(b) $z = \dfrac{20.0 - 18.0}{3.2} = 0.62$, the corresponding area is 0.2324, and the probability is $0.3264 + 0.2324 = 0.5588$.

(c) $0.5000 - 0.2324 = 0.2676$.

9.15 The probability that she will complete the puzzle of newspaper A in 30 minutes is $z = \dfrac{30.0 - 25.2}{3.9} = 1.23$; the corresponding probability is 0.3907; and the probability that she will complete the puzzle is $0.5000 + 0.3907 = 0.8907$. For newspaper B, $z = \dfrac{30.0 - 25.2}{1.9} = 2.53$; the corresponding probability is 0.4943; and the probability that she will complete the puzzle is $0.5000 + 0.4943 = 0.9943$. She should buy newspaper B.

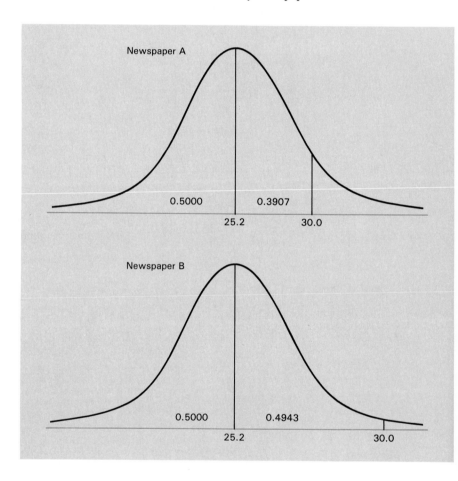

9.16 The entry nearest to 0.4800 is 0.4798 corresponding to $z = 2.05$, so $-2.05 = \dfrac{6.0 - \mu}{0.025}$, $-0.05125 = 6.0 - \mu$, and $\mu = 6.05$.

9.17 (a) $z = \dfrac{29.5 - 36.2}{5.1} = -1.31$ and $z = \dfrac{30.5 - 36.2}{5.1} = -1.12$; the proba-

bility is $0.4049 - 0.3686 = 0.0363$.

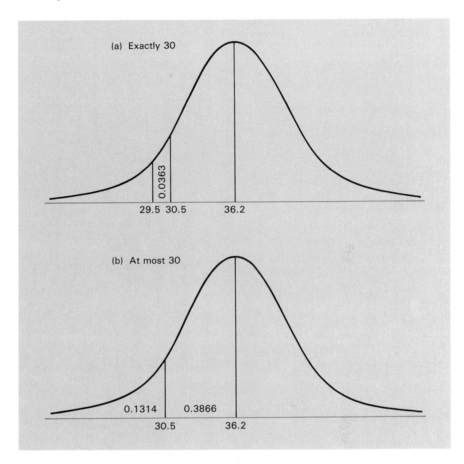

(b) $z = 1.12$; the probability is $0.5000 - 0.3686 = 0.1314$.

9.20 $\mu = 14(0.5) = 7$ and $\sigma = \sqrt{14(0.5)(0.5)} = 1.87$, so that $z = \dfrac{7.5 - 7}{1.87} = $

0.27 and the probability is $2(0.1064) = 0.2128$; Table V shows 0.209.

9.21 $\mu = 160(0.15) = 24$, $\sigma = \sqrt{160(0.15)(0.85)} = 4.52$, $z = \dfrac{29.5 - 24}{4.52} = $

1.22, the corresponding area is 0.3888, and the probability is $0.5000 - 0.3888 = 0.1112$.

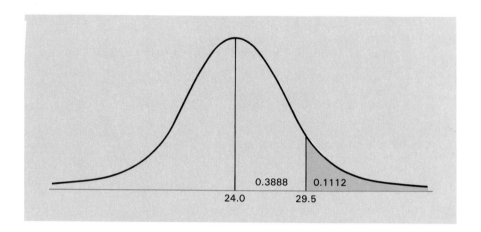

0.3888 | 0.1112

24.0 | 29.5

9.26 (a) $\mu = 100(0.5) = 50$ and $\sigma = \sqrt{100(0.5)(0.5)} = 5$, so that $z = \dfrac{51.5 - 50}{5} = 0.30$, the corresponding area is 0.1179, and the probability is $2(0.1179) = 0.2358$.

(b) $\mu = 10{,}000(0.5) = 5{,}000$ and $\sigma = \sqrt{10{,}000(0.5)(0.5)} = 50$, so that $z = \dfrac{5{,}100.5 - 5{,}000}{50} = 2.01$, the corresponding area is 0.4778, and the probability is $2(0.4778) = 0.9556$.

Chapter 9 The Normal Distribution

Sampling and Sampling Distributions

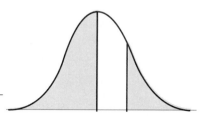

The purpose of most statistical investigations is to make valid generalizations on the basis of samples about the populations from which the samples came. The whole problem of when and under what conditions samples permit such generalizations has no easy solution. For instance, if we want to estimate the average amount of money people spend on their vacations, we would hardly take as our sample the amounts spent by the deluxe-class passengers on a 92-day ocean cruise, nor would we attempt to estimate wholesale prices of all farm products on the basis of the prices of apricots alone. In both cases we would reject estimates based on these samples as ridiculous, but just which vacationers and which farm products we should include in our samples, and how many of them, is not intuitively clear.

In the theory which we shall study in most of the remainder of this book, it will be assumed that we are dealing with **random samples**. This attention to random samples is due to the fact that they permit valid, or logical, generalizations and hence are widely used in actual practice. As we shall see, however, random sampling is not always practical, feasible, or even desirable, and some other sampling procedures will be discussed briefly in Chapter 21.

In this chapter we begin with a formal definition of **random sampling** in Section 10.1. Then, in Section 10.2, we introduce the related concept of a **sampling distribution**, which tells us how quantities determined from samples may vary from sample to sample, and in Sections 10.3 and 10.4 we learn how such variations can be measured.

10.1

Random Sampling

Earlier in this book we distinguished between populations and samples, stating that a population consists of all conceivably or hypothetically possible instances (or observations) of a given phenomenon, while a sample is simply a part of a population. In preparation for the work which follows, let us now distinguish between two kinds of populations—**finite populations** and **infinite populations**. A finite population is one which consists of a finite number, or fixed number, of elements (items, objects, measurements, or observations). Examples of finite populations are the net weights of the 24,000 cans of rust remover in a production lot, the scores made by the 650-person entering class of a technical school on the engineer scale of the Strong-Campbell Interest Inventory, and the outside diameters of a lot of 10,000 precision ball bearings.

In contrast to finite populations, a population is said to be infinite if there is, at least hypothetically, no limit to the number of elements it can contain. The population which consists of the results obtained in all hypothetically possible rolls of a pair of dice is an infinite population, and so is the population which consists of all conceivably possible measurements which could be made of the length of a metal strip.

To introduce the idea of random sampling from a finite population, let us ask the following three questions: (1) "How many distinct samples of size n can be taken from a finite population of size N?" (2) "How is a random sample defined?" (3) "How can a random sample be taken in actual practice?"

To answer the first question, we refer to the rule for combinations on page 122 according to which r objects can be selected from a set of n objects in $\binom{n}{r} = \dfrac{n!}{r!(n-r)!}$ ways. With a change of letters, we can say that the number of distinct samples of size n which can be drawn from a finite population of size N is $\binom{N}{n} = \dfrac{N!}{n!(N-n)!}$.

Chapter 10 Sampling and Sampling Distributions

EXAMPLE 10.1 How many different samples of size n can be drawn from a finite population of size N if

(a) $n = 2$ and $N = 10$

(b) $n = 3$ and $N = 100$

SOLUTION (a) $\binom{10}{2} = \dfrac{10!}{2!(10-2)!} = \dfrac{10 \cdot 9}{2} = 45$

(b) $\binom{100}{3} = \dfrac{100!}{3!(100-3)!} = \dfrac{100 \cdot 99 \cdot 98}{3 \cdot 2} = 161{,}700$ ∎

To answer the second question, we make use of the answer to the first one and define a **simple random sample** (or more briefly, a **random sample**) from a finite population as **a sample which is chosen in such a way that each of the** $\binom{N}{n}$ **possible samples has the same probability,** $1/\binom{N}{n}$**, of being selected**.

For instance, if a finite population consists of the $N = 5$ elements a, b, c, d, and e (which might be the repair costs on five cars), there are $\binom{5}{2} = 10$ possible distinct samples of size $n = 2$; they consist of the elements ab, ac, ad, ae, bc, bd, be, cd, ce, and de. If we choose one of these samples in such a way that each has the probability $\frac{1}{10}$ of being chosen, we call this sample a random sample. For example, we could, in simple cases like the one just given, write each of the $\binom{N}{n}$ possible samples on a slip of paper, put these slips in a hat, shuffle them thoroughly, and then draw one without looking. Such a procedure is obviously impractical, if not impossible, in more realistically complex problems of sampling; we mention it here only to make the point that a random sample is a sample whose selection must depend entirely on chance. With regard to the third question, how to take a random sample in actual practice, fortunately we can take a random sample without actually resorting to the tedious process of listing all possible samples. We can list instead the N individual elements of a finite population, then take a random sample by choosing the elements to be included in the sample one at a time without replacement, making sure that in each of the successive drawings each of the remaining elements of the population has the same chance of being selected. This leads to the same probability, $1/\binom{N}{n}$, for each possible sample. For instance, to take a random sample of

20 past-due accounts from a file of 257 such accounts, we could write each account number on a slip of paper, put the slips in a box and mix them thoroughly, then draw (without looking) 20 slips one after the other without replacement.

Even such a relatively simple procedure as this is often not necessary in practice, where the simplest way to take a random sample is to use a table of **random digits** (or **random numbers**). Published tables of random numbers consist of pages on which the decimal digits 0, 1, 2, . . . , and 9 are set down in much the same fashion as they might appear if they had been generated by a chance or gambling device giving each digit the same probability of $\frac{1}{10}$ of appearing at any given place in the table. Some early tables of random numbers were copied from pages of census data or from tables of 20-place logarithms, but they were found to be deficient in various ways. Nowadays, such tables are made with the use of computers, but it would be possible to generate a table with a perfectly constructed spinner like that shown in Figure 10.1.

Table XII is an excerpt from a published table of random numbers, and we shall illustrate its use by considering the problem of taking a random sample of 10 printing firms from the 562 firms listed in the Yellow Pages of a large city telephone directory. Numbering the firms on the alphabetical list 001, 002, 003, . . . , 561, and 562, we arbitrarily pick a starting place in the table and then move in any direction, reading out three-digit numbers. For instance, if we arbitrarily enter the table on page 876 and read out the digits in the 26th, 27th, and 28th columns starting with the 31st row and going down the page, we find that the sample consists of the 10 firms whose numbers are

$$187 \quad 155 \quad 388 \quad 320 \quad 281 \quad 88 \quad 520 \quad 275 \quad 480 \quad 273$$

In selecting these numbers, we ignored the tabled numbers greater than 562; also, had any number recurred, we would have ignored it, too.

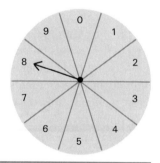

FIGURE 10.1
Spinner

When lists are available and items are, or can readily be, numbered, it is easy to take random samples from finite populations with the aid of random number tables. Unfortunately, however, it is often impossible to proceed in the way we have just described. For example, if we wanted to estimate from a sample the mean protein content of a carload of wheat, it would be impossible to number each of the millions of grains of wheat, choose random numbers, and then locate the corresponding grains. In this and in many similar situations, all one can do is proceed according to the dictionary definition of the word "random," namely, "haphazardly without definite aim or purpose." That is, we must not select or reject any element of a population because of its seeming typicalness or lack of it, nor must we favor or ignore any part of a population because of its accessibility or lack of it, and so on. Such haphazard procedures, it is hoped, will lead to samples which may be treated as though they were, in fact, random samples.

To this point we have been discussing only random samples from finite populations. The concept of a random sample from an infinite population is more difficult to define, but a few simple illustrations will help to explain the basic characteristics of such a sample. For instance, we consider 10 tosses of a coin as a sample from the hypothetically infinite population consisting of all possible tosses of the coin. Then, if the probability of getting heads is the same for each toss and the 10 tosses are independent, we say that the sample is random. Also, we would be sampling from an infinite population if we sample with replacement from a finite population, and our sample would be random if in each draw all elements of the population have the same probability of being selected, and successive draws are independent.

Generally speaking, we assert that the selection of each item in a random sample from an infinite population must be controlled by the same probabilities and that successive selections must be independent of one another. Unless these conditions are satisfied at least approximately, sets of observations drawn from infinite populations cannot legitimately be treated as random samples.

EXERCISES

(Exercises 10.1, 10.3, 10.5, 10.8 are practice exercises. Their complete solutions are given on page 380.)

10.1 How many different samples of size 3 can be selected from a finite population of

(a) size 5

(b) size 10

(c) size 20

10.2 How many different samples of size 4 can be selected from a finite population of

(a) size 12

(b) size 24

(c) size 60

10.3 An employment agency has a client's request for two typists. The agency has five qualified persons available for the positions. List the 10 possible combinations of persons A, B, C, D, and E that could be sent to the job. If each of these samples is assigned the probability $\frac{1}{10}$, show that the probability is $\frac{2}{5}$ that an individual typist will be included in a sample.

10.4 A marketing research manager advises a client firm that any of the following 6 cities are suitable for test marketing a new product: Atlanta, Boston, Chicago, Denver, El Paso, and Fort Worth. If the client firm randomly selects 4 of these cities for test marketing, what is

(a) the probability of each possible sample

(b) the probability that any particular city will be included in the sample

(c) the probability that any specific pair of cities will be included in the sample

10.5 A union president wants to determine the attitude of 576 workers numbered 001 through 576, to a proposed change in their health insurance plan. If the president decides to interview 12 workers concerning the proposed change, which ones would be selected if the sample were chosen by using the first three columns of the random numbers table on page 875 beginning with row 6 and going down the page?

10.6 The sales slips used by a sales associate on a certain day are consecutively numbered 37 to 96. Use columns 9 and 10 of the random numbers table on page 874, beginning with row 11 and going down the page, to select a sample of 10 sales slips for verification by the bookkeeper.

10.7 The manager of a trucking company wants to determine the mileage per gallon of diesel fuel obtained by a sample of 15 trucks from a fleet of 500 trucks. If the trucks are numbered 001, 002, . . . , 500, which ones (by number) will be selected if the manager chooses them by using columns 16, 17, and 18 of the table on page 873 beginning with row 16 and going down the page?

10.8 Explain why each of the following samples may yield misleading information.

(a) To predict the hourly flow of vehicular traffic on a highway, a count is made of the number of vehicles which pass a specified point between 7:00 A.M. and 9:00 A.M. on a Monday.

(b) To predict the outcome of a U.S. presidential election, a poll is made of the readers of the financial newspaper, *The Wall Street Journal*.

(c) To verify that the bottles of liquid detergent are properly filled, an inspector checks every 100th bottle which is filled by a filling machine.

(d) To answer questions about their local public transportation facilities, telephone interviewers communicated with residents at their homes during the day.

(e) To determine the proportion of children who eat flavored gelatin, children are asked, "How often do you eat Jell-O?"

(f) To determine whether psychiatric treatment should be included in a company health plan, an employer asks, "Have you or any member of your family ever had psychiatric treatment?"

10.9 On page 357 we said that a random sample can be drawn from a finite population by choosing the elements to be included in the sample one at a time, making sure that in each of the successive drawings each of the remaining elements of the population has the same chance of being selected. To verify that this will give the correct probability to each sample, let us refer to the example on page 357 where we dealt with random samples of size 3 drawn from the finite population which consists of the elements a, b, c, d, and e. To find the probability of drawing any particular sample (say, b, c, and e), we can argue that the probability of getting one of these three elements on the first draw is $\frac{3}{5}$, the probability of then getting one of the remaining two elements on the second draw is $\frac{2}{4}$, and the probability of then getting the third element on the third draw is $\frac{1}{3}$. Multiplying these three probabilities, we find that the probability of getting the particular sample is $\frac{3}{5} \cdot \frac{2}{4} \cdot \frac{1}{3} = \frac{1}{10}$, and this agrees with the value obtained on page 357.

(a) Use the same kind of argument to verify that for each possible random sample of size 3, drawn one at a time from a finite population of size 100, the probability is $1 / \binom{100}{3} = \frac{1}{161,700}$.

(b) Use the same kind of argument to verify in general that for each possible random sample of size n, drawn one at a time from a finite population of size N, the probability is $1 / \binom{N}{n}$.

10.10 Making use of the fact that among the $\binom{N}{n}$ samples of size n which can be drawn from a finite population of size N there are $\binom{N-1}{n-1}$ which contain a specific element, show that the probability that any specific element of the population will be contained in a random sample of size n is $\frac{n}{N}$.

10.2

Sampling Distributions

Let us now introduce the concept of the **sampling distribution** of a statistic, probably the most basic concept of statistical inference. As we shall see, this concept is related to the idea of chance variation, or chance fluctuations, which we mentioned earlier to emphasize the need for measuring the variability of data. In this chapter we shall concentrate mainly on the sample mean and its sampling distribution, but later on we shall consider the sampling distributions of other statistics.

To introduce the idea of a sampling distribution, let us construct the one for the mean of random samples of size $n = 2$ from the finite population of size $N = 5$, whose elements are the numbers 1, 3, 5, 7, and 9. The mean of this population is

$$\mu = \frac{1 + 3 + 5 + 7 + 9}{5} = 5$$

its variance is

$$\sigma^2 = \frac{1}{5}[(1 - 5)^2 + (3 - 5)^2 + (5 - 5)^2 + (7 - 5)^2 + (9 - 5)^2] = 8$$

and hence, its standard deviation is $\sigma = \sqrt{8}$.

Now, there are $\binom{5}{2} = 10$ random samples of size $n = 2$ which can be drawn from this population; they are

1 and 3	1 and 5	1 and 7	1 and 9	3 and 5
3 and 7	3 and 9	5 and 7	5 and 9	7 and 9

and their means are 2, 3, 4, 5, 4, 5, 6, 6, 7, and 8. Since each sample has the probability $\frac{1}{10}$, we get the following sampling distribution of the mean for random samples of size $n = 2$ from the given population:

$\bar{x}$	Probability
2	1/10
3	1/10
4	2/10
5	2/10
6	2/10
7	1/10
8	1/10

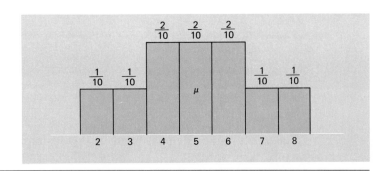

FIGURE 10.2
Sampling
distribution of the
mean

A histogram of this distribution is shown in Figure 10.2.

An examination of this sampling distribution reveals some pertinent information relative to the problem of estimating the mean of the population on the basis of a random sample of two items drawn from the population. For instance, we see that the probability is $\frac{6}{10}$ that a sample mean will not differ from the population mean by more than 1, and that the probability is $\frac{8}{10}$ that a sample mean will not differ from the population mean by more than 2; the first case corresponds to $\bar{x} = 4, 5,$ or 6, and the second to $\bar{x} = 3, 4, 5, 6,$ or 7. Thus, if we did not know the mean of the given population and wanted to estimate it with the mean of a random sample of two observations, this would give us some idea about the potential size of our error.

We can get further useful information about this sampling distribution of the mean by calculating its mean $\mu_{\bar{x}}$ and its standard deviation $\sigma_{\bar{x}}$. (The subscript $\bar{x}$ is used here to distinguish these parameters from those of the original population.) Following the definitions of the mean and the variance of a probability distribution on pages 277 and 279, we get

$$\mu_{\bar{x}} = 2 \cdot \frac{1}{10} + 3 \cdot \frac{1}{10} + 4 \cdot \frac{2}{10} + 5 \cdot \frac{2}{10} + 6 \cdot \frac{2}{10} + 7 \cdot \frac{1}{10} + 8 \cdot \frac{1}{10} = 5$$

and

$$\sigma_{\bar{x}}^2 = (2 - 5)^2 \frac{1}{10} + (3 - 5)^2 \frac{1}{10} + (4 - 5)^2 \frac{2}{10} + (5 - 5)^2 \frac{2}{10}$$
$$+ (6 - 5)^2 \frac{2}{10} + (7 - 5)^2 \frac{1}{10} + (8 - 5)^2 \frac{1}{10} = 3$$

so that $\sigma_{\bar{x}} = \sqrt{3}$.

Observe that at least for this example,

Section 10.2   Sampling Distributions

363

> 1. $\mu_{\bar{x}}$, the mean of the sampling distribution of $\bar{x}$, equals μ, the mean of the population.
> 2. $\sigma_{\bar{x}}$, the standard deviation of the sampling distribution of $\bar{x}$, is smaller than σ, the standard deviation of the population.

The relationships demonstrated in this example are of fundamental importance, and we shall state them formally later. For now, let us merely take note of them and turn to the problem of constructing another sampling distribution of the mean, hoping thereby to gain some further insight into the "behavior" of sample estimates $\bar{x}$ of a population mean μ.

In the preceding example we took a very small sample from a very small population, but it would be difficult to use the same method to construct the sampling distribution of the mean of a large sample from a large population—we would have to enumerate too many possibilities. To construct the sampling distribution of the mean even for random samples of size $n = 5$ from a finite population of size $N = 100$, we would have to list $\binom{100}{5} = 75{,}287{,}520$ possibilities.

So, to get an idea about the sampling distribution of the mean of a larger random sample from a larger finite population, we shall use a **computer simulation**. This means that we shall use a computer to take a number of random samples from the given population, calculate their means, and display the results in the form of a histogram. This histogram will give us some idea about the overall shape and some other key features of the actual sampling distribution of the mean for random samples of the given size from the given population.

EXAMPLE 10.2   Use a computer to generate 100 random samples of size $n = 20$ from the finite population which consists of the integers from 1 to 1,200. Also, calculate the mean of each of the 100 samples, find the overall mean and standard deviation of the 100 sample means, and group the sample means into a distribution with the class marks 25.5, 75.5, . . . , and 475.5.

SOLUTION   Without a computer the reader may picture this kind of simulation as follows: First, the numbers from 1 to 1,200 are written on 1,200 slips of paper (poker chips, small balls, or whatever may lend itself to drawing random samples). Then, a random sample of size $n = 20$ is drawn from this population and the values are recorded, this sample is replaced before the next sample is drawn, and this process is repeated until 100 random samples are obtained.

Actually, using an appropriate computer package, we obtained the printout shown in Figure 10.3. Here "GENE 1 1200, C1" is the instruction to the computer to generate our population, the integers from 1 to 1,200. In the next step, this population is described as having $N = 1,200$, $\mu = 600.50$, and $\sigma = 346.55$. Then the 100 samples of size $n = 20$ are generated and their means are calculated. The printout following the instructions "MEAN C4" and "STDEV C4" tells us that the mean of the 100 means is 605.75 and that their standard deviation is 70.421.

```
MTB > GENE 1 1200,C1
MTB > MEAN C1
    MEAN     =        600.50
MTB > STDEV C1
    ST.DEV. =        346.55
MTB > SET C3
DATA> 4
DATA> END
MTB > STORE
STOR> SAMPLE 20 C1 C2
STOR> LET K1 = AVER(C2)
STOR> JOIN K1 TO C3 PUT IN C3
STOR> ERASE C2
STOR> END
MTB > EXECUTE 100 TIMES
MTB > OMIT ROW WITH 4 IN C3 AND PUT REST IN C4
MTB > MEAN C4
    MEAN     =        605.75
MTB > STDEV C4
    ST.DEV. =         70.421
MTB > HIST C4 25.5 50

Histogram of C4    N = 100

Midpoint    Count
    25.5        0
    75.5        0
   125.5        0
   175.5        0
   225.5        0
   275.5        0
   325.5        0
   375.5        0
   425.5        1    *
   475.5        6    ******
   525.5       17    *****************
   575.5       23    ***********************
   625.5       25    *************************
   675.5       17    *****************
   725.5       10    **********
   775.5        1    *
```

FIGURE 10.3
Computer simulation of a sampling distribution of the mean

Finally, the 100 sample means are grouped into a distribution with the required classes, and this distribution is presented graphically in a form which might be described as a histogram lying on its side. Asked to describe this distribution, we might say that it is fairly symmetrical and bell shaped; in fact, the overall pattern seems to follow quite closely that of a normal curve. All this applies to the distribution which we obtained by means of the computer simulation involving only 100 samples of size $n = 20$ from the population which consists of the integers from 1 to 1,200. It is hoped that it applies also to the actual sampling distribution of the mean, which pertains to all possible samples of size 20 from this population. ■

Note also that the results of this simulation support the two points which were made on page 364. Although the mean of the 100 $\bar{x}$'s does not equal $\mu = 600.5$, its value, 605.75, is very close. Also, the standard deviation of the 100 $\bar{x}$'s, 70.421, is smaller than the population standard deviation, $\sigma = 346.55$.

10.3

The Standard Error of the Mean

In most practical situations we can determine how close a sample mean might be to the mean of the population from which it came by applying two theorems, one given here and the other on page 364, which express essential facts about sampling distributions of the mean. The first of these theorems expresses formally what we discovered in connection with the example on page 364. The mean of the sampling distribution of $\bar{x}$ equals the mean of the population sampled and the standard deviation of the sampling distribution is smaller than the standard deviation of the population. It may be phrased as follows: **For random samples of size n taken from a population having the mean μ and the standard deviation σ, the sampling distribution of $\bar{x}$ has the mean $\mu_{\bar{x}} = \mu$ and the standard deviation**

Standard error of the mean (finite population)

$$\sigma_{\bar{x}} = \frac{\sigma}{\sqrt{n}} \cdot \sqrt{\frac{N-n}{N-1}}$$

for finite populations of size N and

Standard error of the mean (infinite population)

$$\sigma_{\bar{x}} = \frac{\sigma}{\sqrt{n}}$$

for infinite populations.

It is customary to refer to $\sigma_{\bar{x}}$, the standard deviation of the sampling distribution of the mean, as the **standard error of the mean**. Its role in statistics is fundamental, since it measures the extent to which sample means can be expected to fluctuate, or vary, due to chance. Clearly, some knowledge of this variability is essential in determining how well $\bar{x}$ estimates the population mean μ. Intuition leads one (correctly) to feel that the smaller $\sigma_{\bar{x}}$ is (the less the $\bar{x}$'s are spread out), the better the estimate is likely to be, and the larger $\sigma_{\bar{x}}$ is (the more the $\bar{x}$'s are spread out), the poorer the estimate is likely to be. What determines the size of $\sigma_{\bar{x}}$, and hence the goodness of an estimate, can be seen from the preceding formulas. The formula for samples from finite populations shows among other things that (for fixed N) the standard error of the mean *increases* as the variability of the population increases, and *decreases* as the number of items in the sample increases. With respect to the latter, we note that substitution into the formula yields $\sigma_{\bar{x}} = \sigma$ for $n = 1$ and $\sigma_{\bar{x}} = 0$ for $n = N$; in other words, $\sigma_{\bar{x}}$ takes on values between 0 and σ and is 0 only when the sample includes the entire population.

EXAMPLE 10.3 When we sample from an infinite population, what happens to the **standard error of the mean** (and, hence, to the size of the error we are exposed to when we use $\bar{x}$ as an estimate of μ) if the sample size is increased from $n = 50$ to $n = 200$?

SOLUTION The ratio of the two standard errors is

$$\frac{\dfrac{\sigma}{\sqrt{200}}}{\dfrac{\sigma}{\sqrt{50}}} = \frac{\sqrt{50}}{\sqrt{200}} = \frac{1}{2}$$

so that the standard error of the mean is divided by 2, or halved. ∎

The factor $\sqrt{\dfrac{N-n}{N-1}}$ in the first formula for $\sigma_{\bar{x}}$ is called the **finite population correction factor**, for without it the two formulas for $\sigma_{\bar{x}}$ (for finite and infinite populations) are the same. It is usually ignored unless the

EXAMPLE 10.4   Find the value of the finite population correction factor for $n = 100$ and $N = 10,000$.

SOLUTION   Substituting $n = 100$ and $N = 10,000$, we get

$$\sqrt{\frac{N - n}{N - 1}} = \sqrt{\frac{10,000 - 100}{10,000 - 1}} = 0.995$$

This is so close to 1 that the correction factor would ordinarily be ignored in practice. ∎

To get a feeling for the two formulas for $\sigma_{\bar{x}}$, let us return to the two illustrations of the preceding section.

EXAMPLE 10.5   With reference to the illustration on pages 362 and 363 verify that the formula for $\sigma_{\bar{x}}$ for a random sample from a finite population also yields $\sigma_{\bar{x}} = \sqrt{3}$.

SOLUTION   Substituting $n = 2$, $N = 5$, and $\sigma = \sqrt{8}$ into the first of the two formulas for $\sigma_{\bar{x}}$, we get

$$\sigma_{\bar{x}} = \frac{\sqrt{8}}{\sqrt{2}} \cdot \sqrt{\frac{5 - 2}{5 - 1}} = \sqrt{3}$$ ∎

EXAMPLE 10.6   With reference to the computer printout of Figure 10.3, where we had $n = 20$, $N = 1,200$, and $\sigma = 346.55$, what value might we have expected for the standard deviation of the 100 sample means?

SOLUTION   Substituting $n = 20$, $N = 1,200$, and $\sigma = 346.55$ into the first of the two formulas for $\sigma_{\bar{x}}$, we get

$$\sigma_{\bar{x}} = \frac{346.55}{\sqrt{20}} \cdot \sqrt{\frac{1,200 - 20}{1,200 - 1}} = 76.874$$

and this is fairly close to 70.421, the value which we actually obtained. ∎

10.4

The Central Limit Theorem

When we estimate the mean of a population, we usually attach a probability to a measure of the error of our estimate. Using Chebyshev's theorem, we can assert with a probability of at least $1 - 1/k^2$ that the mean of a random sample of size n will differ from the mean of the population from which it came by less than $k \cdot \sigma_{\bar{x}}$. In other words, when we use the mean of a random sample to estimate the mean of a population, we can assert with a probability of at least $1 - 1/k^2$ that our error will be less than $k \cdot \sigma_{\bar{x}}$.

EXAMPLE 10.7   Based on Chebyshev's theorem with, say, $k = 2$, what can we assert about the possible size of our error if we use the mean of a random sample of size $n = 64$ to estimate the mean of an infinite population with $\sigma = 20$?

SOLUTION   Substituting $\sigma = 20$ and $n = 64$ into the second of the two formulas for the standard error of the mean, we get

$$\sigma_{\bar{x}} = \frac{20}{\sqrt{64}} = 2.5$$

and it follows that we can assert with a probability of at least $1 - \frac{1}{2^2} = 0.75$ that the error is less than $k \cdot \sigma_{\bar{x}} = 2(2.5) = 5$. ■

This shows that we can make probability statements about errors of estimates without having to go through the tedious (if not impossible) process of constructing the corresponding sampling distributions.

Chebyshev's theorem applies to any distribution, and it is always possible to use it as in the preceding example. However, there exists another basic theorem of statistics, the **central limit theorem**, which enables us in a great many instances to make much stronger probability statements than we can with Chebyshev's theorem. This is the second theorem referred to on page 366, and it may be stated as follows:

Central limit
theorem

If n (the sample size) is large, the theoretical sampling distribution of the mean can be approximated closely with a normal distribution.

This theorem is of fundamental importance in statistics, since it justifies the use of normal-curve methods in a wide range of problems; it applies to infinite populations and also to populations where n, though large, constitutes but a small portion of the population. It is difficult to say precisely how large n must be so that the central limit theorem applies, but unless the population has a very unusual shape, $n = 30$ is usually regarded as sufficiently large. The distribution of Figure 10.3 is fairly symmetrical and bell shaped, even though the sample size is only $n = 20$. When the population we are sampling has, itself, roughly the shape of a normal curve, the sampling distribution of the mean can be approximated closely with a normal distribution regardless of the size of n.

EXAMPLE 10.8   Based on the central limit theorem, what is the probability that the error will be less than 5 when we use the mean of a random sample of size $n = 64$ to estimate the mean of an infinite population with $\sigma = 20$?

SOLUTION   The probability is given by the area of the white region under the curve in Figure 10.4, that is, by the normal-curve area between

$$z = \frac{-5}{20/\sqrt{64}} = -2 \quad \text{and} \quad z = \frac{5}{20/\sqrt{64}} = 2$$

The entry in Table I corresponding to $z = 2.00$ is 0.4772, so this probability is $0.4772 + 0.4772 = 0.9544$. According to Chebyshev's theorem the probability is "at least 0.75," but we can actually make the much stronger statement that the probability is 0.9544 that the mean of a random sample of size $n = 64$ from the given population will differ from the mean of the population by less than 5. ∎

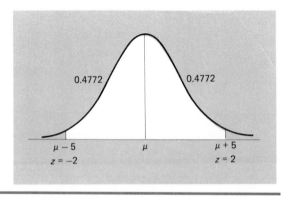

FIGURE 10.4
Sampling
distribution of the
mean

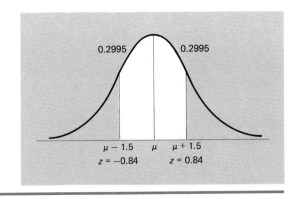

FIGURE 10.5
Sampling
distribution of the
mean

EXAMPLE 10.9　Suppose we use a computer simulation to take 50 random samples of size $n = 5$ from a population with $\sigma = 4$ and find that 31 of their means (or 62 percent) differ from the mean of the population by less than 1.5. Based on the central limit theorem, what is the probability that the difference between the sample mean and the population mean will be less than 1.5, when we take a random sample of size $n = 5$ from an infinite population with $\sigma = 4$?

SOLUTION　The probability is given by the area of the white region under the curve in Figure 10.5; that is, by the normal-curve area between

$$z = \frac{-1.5}{4/\sqrt{5}} = -0.84 \qquad \text{and} \qquad z = \frac{1.5}{4/\sqrt{5}} = 0.84$$

Since the entry in Table I corresponding to $z = 0.84$, is 0.2995, this probability is $0.2995 + 0.2995 = 0.5990$, or about 0.60. This is very close to the 0.62 proportion we got in the simulation.　∎

EXERCISES

(Exercises 10.11, 10.13, 10.17, 10.18, 10.21, 10.22, and 10.23 are practice exercises. Their complete solutions are given on page 380.)

10.11　Random samples of size 2 are taken from the finite population which consists of the numbers 5, 6, 7, 8, 9, and 10.

(a) Show that the mean of this population is $\mu = 7.5$ and that its standard deviation is $\sigma = \sqrt{\dfrac{35}{12}}$.

(b) List the 15 possible random samples of size 2 that can be taken from this finite population and calculate their means.

Section 10.4　The Central Limit Theorem　　　**371**

(c) Use the results of part (b) to construct the sampling distribution of the mean for random samples of size 2 from the given finite population. Assign each possible sample a probability of $\frac{1}{15}$.

(d) Calculate the mean and the variance of the probability distribution obtained in part (c) and verify the results with the use of the theorem on page 366.

10.12 Repeat parts (b), (c), and (d) of Exercise 10.11 for random samples of size 3 from the given population.

10.13 A finite population consisting of the numbers 5, 6, 7, 8, 9, and 10 can be converted into an infinite population if we take a random sample of size 2 by first drawing one element and then replacing it before drawing the second element.

(a) Determine how many different possible samples of size 2 can be drawn from this infinite population and list them.

(b) Determine the means of the samples of part (a). What probability is assigned to each mean? Construct the sampling distribution of the mean for random samples of size 2 drawn from this infinite population.

(c) Calculate the mean and the standard deviation of the probability distribution of part (b) and compare the value of the standard deviation with the corresponding result obtained from the standard error of the mean formula.

10.14 In a simulation of 50 samples the standard deviation of the sampling distribution of the mean is 1.95 and the medians of the 50 samples are

15	18	21	15	17	16	16	14	20	13
14	15	17	16	16	15	16	19	15	15
11	12	14	16	17	18	16	18	16	14
18	15	15	15	17	18	13	17	18	18
16	16	15	16	13	15	13	15	18	16

(a) Calculate the standard deviation of the 50 medians.

(b) Compare the result of part (a) with the standard deviation of the sampling distribution of the mean. On the basis of this information, what can we say about the relative reliability of the medians and the means of the samples in estimating the mean of the given population?

10.15 For random samples of size n from a population having the shape of a normal distribution, the **standard error of the median** (the standard deviation of the sampling distribution of the median) is given by $\sqrt{\frac{\pi}{2}} \cdot \frac{\sigma}{\sqrt{n}}$ or approximately $1.25\frac{\sigma}{\sqrt{n}}$.

(a) How close is the value obtained for the standard deviation of the medians in Exercise 10.14 to the value expected according to this formula with $\sigma = 4$ and $n = 5$?

(b) For large random samples of size n from a large population having the shape of a normal distribution, the **standard error of the standard deviation** (the standard deviation of the standard deviations) is given by $\sigma/\sqrt{2n}$. Find the value of this standard error for the weights, in pounds, of sections of concrete sewer pipe where $\sigma = 12$ pounds and n, the sample size, is 128.

10.16 Referring to the method of Exercise 10.15, if μ is to be estimated by the median of a random sample of size n from a given population having the shape of a normal curve, how large must n be so that this estimate is equally as reliable as another estimate of μ based on the mean of a random sample of size 256?

10.17 When we sample from an infinite population, what happens to the standard error of the mean if the sample size is

(a) increased from 9 to 81

(b) increased from 225 to 400

(c) decreased from 200 to 50

10.18 What is the value of the finite population correction factor when

(a) $n = 5$ and $N = 100$

(b) $n = 500$ and $N = 5,000$

(c) $n = 300$ and $N = 10,000$

10.19 Show that if the mean of a random sample of size n is used to estimate the mean of an infinite population with the standard deviation σ, there is a 50-50 chance that the error (that is, the difference between x and μ) is less than $0.6745 \dfrac{\sigma}{\sqrt{n}}$. This quantity is called the **probable error of the mean**, and is used now mainly in military applications.

10.20 An experimental guided missile is tested by firing a random sample of 49 missiles at a target which is fixed in place. The distances by which the missiles miss the center of the target have a standard deviation of 6.2 feet.

(a) Determine the probable error of the mean.

(b) Explain the meaning of the probable error of the mean.

10.21 Fifty random samples of size $n = 5$ were taken from a population with $\sigma = 4$, and 48 of the sample means (or 96 percent) differed from the mean of the population by less than 3.5. Based on the central limit theorem, what is the probability that the difference between the sample mean and the population mean will be less than 3.5 when we take a random sample of size $n = 5$ from an infinite population with $\sigma = 4$?

10.22 The mean of a random sample of size $n = 100$ is used to estimate the mean of an infinite population having the standard deviation $\sigma = 2$. What can be asserted about the probability that the error will be less than 0.25 using

(a) Chebyshev's theorem

(b) the central limit theorem

10.23 The mean of a random sample of size $n = 36$ is used to estimate the mean sales price of a very large population of residential houses which were sold in a city. The sales prices have a standard deviation of $\sigma = \$6,000$. If we use the central limit theorem, what can we say about the probability that our estimate will be "off" by

(a) less than $600

(b) less than $1,500

10.24 If the distribution of monetary expenditures by all delegates attending a convention has a mean of $1,630 and a standard deviation of $180, what is the probability that the combined expenditures of 36 randomly selected delegates is more than $60,120.

10.5

Technical Note
(Simulating Sampling Experiments)

A table of random numbers, like Table XII, constructed in such a way that each of the digits 0, 1, 2, . . . , and 9 has probability $\frac{1}{10}$ of appearing at any given location in the table, would seem to have limited usefulness. After all, it is just a collection of independent observations of a particular random variable whose probability distribution is known. But, in fact, such a table constitutes a single basic supply of (random) observations which can be used to generate sequences of observations of any other random variable whose distribution is known. By selecting one-digit numbers from the table, we get the integers from 0 to 9; by selecting two-digit numbers, we get the integers from 00 to 99; by selecting three-digit numbers, we get the integers from 000 to 999; and so on. Also, by putting a decimal point in front of the numbers we get the decimal fractions from .0 to .9, from .00 to .99, from .000 to .999, and so on. Now, these numbers, in one form or the other, can be used to sample populations having probability distributions like the binomial or Poisson distributions, populations having continuous distributions like the normal distribution, and also distributions of raw observed data having no known standard form.

For instance, we can play "heads or tails" without ever flipping a coin by letting the digits 0, 2, 4, 6, and 8 represent heads and the digits 1, 3, 5, 7, and 9 represent tails. Then using, for instance, the fourth column of the table on page 873, starting at the top and going down the page, we get 3, 9, 8, 1, 5, 1, 6, 3, 2, 4, . . . , and we interpret this as tail, tail, head, tail, tail, tail, head, tail, head, head,. . . .

Repeated flips of three coins can be simulated in the same way. If we use the first three columns of the table on page 874 starting at the top and going down the page, we read out the random numbers 486, 788, 194, 512, 558, 775, 776, 154, 140, 683, . . . , and we interpret them as 3, 2, 1, 1, 1, 0, 1, 1, 2, 2, . . . , heads. If we did not want to use three columns of random digits and count the number of even digits for this "experiment," we could make use of the fact that the probabilities of getting 0, 1, 2, or 3 heads when flipping three coins are $\frac{1}{8}, \frac{3}{8}, \frac{3}{8}$, and $\frac{1}{8}$, and use the coding

Number of heads	Random digits
0	0
1	1, 2, 3
2	4, 5, 6
3	7

The digits 8 and 9 are ignored whenever they occur, and we would interpret the random numbers 2, 7, 6, 5, 1, 1, 1, 7, 6, 0, . . . , in column 11 on page 873 as representing 1, 3, 2, 2, 1, 1, 1, 3, 2, 0, . . . , heads in repeated tosses of three balanced coins. If we did not want to "waste" any digits, we could have performed this experiment also with three-digit random numbers and the coding shown in the following table:

Number of heads x	Probability of x heads	Probability of x or fewer heads	Random numbers
0	0.125	0.125	000–124
1	0.375	0.500	125–499
2	0.375	0.875	500–874
3	0.125	1.000	875–999

To facilitate the assignment of random numbers to the different values of x we have added the third column to the table. It should be apparent how the cumulative probabilities of x or fewer heads are used in arriving at the entries in the fourth column of the table. With this scheme, the random numbers 213, 109, 915, 657, and 359, for example, represent 1, 0, 3, 2, and 1 heads in five flips of three coins.

Sampling distributions, like that shown in Figure 10.3, are usually made by a computer with appropriate software, although they can also be prepared with the help of a table of random numbers. In recent years, simulation techniques, under the heading of **Monte Carlo methods**, have found wide applications in business research. These simulations are usually done on computers and are used to solve inventory problems, questions arising in connection with waiting lines, advertising, competition, the allocation of resources, scheduling of operations, and situations involving overall planning and organization. Very often, this eliminates the cost of building and operating expensive equipment or facilities, it avoids disrupting ongoing operations, and it enables us to perform experiments which would otherwise cost too much or require too much time.

EXERCISES

(Exercise 10.25 and 10.26 are practice exercises. Their complete solutions are given on page 380.)

10.25 Using three random digits to represent the results obtained in tossing three balanced coins (letting 0, 2, 4, 6, and 8 represent heads and 1, 3, 5, 7, and 9 represent tails), simulate an experiment consisting of 80 tosses of 3 coins. Utilize the table of random numbers beginning on page 873. Go to page 874, begin with row 1, columns 23, 24, and 25, and read down to the bottom of the page; then go to row 1, columns 28, 29, and 30, and read down the page until 80 sets of three digits have been noted. Compare the number of times that 0, 1, 2, and 3 heads occurred with the expected frequencies of 10, 30, 30, and 10 heads.

10.26 Repeat Exercise 10.25 letting 0, 1, 2, and 3 heads be represented by the three-digit random numbers 000–124, 125–499, 500–874, and 875–999.

10.27 Use one-digit random numbers (omitting 7, 8, 9, and 0) to simulate 120 rolls of a balanced die.

10.28 With reference to part (b) of Exercise 10.11 on page 371, label the 15 possible samples 01, 02, 03, . . . , 14, and 15, and use random numbers to simulate an experiment in which 100 random numbers are taken from the given population. Compare the distribution of the means of these samples with the corresponding theoretical sampling distribution obtained in part (c) of Exercise 10.11.

10.29　Suppose that the probabilities are 0.45, 0.27, 0.16, 0.08, and 0.04 that it takes one, two, three, four, or five days in court to settle charges of embezzlement not exceeding $100,000.

(a) Distribute the two-digit random numbers from 00 to 99 to the five values of this random variable, so that they can be used to simulate the time it takes to settle such charges.

(b) Use the results of part (a) and Table XII to simulate the time it takes to settle 25 such embezzlement charges.

10.30　Depending upon the availability of parts, a company can manufacture three, four, five, or six units of a certain item per week with corresponding probabilities of 0.10, 0.40, 0.40, and 0.10. The probabilities of a weekly demand for zero, one, two, three, . . . , or eight units are 0.05, 0.10, 0.30, 0.30, 0.10, 0.05, 0.05, 0.04, and 0.01. If a unit is sold during the week it is made, it will yield a profit of $200; this profit is reduced by $25 for each week that a unit has to be stored. Use random numbers to simulate the operations of this company for 52 weeks and estimate its expected weekly profit on this item.

10.6

A Word of Caution

A point worth repeating is that our examples of the sampling distribution based on all possible sample means and the sampling distribution based on 100 sample means were meant to be teaching aids, designed to convey the idea of a sampling distribution. These examples do not reflect what we do in actual practice, where we ordinarily base an inference on one sample and not 100. In Chapter 11 and subsequent chapters we shall go further into the problem of translating theory concerning sampling distributions into methods of evaluating the goodness of an estimate or the merits or disadvantages of a statistical decision procedure.

　　Another fact worth noting concerns the $\sqrt{n}$ appearing in the denominator of the formula for the standard error of the mean. As we pointed out, as n becomes larger and larger and we gain more and more information, our generalizations should be subject to smaller errors and, in general, our results should be more reliable or more precise. However, the $\sqrt{n}$ in the formulas for $\sigma_{\bar{x}}$ illustrates the fact that gains in precision or reliability are not proportional to increases in the size of the sample. For instance, doubling the size of the sample does not double the reliability of $\bar{x}$ as an estimate of the mean of a population. As is apparent from the formula $\sigma_{\bar{x}} = \sigma/\sqrt{n}$ for samples from infinite populations, we must take four times as large a sample to cut the standard error in half, and nine times as large a sample to triple the reliability, that is, to divide the standard error by 3. This clearly illustrates the fact that it seldom pays to take excessively large samples. For instance, if we increase the sample size from 100 to 10,000 (probably at considerable expense), the size of the error we are exposed to is reduced only by a factor of 10. Similarly, if we increase the sample size from 50 to, say, 20,000, the chance fluctuations we are exposed to are reduced only by a factor of 20, and this may in no way be worth the cost of taking 19,950 additional observations.

10.7

Checklist of Key Terms

Central limit theorem,   369
Computer simulation,   364
Finite population,   356, 357
Finite population correction
   factor,   367
Infinite population,   356
Monte Carlo methods,   376
Probable error of the mean,   373

Random numbers,   358
Random sample,   355, 357
Sampling distribution,   356, 362
Standard error of the mean,   367
Standard error of the median,   372
Standard error of the standard
   deviation,   373

10.8

Review Exercises

10.31   Random samples of size $n = 2$ are drawn from a finite population consisting of the numbers 5, 6, 7, 8, and 9.

(a) Verify that the mean of this population is $\mu = 7$ and the standard deviation is $\sigma = \sqrt{2}$.

(b) List the 10 possible samples of size $n = 2$ that can be drawn without replacement from this population. Calculate their means and assign each mean value the probability $\frac{1}{10}$. Construct the sampling distribution of the mean for these samples.

(c) Calculate the mean and the standard deviation of the sampling distribution of part (b) and verify the results using the theorem for the mean and standard error of the mean of Section 10.3.

10.32 Suppose that in the preceding exercise sampling is with replacement, so that the population is (hypothetically) infinite; that is, there is no limit to the number of observations we could make.

(a) List the 25 possible samples of size $n = 2$ that can be drawn with replacement from the population consisting of the numbers 5, 6, 7, 8, and 9 (counting 6 and 7, for example, and 7 and 6 as different samples). Calculate the sample means and assign each value of the mean the probability $\frac{1}{25}$. Construct the sampling distribution of the mean.

(b) Calculate the mean and the standard deviation of the sampling distribution obtained in part (a), and verify the results using the theorem of Section 10.3.

10.33 The probabilities are 0.14, 0.41, 0.35, and 0.10 that a department store will refer zero, one, two, or three overdue accounts to a collection agency in any given week.

(a) Distribute the two-digit numbers from 00 to 99 to the five values of this random variable so that the corresponding random numbers can be used to simulate the numbers of overdue accounts referred to a collection agency for any period of weeks.

(b) Use the scheme of part (a) to simulate the numbers of overdue accounts referred to a collection agency by the department store during 29 weeks. Use the first and second columns of page 874 starting at the top of the page.

10.34 What is the value of the finite population correction factor when
(a) $n = 18$ and $N = 50$
(b) $n = 25$ and $N = 500$
(c) $n = 12$ and $N = 60$

10.35 What is the probability of each possible sample when a random sample of size $n = 2$ is drawn from a finite sample of size $N = 100$?

10.36 If a sample is taken from an infinite population, what happens to the standard error of the mean if the sample size is
(a) increased from 25 to 225
(b) decreased from 900 to 36

10.37 How many samples of size 3 can be selected from a finite population of
(a) size 5
(b) size 10
(c) size 15

10.38 What is the probability of each possible sample if a random sample of size $n = 4$ is to be drawn from a finite population of $N = 20$?

10.39 List all the possible combinations of two of the following metals which are sold on commodities exchanges: copper, gold, platinum, palladium, and silver.

10.40 If the diameter of an iron casting can be looked upon as a random variable from a population having a normal distribution with $\sigma = 0.25$ millimeters (1 millimeter = about 0.04 inch), what is the probability that the mean of a random sample of size $n = 16$ will differ from the mean of the population by more than 0.10 millimeter?

10.41 If a sample is taken from an infinite population, what happens to the standard error of the mean if the sample size is

(a) increased from 49 to 100

(b) decreased from 100 to 49

10.42 The mean of a random sample of size $n = 50$ is used to estimate the mean time required by a clerk to write a credit card charge slip. Using the central limit theorem and assuming that $\sigma = 30$ seconds for the credit card charge slip time data, with what probability can we assert that the error will be

(a) less than 4 seconds

(b) less than 9 seconds

10.43 The mean of a random sample of size $n = 45$ is used to estimate the mean of a population having a normal distribution with the standard deviation $\sigma = 9$. With what probability can we assert that the error will be less than 4, if we use

(a) Chebyshev's theorem

(b) the central limit theorem

10.44 An auditor wants to check, at random, 10 of 220 items of inventory listed on the monthly inventory report of a sporting goods store. The inventory items are numbered 1 through 220. Which ones, by number, will the auditor check if she uses a random sample by means of random numbers using columns 6, 7, and 8 of the table on 873, starting with the first row and going down the page.

10.9

Solutions of Practice Exercises

10.1 From Table IX, Binomial Coefficients: (a) 10 (b) 120 (c) 1,140

Using formula $\binom{N}{n} = \dfrac{N!}{n!(N-n)!}$, we get

(a) $\binom{5}{3} = \dfrac{5!}{3!(5-3)!} = \dfrac{5 \cdot 4}{2 \cdot 1} = 10$

(b) $\binom{10}{3} = \dfrac{10!}{3!(10-3)!} = \dfrac{10 \cdot 9 \cdot 8}{3 \cdot 2 \cdot 1} = 120$

(c) $\binom{20}{3} = \dfrac{20!}{3!(20-3)!} = \dfrac{20 \cdot 19 \cdot 18}{3 \cdot 2 \cdot 1} = 1{,}140$

10.3 The samples are *AB*, *AC*, *AD*, *AE*, *BC*, *BD*, *BE*, *CD*, *CE*, and *DE*; since each person appears in four of the samples, the probability is $\dfrac{4}{10} = \dfrac{2}{5}$.

10.5 489, 113, 238, 337, 496, 375, 221, 271, 003, 438, 146, and 166

10.8 (a) Traffic may vary by time of day, day of the week, holidays, special events, and so forth.

(b) The opinions of readers of financial newspapers such as *The Wall Street Journal* are not likely to correspond to those of a broader cross section of the U.S. voting public.

(c) There may be a systematic defect where, say, each 10th bottle is improperly filled, so the inspectors sample may show 0 percent defectively filled or 100 percent defectively filled depending on where the cycle is when the first inspection is made.

(d) Employed persons would not be likely to be at home and available for interviews during normal working hours. Also, many people without phones use public transportation but are entirely omitted from the sample.

(e) The question is ambiguous since the word "Jell-O" is a trade mark which is not synonymous with the word "gelatin." There are also Jell-O brand products which are not made of gelatin.

(f) Employees may not provide truthful answers to questions which are personally embarrassing or which could have an adverse effect on their jobs.

10.11 (a) $\mu = \dfrac{5+6+7+8+9+10}{6} = \dfrac{45}{6} = 7.5$ and

$\sigma^2 = \dfrac{(5-7.5)^2 + \cdots + (10-7.5)^2}{6} = \dfrac{17.50}{6} = \dfrac{35}{12}$ and $\sigma = \sqrt{\dfrac{35}{12}}$.

(b) $\binom{6}{2} = 15$ and the samples are 5 and 6, 5 and 7, 5 and 8, 5 and 9, 5 and 10, 6 and 7, 6 and 8, 6 and 9, 6 and 10, 7 and 8, 7 and 9, 7 and 10, 8 and 9, 8 and 10, and 9 and 10.

(c)

Mean	Probability
5.5	1/15
6.0	1/15
6.5	2/15
7.0	2/15
7.5	3/15
8.0	2/15
8.5	2/15
9.0	1/15
9.5	1/15

(d) $\mu_{\bar{x}} = 5.5 \cdot \dfrac{1}{15} + 6.0 \cdot \dfrac{1}{15} + 6.5 \cdot \dfrac{2}{15} + \cdots + 9.5 \cdot \dfrac{1}{15} = \dfrac{112.5}{15}$

$= 7.5$ and $\sigma_{\bar{x}}^2 = (5.5 - 7.5)^2 \left(\dfrac{1}{15}\right) + (6.0 - 7.5)^2 \left(\dfrac{1}{15}\right) + \cdots +$

$(9.5 - 7.5)^2 \left(\dfrac{1}{15}\right) = 1.167$; also $\sigma_{\bar{x}} = \dfrac{\sigma}{\sqrt{n}} \cdot \sqrt{\dfrac{N-n}{N-1}}$, and substituting

into the formula we get $\dfrac{\sqrt{\dfrac{35}{12}}}{\sqrt{2}} \cdot \sqrt{\dfrac{6-2}{6-1}} = \sqrt{\dfrac{35 \cdot 4}{24 \cdot 5}} = \sqrt{\dfrac{140}{120}} = \sqrt{\dfrac{7}{6}}$

and $\sigma_{\bar{x}}^2 = \dfrac{7}{6} = 1.167$.

10.13 (a) The samples are 5 and 5, 5 and 6, 5 and 7, 5 and 8, 5 and 9, 5 and 10, 6 and 5, 6 and 6, 6 and 7, 6 and 8, 6 and 9, 6 and 10, 7 and 5, 7 and 6, 7 and 7, 7 and 8, 7 and 9, 7 and 10, 8 and 5, 8 and 6, 8 and 7, 8 and 8, 8 and 9, 8 and 10, 9 and 5, 9 and 6, 9 and 7, 9 and 8, 9 and 9, 9 and 10, 10 and 5, 10 and 6, 10 and 7, 10 and 8, 10 and 9, 10 and 10; and the means are $\dfrac{5+5}{2} = 5$, $\dfrac{5+6}{2} = 5.5 + \cdots$ and $\dfrac{10+10}{2} = 10$, as shown in part (b).

(b)

Mean	Probability
5.0	1/36
5.5	2/36
6.0	3/36
6.5	4/36
7.0	5/36
7.5	6/36
8.0	5/36
8.5	4/36
9.0	3/36
9.5	2/36
10.0	1/36

(c) $\mu_{\bar{x}} = 5.0 \cdot \dfrac{1}{36} + 5.5 \cdot \dfrac{2}{36} + 6.0 \cdot \dfrac{3}{36} + \cdots + 10 \cdot \dfrac{1}{36} = 7.5$ and

$$\sigma_{\bar{x}}^2 = (5.0 - 7.5)^2 \left(\dfrac{1}{36}\right) + (5.5 - 7.5)^2 \left(\dfrac{2}{36}\right) + (6.0 - 7.5)^2 \left(\dfrac{3}{36}\right) +$$

$$(6.5 - 7.5)^2 \left(\dfrac{4}{36}\right) + (7.0 - 7.5)^2 \left(\dfrac{5}{36}\right) + (7.5 - 7.5)^2 \left(\dfrac{6}{36}\right) +$$

$$(8.0 - 7.5)^2 \left(\dfrac{5}{36}\right) + (8.5 - 7.5)^2 \left(\dfrac{4}{36}\right) + (9.0 - 7.5)^2 \left(\dfrac{3}{36}\right) +$$

$$(9.5 - 7.5)^2 \left(\dfrac{2}{36}\right) + (10.0 - 7.5)^2 \left(\dfrac{1}{36}\right) = \dfrac{52.5}{36} = 1.46, \text{ according}$$

to the theorem $\mu_{\bar{x}} = 7.5$ and $\sigma_{\bar{x}}^2 = \dfrac{35/12}{2} = \dfrac{35}{24} = 1.46$; $\sigma_{\bar{x}} = \sqrt{1.46} = 1.208$.

10.17 (a) $\dfrac{\sigma/\sqrt{81}}{\sigma/\sqrt{9}} = \dfrac{3}{9} = \dfrac{1}{3}$; it is divided by 3.

(b) $\dfrac{\sigma/\sqrt{400}}{\sigma/\sqrt{225}} = \dfrac{15}{20} = \dfrac{3}{4}$; it is divided by $\dfrac{4}{3} = 1\dfrac{1}{3}$.

(c) $\dfrac{\sigma/\sqrt{50}}{\sigma/\sqrt{200}} = \dfrac{14.1421}{7.0711} = 2$; it is multiplied by 2.

10.18 (a) $\sqrt{\dfrac{100 - 5}{100 - 1}} = 0.980$ (b) $\sqrt{\dfrac{5,000 - 500}{5,000 - 1}} = 0.949$

(c) $\sqrt{\dfrac{10,000 - 300}{10,000 - 1}} = 0.985$

10.21 $z = \dfrac{3.5}{4/\sqrt{5}} = 1.96$, and the probability is $2(0.4750) = 0.9500$.

10.22 $\sigma_{\bar{x}} = \dfrac{2}{\sqrt{100}} = \dfrac{2}{10} = 0.20$.

(a) $k = \dfrac{0.25}{0.20} = 1.25$, and the probability is at least $1 - \dfrac{1}{1.25^2} = 0.36$.

(b) $z = \dfrac{0.25}{0.20} = 1.25$, and the probability is $2(0.3944) = 0.7888$.

10.23 $\sigma_{\bar{x}} = \dfrac{6,000}{\sqrt{36}} = 1,000$.

(a) $z = \dfrac{600}{1,000} = 0.60$, and the probability is $2(0.2257) = 0.4514$.

(b) $z = \dfrac{1,500}{1,000} = 1.50$, and the probability is $2(0.4332) = 0.8664$.

Section 10.9   Solutions of Practice Exercises

10.25 The number of heads (even digits) in the 80 sets of three digits are 1, 0, 1, 1,
1, 1, 2, 2, 2, 1, 0, 1, 2, 1, 3, 3, 0, 3, 0, 1, 2, 1, 2, 0, 2, 3, 3, 1, 2, 1, 1, 2, 2,
3, 2, 2, 2, 2, 1, 0, 3, 1, 2, 3, 2, 1, 2, 2, 3, 2, 1, 3, 2, 1, 1, 1, 2, 2, 1, 2, 1, 3,
1, 1, 2, 1, 3, 2, 1, 2, 1, 1, 2, 2, 2, 1, 1, 1, 0, 1.

Number of heads	Observed	Expected
0	7	10
1	32	30
2	29	30
3	12	10
Total	80	80

10.26 The number of heads where 0 heads are the random digits 0–124; 1 head is
the random digits 125–499; 2 heads are the random digits 500–874; and 3
heads are the random digits 875–999.
1, 3, 0, 1, 3, 2, 0, 2, 1, 3, 2, 2, 2, 2, 1, 0, 2, 2, 2, 1, 0, 0, 0, 1, 1, 1, 2, 0, 2,
1, 2, 2, 1, 2, 2, 1, 2, 1, 2, 2, 0, 1, 1, 1, 1, 3, 2, 1, 2, 2, 3, 2, 1, 1, 2, 1, 2, 3,
3, 1, 1, 2, 1, 2, 3, 1, 0, 1, 3, 1, 1, 1, 3, 2, 0, 2, 1, 2, 3, 1.

Number of heads	Observed	Expected
0	10	10
1	30	30
2	29	30
3	11	10
Total	80	80

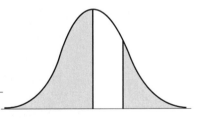

CHAPTER 11

Decision Making: Inferences About Means

Traditionally, statistical inference has been divided into problems of estimation in which we estimate various unknown statistical descriptions of populations, and tests of hypotheses in which we either accept or reject specific assertions about populations or their parameters.

Problems of estimation arise everywhere—in everyday life, in science, and in business. In everyday life, we may want to know how long it takes on the average to iron a shirt, we may be interested in the variation we can expect in a child's performance in a school, and we may want to find out what proportion of all one-car accidents is due to driver fatigue. In science, a psychologist may want to determine the average time that it takes an adult to react to a given stimulus, an engineer may need to know how much variability to expect in the strength of a new alloy, and a biologist may want to determine what percentage of certain insects are born physically defective. In business, a large retailer may want to determine the average income of all families living within 2 miles of a proposed new branch store site, an industrial union official may want to know how much variation there is in the time it takes members to get to work, and a restaurant owner may want to know what proportion of his customers tip at least 15 percent.

In each of these examples interest is centered on determining the "true" value of some quantity, and they are all problems of estimation. However, the business examples would all have been hypothesis-testing problems instead, if the retailer had wanted to know whether the average income of families living within 2 miles of the site exceeds $31,400, if the union official had wanted to determine whether the variation in the time it takes members to get to work actually is $\sigma = 8.2$ minutes, or if the restaurant owner had wanted to investigate the claim that fewer than three-fourths of his customers tip at least 15 percent.

In each of the sets of examples of everyday life, of science, and of business, the first illustration concerns an inference about a mean, the second an inference about a measure of variation, and the third an inference about a percentage or a proportion. Since the statistical treatment of such inferences differs, we shall devote this chapter to inferences about means, and then take up inferences about measures of variation and inferences about proportions in Chapters 12 and 13. In particular, we shall devote Sections 11.1 through 11.4 to the estimation of means, Sections 11.5 through 11.8 to tests of hypotheses concerning means, and Sections 11.9 through 11.11 to tests of hypotheses concerning the means of two populations.

11.1

The Estimation of Means

Given as a single number, an estimate is a value intended to match some characteristic (parameter) of a population. When we say "intended to match" and not "which matches," we mean just that—it is possible for an estimate based on a sample to coincide with the population parameter it is intended to estimate, but this is the exception rather than the rule. This should be clear from our discussion of the sampling distribution of the mean in Chapter 10.

To illustrate some of the problems we face when we estimate a mean, let us refer to a study in which a pharmaceutical manufacturer wants to determine the average (mean) time it takes an adult to open a new type of tamper-resistant aspirin bottle. Available for this purpose are the following experimental data (in seconds) obtained from a random sample of 40 adults who were timed while opening the firm's new aspirin bottle.

Chapter 11 Decision Making: Inferences About Means

23	19	24	18	15	27	27	21	11	20
21	29	25	10	28	21	23	24	30	18
13	18	16	22	33	20	19	26	14	15
20	8	23	29	25	14	17	18	19	21

The mean of this sample is $\bar{x} = \dfrac{824}{40} = 20.6$ seconds, and the pharmaceutical manufacturer could use this figure as an estimate of μ, the true average time it takes an adult to open the tamper-resistant aspirin bottle.

An estimate of this type is called a **point estimate**, since it consists of a single number, or a single point on the real number scale. Although a point estimate is the most common way in which estimates are expressed, this number leaves room for many questions. One might wonder, for instance, on how much information the estimate is based and how much variability there might be in the amounts of time it takes these adults to open the aspirin bottles. Thus, we might supplement the estimate, $\bar{x} = 20.6$ seconds, with the information that this figure is based on $n = 40$ observations, whose standard deviation is $s = 5.71$ seconds, as can be easily verified.

Reports often present sample means together with the values of n and s, but to be meaningful this requires that the "consumer" of the information have some knowledge of statistics. To make this supplementary information meaningful also to the layperson, let us refer to the two theorems of Sections 10.3 and 10.4 on the sampling distribution of the mean. According to the central limit theorem, the sampling distribution of the mean can, for large random samples, be approximated closely with a normal curve. Hence, we can assert with probability $1 - \alpha$ (see Figure 9.12) that a sample mean $\bar{x}$ will differ from the population mean μ by, at most, $z_{\alpha/2}$ standard errors of the mean. Making use of the fact, for large random samples from infinite (or very large) populations, that the sampling distribution of the mean is approximately a normal distribution with

$$\mu_{\bar{x}} = \mu \qquad \text{and} \qquad \sigma_{\bar{x}} = \frac{\sigma}{\sqrt{n}}$$

we find from Figure 11.1 that the probability is $1 - \alpha$ that under the stated conditions $\bar{x}$ will differ from μ by at most $z_{\alpha/2} \cdot \dfrac{\sigma}{\sqrt{n}}$. Since $\bar{x} - \mu$ is the error we make when we use $\bar{x}$ as an estimate of μ, it follows that **the probability is $1 - \alpha$ that $\bar{x}$ will be "off" either way by at most**

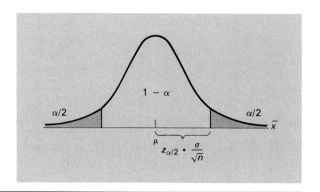

FIGURE 11.1
Sampling
distribution of the
mean.

Maximum error
of estimate

$$E = z_{\alpha/2} \cdot \frac{\sigma}{\sqrt{n}}$$

This result applies when n is large, $n \geq 30$, and the population is infinite (or large enough so that the finite population factor need not be used.) The two values which are most commonly, though not necessarily, used for $1 - \alpha$ are 0.95 and 0.99, and the corresponding values of $\alpha/2$ are 0.025 and 0.005. As the reader was asked to show in Exercise 9.7, $z_{0.025} = 1.96$ and $z_{0.005} = 2.575$.

EXAMPLE 11.1 A team of efficiency experts intends to use the mean of a random sample of size $n = 150$ to estimate the average mechanical aptitude of assembly-line workers in a large industry (as measured by a certain standardized test). If based on experience, the efficiency experts can assume that $\sigma = 6.2$ points on the test scale for such data, what can they assert with probability 0.99 about the maximum error of their estimate?

SOLUTION Substituting $n = 150$ workers, $\sigma = 6.2$ points, and $z_{0.005} = 2.575$ into the formula for the maximum error, we get

$$E = 2.575 \cdot \frac{6.2}{\sqrt{150}} = 1.30$$

Thus, the efficiency experts can assert with probability 0.99 that their error will be, at most, 1.30 points. ∎

Suppose now that the efficiency experts of the preceding example actually collect the necessary data and get $\bar{x} = 52.8$. Can they still assert with 0.99 probability that the error of their estimate, $\bar{x} = 52.8$, is at most 1.30? After all, $\bar{x} = 52.8$ differs from the true (population) mean by at most 1.30 or it does not, and they really have no way of knowing whether it is one or the other. Actually, they can, but it must be understood that the 0.99 probability applies to the method they used to get the estimate and calculate the maximum error (collecting the sample data, determining the value of $\bar{x}$, and using the formula for E) and *not directly* to the parameter they are trying to estimate. In other words, the method they used "works" 99 percent of the time and if they had to bet, 99 to 1 would be fair odds that the error is at most 1.30.

To make this distinction, it has become the custom to use the word **confidence** here instead of probability. In general, we make probability statements about future values of random variables (say, the potential error of an estimate), and we make confidence statements once the data have been obtained. Accordingly, we would say in our example that the efficiency experts can be 99 percent confident that the error of their estimate, $\bar{x} = 52.8$, is at most 1.30.

Use of the formula for E involves one complication. To be able to judge the size of the error we might make when we use $\bar{x}$ as an estimate of μ, we must know σ, the population standard deviation. Since this is not the case in most practical situations, we have no choice but to replace σ with an estimate, usually the sample standard deviation s. In general, this is considered to be reasonable, provided the sample is sufficiently large, and by sufficiently large we mean again $n \geq 30$.

EXAMPLE 11.2 With reference to the illustration on page 386, what can we assert with 95 percent confidence about the maximum error, if the pharmaceutical manufacturer uses $\bar{x} = 20.6$ seconds as an estimate of the average time it takes an adult to open the tamper-resistant aspirin bottle?

SOLUTION Substituting $n = 40$, $s = 5.71$ for σ, and $z_{0.025} = 1.96$ into the formula for E, we find that we can assert with 95 percent confidence that the error is at most

$$E = 1.96 \cdot \frac{5.71}{\sqrt{40}} = 1.77 \text{ seconds} \qquad \blacksquare$$

The formula for E can also be used to determine the sample size that is needed to attain a desired degree of precision. Suppose that we want to use the mean of a large random sample to estimate the mean of a population, and we want to be able to assert with probability $1 - \alpha$ that the error of this estimate will be less than some prescribed quantity E. As before, we write

$E = z_{\alpha/2} \cdot \dfrac{\sigma}{\sqrt{n}}$, and upon solving this equation for n we get

Sample size needed for desired degree of precision

$$n = \left[\frac{z_{\alpha/2} \cdot \sigma}{E} \right]^2$$

EXAMPLE 11.3   With reference to Example 11.1, assume the team of efficiency experts wants to estimate the average mechanical aptitude of a large group of assembly-line workers and wants to be able to assert with probability of 0.99 that the error will be at most 2.0 points. If, based on experience, the efficiency experts can assume that $\sigma = 6.2$ points on the test scale for such data, how large a sample is required?

SOLUTION   Substituting $E = 2.0$ points, $\sigma = 6.2$ points, and $z_{0.005} = 2.575$ into the formula for n, we get

$$n = \left[\frac{(2.575)(6.2)}{2.0} \right]^2 = 64$$

rounded up to the next whole number. Thus a random sample of $n = 64$ workers is required for the estimate. ∎

Note that the result would be the same if we replace ''wants to be able to assert with probability 0.99 that the error *will be* at most 2.0 points'' by ''wants to be able to assert with 99 percent confidence that the error *is* at most 2.0 points.'' The difference is in when the assertion is to be made— before or after the team collects the data.

EXAMPLE 11.4   With reference to the preceding example, suppose that the team of efficiency experts takes a random sample of size $n = 64$ and finds that the average mechanical aptitude of these workers is 53.1 points. If the team uses $\bar{x} = 53.1$ as an estimate of the average mechanical aptitude of all employees of the manufacturing company, what can the team assert about the maximum error?

SOLUTION   The team can assert with 99 percent confidence that the error is at most 2.0 points. ∎

The formula for n cannot be used unless we know (at least approximately) the value of σ, but in Exercise 11.19 we shall see how the method can be modified when we know only that σ does not exceed a certain upper limit.

All the methods of this section are based on the assumption that n is 30 or more. For small samples, a modification in the formula for E will be discussed in Section 11.3.

11.2

Confidence Intervals for Means

Let us now introduce a different way of assessing the error we might make when we use a sample mean to estimate the mean of a population. In what follows, we shall make use of the fact that, for large random samples from infinite populations, the sampling distribution of the mean is approximately normal with the mean μ and the standard deviation $\sigma_{\bar{x}} = \dfrac{\sigma}{\sqrt{n}}$, so that

$$ z = \frac{\bar{x} - \mu}{\sigma/\sqrt{n}} $$

is a value of a random variable having approximately the standard normal distribution. Since the probability is $1 - \alpha$ that a random variable having the standard normal distribution will take on a value between $-z_{\alpha/2}$ and $z_{\alpha/2}$ (see Figure 11.1) or that

$$ -z_{\alpha/2} < z < z_{\alpha/2} $$

we can substitute the foregoing expression for z into this inequality and get

$$ -z_{\alpha/2} < \frac{\bar{x} - \mu}{\sigma/\sqrt{n}} < z_{\alpha/2} $$

If we now apply some relatively simple algebra, we can rewrite this inequality as

$$\bar{x} - z_{\alpha/2} \cdot \frac{\sigma}{\sqrt{n}} < \mu < \bar{x} + z_{\alpha/2} \cdot \frac{\sigma}{\sqrt{n}}$$

and we can assert with probability $1 - \alpha$ that it will be satisfied for any random sample. In other words, we can assert with $(1 - \alpha)100$ percent confidence that the interval from $\bar{x} - z_{\alpha/2} \cdot \frac{\sigma}{\sqrt{n}}$ to $\bar{x} + z_{\alpha/2} \cdot \frac{\sigma}{\sqrt{n}}$, determined on the basis of a large random sample, contains the population mean we are trying to estimate. When σ is unknown but n is large, it is customary to replace σ by the sample standard deviation s.

An interval like this is called a **confidence interval**, its end points are called **confidence limits**, and $1 - \alpha$ is called the **degree of confidence**. As before, the values most commonly used for the degree of confidence are 0.95 and 0.99, and the corresponding values of $z_{\alpha/2}$ are 1.96 and 2.575. In contrast to point estimates, estimates given in the form of confidence intervals are called **interval estimates**.

EXAMPLE 11.5   In the tamper-resistant aspirin bottle illustration on page 386, we had $n = 40$, $\bar{x} = 20.6$, and $s = 5.71$ Construct a 95 percent confidence interval for μ, the true average time in seconds it takes an adult to open a tamper-resistant aspirin bottle.

SOLUTION   Substituting $n = 40$, $\bar{x} = 20.6$, $s = 5.71$ for σ, and $z_{0.025} = 1.96$ into the confidence interval formula, we get

$$20.6 - 1.96 \cdot \frac{5.71}{\sqrt{40}} < \mu < 20.6 + 1.96 \cdot \frac{5.71}{\sqrt{40}}$$
$$18.83 < \mu < 22.37$$

for the true average time in seconds it takes an adult to open a tamper-resistant aspirin bottle. Of course, the interval from 18.83 to 22.37 contains μ or it does not, but we are 95 percent confident that it does. As we have said before, this means that the interval was obtained by a method which "works 95 percent of the time." ∎

¹Since the probability is also $1 - \alpha$ that a random variable having the standard normal distribution will take on a value on the interval from $-z_{\alpha/2}$ to $z_{\alpha/2}$ or that

$$-z_{\alpha/2} \leq z \leq z_{\alpha/2}$$

some authors substitute $\leq$ for $<$ in this confidence interval formula. Practically speaking, this does not make any difference.

FIGURE 11.2
Computer printout
for large-sample
confidence interval
for true average
time required to
open a tamper-
resistant bottle

```
MTB > SET DATA IN C1
DATA> 23 19 24 18 15 27 27 21 11 20
DATA> 21 29 25 10 28 21 23 24 30 18
DATA> 13 18 16 22 33 20 19 26 14 15
DATA> 20  8 23 29 25 14 17 18 19 21
DATA> END
MTB > ZINTERVAL 95 C.I. SIGMA = 5.71 DATA IN C1

THE ASSUMED SIGMA =5.71

            N      MEAN    STDEV   SE MEAN    95.0 PERCENT C.I.
C1         40    20.600    5.710    0.903   ( 18.828,   22.372)

MTB > STOP
```

A computer printout of this example is given in Figure 11.2. It shows the amounts of time taken by each of 40 adults to open a tamper-resistant aspirin bottle, the mean of these times, the standard deviation, and also the standard error of the mean $\frac{5.71}{\sqrt{40}} = 0.90$.

Had we calculated a 99 percent confidence interval in Example 11.5, we would have obtained $18.28 < \mu < 22.92$, and it should be observed that this interval is wider than the 95 percent interval. This illustrates the important fact that when we increase the degree of certainty, namely, the degree of confidence, the confidence interval becomes wider and thus tells us less about the quantity we are trying to estimate. In other words, the surer we want to be, the less we have to be sure of.

11.3

The Estimation of Means (Small Samples)

So far we have assumed not only that the sample size is large enough to treat the sampling distribution of the mean as if it were a normal distribution, but that (when necessary) σ can be replaced with s in the formula for the standard error of the mean. To develop a corresponding theory that applies also to small samples, we must now assume that the population we are sampling has roughly the shape of a normal distribution. We can then base our methods on the statistic

$$t = \frac{\bar{x} - \mu}{s/\sqrt{n}}$$

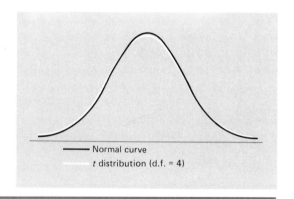

FIGURE 11.3
Standard normal
and *t* distributions

Normal curve
t distribution (d.f. = 4)

whose sampling distribution is called the *t* **distribution**. (More specifically, it is called the **Student-*t* distribution**, as it was first investigated by W. S. Gosset, who published his writings under the pen name "Student.") As is shown in Figure 11.3 the shape of this distribution is very much like that of a normal distribution, and it is symmetrical with zero mean. The exact shape of the *t* distribution depends on the quantity $n - 1$, the sample size less 1, called the **number of degrees of freedom**.[2]

For the standard normal distribution, we defined $z_{\alpha/2}$ in such a way that the area under the curve to its right equals $\alpha/2$ and, hence, the area under the curve between $-z_{\alpha/2}$ and $z_{\alpha/2}$ equals $1 - \alpha$. As is shown in Figure 11.4 the corresponding values for the *t* distribution are $-t_{\alpha/2}$ and $t_{\alpha/2}$. Since these values depend on $n - 1$, the number of degrees of freedom, they must be looked up in a special table, such as Table II at the end of this book; this table contains among others the values of $t_{0.025}$ and $t_{0.005}$ for 1 through 29 degrees of freedom, and it can be seen that $t_{0.025}$ and $t_{0.005}$ approach the corresponding values for the standard normal distribution as the number of degrees of freedom becomes large.

Since the *t* distribution, like the standard normal distribution, is symmetrical about its mean $\mu = 0$ (see Figure 11.4), we can now duplicate the argument on page 389 and thus arrive at the following $(1 - \alpha)\mathbf{100}$ **percent small-sample confidence interval for** μ:

[2]It is hard to explain at this time why one should want to assign a special name to $n - 1$. However, we shall see later in this chapter that there are other applications of the *t* distribution, where the number of degrees of freedom is defined in a different way. The reason for the term "degrees of freedom" lies in the fact that if we know $n - 1$ of the deviations from the mean, then the *n*th is automatically determined. Since the sample standard deviation measures variation in terms of the squared deviations from the mean, we can say that this estimate of σ is based on $n - 1$ independent quantities or that we have $n - 1$ degrees of freedom.

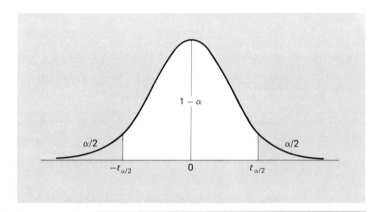

FIGURE 11.4
t distributions

Small-sample confidence interval for μ

$$\bar{x} - t_{\alpha/2} \cdot \frac{s}{\sqrt{n}} < \mu < \bar{x} + t_{\alpha/2} \cdot \frac{s}{\sqrt{n}}$$

The only difference between this confidence interval formula and the large-sample formula (with s substituted for σ) is that $t_{\alpha/2}$ takes the place of $z_{\alpha/2}$.

EXAMPLE 11.6 To test the durability of a new paint for white center lines, a highway department has painted test strips across heavily traveled roads in eight different locations, and automatic counters showed that they deteriorated after having been crossed by (to the nearest hundred) 142,600, 167,800, 136,500, 108,300, 126,400, 133,700, 162,000, and 149,400 cars. Construct a 95 percent confidence interval for the average number of crossings this paint can withstand before it deteriorates.

SOLUTION The mean and the standard deviation of these values are $\bar{x} = 140,800$ and $s = 19,200$ (to the nearest hundred), and since $t_{0.025}$ for $8 - 1 = 7$ degrees of freedom equals 2.365, substitution into the formula yields

$$140,800 - 2.365 \frac{19,200}{\sqrt{8}} < \mu < 140,800 + 2.365 \frac{19,200}{\sqrt{8}}$$

or

$$124,700 < \mu < 156,900$$

```
MTB > SET C1
DATA> 142600 167800 136500 108300 126400 133700 162000 149400
MTB > TINTERVAL WITH 95 PERCENT CONFIDENCE, DATA IN C1

              N      MEAN    STDEV   SE MEAN    95.0 PERCENT C.I.
C1            8     140837   19228    6798   (  124758,   156917)
```

FIGURE 11.5   Computer printout for small-sample confidence interval for μ

This is the desired 95 percent confidence interval for the average amount of traffic (car crossings) the paint can withstand before it deteriorates. ■

A computer printout of the preceding example is shown in Figure 11.5. The difference between the confidence limits given in the printout and those given earlier are due to rounding. Since the original data were given to the nearest hundred, we rounded the mean, the standard deviation, and the confidence limits to the nearest hundred.

The method which we used in Section 11.1 to determine the maximum error we risk when we use a sample mean to estimate the mean of a population can easily be adapted to small samples, provided the population we are sampling has roughly the shape of a normal distribution. All we have to do is substitute s for σ and $t_{\alpha/2}$ for $z_{\alpha/2}$ in the formula for E on page 388.

EXAMPLE 11.7   Ten randomly selected upholstered chairs of a certain design were weighed by the shipping department of their manufacturer and were, on the average, 46.3 pounds each with a standard deviation of 1.2 pounds. What can we assert with 99 percent confidence about the maximum error if we wish to use $\bar{x} = 46.3$ pounds as an estimate of the true average weight of upholstered chairs of this design.

SOLUTION   Substituting $n = 10$, $s = 1.2$, and $t_{0.005} = 3.250$ (the entry in Table II for nine degrees of freedom) into the new formula for E, we get

$$E = t_{\alpha/2} \cdot \frac{s}{\sqrt{n}} = 3.250 \cdot \frac{1.2}{\sqrt{10}} = 1.23 \text{ pounds}$$

Thus, if we use $\bar{x} = 46.3$ pounds as an estimate of the true average weight of a chair, we can be 99 percent confident that the error of this estimate is at most 1.23 pounds. ■

Based on the *t* distribution, we can also modify the method for determining the sample size (see page 000) when *n* turns out to be small. A discussion of this modification may be found in more advanced texts.

11.4

Bayesian Estimation*

In recent years there has been mounting interest in methods of inference in which parameters (for example, the population mean μ or the population standard deviation σ) are looked upon as random variables having **prior distributions** which reflect how a person feels about the different values that a parameter can take. Such prior considerations are then combined with direct sample evidence to obtain **posterior distributions** of the parameters, on which subsequent inferences are based. Since the method used to combine the prior considerations with the direct sample evidence is based on a generalization of Bayes's theorem of Section 8.1, we refer to such inferences as **Bayesian**.

In this section we shall present a Bayesian method of estimating the mean of a population. As we said, our prior feelings about the possible values of μ are expressed in the form of a prior distribution, and like any distribution, this kind of distribution has a mean and a standard deviation. We shall designate these values μ_0 and σ_0 and call them the **prior mean** and the **prior standard deviation**.

If we are sampling a population having the mean μ (which we want to estimate) and the standard deviation σ, if the sample is large enough to apply the central limit theorem (or if the population has a normal distribution), and if the prior distribution of μ has roughly the shape of a normal distribution, it can be shown that the posterior distribution of μ is also a normal distribution with the mean

Posterior mean

$$\mu_1 = \frac{\dfrac{n}{\sigma^2} \cdot \bar{x} + \dfrac{1}{\sigma_0^2} \cdot \mu_0}{\dfrac{n}{\sigma^2} + \dfrac{1}{\sigma_0^2}}$$

*This section may be omitted without loss of continuity. On page 403, exercises pertaining to this section are marked with an asterisk.

and the standard deviation σ_1 given by the formula

$$\frac{1}{\sigma_1^2} = \frac{n}{\sigma^2} + \frac{1}{\sigma_0^2}$$

Since μ_1, the **posterior mean**, may be used as an estimate of the mean of the population, let us examine some of its most important features. We note first that μ_1 is a weighted mean of $\bar{x}$ and μ_0, and that the weights are $\dfrac{n}{\sigma^2}$ and $\dfrac{1}{\sigma_0^2}$, the reciprocals of the variances of the distribution of $\bar{x}$ and the prior distribution of μ. We see also that when no direct information is available and $n = 0$, the weight assigned $\bar{x}$ is 0, the formula reduces to $\mu_1 = \mu_0$, and the estimate is based entirely on the subjective prior information. However, as more and more direct evidence becomes available (that is, as n becomes larger and larger), the weight shifts more and more toward the direct sample evidence, the sample mean $\bar{x}$. Finally, we see that when the subjective feelings about the possible values of μ are vague, that is, when σ_0 is relatively large, the estimate will be based to a greater extent on $\bar{x}$. On the other hand, when there is a great deal of variability in the population we are sampling from, that is, when σ is relatively large, the estimate will be based to a greater extent on μ_0.

EXAMPLE 11.8   An investor who is planning to open a new bowling alley feels most strongly that he should net on the average $\mu_0 = \$2,600$ per month; also, the subjective prior distribution which he attaches to the various possible values of μ has roughly the shape of a normal distribution with the standard deviation $\sigma_0 = \$130$. If during nine months the operation of the bowling alley nets $\$2,810$, $\$2,690$, $\$2,350$, $\$2,400$, $\$2,320$, $\$2,250$, $\$2,430$, $\$2,600$, and $\$2,670$, what is the posterior probability that the bowling alley will net on the average between $\$2,500$ and $\$2,600$ per month?

SOLUTION   The mean and the standard deviation of the sample data are $\bar{x} = 2,502$ and $s = 195$. Using $s = 195$ to estimate the unknown σ, and substituting $n = 9$, $\bar{x} = 2,502$, $s = 195$, $\mu_0 = 2,600$, and $\sigma_0 = 130$ into the formulas for the posterior mean and the **posterior standard deviation**, we get

$$\mu_1 = \frac{\dfrac{9}{195^2} \cdot 2,502 + \dfrac{1}{130^2} \cdot 2,600}{\dfrac{9}{195^2} + \dfrac{1}{130^2}} = \$2,522$$

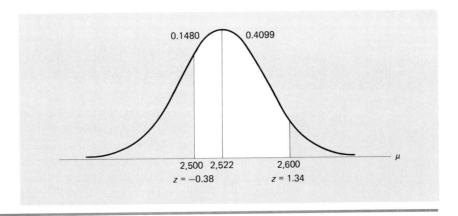

FIGURE 11.6
Posterior
distribution of μ

and

$$\frac{1}{\sigma_1^2} = \frac{9}{195^2} + \frac{1}{130^2} \qquad \text{and} \qquad \sigma_1 = 58.1$$

Having found the mean and the standard deviation of the posterior distribution of μ pictured in Figure 11.6, we must now determine the area of the white region under the curve, the area under the standard normal distribution between $z = \dfrac{2{,}500 - 2{,}522}{58.1} = -0.38$ and $z =$ $\dfrac{2{,}600 - 2{,}522}{58.1} = 1.34$. The entries corresponding to 0.38 and 1.34 in Table I are 0.1480 and 0.4099, so we get $0.1480 + 0.4099 = 0.5579$, or approximately 0.56, for the posterior probability that the bowling alley will net on the average between \$2,500 and \$2,600 per month. ∎

This very brief introduction to **Bayesian inference** should have served to bring out the following two points: (1) In Bayesian statistics the parameter about which an inference is to be made is looked upon as a random variable having a distribution of its own, and (2) this kind of inference permits the use of direct as well as collateral information. To clarify the last point, let us add that in the bowling alley example the subjective prior distribution of the investor may have been based on a subjective evaluation of various factors (business conditions in general, for instance, and indirect information about other bowling alleys), and this evaluation was combined with the figures which were actually observed for the nine months.

EXERCISES

(Exercises 11.1, 11.2, 11.6, 11.7, 11.10(a), 11.11(a), 11.13, 11.15, 11.19, 11.20, and 11.21 are practice exercises. Their complete solutions are given on page 447.)

11.1 To estimate the average daily production of metal containers by a small manufacturer, the shop manager examined a random sample of 56 daily production records, obtaining a mean of 32.5 containers and a standard deviation of 2.9. With 99 percent confidence, what can be said about the maximum error in estimating that the true average daily production is 32.5 containers?

11.2 With the information provided in the preceding exercise, construct a 99 percent confidence interval for the true average daily production of metal containers by the metal products manufacturer.

11.3 In a study of annual apartment rental costs in an eastern city, a random sample of 36 apartments has a mean rental cost of $11,535 per year and a standard deviation of $875.

(a) Construct a 99 percent confidence interval for the true average annual apartment rental cost.

(b) What can be said with 95 percent confidence about the maximum error if the sample mean of $11,535 is used as an estimate of the true average annual apartment rental cost?

11.4 The manager of a grocery store found, on the basis of a random sample of size $n = 60$ taken when the store was crowded, that it took customers an average of $\bar{x} = 13.5$ minutes to go through the checkout counter for ten items or less and for the order to be bagged; the standard deviation of the sample is $s = 3.4$ minutes. What can be asserted, with 98 percent confidence, about the maximum error in the estimate $\bar{x} = 13.5$ minutes of the true average time it takes a customer to check out 10 or fewer items and have the groceries bagged when the store is crowded?

11.5 With the information provided in the preceding exercise, construct a 90 percent confidence interval for the true average time it takes a shopper to go through the checkout counter and the groceries to be bagged when the store is crowded.

11.6 A random sample of the number of minutes required to prepare 100 payroll checks, from a much larger number of payroll checks prepared by the payroll department of a firm, shows that the mean preparation time is 2.75 minutes and the standard deviation is 0.50 minutes. If 2.75 minutes is used as an estimate of the true average time required to prepare a payroll check, with what confidence can we assert that this estimate is off by, at most, 0.25 minutes?

11.7 On page 393 we pointed out that the 99 percent confidence interval calculated for the time needed to open an aspirin bottle is wider than the corresponding 95 percent confidence interval. Calculate the widths of the two intervals and verify that the 99 percent confidence interval is, in fact, about 31 percent wider than the corresponding 95 percent interval. Is this true for *all* 99 percent and 95 percent large-sample confidence intervals of the mean, where both confidence intervals are calculated for the same set of data?

11.8 Verify that, in general, 98 percent large-sample confidence intervals of the mean are about 19 percent wider than the corresponding 95 percent intervals. **Considerations like this are sometimes instrumental in deciding upon the degree of confidence selected for use in practical problems**.

11.9 Verify that for random samples of size $n = 5$ from normal populations, 99 percent confidence intervals of the mean are almost 66 percent wider than the corresponding 95 percent intervals. (Hint: Use values of t table.)

11.10 If a sample constitutes an appreciable portion of a finite population (say, 5 percent or more), the various formulas given in the text should be modified by applying the finite population correction factor. For instance, the formula for E on page 388 becomes

$$E = z_{\alpha/2} \cdot \frac{\sigma}{\sqrt{n}} \sqrt{\frac{N-n}{N-1}}$$

(a) A sample of 100 stockholders selected from 300 stockholders who had attended a stockholders meeting were surveyed to determine their average expenditures to attend the meeting. If the mean of this sample is $\bar{x} = \$125$ and the standard deviation is $s = \$21$, what can we assert with 95 percent confidence about the maximum size of our error if we use $\bar{x} = \$125$ as an estimate of the mean of the population sampled?

(b) A random sample of the labor time used in the production of 36 hand-painted bone china plates, from a production run of 200 such plates, has a standard deviation of 6 minutes and a mean time of 30 minutes. What can we assert with 99 percent confidence about the size of our error if we use $\bar{x} = 30$ as an estimate of the mean production time of all the 200 bone china plates in the production run?

11.11 Use the finite population correction factor $\sqrt{\dfrac{N-n}{N-1}}$ to modify the confidence interval formula on page 392 and thus make it applicable to problems in which a sample constitutes an appreciable portion of a finite population.

(a) A random sample of the odometers in 25 of 98 taxicabs owned by a cab company shows mean weekly mileage of 680, with standard deviation of 176 miles. Construct a 95 percent confidence interval for the weekly mean mileage of all the 98 taxicabs owned by the cab company.

(b) A random sample conducted in a town of 500 families revealed that 50 families had an average annual income of $32,460 with a standard deviation of $5,000. Construct a 90 percent confidence interval for the true average annual income of all the families in this town.

11.12 A security company maintains daily records of the number of burglar alarm warnings flashed on its signal board each day. Assuming that it is reasonable to use a standard deviation of 6.5 alarm warnings, how large a random sample of daily records would be required if the company wished to assert with a probability of 0.99 that the sample mean would be off by at most 2 alarm warnings?

11.13 A railroad supervisor wants to be 99 percent sure that the error is at most 5 minutes in estimating the mean time it takes a passenger train to travel to a nearby city. On how large a sample of trips should the railroad supervisor base this estimate if the standard deviation is
(a) 3.0 minutes
(b) 2.0 minutes
(c) 5.0 minutes

11.14 A bicycle shop wants to know the mean time it takes an employee to assemble a bicycle. Assuming a standard deviation of 4 minutes, how large a sample is needed in order to be able to assert with probability of 0.90 that the sample mean will be off by at most 2 minutes?

11.15 A study by an industrial engineer shows that in a certain shop a random sample of 20 employees left their workstations, on the average, 4.6 times per day, with a standard deviation of 1.1. Construct a 99 percent confidence interval for the average number of times an employee leaves the workstation. (Hint: For 20 employees enter Table II with 19 d.f.)

11.16 A random sample of gasoline sales to 16 passenger cars at an automobile service station shows average sales of 10.2 gallons of gasoline, with a standard deviation of 2.9 gallons. Construct a 95 percent confidence interval for the mean of the population samples.

11.17 Ten typists who have applied for a position in the typing pool of a large office typed a test paragraph in 75, 70, 59, 60, 63, 55, 52, 70, 45, and 85 seconds. If the mean of this sample is used to estimate the average time for a typist to complete this test paragraph, what can we assert with 95 percent confidence about the maximum error?

11.18 Nine chickens randomly selected from a flock of chickens weigh 5.2, 4.4, 4.8, 3.6, 3.1, 6.2, 5.8, 5.1, and 3.2 pounds.
(a) With 90 percent confidence, what can be asserted about the maximum error in estimating the mean weight of the population of all the chickens in the flock?
(b) Construct a 99 percent confidence interval for the mean weight of the chickens in the flock from which this sample came.

11.19 Sometimes we do not know the actual value of σ, but we do know that it will not exceed a certain upper limit. For instance, in Example 11.1 on page 388, it might not be known that $\sigma = 6.2$, but only that it does not exceed 8.0. If such an upper limit is substituted for σ in the formulas for E or n, the resulting values may be unnecessarily large, and we compensate for this by substituting "at least $1 - \alpha$" for "$1 - \alpha$" for the probability or the degree of confidence. For example, if we substitute in Example 11.1, $n = 150$ workers, $\sigma = 8.0$ points, and $z_{0.005}$, we get

$$E = 2.575 \cdot \frac{8.0}{\sqrt{150}} = 1.682$$

and the experts can assert with probability of "at least 0.99" that the error will be, at most, 1.682 points.

Rework Example 11.1 if it is known merely that σ does not exceed 7 percent.

* **11.20** The manager of a chain of fast-food restaurants believes that the prior distribution of the average number of patrons the restaurant will serve per day has a mean of 645 and a standard deviation of 47.5. As far as any one of the restaurants is concerned, the number of patrons it serves changes from day to day, and this variation is measured by a standard deviation of 67.2. If a new restaurant is opened and averages 750 meals served per day during the first 50 days, find a Bayesian estimate of the number of patrons the new restaurant can be expected to serve per day.

* **11.21** With reference to the preceding exercise, what is the posterior probability that the new restaurant will average between 720 and 760 meals per day?

* **11.22** An actuary feels that the prior distribution of the average annual losses for a certain kind of liability coverage has the mean $\mu_0 = \$93.50$ and the standard deviation $\sigma_0 = \$4.30$. He also knows that for any one policy the losses vary from year to year with the standard deviation $\sigma = \$21.72$. If a policy like this averages losses of \$175.36 per year over a period of five years, find a Bayesian estimate of its true average annual losses.

* **11.23** With reference to the preceding exercise, what is the posterior probability that the policy's true average annual losses are between \$100.00 and \$120.00?

11.5

Tests of Hypotheses

All the problems we have studied so far in this chapter were problems of estimation. Later, in Section 13.6, we shall consider problems in which we must decide whether a population is of a particular form. Now, however, we shall consider problems in which we must decide whether a population parameter equals a prescribed value. We call such decision procedures tests of **statistical hypotheses**. Instead of asking, for example, for the mean assessed value of all duplexes in a large city, we may want to decide whether or not the mean assessed value equals some particular value, say, $88,950. At this point it may seem to make little difference how we state the problem, but it will soon become apparent that a number of considerations arise in connection with tests of statistical hypotheses that are not present in problems of estimation.

To illustrate the nature of the situation we face in testing a statistical hypothesis, suppose that a company manufactures a liquid kitchen cleaning wax which it sells in cans marked "300 grams net weight" (about 10.6 ounces). It is known from long experience that the variability of the process is stable and well established at $\sigma = 5$ grams. The cans are filled by machine, and the company makes every effort to control the mean net weight (or the mean "fill") at the 300-gram standard. However, small errors occur in the machine settings and parts wear, for instance, and the mean fill sometimes varies more or less widely from the desired 300 grams. Small departures— on the order of 1 gram or less—from standard are of no consequence, but increasingly larger departures in either direction are of increasingly more concern. Overfilling means giving away product, the value of which in time may amount to the profit on a large volume of sales. Underfilling results in a loss to consumers and also exposes the company to possible punitive action by standards enforcement agencies.

In trying to control the mean fill of the cans at 300 grams, the company has devised the following inspection procedure. Each hour during production runs, the company takes a random sample of 25 cans from the hour's production lot, calculates the sample mean weight $\bar{x}$, and decides on the basis of this value whether or not the process is "in control" (the mean fill is 300 grams, as it is supposed to be) or "out of control" (the mean fill is not 300 grams). To make this decision, the company must have some unambiguous criterion, or rule, to follow. Accordingly, the company has specified this criterion:

> *Consider the process to be out of control if $\bar{x}$ is either 297 grams or less, or if it is 303 grams or more; consider the process to be in control if $\bar{x}$ falls between 297 and 303 grams.*

So far as actions are concerned, when the process is judged to be out of control, it is shut down immediately and a plant engineer is sent in to find out what (if anything) is wrong with it and put it back in control; when the process is judged to be in control, it is allowed to continue in operation without interruption.

In the language of statistics, the company wishes to test, for each submitted lot, the hypothesis that the mean net weight of the wax (the mean fill) is 300 grams against the alternative that the mean fill is not 300 grams. Let us call the hypothesis that the process is in control hypothesis H_0 and we write it as H_0: $\mu = 300$ grams. The **alternative hypothesis** to H_0, designated H_A, is the hypothesis that $\mu \neq 300$ grams. Clearly, hypothesis H_0 is either true or false at any given time, yet the criterion given may lead to its acceptance or to its rejection. Thus, the company may err in one of two ways. First, the company may decide that the process is out of control when, in fact, it is in control. This will happen if the mean (lot) weight per can is actually 300 grams but the sample mean $\bar{x}$ is 297 grams or less, or 303 grams or more. The consequence of this error is that the process operating at the desired level is shut down while an engineer looks for nonexistent trouble. Second, the company may decide that the process is in control when, in fact, it is out of control. This will happen when the mean (lot) weight per can is not 300 grams (is, say, only 290 grams) but the sample mean $\bar{x}$ falls between 297 and 303 grams. The consequence of this error is that the process not operating at the desired level is allowed to continue operating.

The situation described by this example is typical of testing a statistical hypothesis, and it may be summarized as in the following table:

	Accept H_0	Reject H_0
H_0 is true	Correct decision	Type I error
H_0 is false	Type II error	Correct decision

If the hypothesis is true, the decision to accept it is the correct one; conversely, if the hypothesis is false, the decision to reject it is the correct one. On the other hand, if the hypothesis is true and it is rejected, an error has been committed; the error which is committed when one rejects a true hypothesis is called a **Type I error** and the probability of committing it is designated by the lowercase Greek letter α (alpha). Conversely, if the hypothesis is false and it is accepted, an error has been committed; the error which is committed when one accepts a false hypothesis is called a **Type II error**, and the probability of committing it is designated by the Greek letter β (beta).

Let us now direct our attention to the merits of the liquid cleaning wax company's criterion, which we gave on page 404. Specifically, let us calculate the probability α the company faces of rejecting H_0 if it is true and the probabilities β the company faces of accepting H_0 if the mean fill is some one of various possible values other than 300 grams. If these probabilities are satisfactory from an operational standpoint, the criterion may be considered to be a "good" one in the sense that it provides the company with suitable protection against committing one or the other of the two kinds of error.

Recalling the theory of Chapter 10, we observe that the probability α of rejecting hypothesis H_0 if it is true is just the probability of getting a mean of 297 grams or less, or 303 grams or more, in a random sample of size $n = 25$ drawn from a population with the mean $\mu = 300$ and the standard deviation $\sigma = 5$. This probability is represented by the sum of the areas of the white regions of Figure 11.7, and if we use the normal approximation to the sampling distribution of the mean, it is easily found. (We shall assume here that the nature of the data is such that we can use this approximation even though the sample size is only $n = 25$.) According to the theorem on page 366, the standard deviation of this sampling distribution, the standard error of the mean $\sigma_{\bar{x}}$, is given by $\dfrac{\sigma}{\sqrt{n}}$. Hence, we calculate

$$z = \frac{297 - 300}{5/\sqrt{25}} = -3.00 \quad \text{and} \quad z = \frac{303 - 300}{5/\sqrt{25}} = 3.00$$

and it follows from Table I that the area in each tail of the sampling distribution shown in Figure 11.7 is $0.5000 - 0.4987 = 0.0013$. Therefore, the probability that $\bar{x}$ will be 297 or less, or 303 or more, is $0.0013 + 0.0013 = 0.0026$, and this is the probability α of erroneously rejecting the hypothesis that the process is in control. In other words, rounding 0.0026 to 0.003, there

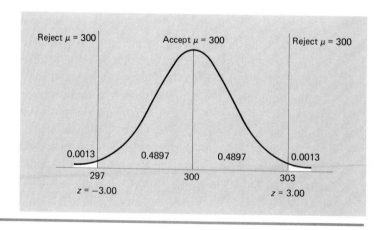

Reject $\mu = 300$ Accept $\mu = 300$ Reject $\mu = 300$

0.0013   0.4897   0.4897   0.0013

297   300   303
$z = -3.00$ $z = 3.00$

FIGURE 11.7
Test criterion

Chapter 11   Decision Making: Inferences About Means

are about 3 chances in 1,000 that the company will commit the error of shutting the process down and looking for trouble which does not exist.

Suppose now that, due to some equipment malfunction, the actual mean fill has shifted and is only 296 grams. Now hypothesis H_0 is false, and the process is out of control. In this case, the sampling distribution of the mean is not as shown in Figure 11.7, but as shown in Figure 11.8. Thus, the probability of not detecting this shift and of accepting the false hypothesis that the process is in control is represented by the area of the white region of Figure 11.8. It is the probability of getting a sample mean between 297 and 303 grams from a population whose mean is $\mu = 296$, and as before, the standard error of the mean is $\sigma_{\bar{x}} = \dfrac{5}{\sqrt{25}}$. Hence, we calculate

$$z = \frac{297 - 296}{5/\sqrt{25}} = 1.00 \qquad \text{and} \qquad z = \frac{303 - 296}{5/\sqrt{25}} = 7.00$$

and it follows from Table I that the area of the white region of Figure 11.8 is $0.5000 - 0.3413 = 0.1587$, since the area under the curve to the right of $z = 7.00$ is negligible. Thus, the probability β of accepting the false hypothesis that the process is in control when actually $\mu = 296$ grams is 0.1587. In other words, there are about 16 chances in 100 that the company will commit the error of letting the process run, thinking that the mean fill is 300 grams when in reality it is only 296 grams.

In computing the probability of accepting hypothesis H_0 when it is false, we supposed that the process mean had shifted from 300 to 296 grams. However, in this filling problem there are an infinite number of possible alternatives for the actual mean weight, and 300 grams represents only one possibility. For each of these possibilities there is a positive probability, β,

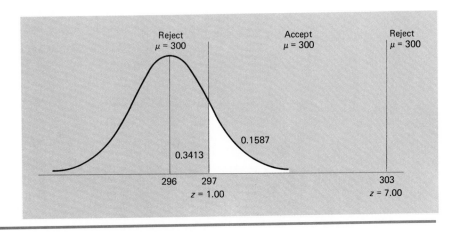

FIGURE 11.8
Test criterion

that the company will accept the hypothesis when it is false. Thus, let us calculate the probability of accepting the hypothesis that the mean weight is 300 grams for several other alternatives, and examine these probabilities to see how well, under various circumstances, the criterion controls the risks facing the company. The procedure is precisely the same as in the case where we supposed that the mean had shifted to 296 grams. The probability of accepting the hypothesis that the mean weight is 300 grams when it is, in fact, say, 305 grams is just the probability that the mean of a sample of 25 weights drawn from a population with mean 305 grams and standard deviation 5 grams will lie between 297 and 303 grams. By drawing a figure like Figure 11.8 with $\mu = 305$ and proceeding as we did above, we find that the probability β (of accepting the false hypothesis that the process is in control when μ is actually 305 grams) is 0.0228.

The third column of the table that follows shows, for 13 possible values of μ, the probabilities of accepting the hypothesis that $\mu = 300$ grams when μ is actually 294, 295, . . . , 305, or 306 grams. When the value of μ is 300, H_0 is true and the probability of accepting it is the probability of not rejecting it, namely, $1 - \alpha = 1 - 0.0026 = 0.9974$. Therefore, the probabilities shown of accepting H_0 are the probabilities β of accepting a false hypothesis with the exception of the probability of 0.9974, which is the probability of avoiding a Type I error. The probabilities of committing a Type II error, shown in the second column, are the same as the corresponding probabilities of accepting H_0 except where $\mu = 300$ grams. In that case, H_0 is true and there is no possibility of committing a Type II error.

Value of μ	Probability of Type II error	Probability of accepting H_0
294	0.0013	0.0013
295	0.0228	0.0228
296	0.1587	0.1587
297	0.5000	0.5000
298	0.8413	0.8413
299	0.9772	0.9772
300	–	0.9974
301	0.9772	0.9772
302	0.8413	0.8413
303	0.5000	0.5000
304	0.1587	0.1587
305	0.0228	0.0228
306	0.0013	0.0013

Chapter 11 *Decision Making: Inferences About Means*

If we plot the probabilities of accepting H_0 as in Figure 11.9 and fit a smooth curve, we get the **operating characteristic curve** of the test criterion, or simply the **OC curve**. An operating characteristic curve provides a good overall picture of the merits of a test criterion. Examination of the curve of Figure 11.9 shows that the probability of accepting hypothesis H_0 is greatest when it is true. For small departures from the 300-gram standard there is a high probability of accepting H_0; that is, when the process deviates only slightly from standard, it will most likely be allowed to continue to operate. But for larger and larger departures from standard in either direction, the probabilities of failing to detect them and accepting H_0 in error become smaller and smaller. This is precisely what the company wants, and any test procedure which did not behave in this way would not be at all suited to its needs.

Of course, the OC curve of Figure 11.9 applies only to the case where the hypothesis $\mu = 300$ grams is accepted if the mean of a random sample of size 25 falls between 297 and 303 grams and rejected otherwise, and σ is known to be 5 grams. If it wishes, the company can change the shape of the OC curve (and hence, change the amount of protection it is getting against committing Type I and Type II errors) by changing the test criterion or the sample size. In fact, OC curves can often be made to assume a particular desired shape by an appropriate choice of the sample size and/or the dividing lines of the test criterion.

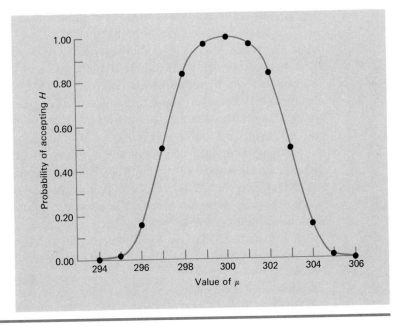

FIGURE 11.9
Operating
characteristic curve

A detailed study of OC curves would go considerably beyond the scope of this text, and the purpose of our illustration was mainly to show how statistical methods can be used to measure and control the risks to which one is exposed in testing hypotheses. Of course, these methods are not limited to problems of quality control in industrial plants. This will become increasingly clear as we proceed.

11.6

Hypothesis Testing: Null Hypotheses and Significance Tests

In the example of the preceding section, we had less trouble with Type I errors than with Type II errors, because we formulated the hypothesis H_0 as a **simple hypothesis** about the parameter μ; that is, we formulated the hypothesis H_0 so that μ took on a single value and the probability of a Type I error could be calculated.[3] Had we formulated instead a **composite hypothesis** about μ, say, the composite hypothesis $\mu \neq 300$ grams, the composite hypothesis $\mu < 300$ grams, or the composite hypothesis $\mu > 300$ grams, where in each case μ can take on more than one possible value, we could not have calculated the probability of a Type I error without specifying how much μ differs from, is less than, or is greater than 300 grams.

To be able to calculate the probability of a Type I error (that is, to know what to expect when a hypothesis is true), it is customary to formulate hypotheses to be tested as simple hypotheses, and in many instances this requires that we hypothesize the opposite of what we hope to prove. For instance, if we want to show that a new copper-bearing steel has a higher yield strength than ordinary steel, we formulate the hypothesis that the two yield strengths are the same. Similarly, if we want to show that one method of teaching computer programming is more effective than another, we hypothesize that the two methods are equally effective, and if we want to show that the proportion of sales slips incorrectly written up in one department of a store is greater than that in another department, we formulate the hypothesis that the two proportions are identical. Since we hypothesize that there is no difference in the yield strength, no difference in the effectiveness of the two methods of teaching computer programming, and no difference

---

[3]Note that we are applying the term "simple hypothesis" to a hypothesis about a parameter; some statisticians use the term "simple hypothesis" only when the hypothesis completely specifies the population.

between the two proportions, we call hypotheses such as these **null hypotheses** and denote them H_0. Nowadays, the term "null hypothesis" is used for any hypothesis set up primarily to see whether it can be rejected. Actually, the idea of setting up a null hypothesis is common even in nonstatistical thinking. It is precisely what we do in criminal proceedings, for example, where an accused is presumed to be innocent until his guilt is proved beyond a reasonable doubt. The presumption that the accused is not guilty is a null hypothesis, and this hypothesis is assumed to be true until it is proven false.

Although a positive probability β of accepting a false hypothesis exists for all values of μ alternative to the test value, we can sometimes sidestep Type II errors altogether. To illustrate how this is done, suppose that a large title search company knows from experience that the mean number of typing errors made on submitted copies of form A by typists preparing these forms is 2.3 per day with a standard deviation of 0.75. In trying to confirm its suspicion that one particular typist makes more errors on the average than the others, the company takes a random sample of nine forms prepared by this typist and tests the null hypothesis that there is no difference between the typist's performance and that of the others (that $\mu = 2.3$ applies to this typist also) by using the following criterion:

> *Reject the null hypothesis $\mu = 2.3$ (and accept the alternative $\mu > 2.3$) if the typist averages 2.7 or more errors per form; otherwise, reserve judgment (perhaps pending further study).*

With this criterion there is no possibility of committing a Type II error; when the hypothesis is tested it may be rejected outright (and the typist presumed to be less proficient than average), but otherwise, the hypothesis is never really rejected on the basis of the given information.

The procedure we have just outlined is called a **significance test**. If the difference between what we expect under the hypothesis and what we observe in a sample is too large to be reasonably attributed to chance, we reject the null hypothesis. If the difference between what we expect and what we observe is so small that it might well be attributed to chance, we say that the result is **not statistically significant** and let it go at that.

With reference to the preceding criterion, the company's suspicion that the typist is worse than average is confirmed if the average number of errors is 2.7 or more; in that case it is felt that the difference between the sample mean and $\mu = 2.3$ is too large to be attributed to chance (see also Exercise 11.32 on page 418). If the sample mean is less than 2.7, the company's suspicion is not confirmed. We do not say that the company's suspicion is wrong, or unjustified, when the sample mean is less than 2.7—we merely say that it is not confirmed. In that case, we may want to continue the investigation, perhaps with a larger sample.

Returning to the cleaning wax filling example of the preceding section, we could convert the criterion on page 404 into that of a significance test by writing

Reject the null hypothesis $\mu = 300$ grams (and consider the process to be out of control) if the mean of the 25 sample fills is 297 grams or less or if it is 303 grams or more; otherwise, reserve judgment.

It should be obvious, though, that there is really no way to reserve judgment in this situation. Once the process is in operation, it must either be allowed to continue in operation or it must be shut down, and no matter how we phrase the criterion, so long as the filling process continues, there is no way possible to avoid the consequences of committing a Type II error.

Whether or not one can afford the luxury of reserving judgment in any given situation depends entirely on the nature of the problem. In general, whenever a decision must be reached one way or the other, we must accept or reject the hypothesis under consideration, and there is no way of avoiding the risk of committing a Type II error.

Since the general problem of testing hypotheses and constructing statistical decision criteria often seems confusing, it will help to proceed systematically as outlined in the following five-step procedure:

1. We formulate a simple null hypothesis and an appropriate alternative hypothesis.

In the cleaning wax filling example the null hypothesis was $\mu = 300$, and the alternative hypothesis was $\mu \neq 300$. We refer to this kind of alternative as a **two-sided alternative**. It is appropriate here because the company wants protection against thinking that the filling process is in control when it is either underfilling or overfilling the cans. In the typist example, the null hypothesis was $\mu = 2.3$ mistakes, and the alternative hypothesis was $\mu > 2.3$. This is called a **one-sided alternative**. It is appropriate here if the burden of proof is on the firm to show (by rejecting the null hypothesis) that the typist is poorer than average. We can also write a one-sided alternative with the inequality sign pointing in the other direction. For instance, if we wanted to determine whether the average time required for production

Chapter 11   Decision Making: Inferences About Means

employees to do a certain job is less than 40 minutes, we might take a random sample of, say, 20 of these times and test the null hypothesis $\mu = 40$ against the alternative $\mu < 40$.

As in the three examples of the preceding paragraph, alternative hypotheses usually specify that the population mean (or whatever other parameter may be of concern) is not equal to, greater than, or less than the value assumed under the null hypothesis. For any given problem, the choice of an appropriate alternative depends mostly on what we hope to be able to show, or better, perhaps, where we want to put the burden of proof.

EXAMPLE 11.9   A company uses a production process designed to make machine components that have an average thickness of 5 inches. The company suspects that the process is not maintaining its intended average.

(a) If the company wants to modify its process if the average thickness is smaller than 5 inches, what null hypothesis and alternative hypothesis should it use?

(b) If the company wants to modify its process if the average thickness is different from 5 inches, what null hypothesis and alternative hypothesis should it use?

SOLUTION   (a) The words "smaller than" suggest that the alternative hypothesis $\mu < 5$ inches is needed together with the null hypothesis $\mu = 5$ inches.

(b) The words "different from" suggest that the alternative hypothesis $\mu \neq 5$ inches is needed together with the null hypothesis $\mu = 5$ inches.   ∎

EXAMPLE 11.10   A shoe manufacturer is considering the purchase of a new automatic machine for stamping out uppers. If μ_1 is the average number of good uppers stamped out by the old machine per hour and μ_2 is the corresponding average for the new machine, the manufacturer wants to test the null hypothesis $\mu_1 = \mu_2$ against a suitable alternative.

(a) What should the alternative be if the manufacturer does not want to buy the new machine unless it is definitely superior to the old one?

(b) What should the alternative be if the manufacturer wants to buy the new machine (which has some other nice features) unless tests prove it to be definitely inferior to the old one?

SOLUTION (a) The manufacturer should use the alternative hypothesis $\mu_1 < \mu_2$ and purchase the new machine only if the null hypothesis can be rejected.

(b) The manufacturer should use the alternative hypothesis $\mu_1 > \mu_2$ and purchase the new machine unless the null hypothesis is rejected. ∎

Having formulated a null hypothesis and a suitable alternative, we then proceed with the following step:

2. We specify the probability of committing a Type I error; if possible, desired, or necessary, we may also make some specifications about the probabilities β of Type II errors for specific alternatives.

The probability of committing a Type I error is usually referred to as the **level of significance** at which a test is performed. Usually, tests are performed at a level of significance of 0.05 or 0.01. Testing a hypothesis at a level of significance of, say, $\alpha = 0.05$ simply means that we are fixing the probability of rejecting the hypothesis if it is true at 0.05. In the past, the choice of 0.05 and 0.01 was dictated in part by practical considerations and in part by the availability of statistical tables. With the advent of computers and an abundance of statistical software, the latter is no longer of any relevance, and there is much greater freedom in the choice of the level of significance. This will be discussed further in Section 11.7.

Once we have set up a pair of hypotheses, the probability of committing a Type I error is absolutely under our control and can be made as small as we like. How small we actually make it in a particular case depends on the consequences (cost, inconvenience, embarrassment, etc.) of rejecting a true null hypothesis. Ordinarily, the more serious the consequences which result from committing a Type I error, the smaller the risk we are willing to take of committing it. However, we are restrained in practice from setting very low probabilities α by the fact that, for a fixed sample size, the smaller we make the probability of rejecting a true hypothesis, the larger the probability β of accepting a false one becomes. For instance, if in the filling problem the probability of shutting down the process when it is in control were reduced from $\alpha = 0.0026$ to $\alpha = 0.0001$, the probability of not detecting that the process is out of control when the mean fill is actually either 296 or 304 grams would be increased from $\beta = 0.1587$ to $\beta = 0.4602$ (see Exercise 11.31 on page 418). What we need in practice is some reasonable balance between the probabilities of committing the two kinds of errors, as dictated for the most part by practical considerations.

Although we generally use a simple hypothesis, we sometimes prefer to use a composite hypothesis for the same set of data. On page 410 we discussed the difference between a simple hypothesis where μ takes on a single value, $\mu = 300$ grams, and a composite hypothesis where μ can take on many values. For example, if we use the composite hypothesis $\mu \neq 300$ grams, the value for μ can be any positive number less than or greater than 300; or if we use the composite hypothesis $\mu < 300$ or $\mu > 300$, the value for μ can be any positive number less than 300 grams, or greater than 300 grams, respectively.

Let us now see what can be done when the null hypothesis is not a simple hypothesis. Referring to the example of the typist on page 410, the null hypothesis is given as $\mu = 2.3$, the alternative hypothesis is $\mu > 2.3$, and from Exercise 11.32 on page 418, the calculated value of $z = 1.60$ and the corresponding α is 0.0548. Suppose, now, that the company wants to allow for the possibility that the number of errors made by typists might average less than 2.3. In this situation we test the null hypothesis $\mu \leq 2.3$ against the alternative hypothesis $\mu > 2.3$. This means that there is no unique probability for α, the probability of a Type I error; but observe that if μ is less than 2.3 the normal curve is shifted to the left and the area to the right of 2.7 (as specified in the example) becomes smaller than 0.0548. Thus, if the null hypothesis is $\mu \leq 2.3$, we say that the probability of a Type I error is, at most, 0.0548. This may be compared with the simple hypothesis $\mu = 2.3$, where we state that the probability of a Type I error is 0.0548.

3. **Using suitable statistical theory, we construct a test criterion for testing the null hypothesis against the alternative hypothesis (both formulated in step 1) at the level of significance (specified in step 2).**

In the cleaning wax filling example, we based the criterion on the normal-curve approximation to the sampling distribution of $\bar{x}$; in general, the criterion depends on the statistic on which the decision is to be based and on its sampling distribution. We call this statistic the **test statistic**. A good portion of the remainder of this book will be devoted to the construction of such criteria. As we shall see, this usually involves choosing an appropriate test statistic, specifying the sample size, and then determining the dividing lines, or critical values, of the criterion. Among the previous examples, we used a **two-sided test** (or **two-tailed test**) with the alternative $\mu \neq 300$ in the cleaning wax filling example, rejecting the null hypothesis for either small or large values of $\bar{x}$. In the example dealing with the number of mistakes made by a typist, we used a **one-sided test** (or **one-tailed test**) with the one-sided alternative $\mu > 2.3$, rejecting the null hypothesis only for large values of $\bar{x}$.

And in the example dealing with the time required to do a certain job, we would use a one-sided test (or one-tailed test) with the alternative $\mu < 40$, rejecting the null hypothesis only for small values of $\bar{x}$. In general, a test is called two sided (or two tailed) if the null hypothesis is rejected when a value of the test statistic falls in either of the two tails of its sampling distribution, and one sided (or one tailed) if the null hypothesis is rejected when a value of the test statistic falls in just one specified tail of its sampling distribution.

> **4. We calculate from the data the value of the statistic on which the decision is to be based**.
>
> **5. We decide whether to reject the null hypothesis, whether to accept it, or whether to reserve judgment**.

As we have said, step 5 depends on whether we must make a decision one way or the other on the basis of the test, or whether the circumstances of the problem are such that we can delay a decision pending further study. Sometimes we may accept a null hypothesis with the hope that we are not exposing ourselves to excessively high risks of committing serious Type II errors. Of course, if it is necessary and we have enough information, we can calculate the probabilities needed to get an overall picture from the OC curve of the test criterion.

Before we discuss various special tests about means in the next few sections, let us point out that the concepts we have introduced here apply equally well to hypotheses concerning proportions, standard deviations, the randomness of samples, relationships among several variables, trends of time series, and so on.

Also, the five steps just outlined may be referred to as the classical approach to tests of significance. With the advent of computers and the general availability of statistical software, the five steps may be modified to allow for more freedom in the choice of the level of significance. As we have already indicated on page 414, this will be explained in Section 11.7. In some instances the modification does not only allow for more freedom in the choice of the level of significance, but it may actually simplify the whole procedure.

To summarize briefly, the following steps are required to implement the five-step procedure.

> **1.** *Hypothesis.* Formulate a null hypothesis and an alternative hypothesis.
>
> **2.** *Level.* Specify the probability of committing a Type I or Type II error.

Chapter 11   Decision Making: Inferences About Means

3. *Criterion.* Construct a test criterion for testing the null hypothesis against the alternative hypothesis at the specified level of significance.

4. *Statistic.* Calculate from the data the value of the statistic on which the decision is to be based.

5. *Conclusion.* Decide whether to reject the null hypothesis. Otherwise, accept the null hypothesis or reserve judgment.

Example 11.11 on page 423 provides a practical format for use in this and in other problems where we can use the five-step procedure.

EXERCISES

(Exercises 11.24, 11.26, 11.28, and 11.34 are practice exercises. Their complete solutions are given on page 447.)

11.24 If we want to test, on the basis of a random sample, the hypothesis that the mean gold content in a short ton (2,000 pounds) of ore is 0.25 troy ounces, under what conditions would we commit

(a) a Type I error
(b) a Type II error

11.25 If we want to test the hypothesis that the use of a cellular car telephone increases the numbers of sales made by real estate salespersons, under what conditions would we commit

(a) a Type I error
(b) a Type II error

11.26 Whether an error is a Type I error or a Type II error depends upon how the hypothesis to be tested is formulated. To illustrate this, reword the hypothesis of the preceding exercise so that a Type I error becomes a Type II error, and vice versa.

11.27 With reference to the filling example, verify the values of the probabilities of Type II errors given in the middle column of the table on page 408.

11.28 Suppose that for a given population with $\sigma = 8.4$ inches we want to test the null hypothesis $\mu = 75.0$ inches against the alternative hypothesis $\mu < 75.0$ inches on the basis of a random sample of size $n = 100$.

(a) If the null hypothesis is rejected when $\bar{x} < 73.0$ inches and otherwise it is accepted, find the probability of a Type I error.

(b) If the hypothesis we want to test had been $\mu \geq 75.0$ inches and the criterion is the same as in part (a), what could we have said about the probability of a Type I error?

11.29 Suppose that in the filling example the criterion is changed so that the hypothesis $\mu = 300$ grams is accepted if the sample mean falls between 298 and 302 grams; otherwise, the hypothesis is rejected.

(a) Show that this will increase the probability of a Type I error from 0.0026 to 0.0456.

(b) Show that this will decrease the probability of a Type II error when $\mu = 296$ from 0.1587 to 0.0228.

11.30 Suppose that in the filling example σ had been 6 grams instead of 5 grams but that everything else remained the same.

(a) Show that this will increase the probability of a Type I error from 0.0026 to 0.0124.

(b) Show that this will increase the probability of a Type II error when $\mu = 296$ from 0.1587 to 0.2033.

11.31 With reference to the filling example, use $z_{0.00005} = 3.9$ and verify that the probability of not detecting that the process is out of control is $\beta = 0.4602$ when $\mu = 296$ and $\alpha = 0.0001$.

11.32 With reference to the typist example on page 411, verify that the probability of committing a Type I error is 0.0548.

11.33 An automatic machine in a food processing plant is supposed to set the lids on pint jars of mayonnaise so that the average "twist" required for a person to loosen the lids ("break the sets") is 30 inch-pounds. It is known from long experience that the variability of the sets is stable and given by $\sigma = 2.0$ inch-pounds. The processor does not want the lids set too loosely since this may cause discoloration and spoilage of the mayonnaise, and he does not want them set too tightly since people resent having to struggle with stubborn lids. Consequently, the processor sets up a hypothesis that the lids are set at 30 inch-pounds on the average (the process is in control) and an alternative that the lids are not set at 30 inch-pounds (the process is out of control). The hypothesis is tested periodically by taking from production lots of sealed jars random samples of 36 jars, determining the mean twist $\bar{x}$ required to break the sets, accepting the hypothesis if $\bar{x}$ is between 29.2 inch-pounds and 30.8 inch-pounds and rejecting it if $\bar{x}$ is either less than 29.2 inch-pounds or greater than 30.8 inch-pounds.

(a) Find the probability of a Type I error.

(b) Find the probabilities of Type II errors for alternative mean sets of 28.5, 29.0, 29.5, 30.5, 31.0, and 31.5 inch-pounds.

(c) Plot the OC curve.

11.34 A business office which owns many computers is considering replacing an old-model printer with a new model. If μ_1 is the average number of lines per minute printed by the old model and μ_2 is the average number of lines per minute printed by the new model, the null hypothesis to be tested is $\mu_1 = \mu_2$.

(a) What alternative hypothesis should the business office use if it does not want to buy the new-model printer unless it prints more lines per minute? Simply stated, the burden of proof is on the new-model printer, which will be purchased only if the null hypothesis can be rejected.

(b) What alternative hypothesis should the business office use if it is anxious to get the new-model printer (which has additional features in its favor) unless it prints fewer lines per minute than the old model? (Note: The burden of proof is now on the old-model printer, which will be kept only if the null hypothesis can be rejected.)

(c) What alternative hypothesis would the business office have to use so that the rejection of the null hypothesis can lead either to keeping the old-model printer or purchasing the new model?

11.35 Suppose that a toxic waste disposal company is studying several methods of disposing of petroleum wastes, and it has a new method which it suspects produces larger amounts of dangerous by-products than the average of all other waste disposal methods which are under study.

(a) The toxic waste disposal company will discontinue its study of the new method, provided its suspicion is confirmed on the basis of observation of the production of dangerous by-products by experiments with the new method. What hypothesis and alternative hypothesis should the toxic waste disposal company set up?

(b) What hypothesis and alternative hypothesis should the toxic waste disposal company set up if it decides to discontinue studying the new method unless it can be proved that it causes smaller amounts of dangerous by-products than the average of all the other petroleum waste disposal methods being studied?

11.36 Suppose that a large supermarket has one checkout clerk whom the manager suspects of making more mistakes than the average of all the clerks. The manager knows that for all clerks in this market, the average number of register mistakes per day per clerk is 18 and the standard deviation is 5. If the manager decides to fire the suspected clerk only if in a random sample of 40 days of work he averages more than 20 mistakes, what is the probability of

(a) firing the clerk when his work is, in fact, of average quality

(b) keeping the clerk if he averages 21 mistakes per day

(c) Suppose that the company wants to allow for the possibility that the average number of mistakes per day per clerk is less than 18. Use this information to recalculate part (a). (Hint: Use $\mu \le 18$, a composite hypothesis.)

11.37 In hypothesis testing, a function whose values are the probabilities of reject-ing a given hypothesis (and accepting the alternative) for various values of the parameter under consideration is called a **power function**. Thus, in the filling example, for all values of μ other than the hypothesized 300 grams, the power function gives the probabilities $1 - \beta$ of not committing a Type II error; for $\mu = 300$, however, it gives the probability α of committing a Type I error. Obviously, the values of the power function are 1 minus the corre-sponding values of the OC curve. Plot the graph of the power function for the filling example and describe this curve.

11.7

Tests Concerning Means

Having used tests concerning means to illustrate the basic principles of hypothesis testing, let us now consider how to proceed in actual practice. Suppose, for instance, that we want to determine, on the basis of the mean $\bar{x}$ of a random sample of size 100, whether or not the average weekly food expenditure of families of three within a certain income range is \$85.00. From information gathered in other pertinent studies, we assume that the variability of such expenditures is given by a standard deviation of $\sigma =$ \$12.20.

Beginning with step 1 on page 412, we formulate the null hypothesis to be tested and the alternative hypothesis, denoted by H_A, as

$$H_0\text{:}\,\mu = \$85.00$$
$$H_A\text{:}\,\mu \neq \$85.00$$

We used the two-sided alternative $\mu \neq \$85.00$ since the "whether or not" earlier suggests that we reject the null hypothesis for values of μ less than or greater than \$85.00. So far as step 2 is concerned, suppose for the sake of argument that we fix the level of significance at $\alpha = 0.05$.

Next, in step 3, we shall depart slightly from the procedures used in the examples of Section 11.6, where we stated the test criteria in terms of values of $\bar{x}$. From now on we shall base our criteria for tests concerning means on the statistic

Statistic for test concerning mean

$$z = \frac{\bar{x} - \mu_0}{\sigma/\sqrt{n}}$$

Chapter 11   Decision Making: Inferences About Means

provided that n is large enough, 30 or more, to approximate the sampling distribution of the mean with a normal distribution. Here μ_0 is the mean of the population sampled when the null hypothesis is true. The reason for working with standard units, or z-values, is that it enables us to formulate criteria which are applicable to a great variety of problems, not just one.

Thus, we can use the test criteria shown in Figure 11.10. Depending on the choice of the alternative hypothesis, the dividing line (or lines) of the

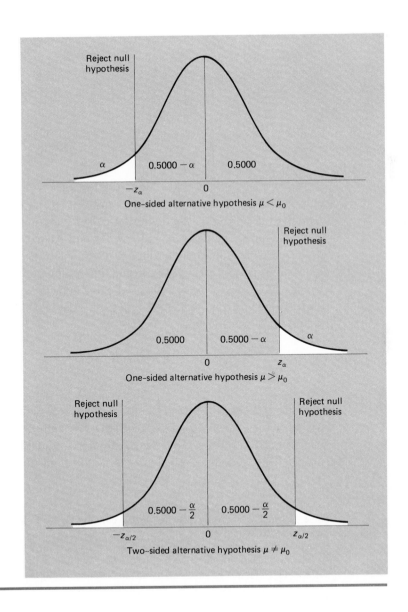

FIGURE 11.10
Test criteria

criterion is $-z_\alpha$ or z_α for the one-sided alternative and $-z_{\alpha/2}$ and $z_{\alpha/2}$ for the two-sided alternative. Once again, z_α and $z_{\alpha/2}$ are such that the areas to their right under the standard normal distribution are α and $\alpha/2$, respectively.

Symbolically, we can formulate these criteria as shown in the following table:[4]

Alternative hypothesis	Reject the null hypothesis if	Accept the null hypothesis or reserve judgment if
$\mu < \mu_0$	$z \leq -z_\alpha$	$z > -z_\alpha$
$\mu > \mu_0$	$z \geq z_\alpha$	$z < z_\alpha$
$\mu \neq \mu_0$	$z \leq -z_{\alpha/2}$ or $z \geq z_{\alpha/2}$	$-z_{\alpha/2} < z < z_{\alpha/2}$

If $\alpha = 0.05$, the dividing lines, or **critical values**, of the criteria are -1.645 or 1.645 for the one-sided alternatives and -1.96 and 1.96 for the two-sided alternative; if $\alpha = 0.01$, the dividing lines of the criteria are -2.33 or 2.33 for the one-sided alternatives, and -2.575 and 2.575 for the two-sided alternative. All these values come directly from Table I.

Returning now to the food expenditures illustration on page 420, suppose that the mean of the sample is 87.80. Then, in step 4 we substitute this value together with $\mu_0 = 85.00$, $\sigma = 12.20$, and $n = 100$ into the foregoing formula for z, and we get

$$z = \frac{87.80 - 85.00}{12.20/\sqrt{100}} = 2.30$$

Since this exceeds 1.96, we reject the null hypothesis in step 5 and conclude that the average weekly food expenditure of the families in question does not equal $85.00. In other words, the difference of $2.80 between the observed mean and the hypothetical value of μ is too large to be accounted for by

---

[4]Some authors substitute $<$ for $\leq$ in the middle column of this table and $\leq$ for $<$ in the right-hand column. In other words, they include the dividing lines of the test criteria among the values for which the null hypothesis is accepted or we reserve judgment. Since the standard normal distribution is a continuous distribution, this is of no practical significance. However, when we are dealing with discrete random variables, as in Chapter 12, the use of certain tables may require that the dividing lines of the test criteria are included among the values for which the null hypothesis is rejected.

chance. It appears from the data that the true average weekly food expenditure is actually greater than $85.00.

If we had used the 0.01 level of significance instead of the 0.05 level, we could not have rejected the null hypothesis $\mu = \$85.00$ since $z = 2.30$ falls between -2.575 and 2.575. This illustrates the important point that the level of significance should be specified before a significance test is actually performed. This will spare us the temptation of later choosing a level of significance which happens to suit our particular objectives.

The procedure we have described in this section is a large-sample test; it is exact only when the population we are sampling has a normal distribution. Also, since σ is often unknown, we may have no choice but to substitute for it the sample standard deviation s.

EXAMPLE 11.11 A large retailer wants to determine whether the mean income of families living within 2 miles of a proposed building site exceeds $24,400. What can he conclude at the 0.05 level of significance, if the mean income of a random sample of $n = 60$ families living within 2 miles of the proposed site is $\bar{x} = \$24,524$ and the standard deviation is $s = \$763$?

SOLUTION
1. H_0: $\mu = \$24,400$.
   H_A: $\mu > \$24,400$.

2. $\alpha = 0.05$.

3. Reject the null hypothesis if $z \geq 1.645$, where

$$z = \frac{\bar{x} - \mu_0}{\sigma/\sqrt{n}}$$

with $s = 763$ substituted for σ; otherwise accept the null hypothesis or reserve judgment.

4. Substituting $\bar{x} = 24,524$, $n = 60$, $\mu_0 = 24,400$, and $s = 763$ for σ into the formula for z, we get

$$z = \frac{24,524 - 24,400}{763/\sqrt{60}} = 1.26$$

5. Since $z = 1.26$ is less than 1.645, the null hypothesis cannot be rejected. In other words, the difference between $24,524 and $24,400 is not large enough to provide evidence at the 0.05 level of significance that average family income in the area exceeds $24,400. In this instance, the retailer may well decide to reserve judgment pending further study rather than to accept the null hypothesis and thus risk committing a Type II error. ∎

EXAMPLE 11.12   A trucking firm suspects that the average lifetime of 25,000 miles claimed for certain tires is too high. To test the claim, the firm puts a random sample of 40 of these tires on its trucks and later finds that their mean lifetime is 24,421 miles and the standard deviation is 1,349 miles. What can it conclude at the 0.01 level of significance?

SOLUTION   Using the five-step procedure outlined in the preceding example we get

1. H_0: $\mu = 25,000$ miles.
   H_A: $\mu < 25,000$ miles.

2. $\alpha = 0.01$.

3. Reject the null hypothesis if $z \leq -2.33$, where

$$z = \frac{\bar{x} - \mu_0}{\sigma/\sqrt{n}}$$

with $s = 1,349$ substituted for σ; otherwise, accept the null hypothesis or reserve judgment.

4. Substituting $\bar{x} = 24,421$, $\mu_0 = 25,000$, $n = 40$, and $s = 1,349$ for σ into the formula for z, we get

$$z = \frac{24,421 - 25,000}{1,349/\sqrt{40}} = -2.71$$

5. Since $z = -2.71$ is actually less than -2.33, the null hypothesis must be rejected. In other words, the trucking firm can conclude that the average lifetime of the tires is not as high as claimed.   ■

To present the modification in the procedure for conducting tests of significance which we mentioned on page 414, let us refer to Example 11.11. Instead of comparing the value of the test statistic, $z = 1.26$, with the dividing line of the test criterion, $z_{0.05} = 1.645$, we compare the probability of getting a value less than or equal to $z = 1.26$ with the specified level of significance, $\alpha = 0.05$. As can be seen from Table I, the area under the standard normal curve to the right of $z = 1.26$ is $0.5000 - 0.3962 = 0.1038$, and since this exceeds $\alpha = 0.05$, the null hypothesis cannot be rejected. This agrees with the result obtained in Example 11.11 on page 423.

The probability which we calculated in the preceding paragraph is called the **P-value**, **prob-value**, **tail probability**, or the **observed level of significance** corresponding to the observed value of the test statistic. In general, P-values may be defined as follows:

Corresponding to an observed value of a test statistic, the *P*-value is the lowest level of significance at which the null hypothesis could have been rejected.

If the alternative hypothesis is $\mu < \mu_0$, the *P*-value is given by the area under the standard normal curve to the left of the observed value of z; if the alternative hypothesis is $\mu > \mu_0$, the *P*-value is given by the area under the standard normal curve to the right of the observed value of z. If the alternative hypothesis is $\mu \neq \mu_0$ and the observed value of z is positive, the *P*-value is given by *twice* the area under the standard normal curve to the right of the observed value of z; if the alternative hypothesis is $\mu \neq \mu_0$ and the observed value of z is negative, the *P*-value is given by *twice* the area under the standard normal curve to the left of the observed value of z. These arguments apply to the large-sample test concerning means, but they can easily be adapted to tests concerning other population parameters based on other test statistics.

If we want to base significance tests on *P*-values, steps 1 and 2 of the five-step procedure remain the same, but steps 3, 4, and 5 must be modified as follows:

3′. We specify the test statistic.

4′. We calculate the value of the test statistic from the sample data, and, based on the sampling distribution of the test statistic, we determine the corresponding P-value.

5′. We decide whether to reject the null hypothesis, whether to accept it, or whether to reserve judgment, by comparing the P-value obtained in step 4′ with the level of significance specified in step 2. (If the *P*-value is less than or equal to α, the null hypothesis must be rejected; otherwise, we accept the null hypothesis or reserve judgment.)[5]

The following illustrates this procedure.

EXAMPLE 11.13   Rework Example 11.12, basing the decision on the *P*-value corresponding to the value obtained for the test statistic.

SOLUTION   Using the five-step procedure we get

1. H_0: $\mu = 25,000$ miles.
H_A: $\mu < 25,000$ miles.

[5]If test criteria are modified as in the footnote to page 000 (that is, if the dividing lines of the test criteria are included among the values for which the null hypothesis is accepted or we reserve judgment), *P*-values must be defined in a different way.

2. $\alpha = 0.01$.

3'. The test statistic is

$$z = \frac{\bar{x} - \mu_0}{\sigma/\sqrt{n}}$$

with s substituted for σ.

4'. The value of z is known from Example 11.12, where we showed that $z = -2.71$. The corresponding P-value is given by the area under the standard normal curve to the left of $z = -2.71$, and we find from Table I that it equals

$$0.5000 - 0.4966 = 0.0034$$

5'. Since 0.0034 is less than $\alpha = 0.01$, the null hypothesis must be rejected. Of course, this agrees with the result obtained before. ∎

As we pointed out on page 423, the level of significance should always be specified in advance to avoid the temptation of later choosing a level of significance which happens to suit one's purpose. Nevertheless, steps 2 and 5' are often omitted in connection with studies that are more of an exploratory nature and there is no real need to reach a decision. In that case, P-values are interpreted as measures of potential or interest. Thus, research workers might say that a small P-value suggests that their results "look promising," without going into any further detail. Of course, this interpretation of P-values is a highly subjective and risky business, but it provides an alternative to some of the abuses connected with tests of significance. We are referring here to the fact that among significance tests of null hypotheses that are true, we can always expect some spuriously "significant" results. For instance, if research workers conduct 400 significance tests at the 0.05 level of significance, when the respective H_0's are true, they can expect $400(0.05) = 20$ totally meaningless "significant" results. How this may be abused is illustrated by the following example and in Exercise 11.67 on page 441.

EXAMPLE 11.14   Suppose that an unscrupulous manufacturer wants "scientific proof" that a totally useless chemical additive will improve the mileage yield of gasoline. If he pays 30 different research groups to test the effectiveness of the additive at the 0.05 level of significance, what is the probability that at least one of them will come up with "significant results" (which the manufacturer will then use to promote the additive with "scientific claims") even though the product is totally ineffective?

SOLUTION   The probability that none of the research groups will reject the true null hypothesis that the additive is totally ineffective is $(1 - 0.05)^{30} = (0.95)^{30}$, and hence, the probability is

$$1 - (0.95)^{30} = 0.79$$

that at least one of them will get the spurious results which the manufacturer wants.   ■

As shown on the last few pages, there are two ways of utilizing P-values. They can be used in decision making, or they can be used in situations where we do not actually make decisions.

P-values can be used in decision making as an alternative and *equivalent* way of conducting tests of significance. Here we compare P-values with levels of significance instead of comparing test statistics with critical values. In connection with this, the P-value approach provides more freedom in the choice of the level of significance. Also, in some cases, the use of P-values will actually simplify the work (as in exact tests concerning percentages, probabilities, or proportions).

P-values are also used where we do not actually make decisions. Here we use P-values as measures of the extent to which data support or refute a null hypothesis. As indicated earlier, this can be a highly subjective, risky procedure which should be used with caution.

11.8

Tests Concerning Means (Small Samples)

When we do not know the value of the population standard deviation and the sample is small, $n < 30$, we shall assume as on page 423 that the population we are sampling has roughly the shape of a normal distribution and base tests of the null hypothesis $\mu = \mu_0$ on the statistic

Statistic for small-sample test concerning mean

$$t = \frac{\bar{x} - \mu_0}{s/\sqrt{n}}$$

whose sampling distribution is the t distribution with $n - 1$ degrees of freedom. The criteria for small-sample tests concerning means based on the t

statistic are like those shown in Figure 11.10 and in the table on page 422, with z replaced by t and z_α and $z_{\alpha/2}$ replaced by t_α and $t_{\alpha/2}$. Here, again, t_α and $t_{\alpha/2}$ are such that the area to their right under the t distribution are α and $\alpha/2$, respectively. For the most commonly used values of α and $\alpha/2$, the dividing lines of these tests may be read from Table II, with the number of degrees of freedom equal to $n - 1$.

EXAMPLE 11.15   Suppose that we want to test, on the basis of a random sample of size 6, whether the average weight of horses in a large herd of American saddle horses exceeds 1,000 pounds. What can we conclude at the 0.01 level of significance if the sample values are 987, 1,146, 995, 1,010, 1,183, and 1,075 pounds?

SOLUTION   Using the previously illustrated format for the five-step procedure, we get

1. H_0: $\mu = 1,000$ pounds.
   H_A: $\mu > 1,000$ pounds.
2. $\alpha = 0.01$.
3. Reject the null hypothesis if $t \geq 3.365$, the value of $t_{0.01}$ for $6 - 1 = 5$ degrees of freedom, where

$$t = \frac{\bar{x} - \mu_0}{s/\sqrt{n}}$$

   Otherwise, state merely that the null hypothesis cannot be rejected (since the formulation of the problem does not specify whether a decision must be reached one way or the other).

4. Calculating the mean and the standard deviation of the sample, we get $\bar{x} = 1,066$ and $s = 83.2$, and substituting these values together with $n = 6$ and $\mu = 1,000$ into the formula for t, we find that

$$t = \frac{1,066 - 1,000}{83.2/\sqrt{6}} = 1.94$$

5. Since $t = 1.94$ is less than 3.365, the null hypothesis cannot be rejected. In other words, we cannot conclude that the average weight of horses in this herd exceeds 1,000 pounds. ■

A computer printout of the preceding small-sample t test concerning the mean is shown in Figure 11.11. The $+1$ following "ALTERNATIVE" is a code for the alternative hypothesis $\mu > \mu_0$, and "P VALUE 0.055" tells us

```
MTB > SET C1
DATA> 987 1146 995 1010 1183 1075
DATA> END
MTB > TTEST MU=1000, ALTERNATIVE +1, ON DATA IN C1

TEST OF MU = 1000.0 VS MU G.T. 1000.0

            N      MEAN    STDEV   SE MEAN       T    P VALUE
C1          6    1066.0     83.2      34.0    1.94      0.055
```

FIGURE 11.11 Computer printout for small-sample t test concerning mean

that the p-value is 0.055. Since 0.055 is greater than 0.01, we conclude, as before, that the null hypothesis cannot be rejected. To use P-values in problems involving the t distribution, it is useful to have suitable statistical software or a calculator, which is preprogrammed to perform the necessary calculations.

11.9

Differences Between Means

There are many statistical problems in which we must decide whether an observed difference between two sample means can be attributed to chance. We may want to decide, for instance, whether there is really a difference in the average gasoline consumption of two kinds of compact cars, if sample data show that one kind averaged 24.8 miles per gallon while, under the same conditions, the other kind averaged 25.6 miles per gallon. Similarly, we may want to decide on the basis of samples whether there actually is a difference in the size of delinquent charge accounts in two branches of a department store, whether men can perform a given task faster than can women, whether one kind of television tube lasts longer than another, and so on.

The method we shall employ to test whether an observed difference between two sample means can be attributed to chance is based on the following theory: If $\bar{x}_1$ and $\bar{x}_2$ are the means of two large independent random samples of size n_1 and n_2, the sampling distribution of the statistic $\bar{x}_1 - \bar{x}_2$ can be approximated closely with a normal curve having the mean $\mu_1 - \mu_2$ and the standard deviation

$$\sqrt{\frac{\sigma_1^2}{n_1} + \frac{\sigma_2^2}{n_2}}$$

where μ_1, μ_2, σ_1, and σ_2 are the means and the standard deviations of the two populations from which the two samples came. It is customary to refer to the standard deviation of this sampling distribution as the **standard error of the difference between two means**.

By "independent" samples we mean that the selection of one sample is in no way affected by the selection of the other. Thus, the theory does not apply to "before and after" kinds of comparisons, nor does it apply, say, to the comparison of the IQs of husbands and wives. A special method for comparing the means of dependent samples is explained in Section 11.11.

In most practical situations σ_1 and σ_2 are unknown, but if we limit ourselves to large samples (neither n_1 nor n_2 should be less than 30), we can use the sample standard deviations s_1 and s_2 as estimates of σ_1 and σ_2, and base the test of the null hypothesis $\mu_1 - \mu_2 = 0$ on the statistic

Statistic for large-sample test concerning difference between two means

$$z = \frac{\bar{x}_1 - \bar{x}_2}{\sqrt{\dfrac{s_1^2}{n_1} + \dfrac{s_2^2}{n_2}}}$$

which has approximately the standard normal distribution. No matter how it looks, this is actually a z-value; we calculate it by subtracting from $\bar{x}_1 - \bar{x}_2$ the mean of its sampling distribution, which under the null hypothesis is $\mu_1 - \mu_2 = 0$, and then dividing this difference by the (estimated) standard error of the difference between two means.

Depending on whether the alternative hypothesis is $\mu_1 - \mu_2 < 0$, $\mu_1 - \mu_2 > 0$, or $\mu_1 - \mu_2 \neq 0$, the criteria on which we base the actual tests are like those shown in Figure 11.10 and in the table on page 422, with $\mu_1 - \mu_2$ substituted for μ and 0 for μ_0.

EXAMPLE 11.16   In a department store's study designed to test whether or not the mean balance outstanding on 30-day charge accounts is the same in its two suburban branch stores, random samples yielded the following results:

$$n_1 = 80 \quad \bar{x}_1 = \$64.20 \quad s_1 = \$16.00$$
$$n_2 = 100 \quad \bar{x}_2 = \$71.41 \quad s_2 = \$22.13$$

where the subscripts denote branch store 1 and branch store 2. Use the 0.05 level of significance to test the null hypothesis $\mu_1 - \mu_2 = 0$ against the alternative hypothesis $\mu_1 - \mu_2 \neq 0$, where μ_1 and μ_2 are the actual mean balances outstanding on all 30-day charge accounts in branch stores 1 and 2.

SOLUTION Using the five-step procedure we get

1. $H_0: \mu_1 - \mu_2 = 0$.
   $H_A: \mu_1 - \mu_2 \neq 0$.
2. $\alpha = 0.05$.
3. Reject the null hypothesis if $z \leq -1.96$ or $z \geq 1.96$, where

$$z = \frac{\bar{x}_1 - \bar{x}_2}{\sqrt{\dfrac{s_1^2}{n_1} + \dfrac{s_2^2}{n_2}}}$$

4. Substituting the given values of n_1, n_2, $\bar{x}_1$, $\bar{x}_2$, s_1, and s_2 into the formula for z, we get

$$z = \frac{64.20 - 71.41}{\sqrt{\dfrac{(16.00)^2}{80} + \dfrac{(22.13)^2}{100}}} = -2.53$$

5. Since $z = -2.53$ is less than -1.96, it follows that the null hypothesis must be rejected. That is, the difference between the two sample means is too large to be attributed to chance, and we conclude that there is a real difference between the two population means. Had we wanted to use the P-value approach in this example, we would have found from Table I that the P-value corresponding to $z = -2.53$ in a two-tailed test is $2(0.5000 - 0.4943) = 0.0114$. Since this value is less than $\alpha = 0.05$, we conclude, as before, that the null hypothesis must be rejected. ∎

11.10

Differences Between Means (Small Samples)

The significance test described in Section 11.9 applies only to large independent random samples. However, as in Section 11.8, a corresponding small-sample test can be based on an appropriate t statistic. For this test, which is used when $n_1 < 30$ or $n_2 < 30$, we must assume that we are dealing with independent random samples from populations having roughly the shape of normal distributions with the same standard deviation. Then, we can base tests of the null hypothesis $\mu_1 - \mu_2 = 0$ on the statistic

*Statistic for
small-sample test
concerning
difference
between two
means*

$$t = \frac{\bar{x}_1 - \bar{x}_2}{\sqrt{\dfrac{(n_1 - 1)s_1^2 + (n_2 - 1)s_2^2}{n_1 + n_2 - 2} \cdot \left(\dfrac{1}{n_1} + \dfrac{1}{n_2}\right)}}$$

whose sampling distribution is the t distribution with $n_1 + n_2 - 2$ degrees of freedom. Depending on whether the alternative hypothesis is $\mu_1 - \mu_2 < 0$, $\mu_1 - \mu_2 > 0$, or $\mu_1 - \mu_2 \neq 0$, the criteria on which we base the small-sample tests for the significance of the difference between two means are like those shown in Figure 11.10 and in the table on page 422, with t substituted for z, $\mu_1 - \mu_2$ substituted for μ, and 0 for μ_0.

EXAMPLE 11.17 The following are measurements of the heat-producing capacity (in millions of calories per ton) of random samples of five specimens each of coal from two mines:

Mine 1:	8,380	8,210	8,360	7,840	7,910
Mine 2:	7,540	7,720	7,750	8,100	7,690

Use the 0.05 level of significance to test whether the difference between the means of these two samples is significant.

SOLUTION Using the five-step procedure we get

1. H_0: $\mu_1 - \mu_2 = 0$.
   H_A: $\mu_1 - \mu_2 \neq 0$.
2. $\alpha = 0.05$.
3. Reject the null hypothesis if $t < -2.306$ or $t > 2.306$, where

$$t = \frac{\bar{x}_1 - \bar{x}_2}{\sqrt{\dfrac{(n_1 - 1)s_1^2 + (n_2 - 1)s_2^2}{n_1 + n_2 - 2} \cdot \left(\dfrac{1}{n_1} + \dfrac{1}{n_2}\right)}}$$

and 2.306 is the value of $t_{0.025}$ for $5 + 5 - 2 = 8$ degrees of freedom; otherwise, simply state that the difference between the two sample means is not significant.

4. The means and the variances of the two samples are $\bar{x}_1 = 8,140$, $\bar{x}_2 = 7,760$, $s_1^2 = 63,450$, and $s_2^2 = 42,650$. Substituting these values together with $n_1 = 5$ and $n_2 = 5$ into the formula for t, we get

FIGURE 11.12

Computer printout
for small-sample t
test concerning
difference between
two means

```
MTB > SET C1
DATA> 8380 8210 8360 7840 7910
DATA> END
MTB > SET C2
DATA> 7540 7720 7750 8100 7690
DATA> END
MTB > TWOSAMPLE C1 C2;
SUBC> POOLED.

TWOSAMPLE T FOR C1 VS C2
           N      MEAN     STDEV    SE MEAN
C1         5      8140      252       113
C2         5      7760      207        92

95 PCT CI FOR MU C1 - MU C2: (44, 716)

TTEST MU C1 = MU C2 (VS NE):  T= 2.61   P=0.031   DF=  8

POOLED STDEV =          230
```

$$t = \frac{8,140 - 7,760}{\sqrt{\frac{4(63,450) + 4(42,650)}{5 + 5 - 2} \cdot \left(\frac{1}{5} + \frac{1}{5}\right)}}$$

$$= 2.61$$

5. Since $t = 2.61$ exceeds 2.306, we find that the null hypothesis must be rejected; in other words, we conclude that the average heat-producing capacity of coal from the two mines is not the same. ∎

A computer printout of the preceding example is given in Figure 11.12. Upon entering the raw data we were provided with the means, standard deviations, and standard errors of the means of the two samples, the 95 percent confidence interval for $\mu_1 - \mu_2$, the P-value, and the number of degrees of freedom. The value $t = 2.61$ is exactly the same as that previously obtained in the example.

11.11

Differences Between Means (Paired Data)

The methods of Sections 11.9 and 11.10 cannot be used when the samples are not independent. As we pointed out on page 430, they cannot be used, for example, when we deal with "before and after" kinds of comparisons, the IQs of husbands and wives, and numerous other situations where the data are naturally paired. To test the null hypothesis $\mu_1 - \mu_2 = 0$ with this kind of data, we work with the (signed) differences of the **paired data** and test whether these differences may be looked upon as a random sample from a population which has the mean $\mu = 0$. If the sample is small and it is reasonable to look upon the differences as a random sample from a population having roughly the shape of a normal distribution, we use the t test of Section 11.8, and for large samples, we use the z test described in Section 11.9. To apply these tests, we must calculate the mean of the differences, the standard deviation (s or σ) of these differences and substitute these values together with n into the formulas for t or z.

EXAMPLE 11.18   The following are the average weekly losses of worker-hours due to accidents in 10 industrial plants before and after a certain safety program was put into operation:

45 and 36	73 and 60	46 and 44	124 and 119	33 and 35,
57 and 51	83 and 77	34 and 29	26 and 24	17 and 11

Use the 0.05 level of significance to test whether the safety program is effective. The differences are 9, 13, 2, 5, -2, 6, 6, 5, 2, and 6, and for these data we perform the following test:

SOLUTION   Using the five-step procedure we get

1. H_0: $\mu = 0$.
   H_A: $\mu > 0$. (The hypothesis that on the average there are more accidents "before" than "after.")
2. $\alpha = 0.05$.
3. Reject the null hypothesis if $t > 1.833$, where

$$t = \frac{\bar{x} - \mu_0}{s/\sqrt{n}}$$

and 1.833 is the value of $t_{0.05}$ for $10 - 1 = 9$ degrees of freedom; otherwise, accept the null hypothesis or reserve judgment (as the situation may demand).

4. First calculating the mean and the standard deviation of the ten differences, we get $\bar{x} = 5.2$ and $s = 4.08$. Then, substituting these values together with $n = 10$ and $\mu_0 = 0$ into the formula for t, we get

$$t = \frac{5.2 - 0}{4.08/\sqrt{10}} = 4.03$$

5. Since $t = 4.03$ exceeds 1.833, the null hypothesis must be rejected; in other words, we have shown that the industrial safety program is effective. ■

Going one step farther, we might determine the *P*-value, which is 0.0015, and conclude that there is *substantial* evidence for the effectiveness of the program.

EXERCISES

(Exercises 11.38, 11.41, 11.44, 11.46, 11.47, 11.52, 11.53, 11.58, 11.59, 11.61, and 11.62 are practice exercises. Their complete solutions are given on page 447.)

11.38 The manager of a power tool rental company wants to know whether the true average number of power tools rented per day is 25.0. If in a random sample of 36 days the average number of power tools rented is 22.8 with a standard deviation of 6.9 rentals, is there, at the 0.05 level of significance, sufficient evidence to reject the null hypothesis $\mu = 25.0$?

11.39 The shipping department manager of a mail-order catalog sales company claims that the average order shipped by the firms weighs 20 pounds. To verify this claim the general manager of the company randomly selects a sample of 100 orders and concludes that they have a mean weight of 18.1 pounds with a standard deviation of 8.1 pounds. Use the 0.05 level of significance to test the null hypothesis $\mu = 20$ pounds against the alternative hypothesis $\mu < 20$.

11.40 Production data concerning assembly workers who had received "on-the-job training" (training provided informally by fellow workers or a supervisor) show that the time it takes these workers to assemble a certain component is a random variable, having a mean of 5.25 minutes and a standard deviation of 0.75 minutes. A randomly selected group of 50 new workers received vestibule training (formal training provided in a classroom or some place other than the actual work area) and, at the conclusion of their training, assembled these components in 4.9 minutes, with the standard deviation unchanged.

(a) Does this constitute evidence at the 0.01 level of significance that following participation in vestibule training, the mean time required by a worker to assemble a component is less?

(b) If the difference in part (a) is significant, is it also important to the manufacturer of the component?

11.41 Investigating the possibility that a coin-operated soda pop vending machine is dispensing too much soda pop, the owner of the machine takes a random sample of 40 "6-fluid-ounce" servings from a large number of servings and finds that the mean is 6.15 fluid ounces with a standard deviation of 0.3 fluid ounce. Is this evidence of overfilling at the 0.01 level of significance?

11.42 An automotive engineer asserts that the mean mileage of a certain type of recreational vehicle is 10 miles per gallon of gasoline. What can one conclude at the level of significance $\alpha = 0.05$ about the engineer's assertion concerning the mileage of these vehicles if a random sample of 60 of the recreational vehicles has a mean mileage of 10.4 miles per gallon with a standard deviation of 2.0 miles per gallon?

11.43 The production manager of a large manufacturing company estimates that the mean age of his employees is 22.8 years. The treasurer of the firm needs a more accurate employee mean age figure in order to estimate the cost of an annuity benefit program being considered for employees. The treasurer takes a random sample of 70 workers and finds that the mean age of the employees sampled is 26.2 years with a standard deviation of 4.6 years. At the 0.01 level of significance, what can the treasurer conclude about the accuracy of the production manager's estimate?

11.44 A production process is designed to add 55 gallons of water to each of numerous batches of a mixture. The mean number of gallons of water occasionally varies, but the standard deviation is considered to be stable and well established at 2.8 gallons. In order to verify that mixtures receive 55 gallons of water, a production engineer closely observes the mixing of a random sample of 100 batches and determines the mean net gallons of water added. For what values of $\bar{x}$ should the production engineer reject the null hypothesis $\mu = 55$ if he uses a two-sided alternative and a level of significance of 0.01?

11.45 (a) Repeat the preceding exercise using the one-sided alternative hypothesis $\mu < 55$ gallons, which might be more appropriate in this example if the mixture were harmed by adding less than 55 gallons of water.

(b) Both producers and consumers can be adversely affected if they get either more or less than a certain standard. Suggest some practical illustrations of this.

11.46 If we wish to test the null hypothesis $\mu = \mu_0$ in such a way that the probability of a Type I error is α, and the probability of a Type II error is β for the specific alternative $\mu = \mu_A$, we must take a random sample of size n, where

$$ n = \frac{\sigma^2(z_\alpha + z_\beta)^2}{(\mu_A - \mu_0)^2} $$

if the alternative is one sided, and

$$ n = \frac{\sigma^2(z_{\alpha/2} + z_\beta)^2}{(\mu_A - \mu_0)^2} $$

if the alternative is two sided.

Suppose, for instance, that for a population with $\sigma = 5$ we want to test the null hypothesis that its mean is 200 pounds against the alternative that its mean is less than 200 pounds. The probability of a Type I error is to be 0.05, and the probability of a Type II error when the mean of the population is 198 pounds is to be 0.20. Substituting into the first of the formulas for n, we get

$$n = \frac{(5^2)(1.645 + 0.84)^2}{(198 - 200)^2} = 38.6$$

so that we must take a sample of size 39, rounding up.

(a) Suppose that we want to test the hypothesis $\mu = \$400$ against the alternative $\mu \neq \$400$ for a population whose standard deviation is $12. If this hypothesis is true, we want to be 95 percent sure of accepting it, and if the true mean differs from $400 by $5 in either direction, we want to be 90 percent sure of rejecting the hypothesis. What is the required sample size? For what values of $\bar{x}$ should the hypothesis be rejected?

(b) Suppose that we want to test the null hypothesis $\mu = 128$ feet against the alternative hypothesis $\mu > 128$ feet for a population whose standard deviation is 6 feet. How large a sample will be required if the probability of a Type I error is to be 0.05 and the probability of a Type II error is to be 0.01 when $\mu = 130$ feet? For what values of $\bar{x}$ should the hypothesis be rejected?

11.47 Ten randomly selected oil wells in a large field of oil wells produced 21, 19, 20, 22, 24, 21, 19, 22, 22, and 20 barrels of crude oil per day. Is this evidence at the 0.01 level of significance that the oil wells are not producing an average of 22.5 barrels of crude oil per day?

11.48 An analysis of the extensive records of an automobile manufacturer shows that 10 orders for an automobile part from a certain supplier were received in 7, 9, 16, 13, 12, 15, 10, 8, 9, and 6 days. Use the 0.01 level of significance to test the claim that on the average such orders are filled by the supplier in 7.5 days. Choose the alternative hypothesis in such a way that rejection of the null hypothesis, $\mu = 7.5$ days, implies that it takes longer than that.

11.49 The proprietor of a greenhouse claims that its pots of lilies average 6.0 buds, with a standard deviation of 0.4 buds. If a random sample of 12 pots of lilies from a large number of pots of lilies has a mean of 5.8 buds, does this deny the proprietor's claim of the mean number of buds at the 0.05 level of significance?

11.50 Advertisements claim that the average nicotine content of a certain kind of cigarette is 0.30 milligram. Suspecting that this figure is too low, a consumer protection service takes a random sample of 15 of these cigarettes from different production lots and finds that their nicotine content has a mean of 0.33 milligram with a standard deviation of 0.018 milligram. Use the 0.05 level of significance to test the null hypothesis $\mu = 0.30$ against the alternative hypothesis $\mu > 0.30$.

Section 11.11   Differences Between Means (Paired Data)   **437**

11.51 An automobile manufacturer claims for a certain kind of car the average mileage per gallon of gasoline is 40. Suspecting this figure is too high, a consumer protection service takes a random sample of 20 of these cars from different automobile assembly plants and determines that their gasoline consumption has a mean of 34 miles per gallon with a standard deviation of 6.3 miles per gallon. Use the 0.05 level of significance to test the null hypothesis $\mu = 40$ against the alternative $\mu < 40$.

11.52 A study was made of the number of gallons of gasoline purchased by customers for their automobiles at two gasoline stations. If 35 randomly selected purchases made in station A average 9.6 gallons with standard deviation of 1.75, and 51 randomly selected sales at station B average 8.3 gallons with a standard deviation of 2.18, test at the level of significance $\alpha = 0.01$ whether the difference between these two sample means is significant.

11.53 A company wants to compare the lifetimes of two stones used in an abrasive process (called "superfinishing"), which produces rapidly a fine microfinish on machined surfaces. In laboratory tests, hot-rolled-steel driveshafts of the same degree of surface roughness are processed for 2 minutes each under specified conditions using both stones. If the average lifetime of 10 stones of the first kind was 60 pieces with a standard deviation of 5 pieces, while the average lifetime of 10 stones of the second kind was 64 pieces with a standard deviation of 3 pieces, is the difference between these two means significant at a level of significance of 0.05?

11.54 To collect information for a water conservation drive on a college campus, sample data are collected which show that 50 showers taken by students in dormitory A used, on the average, 36 gallons of water with standard deviation of 2.5 gallons, while 50 showers taken by students in dormitory B used, on the average, 35.5 gallons of water with standard deviation of 2.3 gallons. Test the null hypothesis $\mu_1 - \mu_2 = 0$ against the alternative hypothesis $\mu_1 - \mu_2 > 0$ at the level of significance $\alpha = 0.01$.

11.55 Following is a random sample of grades achieved on a statistics examination by nine men students in a very large class and a random sample of grades achieved in the same examination by six women students:

| Men students: | 79, | 88, | 64, | 91, | 83, | 66, | 89, | 74, | 68 |
| Women students: | 70, | 51, | 82, | 72, | 90, | 61, | | | |

Use the level of significance $\alpha = 0.01$ to test whether the difference between the means of these two samples is significant.

11.56 Following are the numbers of newspapers sold by eight randomly selected news vendors on the east side of the city and by eight randomly selected news vendors on the west side of the city:

| East side: | 47, | 56, | 32, | 59, | 51, | 34, | 57, | 42, |
| West side: | 38, | 19, | 50, | 40, | 58, | 29, | 36, | 40 |

Use the 0.01 level of significance to test whether news vendors on the east side of the city sell more newspapers than news vendors on the west side.

11.57 In comparing the breaking strength of two brands of similar cotton cord, a testing service found that four pieces of brand *A* had an average breaking strength of 415 pounds with a standard deviation of 29 pounds; while four pieces of brand *B* cord had an average breaking strength of 385 pounds with a standard deviation of 24 pounds. Use the level of significance $\alpha = 0.05$ to test whether the difference between the two sample means is significant.

11.58 In some problems we are interested in testing whether the difference between the means of two populations is equal to, less than, or greater than a given constant. So, we test the null hypothesis $\mu_1 - \mu_2 = \delta\,(delta)$, where δ is the given constant, against an appropriate alternative hypothesis. To perform this kind of test, we substitute $\bar{x}_1 - \bar{x}_2 - \delta$ for $\bar{x}_1 - \bar{x}_2$ in the numerator of the z statistic on page 430, or the t statistic on page 432, and otherwise proceed in the same way as before.

(a) Sample surveys conducted in a large county in 1972 and again in 1992 showed that in 1972 the average height of 400 10-year-old boys was 53.2 inches with a standard deviation of 2.4 inches, while in 1992 the average height of 500 10-year-old boys was 54.5 inches with a standard deviation of 2.5 inches. Use the level of significance $\alpha = 0.05$ to test whether the true average increase in height is at most 0.5 inch.

(b) To test the claim that the resistance of electric wire can be reduced by more than 0.050 ohm by alloying, 25 values obtained for alloyed wire yielded $\bar{x}_1 = 0.083$ ohm and $s_1 = 0.003$ ohm, and 25 values obtained for standard wire yielded $\bar{x}_2 = 0.136$ ohm and $s_2 = 0.002$ ohm. Use the level of significance $\alpha = 0.05$ to determine whether the claim has been substantiated.

11.59 If we want to study the effectiveness of a new diet on the basis of weights "before and after," or if we want to study whatever differences there may be between the IQs of husbands and wives, the methods introduced in this chapter cannot be used. The samples are not independent; in fact, in each case the data are *paired*. To handle data of this kind, we work with the signed differences of the paired data and test whether these differences may be looked upon as a sample from a population for which $\mu = 0$. In this example, the signed difference between 37 and 28 is $+9$, the difference between 45 and 46 is -1, and so forth. If the sample is small, we use the t test; otherwise, we use a large-sample test. Apply this technique to determine the effectiveness of an industrial safety program on the basis of the following data (collected over a period of one year) on the average weekly loss of worker-hours due to accidents in 12 plants "before and after" the program was put into operation:

37 and 28	72 and 59	26 and 24	125 and 120
45 and 46	54 and 43	13 and 15	79 and 75
12 and 18	34 and 29	39 and 35	26 and 24

Use the level of significance $\alpha = 0.05$ to decide whether the safety program is effective.

11.60 In a study of the effectiveness of physical exercise in weight reduction, a group of 16 persons engaged in a prescribed program of physical exercise for one month showed the following results:

Weight before (pounds)	Weight after (pounds)	Weight before (pounds)	Weight after (pounds)
209	196	170	164
178	171	153	152
169	170	183	179
212	207	165	162
180	177	201	199
192	190	179	173
158	159	243	231
180	180	144	140

Use the 0.01 level of significance to test the null hypothesis that the prescribed program of exercise is not effective in reducing weight.

11.61 Determine the P-value (prob-value, tail probability, or the observed level of significance) corresponding to z for the observed level of the statistic in one-tailed tests.

(a) $z = 1.64$ (b) $z = -1.64$

(c) $z = 2.76$ (d) $z = -2.76$

(e) $z = 0.00$ (f) $z = -1.645$

(g) $z = 3.09$ (h) $z = -4.0$

(Hint: Find the area of each z-value from Table I, normal-curve areas, and subtract from 0.5000.)

11.62 Determine the P-value (prob-value, tail probability, or the observed level of significance) corresponding to z for the observed level of the statistic in two-tailed tests.

(a) $z = 2.02$ (b) $z = -2.02$

(c) $z = 1.98$ (d) $z = -1.98$

(e) $z = 0.55$ (f) $z = -2.80$

(g) $z = 0.00$ (h) $z = 5.0$

(Hint: Find the area of each z-value from Table I, normal-curve areas. Subtract this area from 0.5000, as in Exercise 11.61. Multiply the result by 2.)

11.63 Suppose we want to base our decisions on the P-value obtained for the test statistic, with the level of significance $\alpha = 0.01$. Do we reject or do we accept (or reserve judgment) the null hypothesis in the following situations:

(a) $P = 0.0083$ (b) $P = 0.0564$

(c) $P = 0.0198$ (d) $P = 0.0100$

(e) $P = 0.0436$ (f) $P = 0.0500$

(Hint: Reject the null hypothesis if $P \leq 0.01$.)

11.64 Suppose we want to base our decisions on the P-value obtained for the test statistic with the level of significance $\alpha = 0.05$. Do we reject or do we accept (or reserve judgment) the null hypothesis in the following situations:

(a) $P = 0.0083$ (b) $P = 0.0564$

(c) $P = 0.0198$ (d) $P = 0.0100$

(e) $P = 0.0436$ (f) $P = 0.0500$

(Hint: Reject the null hypothesis if $P \leq 0.05$.)

11.65 If the P-value for the power tool Exercise 11.38 is 0.0562, and if we set the level of significance at $\alpha = 0.05$,

(a) should we reject the null hypothesis, or should we accept the null hypothesis (or reserve judgment)?

(b) If the calculated z value for Exercise 11.38 is -1.91, verify that the P-value is 0.0562.

11.66 If the P-value for the mail-order Exercise 11.39 is 0.0094 and if we set the level of significance at $\alpha = 0.05$,

(a) should we reject the null hypothesis, or should we accept the null hypothesis (or reserve judgment)?

(b) If the calculated z-value for Exercise 11.39 is -2.35, verify that the P-value is 0.0094.

11.67 Suppose that the advertisements of a hair shampoo manufacturer claim that its shampoo "washes hair cleaner," when, in fact, its shampoo does not wash hair differently from a competing brand. If 20 testing companies each conduct a significance test of the effectiveness of the advertised shampoo at the 0.05 level of significance, what is the probability that at least one of them will come up with a spuriously significant result which supports the advertiser's claim?

11.12

A Word of Caution

We should note that in statistics the term "significant" is used in a technical sense. If we say that something is "statistically significant," we do not mean to imply that it is necessarily of any practical significance or importance. For instance, a battery manufacturer may find from sample data that a new, expensive additive produces a statistically significant increase in the average useful lifetime of his batteries. However, this average increase in the lifetimes of the batteries may be so small that there is no economic justification for using the costly new additive.

11.13

Checklist of Key Terms

11.14

Review Exercises

11.68 To estimate the machine time requirements for a large order of turned bronze shafts (which are shaped by rotating the shaft against a cutting tool fixed in place on a lathe), a machine shop manager feels the average time to turn a shaft is expressed by a distribution which has the mean $\mu_0 = 5.0$ minutes and the standard deviation $\sigma_0 = 1.0$ minute. If, subsequently, the actual times to turn a random sample of 50 shafts have a mean of 5.45 minutes and a standard deviation of 1.6 minutes, find

(a) the posterior mean and the posterior standard deviation

(b) the posterior probability that μ lies between 5.0 and 6.0 minutes

11.69 To estimate the time required for a garment worker to sew the beads on a beaded garment, a random sample of 36 garment workers is timed in the performance of this task. The mean is 20.4 minutes and the standard deviation is 3.1 minutes. What can we say with 95 percent confidence about the maximum size of the error if we use $\bar{x} = 20.4$ minutes as an estimate of the true average time it takes a garment worker to perform this task?

11.70 A fish processing company claims that a production run of a certain type of fish yields, on the average, 9.64 ounces of fish fillets per pound of fish. Is this figure supported by an industry study in which a random sample of 40 production runs of such fish yielded 9.52 ounces of fish fillets per pound of fish, with a standard deviation of 0.28 ounce? Use the level of significance $\alpha = 0.01$ to test the null hypothesis $\mu = 9.64$ ounces.

11.71 In testing the hypothesis that a new type of luggage is more durable than an older model of luggage, explain under what conditions a Type I error would be committed and the conditions under which a Type II error would be committed.

11.72 For a very large population of lengths of metal strips whose standard deviation is assumed to be 0.10 inch, a buyer wants to test (on the basis of a random sample of strips drawn from the lot) the hypothesis that the true mean length of the strips is 4 inches against the hypothesis that it is less than 4 inches. Consequences of rejecting the hypothesis if it is true and of accepting it if the mean length is actually 3.95 inches are considered to be equally serious, and their risks are both set at 0.02. What sample size should be used, and for what values of $\bar{x}$ should the buyer reject the hypothesis?

11.73 Five measurements of the tar content of a certain kind of cigarette yielded 14.5, 14.2, 14.4, 14.3, and 14.6 mg/cig (milligrams per cigarette). Show that the difference between the mean of this sample, $\bar{x} = 14.4$, and the average tar content claimed by the cigarette manufacturer, $\mu = 14.0$, is significant at $\alpha = 0.05$.

11.74 Suppose that in the preceding exercise the first measurement is recorded incorrectly as 16.0 instead of 14.5. Show that now the difference between the mean of the sample, $\bar{x} = 14.7$, and the average tar content claimed by the cigarette manufacturer, $\mu = 14.0$, is not significant at $\alpha = 0.05$. Explain the apparent paradox that even though the difference between $\bar{x}$ and μ has increased, it is no longer significant.

11.75 Five applicants for a drivers license each take a driving test, and they complete this test, on the average, in $\bar{x} = 10.52$ minutes, with $s = 0.37$ minutes. Construct a 99 percent confidence interval for the true number of minutes it takes an applicant to complete a driving test.

11.76 In 10 randomly selected business days the Alpha St. parking lot had a mean of 2,020 paid parking revenue hours with $s = 139$ paid parking revenue hours, while for 10 randomly selected business days the Beta St. parking lot had a mean of 1,975 paid parking revenue hours with $s = 148$ paid parking revenue hours. Test at the 0.01 level of significance whether the difference between the two sample means is significant.

11.77 A random sample of 48 star sapphires has a mean weight of 3.01 carats and a standard deviation of 0.09 carat. If this mean is used to estimate the true mean weight of the gems from which this sample came, with what probability can we assert that this estimate is "off" by 0.03 carat at most?

11.78 A solid-waste-disposal study based on a sample of 10 of many town dumps in the area yielded a mean weight of 5.1 pounds of solid waste per person per day with a standard deviation of 0.86 pound. If the mean of this sample is used to estimate the corresponding true mean for the whole area, what can we say with 99 percent confidence about the possible size of the error?

11.79 A study conducted by an urban bus company showed that 100 of its randomly selected passengers at a bus stop had to wait, on the average, 10.45 minutes with a standard deviation of $s = 1.90$ minutes for the arrival of their buses. Construct a 95 percent confidence interval for the true average waiting time of one of its passengers for his or her bus at this bus stop.

11.80 The average breaking strength of a certain type of wire rope is 48,000 pounds. Investigating the effectiveness of a new and untested alloy steel, the manufacturing firm wants to test the null hypothesis $\mu = 48,000$ pounds against a suitable alternative, where μ is the average breaking strength of the rope when made of the untested alloy steel.

(a) What alternative hypothesis should the firm use if it does not want to use the new alloy steel wire rope unless it is definitely stronger with respect to breaking strength?

(b) What alternative hypothesis should the firm use if the new process is actually cheaper and the manufacturer wants to use the new alloy steel unless it actually decreases the breaking strength of the wire rope?

11.81 A random sample of 50 households of three persons in city A shows that the average number of motor vehicles owned is 2.9 with a standard deviation of 0.27. A random sample of 50 comparable households in city B shows that the average number of motor vehicles owned is 3.0 with a standard deviation of 0.31. Test at the 0.05 level of significance whether the difference between the two sample means is significant.

11.82 If we want to estimate the average number of days a vacationist rents a room at a certain resort hotel, and it is assumed that $\sigma = 2.0$ days, how large a sample is needed so that it can be asserted with probability of 0.95 that the sample mean will be off by less than 0.5 days?

11.83 With reference to the illustration of Section 11.10, suppose that we had wanted to test whether the heat-producing capacity of the coal from the first mine exceeds that of the coal from the second mine by more than 50 million calories per ton. Use the data of Example 11.17 on page 432 to test the null hypothesis $\mu_1 - \mu_2 = 50$ against the alternative hypothesis $\mu_1 - \mu_2 > 50$ at the level of significance $\alpha = 0.05$. (Hint: Use method of Exercise 11.58.)

11.84 It is desired to test the null hypothesis $\mu = 100$ pounds against the alternative hypothesis $\mu > 100$ pounds on the basis of a random sample of size $n = 64$ from a population with $\sigma = 12$.
(a) If $\alpha = 0.05$, for what values of $\bar{x}$ will the null hypothesis be rejected?
(b) Calculate β for $\mu = 102$, 104, and 106 pounds, and draw a rough sketch of the OC curve.

11.85 The sales data for blouses sold at a women's specialty shop show that for six randomly selected days, the sales of silk blouses are 4.0, 4.6, 4.4, 6.6, 6.0, and 5.0 percent of all the blouses sold. If the mean of this sample is used to estimate the mean percentage of the corresponding population, what can we assert with 90 percent confidence about the size of our error?

11.86 In a tomato packaging plant, the productivity of 20 workers on the day shift was measured and compared with that of 20 workers on the night shift, and it was found that the productivity of the night workers was lower, on the average, by 6.0 percent with a standard deviation of 2.0 percent. Using the level of significance $\alpha = 0.05$, what can we conclude about a claim made by a foreman that the productivity of night workers in this tomato packaging plant is lower, on the average, by at least 8.0 percent?

11.87 The personnel manager of a large manufacturing company who wants to check the claim that production employees have, on the average, completed the 10th grade of schooling, takes a random sample of 40 workers from a large number of workers. Using her results, $\bar{x} = 9.3$ grades of schooling and $s = 2.3$ grades of schooling, test the null hypothesis $\mu = $ 10th grade against the alternative hypothesis $\mu \neq$ 10th grade at the 0.01 level of significance.

11.88 Calculate the P-value for Exercise 11.87 if the z-value is -1.92. Do we reject or do we accept (or reserve judgment on) the null hypothesis where

(a) $\alpha = 0.01$

(b) $\alpha = 0.05$

(c) $\alpha = 0.10$

11.89 Calculate the P-value for Exercise 11.81 if the z-value is -1.72. Do we reject or do we accept (or reserve judgment on) the null hypothesis where

(a) $\alpha = 0.01$

(b) $\alpha = 0.05$

(c) $\alpha = 0.10$

11.90 Calculate the P-value for Exercise 11.39 if the z-value is -2.35. Do we reject or do we accept (or reserve judgment on) the null hypothesis where

(a) $\alpha = 0.01$

(b) $\alpha = 0.05$

(c) $\alpha = 0.10$

11.91 A production manager, using sample data, compares the cost of producing metal stampings on a new type of machine with the cost of producing these stampings on the factory's existing equipment. If the new machine results in a statistically significant reduction in cost, does this finding justify the replacement of the factory's equipment with the new machine?

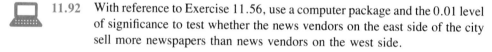

11.92 With reference to Exercise 11.56, use a computer package and the 0.01 level of significance to test whether the news vendors on the east side of the city sell more newspapers than news vendors on the west side.

11.93 With reference to Exercise 11.17 concerning the number of seconds required by 10 typists to type a test paragraph, use a computer package to determine what we can assert with 95 percent confidence about the maximum error.

11.94 Use a computer package to rework

(a) Exercise 11.18(a)

(b) Exercise 11.18(b)

11.95 With reference to Exercise 11.47, use a computer package to determine whether there is evidence at the 0.01 level of significance that the oil wells are not producing an average of 22.5 barrels of crude oil per day.

11.96 With reference to Exercise 11.48, use a computer package and the 0.01 level of significance to test the claim that, on the average, such orders are filled by the supplier in 7.5 days.

Chapter 11   Decision Making: Inferences About Means

With reference to Exercise 11.55, use a computer package and the 0.01 level of significance to test whether the difference between the means of men students and women students on this examination is significant.

11.15

Solutions of Practice Exercises

11.1 With 99 percent confidence, error is at most $2.575 \cdot \dfrac{2.9}{\sqrt{56}} \cong 1.0$ container.

11.2 $32.5 - 2.575 \cdot \dfrac{2.9}{\sqrt{56}} < \mu < 32.5 + 2.575 \cdot \dfrac{2.9}{\sqrt{56}}$,

$32.5 - 1.0 < \mu < 32.5 + 1.0$, and $31.5 < \mu < 33.5$ containers.

11.6 $0.25 = z_{\alpha/2} \cdot \dfrac{0.50}{\sqrt{100}}$, so that $z_{\alpha/2} = \dfrac{0.25\sqrt{100}}{0.50} = 5$; the corresponding entry in Table I is 0.4999997, so that $2(0.4999997) = 0.9999994$, and we can assert with almost 100 percent confidence that the error of estimate is at most 0.25.

11.7 $100\left(\dfrac{2.575 - 1.96}{1.96}\right) = 31.4$ percent.

11.10 (a) With 95 percent confidence, error is at most

$$1.96\,\dfrac{21}{\sqrt{100}} \cdot \sqrt{\dfrac{300 - 100}{300 - 1}} = 4.116 \cdot 0.818 = \$3.37.$$

11.11 (a) $680 - 1.96 \cdot \dfrac{176}{\sqrt{25}} \cdot \sqrt{\dfrac{98 - 25}{98 - 1}} < \mu < 680 + 1.96\,\dfrac{176}{\sqrt{25}} \cdot \sqrt{\dfrac{98 - 25}{98 - 1}}$,

$680 - 59.85 < \mu < 680 + 59.85$, and $620.15 < \mu < 739.85$.

11.13 (a) $n = \left[\dfrac{(2.575) \cdot (3.0)}{5}\right]^2 = 2.39$ rounded up to three trips;

(b) $n = \left[\dfrac{(2.575) \cdot (2.0)}{5}\right]^2 = 1.06$ rounded up to two trips;

(c) $n = \left[\dfrac{(2.575) \cdot (5.0)}{5}\right]^2 = 6.63$ rounded up to seven trips.

11.15 $4.6 - 2.861 \cdot \dfrac{1.1}{\sqrt{20}} < \mu < 4.6 + 2.861 \cdot \dfrac{1.1}{\sqrt{20}}$, $4.6 - 0.704 < \mu < 4.6 + 0.704$, and $3.90 < \mu < 5.30$ times.

11.19 Substituting $n = 150$ workers, $\sigma = 7.0$ points, and $z_{0.005} = 2.575$, we get

$$E = 2.575\frac{7.0}{\sqrt{150}} = 1.477$$

and the experts can assert with probability of "at least 0.99" that the error will be at most 1.4717 points.

11.20 $\mu_1 = \dfrac{\dfrac{50}{(67.2)^2} \cdot 750 + \dfrac{1}{(47.5)^2} \cdot 645}{\dfrac{50}{(67.2)^2} + \dfrac{1}{(47.5)^2}} = 746.0.$

11.21 $\dfrac{1}{\sigma_1^2} = \dfrac{50}{(67.2)^2} + \dfrac{1}{(47.5)^2} = 0.0115$, $\sigma_1^2 = \dfrac{1}{0.0115} = 86.96$, and $\sigma_1 = 9.32$;

also, $z = \dfrac{720 - 746}{9.32} = -2.79$ and $z = \dfrac{760 - 746}{9.32} = 1.50$, and the probability is $0.4974 + 0.4332 = 0.9306$.

11.24 A Type I error would be committed if the hypothesis $\mu = 0.25$ is true and we reject it; a Type II error would be committed if the hypothesis $\mu = 0.25$ is false and we accept it.

11.26 Test the hypothesis that the use of a car phone is not effective in increasing sales.

11.28 (a) $z = \dfrac{73.0 - 75.0}{8.4/\sqrt{100}} = -2.38$ and $\alpha = 0.5000 - 0.4913 = 0.0087$.

(b) Since the probability of a Type I error is greater for $\mu = 75.0$ than for any value of $\mu > 75.0$, the probability of a Type I error is at most 0.0087.

11.34 (a) $\mu_2 > \mu_1$ and buy the new printer only if the hypothesis $\mu_1 = \mu_2$ can be rejected.

(b) $\mu_2 < \mu_1$ and buy the new printer unless the hypothesis $\mu_1 = \mu_2$ can be rejected.

(c) $\mu_2 \neq \mu_1$.

11.38 Using the five-step procedure, we get

1. H_0: $\mu = 25.0$.
   H_A: $\mu \neq 25.0$.

2. $\alpha = 0.05$

3. Reject the null hypothesis if $z < -1.96$ or $z > 1.96$, where $z = \dfrac{\bar{x} - \mu_0}{\sigma/\sqrt{n}}$ with s substituted for σ.

4. Substituting $\bar{x} = 22.8$, $n = 36$, $\mu_0 = 25$, and $s = 2.1$ for σ into the formula for z, we get

$$z = \frac{22.8 - 25.0}{6.9/\sqrt{36}} = -1.91.$$

5. Since -1.91 lies between -1.96 and 1.96 the null hypothesis cannot be rejected. The difference between $\bar{x} = 22.8$ and $\mu = 25.0$ is not significant.

11.41 Using the five-step procedure we get

1. H_0: $\mu = 6.0$ fluid ounces.
H_A: $\mu > 6.0$ ounces.

2. $\alpha = 0.01$.

3. Reject the null hypothesis if $z \geq 2.33$, where $z = \dfrac{\bar{x} - \mu_0}{\sigma/\sqrt{n}}$ with s substituted for σ.

4. Substituting $\bar{x} = 6.15$, $n = 40$, $\mu_0 = 6.0$, and $s = 0.3$ for σ, we get
$$z = \frac{6.15 - 6.0}{0.3/\sqrt{40}} = 3.16.$$

5. Since $z = 3.16$ is greater than 2.33, the null hypothesis must be rejected. The difference between $\bar{x}$ and μ_0 is significant. The machine is overfilling at the 0.01 level of significance.

11.44 Using the five-step procedure we get

1. H_0: $\mu = 55$.
H_A: $\mu \neq 55$.

2. $\alpha = 0.01$.

3. Reject the values of $\bar{x}$ where $\bar{x} \leq \mu_0 - 2.575 \cdot \dfrac{\sigma}{\sqrt{n}}$ or if $\bar{x} \geq \mu_0 + 2.575 \cdot \dfrac{\sigma}{\sqrt{n}}$; otherwise, accept the null hypothesis or reserve judgment.

4. Substituting $z = 2.575$, $n = 100$, $\mu_0 = 55$, and $\sigma = 2.80$ into the formula for z and solving for $\bar{x}$ we get
$$\bar{x} \leq 55 - 2.575 \cdot \frac{2.80}{\sqrt{100}} = 54.28 \text{ and } \bar{x} \geq 55 + 2.575 \cdot \frac{2.80}{\sqrt{100}} = 55.72.$$

5. Reject all values of $\bar{x}$ which are ≤ 54.28 or which are ≥ 55.72. Accept the null hypothesis or reserve judgment for values of $\bar{x}$ which lie between, but are not equal to 54.28 and 55.72.

11.46 (a) $\dfrac{12^2(1.96 + 1.28)^2}{5^2} = 61$ (rounded up); reject if $\bar{x} \leq 400 - 1.96 \cdot \dfrac{12}{\sqrt{61}} =$

$\$396.99$ or $\bar{x} \geq 400 + 1.96 \cdot \dfrac{12}{\sqrt{61}} = \$403.01.$

(b) $\dfrac{6^2(1.645 + 2.33)^2}{(130 - 128)^2} = 142$ (rounded up); reject if $\bar{x} > 128 +$

$1.645 \cdot \dfrac{6}{\sqrt{142}} = 128.83$ feet.

11.47 First solve for $\bar{x}$ which is 21 and for s which is 1.56. Then

1. H_0: $\mu = 22.5$.
   H_A: $\mu \neq 22.5$.
2. $\alpha = 0.01$.
3. Reject the null hypothesis if $t \leq -3.250$ or $t \geq 3.250$ where
   $t = \dfrac{\bar{x} - \mu_0}{\sigma/\sqrt{n}}$ with s substituted for σ.
4. Substituting $\bar{x} = 21.0$, $n = 10$, $\mu_0 = 22.5$, and $s = 1.56$ for σ into the formula for t we get $t = \dfrac{21 - 22.5}{1.56/\sqrt{10}} = -3.04$.
5. Since -3.04 falls between -3.25 and 3.25, the null hypothesis cannot be rejected.

11.52 1. H_0: $\mu_1 - \mu_2 = 0$.
   H_A: $\mu_1 - \mu_2 \neq 0$.
2. $\alpha = 0.01$.
3. Reject the null hypothesis if $z \leq -2.575$ or $z \geq 2.575$, where

$$z = \dfrac{\bar{x}_1 - \bar{x}_2}{\sqrt{\dfrac{s_1^2}{n_1} + \dfrac{s_2^2}{n_2}}}$$

4. Substituting $\bar{x}_1 = 9.6$, $n_1 = 35$, $s_1 = 1.75$, $x_2 = 8.3$, $n_2 = 51$, and $s_2 = 2.18$ into the formula for z, we get

$$z = \dfrac{9.6 - 8.3}{\sqrt{\dfrac{1.75^2}{35} + \dfrac{2.18^2}{51}}} = 3.06.$$

5. Since 3.06 is greater than 2.575, we must reject the null hypothesis. The difference is significant. The two stations do not, on the average, sell the same number of gallons of gasoline per car.

11.53 1. H_0: $\mu_1 - \mu_2 = 0$.
   H_A: $\mu_1 - \mu_2 \neq 0$.
2. $\alpha = 0.05$.
3. Reject the null hypothesis if $t \leq -2.101$ or $t \geq 2.101$ (from Table II with $10 + 10 - 2$ degrees of freedom, under column head $t_{0.025}$), where

$$t = \frac{\bar{x}_1 - \bar{x}_2}{\sqrt{\dfrac{(n-1)s_1^2 + (n_2-1)s_2^2}{n_1 + n_2 - 2} \cdot \left(\dfrac{1}{n_1} + \dfrac{1}{n_2}\right)}}$$

4. Substituting $\bar{x}_1 = 60$, $n_1 = 10$, $s_1 = 5$, $\bar{x}_2 = 64$, $n_2 = 10$, and $s_2 = 3$ into the formula for t, we get

$$t = \frac{60 - 64}{\sqrt{\dfrac{9(5)^2 + 9(3)^2}{10 + 10 - 2} \cdot \left(\dfrac{1}{10} + \dfrac{1}{10}\right)}} = -2.17$$

5. Since $-2.17 \leq -2.101$ the null hypothesis must be rejected. The difference between the average of 60 and 64 is significant.

11.58 (a) 1. H_0: $\mu_1 - \mu_2 = 0.5$.
H_A: $\mu_1 - \mu_2 > 0.5$.

2. $\alpha = 0.05$.

3. Reject the null hypothesis if $z \geq 1.645$ where

$$z = \frac{(\bar{x}_1 - \bar{x}_2) - \delta}{\sqrt{\dfrac{s_1^2}{n_1} + \dfrac{s_2^2}{n_2}}}$$

where s_1 and s_2 are estimates of σ_1 and σ_2.

4. Substituting $\bar{x}_1 = 54.5$, $\bar{x}_2 = 53.2$, $\delta = 0.5$, $s_1 = 2.5$, $s_2 = 2.4$, $n_1 = 500$, and $n_2 = 400$, we get

$$z = \frac{(54.5 - 53.2) - 0.5}{\sqrt{\dfrac{2.5^2}{500} + \dfrac{2.4^2}{400}}} = 4.88$$

5. Since 4.88 is greater than 1.645, the null hypothesis must be rejected. The difference between the two sample means is significant. The average increase in height exceeds 0.5 inch.

(b) 1. H_0: $\mu_1 - \mu_2 = -0.05$.
H_A: $\mu_1 - \mu_2 < -0.05$.

2. $\alpha = 0.05$.

3. Reject the null hypothesis if $t \leq -1.645$, where

$$t = \frac{(\bar{x}_1 - \bar{x}_2) - \delta}{\sqrt{\dfrac{(n_1-1)s_1^2 + (n_2-1)s_2^2}{n_1 + n_2 - 2} \cdot \left(\dfrac{1}{n_1} + \dfrac{1}{n_2}\right)}}$$

4. Substituting $\bar{x}_1 = 0.083$, $n_1 = 25$, $s_1 = 0.003$, $\bar{x}_2 = 0.136$, $n_2 = 25$, and $s_2 = 0.002$ into the formula for t, we get

$$t = \frac{(0.083 - 0.136) - (-0.05)}{\sqrt{\dfrac{24(0.003)^2 + 24(0.002)^2}{25 + 25 - 2}\left(\dfrac{1}{25} + \dfrac{1}{25}\right)}} = -4.16$$

5. Since -4.16 is less than -1.645, the null hypothesis must be rejected. The difference is significant. The claim has been substantiated.

11.59 First, calculate $\bar{x}$ and s for the signed differences. The signed differences are
9, 13, 2, 5, -1, 11, -2, 4, -6, 5, 4, and 2 and $\bar{x} = \dfrac{46}{12} = 3.83$, and $s = \sqrt{\dfrac{325.67}{12 - 1}} = 5.44$.

1. H_0: $\mu = 0$.
   H_A: $\mu > 0$.
2. $\alpha = 0.05$.
3. Reject the null hypothesis where $t \geq 1.796$ when t is $\dfrac{\bar{x} - 0}{\sigma/\sqrt{n}}$ with s substituted for σ; otherwise, accept the null hypothesis or reserve judgment.
4. Substituting $\bar{x} = 3.83$, $s = 5.44$, and $n = 12$, we get $t = \dfrac{3.83 - 0}{5.44/\sqrt{12}} = 2.44$.
5. Since 2.44 is greater than 1.796 the null hypothesis must be rejected. The difference is significant. The safety program appears to be effective.

11.61
(a) $0.5000 - 0.4495 = 0.0505$
(b) $0.5000 - 0.4495 = 0.0505$
(c) $0.5000 - 0.4971 = 0.0029$
(d) $0.5000 - 0.4971 = 0.0029$
(e) $0.5000 - 0.0000 = 0.5000$
(f) $0.5000 - 0.4500 = 0.0500$
(g) $0.5000 - 0.4990 = 0.0010$
(h) $0.50000 - 0.49997 = 0.00003$

11.62
(a) $2(0.5000 - 0.4783) = 0.0434$
(b) $2(0.5000 - 0.4783) = 0.0434$
(c) $2(0.5000 - 0.4761) = 0.0478$
(d) $2(0.5000 - 0.4761) = 0.0478$
(e) $2(0.5000 - 0.2088) = 0.5824$
(f) $2(0.5000 - 0.4974) = 0.0052$
(g) $2(0.5000 - 0.0000) = 1.0000$
(h) $2(0.50000 - 0.4999997) = 0.0000006$

Decision Making: Inferences About Standard Deviations

In Chapter 11 we learned to construct confidence intervals for means and to perform tests of hypotheses concerning the means of one and two populations. As we shall see in this and some of the following chapters, very similar methods can be used for inferences about other population parameters. By studying the sampling distributions of appropriate statistics, statisticians have developed methods of inference about population proportions, standard deviations, medians, quartiles, and the like. In principle, the ideas are always the same, but some of the sampling distributions are mathematically quite involved. Fortunately, this difficulty is resolved by the important result that for large samples, many of these sampling distributions can be approximated with normal curves.

In this chapter we shall concentrate on population standard deviations, and population variances, which are not only important in their own right, but which must sometimes be estimated before we can make inferences about other parameters. This is the case, for example, when we make inferences about population means and must know or estimate the value of σ.

In Section 12.1 we shall be concerned with the estimation of σ, and in Sections 12.2 and 12.3 we shall study tests concerning the standard deviation of one population and the standard deviations of two populations.

12.1

The Estimation of σ

Although there are other methods of estimating the standard deviation of a population (see, for example, Exercise 12.7 on page 458), the sample standard deviation is the most widely used estimator of this parameter. Limiting our discussion to problems in which we use s to make inferences about σ (or s^2 to make inferences about σ^2), let us begin by constructing a confidence interval for σ based on the standard deviation of a random sample of size n. The theory on which such an interval is based requires that the population sampled has roughly the shape of a normal distribution, in which case the statistic called

Chi-square
statistic

$$\chi^2 = \frac{(n-1)s^2}{\sigma^2}$$

"chi-square" has as its sampling distribution an important continuous distribution called the **chi-square distribution**. The mean of this distribution is $n - 1$ and, as with the t distribution, we call this quantity the number of degrees of freedom, or simply the **degrees of freedom**. An example of a chi-square distribution is shown in Figure 12.1 and examples of chi-square distributions with various degrees of freedom are shown in Figure 12.2.

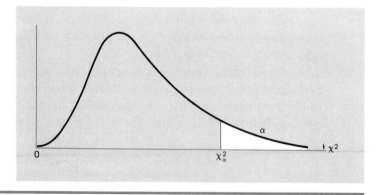

FIGURE 12.1
Chi-square
distribution

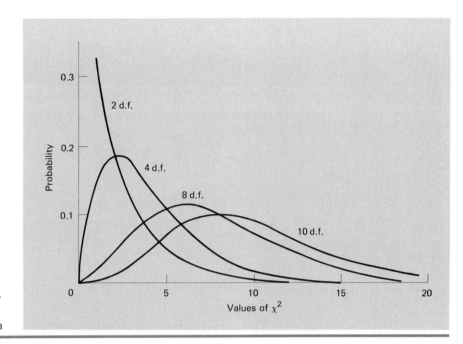

FIGURE 12.2
Chi-square
distributions for 2,
4, 8, and 10
degrees of freedom

Unlike the normal and t distributions, the domain of the chi-square distribution is restricted to the nonnegative real numbers.

As we did with z_α and t_α, we now define χ^2_α as the value for which the area to its right under the chi-square distribution is equal to α. Thus, $\chi^2_{\alpha/2}$ is such that the area to its right under the curve is $\alpha/2$, while $\chi^2_{1-\alpha/2}$ is such that the area to its left under the curve is $\alpha/2$ (see also Figure 12.3). We make this distinction because the chi-square distribution is not symmetrical. Among

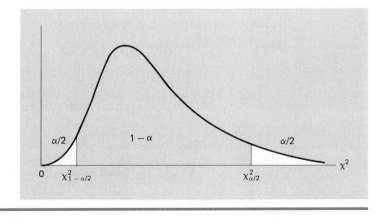

FIGURE 12.3
Chi-square
distribution

others, values of $\chi^2_{0.995}$, $\chi^2_{0.975}$, $\chi^2_{0.025}$, and $\chi^2_{0.005}$ are given in Table III at the end of the book for 1, 2, 3, . . . , and 30 degrees of freedom.

Referring to Figure 12.3, we find that we can assert with probability $1 - \alpha$ that a random variable having the chi-square distribution will take on a value between $\chi^2_{1-\alpha/2}$ and $\chi^2_{\alpha/2}$. Applying this result to the χ^2 statistic given above we can assert with probability $1 - \alpha$ that

$$\chi^2_{1-\alpha/2} < \frac{(n-1)s^2}{\sigma^2} < \chi^2_{\alpha/2}$$

This double inequality can be written as

Confidence interval for σ^2

$$\frac{(n-1)s^2}{\chi^2_{\alpha/2}} < \sigma^2 < \frac{(n-1)s^2}{\chi^2_{1-\alpha/2}}$$

which is a $(1 - \alpha)100$ percent confidence interval for σ^2, the population variance. Also, if we take the square root of each of the three terms of this double inequality, we get a $(1 - \alpha)100$ percent confidence interval for σ, the population standard deviation.

EXAMPLE 12.1   A random sample of $n = 5$ specimens of a certain kind of ice cream has a mean fat content of $\bar{x} = 11.3$ percent and a standard deviation of $s = 0.38$ percent. Construct a 95 percent confidence interval for σ, the standard deviation of the population sampled.

SOLUTION   Since we have $5 - 1 = 4$ degrees of freedom, we find from Table III that $\chi^2_{0.975} = 0.484$ and $\chi^2_{0.025} = 11.143$. Substituting these values together with $n = 5$ and $s = 0.38$ into the confidence-interval formula for σ^2 we get the 95 percent confidence interval for σ^2, the population variance. Thus,

$$\frac{(5-1)(0.38)^2}{11.143} < \sigma^2 < \frac{(5-1)(0.38)^2}{0.484}$$

so that $0.052 < \sigma^2 < 1.193$

Taking their square roots we get

$$0.23 \text{ percent} < \sigma < 1.09 \text{ percent}$$

which is the 95 percent confidence interval for σ, the population standard deviation. ∎

The kind of confidence interval we have just described is often referred to as a **small-sample confidence interval**, since it is used mainly when n is small (and, of course, only when we can assume that the population from which we are sampling has roughly the shape of a normal distribution). Otherwise, we make use of the fact that for large samples of 30 or more the sampling distribution of s can be approximated with a normal distribution having the mean σ and the standard deviation $\frac{\sigma}{\sqrt{2n}}$ (see Exercise 10.15(b) on page 372). So, we can assert with probability $1 - \alpha$ that

$$-z_{\alpha/2} < \frac{s - \sigma}{\dfrac{\sigma}{\sqrt{2n}}} < z_{\alpha/2}$$

and simple algebra leads to the following $(1 - \alpha)100$ percent large-sample confidence interval for the population standard deviation σ.

Large-sample confidence interval for σ

$$\frac{s}{1 + \dfrac{z_{\alpha/2}}{\sqrt{2n}}} < \sigma < \frac{s}{1 - \dfrac{z_{\alpha/2}}{\sqrt{2n}}}$$

EXAMPLE 12.2 With reference to Example 11.5 on page 000 where $s = 5.71$ seconds for $n = 40$ adults to open a new type of tamper-resistant aspirin bottle, construct a 95 percent confidence interval for the population sampled.

SOLUTION Substituting $n = 40$, $s = 5.71$, and $z_{\alpha/2} = 1.96$ into the confidence-interval formula given, we get

$$\frac{5.71}{1 + \dfrac{1.96}{\sqrt{80}}} < \sigma < \frac{5.71}{1 - \dfrac{1.96}{\sqrt{80}}}$$

and

$$4.90 < \sigma < 7.31$$

This means that we are 95 percent confident that the interval from 4.90 to 7.31 contains σ, the true standard deviation of the times required, in seconds, for adults to open the new type of tamper-resistant aspirin bottle. ∎

(Exercises 12.1, 12.3, 12.7(a) are practice exercises. Their complete solutions are given on page 468.)

12.1 With reference to Exercise 11.15 on page 402, construct a 99 percent confidence interval for σ, the true standard deviation of the number of times that employees leave their workstations per day.

12.2 With reference to Exercise 11.16 on page 402, construct a 95 percent confidence interval for σ, the true standard deviation of the number of gallons of gasoline sold to passenger cars at an automobile service station.

12.3 With reference to Exercise 11.17 on page 402, construct a 90 pecent confidence interval for the true variance of the times required by typists to complete the test paragraph.

12.4 With reference to Exercise 11.1 on page 400, construct a 99 percent confidence interval for the true standard deviation of the numbers of metal containers produced per day by the small manufacturer.

12.5 With reference to Exercise 11.3 on page 400, construct a 99 percent confidence interval for the true standard deviation of the annual apartment rental costs.

12.6 With reference to Exercise 11.4 on page 400, construct a 98 percent confidence interval for the true variance of the time it takes for a customer to go through a grocery checkout.

12.7 When we deal with very small samples, good estimates of the population standard deviation can often be obtained on the basis of the sample range (the largest sample minus the smallest). Such quick estimates of σ are given by the sample range divided by the divisor d, which depends on the size of the sample; for samples from populations having roughly the shape of a normal distribution, its values are shown in the following table:

n	2	3	4	5	6	7	8	9	10	11	12
d	1.13	1.69	2.06	2.33	2.53	2.70	2.85	2.97	3.08	3.17	3.26

For instance, in Example 11.6 on page 395, which deals with the durability of paint for highway center lines, we have $n = 8$ and a sample range of $167,800 - 108,300 = 59,500$ crossings. Since $d = 2.85$ for $n = 8$, we find that we can estimate σ, the true standard deviation of the population sampled, as

$$\frac{59,500}{2.85} = 20,877 \text{ crossings}$$

This is somewhat higher than the sample standard deviation $s = 19,200$ crossings, but not knowing the true value of σ, we cannot say which of the two estimates is actually closer.

(a) With reference to Exercise 11.17 on page 402, use this method to estimate the true standard deviation of the time (in seconds) for a typist to complete a test paragraph, and compare the results with the sample standard deviation s.

(b) With reference to Exercise 11.18 on page 402, use this method to estimate the true standard deviation of the weights of the chickens (in pounds) and compare the result with the sample standard deviation s.

12.2

Tests Concerning σ and σ^2

In this section we shall consider the problem of testing the null hypothesis that a population standard deviation equals a specified constant σ_0, or that a population variance equals σ_0^2. This kind of test is required whenever we want to test the uniformity of a product, process, or operation. For instance, we may want to test whether a certain kind of glass is sufficiently homogeneous for making delicate optical equipment, whether the variation in the outside diameter of mass-produced copper tubing is within permissible limits, whether a lack of uniformity in certain workers' performance may call for stricter supervision, and so on.

The test of the null hypothesis $\sigma = \sigma_0$, the hypothesis that a population standard deviation equals a specified constant, is based on the same assumptions, the same statistic, and the same sampling theory as the small-sample confidence interval for σ. Assuming that our random sample comes from a population having roughly the shape of a normal distribution, we base our decision on the statistic

Statistic for test concerning standard deviation

$$\chi^2 = \frac{(n-1)s^2}{\sigma_0^2}$$

where n and s^2 are the sample size and the sample variance and σ_0 is the value of the population standard deviation assumed under the null hypothesis. The sampling distribution of this statistic is the chi-square distribution with $n - 1$ degrees of freedom; hence, the criteria for testing the null hypothesis $\sigma = \sigma_0$ against the alternative hypothesis $\sigma < \sigma_0$, $\sigma > \sigma_0$, or $\sigma \neq \sigma_0$ are as shown in Figure 12.4. For the one-sided alternative $\sigma < \sigma_0$, we reject the null hypothesis for values of χ^2 falling into the left-hand tail of its sampling

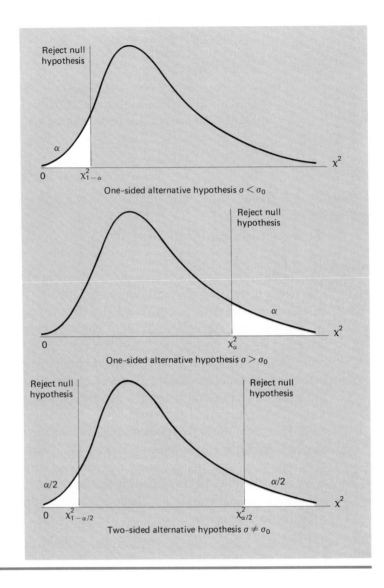

FIGURE 12.4
Test criteria

distribution; for the one-sided alternative $\sigma > \sigma_0$, we reject the null hypothesis for values of χ^2 falling into the right-hand tail of its sampling distribution; and for the two-sided alternative $\sigma \neq \sigma_0$, we reject the null hypothesis for values of χ^2 falling into either tail of its sampling distribution. The quantities χ_α^2, $\chi_{1-\alpha}^2$, $\chi_{\alpha/2}^2$, and $\chi_{1-\alpha/2}^2$ may be read from Table III.

EXAMPLE 12.3   Specifications for mass-produced bearings of a certain type require, among other things, that the standard deviation of their outside diameters should not exceed 0.0050 cm. Use the level of signifi-cance 0.01 to test the null hypothesis $\sigma = 0.0050$ against the alter-native hypothesis $\sigma > 0.0050$ on the basis of a random sample of size $n = 12$ for which $s = 0.0077$ cm.

SOLUTION   Following the five-step procedure explained in Chapter 11, we get

1. H_0: $\sigma = 0.0050$.
   H_A: $\sigma > 0.0050$.

2. $\alpha = 0.01$.

3. Reject the null hypothesis if $\chi^2 > 24.725$ where

$$\chi^2 = \frac{(n-1)s^2}{\sigma_0^2}$$

and otherwise accept the null hypothesis or reserve judgment.

4. Substituting $n = 12$, $s = 0.0077$, and $\sigma_0 = 0.0050$ into the for-mula for χ^2, we get

$$\chi^2 = \frac{11(0.0077)^2}{(0.0050)^2} = 26.09$$

5. Since $\chi^2 = 26.09$ exceeds 24.725, the critical value of $\chi^2_{0.01}$ for $12 - 1 = 11$ degrees of freedom (obtained from Table III for χ^2), the null hypothesis must be rejected. We can conclude that the outside diameter of the ball bearings is larger than 0.0050, or we can reserve judgment.   ■

When n is large $n \geq 30$, we can base tests of the null hypothesis $\sigma = \sigma_0$ on the same theory we used in constructing large-sample confidence inter-vals in the preceding section. That is, we use the statistic

Statistic for large-sample test concerning standard deviation

$$z = \frac{s - \sigma_0}{\sigma_0/\sqrt{2n}}$$

whose sampling distribution is approximately the standard normal distribu-tion, and also use the test criterion of Figure 11.8.

EXAMPLE 12.4   The variability of a store's sales in a random sample of 50 days is measured by the standard deviation $s = \$2,250$. Use the 0.01 level of significance to test the null hypothesis $\sigma = \$3,000$ against the alternative hypothesis $\sigma < \$3,000$ for the population sampled.

SOLUTION   Following the five-step procedure we get

1. H_0: $\sigma = \$3,000$.
   H_A: $\sigma < \$3,000$.

2. $\alpha = 0.01$.

3. Reject the null hypothesis if $z \leq -2.33$, where

$$z = \frac{s - \sigma_0}{\sigma_0 / \sqrt{2n}}$$

otherwise, accept the null hypothesis or reserve judgment.

4. Substituting $n = 50$, $s = 2,250$, and $\sigma_0 = 3,000$ into the formula for z, we get

$$z = \frac{2,250 - 3,000}{3,000/\sqrt{100}} = -2.50$$

5. Since -2.50 is less than $-z_{0.01} = -2.33$, the null hypothesis must be rejected. In other words, we conclude that the sales are less variable than assumed under the null hypothesis, or we can reserve judgment.   ∎

EXAMPLE 12.5   Rework the preceding example, using the 0.004 level of significance instead of 0.01.

SOLUTION   We could determine $z_{0.004}$ in the same way in which we determined $z_{0.01}$ in part (a) of Example 9.12, but let us use P-values instead.

1. H_0: $\sigma = \$3,000$.
   H_A: $\sigma < \$3,000$.

2. $\alpha = 0.004$.

3'. The test statistic is

$$z = \frac{s - \sigma_0}{\sigma_0 / \sqrt{2n}}$$

4'. Substituting $n = 50$, $s = 2,250$, and $\sigma_0 = 3,000$ into the formula for z, we get (as before)

$$z = \frac{2,250 - 3,000}{3,000/\sqrt{100}} = -2.50$$

From Table I, the P-value corresponding to $z = -2.50$ in a one-tailed test is $0.5000 - 0.4938 = 0.0062$.

5'. Since 0.0062 exceeds $\alpha = 0.004$, we find that the null hypothesis cannot be rejected at this level of significance. In other words, we cannot conclude in this case that sales are less variable than assumed under the null hypothesis. ∎

12.3

Tests Concerning Two Standard Deviations

In this section we shall discuss a test concerning the equality of the standard deviations, or variances, or two populations. This test is often used in connection with the small-sample test of the difference between two means, which requires that the variances of the two populations be equal. For instance, in Example 11.17 on page 432 dealing with the heat-producing capacity of the coal from two mines, the two samples had variances of $\dfrac{253{,}800}{4} = 63{,}450$ and $\dfrac{170{,}600}{4} = 42{,}650$, and despite what may seem to be a large difference, we assumed that the population variances were, indeed, equal. We could not discuss the rationale of this assumption at that time, but we actually tested—and were unable to reject—the null hypothesis that the populations had equal variances before we performed the t test for the significance of the difference between the two sample means.

Given independent random samples of size n_1 and n_2 from two populations, we usually base tests of the equality of the two population standard deviations (or variances) on the ratios $\dfrac{s_1^2}{s_2^2}$ or $\dfrac{s_2^2}{s_1^2}$ where s_1 and s_2 are the two sample standard deviations. Assuming that the populations from which the samples came have roughly the shape of normal distributions, it can be shown that the sampling distribution of such a ratio, appropriately called a **variance ratio**, is a continuous distribution called the **F distribution**. This distribution depends on the two parameters $n_1 - 1$ and $n_2 - 1$, the number of degrees of freedom in the sample estimates, s_1^2 and s_2^2, of the unknown population variances. One difficulty with this distribution is that most tables give only values of $F_{0.05}$ (defined in the same way as $z_{0.05}$, $t_{0.05}$, and $\chi^2_{0.05}$) and $F_{0.01}$, so we can work only with the right-hand tail of the distribution. For this reason we base our decision on the equality of two population standard deviations σ_1 and σ_2 (or variances σ_1^2 and σ_2^2) on the statistic

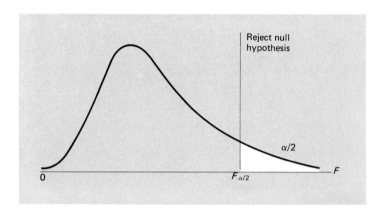

FIGURE 12.5
F distribution

Statistic for test concerning the equality of two standard deviations

$$F = \frac{s_1^2}{s_2^2} \quad or \quad \frac{s_2^2}{s_1^2} \quad \textit{whichever is larger}$$

With this statistic we reject the null hypothesis $\sigma_1 = \sigma_2$ and accept the alternative $\sigma_1 \neq \sigma_2$ when the observed value of F exceeds $F_{\alpha/2}$, where α is the level of significance (see also Figure 12.5). By using a right-hand tail area of $\alpha/2$ instead of α, we compensate for the fact that we always use the larger of the two variance ratios. The necessary values of $F_{\alpha/2}$ for $\alpha = 0.02$ or 0.10, $F_{0.01}$ and $F_{0.05}$, are given in Table IV at the end of the book, where the number of degrees of freedom for the numerator is $n_1 - 1$ or $n_2 - 1$, depending on whether we are using the ratio $\dfrac{s_1^2}{s_2^2}$; or the ratio $\dfrac{s_2^2}{s_1^2}$; correspondingly, the number of degrees of freedom for the denominator is $n_2 - 1$ or $n_1 - 1$.

EXAMPLE 12.6 In the example on the coal from two mines on page 432, we used a *t* test to test the significance of the difference between two sample means. Test at the 0.02 level of significance whether there is any real evidence that the standard deviations of the two populations are not equal.

SOLUTION   Following the five-step procedure, we get

1. H_0: $\sigma_1 = \sigma_2$.
   H_A: $\sigma_1 \neq \sigma_2$.

2. $\alpha = 0.02$.

3. Reject the null hypothesis if $F \geq 16.0$, the critical value for $F_{0.01}$ with $5 - 1 = 4$, and $5 - 1 = 4$ degrees of freedom.

$$F = \frac{s_1^2}{s_2^2} \quad \text{or} \quad \frac{s_2^2}{s_1^2} \quad \text{whichever is larger.}$$

4. Substituting $n_1 = 5$, and $n_2 = 5$, $s_1^2 = 63{,}450$, and $s_2^2 = 42{,}650$, we get

$$F = \frac{s_1^2}{s_2^2} = \frac{63{,}450}{42{,}650} = 1.49$$

5. Since 1.49 falls short of 16.0, the value of $F_{0.01}$ for $5 - 1 = 4$ and $5 - 1 = 4$ degrees of freedom, we find that the null hypothesis cannot be rejected at the 0.02 level of significance. (Note: We use a right-hand tail for $\alpha/2$ instead of α to compensate for the fact that we always use the larger of the two variance ratios and $\dfrac{0.02}{2} = 0.01$.)   ■

Since the test described here is very sensitive to departures from the assumptions, it must be used with considerable caution. We say that the test is not **robust** and, if circumstances permit, replace it with another procedure which is, it is hoped, more robust.

EXAMPLE 12.7   With reference to the preceding example where $F = 1.49$ was much less than $F_{0.01} = 16.0$, what is the least level of significance at which the null hypothesis could have been rejected?

SOLUTION   What we must find here is the P-value corresponding to $F = 1.49$ for $5 - 1 = 4$ and $5 - 1 = 4$ degrees of freedom. Using appropriate statistical software or a suitably preprogrammed calculator we find that for four and four degrees of freedom the probability of getting an F-value greater than or equal to 1.49 is 0.3543, and hence that the P-value is $2(0.3543) = 0.7086$. It follows that unless we had been willing to assume such an absurdly high risk of committing a Type I error, we would not have been able to reject the null hypothesis. This is an indication that these sample values, though exhibiting a large numerical difference, give no substantial evidence against H_0. ■

EXERCISES

(Exercise 12.8, 12.9, 12.12, and 12.15 are practice exercises. Their complete solutions are given on page 468.)

12.8 The manager of a household appliance service company wants to know whether or not the length of time per service call which the company bills to its customers has a standard deviation of 8.5 minutes. What can the manager conclude at the 0.05 level of significance if $s = 10$ minutes for a sample of 21 service calls randomly selected from a large population of service calls?

12.9 Suppose that in Exercise 12.8 the manager of the household appliance service company wants to know whether the population standard deviation, σ, is greater than 8.5 minutes. Using the same data as before, what can be concluded at the 0.05 level of significance?

12.10 The wages paid to a random sample of 24 production workers who are paid on a piece-rate basis have a variance of 6 dollars squared per day. Test the hypothesis $\sigma^2 = 10$ dollars squared per day against the alternative hypothesis $\sigma^2 \neq 10$ dollars squared at the level of significance $\alpha = 0.05$.

12.11 With reference to Exercise 11.50 on page 437, use the 0.05 level of significance to test the null hypothesis $\sigma = 0.010$ against the alternative hypothesis that this figure is too low.

12.12 With reference to Exercise 11.38 on page 435, use the large-sample test at the level of significance $\alpha = 0.05$ to test the null hypothesis $\sigma = 8.9$ rentals against the alternative hypothesis $\sigma < 8.9$ rentals.

12.13 With reference to Exercise 11.42 on page 436, use the large-sample test at the 0.05 level of significance to test the null hypothesis $\sigma = 1.5$ miles per gallon against the alternative hypothesis $\sigma \neq 1.5$ miles per gallon.

12.14 A buyer of American upland cotton specifies that the standard deviation of the length of the cotton fibers should not exceed 0.0625 inch (the decimal equivalent of $\frac{1}{16}$ inch).
   (a) Use the level of significance $\alpha = 0.01$ to test the null hypothesis $\sigma = 0.0625$ inch against the alternative hypothesis $\sigma > 0.0625$ inch on the basis of a random sample of size $n = 40$ for which $s = 0.0750$ inch.
   (b) Using the same data, test the null hypothesis using the level of significance $\alpha = 0.05$.

12.15 Two different techniques of lighting a store's window displays are compared by measuring the intensity of light at selected locations in areas lighted by the two methods. If a random sample of 12 measurements of the intensity of light provided by the first technique has a standard deviation of 2.6 foot-candles and a random sample of 16 measurements of the intensity of light provided by the second technique has a standard deviation of 4.4 foot-candles, test the null hypothesis $\sigma_1 \neq \sigma_2$ at the 0.10 level of significance.

12.16 With reference to Exercise 11.55 on page 438, test at the 0.02 level of significance whether it is reasonable to assume that the two population standard deviations are equal.

12.17 With reference to Exercise 11.57 on page 439, test at the 0.10 level of significance whether it is reasonable to assume that the two population standard deviations are equal.

12.4

Checklist of Key Terms

Chi-square distribution, 454
Chi-square statistic, 454
Degrees of freedom, 454

F distribution, 463
Robust, 465
Variance ratio, 463

12.5

Review Exercises

12.18 In a random sample of 10 drives on a golf driving range, a golfer using a No. 3 iron averages 160 yards per drive with a standard deviation of 4.50 yards. Test the null hypothesis that the consistency of the golfer's drives is actually measured by 3.0 yards, using the 0.01 level of significance and the alternative hypothesis that the drives are actually less consistent.

12.19 A random sample of 25 customers in a gift shop completed their shopping in an average of 19.4 minutes, with a standard deviation of 3.50 minutes. Construct a 95 percent confidence interval for σ.

12.20 A random sample of weekly earnings for 14 production workers in the Detroit plant of a company has a standard deviation of \$21.18, and a random sample of weekly earnings for 10 production workers in the Cleveland plant of this company has a standard deviation of \$29.32. Use the 0.10 level of significance to test the null hypothesis that the weekly earnings of production workers in this company are equally variable in both cities.

12.21 An investment banker who is considering companies as prospects for mergers, consolidations, and acquisitions, analyzes a sample of six companies and finds that these companies have 14.0, 12.5, 11.6, 13.0, 10.5, and 12.8 percent after-tax returns on a discounted cash flow basis.

(a) Calculate s for the data to obtain an estimate of the standard deviation of the population sampled.

(b) Calculate the range of the data and use the table in Exercise 12.7 on page 458 to get another estimate of this population standard deviation, and compare it to the value calculated in part (a).

12.22 In a random sample of 150 accounts receivable from a very large number of such accounts, an auditor determined that the average balance in the accounts is $\bar{x} = 285.93$ and the standard deviation is $s = 41.65$. Construct a 95 percent confidence interval for the standard deviation of the balances in the accounts.

12.23 With reference to Exercise 11.76 on page 444, test at the 0.10 level of significance whether it is reasonable to assume that the two populations sampled have equal standard deviations.

12.24 In a random sample of 35 business days a mail-order catalog company receives an average of 349 orders per day, with a standard deviation of 49 orders per day. Use the 0.05 level of significance to test the claim that, for the population sampled, σ is at least 60 orders.

12.6

Solutions of Practice Exercises

12.1 Since we have $20 - 1 = 19$ degrees of freedom, we find from Table III that $\chi^2_{0.995} = 6.844$ and $\chi^2_{0.005} = 38.582$. Substituting these values together with $n = 20$ and $s = 1.1$ into the confidence interval formula for σ^2,

$$\frac{(n-1)s^2}{\chi^2_{\alpha/2}} < \sigma^2 < \frac{(n-1)s^2}{\chi^2_{1-\alpha/2}}$$

we get $\dfrac{(20-1)(1.1)^2}{38.582} < \sigma^2 < \dfrac{(20-1)(1.1)^2}{6.844}$, so $0.5959 < \sigma^2 < 3.3591$, and taking their square roots, we get $0.77 < \sigma < 1.83$.

12.3 $s = \sqrt{\dfrac{10(41{,}454) - (634)^2}{10(10 - 1)}} = 11.82$ seconds.

Since we have $10 - 1 = 9$ degrees of freedom, we find from Table III that $\chi^2_{0.950} = 3.325$ and $\chi^2_{0.05} = 16.919$. Substituting these values together with $n = 10$ and $s = 11.82$ seconds into the confidence interval formula for σ^2,

$$\frac{(n-1)s^2}{\chi^2_{\alpha/2}} < \sigma^2 < \frac{(n-1)s^2}{\chi^2_{1-\alpha/2}}$$

we get $\dfrac{(10-1)(11.82)^2}{16.919} < \sigma^2 < \dfrac{(10-1)(11.82)^2}{3.325}$, so $74.32 < \sigma^2 < 378.17$.

12.7   Calculate the range by subtracting the smallest value from the largest value. Divide the remainder by the value of d obtained from the table.

(a) $\dfrac{85 - 45}{3.08} = 12.99$ seconds, compared to 11.82 seconds.

(b) $\dfrac{6.2 - 3.1}{2.97} = 1.04$ pounds, compared to $s = 1.11$ pounds.

12.8   **1.** H_0: $\sigma = 8.5$.
         H_A: $\sigma \neq 8.5$.

     2. $\alpha = 0.05$.

     3. Reject the null hypothesis if $\chi^2 \leq 9.591$ or $\chi^2 \geq 34.170$, where

$$\chi^2 = \frac{(n-1)s^2}{\sigma_0^2}$$

and 9.591 is the value $\chi^2_{0.975}$ for $21 - 1 = 20$ degrees of freedom, and 34.170 is the value of $\chi^2_{0.025}$ for $21 - 1 = 20$ degrees of freedom.

     4. Substituting $n = 21$, $s = 10.0$, and $\sigma_0 = 8.5$ into the formula for χ^2, we get

$$\chi^2 = \frac{(21 - 1)(10.0)^2}{8.5^2} = 27.682$$

     5. Since $\chi^2 = 27.682$ lies between 9.591 and 34.170, we cannot reject the null hypothesis.

12.9   **1.** H_0: $\sigma = 8.5$.
         H_A: $\sigma > 8.5$.

     2. $\alpha = 0.05$.

     3. Reject the null hypothesis if $\chi^2_{0.05} \geq 31.410$ when

$$\chi^2 = \frac{(n-1)s^2}{\sigma_0^2}$$

Section 12.6   *Solutions of Practice Exercises*   **469** and 31.410 is the value of $\chi^2_{0.05}$ for $21 - 1 = 20$ degrees of freedom.

4. Substituting $n = 21$, $s = 10.0$, and $\sigma_0 = 8.5$ into the formula for χ^2, we get

$$\chi^2 = \frac{(21 - 1)(10.0)^2}{8.5^2} = 27.682$$

5. Since $\chi^2 = 27.682$ is less than 31.410 we cannot reject the null hypothesis.

12.12 1. H_0: $\sigma = 8.9$ rentals.
H_A: $\sigma \leq 8.9$ rentals.

2. $\alpha = 0.05$.

3. Reject the null hypothesis if $z \leq -1.645$, where

$$z = \frac{s - \sigma_0}{\sigma_0 / \sqrt{2n}}$$

4. Substituting $n = 36$, $s = 6.9$ rentals, and $\sigma_0 = 8.9$ rentals into the formula for z, we get

$$z = \frac{6.9 - 8.9}{8.9 / \sqrt{2 \cdot 36}} = -1.907$$

5. Since -1.907 is less than -1.645, we reject the null hypothesis.

12.15 1. H_0: $\sigma_1 = \sigma_2$.
H_A: $\sigma_1 \neq \sigma_2$.

2. $\alpha = 0.10$.

3. Reject the null hypothesis if $F \geq 2.72$, where

$$F = \frac{s_1^2}{s_2^2} \quad \text{or} \quad \frac{s_2^2}{s_1^2}$$

whichever is larger, and 2.72 is the value of $F_{0.05}$ for $16 - 1 = 15$ degrees of freedom and $12 - 1 = 11$ degrees of freedom.

4. Since s_2^2 is greater than s_1^2, we substitute $s_2 = 4.4$ into the numerator of the variance ratio and $s_1 = 2.6$ into the denominator of the variance ratio, and we get

$$F = \frac{4.4^2}{2.6^2} = 2.86$$

5. Since $F = 2.86$ exceeds 2.72, the null hypothesis must be rejected.

Decision Making: Inferences About Proportions

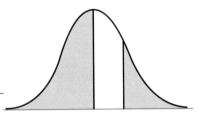

In principle, the work of this chapter will be very similar to that of Chapters 11 and 12. In problems of estimation we shall again construct confidence intervals and determine, or control, the possible size of our error. In tests of hypotheses we shall again formulate null hypotheses and their alternatives, decide between one-tailed tests and two-tailed tests, choose levels of significance, and so forth. The main difference is that we will be concerned with other parameters. Instead of population means, variances, and standard deviations, we will deal with population proportions, percentages, or probabilities.

Section 13.1 deals with the estimation of proportions; Section 13.2 deals with tests concerning proportions; Sections 13.3 and 13.4 deal with tests concerning two or more proportions; in Section 13.5 we shall learn how to analyze data tallied into two-way classifications; and in Section 13.6 we shall learn how to judge whether differences between the frequencies of an observed distribution and corresponding expectations can be attributed to chance.

13.1

The Estimation of Proportions

The information that is usually available for the estimation of a true proportion (percentage, or probability) is a **sample proportion** $\frac{x}{n}$, where x is the number of times that an event has occurred in n trials. For instance, if in a random sample of 800 purchases at a department store 424 were charged to credit cards, then $\frac{x}{n} = \frac{424}{800} = 0.53$, and we can use this figure as a point estimate of the true proportion of purchases made at this store that are charged to credit cards. Similarly, a large finance company might estimate the proportion of its debtors who are at least one installment behind as 0.06, if a random sample of 400 accounts included 24 which were at least one installment behind.

Throughout this section it will be assumed that the situations satisfy (at least approximately) the conditions underlying the binomial distribution; that is, our information will consist of the number of successes observed in a given number of independent trials, and it will be assumed that for each trial the probability of a success—the parameter we want to estimate—has the constant value p. Thus, the sampling distribution of the counts our methods will be based on is the binomial distribution with the mean $\mu = np$ and the standard deviation $\sigma = \sqrt{np(1-p)}$, and we know that this distribution can be approximated with a normal distribution when n is large.[1] It follows that, for large values of n, the statistic

$$z = \frac{x - np}{\sqrt{np(1-p)}}$$

has approximately the standard normal distribution. If we substitute this expression for z into the double inequality $-z_{\alpha/2} < z < z_{\alpha/2}$ and use some simple algebra, we arrive at

---

[1]On page 341 we said that the normal approximation to the binomial distribution may be used when np and $n(1-p)$ are both greater than 5. So, when $n = 50$, for example, the normal-curve methods discussed here and later in this chapter may be used if p lies between 0.10 and 0.90; when $n = 100$ they may be used if p lies between 0.05 and 0.95; and when $n = 200$ they may be used if p lies between 0.025 and 0.975. This illustrates what we mean here by "n being large."

Chapter 13   Decision Making: Inferences About Proportions

$$\frac{x}{n} - z_{\alpha/2} \sqrt{\frac{p(1-p)}{n}} < p < \frac{x}{n} + z_{\alpha/2} \sqrt{\frac{p(1-p)}{n}}$$

This may look like a confidence-interval formula for p, and, indeed, the inequalities will be satisfied with probability $1 - \alpha$, but it cannot be used in this form because the unknown parameter p itself appears in $\sqrt{\frac{p(1-p)}{n}}$ to the left of the first inequality sign and to the right of the other. The quantity $\sqrt{\frac{p(1-p)}{n}}$ is called the **standard error of a proportion**, as it is, in fact, the standard deviation of the sampling distribution of a sample proportion (see Exercise 13.14 on page 478). To get around this difficulty, we substitute the sample proportion $\frac{x}{n}$ for p in $\sqrt{\frac{p(1-p)}{n}}$, and we thus arrive at the following $(1 - \alpha)$ **100 percent large-sample confidence interval** for p:

Large-sample confidence interval for p

$$\frac{x}{n} - z_{\alpha/2} \sqrt{\frac{\frac{x}{n}\left(1 - \frac{x}{n}\right)}{n}} < p < \frac{x}{n} + z_{\alpha/2} \sqrt{\frac{\frac{x}{n}\left(1 - \frac{x}{n}\right)}{n}}$$

There are other methods for constructing confidence intervals for p, but we shall not go into them here. Among them, a method based on special tables was given in earlier editions of this book.

EXAMPLE 13.1   In a random sample of 400 cars stopped at a roadblock, 152 of the drivers were wearing their seat belts. Construct a 95 percent confidence interval for the corresponding true proportion in the population sampled.

SOLUTION   Substituting $n = 400$, $\frac{x}{n} = \frac{152}{400} = 0.38$, and $z_{0.025} = 1.96$ into the large-sample confidence interval formula, we get

$$0.38 - 1.96 \sqrt{\frac{(0.38)(0.62)}{400}} < p < 0.38 + 1.96 \sqrt{\frac{(0.38)(0.62)}{400}}$$

$$0.33 < p < 0.43$$

Clearly, the interval from 0.33 to 0.43 either contains the true proportion p or it does not, and we really don't know which. However, the 95 percent confidence implies that the interval was constructed by a method which leads to correct results 95 percent of the time. Note also that for $n = 400$ and p on the interval from 0.33 to 0.43, np and $n(1 - p)$ are both much greater than 5, so that there can be no question about using the normal approximation to the binomial distribution (see page 340). ∎

The theory presented here can also be used to judge the possible size of the error we may make when we use a sample proportion as a point estimate of a population proportion p. In this case, we can assert with $(1 - \alpha)$ 100 percent confidence that the size of our error will be, at most

Maximum error of estimate

$$E = z_{\alpha/2} \sqrt{\frac{p(1 - p)}{n}} \qquad \text{or approximately} \qquad E = z_{\alpha/2} \sqrt{\frac{\frac{x}{n}\left(1 - \frac{x}{n}\right)}{n}}$$

The first of these two formulas cannot be used in practice since p is the quantity we are trying to estimate, but the second formula can be used provided that n is large enough to justify the normal-curve approximation to the binomial distribution.

EXAMPLE 13.2   In a random sample of 200 vacationers interviewed at a resort, 142 said that they chose the resort mainly because of its climate. With 99 percent confidence, what can we say about the maximum error, if we use $\dfrac{x}{n} = \dfrac{142}{200} = 0.71$ as an estimate of the true proportion of vacationers who choose the resort mainly because of its climate?

SOLUTION   Substituting $n = 200$, $\frac{x}{n} = 0.71$, and $z_{0.005} = 2.575$ into the formula for E, we get

$$E = 2.575 \sqrt{\frac{(0.71)(0.29)}{200}} = 0.08$$

rounded to two decimals. ∎

As in the estimation of means, we can use the expression for the maximum error to determine how large a sample is needed to attain a desired degree of precision. If we want to assert with probability $1 - \alpha$ that a sample proportion will differ from the true proportion p by at most some quantity E, we can solve the equation

Chapter 13   Decision Making: Inferences About Proportions

$$E = z_{\alpha/2} \sqrt{\frac{p(1 - p)}{n}}$$

for n and get

Sample size

$$n = p(1 - p)\left(\frac{z_{\alpha/2}}{E}\right)^2$$

Since this formula involves p, it cannot be used unless we have some information about the possible values that p might assume. Without such information, we make use of the fact that $p(1 - p)$ equals $\frac{1}{4}$ when $p = \frac{1}{2}$ and is smaller than $\frac{1}{4}$ for all other values of p. Hence, if we use the formula

Sample size

$$n = \frac{1}{4}\left(\frac{z_{\alpha/2}}{E}\right)^2$$

our sample size may be larger than necessary, but we can account for this by asserting with a probability of *at least* $1 - \alpha$ that the error in our estimate will not exceed E. In case we do have some information about the possible range of values p might assume in a given problem, we can take this into account in determining n. We substitute for p in the first of the two sample size formulas whichever value within that range is closest to $\frac{1}{2}$.

EXAMPLE 13.3   Suppose that we want to estimate what proportion of gift items purchased at a department store are returned for a refund, and that we want to be "at least 95 percent sure" that the error of our estimate will be, at most, 0.05. How large a sample will we need if
(a) we have no idea what the true proportion might be
(b) we know that the true proportion is anywhere from 0.01 to 0.20

SOLUTION   (a) Substituting $E = 0.05$ and $z_{0.025} = 1.96$ into the formula for n just given, we get

$$n = \frac{1}{4}\left(\frac{1.96}{0.05}\right)^2 = 385$$

rounded up to the nearest integer.

(b) Substituting these same values together with $p = 0.20$ (the value from 0.01 to 0.20 closest to $\frac{1}{2}$) into the first of the two formulas for n, we get

$$n = (0.20)(0.80)\left(\frac{1.96}{0.05}\right)^2 = 246$$

rounded up to the nearest integer. ∎

EXERCISES

(Exercises 13.1, 13.6, and 13.10 are practice exercises. Their complete solutions are given on page 518.)

13.1 In a random sample of 500 high-fashion women's dresses selected from the inventory of a large retailer, 95 dresses were determined to be out of fashion and must therefore be sold at reduced prices. Construct a 99 percent confidence interval for the corresponding population proportion.

13.2 In a random sample survey, 250 commuters to the downtown center of a city are asked whether they commuted to the city by public transportation or by privately owned vehicle. If 88 persons commuted by public transportation, construct a 90 percent confidence interval for the true proportion of commuters who use public transportation.

13.3 In the sample survey of Exercise 13.2, another 100 commuters are asked whether they plan to shop in a department store while in the downtown area. If 48 commuters reply that they plan to shop in a department store, construct a 95 percent confidence interval for the corresponding population proportion.

13.4 In a study conducted by a gasoline service station operator, it was found that among 600 randomly selected purchasers of gasoline at full-service stations whose windshields were deliberately not cleaned by the attendant, 236 purchasers asked for the service. Construct a 95 percent confidence interval for the actual percentage of persons who ask for the service.

13.5 Analysis of 300 randomly selected accounts receivable of a firm by an auditor show that 30 are past due. Construct a 99 percent confidence interval for the actual proportion of accounts receivable which are past due.

13.6 In a random sample of 600 young business executives, 475 revealed that as a result of recent findings linking a high-cholesterol diet and lack of exercise to heart disease, they were utilizing a low-cholesterol diet and regular exercise routine as a priority. What can be asserted with 90 percent confidence about the maximum size of the error if the sample proportion $\frac{475}{600} = 0.79$ is used as an estimate of the actual population proportion?

13.7　In a random sample of 120 persons who attempted to return merchandise at the customer service desk of a department store, it was found that 18 persons were not allowed to do so because the merchandise was worn, damaged, returned late, purchased at another store, or unaccompanied by a sales slip. Construct a 99 percent confidence interval for the proportion of customers not allowed to return merchandise in the population sampled.

13.8　In a study of consumer buying habits, 88 women in a random sample of 400 women, drawn from a large population, reported that they "automatically" buy (when available) the economy size of whatever they need. What can we assert with 98 percent confidence about the maximum size of our error, if we use the sample proportion $\frac{88}{400} = 0.22$, as an estimate of the corresponding proportion in the population sampled?

13.9　In a random sample of 260 defendants in a small claims court, 169 defendants felt that the verdicts of the court were fair and impartial. If $\frac{169}{260} = 0.65$ is used as an estimate of the corresponding true proportion in the population sampled, what can be asserted with 90 percent confidence about the maximum error?

13.10　A large health insurance company wants to estimate, from a sample of its thousands of policyholders, the percentage of its policyholders who will make claims for health insurance benefits during the coming year. How large a sample (from claims made during a year) will be needed so that the insurance company can be at least 95 percent confident that the sample percentage will be in error by, at most, 10 percent?

13.11　With reference to Exercise 13.10, suppose the health insurance company has reason to believe that the actual percentage of its policyholders who will make claims for benefits during the coming year is somewhere between 10 and 20 percent. How large a sample will the insurance company need to be at least 80 percent confident that the sample percentage will be in error by less than 5 percent?

13.12　A manufacturing company considering an incentive pay bonus (more money for those who are on time and take few sick days) wants to estimate the proportion of its employees who would qualify for the bonus. How large a sample will it have to take from its personnel records to be at least 98 percent confident that the sample proportion and true proportion will differ by at most 0.05?

13.13　A men's necktie manufacturer wants to determine what proportion of neckties purchased for wear by men were actually purchased by women. How large a sample will the manufacturer need to be at least 98 percent confident that the sample proportion will be within 0.06 of the population proportion?

13.14   Since the proportion of successes is simply the number of successes divided by n, the mean and the standard deviation of the sampling distribution of the proportion of successes may be obtained by dividing the mean and the standard deviation of the sampling distribution of the number of successes by n. Use this argument to verify the standard error formula given on page 473.

13.15   If a sample constitutes at least 5 percent of a population, and the sample itself is large, we can use the **finite population correction factor** to reduce the width of confidence intervals for p. If we make this correction, the large-sample confidence limits for p become

$$\frac{x}{n} \pm z_{\alpha/2} \sqrt{\frac{\frac{x}{n}\left(1 - \frac{x}{n}\right)}{n}} \cdot \sqrt{\frac{N - n}{N - 1}}$$

where N is, as before, the size of the population sampled.

(a)   Among 500 students taking a course in statistics at a certain college, a random sample of 250 students is interviewed, and it is found that 185 of them have access to a personal computer. Construct a 95 percent confidence interval for the actual proportion of all students in the course who have access to a personal computer.

(b)   The mayor of a town would like to buy a new fire engine, but wants to know what proportion of persons on the town's voting list would oppose this expenditure. If, in a random sample of 100 of the 534 persons on the voting list, 28 oppose the expenditure, find an 80 percent confidence interval for the corresponding proportion of persons on the voting list who oppose the expenditure.

13.2

Tests Concerning Proportions

In this section we shall be concerned with tests of hypotheses which enable us to decide, on the basis of sample data, whether the true value of a proportion (percentage, or probability) equals, is greater than, or is less than a given constant. They will make it possible, for example, to determine whether the true proportion of shoppers who can identify a highly advertised trade mark is 0.40, whether it is true that 10 percent of the shirts "cleaned" by a certain laundry are rejected at final inspection because of inferior work, or whether the true probability is 0.70 that a person plans to buy his next car from the same dealer who sold him his last car.

Questions of this kind are usually decided on the basis of either the observed number or the observed proportion of successes in what are assumed to be n independent trials, each of which has the same probability p of success. In other words, we shall assume that we can use the binomial distribution and that we are, in fact, testing hypotheses about its parameter p.

When n is small, tests concerning true proportions can be based directly on tables of binomial probabilities such as Table V, as is illustrated by the examples which follow.

Some of the following significance tests are based on P-values where we use the alternate five-step procedure explained on page 425 and illustrated in Examples 13.4 and 13.5. Where the significance tests are based on z, we use the five-step procedure explained on page 412 and illustrated in Examples 13.6 and 13.7.

EXAMPLE 13.4 It has been claimed that 40 percent of all shoppers can identify a highly advertised trade mark. If 2 of 12 shoppers interviewed at random can identify the trade mark, test the claim at the 0.05 level of significance (two-tailed criterion).

SOLUTION

1. H_0: $p = 0.40$.
   H_A: $p \neq 0.40$.

2. $\alpha = 0.05$.

3'. Base the test on x, the observed number of successes.

4'. We are given that $x = 2$, and we find from Table V where $n = 12$, $p = 0.40$, and for $x = 0$, 1, and 2 that the probability of 2 or fewer successes is

$$0.002 + 0.017 + 0.64 = 0.083$$

Since the alternative hypothesis is two sided, the P value is $2(0.083) = 0.166$.

5'. Since 0.166 exceeds 0.05, the null hypothesis cannot be rejected. In other words, there is no real evidence that the claim may not be valid. ∎

Figure 13.1 illustrates that the sum of the probabilities of the bars representing $x = 0$ and $x = 1$ will be, at most, $\alpha/2 = 0.025$, and the sum for 9 and 10 will be, at most, $\alpha/2 = 0.025$. We can, therefore, reject the null hypothesis for 0 and 1 and for 9 and 10. As the reader will be asked to verify in Exercise 13.16 on page 484, the test criterion is as shown in Figure 13.1.

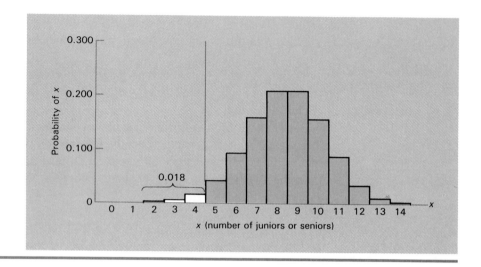

FIGURE 13.1
Binomial
distribution with
$p = 0.40$ and
$n = 12$

The example which follows illustrates the use of a one-tailed criterion in a test concerning a proportion.

EXAMPLE 13.5   It has been claimed that at least 60 percent of the juniors and seniors attending a large university prefer to live off campus. If 3 of 14 juniors or seniors selected at random prefer to live off campus, test the claim at the 0.05 level of significance (one-tailed criterion).

SOLUTION

1. H_0: $p = 0.60$.
   H_A: $p < 0.60$.

2. $\alpha = 0.05$.

3'. Base the test on x, the observed number of successes.

4'. We are given that $x = 3$, and we find from Table V where $n = 14$, $p = 0.60$, and $x = 0, 1, 2$, and 3 that the probability of 3 or fewer successes is

$$0.001 + 0.003 = 0.004$$

Since the alternative hypothesis is one sided, the P-value is 0.004.

5'. Since 0.004 is less than 0.05, the null hypothesis must be rejected. We conclude that less than 60 percent of the juniors

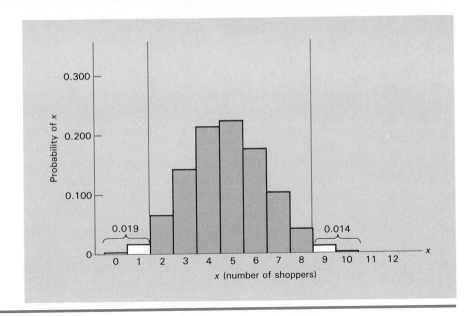

FIGURE 13.2
Binomial
distribution with
$p = 0.60$ and
$n = 14$

and seniors at the given university prefer to live off campus. Figure 13.2 shows the binomial distribution with $p = 0.60$ and $n = 14$. ∎

We used P-values in Examples 13.4 and 13.5 to avoid unnecessary calculations. If we had used steps 3, 4, and 5 (explained on page 480) in Example 13.5, we would have first determined the critical region, namely, the values of x for which the null hypothesis must be rejected. We do this by using Table V, binomial probabilities, where we find for $n = 14$ and $p = 0.60$ the probabilities of getting two or fewer successes, three or fewer successes, four or fewer successes, and five or fewer successes are obtained by adding successive probabilities in the table and are, respectively, 0.001, 0.004, 0.018, and 0.059. Since each of the first three values are less than 0.05 and the fourth value exceeds it, we find that the null hypothesis must be rejected for $x = 0$, $x = 1$, $x = 2$, $x = 3$, or $x = 4$. Then we conclude that since the observed value is $x = 3$, the null hypothesis must be rejected. Note that much of this work is unnecessary when we work with P-values. By contrast, when we used P-values in the solution of Example 13.5, all that we needed was the second of the four probabilities, namely, 0.004 (which is the sum of 0.001 and 0.003 from Table V), and since 0.004 is less than the 0.05 level of significance used to test the claim, the null hypothesis is rejected. In Exercise 13.17, the reader will be asked to show that in Example 13.4 the null hypothesis must be rejected for $x = 0$, $x = 1$, $x = 9$, $x = 10$, and $x = 11$. Again, this requires the determination of many more probabilities than the one probability which is needed when working with P-values, as shown on page 479.

In Examples 13.4 and 13.5, the levels of significance are specified as 0.05, but we ought to refer to these levels of significance as nominal because they are not really the corresponding probabilities of Type I errors. This results from the fact that random variables having binomial distributions are discrete, and most of the time it is impossible to draw the dividing line of a test criterion so that the probability of a Type I error is exactly equal to a specified value such as 0.05 or 0.01. Referring to the results obtained in the preceding paragraph, we thus find that in Example 13.5 the probability of a Type I error is actually

$$0.001 + 0.003 + 0.014 = 0.018$$

and in Exercise 13.18, the reader will be asked to verify that in Example 13.4 the probability of a Type I error is actually 0.033.

When n is large, tests concerning true proportions (percentages, or probabilities) are usually based on the normal-curve approximation to the binomial distribution. Using again the z statistic which led to the large-sample confidence interval for p, we base tests of the null hypothesis $p = p_0$ on the values of

Statistic for large-sample test concerning proportion

$$z = \frac{x - np_0}{\sqrt{np_0(1 - p_0)}}$$

which has approximately the standard normal distribution.[2] The actual test criteria are again like those shown in Figure 11.10 on page 421 and in the table on page 422. For the one-sided alternative $p < p_0$, we reject the null hypothesis when $z \leq -z_\alpha$; for the one-sided alternative $p > p_0$, we reject the null hypothesis when $z \geq z_\alpha$; and for the two-sided alternative $p \neq p_0$, we reject the null hypothesis when $z \leq -z_{\alpha/2}$ or $z \geq z_{\alpha/2}$. As before, α is the level of significance.

EXAMPLE 13.6   It has been claimed that at least 30 percent of all families moving away from California move to Arizona. If a random sample of the records of several large van lines shows that the belongings of 153 of 600 families moving away from California were shipped to Arizona,

[2]Many statisticians make a continuity correction here by substituting $x - \frac{1}{2}$ or $x + \frac{1}{2}$ for x in the formula for z, whichever makes z smaller. However, when n is large the effect of this correction is usually negligible.

Chapter 13   Decision Making: Inferences About Proportions

test the null hypothesis $p = 0.30$ against the alternative hypothesis $p < 0.30$ at the 0.01 level of significance.

SOLUTION **1.** H_0: $p = 0.30$.
H_A: $p < 0.30$.

2. $\alpha = 0.01$.

3. Reject the null hypothesis if $z \le -2.33$, where

$$z = \frac{x - np_0}{\sqrt{np_0(1 - p_0)}}$$

otherwise, accept the null hypothesis or reserve judgment.

4. Substituting $x = 153$, $n = 600$, and $p_0 = 0.30$ into the formula for z, we get

$$z = \frac{153 - 600(0.30)}{\sqrt{600(0.30)(0.70)}} = -2.40$$

5. Since -2.40 is less than -2.33, we find that the null hypothesis must be rejected. In other words, the evidence contradicts the claim and we conclude that less than 30 percent of all families moving away from California move to Arizona. ∎

EXAMPLE 13.7 A large national brokerage firm claims that 80 percent of its customers who sell stock to establish tax losses immediately reinvest the proceeds in other stocks. If a random sample of 320 sales (chosen from a great number of sales known to have been made to establish losses) includes 245 in which the proceeds were immediately reinvested in other stocks, test the null hypothesis $p = 0.80$ against the alternative hypothesis $p \ne 0.80$ at the level of significance $\alpha = 0.075$.

SOLUTION **1.** H_0: $p = 0.80$.
H_A: $p \ne 0.80$.

2. $\alpha = 0.075$.

3′. Use the test statistic

$$z = \frac{x - np_0}{\sqrt{np_0(1 - p_0)}}$$

4′. Substituting $x = 245$, $n = 320$, and $p_0 = 0.80$ into the formula for z, we get

$$z = \frac{245 - 320(0.80)}{\sqrt{320(0.80)(0.20)}} = -1.54$$

From Table I, the probability of getting a z-value less than -1.54 is $0.5000 - 0.4382 = 0.0618$, and, hence, the P-value is $2(0.0618) = 0.1236$ (since the alternative hypothesis is two sided).

5′. Since 0.1236 exceeds 0.075, we find that the null hypothesis cannot be rejected. We conclude that there is no real evidence to refute the claim. ∎

EXERCISES

(Exercises 13.16, 13.19, 13.20, 13.22, 13.24, and 13.29 are practice exercises. Their complete solutions are given on page 518.)

13.16 With reference to Example 13.4 on page 479 (where $n = 12$ and $p = 0.40$), show the probabilities that x, the number of shoppers who can identify the trade mark, is

(a) 1 or fewer, and 9 or more, and that both probabilities are less than 0.025

(b) 2 or fewer, and 8 or more, and that both probabilities are greater than 0.025

13.17 With reference to the preceding Exercise 13.16, verify that the null hypothesis must be rejected for $x = 0$, $x = 1$, $x = 9$, $x = 10$, and $x = 11$ observations.

13.18 Based on the preceding Exercises 13.16 and 13.17, verify that the probability of a Type I error in Example 13.4 is actually 0.033.

13.19 A clerk at a large video store estimates that 70 percent of its video rentals are returned within one day. The manager believes that this estimate is too low. A random sample of 15 rental returns is taken to test the null hypothesis $p = 0.70$ against the alternative hypothesis $p > 0.70$ at the 0.04 level of significance.

(a) For what values of x, the number of rentals returned within one day, must the null hypothesis be rejected?

(b) What is the actual level of significance?

13.20 Suppose that we want to decide on the basis of 15 flips of a coin whether it may be regarded as fair. How many heads would we have to get to be able to reject the null hypothesis that the probability of heads is 0.50 at the level of significance $\alpha = 0.05$?

13.21 A direct mail company claims that at most 10 percent of its catalogs cannot be delivered because addressees have moved, died, gone out of business, or clerical errors or other reasons exist. If catalogs are mailed to 14 randomly selected addressees, how many of them must be undelivered before the null hypothesis $p = 0.10$ can be rejected at the level of significance $\alpha = 0.05$.

13.22 It was reported in the *Harvard Business Review* that 40 percent of black MBA managers say the word *patronizing* best describes the organizational climate at their companies for black managers. If 6 out of 10 randomly selected black MBA managers support this belief, can we reject the null hypothesis $p = 0.40$ against the alternative hypothesis $p \neq 0.40$ at the 0.05 level of significance?

13.23 A medical doctor at a clinic claims that 60 percent of the clinic's patients utilize health insurance to pay their medical bills, but a social worker thinks that this proportion may be too high. In a random sample of 12 medical bills, at least how many must be at least partially covered by health insurance so that the null hypothesis, $p = 0.60$, cannot be rejected at the level of significance $\alpha = 0.05$.

13.24 The service manager for an appliance sales company asserts that 6 percent of the appliances sold are returned to the service department for repair under the warranty, and the sales manager believes that this claim is too high.

(a) Test the service manager's assertion at the 0.05 level of significance if 56 out of a random sample of 1,000 appliance sales are returned to the service department for repair under the warranty.

(b) Calculate the *P*-value for the data of this exercise. Does the *P*-value support your decision at the $\alpha = 0.05$ level?

13.25 In a random sample of 200 complaints about the efficiency of a new type of swimming pool water filter, it is found that 114 complaints were due, at least in part, to owners and operators who, for economic reasons, did not run the filter the recommended number of hours per day.

(a) Use the level of significance $\alpha = 0.05$ to decide whether this supports the claim that 0.65 of the complaints are due to failure of the owners and operators to run the filter the recommended number of hours per day.

(b) Calculate the *P*-value for the data of this exercise. Does this *P*-value support your decision at the $\alpha = 0.05$ level?

13.26 A market researcher wants to know whether automobile owners prefer a new type of automobile floor mat to the old type. What can the market researcher conclude at the level of significance $\alpha = 0.05$ if only 55 out of 100 randomly selected automobile owners prefer the new type of floor mat and the alternative hypothesis is

(a) $p \neq 0.60$

(b) $p < 0.60$

13.27 A random sample of 150 delegates attending a national convention shows that 95 delegates traveled to the convention city by air transportation.

(a) Test at the $\alpha = 0.01$ level of significance the null hypothesis that the corresponding population proportion is $p = 0.55$ against the alternative hypothesis $p > 0.55$.

(b) Calculate the P-value for the data of this exercise. Does the P-value support your decision at the 0.01 level?

13.28 A management consultant conducted a survey of 1,000 workers in the United States and finds that 718 of these workers expect to live as well as they do now when they retire. Test the null hypothesis that the true proportion of workers in the population sampled who feel this way is 0.75 against the alternative hypothesis that this figure is incorrect, using the level of significance

(a) $\alpha = 0.05$

(b) $\alpha = 0.01$

13.29 In the construction of tables of random numbers (see discussion on page 358), there are various ways of detecting possible departures from randomness. For instance, there should be about as many even digits (0, 2, 4, 6, or 8) as there are odd digits (1, 3, 5, 7, or 9). Count the number of even digits among the 350 digits constituting the first 10 rows of the table on page 876, and test at the level of significance $\alpha = 0.05$ whether, on the basis of this criterion, we should be concerned about the possibility that these random numbers are, in fact, not random?

13.30 In order to control the proportion of defectives or other characteristics (attributes) of mass-produced items, quality control engineers take random samples of size n at regular intervals of time and plot the sample proportions on a **control chart** such as that of Figure 13.3. Other quality control charts with special tables are shown in Chapter 18. If the production process is considered to be in control when the true proportion of defectives is p_0, the **central line** of the control chart for the proportion of defectives is at p_0, and the **3-sigma upper and lower control limits** are at

$$p_0 + 3\sqrt{\frac{p_0(1 - p_0)}{n}} \quad \text{and} \quad p_0 - 3\sqrt{\frac{p_0(1 - p_0)}{n}}$$

Now, a process is assumed to be in control as long as the sample proportions, plotted on the control chart, remain between the two control limits.

(a) Construct a control chart for the proportion of defectives obtained in repeated random samples of size 100 from a process which is considered to be in control when $p = 0.20$

(b) Given that 25 consecutive samples of size 100 contained 21, 16, 28, 24, 19, 22, 20, 12, 17, 22, 13, 23, 19, 20, 21, 17, 23, 25, 14, 18, 22, 17, 25, 19, and 24 defectives, plot the sample proportions on the control

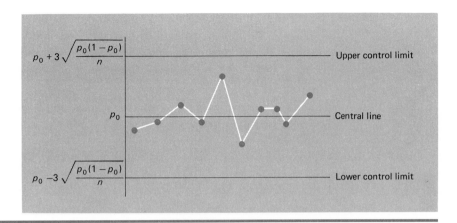

FIGURE 13.3
Control chart

chart constructed in part (a) and comment on the performance of the process.

13.31 Repeated random samples of size 150 are taken from a production process which is considered to be in control when $p = 0.10$.

(a) Construct a control chart (see the preceding exercise) for the proportion of defectives observed in these samples.

(b) Given that 20 consecutive samples of size 150 contained 19, 9, 21, 13, 18, 22, 25, 14, 8, 20, 27, 29, 24, 18, 20, 12, 15, 16, 9, and 11 defectives, plot the sample proportions on the control chart constructed in part (a) and comment on the performance of the process.

13.3

Differences Between Proportions

There are many problems in which we must decide whether the observed difference between two sample proportions can be attributed to chance, or whether it is indicative of the fact that the two corresponding population proportions are unequal. For instance, we may want to decide on the basis of sample data whether one kind of mail-order solicitation will actually yield a greater response than another, or we may want to test on the basis of samples whether two manufacturers of electronic equipment ship equal proportions of defectives.

The method we shall use to test whether an observed difference between two sample proportions can be attributed to chance, or whether it is statistically significant, is based on the following theory: If x_1 and x_2 are the numbers of successes obtained in n_1 trials of one kind and n_2 of another, the trials are all independent, and the corresponding probabilities of a success are p_1 and p_2, then the sampling distribution of $\dfrac{x_1}{n_1} - \dfrac{x_2}{n_2}$ has the mean $p_1 - p_2$ and the standard deviation, called the **standard error of the difference between two proportions**,

$$\sqrt{\frac{p_1(1 - p_1)}{n_1} + \frac{p_2(1 - p_2)}{n_2}}$$

When we test the null hypothesis $p_1 = p_2 (= p)$ against an appropriate alternative hypothesis, the mean of the sampling distribution of the difference between two proportions is $p_1 - p_2 = 0$, and the standard error can be written

$$\sqrt{p(1 - p)\left(\frac{1}{n_1} + \frac{1}{n_2}\right)}$$

where p is usually estimated by **pooling** the data; that is, by substituting for it the combined sample proportion $\dfrac{x_1 + x_2}{n_1 + n_2}$. Then, since for large samples the sampling distribution of the difference between two proportions can be approximated closely with a normal distribution, we base the test on the statistic

Statistic for test concerning difference between two proportions

$$z = \frac{\dfrac{x_1}{n_1} - \dfrac{x_2}{n_2}}{\sqrt{p(1 - p)\left(\dfrac{1}{n_1} + \dfrac{1}{n_2}\right)}} \qquad \text{with} \qquad p = \frac{x_1 + x_2}{n_1 + n_2}$$

which has approximately the standard normal distribution. The test criteria are again those of Figure 11.10 on page 421 with $p_1 - p_2$ substituted for μ and 0 substituted for μ_0. For the one-sided alternative $p_1 < p_2$ we reject the null hypothesis if $z \leq -z_\alpha$, for the one-sided alternative $p_1 > p_2$ we reject the null hypothesis if $z \geq z_\alpha$, and for the two-sided alternative $p_1 \neq p_2$ we reject the null hypothesis if $z \leq -z_{\alpha/2}$ or $z \geq z_{\alpha/2}$.

Chapter 13 Decision Making: Inferences About Proportions

EXAMPLE 13.8 One production process yielded 28 defective pieces in a random sample of size 400 while another yielded 15 defective pieces in a random sample of size 300. Test the null hypothesis $p_1 = p_2$ (that the two processes yield equal proportions of defectives) against the alternative hypothesis $p_1 \neq p_2$ at the 0.05 level of significance.

SOLUTION
1. H_0: $p_1 = p_2$.
   H_A: $p_1 \neq p_2$.

2. $\alpha = 0.05$.

3. Reject the null hypothesis if $z \leq -1.96$ or $z \geq 1.96$ where z is given by the foregoing formula (test concerning difference between two proportions); otherwise, accept the null hypothesis or reserve judgment.

4. Substituting $x_1 = 28$, $n_1 = 400$, $x_2 = 15$, $n_2 = 300$, and
$$\frac{28 + 15}{400 + 300} = 0.061$$
for p into the formula for z we get

$$z = \frac{\dfrac{28}{400} - \dfrac{15}{300}}{\sqrt{(0.061)(0.939)\left(\dfrac{1}{400} + \dfrac{1}{300}\right)}} = 1.10$$

5. Since this value falls between $-z_{0.025} = -1.96$ and $z_{0.025} = 1.96$, we find that the null hypothesis cannot be rejected. In other words we cannot conclude that there is a real difference between the true proportions of defectives. We, therefore, accept the null hypothesis or reserve judgment. ■

13.4

Differences Among k Proportions

There are also many problems in which we must decide whether observed differences among more than two sample proportions can be attributed to chance, or whether they are indicative of the fact that the corresponding population proportions are not all equal. For instance, if 26 of 200 brand A tires, 21 of 200 brand B tires, 17 of 200 brand C tires, and 34 of 200 brand D tires failed to last 30,000 miles, we may want to decide whether the differences among $\frac{26}{200} = 0.13$, $\frac{21}{200} = 0.105$, $\frac{17}{200} = 0.085$, and $\frac{34}{200} = 0.17$ are significant, or whether they may be due to chance.

To illustrate the method we use to analyze this kind of data, suppose that a survey in which independent random samples of 100 men, 130 women, and 90 children were asked whether or not they like the flavor of a new toothpaste, yielded the results shown in the following table:

	Men	Women	Children
Like the flavor	60	67	49
Do not like the flavor	40	63	41
Total	100	130	90

The proportions of persons who like the flavor are $\frac{100}{60} = 0.60$, $\frac{67}{130} = 0.52$, and $\frac{49}{90} = 0.54$ for the three groups, and we want to decide at the 0.05 level of significance whether the differences among them can be attributed to chance.

If we let p_1, p_2 and p_3 denote the true proportions of men, women, and children in the populations sampled who like the flavor, the null hypothesis we want to test is $p_1 = p_2 = p_3$ and the alternative hypothesis is that p_1, p_2, and p_3 are not all equal. If the null hypothesis is true, the three samples come from populations having a common proportion p, and we can combine the three samples and look at them as one sample from one population. Also, we can pool the data, as in the preceding section, and estimate the common proportion of persons who like the flavor to be

$$\frac{60 + 67 + 49}{100 + 130 + 90} = 0.55$$

With this estimate we would expect $100(0.55) = 55$ of the men, $130(0.55) = 71.5$ of the women, and $90(0.55) = 49.5$ of the children to like the flavor of the toothpaste. Subtracting these figures from the totals of their samples, we find that $100 - 55 = 45$ of the men, $130 - 71.5 = 58.5$ of the women, and $90 - 49.5 = 40.5$ of the children would be expected not to like the flavor.

These results are summarized in the following table, where the **expected frequencies** are shown in parentheses below the **observed frequencies**:

	Men	Women	Children
Like the flavor	60 (55)	67 (71.5)	49 (49.5)
Do not like the flavor	40 (45)	63 (58.5)	41 (40.5)

To test the null hypothesis that the p's are all equal in problems like this, we compare the frequencies which were actually observed with the frequencies we would expect if the null hypothesis were true. It stands to reason that the null hypothesis should be accepted if the discrepancies between the observed and the expected frequencies are small. On the other hand, if the discrepancies between the two sets of frequencies are large, the observed frequencies depart substantially from what we would expect to observe, and this suggests that the null hypothesis must be false.

Using the letter o for the observed frequencies and the letter e for the expected frequencies, we base their comparison on the following χ^2 (**chi-square**) **statistic**:

Statistic for test concerning differences among proportions

$$\chi^2 = \sum \frac{(o - e)^2}{e}$$

In words, χ^2 is the sum of the quantities obtained by dividing $(o - e)^2$ by e separately for each **cell** of the table, and for our example we get

$$\chi^2 = \frac{(60 - 55)^2}{55} + \frac{(67 - 71.5)^2}{71.5} + \frac{(49 - 49.5)^2}{49.5} + \frac{(40 - 45)^2}{45}$$
$$+ \frac{(63 - 58.5)^2}{58.5} + \frac{(41 - 40.5)^2}{40.5}$$
$$= 1.65$$

It remains to be seen whether this value is large enough to reject the null hypothesis $p_1 = p_2 = p_3$.

If the null hypothesis that the p's are all equal is true, the sampling distribution of the χ^2 statistic is approximately the chi-square distribution.

Since the null hypothesis will be rejected only when the value obtained for χ^2 is too large to be accounted for by chance, we base our decision on the criterion shown in Figure 13.4, where χ_α^2 is such that the area under the chi-square distribution to its right equals α. The parameter of the chi-square distribution, the number of degrees of freedom, equals $k - 1$ when we compare k sample proportions. Intuitively, we can justify this formula with the argument that once we have calculated $k - 1$ of the expected frequencies in either row of the table, all of the other expected frequencies can be obtained by subtraction from the totals of the rows and columns (see Exercise 13.43 and also the discussion on page 500).

Returning to our illustration, we find that $\chi^2 = 1.65$ does not exceed 5.991, the value of $\chi_{0.05}^2$ for $3 - 1 = 2$ degrees of freedom. Consequently, we either reserve judgment or we accept the hypothesis that equal proportions of men, women, and children like the flavor of the new toothpaste. If there are, in fact, differences among the true proportions for the three groups, we have scanty evidence of it at the 0.05 level of significance.

In general, if we want to compare k sample proportions, we first combine the data and get the following estimate of p:

Estimate of common population proportion

$$\frac{x_1 + x_2 + \cdots + x_k}{n_1 + n_2 + \cdots + n_k}$$

where the n's are the sample sizes, and the x's the numbers of successes, in the k samples. We then multiply the n's by this estimate of p to get the expected frequencies for the first row of the table; after that we subtract these values from the totals of the corresponding samples to get the expected frequencies for the second row of the table. We can also get the expected

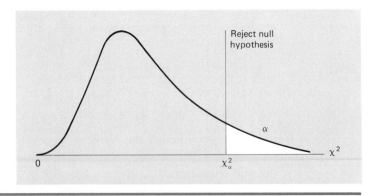

FIGURE 13.4
Test criterion

Chapter 13   Decision Making: Inferences About Proportions

frequency for any one of the cells by multiplying the total of the column to which it belongs by the total of the row to which it belongs, and dividing by the **grand total**, $n_1 + n_2 + \cdots + n_k$, for the entire table (see also page 499).

Next, we calculate χ^2 as just defined, with $\dfrac{(o - e)^2}{e}$ determined separately for each of the $2k$ cells of the table, and reject the null hypothesis $p_1 = p_2 = \cdots = p_k$ if this value of χ^2 exceeds χ^2_α for $k - 1$ degrees of freedom.

EXAMPLE 13.9 The president of a large corporation plans to increase the compensation of the firm's employees and wants to know whether the employees would prefer their increase to be primarily in the form of monetary compensation or principally in an employee benefits package such as a retirement plan, health insurance, life insurance, vacation time, and child care. Independent random samples were taken (within the firm) of 180 production workers, 110 general and administrative employees, 60 executive and managerial personnel, and 50 salespersons which yield the results shown in the following table.

	Production	General and administrative	Managerial and executive	Salespersons	
Monetary compensation	95	60	30	23	208
Employee benefits	85	50	30	27	192
Total	180	110	60	50	400

Test at the 0.01 level of significance whether the differences among the sample proportions of employees who chose monetary compensation, $\dfrac{95}{180} = 0.53$, $\dfrac{60}{110} = 0.54$, $\dfrac{30}{60} = 0.50$, and $\dfrac{23}{50} = 0.46$, respectively, are significant.

SOLUTION
1. H_0: $p_1 = p_2 = p_3 = p_4$.
   H_A: p_1, p_2, p_3, and p_4 are not all equal.
2. $\alpha = 0.01$.
3. Reject the null hypothesis if $\chi^2 \geq 11.345$ where

$$\chi^2 = \sum \frac{(o - e)^2}{e}$$

and 11.345 is the value of $\chi^2_{0.01}$ for $k - 1 = 4 - 1 = 3$ degrees of freedom; otherwise, accept the null hypothesis or reserve judgment.

4. Since the total for the first row *(Monetary compensation)* is $95 + 60 + 30 + 23 = 208$ we get expected frequencies of
$$\frac{208 \cdot 180}{400} = 93.6, \quad \frac{208 \cdot 110}{400} = 57.2, \quad \frac{208 \cdot 60}{400} = 31.2 \text{ for}$$
the first three cells of the first row of the table. Then by subtraction we get $208 - 93.6 - 57.2 - 31.2 = 26.0$ for the fourth cell of the first row. Then, by subtracting these first row expected frequencies from their column totals, we get second row *(Employee benefits)* expected values of $180 - 93.6 = 86.4$, $110 - 57.2 = 52.8$, $60 - 31.2 = 28.8$, and $50 - 26.0 = 24.0$ for the four cells of the second row. The results are summarized in the following table.

	Production	General and administrative	Managerial and executive	Salespersons	
Monetary compensation	95 (93.6)	60 (57.2)	30 (31.2)	23 (26.0)	208
Employee benefits	85 (86.4)	50 (52.8)	30 (28.8)	27 (24.0)	192
Total	180	110	60	50	400

Finally, substituting the expected frequencies together with the observed frequencies into the formula for χ^2, we get

$$\chi^2 = \frac{(95 - 93.6)^2}{93.6} + \frac{(60 - 57.2)^2}{57.2} + \frac{(30 - 31.2)^2}{31.2}$$
$$+ \frac{(23 - 26.0)^2}{26.0} + \frac{(85 - 86.4)^2}{86.4} + \frac{(50 - 52.8)^2}{52.8}$$
$$+ \frac{(30 - 28.8)^2}{28.8} + \frac{(27 - 24.0)^2}{24.0} = 1.15$$

5. Since $\chi^2 = 1.15$ is less than 11.345, the null hypothesis cannot be rejected. There are no significant differences among the employee groups at the 0.01 level of significance. Accept the null hypothesis or reserve judgment. ∎

When we calculate the expected frequencies, we usually round them to the nearest integer or to one decimal. The entries in Table III are given to three decimals, but there is seldom any need to carry more than two decimals in calculating the value of the χ^2 statistic, itself. Also, the test we have been discussing is an approximate test which should not be used when one (or more) of the expected frequencies is less than 5. If this is the case, we can sometimes combine some of the samples in such a way that none of the e's is less than 5.

It is of interest to note that for $k = 2$ the χ^2 statistic of this section actually equals the square of the z statistic of Section 13.3 (see Exercises 13.36 and 13.38 that follow). Thus, for $k = 2$ the two tests are equivalent so long as the alternative hypothesis is $p_1 \neq p_2$; when the alternative hypothesis is $p_1 < p_2$ or $p_1 > p_2$, the method of this section cannot be used.

EXERCISES

(Exercise 13.32, 13.35, and 13.39 are practice exercises. Their complete solutions are given on page 518.)

13.32 A large corporation conducted a study of employee turnover in which 84 employees out of a random sample of 300 newly hired employees in New York left during the first year. In a similar study made by the firm's Los Angeles plant, 32 employees out of a random sample of 100 new employees left during the first year. Use the level of significance $\alpha = 0.05$ to test whether the difference between the two sample proportions of employee turnover is significant.

13.33 A credit bureau conducts an analysis of 500 randomly selected time payment accounts of persons residing in the town of Weston and finds that 45 of them were delinquent at one time or another. A similar study conducted in the town of Easton, where 600 randomly selected accounts were analyzed, finds 36 of the accounts were delinquent at one time or another. Use the level of significance $\alpha = 0.05$ to determine whether the proportion of delinquencies in Weston is higher than that of Easton.

13.34 The following table shows the results of a survey in which random samples of members of two large labor unions were asked whether they were for or against a certain piece of legislation.

	Union A	Union B
For the legislation	980	875
Against the legislation	510	328

Determine at the 0.01 level of significance whether or not a higher proportion of Union A members favor the legislation.

13.35 A commercial greenhouse wants to test the effectiveness of alternative fertilizers on plant growth. One sample of 400 plants is treated with brand A fertilizer and another 400-plant sample is treated with brand B fertilizer. Of the 400 plants treated with brand A, 350 bloom within two weeks, and of the 400 plants treated with brand B, only 210 bloom within two weeks. Based on the method of Section 13.3, can it be concluded at the 0.05 level of significance that the two brands are not equally effective?

13.36 Rework the preceding exercise using the method of Section 13.4 and verify that the value of the χ^2 statistic equals the square of the value of the z statistic.

13.37 In random samples of homes in the communities of Northboro and Southboro, 96 of 300 Northboro homes had electrical garbage disposal units and 162 of 300 Southboro homes had electrical garbage disposal units. Use the method of Section 13.3 and the level of significance $\alpha = 0.01$ to test the null hypothesis $p_1 = p_2$ against the alternative hypothesis $p_1 \neq p_2$.

13.38 Rework the preceding exercise using the method of Section 13.4, and verify that the value obtained for the χ^2 statistic equals the square of the value obtained for the z statistic.

13.39 The following table shows the results of a survey in which randomly selected chief executive officers of major corporations predicted that the profits of their firms would increase during the coming year. At the 0.01 level of significance, are the differences among the sample proportions significant?

	New York	Chicago	Los Angeles	Houston	
Increase profits	139	91	73	117	420
No increase in profits	161	109	77	133	480
Total	300	200	150	250	900

13.40 In an analysis of the production process of a factory, samples of size 100, 150, and 75 of the units produced were taken from a large volume of production. The number of defectives in the samples were 12, 19, and 6, respectively, and all this information is summarized in the following table.

	Sample 1	Sample 2	Sample 3	
Defective	12	19	6	37
Not defective	88	131	69	288
Total	100	150	75	325

Use the level of significance $\alpha = 0.05$ to test the null hypothesis that there are no differences in the population proportions.

13.41 The following table shows that among 100 investment company stock analysts who are surveyed in each of five parts of the United States there are 47, 45, 54, 49, and 40 who predict that stock prices will advance next month.

	Part 1	Part 2	Part 3	Part 4	Part 5	
Prices will advance	47	45	54	49	40	235
Prices will not advance	53	55	46	51	60	265
Total	100	100	100	100	100	500

At the 0.05 level of significance, are differences among the corresponding sample proportions significant?

13.42 Following are the results of a survey in which randomly selected voters in the Middle Atlantic states were asked whether they favored the foreign policy of the president of the United States

	New Jersey	Pennsylvania	New York	
Favor	930	1,305	1,530	3,765
Do not favor	570	795	870	2,235
Total	1,500	2,100	2,400	6,000

Use the level of significance $\alpha = 0.05$ to test the null hypothesis that there are no differences among the population proportions.

13.43 Make use of the fact that the expected numbers of successes for the k samples are obtained by multiplying $\dfrac{x_1 + x_2 + \cdots + x_k}{n_1 + n_2 + \cdots + n_k}$, respectively, by $n_1, n_2, \ldots,$ and n_k, to show that the sum of the expected numbers of successes for the k samples equals the sum of the observed numbers of successes.

13.5

Contingency Tables

The χ^2 statistic plays an important role in many other problems where information is obtained by counting or enumerating rather than measuring. The method we shall describe here for analyzing such **count data** is an extension of the method of the preceding section, and it applies to two distinct kinds of problems which differ conceptually but are analyzed in the same way.

In the first kind of problem we deal with trials permitting more than two possible outcomes. For instance, in the illustration of the preceding section each person might have been asked whether he or she likes the flavor of the new toothpaste, dislikes it, or is indifferent to it, and this might have resulted in the following table:

	Men	Women	Children	
Like the flavor	52	56	45	153
Indifferent	15	23	11	49
Do not like the flavor	33	51	34	118
Total	100	130	90	320

We refer to this kind of table as a 3×3 table, because it contains three rows and three columns; more generally, when there are c samples and each trial permits r alternatives, we refer to the resulting table as an **r × c table** (where $r \times c$ is read "r by c"). Here, as in the example of the preceding section, the column totals (the sizes of the different samples) are fixed. On the other hand, the row totals ($52 + 56 + 45 = 153$, $15 + 23 + 11 = 49$, and $33 + 51 + 34 = 118$) depend on the responses of the persons interviewed, and hence, on chance.

In the second kind of problem, the column totals as well as the row totals are left to chance; in other words; they are contingent on circumstances beyond our control. Suppose, for instance, that we want to investigate whether there really is a relationship between a man's performance in a company training program and his ultimate success in the job. Suppose, furthermore, that a random sample of 400 cases taken from the company's very extensive files of employees who completed the program, yielded the results shown in the following table:

		Performance in training program			
		Below average	Average	Above average	
	Poor	23	60	29	112
Success in job (employer's rating)	Average	28	79	60	167
	Very good	9	49	63	121
	Total	60	188	152	400

This is also a 3 × 3 table, and it is mainly in connection with problems like this that $r \times c$ tables are referred to as **contingency tables**.

Before we demonstrate how $r \times c$ tables are analyzed, let us examine the null hypotheses we want to test. In the problem dealing with the flavor of the toothpaste, we want to test the null hypothesis that the probabilities of getting a favorable reaction, indifference, or an unfavorable reaction are the same for each group. In other words, we want to test the null hypothesis that a person's reaction to the flavor of the toothpaste is independent of his or her being a man, woman, or child. In the problem directly preceding, we are also concerned with a null hypothesis of **independence**; specifically, the null hypothesis that employees' success in their jobs is independent of their performance in the training program.

To illustrate the analysis of an $r \times c$ table, let us refer to the second example and begin by calculating the **expected cell frequencies**. If the null hypothesis of independence is true, the probability of randomly selecting an employee whose performance in the program was below average and who is doing poorly in his job is given by the product of the probability that his performance in the program was below average and the probability that he is doing poorly in his job. Using the totals of the first column and the first row to estimate these two probabilities, we get $\dfrac{23 + 28 + 9}{400} = \dfrac{60}{400}$ for the probability that an employee (randomly selected from among the employees who completed the training program) performed below average in the program, and $\dfrac{23 + 60 + 29}{400} = \dfrac{112}{400}$ for the probability that he is doing poorly in his job. Hence, we estimate the probability of choosing an employee whose performance was below average in the program and who is doing poorly in his job to be $\dfrac{60}{400} \cdot \dfrac{112}{400}$, and in a sample of size 400 we would expect to find

$$400 \cdot \frac{60}{400} \cdot \frac{112}{400} = \frac{60 \cdot 112}{400} = 16.8$$

employees who fit this description.

In this last result, $\dfrac{60 \cdot 112}{400}$ is just the product of the total of the first column and the total of the first row divided by the grand total for the entire table. In general,

> The expected frequency for any cell of a contingency table may be obtained by multiplying the total of the column to which it belongs by the total of the row to which it belongs and then dividing by the grand total for the whole table.

With this rule we get an expected frequency of $\dfrac{188 \cdot 112}{400} = 52.6$ for the second cell of the first row and $\dfrac{60 \cdot 167}{400} = 25.0$ and $\dfrac{188 \cdot 167}{400} = 78.5$ for the first two cells of the second row.

It is not necessary to calculate all the expected cell frequencies in this way, since it can be shown that the sum of the expected frequencies for any row or column must equal the sum of the corresponding observed frequencies. Therefore, we can get some of the expected cell frequencies by subtraction from row and column totals. For instance, for our illustration we get by subtraction

$$112 - 16.8 - 52.6 = 42.6$$

for the third cell of the first row,

$$167 - 25.0 - 78.5 = 63.5$$

for the third cell of the second row, and

$$60 - 16.8 - 25.0 = 18.2$$
$$188 - 52.6 - 78.5 = 56.9$$

and

$$152 - 42.6 - 63.5 = 45.9$$

for the three cells of the third row. These results are summarized in the following table, where the expected frequencies are shown in parentheses below the corresponding observed frequencies:

| | | Performance in training program | | |
		Below average	Average	Above average
	Poor	23 (16.8)	60 (52.6)	29 (42.6)
Success in job (employer's rating)	Average	28 (25.0)	79 (78.5)	60 (63.5)
	Very good	9 (18.2)	49 (56.9)	63 (45.9)

From here on the work is like that of the preceding section; we calculate the χ^2 statistic according to the formula

$$\chi^2 = \sum \frac{(o - e)^2}{e}$$

with $\frac{(o - e)^2}{e}$ calculated separately for each cell of the table. Then we reject the null hypothesis of independence at the level of significance α if the value obtained for χ^2 exceeds the value of χ_α^2 for $(r - 1)(c - 1)$ degrees of freedom, where r is the number of rows and c the number of columns. In our example the number of degrees of freedom is $(3 - 1)(3 - 1) = 4$, and it should be observed that after we had calculated four of the expected cell frequencies, we got all the others by subtraction from the totals of appropriate rows and columns.

EXAMPLE 13.10   Returning to the illustration on page 501, test at the 0.01 level of significance whether success of persons in the job is independent of their performance in the training program.

SOLUTION   **1.** H_0: Performance in the training program and success in the job are independent.

H_A: Performance in the training program and success in the job are not independent.

2. $\alpha = 0.01$.

3. Reject the null hypothesis if $\chi^2 \geq 13.277$ where

$$\chi^2 = \Sigma \frac{(o - e)^2}{e}$$

and 13.277 is the value of $\chi^2_{0.01}$ for $(3 - 1)(3 - 1) = 4$ degrees of freedom; otherwise, accept the null hypothesis or reserve judgment

4. Calculate the expected frequencies and insert in the table as shown on page 501. Then, substituting the observed and expected frequencies from this table into the formula for χ^2 we get

$$\chi^2 = \frac{(23 - 16.8)^2}{16.8} + \frac{(60 - 52.6)^2}{52.6} + \frac{(29 - 42.6)^2}{42.6}$$
$$+ \frac{(28 - 25.0)^2}{25.0} + \frac{(79 - 78.5)^2}{78.5} + \frac{(60 - 63.5)^2}{63.5}$$
$$+ \frac{(9 - 18.2)^2}{18.2} + \frac{(49 - 56.9)^2}{56.9} + \frac{(63 - 45.9)^2}{45.9}$$
$$= 20.34$$

5. Since $\chi^2 = 20.34$ exceeds 13.277 the null hypothesis must be rejected. We have shown that at the 0.01 level of significance, there is a dependence (or relationship) between an employee's performance in the training program and his or her success on the job.   ■

A computer printout of the preceding chi-square analysis is shown in Figure 13.5. The difference between the values of chi-square obtained earlier and in Figure 13.5 is due to rounding.

The MINITAB solution, Figure 13.5, shows the observed frequencies and expected frequencies in the same physical arrangement of columns and rows as those in our manually prepared solution. The computer solution

```
MTB > READ C1 C2 C3
DATA> 23 60 29
DATA> 28 79 60
DATA> 9 49 63
MTB > CHIS C1 C2 C3

Expected counts are printed below observed counts

                C1        C2        C3     Total
         1      23        60        29      112
              16.8      52.6      42.6

         2      28        79        60      167
              25.0      78.5      63.5

         3       9        49        63      121
              18.1      56.9      46.0

     Total      60       188       152      400

   ChiSq =    2.29 +    1.03 +    4.32 +
              0.35 +    0.00 +    0.19 +
              4.61 +    1.09 +    6.30 =  20.18
   df = 4
```

FIGURE 13.5
Computer printout
for analysis of
contingency table

substitutes C1, C2, and C3, replacing our captions Below average, Average, and Above average. The numerals 1, 2, and 3 replace the titles of our rows, Poor, Average, and Very good. Chi-square is calculated in abbreviated form. The *P*-value is shown by some computer programs but is not provided here or in our Table III, values of χ^2.

The method we have used here to analyze the contingency table applies also when the column totals are fixed sample sizes (as in the toothpaste problem) and do not depend on chance. The rule by which we multiply the row total by the column total and then divide by the grand total must be justified in a different way, but this is of no consequence—the expected cell frequencies are determined in exactly the same way (see Exercise 13.52 on page 511 and the following example.)

Example 13.11 illustrates analysis of a contingency table where column totals are fixed sample sizes.

EXAMPLE 13.11   Following are three random samples of salespersons in a large tele-marketing company which are classified by age and sales performance. All sample sizes are fixed at *n* = 60. Test at the 0.05 level of significance whether the sales performance of these persons is independent of their ages.

	Youthful	*Middle age*	*Senior*	
Highest quarter of sales performance	13	17	18	48
Middle half of sales performance	31	30	28	89
Lowest quarter of sales performance	16	13	14	43
Total	60	60	60	180

SOLUTION

1. H_0: Age and sales performance are independent (unrelated).
   H_A: Age and sales performance are not independent (related).

2. $\alpha = 0.05$

3. Reject the null hypothesis if $\chi^2 \geq 9.488$ where

$$\chi^2 = \Sigma \frac{(o - e)^2}{e}$$

and 9.488 is the value of $\chi^2_{0.05}$ for $(3 - 1)(3 - 1) = 4$ degrees of freedom; otherwise, accept the null hypothesis or reserve judgment.

4. Since the total for the first row is $13 + 17 + 18 = 48$, we get expected frequencies of $\frac{48 \cdot 60}{180} = 16.0$ for cell 1, cell 2, and cell 3 of the first row. Since the total for the second row is $31 + 30 + 28 = 89$, we get expected frequencies of $\frac{89 \cdot 60}{180} = 29.7$ for cell 1, cell 2, and cell 3 of the second row. Then, by subtraction, we get $60 - 16.0 - 29.7 = 14.3$ for cell 1, cell 2, and cell 3 of the third row. The observed and expected values are summarized in the following table.

	Youthful	*Middle age*	*Senior*	
Highest quarter of sales performance	13 (16.0)	17 (16.0)	18 (16.0)	48
Middle half of sales performance	31 (29.7)	30 (29.7)	28 (29.7)	89
Lowest quarter of sales performance	16 (14.3)	13 (14.3)	14 (14.3)	43
Total	60	60	60	180

504

Finally, substituting the expected values together with the observed values into the formula for χ^2, we get

$$\chi^2 = \frac{(13 - 16.0)^2}{16.0} + \frac{(17 - 16.0)^2}{16.0} + \frac{(18 - 16.0)^2}{16.0}$$
$$+ \frac{(31 - 29.7)^2}{29.7} + \frac{(30 - 29.7)^2}{29.7} + \frac{(28 - 29.7)^2}{29.7}$$
$$+ \frac{(16 - 14.3)^2}{14.3} + \frac{(13 - 14.3)^2}{14.3} + \frac{(14 - 14.3)^2}{14.3}$$
$$= 1.36$$

5. Since $\chi^2 = 1.36$ does not exceed 9.488 the null hypothesis cannot be rejected; that is, we may conclude at the 0.05 level of significance that there is no relationship between age and sales performance in this telemarketing company. ∎

In Example 13.11 we intentionally sampled a fixed number of persons from each of three age groups, relating them to their sales performances. We, therefore, tested whether these three populations are homogeneous as well as independent. The null hypothesis could therefore have been stated as H_0: The three proportions are homogeneous in their sales performances. This differs from Example 13.9 where we sampled a total of 400 persons and had no way of knowing in advance the number of observations in each column and in each row. Aside from this difference, as previously stated, the expected frequencies are determined in exactly the same way.

Since the χ^2 statistic we are using here has only approximately a chi-square distribution, it should not be used in cases where any of the expected cell frequencies are less than 5. When there are expected frequencies smaller than 5, it is often possible to combine some of the cells, subtract 1 degree of freedom for each cell eliminated, and then perform the test just as it has been described.

13.6

Goodness of Fit

In this section we shall treat a further application of the χ^2 criterion, in which we compare an observed frequency distribution with a distribution we might expect according to theory or assumptions. We refer to such a comparison as a test of **goodness of fit**.

To illustrate, let us consider Table XII, the table of random digits, which is supposed to have been constructed in such a way that each digit is a value of a random variable which takes on the values 0, 1, 2, 3, 4, 5, 6, 7, 8, and 9 with equal probabilities of 0.10. To determine whether it is reasonable to conclude that this is, indeed, the case, we might count how many times each digit appears in the table, or part of the table; specifically, we shall take the 250 digits in the first five columns on page 874. This yields the values shown in the "Observed frequency" column of the following table:

Digit	Probability	Observed frequency o	Expected frequency e
0	0.10	23	25
1	0.10	25	25
2	0.10	20	25
3	0.10	23	25
4	0.10	23	25
5	0.10	22	25
6	0.10	29	25
7	0.10	25	25
8	0.10	33	25
9	0.10	27	25

We got the expected frequencies in the right-hand column by multiplying each of the probabilities of 0.10 by 250, the total number of digits counted.

To test whether the discrepancies between the observed and expected frequencies can be attributed to chance, we use the same chi-square statistic as in the two preceding sections.

Statistic for test of goodness of fit

$$\chi^2 = \sum \frac{(o - e)^2}{e}$$

calculating $\frac{(o - e)^2}{e}$ separately for each class of the distribution. Then, if the value we get for χ^2 exceeds χ_α^2, we reject the null hypothesis on which the expected frequencies are based at the level of significance α; the number

Chapter 13   Decision Making: Inferences About Proportions

of degrees of freedom is $k - m$, where k is the number of terms $\dfrac{(o - e)^2}{e}$ added in the formula for χ^2, and m is the number of quantities we must obtain from the observed data to calculate the expected frequencies.

EXAMPLE 13.12 Based on the observed frequencies given, test at the 0.05 level of significance whether there is any indication that the digits in Table XII, random numbers, may not be regarded as random

SOLUTION 1. H_0: The probability of each digit is 0.10.
   H_A: The probabilities are not all 0.10.

2. $\alpha = 0.05$.

3. Reject the null hypothesis on which the expected frequencies are based if $\chi^2 \geq 16.919$, where

$$\chi^2 = \Sigma \frac{(o - e)^2}{e}$$

and 16.919 is the value of $\chi^2_{0.05}$ for $k - m = 10 - 1 = 9$ degrees of freedom; otherwise, state that there is no indication that the digits in Table XII may not be regarded as random.

4. Substituting the observed and expected frequencies from the preceding table, we get

$$\chi^2 = \frac{(23 - 25)^2}{25} + \frac{(25 - 25)^2}{25} + \frac{(20 - 25)^2}{25} + \frac{(23 - 25)^2}{25}$$
$$+ \frac{(23 - 25)^2}{25} + \frac{(22 - 25)^2}{25} + \frac{(29 - 25)^2}{25} + \frac{(25 - 25)^2}{25}$$
$$+ \frac{(33 - 25)^2}{25} + \frac{(27 - 25)^2}{25} = 5.20$$

5. Since $\chi^2 = 5.20$ does not exceed 16.919, we find that the null hypothesis cannot be rejected. In other words there is no indication that the digits in Table XII may not be regarded as random. ∎

In the illustration dealing with random digits, we find that the null hypothesis cannot be rejected. In other words the table of random numbers has "passed the test." The number of degrees of freedom is nine because there are 10 terms, $\dfrac{(o - e)^2}{e}$, in the formula for χ^2, and the only quantity needed from the observed data to calculate the expected frequencies is the total frequency of 250.

```
MTB > SET EXPECTED NUMBERS INTO C1
DATA> 25 25 25 25 25 25 25 25 25 25
MTB > SET OBSERVED NUMBERS INTO C2
DATA> 23 25 20 23 23 22 29 25 33 27
MTB > SUBTRACT C1 FROM C2, PUT DIFFERENCES INTO C3
MTB > MULT C3 BY C3, PUT IN C4
MTB > DIVIDE C4 BY C1, PUT IN C5
MTB > SUM C5 (CHISQUARE)
   SUM       =       5.2000
MTB > PRINT C1-C5
   ROW     C1     C2     C3     C4     C5

    1      25     23     -2      4    0.16
    2      25     25      0      0    0.00
    3      25     20     -5     25    1.00
    4      25     23     -2      4    0.16
    5      25     23     -2      4    0.16
    6      25     22     -3      9    0.36
    7      25     29      4     16    0.64
    8      25     25      0      0    0.00
    9      25     33      8     64    2.56
   10      25     27      2      4    0.16
```

FIGURE 13.6
Computer printout for Example 13.12, test of goodness of fit

A computer printout of this test for goodness of fit is shown in Figure 13.6, and its chi-square, 5.20, agrees with the answer obtained in the preceding illustration.

The method we have illustrated in this section is used quite generally to test how well distributions we expect (on the basis of theory or assumptions) fit, or describe, observed data. In some of the exercises which follow, we shall test whether it is reasonable to treat an observed distribution as if it had (at least approximately) the shape of a normal distribution, and we shall also test whether given sets of data fit the pattern of binomial and Poisson distributions. As in the tests of the preceding sections, the sampling distribution of the χ^2 statistic is only approximately a chi-square distribution when it is used for tests of goodness of fit. So, if any of the expected frequencies is less than 5, we must again combine some of the data; in this case, we combine adjacent classes of the distribution.

EXERCISES

(Exercises 13.44, 13.46, 13.48, 13.54, and 13.58 are practice exercises. Their complete solutions are given on page 518.)

13.44 Determine the number of degrees of freedom in a contingency table having

(a) two rows and three columns

(b) three rows and three columns

(c) five rows and four columns

(d) four rows and five columns

13.45 Use Table III on page 857, values of χ^2, to obtain values of $\chi^2_{0.05}$ for parts (a), (b), (c), and (d) of the preceding exercise.

13.46 Use the incomplete contingency table provided to perform the following:

35 ( )	50 ( )	( )	105
60 ( )	55 ( )	( )	150
( )	( )	( )	
140	160		370

(a) Calculate the five missing observed values.

(b) Calculate the nine expected values.

(c) Calculate the value of χ^2 using the formula $\chi^2 = \sum \dfrac{(o - e)^2}{e}$.

13.47 Verify the computer printout (Figure 13.7) of the following 3×3 table and decide at the 0.05 level of significance whether the differences in the reactions to the flavor of the new toothpaste are significant.

Consumer Reaction to Flavor of New Toothpaste

	Men	*Women*	*Children*	
Like the flavor	52	56	45	153
Indifferent	15	23	11	49
Do not like the flavor	33	51	34	118
Total	100	130	90	320

13.48 A random sample of 350 inexpensive electronic toys which are produced in Hong Kong, Japan, and Korea are examined by an importer in the United States to determine the quality of the toys, with the following results

```
MTB > READ C1 C2 C3
DATA> 52 56 45
DATA> 15 23 11
DATA> 33 51 34
DATA> CHIS C1 C2 C3
      3 ROWS READ

Expected counts are printed below observed counts

              C1        C2        C3     Total
     1        52        56        45       153
            47.8      62.2      43.0

     2        15        23        11        49
            15.3      19.9      13.8

     3        33        51        34       118
            36.9      47.9      33.2

Total        100       130        90       320

ChiSq =    0.37 +    0.61 +    0.09 +
           0.01 +    0.48 +    0.56 +
           0.41 +    0.20 +    0.02 = 2.74
df = 4
```

FIGURE 13.7
Computer printout
for Exercise 13.47,
3×3 table

Geographical Location

	Hong Kong	Japan	Korea
Acceptable	104	64	79
Imperfect, but salable	29	17	24
Defective	16	10	7

Test at the level of significance $\alpha = 0.01$ whether geographical location of the producer and quality of the toys are independent (no relationship).

13.49 A random sample of 900 household incomes was drawn from four communities by a marketing research company. The results are in number of households.

	Wellshire	Xenton	Yorkville	Zenburg
High income	29	43	49	11
Middle income	123	143	207	82
Low income	48	64	89	12

Chapter 13   Decision Making: Inferences About Proportions

Test at the level of significance $\alpha = 0.05$ whether the communities of residence and levels of income are independent (no relationship).

13.50 The manager of a large hotel wants to know whether the hotel's convention facilities satisfy the needs of small-, medium-, and large-sized conventions. A random sample of 400 convention guests was sampled with the following results.

	Convention Size		
	Small	Medium	Large
Excellent	28	103	100
Adequate	24	56	35
Inadequate	12	27	15

Use the 0.01 level of significance to test the null hypothesis that there is no real relationship between the adequacy of the facilities and the size of the conventions.

13.51 A large national union wants to know the attitudes of its membership toward a proposed collective bargaining agreement, and a random sample of 450 members taken in four local unions yields the following opinions.

	Attitudes of membership		
	In favor	Opposed	Uncertain
Local No. 1	18	30	12
Local No. 2	71	89	20
Local No. 3	51	27	12
Local No. 4	59	42	19

At the 0.05 level of significance, is there a relationship between the attitudes of union members, and the local union to which they belong?

13.52 Use an argument similar to that on page 499 to show that the rule for calculating the expected cell frequencies (dividing the product of the column total and the row total by the grand total) applies also when the column totals are fixed sample sizes and do not depend on chance.

13.53 If the analysis of a contingency table shows that there is a relationship between the two variables under consideration, the strength of the relationship can be measured by the **contingency coefficient**

$$C = \sqrt{\frac{\chi^2}{\chi^2 + n}}$$

where n is the total frequency for the table. This coefficient assumes values between 0 (corresponding to independence) and a maximum value of less than 1 depending on the size of the table. For example, for a $k \times k$ table the maximum value of C is $\sqrt{(k-1)/k}$. The larger C is, the stronger is the relationship between the variables.

(a) What is the maximum value of C for a 3×3 table?

(b) Calculate C for a contingency table with $n = 300$ and $\chi^2 = 25.6$.

(c) Calculate C for the data of Exercise 13.51.

13.54 To determine whether a die is balanced, it is rolled 360 times. The following are the results: 1 showed 57 times, 2 showed 46 times, 3 showed 68 times, 4 showed 52 times, 5 showed 72 times, and 6 showed 65 times. At the 0.05 level of significance, can we reject the null hypothesis that the die is balanced?

13.55 Data collected over a 10-year period in a certain firm show that there were no industrial accidents in 60 months, one accident in 31 months, two accidents in 22 months, and three in 10 months. At the level of significance $\alpha = 0.05$, does this substantiate the claim that the probabilities of 0, 1, 2, or 3 accidents are 0.40, 0.30, 0.20, and 0.10?

13.56 A carbonated beverage manufacturing company produces 12-ounce cans of cola which are marketed in six-packs (six cans to the package). Due to a systematic error in the filling equipment, it is suspected that half the cans may have been defectively filled and contain less than the specified amount of cola. A random sample of 100 six-packs of cola was inspected, and the number of defectively filled cans per six-pack were as follows.

Defective cans per six-pack	Number of six-packs
0	2
1	15
2	21
3	31
4	20
5	8
6	3

At the 0.05 level of significance, does it appear that the data may be looked on as values of a random variable having the binomial distribution $p = 0.50$ and $n = 6$.

13.57 Following is a distribution of the number of minutes spent in a university computer center by a random sample of 200 students:

Minutes spent in computer center	Number of students
20–39	16
40–59	56
60–79	72
80–99	48
100–119	8

The mean and standard deviation of these times, calculated before they were grouped, are $\bar{x} = 67.1$ minutes and $s = 19.9$ minutes.

(a) Find the area under a normal curve with $\mu = 67.1$ and $\sigma = 19.9$ which lies between 19.5 and 39.5, between 39.5 and 59.5, between 59.5 and 79.5, between 79.5 and 99.5, and between 99.5 and 119.5.

(b) Calculate the expected normal-curve frequencies for the five classes of the distribution by multiplying each of the areas found in part (a) by 200.

(c) Test, at the 0.05 level of significance, the null hypothesis that this sample might reasonably have come from a population having approximately the shape of a normal distribution. In making the χ^2 test of the goodness of fit of a normal distribution, the number of degrees of freedom is $k - 3$, where k is the number of classes, and 3 degrees of freedom are lost since the sums of the expected and observed frequencies must agree and the mean and standard deviation of the normal curve had to be estimated from the data.

13.58 Following is the distribution of the number of credit applications received by a furniture store in 300 business days:

Number of credit applications	Frequency (number of days)
0	12
1	60
2	87
3	80
4	40
5	15
6	6

Test at the 0.01 level of significance the hypothesis that the underlying distribution from which this sample came is a Poisson distribution with the parameter $\lambda = 2.5$.

13.7

Checklist of Key Terms

Cell,   491
Chi-square statistic,   491
Contingency coefficient,   511
Contingency table,   499
Count data,   498
Expected cell frequencies,   499
Goodness of fit,   505
Grand total,   493
Independence,   499

Large sample confidence interval
   for p, 473
Observed cell frequencies,   491
$r \times c$ table,   498
Sample proportion,   472
Standard error of a proportion,   473
Standard error of difference
   between two proportions,   488

13.8

Review Exercises

13.59 Three coins are tossed 120 times, and 0, 1, 2, and 3 heads showed 12, 47, 43, and 18 times. At the 0.05 level of significance, is it reasonable to suppose that the coins are balanced?

13.60 A random sample of 250 persons who are now assigned to temporary positions by a temporary employment company shows that 220 of these persons again intend to obtain temporary positions through this firm.

(a) Construct a 95 percent confidence interval for the true proportion of persons who again intend to obtain temporary positions through this firm.

(b) If we use the sample proportion $\frac{220}{250} = 0.88$ to estimate the true proportion, what can we say with 99 percent confidence about the size of our error?

13.61 A major fast-food franchising company has asked all its franchisees to adopt a uniform accounting system. To determine the extent of compliance by the franchisees, the southwestern U.S. regional manager takes a random sample of 50 franchisees in each state from a large number of franchisees in Arizona, New Mexico, Oklahoma, and Texas. If 32 of the franchisees in Arizona, 27 of the franchisees in New Mexico, 35 of the franchisees in Oklahoma, and 36 of the franchisees in Texas have adopted the uniform accounting system, test at the 0.05 level of significance whether the differences among the corresponding sample proportions are real.

13.62 A used car dealer claims that at least 90 percent of the cars which he sells are stored in his used car lot for 25 days or more before being sold. If, in a random sample, 10 of 14 used cars which were sold had to be stored this long, what can we conclude about his claim at the 0.05 level of significance?

13.63 The city council wants to determine what proportion of voters in the city would be opposed to increasing the salary of the mayor. How large a sample is required in order to be able to assert with a probability of at least 0.95 that the sample proportion will be off by less than 0.02?

13.64 With reference to the preceding exercise, how large a sample would be required if the population proportion is presumed to be at most 0.40?

13.65 The director of a charitable organization feels that at least 5 percent of its pledges (promises to pay made by contributors) are never paid. What can we conclude about this claim at the level of significance $\alpha = 0.01$ if a random sample of 500 pledges includes 15 who did not pay?

13.66 A random sample of statements presented to guests for payment at a large hotel showed that 180 out of 300 statements had been paid by credit card. Construct a 99 percent confidence interval for the actual percentage of statements paid at this hotel by credit card.

13.67 A survey of 200 randomly selected stockholders in Boston finds that 94 believe that stock prices will soon decrease, and a random sample of 800 stockholders in New York finds that 230 also believe that stock prices will soon decrease. Use the z statistic to test at the 0.01 level of significance whether there is a real difference between the proportions of stockholders, in the two populations sampled, who believe that stock prices will soon decrease.

13.68 Use the χ^2 statistic to rework the preceding exercise, and verify that the value obtained for the χ^2 statistic equals the square of the value obtained for the z statistic.

13.69 The following table shows how random samples of 50 clerical employees at each of three large corporate offices replied to a question of whether they would continue to work there if comparable employment were available elsewhere

	Office 1	Office 2	Office 3	
Yes	42	34	33	109
No	8	16	17	41
Total	50	50	50	150

Test at the 0.05 level of significance whether the differences among the corresponding proportion of *Yes* answers are significant.

13.70 In a random sample of 300 students at a large urban university, 204 stated that they usually commute to the university by public transportation. Can it be concluded at the 0.05 level that, at most, 65 percent of all students at this university usually commute to the university by public transportation?

13.71 Based on the results of 13 random trials, we want to test the null hypothesis $p = 0.20$ against the alternative hypothesis $p > 0.20$ at the 0.05 level of significance. For what numbers of successes must the null hypothesis be rejected? What is the actual level of significance?

13.72 A *Wall Street Journal*/NBC News poll asked 1,573 adults across the United States the question, ''Do you think the United States should limit imports from the following countries to protect American industry?'' The results are shown in the following table:

	Country		
	Japan	*Mexico*	*Canada*
Limit	1,101	755	582
Not limit	409	676	818
Not sure	63	142	173

Test at the 0.05 level of significance whether the differences in responses concerning Japan, Mexico, and Canada are significant.

13.73 A random sample of 100 automobile emissions tests made by an inspection station showed that 15 automobiles failed the test, while a random sample of 150 automobile exhaust emissions tests made by another inspection station showed that 27 failed the test. Can the null hypothesis $p_1 = p_2$ be rejected against the alternative hypothesis $p_1 < p_2$ at the 0.01 level of significance?

13.74 A study was conducted to test the safety of small bridges in New England which were constructed prior to 1960. Out of a sample of 800 bridges inspected, 480 were found to be below safety standards. If we use $\frac{480}{800} = 0.60$ as an estimate of the true proportion of small bridges in New England that do not meet safety standards, what can we say with 99 percent confidence about the possible size of our error?

13.75 The following table shows the number of daily charters per week made by a yacht captain based in Miami, whose yacht is available for charter 7 days a week, 52 weeks per year.

Number of daily charters per week	Number of weeks
2 or fewer	3
3	12
4	15
5	16
6 or more	6

Use the 0.05 level of significance to test the null hypothesis that the yacht is chartered 60 percent of the time, namely, the number of times the yacht is chartered per week is a random variable having the binomial distribution with $n = 7$ (days per week) and $p = 0.60$.

13.76 In order to determine the degree of compliance with the company's standards for disposal of used motor oil, a national corporation sampled 300 of its service stations in various parts of the country. The results are shown in the following table.

Compliance with used motor oil disposal standards

	Exceeds standards	Meets standards	Below standards
Eastern stations	15	48	28
Midwestern stations	20	56	25
Western stations	23	51	34

Can we conclude at the 0.01 level of significance that a relationship exists between the degree of compliance with used motor oil disposal standards and the geographical location of the service stations?

13.77 In a random sample of 320 car owners who reported car nonstart problems caused, they admitted, by owner neglect, 160 reported that their negligence consisted of leaving their headlights on and running their batteries down.

(a) Verify that $0.445 < p < 0.555$ is a 95 percent confidence interval for the actual proportion of such owners in the population sampled.

(b) Verify that

$$0.50 - 1.75(0.028) < p < 0.50 + 2.33(0.028)$$
$$0.451 < p < 0.565$$

is an alternative 95 percent confidence interval for the same parameter.

(c) Explain in what way the (symmetric) confidence interval of part (a) is preferable to that of part (b).

13.78 In evaluating the acoustical characteristics of a factory production line, a random sample of 50 workers was drawn from among 395 workers, and 38 felt that the noise level was excessive. Construct a 90 percent confidence interval for the corresponding proportion of all the workers in the factory who feel this way. (Hint: Refer to the finite population factor explained in Exercise 13.15.)

13.79 Use a computer package to verify Example 13.9 on page 493 concerning employee preferences for monetary compensation versus an employee benefits package.

13.80 Use a computer package to rework Exercise 13.39 on page 496 concerning the profit predictions of chief executive officers in four cities.

13.81 Use a computer printout to verify Example 13.11 on page 503 concerning whether the sales performance of salespersons in a telemarketing company is independent of their ages.

13.82 Use the data of Figure 13.6 on page 508, computer printout for a test of goodness of fit, to test at the 0.01 level of significance whether there is any indication that the digits in Table XII, random numbers, may not be regarded as random.

13.83 Use a computer package to rework Exercise 13.72 on page 516 relating to *The Wall Street Journal* news poll about limitation of imports from Japan, Mexico, and Canada.

13.84 Use a computer package to rework Exercise 13.76 on page 517 concerning compliance with used motor oil standards by automobile service stations in three regions.

13.9

Solutions of Practice Exercises

13.1 Substituting $n = 500$ and $\dfrac{x}{n} = \dfrac{95}{500} = 0.19$ into the formula for large sample confidence interval for p, we get $0.19 - 2.575 \sqrt{\dfrac{(0.19)(1 - 0.19)}{500}} < p < 0.19 + 2.575 \sqrt{\dfrac{(0.19)(1 - 0.19)}{500}}$, $0.19 - 0.04 < p < 0.19 + 0.04$, and $0.15 < p < 0.23$.

13.6 Substituting $n = 600$, $\dfrac{x}{n} = \dfrac{475}{600} = 0.79$, and $z_{\alpha/2} = 1.645$ into the formula for the maximum error of estimate we get, with 90 percent confidence, error is less than $E = 1.645 \sqrt{\dfrac{(0.79)(1 - 0.79)}{600}} = 0.03$.

13.10 Substituting 0.10 for E and $z_{0.025}$ into the formula for sample size $n = \frac{1}{4}\left(\frac{z_{\alpha/2}}{E}\right)^2$, we get $n = \frac{1}{4}\left(\frac{1.96}{0.10}\right)^2 = 97$ (rounded up).

13.16 (a) From Table V the probability of x for 1 or less is obtained by adding probabilities for $x = 0$ and $x = 1$ and is $0.002 + 0.017 = 0.019$, and the probability for x of 9 or more is obtained by adding probabilities for $x = 9$, $x = 10$, and $x = 11$ and is $0.012 + 0.002 + 0.000 = 0.014$. Both 0.019 and 0.014 are less than 0.025.

(b) The probability of x for 2 or less is obtained by adding the probabilities for $x = 0$, $x = 1$, and $x = 2$ and is $0.002 + 0.017 + 0.064 = 0.083$, and the probability for 8 or more is obtained by adding $x = 8$, $x = 9$, $x = 10$, and $x = 11$ or more and is 0.042, $+ 0.012 + 0.002 + 0.000 = 0.056$. Both 0.083 and 0.056 are greater than 0.025.

13.19 (a) The critical region is $x = 14$ and $x = 15$. (Note: If we also include $x = 13$ for which the probability is 0.092, the total exceeds 0.04.)

(b) From Table V, $x = 14$ and $x = 15$ have probabilities of 0.005 and $0.031 = 0.036$. This sum is the actual level of significance, also called the observed level of significance.

13.20 From Table V, the probability of getting at most three successes is $0.003 + 0.014 = 0.017$, the probability of getting at most 4 successes is $0.003 + 0.014 + 0.042 = 0.059$, the probability of getting 12 or more successes is $0.003 + 0.014 = 0.017$, and the probability of getting 11 or more successes is $0.003 + 0.014 + 0.042 = 0.059$; since the first and third probabilities are less than 0.025 and the second and fourth exceed 0.025, the null hypothesis must be rejected for $x = 0$, 1, 2, 3, 12, 13, 14, or 15 heads.

13.22 Test the null hypothesis $p = 0.40$ against the alternative hypothesis $p \neq 0.40$ at the 0.05 level of significance. From Table V, with $n = 10$, $p = 0.40$, and $x = 6$ the probability of six or fewer successes is $0.006 + 0.040 + 0.121 + 0.215 + 0.251 + 0.201 + 0.111 = 0.945$, and the probability of six or more successes is $0.111 + 0.042 + 0.011 + 0.002 = 0.166$. Since both exceed 0.025, the null hypothesis cannot be rejected.

13.24 (a) **1.** H_0: $p = 0.06$.
H_A: $p < 0.06$.

2. $\alpha = 0.05$.

3. Reject the null hypothesis if $z \leq -1.645$, where

$$z = \frac{x - np_0}{\sqrt{np_0(1 - p_0)}}$$

otherwise, accept the null hypothesis or reserve judgment.

4. Substituting $x = 56$, $n = 1,000$, and $p_0 = 0.06$ into the formula for z we get

$$z = \frac{56 - 1,000(0.06)}{\sqrt{1,000(0.06)(1 - 0.06)}} = -0.53$$

5. Since $z = -0.53$ exceeds -1.645 the null hypothesis cannot be rejected. Accept the null hypothesis or reserve judgment.

(b) $0.5000 - 0.2019 = 0.2981$. Since 0.2981 is greater than $\alpha = 0.05$ the null hypothesis cannot be rejected.

13.29 Test the null hypothesis $p = 0.50$ against the alternative hypothesis $p \neq 0.50$ at the 0.05 level of significance; since $z = \dfrac{174 - 350(0.50)}{\sqrt{350(0.50)(0.50)}} = -0.11$ falls between -1.96 and 1.96, the null hypothesis cannot be rejected. There is no real evidence of a lack of randomness.

13.32 **1.** H_0: $p_1 = p_2$.
H_A: $p_1 \neq p_2$.

2. $\alpha = 0.05$.

3. Reject the null hypothesis if $z \leq -1.96$ or $z \geq 1.96$, where z is given by the formula

$$z = \frac{\dfrac{x_1}{n_1} - \dfrac{x_2}{n_2}}{\sqrt{p(1-p)\left(\dfrac{1}{n_1} + \dfrac{1}{n_2}\right)}} \qquad \text{with} \qquad p = \frac{x_1 + x_2}{n_1 + n_2}$$

otherwise, accept the null hypothesis or reserve judgment.

4. Substituting $x_1 = 84$, $n_1 = 300$, $x_2 = 32$, $n_2 = 100$, and 0.29 for p into the formula for z, we get $\dfrac{84 + 32}{300 + 100} =$

$$z = \frac{\dfrac{84}{300} - \dfrac{32}{100}}{\sqrt{(0.29)(0.71)\left(\dfrac{1}{300} + \dfrac{1}{100}\right)}} = -0.76$$

5. Since $z = -0.76$ falls between -1.96 and 1.96, the null hypothesis cannot be rejected. We accept the null hypothesis or reserve judgment.

13.35 **1.** H_0: $p_1 = p_2$.
H_A: $p_1 \neq p_2$.

2. $\alpha = 0.05$.

3. Reject the null hypothesis if $z \leq -1.96$ or $z \geq 1.96$, where z is given by the formula

$$z = \frac{\dfrac{x_1}{n_1} - \dfrac{x_2}{n_2}}{\sqrt{p(1-p)\left(\dfrac{1}{n_1} + \dfrac{1}{n_2}\right)}} \qquad \text{with} \qquad p = \frac{x_1 + x_2}{n_1 + n_2}$$

otherwise, accept the null hypothesis or reserve judgment.

4. Substituting $x_1 = 350$, $n_1 = 400$, $x_2 = 210$, $n_2 = 400$, and $\dfrac{350 + 210}{400 + 400}$

$= 0.70$ for p into the formula for z, we get

$$z = \frac{\dfrac{350}{400} - \dfrac{210}{400}}{\sqrt{(0.70)(0.30)\left(\dfrac{1}{400} + \dfrac{1}{400}\right)}} = 10.80$$

5. Since $z = 10.80$ exceeds 1.96, the null hypothesis must be rejected. The difference is significant at the 0.05 level.

13.39 **1.** H_0: $p_1 = p_2 = p_3 = p_4$.
H_A: p_1, p_2, p_3, and p_4 are not all equal.

2. $\alpha = 0.01$.

3. Reject the null hypothesis if $\chi^2 \geq 11.345$ where $\chi^2 = \sum \dfrac{(o - e)^2}{e}$

and 11.345 is the value of χ^2 for $(2 - 1)(4 - 1) = 3$ degrees of freedom; otherwise, state that the differences among the sample proportions are not significant.

4. Since the total for the first row is $139 + 91 + 73 + 117 = 420$, we get expected frequencies of $\dfrac{420 \cdot 300}{900} = 140.0$, $\dfrac{420 \cdot 200}{900} = 93.3$, and

$\dfrac{420 \cdot 150}{900} = 70.0$ for the first three cells of the table. Then, by subtraction, we get $420 - 140.0 - 93.3 - 70.0 = 116.7$ for the fourth cell of the first row (increase) and $300 - 140.0 = 160.0$, $200 - 93.3 = 106.7$, $150 - 70.0 = 80.0$, and $250 - 116.7 = 133.3$, for the four cells of the second row (no increase). The foregoing is summarized in the following table

	New York	Chicago	Los Angeles	Houston	
Increase	139 (140.0)	91 (93.3)	73 (70.0)	117 (116.7)	420
No increase	161 (160.0)	109 (106.7)	77 (80.0)	133 (133.3)	480
Total	300	200	150	250	900

Finally, substituting all these values together with the observed frequencies into the formula for χ^2, we get

$$\chi^2 = \frac{(139 - 140.0)^2}{140.0} + \frac{(91 - 93.3)^2}{93.3} + \frac{(73 - 70.0)^2}{70.0} + \frac{(117 - 116.7)^2}{116.7}$$
$$+ \frac{(161 - 160.0)^2}{160.0} + \frac{(109 - 106.7)^2}{106.7} + \frac{(77 - 80.0)^2}{80.0} + \frac{(133 - 133.3)^2}{133.3}$$
$$= 0.36$$

5. Since $\chi^2 = 0.36$ does not exceed 11.345, the null hypothesis cannot be rejected. The differences among the four sample proportions are not significant at the $\alpha = 0.01$ level.

13.44 The number of degrees of freedom is $(r - 1)(c - 1)$.
(a) $(2 - 1)(3 - 1) = 2$ (b) $(3 - 1)(3 - 1) = 4$
(c) $(5 - 1)(4 - 1) = 12$ (d) $(4 - 1)(5 - 1) = 12$

13.46 (a) The marginal value (total) for row 3 is $370 - 150 - 105 = 115$, and the marginal value for column 3 is $370 - 140 - 160 = 70$. By subtraction,

Row 1, cell 3, is $105 - 35 - 50 = 20$.
Row 2, cell 3, is $150 - 60 - 55 = 35$.
Row 3, cell 1, is $140 - 35 - 60 = 45$.
Row 3, cell 2, is $160 - 50 - 55 = 55$.
Row 3, cell 3, is $70 - 20 - 35 = 15$.

(b) For row 1 the expected values are $\dfrac{(105)(140)}{370} = 39.7$, $\dfrac{(105)(160)}{370} =$ 45.4 for cells 1 and 2 of the first row, and, by subtraction, $105 - 39.7 - 45.4 = 19.9$ for cell 3. For row 2, the expected values are $\dfrac{(150)(140)}{370} = 56.8$, $\dfrac{(150)(160)}{370} = 64.9$ for cells 1 and 2, and, by subtraction, $150 - 56.8 - 64.9 = 28.3$ for cell 3. For row 3, by subtraction, we get $140 - 39.7 - 56.8 = 43.5$, $160 - 45.4 - 64.9 = 49.7$, and $70 - 19.9 - 28.3 = 21.8$.

(c) $\chi^2 = \dfrac{(35 - 39.7)^2}{39.7} + \dfrac{(50 - 45.4)^2}{45.4} + \dfrac{(20 - 19.9)^2}{19.9} + \dfrac{(60 - 56.8)^2}{56.8}$
$+ \dfrac{(55 - 64.9)^2}{64.9} + \dfrac{(35 - 28.3)^2}{28.3} + \dfrac{(45 - 43.5)^2}{43.5} + \dfrac{(55 - 49.7)^2}{49.7}$
$+ \dfrac{(15 - 21.8)^2}{21.8} = 7.04$

13.48 **1.** H_0: Geographical location and quality of the toys are independent (the three countries ship toys of equal quality).
H_A: Geographical location and quality of the toys are not independent (the three countries do not ship toys of equal quality).

2. $\alpha = 0.01$.

3. Reject the null hypothesis if $\chi^2 \geq 13.277$, where $\chi^2 = \sum \dfrac{(o - e)^2}{e}$

and 13.277 is the value of $\chi^2_{0.01}$ for $(3 - 1)(3 - 1) = 4$ degrees of freedom; otherwise, accept the null hypothesis or reserve judgment.

4. Since the total for the first row is $104 + 64 + 79 = 247$, we get expected frequencies of $\dfrac{(247)(149)}{350} = 105.2$ and $\dfrac{(247)(91)}{350} = 64.2$ for the first two cells of the first row of the table. Then, by subtraction, we get $247 - 105.2 - 64.2 = 77.6$ for the third cell of the first row. The total for the second row is $29 + 17 + 24 = 70$, and we get $\frac{(70)(149)}{350} = 29.8$ and $\frac{(70)(91)}{350} = 18.2$ for the first two cells of the second row. Then, by subtraction, we get $70 - 29.8 - 18.2 = 22.0$ for the third cell of the second row and $149 - 105.2 - 29.8 = 14.0$, $91 - 64.2 - 18.2 = 8.6$, and $110 - 77.6 - 22.0 = 10.4$ for the three cells of the third row. The results are summarized in the following table.

Geographical location

	Hong Kong	*Japan*	*Korea*	
Acceptable	104 (105.2)	64 (64.2)	79 (77.6)	247
Imperfect, but salable	29 (29.8)	17 (18.2)	24 (22.0)	70
Defective	16 (14.0)	10 (8.6)	7 (10.4)	33
Total	149	91	110	350

Substituting the observed and expected frequencies from the table into the formula for χ^2, we get

$$\chi^2 = \frac{(104 - 105.2)^2}{105.2} + \frac{(64 - 64.2)^2}{64.2} + \frac{(79 - 77.6)^2}{77.6} + \frac{(29 - 29.8)^2}{29.8}$$
$$+ \frac{(17 - 18.2)^2}{18.2} + \frac{(24 - 22.0)^2}{22.0} + \frac{(16 - 14.0)^2}{14.0} + \frac{(10 - 8.6)^2}{8.6}$$
$$+ \frac{(7 - 10.4)^2}{10.4} = 1.95$$

5. Since $\chi^2 = 1.95$ does not exceed 13.277, the null hypothesis of independence cannot be rejected. Geographical location and quality are independent. In other words, the quality may be the same in all of the locations.

13.54 Test the null hypothesis that the die is balanced against the alternative hypothesis that it is not balanced at the 0.05 level of significance. The expected frequencies are all $360 \cdot \frac{1}{6} = 60$ and since $\chi^2 = \frac{(57 - 60)^2}{60} + \frac{(46 - 60)^2}{60} + \cdots + \frac{(65 - 60)^2}{60} = 8.37$ is less than 11.070, the null hypothesis cannot be rejected. There is no real evidence that the die is not balanced.

13.58 **1.** H_0: The population sampled has a Poisson distribution with $\lambda = 2.5$.
H_A: The population sampled has some other distribution.

2. $\alpha = 0.01$.

3. Reject the null hypothesis if $\chi^2_{0.01} \geq 16.812$, where $\chi^2 = \sum \dfrac{(o-e)^2}{e}$

and 16.812 is the value of $\chi^2_{0.01}$ for five degrees of freedom; otherwise, accept the null hypothesis or reserve judgment.

4. The probabilities are $f(0) = \dfrac{2.5^0 \cdot e^{-2.5}}{0!} = 0.082$, $f(1) = \dfrac{2.5(0.082)}{1!} = 0.205$, $f(2) = \dfrac{2.5^2(0.082)}{2!} = 0.256$, $f(3) = \dfrac{2.5^3(0.082)}{3!} = 0.214$,

$f(4) = \dfrac{2.5^4(0.082)}{4!} = 0.133$, $f(5) = \dfrac{2.5^5(0.082)}{5!} = 0.067$, and $f(6) = \dfrac{2.5^6(0.082)}{6!} = 0.028$, and multiplying these probabilties by 300, we

get the expected frequencies 24.6, 61.5, 76.8, 64.2, 39.9, 20.1, and 8.4. Substituting the observed probabilities from the table, and combining them with the probabilities into the formula for χ^2, we get

$$\chi^2 = \frac{(12-24.6)^2}{24.6} + \frac{(60-61.5)^2}{61.5} + \frac{(87-76.8)^2}{76.8} + \frac{(80-64.2)^2}{64.2}$$
$$+ \frac{(40-39.9)^2}{39.9} + \frac{(15-20.1)^2}{20.1} + \frac{(6-8.4)^2}{8.4} = 13.72$$

5. Since $\chi^2 = 13.72$ does not exceed 16.812, the null hypothesis cannot be rejected. The Poisson distribution with $\lambda = 2.5$ provides a good fit.

Decision Making:
Analysis
of Variance

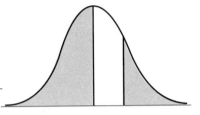

In this chapter we shall consider the problem of deciding whether observed differences among more than two sample means can be attributed to chance, or whether there are real differences among the means of the populations sampled. For instance, we may want to decide on the basis of sample data whether there really is a difference in the effectiveness of three methods of teaching managerial accounting, we may want to compare the average monthly sales of several insurance salesmen, we may want to see whether there really is a difference in the average mileage obtained with four kinds of gasoline, we may want to judge whether there really is a difference in the durability of five kinds of carpet, and so on. The method we shall introduce for this purpose is a powerful statistical tool called **analysis of variance**, or ANOVA for short. A one-way analysis of variance is described in Section 14.2 and a two-way analysis of variance in Section 14.3.

14.1

Differences Among k Means

Suppose that we want to compare the cholesterol contents of four competing diet foods on the basis of the following data (in milligrams per package) which were obtained for three 6-ounce packages of each of the diet foods:

Diet food A:	3.6	4.1	4.0
Diet food B:	3.1	3.2	3.9
Diet food C:	3.2	3.5	3.5
Diet food D:	3.5	3.8	3.8

The means of these four samples are 3.9, 3.4, 3.4, and 3.7, and we want to know whether the differences among them are significant or whether they can be attributed to chance.

In general, in problems like this, if $\mu_1, \mu_2, \ldots,$ and μ_k are the means of k populations from each of which a sample is drawn, we want to test the null hypothesis $\mu_1 = \mu_2 = \ldots = \mu_k$ against the alternative that these means are not all equal.[1] Evidently, this null hypothesis would be supported if the differences among the sample means were small, and the alternative hypothesis would be supported if the differences among the sample means were large. Thus, we need a precise measure of the discrepancies among the $\bar{x}$'s, and with it a rule to follow which tells us when the discrepancies are so large that the null hypothesis should be rejected. An obvious choice of such a measure is the variance of the $\bar{x}$'s, and this is the measure we shall use here. For the diet foods the mean of the four $\bar{x}$'s is

$$\frac{3.9 + 3.4 + 3.4 + 3.7}{4} = 3.6$$

---

[1] In connection with work later in this chapter, it is desirable to write these means as $\mu_1 = \mu + \alpha_1$, $\mu_2 = \mu + \alpha_2, \ldots,$ and $\mu_k = \mu + \alpha_k$. Here

$$\mu = \frac{\mu_1 + \mu_2 + \cdots + \mu_k}{k}$$

is called the **grand mean**, and the α's whose sum is zero (see Exercise 14.11, on page 541), are called the **treatment effects**. In this notation, the null hypothesis becomes $\alpha_1 = \alpha_2 = \cdots = \alpha_k = 0$, and the alternative hypothesis is that the α's are not all equal to zero.

and their variance is

$$s_{\bar{x}}^2 = \frac{(3.9 - 3.6)^2 + (3.4 - 3.6)^2 + (3.4 - 3.6)^2 + (3.7 - 3.6)^2}{4 - 1}$$

$$= 0.06$$

where the subscript $\bar{x}$ is used to show that this is the variance of the sample means.

Let us now make two assumptions which are critical to the method of analysis we shall use: It will be assumed that (1) the populations from which we are sampling can be approximated closely with normal distributions and (2) they all have the same variance σ^2. With these assumptions, we note that, if the null hypothesis $\mu_1 = \mu_2 = \cdots = \mu_k$ is true, we can look upon the k samples as samples from one and the same (normal) population and, hence, upon the variance of their means, $s_{\bar{x}}^2$, as an estimate of $\sigma_{\bar{x}}^2$, the square of the standard error of the mean. Now, since $\sigma_{\bar{x}} = \dfrac{\sigma}{\sqrt{n}}$ for samples from infinite populations, we can look upon $s_{\bar{x}}^2$ as an estimate of $\sigma_{\bar{x}}^2 = \left(\dfrac{\sigma}{\sqrt{n}}\right)^2 = \dfrac{\sigma^2}{n}$ and, therefore, upon $n \cdot s_{\bar{x}}^2$ as an estimate of σ^2. For instance, for our example where $n = 3$ for each sample, we have $n \cdot s_{\bar{x}}^2 = 3(0.06) = 0.18$ as an estimate of σ^2, the common variance of the four populations sampled.

If σ^2 were known, we could compare $n \cdot s_{\bar{x}}^2$ with σ^2 and reject the null hypothesis that the population means are all equal if this value is much larger than σ^2. However, in most practical problems σ^2 is not known and we have no choice but to estimate it on the basis of the sample data. Having assumed that the k samples do, in fact, all come from identical populations, we could use any one of their variances, $s_1^2, s_2^2, \ldots,$ or s_k^2, as a second estimate of σ^2, and we can also use their mean. Averaging, or **pooling**, the four sample variances in our example, we get

$$\frac{s_1^2 + s_2^2 + s_3^2 + s_4^2}{4} = \frac{1}{4}\left[\frac{(3.6 - 3.9)^2 + (4.1 - 3.9)^2 + (4.0 - 3.9)^2}{3 - 1}\right.$$

$$+ \frac{(3.1 - 3.4)^2 + (3.2 - 3.4)^2 + (3.9 - 3.4)^2}{3 - 1}$$

$$+ \frac{(3.2 - 3.4)^2 + (3.5 - 3.4)^2 + (3.5 - 3.4)^2}{3 - 1}$$

$$\left.+ \frac{(3.5 - 3.7)^2 + (3.8 - 3.7)^2 + (3.8 - 3.7)^2}{3 - 1}\right]$$

$$= 0.08$$

Section 14.1   *Differences Among k Means*   527 and we now have two estimates of σ^2,

$$n \cdot s_{\bar{x}}^2 = 0.18 \text{ and } \frac{s_1^2 + s_2^2 + s_3^2 + s_4^2}{4} = 0.08$$

If the first of two such estimates of σ^2 (which is based on the variation among the sample means) is "much" larger than the second estimate (which is based on the variation within the samples and, hence, measures variation due to chance), it stands to reason that the null hypothesis should be rejected. After all, in that case the variation among the sample means would be greater than we would expect it to be if it were due only to chance. To put the comparison of the two estimates of σ^2 on a rigorous basis, we use the statistic

Statistic for test concerning differences among means

$$F = \frac{\textit{estimate of } \sigma^2 \textit{ based on the variation among the } \bar{x}\textit{'s}}{\textit{estimate of } \sigma^2 \textit{ based on the variation within the samples}}$$

which is appropriately called a **variance ratio**.

If the null hypothesis is true and if the assumptions we made are valid, the sampling distribution of this statistic is the F distribution which we introduced in Chapter 12. Since the null hypothesis will be rejected only when F is large (that is, when the variability of the $\bar{x}$'s is too great to be attributed to chance), we base our decision on the criterion of Figure 14.1. Here F_α is such that the area under the curve to its right equals the level of significance α. For $\alpha = 0.05$ or 0.01, the critical values of F_α may be looked up in Table IV at the end of the book, and if we compare the means of k random samples

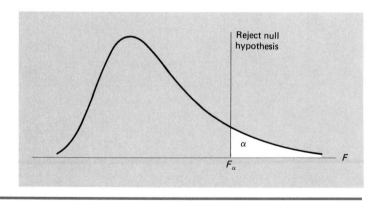

FIGURE 14.1
F distribution

of size n, we have $k - 1$ degrees of freedom for the numerator and $k(n - 1)$ degrees of freedom for the denominator.[2]

Returning to our example, we find that for $k = 4$ and $n = 3$, the numerator and denominator degrees of freedom are $k - 1 = 4 - 1 = 3$ and $k(n - 1) = 4(3 - 1) = 8$ and that $F_{0.05} = 4.07$. Since

$$F = \frac{0.18}{0.08} = 2.25$$

is less than the critical value of 4.07, we find that the null hypothesis cannot be rejected. Although there are what may seem to be substantial differences among the means of the samples, this, we conclude, is due to chance.

The technique we have just described is the simplest form of an analysis of variance. Although we could go ahead and perform F tests for differences among k means without further discussion, it will be instructive to look at the problem from an analysis of variance point of view, and we shall do so in the next section.

14.2

One-Way Analysis of Variance

The basic idea in the analysis of variance is to express a measure of the total variation in a set of data as a sum of terms, which can be attributed to specific sources, or causes, of variation. With regard to the illustration of the preceding section, two such sources of variation might be (1) actual differences in the average cholesterol content of the four diet foods and (2) chance, which in problems of this kind is usually called the **experimental error**. The measure of the total variation in a set of data which we shall use is the **total sum of squares**[3]

$$SST = \sum_{i=1}^{k} \sum_{j=1}^{n} (x_{ij} - \bar{x}..)^2$$

---

[2]In connection with the numerator degrees of freedom, the numerator is $n \cdot s_{\bar{x}}^2$, and $s_{\bar{x}}^2$ is the variance of k means and, hence, has $k - 1$ degrees of freedom in accordance with the terminology introduced in the footnote to page 394. As for the denominator degrees of freedom, the denominator is the mean of k sample variances with each having $n - 1$ degrees of freedom.

[3]The use of double subscripts and double summations is explained briefly in Section 3.10.

where x_{ij} is the jth observation of the ith sample ($i = 1, 2, \ldots, k$ and $j = 1, 2, \ldots, n$), and $\bar{x}..$ is the **grand mean**, the mean of all the kn measurements or observations. Note that if we divided the total sum of squares SST by $kn - 1$, we would get the variance of the data; hence, the total sum of squares of a set of data is interpreted in much the same way as its sample variance.

If we let $\bar{x}_{i\cdot}$ denote the mean of the ith sample, we can now write the following identity, which forms the basis of a **one-way analysis of variance**:[4]

Identity for one-way analysis of variance

$$SST = n \cdot \sum_{i=1}^{k} (\bar{x}_{i\cdot} - \bar{x}..)^2 + \sum_{i=1}^{k} \sum_{j=1}^{n} (x_{ij} - \bar{x}_{i\cdot})^2$$

Looking closely at the two terms into which the total sum of squares SST has been partitioned, we find that the first term is a measure of the variation among the sample means; in fact, if we divide it by $k - 1$ we get the quantity which we earlier denoted $n \cdot s_{\bar{x}}^2$. Similarly, the second term is a measure of the variation within the individual samples, and if we divided this term by $k(n - 1)$ we would get the mean of the variances of the individual samples, the quantity which we put into the denominator of F in the preceding section.

It is customary to refer to the first term, the quantity which measures the variation among the sample means, as the **treatment sum of squares** *SS(Tr)*, and to the second term, which measures the variation within the samples, as the **error sum of squares** *SSE*. This terminology is explained by the fact that most analysis of variance techniques were originally developed in connection with agricultural experiments where different fertilizers, for example, were regarded as different **treatments** applied to the soil. The word "error" in "error sum of squares" pertains to the experimental error, which we also refer to as chance. Although this may sound confusing at first, we shall refer to the four diet foods of our example as four treatments, and in

---

[4]This identity may be derived by writing the total sum of squares as

$$SST = \sum_{i=1}^{k} \sum_{j=1}^{n} (x_{ij} - \bar{x}..)^2$$

$$= \sum_{i=1}^{k} \sum_{j=1}^{n} [(\bar{x}_{i\cdot} - \bar{x}..) + (x_{ij} - \bar{x}_{i\cdot})]^2$$

and then expanding the squares $[(\bar{x}_{i\cdot} - \bar{x}..) + (x_{ij} - \bar{x}_{i\cdot})]^2$ by means of the binomial theorem and simplifying algebraically.

Chapter 14   Decision Making: Analysis of Variance

other problems we may refer to three kinds of packaging as three different treatments, five kinds of advertising campaigns as five different treatments, and so on.

Before we go any further, let us verify the identity $SST = SS(Tr) + SSE$ with reference to the diet foods example of the preceding section. Substituting into the formulas for the different sums of squares, we get

$$
\begin{aligned}
SST = {} & (3.6 - 3.6)^2 + (4.1 - 3.6)^2 + (4.0 - 3.6)^2 \\
& + (3.1 - 3.6)^2 + (3.2 - 3.6)^2 + (3.9 - 3.6)^2 \\
& + (3.2 - 3.6)^2 + (3.5 - 3.6)^2 + (3.5 - 3.6)^2 \\
& + (3.5 - 3.6)^2 + (3.8 - 3.6)^2 + (3.8 - 3.6)^2 \\
= {} & 1.18 \\
SS(Tr) = {} & 3[(3.9 - 3.6)^2 + (3.4 - 3.6)^2 + (3.4 - 3.6)^2 \\
& + (3.7 - 3.6)^2] \\
= {} & 0.54 \\
SSE = {} & (3.6 - 3.9)^2 + (4.1 - 3.9)^2 + (4.0 - 3.9)^2 \\
& + (3.1 - 3.4)^2 + (3.2 - 3.4)^2 + (3.9 - 3.4)^2 \\
& + (3.2 - 3.4)^2 + (3.5 - 3.4)^2 + (3.5 - 3.4)^2 \\
& + (3.5 - 3.7)^2 + (3.8 - 3.7)^2 + (3.8 - 3.7)^2 \\
= {} & 0.64
\end{aligned}
$$

and it can be seen that

$$SS(Tr) + SSE = 0.54 + 0.64 = 1.18 = SST$$

To test the null hypothesis $\mu_1 = \mu_2 = \cdots = \mu_k$ (or $\alpha_1 = \alpha_2 = \cdots = \alpha_k = 0$ in the notation of the footnote to page 526) against the alternative that the treatment means are not all equal (or that the treatment effects are not all zero), we now proceed as in the preceding section and compare $SS(Tr)$ with SSE by means of an F statistic. In practice, we usually exhibit the necessary work in the **analysis of variance table** as follows:

Source of variation	Degrees of freedom	Sum of squares	Mean square	F
Treatments	$k - 1$	$SS(Tr)$	$MS(Tr) = \dfrac{SS(TR)}{k - 1}$	$\dfrac{MS(Tr)}{MSE}$
Error	$k(n - 1)$	SSE	$MSE = \dfrac{SSE}{k(n - 1)}$	
Total	$kn - 1$	SST		

Here the second column lists the degrees of freedom (the number of independent deviations from the mean on which the sums of squares are based), the fourth column lists the **mean squares** $MS(Tr)$ and MSE, which are obtained by dividing the corresponding sums of squares by their degrees of freedom, and the right-hand column gives the value of the F statistic as the ratio of the two mean squares. These two mean squares are, in fact, the two estimates of σ^2 referred to on page 528; the numerator and denominator degrees of freedom for the F test, $k - 1$ and $k(n - 1)$, are shown opposite "Treatments" and "Error" in the "Degrees of freedom" column. The significance test is the same as before; we compare F with F_α for $k - 1$ and $k(n - 1)$ degrees of freedom.

EXAMPLE 14.1   For the diet foods example, test the null hypothesis that the sample means are all equal against the alternative hypothesis that they are not all equal. The number of observations in each of these samples is equal. Use the identity formula for one-way analysis of variance where the first term in the formula represents $SS(Tr)$ and the second term represents SSE. Construct an analysis of variance table to summarize the calculations in the identity formula and to show the calculation of F.

SOLUTION   **1.** H_0: $\mu_1 = \mu_2 = \mu_3 = \mu_4$.
H_A: The μ's are not all equal.

2. $\alpha = 0.05$.

3. Reject the null hypothesis if $F \geq 4.07$, where

$$F = \frac{MS(Tr)}{MSE}$$

$k - 1 = 4 - 1 = 3$ degrees of freedom for the numerator, and $k(n - 1) = 4(3 - 1) = 8$ degrees of freedom for the denominator, and the identity formula for one-way analysis of variance is

$$SST = n \cdot \sum_{i=1}^{k} (\bar{x}_{i\bullet} - \bar{x}_{\bullet\bullet})^2 + \sum_{i=1}^{k} \sum_{j=1}^{n} (x_{ij} - \bar{x}_{i\bullet})^2$$

where the first term represents $SS(Tr)$ and the second term represents SSE.

4. The sums of squares are calculated on page 531 and are $SS(Tr) = 0.54$, $SSE = 0.64$, and $SST = 1.18$, so that $MS(Tr) = \dfrac{SS(Tr)}{k - 1} =$

$$\frac{0.54}{4-1} = 0.18, \ MSE = \frac{SSE}{k(n-1)} = \frac{0.64}{4(3-1)} = 0.08, \text{ and}$$

$F = \frac{MS(Tr)}{MSE} = \frac{0.18}{0.08} = 2.25.$ The results are summarized in the table that follows. It may be observed that the number of degrees of freedom for SST is $kn - 1 = 4.3 - 1 = 11$. This provides a check since it equals the sum of the other two, $3 + 8 = 11$.

Source of variation	Degrees of freedom	Sum of squares	Mean square	F
Treatments	3	0.54	0.18	2.25
Error	8	0.64	0.08	
Total	11	1.18		

5. Since $F = 2.25$ is less than 4.07, the value of $F_{0.05}$ for three and eight degrees of freedom, we find (as before) that the null hypothesis cannot be rejected at the 0.05 level of significance. ∎

The numbers which we used in our illustration were intentionally chosen so that the calculations would be relatively simple. In actual practice, the calculation of the sums of squares can be quite tedious unless we use the following computing formulas, in which $T_{i\bullet}$ denotes the total of the observations for the ith treatment (that is, the sum of the values in the ith sample), and $T_{\bullet\bullet}$ denotes the grand total of all the data.[5]

Computing formulas for sums of squares (sample sizes equal)

$$SST = \sum_{i=1}^{k} \sum_{j=1}^{n} x_{ij}^2 - \frac{1}{kn} \cdot T_{\bullet\bullet}^2.$$

$$SS(Tr) = \frac{1}{n} \cdot \sum_{i=1}^{k} T_{i\bullet}^2 - \frac{1}{kn} \cdot T_{\bullet\bullet}^2.$$

and by subtraction

$$SSE = SST - SS(Tr)$$

[5]Non-computer calculations can also be simplified by coding, that is, by subtracting the same constant from each value and/or multiplying each value by a constant.

EXAMPLE 14.2 For the diet foods example, test the null hypothesis that the means are all equal against the alternative hypothesis that they are not all equal. The number of observations in each of these samples is equal. Use the *computing formulas* provided to calculate *SST, SS(Tr)*, and *SSE*. Steps 1, 2, and 5 are the same as those provided in Example 14.1, step 3 has the computing formulas, but step 4 is simplified through the use of the computing formulas which reduce laborious calculations while providing identical answers.

1. H_0: $\mu_1 = \mu_2 = \mu_3 = \mu_4$.
   H_A: The μ's are not all equal.

2. $\alpha = 0.05$.

3. Reject the null hypothesis if $F \geq 4.07$, where

$$F = \frac{MS(Tr)}{MSE},$$

$k - 1 = 4 - 1 = 3$ degrees of freedom for the numerator, and $k(n - 1) = 4(3 - 1) = 8$ degrees of freedom for the denominator and the computing formulas are

$$SST = \sum_{i=1}^{k} \sum_{j=1}^{n} x_{ij}^2 - \frac{1}{kn} \cdot T_{..}^2.$$

$$SS(Tr) = \frac{1}{n} \cdot \sum_{i=1}^{k} T_{i.}^2 - \frac{1}{kn} \cdot T_{..}^2.$$

$$SSE = SST - SS(Tr)$$

4. Calculating $T_{1.}, T_{2.}, T_{3.}, T_{4.}, T_{..}$, and $\sum \sum x^2$, we first determine that the total for each sample is $T_{1.} = 3.6 + 4.1 + 4.0 = 11.7$, $T_{2.} = 3.1 + 3.2 + 3.9 = 10.2$, $T_{3.} = 3.2 + 3.5 + 3.5 = 10.2$, and $T_{4.} = 3.5 + 3.8 + 3.8 = 11.1$ and their overall total is $T_{..} = 11.7 + 10.2 + 10.2 + 11.1 = 43.2$. Finally, the sum of the individual observations squared is $\sum \sum x^2$ is $3.6^2 + 4.1^2 + 4.0^2 + 3.1^2 + 3.2^2 + 3.9^2 + 3.2^2 + 3.5^2 + 3.5^2 + 3.5^2 + 3.8^2 + 3.8^2 = 156.70$.

Substituting $k = 4$, $n = 3$, $T_{1.} = 11.7$, $T_{2.} = 10.2$, $T_{3.} = 10.2$, $T_{4.} = 11.1$, $T_{..} = 43.2$, and $\sum \sum x^2 = 156.70$ into the formulas, we get

$$SST = 156.70 - \frac{1}{12}(43.2)^2 = 1.18$$

$$SS(Tr) = \frac{1}{3}(11.7^2 + 10.2^2 + 10.2^2 + 11.1^2) - \frac{1}{12}(43.2)^2$$
$$= 0.54$$

and

$$SSE = 1.18 - 0.54 = 0.64$$

Of course these results are identical with those obtained in Example 14.1, and the analysis of variance table which we should construct at this point is also the same. The table shows that

$$MS(Tr) = \frac{SS(Tr)}{k-1} = \frac{0.54}{3} = 0.18, \ MSE = \frac{SSE}{k(n-1)} = \frac{0.64}{8}$$

$= 0.08$, and $F = \dfrac{MS(Tr)}{MSE} = \dfrac{0.18}{0.08} = 2.25$. The reader can re-examine this table on page 533.

5. Since $F = 2.25$ is less than 4.07, the value of $F_{0.05}$ for three and eight degrees of freedom, we find (as before) that the null hypothesis cannot be rejected at the 0.05 level of significance.

∎

A computer printout of our analysis of variance example is shown in Figure 14.2, where the values corresponding to $SST = 1.18$, $SS(Tr) = 0.54$, and $SSE = 0.64$ are given in the column headed "SS." Besides the degrees of freedom, the sums of squares, the mean squares, and the value of F, the printout provides information which permits further comparisons among the population means.

The method we have discussed here applies only when each sample has the same number of observations, but minor modifications make it applicable also to situations where the sample sizes are not all equal. If there are n_i values for the ith treatment, the computing formulas for the sums of squares become

Computing formulas for sums of squares (unequal sample sizes)

$$SST = \sum_{i=1}^{k} \sum_{j=1}^{n_i} x_{ij}^2 - \frac{1}{N} \cdot T_{\bullet\bullet}^2$$

$$SS(Tr) = \sum_{i=1}^{k} \frac{T_{i\bullet}^2}{n_i} - \frac{1}{N} \cdot T_{\bullet\bullet}^2$$
$$SSE = SST - SS(Tr)$$

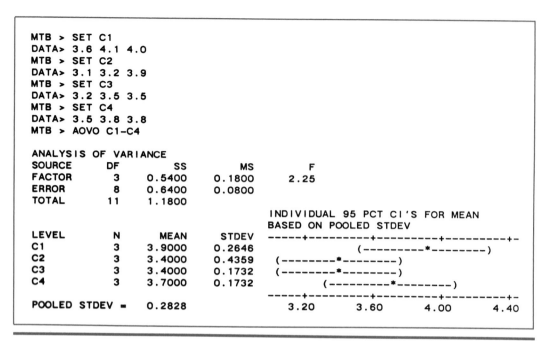

```
MTB > SET C1
DATA> 3.6 4.1 4.0
MTB > SET C2
DATA> 3.1 3.2 3.9
MTB > SET C3
DATA> 3.2 3.5 3.5
MTB > SET C4
DATA> 3.5 3.8 3.8
MTB > AOVO C1-C4

ANALYSIS OF VARIANCE
SOURCE        DF        SS          MS          F
FACTOR         3      0.5400      0.1800      2.25
ERROR          8      0.6400      0.0800
TOTAL         11      1.1800
                                         INDIVIDUAL 95 PCT CI'S FOR MEAN
                                         BASED ON POOLED STDEV
LEVEL          N       MEAN       STDEV   -----+---------+---------+---------+-
C1             3      3.9000      0.2646               (---------*--------)
C2             3      3.4000      0.4359   (--------*--------)
C3             3      3.4000      0.1732   (--------*--------)
C4             3      3.7000      0.1732             (---------*--------)
                                         -----+---------+---------+---------+-
POOLED STDEV =        0.2828           3.20      3.60      4.00      4.40
```

FIGURE 14.2

Computer printout for analysis of variance

where $N = n_1 + n_2 + \cdots + n_k$. The only other change is that the total number of degrees of freedom is $N - 1$ and the degrees of freedom are $k - 1$ for treatments and $N - k$ for error.

EXAMPLE 14.3   A restaurant manager wants to determine whether the sales of steak and shrimp combination dinners depend on how this entree is described on the menu. He has three kinds of menus printed, listing steak and shrimp combination dinners among the other entrees or featuring them as "Chef's Special" and as "Gourmet's Delight," and he intends to use each kind of menu on six different Saturday nights. However, only the following data, showing the numbers of steak and shrimp combination dinners sold on 15 Saturdays, are actually collected:

Listed among other entrees	221, 205, 198, 237, 206, 223
Featured as "Chef's Special"	247, 214, 222, 244, 215, 226
Featured as "Gourmet's Delight"	206, 219, 202

Use the 0.05 level of significance to test the null hypothesis that the different descriptions do not affect the sales of the dinner. (The number of observations in the samples are not all equal.)

SOLUTION **1.** $H_0: \mu_1 = \mu_2 = \mu_3$.

H_A: The μ's are not all equal.

2. $\alpha = 0.05$.

3. Reject the null hypothesis if $F \geq 3.89$, where

$$F = \frac{MS(Tr)}{MSE}$$

$k - 1 = 3 - 1 = 2$ degrees of freedom for the numerator, $N - k = 15 - 3 = 12$ degrees of freedom for the denominator, and $N - 1 = 15 - 1 = 14$ for the total and the computing formulas for sum of squares (unequal sample sizes) are

$$SST = \sum_{i=1}^{k} \sum_{j=1}^{ni} x_{ij}^2 - \frac{1}{N} \cdot T_{\bullet\bullet}^2$$

$$SS(Tr) = \sum_{i=1}^{k} \frac{T_{i\bullet}^2}{n_i} - \frac{1}{N} \cdot T_{\bullet\bullet}^2$$

$$SSE = SST - SS(Tr)$$

4. Calculating $T_{1\bullet}, T_{2\bullet}, T_{3\bullet}, T_{\bullet\bullet}$, and $\sum \sum x^2$, we first determine that the total for each sample is $T_{1\bullet} = 221 + 205 + 198 + 237 + 206 + 223 = 1{,}290$, $T_{2\bullet} = 247 + 214 + 222 + 244 + 215 + 226 = 1{,}368$, and $T_{3\bullet} = 206 + 219 + 202 = 627$ and their overall total is $T_{\bullet\bullet} = 1{,}290 + 1{,}368 + 627 = 3{,}285$. Finally, the sum of the individual observations squared is

$$\Sigma \Sigma x^2 = 221^2 + 205^2 + 198^2 + 237^2 + 206^2 + 223^2 +$$
$$247^2 + 214^2 + 222^2 + 244^2 + 215^2 + 226^2 + 206^2 + 219^2 +$$
$$202^2 = 722{,}531.$$ Substituting these values into the formulas for sums of squares, we get

$$SST = 722{,}531 - \frac{1}{15}(3{,}285)^2 = 722{,}531 - 719{,}415$$
$$= 3{,}116$$

$$SS(Tr) = \frac{1{,}290^2}{6} + \frac{1{,}368^2}{6} + \frac{627^2}{3} - 719{,}415$$
$$= 882$$

and

$$SSE = 3{,}116 - 882 = 2{,}234$$

Also, the mean squares are $MS(Tr) = \dfrac{SS(Tr)}{k-1} = \dfrac{882}{3-1} = 441.0$,

$MSE = \dfrac{SSE}{N-k} = \dfrac{2{,}234}{15-3} = 186.2$, and $F = \dfrac{441}{186.2} = 2.37$.

These results are summarized in the following table.

Source of variation	Degrees of freedom	Sum of squares	Mean square	F
Treatments	2	882	441.0	2.37
Error	12	2,234	186.2	
Total	14	3,116		

5. Since $F = 2.37$ does not exceed 3.89, the value of $F_{0.05}$ for 2 and 12 degrees of freedom, we find that the null hypothesis (that the different descriptions do not affect the sales of the dinners) cannot be rejected. ∎

EXERCISES

(Exercises 14.1, 14.3, 14.4, and 14.5 are practice exercises. Their complete solutions are given on page 555.)

14.1   In performing an F test for the differences among k means, where each sample contains an equal number of items, we have $k-1$ degrees of freedom in the numerator and $k(n-1)$ degrees of freedom in the denominator.

How many degrees of freedom do we have in the numerator, and how many do we have in the denominator of the following?

(a) five randomly selected samples with four items in each sample

(b) four randomly selected samples with five items in each sample

(c) five randomly selected samples with five items in each sample

(d) four randomly selected samples with four items in each sample

14.2   In performing the F test for the differences among k means, if the variance ratio is 3.25 and the level of significance is $\alpha = 0.05$, should the null hypothesis be rejected where

(a) the degrees of freedom for the numerator are 5 and the degrees of freedom for the denominator are 6

(b) the degrees of freedom for the numerator are 15 and the degrees of freedom for the denominator are 11

14.3   An electronics manufacturer wants to test the thickness of the insulation which covers three competing brands of the same type of wire, using a sample of five randomly selected pieces of wire for each brand and carefully measuring the thickness of the insulation in millimeters. The results of these measurements are as follows:

Brand 1:	2.4	2.3	2.2	2.0	2.6
Brand 2:	2.0	2.2	2.5	2.6	2.7
Brand 3:	2.6	2.6	2.6	2.0	2.7

Use the method of Section 14.1 to test, at the 0.01 level of significance, the null hypothesis that the three competing brands of wire are covered with insulation of the same thickness.

14.4   Following are the numbers of patrons who responded to an advertised promotion in four beauty salons of a small chain of beauty salons on five randomly selected days.

Salon 1:	77	68	82	73	80
Salon 2:	75	63	77	74	76
Salon 3:	70	69	81	79	91
Salon 4:	68	60	63	71	63

(a) Use the method of Section 14.1 to test at the 0.05 level of significance the null hypothesis that the four beauty salons have the same number of responses to the advertised promotion.

(b) Perform an analysis of variance as shown in the illustration of Example 14.1 by substituting into the formulas for different sums of squares [SST, $SS(Tr)$, and SSE] and using the analysis of variance table. Compare the resulting F value with that obtained in part (a) of this exercise.

(c) Perform an analysis of variance as shown in Example 14.2, using the computing formulas for the required sums of squares, and compare the resulting F value with the F values obtained in parts (a) and (b) of this exercise.

14.5 In performing an F test for the differences among k means where the sample sizes are not all equal, the total number of degrees of freedom is obtained by $N - 1$, the total number of degrees of freedom for the numerator (treatments) is $k - 1$, and the total number of degrees of freedom for the denominator (error) is $N - k$. How many degrees of freedom do we have in the numerator, how many do we have in the denominator, and how many do we have in total for the following:

(a) three samples with 4, 5, and 6 observations, respectively

(b) four samples with 6, 6, 2, and 2 observations, respectively

(c) five samples with 8, 8, 7, 7, and 12 observations, respectively

14.6 Safety engineers tested three coal mines for the percentage of methane gas in the air by on-the-ground analysis of six randomly selected containers of air from each mine.

First mine:	0.4	1.7	7.2	1.9	4.8	6.1
Second mine:	2.0	1.8	4.0	4.6	1.1	0.9
Third mine:	3.7	1.9	0.6	3.9	3.0	1.4

Use the 0.05 level of significance and the computing formulas for sums of squares (sample sizes equal) to test whether the differences among the means of the three samples are significant.

14.7 The following numbers of boxes of different types of Girl Scout cookies were sold in each of eight communities:

Peanut butter	214	231	227	210	213	247	209	181
Vanilla creme:	210	218	211	198	216	231	240	203
Chocolate mint:	201	261	232	216	228	218	211	199

Use the 0.05 level of significance and the computing formulas for sums of squares (sample sizes equal) to test the null hypothesis that on the average the sales of the three types of cookies are the same.

14.8 Random samples of six students taken from four freshman mathematics sections at a university have the following grades on a common examination.

Section 1:	71	66	49	85	76	58
Section 2:	55	59	38	52	70	57
Section 3:	83	76	84	73	99	86
Section 4:	67	72	58	92	74	55

Use the computing formulas for the sum of squares (sample sizes equal) and the 0.01 level of significance to test whether the differences among the means of the four samples are significant.

14.9 A gasoline station is open 24 hours a day, operating on three 8-hour shifts with the morning shift beginning at midnight, followed by a day shift and night shift. The number of gasoline sales made on 16 randomly selected shifts is as follows:

Morning shift:	31	22	28	30			
Day shift:	28	39	44	32	36	28	30
Night shift:	24	31	22	18	20		

Perform an analysis of variance to test, at the 0.05 level of significance, whether the observed differences among the mean number of sales on the three shifts can be attributed to chance.

14.10 Following are the numbers of marketable apples harvested from randomly selected trees in four sections of a large apple orchard.

Northeast section:	79	48	57	82	69	79	78	92	
Southeast section:	67	75	73	77	52	69	71	82	51
Northwest section:	68	75	84	73	81				
Southwest section:	70	73	68	59	71	49	92	89	91	43

Use the 0.05 level of significance to test whether the differences among the four sample means can be attributed to chance.

14.11 With reference to the notation introduced in the footnote on page 526, show that the sum of the α's, the treatment effects, is equal to zero.

14.3

Two-Way Analysis of Variance

In Examples 14.1 and 14.2, which we used to illustrate a one-way analysis of variance, we were unable to show that there really is a difference in the average cholesterol content of the four diet foods, even though the sample means varied from 3.4 to 3.9 milligrams per package. The results were not statistically significant because there were also considerable differences among the values within each of the samples and, hence, a large experimental error. Since this is the quantity in the denominator of the F statistic, the F ratio was not large enough to lead us to reject the null hypothesis. But, suppose now we learn something that we did not know earlier—the measurements of the cholesterol contents were performed in different laboratories. The first value of each sample, we learn, came from one laboratory, the second value came from another laboratory, and the third value came from a third laboratory. This puts the whole study in a new light and we might picture the original data as follows:

	Laboratory 1	Laboratory 2	Laboratory 3
Diet food A	3.6	4.1	4.0
Diet food B	3.1	3.2	3.9
Diet food C	3.2	3.5	3.5
Diet food D	3.5	3.8	3.8

From these data we find that the means of the cholesterol readings from the three laboratories are 3.35, 3.65, and 3.80 milligrams, and this suggests that what we called chance variation, or experimental error, in our earlier analysis may well have been caused in part by differences in laboratories.

It also suggests that we should perform a **two-way analysis of variance**, in which the total variation of the data is partitioned into one component which we ascribe to possible differences due to one variable (the different treatments), a second component which we ascribe to possible differences due to a second variable—an extraneous variable which causes variations which should not be included in the error sum of squares—and a third component which we ascribe to chance. It is customary to call the categories of such an extraneous variable—the three laboratories in our example—**blocks**, thanks again to the origin of this method in agricultural research.

To formulate the null hypotheses to be tested in a two-way analysis of variance, let us write μ_{ij} for the true mean which corresponds to the ith treatment and the jth block (in our numerical illustration, the true average cholesterol content of the ith diet food as measured by the jth laboratory) and express it as

$$\mu_{ij} = \mu + \alpha_i + \beta_j$$

As in the notation of the footnote on page 526, μ is the grand mean (the average of all the μ_{ij}) and the α_i are the treatment effects (whose sum is zero). Correspondingly, we refer to the β_j as the **block effects** (whose sum is also zero), and write the two null hypotheses we want to test as

$$\alpha_1 = \alpha_2 = \cdots = \alpha_k = 0$$

and

Chapter 14 Decision Making: Analysis of Variance

$$\beta_1 = \beta_2 = \cdots = \beta_n = 0$$

The alternative to the first null hypothesis (which in our illustration amounts to the hypothesis that the true average cholesterol content is the same for the four foods) is that the treatment effects α_i are not all zero. Also, the alternative to the second null hypothesis (which in our illustration amounts to the hypothesis that the use of the different laboratories in performing the measurements has no effect on the results) is that the block effects β_j are not all zero.

To test the second of the null hypotheses, we need a quantity, similar to the treatment sum of squares, which measures the variation in the different block means (3.35, 3.65, and 3.80 milligrams in our example) instead of the variation in the different treatment means. So, if we let $T_{\cdot j}$ denote the total of the values in the jth block, substitute it for $T_{i\cdot}$ in the formula for $SS(Tr)$, sum on j instead of i, and interchange n and k, we obtain, analogous to $SS(Tr)$, the **block sum of squares**

Computing formula for block sum of squares

$$SSB = \frac{1}{k} \cdot \sum_{j=1}^{n} T_{\cdot j}^2 - \frac{1}{kn} \cdot T_{\cdot\cdot}^2.$$

In a two-way analysis of variance we compute SST and $SS(Tr)$ according to the formulas on page 533, SSB according to the formula immediately preceding, and then we get SSE by subtraction. Since

$$SST = SS(Tr) + SSB + SSE$$

we have

Error sum of squares (two-way analysis of variance)

$$SSE = SST - SS(Tr) - SSB$$

Observe that the error sum of squares for a two-way analysis of variance does not equal the error sum of squares for a one-way analysis of variance performed on the same data, even though we denote both with the symbol SSE. In fact, we are now partitioning the error sum of squares for the one-way analysis of variance into two terms: the block sum of squares, SSB, and the remainder which is the new error sum of squares, SSE.

We can now construct the following analysis of variance table for a two-way analysis of variance:

Source of variation	Degrees of freedom	Sum of squares	Mean square	F
Treatments	$k - 1$	$SS(Tr)$	$MS(Tr) = \dfrac{SS(Tr)}{k - 1}$	$\dfrac{MS(Tr)}{MSE}$
Blocks	$n - 1$	SSB	$MSB = \dfrac{SSB}{n - 1}$	$\dfrac{MSB}{MSE}$
Error	$(k - 1)(n - 1)$	SSE	$MSE = \dfrac{SSE}{(k - 1)(n - 1)}$	
Total	$kn - 1$	SST		

The mean squares are again given by the sums of squares divided by their degrees of freedom, and the two F values are given by the mean squares for treatments and blocks divided by the mean square for error. Also, the degrees of freedom for blocks is $n - 1$ (like those for treatments with n substituted for k), and the degrees of freedom for error can be found by subtracting the degrees of freedom for treatments and blocks from $kn - 1$, the total number of degrees of freedom:

$$(kn - 1) - (k - 1) - (n - 1) = kn - k - n + 1$$
$$= (k - 1)(n - 1)$$

Thus, in the significance test for treatments the numerator and denominator degrees of freedom for F are $k - 1$ and $(k - 1)(n - 1)$, and in the significance test for blocks the numerator and denominator degrees of freedom for F are $n - 1$ and $(k - 1)(n - 1)$.

EXAMPLE 14.4   Based on the data of page 542 test at the 0.05 level of significance whether the differences among the means obtained for the different diet foods (treatments) are significant, and also whether the differences among the means obtained for the different laboratories (blocks) are significant.

Chapter 14   Decision Making: Analysis of Variance

	Laboratory 1	Laboratory 2	Laboratory 3
Diet food A	3.6	4.1	4.0
Diet food B	3.1	3.2	3.9
Diet food C	3.2	3.5	3.5
Diet food D	3.5	3.8	3.8

SOLUTION   **1.** H_0's: $\alpha_1 = \alpha_2 = \alpha_3 = \alpha_4 = 0$;
$\qquad\qquad \beta_1 = \beta_2 = \beta_3 = 0$.
$\qquad H_A$: The treatment effects are not equal to zero;
$\qquad\qquad$ the block effects are not equal to zero.

2. $\alpha = 0.05$ for the differences among means obtained for the different diet foods (treatments); $\alpha = 0.05$ for the differences among means obtained for the different laboratories (blocks).

3. For treatments, reject the null hypothesis if $F \geq 4.76$, where F is determined by a two-way analysis of variance and 4.76 is the value of $F_{0.05}$ for $k - 1 = 4 - 1 = 3$ and $(k-1)(n-1) = (4-1)(3-1) = 6$ degrees of freedom. For blocks, reject the null hypothesis if $F \geq 5.14$, where F is determined by a two-way analysis of variance and 5.14 is the value of $F_{0.05}$ for $n - 1 = 3 - 1 = 2$ and $(k-1)(n-1) = (4-1)(3-1) = 6$ degrees of freedom. If either null hypothesis cannot be rejected, accept it or reserve judgment.

4. Substituting $k = 4$, $n = 3$, $T_{1.} = 11.7$, $T_{2.} = 10.2$, $T_{3.} = 10.2$, $T_{4.} = 11.1$, $T_{..} = 43.2$, and $\sum \sum x^2 = 156.70$ and for SSB, $T_{.1} = 13.4$, $T_{.2} = 14.6$, $T_{.3} = 15.2$, we get

$$SST = 156.70 - \frac{1}{12}(43.2)^2 = 1.18$$

$$SS(Tr) = \frac{1}{3}(11.7^2 + 10.2^2 + 10.2^2 + 11.1^2) - \frac{1}{12}(43.2)^2 = 0.54$$

Note that SST and $SS(Tr)$ were previously calculated in Example 14.2 and are reproduced here for convenience.

$$SSB = \frac{1}{k} \cdot \sum_{j=1}^{n} T_{.j}^2 - \frac{1}{kn} \cdot T_{..}^2 = \frac{1}{4}(13.4^2 + 14.6^2 + 15.2^2)$$
$$- \frac{1}{12}(43.2)^2 = 0.42$$

and

$$SSE = 1.18 - (0.54 + 0.42) = 0.22$$

$$MS(Tr) = \frac{0.54}{4 - 1} = 0.18, \ MSB = \frac{0.42}{3 - 1} = 0.21, \text{ and } MSE =$$

$$\frac{0.22}{(3)(2)} = 0.037, \text{ so that for treatments } F = \frac{0.18}{0.037} = 4.86, \text{ and}$$

for blocks $F = \dfrac{0.21}{0.037} = 5.68$. All these results are summarized
in the following analysis of variance table.

Source of variation	Degrees of freedom	Sum of squares	Mean square	F
Treatments	3	0.54	0.18	4.86
Blocks	2	0.42	0.21	5.68
Error	6	0.22	0.037	
Total	11	1.18		

5. Since $F = 4.86$ exceeds 4.76, the value of $F_{0.05}$ for three and
   six degrees of freedom, we find that we must reject the null
   hypothesis that the true average cholesterol content of the four
   diet foods is the same. Also, since $F = 5.68$ exceeds 5.14, the
   value of $F_{0.05}$ for two and six degrees of freedom, we find that
   we must reject the null hypothesis about the laboratories; in
   other words, we have shown that there is a systematic
   difference in the results provided by the three laboratories. This
   may not be of any special interest, but after taking the
   differences among the laboratories into account, it now seems
   evident that there are real differences among the cholesterol
   contents of the four foods. ■

The computer printout of Figure 14.3 is a two-way analysis of variance
for the preceding diet food example. The section at the bottom of the printout
headed "ANALYSIS OF VARIANCE" provides calculations which correspond precisely with those of the analysis of variance table except that the
values for F are not provided.

Caution must be used in the interpretation of the L (letter) plot provided
on the printout, since it does not use the letters of our table correspondingly.

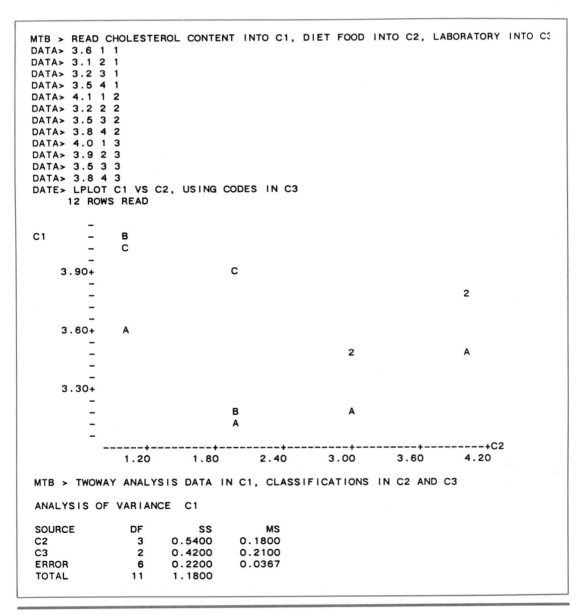

```
MTB > READ CHOLESTEROL CONTENT INTO C1, DIET FOOD INTO C2, LABORATORY INTO C3
DATA> 3.6  1  1
DATA> 3.1  2  1
DATA> 3.2  3  1
DATA> 3.5  4  1
DATA> 4.1  1  2
DATA> 3.2  2  2
DATA> 3.5  3  2
DATA> 3.8  4  2
DATA> 4.0  1  3
DATA> 3.9  2  3
DATA> 3.5  3  3
DATA> 3.8  4  3
DATE> LPLOT C1 VS C2, USING CODES IN C3
      12 ROWS READ


C1        -    B
          -    C
          -
    3.90+                       C
          -                                                  2
          -
          -
          -
    3.60+      A
          -                            2                A
          -
          -
          -
    3.30+
          -
          -                    B               A
          -                    A
          -
         ------+---------+---------+---------+---------+---------+C2
            1.20      1.80      2.40      3.00      3.60      4.20

MTB > TWOWAY ANALYSIS DATA IN C1, CLASSIFICATIONS IN C2 AND C3

ANALYSIS OF VARIANCE   C1

SOURCE        DF       SS         MS
C2             3     0.5400     0.1800
C3             2     0.4200     0.2100
ERROR          6     0.2200     0.0367
TOTAL         11     1.1800
```

FIGURE 14.3   Computer printout for two-way analysis of variance

The diagram assigns the letter A to the cholesterol readings of each of the four diet foods as measured in laboratory 1, the letter B to the cholesterol readings of the foods as measured in laboratory 2, and the letter C to the cholesterol readings of the foods as measured in laboratory 3. Where two laboratories have identical readings for a diet food, this is designated on the diagram with the numeral 2. Imaginary vertical lines drawn from the 1, 2, 3, and 4 of the $\bar{x}$ axis provide columns on which diet foods A, B, C, and D, respectively, are plotted. The y axis shows cholesterol readings in milligrams. If we draw a pencil line connecting all the plotted A values, this line shows us the cholesterol measurements of each of the four diet foods by laboratory 1. This pencil line makes it immediately apparent that laboratory 1 gets consistently lower cholesterol measurements for all the foods it tests, at least in this experiment.

The diet foods data which we just analyzed constitute a **complete-block experiment**. It is complete in the sense that each treatment occurs in each block the same number of times—in our example, each diet food is tested once by each laboratory. In a complete-block experiment, the treatments are our primary concern while the blocks represent an extraneous variable, sometimes called a **nuisance variable**, which we introduce to eliminate the variation caused by it from the error sum of squares.

However, a two-way analysis of variance can also be used in connection with **two-factor experiments**, where both variables are of material concern. This would be the case, for example, in an analysis of the following data collected in an experiment designed to test whether or not the range of a missile flight (in miles) is affected by three different launchers and also by four different fuels (see Exercise 14.18 on page 551):

	Fuel 1	Fuel 2	Fuel 3	Fuel 4
Launcher X	45.9	57.6	52.2	41.7
Launcher Y	46.0	51.0	50.1	38.8
Launcher Z	45.7	56.9	55.3	48.1

Note that we used a different format for the table to distinguish between two-factor and complete-block experiments.

When a two-way analaysis of variance is used in this way, we usually call the two variables **factors A** and **B** (instead of treatments and blocks) and write SSA instead of $SS(Tr)$; we still write SSB, but now B stands for factor B instead of for blocks.

EXERCISES

(Exercises 14.12, 14.14, and 14.17 are practice exercises. Their complete solutions are given on page 555.)

14.12 In a test of significance for two-way analysis of variance, the numerator and denominator degrees of freedom of the F ratio for treatments and for blocks are

	Numerator	Denominator
Treatments	$k - 1$	$(k-1)(n-1)$
Blocks	$n - 1$	$(k-1)(n-1)$

Suppose that in a significance test for two-way analysis of variance, the blocks and treatments are shown here, with each XXX representing an observation

	Block 1	Block 2	Block 3	Block 4	Block 5
Treatment 1	XXX	XXX	XXX	XXX	XXX
Treatment 2	XXX	XXX	XXX	XXX	XXX
Treatment 3	XXX	XXX	XXX	XXX	XXX
Treatment 4	XXX	XXX	XXX	XXX	XXX

Using Table IV and the information provided, determine
(a) the critical value of $F_{0.05}$ for treatments
(b) the critical value of $F_{0.05}$ for blocks

14.13 Use the information and table in Exercise 14.12 to determine
(a) the critical value of $F_{0.01}$ for treatments
(b) the critical value of $F_{0.01}$ for blocks

14.14 The sales manager of a chain of five garden shops wants to know the effectiveness of four different kinds of packaging on the sales of identical grass seed and puts each kind of package in each of the five shops. Perform a two-way analysis of variance on the number of packages sold on a given day to test the null hypothesis that packaging has no effect on sales, at the 0.05 level of significance.

	Store 1	Store 2	Store 3	Store 4	Store 5
Plastic bag	45	37	41	37	50
Paper bag	54	54	56	44	47
Plain box	45	56	58	47	45
Dispenser box	61	55	50	49	52

14.15 Four different, although supposedly equivalent, forms of a standardized achievement test are given to each of four students, and the following are their scores:

	Student C	Student D	Student E	Student F
Form 1	77	62	52	66
Form 2	85	63	49	65
Form 3	81	65	46	64
Form 4	88	72	55	60

Perform a two-way analysis of variance to test at the 0.01 level of significance whether it is reasonable to treat the four forms as equivalent. If the order in which each student takes the four tests is **randomized** by some means, we call the design of this experiment a **randomized block design**. The purpose of this randomization is to take care of such possible extraneous factors as fatigue, or perhaps the experiences gained from repeatedly taking the test.

14.16 In an experiment, American upland cotton seeds provided by three commercial seed companies were planted on equal sized test lots at five agricultural field stations. The resulting cotton linters were weighed, in pounds, with the following results.

	Station 1	Station 2	Station 3	Station 4	Station 5
Seed company 1	40	44	35	45	41
Seed company 2	48	46	49	45	47
Seed company 3	46	49	43	48	44

Perform a two-way analysis of variance, using the 0.05 level of significance for both tests.

14.17 A supermarket chain conducted a study to determine where to place its generic-brand products in order to increase sales. Sales (in thousands of dollars) for one week were as follows:

	Store 1	Store 2	Store 3
High shelf	57	53	49
Eye-level shelf	50	55	53
Low shelf	52	52	56

Perform a two-way analysis of variance, using the level of significance $\alpha = 0.05$.

14.18   With reference to the missile range data on page 548, perform a two-way analysis of variance to test at the 0.05 level of significance whether there are significant differences

(a) among the mean ranges for the three launchers

(b) among the mean ranges for the four fuels

14.4

A Word of Caution

Although the analysis of variance is a very powerful statistical tool, our example shows what can happen when we use the wrong kind of analysis, in this case, a one-way analysis when we should have used a two-way analysis. In addition to this there are many other pitfalls, for it is often difficult to determine whether the necessary assumptions are met. In the two-way analysis we had only one observation from each population, that is, one observation for each combination of diet foods and laboratories. Consequently, it is impossible in this example to determine statistically whether the populations sampled have roughly the shape of normal distributions with the same variance. To aid in such a determination, we might have taken several observations from each population, but there are many situations in which this is neither feasible nor practical.

Furthermore, it should be understood that what we have presented here is merely an introduction to some of the most basic techniques which come under the general heading of analysis of variance. An obvious generalization would be to apply the idea of analyzing the total variation of a set of data to experiments in which there are more than two variables about which we want to test hypotheses. Then there are situations in which the variables under consideration are not independent. Suppose, for instance, that a tire manufacturer is experimenting with variuos treads under various road conditions, and finds that one kind is especially good for dirt roads while another kind is especially good for icy roads. If this is the case, we say that there is an **interaction** between road conditions and the designs of the treads. On the other hand, if each of the treads performed equally under all kinds of road conditions, we would say that there is no interaction and that the two variables (tread design and road conditions) are independent. Here we have studied only the case where there is assumed to be no interaction.

Finally, let us mention the problem of how to interpret the results of an analysis of variance once it has been shown that the populations sampled do not have equal means. For instance, in the example dealing with the four diet foods, A, B, C, and D, the sample means were 3.9, 3.4, 3.4, and 3.7, and the differences among them were shown to be significant, but can we conclude that in general food A contains more cholesterol on the average than the other three? Or can we conclude that foods B and C are really lower in cholesterol content than food D? There exist statistical techniques which provide answers to questions of this kind; they are called **multiple-comparisons tests**, and they may be found in more advanced texts.

14.5

Checklist of Key Terms

Analysis of variance,   525
Analysis of variance table,   531
ANOVA,   525
Block effects,   542
Block sum of squares,   543
Blocks,   542
Complete-block experiment,   548
Degrees of freedom,   529
Error sum of squares,   530
Experimental error,   529
F statistic,   528
Grand mean,   526, 530

Mean squares,   532
Nuisance variable,   548
One-way analysis of variance,   530
Randomized block design,   550
Total sum of squares,   529
Treatment effects,   526
Treatment sum of squares,   530
Treatments,   530
Two-factor experiment,   548
Two-way analysis of variance,   542
Variance ratio,   528

14.6

Review Exercises

14.19 To compare the times required by four experienced assembly workers to assemble a table, the assembling of several identical tables by these workers was timed, in minutes, and the following observations were obtained.

Alice:	22.0	20.3	18.2	23.6	22.4
Bill:	22.9	21.1	23.2	24.8	
Claire:	21.1	18.6	22.2	18.0	19.9	23.0
Dave:	20.9	25.1	20.7	21.8	23.4	

At the 0.05 level of significance, can the differences among the means of the four workers be attributed to chance?

14.20 Three hot-beverage vending machines are thought to be defective and their performances have been recorded over a two-month period. The following data show the numbers of times these machines have failed to operate properly during the period:

	Machine 1	Machine 2	Machine 3
Coffee	22	24	16
Soup	26	25	22
Tea	19	21	17
Hot chocolate	16	20	15

Perform a two-way analysis of variance and test, at the 0.05 level of significance, whether

(a) the differences among the means obtained for the four beverages can be attributed to chance

(b) the differences among the means obtained for the three vending machines can be attributed to chance

14.21 To find the best arrangement of instruments on a control panel of an airplane, three different arrangements were tested by simulating an emergency condition and observing the reaction time required to correct the condition. The reaction times (in tenths of a second) of 12 pilots (randomly assigned to the different arrangements) were as follows:

Arrangement 1:	8	15	10	11
Arrangement 2:	16	11	14	19
Arrangement 3:	12	7	13	8

(a) Use the method of Section 14.1 and the 0.05 level of significance to test whether the differences among the three sample means can be attributed to chance.

(b) Use the computing formulas for SST, $SS(Tr)$, and SSE to determine the values of these sums of the squares for the given data, construct an analysis of variance table, and compare the value of F with that obtained in part (a).

14.22 The following are the miles per gallon of gasoline obtained by four test drivers operating, in turn, three different automobiles.

	Test driver 1	Test driver 2	Test driver 3	Test driver 4
Automobile 1	19.1	19.4	19.7	18.3
Automobile 2	23.8	24.5	26.0	25.0
Automobile 3	29.1	26.9	27.4	28.2

Perform a two-way analysis of variance and test at the 0.01 level of significance whether

(a) the differences among the means obtained by the three automobiles can be attributed to chance

(b) the differences among the means obtained by the four drivers can be attributed to chance

14.23 The sample data in the following table are the wages earned in a certain week, in dollars, by nine randomly selected workers who are engaged in various work activities in three large companies.

	Company 1	Company 2	Company 3
Machine operators	403	395	430
Assemblers	391	370	425
Inspectors	406	402	400

Analyze this two-factor experiment using the 0.05 level of significance.

14.24 The following are the numbers of sales returns made by customers on five randomly selected days at four department stores.

Department store 1:	14	20	18	10	26
Department store 2:	20	28	12	22	18
Department store 3:	26	18	22	26	16
Department store 4:	20	18	14	22	16

Test at the 0.05 level of significance whether the differences among the means of the sales returns at the four sampled department stores can be attributed to chance, using the computing formulas for SST, $SS(Tr)$, and SSE.

14.25 Analysis of the maintenance records of four randomly selected photocopying machines of each of three brands shows the following numbers of downtimes during a year. All machines are new and have had about the same amount of use under similar conditions.

> Copier A: 16   20   10   14
> Copier B: 35   25   31   29
> Copier C: 17   22   21   24

Test at the 0.01 level of significance whether the differences among the three means are significant, using the computing formulas for *SST*, *SS(Tr)*, and *SSE*.

14.26 Use a computer package to rework the *F* test of Example 14.3 where the restaurant manager wants to know whether the sales of steak and shrimp combination dinners depend on how this entree is described on the menu.

14.27 Use a computer package to rework Exercise 14.14 where the manager of a chain of five garden shops wants to know the effectiveness of four different kinds of packaging on the sales of identical grass seed.

14.28 Use a computer package to rework Exercise 14.15 where four different, although supposedly equivalent forms of a standardized achievement test are given to each of four students.

14.29 Use a computer package to rework Exercise 14.20 where three hot-beverage dispensing machines are thought to be defective and their performances have been recorded over a two-month period.

14.30 Use a computer package to rework Exercise 14.22 where three automobiles are driven by four test drivers and the mileages per gallon of gasoline are obtained.

14.7

Solutions of Practice Exercises

14.1 (a) $(k - 1) = (5 - 1) = 4$ degrees of freedom in the numerator, and $k(n - 1) = 5(4 - 1) = 15$ degrees of freedom in the denominator.

(b) $(k - 1) = (4 - 1) = 3$ degrees of freedom in the numerator, and $k(n - 1) = 4(5 - 1) = 16$ degrees of freedom in the denominator.

(c) $(k - 1) = (5 - 1) = 4$ degrees of freedom in the numerator, and $k(n - 1) = 5(5 - 1) = 20$ degrees of freedom in the denominator.

(d) $(k - 1) = (4 - 1) = 3$ degrees of freedom in the numerator, and $k(n - 1) = 4(4 - 1) = 12$ degrees of freedom in the denominator.

14.3 **1.** H_0: $\mu_1 = \mu_2 = \mu_3$.
   H_A: The μ's are not all equal.

2. $\alpha = 0.01$.

3. Reject the null hypothesis if $F \geq 6.93$, where

$$F = \frac{\text{estimate of } \sigma^2 \text{ based on the variation among the } \bar{x}\text{'s}}{\text{estimate of } \sigma^2 \text{ based on the variation within the samples}}$$

$k - 1 = 3 - 1 = 2$ degrees of freedom for the numerator, and $k(n - 1) = 3(5 - 1) = 12$ degrees of freedom for the denominator. Otherwise, accept the null hypothesis or reserve judgment.

4. To obtain the numerator of the variance ratio, first calculate the three means and the grand mean of the three samples, getting $\frac{2.3 + 2.4 + 2.5}{3} = 2.4$. Then, substituting into the formula which defines the sample variance, we get $s_{\bar{x}}^2 =$

$$\frac{(2.3 - 2.4)^2 + (2.4 - 2.4)^2 + (2.5 - 2.4)^2}{3 - 1} = 0.01. \text{ Finally, multiply-}$$

ing by the sample size $n = 5$, we obtain $(5)(0.01) = 0.050$ for the numerator. To obtain the denominator of the variance ratio, we calculate and pool (average) the variances of the three samples as follows.

$$s_1^2 + s_2^2 + s_3^2 =$$

$$\frac{1}{3}\left[\frac{(2.4 - 2.3)^2 + (2.3 - 2.3)^2 + (2.2 - 2.3)^2 + (2.0 - 2.3)^2 + (2.6 - 2.3)^2}{5 - 1}\right.$$

$$+ \frac{(2.0 - 2.4)^2 + (2.2 - 2.4)^2 + (2.5 - 2.4)^2 + (2.6 - 2.4)^2 + (2.7 - 2.4)^2}{5 - 1}$$

$$\left. + \frac{(2.6 - 2.5)^2 + (2.6 - 2.5)^2 + (2.6 - 2.5)^2 + (2.0 - 2.5)^2 + (2.7 - 2.5)^2}{5 - 1}\right]$$

$$= 0.072$$

Combining the numerator and the denominator of the variance ratio, we get $F = \dfrac{0.050}{0.072} = 0.69$.

5. Since $F = 0.69$ does not exceed 6.93, the null hypothesis cannot be rejected. It appears that there is no difference in the thickness of the insulation covering the three brands of wire.

14.4 (a) **1.** $H_0: \mu_1 = \mu_2 = \mu_3 = \mu_4$.
   H_A: The μ's are not all equal.

2. $\alpha = 0.05$.

3. Reject the null hypothesis if $F \geq 3.24$, where

$$F = \frac{\text{estimate of } \sigma^2 \text{ based on the variation among the } \bar{x}\text{'s}}{\text{estimate of } \sigma^2 \text{ based on the variation within the samples}},$$

$k - 1 = 4 - 1 = 3$ degrees of freedom for the numerator, and $k(n - 1) = 4(5 - 1) = 16$ degrees of freedom for the denominator. Otherwise, accept the null hypothesis or reserve judgment.

4. To obtain the numerator of the variance ratio, first calculate the means, and then the grand mean of the $\bar{x}$'s of the four samples getting, for the grand mean

$$\frac{76 + 73 + 78 + 65}{4} = 73$$

Then, substituting into the formula which defines the sample variance, we get

$$s_{\bar{x}}^2 = \frac{(76 - 73)^2 + (73 - 73)^2 + (78 - 73)^2 + (65 - 73)^2}{4 - 1} = 32.67$$

Finally, multiplying by the sample size, $n = 5$, we obtain 163.35 for the numerator.

To obtain the denominator of the variance ratio we calculate and pool (average) the variance of the four samples as follows.

$$\frac{s_1^2 + s_2^2 + s_3^2 + s_4^2}{4} =$$

$$\frac{1}{4}\left[\frac{(77 - 76)^2 + (68 - 76)^2 + (82 - 76)^2 + (73 - 76)^2 + (80 - 76)^2}{5 - 1} \right.$$

$$+ \frac{(75 - 73)^2 + (63 - 73)^2 + (77 - 73)^2 + (74 - 73)^2 + (76 - 73)^2}{5 - 1}$$

$$+ \frac{(70 - 78)^2 + (69 - 78)^2 + (81 - 78)^2 + (79 - 78)^2 + (91 - 78)^2}{5 - 1}$$

$$\left. + \frac{(68 - 65)^2 + (60 - 65)^2 + (63 - 65)^2 + (71 - 65)^2 + (63 - 65)^2}{5 - 1} \right]$$

$$= 41.12$$

5. Since $F = \dfrac{163.35}{41.12} = 3.97$ is greater than 3.24 the null hypothesis must be rejected. The difference is significant. In other words, the μ's are not all equal.

(b) 1. H_0: $\mu_1 = \mu_2 = \mu_3 = \mu_4$.
   H_A: The μ's are not all equal.

2. $\alpha = 0.05$.

3. Reject the null hypothesis if $F \geq 3.24$, where

$$F = \frac{\text{estimate of } \sigma^2 \text{ based on the variation among the } \bar{x}\text{'s}}{\text{estimate of } \sigma^2 \text{ based on the variation within the samples}}$$

$(k - 1) = 4 - 1 = 3$ degrees of freedom for the numerator, and $k(n - 1) = 4(5 - 1) = 16$ degrees of freedom for the denominator.

$kn - 1 = (4 \cdot 5) - 1 = 19$ provides a check as it equals the sum of the other two.

4. Next we calculate SST, $SS(Tr)$, and SSE and insert these values into the analysis of variance table.

$$
\begin{aligned}
SST = {} & (77 - 73)^2 + (68 - 73)^2 + (82 - 73)^2 + (73 - 73)^2 + (80 - 73)^2 \\
& + (75 - 73)^2 + (63 - 73)^2 + (77 - 73)^2 + (74 - 73)^2 + (76 - 73)^2 \\
& + (70 - 73)^2 + (69 - 73)^2 + (81 - 73)^2 + (79 - 73)^2 + (91 - 73)^2 \\
& + (68 - 73)^2 + (60 - 73)^2 + (63 - 73)^2 + (71 - 73)^2 + (63 - 73)^2 \\
= {} & 1148 \\
SS(Tr) = {} & 5\,[(76 - 73)^2 + (73 - 73)^2 + (78 - 73)^2 + (65 - 73)^2] = 490 \\
SSE = {} & (77 - 76)^2 + (68 - 76)^2 + (82 - 76)^2 + (73 - 76)^2 + (80 - 76)^2 \\
& + (75 - 73)^2 + (63 - 73)^2 + (77 - 73)^2 + (74 - 73)^2 + (76 - 73)^2 \\
& + (70 - 78)^2 + (69 - 78)^2 + (81 - 78)^2 + (79 - 78)^2 + (91 - 78)^2 \\
& + (68 - 65)^2 + (60 - 65)^2 + (63 - 65)^2 + (71 - 65)^2 + (63 - 65)^2 \\
= {} & 658
\end{aligned}
$$

and it can be seen that $SS(Tr) + SSE = 490 + 658 = 1{,}148 = SST$. We exhibit $SS(Tr)$, SSE, and SST, and calculate F in an analysis of variance table.

Source of variation	Degrees of freedom	Sum of squares	Mean square	F
Treatments	$(k - 1)$ $4 - 1 = 3$	$SS(Tr)$ 490	$MS(Tr) = \dfrac{SS(Tr)}{k - 1}$ $= \dfrac{490}{4 - 1} = 163.33$	$\dfrac{MS(Tr)}{MSE} =$ $\dfrac{163.33}{41.12} = 3.97$
Error	$k(n - 1)$ $4(5 - 1) = 16$	SSE 658	$MSE = \dfrac{SSE}{k(n - 1)} =$ $\dfrac{658}{4(5 - 1)} = 41.12$	
Total	$3 + 16 = 19$; and $kn - 1 =$ $(4 \cdot 5) - 1 = 19$	$490 + 658 =$ $1{,}148 = SST$		

5. Since $F = 3.97$ is greater than 3.24 the null hypothesis must be rejected. The difference is significant.

(c) 1. H_0: $\mu_1 = \mu_2 = \mu_3 = \mu_4$.
H_A: The μ's are not all equal.
2. $\alpha = 0.05$.

3. Reject the null hypothesis if $F \geq 3.24$ where we use the computing formulas for SST, $SS(Tr)$, and SSE; $(k-1) = 4 - 1 = 3$ degrees of freedom for the numerator; and $k(n-1) = 4(5-1) = 16$ degrees of freedom for the denominator. $kn - 1 = (4 \cdot 5) - 1 = 19$ is a check as it equals the sum of the other two.

4. Substituting $k = 4$, $n = 5$, $T_{1.} = 77 + 68 + 82 + 73 + 80 = 380$, $T_{2.} = 75 + 63 + 77 + 74 + 76 = 365$, $T_{3.} = 70 + 69 + 81 + 79 + 91 = 390$, and $T_{4.} = 68 + 60 + 63 + 71 + 63 = 325$, $T_{..} = 380 + 365 + 390 + 325 = 1,460$, and $\sum \sum x^2 = 77^2 + 68^2 + 82^2 + \cdots + 71^2 + 63^2 = 107,728$ into the formulas we get

$$SST = \sum_{i=1}^{k} \sum_{j=1}^{n} x_{ij}^2 - \frac{1}{kn} \cdot T_{..}^2 = 107,728 - \frac{1}{(4)(5)}(1,460)^2 = 1,148$$

$$SS(Tr) = \frac{1}{n} \cdot \sum_{i=1}^{k} T_{i.}^2 - \frac{1}{kn} \cdot T_{..}^2 = \frac{1}{5} \cdot (380^2 + 365^2 + 390^2 + 325^2)$$
$$- \frac{1}{(4)(5)}(1,460)^2 = 490$$

and by subtraction $SSE = SST - SS(Tr) = 1,148 - 490 = 658$.

Insert the results in the analysis of variance table and calculate $F = 3.97$. Since the values of SST, $SS(Tr)$, and SSE are exactly the same as in part (b) of this exercise, the analysis of variance table for part (c) is also exactly the same.

5. Since $F = 3.97$ is greater than 3.24, the null hypothesis must be rejected. The difference is significant.

Parts (a), (b), and (c) of this exercise have the same solutions.

14.5   (a) Numerator has $k - 1 = 3 - 1 = 2$, denominator has $N - k = 15 - 3 = 12$, and total has $N - 1 = 15 - 1 = 14$ degrees of freedom.

      (b) Numerator has $k - 1 = 4 - 1 = 3$, denominator has $N - k = 16 - 4 = 12$, and total has $N - 1 = 16 - 1 = 15$ degrees of freedom.

      (c) Numerator has $k - 1 = 5 - 1 = 4$, denominator has $N - k = 42 - 5 = 37$, and total has $N - 1 = 42 - 1 = 41$ degrees of freedom.

14.12 (a) Degrees of freedom for numerator are $k - 1 = 4 - 1 = 3$; degrees of freedom for denominator are $(k - 1)(n - 1) = (4 - 1)(5 - 1) = 12$. $F_{0.05}$ for 3 and 12 degrees of freedom is 3.49.

      (b) Degrees of freedom for numerator are $n - 1 = 5 - 1 = 4$; degrees of freedom for denominator are $(k - 1)(n - 1) = (4 - 1)(5 - 1) = 12$. $F_{0.05}$ for 4 and 12 degrees of freedom is 3.26.

14.14 1. H_0's: $\alpha_1 = \alpha_2 = \alpha_3 = \alpha_4 = 0$;
          $\beta_1 = \beta_2 = \beta_3 = \beta_4 = \beta_5 = 0$.
     H_A's: The treatment effects are not all equal to zero; the block effects are not all equal to zero.

2. $\alpha = 0.05$ for both tests.

3. For treatments, reject the null hypothesis if $F \geq 3.49$, where F is determined by a two-way analysis of variance, 3.49 is the value of $F_{0.05}$ for $k - 1 = 4 - 1 = 3$ degrees of freedom (numerator), and $(k - 1)(n - 1) = (4 - 1)(5 - 1) = 12$ degrees of freedom (denominator). For blocks, reject the null hypothesis if $F \geq 3.26$ where F is determined by a two-way analysis of variance, 3.26 is the value of $F_{0.05}$ for $n - 1 = 5 - 1 = 4$ (numerator), and $(k - 1)(n - 1) = (4 - 1)(5 - 1) = 12$ (denominator) degrees of freedom. If either null hypothesis cannot be rejected, accept it or reserve judgment.

4. Substituting $k = 4$, $n = 5$, $T_{1.} = 45 + 37 + 41 + 37 + 50 = 210$, $T_{2.} = 54 + 54 + 56 + 44 + 47 = 255$, $T_{3.} = 45 + 56 + 58 + 47 + 45 = 251$, $T_{4.} = 61 + 55 + 50 + 49 + 52 = 267$; $T_{.1} = 45 + 54 + 45 + 61 = 205$, $T_{.2} = 37 + 54 + 56 + 55 = 202$, $T_{.3} = 41 + 56 + 58 + 50 = 205$, $T_{.4} = 37 + 44 + 47 + 49 = 177$, $T_{.5} = 50 + 47 + 45 + 52 = 194$; $T_{..} = 205 + 202 + 205 + 177 + 194 = 983$; $\sum \sum x^2 = 45^2 + 37^2 + 41^2 + 37^2 + 50^2 + 54^2 + 54^2 + 56^2 + 44^2 + 47^2 + 45^2 + 56^2 + 58^2 + 47^2 + 45^2 + 61^2 + 55^2 + 50^2 + 49^2 + 52^2 = 49{,}167$ into the computing formulas for sums of squares we get

$$SST = \sum_{i=1}^{k} \sum_{j=1}^{n} x_{ij}^2 - \frac{1}{kn} \cdot T_{..}^2 = 49{,}167 - \frac{1}{(4)(5)} \cdot 983^2 = 852.55$$

$$SS(Tr) = \frac{1}{n} \cdot \sum_{i=1}^{k} T_{i.}^2 - \frac{1}{kn} \cdot T_{..}^2 = \frac{1}{5}(210^2 + 255^2 + 251^2 + 267^2) - \frac{1}{20} \cdot 983^2$$
$$= 368.55$$

$$SSB = \frac{1}{k} \cdot \sum_{j=1}^{n} T_{.j}^2 - \frac{1}{kn} \cdot T_{..}^2 = \frac{1}{4}(205^2 + 202^2 + 205^2 + 177^2 + 194^2) - \frac{1}{20} \cdot 983^2$$
$$= 140.30, \text{ and}$$

$$SSE = SST - SS(Tr) - SSB = 852.55 - (368.55 + 140.30) = 343.70.$$

As may be seen in step 3, the degrees of freedom are $k - 1 = 3$, $n - 1 = 4$, $(k - 1)(n - 1) = 12$; and $kn - 1 = 4 \cdot 5 - 1 = 19$ (which is a check for $3 + 4 + 12 = 19$), and we get

$$MS(Tr) = \frac{SS(Tr)}{k - 1} = \frac{368.55}{3} = 122.85; \quad MSB = \frac{SSB}{n - 1} = \frac{140.30}{4} = 35.08$$

$$MSE = \frac{SSE}{(k - 1)(n - 1)} = \frac{343.70}{12} = 28.64; \quad F = \frac{122.85}{28.64} = 4.29 \quad \text{for}$$

treatments and $F = \dfrac{35.08}{28.64} = 1.22$ for blocks, and all these results are summarized in the following analysis of variance table.

Source of variation	Degrees of freedom	Sum of squares	Mean squares	F
Treatments	3	368.55	122.85	4.29
Blocks	4	140.30	35.08	1.22
Error	12	343.70	28.64	
Total	19	852.55		

5. For treatments, since $F = 4.29$ exceeds 3.49, the null hypothesis must be rejected; for blocks, since $F = 1.22$ is less than 3.26, we cannot reject the null hypothesis. In other words, we can reject the null hypothesis that the type of packaging makes no difference. For blocks, since 1.22 does not exceed 3.26, the null hypothesis cannot be rejected. In other words, we cannot reject the null hypothesis that the sales of grass seed are the same in the five stores.

14.17　**1.** H_0's: $\alpha_1 = \alpha_2 = \alpha_3 = 0$;
　　　　　　$\beta_1 = \beta_2 = \beta_3 = 0$.
H_A's: The A factors are not all equal to zero; the B factors are not all equal to zero.

2. $\alpha = 0.05$ for both tests.

3. For A factors, reject the null hypothesis if $F \geq 6.94$ where F is determined by a two-way analysis of variance, 6.94 is the value of $F_{0.05}$ for $k - 1 = 3 - 1 = 2$ degrees of freedom (numerator), and $(k - 1)(n - 1) = (3 - 1)(3 - 1) = 4$ degrees of freedom (denominator). For blocks, reject the null hypothesis if $F \geq 6.94$, where F is determined by a two-way analysis of variance and 6.94 is the value of $F_{0.05}$ for $n - 1 = 3 - 1 = 2$ degrees of freedom (numerator), and $(k - 1)(n - 1) = 4$ (denominator) degrees of freedom. If either null hypothesis cannot be rejected, accept it or reserve judgment.

4. Substituting $k = 3$, $n = 3$, $T_{1.} = 57 + 53 + 49 = 159$, $T_{2.} = 50 + 55 + 53 = 158$, $T_{3.} = 52 + 52 + 56 = 160$, $T_{.1} = 57 + 50 + 52 = 159$, $T_{.2} = 53 + 55 + 52 = 160$, $T_{.3} = 49 + 53 + 56 = 158$, $T_{..} = 159 + 160 + 158 = 477$, and $\sum\sum x^2 = 57^2 + 53^2 + 49^2 + 50^2 + 55^2 + 53^2 + 52^2 + 52^2 + 56^2 = 25{,}337$ into the computing formulas for the sums of squares, we get

$$SST = \sum_{i=1}^{k} \sum_{j=1}^{n} x_{ij}^2 - \frac{1}{kn} \cdot T_{..}^2 = 25{,}337 - \frac{1}{9} \cdot 477^2 = 56.00$$

$$SSA = \frac{1}{n} \cdot \sum_{i=1}^{k} T_{i\cdot}^2 - \frac{1}{kn} \cdot T_{\cdot\cdot}^2 = \frac{1}{3}(159^2 + 158^2 + 160^2) - \frac{1}{9} \cdot 477^2 = 0.67$$

$$SSB = \frac{1}{k} \cdot \sum_{j=1}^{n} T_{\cdot j}^2 - \frac{1}{kn} \cdot T_{\cdot\cdot}^2 = \frac{1}{3}(159^2 + 160^2 + 158^2) - \frac{1}{9} \cdot 477^2 = 0.67$$

$$SSE = SST - SSA - SSB = 56.00 - 0.67 - 0.67 = 54.66$$

Since the degrees of freedom are
$$k - 1 = 3 - 1 = 2, \ n - 1 = 3 - 1 = 2, \ (k - 1)(n - 1) = 4,$$
and $kn - 1 = 9 - 1 = 8$, we then get $MSA = \dfrac{0.67}{2} = 0.34,$

$MSB = \dfrac{0.67}{2} = 0.34$, and $MSE = \dfrac{54.66}{4} = 13.66.$

$F = \dfrac{0.34}{13.67} = 0.02$ for A factors (shelf life), and $F = \dfrac{0.34}{13.67} = 0.02$

for B factors (stores).

5. Since $F = 0.02$ is less than 6.94, the value of $F_{0.05}$ for two and four degrees of freedom, the null hypothesis for shelf life cannot be rejected; also, since $F = 0.02$ is less than 6.94, the value of $F^{0.05}$ for two and four degrees of freedom, the null hypothesis for store location cannot be rejected.

Decision Making: Nonparametric Tests

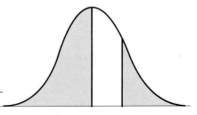

Most of the tests of hypotheses discussed in Chapters 11 through 14 require specific assumptions about the population, or populations, sampled. In many cases, we must assume that the populations have roughly the shape of normal distributions, or that their variances are known or are known to be equal, or that the samples are independent. Since there are many situations where these assumptions cannot be met, statisticians have developed alternative techniques based on less stringent assumptions, which have become known as **nonparametric tests**.

Aside from the fact that nonparametric tests may be used under very general conditions, they are often easier to explain and understand than the standard tests which they replace; moreover, in many of these tests the computational burden is relatively light. For these reasons, nonparametric tests have become quite popular, and extensive literature is devoted to their theory and application.

In Sections 15.1 through 15.5 we shall present the **sign test** (unranked) as a nonparametric alternative to tests concerning differences between means and tests concerning differences between means based upon paired data. In Sections 15.4, 15.5, 15.6, 15.7, and 15.8 we study the sign test, the **U** test, and the **H test**, which are based upon **rank sums**. In Sections 15.9, 15.10, 15.11 we shall learn how to test **randomness** of a sample once the data have been obtained by using the **total number of runs** and **runs above and below the median**. Finally, in Section 15.12 we shall illustrate the calculation of *P*-values in nonparametric tests.

15.1

The One-Sample Sign Test

Except for the large-sample tests, all the standard tests concerning means that we have studied are based on the assumption that the populations sampled have roughly the shape of normal distributions. When in a particular case this assumption is untenable, the standard test can be replaced by one of several nonparametric alternatives, among them the **sign test**, which we shall study in Sections 15.1, 15.2, 15.3, 15.4 and 15.5.

The one-sample sign test applies when we sample a continuous symmetrical population, so that the probability a sample value is less than the mean and the probability a sample value is greater than the mean are both $\frac{1}{2}$.[1] To test the null hypothesis $\mu = \mu_0$ against an appropriate alternative on the basis of a random sample of size n, we replace each sample value greater than μ_0 with a plus sign and each sample value less than μ_0 with a minus sign; then we test the null hypothesis that these plus and minus signs are values of a random variable having the binomial distribution with $p = \frac{1}{2}$. (If a sample value equals μ_0, which is possible since we usually deal with rounded data, we simply discard it.)

To perform the actual test when the sample is small, we can refer directly to tables of binomial probabilities such as Table V, and when the sample is large, we can use the normal approximation to the binomial distribution.

EXAMPLE 15.1   In a given year, the average number of days required by a (small) sample of 15 wholesalers of drugs and drug sundries to convert receivables into cash were 33.9, 35.4, 37.3, 40.9, 27.8, 35.5, 34.6, 41.1, 30.0, 43.2, 33.9, 41.3, 32.0, 37.7, and 35.2 days. Use the one-sample sign test to test the null hypothesis $\mu = 32.0$ days

---

[1]If we cannot assume that the population is symmetrical, we can still use the one sample sign test, but we have to test the null hypothesis $\tilde{\mu} = \tilde{\mu}_0$, where $\tilde{\mu}$ is the population median.

against the alternative hypothesis $\mu > 32.0$ days at the 0.01 level of significance.

SOLUTION   Because one of the sample values is 32.0, it is discarded and the sample size is $n = 14$.

1. H_0: $\mu = 32.0$.
   H_A: $\mu > 32.0$.

2. $\alpha = 0.01$.

3. The criterion may be based on the number of plus signs or the number of minus signs. In this example we use the number of plus signs, denoted by x. We reject the null hypothesis if the probability of getting x or more plus signs is less than or equal to $\alpha = 0.01$; otherwise, accept the null hypothesis or reserve judgment.

4. Replacing each value less than 32.0 with a minus sign, each value greater than 32.0 with a plus sign, and discarding the one value which actually equals 32.0, we get

$$+ + + + - + + + - + + + + +$$

and the question is whether 12 plus signs observed in 14 trials supports the null hypothesis $\mu = 32.0$ or the alternative hypothesis $\mu > 32.0$. From Table V we find that for $n = 14$ and $p = \frac{1}{2}$, the probability of 12 or more successes is $0.006 + 0.001 = 0.007$.

5. Since 0.007 is less than $\alpha = 0.01$, the null hypothesis must be rejected; it appears that for the time period and population studied, wholesalers of drugs and drug sundries took more than 32.0 days on the average to convert receivables into cash. ∎

15.2

The Sign Test (Large Samples)

When np and $n(1 - p)$ are both greater than 5, we can use the normal approximation to the binomial distribution shown on page 340. The large sample test is based on the statistic

$$z = \frac{x - np_0}{\sqrt{np_0(1 - p_0)}}$$

with $p_0 = 0.50$, which has approximately the standard normal distribution. This technique will be illustrated in Example 15.2.

EXAMPLE 15.2   In the beginning of Chapter 11 we gave the following data on a large industrial plant's daily emission of sulfur oxides (in tons):

17	15	20	29	19	18	22	25	27	9
24	20	17	6	24	14	15	23	24	26
19	23	28	19	16	22	24	17	20	13
19	10	23	18	31	13	20	17	24	14

Use the one-sample sign test to test the null hypothesis that the plant's true average daily emission of sulfur oxides is $\mu = 23.5$ tons against the alternative hypothesis $\mu < 23.5$ tons at the 0.05 level of significance.

SOLUTION   **1.** H_0: $\mu = 23.5$ tons.
  H_A: $\mu < 23.5$ tons.

2. $\alpha = 0.05$.

3. If x is the number of plus signs, reject the null hypothesis if $z \leq -1.645$, where

$$z = \frac{x - np_0}{\sqrt{np_0(1 - p_0)}}$$

with $p_0 = \frac{1}{2}$; otherwise, accept it or reserve judgment.

4. Replace each value less than 23.5 with a minus sign, each value greater than 23.5 with a plus sign. There are 11 plus signs and 29 minus signs. Thus, $x = 11$, and we get

$$z = \frac{11 - 40 \cdot \frac{1}{2}}{\sqrt{40 \cdot \frac{1}{2} \cdot \frac{1}{2}}} = -2.85$$

5. Since this is less than $-z_{0.05} = -1.645$, it follows that the null hypothesis must be rejected, and we conclude that the plant's true average daily emission of sulfur oxides is less than 23.5 tons. When n is small in problems like this, it may be desirable to use the continuity correction given in the footnote

```
MTB > SET DATA INTO C1
DATA> 17 15 20 29 19 18 22 25 27 9
DATA> 24 20 17 6 24 14 15 23 24 26
DATA> 19 23 28 19 16 22 24 17 20 13
DATA> 19 10 23 18 31 13 20 17 24 14
MTB > SUBTRACT 23.5 FROM C1, PUT DIFFERENCES INTO C2
MTB > SIGNS OF C2
        29  NEGATIVE VALUES       0  ZERO VALUES       11  POSITIVE VALUES
MTB > STOP
```

FIGURE 15.1
Computer printout providing data for one-sample sign test

to page 482, but if we had substituted $11 + \frac{1}{2} - 20$ instead of $11 - 20$ into the formula for z, we would have obtained $z = -2.69$, and the conclusion would have been the same. ∎

Figure 15.1 is a computer printout of the sulfur oxides data. In this printout the computer subtracts $\mu = 23.5$ from each number in the table and tells us that there are 29 negative, no zero, and 11 positive values. These values are the same as those obtained in the example just given. The computer does not complete this problem, so, as before, we must substitute these values into the formula provided and use the test procedure.

15.3

The Paired-Sample Sign Test

The sign test has important applications in problems involving paired data, as previously mentioned in Exercise 11.59. In these problems, each pair of sample values can be replaced with a plus sign if the first value is greater than the second, a minus sign if the first value is smaller than the second, or be discarded if the two values are equal. Then, we proceed as in Section 15.1.

EXAMPLE 15.3 To determine the effectiveness of a new traffic control system, the numbers of accidents that occurred at a random sample of eight dangerous intersections during the four weeks before and the four weeks following the installation of the new system were observed with the following results:

$$\begin{array}{llll} 9 \text{ and } 5 & 7 \text{ and } 3 & 3 \text{ and } 4 & 16 \text{ and } 11 \\ 12 \text{ and } 7 & 12 \text{ and } 5 & 5 \text{ and } 5 & 6 \text{ and } 1 \end{array}$$

Use the sign test at the level of significance $\alpha = 0.10$ to test the null hypothesis that the new traffic control system is as effective as the old system against the alternative hypothesis that the new system is more effective.

SOLUTION
1. H_0: $\mu_1 = \mu_2$.
   H_A: $\mu_1 > \mu_2$.

2. $\alpha = 0.10$.

3. If x is the number of plus signs, reject the null hypothesis if the probability of getting x or more plus signs is less than or equal to $\alpha = 0.10$; otherwise, accept it or reserve judgment.

4. Replacing each pair of values with a plus sign if the first value is greater than the second, and with a minus sign if the first value is smaller than the second, and discarding equal values, we get

$$+ + - + + + +$$

where $x = 6$. Table V shows that for $n = 7$ and $p = \frac{1}{2}$, the probability of six or more successes is $0.055 + 0.008 = 0.063$.

5. Since $0.063 < 0.10$, the null hypothesis must be rejected. Apparently the new traffic control system is effective. ■

EXERCISES

(Exercises 15.1, 15.3, 15.5, 15.6, and 15.8 are practice exercises. Their complete solutions are given on page 600.)

15.1 In the one-sample sign test we can use the normal approximation to the binomial distribution if np and $n(1-p)$ are both greater than 5. Where $p = \frac{1}{2}$, can we use the normal approximation to the binomial distribution where

(a) $n = 6$

(b) $n = 10$

(c) $n = 12$

15.2 In a sample of 12 randomly selected days, a personnel manager receives 7, 5, 7, 2, 9, 10, 4, 3, 8, 7, 9, and 7 applications for employment. Use the sign test based on Table V and the 0.05 level of significance to test the null hypothesis $\mu = 5$ (that on the average the personnel manager receives 5 applications for employment daily) against the alternative hypothesis $\mu > 5$.

15.3 An efficiency expert using a stopwatch observes that the amounts of time, in seconds, required by a librarian to check out 15 randomly selected books are 10.35, 10.00, 7.50, 8.85, 13.75, 9.50, 11.45, 10.15, 9.25, 9.85, 6.65, 13.85, 15.60, 8.50, and 11.10. Use the sign test in conjunction with Table V, and the level of significance $\alpha = 0.05$ to test the null hypothesis that, on the average, the librarian checks out a book in 9.00 seconds against the alternative that this figure is too low.

15.4 A random sample of nine technicians working in a shop repair 15, 11, 9, 12, 15, 12, 13, 16, and 13 small electrical appliances during a day. Use the sign test at the 0.05 level of significance to test the null hypothesis $\mu = 11$ (that on the average a technician repairs 11 small electrical appliances per day) against the alternative hypothesis $\mu > 11$.

15.5 Use the normal approximation to the binomial distribution to rework Example 15.1 on page 564 which deals with the number of days required by certain wholesalers to convert receivables into cash.

15.6 Twenty-four tablets randomly selected from a large production lot of tablets manufactured by a pharmaceutical company contain the following weights, in milligrams, of a potent medication: 32.04, 31.97, 32.00, 32.01, 32.14, 31.99, 31.94, 32.04, 32.17, 32.29, 31.98, 31.92, 32.18, 32.03, 32.02, 31.80, 32.13, 32.00, 32.01, 31.95, 32.02, 32.29, 31.96, and 32.01. Use the sign test and the level of significance $\alpha = 0.05$ to test the null hypothesis that the true average weight of the medication per tablet in the entire production lot is 32.05 milligrams against the one-sided alternative $\mu < 32.05$.

15.7 Following are the numbers of orders shipped by a steel distributor on 20 randomly selected days: 63, 51, 45, 36, 49, 56, 50, 47, 41, 58, 43, 60, 38, 42, 50, 66, 33, 46, 41, and 49. Use the sign test and the level of significance $\alpha = 0.01$ to test the null hypothesis that, on the average, 42 orders are shipped per day against the alternative hypothesis that this figure is too low.

15.8 The following are the numbers of parking tickets issued to parking law violators by two meter maids, in a random sample of 30 days: 41 and 42, 39 and 44, 39 and 37, 40 and 42, 36 and 37, 38 and 38, 42 and 44, 39 and 41, 42 and 40, 41 and 43, 42 and 45, 47 and 49, 40 and 49, 41 and 43, 38 and 40, 37 and 40, 41 and 43, 40 and 41, 44 and 44, 45 and 41, 42 and 39, 36 and 40, 39 and 43, 38 and 41, 40 and 41, 41 and 45, 43 and 41, 37 and 40, 36 and 42, 40 and 44. Use the sign test at the level of significance $\alpha = 0.01$ to test the null hypothesis that, on the average, the two meter maids issue the same

number of tickets against the alternative that, on the average, the second
meter maid issues more tickets than the first.

15.9   The following are the numbers of employees who are absent from work in two
departments of a large firm, in a random sample of 30 days: 4 and 3, 3 and 1,
4 and 5, 6 and 4, 4 and 4, 5 and 7, 1 and 1, 5 and 0, 5 and 1, 5 and 1, 4 and 2,
3 and 6, 7 and 8, 3 and 0, 1 and 2, 2 and 0, 0 and 2, 6 and 5, 0 and 3, 5 and 7,
5 and 6, 2 and 1, 8 and 1, 5 and 2, 6 and 3, 3 and 0, 3 and 0, 3 and 5, 4 and 1,
and 2 and 0. Use the sign test at the level of significance $\alpha = 0.05$ to test the
null hypothesis that, on the average, there are an equal number of absences
from each department, against the alternative hypothesis that there are more
absences in the first department.

15.10 Over a 15-day period of time, the number of automobiles sold by two agencies was 8 and 7, 7 and 14, 5 and 4, 14 and 8, 13 and 6, 12 and 14, 10 and 11,
8 and 10, 5 and 4, 16 and 8, 12 and 12, 11 and 6, 9 and 15, 11 and 3, and 9
and 5 respectively. Use the sign test together with Table V and the $\alpha = 0.01$
level of significance to test the null hypothesis $\mu_1 = \mu_2$ that, on the average,
the same number of automobiles is sold in both agencies against the alternative $\mu_1 > \mu_2$.

15.11 Use the paired-sample sign test to rework Exercise 11.59 on page 439.

15.4

Rank Sums: The Signed-Rank Test

The sign test is easy to perform and has intuitive appeal, but it is
wasteful of information because it utilizes only the signs of the differences
between the observations and μ_0 in the one-sample case, or the signs of the
differences between the pairs of observations in the paired-sample case. It is
for this reason that an alternative nonparametric test, the **signed-rank test**
also called the **Wilcoxon signed-rank test**, is often preferred.

In this test, we rank the differences without regard to their signs,
assigning rank 1 to the smallest numerical difference (that is, to the smallest
difference in absolute value), rank 2 to the second smallest numerical difference, . . . , and rank n to the largest numerical difference. Zero differences
are again discarded, and if two or more differences are numerically equal, we
assign each one the mean of the ranks which they jointly occupy. Then we
base the test on T^+, the sum of the ranks of the positive differences, T^-, the
sum of the ranks of the negative differences, or T, the smaller of the two.

To illustrate this procedure, let us refer to Example 15.1 on page 564.
We are given the average number of days required by a sample of 15 whole-

salers of drugs and drug sundries to convert receivables into cash, and used the one-sample sign test to test the null hypothesis $\mu = 32$ against the alternative hypothesis $\mu > 32$ at the 0.01 level of significance. The sample of Example 15.1 is shown in the first column of the following table.

Number of days	Differences	Ranks
33.9	1.9	1.5
35.4	3.4	6
37.3	5.3	9
40.9	8.9	11
27.8	-4.2	8
35.5	3.5	7
34.6	2.6	4
41.1	9.1	12
30.0	-2.0	3
43.2	11.2	14
33.9	1.9	1.5
41.3	9.3	13
32.0	0.0	—
37.7	5.7	10
35.2	3.2	5

The differences between the numbers of days in column 1 and $\mu = 32.0$ are given in the second column. In ranking the differences in column 3, we ignore the signs of the differences, so the smallest value is 1.9 (after we discard the zero difference). Where there are ties, we assign the mean of the ranks which they jointly occupy. Thus, since the values 1.9 and 1.9 occupy the first and second ranks, we assign each difference the rank of $\frac{1 + 2}{2} = 1.5$. The ranks are shown in the third column. It follows that $T^+ = 1.5 + 6 + 9 + 11 + 7 + 4 + 12 + 14 + 1.5 + 13 + 10 + 5 = 94$ and $T^- = 8 + 3 = 11$. Since $T^+ = 94$ and $T^- = 11$, then T (the smaller of the two) is 11. Also, since $T^+ + T^-$ is always the sum of the integers from 1 to n, namely, $\frac{n(n + 1)}{2}$, we could have obtained T^+ more easily by subtracting $T^- = 11$ from $\frac{14 \cdot 15}{2} = 105$, and $105 - 11 = 94$ is the value of T^+.

The close relationship between T^+, T^-, and T, is reflected also by their sampling distributions, which are pictured in Figure 15.2 for the special case

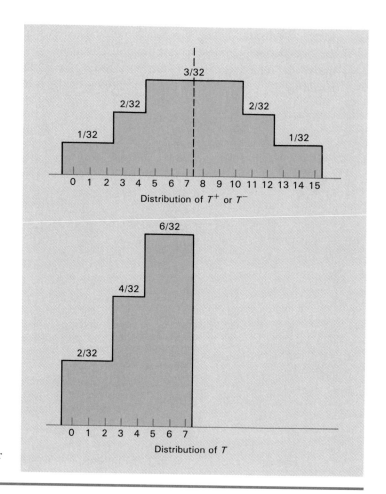

FIGURE 15.2
Distributions of T^+, T^-, and T for $n = 5$

where $n = 5$. To simplify the construction of tables of critical values, we shall base all tests of the null hypothesis $\mu = \mu_0$ on the distribution of T and reject it for values falling into the left-hand tail. We have to be careful, though, to use the right statistic and the right critical value. When $\mu < \mu_0$ then T^+ will tend to be small, so when the alternative hypothesis is $\mu < \mu_0$, we base the test on T^+; when $\mu > \mu_0$, then T^- will tend to be small, so when the alternative hypothesis is $\mu > \mu_0$, we base the test on T^-; and when $\mu \neq \mu_0$ then either T^+ or T^- will tend to be small, so when the alternative hypothesis is $\mu \neq \mu_0$, we base the test on T. All this is summarized in the following table.

Alternative hypothesis	Reject the null hypothesis if	Accept the null hypothesis or reserve judgment if
$\mu < \mu_0$	$T^+ \le T_{2\alpha}$	$T^+ > T_{2\alpha}$
$\mu > \mu_0$	$T^- \le T_{2\alpha}$	$T^- > T_{2\alpha}$
$\mu \ne \mu_0$	$T \le T_\alpha$	$T > T_\alpha$

The necessary values of T_α, which are the largest values of T for which the probability of $T \le T_\alpha$ does not exceed α, may be found in Table XIV at the end of the book; the blank spaces in the table indicate that the null hypothesis cannot be rejected regardless of the value we obtain for the test statistic. Note that the same critical values serve for tests at different levels of significance depending on whether the alternative hypothesis is one sided or two sided.

EXAMPLE 15.4 With reference to the data of Example 15.1 on page 564 which relates to the wholesalers of drugs and drug sundries, use the signed rank test at the 0.01 level of significance to test the null hypothesis $\mu = 32$ against the alternative hypothesis $\mu > 32$.

SOLUTION
1. H_0: $\mu = 32$.
   H_A: $\mu > 32$.

2. $\alpha = 0.01$

3. Reject the null hypothesis if $T^- \le 16$ where 16 is the value of $T_{0.02}$ for $n = 14$; otherwise, accept the null hypothesis or reserve judgment.

4. As shown on page 571, $T^- = 11$.

5. Since $T^- = 11$ is less than 16, the null hypothesis must be rejected. As in Example 15.1 we conclude that the average number of days is greater than 32. ∎

The signed-rank test can also be used in place of the paired-sample sign test. The procedure is exactly the same, but in that case we test the null hypothesis $\mu_1 = \mu_2$ using the criteria shown in the table given earlier, except that the alternative hypotheses are $\mu_1 < \mu_2$, $\mu_1 > \mu_2$, or $\mu_1 \ne \mu_2$ instead of $\mu < \mu_0$, $\mu > \mu_0$, or $\mu \ne \mu_0$.

Rank Sums: The Signed-Rank Test (Large Samples)

When n is 15 or more, it is considered reasonable to assume that the distributions of T^+ and T^- can be approximated closely with normal curves. In that case we can base all tests on either T^+ or T^-, and as it does not matter which one we choose, we shall use here the statistic T^+.

Based on the assumption that each difference is as likely to be positive as negative, it can be shown that the mean and the standard deviation of the sampling distribution of T^+ are

Mean and standard deviation of T^+ statistic

$$\mu_{T+} = \frac{n(n + 1)}{4}$$

and

$$\sigma_{T+} = \sqrt{\frac{n(n + 1)(2n + 1)}{24}}$$

Thus, for large samples, in this case, $n \geq 15$, we can base the signed-rank test on the statistic

Statistic for large-sample signed-rank test

$$z = \frac{T^+ - \mu_{T+}}{\sigma_{T+}}$$

which is a value of a random variable having approximately the standard normal distribution. When the alternative hypothesis is $\mu \neq \mu_0$ (or $\mu_1 \neq \mu_2$), we reject the null hypothesis if $z < -z_{\alpha/2}$ or $z > z_{\alpha/2}$; when the alternative hypothesis is $\mu > \mu_0$ (or $\mu_1 > \mu_2$), we reject the null hypothesis if $z > z_\alpha$; and when the alternative hypothesis is $\mu < \mu_0$ (or $\mu_1 < \mu_2$), we reject the null hypothesis if $z < -z_\alpha$.

EXAMPLE 15.5   Following are the numbers of new loans made by two branches of a finance company, respectively, over a 16-day period: 8 and 8,

9 and 6, 2 and 15, 6 and 4, 15 and 7, 13 and 7, 10 and 15, 10 and 12, 6 and 13, 7 and 6, 18 and 9, 11 and 14, 10 and 6, 3 and 15, 12 and 2, and 14 and 3. Use the large-sample signed-rank test at the $\alpha = 0.05$ level of significance to test whether, on the average, the same number of loans is made by both branches, against the alternative that branch 1 makes more loans than branch 2.

SOLUTION **1.** H_0: $\mu_1 = \mu_2$.
H_A: $\mu_1 > \mu_2$.

2. $\alpha = 0.05$.

3. Reject the null hypothesis if $z \geq 1.645$, where

$$z = \frac{T^+ - \mu_{T^+}}{\sigma_{T^+}}$$

otherwise, accept the null hypothesis or reserve judgment.

4. The differences and the ranks of their absolute values are shown in the following table.

Branch 1	Branch 2	Difference	Rank
8	8	0	—
9	6	3	4.5
2	15	−13	15
6	4	2	2.5
15	7	8	10
13	7	6	8
10	15	−5	7
10	12	−2	2.5
6	13	−7	9
7	6	1	1
18	9	9	11
11	14	−3	4.5
10	6	4	6
3	15	−12	14
12	2	10	12
14	3	11	13

It follows that

$$T^+ = 4.5 + 2.5 + 10 + 8 + 1 + 11 + 6 + 12 + 13 = 68$$

and since (after we discarded the zero difference)

$$\mu_{T+} = \frac{15 \cdot 16}{4} = 60 \qquad \text{and} \qquad \sigma_{T+} = \sqrt{\frac{15 \cdot 16 \cdot 31}{24}} = 17.6$$

we combine the results of the three calculations to get

$$z = \frac{68 - 60}{17.6} = 0.45$$

5. Since 0.45 does not exceed 1.645, we cannot reject the null hypothesis. We accept the null hypothesis that there is no difference in the number of loans made by the two branches or reserve judgment. ∎

EXERCISES

(Exercises 15.12, 15.14, 15.16, 15.20 and 15.22 are practice exercises. Their complete solutions are given on page 600.)

15.12 On what statistic do we base our decision and for what values of the statistic do we reject the null hypothesis, if we have a random sample of size $n = 12$ and are using the signed-rank test at the 0.05 level of significance to test the null hypothesis $\mu = \mu_0$ against the alternative hypothesis

(a) $\mu \neq \mu_0$

(b) $\mu > \mu_0$

(c) $\mu < \mu_0$

15.13 Rework Exercise 15.12 with the level of significance changed to 0.01.

15.14 On what statistic do we base our decision and for what values of the statistic do we reject the null hypothesis, if we have a random sample of $n = 10$ pairs of values and are using the signed-rank test at the 0.01 level of significance to test the null hypothesis $\mu_1 = \mu_2$ against the alternative hypothesis

(a) $\mu_1 > \mu_2$

(b) $\mu_1 \neq \mu_2$

(c) $\mu_1 < \mu_2$

15.15 Rework Exercise 15.14 with the level of significance changed to 0.05.

15.16 In a random sample of 13 weeks, a commercial paper dealer sold 138, 150, 141, 125, 133, 134, 155, 137, 139, 132, 144, 130, and 135 million dollars worth of commercial paper. Use the signed-rank test at the 0.05 level of significance to test the null hypothesis $\mu = 143$ million dollars against the alternative hypothesis

(a) $\mu < \$143$ million

(b) $\mu \neq \$143$ million

15.17 Use the signed-rank test to rework Exercise 15.4 on page 569.

15.18 Following are the number of tons of phosphate rock used by a fertilizer manufacturer on 14 randomly selected days: 11.0, 9.8, 10.9, 13.6, 7.1, 10.0, 12.5, 10.5, 11.0, 8.2, 10.3, 12.6, 10.0, and 10.8.

(a) Use the sign test based on Table V and the 0.05 level of significance to test the null hypothesis $\mu = 10.0$ (that, on the average, the fertilizer factory uses 10.0 tons of phosphate rock per day) against the alternative hypothesis $\mu > 10.0$.

(b) Rework this exercise using the signed-rank test based on Table XIV and the 0.05 level of significance to test the null hypothesis $\mu = 10$ against the alternative hypothesis $\mu > 10.0$.

15.19 A random sample of orders at an automobile supply warehouse took 27, 41, 33, 44, 34, 22, 38, 23, 30, 37, and 32 minutes to assemble for shipment. Use the signed-rank test at the 0.05 level of significance to test whether or not it takes, on the average, 29 minutes to assemble an order for shipment.

15.20 Counts of vehicular traffic on a road between 12:00 noon and 12:30 P.M. on nine randomly selected days showed that northbound and southbound traffic counts were, respectively, 83 and 92, 82 and 92, 88 and 94, 88 and 93, 86 and 91, 89 and 96, 85 and 81, 83 and 81, and 85 and 88. Use the signed-rank test and the 0.05 level of significance to test whether or not there was an equal volume of northbound and southbound traffic.

15.21 Following are the numbers of automobile driver's license examination tests administered by inspectors, on 14 randomly selected days, to men and women applicants, respectively: 14 and 14, 24 and 19, 15 and 9, 22 and 18, 11 and 13, 31 and 13, 16 and 19, 31 and 17, 17 and 10, 23 and 11, 38 and 18, 15 and 9, 16 and 17, 20 and 9. Use the signed-rank test based on Table XIV to test at the 0.05 level of significance whether the testing center averages equally many men and women applicants per day or whether it averages more men applicants.

15.22 Following are the numbers of gallons of diesel fuel used on a certain day by 25 randomly selected trucks of a large truck transportation company: 28.4, 38.3, 26.8, 24.5, 29.1, 27.6, 21.5, 17.9, 32.3, 34.0, 13.6, 21.4, 35.9, 30.6, 34.1, 22.8, 26.7, 28.5, 51.9, 27.2, 35.8, 22.3, 21.0, 49.2, and 31.7. Test at the 0.5 level of significance whether or not the mean daily utilization of diesel fuel by the company's trucks is 23.0 gallons, using

(a) the signed-rank test based on Table XIV

(b) the large-sample signed-rank test

15.23 An advertising agency wants to know whether the number of column inches of classified advertising carried by two competing local newspapers is equal. The number of column inches appearing in both newspapers, respectively, on 20 randomly selected days follows: 595 and 608, 663 and 725, 713 and

806, 626 and 620, 682 and 626, 639 and 595, 651 and 614, 769 and 744, 701 and 719, 723 and 680, 670 and 639, 665 and 602, 639 and 657, 694 and 624, 614 and 614, 651 and 583, 632 and 682, 739 and 657, 657 and 639, and 775 and 745. Use the large-sample signed-rank test, at the 0.05 level of significance, to test whether or not newspaper 1 and newspaper 2 carry equal amounts of classified advertising.

15.6

Rank Sums: The *U* Test

In this section we shall present a nonparametric alternative to the two-sample *t* test for the difference between two means. It is called the **U test**, the **Mann-Whitney test**, or the **Wilcoxon test**, named after the statisticians who contributed to its development. With this test we will be able to test the null hypothesis $\mu_1 = \mu_2$ without having to assume that the populations sampled have roughly the shape of normal distributions; in fact, the test requires only that the populations be continuous (in order to avoid ties), and in practice it does not matter whether this assumption is satisfied or not, so long as the number of ties is small.

To illustrate how the *U* test is performed, suppose that we want to compare the mean lifetimes of two kinds of 9-volt batteries on the basis of the following lifetimes (in hours):

Brand *A*:	6.9	11.2	14.0	13.2	9.1	13.9
	16.1	9.3	2.4	6.4	18.0	11.5
Brand *B*:	15.5	11.1	16.0	15.8	18.2	13.7
	18.3	9.0	17.2	17.8	13.0	15.1

The means of these two random samples are 11.0 and 15.1, and their difference seems large, but it may or may not be significant. Shortcut methods suggest that the variance in the brand *A* batteries is almost three times the variance in the brand *B* batteries, so it may be unreasonable to use the two-sample *t* test, which is based on the assumption that the samples come from populations with equal variability.

We begin the *U* test by arranging the data jointly, as if they comprise one sample, in an increasing order of magnitude. For our data we get

2.4	6.4	6.9	9.0	9.1	9.3
A	A	A	B	A	A

11.1	11.2	11.5	13.0	13.2	13.7
B	A	A	B	A	B

13.9	14.0	15.1	15.5	15.8	16.0
A	A	B	B	B	B

16.1	17.2	17.8	18.0	18.2	18.3
A	B	B	A	B	B

where we indicated for each value whether it belongs to brand A or to brand B. Assigning the data in this order the ranks $1, 2, 3, \ldots$, and 24, we find that the lifetimes of the brand A batteries occupy ranks 1, 2, 3, 5, 6, 8, 9, 11, 13, 14, 19, and 22, while those of brand B occupy ranks, 4, 7, 10, 12, 15, 16, 17, 18, 20, 21, 23, and 24. There are no ties here between values belonging to different samples, but if there were, we would assign each of the tied observations the mean of the ranks which they jointly occupy. For instance, if the third and fourth values were the same, we would assign each the rank $\frac{3+4}{2} = 3.5$, and if the ninth, tenth, and eleventh values were the same, we would assign each the rank $\frac{9 + 10 + 11}{3} = 10$.

The null hypothesis we want to test in a problem like this is that the two samples come from identical populations. If this hypothesis is true, it seems reasonable to suppose that the means of the ranks assigned to the values of the two samples should be more or less the same. The alternative hypothesis is that the means of the populations are not equal, and if this is the case and the difference is pronounced, most of the smaller ranks will go to the values of one sample, while most of the higher ranks will go to those of the other sample.

The test of the null hypothesis that the two samples come from identical populations may either be based on W_1, the sum of the ranks of the values of the first sample, or on W_2, the sum of the ranks of the values of the second sample, and in practice it does not matter which sample we call sample 1 and which we call sample 2. (When the sample sizes are unequal, we usually let the smaller of the two be sample 1; however, this is not required for the work in this book.)

For our example we find that the sum of the ranks of the lifetimes of brand A batteries is

$$W_1 = 1 + 2 + 3 + 5 + 6 + 8 + 9 + 11 + 13 + 14 + 19 + 22$$

$$= 113$$

while the sum of the ranks of the lifetimes of brand B batteries is

$$W_2 = 4 + 7 + 10 + 12 + 15 + 16 + 17 + 18 + 20 + 21 + 23 + 24$$

$$= 187$$

A simplification can be introduced at this point. If the sample sizes are n_1 and n_2, the sum of W_1 and W_2 is the sum of the first $n_1 + n_2$ positive integers, which is known to be

$$\frac{(n_1 + n_2)(n_1 + n_2 + 1)}{2}$$

This formula enables us to find W_2 if we know W_1, and vice versa. For our example we get $W_1 = 113$, n_1 (brand A) $= 12$, and n_2 (brand B) $= 12$, and since the sum of the first 24 positive integers is $\frac{24 \cdot 25}{2} = 300$, it follows that $W_2 = 300 - 113 = 187$, as before.

When the use of **rank sums** was first proposed as a nonparametric alternative to the two-sample t test, the decision was based on W_1 or W_2, but now the decision is based on either of the related statistics[2]

U_1 and U_2
statistics

$$U_1 = W_1 - \frac{n_1(n_1 + 1)}{2}$$

or

$$U_2 = W_2 - \frac{n_2(n_2 + 1)}{2}$$

or on the statistic U, which always equals the smaller of the two. The resulting tests are equivalent to those based on W_1, W_2, or W, but they have the advantage that they lend themselves more readily to the construction of tables of critical values. Not only do U_1 and U_2 take on values on the same interval from 0 to $n_1 n_2$—indeed, their sum is always equal to $n_1 n_2$—but they have identical distributions symmetrical about $\frac{n_1 n_2}{2}$.

[2]These formulas differ from the ones given in previous editions of this book, but they are equivalent except that U_1 and U_2 are interchanged to conform with current usage.

Chapter 15   Decision Making: Nonparametric Tests

The null hypothesis is $\mu_1 = \mu_2$, and we shall base all tests on the sampling distribution of the statistic U and reject it for values falling into the left-hand tail. We have to be careful to use the appropriate statistic and the correct critical value. If $\mu_1 < \mu_2$, then the calculated value of U_1 will tend to be smaller than the calculated value for U_2. Thus, when the alternative hypothesis is $\mu_1 < \mu_2$, we base the test on U_1. Similarly, when $\mu_1 > \mu_2$, then U_2 will tend to be smaller. Thus, when the alternative hypothesis is $\mu_1 > \mu_2$, we base the test on the calculated value for U_2. Finally, where $\mu_1 \neq \mu_2$, we base the test on U, which is the smaller of the calculated values for U_1 or U_2.

The necessary values of U_α, which are the largest values of U for which the probability of $U \leq U_\alpha$ does not exceed α, may be found in Table VII at the end of the book; the blank spaces in the table indicate that the null hypothesis cannot be rejected regardless of the value we obtain for the test statistic. Note that Table VII refers to one-sided alternatives for α's 0.01 and 0.05 and two-sided alternatives for α's 0.01 and 0.05.

EXAMPLE 15.6   With reference to the lifetimes (in hours) of the 9-volt battery data on page 578, use the U test at the 0.05 level of significance to test whether or not the two samples come from populations with equal means.

SOLUTION   **1.** H_0: $\mu_1 = \mu_2$.
H_A: $\mu_1 \neq \mu_2$.

2. $\alpha = 0.05$.

3. Reject the null hypothesis if $U \leq 37$ where 37 is the two-sided value of $U_{0.05}$ for $n_1 = 12$ and $n_2 = 12$; otherwise, accept the null hypothesis or reserve judgment.

4. Having already shown on page 579 that $W_1 = 113$ and $W_2 = 187$, we get $U_1 = 113 - \dfrac{12 \cdot 13}{2} = 35$ and $U_2 = 187 - \dfrac{12 \cdot 13}{2} = 109$, and, hence, $U = 35$. Note that $U_1 + U_2 = 35 + 109 = 144$, which equals $n_1 n_2 = 12 \cdot 12 = 144$.

5. Since $U = 35$ is less than 37, the null hypothesis must be rejected. In other words, we conclude that there is a difference in the mean lifetimes of the two batteries. ∎

EXAMPLE 15.7   Following are the numbers of sales made by two telemarketing sales-persons, Alex and Brenda, on randomly selected days

| Alex: | 23 | 31 | 24 | 35 | 20 | 28 | 17 | 36 | 23 | 32 | 24 | 19 |
| Brenda: | 23 | 27 | 22 | 28 | 16 | 19 | 17 | 31 | 21 | 26 | | |

Use the U test at the 0.05 level of significance to test whether it is reasonable to say that Alex makes a larger number of sales per day, on the average, than Brenda. Alex's mean number of sales per day is 26.0, and Brenda's mean number of sales is 23.0.

SOLUTION

1. $H_0: \mu_1 = \mu_2.$
   $H_A: \mu_1 > \mu_2.$

2. $\alpha = 0.05.$

3. Reject the null hypothesis if $U_2 \leq 34$ where 34 is the value of $U_{0.05}$ for $n_1 = 12$ and $n_2 = 10$, one-sided alternative; otherwise, accept the null hypothesis or reserve judgment.

4. Arranging the data jointly according to size, indicating for each value whether it refers to Alex (A) or Brenda (B), and then ranking the data, we get

16	17	17	19	19	20	21	22	23	23	23
B	B	A	A	B	A	B	B	A	A	B
1	2.5	2.5	4.5	4.5	6	7	8	10	10	10

24	24	26	27	28	28	31	31	32	35	36
A	A	B	B	A	B	B	A	A	A	A
12	13	14	15	16.5	16.5	18.5	18.5	20	21	22

Brenda's values constitute the smaller (second) sample and occupy the ranks

$$W_2 = 1 + 2.5 + 4.5 + 7 + 8 + 10 + 14 + 15 + 16.5 + 18.5$$
$$= 97.0$$

and

$$U_2 = 97 - \frac{10 \cdot 11}{2} = 42$$

5. Since $U_2 = 42$ exceeds 34, the null hypothesis cannot be rejected. There is no evidence of significance at the 0.05 level that the mean number of sales for Alex and Brenda are not equal. ∎

15.7

Rank Sums: The U Test (Large Samples)

The large-sample U test may be based on either U_1 or U_2 as defined on page 580, but since the resulting tests are equivalent and it does not matter which sample we denote sample 1 and which sample we denote sample 2, we shall use here the statistic U_1.

Based on the assumption that the two samples come from identical continuous populations, it can be shown that the mean and the standard deviation of the sampling distribution of U_1 are[3]

Mean and standard deviation of U_1 statistic

$$\mu_{U_1} = \frac{n_1 n_2}{2}$$

and

$$\sigma_{U_1} = \sqrt{\frac{n_1 n_2 (n_1 + n_2 + 1)}{12}}$$

Observe that these formulas remain the same when we interchange the subscripts 1 and 2, but this should not come as a surprise—as we pointed out on page 580, the distributions of U_1 and U_2 are the same.

Furthermore, if n_1 and n_2 are both greater than 8, the sampling distribution of U_1 can be approximated closely by a normal distribution. Thus, we base the test of the null hypothesis $\mu_1 = \mu_2$ on the statistic

Statistic for large-sample U test

$$z = \frac{U_1 - \mu_{U_1}}{\sigma_{U_1}}$$

which has approximately the standard normal distribution. When the alternative hypothesis is $\mu_1 \neq \mu_2$, we reject the null hypothesis if $z < -z_{\alpha/2}$ or $z > z_{\alpha/2}$; when the alternative hypothesis is $\mu_1 > \mu_2$, we reject the null

---

[3]When there are ties in rank the formula for the standard deviation provides only an approximation, but if the number of ties is small, there is usually no need to make any correction.

hypothesis if $z > z_\alpha$; and when the alternative hypothesis is $\mu_1 < \mu_2$, we reject the null hypothesis if $z < -z_\alpha$.

EXAMPLE 15.8 The following are the weight gains (in pounds) of two random samples of young turkeys fed two different diets but otherwise kept under identical conditions:

Diet 1:   16.3 10.1 10.7 13.5 14.9 11.8 14.3 10.2 12.0 14.7 23.6
           15.1 14.5 18.4 13.2 14.0

Diet 2:   21.3 23.8 15.4 19.6 12.0 13.9 18.8 19.2 15.3 20.1 14.8
           18.9 20.7 21.1 15.8 16.2

Use the large-sample U test at the 0.01 level of significance to test the null hypothesis that the two populations sampled are identical against the alternative hypothesis that on the average the second diet produces a greater gain in weight.

SOLUTION   1. H_0: $\mu_1 = \mu_2$.
              H_A: $\mu_1 < \mu_2$.
            2. $\alpha = 0.01$.
            3. Reject the null hypothesis if $z < -2.33$, where

$$z = \frac{U_1 - \mu_{U_1}}{\sigma_{U_1}}$$

otherwise, accept the null hypothesis or reserve judgment.

            4. Ranking the data jointly according to size, we find that the values of the first sample occupy ranks 21, 1, 3, 8, 15, 4, 11, 2, 5.5, 13, 31, 16, 12, 22, 7, and 10. (The fifth and sixth values are both equal to 12.0, so we assign each the rank 5.5.) Thus

$$W_1 = 1 + 2 + 3 + 4 + 5.5 + 7 + 8 + 10 + 11 + 12 + 13$$

$$+ 15 + 16 + 21 + 22 + 31$$

$$= 181.5$$

and

$$U_1 = 181.5 - \frac{16 \cdot 17}{2} = 45.5$$

Since $\mu_{U_1} = \dfrac{16 \cdot 16}{2} = 128$ and $\sigma_{U_1} = \sqrt{\dfrac{16 \cdot 16 \cdot 33}{12}}$

= 26.53, it follows that

$$z = \frac{45.5 - 128}{26.53} = -3.11$$

5. Since $z = -3.11$ is less than -2.33, the null hypothesis must be rejected; conclude that on the average the second diet produces a greater gain in weight. ∎

15.8

Rank Sums: The H Test

The H **test**, or **Kruskal-Wallis test**, is a rank-sum test which serves to test the null hypothesis that k independent random samples come from identical populations against the alternative hypothesis that the means of these populations are not all equal. Unlike the standard test which it replaces, the one-way analysis of variance of Section 14.2, it does not require the assumption that the samples come from populations having roughly the shape of normal distributions.

In the H test the data are ranked jointly from low to high as though they constitute a single sample. Then, if R_i is the sum of the ranks assigned to the n_i values of the ith sample and $n = n_1 + n_2 + \cdots + n_k$, the H test is based on the statistic

Statistic for H test

$$H = \frac{12}{n(n + 1)} \sum_{i=1}^{k} \frac{R_i^2}{n_i} - 3(n + 1)$$

If the null hypothesis is true and each sample has at least five observations, the sampling distribution of H can be approximated closely with a chi-square distribution with $k - 1$ degrees of freedom. Consequently, we can reject the null hypothesis that $\mu_1 = \mu_2 = \cdots = \mu_k$ and accept the alternative that the μ's are not all equal at the level of significance α, if $H \geq \chi_\alpha^2$ for $k - 1$ degrees of freedom. If any sample has fewer than five items, the χ^2 approximation cannot be used, and the test must be based on special tables.

EXAMPLE 15.9   A company's trainees are randomly assigned to groups which are taught a certain industrial inspection procedure by three different methods, and at the end of the instruction period they are tested for inspection performance quality. The following are their scores:

Method E:	94	87	91	74	86	97	
Method F:	85	82	79	84	61	72	80
Method G:	89	67	72	76	69		

Use the H test to determine at the 0.05 level of significance whether the three methods are equally effective.

SOLUTION

1. H_0: $\mu_1 = \mu_2 = \mu_3$.

   H_A: μ_1, μ_2, and μ_3 are not all equal.

2. $\alpha = 0.05$.

3. Reject the null hypothesis if $H \geq 5.991$, which is the value of $\chi^2_{0.05}$ for $3 - 1 = 2$ degrees of freedom; otherwise, accept it or reserve judgment.

4. Arranging the data jointly according to size and indicating for each observation whether it refers to method E, method F, or method G, and then ranking the data, we get

61	67	69	72	72	74	76	79	80
F	G	G	F	G	E	G	F	F
1	2	3	4.5	4.5	6	7	8	9

82	84	85	86	87	89	91	94	97
F	F	F	E	E	G	E	E	E
10	11	12	13	14	15	16	17	18

thus,

$$R_1 = 6 + 13 + 14 + 16 + 17 + 18 = 84$$
$$R_2 = 1 + 4.5 + 8 + 9 + 10 + 11 + 12 = 55.5$$
$$R_3 = 2 + 3 + 4.5 + 7 + 15 = 31.5$$

There is one tie, and the two tied observations which occupy ranks 4 and 5 are both ranked 4.5.

Then, substituting these values of R_1, R_2, and R_3 together with $n_1 = 6$, $n_2 = 7$, and $n_3 = 5$ into the formula for H, we get

$$H = \frac{12}{18 \cdot 19}\left(\frac{84^2}{6} + \frac{55.5^2}{7} + \frac{31.5^2}{5}\right) - 3 \cdot 19$$
$$= 6.67$$

5. Since 6.67 exceeds 5.991, the value of $\chi^2_{0.05}$ for $k - 1 = 3 - 1 = 2$ degrees of freedom, we reject the null hypothesis; that

is, we conclude that the three methods are not equally effective.

EXERCISES

(Exercise 15.24, 15.27, and 15.30 are practice exercises. Their complete solutions are given on page 600.)

15.24   Following are the numbers of defective plastic wastebaskets observed by inspectors in randomly selected production runs, using two different molding machines:

Molding machine 1:   19   27   23   23   18   24
Molding machine 2:   17   19   20   18   15   22

Use the U test at the 0.05 level of significance to test the null hypothesis that the two molding machines average equally many defectives per production run against the alternative hypothesis that they do not average equally many defectives per production run.

15.25   The following are the numbers of minutes it took random samples of 12 men and 15 women to complete applications for employment at the personnel department of a large company:

Men: 20.4   19.5   20.8   19.9   21.0   18.7   19.7   18.9
         19.4   17.7   21.6   17.4
Women: 20.1   19.3   21.9   19.8   17.8   19.2   19.0   17.5
         20.0   17.6   21.1   18.1   20.9   19.6   20.3

Use the U test (based on Table VII) at the 0.05 level of significance to test the null hypothesis that the two samples come from identical populations against the alternative hypothesis that they have unequal means.

15.26   Following are the Rockwell hardness numbers obtained for six aluminum die castings randomly selected from production lot A and for eight aluminum die castings randomly selected from production lot B:

Production lot A: 75   56   63   70   58   74
Production lot B: 63   85   77   80   86   76   72   82

Use the U test at the 0.05 level of significance to test the claim that the average hardness of die castings from the two production lots is the same.

15.27   Following are the weekly wages (rounded to the nearest dollar) of randomly selected repair mechanics in two cities:

City A: 480   476   497   479   464   496   492   432   481   475   496
          498   493   485   470   468   486   499   480   443

City B: 494 493 476 480 471 489 465 471 490 462 460
         486 465 470 483 472 435 455 499 477 495 473
         465 476

Use the U test and the level of significance $\alpha = 0.05$ to test the null hypothesis that there is no difference in the average weekly wages of repair mechanics in the two cities.

15.28 Use the large sample U test to rework Exercise 15.25.

15.29 Following are the annual real estate taxes paid in dollars on a random sample of 10 condominium apartments in each of two large condominium apartment complexes in the same city:

Complex 1: 1,086 1,005 1,053 1,164   979 1,007   978 1,020
             941 1,015

Complex 2:   926 1,051   853 1,081 1,017   931 1,059   965
             937   907

Use the large-sample test at the 0.05 level of significance to test the claim that, on the average, taxes are higher in condominium complex 1 than in condominium complex 2.

15.30 A small motion picture theater shows the same film three times a day and the following is the size of the audience on randomly selected days

First screening: 179 164 181 176 173 178 164

Second screening: 169 177 166 171 181 189

Third screening: 174 167 168 183 169

Use the H test at the 0.05 level of significance to test the claim that there is no difference in the true average size of the audience in the three daily screenings.

15.31 Use the H test to rework Exercise 14.7 on page 540.

15.32 Use the H test to rework Exercise 14.10 on page 541.

15.33 Following are the numbers of tickets sold for 10 performances at each of four movie theaters:

Theater A: 119 215 227 191 212
            186 271 169 199 216

Theater B: 140 190 256 188 111
            189 255 173 200 241

Theater C: 110 187 210 216 141
            204 248 211 181 210

Theater D: 211 215 197 217 117
            257 243 215 185 271

Use the H test at the level of significance $\alpha = 0.05$ to test the null hypothesis that the true average numbers of ticket sales at the four theaters are all equal.

15.9

Tests of Randomness: Runs

All the methods of inference we have discussed so far are based on the assumption that we are dealing with random samples. However, there are many applications in which it is hard to decide whether this assumption is justifiable. This is true particularly when we have little or no control over the selection of the data. For instance, if we want to predict a department store's sales volume for a given month, we have no choice but to use sales data from previous years and, perhaps, collateral information about economic conditions in general. None of this information constitutes a random sample in the strict sense. Also, we have no choice but to rely on whatever records are available if we want to make long-range predictions of the weather, if we want to estimate the mortality rate of a disease, or if we want to study traffic accidents at a dangerous intersection.

Several methods have been developed in recent years which make it possible to judge the randomness of a sample on the basis of the order in which the observations are taken. We can thus test, after the data have been taken, whether patterns that look suspiciously nonrandom may be attributed to chance. The technique we shall describe in this and the following section is based on the **theory of runs**. A **run** is a succession of identical letters (or other kinds of symbols) which is followed, and preceded by different letters or no letters at all. To illustrate, consider the following arrangements of letters typed by a secretary in the given order which do, D, and do not, N, contain erasures:

$$\underline{NNNN} \quad \underline{DDD} \quad \underline{NNNNNNN} \quad \underline{DD} \quad \underline{NN} \quad \underline{DDDD}$$

Using underlines to combine the letters which consitute the runs, we find that first there is a run of four N's, then a run of three D's, then a run of seven N's, then a run of two D's, then a run of two N's, and finally a run of four D's. In all, there are six runs of varying lengths.

The **total number of runs** (represented by u) appearing in an arrangement of this kind is often a good indication of a possible lack of randomness.

If there are too few runs, we might suspect a definite grouping or clustering, or perhaps a trend; if there are too many runs, we might suspect some sort of repeated alternating pattern. In the example there seems to be a definite clustering—the letters with erasures seem to come in groups—but it remains to be seen whether this is significant or whether it can be attributed to chance.

If there are n_1 letters of one kind, n_2 letters of another kind, and u runs, we base this kind of decision on the following criterion:

Reject the null hypothesis of randomness if

$$u \leq u'_{\alpha/2} \qquad \text{or} \qquad u \geq u_{\alpha/2}$$

where $u'_{\alpha/2}$ and $u_{\alpha/2}$ may be read from Table VIII for values of n_1 and n_2 through 15, and $\alpha = 0.05$ and $\alpha = 0.01$.

In the construction of Table VIII, $u'_{\alpha/2}$ is the largest value of u for which the probability of $u \leq u'_{\alpha/2}$ is less than or equal to $\alpha/2$, $u_{\alpha/2}$ is the smallest value of u for which the probability of $u \geq u_{\alpha/2}$ is less than or equal to $\alpha/2$, and the blank spaces indicate that the null hypothesis of randomness cannot be rejected for values in that tail of the sampling distribution of u regardless of the value of u. More extensive tables for the **u test** may be found in handbooks of statistical tables.

EXAMPLE 15.10   With reference to the arrangement of letters typed by a secretary which do, D, and do not, N, contain erasures, use the u test at the 0.05 level of significance to test the null hypothesis of randomness against the alternative hypothesis that the arrangement is not random.

SOLUTION   1. H_0: The arrangement is random.
H_A: The arrangement is not random.

2. $\alpha = 0.05$.

3. Reject the null hypothesis if $\mu \leq 6$ or $u \geq 17$, where 6 and 17 are the values of $u'_{0.025}$ and $u_{0.025}$ for $n_1 = 13$ and $n_2 = 9$; otherwise, accept it or reserve judgment.

4. The total number of runs, by inspection of the data, is $u = 6$.

5. Since $u = 6$ equals the value of $u'_{0.025}$, the null hypothesis must be rejected; we conclude that the letters with erasures seem to come in clusters. (There are too few runs and it appears that the letters with erasures come in clusters.) ■

15.10

Tests of Randomness: Runs (Large Samples)

Under the null hypothesis that n_1 letters of one kind and n_2 letters of another kind are arranged at random, it can be shown that the mean and the standard deviation of u are

Mean and standard deviation of u

$$\mu_u = \frac{2n_1 n_2}{n_1 + n_2} + 1$$

and

$$\sigma_u = \sqrt{\frac{2n_1 n_2 (2n_1 n_2 - n_1 - n_2)}{(n_1 + n_2)^2 (n_1 + n_2 - 1)}}$$

Furthermore, if neither n_1 nor n_2 is less than 10, the sampling distribution of u can be approximated closely with a normal curve, and we can base the test of the null hypothesis of randomness on the statistic

Statistic for large-sample u test

$$z = \frac{u - \mu_u}{\sigma_u}$$

which has approximately the standard normal distribution. If the alternative hypothesis is that the arrrangement is not random, we reject the null hypothesis for $z \le -z_{\alpha/2}$ or $z \ge z_{\alpha/2}$; if the alternative hypothesis is that there is a clustering or a trend, we reject the null hypothesis for $z \le -z_{\alpha}$; and if the alternative hypothesis is that there is an alternating, or cyclical, pattern, we reject the null hypothesis for $z \ge z_{\alpha}$.

EXAMPLE 15.11   The following is an arrangement of 30 men, M, and 18 women, W, lined up to purchase tickets for a rock concert:

M W M W M M M W M W M M M W W M M M M W W M W M
M M W M M M W W W M W M M M W M W M M M M W W M

Test for randomness at the 0.05 level of significance.

SOLUTION   **1.** H_0: Arrangement is random.
H_A: Arrangement is not random.

2. $\alpha = 0.05$.

3. Reject the null hypothesis if $z \leq -1.96$ or $z \geq 1.96$, where

$$z = \frac{u - \mu_u}{\sigma_u}$$

otherwise, accept the null hypothesis or reserve judgment.

4. Since $n_1 = 30$, $n_2 = 18$, and $u = 27$, we get

$$\mu_u = \frac{2 \cdot 30 \cdot 18}{30 + 18} + 1 = 23.5$$

$$\sigma_u = \sqrt{\frac{2 \cdot 30 \cdot 18(2 \cdot 30 \cdot 18 - 30 - 18)}{(30 + 18)^2(30 + 18 - 1)}} = 3.21$$

and, hence

$$z = \frac{27 - 23.5}{3.21} = 1.09$$

5. Since this value falls between -1.96 and 1.96, the null hypothesis cannot be rejected; in other words, there is no real evidence to suggest that the arrangement is not random. ∎

15.11

Tests of Randomness: Runs Above and Below the Median

The method of the preceding section is not limited to tests of the randomness of series of attributes (such as the N's and D's and the M's and W's of our examples). Any sample consisting of numerical measurements or observations can be treated similarly by using the letters a and b to denote values falling above, a, and below, b, the median of the sample. Numbers equal to the median are omitted. The resulting series of a's and b's (representing the data in their original order) can be treated for randomness on the basis of the total number of runs of a's and b's, the total number of **runs above and below the median**.

EXAMPLE 15.12   On 24 successive trips between two cities, a bus carried 24, 19, 32, 28, 21, 23, 26, 17, 20, 28, 30, 24, 13, 35, 26, 21, 19, 29, 27, 18, 26, 14, 21, and 23 passengers. Use the total number of runs above and below the median and the 0.01 level of significance to test whether it is reasonable to treat these data as if they constitute a random sample.

SOLUTION   The median number of passengers is 23.5, so we get the following arrangement of values above and below it

$$a\ b\ a\ a\ b\ b\ a\ b\ b\ a\ a\ a\ b\ a\ a\ b\ b\ a\ a\ b\ a\ b\ a\ b\ b\ b$$

1. H_0: Arrangement is random.
   H_A: Arrangement is not random.
2. $\alpha = 0.01$.
3. Reject the null hypothesis if $u \leq 6$ or $u \geq 20$, where 6 and 20 are the values of $u'_{0.005}$ and $u_{0.005}$ for $n_1 = 12$ and $n_2 = 12$; otherwise, accept the null hypothesis or reserve judgment.
4. $u = 14$ by inspection of the arrangement of a's and b's.
5. Since $u = 14$ falls between 6 and 20, the null hypothesis cannot be rejected; in other words, there is no real evidence to indicate that the data do not constitute a random sample. ∎

EXERCISES

(Exercises 15.34, 15.40, and 15.42 are practice exercises. Their complete solutions are given on page 600.)

15.34   In three separate "experiments" a prestidigitator flips an evenly balanced coin 25 times and the sequence of heads (H) and tails (T) follows:

(a) $H\ T\ H\ T\ H\ T\ H\ T\ H\ T\ H\ T\ H\ T\ H\ T\ H\ T\ H\ T\ H\ T\ H\ T\ H$;
    test for randomness at the 0.05 level of significance.

(b) $H\ H\ H\ H\ H\ H\ H\ H\ H\ H\ H\ H\ H\ T\ T\ T\ T\ T\ T\ T\ T\ T\ T\ T\ T$;
    test for randomness at the 0.05 level of significance.

(c) $H\ T\ T\ H\ H\ H\ T\ H\ T\ H\ T\ H\ T\ H\ T\ H\ T\ T\ H\ T\ H\ H\ H\ T\ T$;
    test for randomness at the 0.05 level of significance.

(d) Examine the data of parts (a), (b), and (c) before performing the required calculations and explain in your own words why or why not each experiment appears to have a random distribution of runs.

15.35   The J. P. Morgan Index measures the value of the U.S. dollar against 15 other currencies and is reported in *The Wall Street Journal*. During a recent 18-month period, the value of the dollar at the end of each month was up (U) or down (D) as shown:

$$D\ U\ D\ D\ D\ D\ U\ U\ D\ D\ U\ U\ U\ U\ D\ D\ D\ D$$

Test for randomness at the 0.05 level of significance.

15.36 While ocean fishing, a fisherman caught 15 mackerel (*M*) and 9 cod (*C*) in the following order:

$$C\,C\,M\,M\,M\,M\,M\,M\,M\,M\,M\,C\,C\,C\,C\,M\,M\,M\,M\,M\,M\,M\,C\,C$$

Test for randomness at the 0.01 level of significance.

15.37 An automatic packaging machine developed a systematic defect and over-filled (*O*) each fourth box of paperclips while correctly filling (*F*) the remaining boxes, resulting in the following arrangement of 48 boxes of paperclips packaged by the machine.

$$F\,F\,F\,O\,F\,F\,F\,O\,F\,F\,F\,O\,F\,F\,F\,O\,F\,F\,F\,O\,F\,F\,F\,O$$
$$F\,F\,F\,O\,F\,F\,F\,O\,F\,F\,F\,O\,F\,F\,F\,O\,F\,F\,F\,O\,F\,F\,F\,O$$

Test for randomness at the 0.05 level of significance.

15.38 Representing each 0, 2, 4, 6, and 8 by the letter *E* (for even) and each 1, 3, 5, 7, and 9 by the letter *O* (for odd), test at the 0.05 level of significance whether the arrangement of the 50 digits in the first column of the random-number table on page 875 may be regarded as random.

15.39 The following is the sequence of 30 buy (*B*) and sell (*S*) orders placed by a stock market speculator:

$$B\,B\,B\,B\,B\,B\,B\,B\,B\,B\,S\,S\,S\,S\,S$$
$$S\,S\,S\,S\,B\,B\,B\,B\,B\,B\,B\,B\,S\,S\,S$$

Test for randomness at the 0.01 level of significance.

15.40 The numbers of automobiles towed each day for 30 consecutive days by an automobile towing service are

19	15	16	16	17	14	16	15	18	18	20	18	17	19	16
15	16	16	14	15	16	18	18	20	18	20	18	17	19	18

After discarding the three values which equal the median, test for randomness at the 0.01 level of significance.

15.41 The closing prices of a certain stock (stock prices are quoted in whole dollars and in eighths, where $\frac{1}{8} = 12\frac{1}{2}$ cents) on the New York Stock exchange for 29 consecutive business days are

$$15\tfrac{7}{8},\ 15\tfrac{1}{4},\ 15\tfrac{1}{8},\ 15\tfrac{1}{2},\ 14\tfrac{7}{8},\ 13\tfrac{1}{2},\ 14\tfrac{1}{4},\ 14\tfrac{1}{2},\ 14,\ 14\tfrac{1}{8},\ 14\tfrac{7}{8},\ 14\tfrac{1}{2}$$

$$15,\ 15\tfrac{1}{4},\ 15,\ 15\tfrac{1}{8},\ 15\tfrac{3}{4},\ 15\tfrac{7}{8},\ 16\tfrac{1}{8},\ 16\tfrac{1}{4},\ 16\tfrac{1}{2},\ 16\tfrac{1}{2},\ 16\tfrac{1}{4},\ 15\tfrac{1}{2}$$

$$15,\ 14\tfrac{1}{2},\ 14\tfrac{1}{4},\ 13\tfrac{7}{8},\ 14\tfrac{1}{8}$$

Use the total number of runs above and below the median to test at the 0.01 level of significance whether it is reasonable to treat these data as though they constitute a random sample.

15.42 The total numbers of retail stores opening for business and also quitting business within 33 recent years in a large city were 108, 103, 109, 107, 125, 142, 147, 122, 116, 153, 144, 162, 143, 126, 145, 129, 134, 137, 143, 150, 148, 152, 125, 106, 112, 139, 132, 122, 138, 148, 155, 146, and 158; the median number is 138. Test at the 0.05 level of significance whether there is a significant upward trend in these data.

15.43 Reading across successive rows in Exercise 2.33 on page 36, test at the 0.05 level of significance whether the data concerning the 100 lot-for-lot inventory orders may be regarded as a random sample.

15.12

P-values for Nonparametric Tests

The *P*-values which we discussed in Chapter 11 can also be used in much the same manner in certain nonparametric tests. To illustrate the calculation and use of *P*-values in problems where we employ Table V, binomial probabilities, we refer to the one-sample sign test of Example 15.1. In this example it is shown that for $n = 14$ and $p = \frac{1}{2}$ the probability of success from Table V is $0.006 + 0.001 = 0.007$. This amount is also the value for *P*. Since 0.007 is less than or equal to $\alpha = 0.01$ (the specified critical value), the null hypothesis must be rejected. This agrees with the previously provided solution to Example 15.1.

Repeating this line of reasoning for the paired-sample data of Example 15.3, we showed that for $n = 7$ and $p = \frac{1}{2}$, the probability of success from Table V is $0.055 + 0.008 = 0.063$. This amount is also the value for *P*. Since 0.063 is less than or equal to $\alpha = 0.10$ (the specified critical value), the null hypothesis must be rejected. This agrees with the previously provided solution to Example 15.3.

P-values can also be calculated for problems where we utilize *z*-values in conjunction with Table I, normal curve areas. In Example 15.2 where the calculated value of $z = -2.85$, its corresponding area in Table I is 0.4978, and subtracting this value from 0.5000, we obtain $P = 0.5000 - 0.4978 = 0.0022$. Since 0.0022 is less than the critical value of $\alpha = 0.05$, the null hypothesis must be rejected. This agrees with the previously provided solution to Example 15.2.

15.13

A Word of Caution

Statistical methods which require no (or virtually no) assumptions about the populations from which we are sampling are usually less efficient than the corresponding standard techniques. To illustrate this point, let us refer to the calculations in Chapter 10 where we showed that, by using Chebyshev's theorem, we can assert with a probability of *at least* 0.75 that the mean of a random sample of size $n = 64$ drawn from an infinite population with $\sigma = 20$ will differ from the population mean μ by less than 5. As we also showed, however, if we can assume that the population from which we are sampling has the shape of a normal distribution, we can make the same assertion with the probability 0.9544 (instead of ''at least'' 0.75). To put it another way, assertions made with equal confidence require larger samples if they are made without knowledge of the form of the underlying distribution than if they are made with such knowledge. It is generally true that the more we are willing to assume, the more we can infer from a sample; however, the more we assume, the more we limit the applicability of our methods.

15.14

Check list of Key Terms

H test, 564, 585
Kruskal-Wallis test, 585
Mann-Whitney test, 578
Nonparametric tests, 563
One-sample sign test, 564
Paired-sample sign test, 567
Randomness, 564
Rank sums, 564, 580
Run, 589
Runs above and below the
     median, 564, 592

Signed-rank test, 563
Sign test, 563, 564
Theory of runs, 564
Total number of runs, 589
u test, 590
U test, 564, 578
Wilcoxon signed-rank test, 570
Wilcoxon test, 578

15.15

Review Exercises

15.44 Following are the times, in minutes, required by a random sample of 18 loan applicants to complete a loan application at a bank: 34, 34, 34, 32, 30, 36, 32, 35, 30, 33, 33, 30, 31, 33, 34, 30, 32, and 33. Use the sign test at the 0.05 level of significance to test the null hypothesis $\mu = 31$ minutes against the alternative $\mu \neq 31$ minutes.

15.45 An electric light bulb manufacturing company claims that its standard 75-watt light bulbs last, on the average, 750 burning hours. A test of twelve 75-watt bulbs by a testing company yields the following burning life data for these bulbs, rounded to the nearest hour: 724, 762, 750, 774, 733, 777, 759, 738, 769, 771, 747, and 788. Use the signed-rank test at the 0.01 level of significance to test the manufacturer's claim against the alternative that the bulbs do not last 750 burning hours.

15.46 In a random sample of 20 weeks, two savings banks opened the following numbers of new savings accounts, respectively: 23 and 38, 34 and 31, 38 and 27, 42 and 37, 41 and 29, 56 and 36, 38 and 48, 47 and 41, 46 and 30, 29 and 31, 49 and 35, 34 and 33, 35 and 28, 32 and 22, 35 and 54, 38 and 55, 45 and 48, 53 and 57, 40 and 48, 41 and 28. Use the large sample signed-rank test at the 0.05 level of significance to test whether or not the two banks, on the average, attract equal numbers of savings accounts.

15.47 Four gold mining claims on a stream which is panned by prospectors yield the following amounts of gold, in troy ounces, on five consecutive days.

Claim 1:	2.27	1.66	2.31	2.39	2.07
Claim 2:	1.68	2.33	1.84	2.32	2.20
Claim 3:	2.02	2.20	1.95	2.56	2.40
Claim 4:	2.13	2.21	2.46	2.49	2.34

Use the H test at the 0.05 level of significance to test the null hypothesis that, on the average, the amounts of gold panned daily at the four claims are the same.

15.48 To test the claim that Inspector 1 finds more defects in a bolt of cloth than Inspector 2, Inspector 1 examines 12 bolts of cloth, following which Inspector 2 examines the same 12 bolts of cloth. Following are the numbers of defects found by the two inspectors in each bolt of cloth: 7 and 5, 12 and 11, 8 and 10, 7 and 6, 14 and 11, 9 and 9, 8 and 7, 10 and 9, 6 and 8, 5 and 4, 7 and 6, and 5 and 6. Use the sign test at the 0.05 level of significance to test the null hypothesis $\mu_1 = \mu_2$ against the alternative hypothesis $\mu_1 > \mu_2$, where μ_1 and μ_2 are the respective means of the numbers of defects found for the populations sampled.

15.49 Following are the numbers of workdays idle, in millions of workdays, from strikes involving 1,000 or more workers in the United States for the years 1965 to 1989, inclusive: 15.1, 16.0, 31.2, 35.6, 29.4, 52.8, 35.5, 16.8, 16.3, 31.8, 17.6, 23.9, 21.3, 23.8, 20.4, 20.8, 16.9, 9.1, 17.5, 8.5, 7.1, 11.9, 4.5, 4.4, and 17.0. Use the large sample test based on runs above and below the median and the 0.05 level of significance to test whether there is a significant trend in this series. The median is 17.5 million days.

15.50 Following are the driving times (in minutes) of 15 loaded coal trucks from the mine tipple to an electric power plant and the driving times of the empty trucks on the return trips: 83 and 88, 79 and 66, 81 and 79, 95 and 88, 86 and 69, 87 and 92, 88 and 87, 68 and 70, 83 and 76, 79 and 65, 66 and 66, 89 and 91, 94 and 79, 77 and 98, and 81 and 90. Use the sign test (based on Table V) and the 0.05 level of significance to test the null hypothesis $\mu_1 = \mu_2$ (that the true average driving times in both directions are equal) against the alternative hypothesis $\mu_1 < \mu_2$.

15.51 Following is the arrangement of wins by the American League (A) and the National League (N) for 60 consecutive All-Star baseball games:

> $A\ A\ A\ N\ A\ N\ A\ N\ A\ A\ A\ N\ A\ A\ A\ A\ N\ N\ N\ N\ A\ N\ N\ A\ A\ N\ A$
> $N\ N\ N\ A\ N\ N\ N\ N\ N\ N\ N\ A\ N\ N\ N\ N\ N\ N\ N\ N\ N\ N\ A$
> $N\ N\ A\ N\ A\ A\ A$

Test for randomness at the level of significance $\alpha = 0.05$ against the alternative hypothesis that there is an alternating or cyclical pattern.

15.52 On six randomly selected days a tire company sells 50, 49, 49, 47, 50, and 52 tires. Use the sign test at the 0.05 level of significance to test the null hypothesis $\mu = 48$ (that the tire company can expect average sales of 48 tires a day) against the alternative $\mu > 48$.

15.53 The following is the sequence in which a speculator buys (B) and sells (S) crude oil futures on the New York Mercantile Exchange:

> $B\ B\ B\ S\ S\ S\ S\ B\ S\ S\ B\ B\ B\ B\ B\ S\ S\ S\ B\ B$

Test for randomness at the 0.05 level of significance.

15.54 In two random samples over a 10-day period the following number of people applied for car loans at two local banks:

> Bank A: 2 3 5 10 6 11 4 8 10 12
> Bank B: 6 7 3 9 1 4 8 7 5 2

Use the large-sample U test at the 0.05 level of significance to test the null hypothesis that on the average the two banks have equally many car loan applicants against the alternative hypothesis that on the average one bank has more applicants than the other.

15.55 Rework the preceding exercise using Table VII instead of the large-sample approximation.

15.56 Following are the final examination grades of six randomly selected students in each of four sections of an elementary accounting class at a university.

> Section 1: 80 85 98 91 83 82
> Section 2: 78 79 72 81 84 69
> Section 3: 71 68 70 87 85 74
> Section 4: 74 77 85 88 81 75

Use the H test at the 0.05 level of significance to test the null hypothesis that the four samples come from identical populations against the alternative that the populations are not all equal.

15.57 The following sequence of 25 arrivals of buses at a bus terminal indicates whether the buses arrived on time (O) or arrived late (L): O O O L L O O O O L L O O O O L L L L O O O O L L. Test at the 0.05 level of significance whether the sequence may be regarded as random.

15.58 The following are the average daily temperatures (in degrees Fahrenheit) recorded in a random sample of 14 days at a popular resort town: 89.1, 90.5, 87.0, 93.6, 96.0, 87.9, 95.1, 90.2, 91.0, 86.4, 92.5, 96.6, 85.0, and 86.9. Use the sign test (based on Table V) and the 0.05 level of significance to test the null hypothesis $\mu = 92.0°F$ (that the true mean temperature in this resort town is 92.0°F) against the alternative hypothesis $\mu \neq 92.0°F$.

15.59 Rework the preceding exercise using the large-sample technique.

15.60 An engineer wants to know whether there is a difference in the breaking strength of wire cable produced to specifications by two suppliers, and the engineer tests random samples of 12 lengths of each supplier's cable. Following is the breaking strength of the two samples, in thousands of pounds:

> Supplier 1: 1.9 1.6 2.1 1.9 1.9 1.8 1.4 1.8 1.7
> 1.9 2.8 2.0
> Supplier 2: 1.7 2.3 1.7 2.2 2.0 2.2 2.4 2.1 2.2
> 1.8 1.6 2.0

Use the U test based on Table VII and the 0.01 level of significance to test whether it is reasonable to conclude that there is no difference in the actual mean breaking strength of the cable from the two suppliers.

15.61 Rework the preceding exercise using the large sample approximation to the sampling distribution of the U statistic.

15.62 The following sequence shows whether a certain store in a chain of seven-day stores generated more than (M) or less than (L) 10 percent of the chain's cash receipts during a 30-day month: L, L, L, M, M, L, L, M, L, L, L, M, M, M, L, M, L, L, M, L, L, L, L, M, L, L, L, L, M, M. Test for randomness at the 0.05 level of significance.

15.16

Solutions of Practice Exercises

15.1 (a) No. $np = 6 \cdot \dfrac{1}{2} = 3$, $n(1 - p) = 6\left(\dfrac{1}{2}\right) = 3$, and they are not greater than 5.

(b) No. $np = 10 \cdot \dfrac{1}{2} = 5$, $n(1 - p) = 10 \cdot \dfrac{1}{2} = 5$, and they are not greater than 5.

(c) Yes. $np = 12 \cdot \dfrac{1}{2} = 6$, $n(1 - p) = 12 \cdot \dfrac{1}{2} = 6$, and they are greater than 5.

15.3 Since none of the values equals 9.00, none is discarded and the sample size is 15.

1. H_O: $\mu = 9.00$.
   H_A: $\mu > 9.00$.

2. $\alpha = 0.05$.

3. The criterion may be based on the number of plus signs or the number of minus signs. Using the number of plus signs denoted by x, reject the null hypothesis if the probability of getting x or more plus signs is less than or equal to 0.05.

4. Replacing each value greater than 9.00 with a plus sign and each value less than 9.00 with a minus sign, we get

$$+ \ + \ - \ - \ + \ + \ + \ + \ + \ + \ - \ + \ + \ - \ +$$

where there are 11 plus signs. Table V shows that for $n = 15$ and $p = 0.50$ the probability of 11 or more plus signs is $0.042 + 0.014 + 0.003 = 0.059$.

5. Since 0.059 exceeds 0.05, the null hypothesis cannot be rejected.

15.5   Since one of the values equals 32.0, it must be discarded and the sample size is only $n = 14$. Thus $z = \dfrac{12 - 14(0.5)}{\sqrt{14(0.5)(0.5)}} = 2.67$, and since this value exceeds 2.33, the null hypothesis must be rejected.

15.6   Since none of the tablets sampled is exactly 32.05 ounces, none is discarded and $n = 24$.

1. H_O: $\mu = 32.05$.
   H_A: $\mu < 32.05$.
2. $\alpha = 0.05$.
3. If x is the number of $+$ signs (tablets containing more than 32.05 milligrams of medication) reject the null hypothesis if $z \leq -1.645$, where

$$z = \frac{x - np_0}{\sqrt{np_0(1 - p_0)}}$$

with $p_0 = 0.50$; otherwise, accept it or reserve judgment.

4. Replacing each positive difference with a plus sign and each negative difference with a minus sign, we get six plus signs (six values greater than 32.05). Thus $x = 6$ and $z = \dfrac{6 - 24(0.5)}{\sqrt{24(0.5)(0.5)}} = -2.45$.

5. Since $z = -2.45$ is less than -1.645, the null hypothesis must be rejected; the mean weight of the medication contained in the entire production lot of tablets is less than 32.05 milligrams.

15.8   Since the difference is zero in each of two pairs, the sample size is reduced to 28.

1. H_0: $\mu_1 = \mu_2$.
   H_A: $\mu_1 < \mu_2$.
2. $\alpha = 0.01$.
3. If x is the number of plus $(+)$ signs (first meter maid issues more parking tickets than second meter maid), reject the null hypothesis if $z \leq -2.33$, where

$$z = \frac{x - np_0}{\sqrt{np_0(1 - p_0)}}$$

with $p = 0.50$; otherwise, accept it or reserve judgment.

4. Replacing each positive difference with a plus sign and each negative difference with a minus sign, we get five positive $(+)$ differences. Thus, $x = 5$ and

$$z = \frac{5 - 28(0.5)}{\sqrt{28(0.5)(0.5)}} = -3.40$$

5. Since -3.40 is less than -2.33, the null hypothesis must be rejected; on the average, the second meter maid issues more parking tickets than the first meter maid.

15.12 (a) $T \leq 14$ (b) $T^- \leq 17$ (c) $T^+ \leq 17$

15.14 (a) $T^- \leq 5$ (b) $T \leq 3$ (c) $T^+ \leq 5$

15.16 (a) **1.** H_0: $\mu = 143$.
H_A: $\mu < 143$.

  2. $\alpha = 0.05$.

  3. Reject the null hypothesis if $T^+ \leq 21$, where 21 is the value of $T_{0.10}$ for $n = 13$; otherwise, accept the null hypothesis or reserve judgment.

4. Sales in millions of dollars	Differences from 143	Ranks
138	-5	4
150	7	6
141	-2	2
125	-18	13
133	-10	9
134	-9	8
155	12	11
137	-6	5
139	-4	3
132	-11	10
144	1	1
130	-13	12
135	-8	7

It follows that

$$T^+ = 6 + 11 + 1 = 18$$

and

$$T^- = 4 + 2 + 13 + 9 + 8 + 5 + 3 + 10 + 12 + 7 = 73$$

  5. Since $T^+ = 18$ is less than 21, we reject the null hypothesis and conclude that the sales are less than 143.

(b) **1.** H_0: $\mu = 143$.
H_A: $\mu \neq 143$.

  2. $\alpha = 0.05$.

  3. Reject the null hypothesis if $T^+ \leq 17$ where 17 is the value of

$T_{0.05}$ for $n = 13$; otherwise, accept the null hypothesis or reserve judgment.

4. From part (a) of this exercise, $T^+ = 18$.

5. Since $T^+ = 18$ is greater than 17, the critical value for $T_{0.05}$, we cannot reject the null hypothesis. We accept the null hypothesis that $\mu = 143$, or reserve judgment.

15.20 1. H_0: $\mu_1 = \mu_2$.
       H_A: $\mu_1 \neq \mu_2$.

2. $\alpha = 0.05$.

3. Reject the null hypothesis if $T \leq 6$, where 6 is the value of $T_{0.05}$ for $n = 9$; otherwise, accept the null hypothesis or reserve judgment.

4.

Northbound	Southbound	Difference	Rank
83	92	−9	8
82	92	−10	9
88	94	−6	6
88	93	−5	4.5
86	91	−5	4.5
89	96	−7	7
85	81	4	3
83	81	2	1
85	88	−3	2

It follows that

$$T^+ = 3 + 1 = 4$$

and

$$T^- = 8 + 9 + 6 + 4.5 + 4.5 + 7 + 2 = 41$$

so

$$T = 4$$

Check: $4 + 41 = 45$, $\dfrac{9 \cdot 10}{2} = 45$

5. Since $T = 4$ is less than 6, the null hypothesis must be rejected. We accept the null hypothesis or reserve judgment.

15.22 (a) 1. H_0: $\mu = 23.0$.
              H_A: $\mu \neq 23.0$.

       2. $\alpha = 0.05$.

3. Reject the null hypothesis if $T \leq 90$ where T is the value of $T_{0.05}$ for $n = 25$; otherwise, accept the null hypothesis or reserve judgment.

4. Their differences and ranks of their absolute values are shown in the following table:

Gallons of diesel fuel	Differences from 23.0	Ranks
28.4	5.4	12
38.3	15.3	23
26.8	3.8	8
24.5	1.5	3.5
29.1	6.1	14
27.6	4.6	10
21.5	−1.5	3.5
17.9	−5.1	11
32.3	9.3	17
34.0	11.0	19
13.6	−9.4	18
21.4	−1.6	5
35.9	12.9	22
30.6	7.6	15
34.1	11.1	20
22.8	−0.2	1
26.7	3.7	7
28.5	5.5	13
51.9	28.9	25
27.2	4.2	9
35.8	12.8	21
22.3	−0.7	2
21.0	−2.0	6
49.2	26.2	24
31.7	8.7	16

It follows that

$$T^{-} = 3.5 + 11 + 18 + 5 + 1 + 2 + 6 = 46.5$$

and

$$T^{+} = 12 + 23 + 8 + 3.5 + 14 + 10 + 17 + 19 + 22 + 15 + 20 + 7 + 13 + 25 + 9 + 21 + 24 + 16 = 278.5$$

and thus

$$T = 46.5$$

Check: $46.5 + 278.5 = 325,$ $\dfrac{25 \cdot 26}{2} = 325$

5. Since $T = 46.5$ is less than 90, the null hypothesis must be rejected. We conclude that the true mean is not equal to 23.0.

(b) 1. Same as part (a).

2. Same as part (a).

3. Reject the null hypothesis if $z \leq -1.96$ or $z \geq 1.96$, where

$$z = \frac{T^+ - \mu_{T^+}}{\sigma_{T^+}}$$

otherwise, accept the null hypothesis or reserve judgment.

4. From part (a), $T^+ = 278.5$, and since

$$\mu_{T^+} = \frac{25 \cdot 26}{4} = 162.5 \quad \text{and} \quad \sigma_{T^+} = \sqrt{\frac{25 \cdot 26 \cdot 51}{24}} = 37.16$$

we finally get

$$z = \frac{278.5 - 162.5}{37.16} = 3.12$$

5. Since 3.12 exceeds 1.96, the null hypothesis must be rejected. We conclude that the true mean is not equal to 23, or we may reserve judgment.

15.24 1. H_0: $\mu_1 = \mu_2$.
H_A: $\mu_1 \neq \mu_2$.

2. $\alpha = 0.05$.

3. Reject the null hypothesis if $U \leq 5$ where 5 is the value of $U_{0.05}$ for $n_1 = 6$ and $n_2 = 6$, using Table VII, two-sided alternative; otherwise, accept the null hypothesis or reserve judgment.

4. Arranging the data jointly as if they comprise one sample in an increasing order of magnitude, we find that those of the first sample occupy ranks 5.5, 12, 9.5, 9.5, 3.5, and 11, and those of the second sample occupy ranks 2, 5.5, 7, 3.5, 1, and 8; then $W_1 = 5.5 + 12 + 9.5 + 9.5 + 3.5 + 11 = 51$, and $W_2 = 2 + 5.5 + 7 + 3.5 + 1 + 8 = 27$. Thus,

$$U_1 = W_1 - \frac{n_1(n_1 + 1)}{2} = 51 - \frac{6(6 + 1)}{2} = 30$$

$$U_2 = W_2 - \frac{n_2(n_2 + 1)}{2} = 27 - \frac{6(6 + 1)}{2} = 6$$

and hence $U = 6$. Note that $U_1 + U_2 = 36$ which equals $n_1 n_2 = 6 \cdot 6 = 36$.

5. Since $U = 6$ is not less than or equal to 5, the critical value from Table VII, the null hypothesis cannot be rejected.

15.27   1. $H_0: \mu_1 = \mu_2$.
$H_A: \mu_1 \neq \mu_2$.

2. $\alpha = 0.05$.

3.   Reject the null hypothesis if $z \leq 1.96$ or $z \geq 1.96$, where

$$z = \frac{U_1 - \mu_{U_1}}{\sigma_{U_1}}$$

otherwise, accept the null hypothesis or reserve judgment.

4.   Arranging the data according to size, we find that $W_1 = 1 + 3 + 7 + 11 + 12.5 + 18 + 20 + 23 + 25 + 25 + 27 + 29 + 30.5 + 34 + 35.5 + 39 + 40 + 41 + 42 + 43.5 = 507$, and since

$$U_1 = W_1 - \frac{n_1(n_1 + 1)}{2} = 507 - \frac{20(20 + 1)}{2} = 297$$

$$\sigma_{U_1} = \sqrt{\frac{n_1 n_2 (n_1 + n_2 + 1)}{12}} = \sqrt{\frac{20 \cdot 24 \cdot 45}{12}} = 42.43$$

$$\mu_{U_1} = \frac{n_1 n_2}{2} = \frac{20 \cdot 24}{2} = 240$$

it follows that

$$z = \frac{U_1 - \mu_{U_1}}{\sigma_{U_1}} = \frac{297 - 240}{42.43} = 1.34$$

5.   Since $z = 1.34$ falls between -1.96 and 1.96, the null hypothesis cannot be rejected.

15.30   1. $H_0: \mu_1 = \mu_2 = \mu_3$.
$H_A: \mu_1, \mu_2$, and μ_3, are not all equal.

2. $\alpha = 0.05$.

3.   Reject the null hypothesis if $H \geq 5.991$ which is the value of χ^2 for $3 - 1 = 2$ degrees of freedom; otherwise, accept it or reserve judgment.

4.   Arranging the data jointly according to size, we get 164, 164, 166, 167, 168, 169, 169, 171, 173, 174, 176, 177, 178, 179, 181, 181, 183, and 189. Assigning the data, in this order, the ranks 1, 2, 3, . . . , 18 we find that

$$R_1 = 14 + 1 + 15.5 + 11 + 9 + 13 + 2 = 65.5$$
$$R_2 = 6.5 + 12 + 3 + 8 + 15.5 + 18 = 63$$
$$R_3 = 10 + 4 + 5 + 17 + 6.5 = 42.5$$

and it follows that

$$H = \frac{12}{n(n+1)} \sum_{i=1}^{k} \frac{R_i^2}{n_i} - 3(n+1) \quad = \frac{12}{18.19}\left(\frac{65.5^2}{7} + \frac{63^2}{6} + \frac{42.5^2}{5}\right) - 3 \cdot 19$$

$$= 0.25$$

5. Since 0.25 is less than 5.991, the value of $\chi^2_{0.05}$ for two degrees of freedom, we cannot reject the null hypothesis. There is no evidence at the 0.05 level of significance that the audiences are not of equal size.

15.34 (a) **1.** H_0: Arrangement is random.
      H_A: Arrangement is not random.
   2. $\alpha = 0.05$.
   3. Reject the null hypothesis if $u \leq 8$ or $u \geq 19$, where 8 and 19 are the values of $u'_{0.025}$ and $u_{0.025}$ for $n_1 = 13$ heads and $n_2 = 12$ tails; otherwise, reject it or reserve judgment.
   4. $u = 25$ by inspection of data.
   5. Since $u = 25$ is greater than 19, the critical value of $u_{0.025}$ the null hypothesis of randomness must be rejected.

(b) **1.** H_0: Arrangement is random.
      H_A: Arrangement is not random.
   2. $\alpha = 0.05$.
   3. Reject the null hypothesis if $u \leq 8$ or $u \geq 19$, where 8 and 19 are the values of $u'_{0.025}$ and $u_{0.025}$ for $n_1 = 13$ heads and $n_2 = 12$ tails; otherwise, accept it or reserve judgment.
   4. $u = 2$ by inspection of data.
   5. Since $u = 2$ is less than 8, the critical value of $u'_{0.025}$, the null hypothesis of randomness must be rejected.

(c) **1.** H_0: Arrangement is random.
      H_A: Arrangement is not random.
   2. $\alpha = 0.05$.
   3. Reject the null hypothesis if $u \leq 8$ or $u \geq 19$, where 8 and 19 are the values of $u'_{0.025}$ and $u_{0.025}$ for $n_1 = 13$ and $n_2 = 12$; otherwise, accept it or reserve judgment.
   4. $u = 18$ by inspection.
   5. Since $u = 18$ falls between $u = 8$ and $u = 19$, the null hypothesis cannot be rejected. There is no evidence of any lack of randomness.

(d) In (a) there are too many runs, in (b) there are two few runs, and in (c) there are many, but not too many runs.

15.40 $\bar{x}$ is 17, so that the arrangement is $a, b, b, b, b, b, b, a, a, a, a, a, b, b, b, b,$ $b, b, b, a, a, a, a, a, a, a, a$, where three values equal to 17 have been discarded.

1. H_0: Arrangement is random.
   H_A: Arrangement is not random.

2. $\alpha = 0.01$.

3. Reject the null hypothesis of $u \leq 7$ or $u \geq 22$ where 7 and 14 are the values of $u'_{0.005}$ and $u_{0.005}$ for $n_1 = 14$ and $n_2 = 13$; otherwise, accept the null hypothesis or reserve judgment.

4. The number of runs is 5, by inspection of the arrangement of a's and b's.

5. Since the number of runs, $u = 5$, is less than the critical value of 7, the null hypothesis must be rejected. There seems to be a definite clustering.

15.42 $x = 138$, so the arrangment is $b, b, b, b, b, a, a, b, b, a, a, a, a, b, a, b, b, b,$ $a, a, a, a, b, b, b, a, b, b, a, a, a, a$, where one value equal to 138 has been discarded.

1. H_0: Arrangement is random.
   H_A: Arrangement is not random.

2. $\alpha = 0.05$.

3. Reject the null hypothesis if $z \leq -1.645$; otherwise, accept the null hypothesis or reserve judgment.

4. Since $n_1 = 16$, $n_2 = 16$, $u = 12$,

$$\mu_u = \frac{2 \cdot 16 \cdot 16}{32} + 1 = 17$$

$$\sigma_u = \sqrt{\frac{2 \cdot 16 \cdot 16(512 - 32)}{32^2 \cdot 31}} = 2.78$$

and

$$z = \frac{12 - 17}{2.78} = -1.80$$

5. Since -1.80 is less than -1.645, the critical value for $\alpha = 0.05$ (one sided, left tail), the null hypothesis must be rejected. There is a trend.

CHAPTER 16

Decision Making: Linear Regression

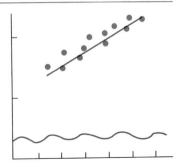

T he main objective of many statistical investigations is to establish relationships which make it possible to predict one or more variables in terms of other variables which are known. For instance, studies are made to predict the future sales of a new product in terms of its price, a woman's weight loss in terms of the number of weeks she will stay on an 800-calorie-per-day diet, family expenditures for housing in terms of family income, the per capita consumption of certain food items in terms of the amount of money spent advertising them on television, and so forth.

It would be ideal, of course, if we could predict one quantity exactly in terms of another, but this is seldom possible; in most instances we must be satisfied with predicting averages or expected values. For instance, we cannot predict exactly how much money a specific college graduate will earn 10 years after graduation, but given suitable data we can predict the average earnings of all college graduates 10 years after graduation. Similarly, we can predict the average yield of a given variety of wheat in terms of the rainfall in the month of July, and we can predict the expected grade-point average of a student starting an M.B.A. program in terms of his undergraduate grade-point average. This problem of predicting the average value of one variable in terms of the known value of another variable (or the known values of other variables) is the problem of **regression**. This term dates back to Francis Galton, who used it first in 1877 in a study that showed that the heights of persons born to tall and short parents will tend to move back or "regress" toward the mean height of the population.

The case where predictions are based on the known value of one variable is treated in Sections 16.1 through 16.3, and the case where predictions are based on the known values of several variables is treated in Section 16.4. Related problems will be taken up in Chapter 20.

16.1

Curve Fitting

Whenever possible, scientists strive to express, or approximate, relationships between known quantities and quantities that are to be predicted in terms of mathematical equations. In physics it is known, for example, that at a constant temperature the relationship between the volume, y, of a gas and its pressure, x, is given by the formula

$$y = \frac{k}{x}$$

where k is a numerical constant; also, in biology, it has been discovered that the size of a culture of bacteria, y, can be expressed in terms of the time, x, it has been exposed to certain favorable conditions by means of the formula

$$y = a \cdot b^x$$

where a and b are numerical constants.

Business and economic statisticians have borrowed and continue to borrow liberally from the tools of the natural sciences. For instance, the first equation, $y = \frac{k}{x}$, is often used to express the relationship between the demand, y, for a commodity and its price, x, and the second equation, $y = a \cdot b^x$, is often used to express, among other things, how a company's production or sales, y, grow with time, x.

In any situation where we want to use observed data to derive a mathematical equation and use it to predict the value of one variable from a given value of another—a procedure known generally as **curve fitting**—there are essentially three problems to be solved. We must decide what kind of "predicting" equation is to be used; then we must find the particular equation which is in some sense the best of its kind; and finally, we must settle certain questions regarding the goodness of the particular equation or of the predictions made from it.

With respect to the first of these problems of curve fitting, there are many different kinds of curves (and their equations) that can be used for predictive purposes. The equations we use are of the form y equals some expression in x, and when a known value of x is substituted into the equation, we can calculate the value of y. Here we designate the variable to be predicted by the letter y and call it the "dependent" variable since its value is determined by the value of x. The predictor variable, x, is the "independent" variable. As we shall see, a **regression equation** may also have more than one independent variable.

Among the many different kinds of curves, we might use a straight line having the equation $y = a + bx$, a parabola given by $y = a + bx + cx^2$, an exponential curve given by $y = a \cdot b^x$, or any one of many other mathematical equations. The choice of one of these is sometimes decided for us by theoretical considerations, but usually it is decided by direct inspection of the data. We plot the data on ordinary (arithmetic) graph paper or sometimes on special graph paper with logarithmic scales. The resulting pattern of points is called a **scatter diagram**, and we can often decide by visual study of such a plot whether there is an overall pattern in the data and upon the kind of curve, if any, which best describes the pattern. Figure 16.1 shows some types of

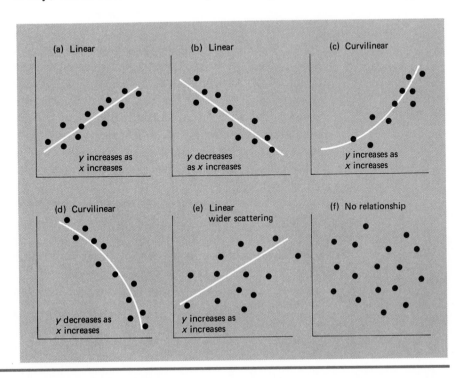

FIGURE 16.1
Possible plots of paired data

patterns we might find in a scatter diagram. The wider the pattern of scattering, the lower the degree of association between the independent and the dependent variable. Notice that portions of curvilinear relationships may take on the appearance of straight lines, but when making predictions beyond the range of the data, it is wise to keep in mind that curves may change direction.

There exist various methods for putting this decision on a more objective basis, but they will not be discussed in this book. As far as the second and third problems of curve fitting are concerned, we shall study the second in some detail in Section 16.2 and the third in Section 16.3.

16.2

Linear Regression

Of the various kinds of equations used to predict values of one variable, y, from associated values of another variable, x, the simplest and most widely used is the **linear equation in two unknowns**, which is of the form

$$y = a + bx$$

where a is the y intercept (the value of y at the point where $x = 0$) and b is the slope of the line (the change in y which accompanies a change of one unit in x). Ordinarily, the numerical constants a and b are estimated from sample data, and once they have been determined, we can substitute a given value of x into the equation and calculate the predicted value of y. Linear equations are useful and important not only because many relationships are actually of this form, but also because they often provide close approximations to relationships which would otherwise be difficult to describe in mathematical terms.

The term "linear equation" arises from the fact that, when plotted on ordinary graph paper (or arithmetic paper), all pairs of values of x and y which satisfy an equation of the form $y = a + bx$ fall on a straight line. Suppose, for instance, that a large mail-order firm wants to predict the number of orders it can expect to receive, y, in terms of the number of catalogs it distributes, x, and that on the basis of past experience it has derived the predicting equation

$$y = 11,400 + 1.8x$$

The graph of this linear equation is shown in Figure 16.2, and any pair of values of x and y which are such that $y = 11,400 + 1.8x$ forms a point (x,y) that falls on the line. We plot the independent variable, x, the number of catalogs distributed on the horizontal axis, and the dependent variable, y, the number of orders expected, on the vertical axis.

Substituting $x = 5,000$, for example, the firm finds that when 5,000 catalogs are distributed, it can expect to receive $11,400 + (1.8)(5,000) = 20,400$ orders, and when $x = 10,000$ catalogs are distributed, it can expect to receive $11,400 + (1.8)(10,000) = 29,400$ orders. The line representing the equation in Figure 16.2 slopes upward. As x takes on large values, y also increases. The constant 1.8 in this equation is the slope, and it is positive.

Once we have decided to fit a straight line, we are faced with the problem of finding the equation of the particular line which in some sense provides the best possible fit to the observed data. To show how this is done, let us consider the following: An automatic vending machine company owns

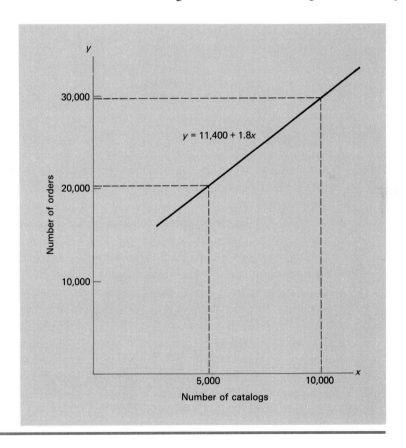

FIGURE 16.2
Graph of linear equation

and controls a very large stock of vending machines of a certain kind. The machines are installed in various locations, and they are of various ages. Company records show, among other things, for each active machine the amount of money spent on its maintenance in its last (full) year of use. From this stock we take a random sample of $n = 10$ machines, and, recording for each its maintenance cost, y, and its last year of use, x, we get [1]

Year x	Maintenance cost (dollars) y
4	148
2	128
3	133
5	154
2	118
3	145
4	143
5	159
4	142
3	127

Plotting these pairs of values on arithmetic paper as in Figure 16.3 we observe that, although the points do not fall on a straight line, the overall pattern of the relationship is reasonably well described by the line. There is no noticeable departure from linearity in the scatter of the points, so we feel justified in deciding that a straight line is a suitable description of the underlying relationship.

We now face the problem of finding the equation of the line which in some sense provides the best fit to the data and which, it is hoped, will later yield the best possible predictions of y from x. Logically, there is no limit to the number of straight lines which can be drawn on a piece of graph paper. Some of these lines would be such obviously poor fits to the data that we could not consider them seriously, but there are many lines which would seem to provide more or less "good" fits, and the problem is to find that one line which fits the data "best" in some well-defined sense. If all the points actually fell on a straight line, the criterion would be self-evident, but this is an extreme case which we rarely encounter in practice. In general, we have to be satisfied with a line having certain desirable, but not perfect, properties.

[1] Here and there, for the sake of simplicity, we shall call this (somewhat loosely) the "age" of a machine.

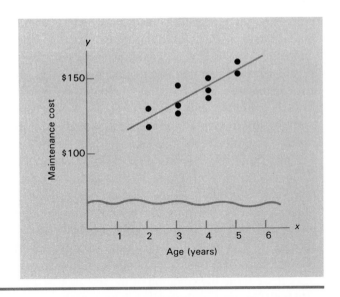

FIGURE 16.3
Data on age and
maintenance cost of
vending machines

The criterion which, nowadays, is used almost exclusively for defining a "best" fit dates back to the early part of the nineteenth century and the French mathematician Adrien Legendre; it is known as the **method of least squares**. As it will be used here, this method requires that the line which we fit to our data be such that the sum of the squares of the vertical deviations of the data points from the estimating line is a minimum.

For the maintenance-cost problem, the method of least squares requires that the sum of the squares of the distances represented by the solid-line segments of Figure 16.4 be as small as possible. To explain the nature of this

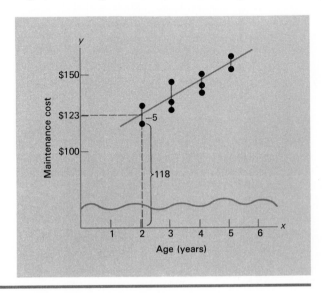

FIGURE 16.4
Line fitted to data
on age and
maintenance of
vending machines

procedure, let us consider one of the vending machines, say, the one whose maintenance cost was $118 during its second year of use. If we mark $x = 2$ on the horizontal scale and read the corresponding value of y off the line of Figure 16.4 we find that this maintenance cost is about $123; therefore, the error in the prediction based on the line, represented by the vertical distance from the point to the line, is $118 - 123 = -5$. Altogether, there are 10 such errors in this example, and the least-squares criterion requires that we minimize the sum of their squares.

To show how a **least-squares line** is actually fitted to a set of data, let us consider n pairs of numbers (x_1, y_1), (x_2, y_2), . . . , (x_n, y_n) which might represent such things as the reading rate and reading comprehension of n financial analysts, the number of labor units per acre and crop yield per acre on n farms, the score on a paper-and-pencil personality test and vocational success of n college graduates, and product advertising expenditures and product sales of n consumer goods manufacturers.

If we write the equation of the line as $\hat{y} = a + bx$, where the symbol $\hat{y}$ ("y-hat") is used to distinguish between observed values of y and the corresponding values $\hat{y}$ on the line, the least-squares criterion requires that we minimize the sum of the squares of the differences between the y's and the $\hat{y}$'s (see Figure 16.5). This means that we must find the numerical values of the constants a and b appearing in the equation $\hat{y} = a + bx$ for which

$$\Sigma(y - \hat{y})^2 = \Sigma \, [y - (a + bx)]^2$$

is as small as possible. We shall not go through the derivation of the two equations, called the **normal equations**, which provide the solution to this

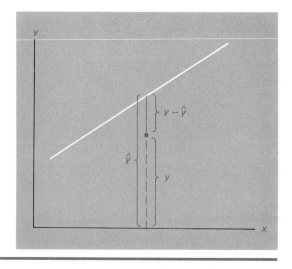

FIGURE 16.5
Least-squares line

Chapter 16   Decision Making: Linear Regression

problem. Instead, we merely state that minimizing $\sum(y - \hat{y})^2$ yields the following system of two linear equations in the unknowns a and b:

Normal equations

$$\sum y = na + b(\sum x)$$
$$\sum xy = a(\sum x) + b(\sum x^2)$$

In these equations, whose solution gives the least-squares value of a and b, n is the number of pairs of observations, $\sum x$ and $\sum y$ are the sums of the observed x's and y's, $\sum x^2$ is the sum of the squares of the x's and $\sum xy$ is the sum of the cross products of the x's and their associated observed values of y.

EXAMPLE 16.1   Fit a least-squares line to the vending machine data on page 614.

SOLUTION   We get the sums needed for substitution into the normal equations by performing the calculations shown in the following table:

Year x	Maintenance cost (dollars) y	x^2	xy
4	148	16	592
2	128	4	256
3	133	9	399
5	154	25	770
2	118	4	236
3	145	9	435
4	143	16	572
5	159	25	795
4	142	16	568
3	127	9	381
35	1,397	133	5,004

Substituting $n = 10$ and the four column totals into the two normal equations, we get

$$1,397 = 10a + 35b$$
$$5,004 = 35a + 133b$$

Section 16.2   Linear Regression

and we must now solve these two simultaneous linear equations for a and b. There are several ways in which this can be done; from elementary algebra we can use either the method of elimination or the method of determinants. In either case, we get $a = 101.5$ and $b = 10.9$. ∎

As an alternative to these procedures, we can solve the two normal equations symbolically for a and b and then substitute the value of n and the various sums obtained from the data into the resulting formulas. Among the various ways in which we can write these formulas, perhaps most convenient is the format where we use as building blocks the quantities

$$S_{xx} = \sum x^2 - \frac{1}{n}(\sum x)^2$$

and

$$S_{xy} = \sum xy - \frac{1}{n}(\sum x)(\sum y)$$

Note in Exercise 3.27 on page 73 we used the first of these quantities in an alternative computing formula for the sample standard deviation.

In this notation, the solutions of the two normal equations can be written as

Solutions of normal equations

$$b = \frac{S_{xy}}{S_{xx}}$$

$$a = \frac{\sum y - b(\sum x)}{n}$$

where we first calculate b and then substitute its value into the formula for a.

EXAMPLE 16.2   Use these formulas to rework the preceding example.

SOLUTION   Substituting $n = 10$ and the various sums shown in the preceding table into these formulas for S_{xx} and S_{xy}, we get

$$S_{xx} = \sum x^2 - \frac{1}{n}(\sum x)^2 = 133 - \frac{1}{10}(35)^2 = 10.5$$

$$S_{xy} = \sum xy - \frac{1}{n}(\sum x)(\sum y) = 5{,}004 - \frac{1}{10}(35)(1{,}397) = 114.5$$

and, as before (except for a slight difference due to rounding),

$$b = \frac{S_{xy}}{S_{xx}} = \frac{114.5}{10.5} = 10.9$$

$$a = \frac{\sum y - b(\sum x)}{n} = \frac{1{,}397 - 10.9(35)}{10} = 101.6 \qquad \blacksquare$$

Computer software exists for fitting least-squares lines. Figure 16.6 shows the solution to our problem obtained by means of such a commercially available program. The values of a and b are 101.533 and 10.905 in the column headed "Coef" (coefficient). The differences between the results are due to rounding.

```
MTB > NAME C1='X' C2='COST'
MTB > PRINT C1 C2

ROW    X    COST

 1     4    148
 2     2    128
 3     3    133
 4     5    154
 5     2    118
 6     3    145
 7     4    143
 8     5    159
 9     4    142
10     3    127

MTB > REGR 'COST' 1 'X'

The regression equation is
cost = 102 + 10.9 x

Predictor       Coef       Stdev      t-ratio       p
Constant      101.533      6.360       15.96     0.000
x              10.905      1.744        6.25     0.000

s = 5.651       R-sq = 83.0%     R-sq(adj) = 80.9%

Analysis of Variance

SOURCE        DF       SS         MS         F        p
Regression     1     1248.6     1248.6     39.09    0.000
Error          8      255.5       31.9
Total          9     1504.1

Unusual Observations
Obs.      x       cost     Fit Stdev.Fit  Residual   St.Resid
 6      3.00    145.00    134.25    1.99     10.75      2.03R

R denotes an obs. with a large st. resid.

MTB > STOP
```

FIGURE 16.6
Computer printout for linear regression of age and maintenance costs of vending machines

EXAMPLE 16.3 Rounding 101.533 to 101.5, use the least-squares line $\hat{y} = 101.5 + 10.9x$ to predict the maintenance cost of one of the vending machines during the second year of use.

SOLUTION   Substituting $x = 2$ into the equation, we get

$$\hat{y} = 101.5 + 10.9(2) = \$123.30$$

and this is the best estimate we can make in the least-squares sense. ■

In the discussion of this section we have considered only the problem of fitting a straight line to paired data. More generally, the method of least squares can also be used to fit other kinds of curves and to derive predicting equations in more than two unknowns. The problem of fitting some curves other than straight lines by the method of least squares will be discussed briefly in Chapter 20; a simple example of a predicting equation in more than two unknowns will be treated later in this chapter.

EXERCISES

(Exercises 16.1, 16.3, and 16.5 are practice exercises. Their complete solutions are given on page 648.)

16.1   A jeans manufacturer knows that a large budget for television advertising of his product will create a demand for it among department store buyers. The following table shows the dollars (in thousands) spent for advertising the fall line of jeans for eight years and the number of pairs of jeans sold (in thousands) in each fall line.

Year	Number of dollars spent on television advertising (thousands) x	Number of pairs of jeans sold (thousands) y
1985	50	45
1986	65	60
1987	75	80
1988	100	95
1989	125	120
1990	140	150
1991	170	145
1992	195	190

(a) Solve the normal equations on page 617 to find the equation of the least-squares line which will enable us to predict the number of pairs of jeans sold, $\hat{y}$, in terms of the dollars spent on television advertising, x.

(b) Use the formulas on page 618 to calculate the values of a and b.

16.2   (a) Use the equation derived in part (a) of the preceding exercise to estimate the number of pairs of jeans which are expected to be sold with a television advertising budget of a quarter of a million dollars.

(b) When the advertising budget is a quarter of a million dollars, what is the expected advertising cost per pair of jeans sold?

16.3   The following table shows the billions of therms (1 therm = 100,000 British thermal units) of natural gas shipped monthly for a year by two natural gas companies.

Company 1 x	Company 2 y
2.0	3.8
1.2	2.4
1.3	2.4
0.4	1.4
0.9	2.1
1.2	2.8
2.8	4.9
0.6	1.2
1.0	2.3
2.6	4.2
0.8	1.9
1.5	3.1

(a) Solve the normal equations on page 617 to find the equation of the least-squares line which will enable us to predict y in terms of x.

(b) Use the formulas on page 618 to check the values of a and b obtained in part (a).

16.4   Use the results of part (b) of the preceding exercise to predict the billions of therms of natural gas shipped by Company 2 if the shipments of Company 1 are 1.4 billion therms.

16.5   The following table shows the weekly labor costs paid (x) and weekly revenues received from bicycle repairs (y) by a bicycle shop for a quarter of a year.

Labor costs x (in hundreds)	Repair revenues y (in thousands)
$7.1	$3.9
2.2	1.7
7.2	3.7
3.1	1.5
3.3	2.2
3.5	1.4
7.7	4.9
4.1	2.5
6.8	4.5
4.7	3.4
5.3	2.3
5.5	3.6
6.1	3.2

(a) Find the equation of the least-squares line which will enable us to predict repair revenues from labor costs of the bicycle shop.

(b) Plot the least-squares line together with the original data on one diagram.

16.6 With reference to the preceding exercise, predict the weekly repair revenues when $5.8 (hundred) is the weekly labor cost.

16.7 The following table shows 10 weeks of sales of two competing brands of athletic shoes (in pairs) at a sporting goods store:

Brand A athletic shoes x	Brand B athletic shoes y
76	172
58	134
63	140
71	159
66	145
55	126
60	132
64	141
69	150
80	178

(a) Find the equation of the least-squares line which will enable us to predict the sales of brand B shoes from the sales of brand A shoes.

(b) Predict the sales of brand B shoes for a week in which the sales of brand A shoes are 65 pairs.

16.8 The following data show the improvement (gain in reading speed in words per minute) of six students in a speed-reading program, and the number of weeks they have been in the program:

Number of weeks x	Speed gain (words per minute) y
4	91
2	50
8	210
6	164
9	241
3	79

(a) Find the least-squares line from which we may predict the speed-reading gain of a person who has been in the program for a given number of weeks.

(b) Use the equation of the least-squares line to predict the increase in reading speed which a person can expect if he is in the program for five weeks.

16.9 A woman wants to open a small fashion boutique business. Before selecting a location, she would like to be able to predict the profit in dollars that the store may be expected to earn per hundred square feet of selling space. She gathers the following information.

Store size (hundreds of square feet) x	Profit (thousands of dollars) y
35	20
22	15
27	17
16	9
28	16
12	7
40	22
32	23

(a) Find the least-squares line from which the woman can predict the store profit in terms of store size. What profit can she expect to earn from a suitable 1,500-square-foot store?

(b) Plot the eight given data points and the least-squares line on one graph, and read the answer to part (a) of this exercise from the graph.

16.10   If, in the preceding exercise, we wanted to predict the store size necessary to produce an expected profit of ten thousand dollars, we could substitute $\hat{y} =$ 10 into the least-squares equation obtained in Exercise 16.9 and solve for x, but this would not be a prediction in the least-squares sense. To make the best possible least-squares estimate of store size required for a given profit, let the profit data be x and the store size data be y.

(a) Find the equation of such a line and use it to predict the store size required to earn a profit of ten thousand dollars.

(b) Use the equation of Exercise 16.9 to calculate the predicted profit from the same store size and compare it with your answer to part (a).

16.3

Regression Analysis

In the preceding section we used a least-squares line to predict the maintenance cost of a vending machine during its second year of use as $123.30, but even if we interpret the line correctly as a **regression line** (that is, treat the predictions made from it as averages, or expected values), several questions remain to be answered.

1. How good are the values we found for the constants a and b in the equation $\hat{y} = a + bx$? After all, $a = 101.5$ and $b = 10.9$ are only estimates based on a random sample, and if we based our work on another sample of 10 of the vending machines, the method of least squares would surely lead to different values of a and b.

2. How good an estimate is $123.30 of the true average maintenance cost of one of the vending machines during its second year?

Also, we might ask

3. How can we obtain limits (two numbers) and an associated degree of confidence which measure the goodness of a

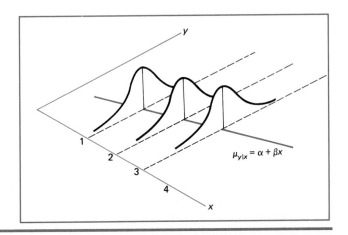

FIGURE 16.7
Distributions of y for given values of x

prediction in the same way in which a confidence interval measures the goodness of, say, an estimate of the mean of a population?

When in the first question, we said that the numbers $a = 101.5$ and $b = 10.9$ are "only estimates based on sample data," we implied the existence of corresponding true values, usually denoted by α and β, and therefore of a true regression line $\mu_{y|x} = \alpha + \beta x$, where $\mu_{y|x}$ is read "the true mean of y for a given value of x." It is customary to refer to α and β as **regression coefficients** and to a and b as the corresponding **estimated regression coefficients.**[2]

To clarify the idea of a true regression line, let us consider Figure 16.7, in which we have drawn the distribution of y for several values of x. With reference to our example, these curves should be looked upon as the distributions of the maintenance costs of such vending machines during their first, second, and third years of use; to complete the picture, we can visualize similar distributions for all other values of x within the range of values under consideration. Note that the means of all the distributions of Figure 16.7 lie on the true regression line given by $\mu_{y|x} = \alpha + \beta x$.

In **linear regression analysis** we assume that the x's are constants, not values of random variables and that for each value of x the variable to be predicted, y, has a certain distribution (as shown in Figure 16.7) whose mean is $\alpha + \beta x$. In **normal regression analysis** we assume, furthermore, that these distributions are all normal distributions having the same standard deviation σ. In other words, the distributions pictured in Figure 16.7 as well as those we imagine, are normal distributions with the means $\alpha + \beta x$ and the standard deviation σ.

[2]The coefficients α and β should not be confused with the probabilities α and β of committing Type I and Type II errors.

Based on these assumptions, it can be shown that the estimated regression coefficients a and b, obtained by the method of least squares, are values of random variables having normal distributions with the means α and β and the standard deviations.

$$\sigma\sqrt{\frac{1}{n} + \frac{\bar{x}^2}{S_{xx}}} \quad \text{and} \quad \frac{\sigma}{\sqrt{S_{xx}}}$$

Note that both of these standard error formulas require that we estimate σ, the common standard deviation of the normal distributions pictured in Figure 16.7. Otherwise, the x's are assumed to be constants, so there is no problem in determining $\bar{x}$ and S_{xx}. The estimate of σ we shall use is called the **standard error of estimate**, and it is denoted by s_e. Its formula is

$$s_e = \sqrt{\frac{\sum(y - \hat{y})^2}{n - 2}}$$

where, again, the y's are the observed values of y and the $\hat{y}$'s are the corresponding values on the least-squares line. Observe the s_e^2 is the sum of the squares of the vertical deviations from the points to the line (namely, the quantity which we minimized by the method of least squares) divided by $n - 2$.

The preceding formula defines s_e, but in practice we calculate its value by means of the computing formula

Standard error of estimate

$$s_e = \sqrt{\frac{S_{yy} - bS_{xy}}{n - 2}}$$

where

$$S_{yy} = \sum y^2 - \frac{1}{n}(\sum y)^2$$

is analogous to the formula for S_{xx} on page 618.

EXAMPLE 16.4 Find s_e for the least-squares line which we fit to the data pertaining to the age of vending machines and their cost of maintenance.

SOLUTION Since $n = 10$ and we have already shown on page 619 that $b = 10.9$

Chapter 16   Decision Making: Linear Regression

and $S_{xy} = 114.5$, the only other quantity needed is S_{yy}. Calculating

$$\Sigma \, y^2 = 148^2 + 128^2 + \cdots + 127^2$$
$$= 196,665$$

and copying $\Sigma \, y = 1,397$ from the table on page 617, we get

$$S_{yy} = \Sigma \, y^2 - \frac{1}{n}(\Sigma \, y)^2 = 196,665 - \frac{1}{10}(1,397)^2 = 1,504.1$$

and, hence,

$$s_e = \sqrt{\frac{S_{yy} - bS_{xy}}{n - 2}} = \sqrt{\frac{1,504.1 - 10.9(114.5)}{10 - 2}} = 5.66 \qquad \blacksquare$$

The result we obtained here can also be read from Figure 16.6. There we find $S = 5.651$, and the difference between the two results is due to rounding. Indeed, if we had rounded the value of b to three decimals and substituted $b = 10.905$ into the formula for s_e, we would also have obtained $s_e = 5.651$. This kind of error can be avoided by using the alternative computing formula for s_e given in Exercise 16.22 on page 634.

Inferences about the regression coefficients α and β can be based on the statistics

Statistics for inferences about regression coefficients

$$t = \frac{a - \alpha}{S_e \sqrt{\dfrac{1}{n} + \dfrac{\bar{x}^2}{S_{xx}}}}$$

$$t = \frac{b - \beta}{S_e / \sqrt{S_{xx}}}$$

whose sampling distributions are t distributions with $n - 2$ degrees of freedom. The quantities in the denominators are estimates of the corresponding standard errors with s_e substituted for σ. It should be noted that these statistics for inferences about regression coefficients require that we, once again, base our work on the assumptions of normal regression analysis given on page 624.

The following example illustrates how we test hypotheses about either of the regression coefficients α and β.

EXAMPLE 16.5 Suppose that someone claims that $\beta = 12.50$ in the vending machine example and that one purpose of the study was to test this claim. Now, β is the slope of the regression line; that is, it is the change in y associated with a change of one unit in x. Hence, the hypothesis asserts that, in the population of vending machines sampled, each year's use adds another \$12.50 on the average to the maintenance cost of a machine. Test this hypothesis against the alternative hypothesis $\beta \neq 12.50$ at the 0.05 level of significance.

SOLUTION 1. H_0: $\beta = 12.5$.
   H_A: $\beta \neq 12.5$.

2. $\alpha = 0.05$.

3. Reject the null hypothesis if $t \leq -2.306$ or $t \geq 2.306$, where

$$t = \frac{b - \beta}{s_e / \sqrt{S_{xx}}}$$

and 2.306 is the value of $t_{0.025}$ for $10 - 2 = 8$ degrees of freedom; otherwise, accept the null hypothesis or reserve judgment.

4. Since we already know from pages 618, 619, and 627 that $b = 10.9$, $S_{xx} = 10.5$, and $s_e = 5.66$, substitution of these values together with $\beta = 12.5$ yields

$$t = \frac{10.9 - 12.5}{5.66 / \sqrt{10.5}} = -0.92$$

5. Since $t = -0.92$ falls on the interval from -2.306 and 2.306, the null hypothesis cannot be rejected; that is, there is no real evidence that the slope is not $\beta = 12.5$. ∎

We could have saved ourselves some work in the preceding example by referring to Figure 16.6. The column headed "Stdev" shows that the estimated standard error, the quantity which goes into the denominator of the t statistic, is 1.744, so we can write directly

$$t = \frac{10.9 - 12.5}{1.744} = -0.92$$

Tests concerning the regression coefficient α are performed in the same way, except that we use the first, instead of the second, of the two t statistics. In many practical applications, however, the regression coefficient α is not of as much interest—it is just the y-intercept, namely, the value of y which corresponds to $x = 0$.

To construct **confidence intervals for the regression coefficients** α **and** β, we substitute into the middle term of $-t_{\alpha/2} < t < t_{\alpha/2}$ the appropriate t statistic from page 627. Then simple algebra leads to the formulas

Confidence limits for regression coefficients

$$a \pm t_{\alpha/2} \cdot s_e \sqrt{\frac{1}{n} + \frac{\bar{x}^2}{S_{xx}}}$$

$$b \pm t_{\alpha/2} \cdot \frac{s_e}{\sqrt{S_{xx}}}$$

where the degree of confidence is $(1 - \alpha)100$ percent and $t_{\alpha/2}$ is the entry in Table II for $n - 2$ degrees of freedom.

EXAMPLE 16.6   Using the data on age and maintenance cost of vending machines, construct a 95 percent confidence interval for β, the amount by which the maintenance cost can be expected to increase as the machine becomes a year older.

SOLUTION   The necessary quantities which have previously been determined are $b = 10.9$, $s_e = 5.66$, $S_{xx} = 10.5$, and $t_{0.025} = 2.306$ for $10 - 2 = 8$ degrees of freedom. Substituting these values into the second of the preceding formulas, we arrive at the confidence limits

$$10.9 \pm 2.306 \frac{5.66}{\sqrt{10.5}}$$

obtaining 10.9 ± 4.0279. Rounding to one decimal we can write the 95 percent confidence interval for β as $6.9 < \beta < 14.9$.   ■

This confidence interval is rather wide, and this is due to two things— the very small size of the sample and the large variation measured by s_e, namely, the large variation in the maintenance costs of vending machines of the same age.

The work we have done here can be simplified greatly by referring, once again, to the computer printout of Figure 16.6. We find that $b = 10.905$ and that the estimate of the standard error, by which we have to multiply $t_{\alpha/2}$, is 1.744. Again using $t_{0.025} = 2.306$, we get the confidence limits

$$10.905 \pm 2.306(1.744)$$

or 10.905 ± 4.022, and we can write the 95 percent confidence interval for β as

$$6.9 < \beta < 14.9$$

EXAMPLE 16.7 The following are the assessed valuations of eight houses and the selling prices of these houses. The data constitute a random sample of all houses assessed and sold in that city. The assessed values, in thousands, are $116.0, $160.8, $103.2, $55.8, $89.6, $65.0, $144.0, and $80.6, and the corresponding selling prices, in thousands, are $185.0, $246.4, $162.2, $97.6, $148.0, $110.4, $236.6, and $126.8. Construct a 95 percent confidence interval for β, where β is the amount (in thousands of dollars) by which the selling price can be expected to increase as the assessed valuation increases by $1,000.

SOLUTION We prepare the following table, from which we take the necessary sums.

Assessed value (thousands of dollars) x	Selling price (thousands of dollars) y	x^2	xy	y^2
116.0	185.0	13,456.00	21,460.00	34,225.00
160.8	246.4	25,856.64	39,621.12	60,712.96
103.2	162.2	10,650.24	16,739.04	26,308.84
55.8	97.6	3,113.64	5,446.08	9,525.76
89.6	148.0	8,028.16	13,260.80	21,904.00
65.0	110.4	4,225.00	7,176.00	12,188.16
144.0	236.6	20,736.00	34,070.40	55,979.56
80.6	126.8	6,496.36	10,220.08	16,078.24
815.0	1,313.0	92,562.04	147,993.52	236,922.52

Using the sums, the sample size $n = 8$, and the appropriate formula, we get

$$S_{xx} = \sum x^2 - \frac{1}{n}\left(\sum x\right)^2 = 92,562.04 - \frac{1}{8}(815.0)^2 = 9,533.915$$

$$S_{yy} = \sum y^2 - \frac{1}{n}(\sum y)^2 = 236{,}922.52 - \frac{1}{8}(1{,}313.0)^2 = 21{,}426.395$$

$$S_{xy} = \sum xy - \frac{1}{n}(\sum x)(\sum y) = 147{,}993.52 - \frac{1}{8}(815.0)(1{,}313.0) = 14{,}231.645$$

Then we get

$$b = \frac{S_{xy}}{S_{xx}} = \frac{14{,}231.645}{9{,}533.915} = 1.4927$$

$$s_e = \sqrt{\frac{S_{yy} - bS_{xy}}{n-2}} = \sqrt{\frac{21{,}426.395 - 1.4927(14{,}231.645)}{8-2}} = 5.5199$$

and since $t_{0.025} = 2.447$ for $8 - 2 = 6$ degrees of freedom we arrive at the confidence limits

$$1{,}4927 \pm 2.447 \cdot \frac{5.5199}{\sqrt{9{,}533.915}}$$

or 1.4927 ± 0.1383. Rounding to three decimals, we can write the 95 percent confidence interval for β as $1.354 < \beta < 1.631$. ∎

The work we have done here can be simplified by using a computer. For our new example we have Figure 16.8, and we find that $b = 1.49274$, and that the estimate of the standard error by which we have to multiply $t_{\alpha/2}$, is 0.05645. Using $t_{0.025} = 2.447$, we thus get the 95 percent confidence limits for β as $1.49274 \pm 2.447(0.05645)$ or 1.49274 ± 0.13813. The print-out also notes that our seventh observation, where $x = 144$ and $y = 236.60$, is out of line with our other observations. This alerts us to the possibility that we may want to verify or delete this item if we believe it to be incorrect.

To answer the second question asked on page 624, the one concerning the estimation, or prediction, of the average value of y for a given value of x, we use a method that is very similar to the one just discussed. Basing our argument on another t statistic, we arrive at the following $(1 - \alpha)100$ percent confidence limits for $\mu_{y|x_0}$, the mean of y when $x = x_0$:

Confidence limits for mean of y when $x = x_0$

$$(a + bx_0) \pm t_{\alpha/2} \cdot s_e \sqrt{\frac{1}{n} + \frac{(x_0 - \bar{x})^2}{S_{xx}}}$$

As before, the number of degrees of freedom is $n - 2$ and the corresponding value of $t_{\alpha/2}$ may be read from Table II.

```
ROW        X          Y

 1      116.0      185.0
 2      160.8      246.4
 3      103.2      162.2
 4       55.8       97.6
 5       89.6      148.0
 6       65.0      110.4
 7      144.0      236.6
 8       80.6      126.8

MTB > REGR 'Y' 1 'X'

The regression equation is
Y = 12.1 + 1.49 X

Predictor         Coef         Stdev       t-ratio
Constant        12.052         6.072          1.98
X              1.49274       0.05645         26.44

s = 5.512        R-sq = 99.1%      R-sq(adj) = 99.0%

Analysis of Variance

SOURCE          DF           SS             MS
Regression       1        21244          21244
Error            6          182             30
Total            7        21426

Unusual Observations
Obs.        X          Y      Fit Stdev.Fit  Residual   St.Resid
  7        144     236.60   227.01     3.07      9.59      2.10R

R denotes an obs. with a large st. resid.
```

FIGURE 16.8   Computer printout for linear regression of assessed value and selling price of houses

EXAMPLE 16.8   Referring again to the data on page 614, suppose that we want to estimate the mean maintenance costs of two-year-old vending machines. Construct a 99 percent confidence interval for this mean.

SOLUTION   Copying $\sum x = 35$, $S_{xx} = 10.5$, $a + bx_0 = 101.5 + 10.9(2) = 123.30$, and $s_e = 5.66$ from pages 617, 618, 620, and 627 and substituting these values together with $n = 10$, $\bar{x} = \dfrac{35}{10} = 3.5$, and $t_{0.005} = 3.355$ (for $10 - 2 = 8$ degrees of freedom) into the confidence interval formula, we get

$$123.30 \pm (3.355)(5.66) \cdot \sqrt{\frac{1}{10} + \frac{(2 - 3.5)^2}{10.5}}$$

or 123.30 ± 10.65. Hence, we can write the 99 percent confidence interval for the mean maintenance cost of two-year-old vending machines as

$$112.65 < \mu_{y|2} < 133.95 \qquad \blacksquare$$

The third question asked on page 624 differs from the other two in that it does not concern the estimation of a population parameter but the prediction of a single future observation. The end points of an interval for which we can assert with a given degree of confidence that it will contain such an observation are called **limits of prediction**, and the calculation of such limits will answer the third kind of question. Basing our argument on yet another t statistic, we arrive at the following $(1 - \alpha)100$ percent limits of prediction for a value of y when $x = x_0$:

Limits of prediction

$$(a + bx_0) \pm t_{\alpha/2} \cdot s_e \sqrt{1 + \frac{1}{n} + \frac{(x_0 - \bar{x})^2}{S_{xx}}}$$

Again, the number of degrees of freedom is $n - 2$ and the corresponding value of $t_{\alpha/2}$ may be read from Table II.

EXAMPLE 16.9   Referring again to the example on page 632, find 99 percent limits of prediction for the maintenance cost of a two-year-old vending machine.

SOLUTION   Noting that the only difference between the limits just given and the confidence limits for $\mu_{y|x_0}$ is that we add 1 to the quantity under the square root sign, we can immediately write the limits of prediction as

$$123.30 \pm (3.355)(5.66) \cdot \sqrt{1 + \frac{1}{10} + \frac{(2 - 3.5)^2}{10.5}}$$

or

$$123.30 \pm 21.77$$

Thus, the 99 percent limits of prediction are 101.53 and 145.07. $\blacksquare$

Let us remind the reader that all these methods are based on the very stringent assumptions of normal regression analysis. Furthermore, if we base more than one inference on the same data, we will run into problems with regard to the level of significance and/or degrees of confidence. The random variables on which the various procedures are based are not independent.

EXERCISES

(Exercises 16.11, 16.12, 16.13, 16.16, and 16.17 are practice exercises. Their complete solutions are given on page 648.)

16.11 With reference to the vending machines data on page 614, use the 0.05 level of significance to test the null hypothesis $\alpha = \$125.00$ against the alternative hypothesis $\alpha < \$125.00$.

16.12 With reference to the vending machines data on page 614, construct a 95 percent confidence interval for the regression coefficient α.

16.13 With reference to Exercise 16.8 on page 623, test the null hypothesis $\beta = 30.0$ against the alternative hypothesis $\beta \neq 30.0$ at the 0.05 level of significance. Also, state in words the hypothesis being tested.

16.14 With reference to Exercise 16.1 on page 620, test the null hypothesis $\beta = 1.00$ against the alternative hypothesis $\beta > 1.00$ at the 0.05 level of significance.

16.15 With reference to Exercise 16.3 on page 621, test the null hypothesis $\beta = 1.6$ against the alternative hypothesis $\beta \neq 1.6$ at the 0.05 level of significance. Also, state in words the hypothesis being tested.

16.16 With reference to Exercise 16.3 on page 621, test the null hypothesis $\alpha = 0.4$ against the alternative hypothesis $\alpha \neq 0.4$ at the 0.01 level of significance. Also, state in words the hypothesis being tested.

16.17 With reference to Exercise 16.8 on page 623, construct a 95 percent confidence interval for the regression coefficient β.

16.18 With reference to Exercise 16.14, construct a 99 percent confidence interval for the regression coefficient β.

16.19 With reference to the preceding exercise, construct a 95 percent confidence interval for the regression coefficient β. Compare it with the 99 percent confidence interval of Exercise 16.18.

16.20 With reference to Exercise 16.8 on page 623 and Exercise 16.13, find a 95 percent confidence interval for the true average speed-reading gain when the course participation is five weeks.

16.21 With reference to the preceding exercise, find 95 percent limits of prediction for the speed reading gain when the course participation is five weeks.

16.22 Verify that the following formula for s_e is equivalent to the one given on page 626:

Chapter 16 Decision Making: Linear Regression

$$s_e = \sqrt{\frac{S_{xx} \cdot S_{yy} - (S_{xy})^2}{(n-2)S_{xx}}}$$

Also use this alternative formula to recalculate the value of s_e given on page 627.

16.4

Multiple Regression[3]

Although there are many problems in which one variable can be predicted quite accurately in terms of another, it stands to reason that predictions should improve if one considers additional relevant information. For instance, we should be able to make better predictions of a company's newly hired salesperson's first-year sales if we consider not only their years of experience, but their sales aptitude, their education, and their personalities. Also, we should be able to make better predictions of the performance of heavy equipment operators if we consider not only their years of experience, but their visual acuity, their ability to judge spatial relations, and their eye-hand coordination.

Many mathematical formulas can serve to express relationships between more than two variables, but most commonly used in statistics (partly for reasons of convenience) are linear equations of the form

$$y = b_0 + b_1 x_1 + b_2 x_2 + \cdots + b_k x_k$$

Here y is the variable which is to be predicted, $x_1, x_2, x_3, \ldots,$ and x_k are the k known variables on which predictions are to be based, and $b_0, b_1, b_2, b_3, \ldots,$ and b_k are numerical constants which must be determined from the observed data.

To illustrate, consider the following equation which was obtained in a study of the demand for different meats

$$\hat{y} = 3.489 - 0.090x_1 + 0.064x_2 + 0.019x_3$$

Here y denotes the total consumption of federally inspected beef and veal in millions of pounds, x_1 denotes a composite retail price of beef in cents per pound, x_2 denotes a composite retail price of pork in cents per pound, and x_3 denotes income as measured by a certain payroll index. With this equation,

[3]The use of the appropriate computer software in the exercises of this section can greatly simplify their solution.

we can predict the total consumption of federally inspected beef and veal on the basis of specified values of x_1, x_2, and x_3.

The main problem in deriving a linear equation in more than two variables which best describes a given set of data is that of finding numerical values of b_0, b_1, b_2, b_3, . . . , and b_k. This is usually done by the method of least squares; that is, we minimize the sum of squares $\Sigma(y - \hat{y})^2$, where, as before, the y's are the observed values and the $\hat{y}$'s are the values calculated by means of the linear equation. In principle, the problem of determining the values of b_0, b_1, b_2, b_3, . . . , and b_k is the same as it is in a two-variable problem; however, manual solutions may be extremely time consuming because the method of least squares requires that we solve as many normal equations as there are unknown constants b_0, b_1, b_2, b_3, . . . , and b_k. For instance, when there are two independent variables x_1 and x_2, and we want to fit the equation $y = b_0 + b_1x_1 + b_2x_2$, we must solve the three normal equations

Normal equations (two independent variables)

$$\Sigma y = n \cdot b_0 + b_1(\Sigma x_1) + b_2(\Sigma x_2)$$
$$\Sigma x_1y = b_0(\Sigma x_1) + b_1(\Sigma x_1^2) + b_2(\Sigma x_1x_2)$$
$$\Sigma x_2y = b_0(\Sigma x_2) + b_1(\Sigma x_1x_2) + b_2(\Sigma x_2^2)$$

Here, Σx_1y is the sum of the cross products of the given values of x_1 and their associated values of y, Σx_1x_2 is the sum of the cross products of the given values of x_1 and their associated values of x_2, and so on.

EXAMPLE 16.10 The following data show the number of bedrooms, the number of baths, and the prices at which eight one-family houses sold recently in a certain community:

Number of bedrooms x_1	Number of baths x_2	Price (dollars) y
3	2	88,800
2	1	84,300
4	3	93,800
2	1	84,200
3	2	89,700
2	2	84,900
5	3	98,400
4	2	92,900

Find a linear equation which will enable us to predict the average sale price of a one-family house in the given community in terms of the number of bedrooms and the number of baths.

SOLUTION   To get the sums needed for substitution into the three normal equations, we perform the calculations shown in the following table:

x_1	x_2	y	$x_1 y$	$x_2 y$	x_1^2	$x_1 x_2$	x_2^2
3	2	88,800	266,400	177,600	9	6	4
2	1	84,300	168,600	84,300	4	2	1
4	3	93,800	375,200	281,400	16	12	9
2	1	84,200	168,400	84,200	4	2	1
3	2	89,700	269,100	179,400	9	6	4
2	2	84,900	169,800	169,800	4	4	4
5	3	98,400	492,000	295,200	25	15	9
4	2	92,900	371,600	185,800	16	8	4
25	16	717,000	2,281,100	1,457,700	87	55	36

Then, substituting the column totals and $n = 8$ into the normal equations, we get

$$717,000 = 8b_0 + 25b_1 + 16b_2$$
$$2,281,100 = 25b_0 + 87b_1 + 55b_2$$
$$1,457,700 = 16b_0 + 55b_1 + 36b_2$$

and the solution of this system of linear equations, rounded to the nearest whole number is $b_0 = 75,192$, $b_1 = 4,133$, and $b_2 = 758$ (see Exercise 16.26 on page 645). Thus, the least-squares equation is

$$\hat{y} = 75,192 + 4,133 x_1 + 758 x_2$$

and this tells us that, in this study, each extra bedroom adds on the average \$4,133, and each bath \$758 to the sale price of a house. To estimate (predict) the average sale price of three-bedroom houses with two baths, for instance, we substitute $x_1 = 3$ and $x_2 = 2$ and get

$$\hat{y} = 75,192 + (4,133)(3) + (758)(2) = \$89,107$$

or approximately \$89,100. ■

Section 16.4   Multiple Regression

The use of a computer is especially valuable in the analysis and solution of multiple regression problems. As the number of independent variables increases, the required calculations become increasingly complex and laborious. It was for this very practical reason that although the theoretical basis for multiple regression was well known, the technique was not widely used for the solution of large numbers of applied problems prior to the widespread availabilty of computers.

The introducton of computers with appropriate software has permitted quick, easy solutions to complicated multiple regression problems, encouraging routine use of this important aspect of statistical analysis.

The tedious calculations of the preceding example are greatly simplified by the use of a computer, as in the computer printout of Figure 16.9. Here we find in the column headed "Coeff" that $b_0 = 75,191.7$, $b_1 = 4,133.3$, and $b_2 = 758.3$. In the line immediately above the coefficients, we find that after rounding, the least-squares equation becomes $y = 75,192 + 4,133x_1 + 758x_2$. The computer printout also shows "R-sq = 99.6 percent," an important quantity which we shall explain where we continue this calculation on page 673.

Most printouts like that of Figure 16.9 also provide information which makes it easy to test hypotheses about the true multiple regression coefficients β_0, β_1, β_2 . . . (the quantities estimated by b_0, b_1, b_2 . . .) or to construct confidence intervals. The following examples show how the computer printout of Figure 16.9 can be used to test hypotheses about regression coefficients.

FIGURE 16.9
Computer printout for the number of bedrooms, the number of baths, and the prices of one-family houses

```
MTB > PRINT 'X1' 'X2' 'Y'
  ROW    X1   X2      Y

   1      3    2    88800
   2      2    1    84300
   3      4    3    93800
   4      2    1    84200
   5      3    2    89700
   6      2    2    84900
   7      5    3    98400
   8      4    2    92900

MTB > REGR 'Y' 2 'X1' 'X2'

The regression equation is
Y = 75192 + 4133 X1 + 758 X2

Predictor        Coef        Stdev      t-ratio
Constant      75191.7        418.0       179.88
X1             4133.3        228.6        18.08
X2              758.3        340.5         2.23

s = 370.4        R-sq = 99.6%       R-sq(adj) = 99.5%
```

Chapter 16   Decision Making: Linear Regression

EXAMPLE 16.11   Suppose it is claimed that $\beta_1 = 3{,}500$ in the bedroom, bathroom, house price example, and one purpose of the study was to test this claim. β_1 is the change in y associated with a change of one unit in x_1. Hence the hypothesis asserts that in the population of houses sampled, each additional bedroom adds another \$3,500 on the average to the price of the house. Test this hypothesis against the alternative hypothesis $\beta_1 \neq 3{,}500$ at the 0.05 level of significance.

SOLUTION   From the regression equation of Figure 16.9 we observe that the predicted value for each additional bedroom, b_1, is \$4,133.3, and its standard error (Stdev) is \$228.6. Combining these values in a significance test for the difference between b_1, and β_1, we get

$$t = \frac{4{,}133.3 - 3{,}500}{228.6} = 2.770$$

This ratio has a t distribution with 8 (number of houses in the sample) $-3 = 5$ degrees of fredoom. (We lose three degrees of freedom because β_0, β_1, and β_2 are replaced by estimates b_0, b_1, and b_2.) Reading the value under $t_{0.025}$ from Table II on page 855 we get $t = 2.571$, and since 2.770 is greater than 2.571, we reject the null hypothesis and accept the alternative hypothesis $\beta_1 \neq 3{,}500$. ■

EXAMPLE 16.12   Suppose it is claimed that $\beta_2 = 725$ in the house price example, and a purpose of the study is to test this claim. β_2 is the change in y associated with a change in one unit of x_2. Hence the hypothesis asserts that in the population of houses sampled, each additional bathroom adds another \$725 on the average to the price of a house. Test this hypothesis against the alternative hypothesis $\beta_2 \neq 725$ at the 0.05 level of significance.

SOLUTION   From the regression equation of Figure 16.9 we observe that the predicted increase in value for each additional bathroom, b_2, is \$758.3 and its standard error (Stdev) is \$340.5. Combining these values in a significance test for the difference between b_2 and β_2, we get

$$t = \frac{758.3 - 725}{340.5} = 0.0979$$

As before, the critical value of $t_{0.025}$ from Table II is 2.571, and since 0.0979 is less than 2.571, we cannot reject the null hypothesis. ■

The following example is also based on Figure 16.9, and it shows how we can construct a confidence interval for the true multiple regression coefficient.

EXAMPLE 16.13   Construct a 95 percent confidence interval for β_1, the true average value each bedroom adds to the sales price of a house in our population.

SOLUTION   Referring to Figure 16.9 we find that $b_1 = 4,133.3$ and that the estimate of standard error by which we multiply $t_{\alpha/2}$ is 228.6. Again using the value of $t_{0.025} = 2.571$ from Table II for five degrees of freedom we get the confidence limits.

$$4,133.3 \pm 2.571(228.6) = 4,133.3 \pm 587.73$$

and the 95 percent confidence interval for β_1 is

$$3,545.57 < \beta_1 < 4,271.03 \qquad \blacksquare$$

In certain cases involving paired data, where the values of y first increase and then decrease, or first decrease and then increase, a **parabola** having the equation

$$\hat{y} = a + bx + cx^2$$

will often provide a good fit. This equation can also be written as

$$\hat{y} = b_0 + b_1 x + b_2 x^2$$

to conform with the notation of this section, and we can thus look upon parabolas as linear equations in two unknowns $x_1 = x$ and $x_2 = x^2$. Thus, fitting a parabola to a set of paired data may be viewed as an application of the method used for multiple regression.

EXAMPLE 16.14   The following are data on the average daily catch of fish, in pounds per crew member, on eight test trips on a fishing boat where the size of the crew was varied.

Trip	Number of crew members	Catch (pounds)
1	5	891
2	1	423
3	9	237
4	6	764
5	3	839
6	7	771
7	8	550
8	4	879

(a) Fit a parabola which, as would appear from Figure 16.10, should be the right kind of curve to fit to the given data.

(b) Use the result of part (a) to predict the average daily catch of fish in pounds per crew member, when the number of crew members is 2.

SOLUTION (a) Use the column totals from the following table to fit a linear

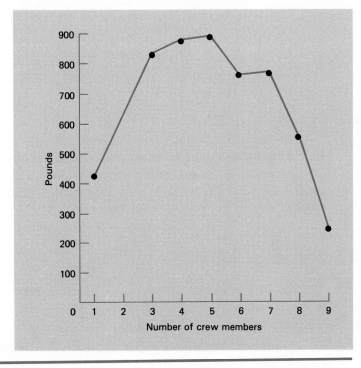

FIGURE 16.10
Average daily catch of fish per crew member

equation of the form $y = b_0 + b_1x_1 + b_2x_2$ to the data provided in the example.

$x_1 = x$	$x_2 = x^2$	y	x_1y	x_2y	x_1^2	x_1x_2	x_2^2
5	25	891	4,455	22,275	25	125	625
1	1	423	423	423	1	1	1
9	81	237	2,133	19,197	81	729	6,561
6	36	764	4,584	27,504	36	216	1,296
3	9	839	2,517	7,551	9	27	81
7	49	771	5,397	37,779	49	343	2,401
8	64	550	4,400	35,200	64	512	4,096
4	16	879	3,516	14,064	16	64	256
43	281	5,354	27,425	163,993	281	2,017	15,317

Thus, the three normal equations are

$$5,354 = 8b_0 + 43b_1 + 281b_2$$
$$27,425 = 43b_0 + 281b_1 + 2,017b_2$$
$$163,993 = 281b_0 + 2,071b_1 + 15,317b_2$$

and it follows that

$$\hat{y} = 146.214 + 321.749x - 34.345x^2$$

(b) Substituting the values of x and x^2 we get

$$\hat{y} = 146.214 + (321.749)(2) - (34.345)(4) = 652.332 \qquad \blacksquare$$

The use of a computer in solving such problems, as illustrated in Figure 16.11, can eliminate the laborious calculations and the numerous opportunities for error. As shown in the computer printout, the coefficients are $b_0 = 146.21$, $b_1 = 321.75$, and $b_2 = -34.345$, and the equation of the parabola is rounded to $y = 146 + 332x_1 - 34.3x_2$.

EXERCISES

(Exercises 16.23 and 16.27 are practice exercises. Their complete solutions are given on page 648.)

16.23   A sales report shows the number of dresses sold, number of hours worked, and months of experience, for 10 randomly selected part-time sales personnel in the women's dress department of a large store.

FIGURE 16.11
Computer printout
for the average
daily catch of fish
in pounds per crew
member, and the
number of crew
members

```
MTB > PRINT 'X1' 'X2' 'Y'
  ROW    X1     X2      Y

    1      5     25     891
    2      1      1     423
    3      9     81     237
    4      6     36     764
    5      3      9     839
    6      7     49     771
    7      8     64     550
    8      4     16     879

MTB > REGR 'Y' 2 'X1' 'X2'

The regression equation is
Y = 146 + 322 X1 - 34.3 X2

Predictor        Coef       Stdev     t-ratio
Constant        146.21      67.84       2.16
X1              321.75      29.16      11.03
X2             -34.345       2.791    -12.31

s = 48.39        R-sq = 97.1%      R-sq(adj) = 95.9%
```

Dresses sold	Hours worked	Months of experience
y	x_1	x_2
4	6	0
2	4	2
16	16	4
10	10	6
12	12	8
8	8	10
14	12	12
18	16	14
16	14	16
3	4	3

(a) Fit an equation of the form $y = b_0 + b_1x_1 + b_2x_2$ to these data.

(b) Use the equation obtained in part (a) to predict the sales by a part-time salesperson who works 5 hours and who has 2.5 months of experience.

16.24   The cost of landscaping newly built houses in a community was provided by a landscaping firm for a sample of 12 houses for which household incomes and the amounts of the real estate mortgages were known. The information, in thousands of dollars, is provided in the following table:

Household	Landscape expenditures y	Household income x_1	Mortgage amount x_2
1	2.7	18.6	24.2
2	3.6	20.4	32.1
3	1.8	19.4	28.2
4	5.4	24.2	36.1
5	5.2	24.0	30.4
6	6.3	28.4	40.1
7	1.3	37.2	48.2
8	8.4	56.8	80.3
9	4.6	26.4	20.1
10	5.9	23.6	32.6
11	7.1	45.4	54.7
12	4.1	24.6	48.2

(a) Fit an equation of the form $y = b_0 + b_1x_1 + b_2x_2$ to these data.

(b) Use the equation obtained in part (a) to estimate the landscape expenditures when household income is 43.2 and the mortgage amount is 51.3 thousands of dollars.

16.25 The following table shows the weekly sales, test scores, and achievement ratings of five salespersons working for a local car dealership:

Salesperson	Weekly sales y	Sales aptitude test score x_1	Mechanical achievement rating x_2
Ms. Walters	11	10	6
Mr. Sullivan	5	4	2
Mr. Obmer	8	1	4
Ms. Smith	12	7	5
Mr. Jones	4	3	1

(a) Fit an equation of the form $y = b_0 + b_1x_1 + b_2x_2$ to these data.

(b) Use the equataation obtained in part (a) to predict the sales of a saleperson with a sales aptitude test score of 2 and a mechanical achievement rating of 3.

16.26 Use the method of elimination or determinants to verify that the solution of the three normal equations on page 637 is $b_0 = 75{,}192$, $b_1 = 4{,}133$, and $b_2 = 758$. (There will most likely be differences in the results due to rounding.)

16.27 The following are data on the ages and incomes of five industrial salespersons working for a large company and the number of years of sales experience each has had with the company:

Age x_1	Sales experience x_2	Income y
31	4	35,400
37	4	41,200
38	5	45,000
42	2	40,300
45	0	36,800

(a) Fit an equation of the form $y = b_0 + b_1x_1 + b_2x_2$ to these data.

(b) Use the equation in part (a) to estimate the average income of a 40-year-old industrial salesperson having four years of sales experience with this company.

16.5

Checklist of Key Terms

16.6

Review Exercises

16.28 An economist wants to estimate the relationship between the annual income of families and their annual savings. The following data are obtained:

Annual income (thousands of dollars) x	Annual savings (thousands of dollars) y
12	0.0
13	0.1
14	0.2
15	0.2
16	0.5
17	0.5
18	0.6
19	0.7
20	0.8

(a) Fit a least-squares line which will enable us to predict the annual savings of a family in terms of its annual income.

(b) Use the equation obtained in part (a) to predict the annual savings of a family whose annual income is $26,000.

16.29 The following are sample data provided by six Boston hospitals. A financial analyst is trying to see if there is a relationship between the number of beds a hospital has, its admissions, and its expenses.

Hospital	Beds x_1	Admissions (thousands) x_2	Expenses (thousands of dollars) y
Massachusetts General Hospital	1,082	31.0	268
Brigham and Women's Hospital	713	29.4	177
New England Deaconess	489	13.4	101
Beth Israel	464	19.2	120
Boston City Hospital	451	16.3	108
New England Medical Center	444	14.7	135

(a) Fit an equation of the form $y = b_0 + b_1x_1 + b_2x_2$ to these data.

(b) Use the equation obtained in part (a) to predict expenses for a particular hospital when the number of beds is equal to 650 and admissions are 30,500.

16.30 The campaign manager for a candidate for president of the United States wanted to find out whether there was a relationship between the number of votes his candidate obtained and the number of hours he spent actively campaigning in different primaries. The results of the primaries were as follows:

Primary	Number of hours campaigning x	Number of votes obtained (thousands) y
Indiana	40	200
New Jersey	26	175
New York	49	415
Massachusetts	48	320
Texas	42	275
Pennsylvania	40	300
California	52	475
Wisconsin	34	125
Illinois	39	400
Ohio	40	315

(a) Fit the least-squares line from which we can predict the number of votes obtained in terms of hours of campaigning.

(b) Use the equation found in part (a) to predict the number of votes that can be obtained when 37 hours are spent campaigning.

16.31 With reference to the preceding exercise, test the null hypothesis $\beta = 12$ against the alternative hypothesis $\beta < 12$ at the 0.01 level of significance. State in words the hypothesis being tested, and also discuss whether it is at all reasonable to perform this test.

16.32 With reference to Exercise 16.1, on page 620, construct a 95 percent confidence interval for the regression coefficient α.

16.33 Use a computer package to rework Exercise 16.1 (a) on page 620 and find the equation of the least-squares line which will enable us to predict the number of pairs of jeans sold (in thousands) in each fall line.

16.34 Use a computer package to rework Exercise 16.5 (a) on page 621, and find the equation of the least-squares line which will enable us to predict the weekly repair revenues from the weekly labor costs of the bicycle shop.

16.35 Use the computer prinout of the multiple regression equation in Figure 16.9 on page 638 to verify that the average sales price of three-bedroom houses with one bath is $88,349.

16.36 Use the computer printout and rounded regression equation of Figure 16.11 on page 643 to verify that the predicted average daily catch of fish, in pounds per crew member, is $146 + 322(3) - 34.3(9) = 803.3$ pounds when the number of crew members is three.

16.7

Solutions of Practice Exercises

16.1 $n = 8$, $\sum x = 920$, $\sum x^2 = 124{,}500$, $\sum y = 885$, and $\sum xy = 119{,}350$:

(a)
$$885 = 8a + 920b$$
$$119{,}350 = 920a + 124{,}500b$$

Multiplying expressions on both sides of the first equation by 115 and subtracting yields $b = 0.940$; then substituting into the first of the two normal equations yields $a = 2.525$; $\hat{y} = 2.525 + 0.940x$.

(b) $S_{xx} = 124{,}500 - \dfrac{1}{8}(920)^2 = 18{,}700$, $S_{xy} = 119{,}350 - \dfrac{1}{8}(920)(885) =$

$17{,}575$, $b = \dfrac{17{,}575}{18{,}700} = 0.940$, and $a = \dfrac{885 - 0.940(920)}{8} = 2.525$.

16.3 (a)
$$32.5 = 12a + 16.3b$$
$$53.24 = 16.3a + 28.39b$$

Using simultaneous equations to solve for a and b, we get $a = 0.732$ and $b = 1.455$.

$$\hat{y} = 0.73 + 1.46x.$$

(b) $S_{xx} = \sum x^2 - \dfrac{1}{n}(\sum x)^2 = 28.39 - \dfrac{1}{12}(16.3)^2 = 6.249$

$S_{xy} = \sum xy - \dfrac{1}{n}(\sum x)(\sum y) = 53.24 - \dfrac{1}{12}(16.3)(32.5) = 9.094$

$b = \dfrac{S_{xy}}{S_{xx}} = \dfrac{9.094}{6.249} = 1.455$

and

$a = \dfrac{\sum y - b(\sum x)}{n} = \dfrac{32.5 - 1.455(16.3)}{12} = 0.732$

16.5 $n = 13$, $\sum x = 66.6$, $\sum y = 38.8$, $\sum x^2 = 379.82$, $\sum xy = 220.95$

(a) $S_{xx} = \sum x^2 - \dfrac{1}{n}(\sum x)^2 = 379.82 - \dfrac{1}{13}(66.6)^2 = 38.623$

$S_{xy} = \sum xy - \dfrac{1}{n}(\sum x)(\sum y) = 220.95 - \dfrac{1}{13}(66.6)(38.8) = 22.175$

$b = \dfrac{S_{xy}}{S_{xx}} = \dfrac{22.175}{38.623} = 0.574$, and

$a = \dfrac{\sum y - b(\sum x)}{n} = \dfrac{38.8 - (0.574)(66.6)}{13} = 0.044$, so

$\hat{y} = a + bx = 0.044 + 0.574x$

(b)

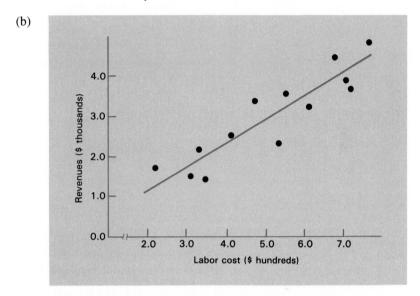

16.11 From the vending machine example we know that $n = 10$, $\bar{x} = 3.5$, $s_e = 5.66$, $S_{xx} = 10.5$, and $a = 101.6$. Test the null hypothesis $\alpha = 125.00$ against the alternative hypothesis $\alpha < 125.00$ at the 0.05 level of signifi-

cance. Since $t = \dfrac{101.5 - 125}{5.66\sqrt{\dfrac{1}{10} + \dfrac{3.5}{10.5}}} = -3.69$ is less than -1.86, the null

hypothesis must be rejected.

16.12 $101.5 - 2.306(5.66) \cdot \sqrt{\dfrac{1}{10} + \dfrac{3.5^2}{10.5}} < \alpha < 101.5 + 2.306(5.66) \cdot$

$\sqrt{\dfrac{1}{10} + \dfrac{3.5^2}{10.5}}$, $101.5 - 14.7 < \alpha < 101.5 + 14.7$, and $86.8 < \alpha < 116.2$.

16.13 Test the null hypothesis $\beta = 30.0$ against the alternative hypothesis $\beta \neq 30.0$ at the 0.05 level of significance. Since $n = 6$, $\sum x = 32$, $\sum x^2 = 210$,

$\sum y = 835$, $\sum xy = 5,534$, $S_{xx} = 39.333$, and $S_{xy} = 1,080.667$ from Exercise 16.8, $\sum y^2 = 146,099$, $S_{yy} = 146,099 - \frac{1}{6}(835)^2 = 29,894.833$, and

$$s_e = \sqrt{\frac{29,894.833 - 27.475(1,080.667)}{4}} = 7.133, \text{ we get}$$

$t = \dfrac{27.475 - 30.000}{\dfrac{7.133}{\sqrt{39.333}}} = -2.22$. Since this value falls between -2.776

and 2.776, the null hypothesis cannot be rejected. The difference between $b = 27.475$ and $\beta = 30.000$ may well be due to chance.

16.16 Test the null hypothesis $\alpha = 0.4$ against the alternative hypothesis $\alpha \neq 0.4$ at the 0.01 level of significance; this is the hypothesis that expected shipments of natural gas by Company 2 are 0.4 billion therms when shipments by Company 1 are zero.

1. H_0: $\alpha = 0.4$.
   H_A: $\alpha \neq 0.4$.

2. $\alpha = 0.01$.

3. Reject the null hypothesis if $t \leq -3.169$ or $t \geq 3.169$ where

$$t = \frac{a - \alpha}{s_e \sqrt{\dfrac{1}{n} + \dfrac{\bar{x}^2}{S_{xx}}}}$$

and 3.169 is the value of $t_{0.01}$ for $12 - 2 = 10$ degrees of freedom; otherwise, accept the null hypothesis or reserve judgment.

4. From the solution to Exercise 16.15, we know that $n = 12$, $s_e = 0.227$, $\bar{x} = \dfrac{16.3}{12} = 1.358$, and $S_{xx} = 6.249$, and hence

$$t = \frac{0.732 - 0.4}{0.227 \sqrt{\dfrac{1}{12} + \dfrac{1.358^2}{6.249}}} = 2.38$$

5. Since 2.38 falls between -3.169 and 3.169, the null hypothesis cannot be rejected.

16.17 Since $n = 6$, $b = 27.475$, $S_{xx} = 39.333$, $S_{xy} = 1,080.667$, and $\sum y = 835$ from Exercise 16.8, $\sum y^2 = 146,099$, $S_{yy} = 146,099 - \frac{1}{6}(835)^2 = 29,894.83$, and $s_e = \sqrt{\dfrac{29,894.833 - 27.475(1,080.667)}{4}} = 7.133$, we get

$27.475 \pm 2.776 \cdot \dfrac{7.133}{\sqrt{39.333}}$ and $24.318 < \beta < 30.632$.

16.23 $n = 10$, $\sum x_1 = 102$, $\sum x_2 = 75$, $\sum y = 103$, $\sum x_1^2 = 1{,}228$, $\sum x_2^2 = 825$, $\sum x_1 x_2 = 912$, $\sum x_1 y = 1{,}288$, and $\sum x_2 y = 989$.

(a) The normal equations are

$$
\begin{aligned}
103 &= 10b_0 + 102b_1 + 75b_2 \\
1{,}288 &= 102b_0 + 1{,}228b_1 + 912b_2 \\
989 &= 75b_0 + 912b_1 + 825b_2
\end{aligned}
$$

and their solution is $b_0 = -2.503$, $b_1 = 1.103$, and $b_2 = 0.207$, so that $\hat{y} = -2.503 + 1.103x_1 + 0.207x_2$.

(b) $\hat{y} = -2.503 + 1.103(5) + 0.207(2.5) = 3.53$ dresses sold.

16.27

x_1	x_2	y	$x_1 y$	$x_2 y$	x_1^2	$x_1 x_2$	x_2^2
31	4	35,400	1,097,400	141,600	961	124	16
37	4	41,200	1,524,400	164,800	1,369	148	16
38	5	45,000	1,710,000	225,000	1,444	190	25
42	2	40,300	1,692,600	80,600	1,764	84	4
45	0	36,800	1,656,000	0	2,025	0	0
193	15	198,700	7,680,400	612,000	7,563	546	61

$n = 5$, $x_1 = 193$, $x_2 = 15$, $y = 198{,}700$, $x_1 y = 7{,}680{,}400$, $x_2 y = 612{,}000$, $x_1^2 = 7{,}563$, $x_1 x_2 = 546$, and $x_2^2 = 61$.

(a) The normal equations are

$$
\begin{aligned}
198{,}700 &= 5b_0 + 193b_1 + 15b_2 \\
7{,}680{,}400 &= 193b_0 + 7{,}563b_1 + 546b_2 \\
612{,}000 &= 15b_0 + 546b_1 + 61b_2
\end{aligned}
$$

and their solution is $b_0 = -6{,}279$, $b_1 = 961$, and $b_2 = 2{,}976$.

(b) $y = -6{,}279 + 961(40) + 2{,}976(4) = \$44{,}065$.

Decision Making: Correlation

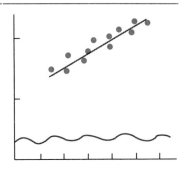

Having learned how to fit a least-squares line to paired data, we turn now to the problem of determining how well such a line actually fits the data. Of course, in the vending machines example we can get some idea of this by drawing and inspecting the diagram of Figure 16.4, but in order to determine this objectively, let us refer to the original data:

Year	Maintenance cost (dollars)
x	*y*
4	148
2	128
3	133
5	154
2	118
3	145
4	143
5	159
4	142
3	127

As can be seen from this table, there are substantial differences among the maintenance costs of the vending machines, the smallest being $118 and the largest being $159. However, we also see that the $118 cost is for a machine in its second year of use, while the $159 is for a machine in its fifth year, and this suggests that the differences among the maintenance costs may well be due, at least in part, to differences in the ages of the machines. These observations raise the following question, which we shall answer in this chapter: Of the total variation among the y's, how much can be attributed to the relationship between the two variables x and y (that is, to the fact that the observed y's correspond to different values of x), and how much can be attributed to chance?

In Section 17.1 we shall introduce the **coefficient of correlation** as a measure of the strength of the linear relationship between two variables, and in Section 17.2 we shall learn how to test its significance. The problems of **rank correlation** and **multiple correlation** will be treated in Sections 17.3 and 17.4.

17.1

The Coefficient of Correlation

With regard to the question just raised, we are faced here with an analysis of variance problem, and a study of Figure 17.1 will help to understand this. Referring to this figure, we see that the deviation of any observed value y from the mean of all the observed values of y, $y - \bar{y}$, can be written as the sum of two parts: $\hat{y} - \bar{y}$, the deviation of the value on the line (corresponding to an observed value of x) from the mean of the y's, and $y - \hat{y}$, the deviation of the observed value of y from the corresponding value on the line. Symbolically, we write

$$y - \bar{y} = (\hat{y} - \bar{y}) + (y - \hat{y})$$

for any observed value of y, and if we square the expressions on both sides of this identity and sum over all n values of y, we find that algebraic simplifications lead to

$$\sum (y - \bar{y})^2 = \sum (\hat{y} - \bar{y})^2 + \sum (y - \hat{y})^2$$

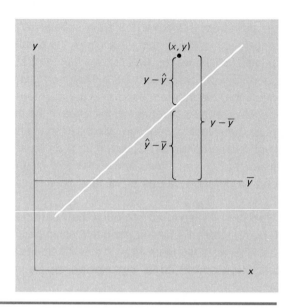

FIGURE 17.1
Illustration that
$y - \bar{y} = (\hat{y} - \bar{y}) + (y - \hat{y})$

As our measure of the total variation of the y's we use the quantity on the left, $\sum (y - \bar{y})^2$, called the **total sum of squares**. This measure is just $n - 1$ times the variance of the y's, and, as the equation shows, it has been partitioned into two additive components. The first of these, $\sum (\hat{y} - \bar{y})^2$, consists of the sum of the squares of the deviations of the values on the line from the mean $\bar{y}$, and it is called the **regression sum of squares**. It measures that portion of the total variation of the y's which would exist if differences in x were the only cause of differences among the y's, or in other words, if all the y's lay directly on the line.

This is hardly ever the case in practice, though, and the fact that all the points do not lie on a regression line is an indication that there are other factors than differences among the x's which affect the values of y. It is customary to lump together all these other factors—not separately considered in a study—under the general heading of "chance." Chance variation thus governs on the amounts by which the points deviate from the line, and its measure, $\sum (y - \hat{y})^2$, is the sum of the squared deviations of the observed y values from their corresponding values $\hat{y}$ on the line. This quantity, the second of the two components into which we partition the total sum of squares, is called the **residual sum of squares**.

To calculate the various sums of squares for the maintenance-cost example, we could substitute the values of y given on page 652, $\bar{y}$, and the values of $\hat{y}$ obtained by substituting the x's into $\hat{y} = 101.5 + 10.9x$ (see page 620), but there are simplifications. First, for $\sum (y - \bar{y})^2$ we have the computing formula

$$S_{yy} = \sum y^2 - \frac{1}{n}(\sum y)^2$$

and on page 627 we show that it equals 1,504.1 for our example. Second, $\sum (y - \hat{y})^2$ is the quantity which we minimized by the method of least squares, and which appears in the numerator of the formula for s_e. Copying the numerator from its computing formula on page 626 we get

$$\sum (y - \hat{y})^2 = S_{yy} - bS_{xy}$$

and $1,504.1 - 10.9(114.5) = 256.05$ for our example. (The values of b and S_{xy} were determined on page 619.) Finally, by subtraction, the regression sum of squares is given by

$$\begin{aligned} \sum (\hat{y} - \bar{y})^2 &= \sum (y - \bar{y})^2 - \sum (y - \hat{y})^2 \\ &= S_{yy} - (S_{yy} - bS_{xy}) \\ &= bS_{xy} \end{aligned}$$

and for our example we get $10.9(114.5) = 1,248.05$.

It is of interest to note that all the quantities we have calculated here could have been obtained directly from Figure 16.6 on page 619. Under "Analysis of variance," in the column headed "SS," we find that the total sum of squares is 1,504.1, the "Error" or residual sum of squares is 255.5, and the regression sum of squares is 1,248.6. The differences between the values shown here and earlier are due to rounding.

We are now ready to examine the sums of squares, and comparing the regression sum of squares with the total sum of squares, we find that

$$\frac{\sum (\hat{y} - \bar{y})^2}{\sum (y - \bar{y})^2} = \frac{1,248.05}{1,504.1} = 0.83$$

is the proportion of the total variation in the maintenance costs that can be attributed to the relationship with x, namely, to differences between the ages of the vending machines. This quantity is referred to as the **coefficient of determination** and it is denoted by r^2. Note that the coefficient of determination is also given in Figure 16.6 on page 619; near the middle of the printout is the information "R-sq = 83.0%."

If we take the square root of the coefficient of determination we get the **coefficient of correlation**, which is denoted by r. Its sign is chosen so that it is the same as that of the estimated regression coefficient b, and for our example, where b is positive, we get

$$r = \sqrt{0.83} = 0.91$$

rounded to two decimals.

It follows from the rule for the sign of r that r is positive when the least-squares line has an upward slope, that is, when the relationship between x and y is such that small values of y tend to go with small values of x and large values of y tend to go with large values of x. Also, r is negative when the least-squares line has a downward slope, that is, when large values of y tend to go with small values of x and small values of y tend to go with large values of x. Geometrically, the ideas of a **positive correlation** and a **negative correlation** are illustrated in the first two diagrams of Figure 17.2; the third diagram illustrates the case where the least-squares line is horizontal, $r = 0$, and there is **no correlation**. These diagrams are similar to some of those shown in Figure 16.1.

Since part of the variation of the y's cannot exceed their total variation, $\sum(y - \hat{y})^2$ cannot exceed $\sum(y - \bar{y})^2$, and it follows from the formula defining r that a correlation coefficient must lie on the interval from -1 to $+1$. If all the points actually fall on a straight line, the residual sum of squares, $\sum (y - \hat{y})^2$, is zero, $\sum (\hat{y} - \bar{y})^2 = \sum (y - \bar{y})^2$, and the resulting value of r, -1 or $+1$, indicates that the fit of the line to the paired observations is perfect. If, however, the scatter of the points is such that the least-squares line is a horizontal line coincident with $\bar{y}$ (that is, a line with slope $b = 0$ which intersects the y axis at height $a = \bar{y}$), then $\sum (y - \hat{y})^2$ equals $\sum (y - \bar{y})^2$ and $r = 0$. In this case none of the variation of the y's can be attributed to their relationship with x, and the fit is so poor that knowledge of x is of no help in predicting y—the predicted value of y is $\bar{y}$ for any x.

The formula which defines r shows clearly the nature of the coefficient of correlation, but in actual practice it is seldom used to determine its value. To derive a computing formula for r, we first substitute $\sum (y - \bar{y})^2 = S_{yy}$ and $\sum (\hat{y} - \bar{y})^2 = bS_{xy}$ from pages 654 and 655 into the formula for r^2, getting

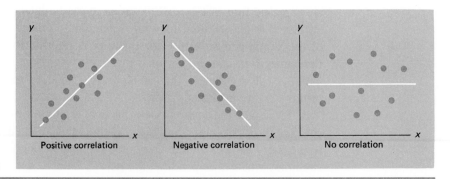

FIGURE 17.2

Types of correlation

Positive correlation   Negative correlation   No correlation

$$r^2 = \frac{bS_{xy}}{S_{yy}}$$

Then, substituting $b = \dfrac{S_{xy}}{S_{xx}}$ from page 619, we arrive at the result that

$$r^2 = \frac{S_{xy}^2}{S_{xx} \cdot S_{yy}}$$

and, hence, the following computing formula:[1]

Computing formula for coefficient of correlation

$$r = \frac{S_{xy}}{\sqrt{S_{xx} \cdot S_{yy}}}$$

For easy reference, let us remind the reader that, as shown on pages 618 and 626,

$$S_{xx} = \sum x^2 - \frac{1}{n}(\sum x)^2$$

$$S_{yy} = \sum y^2 - \frac{1}{n}(\sum y)^2$$

$$S_{xy} = \sum xy - \frac{1}{n}(\sum x)(\sum y)$$

[1]This computing formula follows directly from an alternative, but equivalent, definition of the coefficient of correlation based on the **sample covariance**

$$S_{xy} = \frac{\sum (x - \bar{x})(y - \bar{y})}{n - 1}$$

In this formula, we add the products obtained by multiplying the deviation of each x from $\bar{x}$ by the deviation of the corresponding y from $\bar{y}$ and divide by $n - 1$. In this way we literally measure the way in which the values of x and y vary together. If the relationship between the x's and the y's is such that large values of x tend to go with large values of y, and small values of x with small values of y, the deviations $x - \bar{x}$ and $y - \bar{y}$ tend to be both positive or both negative, so that most of the products $(x - \bar{x})(y - \bar{y})$ and, hence, the covariance, are positive. On the other hand, if the relationship between the x's and y's is such that large values of x tend to go with small values of y and vice versa, the deviations $x - \bar{x}$ and $y - \bar{y}$ tend to be of opposite sign, so most of the products and, hence, the covariance, are negative. Using the covariance and the standard deviations, s_x and s_y, of the x's and the y's, we can define the coefficient of correlation as

$$r = \frac{S_{xy}}{S_x \cdot S_y}$$

Since the sum of products $\sum (x - \bar{x})(y - \bar{y})$ in the formula for the sample covariance is called a **product moment**, this explains why r is often called the **product-moment coefficient of correlation**.

Section 17.1 The Coefficient of Correlation

EXAMPLE 17.1 Use the computing formula to calculate the coefficient of correlation for the vending machine data of page 652.

SOLUTION Substituting the values calculated on pages 618, 619, and 620. $S_{xx} = 10.5$, $S_{xy} = 114.5$, and $S_{yy} = 1,504.1$, into the computing formula for the coefficient of correlation, r, we get

$$r = \frac{114.5}{\sqrt{(10.5)(1,504.1)}} = 0.91$$ ∎

EXAMPLE 17.2 The following are the average straight-time hourly earnings, during a certain month, for selected occupations in Montana and West Virginia:

Occupation	Montana (dollars) x	West Virginia (dollars) y
Secretaries	8.64	9.83
Typists II	6.17	7.77
Receptionists	6.04	5.60
Key entry operators	6.23	7.26
Computer operators	7.30	8.95
Drafters	10.26	10.70
Electronics technicians	13.96	13.55
Maintenance carpenters	12.72	12.47
Maintenance painters	13.29	11.59
Truck drivers	10.88	9.90
Forklift operators	9.91	10.04
Janitors, porters, cleaners	5.89	6.04

Use the computing formula to calculate the coefficient of correlation.

SOLUTION $n = 12$, $\sum x = 111.29$, $\sum y = 113.70$, $\sum x^2 = 1,131.15$, $\sum y^2 = 1,144.39$, $\sum xy = 1,131.63$, so that

$$S_{xx} = 1,131.15 - \frac{1}{12}(111.29)^2 = 99.028$$

$$S_{yy} = 1,144.39 - \frac{1}{12}(113.70)^2 = 67.082$$

$$S_{xy} = 1,131.63 - \frac{1}{12}(111.29)(113.70) = 77.157$$

$$r = \frac{77.157}{\sqrt{(99.028)(67.082)}} = 0.947 \qquad \blacksquare$$

Figure 17.3 is a computer printout of Example 17.2. As can be seen, the points form an upward-sloping pattern like that shown in Figure 17.2 for

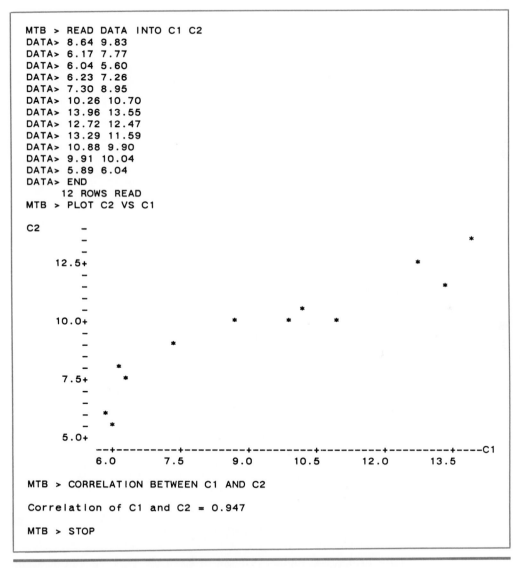

```
MTB > READ DATA INTO C1 C2
DATA> 8.64 9.83
DATA> 6.17 7.77
DATA> 6.04 5.60
DATA> 6.23 7.26
DATA> 7.30 8.95
DATA> 10.26 10.70
DATA> 13.96 13.55
DATA> 12.72 12.47
DATA> 13.29 11.59
DATA> 10.88 9.90
DATA> 9.91 10.04
DATA> 5.89 6.04
DATA> END
      12 ROWS READ
MTB > PLOT C2 VS C1
```

```
C2      -
        -
        -
  12.5+                                              *
        -                                  *
        -                                      *
        -
        -
  10.0+              *        *       *
        -                 *
        -         *
        -
        -
   7.5+      *
        -      *
        -
        -    *
        -    *
   5.0+
        --+---------+---------+---------+---------+---------+----C1
          6.0       7.5       9.0      10.5      12.0      13.5
```

```
MTB > CORRELATION BETWEEN C1 AND C2

Correlation of C1 and C2 = 0.947

MTB > STOP
```

FIGURE 17.3 Computer printout of correlation between average straight-time hourly earnings in Montana and in West Virginia

positive correlation. The coefficient of correlation is printed as 0.947. The absence of a plus or minus sign preceding this number informs us that the correlation is positive.

EXAMPLE 17.3 A men's tie shop ran 10 sales promotions to determine the number of men's neckties of a certain type that customers would buy at various prices. Following are the sales results:

Prices (dollars) x	Number of ties sold y
6.49	187
6.99	149
7.49	155
7.99	148
8.49	130
8.99	132
9.49	90
9.99	99
10.49	69
10.99	51
87.40	1,210

Use the computing formula to calculate the coefficient of correlation.

SOLUTION $n = 10$, $\sum x = 87.40$, $\sum y = 1,210$, $\sum x^2 = 784.501$, $\sum y^2 = 162,686$, $\sum xy = 10,016.40$, so that

$$S_{xx} = 784.501 - \frac{1}{10}(87.40)^2 = 20.625$$

$$S_{yy} = 162,686 - \frac{1}{10}(1,210)^2 = 16,276$$

$$S_{xy} = 10,016.40 - \frac{1}{10}(87.40)(1,210) = -559$$

$$r = \frac{-559}{\sqrt{(20.625)(16,276)}} = -0.965 \qquad \blacksquare$$

Figure 17.4 is a computer printout of Example 17.3. As can be seen, the points of the diagram form a downward-sloping pattern like that shown in Figure 17.2 for negative correlation. The coefficient of correlation is calcu-

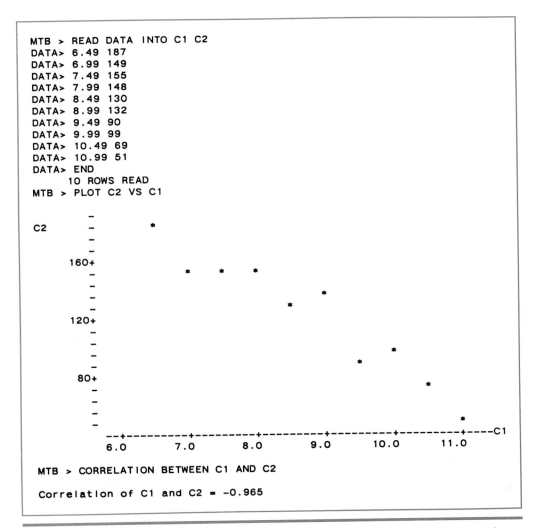

```
MTB > READ DATA INTO C1 C2
DATA> 6.49 187
DATA> 6.99 149
DATA> 7.49 155
DATA> 7.99 148
DATA> 8.49 130
DATA> 8.99 132
DATA> 9.49 90
DATA> 9.99 99
DATA> 10.49 69
DATA> 10.99 51
DATA> END
      10 ROWS READ
MTB > PLOT C2 VS C1
```

MTB > CORRELATION BETWEEN C1 AND C2

Correlation of C1 and C2 = -0.965

FIGURE 17.4 Computer printout of correlation between number of men's neckties and various prices at which they were sold

lated as -0.965, and the minus sign preceding the number means that the correlation is negative.

As we have defined r, the coefficient of correlation, $100r^2$ gives the percentage of the total variation of the y's which is explained by, or is due to, their relationships with x. This itself is a very important measure in the study of relationships between two variables; beyond this, $100r^2$ also permits valid comparisons to be made among several relationships of this kind. If, for instance, in one study $r = 0.80$, then 64 percent of the variation in y is accounted for by its relationship with x; if in another study $r = 0.40$, only 16

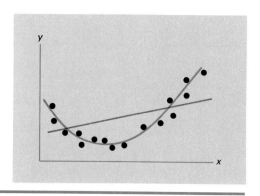

percent of the variation in y is accounted for by its relationship with x. Thus, in the sense of "percentage of variation accounted for" we can say that a correlation of 0.80 is four times as strong as a correlation of 0.40. In the same way, we say that a correlation of 0.60 is nine times as strong as a correlation of 0.20, and so on.

In interpreting a correlation coefficient it is sometimes assumed that a numerically high value of r establishes a cause-and-effect relationship running from the independent variable x to the dependent variable y. We want to make it clear that this is not so. There are cases in which changes in one variable are considered to be "the cause" of changes in another variable (called its "effect"), but only logical argument, not a high value of r, can establish such a relationship. This is discussed further in Section 17.5.

We also want to make it clear that r measures only the strength of linear relationships. The value of r calculated for the data of Figure 17.5, for example, is near zero even though the points are all very close to the curve fitted to these points. There is an obvious strong curvilinear relationship between the two variables, but virtually no linear relationship.

17. 2

A Significance Test for r

When r is calculated on the basis of sample data, we may get a strong positive or negative correlation purely by chance, even though there is actually no linear relationship whatever between the two variables in the population from which the sample came.

Suppose, for instance, that we take two dice, one red and one green, roll them five times, and get the results shown in the following table:

Red die	Green die
x	y
4	5
2	2
4	6
2	1
6	4

Presumably there is no relationship between x and y, the numbers of points showing on the two dice. It is hard to see why, for example, large values of x should be associated with large values of y and small values of x with small values of y. But calculating r, we get the surprisingly high value $r = 0.66$. This raises the question of whether something is wrong with the presumption that there is no relationship between x and y, and to answer it we shall have to see whether the high value of r may be attributed to chance.

When a correlation coefficient is calculated from sample data, as in the foregoing example, the value we obtain for r is only an estimate of a corresponding parameter, the **population correlation coefficient**, which we denote by the Greek letter ρ (rho). What r measures for a sample, ρ measures for a population.

There are several ways of testing the null hypothesis of no correlation, the null hypothesis $\rho = 0$. Here we shall make the same assumptions as in Section 16.3, except that x is also a random variable having a normal distribution. Referring to Table VI,

We reject the null hypothesis of no correlation at the level of significance α if the value of r calculated for a set of paired data exceeds $r_{\alpha/2}$ or is less than $-r_{\alpha/2}$; otherwise, we accept the null hypothesis.

With Table VI, we can perform this test at the 0.05, 0.02, and 0.01 levels of significance.

EXAMPLE 17.4 Use the 0.05 level of significance to test the null hypothesis of no correlation for the example where we rolled a pair of dice five times and got $r = 0.66$.

SOLUTION Since $r = 0.66$ does not exceed 0.878, the value of $r_{0.025}$ for $n = 5$, we find that the null hypothesis cannot be rejected; in other words, the correlation coefficient of 0.66 obtained for the pair of dice is not significant. ∎

EXAMPLE 17.5 Use the 0.01 level of significance to test the null hypothesis of no correlation for the maintenance-cost example where we had $n = 10$ and $r = 0.91$.

SOLUTION Since $r = 0.91$ exceeds 0.765, the value of $r_{0.005}$ for $n = 10$, the null hypothesis must be rejected; in fact, it appears virtually certain that the two variables—machine age and maintenance cost—are related. ∎

EXERCISES

(Exercises 17.1 and 17.6 are practice exercises. Their complete solutions are given on page 681.)

17.1 Following are the numbers of sales contacts made by 10 salespersons during a week and the number of sales made.

Sales contacts x	Sales y
71	25
64	16
100	37
105	40
75	18
59	10
82	22
68	14
111	42
90	19

Calculate r for the data, and test the null hypothesis of no correlation at the 0.05 level of significance.

17.2 The following information is provided by a company with catalog outlets in 12 cities.

Number of catalogs distributed (in thousands) x	Number of orders received (in thousands) y
6	20
2	14
5	20
1	14
10	28
7	23
15	36
3	16
11	32
13	33
2	13
12	30

Calculate r for these data, and test the null hypothesis of no correlation at the 0.05 level of significance.

17.3 Since r does not depend on the scales of x and y, its calculation can often be simplified by adding a suitable positive or negative number to each x, each y, or both. Rework Exercise 17.1 after subtracting 59 from each x and 10 from each y.

17.4 With reference to Exercise 16.5 of page 621,
(a) Calculate r for the given data.
(b) Use the 0.05 level of significance to test whether there is a real relationship between labor costs and repair revenues, and discuss whether it is reasonable to perform this test.

17.5 Following are data for the production of rye, x, and the production of grapefruit, y, in the United States for the years 1984 through 1989. It can be seen by inspection that as the production of rye declines, the production of grapefruit increases, and the regression line must therefore be negative (slopes downward from left to right when plotted on a graph).

Rye (millions of bushels)	Grapefruit (millions of boxes)
32.4	53.8
20.3	56.1
19.5	57.4
19.5	63.7
14.7	68.7
13.5	69.5

(a) If we find that there is a strong correlation (either positive or negative) in this exercise, can we assume that there exists a "real" relationship between the production of rye and the production of grapefruit?

(b) Calculate r for the production of rye and the production of grapefruit.

(c) Find the percentage of total variation in the production of grapefruit which appears to be accounted for by differences in the production of rye.

(d) Use the 0.05 level of significance to test the null hypothesis of no correlation between the two variables.

17.6   The following table shows the number of guests registered weekly at a health spa and the weekly wage expense for general maintenance workers of the spa's buildings and grounds during an eight-week period.

Number of guests (in hundreds) x	Weekly wage expense (thousands of dollars) y
3.2	6.8
2.9	7.0
3.7	7.1
2.5	7.8
3.3	6.3
2.7	7.6
2.9	5.8
3.4	7.2

(a) Calculate r for these data.

(b) Test the null hypothesis of no correlation at the 0.01 level of significance to determine whether there is a real relationship between the two variables.

17.7   With reference to Exercise 17.6, what percentage of the total variation in wages paid is accounted for by the number of guests?

17.8   If $r = 0.75$ for one set of paired data and $r = 0.50$ for another set of paired data, compare the strength of the two relationships.

17.9   If we calculate r for each of the following sets of data, should we be surprised if we get $r = 1$ and $r = -1$? Explain your answer.

(a)	x	y	(b)	x	y
	20	5		5	15
	8	2		10	6

17.10 With reference to Exercise 16.25 on page 644, calculate r for each of the following pairs of variables:

(a) weekly sales and sales aptitude test scores

(b) weekly sales and mechanical achievement ratings

(c) sales aptitude test scores and mechanical achievement ratings

17.11 Test in each case whether the value of r is significant at the 0.05 level of significance:

(a) $n = 12$ and $r = -0.401$.

(b) $n = 8$ and $r = 0.834$.

(c) $n = 6$ and $r = 0.820$.

17.12 Test in each case whether the value of r is significant at the 0.01 level of significance:

(a) $n = 10$ and $r = 0.715$.

(b) $n = 15$ and $r = -0.603$.

(c) $n = 20$ and $r = 0.582$.

17.13 Correlation methods are sometimes used to study the relationship between two (time) series of data which are recorded annually, monthly, weekly, daily, and so on. Suppose, for instance, that in the years 1979–1992 a large textile manufacturer spent 0.8, 0.5, 0.8, 1.0, 1.0, 0.9, 0.8, 1.2, 1.0, 0.9, 0.8, 1.0, 1.0, and 0.8 million dollars on research and development and that in these years its share of the market was 20.4, 18.6, 19.1, 18.0, 18.2, 19.6, 20.0, 20.4, 19.2, 20.5, 20.8, 18.9, 19.0, and 19.8 percent. To see whether and how the company's share of the market in a given year may be related to its expenditures on research and development in prior years, let x_t denote the company's research and development expenditures and y_t its market share in the year t, and

(a) Calculate the correlation coefficient for y_t and x_{t-1}.

(b) Calculate the correlation coefficient for y_t and x_{t-2}.

(c) Calculate the correlation coefficient for y_t and x_{t-3}.

(d) Calculate the correlation coefficient for y_t and x_{t-4}.

For instance, in part (a) calculate r after pairing the 1980 percentage share of the market with the 1979 expenditures on research and development, the 1981 market share with the 1980 expenditures, and so on, . . . , and in part (d) calculate r after pairing the 1983 percentage share of the market with the 1979 expenditures on research and development, the 1984 market share with the 1980 expenditures, and so on. These time-lag correlations are called **cross correlations**. To continue,

(e) Test, at the level of significance 0.05, whether the correlation coefficients obtained in parts (a) through (d) are significant.

(f) Discuss the apparent duration of the effect of expenditures on research and development on the company's share of the market.

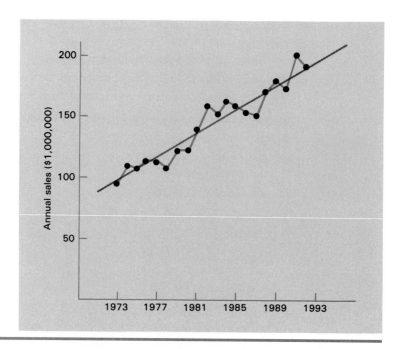

FIGURE 17.6
Diagram for
Exercise 17.14

17.14 Correlation methods are sometimes used to study the internal structure (or systematic patterns) in series of data (time series) which are recorded on an annual, monthly, weekly, . . . , basis. Consider, for example, the diagram of Figure 17.6, which shows a line chart of a company's annual sales for the years 1973–1992. There is an obvious linear trend in the series as shown by the least-squares line, and to look for further patterns, we can study the deviations from the line, $y - \hat{y}$, which are $-2, 6, 0, 3, -2, -13, -5, -10,$ 1, 18, 6, 10, 1, $-8, -15, 0, 3, -7, 15,$ and 0 million dollars for the years 1973–1992. Letting y_t denote the deviation from the line in the year t,

(a) Calculate the correlation coefficient for y_t and y_{t-1}.

(b) Calculate the correlation coefficient for y_t and y_{t-2}.

(c) Calculate the correlation coefficient for y_t and y_{t-3}.

(d) Calculate the correlation coefficient for y_t and y_{t-4}.

(e) Calculate the correlation coefficient for y_t and y_{t-5}.

For instance, in part (a) calculate r after pairing the 1974 deviation from the line with the 1973 deviation from the line, the 1975 deviation from the line with the 1974 deviation from the line, and so on, . . . , and in part (e) calculate r after pairing the 1978 deviation from the line with the 1973 deviation from the line, the 1979 deviation from the line with the 1974 deviation from the line, and, finally, the 1992 deviation from the line with the 1987 deviation from the line. These lag-time correlations are also called **autocorrelations**. To continue,

(f) Test at the 0.05 level of significance whether the correlation coefficients obtained in parts (a) through (e) are significant.

(g) Discuss the possible existence of a cyclical (or repeating) pattern in the series.

17.15 On pages 654 and 655 we calculated for the maintenance-cost example the total sum of squares and the residual sum of squares by using a computing formula to obtain $\sum (y - \bar{y})^2$ and $\sum (y - \hat{y})^2$. However, it can also be shown that

$$\sum (y - \bar{y})^2 = \sum y^2 - n \cdot \bar{y}^2, \text{ and}$$

$$\sum (y - \hat{y})^2 = \sum y^2 - a(\sum y) - b(\sum xy)$$

where a and b are the y intercept and the slope of the least-squares line. Use these formulas to recalculate the two sums of squares for the maintenance-cost example. As will be seen, substantial differences may arise due to rounding the estimated regression coefficients.

17.3

Rank Correlation

Since the significance test for r of the preceding section is based on fairly stringent assumptions, it is sometimes preferable to use a nonparametric alternative which can be applied under much more general conditions. This test of the null hypothesis of no correlation is based on the **rank correlation coefficient** (often called **Spearman's rank correlation coefficient**), which is essentially the coefficient of correlation for the ranks of the x's and the y's within the two samples. As we shall see, the rank correlation coefficient has the added advantage that it is usually easier to determine than the product-moment coefficient of correlation when no calculator is available.

To calculate the rank correlation coefficient, we first rank the x's among themselves, giving rank 1 to the largest (or smallest) value, rank 2 to the second largest (or second smallest), and so on; then we rank the y's similarly among themselves, find the sum of the squares of the differences, d, between the ranks of the x's and y's, and substitute into the formula

Rank correlation coefficient

$$r_s = 1 - \frac{6(\sum d^2)}{n(n^2 - 1)}$$

where n is the number of pairs of observations. When there are ties in rank, we assign to each of the tied observations the mean of the ranks which they jointly occupy. For instance, if the third and fourth largest values of a variable are the same, we assign each the rank $\dfrac{3+4}{2} = 3.5$, and if the fifth, sixth, and seventh largest values of a variable are the same, we assign each the rank $\dfrac{5+6+7}{3} = 6$.

EXAMPLE 17.6 The number of hours of study for an examination and the grades received by a random sample of 10 students are:

Number of hours studied x	Grade in examination y
8	56
5	44
11	79
13	72
10	70
5	54
18	94
15	85
2	33
8	65

Calculate r_S.

SOLUTION Ranking the x's among themselves from low to high, and also the y's, we get the ranks shown in the first two columns of the table:

Rank of x	Rank of y	d	d^2
4.5	4	0.5	0.25
2.5	2	0.5	0.25
7	8	−1.0	1.00
8	7	1.0	1.00
6	6	0.0	0.00
2.5	3	−0.5	0.25
10	10	0.0	0.00
9	9	0.0	0.00
1	1	0.0	0.00
4.5	5	−0.5	0.25
		Total	3.00

Then, determining the d's and their squares, and substituting $n = 10$ and $\sum d^2 = 3.00$ into the formula for r_S, we get

$$r_S = 1 - \frac{6 \cdot 3}{10(10^2 - 1)} = 0.98$$

If we calculate r for these data (the original x's and y's), we get 0.96, so that the difference between r and r_S is very small in this case.

∎

When there are no ties, r_S equals the correlation coefficient r calculated for the two sets of ranks; when ties exist, there will be a small (but usually negligible) difference. By using ranks, we naturally lose some information, but as we said, r_S is usually easier to dermine than r when no computer or calculator is available. Mainly, though, rank correlation methods have the advantage that they can be used to measure relationships in problems where items cannot be measured but can be ranked (see, for instance, Exercises 17.23 and 17.24) and that tests of significance based on them are relatively unrestrictive.

Figure 17.7, on page 672, is a computer printout of the preceding example. Although it cannot be seen on the printout, the computer has ranked the data. The printed coefficient of correlation is 0.982.

In testing the null hypothesis of no correlation between two variables x and y, we do not have to make any assumptions about the nature of the populations from which the samples came. Under the null hypothesis of no correlation (indeed, the null hypothesis that the x's and y's are randomly matched), the sampling distribution of r_S has the mean 0 and the standard deviation.[2]

$$\sigma_{r_s} = \frac{1}{\sqrt{n - 1}}$$

Since this sampling distribution can be approximated with a normal distribution even for relatively small values of n, we base the test of the null hypothesis on the statistic

Statistic for testing significance of r_S

$$z = \frac{r_S - 0}{1/\sqrt{n - 1}} = r_S\sqrt{n - 1}$$

[2]There exists a correction for σ_{r_s} that accounts for ties in rank, but it is seldom used unless the number of ties is large.

Section 17.3   Rank Correlation

```
MTB > READ NUMBER OF HOURS STUDIED INTO C1, GRADE IN EXAMINATION INTO C2
DATA> 8 56
DATA> 5 44
DATA> 11 79
DATA> 13 72
DATA> 10 70
DATA> 5 54
DATA> 18 94
DATA> 15 85
DATA> 2 33
DATA> 8 65
     10 ROWS READ
MTB > RANK NUMBER OF HOURS STUDIED IN C1, PUT RANKS INTO C11
MTB > RANK GRADE IN EXAMINATION IN C2, PUT RANKS INTO C12
MTB > CORRELATION BETWEEN C11 AND C12

Correlation of C11 and C12 = 0.982
```

FIGURE 17.7 Computer printout of rank correlation between number of hours studied and grades in examinations

which has approximately the standard normal distribution.

EXAMPLE 17.7 With reference to Example 17.6 where we had $n = 10$ and $r_S = 0.98$, test the significance of this value of r_S at the 0.01 level of significance.

SOLUTION Substituting $n = 10$ and $r_S = 0.98$ into the formula for z, we get

$$z = 0.98\sqrt{10 - 1} = 2.94$$

Since this value exceeds $z_{0.005} = 2.575$, we reject the null hypothesis of no correlation and conclude at the 0.01 level of significance that there is, in fact, a real (positive) relationship between study time and grades in the population sampled. ∎

17.4

Multiple Correlation

In the beginning of this chapter we introduced the correlation coefficient as a measure of the goodness of the fit of a least-squares line to a set of paired data. If predications are to be made with equations of the form

$$\hat{y} = b_0 + b_1 x_1 + b_2 x_2 + \cdots + b_k x_k$$

as in Section 16.4, we define the **multiple correlation coefficient** in the same way we originally defined r. We take the square root of the quantity

$$1 - \frac{\Sigma (y - \hat{y})^2}{\Sigma (y - \bar{y})^2}$$

which is the proportion of the total variation of the y's that can be attributed to the relationship with the x's. The only difference is that we now calculate $\hat{y}$ by means of the multiple regression equation instead of the equation $\hat{y} = a + bx$.

EXAMPLE 17.8   In Example 16.10, page 637, where we derived the equation $\hat{y} = 75{,}192 + 4{,}133 x_1 + 758 x_2$, we find that $\Sigma (y - \hat{y})^2 = 685{,}851$ and $\Sigma (y - \bar{y})^2 = 185{,}955{,}000$. What is the value of the multiple correlation coefficient?

SOLUTION   Since

$$1 - \frac{\Sigma (y - \hat{y})^2}{\Sigma (y - \bar{y})^2} = 1 - \frac{685{,}851}{185{,}955{,}000} = 0.9963$$

it follows that the multiple correlation coefficient is $\sqrt{0.9963} = 0.998$.   ■

The preceding example also serves to illustrate that adding more independent variables in a correlation study is not always sufficiently productive to justify the extra work. The value of r for y and x_1 alone is actually 0.996, so very little seems to be gained by considering x_2 also. In this example, predictions based on the number of bedrooms alone are virtually as good as predictions which also take into account the number of baths. However, the situation could be quite different where one independent variable accounts for a low percentage of the total variation, and adding more variables helps to account for a much greater percentage of the total variation.

Multiple correlation quantities may be calculated along with multiple regression quantities when using certain types of computer software. The computer printout of Figure 16.9, for example, provides "R-sq = 99.6%," which, although stated in percentage terms, is the same as our calculated value of $r_2 = 0.9963$ in the example just given.

(Exercises 17.16, 17.22, 17.24, 17.25, and 17.26 are practice exercises. Their complete solutions are given on page 681.)

17.16   Calculate r_S for the data of Exercise 16.1 on page 620, and test the null hypothesis of no correlation at the 0.05 level of significance.

17.17   Calculate r_S for the data of Exercise 17.2 on page 664, and compare it with the value of r obtained in that exercise.

17.18   Calculate r_S for the data of Exercise 16.5 on page 621, and test the null hypothesis at the 0.01 level of significance.

17.19   Calculate r_S for the data of Exercise 17.6 on page 666, and test the null hypothesis of no correlation at the 0.01 level of significance.

17.20   Using the formula $z = r_S \sqrt{n - 1}$, is the value of r_S significant where
(a) $r_S = 0.88$ and $n = 10$ at the 0.01 level of significance
(b) $r_S = 0.75$ and $n = 10$ at the 0.01 level of significance
(c) $r_S = -0.60$ and $n = 10$ at the 0.05 level of significance
(d) $r_S = -0.70$ and $n = 10$ at the 0.05 level of significance

17.21   The following table shows how a panel of nutrition experts and a panel of heads of household ranked 15 breakfast foods on their palatability:

Breakfast foods	Nutrition experts	Heads of household
A	3	5
B	7	4
C	11	8
D	9	14
E	1	2
F	4	6
G	10	12
H	8	7
I	5	1
J	13	15
K	12	9
L	2	3
M	15	10
N	6	11
O	14	13

Calculate r_S as a measure of the consistency of the two rankings.

17.22 The following table shows how two potential customers ranked the importance of various features of condominiums.

	Mr. Jones	Ms. Brown
Price	1	1
Interest rate	3	7
Neighborhood	7	2
Schools	6	3
Landscaping	8	5
Security	4	4
Parking	5	8
Transportation to work	2	9
Nearness of shopping center	9	6

(a) Find r_S as a measure of the consistency of the two rankings.

(b) Test whether the value of r_S is significant at the 0.05 level.

17.23 The following table shows how a panel of advertising account managers and another panel of television producers ranked 15 ideas for a new television show.

Television producers	Advertising account managers
9	12
11	6
6	4
15	13
1	5
7	8
2	1
5	3
4	7
8	11
13	14
10	15
3	2
12	10
4	9

Calculate r_S as a measure of the consistency of the two rankings.

17.24 Following are the rankings which three managers gave to 12 applicants for a supervisory position:

Manager 1	Manager 2	Manager 3
9	8	7
10	7	9
1	2	4
5	5	8
3	4	2
8	6	5
11	12	10
4	3	6
12	10	12
7	11	11
2	1	3
6	9	1

Calculate r_S for each pair of rankings and determine which pair of rankings is

(a) most consistent

(b) least consistent

17.25 In a multiple regression problem, the residual sum of squares is $\sum (y - \hat{y})^2 = 75{,}240$, and the total sum of squares is $\sum (y - \bar{y})^2 = 112{,}550$. Find the value of the multiple correlation coefficient.

17.26 Use the least-squares equation of Exercise 16.23 on page 642 to calculate $\hat{y}$ for each of the 10 sales personnel, determine the two sums of squares $\sum (y - \hat{y})^2$ and $\sum (y - \bar{y})^2$, and calculate the multiple correlation coefficient.

17.27 Use the least-squares equation derived in Exercise 16.24 on page 643 and the computing formula on page 673 to calculate the multiple correlation coefficient.

17.28 Use the least-squares equation derived in Exercise 16.25 on page 644 and the computing formula on page 673 to calculate the multiple correlation coefficient.

17.5

A Word of Caution

One must always take special care in interpreting the results of correlation studies. We call attention again to the fact that the correlation coefficient r measures only the strength of linear relationships (see Figure 17.5) and that it is possible to find a high degree of correlation in sample data when actually there is no relationship whatever in the population sampled.

We also call attention again to the danger of presuming that a high correlation coefficient implies a cause-and-effect relationship between two variables x and y. For instance, a high positive correlation has been observed in the study of the relationship between teachers' salaries and liquor consumption, and a high negative correlation has been observed in a study of the annual per capita consumption of chewing tobacco in the United States and the number of automobile thefts reported in a sample of urban areas in the same years. Moreover, in another study, a strong positive correlation was observed between the number of storks seen nesting in English villages and the number of children born in these same villages. We leave it to the reader's ingenuity to explain why there might be strong correlations observed in these instances in the absence of any cause-and-effect relationships.

Finally, we note that in a study devoted to various consequences of retail advertising a significantly high positive correlation was observed between the advertising expenses, x, of a sample of sporting goods stores and the net operating profits, y, of the stores. But which way, if either, should we argue? Do high advertising outlays lead to high profits, or do high profits lead to high advertising outlays?

17.6

Checklist of Key Terms

17.7

Review Exercises

17.29 If $r = 0.40$ for one set of data and $r = -0.80$ for another, compare the strength of the two relationships.

17.30 Following are data for fall 1988 enrollment and teachers in full-time elementary and secondary schools of the Atlantic Ocean coastal states in the United States.

State	Enrollment (in 100,000's) x	Teachers (in 10,000's) y
Connecticut	4.63	3.55
Delaware	0.96	0.59
Florida	17.21	10.04
Georgia	11.07	5.99
Maine	2.13	1.46
Maryland	6.89	4.09
Massachusetts	8.23	6.01
New Hampshire	1.69	1.04
New Jersey	10.81	7.97
New York	25.74	17.28
North Carolina	10.83	6.19
Pennsylvania	16.60	10.44
Rhode Island	1.34	0.92
South Carolina	6.16	3.59
Virginia	9.82	6.09

Calculate r_S.

17.31 If a set of $n = 10$ paired observations yields $r = 0.65$, test the null hypothesis of no correlation
(a) at the 0.05 level of significance
(b) at the 0.01 level of significance

17.32 Following are the rankings made by two executives of eight applicants for appointments to a training program.

First executive	Second executive
x	y
4	6
5	3
1	2
3	1
2	5
7	4
8	7
6	8

Calculate r_S as a measure of consistency of the two rankings.

17.33 For the data of the preceding exercise, test the null hypothesis of no correlation at the 0.05 level of significance.

17.34 In a multiple regression problem the residual sum of squares is $\sum (y - \hat{y})^2 = 576$, and the total sum of squares is $\sum (y - \bar{y})^2 = 952$. Find the value of the multiple correlation coefficient.

17.35 For the following sample data

x	y
4	3
2	4
1	2
3	1

verify that $r = 0$ and that the least-squares line which fits these data best is a horizontal line coincident with $\bar{y}$.

17.36 In a random sample of 20 officers of a bank, the correlation coefficient for their ages, x, and the number of years of their banking experience, y, is 0.64. What percentage of the differences in the number of years of banking experience can be attributed to the ages of the bank officers?

17.37 Calculate r for the data of Exercise 16.28 on page 646, and test the null hypothesis of no correlation at the 0.05 level of significance.

17.38 Use the least-squares equation of Exercise 16.29 on page 646 to calculate $\hat{y}$ for each of the hospitals, determine the two sums of squares $\sum (y - \hat{y})^2$ and $\sum (y - \bar{y})^2$, and calculate the multiple correlation coefficient.

17.39 Following are the ways two gourmets ranked seven fine restaurants in a city:

Restaurant	Gourmet 1 x	Gourmet 2 y
A	7	6
B	1	3
C	5	5
D	3	7
E	4	2
F	2	1
G	6	4

Calculate r_S as a measure of consistency.

17.40 Following are the numbers of inquiries which an investment company received in 10 weeks concerning its Aggressive Growth Mutual Fund, x, and its Balanced Portfolio Mutual Fund, y.

Growth Fund x	Balanced Fund y
38	63
45	74
47	78
23	59
35	40
12	18
28	43
37	51
52	75
50	12

Calculate r and test the null hypothesis of no correlation at the 0.05 level of significance.

17.41 If a random sample of $n = 20$ pairs of observations yielded $r_S = 0.55$, is this rank correlation significant

(a) at the 0.05 level

(b) at the 0.01 level

17.42 Interpret, in your own words, the meaning of Figure 17.3, computer printout of correlation between average straight-time hourly earnings in Montana and West Virginia.

17.43 Use a computer package to rework Exercise 17.2 on page 664 where we calculate the coefficient of correlation, r for the number of catalogs distributed and the number of orders received in 12 cities.

17.44 Use a computer package to rework Exercise 17.5(b) on page 666 where we calculate the coefficient of correlation, r, for the production of rye and the production of grapefruit in the United States for the years 1984 through 1989.

17.45 Use a computer package to rework Exercise 17.16 on page 674 where we calculate the coefficient of correlation, r_S, for the number of dollars spent on television advertising and the number of pairs of jeans sold during the years 1985 through 1992.

17.46 Use a computer package to rework Exercise 17.17 on page 674 where we calculate the coefficient of correlation, r_S, for the number of catalogs distributed and the number of orders received in 12 cities.

17.47 Use a computer package to rework Exercise 17.19 on page 674 where we calculate the coefficient of correlation, r_S, for the number of guests registered weekly at a health spa and the weekly wage expense for general maintenance workers of the spa's buildings and grounds.

17.8

Solutions of Practice Exercises

17.1

x	x^2	y	y^2	xy
71	5,041	25	625	1,775
64	4,096	16	256	1,024
100	10,000	37	1,369	3,700
105	11,025	40	1,600	4,200
75	5,625	18	324	1,350
59	3,481	10	100	590
82	6,724	22	484	1,804
68	4,624	14	196	952
111	12,321	42	1,764	4,662
90	8,100	19	361	1,710
825	71,037	243	7,079	21,767

$n = 10$, $\sum x = 825$, $\sum x^2 = 71{,}037$, $\sum y = 243$, $\sum y^2 = 7{,}079$, and $\sum xy = 21{,}767$. Since $S_{xx} = 71{,}037 - \dfrac{1}{10}(825)^2 = 2{,}974.5$, $S_{xy} = 21{,}767$

$- \dfrac{1}{10}(825)(243) = 1{,}719.5$, and $S_{yy} = 7{,}079 - \dfrac{1}{10}(243)^2 = 1{,}174.1$, then

$b = \dfrac{S_{xy}}{S_{xx}} = \dfrac{1{,}719.5}{2{,}974.5} = 0.578$, and we get $r = \dfrac{1{,}719.5}{\sqrt{2{,}974.5 \cdot 1{,}174.1}} =$
0.92.

Since $r = 0.92$ exceeds 0.62, the value of $r_{0.025}$ for $n = 10$ from Table VI, Values of r, the null hypothesis of no correlation must be rejected. $r = 0.92$ is signifcant.

17.6 (a)

x	x^2	y	y^2	xy
3.2	10.24	6.8	46.24	21.76
2.9	8.41	7.0	49.00	20.30
3.7	13.69	7.1	50.41	26.27
2.5	6.25	7.8	60.84	19.50
3.3	10.89	6.3	36.69	20.79
2.7	7.29	7.6	57.76	20.52
2.9	8.41	5.8	33.64	16.82
3.4	11.56	7.2	51.84	24.48
24.6	76.74	55.6	389.42	170.44

From the table $\sum x = 24.6$, $\sum x^2 = 76.74$, $\sum y = 55.6$, $\sum y^2 = 389.42$, and $\sum xy = 170.44$.

$$S_{xx} = \sum x^2 - \frac{1}{n}(\sum x)^2 = 76.74 - \frac{1}{8}(24.6)^2 = 1.095$$

$$S_{yy} = \sum y^2 - \frac{1}{n}(\sum y)^2 = 389.42 - \frac{1}{8}(55.6)^2 = 3.0$$

$$S_{xy} = \sum xy - \frac{1}{n}(\sum x)(\sum y) = 170.44 - \frac{1}{8}(24.6)(55.6) = -0.53$$

$$r = \frac{S_{xy}}{\sqrt{S_{xx} \cdot S_{yy}}} = \frac{-0.53}{\sqrt{(1.095)(3.0)}} = -0.292$$

(b) Since -0.292 falls betweeen -0.834 and 0.834, the values of $-r_{0.005}$ and $r_{0.005}$ for $n = 8$ from Table VI, the null hypothesis cannot be rejected. We accept the null hypothesis or reserve judgment. The difference is not significant.

17.16

x	y	Rank of x	Rank of y	d	d^2
50	45	1	1	0	0
65	60	2	2	0	0
75	80	3	3	0	0
100	95	4	4	0	0
125	120	5	5	0	0
140	150	6	7	-1	1
170	145	7	6	1	1
195	190	8	8	0	0
				Total	2

$$\sum d^2 = 2$$
$$r_S = 1 - \frac{6 \cdot 2}{8 \cdot 63} = 0.98$$

Since $z = 0.98\sqrt{8-1} = 2.593$ exceeds 1.96, the null hypothesis of no correlation must be rejected.

17.22

x	y	d	d^2
1	1	0	0
3	7	-4	16
7	2	5	25
6	3	3	9
8	5	3	9
4	4	0	0
5	8	-3	9
2	9	-7	49
9	6	3	9
	Total		126

(a) $r_S = 1 - \dfrac{6(\sum d^2)}{n(n^2 - 1)} = 1 - \dfrac{6 \cdot 126}{9(81 - 1)} = -0.05.$

(b) Since $z = -0.05\sqrt{9-1} = -0.14$ falls between -1.96 and 1.96, the null hypothesis of no correlation cannot be rejected.

Mgr. 1	Mgr. 2	Mgr. 3	d 1 and 2	d² 1 and 2	d 1 and 3	d² 1 and 3	d 2 and 3	d² 2 and 3
9	8	7	1	1	2	4	1	1
10	7	9	3	9	1	1	−2	4
1	2	4	−1	1	−3	9	−2	4
5	5	8	0	0	−3	9	−3	9
3	4	2	−1	1	1	1	2	4
8	6	5	2	4	3	9	1	1
11	12	10	−1	1	1	1	2	4
4	3	6	1	1	−2	4	−3	9
12	10	12	2	4	0	0	−2	4
7	11	11	−4	16	−4	16	0	0
2	1	3	1	1	−1	1	−2	4
6	9	1	−3	9	5	25	8	64
			Total	48		80		108

$\sum d^2$ for 1 and 2 is 48; for 1 and 3 is 80; for 2 and 3 is 108.

$r_S = 1 - \dfrac{6(\sum d^2)}{n(n^2 - 1)}$, and $r_S = 1 - \dfrac{6 \cdot 48}{12 \cdot 143} = 0.83$ for managers 1 and 2,

$r_S = 1 - \dfrac{6 \cdot 80}{12 \cdot 143} = 0.72$ for managers 1 and 3, and $r_S = 1 - \dfrac{6 \cdot 108}{12 \cdot 143} = 0.62$ for managers 2 and 3.

(a) Managers 1 and 2 are most consistent.

(b) Managers 2 and 3 are least consistent.

17.25 $\sqrt{1 - \dfrac{75{,}240}{112{,}550}} = 0.58$.

17.26 Since $\hat{y} = -2.503 + 1.103x_1 + 0.207x_2$ from Exercise 16.23, we get

$$\hat{y} = -2.503 + 1.103(6) + 0.207(0) = 4.115$$
$$\hat{y} = -2.503 + 1.103(4) + 0.207(2) = 2.323$$
$$\hat{y} = -2.503 + 1.103(16) + 0.207(4) = 15.973$$
$$\hat{y} = -2.503 + 1.103(10) + 0.207(6) = 9.769$$
$$\hat{y} = -2.503 + 1.103(12) + 0.207(8) = 12.389$$
$$\hat{y} = -2.503 + 1.103(8) + 0.207(10) = 8.391$$
$$\hat{y} = -2.503 + 1.103(12) + 0.207(12) = 13.217$$
$$\hat{y} = -2.503 + 1.103(16) + 0.207(14) = 18.043$$
$$\hat{y} = -2.503 + 1.103(14) + 0.207(16) = 16.251, \text{ and}$$
$$\hat{y} = -2.503 + 1.103(4) + 0.207(3) = 2.530, \text{ so that}$$

y	$\hat{y}$	$y - \hat{y}$	$(y - \hat{y})^2$
4	4.115	−0.115	0.0132
2	2.323	−0.323	0.1043
16	15.973	0.027	0.0007
10	9.769	0.231	0.0534
12	12.389	−0.389	0.1513
8	8.391	−0.391	0.1529
14	13.217	0.783	0.6131
18	18.043	−0.043	0.0018
16	16.251	−0.251	0.0630
3	2.530	0.470	0.2209

$\sum y = 103$

$\sum (y - \hat{y})^2 = 1.375$

Also, since $\sum (y - \bar{y})^2 = 1{,}369 - \dfrac{1}{10}(103)^2 = 308.1$, we find that the

multiple correlation coefficient is $\sqrt{1 - \dfrac{1.375}{308.1}} = 1.0$.

18

Quality Control

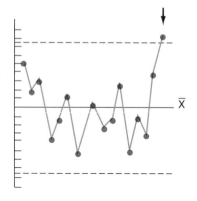

Although there may be a tendency to think of quality control as a recent development, there is really nothing new about the idea of making a quality product characterized by a high degree of uniformity. For centuries, highly skilled artisans have striven to make products distinctive through superior quality, and once a standard of quality was achieved, to eliminate insofar as possible all variability between products that were nominally alike.

However, the idea that statistics might be instrumental in controlling the quality of manufactured products is relatively new, going back no farther than the work of Dr. Walter Shewhart of the Bell Laboratories in the 1920s, and the widespread use of what is now called **statistical quality control** (or *quality control*, or *Q.C.,* for short) is even more recent than that. Although the new methods were readily accepted in Great Britain, it was not until World War II that statistical quality control methods were used on any great scale in the United States. As a result of the war, it became necessary for many different industries to devote themselves to an all-out production effort, requiring the production of tremendous amounts of war materiel made to more exacting specifications than ever before and, in many cases, made by new methods, with substitute materials, poorly trained help, on machines designed for other purposes; it was this exigency which led to the wide acceptance of statistical quality control in this country.

Despite the claims of a few enthusiasts, quality control did not win the war single-handedly, but it undoubtedly made a substantial contribution. Like any other statistical tool, there are certain things that QC can do and some that it cannot. Obviously, the problem of designing machines capable of making products to very exact specifications is an engineering problem and not a statistical one. But like other statistical tools properly used, quality control proved to be extremely helpful in a wide variety of situations, and it was only natural that its success during the war should be followed by its continued and expanded use in the postwar period. At the present time, statistical quality control is used to some extent in virtually every kind of industry in existence and in virtually every country having an industry within its borders, notably in Japan, where it has been widely utilized. Precisely what economies are being achieved by these methods through reductions in time and manpower requirements, waste, scrap, rework, and inspection cost, is impossible to determine, but they are undoubtedly large.

Shortly after the end of World War II in 1945, Japanese industry embarked upon an era of truly remarkable reconstruction and development. History records several major contributors to the intellectual foundations that underlay the industrial transformation of this nation. Perhaps the best known figure is that of W. Edwards Deming (of the United States) who brought a new theory of management to Japan. His theory of management focuses upon quality and, to this end, integrates human relations management and other factors with statistical quality control. Quality control is not entirely quantitative, and is not the exclusive domain of the statistician.

At the heart of Deming's philosophy are his well known 14 Points. These have been widely discussed and, although not universally agreed upon, provide a new foundation for management. With permission of the authors, W. E. Deming's[1] 14 Points and M. Walton's[2] commentary are quoted here, verbatim. Brevity requires that we omit discussion of the *Seven Deadly Diseases,* and the *Obstacles,* which supplement and illuminate the points.

1. *Create and publish to all employees a statement of the aims and purposes of the company or other organization. Their management must demonstrate constantly their commitment to this statement.*

   Dr. Deming suggests a radical new definition of a company's role: Rather than to make money, it is to stay in business and provide jobs through innovation, research, constant improvement and maintenance.

---

[1]Deming's 14 Points (January 1990 revision) reprinted from *Out of the Crisis* by W. Edwards Deming by permission of MIT and W. Edwards Deming. Published by MIT, Center for Advanced Engineering Study, Cambridge, MA 02139. Copyright 1986 by W. Edwards Deming.

[2]Walton, M., *Deming Management at Work.* New York: G. P. Putnam's Sons, 1991.

2. *Learn the new philosophy, top management and everybody.*

Americans are too tolerant of poor workmanship and sullen service. We need a new religion in which mistakes and negativism are unacceptable.

3. *Understand the purpose of inspection, for improvement of processes and reduction of cost.*

American firms typically inspect a product as it comes off the assembly line or at major stages along the way; defective products are either thrown out or reworked. Both practices are unnecessarily expensive. In effect, a company is paying workers to make defects and to correct them. Quality comes not from inspection but from improvement of the process. With instruction, workers can be enlisted in this improvement.

4. *End the practice of awarding business on the basis of price tag alone.*

Purchasing departments customarily operate on orders to seek the lowest priced vendor. Frequently, this leads to supplies of low quality. Instead, buyers should seek the best quality in a long-term relationship with a single supplier for any one item.

5. *Improve constantly and forever the system of production and service.*

Improvement is not a one-time effort. Management is obligated to continually look for ways to reduce waste and improve quality.

6. *Institute training.*

Too often, workers have learned their job from another worker who was never trained properly. They are forced to follow unintelligible instructions. They can't do their jobs well because no one tells how to do so.

7. *Teach and institute leadership.*

The job of a supervisor is not to tell people what to do nor punish them but to lead. Leading consists of helping people to do a better job of learning by objective methods who is in need of individual help.

8. *Drive out fear. Create trust. Create a climate for innovation.*

Many employees are afraid to ask questions or take a position, even when they do not understand what their job is or what is right or wrong. They will continue to do things the wrong way, or not to do them at all. The economic losses from fear are appalling. To assure better quality and productivity, it is necessary that people feel secure.

9. *Optimize toward the aims and purposes of the company.*

Often a company's departments or units are competing with each other or have goals that conflict. They do not work as a team so they can solve or foresee problems. Worse, one department's goals may cause troubles for another.

10. *Eliminate exhortations for the work force.*

These never helped anybody do a good job. Let workers formulate their own slogans.

11. (a) *Eliminate numerical quotas for production. Instead, learn and institute methods for improvement.*

(b) *Eliminate M.B.O. (Management by Objectives). Instead, learn the capabilities of processes, and how to improve them.* Quotas take into account only numbers, not quality or methods. They are usually a guarantee of inefficiency and high cost. A person, to hold a job, meets a quota at any cost, without regard to damage to his company.

12. *Remove barriers that rob people of pride of workmanship.*

People are eager to do a good job and distressed when they cannot. Too often, misguided supervisors, faulty equipment and defective materials stand in the way of good performance. These barriers must be removed.

13. *Encourage education and self-improvement for everyone.*

Both management and the work force will have to be educated in the new methods, including teamwork and statistical techniques.

14. *Take action to accomplish the transformation.*

It will require a special top management team with a plan of action to carry out the quality mission. Workers cannot do it on their own, nor can managers. A critical mass of people in the company must understand the fourteen points, the *Seven Deadly Diseases* and the *Obstacles.*

Statistical quality control, which was once viewed by some with distrust and even alarm, has passed its qualifying tests with distinction, and there is no apparent limit to its use in the years ahead.

18.1

Some Preliminary Remarks

Many problems arising in the manufacture of a product are amenable to statistical treatment. (Some of them have already been treated in earlier parts of this book.) In a broad sense, what is sometimes called **industrial statistics** embraces all the statistical techniques which can be used anywhere in the solution of these problems. Thus, quality control is merely one branch of industrial statistics and is not, as is sometimes thought, synonymous with industrial statistics.

When we speak of (statistical) quality control, we are referring to two specific statistical techniques—the control chart and acceptance sampling—used as aids in assuring that desired quality standards are being met as economically as possible. Used technically, as in this discussion, the **quality** of a product refers to some property of the product such as the outside diameter of a ball bearing, the breaking strength of yarn, the drained weight of a No. $2\frac{1}{2}$ can of fruit salad, or the potency of a drug product.

It may surprise some persons to learn that two apparently identical parts made under carefully controlled conditions, from the same batch of raw material, and only seconds apart by the same machine, can nevertheless be quite different in many respects. This is due to the fact that it is seldom, if ever, possible to duplicate the exact conditions existing at a given time, no matter how great an effort is made. Thus, any manufacturing process, however good, is characterized by a certain amount of variability which is of the same chance or random nature as the variation we might find between repeated rolls of a pair of dice. Chance variation is an inherent and inevitable part of any process and there is no way in which it can be completely eliminated. When the variability present in a production process is confined to chance variation, the process is said to be in a state of statistical control.

Statistical control is usually achieved in a process by finding and eliminating trouble of the sort causing another kind of variation called **assignable variation**. Under this heading we include variations in a process due to poorly trained operators, substandard or poor quality raw materials, faulty machine settings, broken or worn parts, and the like. Inasmuch as manufacturing processes are rarely free from troubles of this sort for any length of time, it is important to have some systematic method of detecting serious deviations from a state of statistical control when, or if possible before, they occur. It is to this end that **control charts**, the subject matter of the next few sections, are principally used.

18.2

The Control Chart

A control chart is a simple chart characterized essentially by three horizontal lines—a **central line** to indicate the desired standard, or level, of the process and an **upper and a lower control limit** (see Figure 18.1). By plotting results obtained from samples taken periodically at frequent intervals (for example, each hour, half-day, or day), it is possible to check by means of such a chart whether the variation between the samples may be attributed to chance or whether trouble of the sort just indicated has entered the process. The upper and lower control limits serve as the decision criteria. When a sample point falls beyond them, one looks for trouble, that is, for sources of assignable variation; otherwise, the process is left alone. The detection of "lack of control" is a very important use of control charts, but it is not the only one. If a process is known to be in control, it is possible to indicate by means of a control chart the process capability, namely, the average level at which the process is capable of operating, and also the amount of chance variation that is inherent in the process. In short, control charts constitute powerful tools which provide management with logical bases for many important actions.

Since the word "quality" is used in a general way to refer to any characteristic, or property, of a product, let us distinguish between those characteristics which are measurable and those which are merely noted or

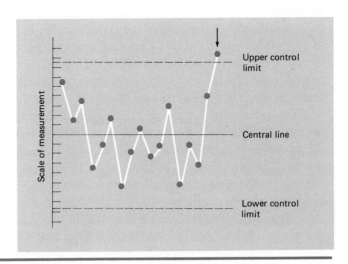

FIGURE 18.1
The control chart

observed. If the relevant quality characteristic is the length of a bolt, the initial angle of a torsion spring, the bore of a ball bearing, the seam strength of a shirt, the weight of a bag of coffee, . . . , this characteristic can in some way be assigned a numerical value. Control charts designed to control such measurable characteristics are called **control charts for variables**.

In contrast, there are properties of products that are not measurable, referring to differences in kind rather than differences in degree. Bolts do or do not have heads, canned foods do or do not have labels, shirts do or do not have all the necessary buttons, and, more generally, items are classified as nondefective or defective, satisfactory or unsatisfactory. Charts designed to control such quality characteristics as these are called **control charts for attributes**; they will be treated briefly in Section 18.5. Control charts for variables will be discussed in Sections 18.3 and 18.4.

If the reader understands the principles underlying statistical estimation and tests of hypotheses (see Chapter 11), the logic of a control chart, its construction, and the reason why it works, will be fairly obvious. A control chart simply provides a convenient way of repeatedly testing hypotheses relative to the quality of a manufactured product. The purpose of these tests is to decide on the basis of relatively few observations whether a desired standard of quality is actually being met. The hypothesis being tested is that the process is "in control." If the hypothesis is accepted and the process is allowed to continue without modification, it is presumed that the process is operating satisfactorily or, in other words, that whatever variability there is can be attributed to chance. If the hypothesis is rejected, it is presumed that there is trouble of some sort, that the process is "out of control," and a search is made to detect the source (or sources) of assignable nonrandom variations.

As always in the testing of statistical hypotheses, there is the possibility of committing errors and this accounts for the use of the word "presume" in the preceding paragraph. If we reject the hypothesis that the process is in control when it should actually be accepted, we will be committing a Type I error (see page 405). The consequences of such a Type I error are that we look for nonexistent trouble, and such a search can easily lead to an increase in cost owing to loss in time and production. If we accept the hypothesis that the process is in control when actually it is not, we will be committing a Type II error. The consequences of such a Type II error are that we fail to look for existing trouble and thus may manufacture and ship products which fail to meet required standards.

Naturally, manufacturers would like to avoid these errors completely and always follow the right course of action, but, as we have seen, this is generally impossible. In practice, there is no choice but to seek an economic balance between the possible risks (losses) associated with the two kinds of errors, and in this country it has become more or less accepted practice to use **3-sigma control limits**, that is, charts on which the upper and lower control limits are drawn three standard deviations (standard errors) above and below the central line. When dealing with sampling distributions that can be approximated closely with normal curves, the probability of committing a Type I error is just 0.003 since 99.7 percent of the area under the normal curve lies between $z = -3$ and $z = 3$. The use of 3-sigma control limits does not provide any guarantee, or for that matter any information, about the probabilities of committing Type II errors. As we saw in Chapter 11, questions about Type II errors can be decided only by studying operating characteristic curves (see page 409). Nevertheless, the use of 3-sigma control limits can be justified on the grounds of long experience and satisfactory performance in practice, and it is recommended that they be used unless there are very good reasons why other control limits should be preferred.

18.3

$\overline{X}$- and R-Charts

In this and in subsequent sections of this chapter, we shall use the notation that is generally found in the literature on quality control. It is important to observe that this notation differs somewhat from that which has become standard in many other branches of statistics and which we use in other parts of this book.

To illustrate the construction of control charts for variables, let us assume that an engine manufacturer has started producing a new type of crankshaft and wishes to set up a control procedure for the diameter of the crankshaft, specifications for which are 1.000 inch ± 0.005 inch. Its objective is twofold: The company not only wants to know whether the production process designed for the new crankshaft is under control and in accordance with specifications, but it also wants to use control charts in the future to keep a continual check on the process.

In the beginning the company plans to set up control procedures for both the average and the variability of the diameters. Later on it may prove possible to dispense with one or the other. Generally speaking, a continual check on the quality of a product requires that we take samples at frequent intervals of time, calculate certain statistics, and decide on the basis of the values thus obtained whether or not the process may be presumed to be under control. In quality control it is customary to refer to such samples as "subgroups," or as "rational subgroups," if they are such that the variation within a sample can be due only to chance while the variation between samples can be due either to chance or to assignable causes of variation. Time, order of production, or source of production, are common bases used for forming rational subgroups, and frequent small subgroups of four or five are usually better and more informative than infrequent larger groups. It is generally recommended that at least 25 subgroups be used in the construction of trial control limits.

To check on average quality, it is customary in quality control to use the mean, $\overline{X}$, of the observations within each subgroup, and to check on variability, it is customary to use either the standard deviation, σ, or the range, R. The standard deviation is in many respects a more desirable measure of variation than the range, but, as we pointed out on page 67, the range is an adequate measure of variation when the sample size is small, and it is much easier to find. Since we have only to subtract the smallest sample value from the largest, the range is often used in problems of quality control where it is important to obtain results quickly and with a minimum of arithmetic.

To return now to the problem of the engine manufacturer, let us suppose that samples of size 5 have been taken from each hour's production for 30 hours and that the diameters of the crankshafts are measured to the nearest thousandth of an inch. To simplify our notation, we shall "code" these measurements by writing each as so many thousandths of an inch above or below 1 inch. We shall thus write 2 instead of 1.002 inch, -1 instead of 0.999 inch, 0 instead of 1.000 inch, and, in this notation, the original specifications become 0 ± 5. The table which follows contains the (coded) measurements obtained in 30 samples (subgroups), and since we shall construct control charts based on the mean and the range, the values of these statistics are shown below the respective samples:

Subgroup:	1	2	3	4	5	6	7	8	9	10	11	12	13	14	15
	−1	0	1	1	0	−2	2	1	−1	1	2	1	0	2	1
	−1	1	1	−2	3	−2	1	−2	2	−1	−1	−3	0	−1	−1
	0	−3	2	−1	−2	1	−1	−1	1	0	−2	−2	−1	−1	2
	−2	2	−1	0	−2	1	0	−1	1	0	−1	1	0	0	0
	1	1	0	−1	1	2	0	0	2	−1	−1	0	1	−2	−2
$\overline{X}$	−0.6	0.2	0.6	−0.6	0	0	0.4	−0.6	1.0	−0.2	−0.6	−0.6	0	−0.4	0
R	3	5	3	3	5	4	3	3	3	2	4	4	2	4	4

Chapter 18   Quality Control

Subgroup:	16	17	18	19	20	21	22	23	24	25	26	27	28	29	30
	2	1	0	−2	−3	1	−2	2	1	3	2	1	1	2	0
	−1	1	0	1	3	1	1	2	0	−1	0	−2	0	0	0
	0	0	1	2	1	0	3	−1	1	0	0	−2	0	3	2
	0	0	−2	0	2	−1	1	1	2	1	1	1	1	−2	1	1
	1	1	−1	1	0	2	−3	0	−2	−1	1	1	−1	−2	−1
$\bar{X}$	0.4	0.6	−0.4	0.4	0.6	0.6	0	0.8	0.4	0.4	0.8	−0.2	−0.4	0.8	0.4
R	3	1	3	4	6	3	6	3	4	4	2	3	3	5	3

To estimate the true average of the (coded) diameters of the crankshafts produced by the new process, we shall use the mean of the 30 $\bar{X}$'s, which, in the notation of quality control, is written as $\bar{\bar{X}}$. In general, if we have k subgroups whose means are $\bar{X}_1, \bar{X}_2, \ldots,$ and $\bar{X}_k$, the overall mean, which will serve as the **central line of the control chart for the mean**, is given by the formula

Overall mean

$$\bar{\bar{X}} = \frac{\bar{X}_1 + \bar{X}_2 + \cdots + \bar{X}_k}{k}$$

EXAMPLE 18.1 Using the data of the engine manufacturer shown in the preceding table, and using the formula for the overall mean, calculate $\bar{\bar{X}}$ for the 30 samples. The $\bar{\bar{X}}$ which we calculate here serves as the central line of the control chart for the mean, Figure 18.2.

SOLUTION Substituting the means of the 30 subgroups given in the preceding table into the formula for the overall mean,

$$\bar{\bar{X}} = \frac{\bar{X}_1 + \bar{X}_2 + \cdots + \bar{X}_k}{k}$$

we get

$$\bar{\bar{X}} = (-0.6 + 0.2 + 0.6 - 0.6 + 0 + 0 + 0.4 - 0.6 + 1.0 - 0.2 - 0.6$$
$$- 0.6 + 0 - 0.4 + 0 + 0.4 + 0.6 - 0.4 + 0.4 + 0.6 + 0.6 + 0$$
$$+ 0.8 + 0.4 + 0.4 + 0.8 - 0.2 - 0.4 + 0.8 + 0.4)/30 = 0.13 \quad \blacksquare$$

The **average range** that can be expected for samples (of the given size) from this process is estimated by means of the formula

$$\overline{R} = \frac{R_1 + R_2 + \cdots + R_k}{k}$$

where $R_1, R_2, \ldots$, and R_K are the ranges of the individual subgroups. In our example, this average range will serve as the central line of the control chart for the range.

EXAMPLE 18.2   Using the data of the engine manufacturer shown in the preceding table, and using the formula for the average range, calculate $\overline{R}$ for the 30 samples. The $\overline{R}$ which we calculate here serves as the central line of the control chart for the range, Figure 18.2.

SOLUTION   Substituting the ranges of the 30 subgroups given in the preceding table into the formula for the average range,

$$\overline{R} = \frac{R_1 + R_2 + \cdots + R_k}{k}$$

we get

$$\overline{R} = (3 + 5 + 3 + 3 + 5 + 4 + 3 + 3 + 3 + 2 + 4 + 4 + 2 + 4 + 4$$
$$+ 3 + 1 + 3 + 4 + 6 + 3 + 6 + 3 + 4 + 4 + 2 + 3 + 3 + 5 + 3)/30$$
$$= 3.50$$

■

To construct upper and lower control limits for $\overline{X}$ and R, namely, criteria for testing hypotheses about the mean and variation of the population from which these samples were obtained, we shall, as always (see Chapter 12), have to investigate the sampling distributions of the given statistics. Leaving all theoretical considerations about these sampling distributions aside, let us merely state that the required **3-sigma control limits for the mean** are usually calculated by means of the formula

Three-sigma control limits for mean

$$\overline{\overline{X}} \pm A_2 \overline{R}$$

where A_2 is a constant which depends on the size of the sample (subgroup) and which can be looked up in Table XIII on page 877. Similarly, the **3-sigma control limits for the range** are usually calculated by means of the formulas

$$D_4 \bar{R} \quad \text{and} \quad D_3 \bar{R}$$

where D_4 and D_3 are also given in Table XIII.

EXAMPLE 18.3   Calculate the 3-sigma control limits for the mean diameter of the crankshafts produced by the engine manufacturer. The control limits which we calculate here serve as the control limits of the control chart for the mean, Figure 18.2.

SOLUTION $\bar{\bar{X}} = 0.13$ is obtained from Example 18.1, $\bar{R} = 3.50$ is obtained from Example 18.2, and A_2 is obtained from Table XIII on page 877. To obtain the value of A_2 from the table of control chart constants we read down the column headed A_2, and across the row where 5 is the number of observations in the sample, getting the value 0.577. Substituting these values into the formula for 3-sigma control limits for mean, we get

$$\bar{\bar{X}} \pm A_2 \bar{R} = 0.13 \pm (0.577)(3.50)$$

obtaining an upper control limit of 2.15 and lower control limit of -1.89. ∎

EXAMPLE 18.4   Calculate the 3-sigma control limits for the ranges of the diameters of the crankshafts produced by the engine manufacturer. The control limits which we calculate here serve as the control limits of the control chart for the range, Figure 18.2.

SOLUTION $\bar{R} = 3.50$, which is obtained from Example 18.2. D_4 and D_3 are obtained from Table XIII, control chart constants. To obtain the value of D_4 from this table, we read down the column headed D_4, and across the row where 5 is the number of observations in the sample, getting 2.115. We use the same procedure to obtain the value of D_3, getting zero. Substituting $\bar{R} = 3.50$, $D_4 = 2.115$, and $D_3 = 0$ into the two formulas, we get

$$D_4 \bar{R} = (2.115)(3.50) = 7.40$$

which is the upper control limit for the range, and

$$D_3 \bar{R} = (0)(3.50) = 0$$

which is the lower control limit for the range. ∎

The upper and lower conrol limits for the mean which are calculated in Example 18.3 and the upper and lower control limits for the range which are calculated in Example 18.4 are plotted together with the corresponding $\overline{\overline{X}}$ and $\overline{R}$ to create the two control charts of Figure 18.2. The points which are plotted on these charts are the $\overline{X}$'s and R's of the 30 subgroups shown on pages 694 and 695.

The fact that on both charts all sample points fall within the 3-sigma control limits can be interpreted as implying that the process is in a state of statistical control or, in other words, that the only kind of variation present is chance variation. Had the charts indicated that at one time or another the process was not in control, it would have been necessary to eliminate the out-of-control data, recalculate $\overline{\overline{X}}$ and $\overline{R}$ on the basis of the remaining samples, and establish new control limits.

As we pointed out earlier, the purpose of constructing control charts is not only to check whether there is any assignable variation, but also to see whether the process will meet specifications. To answer this kind of question, we shall have to estimate the true mean and standard deviation of the diameters of crankshafts produced by the process and in the notation of quality control, these quantities are written as $\overline{X}'$ and σ'. (In the notation used otherwise in this book we call these population values μ and σ.) Although there are other, and perhaps better, ways in which to estimate these values, it is customary in quality control problems of this kind to estimate $\overline{X}'$ by means of $\overline{\overline{X}}$, and σ' by means of $\overline{R}/d_2$, where d_2 is another constant which can be looked up in Table XIII. Since $d_2 = 2.326$ for samples of size 5 and $\overline{\overline{X}}$ and $\overline{R}$ equaled 0.13 and 3.5, we shall thus estimate the true mean of the (coded) diameters of the crankshafts as 0.13 and their standard deviation as

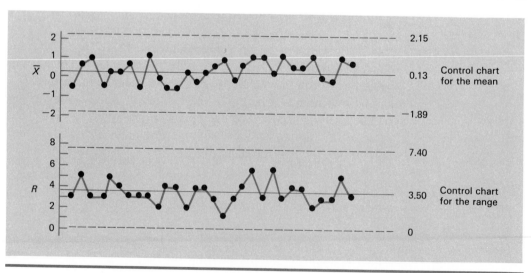

FIGURE 18.2   Control charts for crankshafts

$3.5/2.326 = 1.50$. Assuming that the diameters of the crankshafts produced by the given process are normally distributed with the mean and standard deviation just given, we can say that 99.7 percent of the crankshafts will have (coded) diameters lying between their mean plus and minus three standard deviations and, hence, between $0.13 - 3(1.50) = -4.37$ and $0.13 + 3(1.50) = 4.63$. Since the specifications in terms of the coded data read 0 ± 5, it appears that almost all of the product will meet specifications so long as the process continues to operate at the same level and with the same amount of variability.

To keep a continual check on the process, we simply extend the control lines of Figure 18.2 and plot, as before, the means and ranges obtained from repeated (hourly or daily) samples of five observations. If at any time in the future a point falls outside the control limits, appropriate actions will have to be taken to search for possible sources of assignable variation. Of course, it is possible to obtain a point outside the control limits by chance, but the probability of this happening is less than 0.003. It should also be remembered that the control limits which we established are really only estimates and after more information has been obtained it may well become desirable to recalculate and, if necessary, adjust them. Furthermore, it could happen that changes will take place in the process itself later on, and such changes, of course, would make it necessary to calculate new control limits.

Control charts are not only watched for points falling outside the control limits; they are also scrutinized for unusual patterns suggesting trouble. For instance, a run of 7 successive points on the same side of the central line of an $\overline{X}$-chart is looked upon as roughly equivalent to a point outside the control limits, and it is usually interpreted to mean that the process average has shifted or that the process will soon go out of control. In this way, impending trouble can often be detected and prevented at considerable savings. Other patterns which are a cause for concern are a trend of 6 or more points, cyclical patterns of points, large numbers of points too close to upper or lower control limits, large numbers of points too close to the central line (indicating possible tampering with the data), a run of 10 of 12 points on one side of the central line, and any other aberrations.

18.4

Median and Range Control Charts

Median and range control charts are calculated in much the same manner and are useful for the same purposes as the more widely used mean and range control charts which we explained in Section 18.3. One difference is that the median of the subgroup medians (or, sometimes, the mean of the subgroup medians) is employed as the **central line of the control chart for the median**. Another difference is that the median of the subgroup ranges is used as the central line of the control chart for the range.

The control chart for the median possesses two advantages. Since the values of the medians of the subgroups are unaffected by extreme values, these medians avoid giving false out-of-control signals based on an occasional very large or very small value. Another advantage is its simplicity of calculation, making it especially useful where quality control data are collected by mathematically unskilled workers on the shop floor. When the subsets consist of an odd number of items, for example, no calculations are required to obtain the median. The median is, of course, the value of the middle item when the values are arranged according to size. The subgroup medians may, therefore, be determined by inspection from the 30 subgroups of crankshaft data on page 694 and are as follows: $-1, 1, 1, -1, 0, 1, 0, -1,$ $1, 0, -1, 0, 0, -1, 0, 0, 1, 0, 1, 1, 1, 1, 1, 1, 0, 1, 1, 0, 1,$ and 0. The grand median of the 30 subgroups is the arithmetic mean of the two central values (15th and 16th) when the 30 subgroup medians are arranged according to size and is $\tilde{\tilde{X}} = \dfrac{0+0}{2}$. Zero is thus the value of the central line of the control chart for the median, as shown in Figure 18.3.

The ranges of the 30 subgroups of the crankshaft data are shown on the table on page 694 and are $3, 5, 3, 3, 5, 4, 3, 3, 3, 2, 4, 4, 2, 4, 4, 3, 1, 3, 4,$ $6, 3, 6, 3, 4, 4, 2, 3, 3, 5,$ and 3. The **range median** of the 30 subgroups is the arithmetic mean of the two central values (15th and 16th) when the 30 subgroup ranges are arranged according to size and is $\dfrac{3+3}{2} = 3.00$.

Thus, 3.00 is the value of the control chart for the range, as shown in Figure 18.3.

The upper and lower limits, the **3-sigma control limits for the median**, are found by the formulas

Three-sigma control limits for median

$$\tilde{\tilde{X}} + \tilde{A}_2\tilde{R} \qquad \text{and} \qquad \tilde{\tilde{X}} - \tilde{A}_2\tilde{R}$$

where A_2 is obtained from the summary table that follows.

The upper and lower limits of the control chart for the range, the **3-sigma control limits for the range**, are found by the formulas

Chapter 18   Quality Control

$$\tilde{D}_4 \tilde{R} \qquad \text{and} \qquad \tilde{D}_3 \tilde{R}$$

where $\tilde{D}_4$ and $\tilde{D}_3$ are obtained from the summary table provided. We need this new table of control chart constants for the median since these are mostly different for the median than for the mean. A summary table for use with the median is shown below, but the complete table can be found in most textbooks on quality control or from the ASTM-STP 15 D, the American Society for Testing and Materials.

Summary Table of
Constants
for Median Charts

n	$\tilde{A}_2$	$\tilde{D}_4$	$\tilde{D}_3$
2	2.22	3.87	0
3	1.27	2.75	0
4	0.83	2.38	0
5	0.71	2.18	0
6	0.56	2.06	0
7	0.52	1.97	0.08
8	0.44	1.90	0.14
9	0.42	1.85	0.19
10	0.37	1.81	0.23

EXAMPLE 18.5 Calculate the 3-sigma control limits for the medians of the diameters of the crankshafts produced by the engine manufacturer. The control limits which we calculate here serve as the control limits of the control chart for the median, Figure 18.3.

SOLUTION $\tilde{\tilde{X}} = 0.00$ from the calculation of the grand median on page 700. $\tilde{R} = 3.00$ from the calculation of the range median on page 700. $\tilde{A}_2$ for sample size of 5 is 0.71 from the summary table of constants. Substituting $\tilde{\tilde{X}} = 0.00$, $\tilde{R} = 3.00$, and $\tilde{A}_2 = 0.71$ into the formula for the upper control limit (UCL) and the formula for the lower control limit (LCL), we get

$$\text{UCL} = \tilde{\tilde{X}} + \tilde{A}_2 \tilde{R} = 0.00 + 0.71(3.00) = 2.13$$

and

$$LCL = \tilde{\tilde{X}} - \tilde{A}_2\tilde{R} = 0.00 - 0.71(3.00) = -2.13 \quad \blacksquare$$

EXAMPLE 18.6   Calculate the 3-sigma control limits for the ranges of the diameters of the crankshafts produced by the engine manufacturer. The control limits which we calculate here serve as the control limits of the control chart for the range, Figure 18.3.

SOLUTION $\tilde{R} = 3.00$ from the calculation of the range median on page 700, $\tilde{D}_4$ for sample size of 5 is 2.18 from the above summary table of constants, and $\tilde{D}_3$ for sample size of 5 is 0 from the above summary table of constants. Substituting $\tilde{R} = 300$, $\tilde{D}_4 = 2.18$, and $\tilde{D}_3 = 0$ into the formula for the upper control limit and the formula for the lower control limit, we get

$$UCL = \tilde{D}_4\tilde{R} = 2.18(3.00) = 6.54$$

and

$$LCL = \tilde{D}_3\tilde{R} = 0(3.00) = 0 \quad \blacksquare$$

The upper and lower control limits for the median which are calculated in Example 18.5 and the upper and lower control limits for the range which are calculated in Example 18.6 are plotted together with the corresponding $\tilde{\tilde{X}}$ and $\tilde{R}$ to create the two control charts of Figure 18.3. The points which are

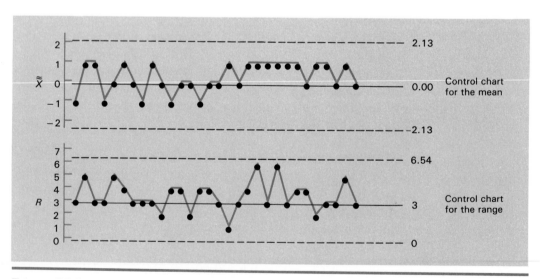

FIGURE 18.3   Control charts for crankshafts

plotted on these charts are the $\tilde{X}$'s and R's of the 30 subgroups shown on page 700.

18.5

$\overline{X}$- and σ-Charts

Although sample ranges are very easy to compute and, for this reason, are used in many problems of quality control, a standard deviation will generally provide more information about the variability of a set of data. For samples of size 10 or fewer, there is relatively little to gain by using the standard deviation instead of the range, and for $n = 2$, there is no gain at all, but when n is greater than 10 it is recommended that the standard deviation be used instead of the range. In quality control, sample standard deviations are defined by means of the formula

Sample standard deviations

$$\sigma = \sqrt{\frac{\sum_{i=1}^{n}(X_i - \overline{X})^2}{n}}$$

where the X's are the individual observations. The use of σ in connection with sample standard deviations is frowned upon in some branches of statistics, but it has become more or less established in quality control work.

If we have k samples (subgroups) whose standard deviations are σ_1, σ_2, . . . , and σ_k, we write their means as

Means of standard deviations

$$\overline{\sigma} = \frac{\sigma_1 + \sigma_2 + \cdots + \sigma_k}{k}$$

In terms of $\overline{\overline{X}}$ and $\overline{\sigma}$, the control limits of the $\overline{X}$-chart become

Control limits of $\overline{X}$-chart (in terms of $\overline{\overline{X}}$ and $\overline{\sigma}$)

$$\overline{\overline{X}} \pm A_1\overline{\sigma}$$

while the central line is again $\overline{\overline{X}}$. The constant A_1 can also be looked up in Table XIII. To control variability, we now use a σ-**chart** whose central line is $\overline{\sigma}$ and whose upper and lower control limits are

Control limits of
σ-chart (central
line is $\overline{\sigma}$)

$$B_4\overline{\sigma} \quad \text{and} \quad B_3\overline{\sigma}$$

where B_4 and B_3 are given in Table XIII. It will be left as an exercise for the reader to construct such $\overline{X}$- and σ-charts for the data of the preceding section.

The methods which we have illustrated so far are designed to establish control limits and central lines when $\overline{X}'$ and σ', the true mean and standard deviation, are unknown. If we wanted to construct control charts for processes for which these quantities are known or specified, we could write the central line and control limits for $\overline{X}$ as $\overline{X}'$ and $\overline{X}' \pm A\sigma'$ and those for σ as $c_2\sigma'$, $B_2\sigma'$, and $B_1\sigma'$. All these constants are given in Table XIII.

EXERCISES

(Exercise 18.1, 18.2, and 18.5 are practice exercises. Their complete solutions are given on page 720.)

18.1 It is proposed to establish control over a machine which turns out some 4,000 compression springs an hour. Subgroups of 5 springs are taken from each hour's production, and the free lengths of the springs are measured. The following are the means and ranges (in inches) obtained in 20 subgroups:

Subgroup:	1	2	3	4	5	6	7
$\overline{X}$	1.510	1.495	1.521	1.505	1.524	1.520	1.488
R	0.025	0.030	0.033	0.041	0.039	0.028	0.035

Subgroup:	8	9	10	11	12	13	14
$\overline{X}$	1.465	1.529	1.444	1.531	1.502	1.490	1.531
R	0.060	0.020	0.029	0.028	0.040	0.054	0.038

Subgroup:	15	16	17	18	19	20
$\overline{X}$	1.475	1.478	1.522	1.491	1.491	1.482
R	0.032	0.027	0.041	0.037	0.028	0.043

Calculate control limits for $\overline{X}$ and R, plot the given data, and determine whether or not the process may be considered to be in control.

18.2 The following data refer to the bursting strength of a certain type of corrugated box. The values are computed from subgroups of 10 taken from the production of 25 consecutive periods.

Subgroup:	1	2	3	4	5	6	7	8
$\overline{X}$	83.9	78.6	89.2	85.3	99.8	83.0	73.6	78.8
σ	7.7	6.7	8.2	10.9	16.4	9.1	8.9	8.2

Subgroup:	9	10	11	12	13	14	15	16
$\overline{X}$	92.0	90.0	86.5	93.1	90.6	75.0	80.1	75.4
σ	8.3	12.0	9.0	11.9	7.8	8.9	8.4	10.8

Subgroup:	17	18	19	20	21	22	23	24	25
$\overline{X}$	76.6	79.2	75.0	94.6	92.0	88.8	87.9	89.8	101.2
σ	7.9	11.5	10.2	16.3	22.9	18.4	7.2	10.1	17.3

Construct $\overline{X}$- and σ-charts, plot the given data, and determine to what extent the process is under statistical control. If there are out-of-control samples, eliminate them from the data and recalculate the control values.

18.3 The following uncoded data are for the thicknesses of rubber coating applied to wire and measured in millimeters. The values are subgroups of size 5 taken from the production of 25 periods.

Subgroup:	1	2	3	4	5	6	7	8	9	10	11	12	13
	1.20	1.07	1.10	0.99	1.19	1.18	1.35	0.91	1.20	0.82	1.24	1.07	1.33
	0.96	1.03	1.27	1.29	1.10	1.25	1.04	1.15	1.15	1.07	1.20	1.16	1.25
	1.06	0.89	0.99	1.30	0.92	0.99	1.03	1.19	1.04	1.30	1.17	1.14	1.14
	1.26	1.09	0.95	1.12	1.01	1.33	0.99	1.03	1.26	1.43	1.04	1.25	1.15
	1.20	1.11	1.14	1.07	1.24	1.13	1.13	1.05	1.19	1.09	1.01	1.39	1.12
$\overline{X}$	1.14	1.04	1.09	1.15	1.09	1.18	1.11	1.07	1.17	1.14	1.13	1.20	1.20
R	0.30	0.22	0.32	0.31	0.32	0.34	0.36	0.28	0.22	0.61	0.23	0.32	0.21

Subgroup:	14	15	16	17	18	19	20	21	22	23	24	25
	1.22	1.13	1.00	1.07	1.09	1.11	1.08	1.14	1.31	0.95	1.12	1.03
	1.11	1.09	1.04	1.30	1.25	1.15	1.24	1.07	1.15	1.03	0.89	0.99
	1.06	1.15	0.97	1.13	1.14	1.17	1.03	1.11	1.23	1.06	1.12	1.12
	1.05	0.71	1.18	1.17	1.28	1.21	0.95	0.93	1.13	1.26	1.06	1.26
	1.29	1.07	1.16	1.15	1.10	1.04	1.16	1.06	1.04	1.28	1.02	1.09
$\overline{X}$	1.15	1.03	1.07	1.16	1.17	1.14	1.09	1.06	1.17	1.12	1.04	1.10
R	0.24	0.44	0.21	0.23	0.19	0.17	0.29	0.21	0.27	0.33	0.23	0.27

(a) Calculate a central control line of the control chart for the mean, its upper control limit, and its lower control limit.

(b) Comment on the state of control of the subgroup means.

18.4 Using the data of Exercise 18.3,

(a) Calculate a central control line of the control chart for the range, its upper control limit, and lower control limit.

(b) Comment on the state of control of the subgroup ranges.

18.5 Using the data of Exercise 18.3,

(a) Calculate a central control line of the control chart for the median, its upper control limit, and lower control limit.

(b) Comment on the state of control of the subgroup medians.

18.6 Using the data of Exercise 18.3,

(a) Calculate a central control line of the control chart for the range (where $\tilde{R}$ is the central line), its upper control limit, and lower control limit.

(b) Comment on the state of control of the subgroup ranges.

18.7 Given that $\bar{\sigma}$, the mean of the standard deviations of the 30 subgroups on page 694, is 1.30, construct $\bar{X}$- and σ-charts for the coded outside diameters of the crankshafts. Plot the means of the 30 subgroups on the $\bar{X}$-chart and comment on the state of control.

18.8 In order to determine whether or not a process producing silver castings is in control, 30 subgroups of size 6 are taken. The quality characteristic of interest is the weight of the silver castings, and it is found that $\bar{\bar{X}} = 3.126$ ounces and $\bar{R} = 0.009$ ounce.

(a) Estimate σ', the true standard deviation of the weights of the silver castings.

(b) Assuming that the process is in control, find upper and lower control limits for the subgroup means in terms of $\bar{\bar{X}}$ and σ'.

(c) Calculate the 3-sigma control limits for the mean in terms of $\bar{\bar{X}}$ and $A_2\bar{R}$, and compare answer with part (b) of this exercise.

(d) Assuming that the process is in control, find upper and lower control limits for the subgroup ranges.

(e) Using the results of part (a), within what limits would you expect 99.7 percent of all individual measurements to fall?

18.6

Control Charts for Attributes

To illustrate the construction of **control charts for attributes**, let us construct a **p-chart for fraction defective**. Suppose that a manufacturer produces small electric light bulbs of the type commonly used for Christmas tree lighting. A simple testing procedure determines whether the bulbs will light or not, and the tested bulbs are classified as either satisfactory or defective. To set up a control chart for the proportion of defective bulbs, called the **fraction defective**, samples of size 100 are tested from, say, each half-day's production until 30 such groups are on hand. It is not always possible for the samples to be exactly the same size, and when sample sizes differ, so do control limits. In practice, however, samples which vary in size by no more than plus or minus 25 percent are usually acceptable. Also, to establish control charts for attributes it is usually recommended that the size of the samples be 50 or more, and that there be 25 or more subgroups. Following are the results obtained in 30 samples:

Lot number	Sample size	Number of defectives	Fraction defective
1	100	5	0.05
2	100	2	0.02
3	100	4	0.04
4	100	6	0.06
5	100	3	0.03
6	100	2	0.02
7	100	0	0.00
8	100	9	0.09
9	100	15	0.15
10	100	3	0.03
11	100	2	0.02
12	100	2	0.02
13	100	0	0.00
14	100	6	0.06
15	100	3	0.03
16	100	4	0.04
17	100	2	0.02
18	100	0	0.00
19	100	5	0.05
20	100	4	0.04
21	100	2	0.02
22	100	1	0.01
23	100	1	0.01
24	100	2	0.02
25	100	1	0.01
26	100	0	0.00
27	100	1	0.01
28	100	2	0.02
29	100	2	0.02
30	100	1	0.01
Total	3,000	90	

Section 18.6 Control Charts for Attributes

To estimate the true proportion of defectives, we combine all of the samples, getting 90 defectives among 3,000 bulbs tested and an estimate of $90/3,000 = 0.03$. The symbol used for this estimate, which provides the central line for the control chart of the fraction defective, is $\bar{p}$. To construct 3-sigma control limits, we use the fact that when n, the sample size, is large, the sampling distribution of a proportion can be approximated closely with a normal curve having the mean p' and the standard deviation $\sqrt{\dfrac{p'(1-p')}{n}}$, where p' is the true proportion of defectives (see Exercise 13.30 on page 486). Substituting $\bar{p}$ for p', the upper and lower control limits become

Three-sigma control limits for fraction defective

$$\bar{p} \pm 3 \sqrt{\frac{\bar{p}(1-\bar{p})}{n}}$$

EXAMPLE 18.7   Calculate the 3-sigma control limits for fraction defective of the small electric light bulbs data of page 707. The control limits which we calculate here serve as the control limits of the control chart for fraction defective, Figure 18.4.

SOLUTION   From the above narrative following the table on page 707 we get $\bar{p} = \dfrac{90}{3,000} = 0.03$. Substituting this value into the formula for 3-sigma control limits for fraction defective,

$$\bar{p} \pm 3 \sqrt{\frac{\bar{p}(1-\bar{p})}{n}}$$

we get

$$0.03 + 3 \sqrt{\frac{(0.03)(0.97)}{100}} = 0.081 \text{ and } 0.03 - 3 \sqrt{\frac{(0.03)(0.97)}{100}}$$
$$= -0.021$$

For the latter value, -0.021, we will substitute zero since there can obviously not be a negative proportion of defectives. ∎

Converting these control limits as well as the central line into percentages, we get the control chart shown in Figure 18.4. As can be seen from this diagram, the points representing samples from lots 8 and 9 are above the upper control limits and, hence, indications of a possible lack of control. For

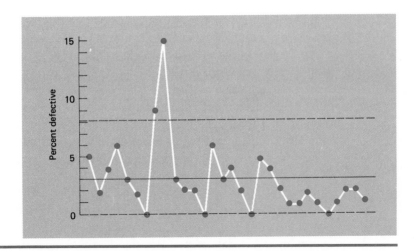

FIGURE 18.4
Control chart for
fraction defective

the sake of argument, let us suppose that an investigation revealed an assignable cause of variation present at these times, namely, a breakdown which the operator failed to record. For maintaining control in the future, a new control chart will have to be constructed, in the calculation of whose central line and control limits the two out-of-control samples will have to be eliminated. It will be left as an exercise for the reader to show that the remaining 28 samples yield a central line of 2.4 percent, an upper control limit of 6.9 percent, and a lower control limit of 0. It should also be observed that the remaining 28 points all fall within these new limits.

The interpretation of a control chart for fraction (or percentage) defective is the same as that of the control charts of the preceding sections. Any sample point falling outside the control limits is evidence of a possible lack of control inasmuch as the probability of getting such a value by chance is less than 0.003. It should be noted that in our illustration there seems to be a downward trend in the proportion of defectives, and this suggests that it would probably be wise to recalculate the control limits after more data have been obtained.

To simplify the work of the inspector who plots the necessary points on control charts, we could modify the chart of Figure 18.4 so that this person can directly plot the number, rather than the fraction or percentage of defectives. Multiplying the central line as well as the control limits by the sample size n, the central line of the control chart for the number of defectives becomes $n\bar{p}$ while the control limits become

Three-sigma
control limits for
number defective

$$n\bar{p} \pm 3\sqrt{n\bar{p}(1 - \bar{p})}$$

Section 18.6   Control Charts for Attributes

In the preceding formulas of this section we estimate p', the true proportion of defectives, with $\bar{p}$. If p' were known or specified, we could construct appropriate control limits and central lines with the same formulas as before, but with p' substituted for $\bar{p}$.

There are some quality control problems concerned with counting numbers of defectives which cannot be handled with the methods just described, because n, the sample size, is essentially unspecified though presumably very large. This happens, for example, if we count the number of imperfections in a piece of cloth, the number of blemishes in a sheet of paper, or the number of air bubbles in a piece of glass. Visualizing such a piece of cloth (sheet of paper, or piece of glass) as subdivided into many small squares, each being perfect or having an imperfection, we are faced with a situation in which the sampling distribution of the total number of imperfections can be approximated closely with a Poisson distribution, and we can construct a c chart for the number of defects. Letting c stand for the number of defects counted in 1 unit of cloth (paper, glass, or whatever) and $\bar{c}$ for the mean of the defects counted in several (usually 25 or more) such units of cloth, the central line of the **control chart for c** is $\bar{c}$ and the 3-sigma control limits are

Three-sigma control limits for $\bar{c}$

$$\bar{c} \pm 3\sqrt{\bar{c}}$$

These formulas are based on a normal-curve approximation to the Poisson distribution.

To illustrate this last technique, let us suppose that 25 pieces (units) of cloth contained, respectively, 2, 4, 3, 6, 5, 4, 8, 1, 4, 2, 3, 5, 6, 4, 2, 2, 1, 7, 5, 3, 2, 1, 5, 6, and 4 imperfections. Getting $\bar{c} = \dfrac{95}{25} = 3.80$, we find that the upper and lower control limits for the number of imperfections per unit of cloth becomes $3.80 + 3\sqrt{3.80} = 9.65$ and $3.80 - 3\sqrt{3.80} = -2.05$. The latter value will again be replaced by 0. The resulting control chart containing the points representing the given data is shown in Figure 18.5. Since none of the points falls outside the control limits, it may be presumed that the process is in a state of statistical control. If the given level of quality, on the average 3.8 imperfections per unit of cloth, is satisfactory, the control chart which we have constructed may be used in the future to keep a continual check on the process.

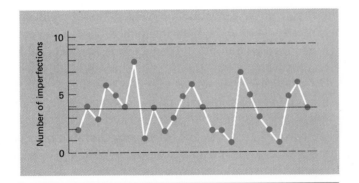

FIGURE 18.5
Control chart for c, the number of imperfections

18.7

Acceptance Sampling

Control chart techniques are by no means suited to all types of problems that arise in maintaining the quality of manufactured products. Suppose, for example, that a manufacturer has contracted to buy parts of a certain standard of quality and that these parts are shipped to him in large lots. For simplicity, let us confine our discussion of so-called **acceptance sampling** to **lot-by-lot sampling inspection** and let us suppose that the quality characteristic in which we are interested is an attribute, rather than a variable. Individual items in a lot are thus nondefective or defective depending on whether they possess a certain characteristic. The buyer of these parts is, of course, interested in making sure that when he accepts and pays for a lot, the product meets quality standards agreed upon. He would like to accept all good lots and reject all bad ones, using some inspection scheme to decide which lots are good and which ones are bad.[3] Naturally, the buyer is also interested in making this decision as economically as possible within the limitations imposed by his desire for accuracy.

In some cases it may be possible to inspect each item in a lot and to reject those which do not conform to specifications. This type of 100 percent inspection is called "screening," and although it may be appropriate in some instances, it is often impractical or impossible. If the testing is destructive,

---

[3]When we say that a lot is "good," this is not meant to imply that it cannot contain any defectives at all. Some defectives in submitted lots are generally inevitable, and the buyer, recognizing this, sets a practical limit on the proportion of defectives he is willing to accept at the price he is paying for the product.

100 percent inspection can obviously not be used. Moreover, screening is generally wasteful of both time and money, and, because neither men nor machines are infallible, it cannot even guarantee that all defective items will be eliminated.

As its name implies, lot-by-lot sampling inspection, which is widely used in industry, involves taking samples and deciding on the basis of the items they contain whether to accept or reject entire lots. Since generalizations from samples to lots (populations) cannot be expected to be infallible, there is the possibility that in lot-by-lot sampling inspection a good lot will be rejected or a bad lot accepted.

It stands to reason that both the producer and the consumer, the seller and the buyer, want to know the risks they are exposed to by an inspection plan before agreeing to it as an acceptance criterion. They want to know the probability of rejecting a good lot, and the probability of accepting a bad one, or, in other words, the probability of committing a Type I error (called the "producer's risk") and the probability of committing a Type II error (called the "consumer's risk").

If the producer and consumer specify these probabilities as well as the proportion of defectives above which a lot is considered to be bad and the proportion of defectives below which a lot is considered to be good, it is possible to construct inspection plans which will meet these requirements. For instance, if we wanted the probability of rejecting a lot with 2 percent or fewer defectives to be less than or equal to 0.05 and the probability of accepting a lot with 6 percent or more defectives to be also less than or equal to 0.05, we could refer to a suitable table and come up with the following inspection plan: take a sample of 235 items from each lot and accept it if the number of defectives is 8 or less, reject it if the number of defectives is 9 or more. (It is assumed here that the lots are so large that for all practical purposes they may be looked upon as infinite populations.)

Numerous tables are available for the construction of acceptance sampling plans based on such things as the acceptable quality level (AQL), the worst quality at which the consumer is willing to accept a lot with a specified high probability; the lot tolerance percent defective (LTPD), the quality above which there is only a specified small probability that a lot will be accepted; the average outgoing quality limit (AOQL), the maximum quality that can be expected in the long run when all rejected lots are subjected to 100 percent inspection, with all defectives removed and replaced with good items; and other criteria.

Reduction in the cost of inspection can be effected by using double or multiple sampling plans. It is also feasible at times to use an item-by-item sequential plan, deciding whether to accept, reject, or continue sampling after each item is inspected. All these plans are nowadays used quite widely in the inspection of the quality of manufactured products and also, with considerable success, in such nonmanufacturing problems as auditing and controlling clerical accuracy.

The term **single sampling** is used when we make an estimate or test a hypothesis on the basis of one sample whose size is determined before any data are actually collected. The disadvantage of single sampling lies in the fact that the predetermined sample size is often unnecessarily large. Let us suppose, for instance, that a public opinion poll wants to predict a gubernatorial election and that it is decided to use a sample of size 1,000. If the contest turned out to be very one sided, it could well be that a sample of size 200 or 400 would have sufficed.

The sampling plans we shall discuss in this section have the advantage that, since the data are collected in several stages, we can often reach decisions on the basis of smaller samples and, hence, at a lower cost. First, let us consider **double sampling**. To illustrate the meaning of this term, let us suppose that we want to inspect lots of manufactured products and that we decide to use the following scheme: we first take a random sample of size 50, accepting the lot if the number of defectives is 2 or less, rejecting the lot if the number of defectives is 7 or more, and taking an additional sample of size 100 if the number of defectives is 3, 4, 5, or 6. If the second sample is needed, we combine the two samples, accepting the lot if the total number of defectives is 6 or less, rejecting it if the total number of defectives is 7 or more.

In double sampling we thus begin with a relatively small sample and if the results are not decisive we supplement it with another. The advantage of this procedure is that if the quality of a lot is very high or very low, this will immediately become apparent on the basis of a relatively small first sample and the second sample will not be needed.

In a handbook of industrial statistics, the typical double sampling criterion which we described might be presented, formally, in the following fashion:

DOUBLE SAMPLING PLAN

| Sample | Sample size | Combined Samples | | |
		Size	Acceptance number	Rejection number
First	50	50	2	7
Second	100	150	6	7

In the double sampling plan shown here, first a sample of size $n = 50$ is taken. If the number of defectives is equal to or greater than 7, we reject the lot. If the number of defectives is more than 2 or fewer than 7, a second sample of size 100 is taken, and if the number of defectives from the total in the first and second sample is fewer than or equal to 6, the lot is accepted. If the number of defectives is 7 or more, the lot is rejected. The procedure ends at this point, since we do not use more than two samples in a double sampling plan.

A further refinement which can produce even greater savings consists of beginning with a small sample and adding further samples until a decision can be reached. Such a procedure is referred to as **multiple sampling**. In the industrial example, we might use the multiple sampling scheme shown in the following table:

MULTIPLE SAMPLING PLAN

		Combined Samples		
Sample	Sample size	Size	Acceptance number	Rejection number
First	20	20		3
Second	20	40	1	4
Third	20	60	2	5
Fourth	20	80	3	6
Fifth	20	100	5	7
Sixth	20	120	6	8
Seventh	20	140	7	8

We begin with a sample of size 20, rejecting the lot if the number of defectives is 3 or more and continuing with a second sample if the number of defectives is fewer than 3. The blank space in the acceptance number column indicates that no acceptance is possible in the first sample. If the second sample is needed, we combine the two samples, accepting the lot if the total number of defectives is 1 or less, rejecting it if the total number of defectives is 4 or more, and continuing with a third sample if the total number of defectives is 2 or 3. We thus proceed until the lot is either accepted or rejected.

Carrying the ideas presented in this section one step farther, we could take observations one at a time, deciding after each observation whether to accept the hypothesis which we are testing, whether to reject it, or whether to continue sampling. Such a procedure is referred to as **sequential sampling**. An appropriate sequential sampling plan for our industrial example would be similar in form to the double and multiple sampling plans, although we would have to give acceptance and rejection numbers corresponding to each additional observation. More detailed treatments of the sampling plans discussed in this section are referred to in the special topics section of the bibliography. Any of the plans discussed in this section may be set up in such a way that a hypothesis is tested against a given alternative with specified probabilities of committing Type I and Type II errors.

EXERCISES

(Exercises 18.9, 18.10, 18.13 and 18.14 are practice exercises. Their complete solutions are given on page 720.)

18.9 Recalculate the control limits for the small electric light bulbs data on page 707 after the two out-of-control samples are eliminated.

18.10 A manufacturer of transistors found the following number of defectives in 25 subgroups of 50 transistors: 3, 5, 4, 2, 3, 2, 7, 0, 2, 4, 2, 3, 4, 1, 2, 4, 8, 2, 4, 2, 6, 4, 3, 1, and 4. Construct a control chart for the fraction defective, plot the sample data on this chart, and comment on the state of control.

18.11 A manufacturer of charcoal briquets of the type used in barbecue grills desires to establish control of the production process at a level $p' = 0.05$. Using this value of p', construct a control chart for the number of defectives in subgroups of size 200. Given that 20 consecutive samples of this size contained 10, 16, 20, 3, 4, 12, 12, 14, 12, 14, 11, 13, 9, 8, 9, 8, 7, 8, 10, and 5 defectives, plot these sample values on the chart and comment on the possibility of establishing control at the desired level.

18.12 For the past three months, a production department completed 500 units a day. The average number of defective parts was 30, though on some days there were only 15 defectives and on others there were as many as 46. Is this evidence of a possible lack of control? Base your argument on 3-sigma control limits.

18.13 The following are the number of defects noted in the final inspection of 30 bolts of woolen cloth: 0, 3, 1, 4, 2, 2, 1, 3, 5, 0, 2, 0, 0, 1, 2, 4, 3, 0, 0, 0, 1, 2, 4, 5, 0, 9, 4, 10, 0, and 3. Construct a control chart for c, the number of defects, plot the given data, and comment on the state of control.

18.14 Suppose an automobile manufacturer receives a large shipment of hubcaps and decides to accept or reject the shipment based on the multiple sampling plan illustrated on page 714, with sample size $n = 20$.
(a) If the first sample contains three defective hubcaps, should we accept or reject the shipment?
(b) If we must take an additional sample and it contains two defects, should we accept or reject the shipment?
(c) If we must take an additional sample and it contains no defects, should we accept or reject the shipment?

18.8

Checklist of Key Terms

18.9

Review Exercises

18.15 (a) Construct $\overline{X}$- and R-charts for the uncoded data of the thicknesses of rubber coating applied to wire given in Exercise 18.3 on page 705.

(b) Plot the uncoded data on the charts of part (a) and comment on the state of control.

18.16 To establish a control chart for the attribute, loose frying pan handles, a kitchenware manufacturer inspected 200 frying pans each day for 25 days. Following are the results obtained:

Lot number	Sample size	Number of defectives
1	200	9
2	200	8
3	200	6
4	200	6
5	200	4
6	200	7
7	200	10
8	200	9
9	200	8
10	200	5
11	200	8
12	200	16
13	200	5
14	200	12
15	200	8
16	200	9
17	200	8
18	200	7
19	200	9
20	200	13
21	200	4
22	200	6
23	200	9
24	200	7
25	200	7

(a) Calculate the proportion defective, and determine the center line and control limits of a control chart for fraction defective.

(b) Construct a control chart for the fraction defective and plot the 25 subgroups.

(c) Comment on the state of control.

(d) Eliminate any out-of-control lots (subgroups) and calculate a new central line and control limits.

18.17   It is proposed to establish control over a machine which turns out some 5,000 nails per hour. Subgroups of 10 nails are taken from each hour's production, and the lengths of the nails are measured. Following are the means and ranges (in inches) obtained in 20 subgroups:

Subgroup:	1	2	3	4	5	6	7
$\overline{X}$	1.524	1.520	1.488	1.521	1.505	1.510	1.495
R	0.039	0.028	0.035	0.033	0.041	0.025	0.030

Subgroup:	8	9	10	11	12	13	14
$\overline{X}$	1.491	1.491	1.482	1.475	1.478	1.522	1.531
R	0.037	0.028	0.043	0.032	0.027	0.041	0.038

Subgroup:	15	16	17	18	19	20
$\overline{X}$	1.531	1.502	1.490	1.465	1.529	1.444
R	0.028	0.040	0.054	0.060	0.020	0.029

Calculate control limits for $\overline{X}$ and R, plot the given data, and determine whether or not the process may be considered to be in control.

18.18 Tests of the breaking strength of a certain type of worsted yarn yielded the following (coded) data. The values given here are computed from subgroups of size 10 taken from the production of 30 consecutive periods.

Subgroup:	1	2	3	4	5	6	7	8	9	10
$\overline{X}$	9.12	8.57	9.43	7.81	8.96	9.32	8.34	7.81	9.23	10.36
σ	1.19	7.00	1.64	1.13	1.29	2.19	0.79	1.14	1.20	1.10

Subgroup:	11	12	13	14	15	16	17	18	19	20
$\overline{X}$	10.52	7.76	8.20	8.97	8.54	9.06	8.56	7.73	9.31	8.56
σ	1.78	0.91	0.93	1.30	0.89	1.02	1.45	0.80	1.62	0.71

Subgroup:	21	22	23	24	25	26	27	28	29	30
$\overline{X}$	9.53	7.49	9.07	7.85	8.14	8.81	8.43	9.12	7.95	8.10
σ	2.30	1.01	0.78	1.12	0.84	1.00	1.12	0.84	0.65	1.07

Construct $\overline{X}$- and σ- charts, plot the given data, and determine to what extent the process is under statistical control. If there are out-of-control samples, eliminate them from the data and recalculate the control values.

18.19 The following data refer to measurements of the inside diameter of short lengths of copper tubing. The values given are computed from subgroups of 7 taken from the production of 29 consecutive periods. Data are in hundredths of an inch.

Subgroup:	1	2	3	4	5	6	7	8	9	10
$\tilde{X}$	26	25	27	24	24	23	24	26	23	25
R	9	8	8	6	7	4	6	4	3	4

Subgroup:	11	12	13	14	15	16	17	18	19	20
$\tilde{X}$	24	23	25	29	26	25	27	24	24	23
R	6	6	3	6	3	4	5	10	4	8

Subgroup:	21	22	23	24	25	26	27	28	29
$\tilde{X}$	24	26	23	25	25	24	27	23	28
R	5	12	6	4	5	7	4	5	6

Construct $\tilde{X}$- and R-charts, plot the given data, and determine if there are any out-of-control samples.

18.20 Comment on the state of control of the $\overline{X}$-charts in Figure 18.6.

18.21 Suppose that a clothing manufacturer receives a large shipment of zippers and decides to accept or reject the shipment based on the double sampling plan shown on page 713, with sample size $n = 50$ for the first sample and $n = 100$ for the second sample.

(a) If the first sample contains four defective zippers, what should the clothing manufacturer do?

(b) If we must take an additional sample and it contains two defective zippers, should the manufacturer accept or reject the shipment?

(c) Suppose the first sample contained two defective zippers, should the manufacturer take an additional sample?

(d) Suppose the first sample contained seven defective zippers, should the manufacturer take an additional sample?

18.22 Suppose that a manufacturer of table lamps decides to accept or reject a shipment of lamp bases based on the multiple sampling plan shown on page 714, with sample size $n = 20$.

(a) If the first sample ($n = 20$) contains no defective lamp bases, should the manufacturer accept the shipment, reject it, or take another sample?

(b) If the first sample ($n = 20$) contains one defective lamp base, what should the manufacturer do?

(c) Following part (b) of this exercise where the first sample ($n = 20$) contains one defective lamp base, suppose the manufacturer takes another sample of the same size and gets no additional defective lamp bases. What should the manufacturer do?

(d) Following part (b) of this exercise where the first sample contains one

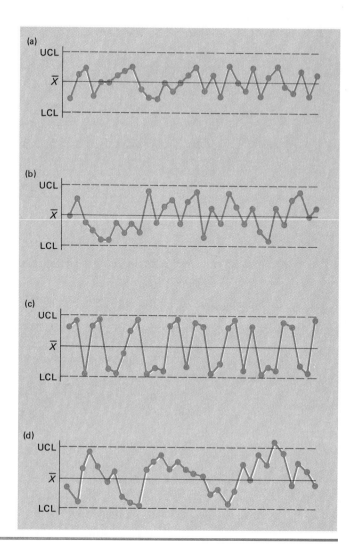

FIGURE 18.6
$\bar{X}$-charts

defective lamp base, suppose the manufacturer takes another sample of the same size and gets three defective lamp bases. What should the manufacturer do?

18.23 Use a computer package and the data of Example 18.1 on page 695 to
(a) verify the $\bar{\bar{X}}$ for the central line of the control chart for the mean
(b) verify the upper and lower limits for the mean
(c) construct the control chart for the mean and plot the sample means.

Note: The computer package uses a methodology that may yield slightly different answers from those obtained manually.

18.24 Use a computer package and the data of Example 18.2 on page 696 to
(a) verify the $\bar{R}$ for the central line of the control chart for the range

(b) verify the upper and lower control limits for the range

(c) construct the control chart for the range and plot the sample ranges.

Note: The computer package uses a methodology that may yield slightly different answers from those obtained manually.

 18.25 Based upon the computer printouts of the control charts for the above Exercises 18.23 and 18.24, is the process in a state of statistical control? That is, does it appear that the only kind of variation present is chance variation?

18.10

Solutions of Practice Exercises

18.1 The central line for $\overline{X}$ is the mean of the 20 $\overline{X}$'s, which is 1.4997.

The central line for R is the mean of the 20 R's, which is 0.0354.

The control limits for $\overline{X}$ are $1.4997 \pm 0.577(0.0354)$, namely 1.4793 and 1.5201.

The control limits for R are $0(0.0354) = 0$ and $2.115(0.0354) = 0.0749$.

18.2 The central line for $\overline{X}$ is the mean of the 25 $\overline{X}$'s, which is 85.600.

The central line for σ is the mean of the 25 σ's, which is 11.000.

The control limits for $\overline{X}$ are $\overline{\overline{X}} \pm A_1\overline{\sigma} = 85.60 \pm 1.028(11.00)$, namely, 74.292 and 96.908.

The control limits for σ are $B_3\overline{\sigma} = 0.284(11.000) = 3.124$ and $B_4\overline{\sigma} = 1.716(11.000) = 18.876$.

18.5 (a) The medians of the 25 subgroups are 1.20, 1.07, 1.10, 1.12, 1.10, 1.18, 1.04, 1.05, 1.19, 1.09, 1.17, 1.16, 1.15, 1.11, 1.09, 1.04, 1.15, 1.14, 1.15, 1.08, 1.07, 1.15 1.06, 1.06, and 1.09. Arranging the subgroup medians according to size, we have 1.04, 1.04, 1.05, 1.06, 1.06, 1.07, 1.07, 1.08, 1.09, 10.9, 1.09, 1.10, 1.10, 1.11, 1.12, 1.14, 1.15, 1.15, 1.15, 1.15, 1.16, 1.17, 1.18, 1.19, and 1.20, and the value of the middle item is 1.10. Thus $\tilde{\tilde{X}} = 1.10$ is the central line for the median.

The subgroup ranges are provided in the exercise, and arranging them according to size, we have 0.17, 0.19, 0.21, 0.21, 0.21, 0.22, 0.22, 0.23, 0.23, 0.23, 0.24, 0.27, 0.27, 0.28, 0.29, 0.30, 0.31, 0.32, 0.32, 0.32, 0.33, 0.34, 0.36, 0.44, and 0.61, and the value of the middle item is 0.27. Thus, $\tilde{R} = 0.27$ is the central line for the range. Substituting $\tilde{\tilde{X}} = 1.10$, $\tilde{R} = 0.27$, and $\tilde{A}_2 = 0.71$ (for sample size 5 from table of constants for medians) into the formula for 3-sigma control limits for the median, we get $\tilde{\tilde{X}} + \tilde{A}_2\tilde{R} = 1.10 + 0.71(0.27) = 1.29$ and $\tilde{\tilde{X}} - \tilde{A}_2\tilde{R} = 1.10 - 0.71(0.27) = 0.91$.

(b) The medians of all the subgroups are in control.

18.9 Lot numbers 8 and 9 are out of control. The central line is the mean of the remaining lots after lots 8 and 9 have been eliminated, which is 0.0236. The control limits are $0.0236 \pm 3 \sqrt{\dfrac{(0.0236)(0.9764)}{100}}$, namely, 0 and 0.0691.

18.10 Since the total number of items sampled is $25 \cdot 50 = 1{,}250$ and the total number of defectives is 82, the central line is $\dfrac{82}{1{,}250} = 0.0656$. The control limits are $0.0656 \pm 3 \sqrt{\dfrac{(0.0656)(0.934)}{50}}$, namely, 0 and 0.171.

For the fraction defective we divide the number of defectives in each subgroup by 50, getting 0.06, 0.10, 0.08, 0.04, 0.06, 0.04, 0.14, 0.00, 0.04, 0.08, 0.04, 0.06, 0.08, 0.02, 0.04, 0.08, 0.16, 0.04, 0.08, 0.04, 0.12, 0.08, 0.06, 0.02, and 0.08. All lots sampled are in control.

18.13 The central line for c is the mean number of defects in the 30 bolts of woolen cloth, which is 2.37. The control limits are $2.37 \pm 3\sqrt{2.37}$, namely, 0 and 6.99. The bolts with 9 and 10 defects are above the upper control limit.

18.14 Use the multiple sampling plan to (a) reject, (b) reject, and (c) reject.

Index Numbers

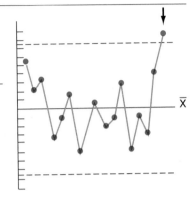

Index numbers are used to measure, or indicate, how much something has changed from one time to another or how something compares with something else. For instance, the following information was obtained from a detailed price index published by the U.S. Department of Commerce concerning prices in the United States during the first half of the year 1991. Prices increased at an annual rate of 2.7 percent, which was modest by comparison with a 6.1 percent increase for the year 1990. College tuition rose by a very substantial 10.9 percent, while personal expenditures such as legal service fees, financial services, and funeral expenses rose by a slightly smaller annual rate of 8.7 percent. The housing index, which had previously experienced great increases, declined to a moderate 3.5 percent increase. But petroleum-based energy products (fuel oil and motor fuels) incurred serious declines, fuel oil prices dropping precipitously by 44.7 percent and motor fuel declining by 29.1 percent. It was, therefore, not surprising to note that airline fares, which are affected by fuel costs, declined by 15.5 percent. Food prices advanced by 5.0 percent, partially because the price of oranges (other crops were also affected) soared by 37.2 percent in January, the largest monthly increase ever recorded for this index. Drastic shortages of these food products resulted from an exceptionally severe freeze in California during the month of December.

Following some preliminary remarks on index numbers in Section 19.1, we shall discuss in Section 19.2 the basic problems which arise in their construction. In Sections 19.3 and 19.4, we shall present some general index number formulas and then devote Section 19.5 to a discussion of some very important indexes and Section 19.6, the concluding section, to some special applications of index numbers.

19.1

Some Preliminary Remarks

Percentages that compare two things—such as the percentage that compares the state and local taxes that Americans paid in 1991 and 1992—are simple examples of index numbers. We call them "simple" because there are also index numbers which are intended to indicate changes in such complicated phenomena as industrial production, business activity, stock prices, transportation costs, consumer confidence, consumer buying plans, and in the prices consumers pay for the "basic necessities" of life (food, housing, energy, and health care) and also for all goods and services. In fact, there are sometimes many different indicators of the same phenomenon. There are, for instance at least 16 different indicators of the condition of stocks on the New York Stock Exchange, or of the direction the market is heading, and many different indicators of the state of the nation's business in general. Among the latter indexes, some which tend to anticipate, or lead, future movements of business activity are of absolutely basic importance to both government and business. Indeed, the Bureau of Economic Analysis, in the U.S. Department of Commerce, constructs a single composite "Index of Leading Economic Indicators" which measures the overall change in such individual leading indicators as contracts and orders for new plants and equipment, the average workweek, the layoff rate, building permits, sensitive raw material prices, stock prices, new orders for consumer goods, and the nation's money supply and its total liquid assets.

The principal use of index numbers in business and economics is to make comparisons between two different time periods, and many companies construct indexes to measure changes through time in their own raw material, labor, energy, and transportation costs. However, index numbers can also be used to make other kinds of comparisons, such as a comparison of the 1992 warranty costs of automobiles built in one assembly plant with the 1992 warranty costs of automobiles built in another, and a comparison of the 1992 production of cotton in Texas with the 1992 production of cotton in California.

Although index numbers are commonly associated with business and economics, they are also widely used in other fields. Psychologists measure intelligence quotients which are essentially index numbers comparing a person's intelligence with that of an average for the person's age, health authorities prepare indexes to show changes in the adequacy of hospital and other health care facilities, state boards of education construct indexes to measure the effectiveness of school systems, sociologists construct indexes measuring population changes, the National Weather Service has devised a "discomfort index" to measure the combined effect of heat and humidity on individuals, and so on.

In recent years the use of index numbers has been extended to so many fields of human activity that some knowledge of these measures really belongs under the heading of "general education." Index numbers showing changes in consumer prices, and the effect of these changes on purchasing power, are of tremendous importance to all consumers, and the Bureau of Labor Statistics' two Consumer Price Indexes are watched by many. The movements of these indexes are vital to millions of workers covered by collective bargaining agreements containing escalator clauses which provide for automatic wage (and sometimes pension benefit) increases when the appropriate Consumer Price Index rises by a specified amount, and to millions of others, too—social security beneficiaries, retired military and government personnel, postal workers, and food stamp recipients, for instance—whose incomes are, by statute, affected by changes in the level of these indexes. Index numbers are of great concern to farmers whose subsidies depend on the Parity Index of the federal government, as well as the parties in alimony agreements and the recipients of trust fund payments, which by "indexing" have been made to vary with an index of the purchasing power of the dollar. Serious suggestions have recently been made that not only wages and salaries, but taxes, interest rates, and various other economic realities be tied to a consumer price index. Aside from major problems connected with the exact nature of the index, or indexes, to be used as the escalator in such a system, many basic questions, all of them outside the scope of our study, arise as to the short- and long-range effect—good or bad—such a move would have on the economy.

19.2

Basic Problems

Like other statistical measures, index numbers are usually constructed to serve definite purposes. Sometimes, the stated purpose of an index is such that the only problem which arises in its construction is that of locating the necessary data. For instance, in a research report it was desired to show, in compact form, the year-to-year changes in the sales of major U.S. corporations. As we will see in Chapter 21, there are numerous private and public sources of general and highly specialized business data. But for this research report, the data were taken from a study of the 500 largest industrial corporations, published annually by *Fortune,* a highly regarded financial magazine. For a certain year (1990) sales of these 500 corporations were reported to be $2,304.3 billion, and for the preceding year they were reported to be $2,164.8 billion, so their index was

$$\text{index} = \frac{2,304.3}{2,164.8} = 1.064 \qquad \text{or} \qquad 106.4 \text{ percent}$$

In contrast, there are many situations in which some very complex problems arise as soon as the purpose of an index has been stated. The most critical among these are (1) the availability and comparability of data, (2) the selection of items to be included in the comparison(s), (3) the choice of time periods (localities and so on) to be compared, (4) the selection of appropriate weights measuring the relative importance of the various items which enter into the index, and (5) the choice of a suitable formula for combining the data into an index number. Some aspects of these basic problems are discussed in the paragraphs that follow.

The availability and comparability of data.   It is hardly necessary to point out that comparisons cannot be made and index numbers cannot be constructed unless the required data can be collected. On various occasions research workers have found that sales data needed by brand were available only by type of merchandise, that insurance losses were given per risk and not per claim, and so on. The problem of availability of data also arises if we want to make a comparison of commodity prices in 1992 with those of 1914. Television sets, computers, some major appliances, contact lenses, frozen foods, transistorized devices, and many other items now widely used were not sold commercially in 1914.

The question of comparability of data can also be quite troublesome. In congressional hearings, some labor organizations and others have complained that, to some extent, the consumer price indexes reflect deterioration in quality rather than an actual change in prices. It does not matter here whether this criticism is valid, but we must always make sure that in price comparisons the prices are actually comparable; that is, they must be the prices of goods and services which, for all practical purposes, are identical in quality. If they are not, this must be taken into account in some way.

The comparability of statistical data may also be questioned when there is a possibility of confusion due to the use of different definitions or when parts of the data come from different sources. For instance, it is very confusing to read in the same edition of a financial paper that the nation's money supply in July was up 5 percent from the year earlier figure, and also that it was up 10.2 percent from the year earlier figure. Actually, both statements are correct, but in the first the money supply is understood to be currency in circulation plus money on deposit in checking accounts, (what the Federal Reserve calls M-1), whereas in the second the supply includes also savings accounts and other bank time deposits except large certificates of deposit and nonbank thrift deposits (what the Federal Reserve calls M-3).

So far as data from different sources are concerned, consider the following table, based on figures published by the United Nations, which shows the importers' and exporters' versions of how many metric tons of four commodities the second country received from the first in a given year:

Commodity	Exporters' data		Importers' data	
Butter	France	5,005	United Kingdom	3,787
Eggs	Denmark	63,534	West Germany	51,273
Coffee	El Salvador	38,153	United States	27,693
Wheat	Canada	288,535	Netherlands	164,578

These figures were deliberately selected to illustrate our point, but major discrepancies are often found in employment and production figures quoted by different sources, in sickness and accident data supplied by different agencies, and in other kinds of data. Whether such instances are the exception or the rule, they illustrate the seriousness of the problem of locating relevant and comparable data.

The selection of items to be included in the comparison. If an index is designed for the special purpose of comparing the price of a commodity at two different times, there is no question as to what figures should be included. However, the situation is entirely different in the construction of general-purpose indexes; for instance, those designed to measure general changes in consumer prices. It is physically impossible to include in such a comparison all commodities and all services, and to include, furthermore, all prices at which these commodities and services are traded in every single transaction throughout the country. The only thing index makers or sponsors can do is to take samples in such a way that, in their professional judgment, the items and transactions included adequately reflect the overall phenomenon being described. For example, one of the Consumer Price Indexes we spoke of is based on 382 entry-level items which play a significant role in the typical budget of persons belonging to a certain population group. These index items constitute a sample of the many goods and services people buy each day, and their prices are collected from a sample of the nation's cities and of the sellers in these cities.

The choice of time periods that are to be compared. If an index number is designed for the specific purpose of comparing 1992 figures with those of say, 1982, it is customary to refer to 1992 as the **given year** and to 1982 as the **base year**, indicating the latter by writing 1982 = 100. In general, the year or period whose data are to be compared with those of another period is called the given year or **given period**, and the year or period with reference to which the comparison is made is called the base year or **base period**.

The choice of a base year or base period presents no problem if an index is to be constructed to make a specific comparison. So far as general-purpose indexes describing complex phenomena are concerned, it is desirable to base the comparison on a relatively recent period of relative economic stability— if such a thing exists. The reason for choosing a stable period is that during times of abnormal economic conditions (during a war, for example), there may be no free trading of some commodities, there may be black markets, and the buying habits of the public may be irregular due to shortages of products that would otherwise be readily available. A major reason for choosing a relatively recent period is that it facilitates the construction of series for important new products (desktop computers, cellular telephones, or recordings on compact disks, for example) for which price and production data are not available for earlier years.

With some exceptions, the federal government has made it a practice to update standard reference base periods of its various published index numbers about every 10 years. Beginning with January 1987, for example, a new standard reference base period with 1982–1984 = 100 was established for the important consumer price indexes (to be discussed in Section 19.5). The selection of a base period does not imply that the period was "normal," since a base year or period is merely a convenient and necessary reference point if comparisons are to be made.

The choice of appropriate weights. There are many situations, particularly in index-number construction, in which figures cannot be meaningfully averaged without paying due attention to the relative importance of each item. Suppose, for example, that a manufacturer wants to construct an index comparing the 1992 and 1988 prices of replacement parts required for machines of a certain type and that he chooses parts AX345 and AX765 to represent the

Chapter 19   Index Numbers

changes in these prices. Suppose, further, that for part AX345 the index with 1988 = 100 is ($5.40/$3.60) · 100 = 150 percent, and for part AX765 it is ($9.60/$4.80) · 100 = 200 percent. On the basis of these figures alone, we might assert that the price of replacement parts in 1992 was (150 + 200)/2 = 175 percent of what it was in 1988. This result would be valid if the same numbers of each of the two parts were replaced, but if in 1992 the company actually replaced, say, 40 times as many parts AX765 as parts AX345, then the two price changes are clearly not equally important. Generally speaking, valid comparisons of price changes require that prices be weighted in some way so as to account for their relative importance in practice. As it is virtually impossible to explain weighting schemes without referring to specific index-number formulas, we shall defer discussion of this matter until we study weighted index numbers.

The choice of a suitable formula. There are various ways in which the average of a set of data can be described, and there are also various ways in which relative changes in prices or quantities can be described. In the next two sections we shall treat some of the simpler index-number formulas, and this discussion should make it clear that any choice among different formulas must ultimately depend on practical considerations and on some of their mathematical niceties. In the notation used in the remainder of this chapter, we refer to index numbers as I, to base-year prices as p_0, to given-year prices as p_n, to base-year quantities as q_0, and to given-year quantities as q_n.

19.3

Unweighted Index Numbers

To illustrate some of the simpler methods used in index-number construction, let us begin with the **simple aggregative method**. The formula for the index it leads to, called a **simple aggregative index**, is

*Simple
aggregative index*

$$I = \frac{\sum p_n}{\sum p_0} \cdot 100$$

where $\sum p_n$ is the sum of the given-year prices, $\sum p_0$ is the sum of the base-year prices, and the ratio of the first to the second is multiplied by 100 to express the index as a percentage.

EXAMPLE 19.1   The prices shown in the following table are the prices in dollars per pound of four nonferrous metals in the years 1988 and in 1989.

| | Price (cents per pound) | |
Metal	1988	1989
Aluminum	110	88
Copper	121	131
Lead	37	39
Zinc	60	82

Construct a simple aggregative index comparing the year 1989 prices of these nonferrous metals with their prices in the year 1988.

SOLUTION   Dividing the sum of the year 1989 prices by the sum of the year 1988 prices and multiplying by 100, we get

$$I = \frac{88 + 131 + 39 + 82}{110 + 121 + 37 + 60} \cdot 100$$

$$= \frac{340}{328} \cdot 100$$

$$= 103.7 \text{ percent}$$

This tells us that the combined-year 1989 prices of the four nonferrous metals are 103.7 percent of their combined prices in year 1988 or, in other words, that prices increased by 3.7 percent over the year. The usual way to express this change is to say that with 1988 = 100, the index stood at 103.7 for the year 1989.   ■

A simple aggregative index is easy to construct and easy to understand, but it does not meet a criterion of adequacy called the **units test**. This test requires that the index yield the same results regardless of the units for which the prices of the various items are quoted. For instance, if in the preceding example we compare the combined prices of 100 pounds of aluminum, 2,000 pounds of copper, 1,000 pounds of lead, and 500 pounds of zinc at the same two time periods as before, we find that the index stands at 109.6 instead of 103.7. Largely for this reason, simple aggregative indexes are not widely used today.

Another way to compare two sets of prices is to first calculate a separate index for each item and then average all these indexes, or **price relatives**, using some measure of central location. If we use the arithmetic mean, we get the **arithmetic mean of price relatives**; symbolically, its formula is

Arithmetic mean of price relatives

$$I = \frac{\sum \frac{p_n}{p_0} \cdot 100}{k}$$

where k is the number of items whose price relatives are being combined into an index. In principle, price relatives can be averaged with any measure of central location, but in practice the arithmetic mean and the geometric mean are most widely used.

EXAMPLE 19.2   Based on the data of Example 19.1, construct an arithmetic mean of price relatives measuring the overall change in the prices of the four nonferrous metals from the year 1988 to the year 1989.

SOLUTION   Dividing the 1989 price of each metal by its 1988 price and multiplying by 100, we get

Metal	Price relative
Aluminum	$\frac{88}{110} \cdot 100 = 80.0$
Copper	$\frac{131}{121} \cdot 100 = 108.3$
Lead	$\frac{39}{37} \cdot 100 = 105.4$
Zinc	$\frac{82}{60} \cdot 100 = 136.7$

Then, calculating the arithmetic mean of these price relatives, we get

$$I = \frac{80.0 + 108.3 + 105.4 + 136.7}{4} = 107.6 \text{ percent} \quad \blacksquare$$

It is a matter of historical interest that the earliest index number on record is an arithmetic mean of price relatives. In the middle of the eighteenth century, G. R. Carli, an Italian, calculated the effect of the import of silver on the value of money, using a formula like the one just given to compare the 1750 prices of oil, grain, and wine with those of the year 1500.

The formulas we have given in this section are all price index formulas. However, if we replace the p's by q's we get **quantity indexes**—index numbers which compare, for example, quantities put into trade during one period with those put into trade during another period.

19.4

Weighted Index Numbers

Today the need for weighting index items has been almost universally accepted, and few indexes are actually computed without using weights. Prior to 1914, the Wholesale Price Index (precursor of Producer Price Index) of the Bureau of Labor Statistics was computed as an arithmetic mean of the price relatives of about 250 commodities. As a result of an important study by W. C. Mitchell in 1915, which has affected index-number construction since that time, the index was changed to a weighted index. Among the important government indexes only the daily Index of Spot Market Prices is still calculated as an unweighted (geometric) mean of price relatives.

In order to construct an index number which reflects differences in importance of the index items, we note first that the importance of changes in the price of a commodity in trade or use is best determined by the quantity of the commodity which is bought or sold, or produced or consumed. Hence, we can construct an index measuring the overall change in the index items by weighting the prices of the items by the corresponding quantities produced in the base year, the given year, or in some other year or period. Such an index, which is 100 times the ratio of the weighted mean of the given year prices to the weighted mean of the base-year prices, is called a **weighted aggregative index**. If we use base-year weights, it is also called a **Laspeyres index**, named after the statistician who first suggested its use. Canceling the denominators of the two weighted means, $\sum q_0$, we can write the general formula for a Laspeyres index as

Laspeyres index

$$I = \frac{\sum p_n q_0}{\sum p_0 q_0} \cdot 100$$

Clearly, this kind of index reflects changes in prices alone—the same quantities of goods (the base-year quantities) are priced at two different times, and any difference between the given-year total (the quantity in the numerator of the index) and the base-year total (the quantity in the denominator of the index) must be accounted for by changes in price.

EXAMPLE 19.3   The following table shows farm prices (per bushel) and quantities produced (in billions of bushels) of three kinds of grain produced in the United States during the years 1987, 1988, and 1989.

	Price per bushel			Quantity of bushels (in billions)		
	1987	1988	1989	1987	1988	1989
Corn	1.94	2.55	2.35	7.1	4.9	7.5
Wheat	2.57	3.72	3.72	2.1	1.8	2.0
Oats	1.56	2.61	1.49	0.4	0.2	0.4

With 1988 as the base year, and using base-year quantities as weights, construct a weighted aggregative (Laspeyres) index which measures the change in the prices of these grains from 1988 to 1989.

SOLUTION   Substituting into the Laspeyres formula,

$$I = \frac{\sum p_n q_0}{\sum p_0 q_0} \cdot 100$$

we get

$$I = \frac{(2.35)(4.9) + (3.72)(1.8) + (1.49)(0.2)}{(2.55)(4.9) + (3.72)(1.8) + (2.61)(0.2)} \cdot 100 = 93.9 \qquad ■$$

We cannot construct a price index by weighting the given-year prices with given-year quantities and the base-year prices with base-year quantities. Since $\sum p_n q_n$ is the total value of the goods in the given year and $\sum p_0 q_0$ is the total value of the goods in the base year, the ratio of $\sum p_n q_n$ to $\sum p_0 q_0$ reflects changes in value rather than changes in price; that ratio is, in fact, a **value index**. We can, however, use given-year quantities to weight both the base-year prices and the given-year prices (that is, price the given-year quantities at the two different times), and construct a weighted aggregative index with given-year weights. Sometimes called a **Paasche index**, the formula is

Paasche index

$$I = \frac{\sum p_n q_n}{\sum p_0 q_n} \cdot 100$$

EXAMPLE 19.4   Using the data of Example 19.3 with 1988 as the base year, and using given-year quantities as weights, construct a weighted aggregative (Paasche) index which measures the change in the price of these grains from 1988 to 1989.

SOLUTION   Substituting the data of Example 19.3 into the Paasche formula,

$$I = \frac{\sum p_n q_n}{\sum p_0 q_n} \cdot 100$$

we get

$$I = \frac{(2.35)(7.5) + (3.72)(2.0) + (1.49)(0.4)}{(2.55)(7.5) + (3.72)(2.0) + (2.61)(0.4)} \cdot 100 = 92.9 \qquad \blacksquare$$

Most of the important index numbers constructed by the federal government are published **in series**, that is, regularly every day, every week, every month, or every year. For these it would be highly impractical to use the Paasche formula, because new quantity weights would be required for each new day, week, month, or year. An index that is currently in great favor is the **fixed-weight aggregative index**, whose formula is

Fixed-weight aggregative index

$$I = \frac{\sum p_n q_a}{\sum p_0 q_a} \cdot 100$$

where the weights are quantities for some other period than the base year 0 or the given year n.

In addition to weighted aggregative indexes of the sort we have discussed, we can also obtain weighted indexes by weighting the individual price relatives. The formula for a **weighted arithmetic mean of price relatives** is

Weighted arithmetic mean of price relatives

$$I = \frac{\sum \dfrac{p_n}{p_0} \cdot w}{\sum w} \cdot 100$$

where the w's are suitable weights assigned to the individual price relatives of the index items, which are written as proportions, not as percentages.

Since the importance of the relative change in the price of a commodity is most reasonably reflected by the total amount of money spent on it, it is customary to use **value weights** for the w's of the last formula. This raises the question of whether to use the values (prices times quantities) of the base year, those of the given year, or perhaps some other fixed-value weights. Actually, if base-year value weights $p_0 q_0$ are used, we do not get a new index, for with these weights, the formula just given reduces to that of a weighted aggregative index with base-year weights, the Laspeyres index.

EXAMPLE 19.5   Using the data of Example 19.3 on page 733 with 1988 as the base year and employing year 1987 value weights, construct a weighted arithmetic mean of price relatives index which measures the change in the price of these grains from 1988 to 1989.

SOLUTION   Calculating first the price relatives $\dfrac{p_n}{p_0} = \dfrac{p_{89}}{p_{88}}$ and the value weights $w = p_a q_a = p_{87} q_{87}$ (in billions of dollars), we get price relative for corn, $\dfrac{2.35}{2.55} = 0.92$; price relative for wheat, $\dfrac{3.72}{3.72} = 1.00$; price relative for oats, $\dfrac{1.49}{2.61} = 0.57$; value weight for corn, $(1.94)(7.1) = 13.77$; value weight for wheat, $(2.57)(2.1) = 5.40$; and value weight for oats, $(1.56)(0.4) = 0.62$. Then, substituting these values into the formula for weighted arithmetic mean of price relatives,

$$I = \frac{\sum \dfrac{p_n}{p_0} \cdot w}{\sum w} \cdot 100$$

we get

$$I = \frac{(0.92)(13.77) + (1.00)(5.40) + (0.57)(0.62)}{13.77 + 5.40 + 0.62} \cdot 100 = 93.1 \quad \blacksquare$$

We now have three measures of, or indicators of change in, the price of these grains produced in the United States from 1988 to 1989: the Laspeyres index of 93.9, the Paasche index of 92.9, and the weighted arithmetic mean of price relatives index (with 1987 value weights) of 93.1. This illustrates the fact that different methods applied to measurements of the same phenomenon can lead to different results. The differences here may not seem large, but, in practice, where often millions of dollars ride on a change of less than one point (as in labor-management agreements containing escalator clauses) the question of choosing an appropriate index is a serious one indeed.

EXERCISES

(Exercises 19.1, 19.2, 19.5, 19.9, and 19.15 are practice exercises. Their complete solutions are given on page 756.)

19.1 Following are the stumpage prices in dollars per 1,000 board feet of softwoods, based on sales of sawtimber from national forests in the years 1988, 1989, and 1990.

Species	1988	1989	1990
Douglas fir	190.20	256.00	389.90
Southern pine	135.70	141.90	131.40
Sugar pine	287.60	260.40	289.10
Ponderosa pine	209.30	182.10	292.00
Western hemlock	105.40	162.90	223.30

Calculate the 1988, 1989, and 1990 values of a simple aggregative index with 1988 = 100 for the overall price change of softwood sawtimber.

19.2 With reference to the preceding exercise, find the arithmetic mean of price relatives comparing the 1990 prices with those of 1988.

19.3 Following are aluminum mill products data in millions of pounds for the years 1988 and 1989.

Product	1988	1989
Plate, sheet and foil	8,333	8,499
Extruded shapes and tubing	2,947	2,835
Powder, flake and paste	90	92
Forgings and impacts	166	159

(a) Calculate a simple aggregative index comparing 1989 production with that of 1988.

(b) Find the arithmetic mean of the four relatives comparing the 1989 production with that of 1988.

19.4 Following are U.S. prices per pound, in dollars, of three selected metal products for the years 1987, 1988, and 1989.

Metal	1987	1988	1989
Nickel	2.28	6.25	6.05
Tin	4.19	4.41	5.20
Cobalt	6.56	7.09	7.64

(a) Find the 1989, 1988, and 1987 values of the simple aggregative index using 1987 = 100.

(b) Find a simple aggregative index comparing the 1989 prices with those of 1988.

(c) Find for 1988 and 1989 the arithmetic mean of price relatives using 1987 = 100.

19.5 With reference to the preceding exercise, compare the 1989 prices of nickel and tin with those of 1988 by finding

(a) the arithmetic mean of the price relatives

(b) the geometric mean of the price relatives

19.6 Manufacturers shipments of color TV sets in the United States during the years 1985–1989 were 16.9, 18.8, 18.5, 19.2, and 21.0 million units. Construct an index series showing changes in these shipments during the years 1985 through 1989 with 1987 = 100.

19.7 Domestic coins (millions of dollars) were produced by the U.S. Mint in the following cities during a certain year:

City	Half-dollars	Quarter-dollars	Dimes	Five-cent pieces	One-cent pieces
Philadelphia	13.0	169.1	85.7	37.3	61.1
Denver	13.1	136.6	70.5	25.9	55.7
West Point	0	0	0	0	20.4

(a) Construct a simple aggregative index for the mints in each of the cities, comparing the total coinage manufactured by each with that of Philadelphia.

(b) Find the arithmetic mean of the relatives comparing the total coinage manufactured in Philadelphia with that of Denver.

19.8 Calculate the geometric mean of the relatives of the four nonferrous metals given on page 731.

19.9 Refer to the prices of nonferrous metals in Example 9.1 on page 730.

(a) Verify the value of 109.6 given for an index based upon the prices of 100 pounds of aluminum, 2,000 pounds of copper, 1,000 pounds of lead, and 500 pounds of zinc.

(b) What value would we get if we compare the combined prices of 100 pounds each of aluminum, copper, lead, and zinc?

(c) What value would we get if we compare the combined prices of 100 pounds each of aluminum, copper, lead and 5,000 pounds of zinc?

19.10 Verify that the Paasche index number for grains referred to in Example 19.4 is 92.9.

19.11 Show that if we substitute base-year value weights into the formula for a weighted arithmetic mean of price relatives, we obtain the formula for the Laspeyres index.

19.12 It is interesting to note that the Laspeyres formula can generally be expected to overestimate price changes, while the Paasche formula will generally do just the opposite. Explain why this is so, using as an illustration a consumer price index intended to measure changes in the prices of a market basket consisting of several hundred consumer goods and services.

19.13 In the **Ideal Index**, which has never been widely used for practical reasons, the upward and downward biases of the Laspeyres index and the Paasche index computed from the same data (see Exercise 19.12) will be more or less averaged out by taking the geometric mean of the two indexes. If a Laspeyres index stands at 134.0 and a Paasche index calculated from the same data stands at 132.5, what is the Ideal Index for this specific comparison?

19.14 Write a general formula for the Ideal Index (see the preceding exercise).

19.15 The following table shows the average prices paid for electricity in cents per kilowatt-hour by residential, commercial, and industrial customers and sales of electricity in billions of kilowatt-hours to these customers for the years 1987, 1988, and 1989.

Category	Price			Quantity		
	1987	1988	1989	1987	1988	1989
Residential	7.45	7.48	7.64	850	660	858
Commercial	7.08	7.04	7.21	893	699	896
Industrial	4.77	4.70	4.72	904	724	915

(a) Use the 1987 quantities as weights and 1987 = 100 to find weighted aggregative indexes for 1988 and 1989 prices.

(b) Calculate a weighted aggregative index comparing the 1989 prices of electricity with those of 1987, using the 1989 quantities as weights.

(c) Calculate a weighted aggregative index comparing the 1989 prices of electricity with those of 1987 using the averages of 1988 and 1989 quantities as weights.

(d) With 1987 = 100, calculate for 1989 the weighted arithmetic mean of price relatives, using the base-year values as weights.

(e) With 1987 = 100, calculate for 1989 the weighted arithmetic mean of price relatives, using the given-year values as weights.

(f) Interchanging the p's and q's in the formula used in part (e), construct an index comparing the 1989 quantities of the three categories with those of 1987.

19.16 Following are the prices of four nonferrous metals and the quantities produced in the United States. Prices are in dollars per pound and production data are in thousands of metric tons.

	Price			Quantity		
Nonferrous metal	1986	1987	1988	1986	1987	1988
Aluminum	0.5587	0.7230	1.1009	4,810	5,329	6,066
Copper	0.6605	0.8250	1.2051	2,221	2,372	2,826
Lead	0.2205	0.3594	0.3717	340	311	385
Zinc	0.3800	0.4192	0.6020	270	220	194

(a) Use 1986 quantities as weights to construct aggregative indexes comparing the 1987 and 1988 prices with those of 1986.

(b) Use 1987 quantities as weights to construct aggregative indexes comparing the 1987 and 1988 prices with those of 1986.

(c) Use 1988 quantities as weights to construct an aggregative index comparing the 1988 prices with those of 1986.

(d) Use the means of the 1986 and 1988 quantities as weights to construct an aggregative index comparing the 1988 prices with those of 1986.

(e) With 1986 = 100, calculate for 1988 the weighted arithmetic mean of price relatives using base-year values as weights. Compare this result with the 1988 index number calculated in part (a).

(f) With 1986 = 100, calculate for 1988 the weighted arithmetic mean of the price relatives, using given-year values as weights.

19.17 Compare the year 1988 prices of the four nonferrous metals of Exercise 19.16 with those of the year 1986 by means of the Ideal Index explained in Exercise 19.13.

19.18 Show that the formula for the weighted arithmetic mean of price relatives with value weights of the form $w = p_0 q_a$ reduces to the formula for a fixed-weight aggregative index.

19.5

Some Important Indexes

Some of the many important indexes intended to describe assorted phenomena are prepared by private organizations. Financial institutions, utility companies, and university bureaus of research, for example, often prepare indexes of such things as employment, factory hours and wages, and retail sales for the regions they serve; trade associations prepare indexes of price and quantity changes vital to their particular interests; and so on. Many of these indexes are widely used and highly respected indicators of the items they describe. However, by far the most widely circulated and widely used indexes are those prepared by the federal government. Of the many important government indexes, we shall describe briefly the Consumer Price Indexes and the Producer Price Index and a quantity index prepared by the Federal Reserve Board called the Index of Industrial Production.

The so-called "Consumer Price Index" is, in actuality, two somewhat different indexes serving two different populations: the **Consumer Price Index for All Urban Consumers (CPI-U)** and the **Consumer Price Index for Urban Wage Earners and Clerical Workers (CPI-W)**. The first index covers about 80 percent of the total population, and the second, about 32 percent of the total population. Both indexes are published by the Bureau of Labor Statistics and are intended to measure price changes in food, clothing, shelter, fuel, drugs, transportation fares, doctors' and dentists' services, and other goods and services that people buy for day-to-day living.

The CPI originated during World War I, but it was not until 1921 that the Bureau of Labor Statistics began regular publication of a national index. The CPI-W is a continuation of this 60-plus-year-old index.

As new uses were developed for the consumer price index, the need for a broader and more representative index became apparent and the CPI-U was introduced in 1978. This index represents the buying habits of a much wider segment of the population and includes professional and salaried workers, part-time workers, the self-employed, the unemployed, and retired people in addition to wage earners and clerical workers. The two indexes, therefore, differ chiefly in the weighting used, which is dependent on the differences in spending patterns of the two populations sampled. The U.S. government updates and revises its indexes every few years. Most recently, the consumer price indexes were revised in 1987 and now use the base period 1982–1984 = 100.

The consumer price indexes are derived from a "market basket" of fixed quantities of items representing all goods and services purchased for consumption, including necessities and luxuries. Specifically excluded are personal life insurance expenses and income and personal property taxes. Included are real estate, sales, and excise taxes. The indexes currently classify data by general household categories of consumption: food and beverages, housing, apparel and upkeep, transportation, medical care, entertainment, commodities, and services.

The CPI Detailed Report is a monthly publication of the Bureau of Labor Statistics showing consumer price movements, statistical tables, and technical notes. This publication includes both the CPI-U and CPI-W and contains a wealth of highly detailed information, such as the relative importance of each reported item, individual indexes for each item, percentage changes in the indexes of each item from the previous month, and annual percentage changes in the indexes of individual items from the corresponding month one year ago (both unadjusted and seasonally adjusted). Detailed information concerning the CPI-U and CPI-W is also published in a less comprehensive format in the widely circulated *Monthly Labor Review,* also a publication of the Bureau of Labor Statistics.

In addition to the publication in the two indexes of data for the United States as a whole, data are also shown for 27 urban areas. These series are compiled and published for the base period 1982–1984 = 100, and for their previous reference base 1967 = 100. Unlike the U.S. indexes, the indexes for the urban areas do not show absolute levels of prices which can be compared directly to one another. They show changes in prices in the same urban area relative to a fixed base time. Prices can, therefore, be higher in an urban area with a lower index figure than in another with a higher index figure. Thus, an index in a specific urban area of, say, 150 for a given month means that consumer prices for that area in that month averaged 50 percent higher than in the base period 1982–1984. If the consumer price index then rises from 150 to 180 in a later month, the prices in the second month average 80 percent higher than in the base period 1982–1984 and 20 percent higher than in the earlier month when the index was 150. The latter figure was obtained by the following calculation:

$$\frac{180 - 150}{150} \cdot 100 = 20 \text{ percent}$$

The Consumer Price Indexes are fixed-quantity price indexes and are a ratio of the costs of purchasing a set of items of constant quality and constant quantity in two different time periods. If the expenditure base and reference periods coincided, this would be the familiar Laspeyres price index formula. But this has been adjusted to make allowances for a new base period for expenditure weights, primarily 1982, 1983, and 1984, based upon the data tabulated from the *Consumer Expenditure Surveys* of these three years.

The index has undergone a number of important revisions, the first in 1940; others in the years 1953, 1964, and 1978; and the current major revision. In addition to changes in expenditure weights, the current revision of the Consumer Price Indexes includes a greatly enhanced housing survey and further advances in methodological and sampling techniques.

Some important uses of the CPIs include the use of the indexes as measures of price change. During periods of price rise, it is a measure of inflation and serves as an indicator of the success or failure of government and Federal Reserve Bank policies designed to curb inflation. Another common use of the CPI is as a deflator of other price series, such as retail sales, earnings, consumption expenditures, and gross national product. The CPI is also used as an escalator to adjust wages and pensions paid under collective bargaining agreements or mandated by legislative acts pertaining to social security payments, veterans' benefits, school lunches under the National School Lunch Act and the Child Nutrition Act, and changes in the income tax structure.

Also constructed by the Bureau of Labor Statistics is the **Producer Price Index**, formerly called the Wholesale Price Index. The origins of the PPI can be found in an 1891 U.S. Senate resolution authorizing the Senate Committee on Finance to investigate the effects of tariff laws upon "the imports and exports, the growth, development, production and prices of agricultural and manufactured articles at home and abroad." The index was first published in 1902. Since that time many changes have been made in the sample of commodities, the base period, and in the method of calculating the index. The index is now intended to measure average changes in the prices received in primary markets of the United States by producers of commodities in all stages of processing. Most of the prices used are those quoted on organized exchanges or markets, or actual transaction prices received by manufacturers and other producers.

Like other comprehensive indexes, the Producer Price Index is based on a sample. Because of the importance of wholesale price movements in the many subdivisions of the economy, about 3,200 items are presently being priced (usually on Tuesday of the week containing the 13th of the month) to get the prices used in the index.

Components of the Producer Price Index are calculated separately by **stage of production** and by **commodity**. The stage of production methodology organizes products by class of buyer and by stages of production: finished goods, intermediate goods, and crude materials (see Figure 19.1). The all-commodities index is comprised of two major commodity groupings: the Farm Products and Processed Foods and Feeds Indexes and the Industrial

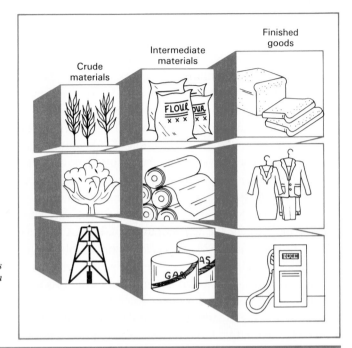

FIGURE 19.1
Stages of
production for
components of the
Producer Price
Indexes
Source: *Producer Prices
and Price Indexes, Data
for September 1991,*
published by the U.S.
Department of Labor,
Bureau of Labor
Statistics.

Commodities Index. Each major commodity grouping includes subgroups, product classes, and other subdivisions for which indexes have been calculated. To illustrate, the Farm Products and Processed Foods and Feeds Index is divided into separate classifications for farm products and for processed foods and feeds. The farm products category is separated into nine products: fresh and dried fruits and vegetables, grains, livestock, live poultry, plant and animal fibers, fluid milk, eggs, hayseed and oilseed, and other farm products. The processed foods and feeds category is similarly subdivided into nine specific items. In like fashion the Industrial Products Index is divided into the main categories of textile products and apparel, hides-skins-leather and related products, fuels and related products and power, chemicals and allied products, rubber and plastic products, lumber and wood products, pulp-paper and allied products, metals and metal products, machinery and equipment, furniture and household durables, nonmetallic minerals products, transportation equipment, and miscellaneous products. Each of these is further subdivided. Chemicals and allied products, for example (which are in the preceding listing), are subdivided into industrial chemicals, prepared paint, paint materials, drugs and pharmaceuticals, fats and oils—inedible, agricultural chemicals and chemical products, plastic resins and materials, and other chemicals and allied products.

Basically, although not strictly, the Producer Price Index is calculated as a weighted, or Laspeyres index. However, this type of index is identical to one in which price relatives p_n/p_0 are weighted with value weights p_0q_a. The weights used in calculating the index represent the total net selling value of commodities produced in, processed in, or imported into the United States and flowing into primary markets. For technical reasons the formula used to calculate the index is a variation of the second one on page 734, with $w = p_0q_a$. Effective with the publication of 1988 data, many important PPI series (including all stage-of-processing groupings and most commodity groups and individual items) were placed on a new reference base, 1982 = 100, to coincide with the new reference year of shipment weights. The new reference base is not used for indexes with a base date later than December 1981 or for indexes for the net output of industries and their products.

Producer Price Indexes is a monthly publication of the Bureau of Labor Statistics which shows producer price movements, statistical tables, and technical notes. This publication includes the Producer Price Index by stage of processing and the Producer Price Index by commodity groupings. Also included are the Standard Industrial Classification (SIC) codes for each commodity, the relative importance of each reported item, individual indexes for each reported item, percentage changes of the indexes of each item from the previous month, annual percentage changes in the indexes of the individual items from the corresponding month of the previous year (both unadjusted and seasonally adjusted), and much other important information. Detailed information concerning the PPIs is also published in the *Monthly Labor Review,* a publication of the Bureau of Labor Statistics mentioned earlier.

Unlike indexes measuring changes in prices, the Federal Reserve Board's **Index of Industrial Production** measures changes in the physical volume or quantity of output of the nation's factories, mines, and electric and gas utilities. Forerunners of the current index appeared in 1919 and 1922 and were succeeded in 1927 by the "New Index of Industrial Production." Based on 60 series for manufactured goods and mineral products, this index represented, either directly or indirectly, about 80 percent of the nation's production of these goods and products. In an effort to keep pace with the output of a rapidly expanding economy, major revisions of the index were made in 1940, 1953, 1959, 1971, 1976, 1985, and 1990. The 1990 revision was the first since 1985 and the seventh since the 1920s. The most recent revision updates and improves the index in many ways, and the base year was changed to 1987 = 100.

The monthly composite index showing changes in the nation's industrial production is arrived at by combining 252 individual monthly series into a number of different groups and then combining the various group indicators into one overall figure. One such grouping of individual series is the

"Major Industry" grouping, whose main components are mining and utilities along with manufacturing. Mining is further subdivided into metal, coal, oil and gas extraction, and stone and earth minerals. Utilities have only two subdivisions, electric and gas. Manufacturing is divided into nondurable and durable categories. The nondurable manufactures group consists of 10 subgroups, including food, tobacco products, textile mill products, apparel products, paper and products, printing and publishing, chemicals and products, petroleum products, rubber and plastic products, and leather and products. The durable manufactures group consists of 10 subgroups, including lumber and products, furniture and fixtures, clay-glass-stone products, primary metals, fabricated metal products, nonelectrical machinery, electrical machinery, transportation equipment, instruments, and miscellaneous manufactures. The earlier-mentioned primary metals and transportation equipment are further subdivided.

The Index of Industrial Production is accompanied by important data concerning capacity utilization rates (percent) in many of the foregoing series. For example, in March 1992 electric utilities were utilizing 88.6 percent of capacity, while manufacturing was using 77.0 percent of capacity.

The Index of Industrial Production is of importance since it measures the output of the United States on an annual basis. Examination of the detailed components of the index serves to disclose basic structural changes which occur in the economy. Additionally, this index discloses an important part of the variation in output over the business cycle.

One special problem which relates to the index is the difficulty of accounting for changes in quality resulting from technological change. An official comment concerning the computer industry states, "Equipment of essentially the same size and price as a piece several years older often offers a marked improvement in capability; this increase in 'quality' (broadly defined) implies a reduction in the price per operation of a magnitude that is difficult to assess."

Another special problem relating to the index is the importance of seasonal adjustments. Adjustments for seasonal factors are not uncommon in other indexes, but are of exceptional importance to the Index of Industrial Production, where some of the component indexes fluctuate by 40 percent or more during a calendar year. The important automobile industry presents a special challenge since automobile assembly plants close down annually for retooling, but not necessarily at the same time each year.

We shall not describe in detail the fairly complicated way in which the individual series are combined into group indexes and eventually into the overall production index. We observe, however, that for the total index the calculations actually performed lead to a fixed-weight aggregative index.

Unlike the consumer and producer price indexes, the Index of Industrial Production is intended to be a measure of current business conditions, and this sensitive, comprehensive business indicator furnishes fundamentally important direction to many persons and institutions whose current activities and future plans are in some way affected by the ever-changing overall business conditions.

The Index of Industrial Production is published in the *Federal Reserve Bulletin,* a monthly publication of the Board of Governors of the Federal Reserve System. Individual indexes are provided for each item in each of the 12 preceding months for which the information has been compiled, as well as average indexes of the items for the preceding year.

19.6

Some Special Applications

Many studies made, and polls taken, in the last few years have shown that the consensus feeling of the American people is that price inflation, in spite of recent declines, is still a very serious problem. In times of inflation, prices rise faster, often much faster, than personal incomes, with the result that a dollar loses some of its value and buys less than it would have bought at an earlier time. It is this "shrinking value of the dollar" which so troubles producers and consumers and governments alike. Of course, there are all sorts of "dollars"—dollars spent for energy, for food, for housing, for medical care, and so on—and their values do not necessarily all move in the same direction at the same time; the value of the hand-held calculator dollar, for example, has increased dramatically in recent years while the value of the medical cost dollar has dropped sharply.

It is easy to show how the value of some single-commodity dollar is measured. If a baker paid $5.20 in 1982 for a fixed quantity of honey and paid $10.40 for the same quantity of the same honey in 1992, the 1992 value of the "honey dollar" has been cut in half and is only 50 cents compared to its 1982 value. This follows from the fact that the honey price has doubled and that it takes two dollars in 1992 to buy what one dollar bought in 1982. Generally speaking, the value, or the purchasing power, of a dollar relative to some period in time is the reciprocal of an appropriate price index (written as a proportion). If prices have doubled since some reference period, the price index on that base is 2.00 (or 200 percent) and the dollar will buy only $\frac{1}{2.00} = \frac{1}{2}$ of what it would have bought in the earlier period. In other words, the purchasing power of the dollar is one-half of what it was, or 50 cents. Similarly, if prices have risen by 50 percent, the price index stands at 150 and the purchasing power is $\frac{1}{1.50} = \frac{2}{3}$ of what it was, or about 67 cents.

The same argument applies also when we speak of the purchasing power of, say, a construction dollar, a food dollar, a rent dollar, or a medical care dollar, none of which refers to a single commodity. Comprehensive indexes of construction, food, rent, and medical care prices are available, so we just take their reciprocals to arrive at the purchasing powers of the different dollars. To get an estimate of the purchasing power of what is the nearest thing to an omnibus dollar used to buy the full range of goods and services available in the economy, called "the" dollar, the reciprocals of such comprehensive indexes as the Consumer Price Index CPI-U or the Producer Price Index is usually used. Figures giving the purchasing power of the dollar, based on these indexes, are regularly published by the government.

Another important application of price indexes is in the calculation of "real wages" as distinct from "money wages." Since money is not an end in itself, wage earners are usually interested in what their wages will buy, and this depends on two things: how much they earn and the prices of the things they want to buy. Clearly, persons would be worse off this year than last year if their money wages have doubled over this period but the prices of the things they want to buy have tripled.

To calculate real wages, we can either multiply actual money wages by a quantity measuring the purchasing power of the dollar, or better, divide money wages by an appropriate price index. This process is called **deflating**, and the price index used as a divisor is called a **deflator**.

EXAMPLE 19.6 From 1990 to 1992 the average weekly wages of one class of city maintenance workers in a large city increased from $386.40 to $417.60. Over the same period an index of consumer prices in that city increased 12.0 percent. Calculate the real average weekly wages of these employees for 1992.

SOLUTION The second column of the accompanying table shows the 1990 and 1992 money wages, and the third column shows the consumer price index with 1990 = 100.

Year	Average weekly wages	Consumer prices (1990 = 100)	Real wages
1990	$386.40	100.0	$386.40
1992	417.60	112.0	372.86

Based on these figures, we get the values in the fourth column, the real wages, by dividing the index numbers (expressed as proportions) into the corresponding actual wages. For 1992 this is $\frac{417.60}{1.12} = 372.86$.

Over the period covered in this example, the money wages (average weekly wages) increased by $\left(\frac{417.60}{386.40} - 1\right)100 = 8.1$ percent. If prices had remained unchanged during this period, real wages would have increased by precisely the same amount as money wages. Prices, however, increased by 12 percent. As a result, real wages actually decreased by $\left(\frac{372.86}{386.40} - 1\right)100 = 3.5$ percent.

Since $1.00 in 1992 could purchase only $\frac{100.0}{112.0} = 0.893$ of what the 1990 dollar could purchase, the purchasing power of the dollar decreased by $1.00 - $0.893 = $0.107, or 10.7 cents. Thus, the larger number of dollars received in wages in 1992 actually provided less purchasing power than was obtainable with the smaller number of dollars received in 1990. ∎

The procedure we have illustrated here is frequently used to deflate individual values, value series, or value indexes. It is used, for example, in analyzing the movements through time of dollar sales or dollar inventories (which vary in response to both price and quantity changes) of manufacturers, wholesalers, and retailers; the total values of construction contracts or construction put in place; money incomes; and money wages. The only real problem in deflating series such as these is that of finding appropriate deflators.

EXERCISES

(Exercises 19.24, 19.27, and 19.31 are practice exercises. Their complete solutions are given on page 756.)

19.19 Would it be possible for the revised Consumer Price Index for All Urban Consumers to reach an all-time high in a given month when at the same time prices on the New York Stock Exchange and industrial production were falling sharply and unemployment had reached a record high and was still increasing?

19.20 An elderly couple, planning to move from Pittsburgh to either Houston or Cleveland, finds from a government publication that the value of the revised Consumer Price Index for All Urban Consumers for Cleveland stands at

374.7, while that for Houston is 337.6. Comment on their conclusion that it would cost them 11.0 percent more to live in Cleveland than in Houston.

19.21 Comment on the following statements, both of which are wrong:
(a) ''Probably the most important use of the Producer Price Indexes is in forecasting later movements in the Consumer Price Indexes.''
(b) ''A direct comparison of the producer price indexes and the consumer price indexes gives a very close estimate of the profit margins between primary markets and other distributive levels.''

19.22 It has been said that in a dynamic economy production indexes, like the Federal Reserve Board's Index of Industrial Production, always understate production. Why is a downward bias inherent in production indexes?

19.23 For the year 1992 relative to the year 1991 the number of personal bankruptcies decreased by 14 percent in city A and increased by 5 percent in city B. Is it reasonable to conclude that for 1992 the number of bankruptcies in A was 19 percent lower than in B?

19.24 It is often desirable or necessary to change the point of reference, or **shift the base**, of an index number series from one period to another. Ordinarily, this is done by simply dividing each value in the series by the original index number for the period which is to be the new base, then multiplying by 100. For instance, to shift the revised CPI-U for the years 1985 through 1990 from 1982–1984 = 100 to 1985 = 100, we divide each of the six yearly values by 288.6, the original value of the series for 1985.
    Following are the average weekly wages of part-time legal office employees in a large city for the years 1985 through 1990: 187.55, 196.92, 203.82, 217.88, 239.67, and 252.85 dollars.
(a) Construct an index showing the changes in these wages from the base year 1985.
(b) Shift the base of the index in part (a) to the year 1988.
(c) If a consumer price index for this city showed an increase of 10 percent from 1988 to 1990 how much did these employees earn in 1990 in real wages (constant 1988 dollars)?

19.25 In the years 1985–1989, 49.3, 51.5, 53.0, 58.4, and 63.4 millions of troy ounces of gold were produced throughout the world.
(a) Construct an index of world gold production for this five-year period with 1985 = 100.
(b) Shift the base of the index of part (a) to 1989.

19.26 For the months of January through December of 1992, a department store had sales of 179, 166, 231, 244, 244, 243, 222, 302, 263, 273, 321, and 536 thousands of dollars.
(a) Construct a monthly index of these sales using January 1992 as the base month.
(b) Shift the base of the index of part (a) to July 1992.

19.27 The average weekly earnings of production workers in manufacturing industries of the United States during the years 1985–1989 were 386.37, 396.01, 406.31, 418.81, and 430.09 dollars. For the same years, 1985–1989, the Consumer Price Index for all Urban Consumers was 107.6, 109.6, 113.6, 118.3, and 124.0, with 1982–1984 = 100.

    (a) Shift the base of the index to 1985; then use these index values to express the actual earnings in constant 1985 dollars. (That is, deflate the actual earnings.)

    (b) Construct an index of the purchasing power of the dollar for this period with 1985 = 100.

    (c) What were the percentage changes from 1985 through 1989 in money earnings, real earnings, living costs, and purchasing power.

19.28 Suppose that in the preceding exercise the gross average weekly earnings of a certain worker remained constant, and was in the amount of $225.55 for each of the five years. Use the indexes calculated in part (a) of the preceding exercise with the base of the index 1985 = 100 to express the *real* wages of the worker for each of the five years.

19.29 In 1990 a salesman residing in a certain city earned a salary of $35,000 and in 1992 earned a salary of $36,000. During the same years the CPI-W for that city increased from 135.4 to 144.6, with 1982–1884 = 100. How well did the salesman's actual earnings gain protect him against inflation in living costs as measured by the CPI-W?

19.30 When we deflate the 1992 value of a single commodity to, say, 1987 prices, we divide its value by an index expressing the 1992 price of the commodity as a relative of the 1987 price. Show symbolically that this process leads to the value of the commodity in 1992 at 1987 prices. (Although this argument does not apply strictly when we deflate an aggregate of the values of several commodities, we are in a sense estimating the total value of the same goods at base-year prices.)

19.31 Since index numbers are designed to compare two sets of figures, it seems reasonable that if an index for 1992 with the base year 1978 stands at 200, the same index for 1978 with the base year 1992 should be equal to 50. (If one thing is twice as big as another, the second should be half as big as the first.) To test whether an index meets this criterion, called the **time-reversal test**, we need only interchange the subscripts 0 and n wherever they appear in the formula and then see whether the resulting index (written as a proportion) is the reciprocal of the first. Determine which indexes among the simple aggregative index, the weighted aggregative index, the arithmetic mean of price relatives, the geometric mean of price relatives, and the Ideal Index (see Exercise 19.13 on page 738) satisfy this criterion.

19.32 As has been suggested in the text, price index formulas can be changed into quantity index formulas simply by replacing the p's with q's and the q's with p's. Using this relationship between the formula for a price index and the corresponding formula for a quantity index, the **factor-reversal test** requires that the product of the two (written as proportions) equal the value index $\sum p_n q_n / \sum p_0 q_0$. Show that this criterion is satisfied if we compare the prices, quantities, and values of a single commodity and for the Ideal Index (see Exercise 19.13 on page 738) but not for any of the other index number formulas given in this chapter.

19.7

A Word of Caution

We now add to our discussion of index numbers a word of caution about their use and interpretation. Trouble always arises when attempts are made to generalize beyond the stated purpose of an index to phenomena it was never intended to describe. The word "general" serves well enough to distinguish more or less comprehensive general-purpose indexes from those that are narrowly limited, or "special," in scope, but it is quite misleading in another sense: most "general-purpose" indexes are themselves strictly limited in purpose and scope.

Perhaps the most widely misunderstood index of all are the revised consumer price indexes (CPI-U and CPI-W) of the Bureau of Labor Statistics. These indexes are widely thought to measure not only the cost of living for everybody everywhere, but also to measure current business conditions—neither of which they do. In view of the government's many careful explanations of just what the Consumer Price Indexes are and are not intended to measure, this is hard to understand. Whatever remote or indirect connection may exist between the phenomena described by the indexes and business conditions in general is unintended. Moreover, there is little basis for thinking of the indexes as a measure of everyone's cost of living, even though for years the former index which the CPI succeeded was officially called a cost-of-living index. Actually, as the government is now careful to point out, the indexes measure the effect of price changes of a (fixed) market basket of goods and services on the cost of living of the families and individuals to which they apply. But a person's cost of living depends to some extent on his or her level of living, and changes in the level of living are not reflected in the indexes because purchases are held constant. Also, the indexes do not take into account, among other things, federal and state income taxes, social security taxes, and such noncash consumption items as food grown at home. Unfortunately, no true cost-of-living index—one which, for example, would measure changes while holding satisfaction or utility, rather than purchases, constant—exists for this country. Nevertheless, some professionals have asserted that, under "normal" conditions, whatever they may be, the revised Consumer Price Indexes can be considered to be a good approximation to changes in the cost of living; just how good no one knows.

There are some persons who would like to see the government develop bigger, better, and more general indexes, say, a truly general "all-consumer" price index (or even a cost-of-living index) covering all families and all goods and services. Others feel that the worth of an index decreases more or less in proportion to the increase in its scope. From the latter point of view, such phenomena as changing retail prices, wholesale prices, industrial production, and so on are far too broad ever to be described in terms of a single number. No matter how one feels about this problem, it is true that the reduction of a large set of data to a single number often entails the loss of such a tremendous amount of information that the whole procedure may have little practical value, if any. There are, indeed, some formidable problems connected both with the construction of index numbers by the professional and their use and interpretation by the layperson. As one economist has pointed out,

It ought to be conceded that index numbers are essentially arbitrary. Being at best rearrangements of data wrenched out of original market and technological contexts, they strictly have no economic meaning. Changes in tastes, technology, population composition, etc., over time increase their arbitrariness. But, of course, there is no bar to the use of indexes 'as if' they did have some unequivocal meaning provided that users remember that they themselves made up the game and do not threaten to "kill the umpire" when the figures contradict expectations.[1]

In any case, professionals must continue to construct indexes, and yesterday's platoon of layperson index watchers has now reached battalion strength and is increasing at such a rate that it is sure to become an army soon.

19.8

Checklist of Key Terms

Arithmetic mean of price
  relatives,   731
Base year (or period),   728
Consumer Price Index-U,   740

Consumer Price Index-W,   740
Deflating,   747
Deflator,   747
Factor-reversal test,   751

[1] I. H. Siegel, in a letter to the editor of *The American Statistician,* February 1952.

19.9

Review Exercises

19.33 For the years 1987 through 1991, the dividends paid per share of common stock of the Atlanta Gas Light Company were 1.60, 1.76, 1.88, 1.96, and 2.04 dollars.

(a) Construct an index with 1987 = 100 to measure the changes in the dividends paid.

(b) Shift the base of this index to 1991.

19.34 A manufacturing company buys replacement parts C305, RM22, and SC-1 for use in robotic machines. Following are the unit prices in dollars the company paid for the parts in 1978, 1986, and 1992 and the quantities of each it used in those years:

	Price			Quantity		
Part no.	1978	1986	1992	1978	1986	1992
C305	0.50	0.95	1.48	260	245	256
RM22	1.10	2.00	3.05	110	124	118
SC-1	0.80	0.92	1.22	48	45	52

(a) Using the 1978 quantities as weights, construct aggregative indexes comparing the 1986 and 1992 prices of the parts with those of 1978.

(b) Using the 1992 quantities as weights, construct aggregative indexes comparing the 1986 and 1992 prices of the parts with those of 1978.

(c) Construct an aggregative index comparing the 1992 prices of the parts with the 1978 prices, in which the weights are the quantities of the parts used in 1986.

(d) With 1978 = 100, calculate for 1992 the weighted arithmetic mean of price relatives using base-year values as weights.

(e) With 1978 = 100, calculate for 1992 the weighted arithmetic mean of price relatives using given-year values as weights.

(f) Interchanging the p's and q's in the formula used in part (a), construct an index comparing the 1992 use of the three parts with that of 1978.

19.35 If in 1992 average factory wages in one region were 118 percent of what they were in 1990 and a consumer price index for that region stood at 80 in 1990 with 1992 = 100, did wages keep up with inflation?

19.36 In the years 1986 through 1991, net sales of Walgreen Co. (a national drugstore chain) in billions of dollars were 3.66, 4.28, 4.88, 5.38, 6.05, and 6.73.

(a) Construct an index measuring the year-to-year change in the amounts of net sales (in billions of dollars) using 1986 as the base year.

(b) Shift the base of the index of part (a) to the year 1990.

19.37 Following are the prices (in dollars) of one pound each of selected fruits and vegetables in the years 1988 and 1989.

Fruits and vegetables	1988	1989
Apples, red Delicious	0.71	0.57
Pears, Anjou	0.64	0.76
Tomatoes, field grown	0.81	0.90
Lettuce, iceberg	0.77	0.52
Potatoes, white	0.31	0.31

(a) Construct a simple aggregative price index comparing the prices of the selected fruits and vegetables in 1989 with their prices in 1988.

(b) Find the arithmetic mean of relatives comparing the 1989 prices with those of 1988.

19.38 The following table provides production data (in millions of short tons) and sales value (in millions of dollars) for stone as well as sand and gravel in the years 1986 and 1988

	Production		Value	
	1986	1988	1986	1988
Stone	1,024	1,248	4,428	5,558
Sand and gravel	910	952	3,107	3,514

Construct a simple aggregative index measuring the change in the overall prices of these two items from 1986 to 1988.

19.39 At present the base period for Consumer Price Indexes is the period 1982–1984 = 100, but the index for "all items" continues to be reported for both the base-period 1982–1984 = 100 and the prior base year 1967 = 100. For August 1991, for example, the CPI-U was reported as 136.6 for all items with 1982–1984 = 100 and was also reported as 409.2 with 1967 = 100. The following data are copied directly from a Bureau of Labor Statistics publication where the CPI-U has the base year 1967 = 100. Perform the following calculations, based upon the data provided in the table following.

Consumer Price Index
All Urban Consumers (CPI-U)
U.S. City Average
(1967 = 100)

All Items

Year	Jan.	Feb.	Mar.	Apr.	May	June	July	Aug.
1986	328.4	327.5	326.0	325.3	326.3	327.9	328.0	328.6
1987	333.1	334.4	335.9	337.7	338.7	340.1	340.8	342.7
1988	346.7	347.4	349.0	350.8	352.0	353.5	354.9	356.6
1989	362.7	364.1	366.2	368.8	370.8	371.7	372.7	373.1
1990	381.5	383.3	385.5	386.2	386.9	389.1	390.7	394.1

All Items

Sep.	Oct.	Nov.	Dec.	Ann. Avg.	Percentage change Dec.–Dec.	Percentage change Avg.–Avg.
330.2	330.5	330.8	331.1	328.4	1.1	1.9
344.4	345.3	345.8	345.7	340.4	4.4	3.7
358.9	360.1	360.5	360.9	354.3	4.4	4.1
374.6	376.2	377.0	377.6	371.3	4.6	4.8
397.5	400.0	400.7	400.9	391.4	6.2	5.4

(a) Verify the annual averages for 1986, 1987, 1988, 1989, and 1990.

(b) Verify the December to December percentage changes for 1987, 1988, 1989, and 1990.

(c) Verify the percentage change for annual average to average for the years 1987, 1988, 1989, and 1990.

19.40 Dividing the 25-year period 1966–1990 into 5-year intervals, we obtain the following percentage increases of the Consumer Price Index All Urban Consumers (CPI-U), 1967 = 100. The data reflect substantial price inflation.

Section 19.9 Review Exercises   **755**

Years	Percentage increase
1966–1970	24.8
1971–1975	39.6
1976–1980	55.4
1981–1985	26.7
1986–1990	22.4

Further analysis of the data shows that a high proportion of the increases were accounted for by the rising prices of energy, food, housing, and medical care. Why should the prices of these four items be of great concern to all consumers?

19.10

Solutions of Practice Exercises

19.1
$$\frac{190.20 + 135.70 + 287.60 + 209.30 + 105.40}{190.20 + 135.70 + 287.60 + 209.30 + 105.40} \cdot 100 = 100.0 \text{ for } 1988,$$

$$\frac{256.00 + 141.90 + 260.40 + 182.10 + 162.90}{928.20} \cdot 100 = 108.1 \text{ for } 1989,$$

$$\frac{389.90 + 131.40 + 289.10 + 292.00 + 223.30}{928.20} \cdot 100 = 142.8 \text{ for } 1990.$$

19.2
$$\frac{389.90}{190.20} \cdot 100 = 205.0 \text{ for Douglas fir,}$$

$$\frac{131.40}{135.70} \cdot 100 = 96.8 \text{ for Southern pine,}$$

$$\frac{289.10}{287.60} \cdot 100 = 100.5 \text{ for Sugar pine,}$$

$$\frac{292.00}{209.30} \cdot 100 = 139.5 \text{ for Ponderosa pine, and}$$

$$\frac{223.30}{105.40} \cdot 100 = 211.9 \text{ for Western hemlock, so that}$$

$$I = \frac{205.0 + 96.8 + 100.5 + 139.5 + 211.9}{5} = 150.7 \text{ for } 1990.$$

19.5
$$I = \frac{\frac{6.05}{6.25} \cdot 100 + \frac{5.20}{4.41} \cdot 100}{2} = 107.4.$$

$$GM = \sqrt{\left(\frac{6.05}{6.25} \cdot 100\right)\left(\frac{5.20}{4.41} \cdot 100\right)} = 106.8.$$

19.9 (a) $I = \dfrac{100(88) + 2{,}000(131) + 1{,}000(39) + 500(82)}{100(110) + 2{,}000(121) + 1{,}000(37) + 500(60)} \cdot 100 = 109.6.$

(b) $I = \dfrac{100(88) + 100(131) + 100(39) + 100(82)}{100(110) + 100(121) + 100(37) + 100(60)} \cdot 100 = 103.7,$ which

is the same answer as in Example 19.1

(c) $I = \dfrac{100(88) + 100(131) + 100(39) + 5{,}000(82)}{100(110) + 100(121) + 100(37) + 5{,}000(60)} \cdot 100 = 133.4.$

19.15 (a) $I = \dfrac{7.48(850) + 7.04(893) + 4.70(904)}{7.45(850) + 7.08(893) + 4.77(904)} \cdot 100 = 99.6$ for 1988, and

$I = \dfrac{7.64(850) + 7.21(893) + 4.72(904)}{16{,}967.02} \cdot 100 = 101.4$ for 1989.

(b) $I = \dfrac{7.64(858) + 7.21(896) + 4.72(915)}{7.45(858) + 7.08(896) + 4.77(915)} \cdot 100 = 101.4$ for 1989.

(c) Since the averages are $\dfrac{660 + 858}{2} = 759.0,$ $\dfrac{699 + 896}{2} = 797.5,$ and

$\dfrac{724 + 915}{2} = 819.5$ we get

$I = \dfrac{7.64(759.0) + 7.21(797.5) + 4.72(819.5)}{7.45(759.0) + 7.08(797.5) + 4.77(818.5)} \cdot 100 = 101.4$

(d) Since base-year values are $7.45(850) = 6{,}332.50,$ $7.08(893) = 6{,}322.44,$ and $4.77(904) = 4{,}312.08,$ we get

$I = \dfrac{\left(\frac{7.64}{7.45}\right)6{,}332.50 + \left(\frac{7.21}{7.08}\right)6{,}322.44 + \left(\frac{4.72}{4.77}\right)4{,}312.08}{6{,}332.50 + 6{,}322.44 + 4{,}312.08} \cdot 100 = 101.4$

(e) Since given-year values are $7.64(858) = 6{,}555.12,$ $7.21(896) = 6{,}460.16,$ and $4.72(915) = 4{,}318.80,$ we get

$I = \dfrac{\left(\frac{7.64}{7.45}\right)(6{,}555.12) + \left(\frac{7.21}{7.08}\right)(6{,}460.16) + \left(\frac{4.72}{4.77}\right)(4{,}318.80)}{6{,}555.12 + 6{,}460.16 + 4{,}318.80} \cdot 100 =$

101.4

(f) $I = \dfrac{\left(\frac{858}{850}\right)(6{,}555.12) + \left(\frac{896}{893}\right)(6{,}460.16) + \left(\frac{915}{904}\right)(4{,}318.80)}{6{,}555.12 + 6{,}460.16 + 4{,}318.80} \cdot 100 =$

100.8.

19.24 (a) Dividing each value of the index by 187.55 and multiplying by 100, we get 100.0, 105.0, 108.7, 116.2, 127.8, and 134.8.

(b) Dividing each value by 116.2 and multiplying by 100, we get 86.1, 90.4, 93.5, 100.0, 110.0, and 116.0.

(c) $\dfrac{252.85}{1.10} = 229.86$.

19.27 (a) Dividing each value by the index 107.6 and multiplying by 100, we get $\dfrac{107.6}{107.6} \cdot 100 = 100.0$, $\dfrac{109.6}{107.6} \cdot 100 = 101.9$, $\dfrac{113.6}{107.6} \cdot 100 = 105.6$, $\dfrac{118.3}{107.6} \cdot 100 = 109.9$, and $\dfrac{124.0}{107.6} \cdot 100 = 115.2$. The earnings in 1985 dollars are $\dfrac{386.37}{100.0} \cdot 100 = 386.37$, $\dfrac{396.01}{101.9} \cdot 100 = 389.01$, $\dfrac{406.31}{105.6} \cdot 100 = 384.76$, $\dfrac{418.81}{109.9} \cdot 100 = 381.08$, and $\dfrac{430.09}{115.2} \cdot 100 = 373.34$.

(b) $\dfrac{107.6}{107.6} \cdot 100 = 100.0$, $\dfrac{107.6}{109.6} \cdot 100 = 98.18$, $\dfrac{107.6}{113.6} \cdot 100 = 94.72$, $\dfrac{107.6}{118.3} \cdot 100 = 90.96$, and $\dfrac{107.6}{124.0} \cdot 100 = 86.77$.

(c) $\dfrac{430.09}{386.37} = 1.113$, so that money earnings are up 11.3 percent, $\dfrac{373.34}{386.67} = 0.966$, so that real earnings are down 3.4 percent, $\dfrac{124.0}{107.6} = 1.152$, so that living costs are up 15.2 percent, $\dfrac{107.6}{124.0} = 0.867$, so that purchasing power is down 13.3 percent.

19.31 The simple aggregative index, the geometric mean of price relatives, and the Ideal Index satisfy the time-reversal test, but the weighted aggregative index and the arithmetic mean of price relatives do not. For the simple aggregative index, for example,

$$\frac{\sum p_n}{\sum p_0} \cdot \frac{\sum p_0}{\sum p_n} = 1$$

but for the Laspeyres index,

$$\frac{\sum p_n q_0}{\sum p_0 q_0} \cdot \frac{\sum p_0 q_n}{\sum p_n q_n} \neq 1$$

Time-Series Analysis

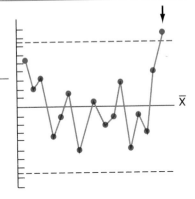

It has been said in many different ways that the future belongs to those who plan for it best. This is certainly true in business and economics where, in planning for an uncertain future, many important, powerful, and often necessary tools are available for help. These include, among others, the ones we have already studied in this book—index numbers, estimation, tests of hypotheses, analysis of variance, regression and correlation, and the rest. We come now to a new tool of absolutely basic importance in business planning. Called time-series analysis, it is essentially a study of the way in which such things as work force, production, sales, and profits move through time. In Section 20.1 we begin our study with some introductory remarks on looking backward and looking ahead, then in Section 20.2 we discuss in some detail the components of a time series. In Sections 20.3 through 20.7 we learn how to measure these components, that is, how to describe them statistically, and in Sections 20.8 and 20.9 we present some special applications.

20.1

Some Preliminary Remarks

Business planning is not an end in itself, but organized planning utilizing various statistical techniques (intended to assess past performance and estimate the success or failure of proposed strategies) seems to have everything in its favor. Aside from its intuitive appeal, there are the achievement records of many highly successful companies which treat planning as an organized activity and analyze exhaustively the many factors bearing on planning decisions. Marketing strategy is often planned in great detail for several years ahead, with enough flexibility built in to allow for whatever changes market conditions may require. Financial strategy is also carefully planned, so that operating plans can be carried out and a proper balance maintained between distributed earnings and retained earnings necessary for future growth. Many manufacturing companies attempt to make their long-range planning (for example, beyond a year) more effective by maintaining projections of 10 years or longer on sales, profits, cash needs, and so on, for all of their major product groups. No intelligent planning of future needs for raw materials and production facilities, for instance, can be done without predictions of such basic variables as product or service demand, production costs, and restrictions on capacity.

Predictions of the sort that involve explaining events which will occur at some future time are called **forecasts**, and the process of arriving at such explanations is called **forecasting**. There are various ways of forecasting the future values of economic variables, including the **intrinsic method**, in which the future values of variables are predicted from their past values. One important statistical technique included in the intrinsic method is **time-series analysis**. By a **time series** we mean statistical data that are collected, observed, or recorded at regular intervals of time. The term "time series," or simply "series," applies, for example, to data recorded periodically showing the total annual sales of retail stores, the total quarterly value of construction contracts awarded, the total amount of unfilled orders in durable goods industries at the end of each month, and the daily clearings in the Chicago Clearing House. We shall restrict ourselves to the analysis of business and economic data, but neither the term "time series" nor the methods of analysis we shall discuss are limited to these kinds of data.

Although in forecasting our concern is with the future, time-series analysis begins by looking backward. After all, it would be silly not to put relevant experience from the past to use in planning for an uncertain future. Thus, we search for observable regularities and patterns in historical series which are so persistent that they cannot be ignored. If we subsequently base our forecasts on such regularities and patterns, we are simply expressing the feeling that the future follows the past with some degree of consistency, that what has happened in the past will, to a greater or lesser extent, continue to happen or will happen again in the future.

20.2

The Components of a Time Series

Sometimes, when we look at the graph of a time series, we get the impression that it has been scrawled by a small child, and it is hard to believe that any kind of analysis could bring order into the seemingly haphazard movement of the data through time. Nevertheless, if we make some simplifying assumptions it becomes possible to identify, explain, and measure the fluctuations that appear in time series. Specifically, let us assume that there are four basic types of variation in a series which, superimposed and acting in concert, account for the observed changes over a period of time and give the series its erratic appearance. These four **components** are

1. Secular trend
2. Seasonal variation
3. Cyclical variation
4. Irregular variation

We shall assume further that there is a multiplicative relationship between these four components; that is, any particular value in a series is the product of factors which can be attributed to the four components.

This is the traditional approach to time-series analysis, but it is only one of many possible models (or schemes) which might be used in studying time series. Although it ignores the hidden interactions and interrelationships in the data and the entire "complex of individually small shifts and nuances," this approach has been and continues to be widely used in practice where, in many instances, it provides entirely satisfactory results. It is possible to construct mathematically sophisticated forecasting models, but there is much of fundamental importance to be learned about the movements of data through time from a study of the traditional methods.

By the **secular trend**, or long-term trend, of a time series we mean the smooth or regular underlying movement of a series over a fairly long period of time. Intuitively speaking, the trend of a time series characterizes the gradual and consistent pattern of changes in the series which are thought to result from persistent forces affecting growth or decline (changes in population, income, and wealth, changes in the level of education and technology, etc.) that exert their influence more or less slowly. For example, Figure 20.1 shows the overall upward trend in the public debt of the United States from 1975 to 1990 (data from U.S. Treasury Department). Figure 20.2 shows the persistent downward trend in shipments of singles records from 1979 to 1990 (data from Recording Industry of America, Inc.). The dramatic decline in shipments of singles records resulted from the greatly increased popularity of personal cassette players and from the introduction of compact disks.

The problem in trend analysis is to describe the underlying movement or general sweep of a time series in quantitative terms. In many series the patterns of gradual growth or decline can be described reasonably well by means of a straight line, but in others more complicated curves are required. For example, the series on imports of jeans by Blue-J Imports, Inc., shown in Figure 20.3 has the general shape of an elongated letter S, and its trend is not well described by a straight line. The curve shown fitted to these data is one of the so-called **growth curves**, and it reflects a type of growth that is frequently observed in time series.

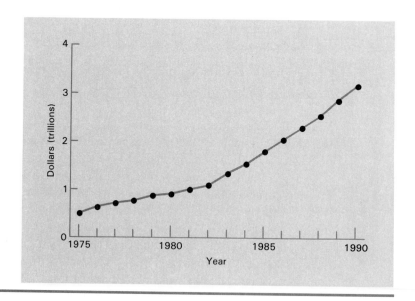

FIGURE 20.1
Public debt of the
United States

Chapter 20   Time-Series Analysis

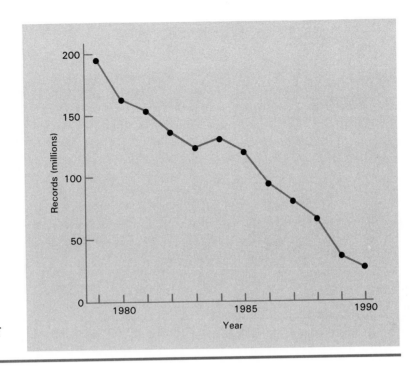

FIGURE 20.2
U.S. shipments of
single records

Strictly speaking, **seasonal variation** is the movements in a time series, like those shown in Figure 20.4, which recur year after year in the same months (or the same quarters) of the year with more or less the same

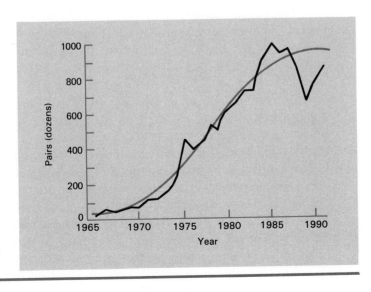

FIGURE 20.3
Growth curve fitted
to imports of jeans

Section 20.2   The Components of a Time Series   **763**

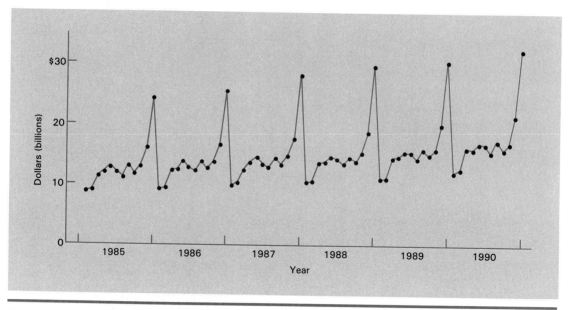

FIGURE 20.4   Retail sales of nondurable general merchandise in the United States

intensity. Thus, the month-to-month variation observed in retail sales is an example of seasonal variation in time series. Sometimes the term "seasonal variation" is also applied to other inherently periodic movements, such as those occurring within a day or week or month, whose period is at most one year. In any case, the movement described is a most obvious one.

Few businesses are free of the effects of seasonal variation. The examination of almost any series of economic data recorded on a quarterly, monthly, weekly, daily, or hourly basis shows movements within the series which seem to occur period after period with some definite degree of regularity. About two-thirds to three-fourths of the total annual business in the jewelry trade is done in the two months before Christmas; except for the holiday season, airline passenger traffic normally drops during the winter months, electric power and natural gas consumption is normally higher in many places during the winter months, city traffic on workdays is always heaviest in the early morning and late afternoon, and so on. To business executives responsible for realistic planning of such activities as production, purchasing, inventory, personnel, advertising, and sales, an understanding of seasonal patterns is of primary concern. Even in cases where the seasonal variation is not of basic concern, it must often be measured statistically in order to facilitate the study of other types of variation.

After the trend and seasonal variation have been eliminated statistically from a time series, in the model we are discussing here there remain the **cyclical** and **irregular variations**. Irregular variations in time series are of two types: (1) variations which are caused by such readily identifiable special events as elections, wars, floods, earthquakes, strikes, and bank failures and (2) random or chance variations whose causes cannot be definitely assigned. Most of the time, irregular variations resulting from the occurrence of special events can be easily recognized and identified with the phenomena which caused them; then the data reflecting their impact can simply be eliminated before measuring the other time-series components. As for those essentially random kinds of fluctuations, there is little to be said except that they usually tend to average out in the long run.

It is conceivable that in any given time series which one is studying there are really no systematic movements of any sort, that all the observed fluctuations in the series are in fact irregular ones. Ordinarily, before attempting to measure, say, a trend, we like to test whether or not there actually is a significant movement of this kind in the series. There are several tests of significance which can be applied in these cases. One of them, the test based on runs above and below the median, was described in Chapter 17.

Cyclical variation is sometimes defined as the variation which remains in a time series after the trend, seasonal, and irregular variations have been eliminated. Actually, there is much more to it than that, but in classical time-series analysis such a process of elimination is the usual way of measuring (business) cyclical variation, or **business cycles**. Generally speaking, business cycles consist of recurring up and down movements of business or economic activity which differ from seasonal variations in that they extend over longer periods of time and, supposedly, result from an entirely different set of causes. The recurring periods of prosperity, recession, depression, and recovery, which constitute the four phases of a complete business cycle, are considered to be due to factors other than the weather, social customs, and so on, which account for seasonal variations. Because of the great importance of cyclical swings of business to the economic and social life of this country, an enormous amount of effort has been spent in studying the business cycle. Many theories have been proposed to account for it, but no generally accepted explanation of this complicated phenomenon has appeared.

20.3

Linear Trends

The most widely used method of fitting trend lines to time series is the method of least squares. As we have seen, the problem of fitting a least-squares line $\hat{y} = a + bx$ is essentially that of determining values of a and b

which, for a given set of data, make $\sum (y - \hat{y})^2$ as small as possible. We can find these two quantities in any problem by solving the two normal equations,

$$\sum y = na + b(\sum x)$$
$$\sum xy = a(\sum x) + b(\sum x^2)$$

or by using formulas derived from them.

In time-series analysis, however, the x's practically always refer to successive periods (usually years) and where this is the case we can simplify the work of fitting a least-squares trend line by performing a change of scale, or **coding** the x's, so that in the new scale the sum of the x's is zero. If the series has an odd number of years, we count from the middle of the period in units of one year, assigning $x = 0$ to the middle year and 1, 2, 3, . . . to the following years and $-1, -2, -3, . . .$ to the preceding years. If the series has an even number of years, though, there are two middle years, not one, and the midpoint of the series falls between them. Assigning $x = 0$ to this point in time and counting from here in units of six months (or half-years), the x's are 1, 3, 5, . . . for the following years and $-1, -3, -5, . . .$ for the preceding years. In either case (an odd number or an even number of years in the series) $\sum x = 0$, and substituting this into the two normal equations and solving for a and b, we get

Computing formulas for a and b (with coding)

$$a = \frac{\sum y}{n} \quad \text{and} \quad b = \frac{\sum xy}{\sum x^2}$$

The advantage of this kind of coding is evident.

EXAMPLE 20.1   For the years 1980 through 1990, U.S. motion picture box office receipts (in millions of dollars) were 2,748, 2,966, 3,453, 3,766, 4,031, 3,749, 3,778, 4,253, 4,458, 5,033, and 5,022. Fit a least-squares trend line of the form $\hat{y} = a + bx$ to this series.

SOLUTION   Since we have data for 11 (an odd number) years, we set $x = 0$ opposite 1985, the middle year, and count both backward and forward from that origin in full years. We show the coded x-values in the second column below and develop the sums we need to find a and b in the third, fourth, and fifth columns.

Box office receipts

Year	x	y	xy	x^2
1980	-5	2,748	$-13,740$	25
1981	-4	2,966	$-11,864$	16
1982	-3	3,453	$-10,359$	9
1983	-2	3,766	$-7,532$	4
1984	-1	4,031	$-4,031$	1
1985	0	3,749	0	0
1986	1	3,778	3,778	1
1987	2	4,253	8,506	4
1988	3	4,458	13,374	9
1989	4	5,033	20,132	16
1990	5	5,022	25,110	25
Total	0	43,257	23,374	110

Substituting $n = 11$, $\sum y = 43,257$, $\sum xy = 23,374$, and $\sum x^2 = 110$ into the new formulas for a and b, we get

$$a = \frac{\sum y}{n} = \frac{43,257}{11} = 3,932.5$$

$$b = \frac{\sum xy}{\sum x^2} = \frac{23,374}{110} = 212.5$$

and, hence, $\hat{y} = 3,932.5 + 212.5x$ for the equation of the trend line. ∎

To avoid confusion over what a trend equation really says, it is always advisable to add a **legend** stating precisely the origin of x and the units of both x and y. In the preceding example, the year 1985 is the origin (corresponding to the zero in the x-scale), the units are full years, and the y's are annual box office receipts in millions of dollars. So we write the trend equation and its legend as

$$\hat{y} = 3,932.5 + 212.5x$$
(origin, 1985; x units, one year; y, annual box
office receipts in millions of dollars)

All of this makes it clear that the trend value for 1985 is $3,932.5 million and that the **annual trend increment** (the year-to-year growth in box office receipts) is estimated to be \$212.5 million for this period.

Once we have calculated a trend equation, we can use it to determine the trend value for any year by substituting into the equation the value of x corresponding to that year.

EXAMPLE 20.2   Based on the results of the preceding example, find the 1980 and 1990 trend value of motion picture box office receipts.

SOLUTION   Substituting $x = -5$ into the trend equation, we get

$$\hat{y} = 3{,}932.5 + 212.5(-5) = 2{,}870 \text{ for } 1980,$$
$$\text{and substituting } x = 5, \text{ we get}$$
$$\hat{y} = 3{,}932.5 + 212.5(5) = \$4{,}995 \text{ million for } 1990.$$

If we now plot these two trend values and join them by a straight line, we get the least-squares trend line drawn through the original series in Figure 20.5.   ■

It is sometimes desirable, or necessary, to modify a trend equation like the one just given so that it can be used with monthly data, so that the x's refer to successive months instead of successive years, or so that the origin of

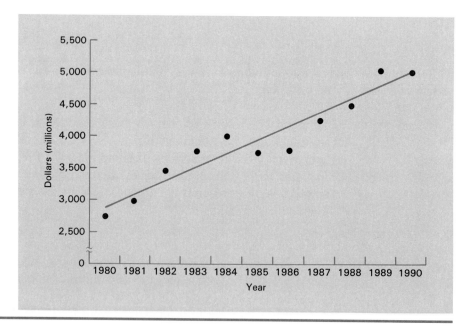

FIGURE 20.5
Motion picture box
office receipts

x is the middle of a month instead of the middle of a year. In the three examples that follow, we show how modifications such as these can be made, using for illustration the motion picture box office series of Example 20.1.

EXAMPLE 20.3 Change the y units in the equation $\hat{y} = 3{,}932.5 + 212.5x$ from annual box office receipts in millions of dollars to monthly box office receipts in millions of dollars.

SOLUTION Since the average monthly figures for the 11 years are one-twelfth the corresponding annual figures (that is, $\dfrac{y}{12}$), we must write a new equation with a and b replaced by $\dfrac{a}{12}$ and $\dfrac{b}{12}$. The modified equation and its legend are

$$\hat{y} = 327.7 + 17.7x$$
(origin, 1985; x units, 1 year;
y, average monthly box office receipts
in millions of dollars) ∎

EXAMPLE 20.4 Modify the trend equation obtained in Example 20.3 so that the x's refer to successive months instead of successive years.

SOLUTION Since b measures the trend increment, the increase or decrease of trend values corresponding to one unit of x, we must divide b by 12, changing it from an annual trend increment to a **monthly trend increment**. Leaving a unchanged, we thus get

$$\hat{y} = 327.7 + 1.5x$$
(origin, 1985, x units, 1 month;
y, average monthly box office receipts
in millions of dollars) ∎

The equation obtained in the preceding example can be used with monthly data just as it stands. The origin is at the end of June (the instant when June becomes July) 1985, but to complete the modification, we often shift the origin from the middle of a year to the middle of a month.

EXAMPLE 20.5 Shift the origin of the trend equation obtained in Example 20.4 from June–July 1985 to the middle of January 1985.

SOLUTION The middle of January 1985 is $5\frac{1}{2}$ months earlier than the middle of the year 1985. Therefore, we must subtract 5.5 monthly trend increments from the 1985 trend value of 327.7, getting $327.7 - (5.5)(1.5) = 319.4$ (accuracy can be improved slightly by using more decimal places). Finally,

$$\hat{y} = 319.4 + 1.5x$$
(origin, January 1985; x units, 1 month;
y, average monthly box office receipts
in millions of dollars) ∎

20.4

Nonlinear Trends

When the data seem to depart more or less widely from linearity in regression or time-series analysis, we must consider fitting some curve other than a straight line. One of the most useful of these other curves is the **parabola** whose equation is

$$\hat{y} = a + bx + cx^2$$

In fitting a parabola by the method of least squares, we must determine a, b, and c so that $\sum(y - \hat{y})^2 = \sum (y - a - bx - cx^2)^2$ is a minimum. To this end we look at the parabola as a multiple regression equation of the form

$$y = a + bx_1 + cx_2$$

with $x_1 = x$ and $x_2 = x^2$. Thus the method of Section 16.2 leads to the normal equations

$$\sum y = na + b(\sum x) + c(\sum x^2)$$
$$\sum xy = a(\sum x) + b(\sum x^2) + c(\sum x^3)$$
$$\sum x^2 y = a(\sum x^2) + b(\sum x^3) + c(\sum x^4)$$

When the values in a series are equally spaced, the solution of these equations for a, b, and c can be simplified appreciably by using the same coding as in the preceding section. Putting the zero of the new scale at the middle of

770 *Chapter 20 Time-Series Analysis*

the series and observing the conventions for coding an odd number of periods and an even number of periods will make $\sum x = 0$ and $\sum x^3 = 0$, and the normal equations reduce to

Normal equations for fitting parabola (with coding)

$$\sum y = na + c(\sum x^2)$$
$$\sum xy = b(\sum x^2)$$
$$\sum x^2 y = a(\sum x^2) + c(\sum x^4)$$

We can then find b directly from the second equation,

$$b = \frac{\sum xy}{\sum x^2}$$

and we can find a and c by solving the first and third equations simultaneously. Parabolas are also referred to as **second-degree polynomial equations,** and polynomial equations of higher degree in x than two, such as $\hat{y} = a + bx + cx^2 + dx^3$ and $\hat{y} = a + bx + cx^2 + dx^3 + ex^4$, can also be fitted by the method of least squares.

EXAMPLE 20.6 According to the Energy Information Administration, *Annual Energy Review, 1991,* production of petroleum by the Organization of the Petroleum Exporting Countries (OPEC) in millions of barrels per day from 1980 to 1990 was as follows: 27.0, 22.8, 19.2, 17.9, 17.9, 16.6, 18.7, 18.8, 20.8, 22.7, and 23.7.

(a) Fit a parabolic trend curve of the form $\hat{y} = a + bx + cx^2$ to this series.

(b) Calculate the trend values for 1980, 1982, and 1991.

(c) Plot the graph of the parabola together with the original series of data.

SOLUTION (a) In order to calculate a, b, and c from the reduced normal equations, we must find n, $\sum y$, $\sum xy$, $\sum x^2 y$, $\sum x^2$, and $\sum x^4$. In the second column of the following table we show the production figures (the y-values) and in the five columns to its right we show the work we do to find the required sums:

Year	Production y	x	xy	x^2y	x^2	x^4
1980	27.0	−5	−135.0	675.0	25	625
1981	22.8	−4	−91.2	364.8	16	256
1982	19.2	−3	−57.6	172.8	9	81
1983	17.9	−2	−35.8	71.6	4	16
1984	17.9	−1	−17.9	17.9	1	1
1985	16.6	0	0.0	0.0	0	0
1986	18.7	1	18.7	18.7	1	1
1987	18.8	2	37.6	75.2	4	16
1988	20.8	3	62.4	187.2	9	81
1989	22.7	4	90.8	363.2	16	256
1990	23.7	5	118.5	592.5	25	625
	226.1	0	−9.5	2,538.9	110	1,958

Now, with all this done, we can find b directly by substituting into the formula, and we get

$$b = \frac{\sum xy}{\sum x^2} = \frac{-9.5}{110} = -0.86$$

Then, substituting $n = 11$ together with the totals of the y, x^2y, x^2, and x^4 columns into the first and third reduced normal equations, we get

$$226.1 = 11a + 110c$$
$$2,538.9 = 110a + 1,958c$$

Solving these two equations by the method of elimination or by determinants, we find that $a = 17.316$ and $c = 0.324$. Accordingly, we write the following trend equation and its legend:

$$\hat{y} = 17.316 - 0.086x + 0.324x^2$$
(origin, 1985; x units, one year; y, production
of crude oil by OPEC nations in millions of
barrels per day)

In this parabolic equation which describes the trend in the production of crude oil in the OPEC countries over the 1980–1990 period, $a = 17.3$ (rounded) is the trend value for 1985, $b = -0.086$ is the slope of the curve at $x = 0$ (the origin), and $2c = 0.648$ is the constant rate at which the slope changes at this particular point.

(b) To find the trend value on a parabolic curve for any year, we merely substitute the appropriate value of x into the trend equation. For 1980 we substitute $x = -5$ and get

$$\hat{y} = 17.316 - 0.086(-5) + 0.324(25) = 25.846$$

which may be rounded to 25.8. For 1982 we substitute $x = -3$ and get

$$\hat{y} = 17.316 - 0.086(-3) + 0.324(9) = 20.5$$

And for 1991 (one year beyond the end of the series), we substitute $x = 6$ and get

$$y = 17.316 - 0.086(6) + 0.324(36) = 28.5$$

(c) To plot a parabolic trend we need at least three points. Thus, using the results of part (b) together with the information that the 1985 trend value is $a = 17.3$, we obtain the curve shown in Figure 20.6. ■

Often a set of data which does not seem linear when plotted on ordinary graph paper (**arithmetic paper**) appears to "straighten out" when plotted on

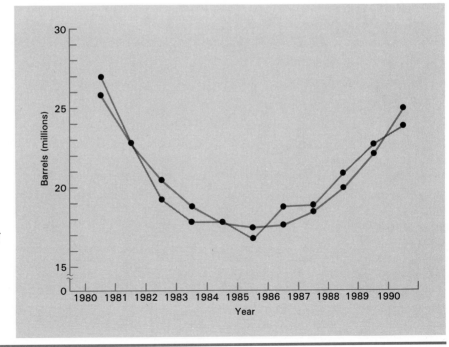

FIGURE 20.6
Daily production of crude oil by the Organization of the Petroleum Exporting Countries, 1980–1990

paper with a logarithmic vertical scale (**semilog paper** or **ratio paper**). The following series showing for the years 1960, 1965, 1970, 1975, 1980, 1985, and 1990 the daily average number of shares of stock traded on the New York Stock Exchange is a good illustration of such data.

Year	Stocks traded (thousands of shares)
1960	3,042
1965	6,176
1970	11,564
1975	18,551
1980	44,871
1985	109,169
1990	156,777

As Figure 20.7 (the plot on arithmetic paper) shows, the path of the data is certainly not well described by a straight line. On the other hand, Figure 20.8 (the plot on semilog paper) shows that it is straightened out remarkably well when we use a logarithmic scale for *y*.

On arithmetic paper, equal intervals on the vertical scale represent

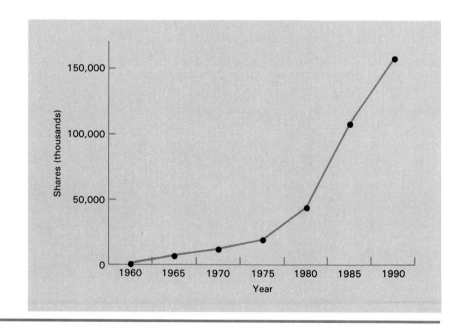

FIGURE 20.7
Daily average shares of stock traded on New York Stock Exchange, 1960–1990, plotted on ordinary graph paper

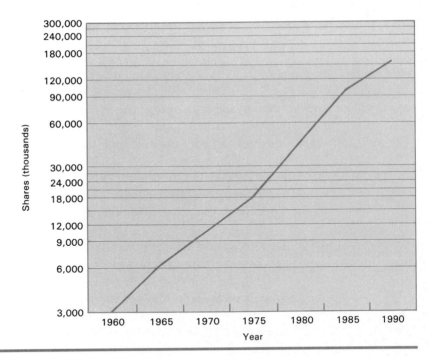

FIGURE 20.8
Daily average
shares of stock
traded on New
York Stock
Exchange, 1960–
1990, plotted on
semilog graph
paper

equal *amounts* of change and the $\hat{y}$-values calculated from the equation $\hat{y} = a + bx$ plot as a straight line on arithmetic paper. On ratio paper, however, equal intervals on the vertical scale represent equal *rates* of change and the $\hat{y}$-values calculated from the equation

$$\hat{y} = a \cdot b^x$$

plot as a straight line on ratio paper. This latter curve is called **exponential** since the x appears in the equation as the exponent of b, and the trends of time series which appear linear when plotted on ratio paper are called **exponential trends**.

Taking the logarithm of the expressions on both sides of the equation $\hat{y} = a \cdot b^x$, we have

$$\log \hat{y} = \log a + x \cdot \log b$$

which is a linear equation in x and $\log \hat{y}$. (Writing A, B, and Y for $\log a$, $\log b$, and $\log \hat{y}$, the equation becomes $Y = A + Bx$, which is the usual equation of a straight line.) In order to fit an exponential trend by the method of least squares (that is, to fit a straight line to the logarithms of the y values), we find numerical values for $\log a$ and $\log b$ from the formulas

$$\log a = \frac{\Sigma \log y}{n} \quad \text{and} \quad \log b = \frac{\Sigma (x \cdot \log y)}{\Sigma x^2}$$

provided that, by the usual change of scale, we make $\Sigma x = 0$; then we find a and b. The work proceeds exactly the same as in fitting a straight line to the y-values themselves, with the exception that we use $\log y$ instead of y.

EXAMPLE 20.7 Fit an exponential curve to the 1960, 1965, 1970, 1975, 1980, 1985, and 1990 daily average number of shares of stock traded on the New York Stock Exchange given on page 774.

SOLUTION There is an odd number of data points in the period, so we code the data by setting the zero of a new x-scale at the middle of the period, which is the year 1975, and count backward and forward from there in units of 5-years. In other words, we code the 5-year periods as $-3, -2, -1, 0, 1, 2,$ and 3. Taking the logarithms needed for the work from Table XI on page 871, we develop the sums needed to find $\log a$ and $\log b$ in the following table:

Year	x	Shares traded (thousands) y	$\log y$	$x \cdot \log y$	x^2
1960	-3	3,042	3.4832	-10.4496	9
1965	-2	6,176	3.7907	-7.5814	4
1970	-1	11,564	4.0631	-4.0631	1
1975	0	18,551	4.2684	0.0000	0
1980	1	44,871	4.6519	4.6519	1
1985	2	109,169	5.0381	10.0762	4
1990	3	156,777	5.1953	15.5859	9
	Total		30.4907	8.2199	28

Substituting the appropriate column totals and $n = 7$ into the formulas for $\log a$ and $\log b$, we get

$$\log a = \frac{30.4907}{7} = 4.3558$$

$$\log b = \frac{8.2199}{28} = 0.2936$$

and we write the trend equation in its logarithmic form and its legend as

$$\log \hat{y} = 4.3558 + 0.2936x$$
(origin 1975; x units, 5 years;
y, daily average shares traded
in thousands of shares)

Table XI shows that the numbers whose logarithms are 4.3558 and 0.2936 are 22,690 and 1.97, so we write the exponential trend equation as

$$\hat{y} = 22,690(1.97)^x$$

In this form, 22,690 is the trend value for 1975, and 1.97 is 1 plus the average 5-year growth of shares traded daily on the New York Stock Exchange over the 30-year period. Hence, the average growth is 0.97 or 97 percent.

For most practical purposes the logarithmic form of the exponential trend equation is more convenient. For instance, to estimate the number of shares traded in 1995, we substitute $x = 4$ into the logarithmic form of the equation and get

$$\log \hat{y} = 4.3558 + (0.2936)(4) = 5.5302$$

Turning to Table XI once again, we find that $\hat{y}$ itself is 339,000. Thus, the estimated average number of shares traded daily in 1995 (based on the 1960–1990 trend) is 339,000,000   ■

If the series has an even number of data points (decades, five-year periods, years, months), we can perform the coding procedure described on page 766.

EXAMPLE 20.8   Fit an exponential curve to the 1965, 1970, 1975, 1980, 1985, and 1990 daily average number of shares of stock traded data shown on page 774. This is the same problem as in Example 20.7, except that the 1960 figure has been deleted.

SOLUTION   There is an even number of data points in the series, so we code the data by setting the zero of a new x-scale halfway between the years 1975 and 1980. In other words, we code the years -5, -3, -1, 1, 3, and 5. Taking the logarithms needed for the work from Table XI, we develop the sums needed to find $\log a$ and $\log b$ in the following table.

Year	x	Shares traded (thousands) y	log y	x · log y	x^2
1965	−5	6,176	3.7907	−18.9535	25
1970	−3	11,564	4.0631	−12.1893	9
1975	−1	18,551	4.2684	−4.2684	1
1980	1	44,871	4.6519	4.6519	1
1985	3	109,169	5.0381	15.1143	9
1990	5	156,777	5.1953	25.9765	25
		Total	27.0075	10.3315	70

Substituting the appropriate column totals and $n = 6$ into the formulas for log a and log b, we get

$$\log a = \frac{27.0075}{6} = 4.5012$$

$$\log b = \frac{10.3315}{70} = 0.1476$$

and we write the trend equation in its logarithmic form and its legend as

$$\log y = 4.5012 + 0.1476x$$
(origin, 1975–1980; x units, half of
5-year period; y, daily average shares
traded, in thousands of shares)

Log y and y, the actual trend values for the year 1965–1990, are readily calculated and are shown as follows:

Year	log y	y
1965	3.7632	5,797
1970	4.0584	11,440
1975	4.3536	22,570
1980	4.6488	44,540
1985	4.9440	87,900
1990	5.2392	173,500

∎

There are various other ways trends can be described mathematically, but even though no two series may be exactly alike, most of them can be handled by the methods we have described here. In each case, our goal is to select that equation or that method of measuring trend which best describes the gradual and consistent pattern of growth.

EXERCISES

(Exercises 20.1, 20.2, 20.5, 20.8, and 20.12 are practice exercises. Their complete solutions are given on page 813.)

20.1 According to the Bureau of Mines, U.S. Interior Department, exports of aluminum (in thousands of metric tons) from 1984 to 1988 were 908, 753, 917, 1,247, and 1,613, respectively.

(a) Plot this series on arithmetic paper.

(b) Fit a least-squares line to the data, and plot it on the chart showing the original data.

20.2 Following are sales in hundreds of millions of dollars as shown in the 1991 annual report of Gerber Products Company and subsidiaries (manufacturers of baby foods and products) for the years 1986 through 1991: 7.31, 8.00, 9.34, 10.33, 11.36, and 11.79.

(a) Plot the series on arithmetic paper.

(b) Fit a least-squares line to this series and plot it on the chart drawn in part (a).

20.3 Following are annual fire losses in the United States in billions of dollars for the years 1980 through 1988, as reported by the Insurance Information Institute, New York: 5.58, 5.62, 5.89, 6.32, 7.60, 7.75, 8.49, 8.63, and 9.63.

(a) Plot the series on arithmetic paper.

(b) Fit a least-squares line to the data, and plot it on the chart of part (a).

(c) Modify the trend equation by shifting the origin of x to the year 1988.

20.4 Following are the profits, in millions of dollars, of a specialty chemical manufacturer for the years 1984–1992: 31.6, 35.9, 40.7, 46.5, 41.1, 45.2, 43.3, 40.9, and 46.5.

(a) Plot the series on arithmetic paper.

(b) Fit a least-squares trend line to these revenues and plot the line on the chart drawn in part (a).

(c) Modify the equation obtained in part (b) for use with monthly data and shift the origin to January 1988.

20.5 Following are the numbers (in thousands) of fishermen employed in U.S. fisheries, as reported in *Fishery Statistics of the United States* (annual) for the years 1980–1988: 193, 198, 216, 223, 230, 239, 247, 256, and 274.

(a) Fit a least-squares trend line to this employment data.

(b) Modify the equation of the trend line obtained in part (a) by shifting the origin to the middle of the year 1987.

(c) Modify the equation of the trend of part (a) by shifting the origin to the end of the year 1982.

(d) Plot the employment series on arithmetic paper, and add the trend obtained in part (a).

20.6 The equation of the least-squares trend line to fit the total value of running shoes sold by an athletic shoe manufacturer for the years 1982–1992 is

$$\hat{y} = 9.40 + 0.60x$$

(origin, 1987; x units, 1 year; annual amounts in millions of dollars)

Modify this trend equation for use with monthly data and shift the origin of the equation to January 1987.

20.7 The equation of a least-squares trend line to fit the annual revenues of The Printing Applications Corporation for the years 1983–1992 is

$$\hat{y} = 995.6 + 32.3x$$

(origin, 1987–1988; x units, 6 months; y, total annual revenues in thousands of dollars)

Modify this trend equation for use with monthly data and shift the origin of x to January 1989.

20.8 In order to calculate the trend values $\hat{y} = a + bx + cx^2$ of a parabolic trend, we can make up a table with columns headed *year*, x, $a + bx$, cx^2, and $\hat{y}$, then calculate $a + bx$ and cx^2 separately for each x and add them to get $\hat{y}$. Turn to Example 20.6 on page 771, and calculate the trend values for the 11 years of the series showing the production of petroleum by the Organization of the Petroleum Exporting Countries.

20.9 Following is the circulation data, in millions of copies, of daily evening newspapers in the United States for the years 1940–1990.

Year	Circulation (in millions of copies)
1940	25.0
1945	29.1
1950	32.6
1955	34.0
1960	34.9
1965	36.3
1970	36.2
1975	36.2
1980	32.8
1985	26.4
1990	21.0

(a) Fit a parabolic trend to this series.

(b) Plot this series and its trend on arithmetic paper.

20.10 Following are the net earnings of UST, Inc. (a publicly traded corporation), for the years 1982–1990.

Year	Net earnings (in millions)
1982	$55
1983	71
1984	84
1985	94
1986	104
1987	131
1988	162
1989	190
1990	223

(a) Plot this series on arithmetic paper.

(b) Fit a parabola to this series by the method of least squares.

(c) What is the trend value for the year 1990?

20.11 With reference to the earnings of UST, Inc., in Exercise 20.10, calculate the yearly trend values for the net earnings of the corporation. Plot them on the chart drawn in part (a) of Exercise 20.10, and draw a smooth curve through these points to indicate the parabolic trend.

20.12 The net earnings series of UST, Inc., in Exercise 20.10 straighten out reasonably well when plotted on ratio paper.

(a) Fit a least-squares line to the logarithms of the values of this series.

(b) From the least-squares equation of part (a) find the logarithms of the trend values for the years 1982–1990; then find the trend values themselves.

(c) Plot the trend values on the chart of the preceding exercise, draw a smooth curve through them to indicate the exponential trend, and then compare visually the parabolic and exponential trends.

(d) What was the average annual percentage growth in net earnings over the nine-year period under consideration.

20.13 Following are annual U.S. exports of goods and services and income in billions of dollars (given at five-year intervals). The data exclude transfers under U.S. military grant programs.

Year	*Exports (in billions)*
1960	$ 31
1965	43
1970	68
1975	158
1980	343
1985	366
1990	652

(a) Fit an exponential curve to these data.

(b) Calculate the yearly trend values for the series.

20.14 Choose what seems to be the best mathematical description of the trend of the following short series; then fit the least-squares trend in the most economical way you can.

(a) In 1990, 1991, and 1992 a bookstore sold 10,000, 11,000, and 12,000 books, respectively.

(b) In 1990, 1991, and 1992 a bookstore sold 5,000, 10,000, and 20,000 books, respectively.

20.15 Comment on the following statement: The use of a least-squares line eliminates all subjectivity in measuring the trend in a time series since, for a given series of data, there is only one line for which $\sum(y - \hat{y})^2$ is a minimum.

20.5

Moving Averages

A secular trend is often considered to be an indication of the "general sweep" of the development of a time series. If it is uncertain whether the trend is linear or whether it might be better described by some other kind of curve, if we are not sure whether we are actually dealing with a trend or part of a cycle, and if we are not really interested in obtaining a mathematical equation, we can describe the overall "behavior" of a time series quite well by means of an artificial series called a **moving average**. A moving average is constructed by replacing each value in a series by the mean of itself and some of the values directly preceding and directly following it. For instance, in a 3-year moving average calculated for annual data, each annual figure is replaced by the mean of itself and the annual figures for the two adjacent years; in a 5-year moving average, each annual figure is replaced by the mean of itself, those of the two preceding years and those of the two following years. If the averaging is done over an even number of periods, say, 4 years or 12 months, the moving average will initially fall between successive years or months. In such cases, the values are customarily brought "back in line" (or "centered") by taking a subsequent 2-year (or 2-month) moving average. We shall use this procedure later in measuring seasonal variation.

The basic problem in constructing a moving average is choosing an appropriate period for the average. This choice depends largely on the nature of the data and the purpose for which the average is constructed. Ordinarily, the purpose of fitting a moving average is to eliminate, insofar as possible, some sort of unwanted or distracting fluctuations in the data. In describing the trend of annual data by a moving average, for example, the main problem is to eliminate those up and down departures of the data from the basic trend which result from business cyclical influences. If all business cycles were exactly alike both in duration and amplitude, their influences could be easily removed from (averaged out of) a series because any absolutely uniform periodic movements are completely eliminated by a moving average whose period is equal to (or a multiple of) the period of the movement. This means also that, if the seasonal movements in a series of monthly data were exactly uniform, the seasonal (and also most of the irregular) variations could be removed from the series by fitting to it a 12-month moving average. However, uniformly periodic cyclical, seasonal, and irregular movements do not appear in economic time series, so the effect of fitting moving averages to series is to smooth out, but not eliminate completely, certain fluctuations in the series.

Computer programs are available to calculate moving averages. These programs can greatly reduce the amount of repetitive arithmetic and reduce the possibility of error.

EXAMPLE 20.9   Construct a five-year moving average for the years 1959–1990 to smooth the series consisting of pretax corporate profits in the United States in billions of dollars.

SOLUTION   We show the original data in the second column of the following table.

Year	Corporate profits before tax	Five-year moving total	Five-year moving average
1959	53.4		
1960	51.1		
1961	51.0	273.1	54.6
1962	56.4	287.7	57.5
1963	61.2	315.4	63.1
1964	68.0	349.5	69.9
1965	78.8	374.9	75.0
1966	85.1	404.3	80.9
1967	81.8	425.3	85.1
1968	90.6	424.9	85.0
1969	89.0	429.9	86.0
1970	78.4	452.6	90.5
1971	90.1	492.9	98.6
1972	104.5	546.7	109.3
1973	130.9	608.7	121.7
1974	142.8	692.3	138.5
1975	140.4	791.1	158.2
1976	173.7	898.1	179.6
1977	203.3	1,016.7	203.3
1978	237.9	1,117.2	223.4
1979	261.4	1,172.4	234.5
1980	240.9	1,145.4	229.1
1981	228.9	1,118.2	223.6
1982	176.3	1,097.3	219.5
1983	210.7	1,081.4	216.3
1984	240.5	1,070.3	214.1
1985	225.0	1,181.9	236.4
1986	217.8	1,318.7	263.7
1987	287.9	1,422.7	284.5
1988	347.5	1,530.0	306.0
1989	344.5		
1990	332.3		

In the third column we show the five-year **moving totals** which consist, for each total shown, of the sum of that year's figure and the figures for the two preceding and the two following years. We get the five-year moving averages shown in the last column by dividing each moving total by 5 (or multiplying it by $\dfrac{1}{5} = 0.20$). ∎

Figure 20.9 is a computer printout of the previous example concerning pretax corporate profits in the United States in billions of dollars. The computer printout is in the same format and the solution is identical to that shown in Example 20.9, but the amount of labor required to calculate and display the answer is greatly reduced.

Both the original series and the five-year moving average are shown in Figure 20.10, and it is evident from this figure that the moving average has substantially reduced the fluctuations in the series and given it a much smoother appearance. The missing values at the beginning and at the end of the artificial series are characteristic of moving averages of this sort: We lose one value at each end for a three-year moving average, two for a five-year moving average, three for a seven-year moving average, and so on. This is

Year	Corporate Profits Before tax	Five year Moving Totals	Five year Moving Averages
1959	53.4		
1960	51.1		
1961	51.0	273.1	54.6
1962	56.4	287.7	57.5
1963	61.2	315.4	63.1
1964	68.0	349.5	69.9
1965	78.8	374.9	75.0
1966	85.1	404.3	80.9
1967	81.8	425.3	85.1
1968	90.6	424.9	85.0
1969	89.0	429.9	86.0
1970	78.4	452.6	90.5
1971	90.1	492.9	98.6
1972	104.5	546.7	109.3
1973	130.9	608.7	121.7
1974	142.8	692.3	138.5
1975	140.4	791.1	158.2
1976	173.7	898.1	179.6
1977	203.3	1016.7	203.3
1978	237.9	1117.2	223.4
1979	261.4	1172.4	234.5
1980	240.9	1145.4	229.1
1981	228.9	1118.2	223.6
1982	176.3	1097.3	219.5
1983	210.7	1081.4	216.3
1984	240.5	1070.3	214.1
1985	225.0	1181.9	236.4
1986	217.8	1318.7	263.7
1987	287.9	1422.7	284.5
1988	347.5	1530.0	306.0
1989	344.5		
1990	332.3		

FIGURE 20.9

Computer printout for pretax corporate profits in the United States

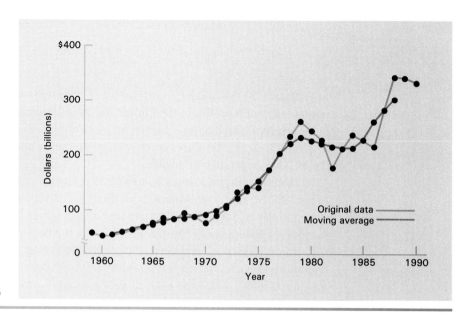

FIGURE 20.10
Pretax corporate
profits, 1959–1990

often of no consequence, but it may cause a problem if a series is very short or if values are needed for each year for further calculations.

20.6

Exponential Smoothing

Moving averages have been widely used for many years to smooth certain unwanted fluctuations out of time series and, hence, describe their underlying nature. A more recently developed smoothing technique—called **exponential smoothing**—is now also available for this purpose. In addition, exponential smoothing is ideally suited to short-run forecasting for inventory control; indeed, the technique was originally used in business mainly to provide an efficient and economical way to forecast item-by-item demand for items covered by automated inventory control systems. This is particularly important in large companies where, often, literally thousands and thousands of items are stocked and it is necessary to make routine forecasts of, say, the week-to-week, or month-to-month, demand for each item.

Exponential smoothing is a particular kind of moving average, but its nature is quite different from the conventional moving average process described in the preceding section. In calculating a conventional moving average, each item in the averaging period is given a weight and all items outside the period are given no weight at all. For instance, as we proceed through the calculation of a five-year moving average using equal weights, each item in each set of five items being averaged is weighted 1 and all the other items not included in the set are weighted 0.

In exponential smoothing, the smoothed value at time t, S_t, is a weighted average of the observed value at time t, y_t, and all the other past (historical) values in the series: $y_{t-1}, y_{t-2}, \ldots$, and y_1. This is not immediately apparent from the way in which the smoothed values are calculated. In practice, we begin by setting S_1, the first value in the series of smoothed values, equal to y_1, the first actual value in the series. Then, as we move forward, at each new time period the new smoothed value is α times the current observed value of y plus $1 - \alpha$ times the previous smoothed value of y, where α, the **smoothing constant**, is a fraction between 0 and 1 which we may choose at our discretion. Hence, the second smoothed value is

$$S_2 = \alpha y_2 + (1 - \alpha)S_1$$

the third smoothed value is

$$S_3 = \alpha y_3 + (1 - \alpha)S_2$$

and in general the smoothed value for time period t is

Exponential smoothing

$$S_t = \alpha y_t + (1 - \alpha)S_{t-1}$$

To show that S_t does, indeed, depend on all the past values in the series, we write $S_{t-1} = \alpha y_{t-1} + (1 - \alpha)S_{t-2}$, and, substituting into the formula for S_t, we get

$$\begin{aligned} S_t &= \alpha y_t + (1 - \alpha)[\alpha y_{t-1} + (1 - \alpha)S_{t-2}] \\ &= \alpha y_t + \alpha(1 - \alpha)y_{t-1} + (1 - \alpha)^2 S_{t-2} \end{aligned}$$

Then we write $S_{t-2} = \alpha y_{t-2} + (1 - \alpha)S_{t-3}$, and, substituting into the result just obtained, we get

$$S_t = \alpha y_t + \alpha(1 - \alpha)y_{t-1} + (1 - \alpha)^2[\alpha y_{t-2} + (1 - \alpha)S_{t-3}]$$
$$= \alpha y_t + \alpha(1 - \alpha)y_{t-1} + \alpha(1 - \alpha)^2 y_{t-2} + (1 - \alpha)^3 S_{t-3}$$

Repeating this process $t - 4$ more times, we finally arrive at the result that

$$S_t = \alpha y_t + \alpha(1 - \alpha)y_{t-1} + \alpha(1 - \alpha)^2 y_{t-2} + \alpha(1 - \alpha)^3 y_{t-3} + \cdots$$
$$+ (1 - \alpha)^{t-1} y_1$$

We see from this that the weight assigned to each observed value in the series decreases exponentially, and this is why we refer to the process as exponential smoothing. Depending on the value of α, the weights assigned to the earlier values in the series decrease more or less rapidly, and, if the averaging process is carried far enough forward, a time comes when the earliest values have very little effect on the current smoothed value.

At the level of this book, we cannot discuss the mathematics of choosing an optimum smoothing constant to meet a particular objective. It is clear, however, that if α is too large, we give too much weight to the current values as they occur, and we will not adequately smooth out the irregular variations. On the other hand, if α is too small, we give too little weight to the current values in the series, and the moving average is insensitive to changes that may actually be taking place.

EXAMPLE 20.10   A real estate development corporation keeps voluminous statistical data on various areas and properties which seem to have above average potential for future purchase or development of one sort or another. Among these data are the annual amounts of snowfall (in feet) during the snow season at the site of a proposed winter resort. The snowfall amounts for the 26-year period 1967–1992 are shown in the second column of the table on page 789, and the graph of the series is shown in Figure 20.11. From an inspection of the data in the table and its graph no trend is apparent, but there is obviously a good deal of irregular, or random, year-to-year variation, and this is what we want to smooth (or average) out. Smooth the series using exponential smoothing, first with the smoothing constant $\alpha = 0.2$ and then with the smoothing constant $\alpha = 0.5$.

SOLUTION   The third column of the table shows the exponentially smoothed values calculated with the constant $\alpha = 0.2$, and the fourth column shows the smoothed values calculated with $\alpha = 0.5$.

Year	Annual snow-fall, y_t	S_t ($\alpha = 0.2$)	S_t ($\alpha = 0.5$)
1967	9.9	9.9	9.9
1968	22.2	12.4	16.0
1969	11.4	12.2	13.7
1970	14.8	12.7	14.2
1971	19.7	14.1	17.0
1972	14.9	14.3	16.0
1973	15.9	14.6	16.0
1974	13.4	14.4	14.7
1075	12.0	13.9	13.4
1976	7.9	12.7	10.6
1977	12.9	12.7	11.8
1978	16.8	13.5	14.3
1979	11.6	13.1	13.0
1980	14.9	13.5	14.0
1981	13.3	13.5	13.6
1982	20.2	14.8	17.0
1983	14.3	14.7	15.6
1984	20.4	15.8	18.0
1985	13.0	15.2	15.6
1986	10.0	14.2	12.8
1987	15.9	14.5	14.4
1988	17.4	15.1	15.9
1989	18.7	15.8	17.3
1990	14.3	15.5	15.8
1991	16.2	15.6	16.0
1992	21.1	16.7	18.6

In this example, we took the first year's snowfall, 9.9 feet, for the first value, S_1, of both smoothed series. Then, with $\alpha = 0.2$, the second value is

$$S_2 = (0.2)(22.2) + (0.8)(9.9) = 12.4$$

the third value is

$$S_3 = (0.2)(11.4) + (0.8)(12.4) = 12.2$$

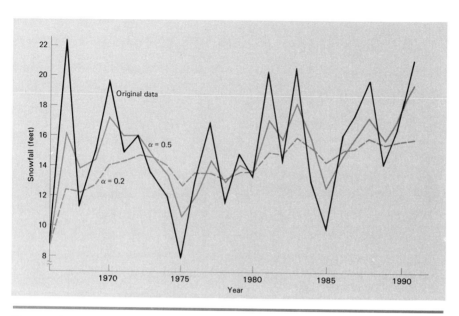

FIGURE 20.11   Exponentially smoothed time series

the fourth value is

$$S_4 = (0.2)(14.8) + (0.8)(12.2) = 12.7$$

and so on. The values in the series with the smoothing constant $\alpha = 0.5$ are calculated in the same way.   ■

It can be seen from the plot of the original data and the two smoothed series in Figure 20.11 that the choice of the smoothing constant has a pronounced effect on the extent of the smoothing. The series with $\alpha = 0.2$ is a good deal more stable than the series with $\alpha = 0.5$, and this is what we want when our objective is to average out the year-to-year changes in the data (which we presume are merely random fluctuations) rather than to respond to them the way the series with $\alpha = 0.5$ does. Of course, when we use exponential smoothing to help predict, say, the market demand for an item at a later time, we want quick responses to whatever actual changes may occur in the level of demand (for instance, an anticipated large stepwise increase resulting from an intensive advertising campaign); this suggests that, at least for a time, we use a relatively large value of α.

Chapter 20   Time-Series Analysis

(Exercises 20.16 and 20.21 are practice exercises. Their complete solutions are given on page 813.)

20.16 Following are the billions of square yards of cotton cloth produced in the United States from 1971 to 1990: 6.1, 5.6, 5.1, 4.7, 4.1, 4.7, 4.4, 4.0, 3.9, 4.5, 3.9, 3.8, 4.2, 4.0, 3.9, 4.4, 4.7, 4.5, 4.6, and 4.5.

(a) Construct a three-year moving average.

(b) Construct a five-year moving average.

(c) Plot the original data, the three-year moving average, and the five-year moving average as shown in Figure 20.10.

20.17 Following are the numbers of automobiles sold by a dealer for the years 1963–1992: 144, 132, 120, 132, 168, 156, 168, 168, 180, 204, 216, 252, 216, 288, 276, 324, 336, 336, 348, 408, 360, 372, 444, 420, 384, 420, 384, 396, 300, and 348.

(a) Construct a three-year moving average and draw a graph showing this moving average together with the original data.

(b) Construct a five-year moving average, add it to the graph of part (a), and compare the two moving averages.

20.18 Following are profits after taxes, in billions of dollars, of corporations in the United States for the years 1970–1990: 44.0, 52.4, 62.6, 81.6, 91.0, 89.5, 109.5, 130.3, 154.4, 173.4, 156.1, 147.8, 113.2, 133.5, 146.4, 128.5, 111.3, 160.8, 210.5, 206.6, and 197.0.

(a) Calculate a three-year moving average and draw a graph showing this moving average together with the original data.

(b) Calculate a five-year moving average, add it to the graph of part (a), and compare the two moving averages.

20.19 Following are the highest prices paid (in dollars per share) for a speculative stock in 26 consecutive months: 34, 20, 44, 45, 32, 41, 38, 29, 31, 28, 22, 43, 26, 25, 27, 30, 37, 21, 33, 36, 42, 23, 24, 39, 40, and 35. Calculate a three-month moving average for the series, and draw a graph showing it together with the original data.

20.20 The following data show total factory sales of cars, trucks, and buses in millions of vehicles, from 1974 to 1990: 10.0, 9.0, 11.5, 12.6, 12.8, 11.5, 8.0, 8.0, 7.0, 9.2, 10.7, 11.4, 10.9, 10.9, 11.2, 10.9, and 9.8. Calculate a five-year moving average for these data, and draw a graph showing it together with the original data.

20.21 The following series shows the number of requests for washing machine repairs at an appliance service company on 10 consecutive business days:

25, 34, 23, 20, 25, 17, 19, 31, 15, and 11. Smooth this series using

(a) the smoothing constant $\alpha = 0.2$

(b) the smoothing constant $\alpha = 0.4$

20.22 Use the formula on page 787 to express S_4 in terms of α, y_4, y_3, y_2, and y_1, and use this result to verify the answers to the preceding exercise.

20.23 The following series shows U.S. exports of tires and tubes (in hundreds of millions of dollars) from 1984 to 1989: 3.9, 3.4, 3.2, 5.1, 7.7, and 8.6. Smooth this series using

(a) the smoothing constant $\alpha = 0.1$

(b) the smoothing constant $\alpha = 0.4$

20.24 The exponential smoothing process with smoothing constant α produces an average which is statistically similar to a $[(2/\alpha) - 1]$-term conventional moving average. For instance, if $\alpha = 0.5$, an exponentially smoothed average is statistically similar to a $(2/0.5) - 1 = 3$-term moving average; and if $\alpha = 0.01$, the exponentially smoothed average is similar to a $(2/0.01) - 1 = 199$-term moving average. This helps explain why a small value of α produces a more stable exponentially smoothed series than a larger value of α does.

(a) If $\alpha = 0.2$, what is the equivalent number of terms being averaged in a conventional moving average?

(b) For what value of α is an exponentially smoothed series equivalent to a 19-term moving average?

By statistical similarity we mean that the variabilities in the exponentially smoothed series and the moving average, not the corresponding terms in the two series, are equivalent.

20.25 When we use exponential smoothing in making short-range predictions, we take the smoothed value at period t, S_t, as the estimate of y at period $t + 1$. Designating this estimate y'_{t+1}, we have

$$y'_{t+1} = S_t = \alpha y_t + (1 - \alpha)S_{t-1}$$

and since $S_{t-1} = y'_t$,

$$y'_{t+1} = \alpha y_t + (1 - \alpha)y'_t$$

As before, we may set the smoothed value at period 1, S_1 (and consequently, the estimated value at period 2, y'_2), equal to y_1; if we prefer, we may assign the average of some recent values to S_1 and y'_2. If, for instance, we want to use an exponential smoothing formula which is statistically equivalent to a 15-term moving average, we can set S_1 and y'_2 equal to the average of the 15 most recent values of y. Estimates for succeeding periods may then be made by using either of the smoothing formulas above with the appropriate α each time the new value y_t becomes available.

(a) A large manufacturer wants to estimate at the end of each week the number of replacement parts of a particular kind which will be demanded the following week for one group of machines. No trend has been observed in the demand for the part for some time and none is anticipated in the near future, nor is there any periodic variation in the demand. The following are the numbers of parts demanded in weekly periods 1–14: 24, 20, 16, 20, 25, 24, 26, 19, 16, 22, 20, 24, 19, and 23. Choose a smoothing formula which is equivalent to a four-term moving average, set $S_1 = y_2' = 19$ (the average demand in the four weeks preceding period 1), and estimate the demand for the remaining periods.

(b) With reference to part (a), set $S_1 = y_1 = 24$ (the actual demand in period 1) and estimate the demand for the remaining periods using $\alpha = 0.2$.

20.7

Seasonal Variation

Let us now consider the problem of measuring those movements in a time series which recur more or less regularly in the same months of successive years. We call the measures of this seasonal variation an **index of seasonal variation**, or a **seasonal index**. For monthly data a seasonal index consists of 12 numbers, one for each month, each of which expresses that particular month's activity as a percentage of the average month's activity. For instance, if the June seasonal index of sales of a wholesaler is 92, this means that June sales are typically 92 percent of sales in the average month. We used the word "typically" here because the actual percentage for a given month varies more or less widely from year to year, and 92 percent is an average of these percentages.

Although seasonal indexes are usually calculated monthly, they can be prepared for other subdivisions of a year, say, quarterly or weekly. For quarterly data a seasonal index consists of 4 numbers, each of which expresses that quarter's activity as a percentage of the average quarter's activity. For weekly data the index consists of 52 numbers, each of which expresses that particular week's activity as a percentage of the average week's activity. In this chapter we focus primarily upon monthly seasonals to avoid unnecessary repetition of the basic concepts, since the procedure shown for monthly indexes can readily be adapted to other time periods.

There are many ways in which seasonal variation can be measured or a seasonal index can be constructed. These range from rather crude measures based on very simple calculations to highly refined measures based on involved computer techniques. We shall illustrate the construction of a seasonal index by using the basic **ratio-to-moving-average**, or **percentage-of-moving-average**, method. Until certain refinements were made possible by the use of high-speed computers, this basic method was probably the most widely used and the most generally satisfactory one available. Today, it is still the best introduction to one's study of seasonal variation.

In constructing a seasonal index all our efforts are aimed at eliminating trend, cyclical, and irregular variations from the series. The way this is done in the basic ratio-to-moving-average method is relatively simple. We begin by calculating a 12-month moving average of the data in order to remove the seasonal movements from the series. Since an n-period moving average will completely eliminate any absolutely uniform n-period recurring movement, a 12-month moving average would eliminate all the seasonal movements from the series, provided these movements recurred with complete regularity year after year. Of course, in actual practice seasonal patterns vary somewhat from year to year, so the moving average cannot be expected to eliminate all of the seasonal variation. It will eliminate most of it, however, as well as most of the irregular variation, so the 12-month moving average is an estimate of the trend and cyclical components of the series. In the classical model we are discussing, each value in the original series is assumed to be the product of factors attributed to the four basic components (secular trend, seasonal variation, cyclical variation, and irregular variation). Therefore, dividing each value by the corresponding value of the 12-month moving average gives an estimate of the seasonal and irregular components in the series. In other words, dividing $T \cdot S \cdot C \cdot I$ by $T \cdot C$ leaves us with $S \cdot I$, the product of the factors attributed to seasonal and irregular variations. All that is left to do then is to eliminate, insofar as possible, the irregular fluctuations.

When one knows a good deal about the series under study, it may be possible to identify and eliminate directly the monthly $S \cdot I$ values which reflect the impact of extraordinary events (for example, a crippling nine-day fog or a strike in a supplier's plant). Irregular variations of this sort, as well as those which are due to chance (nonassignable causes) can also be effectively eliminated by averaging, in some way, the $S \cdot I$ figures for the different Januaries, for the different Februaries, and so on. We can, for instance, reduce the effect of the irregular forces by using the median of the values given for each month, or perhaps by using the **modified (arithmetic) mean** which is the mean of the values remaining after the smallest and largest values have been cast out. Moving averages can also be used for smoothing out the irregular variations remaining at this stage of the calculation. In any case, by some sort of averaging process, we finally arrive at an estimate of the way seasonal factors alone influence the values of a series. This estimate, consisting of the 12 monthly values, is the seasonal index.

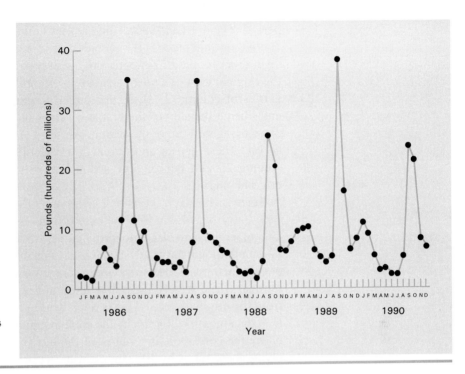

FIGURE 20.12
Receipts of rough rice from producers by southern states' mills

To illustrate the calculation of a seasonal index we shall make use of the series showing receipts of rough rice from producers by southern states' (Louisiana, Texas, Arkansas, Mississippi, and Tennessee) mills. The original data, plotted in Figure 20.12 and given in column 1 of the table on pages 796–797, are the monthly receipts in hundreds of millions of pounds for the years 1986–1990. This is a period which, for purposes of this discussion, we consider to be typical of the way such receipts of rough rice vary from month to month. The pronounced seasonal pattern in the receipts, with no major discernible trend, is evident from the graph.

EXAMPLE 20.11   Calculate a seasonal index for receipts of rough rice by using the basic ratio-to-moving-average method.

SOLUTION   The first step in the procedure is to calculate the 12-month moving totals shown in column 2. The first entry in this column, 102.0, is the sum of the 12 monthly receipts for 1986, and it is recorded at the middle of the period, between June and July 1986. The second entry in this column, 102.1, is obtained by subtracting the January 1986 figure from 102.0 and adding the January 1987 figure; in other words, 102.1 is the sum of the 12 monthly receipts from February 1986 through January 1987, and it is recorded at the middle of this period. The third and succeeding entries in the column are found by continuing this process of subtracting and adding monthly values.

In order to get a 12-month moving average which is centered on the original data, we next calculate two-month moving totals of the entries of column 2. These are shown in column 3, with the first entry being the sum of the first two values in column 2, the second entry being the sum of the second and third values in column 2, and so on. These entries in column 3 are recorded between those of column 2, and, hence, they are in line with (or centered on) the original data.

Since each entry of column 2 is the sum of 12 monthly figures and each entry of column 3 is the sum of two entries of column 2, or altogether the sum of 24 monthly figures, we finally get the centered 12-month moving average shown in column 4 by dividing each entry of column 3 by 24. These moving average values are the trend-cycle estimates, and we use them now to eliminate the $T \cdot C$ components from the original series. This is done by dividing the original $T \cdot S \cdot C \cdot I$ data month by month by the corresponding $T \cdot C$ estimates (that is, by the corresponding values of the moving average) and multiplying these ratios by 100. In this way, we arrive at the percentages of moving average shown in column 5.

Receipts of Rough Rice from Producers by Southern States' Mills* (hundreds of millions of pounds)

Year	Month	Receipts (1)	12-month moving total (2)	2-month moving total (3)	Centered 12-month moving average (4)	Percentages of 12-month moving average (5)
1986	January	2.1				
	February	2.0				
	March	1.5				
	April	4.5				
	May	6.9				
	June	4.9				
	July	3.9	102.0	204.1	8.5	45.9
	August	11.7	102.1	207.3	8.6	136.0
	September	35.2	105.2	213.2	8.9	395.5
	October	11.6	108.0	215.9	9.0	128.9
	November	7.8	107.9	212,5	8.8	88.6
	December	9.9	104.6	208.5	8.7	113.8
1987	January	2.2	103.9	206.6	8.6	25.6
	February	5.1	102.7	201.5	8.4	60.7

Chapter 20   Time-Series Analysis

	March	4.3	98.8	197.5	8.2	52.4
	April	4.4	98.7	195.5	8.1	54.3
	May	3.6	96.8	194.4	8.1	44.4
	June	4.2	97.6	193.0	8.0	52.5
	July	2.7	95.4	195.1	8.1	33.3
	August	7.8	99.7	200.3	8.3	94.0
	September	35.1	100.6	201.1	8.4	417.8
	October	9.7	100.5	199.4	8.3	116.9
	November	8.6	98.9	196.8	8.2	104.9
	December	7.7	97.9	194.4	8.1	95.1
1988	January	6.5	96.5	191.9	8.0	81.2
	February	6.0	95.4	187.6	7.8	76.9
	March	4.2	92.2	175.0	7.3	57.5
	April	2.8	82.8	176.5	7.4	37.8
	May	2.6	93.7	185.2	7.7	33.8
	June	2.8	91.5	181.4	7.6	36.8
	July	1.6	89.9	181.1	7.5	21.3
	August	4.6	91.2	186.0	7.8	59.0
	September	25.7	94.8	195.4	8.1	317.3
	October	20.6	100.6	208.8	8.7	236.8
	November	6.4	108.2	220.1	9.2	69.6
	December	6.1	111.9	226.2	9.4	64.9
1989	January	7.8	114.3	231.3	9.6	81.2
	February	9.6	117.0	235.0	9.8	98.0
	March	10.0	118.0	248.9	10.4	96.2
	April	10.4	130.9	257.7	10.7	97.2
	May	6.3	126.8	253.7	10.6	59.4
	June	5.2	126.9	256.2	10.7	48.6
	July	4.3	129.3	262.0	10.9	39.4
	August	5.6	132.7	265.3	11.0	50.9
	September	38.6	132.6	260.7	10.9	354.1
	October	16.5	128.1	248.8	10.4	158.6
	November	6.5	120.7	238.5	9.9	65.7
	December	8.5	117.8	232.8	9.7	87.6
1990	January	11.2	115.0	228.1	9.5	117.9
	February	9.5	113.1	226.2	9.4	101.1
	March	5.5	113.1	211.6	8.8	62.5
	April	3.0	98.5	202.0	8.4	35.7
	May	3.4	103.5	208.8	8.7	39.1
	June	2.4	105.3	208.9	8.7	27.6
	July	2.4	103.6			
	August	5.6				
	September	24.0				
	October	21.5				
	November	8.3				
	December	6.8				

*Louisiana, Texas, Arkansas, Mississippi, and Tennessee.

All that remains to be done is to eliminate the irregular variations as best we can, and to this end we arrange the entries of column 5 in the five dated columns of the following table.

From the various ways we could use to average the figures given for each month, we choose the median here. (In this case, where we have four values for each month, the median is, in fact, equivalent to the modified mean.) The 12 medians are shown in the second column from the right. Now, since the seasonal index for each month is supposed to be a percentage of the average month, the sum of the 12 values should equal 1,200. Actually, the medians total 1,161.1, and so we adjust for this by multiplying each of the medians by 1,200/ 1,161.1 = 1.0335 and the sum of the seasonal indexes is 1,200.

Month	1986	1987	1988	1989	1990	Median	Seasonal index
January		25.6	81.2	81.2	117.9	81.2	83.9
February		60.7	76.9	98.0	101.1	87.4	90.3
March		52.4	57.5	96.2	62.5	60.0	62.0
April		54.3	37.8	97.2	35.7	46.0	47.5
May		44.4	33.8	59.4	39.1	41.8	43.2
June		52.5	36.8	48.6	27.6	42.7	44.1
July	45.9	33.3	21.3	39.4		36.4	37.6
August	136.0	94.0	59.0	50.9		76.5	79.1
September	395.5	417.8	317.3	354.1		374.8	387.4
October	128.9	116.9	236.8	158.6		143.8	148.6
November	88.6	104.9	69.6	65.7		79.1	81.8
December	113.8	95.1	64.9	87.6		91.4	94.5
					Total	1,161.1	1,200.0

In some cases the adjustment to obtain the seasonal index is much greater than that needed for this example. This can be seen in Exercise 20.26 on page 804. ■

The interpretation of seasonal indexes is straightforward. For instance, in our example January receipts of rough rice from producers are typically 83.9 percent of those of the average month, receipts of rough rice are usually lowest in July, by far the highest in September and in October receipts are usually 48.6 percent above receipts of the average month.

Observe, however, that in using a seasonal index for any purpose, we must always be mindful of its limitations. An index is based on historical (past) data, and we cannot reasonably expect seasonal patterns to remain completely constant over long periods of time. The method we have illustrated here applies to the description of constant seasonal patterns or seasonal patterns which do not change very much. If there are pronounced changes in the seasonal pattern with the passage of time, the sort of index we have discussed will not be suitable.

20.8

Seasonally Adjusted Data

Seasonal indexes are extremely important in various practical applications. We shall briefly explain two of these, the first in **deseasonalizing** data and the second in **forecasting**. Leaving the use of seasonal indexes in forecasting to the section which follows, let us now describe the process of removing seasonal influences from a given set of data, or deseasonalizing a series. Of course, when seasonal fluctuations have actually occurred, nobody knows how things would have been if a series had been uninfluenced by seasonal factors. So, when we speak of what things would have been like without seasonal fluctuations, we are speaking rather loosely. Nevertheless, the notion of a series of data free from seasonal influences is a useful way of understanding the concept.

The process of removing seasonal variation, or deseasonalizing data, consists merely of dividing each value in a series by the corresponding value of the seasonal index and multiplying the result by 100 (or by dividing by the corresponding value of the seasonal index written as a proportion). The logic of this process is quite simple: If October receipts of rough rice from producers are 148.7 percent of the average month, taking $\frac{100}{148.7} = 67.2$ percent of the August receipts would tell us what these receipts should have been if there had been no seasonal variation.

EXAMPLE 20.12   Deseasonalize the 1990 receipts of rough rice from producers by southern states' mills, using the index constructed earlier.

SOLUTION   In the table which follows, the receipts data and the seasonal index are copied from pages 797 and 798 with values of the seasonal index given as proportions and rounded to two decimals. The values in the right-hand column are the deseasonalized receipts and they are computed by dividing each month's actual receipts by the corresponding value of the seasonal index.

Month	1990 Receipts	Seasonal index	Deseasonalized receipts
January	11.2	0.84	13.3
February	9.5	0.90	10.6
March	5.5	0.62	8.9
April	3.0	0.48	6.2
May	3.4	0.43	7.9
June	2.4	0.44	5.4
July	2.4	0.38	6.3
August	5.6	0.79	7.1
September	24.0	3.87	6.2
October	21.5	1.49	14.4
November	8.3	0.82	10.1
December	6.8	0.94	7.2
Total		12.00	

Inspecting this table we find several interesting facts. For instance, there was an increase of 18.4 hundred million pounds in receipts of rough rice from August to September. This was nothing to rejoice over, however, since the deseasonalized data show that this increase is actually less than might have been expected in accordance with typical seasonal patterns. Receipts were exactly the same in June and July, but July was a better month than June if deseasonalized receipts are compared. Also, there was a drop of 2.5 hundred million pounds from September to October. This was no cause for alarm since October was a much better month than September if deseasonalized receipts are compared. The need for taking seasonal variation into account in the analysis of business and economic time series should be apparent from these observations. ∎

The principal source of seasonally adjusted (deseasonalized) series is the federal government. In constructing these series, seasonal indexes are derived by highly sophisticated computer methods which are essentially a refinement and an extension of the basic ratio-to-moving-average method. The computational burden in this work is tremendous, and without the great arithmetic ability of digital computers, the necessary calculations could never be made for a large number of series within any reasonable limits of time and cost. The Bureau of the Census, however, has developed computer methods to the point where it can now virtually mass produce seasonally adjusted series of a high order of quality for almost all important series of data. Other computer approaches to the seasonal adjustment problem, including further refinements in the ratio-to-moving-average technique and, what is an entirely different concept, seasonal adjustments based on regression analysis, may result in still further improvements in seasonally adjusted series.

20.9

Forecasting

Now that we are familiar with time series and know how to measure some of their components, let us discuss briefly the tremendously complicated problem of business forecasting. The rationale of basing forecasts on time series is that, having observed some regularity in the movement of data through time, we are hopeful that "what has happened in the past will, to a greater or lesser extent, continue to happen or will happen again in the future." Thus, the obvious way to forecast the trend of a time series is to extrapolate from the trend equation describing the historical data. By "extrapolate" we mean extend the trend into the future so as to estimate a value that lies beyond the range of the values used to derive the trend equation.

EXAMPLE 20.13   The following trend equation, calculated by the method of least squares from company sales data extending back over a long period of years, describes the long-term growth in sales of a paint manufacturer:

$$\hat{y} = 64.4 + 2.88x$$
(origin, 1991; x units, 1 year; y, total annual
sales in millions of dollars)

Estimate total sales for the year 1995 and based on a seasonal index to be given shortly, estimate monthly sales for that year.

SOLUTION   The 1991 trend value is $64.4 million and the growth forces are estimated to be producing a $2.88 million increase in sales per year. Substituting $x = 4$ into the trend equation, we find that, based on the long-term growth forces alone, the 1995 expected total sales are $\hat{y} =$ 64.4 + 2.88(4) = 75.92, or $75,920,000.

If the manufacturer's sales were uninfluenced by seasonal fluctuations, we could estimate 1995 monthly sales in precisely the same way. Modifying the trend equation for use with monthly data by dividing a by 12 and b by 144 (by 12 and then 12 again) and then shifting the origin to January 1995 (advancing the origin 42.5 months from the middle of 1991 to the middle of January 1995), we get

$$\hat{y} = 6.22 + 0.02x$$
(origin, January 1995; x units, 1 month; y, average monthly sales in millions of dollars)

Hence, $6.22 million is the trend value for January 1995, and substituting $x = 1, 2, 3, \ldots$, and 11 into this equation we get the trend values for the other 11 months of 1995, all these values are shown in the "Trend values" column of the following table:

Month	Trend value	Seasonal index	Predicted monthly sales for 1995
January	6.22	0.77	4.79
February	6.24	0.73	4.56
March	6.26	1.02	6.39
April	6.28	1.25	7.85
May	6.30	1.40	8.82
June	6.32	1.20	7.58
July	6.34	1.00	6.34
August	6.36	1.05	6.68
September	6.38	0.98	6.25
October	6.40	1.04	6.66
November	6.42	0.81	5.20
December	6.44	0.75	4.83

However, there is a very pronounced variation in the manufacturer's sales, which results from seasonal influences. Sales are typically quite low in November, December, January, and February and quite high in April, May, and June. In fact, a seasonal index calculated from recent historical data by the ratio-to-moving-average method shows that, for example, January sales are only 77 percent and May sales are 140 percent of what they would be if there were no seasonal variation. The complete seasonal index, written as proportions, is shown in the third column of the table.

Assuming that the seasonal pattern is not changing and is adequately described by the seasonal index, we complete the solution of this example by multiplying the trend value for each of the 12 months by the seasonal index for that month. That is, we multiply the January trend value by 0.77, the February trend value by 0.73, and so on, getting the predicted monthly sales (in millions of dollars) shown in the last column of the table. If there were no seasonal variation, we would expect May sales to be $\frac{6.30}{6.22} = 1.013$, or 1.3 percent higher than January sales because of the upward trend in sales; taking into account the seasonal influences, though, May sales are projected at $\frac{8.82}{4.79} = 1.841$, or 84.1 percent higher than January sales. ■

What we have done in arriving at these monthly sales predictions is precisely the opposite of deseasonalizing data. We have introduced the seasonal patterns into the data (rather than removed them from it) by multiplying the trend values by the corresponding values of the seasonal index, written as proportions. These products of a measure of the trend and of the seasonal, or $T \cdot S$, are the values we would expect if trend and seasonal forces were the only factors influencing the values of a series, and they are often called the **normal values**.

In the predicted sales values, we have taken into account the effect of trend and seasonal patterns on the manufacturer's sales, but we have not yet considered the possible effects of cyclical and irregular influences. The latter, we have said, are essentially unpredictable; in the manufacturer's case, a large freight shipment of raw materials lost in transit for five weeks, for instance, or a fire which closes a competing manufacturer's plant for six months cannot be foreseen. The effects of such events may tend to average out in the long run, but they can substantially affect sales in particular months and cause even the most careful forecasts to go astray. In connection with the major problems of forecasting both short-run and long-run business cycles and their effect at the level of the economy as a whole and at industry and firm levels, we shall only remark that much help is available to everyone from both private and public sources. Two very important aids are the *Survey of Current Business*, a monthly publication of the Department of Commerce, and *Economic Indicators*, a monthly publication of the U.S. Congress, Joint Economic Committee. Among the wealth of information contained in these publications are various economic indicators. These are series of data which tend to turn up or down before overall economic activity does, the **leading indicators**; series which tend to move at about the same time as overall activity, the **roughly coincident indicators**; and series which tend to move somewhat behind overall activity, the **lagging indicators**, and hence to confirm or refute the earlier directional signals.

EXERCISES

(Exercises 20.26, 20.27, 20.34, and 20.36 are practice exercises. Their complete solutions are given on page 813.)

20.26 In constructing a seasonal index of gasoline sales for a major petroleum products company by the ratio-to-moving-average method, the following medians were obtained (in the same way that we arrived at the values in the column headed "Median" on page 798): 97.1, 84.3, 90.8, 104.3, 106.4, 109.2, 107.7, 111.1, 102.9, 84.6, 98.0, and 92.3. Complete the calculation of the seasonal index.

20.27 The *Survey of Current Business* shows the following monthly sales (hundreds of thousands of dollars) of liquor stores in the United States for a recent four-year-period:

	Year			
Month	1987	1988	1989	1990
January	1,462	1,438	1,425	1,478
February	1,355	1,344	1,335	1,421
March	1,436	1,457	1,499	1,606
April	1,501	1,524	1,509	1,575
May	1,632	1,593	1,645	1,693
June	1,596	1,624	1,675	1,778
July	1,700	1,684	1,725	1,794
August	1,631	1,582	1,674	1,820
September	1,557	1,512	1,610	1,666
October	1,648	1,508	1,552	1,694
November	1,633	1,574	1,617	1,785
December	2,307	2,303	2,254	2,501

Compute a seasonal index for this series by the ratio-to-moving-average method, using the median to average the percentages of moving average for the individual months.

20.28 Use the seasonal index calculated in the preceding exercise to deseasonalize all of the monthly sales data shown in the exercise. Plot the deseasonalized data together with the original data on one chart.

20.29 With reference to Exercise 20.27, fit a least-squares trend line to the total annual liquor sales for all the years.

20.30 The following table shows the total production of electric utilities in the United States in billions of kilowatt-hours, for the years 1986–1990.

			Year		
Month	1986	1987	1988	1989	1990
January	217	223	238	231	237
February	192	194	217	219	213
March	197	202	214	226	226
April	186	189	196	208	211
May	197	206	208	219	222
June	215	226	232	253	249
July	243	248	257	257	266
August	225	248	267	258	286
September	207	213	220	227	237
October	198	203	210	219	225
November	196	200	209	219	214
December	214	220	232	259	237

Compute the seasonal index for these data by the ratio-to-moving-average method; use the modified mean to average the percentages of moving average for the individual months.

20.31 Use the seasonal index of the preceding exercise to deseasonalize the 1990 production of electric utilities in the United States.

20.32 With reference to Exercise 20.30, fit a trend line by the method of least squares to the total production of electric utilities in the United States for the years 1986–1990.

20.33 Deseasonalized data are often multiplied by 12 and then referred to as **annual rates**. The use of seasonally adjusted annual rates is particularly helpful in facilitating the analysis of month-to-month changes in series of data which are best understood on an annual basis, such as GDP, new housing starts, and various other production series. Accordingly, we often see reported such statements as, ''Americans had more money income in June on an annual rate basis than in any other month in history.'' Based on the seasonally adjusted figure for March 1990 calculated in Exercise 20.31, at what annual rate was total production of electric utilities then running?

20.34 A company selling swimming pool supplies had sales of $20,000 and

$24,000 in March and April of 1992. The company's seasonal index for these two months stands at 105 and 140. The president of the company expressed disappointment in the March-to-April performance and estimated that the total 1992 sales would be only $217,000, a figure substantially less than the sales manager's estimate of $264,000. Is there any real reason to be disappointed with the $4,000 sales increase from March to April? How do you suppose the sales manager and the president arrived at their estimates? Which one seems more reasonable?

20.35 The seasonal index for a clothing manufacturer's sales for the 12 months January through December is 71, 91, 102, 100, 111, 119, 108, 143, 114, 93, 73, and 75. If the company expects its total 1993 sales to be $11,100,000, prepare a schedule of the company's anticipated monthly revenues for 1993, ignoring the possible existence of a trend.

20.36 Suppose that there is, in fact, an upward trend in the sales of the clothing manufacturer referred to in the preceding exercise, as shown by the following trend equation

$$\hat{y} = 7,500,000 + 720,000x$$
(origin, 1988; x units, 1 year; y, total annual sales in dollars)

(a) Use this equation, suitably modified, to calculate the trend values for monthly sales for the 12 months of 1993.

(b) Draw up a revised monthly sales budget for 1993 which takes into account the trend in clothing sales.

20.37 The manager of a sporting goods store in northern Vermont finds that the equation which describes the trend in sales for the store is $\hat{y} = 230 + 6.9x$ (origin, 1988; x units, 1 year; y, total annual sales in thousands of dollars). The seasonal index of sales is 171, 128, 83, 80, 78, 69, 64, 65, 67, 74, 104, and 217 for the months January–December. Draw up a monthly sales forecast for the store for 1993.

20.10

A Word of Caution

The real trouble in forecasting and planning for the future is that there are altogether too many variables which need to be taken into account. Some of these are at least quantifiable and essentially predictable, but some are not. In analyzing rates of return on various capital investments, for instance, such inputs to the problem as the net installed cost of a machine and earnings from new equipment can often be determined or estimated reasonably well. But sound capital budgeting forces companies also to take into account such things as government policies which might affect the availability and price of money, changes in leasing opportunities, and possible revisions of depreciation and depletion laws as well as future tax decisions on these rates and allowances. Waiting is not much help, either, since there is no possibility of waiting until all, or sometimes even any, of the basic questions are settled finally. The projection of past experience to the uncertain future is speculative and hazardous, but at some time decisions must be made on the basis of the available incomplete knowledge; otherwise, nothing gets done.

Except for a few irreversible decisions, however, no one is irrevocably committed to a forecast, to survive or perish with it once it has been made. For instance, a large department store in a shopping center may have to make adjustments in its sales forecasts to take account of improved area transportation facilities, the opening of a new competing store nearby, an increase in the sales tax, and other things which could not be foreseen at the time the forecasts were made. Actually, forecasts are tentative things—special kinds of hypotheses, so to speak—which can be modified or revised in response to changing conditions. When forecasts are revised in the light of new information, all those concerned must take whatever steps are necessary to translate revised production, sales, or other goals into action. Intelligent forecasting and planning demand one's continued attention to changing conditions.

Generally speaking, it seems clear that realistic forecasts, which contribute greatly both to individual success and to the stability of the economy, are the results of applying sound business experience and judgment to relevant and timely statistical analyses.

20.11

Checklist of Key Terms

20.12

Review Exercises

20.38 The following data show the amounts of scrap metal resulting from the operations of a small machine shop during the years 1987–1992.

Year	Tons
1987	4.0
1988	6.0
1989	5.0
1990	7.0
1991	8.0
1992	7.5

(a) Plot the series on arithmetic paper.

(b) Fit a least-squares trend line to the data and plot the line on the chart showing the original data.

(c) Modify the trend equation by shifting the origin of x to the year 1991.

20.39 In calculating a seasonal index for a production series, a statistician has arrived at the following medians (in the same way we arrived at the values in the column headed "Median" on page 798): 58.1, 60.1, 73.8, 95.2, 116.8, 125.3, 120.6, 126.1, 123.1, 108.0, 103.1, and 71.8. Complete the calculation of this seasonal index.

20.40 The equation of a least-squares trend line fit to the total annual revenues of an electronics company for the years 1984–1992 is $\hat{y} = 1{,}210.2 + 105.6x$ (origin, 1988; x units, 1 year; y, total annual revenues in thousands of dollars). Modify the trend equation for use with monthly data and shift the origin of the equation to January 1988.

20.41 The following are the net sales (in millions of dollars) of a mining company in the years 1983–1992: 173, 398, 451, 413, 352, 297, 385, 448, 480, and 548. Smooth the series using the exponential smoothing constant $\alpha = 0.3$.

20.42 We have a series in which the raw data are the total annual sales volumes in millions of dollars of a large electronics chain, but we are interested in quantity changes alone, not price changes. Would any sort of statistical adjustment to the raw data seem to be in order before analysis, and if so, what sort of adjustment?

20.43 The equation describing the trend in the sales of a manufacturing company is $\hat{y} = 3{,}600 + 108x$ (origin, 1982; x units, 6 months; y, total annual unit sales). The company's seasonal index for the months of January through December is 84, 72, 101, 120, 100, 99, 88, 96, 108, 96, 96, and 139. Draw up a monthly sales forecast for the year 1993.

20.44 Following is the residential and commercial consumption of coal in the United States from 1950–1990, in millions of short tons per year.

Year	Tons per year (millions)
1950	114.6
1955	68.4
1960	40.9
1965	25.7
1970	16.1
1975	9.4
1980	6.5
1985	7.8
1990	6.3

(a) Plot the series on arithmetic paper.
(b) Fit a parabola to the data by the method of least squares and plot the curve on the graph of part (a).
(c) What is the trend value for the year 1975?
(d) What is the slope of the trend curve at $x = 0$?

20.45 Rounding the series in the preceding exercise to the nearest million short tons per year and plotting the data on semilog paper, we find that the series seems to straighten out quite well.
(a) Fit an exponential curve to these rounded data.
(b) Plot the exponential curve on the graph of part (b) of the preceding exercise and judge by inspection whether the exponential curve or the parabola fits the data better.
(c) What is the average annual rate of growth or decline in consumption?

20.46 Many time series of such things as income, production, and consumption are often published in per capita (for each person) form, not as totals for an entire population. Coffee and tea consumption, for instance, are often reported in pounds consumed per person in the adult population. Why do you suppose this adjustment is made to these series?

20.47 In a study of its sales of one kind of electrical motor, a manufacturer calculates the following least-squares trend equation:

$$\hat{y} = 2{,}800 + 200x$$
(origin, 1991; x units, 1 year; y, total number of
units sold annually)

The company has physical facilities to produce only 3,600 units a year, and it believes that it is reasonable to assume that, at least for the next decade, the trend will continue as before.

(a) What is the expected annual increase in the number of units sold?

(b) By what year will the company's expected sales have equaled its present physical capacity?

(c) How much in excess of the company's present capacity is the estimated 1997 sales figure?

20.48 Following are U.S. air carriers' passenger-mile revenues (in billions of dollars) for four recent years:

	Year			
Month	1	2	3	4
January	3.90	4.12	3.40	3.71
February	3.05	3.43	2.92	2.93
March	3.76	4.08	3.36	3.42
April	3.99	4.08	3.84	3.83
May	4.34	4.57	4.41	4.26
June	5.08	5.19	4.80	4.70
July	5.78	5.99	5.52	5.36
August	6.49	6.34	5.87	5.59
September	4.92	4.77	4.58	4.51
October	4.42	4.25	4.20	4.91
November	3.74	3.62	3.38	3.25
December	4.00	3.88	3.68	3.57

Compute a seasonal index of these data by the ratio-to-moving-average method, using the median to average the percentages for moving average for the individual months.

20.49 Use the seasonal data calculated in the preceding exercise to deseasonalize the data, and plot the deseasonalized data together with the original data on one chart.

20.50 The following is a trend equation fit by the method of least squares to the U.S. air carrier revenue data of Exercise 20.48:

$$\hat{y} = 4.204 - 0.010x$$

(origin, January of the fourth year; x units, 1 month; y, average monthly revenues in billions of dollars)

Use this equation and the seasonal index computed in Exercise 20.48 to forecast monthly revenues in the fourth year.

20.51 The number of work stoppages in the United States involving 1,000 or more workers from 1981 to 1989 were 145, 96, 81, 62, 54, 69, 46, 40, and 51. Fit a least-squares line to the series and plot the trend together with the original series on arithmetic paper.

20.52 Following are the numbers of automobiles, in millions, imported by the United States from Japan during 1978–1990: 1.4, 1.8, 1.9, 1.9, 1.8, 1.9, 1.9, 2.2, 2.4, 2.2, 2.0, 1.9, and 1.7. Construct a three-year moving average and draw a diagram showing the moving average together with the original data.

20.53 In addition to the moving averages we have discussed in Section 20.5 there are also **weighted moving averages**. The advantage of these is that by a suitable choice of weights we can exert a great degree of control over the extent to which a series is smoothed. The weights used in weighted moving averages are often based on binomial coefficients such as 1, 2, and 1; 1, 4, 6, 4 and 1; or 1, 6, 15, 20, 15, 6, and 1. For example, with weights of 1, 2, and 1 we get $(1 \cdot y_1 + 2 \cdot y_2 + 1 \cdot y_3)/4$ for the first value of the moving average, and so on.

(a) Use the series 130, 149, 144, 175, 175, 161, and 158 to verify that we obtain a five-year moving average with weights, 1, 2, 3, 2, and 1 by taking a three-year moving average of a three-year moving average.

(b) Verify that the centered 12-month moving average we used in the ratio-to-moving-average method of calculating a seasonal index is actually a weighted 13-month moving average with weights, 1, 2, 2, 2, 2, 2, 2, 2, 2, 2, 2, 2, and 1.

20.54 Following are quarterly data showing the operating revenues from international operations of air passenger carriers in millions of dollars for four recent years:

	Quarter			
Year	1	2	3	4
First	1,134	1,354	1,673	1,414
Second	1,449	1,603	1,992	1,574
Third	1,329	1,627	1,932	1,501
Fourth	1,366	1,601	1,912	1,494

(a) Draw a chart of these revenues to verify that there is, indeed, a consistent seasonal pattern.

(b) Calculate the centered four-quarter moving average.

(c) Use the results of part (b) to compute a quarterly seasonal index for the revenue figures by the ratio-to-moving-average method.

20.55 With reference to the preceding exercise, use the seasonal index obtained in part (c) to deseasonalize the sales data.

20.56 Assuming a linear trend in the operating revenues of Exercise 20.54, forecast the operating revenues for the four quarters of the sixth year.

20.57 In time-series analysis we sometimes deal with published series of data extending back 50 years or more. Over such long periods of time, though, changes of various kinds often occur which makes the figures in a series not strictly comparable. Using chain store sales as an example, suggest some changes in the reporting of these data down through the years which may make historical comparisons more approximate than exact.

20.58 In the classical time-series model each original value in a series of monthly values is presumed to be the product of the trend, seasonal, cyclical, and irregular components, or $y = T \times S \times C \times I$. In Section 20.9 we called the products we used there, $T \times S$, the "normal values." If now we divide the original values by the normal values, we get the values $C \times I$, called the "cyclical-irregulars." Since $\dfrac{C \times I}{I} = C$, it appears that we can get a measure of the cyclical components alone for each month simply by dividing out the irregular component.

(a) Explain why it is not feasible to isolate the cyclical effect in this way.

(b) Suggest a way in which the irregular effects can be eliminated from the cyclical-irregulars leaving, as a residual, a measure of the cyclical variation alone.

20.59 Use a computer package to rework Exercise 20.16 on page 791 concerning the production of cotton cloth from 1971 to 1990. Do not prepare the graph.

20.60 Use a computer package to rework Exercise 20.17 on page 791 concerning the number of automobiles sold by a dealer for the years 1963–1992. Do not prepare the graph.

20.61 Use a computer package to rework Exercises 20.18(a) and (b) on page 791 concerning profits after taxes of corporations in the United States. Do not prepare the graph.

20.62 Use a computer package to rework Exercise 20.19 on page 791 concerning the highest price paid for a speculative stock in 26 consecutive months. Do not prepare the graph.

20.63 Use a computer package to rework Exercise 20.20 on page 791 concerning the total factory sales of cars, trucks, and buses from 1974 to 1990. Do not prepare the graph.

20.64 Use a computer package to rework Exercise 20.30 on page 805 concerning production of electric utilities for the years 1986–1990.

20.13

Solutions of Practice Exercises

20.1

Year	x	y	xy	x^2
1985	-2	908	$-1,816$	4
1986	-1	753	-753	1
1987	0	917	0	0
1988	1	1,247	1,247	1
1989	2	1,613	3,226	4
Total		5,438	1,904	10

$a = \dfrac{5,438}{5} = 1,087.6$ and

$b = \dfrac{1,904}{10} = 190.4$

$\hat{y} = 1,087.6 + 190.4x$

(origin, 1987; x units, 1 year; y, exports of aluminum in thousands of metric tons)

Substituting the value of x into the trend equation for 1985, we get $\hat{y} = 1,087.6 + 190.4(-2) = 706.8$. Repeating this procedure for the following years, we get 897.2, 1,087.6, 1,278.0, and 1,468.4.

The graph for parts (a) and (b) follows.

20.2

Year	x	y	xy	x^2
1986	-5	7.31	-36.55	25
1987	-3	8.00	-24.00	9
1988	-1	9.34	-9.34	1
1989	1	10.33	10.33	1
1990	3	11.36	34.08	9
1991	5	11.79	58.95	25
Total		58.13	33.47	70

$a = \dfrac{58.13}{6} = 9.69$ and

$b = \dfrac{33.47}{70} = 0.48$

$\hat{y} = 9.69 + 0.48x$

(origin, 1988–1989; x units, 6 months; y, annual sales in hundreds of millions of dollars)

Substituting the value of x into the trend equation for 1986, we get $\hat{y} = 9.69 + 0.48(-5) = 7.29$. Repeating this procedure for the following years, we get 8.25, 9.21, 10.17, 11.13, and 12.09.

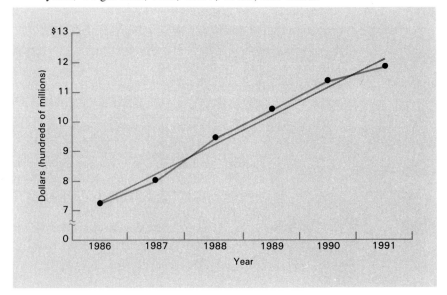

20.5 (a)

Year	x	y	xy	x^2
1980	-4	193	-772	16
1981	-3	198	-594	9
1982	-2	216	-432	4
1983	-1	223	-223	1
1984	0	230	0	0
1985	1	239	239	1
1986	2	247	494	4
1987	3	256	768	9
1988	4	274	1,096	16
Total		2,076	576	60

$a = \dfrac{2,076}{9} = 230.7$ and

$b = \dfrac{576}{60} = 9.6$

$\hat{y} = 230.7 + 9.6x$

(origin, 1984; x units, 1 year; y, fishermen employed in thousands)

Substituting the value of $x = -4$ into the trend equation for 1980, we get $\hat{y} = 230.7 + 9.6(-4) = 192.3$. Repeating this procedure with x values for 1981, 1982, 1983, 1984, 1985, 1986, 1987, and 1988, we get 201.9, 211.5, 221.1, 230.7, 240.3, 249.9, 259.5, and 269.1.

(b) $\hat{y} = 230.7 + 9.6(3) + 9.6x$
$= 259.5 + 9.6x$

(origin, 1987; x units, 1 year; y, number of fishermen employed in thousands)

(c) $\hat{y} = 230.7 + (9.6)(-1.5) + 9.6x$
$= 216.3 + 9.6x$

(d)

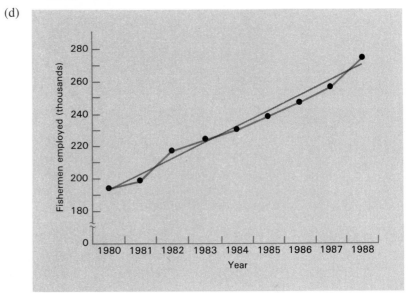

20.8

Year	x	$a + bx$	cx^2	$\hat{y}$
1980	-5	17.746	8.100	25.846
1981	-4	17.660	5.184	22.844
1982	-3	17.574	2.916	20.490
1983	-2	17.488	1.296	18.784
1984	-1	17.402	0.324	17.726
1985	0	17.316	0.0	17.316
1986	1	17.230	0.324	17.554
1987	2	17.144	1.296	18.440
1988	3	17.058	2.916	19.974
1989	4	16.972	5.184	22.156
1990	5	16.886	8.100	24.986

20.12

Year	x	y	log y	x(log y)	x^2	log $\hat{y}$	$\hat{y}$
1982	−4	55	1.7404	−6.9616	16	1.7559	57.00
1983	−3	71	1.8513	−5.5539	9	1.8297	67.57
1984	−2	84	1.9243	−3.8486	4	1.9035	80.08
1985	−1	94	1.9731	−1.9731	1	1.9773	94.90
1986	0	104	2.0170	0.0	0	2.0511	112.49
1987	1	131	2.1173	2.1173	1	2.1249	133.31
1988	2	162	2.2095	4.4190	4	2.1987	158.00
1989	3	190	2.2788	6.8364	9	2.2725	187.29
1990	4	223	2.3483	9.3932	16	2.3463	221.95
	Total		18.4600	4.4287	60		

$$\log a = \frac{18.4600}{9} = 2.0511$$

$$\log b = \frac{4.4287}{60} = 0.0738$$

$\log \hat{y} = 2.0511 + 0.0738x$, ($\hat{y}$ is antilog of log $\hat{y}$)

(origin, 1986; x units, 1 year; y, logarithms of net earnings of UST, Inc., in millions of dollars.)

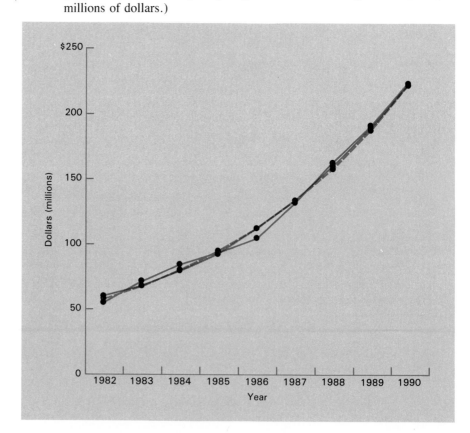

The curves representing the parabolic trend and the exponential trend are virtually identical.

(d) Since $\log b = 0.0738$, $b = 1.185$ and the average growth rate is 18.5 percent.

20.16 (a) For 1972–1989, the three-year moving totals are 16.8, 15.4, 13.9, 13.5, 13.2, 13.1, 12.3, 12.4, 12.3, 12.2, 11.9, 12.0, 12.1, 12.3, 13.0, 13.6, 13.8, and 13.6; for the same years, the three-year moving averages are 5.6, 5.1, 4.6, 4.5, 4.4, 4.4, 4.1, 4.1, 4.1, 4.1, 4.0, 4.0, 4.0, 4.1, 4.3, 4.5, 4.6, and 4.5.

(b) For 1973–1988, the five-year moving totals are 25.6, 24.2, 23.0, 21.9, 21.1, 21.5, 20.7, 20.1, 20.3, 20.4, 19.8, 20.3, 21.2, 21.5, 22.1, and 22.7; for the same years, the five-year moving averages are 5.1, 4.8, 4.6, 4.4, 4.2, 4.3, 4.1, 4.0, 4.1, 4.1, 4.0, 4.1, 4.2, 4.3, 4.4, and 4.5.

(c)

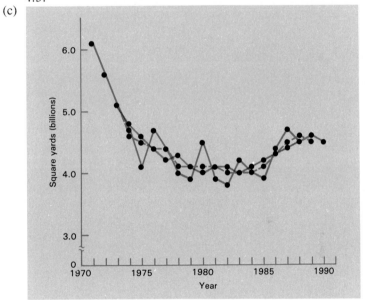

20.21 (a)

y_t	S_t
25	25
34	$(0.2)(34) + (0.8)(25.00) = 26.80$
23	$(0.2)(23) + (0.8)(26.80) = 26.04$
20	$(0.2)(20) + (0.8)(26.04) = 24.83$
25	$(0.2)(25) + (0.8)(24.83) = 24.86$
17	$(0.2)(17) + (0.8)(24.86) = 23.29$
19	$(0.2)(19) + (0.8)(23.29) = 22.43$
31	$(0.2)(31) + (0.8)(22.43) = 24.14$
15	$(0.2)(15) + (0.8)(24.14) = 22.31$
11	$(0.2)(11) + (0.8)(22.31) = 20.05$

817

20.26 The sum of the 12 values is 1,188.7. Multiplying each value by $\dfrac{1,200}{1,188.7} =$ 1.00951, we get the seasonal index 98.0, 85.1, 91.7, 105.3, 107.4, 110.2, 108.7, 112.2, 103.9, 85.4, 98.9, and 93.2.

20.27 For July 1987 to June 1990, the centered 12-month moving averages are 1,620, 1,619, 1,619, 1,621, 1,621, 1,620, 1,621, 1,618, 1,614, 1,606, 1,598, 1,595, 1,595, 1,594, 1,595, 1,596, 1,598, 1,602, 1,606, 1,612, 1,619, 1,625, 1,629, 1,629, 1,629, 1,635, 1,643, 1,650, 1,655, 1,661, 1,668, 1,677, 1,686, 1,694, 1,707, and 1,724. For the same months, the percentages of moving averages are 104.9, 100.7, 96.2, 101.7, 100.7, 142.4, 88.7, 83.1, 90.3, 94.9, 99.7, 101.8, 105.6, 99.2, 94.8, 94.5, 98.5, 143.8, 88.7, 82.8, 92.6, 92.9, 101.0, 102.8, 105.9, 102.4, 98.0, 94.1, 97.7, 135.7, 88.6, 84.7, 95.3, 93.0, 99.2, and 103.1.

Month	1987	1988	1989	1990	Median	Seasonal index
J		88.7	88.7	88.6	88.7	88.9
F		83.1	82.8	84.7	83.1	83.2
M		90.3	92.6	95.3	92.6	92.8
A		94.9	92.9	93.0	93.0	93.2
M		99.7	101.0	99.2	99.7	99.9
J		101.8	102.8	103.1	102.8	103.0
J	104.9	105.6	105.9		105.6	105.8
A	100.7	99.2	102.4		100.7	100.9
S	96.2	94.8	98.0		96.2	96.4
O	101.7	94.5	94.1		94.5	94.7
N	100.7	98.5	97.7		98.5	98.7
D	142.4	143.8	135.7		142.4	142.7
				Total	1,197.8	1,200.2

Correction factor is 1.0018, which is multiplied by monthly medians to provide monthly seasonal indexes. The sum of the corrected seasonal indexes is 1,200.2, which is very close to 1,200.

20.34 The deseasonalized March and April sales are $\dfrac{20,000}{1.05} = \$19,048$ and $\dfrac{24,000}{1.40} = \$17,143$, so there is reason for disappointment. The sales manager ignored the seasonal variation and estimated the annual sales as $12\left(\dfrac{20,000 + 24,000}{2}\right) = \$264,000$; the president took the seasonal variation into account, which is more reasonable and calculated that sales were running at an annual rate of $12\left(\dfrac{19{,}048 + 17{,}143}{2}\right) = \$217{,}146$, or \$217,000 rounded to nearest thousand.

20.36 $\hat{y} = \dfrac{7{,}500{,}000}{12} + \dfrac{720{,}000}{144}x = 625{,}000 + 5{,}000x$

$= 625{,}000 + 5{,}000(54.5) + 5{,}000x$

$= 897{,}500 + 5{,}000x$

(origin, January, 1993; x units, 1 month; y, average monthly sales in dollars)

	1993 trend values	Index	Predicted 1993 sales
J	897,500	71	637,225
F	902,500	91	821,275
M	907,500	102	925,650
A	912,500	100	912,500
M	917,500	111	1,018,425
J	922,500	119	1,097,775
J	927,500	108	1,001,700
A	932,500	143	1,333,475
S	937,500	114	1,068,750
O	942,500	93	876,525
N	947,500	73	691,675
D	952,500	75	714,375

Planning Business Research

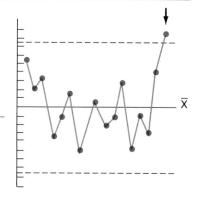

R egardless of whether we merely describe things numerically or whether we generalize beyond our data, locating, assembling, or collecting data can raise many problems. This is a serious matter because access to a good supply of high-quality data is fundamental to all of statistics.

So, we shall begin this chapter with a discussion of sources of business data in Section 21.1, and in connection with this it is important to recognize that much of the published information available from government and private sources (indeed, much of the world's knowledge) is actually based on samples. Since the word "sample" is used somewhat loosely in everyday language, let us observe again that in statistics it has a very special meaning—a sample is a set of data that can reasonably serve to make generalizations, or inferences, about the population from which it came. In Sections 21.2 through 21.6 we shall continue the discussion of Section 10.1 and see how such data can be obtained, particularly in situations where simple random sampling is impractical or not feasible.

Finally, in Sections 21.7 and 21.8 we shall discuss some aspects of the design of experiments, of planning every detail, so that, with reasonable assurance, the data we get will ultimately serve their purpose.

21.1

Sources of Business Data

Data required to solve practical everyday business problems can come from many sources, sometimes broadly classified as **internal** and **external**. Internal data are generated from the activities within a firm; they may be taken from a firm's order book or inventory, payroll, personnel, service, inspection, or accounting records; they may be collected in experiments and tests of product quality characteristics, or they may be gathered by agents, by telephone, or by questionnaires from customers as well as suppliers. External data are obtained from sources outside the firm; they may come from records of state, local, and national governments and their agencies and regulatory bodies, from trade associations, private institutions, other firms, and so on. Some problems require the combination of internal and external data, say, when a company compares its own operating performance with that of its competitors or the industry as a whole.

External data are sometimes classified as **primary**, meaning that the organization gathering the data also publishes or releases them, or as **secondary**, meaning that the data are published by an organization other than the one which gathered them. There are many important and highly respected sources of primary as well as secondary data. Among the nongovernmental sources we find private statistical services, trade associations, trade publications, university research bureaus, commercial and financial periodicals, and specialized reporting agencies. From these sources come data on employment, farm prices and marketings, construction contracts, store sales, bank debits, and the like, often broken down on a regional, state, county, or city basis. In addition, there are reports on prices, production, sales, employment, and the like in different industries, and all this information is supplied to fill the needs of individuals and groups for reliable statistics.

By far the biggest collector and publisher of business data, and generally the most important single source of external data, is the federal government. Within the great mass of statistical material flowing from the government it is possible to find information relating to virtually every aspect of the life of the nation. For instance, the Department of Commerce publishes each year the *Statistical Abstract of the United States,* an immense storehouse of data referring to many things and gathered from many sources. Through the Bureau of the Census, the Commerce Department periodically takes and publishes the results of censuses of population, manufactures, distribution, housing, and agriculture, and also publishes monthly trade reports giving data on inventories, sales, and so on, in various wholesale and retail lines of business for the entire country and for selected cities. The Office of Trade and Investment Analysis and the International Trade Administration of the Commerce Department collect and publish data on the trade of the United States and other countries. Through the Bureau of Economic Analysis, the Department of Commerce issues one of the most important of all statistical publications, the monthly *Survey of Current Business* (which is supplemented by weekly data on some of the major series of data). The S-pages of the regular monthly issues contain indicators of general business conditions and series relating to wholesale and retail commodity prices and trade, construction activity, population and employment, payrolls, wages and hours, finance, foreign trade, transportation, and so on. In addition, the Bureau publishes *Business Statistics,* a biennial supplement to the *Survey of Current Business,* which presents historical data for the series appearing in the monthly S-pages. Without much doubt, these publications constitute two of the most valuable collections of current and historical data.

Other important statistics are collected and published by the Department of Labor, whose Bureau of Labor Statistics issues the *Monthly Labor Review,* the primary source for the indexes of consumer prices and wholesale prices, and data on construction contracts and costs, employment, payrolls, wages and hours, and work stoppages. In addition to the publications of many other departments, agencies, and commissions of the government, the Board of Governors of the Federal Reserve System publishes monthly the *Federal Reserve Bulletin* and the *Federal Reserve Chart Book on Financial and Business Statistics* and releases other data periodically. Besides containing a wealth of financial information, the *Bulletin* is the primary source of the Index of Industrial Production.

The problem of how to keep up with the continuing, massive flow of government data, and where to find needed information, has long bothered users of statistical data, since no single central reference source to the government's statistical output exists. In 1973, however, the Congressional Information Service, Inc., a private organization, began publication of a much needed master index to government statistics dealing with the American people (population and housing; demographic characteristics; consumer prices and expenditures; work force, employment, and earnings; and so on). Called the *American Statistics Index,* it indexes the output of over 100 government agencies, congressional committees, and statistics-producing programs which produce statistics about the American people, and these data constitute half of the government's total statistical production. The Congressional Information Service, Inc., produces the *Statistical Masterfile,* which contains three important indexes: the previously cited *American Statistics Index* (ASI), the *Statistical Reference Index* (SRI), and the Index to International Statistics (IIS).

Most of the data collcted by the government are needed by the government itself in discharging its many responsibilities; data relative to some phenomena are not needed specifically by the government, but are collected and published in response to the needs of such large groups of individuals as to justify their collection at public expense.

Sections D and E of the Bibliography provide a selected, extensive list of sources of business data. The list includes public and private sources available as printed material, on microfiche, and in the form of CD-ROMS, computer tapes, diskettes, and online for use with computers. Some major sources of business data are published in multiple formats for the convenience of users. Many are available free of charge at numerous U.S. Government Document Centers located in university libraries and in other accessible locations throughout the United States.

EXERCISES

(Exercises 21.1 and 21.2 are practice exercises. Their complete solutions are given on page 848.)

21.1   Determine whether the *Federal Reserve Bulletin*, published monthly by the Board of Governors of the Federal Reserve System, is a primary source or a secondary source for the following data:

(a) U.S. balance of payments

(b) margin requirements

(c) member bank reserves

(d) hours and earnings of production workers in manufacturing industries

21.2   Answer each of the following questions for which numerical data and other information are summarized (from various sources) in *Business Statistics*.

(a) What is the definition of ''personal consumption expenditures''?

(b) What factors account for changes in the U.S. gold stock?

(c) What procedure is used in compiling export and import statistics for low-valued shipments?

(d) Does the labor force include the unemployed?

(e) How many gallons are there in a barrel of beer?

21.3   Find in the *Monthly Labor Review*

(a) the number of persons employed in mining for the past five years

(b) the annual values of the Producer Price Index for the same period

21.4 Refer to the *Statistical Abstract of the United States* to determine the sources of the following:

(a) population of the world

(b) amount of workers' compensation payments made in California

21.5 According to the *Federal Reserve Bulletin,* what were the total U.S. reserve assets (in millions of dollars) at the end of the last year for which data are published?

21.6 Find in the *Handbook of Labor Statistics* where the Bureau of the Census obtains its data for consumer income. Are the data completely reliable?

21.7 As of the most recent date or period for which you can locate data, determine

(a) the total amount of capital expenditures made by the paper industry for abatement of air and water pollution

(b) member bank reserve requirements of the Federal Reserve System

(c) mine production of recoverable zinc, by state

(d) national income of the United States

21.2

Samples and Sample Designs

Broadly speaking, there are two different types of samples: **probability samples** and **judgment samples**. By a probability sample from a finite population we mean a sample chosen in such a way that each element of the population has a known, though not necessarily equal, probability of being included in the sample. Simple random samples of size n drawn from populations of size N are probability samples, since each element of the population has a known probability n/N of being included in the sample. There are still other ways to take probability samples from populations and all such samples possess one great advantage: Only probability samples enable us to calculate sampling errors and, hence, judge the "goodness" of estimates or decisions to which statistical analyses lead.

In contrast to probability samples, we shall refer to samples as judgment samples if, in addition to (or instead of) chance, personal judgment plays a significant role in their selection. There are many situations where, for practical reasons, investigators use judgment samples to gain needed information. One important use of such sampling is in testing markets for new products. Because of the tremendous cost of market testing on a national scale, many products are first tested in one or a few cities. Such test cities are usually not selected at random; instead they are carefully chosen because in someone's considered judgment they are "typical" or "average" American cities. Subsequently, when generalizations are made to national markets, samples of public reaction to advertising, packaging, palatability, and the like constitute judgment samples.

Regardless of how the conclusions or actions based on judgment samples ultimately turn out, judgment samples have the undesirable feature that standard statistical theory cannot be applied to evaluate the accuracy and reliability of estimates or to calculate the probabilities of making various kinds of erroneous decisions. Whenever elements of judgment enter in the selection of a sample, the evaluation of the "goodness" of estimates or decisions based on the sample is again largely a matter of personal judgment.

There are a great many ways to select a sample from a population, and there is an extensive literature devoted to the subject of designing sampling procedures. In statistics, a **sample design** is a definite plan, completely determined before any data are collected, for obtaining a sample from a given population. Thus, a plan to take a simple random sample from among the 268 members of a trade association by using a table of random numbers in a prescribed way constitutes a sample design. Of the many ways in which a sample can be taken from a given population, some are quite simple while others are relatively involved. In what follows, we shall discuss briefly some of the most important kinds of sample designs.

21.3

Systematic Sampling

In many situations the most practical way of sampling is to select, say, every 10th voucher in a file, every 20th name on a list, every 50th piece coming off an assembly line, and so forth. Sampling of this sort is referred to as **systematic sampling**, and an element of randomness is usually introduced into this kind of sampling by using random numbers to pick the unit with which to start. Although a systematic sample may not be a random sample in accordance with our definition, it is often reasonable to treat systematic samples as if they were random samples. Whether or not this is justified depends entirely on the structure (order) of the list, or arrangement, the sample comes from. In many instances, systematic sampling actually provides an improvement over simple random sampling inasmuch as the sample is spread more evenly over the entire population.

The real danger in systematic sampling lies in the possible presence of hidden periodicities. For instance, if we inspect every 40th piece made by a particular machine, our results would be biased if, because of a regularly recurring failure, every 20th piece was blemished. Also, a systematic sample might yield biased results if we interviewed the residents of every 10th house along a certain route and it so happened that every 10th house selected was a corner house on a double lot.

21.4

Stratified Sampling

As we have seen, the goodness of a generalization or the closeness of an estimate depends largely on the standard error of the statistic being used, which, in turn, depends on both the sample size and the population variability. In theory, at least, we can increase the precision of a generalization by increasing the sample size and in practice, if the cost of sampling is largely overhead and the items to be sampled are readily at hand, it may be about as easy to take a sample of size 200 as it is to take a sample of size 50. On the other hand, if the cost of sampling is more or less proportional to the size of the sample (for instance, in destructive testing where the cost of sampling is largely the cost of the items tested), it may be very costly to increase the sample size. Moreover, a sample four times as large as another yields estimates which are only twice as reliable as those based on the smaller sample.

One relatively simple scheme for reducing the size of the standard error of a statistic is **stratification**. This is a procedure which consists of stratifying (or dividing) the population into a number of nonoverlapping subpopulations, or **strata** and then taking a sample from each stratum. If the items selected from each stratum constitute a simple random sample, the entire procedure (first stratification and then simple random sampling) is called **stratified (simple) random sampling**. Samples chosen in this way are probability samples.

Although the concept of stratifying is relatively simple, several substantial problems immediately arise: What should be the basis of stratification? How many strata should be formed? What sample sizes should be allocated to the different strata? How should the samples within the strata be taken? Stratification does not guarantee good results, but if properly executed, a stratified sample will generally lead to a higher degree of precision, or reliability, than a simple random sample of the same size drawn from the whole population.

Suppose, for instance, that we want to estimate the mean weight of four persons on the basis of a sample of size 2; the weights of the four persons are 110, 130, 180, and 200 pounds, so that μ, the mean weight we want to estimate, is 155 pounds. If we take an ordinary random sample of size 2 from this population and weigh these two persons, $\bar{x}$ can vary from 120 to 190. In fact, the $\binom{4}{2} = 6$ possible samples of size 2 that can be taken from this population have the means 120, 145, 155, 155, 165, and 190, so that $\sigma_{\bar{x}} = 21.0$ (see Exercise 21.9 on page 832).

Now suppose we know that the four persons consist of two men (who weigh 180 and 200 pounds) and two women (who weigh 110 and 130 pounds) and we stratify our sample by sex, then randomly select one of the two women and one of the two men. We now find that $\bar{x}$ varies on the much smaller interval from 145 to 165. In fact, the means of the four possible samples are 145, 155, 155, and 165, and $\sigma_{\bar{x}} = 7.1$ (see Exercise 21.9 on page 832). This illustrates how, by stratifying the sample, we are able to reduce $\sigma_{\bar{x}}$ from 21.0 to 7.1.

Essentially, the goal of stratification is to form strata in such a way that there is some relationship between being in a particular stratum and the answers sought in the statistical study and that within the separate strata there is as much homogeneity (uniformity) as possible. In our example there is such a connection between sex and weight, and there is much less variability in weight within the two groups than there is in the entire population.

In the preceding example we used what is called **proportional allocation** in selecting the sample, which means that the sizes of the individual samples were proportional to the sizes of the respective strata. In general, if we divide a population of size N into k strata of size $N_1, N_2, \ldots,$ and N_k, and take a sample of size n_1 from the first stratum, a sample of size n_2 from the second stratum, . . . , and a sample of size n_k from the kth stratum, we say that allocation is proportional if

$$\frac{n_1}{N_1} = \frac{n_2}{N_2} = \cdots = \frac{n_k}{N_k}$$

or if these ratios are as nearly equal as possible. In the example dealing with the weights we have $N_1 = 2$, $N_2 = 2$, $n_1 = 1$, and $n_2 = 1$, so that

$$\frac{n_1}{N_1} = \frac{n_2}{N_2} = \frac{1}{2}$$

and the allocation is, indeed, proportional.

It can easily be shown (see Exercise 21.12 on page 833) that allocation is proportional if

(see Exercise 21.12 on page 833)

Sample sizes for proportional allocation

$$n_i = \frac{N_i}{N} \cdot n \qquad \textit{for } i = 1, 2, \ldots, \textit{and } k$$

where n is the total size of the sample; that is, $n = n_1 + n_2 + \cdots + n_k$. When necessary, we use the integers closest to the values given by this formula.

EXAMPLE 21.1 A stratified sample of size $n = 60$ is to be taken from a population of size $N = 4,000$, which consists of three strata of size $N_1 = 2,000$, $N_2 = 1,200$, and $N_3 = 800$. If the allocation is to be proportional, how large a sample must we take from each stratum?

SOLUTION Substituting into the formula, we get $n_1 = \frac{2,000}{4,000} \cdot 60 = 30$, $n_2 = \frac{1,200}{4,000} \cdot 60 = 18$, and $n_3 = \frac{800}{4,000} \cdot 60 = 12$. ∎

After we have taken a sample of size n_1 from the first stratum, a sample of size n_2 from the second stratum, . . . , we calculate the means of the k samples, $\bar{x}_1, \bar{x}_2, \ldots,$ and $\bar{x}_k$, then estimate the mean of the whole population as

$$\bar{x}_w = \frac{N_1\bar{x}_1 + N_2\bar{x}_2 + \cdots + N_k\bar{x}_k}{N_1 + N_2 + \cdots + N_k}$$

This is a weighted mean of the individual $\bar{x}$'s, and the weights are the sizes of the strata. Actually, this formula applies regardless of how we allocate parts of the total sample to the strata, but when allocation is proportional, we can replace the N's with the n's and $\bar{x}_w$ is simply the mean of all the data combined; for this reason proportional allocation is said to be **self-weighting**.

In proportional allocation the importance of different strata sizes is taken into account by the fact that the larger strata contribute relatively more items to the sample. However, strata differ not only in size but also in internal variability, and it might seem reasonable to take somewhat smaller samples from the less variable strata and somewhat larger samples from the more variable strata. We can take into account both the size and the internal variability of strata by taking from each stratum a sample whose size is proportional to the product of the stratum size and the stratum standard deviation. If we denote the standard deviations of the strata as $\sigma_1, \sigma_2, \ldots,$ and σ_k, this kind of allocation requires that we make

$$\frac{n_1}{N_1 \sigma_1} = \frac{n_2}{N_1 \sigma_2} = \cdots = \frac{n_k}{N_k \sigma_k}$$

or make these ratios as nearly equal as possible. In this way, the larger and the more variable strata will contribute relatively more items to the total sample. This method of allocation is called **optimum allocation**, since for a fixed sample size, the sample chosen in this way will have the smallest possible standard error for the estimate of the population mean. To take a sample which meets the foregoing requirement, we find the sample sizes for the different strata by using the formula

Sample sizes for optimum allocation

$$n_i = \frac{n \cdot N_i \sigma_i}{N_1 \sigma_1 + N_2 \sigma_2 + \cdots + N_k \sigma_k} \qquad for\ i = 1, 2, \ldots, and\ k$$

EXAMPLE 21.2 With reference to the preceding example, suppose that $\sigma_1 = 8$, $\sigma_2 = 15$, and $\sigma_3 = 32$. For optimum allocation, how large a sample must we take from each stratum?

SOLUTION Substituting $n = 60$, $N_1 = 2{,}000$, $N_2 = 1{,}200$, $N_3 = 800$, $\sigma_1 = 8$, $\sigma_2 = 15$, and $\sigma_3 = 32$ into the formula for n_1, we get

$$n_1 = \frac{60 \cdot (2{,}000)(8)}{(2{,}000)(8) + (1{,}200)(15) + (800)(32)}$$

which gives $n_1 = 16$, and similarly we find that $n_2 = 18$ and $n_3 = 26$. Note that because of the large variability of the third stratum, n_3 is now larger than n_1 and n_2. ∎

One problem in using optimum allocation is that we must know the standard deviations of the different strata. Another problem arises if we want to estimate several population characteristics from the same set of sample data, since what is optimum for one characteristic may not be optimum for another. In situations like these, it may be better to use proportional allocation. Indeed, the gain in reliability due to optimum allocation is often not large enough to offset the obvious practical advantages of (self-weighting) proportional allocation.

Stratification is not restricted to a single variable of classification, or characteristic, and populations are often stratified according to several characteristics. In a systemwide survey designed to determine the attitude of its students toward, say, a new tuition plan, a state college system with 17 colleges might stratify the students with respect to class standing, sex, major, and college. So, part of the sample would be allocated to sophomore women majoring in English in college A, part to senior men majoring in engineering at college N, and so on. Up to a point, stratification like this, called **cross stratification**, will often increase the precision (reliability) of estimates, and it is widely used, particularly in opinion sampling and market surveys.

21.5

Quota Sampling

In stratified sampling, the cost of taking random samples from the individual strata is often so expensive that interviewers are simply given quotas to be filled from the different strata, with few (if any) restrictions on how they are to be filled. For instance, in determining voters' attitudes toward increased tax refunds to elderly persons, an interviewer working a certain area might be told to interview 5 male self-employed homeowners under 30 years of age, 10 female wage earners in the 50- to 60-year bracket who live in apartments, 4 retired males over 60 who live in mobile homes, and so on, with the actual selection of the individuals being left to the interviewer's discretion. This is called **quota sampling**, and it is a convenient, relatively inexpensive, and often a necessary procedure, but as it is executed, the resulting samples are usually not probability samples.

In the absence of firm restrictions on their choice, interviewers naturally tend to select individuals who are most readily available—persons who work in the same building, shop in the same store, or perhaps reside in the same general area. Quota samples are thus essentially judgment samples, and although it may be possible to guess at sampling errors by using experience or corollary information, quota samples generally do not lend themselves to any sort of formal statistical evaluation.

21.6

Cluster Sampling

To illustrate another important kind of sampling, suppose that a large foundation wants to study the changing patterns of family expenditures in the Los Angeles area. In attempting to complete schedules for 2,000 families, the foundation finds that simple random sampling is practically impossible, since suitable lists are not available and the cost of contacting families scattered over a wide area (with possibly two or three callbacks for the not-at-homes) is very high. One way in which a sample can be taken in this case is to divide the total area of interest into a number of smaller, nonoverlapping areas, say, city blocks. A number of these blocks is then randomly selected, with the ultimate sample consisting of all (or samples of) the families residing in these blocks. Generally speaking, in this kind of sampling, called **cluster sampling**, the total population is divided into a number of relatively small subdivisions, which are themselves clusters of still smaller units, and then some of these subdivisions, or clusters, are randomly selected for inclusion in the overall sample. If the clusters are geographic subdivisions, as in our example, this kind of sampling is also called **area sampling**.

To give two further illustrations of cluster sampling, suppose that the management of a large chain store organization wants to interview a sample of its employees to determine their attitudes toward a proposed pension plan. If random methods are used to select, say, five stores from the list, and if some or all employees of these five stores are interviewed, the resulting sample is a cluster sample. Also, if the dean of students of a university wants to know how fraternity men at the school feel about a certain new regulation, he can take a cluster sample by interviewing some or all of the members of several randomly selected fraternities.

Although estimates based on cluster samples are usually not as reliable as estimates based on simple random samples of the same size (see Exercise 21.10 on page 832), they are usually more reliable per unit cost. Referring again to the survey of family expenditures in the Los Angeles area, it is easy to see that it may well be possible to take a cluster sample several times the size of a simple random sample for the same cost. It is much cheaper to visit and interview families living close together in clusters than families selected at random over a wide area.

In practice, several of the methods we have discussed may well be used in the same survey. For instance, if government statisticians wanted to study the attitude of American farmers toward marketing cooperatives, they might first stratify the country by states or some other geographic subdivision. To take a sample from each stratum, they might then use cluster sampling, subdividing each stratum into a number of smaller geographic subdivisions, and finally they might use simple random sampling or systematic sampling to select a sample of farmers within each cluster.

EXERCISES

(Exercises 21.8, 21.10, 21.12, 21.16, and 21.19 are practice exercises. Their complete solutions are given on page 848.)

21.8   Following are the numbers of automobiles per capita by states, listed by rows in alphabetical order. Washington, D.C., with 0.40 cars per capita has been omitted.

0.65	0.43	0.55	0.38	0.57	0.69	0.77	0.59	0.70	0.57
0.57	0.60	0.55	0.56	0.65	0.55	0.50	0.45	0.58	0.61
0.56	0.60	0.59	0.54	0.53	0.54	0.55	0.46	0.66	0.66
0.52	0.48	0.55	0.56	0.71	0.51	0.63	0.52	0.55	0.57
0.58	0.70	0.50	0.46	0.60	0.61	0.60	0.43	0.55	0.59

(a)   List the 5 possible systematic samples of size 10 that can be taken from this list by starting with one of the first 5 numbers and then taking each 5th number on the list.

(b)   Calculate the means of the 5 samples obtained in part (a). Assuming that the starting point is randomly selected among the first 5 numbers, show that the mean of this sampling distribution of $\bar{x}$ equals the population mean, μ, the mean of the 50 numbers.

21.9   Verify that

(a) $\sigma_{\bar{x}} = 21.0$ for the six sample means on page 827 which are assigned equal probabilities of $\frac{1}{6}$

(b) $\sigma_{\bar{x}} = 7.1$ for the four sample means on page 827 which are assigned equal probabilities of $\frac{1}{4}$

21.10   Suppose that in a group of six athletes there are three ice hockey players whose weights are 210, 220, and 230 pounds and three field hockey players whose weights are 140, 150, and 160 pounds.

(a)   List all the possible random samples of size 2 which may be taken from this population; calculate the means of these samples and show that $\sigma_{\bar{x}} = 22.7$ pounds.

(b)   List all the possible stratified random samples of size 2 which may be taken by selecting one ice hockey player and one field hockey player; calculate the means of these samples and show that $\sigma_{\bar{x}} = 5.8$ pounds.

(c)   Suppose that the six athletes are divided into clusters according to their sports, each cluster is assigned a probability of $\frac{1}{2}$ and a random sample of size 2 is taken from one of the randomly chosen clusters. List all the possible samples, calculate their means, and show that $\sigma_{\bar{x}} = 35.2$ pounds.

(d) Compare and discuss the results obtained for $\sigma_{\bar{x}}$ in parts (a), (b), and (c).

21.11 In a certain industry there were 80 work stoppages including 40 which lasted 1–6 days, 30 which lasted 7–29 days, and 10 which lasted more than 29 days. Using proportional allocation, in how many ways can we choose a 10 percent stratified sample of the 80 work stoppages?

21.12 Verify that if the formula $n_i = \dfrac{N_i}{N} \cdot n$ is used to determine the sample sizes allocated to the strata, then

(a) the allocation is proportional (that is, the ratios n_i/N_i all equal the same constant)

(b) the sum of the n_i is equal to n

21.13 A stratified sample of size $n = 50$ is to be taken from a population of size $N = 20{,}000$, which consists of three strata of size $N_1 = 4{,}000$, $N_2 = 10{,}000$, and $N_3 = 6{,}000$. If the allocation is to be proportional, how large a sample must be taken from each stratum?

21.14 A stratified sample of size $n = 78$ is to be taken from a population of size $N = 60{,}000$, which consists of two strata for which $N_1 = 20{,}000$, $N_2 = 40{,}000$, $\sigma_1 = 12$, and $\sigma_2 = 20$. How large a sample must be taken from each stratum if the allocation is to be

(a) proportional

(b) optimal

21.15 A stratified sample of size $n = 300$ is to be taken from a population of size $N = 60{,}000$ which consists of five strata for which $N_1 = 25{,}000$, $N_2 = 15{,}000$, $N_3 = 10{,}000$, $N_4 = 8{,}000$, and $N_5 = 2{,}000$. If the allocation is to be proportional, how large a sample must be taken from each stratum?

21.16 A stratified sample of size $n = 70$ is to be taken from a population of size $N = 50{,}000$ which consists of three strata for which $N_1 = 5{,}000$, $N_2 = 5{,}000$, $N_3 = 40{,}000$, $\sigma_1 = 8$, $\sigma_2 = 22$, and $\sigma_3 = 5$. How large a sample must be taken from each stratum if the allocation is to be

(a) proportional

(b) optimal

21.17 Suppose that we want to estimate the mean weight of six persons on the basis of a sample size of three. The weights of the six persons are 135, 141, 159, 165, 171, and 267 pounds. The mean of these six weights is $\mu = 173$. If, furthermore, the first four of these weights are weights of women and the other two weights are weights of men, and we stratify according to sex, show that

(a) proportional allocation leads to $n_1 = 2$ and $n_2 = 1$

(b) optimal allocation leads to $n_1 = 1$ and $n_2 = 2$

21.18 With reference to the preceding exercise, show that if the allocation is proportional, there are 12 possible samples for which $\sigma_{\bar{x}} = 16.7$ (provided that the selection within each stratum is random).

21.19 If $\bar{x}$ is the mean of a stratified random sample of size n obtained by proportional allocation from a finite population of size N, which consists of k strata of size $N_1, N_2, \ldots,$ and N_k, then

$$\sigma_{\bar{x}}^2 = \sum_{i=1}^{k} \frac{(N-n)N_i^2}{nN^2(N_i - 1)} \cdot \sigma_i^2$$

where $\sigma_1^2, \sigma_2^2, \ldots,$ and σ_k^2 are the corresponding variances for the individual strata.

(a) Use this formula to verify the value $\sigma_{\bar{x}} = 7.1$, actually $\sqrt{50}$, given in the illustration on page 827.

(b) Use this formula to verify the value $\sigma_{\bar{x}} = 5.8$, actually $\sqrt{\dfrac{100}{3}}$, given in part (b) of Exercise 21.10 on page 832.

This standard error formula, by itself, does not enable us to judge the effectiveness of stratification; this depends on whether or not the variances σ_1^2, $\sigma_2^2, \ldots,$ and σ_k^2 are appreciably smaller than the corresponding variance σ^2 for the entire population.

21.7

Planning Experiments

Even people who have never done any research should be able to visualize some of the problems involved in planning an experiment so that it can actually serve the purpose it is designed for. It happens all too often that an experiment intended to test one thing tests another, or that a poorly designed experiment tests nothing of any interest whatever. Suppose, for instance, that in order to compare the cleansing action of two detergents, someone has soiled 10 swatches of white cloth equally with India ink and oil and then washed 5 swatches in an agitator-type machine using a cup of detergent Q and the other 5 swatches in the same machine using a cup of detergent R. Following this, whiteness readings were made on the swatches with the following results:

Detergent Q	76	85	82	80	77
Detergent R	72	58	74	66	70

Treating these data as independent random samples from two (conceptually infinite) populations of such readings, we want to test, say, at the level of significance 0.01, whether the difference between 80 and 68, the two sample means, is significant. So, we formulate the hypothesis $\mu_1 = \mu_2$ and the alternative hypothesis $\mu_1 \neq \mu_2$, where μ_1 and μ_2 are the "true" average whiteness readings for the two populations. Calculating t for the small-sample test concerning the difference between two means (see page 432) we get $t = 3.67$, and since this exceeds $t_{0.005} = 3.355$ for eight degrees of freedom, we reject the null hypothesis. In other words, we conclude that there is a real difference in the actual average whiteness in the two populations.

Interpreting this result, we might arrive at the perfectly natural conclusion that detergent Q is superior in cleansing action to detergent R. However, a moment's reflection will make us realize that we have no real basis for such a conclusion. For all we know, the water temperature could have been different when testing the two detergents, one detergent could have been used in soft water and the other in hard water, the washing times could have differed substantially, and even the instrument used to determine the whiteness readings could have gone out of adjustment after the readings were taken for the first detergent. Thus, what may have seemed an obvious conclusion at first turns out to be highly questionable. It is entirely possible, of course, that the difference between the two means is due to quality differences in the two detergents, but we have just listed several other factors which could be responsible. In fact, we could go on indefinitely listing possible causes, any of which—either singly or in combination with others—might have accounted for the results. The significance test which we have performed convinces us that the difference is too large to be attributed to chance, but it does not tell us why this difference has occurred.

In general, if we want to show that one factor (among various others) can definitely be considered the cause of an observed phenomenon, we must make sure somehow that none of the other factors could possibly be held responsible. One way to handle this is to perform a rigorously controlled experiment in which all variables except the one of concern are held fixed. To do this in the example just given, we might always use the same washing time, water of exactly the same temperature and hardness, and we might inspect the testing equipment after each use. Under these rigid conditions, we know that a significant difference between the (whiteness) means is not due to differences in washing times, water temperature or hardness, or testing equipment. On the positive side, we know that one detergent performs better than the other if it is used in this narrowly restricted way, but we do not know whether the same difference would exist if the washing time were longer or shorter, if the water had a different temperature or hardness, and so on. Generally speaking, this kind of "overcontrolled" experiment does not really provide us with the kind of information we want.

Another way to handle this kind of problem is to plan the experiment in such a way that we can compare the merits of two treatments under more general conditions and also test whether other important variables might affect the results. To continue with the example, suppose that we want to investigate the effects of four factors on the cleanliness of swatches of white cloth washed in an agitator-type machine: the detergent used, the washing time, the water temperature, and the water hardness. (Such other factors as water level are assumed to be rigorously controlled in the experiment.) Letting Q and R stand for a cup each of the detergents, S and L for washing times of 10 minutes and 20 minutes, W and H for warm and hot water, and E and F for soft and hard water, there are altogether $2 \cdot 2 \cdot 2 \cdot 2 = 16$ ways in which these four factors can be combined. Using identical samples of cloth and testing equipment that is rigorously checked, we might conduct the following series of test washings in which each of the 16 possible combinations is included once:

Test washing	Detergent	Time	Temperature	Hardness
1	R	L	W	E
2	R	L	H	F
3	Q	L	W	E
4	R	S	W	F
5	Q	S	H	F
6	Q	S	W	E
7	R	S	W	E
8	Q	L	H	F
9	R	S	H	F
10	Q	S	H	E
11	Q	L	W	F
12	Q	S	W	F
13	R	L	H	E
14	R	S	H	E
15	Q	L	H	E
16	R	L	W	F

This means that the first test washing is performed with detergent R, a washing time of 20 minutes, and warm soft water; the second test washing is performed with detergent R, a washing time of 20 minutes, and hot hard water; and so on.

An experiment such as this is said to be a **complete factorial experiment**, complete because each **level** of each factor (Q and R, S and L, W and H, and E and F) is used once with each possible combination of the levels of the other factors. The importance of this kind of experiment is that it permits an analysis of variance for testing the effect of each factor and even some of their **interactions**, that is, some of their joint effects.

The seeming lack of order in the arrangement of the 16 tests in the example is by no means accidental. When we first wrote down the possible combinations of detergents, times, temperatures, and hardnesses, we filled the "Detergent" column by writing eight Q's followed by eight R's; then we filled the "Time" column by alternately writing down four L's and four S's, the "Temperature" column by alternately writing down two W's and two H's, and the "Hardness" column by alternating E's and F's. If we actually performed the tests in this order, we would run the first eight tests with detergent Q, the other eight with detergent R, and extraneous factors might conceivably upset the results. For instance, there might be a progressive deterioration in machine efficiency which could not be detected by inspection. Similarly, we might get in trouble if we deliberately conducted the first eight test washings using the shorter washing time, the hot water, or the soft water. We protect ourselves against biases which might inadvertently invalidate the results by **randomizing** the order of the tests—after writing down the 16 possible combinations of the levels of four factors, we selected the order shown in the table with the use of random numbers.

Another important consideration in the planning of experiments is that of **replication** (or repetition). Any time we want to decide whether an observed difference between sample means is significant or whether a sample mean differs significantly from some assumed value, we must estimate the size of chance fluctuations. In experiments of the sort we have just described, as in those described in Chapter 14, this kind of variation is called the **experimental error**, and, when necessary, it is estimated by repeating all (or part) of the entire experiment a number of times. Whether or not replication is needed in the example would depend on how many different hypotheses we want to test; if there is not enough information (degrees of freedom) for estimating the experimental error, we might conduct the 16 test washings in the given order, then rerandomize the order and conduct 16 more tests. The 32 tests thus made, including two each of the 16 possible combinations, would permit a rather detailed analysis of the effects and interactions of the four variables on the whiteness of swatches of cloth washed with the given kind of equipment.

The purpose of this section has been to introduce some of the basic ideas of **experimental design**. Generally speaking, the analysis of an experiment depends partly on the design itself, and partly on assumptions concerning the populations from which the data are obtained. Specification of these assumptions (for example, that the populations from which the data are obtained have normal distributions) thus constitutes another important aspect of the proper use of statistics in experimentation. The analysis of a four-factor experiment such as the one described is fairly complicated, but it is similar, in principle, to the analysis of variance techniques described in Chapter 14.

21.8

Further Considerations

The main problem that arises with complete factorial experiments is that they may require a very large number of observations. For instance, if we wanted to compare the breaking strength of six kinds of linen thread, and the measurements are made by five different technicians with four different instruments, a complete factorial experiment, requiring that each kind of thread be measured by each technician with each instrument, would take $6 \cdot 5 \cdot 4 = 120$ measurements.

To show how the number of measurements can sometimes be reduced, suppose that a market research organization wants to study the potential market for a new breakfast food; in particular, it wants to try it out in four different cities, with four different kinds of packaging, and with four different advertising campaigns. In other words, the organization wants to determine not only whether there is a difference in the demand for the product in the four cities, but also whether the demand is affected by the differences in packaging and/or the differences in advertising. Although a complete factorial experiment would require $4 \cdot 4 \cdot 4 = 64$ observations (representing all possible combinations of cities, packaging, and advertising), it is of interest to note that with proper planning 16 observations would suffice. To illustrate, let us refer to the four cities as 1, 2, 3, and 4; the four kinds of packaging as I, II, III, and IV; and the four kinds of advertising as A, B, C, and D. Then, let us consider the following arrangement, called a **Latin square**:

	Packaging			
	I	*II*	*III*	*IV*
1	*A*	*B*	*C*	*D*
2	*B*	*C*	*D*	*A*
3	*C*	*D*	*A*	*B*
4	*D*	*A*	*B*	*C*

City (labels the rows 1, 2, 3, 4)

In general, a Latin square is a square array of the letters $A, B, C, D, \ldots,$ of the English (Latin) alphabet, which is such that each letter occurs once and only once in each row and in each column.

The Latin square, looked upon as an experimental design, suggests that advertising A be used in city 1 with packaging I, in city 2 with packaging IV, in city 3 with packaging III, and in city 4 with packaging II; that advertising B be used in city 1 with packaging II, in city 2 with packaging I, in city 3 with packaging IV, and in city 4 with packaging III; and so on. Note that each kind of advertising is used once in each city and once for each kind of packaging, each kind of packaging is used once in each city and once with each kind of advertising, and each city is used once for each kind of packaging and once for each kind of advertising.

The analysis of a Latin square experiment is very similar to the two-way analysis of variance of Chapter 14; however, we must find an extra sum of squares which measures the variability that is due to the variable represented by the letters $A, B, C, D, \ldots.$

Finally, let us mention the widely used **incomplete block designs**, which apply when it is impossible to have each treatment in each block.

EXAMPLE 21.3   For instance, if we want to compare 13 kinds of tires but can put only four on a test car at the same time, we might use the following experimental design, where the tires are numbered 1 through 13:

SOLUTION

Test run	Kinds of tires			
1	1	2	4	10
2	2	3	5	11
3	3	4	6	12
4	4	5	7	13
5	5	6	8	1
6	6	7	9	2

7		7	8	10	3
8		8	9	11	4
9		9	10	12	5
10		10	11	13	6
11		11	12	1	7
12		12	13	2	8
13		13	1	3	9

There are 13 test runs, or blocks, and since each kind of tire appears together with each other kind of tire once within the same block, the design is referred to as a **balanced incomplete block design**. ∎

The fact that each kind of tire appears together with each other kind of tire once within the same block is important; it facilitates the statistical analysis because it assures that we have the same amount of information for comparing each pair of tires. In general, the analysis of incomplete block designs is fairly complicated, and we shall not go into it here, as it has been our purpose only to demonstrate what can be accomplished by the careful design of an experiment.

EXERCISES

(Exercises 21.20, 21.23, and 21.25 are practice exercises. Their complete solutions are given on page 848.)

21.20 A market research company retained by a manufacturer of personal computers plans to test market four different models, A, B, C, and D; with two different price structures, α and β; and three different kinds of sales promotions, I, II, and III. List the 24 tests which must be performed if each model is to be used once with each combination of price structures and promotions.

21.21 Suppose that a large fast-food restaurant chain wants to train three store managers, Albert, Bertha, and Charles; under the guidance of two district supervisors, David and Ellen; in three different restaurant locations, Fairville, Gainsboro, and Holton. List the 18 training sessions required if each trainee is to meet once with each district supervisor in each restaurant location.

21.22 A midwestern potato farmer wants to compare the yield of four varieties of potatoes, and at the same time study the effect of six different methods of fertilization and two methods of irrigation. How many test plots must he plant for a complete factorial experiment with only one observation of each kind?

21.23 Suppose that a clothing manufacturer wants to compare three different kinds of sewing machines, *A*, *B*, and *C*, and that she wants to know, in particular, how they perform with three different kinds of needles, *a*, *b*, and *c*, and three kinds of threads I, II, and III.

(a) Construct a 3×3 Latin square.

(b) Use the Latin square of part (a) to design an experiment in which three of the nine possible combinations of needles and threads are assigned to each sewing machine, so that each sewing machine will be used once with each kind of needle and once with each kind of thread.

(c) Suppose that the clothing manufacturer wants to use in the experiment three sewing machine operators, *P*, *Q*, and *R*. With reference to the Latin square design of part (b), indicate how she might assign three of the nine combinations of needles and threads to each of these operators, so that each operator works once with each machine, once with each kind of needle, and once with each kind of thread. (There exists a systematic way of planning this kind of experiment, but use trial and error here to make the assignment.)

21.24 Use the fact that each of the letters must occur once and only once in each column and in each row to complete the following Latin square:

B	A		
	C		
		D	C
			A

21.25 Among the nine persons interviewed in a poll, three are Easterners, three are Southerners, and three are Westerners. By profession, three of them are teachers, three are lawyers, and three are doctors, and no two of the same profession come from the same part of the United States. Also, three are Democrats, three are Republicans, and three are Independents, and no two of the same political affiliation are of the same profession or come from the same part of the United States. If one of the teachers is an Easterner and an Independent, another teacher is a Southerner and a Republican, and one of the lawyers is a Southerner and a Democrat, what is the political affiliation of the doctor who is a Westerner? (Hint: Construct a 3×3 Latin square; this exercise is a simplified version of a famous problem posed by R. A. Fisher in his classical work *The Design of Experiments.*)

21.26 To compare three different golf ball designs, B_1, B_2, B_3, each kind was driven by each of three golf pros, *A, B, C,* using each of three drivers D_1, D_2, D_3. The distances from the tees to the points where the balls came to rest (in yards) were as shown in the following Latin square:

	D_1	D_2	D_3
B_1	B 226	A 246	C 234
B_2	C 241	B 233	A 247
B_3	A 245	C 239	B 226

(a) Calculate the means of the distances obtained with the three golf ball designs, the means of the distances obtained with the three drivers, and the means of the distances obtained by the three golf pros.

(b) What do these means suggest about the effects on distance of any of the three variables under consideration: design, pro, driver?

21.27 A university has seven faculty members who are assigned to its various administrative committees as shown in the following table:

Committee	Professors
Educational Policy	Stout, Wood, Mason, Webb
Faculty Life	Gross, Castro, Mason, Webb
Promotion, Tenure, and Reappointment	Gross, Spires, Wood, Webb
Academic Support Services	Gross, Spires, Stout, Mason
Graduate Admissions	Spires, Castro, Wood, Mason
Graduate Curriculum	Gross, Stout, Castro, Wood
Undergraduate Curriculum	Spires, Stout, Castro, Webb

(a) Verify that this arrangement is a balanced incomplete block design. (In a situation such as this, the balance of the arrangement may not seem too important, yet it may well prevent a clique from assuming an undue amount of control.)

(b) If Stout, Gross, and Spires are (in that order) appointed chairmen of the first three committees, how will the chairmen of the other four committees have to be chosen so that each of the seven professors is chairman of one of the committees? How many different solutions are there to this problem?

21.28 Each day of the week a restaurant features as "specials" three of its seven main courses. Complete the following schedule, in which the main courses are numbered 1–7, so that each main course is featured three times per week, and each main course is featured together with each other main course once per week.

Day	Main courses		
Monday	7	1	
Tuesday	2	4	1
Wednesday	5		3
Thursday	3	4	
Friday	5	7	4
Saturday		6	
Sunday		2	6

21.9

A Word of Caution

In view of the fantastic amount of "statistical" information that is disseminated to the public for one reason or another, we cannot overemphasize the point that such information must always be treated with extreme caution. To avoid serious mistakes in the use of published data, it is essential to check the precise definition of all terms (e.g., "employment," "sales," "shipments"), and this usually requires looking behind the words themselves. A careful search is often necessary to discover not only what the data are supposed to represent, but also what units are being used, how these units are defined, and whether the definitions are consistent throughout so that comparisons can be made. The availability of just such information as this is one of the most valuable features of data published by the federal government. For all series published by the government, it is possible to find somewhere a complete description of what data (rigorously defined) are contained, how, when, and where they were gathered, how they were processed, and so on. Unfortunately, such information is often unavailable for data supplied by other sources, in which case it is always advisable to proceed with extra care.

Another area in which one must proceed cautiously is the area of public opinion sampling. There are in the United States a number of highly reputable polls—the Gallup Poll, the Harris Survey, and the California Poll, for example—based on carefully designed and executed statistical surveys. The past few years, however, have seen a phenomenal growth of polls of all sorts, and there are now literally hundreds of polls whose existence is hard to justify. In countless radio station and newspaper polls people are invited to phone or write in and register votes for their favorite presidential candidate, and interviewers stationed at busy downtown locations ask people for their preferences. In "popcorn" polls, theatergoers "vote" for their choice by buying popcorn in bags displaying their candidate's picture; in "ice cream" polls, a purchase of chocolate ice cream in a supermarket is recorded as a vote for candidate A while a purchase of vanilla ice cream is recorded as a vote for candidate B. Actually, this might all come under the heading of good fun if it were not for the tremendous and growing influence of public opinion sampling on political issues.

21.10

Checklist of Key Terms

Area sampling, 831
Balanced incomplete block
  design, 840
Cluster sampling, 831
Complete factorial experiment, 837
Cross stratification, 830
Experimental error, 837
External data, 821
Incomplete block design, 839
Internal data, 821
Judgment sample, 824
Latin square, 838

Optimum allocation, 829
Primary data, 821
Probability sample, 824
Proportional allocation, 827
Quota sampling, 830
Randomizing, 837
Replication, 837
Sample design, 825
Secondary data, 821
Stratified sampling, 826
Systematic sampling, 825

21.11

Review Exercises

21.29 Among 36 workers on a construction job 20 are carpenters, 12 are electricians, and 4 are laborers. In how many ways can a 25 percent sample be chosen from each group, if
 (a) one-third of the sample is to be allocated to each group
 (b) the allocation is to be proportional

21.30 Determine whether the *Survey of Current Business* is a primary or secondary source for
 (a) U.S. merchandise trade
 (b) newspaper advertising linage
 (c) U.S. international transactions
 (d) total life insurance premiums collected
 (e) employees on payrolls of nonagricultural establishments

21.31 A stratified sample of size $n = 60$ is to be taken from a population of size $N = 13,000$, which consists of three strata for which $N_1 = 6,000$, $N_2 = 3,000$, $N_3 = 4,000$, $\sigma_1 = 15$, $\sigma_2 = 18$, and $\sigma_3 = 5$. If we use optimum allocation, how large a sample will we take from each stratum?

21.32 Determine from the *Statistical Abstract of the United States* the source for the number of municipal and county 9- and 18-hole golf courses in the United States.

21.33 Making use of the fact that each letter must occur once and only once in each row and in each column, complete the following Latin square using the letters *A, B,* and *C.*

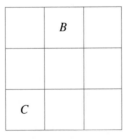

21.34 Answer each of the following questions for which numerical data and other information are summarized (from various sources) in *Business Statistics*:
 (a) What constitutes long-term unemployment?
 (b) Do world production figures for gold include production in the Commonwealth of Independent States?

(c) Does the total labor force include the armed forces of the United States?

21.35 The manager of a women's dress shop wants to display 4 of 13 styles of dresses in the store window, changing the display daily to assure that all the styles are displayed. Complete the following display schedule, in which the dress styles are numbered 1–13, so that each of the dress styles appears in the window once with each of the other dress styles:

Display	Dress styles			
First	8	2		12
Second	5	12	10	9
Third	2	9		6
Fourth	12	6	4	3
Fifth	9	3	1	13
Sixth	6	13		10
Seventh		10	8	7
Eighth	13	7		4
Ninth	10	4	2	1
Tenth	7	1	12	11
Eleventh	4	11	9	
Twelfth		8	6	5
Thirteenth	11	5	3	2

21.36 The following are the sizes of 25 consecutive photocopying orders (in pages) received by a photocopying service store: 1, 12, 20, 5, 18, 23, 25, 30, 17, 15, 25, 16, 12, 15, 100, 39, 4, 5, 19, 12, 90, 24, 10, 15, and 18.
   (a) List the five possible systematic samples of size $n = 5$ that can be taken from this list by starting with one of the first five numbers and then taking each fifth number on the list.
   (b) Calculate the mean of each of the five samples obtained in part (a) and verify that their mean equals the average (mean) number of pages per photocopying order.

21.37 In experiments with four additives which are supposed to improve the performance of a battery, we use the number 1 to indicate that an additive is not used, and the letters a, b, c, and d to indicate that they are used. Thus $1 \cdot b \cdot c \cdot 1 = bc$ means that only the second and third additives are used, and $a \cdot 1 \cdot c \cdot d = acd$ means that only the first, third, and fourth additives are used. Use this notation to list the 16 different experiments that can be performed with or without the individual additives.

21.38 A stratified sample of $n = 1,000$ is to be taken from 248.7 million people in the United States, in which the regional populations are as follows:

Region	Population (millions)
Northeast	50.8
Midwest	59.7
South	85.4
West	52.8
Total	248.7

If the allocation is to be proportional, what part of the sample should be allocated to the four strata?

21.39 A small automobile rental company owns three automobiles. If A, B, and C denote that the three automobiles are rented, and a, b, and c denote that they are not rented, then ABc denotes that the first and second automobiles are rented, but the third automobile is not rented. List the eight possible ways in which the automobile rental company may or may not rent these three vehicles.

21.40 Verify symbolically that for stratified sampling with proportional allocation the weighted mean given by the formula on page 828 equals the mean of the combined data obtained for all the strata.

21.41 A produce dealer received 3,000 pumpkins in two shipments. The first shipment contained 2,000 smaller pumpkins, all of which weigh 10 pounds or less. The second shipment contains 1,000 pumpkins, which weigh more than 10 pounds. To estimate the average weight of all of the pumpkins, a worker takes a 1 percent sample by weighing randomly selected pumpkins, proportionally allocated to the two strata, with the following results (rounded to the nearest pound):

Small pumpkins	4	5	3	8	5	8	6	3	9	10
	8	9	7	10	7	5	7	6	8	9
Large pumpkins	14	29	12	19	25	22	24	17	28	27

(a) Find the means of these two samples and then determine their weighted mean, using as weights the respective sizes of the two strata.

(b) Verify that the result of part (a) equals the ordinary mean weight of the 30 pumpkins; that is, verify for this example that proportional allocation is self-weighting.

21.12

Solutions of Practice Exercises

21.1   (a) secondary

       (b) primary

       (c) primary

       (d) secondary

21.2   (a) Goods and services purchased by individuals; operating expenses of nonprofit institutions; and the value of food, clothing, rental of dwellings, and financial services received in kind by individuals.

       (b) Domestic production of gold, net gold imports or exports, and changes in the amount of gold under earmark.

       (c) The value reported in export statistics is defined as the value at the U.S. port of export, based on the selling price, including inland freight, insurance, and other charges to the U.S. port of export. The value as defined is equivalent to an F.A.S. (free alongside ship) value, excluding the cost of loading the goods aboard the exporting carrier and transportation or other costs beyond the port of export. The import values are custom import values. They may be based on foreign market value, export value, constructed value, American selling price, and so on and generally represent a value in the foreign country. They therefore exclude U.S. import duties, freight, insurance, and other charges incurred in bringing the merchandise to the United States.

21.8   (a) 0.65, 0.69, 0.57, 0.55, 0.56, 0.54, 0.52, 0.51, 0.58, and 0.61; 0.43, 0.77, 0.60, 0.50, 0.60, 0.55, 0.48, 0.63, 0.70, and 0.60; 0.55, 0.59, 0.55, 0.45, 0.59, 0.46, 0.55, 0.52, 0.50, and 0.43; 0.38, 0.70, 0.56, 0.58, 0.54, 0.66, 0.56, 0.55, 0.46, and 0.55; 0.57, 0.57, 0.65, 0.61, 0.53, 0.66, 0.71, 0.57, 0.60, and 0.59.

       (b) 0.58, 0.59, 0.52, 0.55, and 0.61; the mean of the five sample means is $\frac{2.85}{5} = 0.57$, and μ is $\frac{28.43}{50} = 0.57$.

21.10 (a) The $\binom{6}{2} = 15$ samples are 210 and 220, 210 and 230, 210 and 140, 210 and 150, 210 and 160, 220 and 230, 220 and 140, 220 and 150, 220 and 160, 230 and 140, 230 and 150, 230 and 160, 140 and 150, 140 and 160, and 150 and 160. The means of the 15 samples are 215, 220, 175, 180, 185, 225, 180, 185, 190, 185, 190, 195, 145, 150, and 155; $\mu = 185$; $\sigma_{\bar{x}}^2 = \frac{521,125}{15} - \left(\frac{2,775}{15}\right)^2 = 516.67$; and $\sigma_{\bar{x}} = 22.7$.

       (b) The nine stratified samples are 140 and 210, 140 and 220, 140 and 230,

150 and 210, 150 and 220, 150 and 230, 160 and 210, 160 and 220, and 160 and 230; their means are 175, 180, 185, 180, 185, 190, 185, 190, and 195; also, $\sigma_{\bar{x}}^2 = \dfrac{308{,}325}{9} - \left(\dfrac{1{,}665}{9}\right)^2 = 33.3$, and $\sigma_{\bar{x}} = 5.8$.

(c) The six cluster samples are 140 and 150, 140 and 160, 150 and 160, 210 and 220, 210 and 230, and 220 and 230; 145, 150, 155, 215, 220, and 225; also $\sigma_{\bar{x}}^2 = \dfrac{212{,}800}{6} - \left(\dfrac{1{,}110}{6}\right)^2 = 1{,}241.67$, and $\sigma_{\bar{x}} = 35.2$.

21.12 (a) If $n_i = \dfrac{N_i}{N} \cdot n$, then $\dfrac{n_i}{N_i} = \dfrac{n}{N} = $ constant.

(b) $\sum n_i = \sum \dfrac{N_i}{N} \cdot n = \dfrac{n}{N}(\sum N_i) = \dfrac{n}{N} \cdot N = n$.

21.16 (a) $\dfrac{5{,}000}{50{,}000} \cdot 70 = 7$, $\dfrac{5{,}000}{50{,}000} \cdot 70 = 7$, and $\dfrac{40{,}000}{50{,}000} \cdot 70 = 56$; $7 + 7 + 56 = 70$.

(b) $\dfrac{(70)(5{,}000)(8)}{(5{,}000)(8) + (5{,}000)(22) + (40{,}000)(5)} = 8$,

$\dfrac{(70)(5{,}000)(22)}{350{,}000} = 22$, and $\dfrac{(70)(40{,}000)(5)}{350{,}000} = 40$; $8 + 22 + 40 = 70$.

21.19 (a) $\sigma_{\bar{x}}^2 = \dfrac{(4-2) \cdot 2^2}{2 \cdot 4^2(2-1)} \cdot 10^2 + \dfrac{(4-2) \cdot 2^2}{2 \cdot 4^2(2-1)} \cdot 10^2 = 50$, and $\sigma_{\bar{x}} = 7.1$.

(b) $\sigma_{\bar{x}}^2 = \dfrac{(6-2) \cdot 3^2}{2 \cdot 6^2(3-1)} \cdot \dfrac{200}{3} + \dfrac{(6-2) \cdot 3^2}{2 \cdot 6^2(3-1)} \cdot \dfrac{200}{3} = 33.3$, and $\sigma_{\bar{x}} = 5.8$.

21.20 The $4 \cdot 2 \cdot 3 = 24$ tests are $A\alpha$I, $A\alpha$II, $A\alpha$III, $A\beta$I, $A\beta$II, $A\beta$III, $B\alpha$I, $B\alpha$II, $B\alpha$III, $B\beta$I, $B\beta$II, $B\beta$III, $C\alpha$I, $C\alpha$II, $C\alpha$III, $C\beta$I, $C\beta$II, $C\beta$III, $D\alpha$I, $D\alpha$II, $D\alpha$III, $D\beta$I, $D\beta$II, and $D\beta$III.

21.23 (a) One possibility is

	a	b	c
I	A	B	C
II	C	A	B
III	B	C	A

(b) IaA, IbB, IcC, IIaC, IIbA, IIcB, IIIaB, IIIbC, and IIIcA.

(c) One possibility is to assign IaA, IIcB, and IIIbC to P; IbB, IIaC, and IIIcA to Q; and IcC, IIbA, and IIIaB to R.

21.25 The given information is

	E	S	W
T	I	R	
L		D	
D			

and completing the Latin square yields

	E	S	W
T	I	R	D
L	R	D	I
D	D	I	R

Thus, the Western doctor must be a Republican.

Statistical Tables

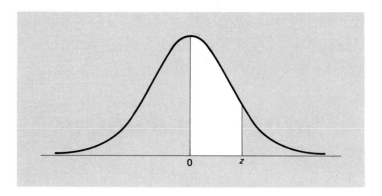

The entries in Table I are the probabilities that a random variable having the standard normal distribution will take on a value between 0 and z; they are given by the area of the white region under the curve in the figure shown.

TABLE I Normal-Curve Areas

z	.00	.01	.02	.03	.04	.05	.06	.07	.08	.09
0.0	0.0000	0.0040	0.0080	0.0120	0.0160	0.0199	0.0239	0.0279	0.0319	0.0359
0.1	0.0398	0.0438	0.0478	0.0517	0.0557	0.0596	0.0636	0.0675	0.0714	0.0753
0.2	0.0793	0.0832	0.0871	0.0910	0.0948	0.0987	0.1026	0.1064	0.1103	0.1141
0.3	0.1179	0.1217	0.1255	0.1293	0.1331	0.1368	0.1406	0.1443	0.1480	0.1517
0.4	0.1554	0.1591	0.1628	0.1664	0.1700	0.1736	0.1772	0.1808	0.1844	0.1879
0.5	0.1915	0.1950	0.1985	0.2019	0.2054	0.2088	0.2123	0.2157	0.2190	0.2224
0.6	0.2257	0.2291	0.2324	0.2357	0.2389	0.2422	0.2454	0.2486	0.2517	0.2549
0.7	0.2580	0.2611	0.2642	0.2673	0.2704	0.2734	0.2764	0.2794	0.2823	0.2852
0.8	0.2881	0.2910	0.2939	0.2967	0.2995	0.3023	0.3051	0.3078	0.3106	0.3133
0.9	0.3159	0.3186	0.3212	0.3238	0.3264	0.3289	0.3315	0.3340	0.3365	0.3389
1.0	0.3413	0.3438	0.3461	0.3485	0.3508	0.3531	0.3554	0.3577	0.3599	0.3621
1.1	0.3643	0.3665	0.3686	0.3708	0.3729	0.3749	0.3770	0.3790	0.3810	0.3830
1.2	0.3849	0.3869	0.3888	0.3907	0.3925	0.3944	0.3962	0.3980	0.3997	0.4015
1.3	0.4032	0.4049	0.4066	0.4082	0.4099	0.4115	0.4131	0.4147	0.4162	0.4177
1.4	0.4192	0.4207	0.4222	0.4236	0.4251	0.4265	0.4279	0.4292	0.4306	0.4319
1.5	0.4332	0.4345	0.4357	0.4370	0.4382	0.4394	0.4406	0.4418	0.4429	0.4441
1.6	0.4452	0.4463	0.4474	0.4484	0.4495	0.4505	0.4515	0.4525	0.4535	0.4545
1.7	0.4554	0.4564	0.4573	0.4582	0.4591	0.4599	0.4608	0.4616	0.4625	0.4633
1.8	0.4641	0.4649	0.4656	0.4664	0.4671	0.4678	0.4686	0.4693	0.4699	0.4706
1.9	0.4713	0.4719	0.4726	0.4732	0.4738	0.4744	0.4750	0.4756	0.4761	0.4767
2.0	0.4772	0.4778	0.4783	0.4788	0.4793	0.4798	0.4803	0.4808	0.4812	0.4817
2.1	0.4821	0.4826	0.4830	0.4834	0.4838	0.4842	0.4846	0.4850	0.4854	0.4857
2.2	0.4861	0.4864	0.4868	0.4871	0.4875	0.4878	0.4881	0.4884	0.4887	0.4890
2.3	0.4893	0.4896	0.4898	0.4901	0.4904	0.4906	0.4909	0.4911	0.4913	0.4916
2.4	0.4918	0.4920	0.4922	0.4925	0.4927	0.4929	0.4931	0.4932	0.4934	0.4936
2.5	0.4938	0.4940	0.4941	0.4943	0.4945	0.4946	0.4948	0.4949	0.4951	0.4952
2.6	0.4953	0.4955	0.4956	0.4957	0.4959	0.4960	0.4961	0.4962	0.4963	0.4964
2.7	0.4965	0.4966	0.4967	0.4968	0.4969	0.4970	0.4971	0.4972	0.4973	0.4974
2.8	0.4974	0.4975	0.4976	0.4977	0.4977	0.4978	0.4979	0.4979	0.4980	0.4981
2.9	0.4981	0.4982	0.4982	0.4983	0.4984	0.4984	0.4985	0.4985	0.4986	0.4986
3.0	0.4987	0.4987	0.4987	0.4988	0.4988	0.4989	0.4989	0.4989	0.4990	0.4990

Also, for $z = 4.0$, 5.0, and 6.0, the areas are 0.49997, 0.4999997, and 0.499999999.

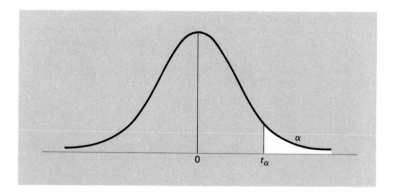

The entries in Table II are values for which the area to their right under the t distribution with given degrees of freedom (the white area in the figure shown above) is equal to α.

Statistical Tables

TABLE II Values of t

d.f.	$t_{.050}$	$t_{.025}$	$t_{.010}$	$t_{.005}$	d.f.
1	6.314	12.706	31.821	63.657	1
2	2.920	4.303	6.965	9.925	2
3	2.353	3.182	4.541	5.841	3
4	2.132	2.776	3.747	4.604	4
5	2.015	2.571	3.365	4.032	5
6	1.943	2.447	3.143	3.707	6
7	1.895	2.365	2.998	3.499	7
8	1.860	2.306	2.896	3.355	8
9	1.833	2.262	2.821	3.250	9
10	1.812	2.228	2.764	3.169	10
11	1.796	2.201	2.718	3.106	11
12	1.782	2.179	2.681	3.055	12
13	1.771	2.160	2.650	3.012	13
14	1.761	2.145	2.624	2.977	14
15	1.753	2.131	2.602	2.947	15
16	1.746	2.120	2.583	2.921	16
17	1.740	2.110	2.567	2.898	17
18	1.734	2.101	2.552	2.878	18
19	1.729	2.093	2.539	2.861	19
20	1.725	2.086	2.528	2.845	20
21	1.721	2.080	2.518	2.831	21
22	1.717	2.074	2.508	2.819	22
23	1.714	2.069	2.500	2.807	23
24	1.711	2.064	2.492	2.797	24
25	1.708	2.060	2.485	2.787	25
26	1.706	2.056	2.479	2.779	26
27	1.703	2.052	2.473	2.771	27
28	1.701	2.048	2.467	2.763	28
29	1.699	2.045	2.462	2.756	29
inf.	1.645	1.960	2.326	2.576	inf.

Source: Richard A. Johnson and Dean W. Wichern, *Applied Multivariate Statistical Analysis,* © 1982, p. 582. Adapted by permission of Prentice-Hall, Inc., Englewood Cliffs, N.J.

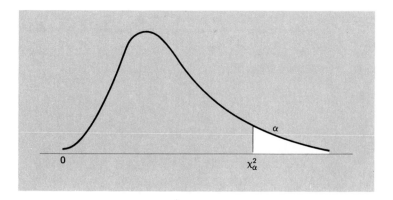

The entries in Table III are values for which the area to their right under the chi-square distribution with given degrees of freedom (the white area in the figure shown) is equal to α.

TABLE III Values of χ^2

d.f.	$\chi^2_{.995}$	$\chi^2_{.99}$	$\chi^2_{.975}$	$\chi^2_{.95}$	$\chi^2_{.05}$	$\chi^2_{.025}$	$\chi^2_{.01}$	$\chi^2_{.005}$	d.f.
1	0.0000393	0.000157	0.000982	0.00393	3.841	5.024	6.635	7.879	1
2	0.0100	0.0201	0.0506	0.103	5.991	7.378	9.210	10.597	2
3	0.0717	0.115	0.216	0.352	7.815	9.348	11.345	12.838	3
4	0.207	0.297	0.484	0.711	9.488	11.143	13.277	14.860	4
5	0.412	0.554	0.831	1.145	11.070	12.832	15.086	16.750	5
6	0.676	0.872	1.237	1.635	12.592	14.449	16.812	18.548	6
7	0.989	1.239	1.690	2.167	14.067	16.013	18.475	20.278	7
8	1.344	1.646	2.180	2.733	15.507	17.535	20.090	21.955	8
9	1.735	2.088	2.700	3.325	16.919	19.023	21.666	23.589	9
10	2.156	2.558	3.247	3.940	18.307	20.483	23.209	25.188	10
11	2.603	3.053	3.816	4.575	19.675	21.920	24.725	26.757	11
12	3.074	3.571	4.404	5.226	21.026	23.337	26.217	28.300	12
13	3.565	4.107	5.009	5.892	22.362	24.736	27.688	29.819	13
14	4.075	4.660	5.629	6.571	23.685	26.119	29.141	31.319	14
15	4.601	5.229	6.262	7.261	24.996	27.488	30.578	32.801	15
16	5.142	5.812	6.908	7.962	26.296	28.845	32.000	34.267	16
17	5.697	6.408	7.564	8.672	27.587	30.191	33.409	35.718	17
18	6.265	7.015	8.231	9.390	28.869	31.526	34.805	37.156	18
19	6.844	7.633	8.907	10.117	30.144	32.852	36.191	38.582	19
20	7.434	8.260	9.591	10.851	31.410	34.170	37.566	39.997	20
21	8.034	8.897	10.283	11.591	32.671	35.479	38.932	41.401	21
22	8.643	9.542	10.982	12.338	33.924	36.781	40.289	42.796	22
23	9.260	10.196	11.689	13.091	35.172	38.076	41.638	44.181	23
24	9.886	10.856	12.401	13.848	36.415	39.364	42.980	45.558	24
25	10.520	11.524	13.120	14.611	37.652	40.646	44.314	46.928	25
26	11.160	12.198	13.844	15.379	38.885	41.923	45.642	48.290	26
27	11.808	12.879	14.573	16.151	40.113	43.194	46.963	49.645	27
28	12.461	13.565	15.308	16.928	41.337	44.461	48.278	50.993	28
29	13.121	14.256	16.047	17.708	42.557	45.722	49.588	52.336	29
30	13.787	14.953	16.791	18.493	43.773	46.979	50.892	53.672	30

Source: Based on Table 8 of *Biometrika Tables for Statisticians,* Vol. I (Cambridge: Cambridge University Press, 1954) by permission of the *Biometrika* trustees.

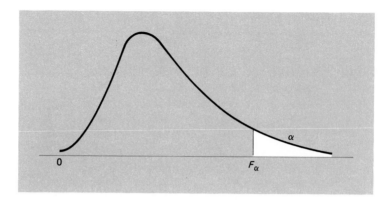

The entries in Table IV are values for which the area to their right under the F distribution with given degrees of freedom (the white area in the figure shown) is equal to α.

TABLE IV Values of $F_{0.05}$

DEGREES OF FREEDOM FOR NUMERATOR

Denominator	1	2	3	4	5	6	7	8	9	10	12	15	20	24	30	40	60	120	∞
1	161	200	216	225	230	234	237	239	241	242	244	246	248	249	250	251	252	253	254
2	18.5	19.0	19.2	19.2	19.3	19.3	19.4	19.4	19.4	19.4	19.4	19.4	19.4	19.5	19.5	19.5	19.5	19.5	19.5
3	10.1	9.55	9.28	9.12	9.01	8.94	8.89	8.85	8.81	8.79	8.74	8.70	8.66	8.64	8.62	8.59	8.57	8.55	8.53
4	7.71	6.94	6.59	6.39	6.26	6.16	6.09	6.04	6.00	5.96	5.91	5.86	5.80	5.77	5.75	5.72	5.69	5.66	5.63
5	6.61	5.79	5.41	5.19	5.05	4.95	4.88	4.82	4.77	4.74	4.68	4.62	4.56	4.53	4.50	4.46	4.43	4.40	4.37
6	5.99	5.14	4.76	4.53	4.39	4.28	4.21	4.15	4.10	4.06	4.00	3.94	3.87	3.84	3.81	3.77	3.74	3.70	3.67
7	5.59	4.74	4.35	4.12	3.97	3.87	3.79	3.73	3.68	3.64	3.57	3.51	3.44	3.41	3.38	3.34	3.30	3.27	3.23
8	5.32	4.46	4.07	3.84	3.69	3.58	3.50	3.44	3.39	3.35	3.28	3.22	3.15	3.12	3.08	3.04	3.01	2.97	2.93
9	5.12	4.26	3.86	3.63	3.48	3.37	3.29	3.23	3.18	3.14	3.07	3.01	2.94	2.90	2.86	2.83	2.79	2.75	2.71
10	4.96	4.10	3.71	3.48	3.33	3.22	3.14	3.07	3.02	2.98	2.91	2.85	2.77	2.74	2.70	2.66	2.62	2.58	2.54
11	4.84	3.98	3.59	3.36	3.20	3.09	3.01	2.95	2.90	2.85	2.79	2.72	2.65	2.61	2.57	2.53	2.49	2.45	2.40
12	4.75	3.89	3.49	3.26	3.11	3.00	2.91	2.85	2.80	2.75	2.69	2.62	2.54	2.51	2.47	2.43	2.38	2.34	2.30
13	4.67	3.81	3.41	3.18	3.03	2.92	2.83	2.77	2.71	2.67	2.60	2.53	2.46	2.42	2.38	2.34	2.30	2.25	2.21
14	4.60	3.74	3.34	3.11	2.96	2.85	2.76	2.70	2.65	2.60	2.53	2.46	2.39	2.35	2.31	2.27	2.22	2.18	2.13
15	4.54	3.68	3.29	3.06	2.90	2.79	2.71	2.64	2.59	2.54	2.48	2.40	2.33	2.29	2.25	2.20	2.16	2.11	2.07
16	4.49	3.63	3.24	3.01	2.85	2.74	2.66	2.59	2.54	2.49	2.42	2.35	2.28	2.24	2.19	2.15	2.11	2.06	2.01
17	4.45	3.59	3.20	2.96	2.81	2.70	2.61	2.55	2.49	2.45	2.38	2.31	2.23	2.19	2.15	2.10	2.06	2.01	1.96
18	4.41	3.55	3.16	2.93	2.77	2.66	2.58	2.51	2.46	2.41	2.34	2.27	2.19	2.15	2.11	2.06	2.02	1.97	1.92
19	4.38	3.52	3.13	2.90	2.74	2.63	2.54	2.48	2.42	2.38	2.31	2.23	2.16	2.11	2.07	2.03	1.98	1.93	1.88
20	4.35	3.49	3.10	2.87	2.71	2.60	2.51	2.45	2.39	2.35	2.28	2.20	2.12	2.08	2.04	1.99	1.95	1.90	1.84
21	4.32	3.47	3.07	2.84	2.68	2.57	2.49	2.42	2.37	2.32	2.25	2.18	2.10	2.05	2.01	1.96	1.92	1.87	1.81
22	4.30	3.44	3.05	2.82	2.66	2.55	2.46	2.40	2.34	2.30	2.23	2.15	2.07	2.03	1.98	1.94	1.89	1.84	1.78
23	4.28	3.42	3.03	2.80	2.64	2.53	2.44	2.37	2.32	2.27	2.20	2.13	2.05	2.01	1.96	1.91	1.86	1.81	1.76
24	4.26	3.40	3.01	2.78	2.62	2.51	2.42	2.36	2.30	2.25	2.18	2.11	2.03	1.98	1.94	1.89	1.84	1.79	1.73
25	4.24	3.39	2.99	2.76	2.60	2.49	2.40	2.34	2.28	2.24	2.16	2.09	2.01	1.96	1.92	1.87	1.82	1.77	1.71
30	4.17	3.32	2.92	2.69	2.53	2.42	2.33	2.27	2.21	2.16	2.09	2.01	1.93	1.89	1.84	1.79	1.74	1.68	1.62
40	4.08	3.23	2.84	2.61	2.45	2.34	2.25	2.18	2.12	2.08	2.00	1.92	1.84	1.79	1.74	1.69	1.64	1.58	1.51
60	4.00	3.15	2.76	2.53	2.37	2.25	2.17	2.10	2.04	1.99	1.92	1.84	1.75	1.70	1.65	1.59	1.53	1.47	1.39
120	3.92	3.07	2.68	2.45	2.29	2.18	2.09	2.02	1.96	1.91	1.83	1.75	1.66	1.61	1.55	1.50	1.43	1.35	1.25
∞	3.84	3.00	2.60	2.37	2.21	2.10	2.01	1.94	1.88	1.83	1.75	1.67	1.57	1.52	1.46	1.39	1.32	1.22	1.00

DEGREES OF FREEDOM FOR DENOMINATOR

Source: M. Merrington and C. M. Thompson, "Tables of percentage points of the inverted beta (*F*) distribution," *Biometrika,* Vol. 33 (1943), by permission of the *Biometrika* trustees.

Statistical Tables

TABLE IV Values of $F_{0.01}$

DEGREES OF FREEDOM FOR NUMERATOR

Denominator	1	2	3	4	5	6	7	8	9	10	12	15	20	24	30	40	60	120	∞
1	4052	5000	5403	5625	5764	5859	5928	5982	6023	6056	6106	6157	6209	6235	6261	6287	6313	6339	6366
2	98.5	99.0	99.2	99.2	99.3	99.3	99.4	99.4	99.4	99.4	99.4	99.4	99.4	99.5	99.5	99.5	99.5	99.5	99.5
3	34.1	30.8	29.5	28.7	28.2	27.9	27.7	27.5	27.3	27.2	27.1	26.9	26.7	26.6	26.5	26.4	26.3	26.2	26.1
4	21.2	18.0	16.7	16.0	15.5	15.2	15.0	14.8	14.7	14.5	14.4	14.2	14.0	13.9	13.8	13.7	13.7	13.6	13.5
5	16.3	13.3	12.1	11.4	11.0	10.7	10.5	10.3	10.2	10.1	9.89	9.72	9.55	9.47	9.38	9.29	9.20	9.11	9.02
6	13.7	10.9	9.78	9.15	8.75	8.47	8.26	8.10	7.98	7.87	7.72	7.56	7.40	7.31	7.23	7.14	7.06	6.97	6.88
7	12.2	9.55	8.45	7.85	7.46	7.19	6.99	6.84	6.72	6.62	6.47	6.31	6.16	6.07	5.99	5.91	5.82	5.74	5.65
8	11.3	8.65	7.59	7.01	6.63	6.37	6.18	6.03	5.91	5.81	5.67	5.52	5.36	5.28	5.20	5.12	5.03	4.95	4.86
9	10.6	8.02	6.99	6.42	6.06	5.80	5.61	5.47	5.35	5.26	5.11	4.96	4.81	4.73	4.65	4.57	4.48	4.40	4.31
10	10.0	7.56	6.55	5.99	5.64	5.39	5.20	5.06	4.94	4.85	4.71	4.56	4.41	4.33	4.25	4.17	4.08	4.00	3.91
11	9.65	7.21	6.22	5.67	5.32	5.07	4.89	4.74	4.63	4.54	4.40	4.25	4.10	4.02	3.94	3.86	3.78	3.69	3.60
12	9.33	6.93	5.95	5.41	5.06	4.82	4.64	4.50	4.39	4.30	4.16	4.01	3.86	3.78	3.70	3.62	3.54	3.45	3.36
13	9.07	6.70	5.74	5.21	4.86	4.62	4.44	4.30	4.19	4.10	3.96	3.82	3.66	3.59	3.51	3.43	3.34	3.25	3.17
14	8.86	6.51	5.56	5.04	4.70	4.46	4.28	4.14	4.03	3.94	3.80	3.66	3.51	3.43	3.35	3.27	3.18	3.09	3.00
15	8.68	6.36	5.42	4.89	4.56	4.32	4.14	4.00	3.89	3.80	3.67	3.52	3.37	3.29	3.21	3.13	3.05	2.96	2.87
16	8.53	6.23	5.29	4.77	4.44	4.20	4.03	3.89	3.78	3.69	3.55	3.41	3.26	3.18	3.10	3.02	2.93	2.84	2.75
17	8.40	6.11	5.19	4.67	4.34	4.10	3.93	3.79	3.68	3.59	3.46	3.31	3.16	3.08	3.00	2.92	2.83	2.75	2.65
18	8.29	6.01	5.09	4.58	4.25	4.01	3.84	3.71	3.60	3.51	3.37	3.23	3.08	3.00	2.92	2.84	2.75	2.66	2.57
19	8.19	5.93	5.01	4.50	4.17	3.94	3.77	3.63	3.52	3.43	3.30	3.15	3.00	2.92	2.84	2.76	2.67	2.58	2.49
20	8.10	5.85	4.94	4.43	4.10	3.87	3.70	3.56	3.46	3.37	3.23	3.09	2.94	2.86	2.78	2.69	2.61	2.52	2.42
21	8.02	5.78	4.87	4.37	4.04	3.81	3.64	3.51	3.40	3.31	3.17	3.03	2.88	2.80	2.72	2.64	2.55	2.46	2.36
22	7.95	5.72	4.82	4.31	3.99	3.76	3.59	3.45	3.35	3.26	3.12	2.98	2.83	2.75	2.67	2.58	2.50	2.40	2.31
23	7.88	5.66	4.76	4.26	3.94	3.71	3.54	3.41	3.30	3.21	3.07	2.93	2.78	2.70	2.62	2.54	2.45	2.35	2.26
24	7.82	5.61	4.72	4.22	3.90	3.67	3.50	3.36	3.26	3.17	3.03	2.89	2.74	2.66	2.58	2.49	2.40	2.31	2.21
25	7.77	5.57	4.68	4.18	3.86	3.63	3.46	3.32	3.22	3.13	2.99	2.85	2.70	2.62	2.53	2.45	2.36	2.27	2.17
30	7.56	5.39	4.51	4.02	3.70	3.47	3.30	3.17	3.07	2.98	2.84	2.70	2.55	2.47	2.39	2.30	2.21	2.11	2.01
40	7.31	5.18	4.31	3.83	3.51	3.29	3.12	2.99	2.89	2.80	2.66	2.52	2.37	2.29	2.20	2.11	2.02	1.92	1.80
60	7.08	4.98	4.13	3.65	3.34	3.12	2.95	2.82	2.72	2.63	2.50	2.35	2.20	2.12	2.03	1.94	1.84	1.73	1.60
120	6.85	4.79	3.95	3.48	3.17	2.96	2.79	2.66	2.56	2.47	2.34	2.19	2.03	1.95	1.86	1.76	1.66	1.53	1.38
∞	6.63	4.61	3.78	3.32	3.02	2.80	2.64	2.51	2.41	2.32	2.18	2.04	1.88	1.79	1.70	1.59	1.47	1.32	1.00

DEGREES OF FREEDOM FOR DENOMINATOR

Source: M. Merrington and C. M. Thompson, "Tables of percentage points of the inverted beta (*F*) distribution," *Biometrika,* Vol. 33 (1943), by permission of the *Biometrika* trustees.

TABLE V   Binomial Probabilities*

							p					
n	x	0.05	0.1	0.2	0.3	0.4	0.5	0.6	0.7	0.8	0.9	0.95
2	0	0.902	0.810	0.640	0.490	0.360	0.250	0.160	0.090	0.040	0.010	0.002
	1	0.095	0.180	0.320	0.420	0.480	0.500	0.480	0.420	0.320	0.180	0.095
	2	0.002	0.010	0.040	0.090	0.160	0.250	0.360	0.490	0.640	0.810	0.902
3	0	0.857	0.729	0.512	0.343	0.216	0.125	0.064	0.027	0.008	0.001	
	1	0.135	0.243	0.384	0.441	0.432	0.375	0.288	0.189	0.096	0.027	0.007
	2	0.007	0.027	0.096	0.189	0.288	0.375	0.432	0.441	0.384	0.243	0.135
	3		0.001	0.008	0.027	0.064	0.125	0.216	0.343	0.512	0.729	0.857
4	0	0.815	0.656	0.410	0.240	0.130	0.062	0.026	0.008	0.002		
	1	0.171	0.292	0.410	0.412	0.346	0.250	0.154	0.076	0.026	0.004	
	2	0.014	0.049	0.154	0.265	0.346	0.375	0.346	0.265	0.154	0.049	0.014
	3		0.004	0.026	0.076	0.154	0.250	0.346	0.412	0.410	0.292	0.171
	4			0.002	0.008	0.026	0.062	0.130	0.240	0.410	0.656	0.815
5	0	0.774	0.590	0.328	0.168	0.078	0.031	0.010	0.002			
	1	0.204	0.328	0.410	0.360	0.259	0.156	0.077	0.028	0.006		
	2	0.021	0.073	0.205	0.309	0.346	0.312	0.230	0.132	0.051	0.008	0.001
	3	0.001	0.008	0.051	0.132	0.230	0.312	0.346	0.309	0.205	0.073	0.021
	4			0.006	0.028	0.077	0.156	0.259	0.360	0.410	0.328	0.204
	5				0.002	0.010	0.031	0.078	0.168	0.328	0.590	0.774
6	0	0.735	0.531	0.262	0.118	0.047	0.016	0.004	0.001			
	1	0.232	0.354	0.393	0.303	0.187	0.094	0.037	0.010	0.002		
	2	0.031	0.098	0.246	0.324	0.311	0.234	0.138	0.060	0.015	0.001	
	3	0.002	0.015	0.082	0.185	0.276	0.312	0.276	0.185	0.082	0.015	0.002
	4		0.001	0.015	0.060	0.138	0.234	0.311	0.324	0.246	0.098	0.031
	5			0.002	0.010	0.037	0.094	0.187	0.303	0.393	0.354	0.232
	6				0.001	0.004	0.016	0.047	0.118	0.262	0.531	0.735
7	0	0.698	0.478	0.210	0.082	0.028	0.008	0.002				
	1	0.257	0.372	0.367	0.247	0.131	0.055	0.017	0.004			
	2	0.041	0.124	0.275	0.318	0.261	0.164	0.077	0.025	0.004		
	3	0.004	0.023	0.115	0.227	0.290	0.273	0.194	0.097	0.029	0.003	
	4		0.003	0.029	0.097	0.194	0.273	0.290	0.227	0.115	0.023	0.004
	5			0.004	0.025	0.077	0.164	0.261	0.318	0.275	0.124	0.041
	6				0.004	0.017	0.055	0.131	0.247	0.367	0.372	0.257
	7					0.002	0.008	0.028	0.082	0.210	0.478	0.698
8	0	0.663	0.430	0.168	0.058	0.017	0.004	0.001				
	1	0.279	0.383	0.336	0.198	0.090	0.031	0.008	0.001			
	2	0.051	0.149	0.294	0.296	0.209	0.109	0.041	0.010	0.001		
	3	0.005	0.033	0.147	0.254	0.279	0.219	0.124	0.047	0.009		
	4		0.005	0.046	0.136	0.232	0.273	0.232	0.136	0.046	0.005	
	5			0.009	0.047	0.124	0.219	0.279	0.254	0.147	0.033	0.005
	6			0.001	0.010	0.041	0.109	0.209	0.296	0.294	0.149	0.051
	7				0.001	0.008	0.031	0.090	0.198	0.336	0.383	0.279
	8					0.001	0.004	0.017	0.058	0.168	0.430	0.663

*All values omitted in this table are 0.0005 or less.

TABLE V   Binomial Probabilities *(continued)*

n	x	0.05	0.1	0.2	0.3	0.4	0.5	0.6	0.7	0.8	0.9	0.95
9	0	0.630	0.387	0.134	0.040	0.010	0.002					
	1	0.299	0.387	0.302	0.156	0.060	0.018	0.004				
	2	0.063	0.172	0.302	0.267	0.161	0.070	0.021	0.004			
	3	0.008	0.045	0.176	0.267	0.251	0.164	0.074	0.021	0.003		
	4	0.001	0.007	0.066	0.172	0.251	0.246	0.167	0.074	0.017	0.001	
	5		0.001	0.017	0.074	0.167	0.246	0.251	0.172	0.066	0.007	0.001
	6			0.003	0.021	0.074	0.164	0.251	0.267	0.176	0.045	0.008
	7				0.004	0.021	0.070	0.161	0.267	0.302	0.172	0.063
	8					0.004	0.018	0.060	0.156	0.302	0.387	0.299
	9						0.002	0.010	0.040	0.134	0.387	0.630
10	0	0.599	0.349	0.107	0.028	0.006	0.001					
	1	0.315	0.387	0.268	0.121	0.040	0.010	0.002				
	2	0.075	0.194	0.302	0.233	0.121	0.044	0.011	0.001			
	3	0.010	0.057	0.201	0.267	0.215	0.117	0.042	0.009	0.001		
	4	0.001	0.011	0.088	0.200	0.251	0.205	0.111	0.037	0.006		
	5		0.001	0.026	0.103	0.201	0.246	0.201	0.103	0.026	0.001	
	6			0.006	0.037	0.111	0.205	0.251	0.200	0.088	0.011	0.001
	7			0.001	0.009	0.042	0.117	0.215	0.267	0.201	0.057	0.010
	8				0.001	0.011	0.044	0.121	0.233	0.302	0.194	0.075
	9					0.002	0.010	0.040	0.121	0.268	0.387	0.315
	10						0.001	0.006	0.028	0.107	0.349	0.599
11	0	0.569	0.314	0.086	0.020	0.004						
	1	0.329	0.384	0.236	0.093	0.027	0.005	0.001				
	2	0.087	0.213	0.295	0.200	0.089	0.027	0.005	0.001			
	3	0.014	0.071	0.221	0.257	0.177	0.081	0.023	0.004			
	4	0.001	0.016	0.111	0.220	0.236	0.161	0.070	0.017	0.002		
	5		0.002	0.039	0.132	0.221	0.226	0.147	0.057	0.010		
	6			0.010	0.057	0.147	0.226	0.221	0.132	0.039	0.002	
	7			0.002	0.017	0.070	0.161	0.236	0.220	0.111	0.016	0.001
	8				0.004	0.023	0.081	0.177	0.257	0.221	0.071	0.014
	9				0.001	0.005	0.027	0.089	0.200	0.295	0.213	0.087
	10					0.001	0.005	0.027	0.093	0.236	0.384	0.329
	11							0.004	0.020	0.086	0.314	0.569
12	0	0.540	0.282	0.069	0.014	0.002						
	1	0.341	0.377	0.206	0.071	0.017	0.003					
	2	0.099	0.230	0.283	0.168	0.064	0.016	0.002				
	3	0.017	0.085	0.236	0.240	0.142	0.054	0.012	0.001			
	4	0.002	0.021	0.133	0.231	0.213	0.121	0.042	0.008	0.001		
	5		0.004	0.053	0.158	0.227	0.193	0.101	0.029	0.003		
	6			0.016	0.079	0.177	0.226	0.177	0.079	0.016		
	7			0.003	0.029	0.101	0.193	0.227	0.158	0.053	0.004	
	8			0.001	0.008	0.042	0.121	0.213	0.231	0.133	0.021	0.002
	9				0.001	0.012	0.054	0.142	0.240	0.236	0.085	0.017
	10					0.002	0.016	0.064	0.168	0.283	0.230	0.099
	11						0.003	0.017	0.071	0.206	0.377	0.341
	12							0.002	0.014	0.069	0.282	0.540

TABLE V Binomial Probabilities *(continued)*

n	x	0.05	0.1	0.2	0.3	0.4	0.5	0.6	0.7	0.8	0.9	0.95
13	0	0.513	0.254	0.055	0.010	0.001						
	1	0.351	0.367	0.179	0.054	0.011	0.002					
	2	0.111	0.245	0.268	0.139	0.045	0.010	0.001				
	3	0.021	0.100	0.246	0.218	0.111	0.035	0.006	0.001			
	4	0.003	0.028	0.154	0.234	0.184	0.087	0.024	0.003			
	5		0.006	0.069	0.180	0.221	0.157	0.066	0.014	0.001		
	6		0.001	0.023	0.103	0.197	0.209	0.131	0.044	0.006		
	7			0.006	0.044	0.131	0.209	0.197	0.103	0.023	0.001	
	8			0.001	0.014	0.066	0.157	0.221	0.180	0.069	0.006	
	9				0.003	0.024	0.087	0.184	0.234	0.154	0.028	0.003
	10				0.001	0.006	0.035	0.111	0.218	0.246	0.100	0.021
	11					0.001	0.010	0.045	0.139	0.268	0.245	0.111
	12						0.002	0.011	0.054	0.179	0.367	0.351
	13							0.001	0.010	0.055	0.254	0.513
14	0	0.488	0.229	0.044	0.007	0.001						
	1	0.359	0.356	0.154	0.041	0.007	0.001					
	2	0.123	0.257	0.250	0.113	0.032	0.006	0.001				
	3	0.026	0.114	0.250	0.194	0.085	0.022	0.003				
	4	0.004	0.035	0.172	0.229	0.155	0.061	0.014	0.001			
	5		0.008	0.086	0.196	0.207	0.122	0.041	0.007			
	6		0.001	0.032	0.126	0.207	0.183	0.092	0.023	0.002		
	7			0.009	0.062	0.157	0.209	0.157	0.062	0.009		
	8			0.002	0.023	0.092	0.183	0.207	0.126	0.032	0.001	
	9				0.007	0.041	0.122	0.207	0.196	0.086	0.008	
	10				0.001	0.014	0.061	0.155	0.229	0.172	0.035	0.004
	11					0.003	0.022	0.085	0.194	0.250	0.114	0.026
	12					0.001	0.006	0.032	0.113	0.250	0.257	0.123
	13						0.001	0.007	0.041	0.154	0.356	0.359
	14							0.001	0.007	0.044	0.229	0.488
15	0	0.463	0.206	0.035	0.005							
	1	0.366	0.343	0.132	0.031	0.005						
	2	0.135	0.267	0.231	0.092	0.022	0.003					
	3	0.031	0.129	0.250	0.170	0.063	0.014	0.002				
	4	0.005	0.043	0.188	0.219	0.127	0.042	0.007	0.001			
	5	0.001	0.010	0.103	0.206	0.186	0.092	0.024	0.003			
	6		0.002	0.043	0.147	0.207	0.153	0.061	0.012	0.001		
	7			0.014	0.081	0.177	0.196	0.118	0.035	0.003		
	8			0.003	0.035	0.118	0.196	0.177	0.081	0.014		
	9			0.001	0.012	0.061	0.153	0.207	0.147	0.043	0.002	
	10				0.003	0.024	0.092	0.186	0.206	0.103	0.010	0.001
	11				0.001	0.007	0.042	0.127	0.219	0.188	0.043	0.005
	12					0.002	0.014	0.063	0.170	0.250	0.129	0.031
	13						0.003	0.022	0.092	0.231	0.267	0.135
	14							0.005	0.031	0.132	0.343	0.366
	15								0.005	0.035	0.206	0.463

TABLE VI Values of r

n	$r_{.025}$	$r_{.010}$	$r_{.005}$		n	$r_{.025}$	$r_{.010}$	$r_{.005}$
3	0.997				18	0.468	0.543	0.590
4	0.950	0.980	0.999		19	0.456	0.529	0.575
5	0.878	0.934	0.959		20	0.444	0.516	0.561
6	0.811	0.882	0.917		21	0.433	0.503	0.549
7	0.754	0.833	0.875		22	0.423	0.492	0.537
8	0.707	0.789	0.834		27	0.381	0.445	0.487
9	0.666	0.750	0.798		32	0.349	0.409	0.449
10	0.632	0.715	0.765		37	0.325	0.381	0.418
11	0.602	0.685	0.735		42	0.304	0.358	0.393
12	0.576	0.658	0.708		47	0.288	0.338	0.372
13	0.553	0.634	0.684		52	0.273	0.322	0.354
14	0.532	0.612	0.661		62	0.250	0.295	0.325
15	0.514	0.592	0.641		72	0.232	0.274	0.302
16	0.497	0.574	0.623		82	0.217	0.256	0.283
17	0.482	0.558	0.606		92	0.205	0.242	0.267

TABLE VII   Critical Values for the U Test

n_2 / n_1	\multicolumn{14}{c}{Two-sided alternative ($\alpha = 0.05$)}

n_1	2	3	4	5	6	7	8	9	10	11	12	13	14	15
2							0	0	0	0	1	1	1	1
3			0	1	1	2	2	3	3	4	4	5	5	
4		0	1	2	3	4	4	5	6	7	8	9	10	
5	0	1	2	3	5	6	7	8	9	11	12	13	14	
6	1	2	3	5	6	8	10	11	13	14	16	17	19	
7	1	3	5	6	8	10	12	14	16	18	20	22	24	
8	0	2	4	6	8	10	13	15	17	19	22	24	26	29
9	0	2	4	7	10	12	15	17	20	23	26	28	31	34
10	0	3	5	8	11	14	17	20	23	26	29	30	36	39
11	0	3	6	9	13	16	19	23	26	30	33	37	40	44
12	1	4	7	11	14	18	22	26	29	33	37	41	45	49
13	1	4	8	12	16	20	24	28	30	37	41	45	50	54
14	1	5	9	13	17	22	26	31	36	40	45	50	55	59
15	1	5	10	14	19	24	29	34	39	44	49	54	59	64

n_2 / n_1	\multicolumn{14}{c}{One-sided alternative ($\alpha = 0.05$)}

n_1	2	3	4	5	6	7	8	9	10	11	12	13	14	15
2				0	0	0	1	1	1	1	2	2	3	3
3		0	0	1	2	2	3	4	4	5	5	6	7	7
4		0	1	2	3	4	5	6	7	8	9	10	11	12
5	0	1	2	4	5	6	8	9	11	12	13	15	16	18
6	0	2	3	5	7	8	10	12	14	16	17	19	21	23
7	0	2	4	6	8	11	13	15	17	19	21	24	26	28
8	1	3	5	8	10	13	15	18	20	23	26	28	31	33
9	1	4	6	9	12	15	18	21	24	27	30	33	36	39
10	1	4	7	11	14	17	20	24	27	31	34	37	41	44
11	1	5	8	12	16	19	23	27	31	34	38	42	46	50
12	2	5	9	13	17	21	26	30	34	38	42	47	51	55
13	2	6	10	15	19	24	28	33	37	42	47	51	56	61
14	3	7	11	16	21	26	31	36	41	46	51	56	61	66
15	3	7	12	18	23	28	33	39	44	50	55	61	66	72

Source: This table is based on Table 11.4 of D. B. Owen, *Handbook of Statistical Tables,* ©1962, U.S. Department of Energy. Published by Addison-Wesley Publishing Company, Inc., Reading, Mass. Reprinted with permission of the publisher.

TABLE VII   Critical Values for the U Test *(continued)*

Two-sided alternative ($\alpha = 0.01$)

n_1 \ n_2	3	4	5	6	7	8	9	10	11	12	13	14	15
3							0	0	0	1	1	1	2
4				0	0	1	1	2	2	3	3	4	5
5			0	1	1	2	3	4	5	6	7	7	8
6		0	1	2	3	4	5	6	7	9	10	11	12
7		0	1	3	4	6	7	9	10	12	13	15	16
8		1	2	4	6	7	9	11	13	15	17	18	20
9	0	1	3	5	7	9	11	13	16	18	20	22	24
10	0	2	4	6	9	11	13	16	18	21	24	26	29
11	0	2	5	7	10	13	16	18	21	24	27	30	33
12	1	3	6	9	12	15	18	21	24	27	31	34	37
13	1	3	7	10	13	17	20	24	27	31	34	38	42
14	1	4	7	11	15	18	22	26	30	34	38	42	46
15	2	5	8	12	16	20	24	29	33	37	42	46	51

One-sided alternative ($\alpha = 0.01$)

n_1 \ n_2	2	3	4	5	6	7	8	9	10	11	12	13	14	15
2												0	0	0
3						0	0	1	1	1	2	2	2	3
4				0	1	1	2	3	3	4	5	5	6	7
5			0	1	2	3	4	5	6	7	8	9	10	11
6			1	2	3	4	6	7	8	9	11	12	13	15
7		0	1	3	4	6	7	9	11	12	14	16	17	19
8		0	2	4	6	7	9	11	13	15	17	20	22	24
9		1	3	5	7	9	11	14	16	18	21	23	26	28
10		1	3	6	8	11	13	16	19	22	24	27	30	33
11		1	4	7	9	12	15	18	22	25	28	31	34	37
12		2	5	8	11	14	17	21	24	28	31	35	38	42
13	0	2	5	9	12	16	20	23	27	31	35	39	43	47
14	0	2	6	10	13	17	22	26	30	34	38	43	47	51
15	0	3	7	11	15	19	24	28	33	37	42	47	51	56

TABLE VIII   Values of u

n_1 \ n_2	VALUES OF $u_{0.025}$											
	4	5	6	7	8	9	10	11	12	13	14	15
4		9	9									
5	9	10	10	11	11							
6	9	10	11	12	12	13	13	13	13			
7		11	12	13	13	14	14	14	14	15	15	15
8		11	12	13	14	14	15	15	16	16	16	16
9			13	14	14	15	16	16	16	17	17	18
10			13	14	15	16	16	17	17	18	18	18
11			13	14	15	16	17	17	18	19	19	19
12			13	14	16	16	17	18	19	19	20	20
13				15	16	17	18	19	19	20	20	21
14				15	16	17	18	19	20	20	21	22
15				15	16	18	18	19	20	21	22	22

n_1 \ n_2	VALUES OF $u'_{0.025}$													
	2	3	4	5	6	7	8	9	10	11	12	13	14	15
2											2	2	2	2
3						2	2	2	2	2	2	2	2	3
4				2	2	2	3	3	3	3	3	3	3	3
5			2	2	3	3	3	3	3	4	4	4	4	4
6		2	2	3	3	3	3	4	4	4	4	5	5	5
7		2	2	3	3	3	4	4	5	5	5	5	5	6
8		2	3	3	3	4	4	5	5	5	6	6	6	6
9		2	3	3	4	4	5	5	5	6	6	6	7	7
10		2	3	3	4	5	5	5	6	6	7	7	7	7
11		2	3	4	4	5	5	6	6	7	7	7	8	8
12	2	2	3	4	4	5	6	6	7	7	7	8	8	8
13	2	2	3	4	5	5	6	6	7	7	8	8	9	9
14	2	2	3	4	5	5	6	7	7	8	8	9	9	9
15	2	3	3	4	5	6	6	7	7	8	8	9	9	10

Source: Adapted, by permission, from F. S. Swed and C. Eisenhart, "Tables for testing randomness of grouping in a sequence of alternatives," Annals of Mathematical Statistics, Vol. 14 (1943).

TABLE VIII   Values of *u* (continued)

n_2 n_1	VALUES OF $u_{0.005}$										
	5	6	7	8	9	10	11	12	13	14	15
5		11									
6	11	12	13	13							
7		13	13	14	15	15	15				
8		13	14	15	15	16	16	17	17	17	
9			15	15	16	17	17	18	18	18	19
10			15	16	17	17	18	19	19	19	20
11			15	16	17	18	19	19	20	20	21
12				17	18	19	19	20	21	21	22
13				17	18	19	20	21	21	22	22
14				17	18	19	20	21	22	23	23
15					19	20	21	22	22	23	24

n_2 n_1	VALUES OF $u'_{0.005}$												
	3	4	5	6	7	8	9	10	11	12	13	14	15
3										2	2	2	2
4						2	2	2	2	2	2	2	3
5				2	2	2	2	3	3	3	3	3	3
6			2	2	2	3	3	3	3	3	3	4	4
7			2	2	3	3	3	3	4	4	4	4	4
8		2	2	3	3	3	3	4	4	4	5	5	5
9		2	2	3	3	3	4	4	5	5	5	5	6
10		2	3	3	3	4	4	5	5	5	5	6	6
11		2	3	3	4	4	5	5	5	6	6	6	7
12	2	2	3	3	4	4	5	5	6	6	6	7	7
13	2	2	3	3	4	5	5	5	6	6	7	7	7
14	2	2	3	4	4	5	5	6	6	7	7	7	8
15	2	3	3	4	4	5	6	6	7	7	7	8	8

TABLE **IX**   Binomial Coefficients

n	$\binom{n}{0}$	$\binom{n}{1}$	$\binom{n}{2}$	$\binom{n}{3}$	$\binom{n}{4}$	$\binom{n}{5}$	$\binom{n}{6}$	$\binom{n}{7}$	$\binom{n}{8}$	$\binom{n}{9}$	$\binom{n}{10}$
0	1										
1	1	1									
2	1	2	1								
3	1	3	3	1							
4	1	4	6	4	1						
5	1	5	10	10	5	1					
6	1	6	15	20	15	6	1				
7	1	7	21	35	35	21	7	1			
8	1	8	28	56	70	56	28	8	1		
9	1	9	36	84	126	126	84	36	9	1	
10	1	10	45	120	210	252	210	120	45	10	1
11	1	11	55	165	330	462	462	330	165	55	11
12	1	12	66	220	495	792	924	792	495	220	66
13	1	13	78	286	715	1287	1716	1716	1287	715	286
14	1	14	91	364	1001	2002	3003	3432	3003	2002	1001
15	1	15	105	455	1365	3003	5005	6435	6435	5005	3003
16	1	16	120	560	1820	4368	8008	11440	12870	11440	8008
17	1	17	136	680	2380	6188	12376	19448	24310	24310	19448
18	1	18	153	816	3060	8568	18564	31824	43758	48620	43758
19	1	19	171	969	3876	11628	27132	50388	75582	92378	92378
20	1	20	190	1140	4845	15504	38760	77520	125970	167960	184756

If necessary, use the identity $\binom{n}{k} = \binom{n}{n-k}$.

TABLE X Values of e^{-x}

x	e^{-x}	x	e^{-x}	x	e^{-x}	x	e^{-x}
0.0	1.000	2.5	0.082	5.0	0.0067	7.5	0.00055
0.1	0.905	2.6	0.074	5.1	0.0061	7.6	0.00050
0.2	0.819	2.7	0.067	5.2	0.0055	7.7	0.00045
0.3	0.741	2.8	0.061	5.3	0.0050	7.8	0.00041
0.4	0.670	2.9	0.055	5.4	0.0045	7.9	0.00037
0.5	0.607	3.0	0.050	5.5	0.0041	8.0	0.00034
0.6	0.549	3.1	0.045	5.6	0.0037	8.1	0.00030
0.7	0.497	3.2	0.041	5.7	0.0033	8.2	0.00028
0.8	0.449	3.3	0.037	5.8	0.0030	8.3	0.00025
0.9	0.407	3.4	0.033	5.9	0.0027	8.4	0.00023
1.0	0.368	3.5	0.030	6.0	0.0025	8.5	0.00020
1.1	0.333	3.6	0.027	6.1	0.0022	8.6	0.00018
1.2	0.301	3.7	0.025	6.2	0.0020	8.7	0.00017
1.3	0.273	3.8	0.022	6.3	0.0018	8.8	0.00015
1.4	0.247	3.9	0.020	6.4	0.0017	8.9	0.00014
1.5	0.223	4.0	0.018	6.5	0.0015	9.0	0.00012
1.6	0.202	4.1	0.017	6.6	0.0014	9.1	0.00011
1.7	0.183	4.2	0.015	6.7	0.0012	9.2	0.00010
1.8	0.165	4.3	0.014	6.8	0.0011	9.3	0.00009
1.9	0.150	4.4	0.012	6.9	0.0010	9.4	0.00008
2.0	0.135	4.5	0.011	7.0	0.0009	9.5	0.00008
2.1	0.122	4.6	0.010	7.1	0.0008	9.6	0.00007
2.2	0.111	4.7	0.009	7.2	0.0007	9.7	0.00006
2.3	0.100	4.8	0.008	7.3	0.0007	9.8	0.00006
2.4	0.091	4.9	0.007	7.4	0.0006	9.9	0.00005

TABLE XI   Logarithms

N	0	1	2	3	4	5	6	7	8	9
10	0000	0043	0086	0128	0170	0212	0253	0294	0334	0374
11	0414	0453	0492	0531	0569	0607	0645	0682	0719	0755
12	0792	0828	0864	0899	0934	0969	1004	1038	1072	1106
13	1139	1173	1206	1239	1271	1303	1335	1367	1399	1430
14	1461	1492	1523	1553	1584	1614	1644	1673	1703	1732
15	1761	1790	1818	1847	1875	1903	1931	1959	1987	2014
16	2041	2068	2095	2122	2148	2175	2201	2227	2253	2279
17	2304	2330	2355	2380	2405	2430	2455	2480	2504	2529
18	2553	2577	2601	2625	2648	2672	2695	2718	2742	2765
19	2788	2810	2833	2856	2878	2900	2923	2945	2967	2989
20	3010	3032	3054	3075	3096	3118	3139	3160	3181	3201
21	3222	3243	3263	3284	3304	3324	3345	3365	3385	3404
22	3424	3444	3464	3483	3502	3522	3541	3560	3579	3598
23	3617	3636	3655	3674	3692	3711	3729	3747	3766	3784
24	3802	3820	3838	3856	3874	3892	3909	3927	3945	3962
25	3979	3997	4014	4031	4048	4065	4082	4099	4116	4133
26	4150	4166	4183	4200	4216	4232	4249	4265	4281	4298
27	4314	4330	4346	4362	4378	4393	4409	4425	4440	4456
28	4472	4487	4502	4518	4533	4548	4564	4579	4594	4609
29	4624	4639	4654	4669	4683	4698	4713	4728	4742	4757
30	4771	4786	4800	4814	4829	4843	4857	4871	4886	4900
31	4914	4928	4942	4955	4969	4983	4997	5011	5024	5038
32	5051	5065	5079	5092	5105	5119	5132	5145	5159	5172
33	5185	5198	5211	5224	5237	5250	5263	5276	5289	5302
34	5315	5328	5340	5353	5366	5378	5391	5403	5416	5428
35	5441	5453	5465	5478	5490	5502	5514	5527	5539	5551
36	5563	5575	5587	5599	5611	5623	5635	5647	5658	5670
37	5682	5694	5705	5717	5729	5740	5752	5763	5775	5786
38	5798	5809	5821	5832	5843	5855	5866	5877	5888	5899
39	5911	5922	5933	5944	5955	5966	5977	5988	5999	6010
40	6021	6031	6042	6053	6064	6075	6085	6096	6107	6117
41	6128	6138	6149	6160	6170	6180	6191	6201	6212	6222
42	6232	6243	6253	6263	6274	6284	6294	6304	6314	6325
43	6335	6345	6355	6365	6375	6385	6395	6405	6415	6425
44	6435	6444	6454	6464	6474	6484	6493	6503	6513	6522
45	6532	6542	6551	6561	6571	6580	6590	6599	6609	6618
46	6628	6637	6646	6656	6665	6675	6684	6693	6702	6712
47	6721	6730	6739	6749	6758	6767	6776	6785	6794	6803
48	6812	6821	6830	6839	6848	6857	6866	6875	6884	6893
49	6902	6911	6920	6928	6937	6946	6955	6964	6972	6981
50	6990	6998	7007	7016	7024	7033	7042	7050	7059	7067
51	7076	7084	7093	7101	7110	7118	7126	7135	7143	7152
52	7160	7168	7177	7185	7193	7202	7210	7218	7226	7235
53	7243	7251	7259	7267	7275	7284	7292	7300	7308	7316
54	7324	7332	7340	7348	7356	7364	7372	7380	7388	7396

TABLE **XI** Logarithms (*continued*)

N	0	1	2	3	4	5	6	7	8	9
55	7404	7412	7419	7427	7435	7443	7451	7459	7466	7474
56	7482	7490	7497	7505	7513	7520	7528	7536	7543	7551
57	7559	7566	7574	7582	7589	7597	7604	7612	7619	7627
58	7634	7642	7649	7657	7664	7672	7679	7686	7694	7701
59	7709	7716	7723	7731	7738	7745	7752	7760	7767	7774
60	7782	7789	7796	7803	7810	7818	7825	7832	7839	7846
61	7853	7860	7868	7875	7882	7889	7896	7903	7910	7917
62	7924	7931	7938	7945	7952	7959	7966	7973	7980	7987
63	7993	8000	8007	8014	8021	8028	8035	8041	8048	8055
64	8062	8069	8075	8082	8089	8096	8102	8109	8116	8122
65	8129	8136	8142	8149	8156	8162	8169	8176	8182	8189
66	8195	8202	8209	8215	8222	8228	8235	8241	8248	8254
67	8261	8267	8274	8280	8287	8293	8299	8306	8312	8319
68	8325	8331	8338	8344	8351	8357	8363	8370	8376	8382
69	8388	8395	8401	8407	8414	8420	8426	8432	8439	8445
70	8451	8457	8463	8470	8476	8482	8488	8494	8500	8506
71	8513	8519	8525	8531	8537	8543	8549	8555	8561	8567
72	8573	8579	8585	8591	8597	8603	8609	8615	8621	8627
73	8633	8639	8645	8651	8657	8663	8669	8675	8681	8686
74	8692	8698	8704	8710	8716	8722	8727	8733	8739	8745
75	8751	8756	8762	8768	8774	8779	8785	8791	8797	8802
76	8808	8814	8820	8825	8831	8837	8842	8848	8854	8859
77	8865	8871	8876	8882	8887	8893	8899	8904	8910	8915
78	8921	8927	8932	8938	8943	8949	8954	8960	8965	8971
79	8976	8982	8987	8993	8998	9004	9009	9015	9020	9025
80	9031	9036	9042	9047	9053	9058	9063	9069	9074	9079
81	9085	9090	9096	9101	9106	9112	9117	9122	9128	9133
82	9138	9143	9149	9154	9159	9165	9170	9175	9180	9186
83	9191	9196	9201	9206	9212	9217	9222	9227	9232	9238
84	9243	9248	9253	9258	9263	9269	9274	9279	9284	9289
85	9294	9299	9304	9309	9315	9320	9325	9330	9335	9340
86	9345	9350	9355	9360	9365	9370	9375	9380	9385	9390
87	9395	9400	9405	9410	9415	9420	9425	9430	9435	9440
88	9445	9450	9455	9460	9465	9469	9474	9479	9484	9489
89	9494	9499	9504	9509	9513	9518	9523	9528	9533	9538
90	9542	9547	9552	9557	9562	9566	9571	9576	9581	9586
91	9590	9595	9600	9605	9609	9614	9619	9624	9628	9633
92	9638	9643	9647	9652	9657	9661	9666	9671	9675	9680
93	9685	9689	9694	9699	9703	9708	9713	9717	9722	9727
94	9731	9736	9741	9745	9750	9754	9759	9763	9768	9773
95	9777	9782	9786	9791	9795	9800	9805	9809	9814	9818
96	9823	9827	9832	9836	9841	9845	9850	9854	9859	9863
97	9868	9872	9877	9881	9886	9890	9894	9899	9903	9908
98	9912	9917	9921	9926	9930	9934	9939	9943	9948	9952
99	9956	9961	9965	9969	9974	9978	9983	9987	9991	9996

TABLE XII Random Numbers

04433	80674	24520	18222	10610	05794	37515
60298	47829	72648	37414	75755	04717	29899
67884	59651	67533	68123	17730	95862	08034
89512	32155	51906	61662	64130	16688	37275
32653	01895	12506	88535	36553	23757	34209
95913	15405	13772	76638	48423	25018	99041
55864	21694	13122	44115	01601	50541	00147
35334	49810	91601	40617	72876	33967	73830
57729	32196	76487	11622	96297	24160	09903
86648	13697	63677	70119	94739	25875	38829
30574	47609	07967	32422	76791	39725	53711
81307	43694	83580	79974	45929	85113	72268
02410	54905	79007	54939	21410	86980	91772
18969	75274	52233	62319	08598	09066	95288
87863	82384	66860	62297	80198	19347	73234
68397	71708	15438	62311	72844	60203	46412
28529	54447	58729	10854	99058	18260	38765
44285	06372	15867	70418	57012	72122	36634
86299	83430	33571	23309	57040	29285	67870
84842	68668	90894	61658	15001	94055	36308
56970	83609	52098	04184	54967	72938	56834
83125	71257	60490	44369	66130	72936	69848
55503	52423	02464	26141	68779	66388	75242
47019	76273	33203	29608	54553	25971	69573
84828	32592	79526	29554	84580	37859	28504
68921	08141	79227	05748	51276	57143	31926
36458	96045	30424	98420	72925	40729	22337
95752	59445	36847	87729	81679	59126	59437
26768	47323	58454	56958	20575	76746	49878
42613	37056	43636	58085	06766	60227	96414
95457	30566	65482	25596	02678	54592	63607
95276	17894	63564	95958	39750	64379	46059
66954	52324	64776	92345	95110	59448	77249
17457	18481	14113	62462	02798	54977	48349
03704	36872	83214	59337	01695	60666	97410
21538	86497	33210	60337	27976	70661	08250
57178	67619	98310	70348	11317	71623	55510
31048	97558	94953	55866	96283	46620	52087
69799	55380	16498	80733	96422	58078	99643
90595	61867	59231	17772	67831	33317	00520
33570	04981	98939	78784	09977	29398	93896
15340	93460	57477	13898	48431	72936	78160
64079	42483	36512	56186	99098	48850	72527
63491	05546	67118	62063	74958	20946	28147
92003	63868	41034	28260	79708	00770	88643
52360	46658	66511	04172	73085	11795	52594
74622	12142	68355	65635	21828	39539	18988
04157	50079	61343	64315	70836	82857	35335
86003	60070	66241	32836	27573	11479	94114
41268	80187	20351	09636	84668	42486	71303

Source: Based on parts of *Table of 105,000 Random Decimal Digits* (Washington, D.C.: Interstate Commerce Commission, Bureau of Transport Economics and Statistics, 1949).

TABLE XII   Random Numbers *(continued)*

48611	62866	33963	14045	79451	04934	45576
78812	03509	78673	73181	29973	18664	04555
19472	63971	37271	31445	49019	49405	46925
51266	11569	08697	91120	64156	40365	74297
55806	96275	26130	47949	14877	69594	83041
77527	81360	18180	97421	55541	90275	18213
77680	58788	33016	61173	93049	04694	43534
15404	96554	88265	34537	38526	67924	40474
14045	22917	60718	66487	46346	30949	03173
68376	43918	77653	04127	69930	43283	35766
93385	13421	67957	20384	58731	53396	59723
09858	52104	32014	53115	03727	98624	84616
93307	34116	49516	42148	57740	31198	70336
04794	01534	92058	03157	91758	80611	45357
86265	49096	97021	92582	61422	75890	86442
65943	79232	45702	67055	39024	57383	44424
90038	94209	04055	27393	61517	23002	96560
97283	95943	78363	36498	40662	94188	18202
21913	72958	75637	99936	58715	07943	23748
41161	37341	81838	19389	80336	46346	91895
23777	98392	31417	98547	92058	02277	50315
59973	08144	61070	73094	27059	69181	55623
82690	74099	77885	23813	10054	11900	44653
83854	24715	48866	65745	31131	47636	45137
61980	34997	41825	11623	07320	15003	56774
99915	45821	97702	87125	44488	77613	56823
48293	86847	43186	42951	37804	85129	28993
33225	31280	41232	34750	91097	60752	69783
06846	32828	24425	30249	78801	26977	92074
32671	45587	79620	84831	38156	74211	82752
82096	21913	75544	55228	89796	05694	91552
51666	10433	10945	55306	78562	89630	41230
54044	67942	24145	42294	27427	84875	37022
66738	60184	75679	38120	17640	36242	99357
55064	17427	89180	74018	44865	53197	74810
69599	60264	84549	78007	88450	06488	72274
64756	87759	92354	78694	63638	80939	98644
80817	74533	68407	55862	32476	19326	95558
39847	96884	84657	33697	39578	90197	80532
90401	41700	95510	61166	33757	23279	85523
78227	90110	81378	96659	37008	04050	04228
87240	52716	87697	79433	16336	52862	69149
08486	10951	26832	39763	02485	71688	90936
39338	32169	03713	93510	61244	73774	01245
21188	01850	69689	49426	49128	14660	14143
13287	82531	04388	64693	11934	35051	68576
53609	04001	19648	14053	49623	10840	31915
87900	36194	31567	53506	34304	39910	79630
81641	00496	36058	75899	46620	70024	88753
19512	50277	71508	20116	79520	06269	74173

TABLE XII Random Numbers *(continued)*

24418	23508	91507	76455	54941	72711	39406
57404	73678	08272	62941	02349	71389	45605
77644	98489	86268	73652	98210	44546	27174
68366	65614	01443	07607	11826	91326	29664
64472	72294	95432	53555	96810	17100	35066
88205	37913	98633	81009	81060	33449	68055
98455	78685	71250	10329	56135	80647	51404
48977	36794	56054	59243	57361	65304	93258
93077	72941	92779	23581	24548	56415	61927
84533	26564	91583	83411	66504	02036	02922
11338	12903	14514	27585	45068	05520	56321
23853	68500	92274	87026	99717	01542	72990
94096	74920	25822	98026	05394	61840	83089
83160	82362	09350	98536	38155	42661	02363
97425	47335	69709	01386	74319	04318	99387
83951	11954	24317	20345	18134	90062	10761
93085	35203	05740	03206	92012	42710	34650
33762	83193	58045	89880	78101	44392	53767
49665	85397	85137	30496	23469	42846	94810
37541	82627	80051	72521	35342	56119	97190
22145	85304	35348	82854	55846	18076	12415
27153	08662	61078	52433	22184	33998	87436
00301	49425	66682	25442	83668	66236	79655
43815	43272	73778	63469	50083	70696	13558
14689	86482	74157	46012	97765	27552	49617
16680	55936	82453	19532	49988	13176	94219
86938	60429	01137	86168	78257	86249	46134
33944	29219	73161	46061	30946	22210	79302
16045	67736	18608	18198	19468	76358	69203
37044	52523	25627	63107	30806	80857	84383
61471	45322	35340	35132	42163	69332	98851
47422	21296	16785	66393	39249	51463	95963
24133	39719	14484	58613	88717	29289	77360
67253	67064	10748	16006	16767	57345	42285
62382	76941	01635	35829	77516	98468	51686
98011	16503	09201	03523	87192	66483	55649
37366	24386	20654	85117	74078	64120	04643
73587	83993	54176	05221	94119	20108	78101
33583	68291	50547	96085	62180	27453	18567
02878	33223	39199	49536	56199	05993	71201
91498	41673	17195	33175	04994	09879	70337
91127	19815	30219	55591	21725	43827	78862
12997	55013	18662	81724	24305	37661	18956
96098	13651	15393	69995	14762	69734	89150
97627	17837	10472	18983	28387	99781	52977
40064	47981	31484	76603	54088	91095	00010
16239	68743	71374	55863	22672	91609	51514
58354	24913	20435	30965	17453	65623	93058
52567	65085	60220	84641	18273	49604	47418
06236	29052	91392	07551	83532	68130	56970

TABLE XII   Random Numbers *(continued)*

94620	27963	96478	21559	19246	88097	44926
60947	60775	73181	43264	56895	04232	59604
27499	53523	63110	57106	20865	91683	80688
01603	23156	89223	43429	95353	44662	59433
00815	01552	06392	31437	70385	45863	75971
83844	90942	74857	52419	68723	47830	63010
06626	10042	93629	37609	57215	08409	81906
56760	63348	24949	11859	29793	37457	59377
64416	29934	00755	09418	14230	62887	92683
63569	17906	38076	32135	19096	96970	75917
22693	35089	72994	04252	23791	60249	83010
43413	59744	01275	71326	91382	45114	20245
09224	78530	50566	49965	04851	18280	14039
67625	34683	03142	74733	63558	09665	22610
86874	12549	98699	54952	91579	26023	81076
54548	49505	62515	63903	13193	33905	66936
73236	66167	49728	03581	40699	10396	81827
15220	66319	13543	14071	59148	95154	72852
16151	08029	36954	03891	38313	34016	18671
43635	84249	88984	80993	55431	90793	62603
30193	42776	85611	57635	51362	79907	77364
37430	45246	11400	20986	43996	73122	88474
88312	93047	12088	86937	70794	01041	74867
98995	58159	04700	90443	13168	31553	67891
51734	20849	70198	67906	00880	82899	66065
88698	41755	56216	66852	17748	04963	54859
51865	09836	73966	65711	41699	11732	17173
40300	08852	27528	84648	79589	95295	72895
02760	28625	70476	76410	32988	10194	94917
78450	26245	91763	73117	33047	03577	65299
50252	56911	62693	73817	98693	18728	94741
07929	66728	47761	81472	44806	15592	71357
09030	39605	87507	85446	51257	89555	75520
56670	88445	85799	76200	21795	38894	58070
48140	13583	94911	13318	64741	64336	95103
36764	86132	12463	28385	94242	32063	45233
14351	71381	28133	68269	65145	28152	39087
81276	00835	63835	87174	42446	08882	27067
55524	86088	00069	59254	24654	77371	26409
78852	65889	32719	13758	23937	90740	16866
11861	69032	51915	23510	32050	52052	24004
67699	01009	07050	73324	06732	27510	33761
50064	39500	17450	18030	63124	48061	59412
93126	17700	94400	76075	08317	27324	72723
01657	92602	41043	05686	15650	29970	95877
13800	76690	75133	60456	28491	03845	11507
98135	42870	48578	29036	69876	86563	61729
08313	99293	00990	13595	77457	79969	11339
90974	83965	62732	85161	54330	22406	86253
33273	61993	88407	69399	17301	70975	99129

TABLE XIII Control Chart Constants

Number of observations in sample, n	CHART FOR AVERAGES			CHART FOR STANDARD DEVIATIONS					CHART FOR RANGES				
	Factors for control limits			Factors for central line	Factors for control limits				Factors for control limits	Factors for control limits			
	A	A_1	A_2	c_2	B_1	B_2	B_3	B_4	d_2	D_1	D_2	D_3	D_4
2	2.121	3.760	1.880	0.5642	0	1.843	0	3.267	1.128	0	3.686	0	3.267
3	1.732	2.394	1.023	0.7236	0	1.858	0	2.568	1.693	0	4.358	0	2.575
4	1.500	1.880	0.729	0.7979	0	1.808	0	2.266	2.059	0	4.698	0	2.282
5	1.342	1.596	0.577	0.8407	0	1.756	0	2.089	2.326	0	4.918	0	2.115
6	1.225	1.410	0.483	0.8686	0.026	1.711	0.030	1.970	2.534	0	5.078	0	2.004
7	1.134	1.277	0.419	0.8882	0.105	1.672	0.118	1.882	2.704	0.205	5.203	0.076	1.924
8	1.061	1.175	0.373	0.9027	0.167	1.638	0.185	1.815	2.847	0.387	5.307	0.136	1.864
9	1.000	1.094	0.337	0.9139	0.219	1.609	0.239	1.761	2.970	0.546	5.394	0.184	1.816
10	0.949	1.028	0.308	0.9227	0.262	1.584	0.284	1.716	3.078	0.687	5.469	0.223	1.777
11	0.905	0.973	0.285	0.9300	0.299	1.561	0.321	1.679	3.173	0.812	5.534	0.256	1.744
12	0.866	0.925	0.266	0.9359	0.331	1.541	0.354	1.646	3.258	0.924	5.592	0.284	1.716
13	0.832	0.884	0.249	0.9410	0.359	1.523	0.382	1.618	3.336	1.236	5.646	0.308	1.692
14	0.802	0.848	0.235	0.9453	0.384	1.507	0.406	1.594	3.407	1.121	5.693	0.329	1.671
15	0.775	0.816	0.223	0.9490	0.406	1.492	0.428	1.572	3.472	1.207	5.737	0.348	1.652

TABLE XIII   Control Chart Constants (*continued*)

Statistic	STANDARDS GIVEN		ANALYSIS OF PAST DATA	
	Central line	Limits	Central line	Limits
$\overline{X}$	$\overline{X}'$	$\overline{X}' \pm A\sigma'$	$\overline{\overline{X}}$	$\overline{\overline{X}} \pm A_1\overline{\sigma}$ or $\overline{\overline{X}} \pm A_2\overline{R}$
σ	$c_2\sigma'$	$B_1\sigma'$, $B_2\sigma'$	$\overline{\sigma}$	$B_3\overline{\sigma}$, $B_4\overline{\sigma}$
R	$d_2\sigma'$	$D_1\sigma'$, $D_2\sigma'$	$\overline{R}$	$D_3\overline{R}$, $D_4\overline{R}$

Source: ASTM Manual on Quality Control of Materials, American Society for Testing and Materials, Philadelphia, Pa., 1951; by permission.

TABLE XIV   Critical Values of T*

n	$T_{0.10}$	$T_{0.05}$	$T_{0.02}$	$T_{0.01}$
4				
5	1			
6	2	1		
7	4	2	0	
8	6	4	2	0
9	8	6	3	2
10	11	8	5	3
11	14	11	7	5
12	17	14	10	7
13	21	17	13	10
14	26	21	16	13
15	30	25	20	16
16	36	30	24	19
17	41	35	28	23
18	47	40	33	28
19	54	46	38	32
20	60	52	43	37
21	68	59	49	43
22	75	66	56	49
23	83	73	62	55
24	92	81	69	61
25	101	90	77	68

*From F. Wilcoxon and R. A. Wilcox, *Some Rapid Approximate Statistical Procedures,* American Cyanamid Company, Pearl River, N.Y., 1964. Reproduced with permission of American Cyanamid Company.

Answers to Odd-Numbered Exercises

In exercises involving extensive calculations, the reader may well get answers differing somewhat from those given here due to rounding at various intermediate stages.

CHAPTER 2

2.1   See Practice Exercises.

2.3   See Practice Exercises.

2.5   The class limits are 10.0–14.9, 15.0–19.9, 20.0–24.9, 25.0–29.9, 30.0–34.9, and 35.0–39.9. The class marks are 12.45, 17.45, 22.45, 27.45, 32.45, and 37.45.

2.7   (a) The class frequencies are 4, 8, 16, 30, 35, 13, 3, and 1.
      (b) The cumulative ''less than'' frequencies are 0, 4, 12, 28, 58, 93, 106, 109, and 110.

2.9   (a) Frequencies are 3, 4, 5, 11, 11, 6, and 2.
      (b) Percentages are 7.1, 9.5, 11.9, 26.2, 26.2, 14.3, and 4.8.

2.11

Grades per Transcript	Number
A	4
B	13
C	18
D	4
F	1
Total	40

2.13

21	6	5	0					
22	4	8	9	1	8	3	2	
23	5	5	0	6	7	3	1	0	0
24	0	4	9	0	4	5		
25	2	3	6	5				
26	9							

2.15   (a) 90, 99, 95, 93, 94.

(b) 278, 274, 277, 275, 271.

(c) 615, 645, 630, 695, 600.

(d) 2.14, 2.18, 2.17, 2.17, 2.15.

2.17   See Practice Exercises.

2.19   See Practice Exercises.

2.21   (a)

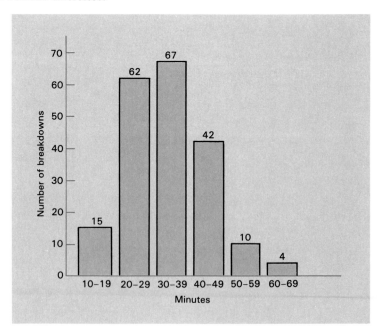

(b)

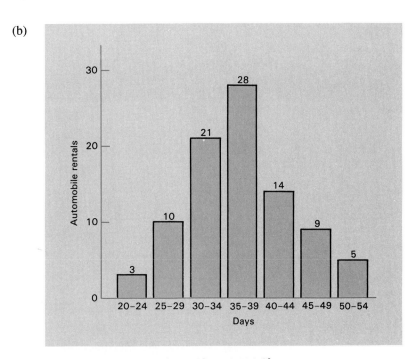

2.23   The central angles are 203.5°, 41.7°, and 114.8°.

2.25   (a) An example of a complete title is, Automobile Production in the United
            States, 1990–1993. The title is complete since it answers three ques-
            tions: what, where, and when. What: automobile production. Where: in
            the United States. When: 1990–1993.

       (b) Some possible headnotes or footnotes might be "excludes military vehi-
            cles"; "includes automobiles manufactured in the United States by for-
            eign firms"; "excludes recreational vehicles"; "includes light trucks";
            "excludes automobiles manufactured in foreign countries by U.S.
            firms."

       (c) Some sources might be considered unreliable by readers. Also, the
            focus of the data might be different if prepared by disparate groups such
            as a manufacturers organization, an automobile manufacturer, an envi-
            ronmental organization, a labor union, or an agency of the U.S. gov-
            ernment.

2.27

```
MTB > SET C1
DATA> 41 37 52 41 46 50 47 36 44 51
DATA> 37 38 44 56 30 34 28 40 39 41
DATA> 40 38 36 49 43 46 31 31 43 29
DATA> 31 33 46 37 35
DATA> END
MTB > STEM-AND-LEAF OF C1;
SUBC> INCREMENT 5.

Stem-and-leaf of C1        N = 35
Leaf Unit = 1.0

     2     2 89
     8     3 011134
    17     3 566777889
    (9)    4 001113344
     9     4 66679
     4     5 012
     1     5 6

MTB > STOP
```

2.29

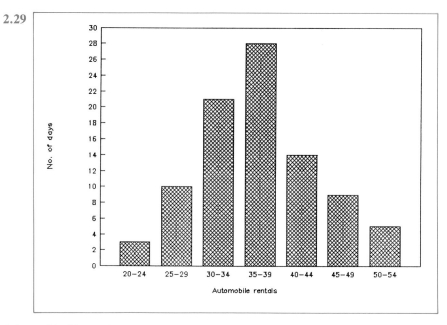

2.31 (a) Yes; (b) no; (c) no; (d) yes.

2.33 Frequencies are 4, 12, 18, 26, 20, 14, and 6.

2.35 (a) Class boundaries are -0.5–49.5, 49.5–99.5, 99.5–149.5, and 149.5–199.5 photocopies.

(b) Class markes are 24.5, 74.5, 124.5, and 174.5 photocopies.

(c) Class interval is 50 photocopies.

2.37

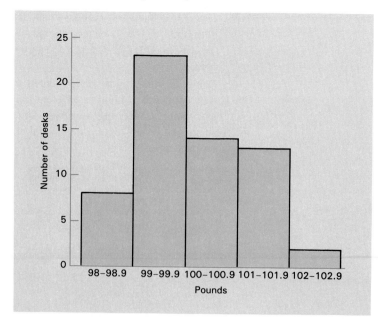

2.39 A year in which 11 ships depart in July is not accommodated; a year in which 23 ships depart in July falls into two overlapping classes, 18–23 and 23–30; a year in which ships depart every day in July is not accommodated; classes of unequal length; fewer than six classes.

2.41 Frequencies for comedy, special interest, drama, science fiction, horror, and action/adventure are 10, 4, 16, 5, 7, and 8, respectively. Corresponding central angles are 72°, 28.8°, 115.2°, 36.0°, 50.4°, and 57.6°.

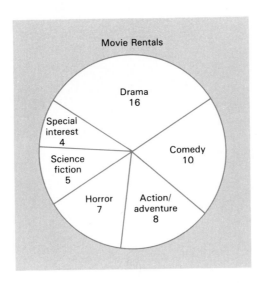

2.43 (a)

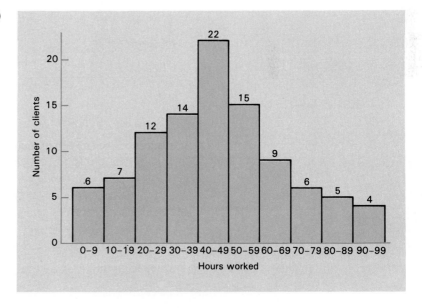

(b)

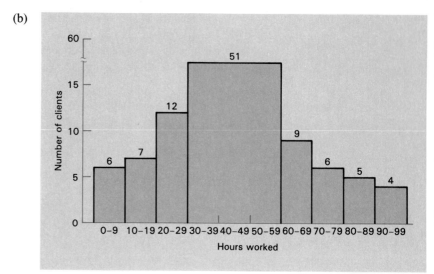

2.45

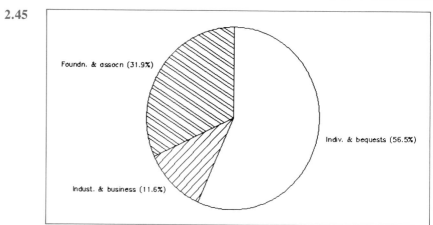

CHAPTER 3

3.1   (a) If we are interested only in the numbers of Class A, Class B, and Class C fires fought by this department for this month, the data constitute a population.

(b) If we want to generalize about this fire department's Class A, Class B, and Class C fires in other months, or generalize about other fire departments in the region or nation at this or at other times, the data constitute a sample.

3.3   See Practice Exercises.

3.5   See Practice Exercises.

3.7   See Practice Exercises.

3.9 See Practice Exercises.

3.11 (a) 40 inches; (b) 29 inches and 46 inches; (c) 42 inches.

3.13 The statement is simplistic. More information would be useful to get a good description of the freshman population in quantitative terms. The measures of location which were provided do not tell us how widely the data are scattered. For example, freshman ages may be compactly grouped, say, from 17 to 19, or widely scattered from ages 15 to 80; the proportion of unmarried students may be 51 percent or 100 percent; the SAT scores may be 1,176 ± 25 points, or they may be 1,176 + 400 points or more, and so on. Also the term *unmarried* is not defined, and its measure of location is the mode; the SAT score is probably a mean or median; the *18 year* age may be a mean, median, or mode. As noted, some terms need to be defined. Does unmarried mean never married (there are other possibilities)? What are the upper and lower bounds for an upper-middle-income family? What is a family? What is full-time employment?

3.15 See Practice Exercises.

3.17 52.8 heads.

3.19 5.6 single-family homes.

3.21 5.2 minutes.

3.23 See Practice Exercises.

3.25 See Practice Exercises.

3.27 (a) 2.85 gallons; (b) 2.85 gallons; (c) 2.85 gallons.

3.29 (a) range, 21 stories; s, 6.5 stories.
(b) range, 12 stories; s, 4.0 stories.

3.31

Kind of nut	Mean (percent)	Range (percent)	Standard deviation (percent)
Almonds	13.4	3.7	1.6
Brazil nuts	10.7	2.4	0.9
Cashews	31.4	4.9	1.8
Peanuts	24.7	4.6	1.9
Walnuts	19.9	3.1	1.2

3.33 Range is 51 inches, s is 13.8 inches.

3.35 (a) $s = \sqrt{\dfrac{7(220) - (-14)^2}{7 \cdot 6}} = 2\sqrt{8}$

(b) The modified data are -49, 32, 0 and 17 so that

$$s = \sqrt{\frac{4(3{,}714) - 0^2}{4 \cdot 3}}$$

$= 35.185$ which, divided by $10 = 3.518$. If s is calculated from the original data the results are identical.

3.37 See Practice Exercises.

3.39 (a) $\frac{3}{4}$; (b) 15 minutes and 45 minutes.

3.41 (a) 25.6 percent.
(b) 37.3 percent.
(c) Sales are more variable than mileage (37.3 is greater than 25.6).
(d) The data for age are more variable than the data for weight (14.4 is greater than 11.8).

3.43 See Practice Exercises.

3.45 $\bar{x} = 43.8$ years, and $s = 15.5$ years.

3.47 0.1.

3.49 (a) 36.8 rentals; (b) 36.5 rentals; (c) 7.2 rentals; (d) 0.125.

3.51 (a) Mean is 22.5 patient contacts and median is 22.4 patient contacts.
(b) s is 8.5 patient contacts.
(c) Q_1 and Q_3 are 16.4 and 28.9 patient contacts.
(d) D_2 and D_8 are 15.0 and 30.6 patient contacts.
(e) P_{15} and P_{85} are 12.7 and 32.4 patient contacts.

3.53 See Practice Exercises.

3.57 See Practice Exercises.

3.59 (a) 18; (b) 102; (c) 6; (d) 46; (e) 64; (f) 12.

3.61 (a) 8; (b) 54; (c) 252.

3.63 (a) No; substituting $n = 2$ we get

$$\left(\sum_{i=1}^{2} x_i \right)^2 = (x_1 + x_2)^2 = x_1^2 + 2x_1 x_2 + x_2^2 \neq x_1^2 + x_2^2 = \sum_{i=1}^{2} x_i^2$$

except where x_1 or $x_2 = 0$.

(b) $\bar{x} = \dfrac{\sum\limits_{i=1}^{n} x_1}{n}$; $\bar{x}_w = \dfrac{\sum\limits_{i=1}^{n} w_i x_i}{\sum\limits_{i=1}^{n} w_i}$; $\bar{\bar{x}} = \dfrac{\sum\limits_{i=1}^{k} n_i \bar{x}_i}{\sum\limits_{i=1}^{k} n_i}$

3.65 (a) 75 percent; (b) 84.0 percent; (c) 88.9 percent.

3.67 (a) \$0.01 per car mile traveled; (b) \$0.0005 per ton mile.

3.69   Distribution A: mean, yes; median, yes.
        Distribution B: mean, no; median, yes.
        Distribution C: mean, no; median, no.

3.71 $\bar{x} = 42.8$ miles (thousands); $s = 21.8$ miles (thousands).

3.73   0.1.

3.75   (a) If we are interested only in the grade point averages of students in this
            college for a certain year, the data constitute a population.
        (b) If we use the data to generalize about the grade point averages of other
            colleges, or if we generalize from the given data to the grade point
            averages of this college in other years, the data constitute a sample.

3.77   (a) \$497.80 per television set.
        (b) \$510.29 per television set.
        (c) \$473.68 per television set.

3.79   7 bulbs.

3.81   \$1.52.

3.83   Mean is 15.2 prescriptions; median is 15.5 prescriptions; mode is 17.0 pre-
        scriptions; s is 6.1 prescriptions.

3.85   (a) 31.25 pints; (b) 0.625 pints, or 20 ounces.

3.87   (a) $\bar{x} = -3$, or 3 days early; $\tilde{x} = -2$, or 2 days early; range = 12 days.

3.89   (a) 24.1; (b) 7.3; (c) 7.0.

3.91   (a) $\frac{2}{3}$; (b) 5,000.

3.93   (a) When $n = 13$ the location of the median is 7, the location of the lower
            hinge is 4, and the location of the upper hinge is 10. This satisfies
            property 1, does not satisfy property 2, does not satisfy property 3.
        (b) When $n = 14$ the location of the median is 7.5, the location of the lower
            hinge is 4, and the location of the upper hinge is 12. This does not satisfy
            property 1, satisfies property 2, does not satisfy property 3.

3.95   (a) 2, 2, 3, 5, 6, 7, 8, 8, 10, 14, 15, 20.
            $1 \cdot \frac{12 + 1}{4} = 3\frac{1}{4}$ item, and its value is 3.5.
            $3 \cdot \frac{12 + 1}{4} = 9\frac{3}{4}$th item, and its value is 13.
        (b) $Q_1 = 28.5''$, and $Q_3 = 50.5''$.

3.97

```
MTB > # 1 FOR CHARGE ACCOUNT, 3 FOR CASH
MTB > # 2 FOR CREDIT CARD, 4 FOR CHECK
MTB > SET C1
DATA> 1 1 2 3 4 3 4 3 1 3
DATA> 3 1 3 4 3 4 3 2 1 1
DATA> 3 1 1 3 1 2 2 1 3 4
DATA> 3 3 1 2 4 4 3 1 4 2
DATA> END
MTB > TALLY C1

        C1  COUNT
         1    12
         2     6
         3    14
         4     8
        N=    40

MTB > STOP
```

3.99

```
MTB > SET C1
DATA> 10.9 19.3 14.7 13.8 15.3 11.4 12.6
MTB > STDEV C1
    ST.DEV. =        2.8472
MTB > STOP
```

3.101

```
MTB > NAME C4 = 'RANGE'
MTB > SET C1
DATA> 2.52 2.52 2.51 2.49 2.50 2.45 2.53 2.52 2.48 2.48
MTB > MEAN C1
    MEAN      =       2.5000
MTB > MAX C1 AS C2
    MAXIMUM =        2.5300
MTB > MIN C1 AS C3
    MINIMUM =        2.4500
MTB > DIFF C2 C3 AS C4
MTB > PRINT C4

RANGE
  0.08

MTB > STDEV C1
    ST.DEV. =      0.024944
MTB > STOP
```

CHAPTER 4

4.1   See Practice Exercises.

4.3 (a)

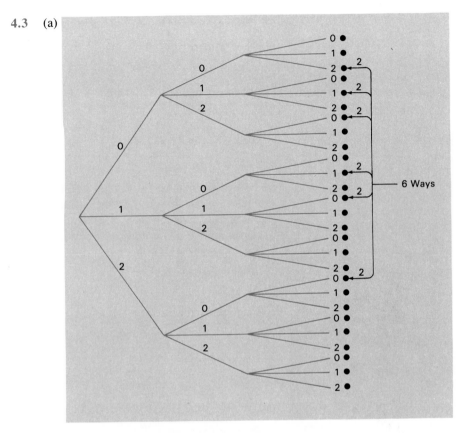

6 Ways

(b) 3 ways;   (c) 6 ways.

4.5

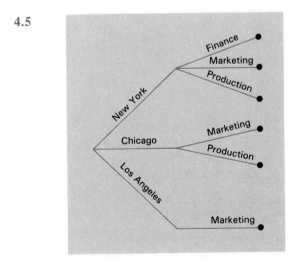

4.7   See Practice Exercises.

4.9   (a) 16 ways;   (b) 625 ways.

4.11   280 categories.

4.13   See Practice Exercises.

4.15   See Practice Exercises.

4.17   (a) 6 ways;   (b) 1 way.

4.19   See Practice Exercises.

4.21   (a) To find the number of ways in which n objects can be arranged in a circle, we can arbitrarily fix the position within the circle of any one of the objects. We can then calculate the number of ways in which the remaining $n - 1$ positions may be filled. The number of circular permutations is $(n - 1)!$.

       (b) 3,628,800 ways.

       (c) 24 ways.

4.23   See Practice Exercises.

4.25   27,405.

4.27   See Practice Exercises.

4.29   (a) 286 ways;   (b) 156 ways;   (c) 13 ways.

4.31   (b) 1, 6, 15, 20, 15, 6, and 1; 1, 7, 21, 35, 35, 21, 7, and 1.

4.33   See Practice Exercises.

4.35 $\frac{1}{8}, \frac{3}{8}, \frac{3}{8}$, and $\frac{1}{8}$.

4.37   (a) $\frac{1}{3}$;   (b) $\frac{1}{2}$.

4.39   (a) 0.29;   (b) 0.001.

4.41   (a) 0.3;   (b) 0.07.

4.43   0.75.

4.45   (a) The theoretical probability of the number of heads is $\frac{1}{2}$. Our simulation is affected by the law of large numbers, which states that, if a situation, trial, or experiment is repeated again and again, the proportion of successes will tend to approach the probability that any one outcome will be a success. The computer will provide random results, so each computer printout can be reasonably expected to be different.

4.47   See Practice Exercises.

4.49   (a) $0.00; yes, it is a fair game.

       (b) −$4.41, which favors the gambler.

4.51   See Practice Exercises.

4.53   See Practice Exercises.

4.55   1.45 absentees.

4.57 $E = \$3.50$; it is not rational to pay \$4 for randomly selecting one of the packages.

4.59   See Practice Exercises.

4.61   (a) apartment building;   (b) office building.

4.63   720 ways.

4.65   720 ways.

4.67   (a)

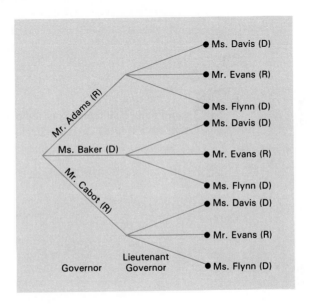

      (b) 5.

4.69   0.18.

4.71   60 ways.

4.73   \$105,850.

4.75 $\frac{1}{6}$.

4.77   (a) 15 ways;   (b) 16 ways.

4.79   5,040 ways.

4.81   2,520 ways.

5.1   See Practice Exercises.

5.3   See Practice Exercises.

5.5   See Practice Exercises.

5.7   (a)

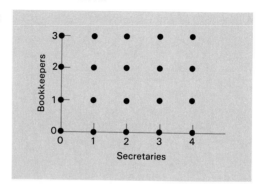

(b) D is the event that at least five temporary personnel are hired. E is the event that equal numbers of temporary secretaries and temporary book-keepers are hired. F is the event that we hire more bookkeepers than secretaries. G is the event that three temporary personnel are hired.

5.9   (a)

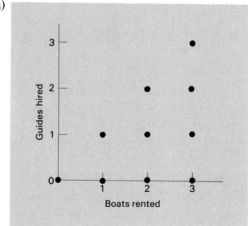

(b) $H = \{(2, 2), (3, 2), (3, 3)\}$; $I = \{(1, 0), (1, 1)\}$; and $J = \{(0, 0), (1, 1), (2, 2), (3, 3)\}$.

(c) $H' = \{(1, 0), (2, 0), (2, 1), (3, 0), (3, 1), (3, 2)\}$ is the event that not all of the rented boats have hired guides. $J \cap I = \{(1, 1)\}$ is the event that only one boat is rented and it has a hired guide.

(d) H and I are mutually exclusive; H and J are not mutually exclusive; I and J are not mutually exclusive.

5.11   (a) Not mutually exclusive;   (b) mutually exclusive;
       (c) not mutually exclusive;   (d) mutually exclusive.

5.13   See Practice Exercises.

5.15   Region 1 represents the event that an investor in the stock market hired an investment counselor and that the investor made capital gains on her investments. Region 2 represents the event that the investor hired an investment counselor, but she did not make capital gains on her investments. Region 3 represents the event that the investor made capital gains on her investments, but she did not hire an investment counselor. Region 4 represents the event that the investor did not hire an investment counselor, and she did not make capital gains on her investments.

5.17   (a) The engine's gasoline consumption will be low, its maintenance cost will be low, but it cannot be sold at a profit.
       (b) The engine's gasoline consumption will be low, and it can be sold at a profit.
       (c) The engine's maintenance cost will be low, but it cannot be sold at a profit.
       (d) The engine's gasoline consumption will be low or it can be sold at a profit, but its maintenance cost will not be low.
       (e) The engine cannot be sold at a profit.

5.19   (a) Region 1 is the event that the soil study group, the water study group, and the wildlife study group will all be established.
       (b) Region 5 is the event that the water study group will be established (but not the soil or the wildlife study groups).
       (c) Region 8 is the event that none of the three study groups will be established.
       (d) Regions 3 and 5 together is the event that a water study group and a wildlife study group will be established, but not a soil study group.
       (e) Regions 1 and 4 together is the event that a wildlife study group and a soil study group will be established.
       (f) Regions 3, 5, and 8 together mean that a soil study group will not be established.

5.21   See Practice Exercises.

5.23   See Practice Exercises.

5.25   (a) 0.65;   (b) 0.60;   (c) 0.40.

5.27   0.73.

5.29   (a) $0.25 + 0.10 = 0.35$.
       (b) $0.25 + 0.15 = 0.40$.
       (c) $0.30 + 0.15 + 0.10 + 0.25 = 0.80$.

5.31   (a) 0.470;   (b) 0.830;   (c) 0.470.

5.33   0.30.

5.35   (a) 0.32;   (b) 0.24.

5.37   See Practice Exercises.

5.39   See Practice Exercises.

5.41   9 to 1.

5.43   See Practice Exercises.

5.45   Less than $\frac{1}{4}$.

5.47   Greater than 0.88 but, at most, 0.90.

5.49   The probability that the first contractor will be awarded the contract is $\dfrac{1}{1+3} = \dfrac{1}{4}$, the probability that the second contractor will be awarded the contract is $\dfrac{1}{1+4} = \dfrac{1}{5}$, so that the probability that either contractor will be awarded the contract is $\dfrac{1}{4} + \dfrac{1}{5} = \dfrac{9}{20}$; hence the odds that neither will be awarded the contract are 11 to 9.

5.51   See Practice Exercises.

5.53   (a) $P(A|B) = P(A) = 0.30$.
    (b) $P(A) \cdot P(B) = (0.30) \cdot (0.60) = 0.18$.
    (c) $P(A \cup B) = P(A) + P(B) - P(A \cap B) = 0.30 + 0.60 - 0.18 = 0.72$.
    (d) $1 - 0.72 = 0.28$.

5.55

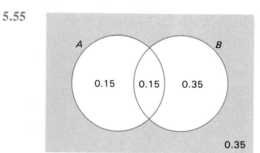

    (a) $P(A|B) = \frac{0.15}{0.50} = 0.30 = P(A)$.
    (b) $P(A|B') = \frac{0.15}{0.50} = 0.30 = P(A)$.
    (c) $P(B|A) = \frac{0.15}{0.30} = 0.50 = P(B)$.
    (d) $P(B|A') = \frac{0.35}{0.70} = 0.50 = P(B)$.

5.57 See Practice Exercises.

5.59 $\dfrac{0.60}{0.90} = 0.67$.

5.61 $P(H|A) = \dfrac{0.03}{0.20} = 0.15 = P(H)$, so that H is also independent of A.

5.63 $\dfrac{5}{6}$.

5.65 $\dfrac{1}{6} \cdot \dfrac{1}{6} = \dfrac{1}{36}$.

5.67 $\dfrac{13}{52} \cdot \dfrac{13}{52} \cdot \dfrac{13}{52} \cdot \dfrac{13}{52} = \dfrac{1}{256}$.

5.69 (a) See Practice Exercises   (d) 0.14
(b) See Practice Exercises   (e) 0.048, 0.096, and 0.760
(c) 0.08   (f) 0.729, 0.0625, 0.844

5.71 (a) The odds are $\dfrac{3}{5}$ to $\dfrac{2}{5}$ or 3 to 2. (The probability was obtained by subtracting the product $\dfrac{4}{6} \cdot \dfrac{3}{5} = \dfrac{2}{5}$ from 1.)
(b) The odds are $\dfrac{4}{5}$ to $\dfrac{1}{5}$ or 4 to 1 that any one clerical worker will be selected or 1 to 4 that the worker will not be selected.

5.73 Events A and C are not mutually exclusive; events B and D are mutually exclusive.

5.75 $0.25 \cdot 0.25 \cdot 0.25 = 0.016$.

5.77 $(0.42)(0.27) = 0.1134$, so events B and C are independent.

5.79 (a) $A' = \{5, 6\}$ is the event the buyer thinks the wool fiber is llama or vicuna.
(b) $A \cup B = \{1, 2, 3, 4, 5\}$ is the event the buyer thinks the wool fiber is not vicuna.
(c) $A \cap B = \{2, 3, 4\}$ is the event the buyer thinks the wool fiber is angora/cashmere, camel, or alpaca.
(d) $A \cap B' = \{1\}$ is the event the buyer thinks the wool fiber is sheep/lamb.

5.81 $0.20 + 0.10 + 0.40 = 0.70$.

5.83 $\dfrac{0.50}{0.75} = \dfrac{2}{3}$, or 0.67.

5.85 (a) $\dfrac{207}{360} = 0.58$;   (b) $\dfrac{245}{360} = 0.68$;   (c) $\dfrac{19}{360} = 0.05$;

(d) $\dfrac{57}{360} = 0.16$;   (e) $\dfrac{19}{207} = 0.09$;   (f) $\dfrac{57}{245} = 0.23$.

	F	F'	
Under 45	19	96	115
45 or older	188	57	245
	207	153	360

5.87 (a) $1 - 0.33 = 0.67$; (b) $1 - 0.59 = 0.41$;
(c) $0.33 + 0.59 = 0.92$; (d) $1 - 0.92 = 0.08$.

5.89 1. The bank is ranked among the 20 largest in the United States and the world.
2. The bank is ranked among the 20 largest in the United States but not in the world.
3. The bank is ranked among the 20 largest in the world but not in the United States.
4. The bank is not ranked among the 20 largest in either the United States or in the world.

5.91 $0.60 \cdot 0.10 = 0.06$.

5.93 $\left(\frac{1}{2}\right)^3 = \frac{1}{8}$.

5.95 (a) A mutual fund invests in corporate bonds, but not in municipal or U.S. government bonds.
(b) A mutual fund invests in corporate bonds and municipal bonds; or corporate bonds, municipal bonds, and U.S. government bonds.
(c) A mutual fund invests in corporate bonds; or corporate bonds and municipal bonds; but not in U.S. government bonds.
(d) A mutual fund invests in corporate bonds, U.S. government bonds, or both, but not in municipal bonds.
(e) A mutual fund does not invest in municipal bonds or U.S. government bonds. It invests in corporate bonds or in no bonds.

CHAPTER 6

6.1 See Practice Exercises.

6.3 (a)

		Driver goes to		
		1	2	3
Driver should go to	1	5	12	20
	2	8	9	18
	3	13	15	12

(b)

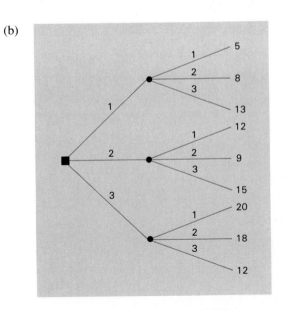

6.5   (a)

	Boston	N.Y.	Phila.
Low	23	26	24
Normal	30	32	31
High	36	37	39

(b)

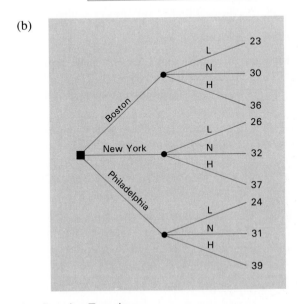

6.7   See Practice Exercises.

6.9   See Practice Exercises.

6.11   See Practice Exercises.

6.13   (a) Stock 1 (the maximin profit is −$4).

   (b) Stock 4 (the maximax profit is $24).

   (c) Stock 3 (see opportunity-loss table below).

		Stock			
		1	*2*	*3*	*4*
	0	0	4	8	12
	1	0	4	8	12
	2	6	0	4	8
Demand	*3*	12	6	0	4
	4	18	12	6	0
5 or more		18	12	6	0

For stock 1, 2, 3, or 4, maximum opportunity losses are 18, 12, 8, and 12, respectively, and the minimax loss of opportunity is, therefore, 8 (stock 3).

6.15   (a) Inspect both;   (b) inspect neither.

6.17   See Practice Exercises.

6.19   (a) The maximum values of the columns are 2, 1, and 3, and the minimum values of the rows are 1, −2, and −5; the saddle point corresponds to A_2 and E_1 (1 is the maximum value of its column and the minimum value of its row).

   (b) The maximum values of the columns are 1, 1, 3, and 5, and the minimum values of the rows are −2, −1, 1, and 1; there are saddle points corresponding to A_1 and E_3, A_1 and E_4, A_2 and E_3, and A_2 and E_4. In each case 1 is the maximum value of its column and the minimum value of its row.

6.21   There is a saddle point (optimum strategy) corresponding to the first strategy of the decision maker and the second strategy of the competitor (the first 0 in the second row is the maximum value of its column and the minimum value of its row).

(a) and (b) It does not seem irrational at all for the competitor to choose his second strategy if he knows that the decision maker bases his decision on the minimax criterion and will choose his first alternative. It seems reasonable for the competitor to choose his first strategy if the decision maker does not always act rationally or is incapable of analyzing the situation intelligently, and the (remote?) possibility of winning 200 units outweighs the risk of losing 2 units.

6.23 See Practice Exercises.

6.25 $\frac{1}{7}$, 0, and $\frac{6}{7}$.

6.27 (a) First station owner should lower his price.
(b) They might take turns lowering their prices on alternate days.

6.29 See Practice Exercises.

6.31 $50p - 30(1 - p) = -20p + 5(1 - p)$ so that $p = 0.333$. They could be off by $0.33 - 0.25 = 0.08$.

6.33 The expectation is maximized if the vendor stocks 3.

6.35 See Practice Exercises.

6.37 (a) The decision would be changed to expanding now.
(b) The decision would be changed to delaying expansion.

6.39 (a) $pb + (1 - p)c$.
(b) EVPI $= bp + c(1 - p) - [ap + c(1 - p)] = (b - a)p$ corresponding to A_1 and EVPI $= bp + c(1 - p) - [bp + d(1 - p)] = (c - d)(1 - p)$ corresponding to A_2.
(c) $p(b - a)$ and $(1 - p)(c - d)$.
(d) By inspection, EVPI $=$ EOL $= (b - a)p$ if A_1 is optimal, and EVPI $=$ EOL $= (c - d)(1 - p)$ if A_2 is optimal.

6.41 See Practice Exercises.

6.43 4.

6.45 Approximately 1.5.

6.47 -110, 0, 90, and 160.

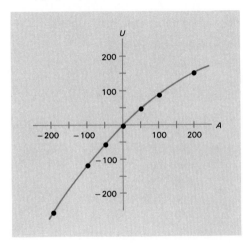

6.49 See Practice Exercises.

6.51

	First sew on:	
Then sew on:	*Gold*	*Silver*
Gold	11	13
Silver	15	9

6.53 (a) She should first order the tailor to sew the gold buttons on the jacket.

(b) She should first order the tailor to sew the silver buttons on the jacket.

(c) It does not matter which buttons she orders the tailor to sew on first.

6.55 (a)

	New script	*No new script*
Leading actress	$480,000	$220,000
No leading actress	−$80,000	$ 40,000

(b)

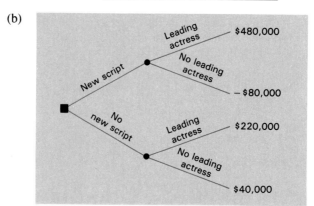

6.57 They should not rewrite the script ($78,000 is less than $84,000).

6.59 $U > 30(0.2) + 0(0.8) = 6$.

6.61 (a)

	Buy reduced-fare ticket	*Buy full-fare ticket*
Takes the flight	100	0
Does not take flight	−400	0

(b) Buy the reduced-fare ticket.

(c)

	Buy reduced- fare ticket	Buy full- fare ticket
Takes the flight	0	100
Does not take flight	400	0

The expected opportunity losses are $0(0.9) + 400(0.1) = 40$ if he buys the reduced-fare ticket and $100(0.9) + 0(0.1) = 90$ if he buys the full-fare ticket; since EVPI equals the minimum EOL, he should be willing to spend, at most, $40.

(d) Buy the full-fare ticket.

6.63 (a) $\dfrac{6}{11}$ and $\dfrac{5}{11}$.

(b) $\dfrac{7}{11}$ and $\dfrac{4}{11}$.

6.65 $200(0.75) + U(0.25) = 1,000$ so that $U(0.25) = 850$ and $U = \dfrac{850}{0.25} = $3,400$.

CHAPTER 7

7.1 See Practice Exercises.

7.3 See Practice Exercises.

7.5 (a) $\dbinom{12}{10}(0.8)^{10}(0.2)^2 = 66(0.1074)(0.04) = 0.28$;

(b) For $n = 12$, $x = 2$, and $p = 0.2$ the value given in the Table is 0.283.

(c)

```
MTB > PDF;
SUBC> BINOMIAL N=12 P=.8.

     BINOMIAL WITH N =   12   P = 0.800000
         K              P( X = K)
         2               0.0000
         3               0.0001
         4               0.0005
         5               0.0033
         6               0.0155
         7               0.0532
         8               0.1329
         9               0.2362
        10               0.2835
        11               0.2062
        12               0.0687
MTB > STOP
```

7.7   See Practice Exercises.

7.9   See Practice Exercises.

7.11 (a) 0.024; (b) zero; (c) 0.403; (d) 0.563.

7.13 0.001, 0.010, 0.044, 0.117, 0.205, 0.246, 0.205, 0.117, 0.044, 0.010, and 0.001.

7.15 See Practice Exercises.

7.17 0.326.

7.19 0.494.

7.21 $f(0) = 0.393; f(1) = 0.471; f(2) = 0.129;$ and $f(3) = 0.007.$

7.23 (a) 0.138; (b) 0.135; (c) the error is 0.003.

7.25 See Practice Exercises.

7.27 $np = 5.1; f(8) = 0.069; f(8)$ is read directly and is 0.0692.

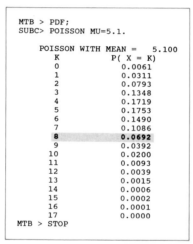

```
MTB > PDF;
SUBC> POISSON MU=5.1.

     POISSON WITH MEAN =    5.100
        K            P( X = K)
        0              0.0061
        1              0.0311
        2              0.0793
        3              0.1348
        4              0.1719
        5              0.1753
        6              0.1490
        7              0.1086
        8              0.0692
        9              0.0392
       10              0.0200
       11              0.0093
       12              0.0039
       13              0.0015
       14              0.0006
       15              0.0002
       16              0.0001
       17              0.0000
MTB > STOP
```

7.29 (a) 0.030; (b) 0.970; (c) 0.184; (d) 0.188.
      Computer solution is (a) 0.0302; (b) 0.9698; (c) 0.1850; (d) 0.1888.

```
MTB > PDF;
SUBC> POISSON MU=3.5.

     POISSON WITH MEAN =    3.500
        K            P( X = K)
        0              0.0302
        1              0.1057
        2              0.1850
        3              0.2158
        4              0.1888
        5              0.1322
        6              0.0771
        7              0.0385
        8              0.0169
        9              0.0066
       10              0.0023
       11              0.0007
       12              0.0002
       13              0.0001
       14              0.0000
MTB > STOP
```

7.31   See Practice Exercises.

7.33   See Practice Exercises.

7.35   See Practice Exercises.

7.37   (a) 1;   (b) 1.

7.39   (a) $\mu = 1.40$ and $\sigma = 1.054$.
        (b) $\mu = 1.40$ and $\sigma = 1.058$.

7.41   (a) $\mu = 288$ and $\sigma = 12.00$.
        (b) $\mu = 106$ and $\sigma = 9.399$.
        (c) $\mu = 487.5$ and $\sigma = 3.062$.
        (d) $\mu = 18.75$ and $\sigma = 3.992$.
        (e) $\mu = 425$ and $\sigma = 18.782$.

7.43   See Practice Exercises.

7.45   See Practice Exercises.

7.47   (a) $\mu = 3.997$, which is very close to $\lambda = 4$.
        (b) $\sigma^2 = 4.003$, which is very close to $\lambda = 4$; also $\sigma = \sqrt{4} = 2$.

7.49   See Practice Exercises.

7.51   (a) At least $\dfrac{35}{36}$;   (b) at least $\dfrac{35}{36}$.

7.53   (a) $f(4) = 0.500$;   (b) $f(4) + f(5) + f(6) = 0.833$.

7.55   0.94 houses sold.

7.57   (a) 0.09;   (b) 0.009;   (c) 0.0009.

7.59   (a) $\dfrac{495}{3,060}, \dfrac{1,320}{3,060}, \dfrac{990}{3,060}, \dfrac{240}{3,060}$, and $\dfrac{15}{3,060}$.

        (b) $0 \cdot \dfrac{495}{3,060} + 1 \cdot \dfrac{1,320}{3,060} + 2 \cdot \dfrac{990}{3,060} + 3 \cdot \dfrac{240}{3,060} + 4 \cdot \dfrac{15}{3,060} = \dfrac{4,080}{3,060} =$
        $\dfrac{4}{3} = 1.333$.

        (c) $\mu = 1.333$. The means are the same.

7.61   (a) 0.841; (b) 0.84.

7.63   (a) The probability is at least 0.89 that the student will get between $24.5 - 3(3.5)$, or 14 questions, and $24.5 + 3(3.5)$, or 35 questions correct.
        (b) At least 0.938.

7.65   (a) 0.110;   (b) 0.336;   (c) 0.889.

7.67   The probability is at least 0.75.

7.69   (a) $f(3) = 0.117$.

       (b) $f(0) = 0.129$.

       (c) $f(5) = 0.000$.

       (d) 0.871 or 0.870.

7.71   (a) 0.292, 0.525, 0.175, and 0.008.

       (b) $\dfrac{9}{10}$ (or 0.9) counterfeits.

       (c) The odds against are 13 to 7.

7.73   Computer solution. (a) 0.0515; (b) $0.0010 + 0.0001 = 0.0011$.

       (c) $0.0001 + 0.0016 + 0.0090 + 0.0318 + 0.0780 + 0.1404 = 0.2609$.

       (d) $0.1914 + 0.2013 + 0.1647 + 0.1048 = 0.6622$.

```
MTB > PDF;
SUBC> BINOMIAL N=15 P=0.45.

   BINOMIAL WITH N =  15   P = 0.450000
       K            P( X = K)
       0              0.0001
       1              0.0016
       2              0.0090
       3              0.0318
       4              0.0780
       5              0.1404
       6              0.1914
       7              0.2013
       8              0.1647
       9              0.1048
      10              0.0515
      11              0.0191
      12              0.0052
      13              0.0010
      14              0.0001
      15              0.0000
MTB > STOP
```

7.75   Computer solution. Probabilities of 0, 1, 2, . . . , 10 are 0.0002, 0.0024, 0.0147, 0.0540, 0.1304, 0.2162, 0.2488, 0.1963, 0.1017, 0.0312, and 0.0043.

```
MTB > PDF;
SUBC> BINOMIAL N=10 P=.42.

   BINOMIAL WITH N =  10   P = 0.420000
       K            P( X = K)
       0              0.0043
       1              0.0312
       2              0.1017
       3              0.1963
       4              0.2488
       5              0.2162
       6              0.1304
       7              0.0540
       8              0.0147
       9              0.0024
      10              0.0002
MTB > STOP
```

8.1   See Practice Exercises.

8.3   0.66.

8.5   (a) $\dfrac{19}{60}$; (b) $\dfrac{18}{19}$; (c) $\dfrac{14}{41}$.

8.7   See Practice Exercises.

8.9   See Practice Exercises.

8.11   See Practice Exercises.

8.13   0, 0.12, 0.12, 0.18, 0.59.

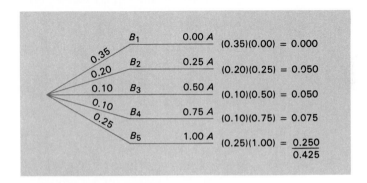

8.15   (a) 0.760, 0.173, and 0.067.
       (b) He should not check.
       (c) $4.55.

8.17   See Practice Exercises.

8.19   See Practice Exercises.

8.21   (a) 0.357; (b) 0.643.

8.23   0.51.

8.25   (a) The probability that economic conditions will remain good increases
       from $\dfrac{1}{3}$ to $\dfrac{4}{9}$, and the probability that there will be a recession decreases
       from $\dfrac{2}{3}$ to $\dfrac{5}{9}$.
       (b) Expand now. E.O.L. is $60,000 if he expands now, and $84,000 if he
       delays expansion.

8.27 $P(B_1|A) = 0.692$ and $P(B_2|A) = 0.308$. The store manager's assessment is
       $\dfrac{0.692}{0.308} = 2.25$ times as likely as the merchandise buyer.

8.29 $P(B_1|A) = 0.66$; $P(B_2|A) = 0.27$; $P(B_3|A) = 0.07$.

8.31 (a) Buy.

   (b) Buy.

CHAPTER 9

9.1 See Practice Exercises.

9.3 (a) 0.4714; (b) 0.6902; (c) 0.2314; (d) 0.1785.

9.5 See Practice Exercises.

9.7 See Practice Exercises.

9.9 (a) 0.5000; (b) 0.3000; (c) 0.2000; (d) 38.46; (e) 0.2422; (f) 0.2578.

9.11 See Practice Exercises.

9.13 (a) 24.8 percent of the trees are less than 38 feet.

   (b) 40.9 percent of the trees are at least 40 feet.

   (c) 34.3 percent of the trees are between 38 feet and 40 feet.

   (d) $x = 38.4$ feet.

   (e) $x = 40.6$ feet.

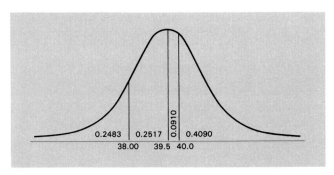

9.15 See Practice Exercises.

9.17 See Practice Exercises.

9.19 (a) 0.4404; (b) 0.0934.

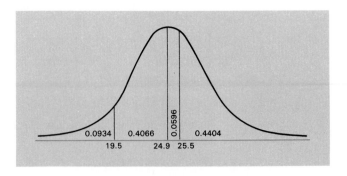

9.21   See Practice Exercises.

9.23   0.0084.

9.25   (a) 0.0526;   (b) 0.0526.

9.27   (a) 0.0239;   (b) 0.3446;   (c) 0.5384.

9.29   (a) 0.2967;   (b) 0.9306;   (c) 0.9821;   (d) 0.0179;   (e) 0.1587.

9.31   (a) 2.05;   (b) 1.28.

9.33   (a) $\frac{1}{16}$;   (b) $\frac{3}{4}$;   (c) $\frac{1}{4}$.

9.35   0.0347.

9.37   (a) 0.4744;   (b) 0.5468;   (c) 0.0819;   (d) 0.6776;   (e) 0.2946.

9.39   (a) -1.25;   (b) 0.61;   (c) -2.04;   (d) -2.50.

9.41   (a) 0.0316;   (b) 0.9605;   (c) 0.0395;   (d) 0.0711.

CHAPTER 10

10.1   See Practice Exercises.

10.3   See Practice Exercises.

10.5   See Practice Exercises.

10.7   108, 233, 041, 443, 261, 296, 295, 057, 255, 177, 138, 282, 041, 328, and 096

10.9   (a) $\dfrac{3}{100} \cdot \dfrac{2}{99} \cdot \dfrac{1}{98} = \dfrac{1}{161,700}$

       (b) $\dfrac{n}{N} \cdot \dfrac{n-1}{N-1} \cdot \;\cdots\; \cdot \dfrac{1}{N-n+1} =$

$$\frac{n!}{N(N-1) \cdot \;\cdots\; \cdot (N-n+1)} \cdot \frac{(N-n)!}{(N-n)!} =$$

$$\frac{n! \cdot (N-n)!}{N!} = \frac{1}{\dbinom{N}{n}}$$

10.11   See Practice Exercises.

10.13   See Practice Exercises.

10.15   (a) The observed value is 1.97 and the expected value is $1.25 \cdot \dfrac{4}{\sqrt{5}} = 2.24$.

       (b) $\sigma_s = \dfrac{12}{\sqrt{2 \cdot 128}} = 0.75$.

10.17   See Practice Exercises.

10.19 The entries nearest to 0.2500 are 0.2486 and 0.2517 corresponding to $z = 0.67$ and $z = 0.68$. Interpolation yields $\dfrac{x}{0.01} = \dfrac{0.0014}{0.0031}$ and $x = 0.0045$, and it follows that $z = 0.67 + 0.0045 = 0.6745$.

10.21 See Practice Exercises.

10.23 See Practice Exercises.

10.25 See Practice Exercises.

10.27 Answers will vary.

10.29 (a) 00–44, 45–71, 72–87, 88–95, and 96–99.

10.31 (a) $\mu = 7$; $\sigma = \sqrt{2}$.

(b) The samples are 5 and 6, 5 and 7, 5 and 8, 5 and 9, 6 and 7, 6 and 8, 6 and 9, 7 and 8, 7 and 9, and 8 and 9; the sample means are 5.5, 6.0, 6.5, 7.0, 6.5, 7.0, 7.5, 7.5, 8.0, and 8.5, respectively.

Sampling
Distribution of the Mean

$\bar{x}$	Probability
5.5	$\frac{1}{10}$
6.0	$\frac{1}{10}$
6.5	$\frac{2}{10}$
7.0	$\frac{2}{10}$
7.5	$\frac{2}{10}$
8.0	$\frac{1}{10}$
8.5	$\frac{1}{10}$

(c) $\mu_{\bar{x}} = 7.0$; $\sigma_{\bar{x}} = 0.866$. According to the theorem,
$$\sigma_{\bar{x}} = \frac{\sqrt{2}}{\sqrt{2}} \cdot \sqrt{\frac{5-2}{5-1}} = \frac{\sqrt{3}}{2} = 0.866.$$

10.33 (a) 00–13, 14–54, 55–89, 90–99.

(b)

x	Random numbers	Observed random numbers	Frequency
0	00–13	09, 04, 06	3
1	14–54	48, 19, 51, 15, 14, 21, 41, 23, 48, 33, 32	11
2	55–89	78, 55, 77, 77, 68, 86, 65, 59, 82, 83, 61	11
3	90–99	93, 93, 90, 97	4

10.35 0.0002.

10.37 (a) 10; (b) 120; (c) 455.

10.39 The $\binom{5}{2} = 10$ possible combinations are copper and gold, copper and platinum, copper and palladium, copper and silver, gold and platinum, gold and palladium, gold and silver, platinum and palladium, platinum and silver, palladium and silver.

10.41 (a) The standard error of the mean is multiplied by $\frac{7}{10}$ or 0.7.

(b) The standard error of the mean is multiplied by $\frac{10}{7}$ or 1.43.

10.43 (a) 0.89; (b) 0.9972.

CHAPTER 11

11.1 See Practice Exercises.

11.3 (a) $\$11,159 < \mu < \$11,191$; (b) $286.

11.5 $12.78 < \mu < 14.22$ minutes.

11.7 See Practice Exercises.

11.9 $100 \left(\dfrac{4.604 - 2.776}{2.776} \right) = 65.8\%$. ($t_{0.005}$ for 4 d.f. = 4.604; $t_{0.025}$ for 4 d.f. = 2.776).

11.11 See Practice Exercises.

11.13 See Practice Exercises.

11.15 See Practice Exercises.

11.17 8.45 seconds.

11.19 See Practice Exercises.

11.21 See Practice Exercises.

11.23 0.9608.

11.25 (a) A Type I error would be committed if we reject the hypothesis (that the use of a car phone increases the number of sales) when it really is effective in increasing the number of sales.

(b) A Type II error would be committed if the hypothesis (that the use of a car phone increases the number of sales) is accepted when it is not really effective in increasing the number of sales.

11.27 $\sigma_{\bar{x}} = \dfrac{5}{\sqrt{25}} = 1$; $z = \dfrac{297 - 294}{1} = 3.00$ and $z = \dfrac{303 - 294}{1} = 9.00$, so that $\beta = 0.5000 - 0.4987 = 0.0013$ when $\mu = 294$ (and by symmetry also when $\mu = 306$); $z = \dfrac{297 - 295}{1} = 2.00$ and $z = \dfrac{303 - 295}{1} = 8.00$, so that

$\beta = 0.5000 - 0.4772 = 0.0228$ when $\mu = 295$ (and by symmetry also when $\mu = 305$); $z = \dfrac{297 - 296}{1} = 1.00$ and $z = \dfrac{303 - 296}{1} = 7.00$, so that

$\beta = 0.5000 - 0.3413 = 0.1587$ when $\mu = 296$ (and by symmetry also when $\mu = 304$); $z = \dfrac{297 - 297}{1} = 0.00$ and $z = \dfrac{303 - 297}{1} = 6.00$, so that

$\beta = 0.5000$ when $\mu = 297$ (and by symmetry also when $\mu = 303$); $z =$ $\dfrac{297 - 298}{1} = -1.00$ and $z = \dfrac{303 - 298}{1} = 5.00$, so that $\beta = 0.5000 +$

$0.3413 = 0.8413$ when $\mu = 298$ (and by symmetry also when $\mu = 302$);

$z = \dfrac{297 - 299}{1} = -2.00$ and $z = \dfrac{303 - 299}{1} = 4.00$, so that $\beta = 0.5000 +$

$0.4772 = 0.9772$.

11.29 (a) $\alpha = 0.0456$; (b) $\beta = 0.0228$.

11.31 $\beta = 0.4602$.

11.33 (a) 0.0164.

(b) 0.0179, 0.2743, and 0.8159.

11.35 (a) The null hypothesis is that the experiments with the suspected new method average as much of the dangerous by-products as the other petroleum waste product disposal methods being studied, and the alternative hypothesis is that the experiments with the suspected new method average more of the dangerous by-products than the other petroleum waste disposal methods being studied.

(b) The null hypothesis is that the experiments with the suspected new method average as much of the dangerous by-products as the other petroleum waste product disposal methods being studied, and the alternative hypothesis is that the experiments with the suspected new method average fewer of the dangerous by-products than the other petroleum waste disposal methods being studied.

11.39 Since -2.35 is less than -1.645, the null hypothesis must be rejected. The difference between $\bar{x} = 18.1$ and $\mu_0 = 20$ is significant.

11.41 See Practice Exercises.

11.43 Since 6.18 is greater than 2.33, the null hypothesis must be rejected. The difference between $\bar{x} = 26.2$ and $\mu_0 = 22.8$ is significant. There is substantial evidence against the production manager's estimate.

11.45 (a) Reject all values of $\bar{x}$ which are ≤ 54.35, and otherwise accept the null hypothesis or reserve judgment.

11.47 See Practice Exercises.

11.49 Since -1.73 lies between -2.201 and 2.201, the null hypothesis cannot be rejected. The difference between 5.8 and 6.0 is not significant.

11.51 Since -4.26 is less than -1.729, the null hypothesis must be rejected. The difference between $\bar{x} = 34$ and $\mu = 40$ is significant.

11.53 See Practice Exercises.

11.55 Since 1.11 lies between -3.012 and 3.012, the null hypothesis cannot be rejected. The difference between the two sample means is not significant.

11.57 Since 1.59 falls between -2.447 and 2.447, the difference between the two sample means is not significant.

11.59 See Practice Exercises.

11.61 See Practice Exercises.

11.63 (a) reject   (b) accept or reserve judgment
      (c) accept or reserve judgment   (d) reject
      (e) accept or reserve judgment   (f) accept or reserve judgment

11.65 (a) Since the P-value of 0.0562 is greater than $\alpha = 0.05$, the null hypothesis cannot be rejected. We therefore accept the null hypothesis or reserve judgment.
      (b) 0.0562.

11.67 0.64.

11.69 1.01 minute.

11.71 A Type I error is committed if the hypothesis that the new type of luggage is more durable than the older model is erroneously rejected. A Type II error is committed if the hypothesis that the new type of luggage is more durable than the old model is erroneously accepted.

11.73 5.66 is greater than 2.776, so the null hypothesis must be rejected. The difference between $\bar{x} = 14.4$ and $\mu = 14.0$ is significant.

11.75 9.76 minutes $< \mu < 11.28$ minutes.

11.77 0.0208.

11.79 10.08 minutes $< \mu < 10.82$ minutes.

11.81 Since -1.72 lies between -1.96 and 1.96, we cannot reject the null hypothesis. The difference between the two sample means is not significant.

11.83 Since 2.27 is greater than 1.860, the null hypothesis must be rejected. We conclude that the average heat capacity of coal from the first mine exceeds that of the coal from the second mine by more than 50 million calories per ton.

11.85 0.82 percent.

11.87 Since $z = -1.92$ lies between -2.575 and 2.575, we cannot reject the null hypothesis. The difference is not significant, and we must accept the null hypothesis or reserve judgment.

11.89 (a) Since $P = 0.0854$ is greater than $\alpha = 0.01$, we accept the null hypothesis or reserve judgment.

(b) Since $P = 0.0854$ is greater than $\alpha = 0.05$, the null hypothesis cannot be rejected. We accept the null hypothesis or reserve judgment.

(c) Since $P = 0.0854$ is less than $\alpha = 0.10$, the null hypothesis must be rejected.

11.91 Not necessarily. The difference may be statistically significant, but it may not be important enough to be economically justifiable.

11.93

```
MTB > SET C1
DATA> 75 70 59 60 63 55 52 70 45 85
DATA> END
MTB > TINTERVAL 95 C1

                N       MEAN      STDEV   SE MEAN    95.0 PERCENT C.I.
  C1           10       63.40     11.82     3.74   (    54.94,     71.86)

MTB > STOP
```

Since the maximum error is half the confidence interval, it is $\dfrac{71.86 - 54.94}{2} = 8.46$.

11.95

```
MTB > SET C1
DATA> 21 19 20 22 24 21 19 22 22 20
MTB > TTEST 22.5 C1

TEST OF MU = 22.500 VS MU N.E. 22.500

                N       MEAN      STDEV   SE MEAN        T     P VALUE
  C1           10     21.000      1.563     0.494    -3.03       0.014

MTB > STOP
```

Since $t = -3.03$ falls between $t = -3.25$ and 3.25 (obtained from Table II for $t = 0.005$ for $10 - 1 = 9$ degrees of freedom), we cannot reject the null hypothesis.

11.97

```
MTB > SET C1
DATA> 79 88 64 91 83 66 89 74 68
DATA> END
MTB > SET C2
DATA> 70 51 82 72 90 61
DATA> END
MTB > TWOSAMPLE [99] C1 C2;
SUBC> POOLED.

TWOSAMPLE T FOR C1 VS C2
           N       MEAN       STDEV     SE MEAN
   C1     9        78.0       10.4         3.5
   C2     6        71.0       14.0         5.7

   99 PCT CI FOR MU C1 - MU C2: (-12.0, 26.0)

   TTEST MU C1 = MU C2 (VS NE): T= 1.11    P=0.29    DF=  13

   POOLED STDEV =           11.9

   MTB > STOP
```

Since $t = 1.11$ lies between -3.012 and 3.012 (obtained from Table II for t with $n_1 + n_2 - 2$ degrees of freedom under column headed $t_{.005}$, the null hypothesis cannot be rejected. The difference between the two means is not significant.

CHAPTER 12

12.1 See Practice Exercises.

12.3 See Practice Exercises.

12.5 $671.29 < \sigma < 1,256.22$.

12.7 See Practice Exercises.

12.9 See Practice Exercises.

12.11 Since 45.36 is greater than 23.685, we must reject the null hypothesis.

12.13 Since 3.652 is greater than 1.96, we reject the null hypothesis.

12.15 See Practice Exercises.

12.17 Since $F = 1.460$ is less than 9.28, we cannot reject the null hypothesis. (We can calculate the two-sample t test of Exercise 11.57.)

12.19 $2.73 < \sigma < 4.87$.

12.21 (a) 1.212 percent.
    (b) $s = 1.383$ percent. The difference between the calculated s and the s obtained from the table is only $1.383 - 1.212 = 0.171$ percent.

12.23 Since $F = 1.134$ is less than 3.18, we cannot reject the null hypothesis.

CHAPTER 13

13.1 See Practice Exercises.

13.3 $0.38 < p < 0.58$.

13.5 $0.06 < p < 0.14$.

13.7 $0.07 < p < 0.23$.

13.9 $E = 0.05$.

13.11 $n = 105$ (rounded up).

13.13 $n = 378$ (rounded up).

13.15 (a) $0.70 < p < 0.78$; (b) $0.23 < p < 0.33$.

13.17 Since all of these probabilities are less than $\alpha = \dfrac{0.05}{2} = 0.025$, the null hypothesis must be rejected for all.

13.19 See Practice Exercises.

13.21 The null hypothesis must be rejected for 4, 5, 6, and greater than 6.

13.23 The null hypothesis must be rejected for $x = 0$, $x = 1$, $x = 2$, and $x = 3$. The null hypothesis cannot be rejected if the number of patients using health insurance is 4 or more.

13.25 (a) Since $z = -2.37$ is less than -1.96, we find that the null hypothesis must be rejected. In other words, the true proportion does not equal 0.65.

(b) The null hypothesis must be rejected since $p = 2(0.0089) = 0.0178$ is less than $\alpha = 0.05$.

13.27 (a) Since $z = 2.05$ is less than 2.33, the null hypothesis cannot be rejected.

(b) The null hypothesis cannot be rejected since 0.0202 exceeds $\alpha = 0.01$. The decision is the same as in part (a).

13.29 See Practice Exercises.

13.31 (a) Central line $= 0.10$, the LCL $= 0.027$, and the UCL $= 0.173$.
(b) Out-of-control samples are 11 and 12.

13.33 Since $z = 1.88$ is greater than 1.645, the null hypothesis must be rejected. The difference is significant at the 0.05 level.

13.35 See Practice Exercises.

13.37 Since $z = -5.45$ is less than -2.575, the null hypothesis must be rejected. The difference is significant.

Answers to Odd-Numbered Exercises

13.39 See Practice Exercises.

13.41 Since $X^2 = 4.26$ does not exceed 9.488 the null hypothesis cannot be rejected. The differences among the sample proportions are not significant.

13.43
$$\frac{x_1 + x_2 + \cdots + x_k}{n_1 + n_2 + \cdots + n_k} \cdot n_1 + \cdots + \frac{x_1 + x_2 + \cdots + x_k}{n_1 + n_2 + \cdots + n_k} \cdot n_k$$

$$= \frac{x_1 + x_2 + \cdots + x_k}{n_1 + n_2 + \cdots + n_k}(n_1 + n_2 + \cdots + n_k)$$

$$= x_1 + x_2 + \cdots + x_k.$$

13.45 5.991, 9.488, 21.026, and 21.026.

13.47 Since 2.77 is less than 9.488 the null hypothesis cannot be rejected.

13.49 Since $X^2 = 15.76$ exceeds 12.592 the null hypothesis of independence must be rejected. The difference is significant, and there is a relationship. In other words the income levels are not all the same for the four communities.

13.51 Since $X^2 = 18.18$ exceeds 12.592, the null hypothesis must be rejected. That is, there is a relationship between the local business unions and the attitudes of their members. Local unions do not all have the same attitude toward the collective bargaining agreement.

13.53 (a) $\sqrt{\frac{2}{3}}$; (b) 0.28; (c) 0.20.

13.55 Since $X^2 = 4.02$ does not exceed 7.815, the null hypothesis cannot be rejected. The probability distribution appears to be correct.

13.57 (a) 0.0739, 0.2697, 0.3804, 0.2160, and 0.0473.
(b) 14.78, 53.94, 76.08, 43.20, and 9.46.
(c) Since $X^2 = 1.16$ is less than 5.991, the null hypothesis cannot be rejected. The normal distribution with $\mu = 67.1$ and $\sigma = 19.9$ provides a good fit.

13.59 Since $X^2 = 1.38$ does not exceed 7.815, the null hypothesis must be rejected. There is no evidence that the coins are not balanced.

13.61 Since $X^2 = 4.31$ does not exceed 7.815, the null hypothesis cannot be rejected. The populations appear to be homogeneous insofar as the adoption of the accounting system is concerned. The differences among the sample proportions are not significant at the 0.05 level.

13.63 2,401.

13.65 Since -2.05 exceeds -2.33, the null hypothesis cannot be rejected at the 0.01 level of significance. The difference is not significant. The director may not have overstated the proportion of pledges which were not paid.

13.67 Since $z = 4.93$ is greater than 2.575, the null hypothesis must be rejected.

13.69 Since $X^2 = 4.89$ does not exceed 5.991, the null hypothesis cannot be rejected at the 0.05 level of significance. There is no evidence that the difference is significant.

13.71 The null hypothesis must be rejected for $x = 6, 7, 8, 9, 10, 11, 12$, and 13; the actual level of significance is 0.030.

13.73 Since $z = -0.61$ exceeds -2.33, the null hypothesis cannot be rejected. Accept the null hypothesis or reserve judgment.

13.75 Since 2.22 does not exceed 9.488 the null hypothesis cannot be rejected. We can conclude that the binomial distribution with $p = 0.60$ and $n = 7$ provides a good fit.

13.77 (a) $0.445 < p < 0.555$.

(b) $0.451 < p < 0.565$.

(c) The width of the confidence interval of part (a) is $0.555 - 0.445 = 0.110$ and that of the confidence interval of part (b) is $0.565 - 0.451 = 0.114$; the narrower interval is more specific about the quantity we are trying to estimate.

13.79

```
MTB > READ C1 C2 C3 C4
DATA> 95 60 30 23
DATA> 85 50 30 27
DATA> END
MTB > CHIS C1 C2 C3 C4
Expected counts are printed below observed counts
            C1        C2        C3        C4     Total
   1        95        60        30        23       208
          93.60     57.20     31.20     26.00
   2        85        50        30        27       192
          86.40     52.80     28.80     24.00

Total      180       110        60        50       400
ChiSq =  0.021 +   0.137 +   0.046 +   0.346 +
         0.023 +   0.148 +   0.050 +   0.375 = 1.146
df = 3
MTB > STOP
```

Since $X^2 = 1.146$ is less than 11.345 (from Table III with $X^2_{.01}$ and d.f. $= 3$) the null hypothesis cannot be rejected. There are no significant differences among employee groups at the 0.01 level of significance.

13.81

```
MTB > READ C1 C2 C3
DATA> 13 17 18
DATA> 31 30 28
DATA> 16 13 14
DATA> END
     3 ROWS READ
MTB > CHIS C1 C2 C3

Expected counts are printed below observed counts

            C1        C2        C3     Total
   1        13        17        18        48
          16.00     16.00     16.00

   2        31        30        28        89
          29.67     29.67     29.67

   3        16        13        14        43
          14.33     14.33     14.33

Total       60        60        60       180

ChiSq =  0.562 +   0.062 +   0.250 +
         0.060 +   0.004 +   0.094 +
         0.194 +   0.124 +   0.008 = 1.358
df = 4
MTB > STOP
```

Since $\chi^2 = 1.3548$ does not exceed 9.488 (from Table II with $\chi^2_{.05}$ and d.f. = 4) the null hypothesis cannot be rejected. We may conclude, at the 0.05 level of significance, that there is no relationship between age and sales performance.

13.83

```
MTB > READ C1 C2 C3
DATA> 1101 755 582
DATA>  409 676 818
DATA>   63 142 173
DATA> END
        3 ROWS READ
MTB > CHIS C1 C2 C3

Expected counts are printed below observed counts

              C1        C2        C3     Total
    1       1101       755       582      2438
           812.67    812.67    812.67

    2        409       676       818      1903
           634.33    634.33    634.33

    3         63       142       173       378
           126.00    126.00    126.00

  Total     1573      1573      1573      4719

ChiSq =102.300 +   4.092 + 65.472 +
        80.045 +   2.737 + 53.179 +
        31.500 +   2.032 + 17.532 = 358.889
  df = 4
MTB > STOP
```

Since $\chi^2 = 358.889$ is greater than 9.488 (from Table II with $\chi^2_{0.05}$ and d.f. 4) the null hypothesis must be rejected. There appears to be a pronounced difference in attitude.

CHAPTER 14

14.1 See Practice Exercises.

14.3 See Practice Exercises.

14.5 See Practice Exercises.

14.7 Since $F = 0.17$ is less than 3.47, the value of $F_{0.05}$ for 2 and 21 degrees of freedom, the null hypothesis cannot be rejected.

14.9 Since 6.18 exceeds 3.81, the value of $F_{0.05}$ for 2 and 13 degrees of freedom, the null hypothesis must be rejected. The observed differences among the mean number of sales on the three shifts cannot be attributed to chance.

14.11 $\mu_i = \mu + \alpha_i$, so that $\sum \mu_i = \sum (\mu + \alpha_i) = \sum \mu + \sum \alpha_i$, since $\sum \mu_i / k = \mu$, $k\mu = k\mu + \sum \alpha_i$, and $\sum \alpha_i = 0$.

14.13 (a) As in Exercise 14.12(a), the degrees of freedom are 3 and 12. The critical value for $F_{0.01}$ from Table IV is 5.95.

(b) As in Exercise 14.12(b), the degrees of freedom are 4 and 12. The critical value for $F_{0.01}$ from Table IV is 5.41.

14.15 For treatments, since $F = 1.24$ is less than 6.99, the null hypothesis cannot be rejected; for blocks, $F = 45.62$ exceeds 6.99, so the null hypothesis must be rejected.

14.17 See Practice Exercises.

14.19 Since 1.74 does not exceed 3.24, the value of $F_{0.05}$ for $4 - 1 = 3$ and $20 - 4 = 16$ degrees of freedom, we cannot reject the null hypothesis.

14.21 (a) Since $F = \dfrac{28}{86/9} = 2.93$ is less than 4.26, the value of $F_{0.05}$ for 2 and 9 degrees of freedom, the null hypothesis cannot be rejected.

(b) Since $F = 2.93$ is less than 4.26, the value of $F_{0.05}$ for 2 and 9 degrees of freedom, the null hypothesis cannot be rejected.

14.23 Since $F = 0.64$ does not exceed 6.94, the value of $F_{0.05}$ for 2 and 4 degrees of freedom, the null hypothesis cannot be rejected for the A factors (various work activities); and since $F = 2.88$ does not exceed 6.94, the value of $F_{0.05}$ for 2 and 4 degrees of freedom, the null hypothesis cannot be rejected for the B factors (the companies).

14.25 Since 15.79 exceeds 8.02, the value of $F_{0.01}$ for 2 and 9 degrees of freedom, the null hypothesis must be rejected.

14.27

```
MTB > NAME C1='SALES' C2='TRTMENT' C3='BLOCKS'
MTB > PRINT C1 C2 C3

ROW   SALES   TRTMENT   BLOCKS

  1     45       1         1
  2     37       1         2
  3     41       1         3
  4     37       1         4
  5     50       1         5
  6     54       2         1
  7     54       2         2
  8     56       2         3
  9     44       2         4
 10     47       2         5
 11     45       3         1
 12     56       3         2
 13     58       3         3
 14     47       3         4
 15     45       3         5
 16     61       4         1
 17     55       4         2
 18     50       4         3
 19     49       4         4
 20     52       4         5

MTB > TWOWAY 'SALES' 'TRTMENT' 'BLOCKS'

ANALYSIS OF VARIANCE   SALES

SOURCE          DF        SS        MS
TRTMENT          3       368.5     122.8
BLOCKS           4       140.3      35.1
ERROR           12       343.7      28.6
TOTAL           19       852.5

MTB > STOP
```

For treatments, $F = \dfrac{122.8}{28.6} = 4.29$.

For blocks, $F = \dfrac{35.1}{28.6} = 1.23$.

For treatments, since $F = 4.29$ exceeds 3.49 (from Table IV, $F_{0.05}$ and d.f. of 3 for numerator and 12 for denominator), the null hypothesis must be rejected; for blocks, since $F = 1.23$ is less than 3.26 (from Table IV, $F_{0.05}$ and d.f. of 4 for numerator and 12 for denominator), we cannot reject the null hypothesis. In other words, we can reject the null hypothesis that the type of packaging makes no difference. For blocks, since 1.23 does not exceed 3.26, the null hypothesis cannot be rejected. In other words we cannot reject the null hypothesis that the sales of grass seed are the same in the five stores.

14.29

```
MTB > NAME C1='SALES' C2='M/C' C3= 'BEV'
MTB > PRINT C1 C2 C3

ROW   SALES   M/C   BEV

 1     22     1     1
 2     26     1     2
 3     19     1     3
 4     16     1     4
 5     24     2     1
 6     25     2     2
 7     21     2     3
 8     20     2     4
 9     16     3     1
10     22     3     2
11     17     3     3
12     15     3     4

MTB > TWOWAY 'SALES' 'M/C' 'BEV'

ANALYSIS OF VARIANCE   SALES

SOURCE      DF       SS        MS
M/C          2     51.50     25.75
BEV          3     86.92     28.97
ERROR        6     13.83      2.31
TOTAL       11    152.25

MTB > STOP
```

Using values provided by the printout we get $F = \dfrac{28.97}{2.31} = 12.54$ for beverages, and $F = \dfrac{25.75}{2.31} = 11.15$ for vending machines (with differences from Exercise 14.20 due to rounding). Then, employing the method for testing the null hypothesis shown in Exercise 14.20, both null hypotheses are rejected.

15.1   See Practice Exercises.

15.3   See Practice Exercises.

15.5   Since $z = 2.67$ exceeds 2.33 the null hypothesis must be rejected.

15.7   Since $z = 2.06$ does not exceed 2.33, the null hypothesis cannot be rejected.

15.9   Since $z = 1.51$ does not exceed 1.645, the null hypothesis cannot be rejected.

15.11   Since 0.073 (from Table V) exceeds 0.05, the null hypothesis cannot be rejected.

15.13   (a) $T \leq 7$;   (b) $T^- \leq 10$;   (c) $T^+ \leq 10$.

15.15   (a) $T^- \leq 11$;   (b) $T \leq 8$;   (c) $T^+ \leq 11$.

15.17   Since $T^- = 4$ is less than 6, the null hypothesis must be rejected, and we conclude (or reserve judgment) that a technician repairs, on the average, more than 11 small appliances per day.

15.19   Since $T = 15$ is greater than 11, we cannot reject the null hypothesis. Accept the null hypothesis that $\mu = 29$ or reserve judgment.

15.21   Since $T^- = 6$ is less than 21, the null hypothesis must be rejected. We conclude that, at this testing center, there are larger numbers of men than women applicants (or we may reserve judgment).

15.23   Since 1.61 falls between -1.96 and 1.96, we cannot reject the null hypothesis. We accept the null hypothesis of no difference between the numbers of column inches of classified advertisements or reserve judgment.

15.25   Since $U = 88$ is not less than or equal to 49, the null hypothesis cannot be rejected.

15.27   See Practice Exercises.

15.29   Since $z = 1.51$ does not exceed 1.645, the null hypothesis cannot be rejected. There is no evidence at the 0.05 level of significance that the real estate taxes are higher in condominium complex 1 than in condominium complex 2.

15.31   Since $H = 0.28$ is less than 5.991, the null hypothesis cannot be rejected.

15.33   Since 2.38 does not exceed 7.815, the null hypothesis cannot be rejected.

15.35   Since 7 falls between the critical values of 5 and 14, the null hypothesis cannot be rejected.

15.37   Since $z = 1.96$ equals the critical value for $\alpha = 0.05$, the null hypothesis of randomness must be rejected.

15.39 Since $z = -4.42$ is less than -2.575, the critical value for $\alpha = 0.01$, the null hypothesis must be rejected.

15.41 Since $\mu = 4$ is less than 7, the null hypothesis must be rejected. There appears to be a definite clustering.

15.43 Since $z = -0.30$ lies between -1.96 and 1.96, the null hypothesis cannot be rejected. There is no evidence at the 0.05 level of significance that the sample is not random.

15.45 Since $T^+ = 47.5$ is greater than 7, we cannot reject the null hypothesis. Accept the manufacturer's claim or reserve judgment.

15.47 Since $H = 2.65$ does not exceed 7.815, the critical value for $\chi^2_{0.05}$, the null hypothesis cannot be rejected. There is no real evidence that the amounts of gold panned per day at the four claim sites are not all equal.

15.49 Since $\mu = 5$ falls below the critical value of 6, the null hypothesis must be rejected. There is a trend.

15.51 Since $z = -1.20$ falls on the interval from -1.96 to 1.96, the null hypothesis cannot be rejected; in other words there is no evidence to indicate that the arrangement is not random.

15.53 Since $\mu = 7$ falls between the critical values of 6 and 16, the critical values from Table VII, the null hypothesis cannot be rejected.

15.55 Since $U = 34$ exceeds 23, the null hypothesis cannot be rejected.

15.57 Since $\mu = 8$ falls between the critical values of 7 and 18, the null hypothesis cannot be rejected. The arrangement may be random.

15.59 Since $z = -1.069$ falls between -1.96 and 1.96, the null hypothesis cannot be rejected.

15.61 Since $z = 1.33$ falls between -2.575 and 2.575, the null hypothesis cannot be rejected.

15.63

```
MTB > SET C1
DATA> 7 5 7 2 9 10 4 3 8 7 9 7
MTB > SUB 5 FROM C1 PUT DIFF IN C2
MTB > SIGNS OF C2
        3  NEGATIVE VALUES        1  ZERO VALUES        8  POSITIVE
VALUES

MTB > STOP
```

Discarding the zero values, we have $3 + 8 = 11$ values, 8 of which have plus signs. Thus, $x = 8$ and Table V shows that for $n = 11$ and $p = \frac{1}{2}$ the probability of 8 or more plus signs is $0.081 + 0.027 + 0.005 = 0.113$. Since 0.113 exceeds 0.050 the null hypothesis cannot be rejected.

15.65

```
MTB > NAME C1='SALES' C2='LEVEL'
MTB > PRINT C1 C2

 ROW   SALES   LEVEL

   1     119      1
   2     215      1
   3     227      1
   4     191      1
   5     212      1
   6     186      1
   7     271      1
   8     169      1
   9     199      1
  10     216      1
  11     140      2
  12     190      2
  13     256      2
  14     188      2
  15     111      2
  16     189      2
  17     255      2
  18     173      2
  19     200      2
  20     241      2
  21     110      3
  22     187      3
  23     210      3
  24     216      3
  25     141      3
  26     204      3
  27     248      3
  28     211      3
  29     181      3
  30     210      3
  31     211      4
  32     215      4
  33     197      4
  34     217      4
  35     117      4
  36     257      4
  37     243      4
  38     215      4
  39     185      4
  40     271      4
```

```
MTB > KRUSKAL-WALLIS DATA IN C1 LEVEL IN C2

 LEVEL     NOBS    MEDIAN   AVE. RANK    Z VALUE
    1        10     205.5      20.9        0.12
    2        10     189.5      18.2       -0.72
    3        10     207.0      17.9       -0.81
    4        10     215.0      25.0        1.41
OVERALL      40                20.5

H = 2.38   d.f. = 3   p = 0.499
H = 2.38   d.f. = 3   p = 0.498  (adj. for ties)

MTB > STOP
```

The computer printout shows that $H = 2.38$ with 2 d.f. Since 2.38 does not exceed 7.815, the null hypothesis cannot be rejected.

16.1   See Practice Exercises.

16.3   See Practice Exercises.

16.5   See Practice Exercises.

16.7   (a) $\hat{y} = 5.635 + 2.146x$.

(b) 145 pairs of brand B shoes.

16.9   (a) $\hat{y} = 0.834 + 0.577x$; $9,489.

(b)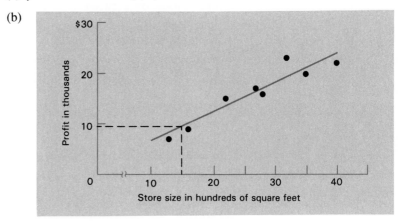

16.11   See Practice Exercises.

16.13   See Practice Exercises.

16.15   Since $t = -1.61$ falls between -2.228 and 2.228, the null hypothesis cannot be rejected.

16.17   See Practice Exercises.

16.19 $0.754 < \beta < 1.126$.

16.21   108.594 and 151.422.

16.23   See Practice Exercises.

16.25   (a) $\hat{y} = 2.096 + 0.054x_1 + 1.565x_2$.

(b) 6.9 car sales per week.

16.27   See Practice Exercises.

16.29   (a) $\hat{y} = 0.556 + 0.219x_1 + 0.874x_2$.

(b) 169.563 (thousands of dollars).

16.31   Since $t = -0.149$ is not less than -2.896, the null hypothesis cannot be rejected. This is the null hypothesis that each additional hour spent campaigning increases the number of votes obtained by 12,000.

16.33

```
MTB > NAME C1='YEAR' C2='X' C3='Y'
MTB > PRINT C1 C2 C3

ROW     YEAR        X        Y

  1     1985       50       45
  2     1986       65       60
  3     1987       75       80
  4     1988      100       95
  5     1989      125      120
  6     1990      140      150
  7     1991      170      145
  8     1992      195      190

MTB > REGR C3 1 C2

The regression equation is
Y = 2.54 + 0.940 X

Predictor          Coef        Stdev     t-ratio          p
Constant          2.543        9.526        0.27      0.798
X               0.93984      0.07636       12.31      0.000

s = 10.44          R-sq = 96.2%       R-sq(adj) = 95.6%

Analysis of Variance

SOURCE           DF          SS          MS          F          p
Regression        1       16518       16518     151.49      0.000
Error             6         654         109
Total             7       17172

MTB > STOP
```

From the computer printout, the regression equation is $Y = 2.54 + 0.940x$.

16.35 Substituting $x_1 = 3$ and $x_2 = 1$ into the regression equation we get $75,192 + 4,133(3) + 758(1) = 88,349$.

CHAPTER 17

17.1 See Practice Exercises.

17.3 $r = 0.92$.

17.5 (a) Offhand, it does not make sense. There is no obvious reason to believe that there is a relationship between the production of rye and the production of grapefruit.

(b) $r = -0.83$.

(c) 68.89 percent.

(d) Since $-0.83 \leq 0.811$, the value of $r_{0.025}$ for $n = 6$ from Table VI, the null hypothesis of no correlation must be rejected. This must be used with great caution, if at all, since there is no apparent relationship between the two variables.

17.7 8.5 percent.

17.9 No, we can always draw a straight line through two points. In part (a) the line has a positive slope and $r = +1$, and in part (b) the line has a negative slope and $r = -1$.

17.11 (a) Since $r = -0.401$ falls between -0.576 and 0.576, where 0.576 is the value of $r_{0.025}$ for $n = 12$ from Table VI, it is not significant.

(b) Since $r = 0.834$ is greater than 0.707, the value of $r_{0.025}$ for $n = 8$ from Table VI, it is significant.

(c) Since $r = 0.820$ is greater than 0.811, the value of $r_{0.025}$ for $n = 6$ from Table VI, it is significant.

17.13 (a) 0.13.

(b) 0.81.

(c) 0.61.

(d) -0.18.

(e) Only those parts of (b) and (c) are significant.

(f) The impact seems to appear after two years and then taper off after the third year.

17.15 $\sum (y - \bar{y})^2 = 196{,}665 - 10\left(\dfrac{1{,}397}{10}\right)^2 = 1{,}504.1; \sum (y - \hat{y})^2 =$
$196{,}665 - 101.5(1{,}397) - 10.9(5{,}004) = 325.9.$

17.17 $r_S = 0.98.$

17.19 Since $z = -0.84$ falls between -2.575 and 2.575, the critical values for the 0.01 level of significance, we cannot reject the null hypothesis of no correlation.

17.21 $r_S = 0.75.$

17.23 $r_S = 0.75.$

17.25 See Practice Exercises.

17.27 The multiple correlation coefficient is 0.59.

17.29 The second relationship is four times as strong as the first.

17.31 (a) Since $r = 0.65$ exceeds 0.632, the null hypothesis of no correlation must be rejected.

(b) Since $r = 0.65$ does not exceed 0.765, the null hypothesis of no correlation cannot be rejected.

17.33 Since $z = 1.51$ is less than 1.96, the null hypothesis of no correlation cannot be rejected.

17.35 $r = 0$, $b = 0$, $a = 2.5$, and since $\bar{y} = 2.5$, the equation of the least-squares line is $\hat{y} = \bar{y}$.

17.37 Since $r = 0.98$ exceeds 0.666, the value of $r_{0.025}$ for $n = 9$ from Table VI, the null hypothesis of no correlation must be rejected. $r = 0.98$ is significant.

17.39 $r_S = 0.46$.

17.41 (a) Since $z = 2.40$ exceeds 1.96, we reject the null hypothesis of no correlation. $r_S = 0.55$ is significant.

(b) Since $z = 2.40$ falls between -2.575 and 2.575, the null hypothesis of no correlation cannot be rejected. $r_S = 0.55$ is not significant.

17.43 From the computer printout, the correlation of X and Y = 0.991, and since 0.991 greatly exceeds 0.576, the value of $r_{0.025}$ for $n = 12$ (from Table VI, Values of r), the null hypothesis of no correlation must be rejected.

```
MTB > NAME C1='X' C2='Y'
MTB > PRINT C1 C2

ROW      X      Y

  1      6     20
  2      2     14
  3      5     20
  4      1     14
  5     10     28
  6      7     23
  7     15     36
  8      3     16
  9     11     32
 10     13     33
 11      2     13
 12     12     30

MTB > CORR C1 C2

Correlation of X and Y = 0.991

MTB > STOP
```

17.45 From the computer printout, the correlation of rank X and rank Y is 0.976. Since $z = 0.976\sqrt{8 - 1} = 2.58$ exceeds 1.96, the null hypothesis of no correlation must be rejected.

```
MTB > NAME C1='YEAR' C2='X' C3='Y'
MTB > PRINT C1 C2 C3

ROW     YEAR      X      Y

  1     1985     50     45
  2     1986     65     60
  3     1987     75     80
  4     1988    100     95
  5     1989    125    120
  6     1990    140    150
  7     1991    170    145
  8     1992    195    190

MTB > RANK C2 PUT IN C11
MTB > RANK C3 PUT IN C12
MTB > NAME C11='RANK X' C12='RANK Y'
MTB > CORR C11 C12

Correlation of RANK X and RANK Y = 0.976

MTB > STOP
```

17.47 From the computer printout, the correlation of rank X and rank Y is -0.323.

```
MTB > NAME C1='X' C2='Y'
MTB > RANK C1 PUT IN C3
MTB > RANK C2 PUT IN C4
MTB > NAME C3='RANK X' C4='RANK Y'
MTB > PRINT C1 C2 C3 C4

ROW       X       Y    RANK X   RANK Y

  1      3.2     6.8     5.0       3
  2      2.9     7.0     3.5       4
  3      3.7     7.1     8.0       5
  4      2.5     7.8     1.0       8
  5      3.3     6.3     6.0       2
  6      2.7     7.6     2.0       7
  7      2.9     5.8     3.5       1
  8      3.4     7.2     7.0       6


MTB > CORR 'RANK X' 'RANK Y'

Correlation of RANK X and RANK Y = -0.323

MTB > STOP
```

CHAPTER 18

18.1 See Practice Exercises.

18.3 (a) The central line for X is the mean of the 25 X's, which is 1.12, and $\bar{R}$ is the mean of the 25 R's, which is 0.2848; the control limits for $\bar{X}$ are $1.12 \pm 0.577(0.2848)$, namely, 0.96 and 1.28.

(b) The means of all the subgroups are in control.

18.5 See Practice Exercises.

18.7 The central line for $\bar{X}$ is 0.13. The control limits are 2.20 and -1.94. The central line for σ is 1.30; the control limits are 2.72 and zero.

18.9 See Practice Exercises.

18.11 The central line is 10; the control limits are 19.24 and 0.76. Sample 3 is out of control.

18.13 See Practice Exercises.

18.15 (a) For mean chart central line is 1.12, UCL is 1.28, and LCL is 0.96; for range chart central line is 0.285, UCL is 0.60, and LCL is zero.

(b) Mean chart is in control. Range chart subgroup 10 is above UCL and is out of control.

18.17 The central line for $\bar{X}$ is the mean of the 20 $\bar{X}$'s, which is 1.4997; the central line for R is the mean of the 20 R's, which is 0.0354; the control limits for $\bar{X}$

are 1.4997 ± 0.308(0.0354), namely, 1.489 and 1.511; and the control limits for R are 0.223(0.0354) = 0.008 and 1.777(0.0354) = 0.063. Subgroups 1, 2, 3, 4, 10, 11, 12, 13, 14, 15, 18, 19, and 20 are out of control.

18.19 The central line for median is 25, the central line for range is 6; UCL for median is 28.12, and LCL for median is 21.88; UCL for range is 11.82, and LCL for range is 0.48. Out-of-control samples are number 14 from control chart for median and number 22 from control chart for range.

18.21 (a) Take another sample of $n = 100$.

      (b) Accept the shipment.

      (c) No, accept the sample.

      (d) No, reject the sample.

18.23

```
MTB > PRINT C1

C1
  -1   -1    0   -2    1    0    1   -3    2    1    1    1    2
  -1    0
   1   -2   -1    0   -1    0    3   -2   -2    1   -2   -2    1
   1    2
   2    1   -1    0    0    1   -2   -1   -1    0   -1    2    1
   1    2
   1   -1    0    0   -1    2   -1   -2   -1   -1    1   -3   -2
   1    0
   0    0   -1    0    1    2   -1   -1    0   -2    1   -1    2
   0   -2
   2   -1    0    0    1    1    1    0    0    1    0    0    1
  -2   -1
  -2    1    2    0    1   -3    3    1    2    0    1    1    0
  -1    2
  -2    1    3    1   -3    2    2   -1    1    0    1    0    1
   2   -2
   3   -1    0    1   -1    2    0    0    1    1    1   -2   -2
   1    1
   1    0    0   -2   -1    2    0    3    1   -2    0    0    2
   1   -1
```

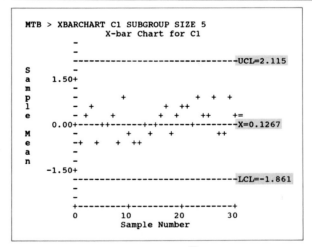

The computer printout shows that $\bar{\bar{X}} = 0.1267$, UCL = 2.115, and LCL = 1.861. These results, together with the sample means, are plotted on the control chart for the mean. Differences are due to the method for calculation used by computer software.

18.25   Yes, by observation.

CHAPTER 19

19.1   See Practice Exercises.

19.3   (a) 100.4 for 1989.
        (b) 99.0 for 1989.

19.5   See Practice Exercises.

19.7   (a) 100, 82.4, and 5.6.
        (b) 119.7.

19.9   See Practice Exercises.

19.11 $I = \dfrac{\sum \dfrac{p_n}{p_0} \cdot p_0 q_0}{\sum p_0 q_0} \cdot 100 = \dfrac{\sum p_n q_0}{\sum p_0 q_0} \cdot 100$

19.13   133.2.

19.15   See Practice Exercises.

19.17   190.8.

19.19   Yes. There may be a remote and indirect connection between general business conditions and the limited phenomenon the CPI-U is intended to describe, but it is not intentional. Prices are said to be "sticky" and tend to fall more slowly than some indicators of worsening business conditions. Stock prices, of course, are not covered by the CPI-U.

19.21   (a) Superficially, this seems reasonable, but (in the short run especially), the PPI's are not good predictors of movements of the CPIs because many components of the PPI's (machinery, for example) do not enter the retail markets at all and many components of the CPIs (physicians and dentists's services, and residential rents, for example) are not included in the PPIs.
        (b) Neither the CPIs nor the PPIs were designed to facilitate the measurement of profit margins between primary markets and other distribution levels.

19.23   No. For instance, the number of personal bankruptcies might have decreased from 200 to 172 in city A and increased from 100 to 105 in city B. Obviously, 172 is not 19 percent lower than 105.

19.25   (a) 100.0, 104.5, 107.5, 118.5, and 128.6.
        (b) 77.8, 81.3, 83.6, 92.1, and 100.0.

19.27   See Practice Exercises.

19.29   His real salary declined by $1,288.98.

19.31   See Practice Exercises.

19.33   (a) 100.0, 110.0, 117.5, 122.5, 127.5.
        (b) 78.4, 86.3, 92.2, 96.1, 100.0.

19.35   Wages did not keep up with inflation.

19.37   (a) 94.4;   (b) 95.5.

19.39   (a) Sum the 12 indexes for year 1986, then divide by 12 to obtain annual
            average for 1986. Repeat procedure for subsequent years.

        (b) $\dfrac{345.7 - 331.1}{331.1} \cdot 100 = 4.4$; $\dfrac{360.9 - 345.7}{345.7} \cdot 100 = 4.4$;

            $\dfrac{377.6 - 360.9}{360.9} \cdot 100 = 4.6$; $\dfrac{400.9 - 377.6}{377.6} \cdot 100 = 6.2$.

        (c) $\dfrac{340.4 - 328.4}{328.4} \cdot 100 = 3.7$; $\dfrac{354.3 - 340.4}{340.4} \cdot 100 = 4.1$;

            $\dfrac{371.3 - 354.3}{354.3} \cdot 100 = 4.8$; $\dfrac{391.4 - 371.3}{371.3} \cdot 100 = 5.4$.

CHAPTER 20

20.1   See Practice Exercises.

20.3   (a)

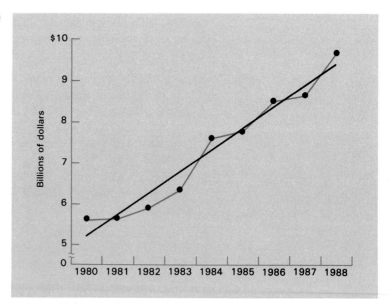

        (b) $\hat{y} = 7.28 + 0.53x$ (origin, 1984; x units, 1 year; y, annual fire losses in
            billions of dollars).

(c) $\hat{y} = 9.40 + 0.53x$ (origin 1988; x units, 1 year; y, annual fire losses in billions of dollars).

20.5 See Practice Exercises.

20.7 $88.580 + 0.449x$ (origin, January, 1989; x units, 1 month; y, average monthly revenues of Printing Applications Corporation in thousands of dollars).

20.9 (a) $\hat{y} = 36.76 - 0.22x - 0.54x^2$ (origin 1965; x units, 5 years; y, circulation of newspapers in millions of copies per day).

(b)

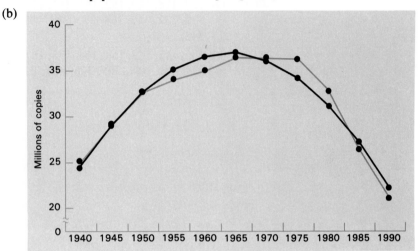

20.11 59.84, 67.05, 78.02, 92.75, 111.24, 133.49, 159.50, 189.27, 222.80.

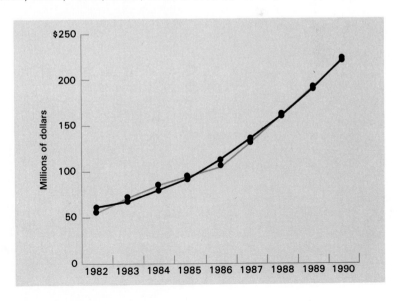

20.13 (a) $\log \hat{y} = 2.1527 + 0.2333x$ [or $\hat{y} = 1.421(1.71)^x$] (origin, 1975; x units, 5 years; y, exports in billions of dollars).

(b) 28.37, 48.54, 83.06, 142.13, 243.22, 416.20, and 712.17.

20.15 The use of a least-squares line does not eliminate all subjectivity in measuring a trend. The decision to fit a straight line is itself subjective, and so is the choice of the least-squares criterion instead of some other method (semi-averages, for example); how many years to use is also a subjective criterion.

20.17 (a) 132, 128, 140, 152, 164, 164, 172, 184, 200, 224, 228, 252, 260, 296, 312, 332, 340, 364, 372, 380, 392, 412, 416, 408, 396, 400, 360, and 348.

(b) 139, 142, 149, 158, 168, 175, 187, 204, 214, 235, 250, 271, 288, 312, 324, 350, 358, 365, 386, 401, 396, 408, 410, 401, 377, and 370.

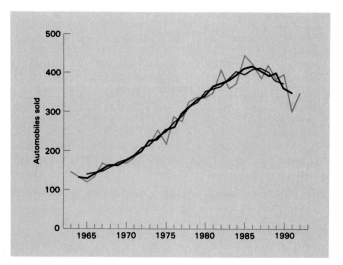

20.19 33, 36, 40, 39, 37, 36, 33, 29, 27, 31, 30, 31, 26, 27, 31, 29, 30, 30, 37, 34, 30, 29, 34, and 38.

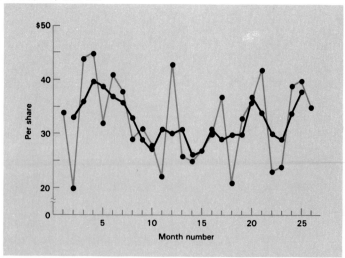

20.21   See Practice Exercises.

20.23   (a) 3.9, 3.8, 3.7, 3.8, 4.2, and 4.6.

(b) 3.9, 3.7, 3.5, 4.1, 5.5, and 6.7.

20.25   (a) 19, 19.4, 18.0, 18.8, 21.3, 22.4, 23.8, 21.9, 19.5, 20.5, 20.3, 21.8, 20.7, 21.6.

(b) 24, 23.2, 21.8, 21.4, 22.1, 22.5, 23.2, 22.4, 21.1, 21.3, 21.0, 21.6, 21.1, 21.5.

20.27   See Practice Exercises.

20.29 $\hat{y} = 19{,}733 + 221.8x$ (origin, years 1988–1989; x units, 6 months; y, total annual sales in hundreds of thousands of dollars).

20.31   227, 227, 235, 237, 234, 235, 231, 253, 241, 240, 229, and 232.

20.33   2,820 billions of kilowatt-hours.

20.35   656,750; 841,750; 943,500; 925,000; 1,026,750; 1,100,750; 999,000; 1,322,750; 1,054,500; 860,250; 675,250; 693,750.

20.37   37.254, 27.948, 18.162, 17.544, 17.143, 15.198, 14.127, 14.379, 14.854, 16.441, 23.157, 48.421.

20.39   59.0, 61.0, 74.9, 96.7, 118.6, 127.2, 122.4, 128.0, 125.0, 109.6, 104.7, 72.9.

20.41   173, 240.50, 303.65, 336.46, 341.12, 327.88, 345.02, 375.91, 407.14, 449.40.

20.43   411.4, 353.7, 497.7, 593.1, 495.8, 492.3, 438.9, 480.2, 541.9, 483.1, 484.6, 703.7.

20.45   (a) $\log \hat{y} = 1.2821 - 0.1675x$, [or $\hat{y} = 1.915(1.471)^x$] (origin, 1970; x units, 5 years; y, annual consumption in millions of short tons).

(b) Plotted on graph of part (a).

(c) 47.1 percent.

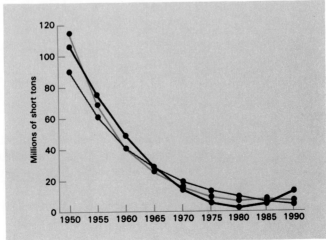

20.47 (a) 200.

(b) year 1995.

(c) 400 units.

20.49

Year	Jan.	Feb.	Mar.	Apr.	May	June
1	4.39	4.33	4.55	4.37	4.26	4.44
2	4.63	4.87	4.93	4.47	4.49	4.54
3	3.82	4.14	4.06	4.21	4.33	4.20
4	4.17	4.16	4.14	4.19	4.18	4.11

Year	July	Aug.	Sept.	Oct.	Nov.	Dec.
1	4.38	4.56	4.53	4.53	4.56	4.55
2	4.54	4.46	4.39	4.35	4.41	4.41
3	4.18	4.13	4.21	4.30	4.12	4.19
4	4.06	3.93	4.15	5.03	3.96	4.06

20.51 $\hat{y} = 71.6 - 10.1x$ (origin, 1985; x units, 1 year; y, number of work stoppages annually).

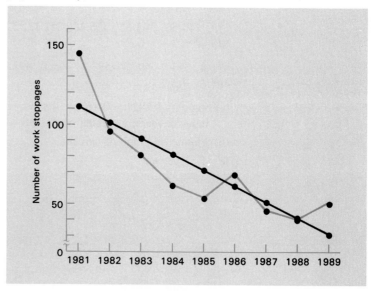

20.53 (a) Corresponding to the third, fourth, and fifth values of the series the values of the weighted moving average are
$$\frac{130 + 2(149) + 3(144) + 2(175) + 175}{9} = 153\frac{8}{9}, \ 163\frac{6}{9}, \text{ and } 166\frac{5}{9};$$
corresponding to the second through sixth values of the series, the val-

ues of the three-year moving average are 141, 156, $164\frac{2}{3}$, $170\frac{1}{3}$, and

$164\frac{2}{3}$; corresponding to the third, fourth, and fifth values of the series, the values are $\frac{1}{3}(141 + 156 + 164\frac{2}{3}) = 153\frac{8}{9}$, $163\frac{6}{9}$, and $166\frac{5}{9}$.

(b) At the start we add to the first 12-month moving total the second so that we have the first and second J figures added-in once each, and the F, M, . . . , and D figures added in twice; the same pattern continues.

20.55

Deseasonalized Quarterly Data

Year	1	2	3	4
1	1,328	1,350	1,390	1,506
2	1,697	1,598	1,654	1,676
3	1,556	1,622	1,605	1,598
4	1,600	1,596	1,588	1,591

20.57 Over long periods of time data are sometimes gathered and reported by different agencies. Also, from time to time definitions are changed, and this year's chain store, department store, or farm, for example, is not necessarily the same as last year's. A government agency at one time developed a definition of a chain store based on volume of sales; under this definition a single large store might be classified as a "chain" store and a chain of 12 small stores excluded from the classification. Other definitions might drop the sales requirement and identify chain stores instead by certain qualitative characteristics, or by a minimum number of employees. Furthermore, changes in the sample coverage and the manner of reporting may affect the comparability of data in a series. Monthly data may at one time be given as average sales per sales day and at another time as total sales for the month. The effect of these changes and others is to make many reported figures not really comparable.

20.59

Year	Cloth Prod. (Billions) (sq. yds)	Three year Moving Totals	Three year Moving Averages	Five year Moving Totals	Five year Moving Averages
1971	6.1				
1972	5.6	16.8	5.6		
1973	5.1	15.4	5.1	25.6	5.1
1974	4.7	13.9	4.6	24.2	4.8
1975	4.1	13.5	4.5	23.0	4.6
1976	4.7	13.2	4.4	21.9	4.4
1977	4.4	13.1	4.4	21.1	4.2
1978	4.0	12.3	4.1	21.5	4.3
1979	3.9	12.4	4.1	20.7	4.1
1980	4.5	12.3	4.1	20.1	4.0
1981	3.9	12.2	4.1	20.3	4.1
1982	3.8	11.9	4.0	20.4	4.1
1983	4.2	12.0	4.0	19.8	4.0
1984	4.0	12.1	4.0	20.3	4.1
1985	3.9	12.3	4.1	21.2	4.2
1986	4.4	13.0	4.3	21.5	4.3
1987	4.7	13.6	4.5	22.1	4.4
1988	4.5	13.8	4.6	22.7	4.5
1989	4.6	13.6	4.5		
1990	4.5				

20.61

Year	Profit After tax ($ Billion)	Three year Moving Totals	Three year Moving Averages	Five year Moving Totals	Five year Moving Averages
1970	44.0				
1971	52.4	159.0	53.0		
1972	62.6	196.6	65.5	331.6	66.3
1973	81.6	235.2	78.4	377.1	75.4
1974	91.0	262.1	87.4	434.2	86.8
1975	89.5	290.0	96.7	501.9	100.4
1976	109.5	329.3	109.8	574.7	114.9
1977	130.3	394.2	131.4	657.1	131.4
1978	154.4	458.1	152.7	723.7	144.7
1979	173.4	483.9	161.3	762.0	152.4
1980	156.1	477.3	159.1	744.9	149.0
1981	147.8	417.1	139.0	724.0	144.8
1982	113.2	394.5	131.5	697.0	139.4
1983	133.5	393.1	131.0	669.4	133.9
1984	146.4	408.4	136.1	632.9	126.6
1985	128.5	386.2	128.7	680.5	136.1
1986	111.3	400.6	133.5	757.5	151.5
1987	160.8	482.6	160.9	817.7	163.5
1988	210.5	577.9	192.6	886.2	177.2
1989	206.6	614.1	204.7		
1990	197.0				

20.63

Year	Factory Sales (in Million)	Five year Moving Totals	Five year Moving Averages
1974	10.0		
1975	9.0		
1976	11.5	55.9	11.2
1977	12.6	57.4	11.5
1978	12.8	56.4	11.3
1979	11.5	52.9	10.6
1980	8.0	47.3	9.5
1981	8.0	43.7	8.7
1982	7.0	42.9	8.6
1983	9.2	46.3	9.3
1984	10.7	49.2	9.8
1985	11.4	53.1	10.6
1986	10.9	55.1	11.0
1987	10.9	55.3	11.1
1988	11.2	53.7	10.7
1989	10.9		
1990	9.8		

CHAPTER 21

21.1 See Practice Exercises.

21.9 (a) $\sigma_{\bar{x}} = \sqrt{\dfrac{(120 - 155)^2 + (145 - 155)^2 + \cdots + (190 - 155)^2}{6}}$

$= 21.0$.

(b) $\sigma_{\bar{x}} = \sqrt{\dfrac{(145 - 155)^2 + (155 - 155)^2 + \cdots + (165 - 155)^2}{4}}$

$= 7.1$.

21.11 3.71 billion ways.

21.13   10, 25, 15, and 50.

21.15   125, 75, 50, 40, and 10.

21.17   (a) $n_1 = 2$; $n_2 = 1$.
(b) $\sigma_{\bar{x}} = \sqrt{153}$ for the four women and $\sigma_{\bar{x}} = \sqrt{2,304}$ for the two men. $n_1 = 1$ and $n_2 = 2$.

21.19   See Practice Exercises.

21.21   Letting A represent Albert; B, Bertha; C, Charles; D, David; E, Ellen; F, Fairville; G, Gainsboro; and H, Holton, the tests are *ADF, ADG, ADH, AEF, AEG, AEH, BDF, BDG, BDH, BEF, BEG, BEH, CDF, CDG, CDH, CEF, CEG, CEH.*

21.23   See Practice Exercises.

21.25   See Practice Exercises.

21.27   (b) There are two solutions: Mason, Academic Support Services; Webb, Undergraduate Curriculum; Castro, Graduate Admissions or Graduate Curriculum; Wood, Graduate Curriculum or Graduate Admissions.

21.29   (a) 1,003,200.
(b) 13,643,520.

21.31 $n_1 = 33$, $n_2 = 20$, and $n_3 = 7$.

21.33

A	B	C
B	C	A
C	A	B

21.35   First display, 13; third display, 7; sixth display, 11; seventh display, 3; eighth display, 5; eleventh display, 8; twelfth display, 1.

21.37   1, *a, b, c, d, ab, ac, ad, bc, bd, cd, abc, abd, acd, bcd,* and *abcd.*

21.39   *ABC, ABc, AbC, Abc, aBC, aBc, abC,* and *abc.*

21.41   (a) $\bar{x}_1 = \dfrac{137}{20} = 6.8$ pounds and $\bar{x}_2 = \dfrac{217}{10} = 21.7$ pounds;

$$\bar{x}_w = \frac{2,000(6.8) + 1,000(21.7)}{2,000 + 1,000} = 11.8 \text{ pounds.}$$

(b) $\bar{x} = \dfrac{4 + 5 + 3 + \cdots + 17 + 28 + 27}{30} = \dfrac{354}{30} = 11.8$ pounds.

Bibliography

A

Some Books on the Theory of Probability and Statistics

BARR, D. R., and ZEHNA, P. W., *Probability: Modeling Uncertainty*. Reading, Mass.: Addison-Wesley Publishing Company, Inc., 1983.

FREUND, J. E., *Introduction to Probability*. Encino, Calif.: Dickenson Publishing Co., Inc., 1973.

FREUND, J. E., and WALPOLE, R. E., *Mathematical Statistics*, 4th ed. Englewood Cliffs, N.J.: Prentice-Hall, Inc, 1987.

GARVIN, A. D., *Probability in Your Life*. Portland, Me.: J. Weston Walch, Publisher, 1978.

GOLDBERG, S., *Probability—An Introduction*. New York: Dover Publications, Inc., 1987.

HODGES, J. L., and LEHMANN, E. L., *Elements of Finite Probability*. San Francisco: Holden-Day, Inc., 1970.

HOEL, P., *Introduction to Mathematical Statistics*, 5th ed. New York: John Wiley & Sons, Inc., 1984.

KENDALL, M. G., and STUART, A., *The Advanced Theory of Statistics*, 5th ed. London: Griffin, 1987.

KOTZ, S., and STROUP, D. E., *Educated Guessing: How to Cope in an Uncertain World*. New York: Marcel Dekker, Inc., 1983.

LARSEN, R. L., and MARX, M. L., *An Introduction to Mathematical Statistics and Its Applications*, 2nd ed. Englewood Cliffs, N.J.: Prentice-Hall, Inc., 1986.

MENDENHALL, W., SCHAEFFER, R. L., and WACKERLY, D. D., *Mathematical Statistics with Applications*, 3rd ed. Boston: Duxbury Press, 1986.

MOSTELLER, F., *Fifty Challenging Problems in Probability, with Solutions*. New York: Dover Publications, Inc., 1987.

NEFT, D. S., COHEN, R. M., and DEUTCH, J. A., *The World Book of Odds*. New York: Grossett & Dunlap, Inc., 1978.

ROSS, SHELDON M., *A First Course in Probability*, 2nd ed. New York: Macmillan Publishing Company, Inc., 1984.

SCHAEFFER, R. L., *Introduction to Probability and Its Applications*. Boston: PWS-Kent Publishing Co., 1990.

WEAVER, W., *Lady Luck: The Theory Of Probability*. New York: Dover Publications, Inc., 1982.

B

Some Books Dealing with Special Topics

ABRAHAM, B., and LEDOLTER, J., *Statistical Methods for Forecasting*. New York: John Wiley & Sons, Inc., 1983.

ANDERSON, T. W., *An Introduction to Multivariate Statistical Analysis*, 2nd ed. New York: John Wiley & Sons, Inc., 1984.

ANDERSON, V. L., and McCLEAN, R. A., *Design of Experiments: A Realistic Approach*. New York: Marcel Dekker, Inc., 1974.

A.T.&T., *Statistical Quality Control Handbook*. Indianapolis, Ind.: A.T.&T. Technologies, 1956.

BEHN, R. D., and VAUPEL, J. W., *Quick Analysis for Busy Decision Makers*. New York: Basic Books, Inc., 1982.

BERGER, J. O., *Statistical Decision Theory and Bayesian Analysis*, 2nd ed. New York: Springer Verlag of New York, Inc., 1985.

BILLINGSLEY, P., CROFT, D. J., HUNTSBERGER, D. V., and WATSON, W., *Statistical Inference for Management and Economics*. Boston: Allyn & Bacon, Inc., 1986.

BOWERMAN, B. L., and O'CONNELL, R. T., *Forecasting and Time Series*, 2nd ed. North Scituate, Mass.: Duxbury Press, 1986.

BOX, G. E. P., HUNTER, W. G., and HUNTER, J. S., *Statistics for Experimenters*. New York: John Wiley & Sons, Inc., 1978.

BOX, G. E. P., and JENKINS, G. M., *Time Series Analysis: Forecasting and Control*, 2nd ed. San Francisco: Holden-Day, Inc., 1977.

BROOK, R. J., ARNOLD, G. C., HASSARD, T. H., and PRINGLE, R. M., ed., *The Fascination of Statistics*. New York: Marcel Dekker, Inc., 1986.

CHAMBERS, J. M., CLEVELAND, W. S., KLEINER, B., and TUKEY, P. A., *Graphical Methods for Data Analysis*. Pacific Grove, Calif: Brooks/Cole, 1983.

CLEVELAND, W. S., *The Elements of Graphing Data*. Monterey, Calif.: Wadsworth Advanced Books and Software, 1985.

CHATTERJEE, S., and PRICE, B., *Regression Analysis by Example*. New York: John Wiley & Sons, Inc., 1977.

CHILDRESS, R. L., *Mathematics for Managerial Decisions*. Englewood Cliffs, N.J.: Prentice-Hall, Inc., 1974.

COCHRAN, W. G., *Sampling Techniques*, 3rd ed. New York: John Wiley & Sons, Inc., 1977.

CONOVER, W. J., *Practical Nonparametric Statistics*, 2nd ed. New York: John Wiley & Sons, Inc., 1980.

DEMING, W. E., *Sample Design in Business Research*. New York: John Wiley & Sons, Inc., 1990.

DEMING, W. E., *Out of the Crisis*. Cambridge, Mass.: Massachusetts Institute of Technology Center of Advanced Engineering Study, 1986.

DEMING, W. E., *Quality, Productivity, and Competitive Position*. Cambridge, Mass.: Massachusetts Institute of Technology, 1982.

DIXON, W. J. (ed.), *BMDP: Statistical Software Manual*. Berkeley: University of California Press, 1990.

DRAPER, N. R., and SMITH, H., *Applied Regression Analysis*, 2nd ed. New York: John Wiley & Sons, Inc., 1981.

DUNCAN, ACHESON J., *Quality Control and Industrial Statistics*, 5th ed. Homewood, Ill.: Richard D. Irwin, Inc., 1986.

EPPEN, G. D., GOULD, F. J., and SCHMIDT, C. P., *Introductory Management Science*, 3rd ed. Englewood Cliffs, N.J.: Prentice-Hall, Inc., 1991.

EZEKIAL, M., and FOX, K. A., *Methods of Correlation and Regression Analysis*, 4th ed. New York: John Wiley & Sons, Inc., 1988.

FEIGENBAUM, A. V., *Total Quality Control*. New York: McGraw-Hill Book Company, 1983.

FISCHER, R. A., *The Design of Experiments*, 8th ed. Edinburgh: Oliver & Boyd, 1966.

GIBBONS, J. D., *Nonparametric Statistical Inference*, 2nd ed. New York: McGraw-Hill Book Company, 1985.

GRANT, E. L., and LEAVENWORTH, R., *Statistical Quality Control*, 6th ed. New York: McGraw-Hill Book Company, 1988.

GUENTHER, W. C., *Sampling Inspection in Statistical Quality Control*. New York: Oxford University Press, 1987.

HARRIS, R. J., *A Primer of Multivariate Statistics*, 2nd ed. San Diego, Calif.: Academic Press, 1985.

HARTWIG, F., and DEARING, B. E., *Exploratory Data Analysis*. Beverly Hills, Calif.: Sage Publications, Inc., 1979.

HOAGLIN, D. C., MOSTELLER, F., and TUKEY, J. W., *Understanding Robust and Exploratory Data Analysis*. New York: John Wiley & Sons, Inc., 1983.

HOLLANDER, M., and PROSCHAN, F., *The Statistical Exorcist*: Dispelling Statistics Anxiety. New York: Marcel Dekker, Inc., 1984.

HOOKE, R., *How to Tell the Liars from the Statisticians*. New York: Marcel Dekker, Inc., 1983.

JEFFREY, R. C., *The Logic of Decision*, 3rd ed. Chicago: University of Chicago Press, 1990.

JOHNSTON, J., *Econometric Methods*, 3rd ed. New York: McGraw-Hill Book Company, 1984.

KENDALL, M. G., and STUART, A., *The Advanced Theory of Statistics*, 5th ed. London: Griffin, 1987.

LARSEN, R. J., and STROUP, D. F., *Statistics in the Real World*. New York: Macmillan Publishing Company, Inc., 1976.

LEHMANN, E. L., *Nonparametrics*: Statistical Methods Based on Ranks. San Francisco: Holden-Day, Inc., 1975.

McRAE, T. W., *Statistical Sampling for Audit and Control*. New York: John Wiley & Sons, Inc., 1974.

MENDENHALL, W., and McCLAVE, J., *A Second Course in Statistics*: Regression Analysis. Santa Clara, Calif.: Dellen Publishing Co., 1981.

MENDENHALL, W., and REINMUTH, J. E., *Statistics for Management and Economics*, 4th ed. Belmont, Calif.: Duxbury Press, 1982.

MONTGOMERY, D. C., *Design and Analysis of Experiments*, 2nd ed. New York: John Wiley & Sons, Inc., 1984.

MONTGOMERY, D. C., and PECK, E. A., *Introduction to Linear Regression Analysis*. New York: John Wiley & Sons, Inc., 1982.

MOORE, P. G., *The Business of Risk*. Cambridge: Cambridge University Press, 1984.

MOSTELLER, F., and ROURKE, R. E. K., *Sturdy Statistics, Nonparametrics and Order Statistics*. Reading, Mass.: Addison-Wesley Publishing Company, Inc., 1977.

MOSTELLER, F., and TUKEY, J. W., *Data Analysis and Regression*. Reading, Mass.: Addison-Wesley Publishing Company, Inc., 1977.

MUDGETT, B. D., *Index Numbers*. New York: John Wiley & Sons, Inc., 1951.

NEFT, D. S., COHEN, R. M., and DEUTCH, J. A., *The World Book of Odds*. New York: Grosset & Dunlap, Inc., 1978.

NELSON, C. R., *Applied Time Series Analysis for Managerial Forecasting*. San Francisco: Holden-Day, Inc., 1973.

NETER, J. W., WASSERMAN, W., and KUTNER, M. H., *Applied Linear Statistical Models*, 2nd ed. Homewood, Ill.: Richard D. Irwin, Inc., 1985.

RUNYON, R. P., *Winning with Statistics*. Reading, Mass.: Addison-Wesley Publishing Company, Inc., 1977.

SCHEAFFER, R. L., MENDENHALL, W., and OTT, L., *Elementary Survey Sampling*, 4th ed. Boston: PWS-Kent Publishing Co., 1990.

SCHLAIFFER, R., *Probabililty and Statistics for Business Decisions*: *An Introduction to Managerial Economics Under Uncertainty*. New York: McGraw-Hill Book Company, 1981.

SCHMID, C. F., *Statistical Graphics*. New York: John Wiley & Sons, Inc., 1983.

SHEWHART, W. A., *Economic Control of Quality of Manufactured Product*. New York: Van Nostrand-Reinhold Company, 1931. Reprinted by American Society for Quality Control.

SIEGEL, S., and CASTELLAN, N. J., Jr., *Nonparametric Statistics for the Behavioral Sciences*, 2nd ed. New York: McGraw-Hill Book Company, 1988.

SNEDECOR, G. W., and COCHRAN, W. G., *Statistical Methods*, 8th ed. Ames: Iowa State University Press, 1989.

STIGLER, S. M., *The History of Statistics*. Cambridge, Mass.: Harvard University Press, 1986.

STUART, A., *The Ideas of Sampling*, 3rd ed. London: Oxford University Press, 1987.

TANUR, J. M., ed., *Statistics*: *A Guide to the Unknown*. San Francisco: Holden-Day, Inc., 1972.

TATSUOKA, M. M., *Multivariate Analysis*, 2nd ed. New York: Macmillan Publishing Company, Inc., 1987.

TUFTE, E. R., *The Visual Display of Quantitative Information*. Cheshire, Conn.: Graphics Press, 1985.

TUKEY, J. W., *Exploratory Data Analysis*. Reading, Mass.: Addison-Wesley Publishing Company, Inc., 1977.

VON NEUMANN, J., and MORGENSTERN, O., *Theory of Games and Economic Behavior*, 3rd ed. Princeton, N.J.: Princeton University Press, 1980.

WADSWORTH, H. M., STEPHENS, K. S., and GODFREY, A. B., *Modern Methods for Quality Control and Improvement*. New York: John Wiley & Sons, Inc., 1986.

WALTON, M., *The Deming Management Method*. New York: Perigee Books, Putnam Publishing Group, 1986.

WEISBERG, S., *Applied Linear Regression*, 2nd ed. New York: John Wiley & Sons, Inc., 1985.

C

Some General Reference Works and Tables

BEYER, W. H., ed., *CRC Handbook of Tables for Probability and Statistics*. Boca Raton, Fla.: CRC Press, 1991.

DANIELLS, L. M., *Business Information Sources*, rev. Berkeley: The University of California Press, 1985.

FREUND, J. E., and WILLIAMS, F. J., *Dictionary/Outline of Basic Statistics*. New York: McGraw-Hill Book Company, 1966.

JURAN, J. M., ed., *Quality Control Handbook*, 3rd ed. New York: McGraw-Hill Book Company, 1974.

LEE, I., and MAYKOVICH, M. K., *Minitab Manual for Prentice-Hall Statistics*. Englewood Cliffs, N.J.: Prentice-Hall, Inc., 1991.

LEE, I., and MAYKOVICH, M. K., *SAS Manual for Prentice-Hall Statistics*. Englewood Cliffs, N.J.: Prentice-Hall, Inc., 1991.

MARRIOTT, F. H. C., ed., *A Dictionary of Statistical Terms*, 5th ed. New York: John Wiley & Sons, Inc., 1990.

NATIONAL BUREAU OF STANDARDS, *Tables of the Binomial Probability Distribution*. Washington, D.C.: U.S. Government Printing Office, 1950.

NORUSSIS, M., *SPSS/PC for the IBM PC/XT/AT*. Chicago: SPSS, Inc., 1986.

NORUSSIS, M., *Advanced Statistics Guide SPSSX*. New York: McGraw-Hill Book Company, 1985.

NORUSSIS, M., *Introductory Statistics Guide SPSSX*. New York: McGraw-Hill Book Company, 1983.

PEARSON, E. S., and HARTLEY, H. O., *Biometrika Tables for Statisticians*. Cambridge: Cambridge University Press, 1976.

RAND CORPORATION, *A Million Random Digits with 100,000 Normal Deviates*. New York: The Free Press, 1966.

RYAN, T. A., JOINER, B. L., and RYAN, B. F., *Minitab Student Handbook*, 2nd ed. North Scituate, Mass.: Duxbury Press, 1985.

STATGRAPHICS Users Guide. Rockville, Md.: STSC, Inc., 1986.

WASSERMAN, P., *Statistics Sources*, 16th ed. Detroit: Gale Research Co., 1992.

D

Some Sources of Statistical Data (Primarily Monthly or Annual)

Agricultural Statistics. Washington, D.C.: U.S. Department of Agriculture.

Business Statistics. Washington, D.C.: U.S. Department of Commerce (biennial).

CRB Commodity Yearbook. Jersey City, N.J.: Commodity Research Bureau, Inc.

Demographic Yearbook. New York: Statistical Office of the United Nations.

Economic Indicators. Washington, D.C.: Joint Economic Committee.

Editor and Publisher Market Guide. New York: Editor and Publisher Co., Inc.

Facts and Figures on Government Finance. New York: Tax Foundation, Inc.

Federal Reserve Bulletin. Washington, D.C.: Board of Governors of the Federal Reserve System.

Handbook of Basic Economic Statistics. Washington, D.C.: Economic Statistics Bureau of Washington, D.C.

Mineral Yearbook. Washington, D.C.: U.S. Bureau of Mines.

Monthly Labor Review. Washington, D.C.: U.S. Bureau of Labor Statistics.

Predicasts Basebook. Cleveland: Predicasts, Inc.

Standard & Poor's Trade and Securities: Statistics. New York: Standard & Poor's.

Statistical Abstract of the United States. Washington, D.C.: U.S. Census Bureau.

Statistical Yearbook. New York: Statistical Office of the United Nations.

Statistics of Income. Washington, D.C.: U.S. Internal Revenue Service.

Survey of Buying Power. New York: Sales and Marketing Management.

Survey of Current Business. Washington, D.C.: U.S. Department of Commerce.

The World Almanac. New York: Newspaper Enterprise Association, Inc.

U.S. Industrial Outlook. Washington, D.C.: U.S. Bureau of Census, Industry and Trade Administration.

U.S. Bureau of the Census. Bureau publications are issued variously at monthly, annual, five-year, and ten-year intervals. Current publications include:

> *Census of Agriculture—1987*
> *Census of Construction Industries—1987*
> *Census of Housing—1990*
> *Census of Manufactures—1987* (annual survey for noncensus years)
> *Census of Population—1990*
> *Census of Retail Trade—1987*
> *Census of Wholesale Trade—1987*
> *County and City Data Book—*five-year intervals
> *County Business Patterns—*annual
> *Current Industrial Reports*
> *Current Population Reports*
> *FT* (foreign trade) *Series*

References to years in the above bibliography will be superseded by later dates as these publications are updated periodically.

E

Some Sources of Statistical Data on CD-ROMS—For Use on the Computer

Following is a selected list of statistical data on CD-ROMS available from your local U.S. Government Documents Center. There is no charge for the use of these disks, and they can be copied (downloaded) onto your privately owned floppy disks. U.S. government publications can be used freely, but the use of privately prepared data is regulated by copyright laws.

Census of Agriculture—1987. Washington, D.C.: Bureau of the Census. Contains statistics about the nation's agricultural production. Volume I contains geographic area series and county data files. The disk also includes U.S. totals.

Census of Population and Housing—1990. Washington, D.C.: U.S. Bureau of the Census. Two sets of data are available. First, the congressional redistricting data are accessible on the PL94-171 disk. Second, information regarding race, housing, age, and other population characteristics can be obtained by using the STF1A CD.

County and City Data Book, 1988. Washington, D.C.: Bureau of the Census. Contains statistical data for states, counties, cities of 25,000 or more, and places of 2,500 or more.

County Business Patterns. Washington, D.C.: U.S. Bureau of the Census. Covers employment, payrolls, size of establishments, and other data by detailed industry.

Economic Censuses—1987. Washington, D.C.: Bureau of the Census. Volume I, release 1D, includes retail trade, wholesale trade, service industries, mineral industries, construction industries, manufactures, and transportation. Volume II, release 2A, provides statistics, by zip code, for retail trade and service industries.

Index to United Nations Documents and Publications. New Canaan, Conn.: Newsbank/Readex Corp. Contains the years 1990, 1991, and the present.

National Trade Databank. Washington, D.C.: U.S. Department of Commerce. Provides information on foreign trade and international economic statistics. There are two programs available on this CD: the National Trade Databank and the Foreign Trader's Index.

Statistical Masterfile. Bethesda, Md.: Congressional Information Service. This CD contains three indexes: *American Statistics Index* (ASI), *Statistical Reference Index* (SRI), and *Index* to *International Statistics* (IIS).

U.S. Imports of Merchandise/U.S. Exports of Merchandise. Washington, D.C.: Bureau of the Census. Contains International Harmonized System Commodity Classification by Country and Customs District. Statistics for U.S. imports/exports by commodity and port.

It may be noted that some of the foregoing titles appear in sets of several disks. Many major statistical references, including the titles named, appear in more than one format such as in printed reports, microfiche, computer tapes, online, and diskettes. Some publications appear in one or more of these formats, but not as CD-ROMS. U.S. Government Documents Centers can provide this information. All the titles listed appear periodically (monthly, annually, or at 5- or 10-year intervals). The references to years in this bibliography of CD-ROMs will be superseded by later dates as all these publications are updated periodically.

Index

Problems of Estimation

Mean (large sample, σ known or estimated by s)

$$\bar{x} - z_{\alpha/2} \cdot \frac{\sigma}{\sqrt{n}} < \mu < \bar{x} + z_{\alpha/2} \cdot \frac{\sigma}{\sqrt{n}}$$

Mean (small sample)

$$\bar{x} - t_{\alpha/2} \cdot \frac{s}{\sqrt{n}} < \mu < \bar{x} + t_{\alpha/2} \cdot \frac{s}{\sqrt{n}}$$

Proportion (large sample)

$$\frac{x}{n} - z_{\alpha/2} \sqrt{\frac{\frac{x}{n}\left(1 - \frac{x}{n}\right)}{n}} < p < \frac{x}{n} + z_{\alpha/2} \sqrt{\frac{\frac{x}{n}\left(1 - \frac{x}{n}\right)}{n}}$$

Standard deviation (large sample)

$$\frac{s}{1 + \dfrac{z_{\alpha/2}}{\sqrt{2n}}} < \sigma < \frac{s}{1 - \dfrac{z_{\alpha/2}}{\sqrt{2n}}}$$

Estimation of mean

$$E = z_{\alpha/2} \cdot \frac{\sigma}{\sqrt{n}}$$

Estimation of proportion

$$E = z_{\alpha/2} \sqrt{\frac{\frac{x}{n}\left(1 - \frac{x}{n}\right)}{n}}$$

Estimation of mean

$$n = \left[\frac{z_{\alpha/2} \cdot \sigma}{E}\right]^2$$

Estimation of proportion

$$n = p(1 - p)\left[\frac{z_{\alpha/2}}{E}\right]^2 \quad \text{or} \quad n = \frac{1}{4}\left[\frac{z_{\alpha/2}}{E}\right]^2$$